D1474133

THE BUILDINGS OF ENGLAND

FOUNDING EDITOR: NIKOLAUS PEVSNER

YORKSHIRE WEST RIDING:
SHEFFIELD AND THE SOUTH

RUTH HARMAN AND NIKOLAUS PEVSNER

Yorkshire West Riding (South)

Boundary of West Riding of Yorkshire

Sheffield; see map pp.550–1 for suburbs

'A' roads

Motorways

Boundary with area covered in Yorkshire West Riding (North) volume

0 ___ 5 ___ 10 ___ 15 miles
0 ___ 10 ___ 20 km

River Aire

Queensbury

Bradshaw

Hebden Bridge

Heptonstall

Blackshaw Head

Shelf

Coley

Hipperholme

Gomersal

Stanley

Northowram

Mytholmroyd

Luddenden

River Calder

Warley

Halifax

Cleckheaton

Birstall

Heckmondwike

Altofts

Todmorden

Sowerby Bridge

Southowram

Lightcliffe

Liversedge

Batley

Hanging Heaton

Outwood

Wrenthorpe

Sowerby

Norland

Brighouse

Clifton

Hartshead

Dewsbury

LANCASHIRE

Soyland

Copley

West Vale

Kirklees Park

Alverthorpe

Kirkthorpe

Ripponden

Greetland

Elland

Rastrick

Ravensthorpe

Earlsheaton

Wakefield

Heath

Rishworth

Barkisland

Stainland

Mirfield

Thornhill

Ossett

Crofton

Scammonden

U. Hopton

Kirkheaton

Whitley Lower

Middletown

Horbury

Sandal Magna

Walton

M62

Golcar

Almondbury

Lepton

Netherton

Flockton

Crigglestone

Newmiller-dam

Ryhill

Slaithwaite

Armitage Br.

Farnley Tyas

Fenay Bridge

Chapelthorpe

Denshaw

Linthwaite

Marsden

S. Crosland

Honley

Shelley

Emley

Woolley

Bretton Hall

Royston

Friarmere

Meltham

Thurstonland

Kirkburton

Scissett

Clayton West

Darton

Carlton

Delph

Netherthong

Skelmanthorpe

High Hoyland

Monk Bretton

A62

Dobcross

Wilshaw

New Mill

Cumberworth

Cawthorne

Ardsley

Scouthead

Uppermill

Holmfirth

Denby Dale

Barnsley

Greenfield

Upper Denby

Gunthwaite

Silkstone

Dodworth

Wombwell

Lydgate

Friezland

Holmbridge

Wooldale

Hoylandswaine

A629

Hepworth

Thurlstone

Wentworth

Cas.

Worsbrough

Carlecotes

Penistone

Thurgoland

Hoyland Nether

Elsecar

Langsett

Hunshelf

Tankersley

A628

Midhopestones

Wortley

High Green

Stocksbridge

Chapeltown

Bolsterstone

Thorpe Hesley

Oughtibridge

Ecclesfield

Bradfield

Grenoside

Worrall

CHESHIRE

DERBYSHIRE

SHEFFIELD

Ringinglow

Fox House

A61

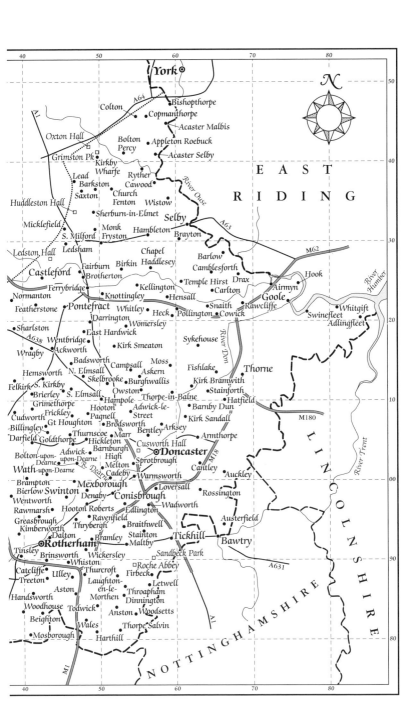

PEVSNER ARCHITECTURAL GUIDES

The *Buildings of England* series was created and largely written by Sir Nikolaus Pevsner (1902–83). First editions of the county volumes were published by Penguin Books between 1951 and 1974. The continuing programme of revisions and new volumes was supported between 1994 and 2011 by research financed through the Pevsner Books Trust. That responsibility has now been assumed by the Paul Mellon Centre for Studies in British Art.

The research and publication of this volume
has been generously supported by

FITZWILLIAM (WENTWORTH) ESTATES

Yorkshire West Riding: Sheffield and the South

BY

RUTH HARMAN

AND

NIKOLAUS PEVSNER

WITH CONTRIBUTIONS FROM

ROGER HARPER
CLARE HARTWELL
PETER LEACH
JOHN MINNIS
JOSEPH SHARPLES
AND
HUMPHREY WELFARE

THE BUILDINGS OF ENGLAND

YALE UNIVERSITY PRESS
NEW HAVEN AND LONDON

YALE UNIVERSITY PRESS
NEW HAVEN AND LONDON

302 Temple Street, New Haven CT 06511
47 Bedford Square, London WC1B 3DP
www.pevsner.co.uk
www.lookingatbuildings.org.uk
www.yalebooks.co.uk
www.yalebooks.com

Published by Yale University Press 2017
2 4 6 8 10 9 7 5 3 1

ISBN 978 0 300 22468 9

Printed in China
through World Print
Set in Monotype Plantin

FOR MY FAMILY
AND EVERYONE WHO HELPED ME

CONTENTS

LIST OF TEXT FIGURES AND MAPS

Every effort has been made to trace or contact all copyright holders. The publishers will be glad to make good any errors or omissions brought to our attention in future editions.

MAPS

PHOTOGRAPHIC ACKNOWLEDGEMENTS

The photographs for this book were mostly taken by Alun Bull (© Alun Bull) and Andrew Caveney (© Andrew Caveney), as shown below. We are grateful for permission to reproduce the remaining photographs as indicated.

Alun Bull: 8, 9, 10, 13, 16, 17, 21, 22, 24, 25, 26, 27, 28, 30, 32, 34, 44, 45, 46, 48, 50, 51, 52, 53, 54, 56, 58, 61, 69, 72, 91, 92, 97, 99, 108, 117

Andrew Caveney: 1, 2, 3, 4, 5, 6, 7, 11, 12, 14, 15, 18, 19, 20, 23, 29, 31, 35, 36, 37, 38, 39, 40, 42, 43, 47, 49, 57, 59, 60, 62, 64, 65, 67, 68, 71, 74, 75, 76, 77, 79, 81, 82, 83, 84, 85, 87, 89, 90, 93, 94, 95, 96, 100, 101, 102, 105, 107, 111, 113, 114, 115, 118

Carter Jonas LLP: 41

© Historic England Archive: 33, 66, 73, 78, 80, 86, 88, 98, 104, 106, 110, 112, 116

© National Trust Images / Andreas von Einsiedel: 55

Rob Ford / Alamy Stock Photo: 63

Sheffield City Council: 103

Shutterstock / Alastair Wallace: 70

University of Sheffield: 109

MAP AND ILLUSTRATION REFERENCES

The numbers printed in italic type in the margin against the place names in the gazetteer of the book indicate the position of the place in question on the INDEX MAP (pp. ii–iii), which is divided into sections by the 10-kilometre reference lines of the National Grid. The reference given here omits the two initial letters which in a full grid reference refer to the 100-kilometre squares into which the county is divided. The first two numbers indicate the *western* boundary, and the last two the *southern* boundary, of the 10-kilometre square in which the place in question is situated. For example, Acaster Malbis (reference 5040) will be found in the 10-kilometre square bounded by grid lines 50 (on the *west*) and 60, and 40 (on the *south*) and 50; Wrenthorpe (reference 3020) in the square bounded by the grid lines 30 (on the *west*) and 40, and 20 (on the *south*) and 30.

The map contains all those places, whether towns, villages or isolated buildings, which are the subject of separate entries in the text.

ILLUSTRATION REFERENCES are given as marginal numbers for photographs, and as marginal *italic* cross-references for images on other pages of the text.

FOREWORD AND ACKNOWLEDGEMENTS

This guide completes the two-volume revision of Nikolaus Pevsner's *Yorkshire: the West Riding*, and is the companion to *Yorkshire West Riding: Leeds, Bradford and the North* by Peter Leach (2009). Pevsner's volume was published in 1959, and a second edition of 1967, revised by Enid Radcliffe, provided an extensive addenda section. Covering a county as large and as varied in its architecture as the West Riding in one volume was only achieved by extreme conciseness, sometimes even at the expense of whole places, like Mytholmroyd. The division into two volumes, which retain Pevsner's writing wherever possible, has allowed more comprehensive coverage of its area, but, as the range of buildings that now falls within the scope of these volumes has greatly increased and so much more information about the West Riding's architecture has become available in the last half century, the entries are still, of necessity, selective and discriminating. The omission of a building should not, therefore, be taken to imply that it is necessarily of no architectural interest.

For many centuries the West Riding was the largest of the three separate counties, or ridings, which, with the City of York, formed Yorkshire. It was abolished in the local government reorganization of 1974 and is now no more real to most people than Barsetshire or Borsetshire. Confusion about its extent abounds. Its southern half, covered by this volume, falls into all the four new Yorkshire counties, with a small western part lost to Greater Manchester. The largest parts form the whole of South Yorkshire, with its four districts of Barnsley, Doncaster, Rotherham and Sheffield, and more than half of West Yorkshire, comprising the districts of Calderdale (which includes Halifax), Kirklees (which includes Dewsbury and Huddersfield), and Wakefield, which includes the West Riding's county town. Also in West Yorkshire are Queensbury, which is in Bradford district, and Ledsham, Ledston Hall and Micklefield, which are in Leeds. The Selby area is a district in North Yorkshire; Acaster Malbis, Bishopthorpe and Copmanthorpe to the north of Selby are in the City of York. Goole and a dozen villages to its west and east are part of the East Riding of Yorkshire as it was created in 1996, having been in Humberside from 1974. The Saddleworth valley is in Oldham district in the county of Greater Manchester. Earlier boundary changes deserving mention are the transfer of a sliver of west Todmorden and its area from Lancashire to the West Riding in 1888 and the southern boundary extensions of Sheffield that took in parts of north Derbyshire in 1935 and 1967.

Help with this volume came from many quarters, firstly in contributions from others to the new text, for which I am very grateful. The gazetteer entries for Dewsbury and Huddersfield are by Joseph Sharples, and those for Uppermill and the other Saddleworth valley villages are by Clare Hartwell. The entries for some two dozen places east and north-east of Leeds and towards York, including Bishopthorpe, Bolton Percy, Ledsham, Ledston Hall and Sherburn in Elmet are by Peter Leach. The entry for Sheffield incorporates the edited text of *Sheffield*, the City Guide in this series by Ruth Harman and John Minnis (2004) but updated to record changes of the last decade and expanded to cover the outer suburbs. Humphrey Welfare wrote the entries for sites of archaeological interest (denoted (HW) in the gazetteer) and the specialist Archaeology section of the Introduction.

Many people kindly welcomed me as a visitor to see their houses, churches, chapels, institutions and other buildings; the generosity of their time and their hospitality are greatly appreciated. It must, however, be emphasized that the description of a building in the text does not imply that it is open to the public. The incumbents, priests, ministers, churchwardens and other church and chapel members are too numerous to mention individually. Among owners and custodians are John Adams, Caroline Carr-Whitworth, Father George Guiver CR, Vicky Davies and Christian Harvey, Clive and Virginia Lloyd, Lord and Lady Scarbrough, and Woodsome Hall Golf Club; some other owners wish not to be named. Where access was not possible, the description appears in brackets. Information derived solely from the List description is indicated NHLE.

Thanks are due to those who sent comments and corrections to the second edition, some many decades ago; among them Harry Battye, John Bird, the late Michael Brooke and John Martin Robinson deserve special mention.

Many people have kindly provided information, shared their own researches, answered queries or helped with expert comment. Christopher Marsden, David Griffiths and Hilary Haigh shared their deep knowledge of Huddersfield and its buildings; Diana Terry, Anthony Littlewood and Mike Buckley similarly helped with Saddleworth. I would like to thank: Wendy and Barrie Armstrong, Julie Banham, Brian Barber (Doncaster), Leonard Bartle, Valerie Bayliss, Sue Behrens and the NADFAS Church Recording Groups, Clyde Binfield, Geoff Brandwood, Michael Breen, Alan Brooke (for his research on Huddersfield mills), Paul Buckland, the Rev. Edward Bundock (Sir Charles Nicholson), David Cant of the Yorkshire Vernacular Buildings Study Group, Richard Carr-Archer, Roger Carr-Whitworth, Gillian Cookson, Alison Cotterill, Lyn Crawford (RBS Archives), Peter Draper, Robert Drake, Patrick Eyres, Patrick Farman (church brasses), Geoffrey Fisher (C17–C18 church monuments; his attributions are indicated (GF) in the gazetteer), Ron Fitzgerald (Dean Clough), Colum Giles, Vera Grand, Judy and Graham Hague, Michael Hall (Bodley), Chris Hammond, Graham Hardy, Roger Harper, Stuart Hartley, Elain Harwood, Richard Hewlings, Mark

Hide (Dean Clough), Mike Higginbottom, David Hill, Julian Holder, the late Derek Holland, Edward Holland, Peter Howell, Mel and Joan Jones, Michael Kerney (stained glass), Anne Kirker, Gill MacGregor, Andrew Martindale, Christoph von Mickwitz, Diana Monahan, James Mortlock (HSBC archives), the late Jean Moulson, the late Tony Munford (Rotherham), Tony Murphy, Arnold Pacey (especially vernacular buildings and panelled church ceilings), the Pennine Horizons Digital Archive volunteers at Hebden Bridge, Sue and Ken Powell, Arthur Quarmby, the Rev. Mary Railton-Crowder, Tony Rigby, Alice Rodgers, Peter Ryder, Andrew Shepherd, the late Tanya Schmoller, Pete Smith, Michael Swift (stained glass), the late Kate Taylor, Sylvia Thomas, Robert Thorne, Chris Wakeling, Paul Walker (Roman Catholic churches), Malcolm Warburton, Andrea Waterhouse (Barclays Group Archives), Chris Webb, Christopher Webster (William Wallen), Josephine Wesley and the late Tom Wesley, Andrew Whitham, Rita Wood (Romanesque Sculpture), Malcolm Woodcock and Mary Wragg. I ask others who are not named individually to forgive me for their omission.

The printed and written sources of information necessary for research about the area are spread across a large number of local studies and reference libraries and archive offices and I am very grateful for assistance in using them from staff at: Barnsley Archives and Local Studies, Batley Library, Dewsbury Library, Doncaster Archives and Doncaster Local Studies Library, Goole Library, Halifax Library, Huddersfield Library, the University Archives at Huddersfield, Leeds City Library, the Henry Moore Institute Library at Leeds, Pontefract Library, Rotherham Library and Archives, Selby Library, Sheffield Reference and Local Studies Libraries, Sheffield Archives, the Adsetts Centre at Sheffield Hallam University, Western Bank Library at Sheffield University, Wakefield Library, York City Library, York Minster Library, the King's Manor and J. B. Morrell Libraries, and the Borthwick Institute at the University of York, and the West Yorkshire Archive Service offices for Calderdale, Kirklees, Leeds and Wakefield. I was also helped by Jason Dodds at the West Yorkshire Historic Environment Record.

Most of my travelling was by public transport but for visiting less accessible places I relied on an intrepid band of friends who drove me about. I am very grateful to Brian and Rosemary Barber, Pauline Ford, Shirley Foster, Roger Harper, Eleanor Magilton, Eileen Marshall, Judith Phillips and Jude Warrender for their good company, enthusiasm and willingness to cope with steep hills, tight corners and dead ends.

The staff at Yale University Press have been a pleasure to work with; their consummate professionalism is matched by their patience, good humour, tolerance and kindness. My greatest thanks are to Charles O'Brien, as editor, for his inexhaustible patience, support and encouragement; his especial help in getting me to the finishing linc included assistance in preparing sections of the introduction. The commissioning editor was Sally Salvesen, the production editor was Linda McQueen, the picture researcher

Elizabeth O'Rafferty, the copy-editor Hester Higton, proofreader Charlotte Chapman and indexer Judith Wardman. The maps and plans have been prepared by Martin Brown. Most of the photographs were taken by Alun Bull and Andrew Caveney.

It has been a great privilege to undertake this revision and I have done my very best to do justice to this wonderfully rich and varied, but often misunderstood, part of the great county that is Yorkshire. It has been a much longer and more demanding task than I ever anticipated and I could not have completed it without the support and care of my family and my much-neglected friends; to all of them I give my heartfelt thanks. I look forward to seeing more of them and the wider world now my days of 'Pevsner purdah' are ended.

As always, the authors and publishers will be glad to receive notice of errors.

Ruth Harman
June 2017

INTRODUCTION

The southern part of the West Riding is not for the faint-hearted. In the first place it is very big. Until its abolition in the local government reorganization of 1974 the whole county was the largest in area of all the English counties, equal to Gloucestershire, Worcestershire and Herefordshire, or Leicestershire, Northamptonshire and Nottinghamshire, put together. Our part is still vast, stretching some sixty miles across, from Todmorden on the border with Lancashire in the west to the eastern extremity where the River Humber begins, and forty miles from Bishopthorpe on the outskirts of York in the north down to the Derbyshire border south of Sheffield. Secondly, it is one of the most varied of areas covered in one volume in this series, and the diversity and contrasts of both its landscape and its buildings are exhilarating and overwhelming by turns.

Much of the area has great natural beauty, a quality that is too often forgotten when the perception of the area as urban and industrial predominates. Its landscape ranges from the Pennine moors of Millstone Grit and the deep-cut valleys on the west side to the limestone lowlands down the east side and the marshlands beyond. Flowing from the hills are the area's great arteries, in the north the River Calder, with its major tributaries of the Colne and Holme, which joins the Aire towards the east; in the south the Don, later joined by the Dearne, which crosses the middle. The River Ouse forms the area's NE boundary and takes the waters of the Aire and Don eastward from Goole to its eastern extremity where the River Humber starts. Within our part of the West Riding are not only busy and densely populated urban areas with great concentrations of buildings, including the two cities of Wakefield and Sheffield and the large towns of Barnsley, Dewsbury, Doncaster, Halifax, Huddersfield and Rotherham, but also the tranquil countryside and villages of the east side and the scattered settlements and the vast and sometimes bleak grandeur of the moorlands of the west.

The medieval pattern of SETTLEMENTS shows much greater population on the lower eastern side than in the less hospitable and accessible uplands. Of the towns Doncaster has a link with the Roman town, and Conisbrough, Pontefract, Sheffield and Tickhill have Anglo-Saxon origins, their status reinforced after 1066 by their great Norman castles. Far to the west the de Lacys' efforts to develop a town beside their castle at Almondbury were notably unsuccessful and on this side population growth came

later, with expansion of the textile industry. In the C16 to C18
handloom weaving alongside agriculture was the mainstay of the
scattered but populous settlements on the hills and high plateaux,
linked by ancient packhorse routes to markets in Halifax and
Huddersfield and to Wakefield further east. The introduction of
steam power and mechanization from the late C18 and the development of canals and railways saw the expansion of existing
industrial centres such as Sheffield and Rotherham, and the
development of towns like Batley, Dewsbury and Huddersfield,
as well as the movement of the west upland population to the
valley bottoms and the transformation of villages like Hebden
Bridge, Slaithwaite and Todmorden into towns. In the C19 too,
coal mining brought expansion of towns such as Barnsley, Normanton and Wath-upon-Dearne, while the development of deep
mining technology in the early C20 saw new settlements much
further east, as at Maltby and Rossington. Today the population
of the area is nearly 2,400,000, which is not far off half the population of the whole of Yorkshire, so the range and quantity of
buildings to see is enormous, and only seaside architecture is
79, 2   absent, though there is a port (Goole), a lighthouse (Whitgift)
and a promenade (Halifax). Most will associate the area with C19
and C20 architecture, especially town halls and other civic buildings, churches and chapels, industrial buildings, model and social
housing, and structures by skilled engineers. These make it easy
to forget that much of the area was prosperous and populous for
centuries beforehand, and it is still surprisingly rich in medieval
churches, country houses and vernacular buildings.

With all this goes the third hallmark of the area: that is, the
relentless pace of change that especially characterizes the last
two centuries, and continues today. From the late C18, manufacturing industries and coal mining and the population and

Goole, docks.
Engraving by J. Rogers after N. Whittock, c.1830

infrastructure that supported them transformed large parts of it; more recently, many of those industries have declined or changed or, like coal mining, effectively vanished. Kellingley Colliery, the last deep mine in Yorkshire, closed in 2015, and one of the greatest differences between the county that Pevsner saw in the 1950s, when the Yorkshire coalfield had over a hundred working pits, and the area now is the disappearance of the mines and the reclamation of their sites and great waste tips as farmland, landscaped country parks or new industrial, business or distribution centres. With the inventiveness, resourcefulness and busyness of the area and the decline, renewal and reinvention of some parts inevitably comes some messiness and degradation, and sometimes one cannot avoid coming face-to-face with the blood and guts of the industrial revolution and its post-industrial aftermath. On this account the area is too often dismissed or disparaged and it is hardly noticed by most tourist guide books. Yet that is part of its robust character too, and, for those with open minds prepared to take it warts and all, the rewards are great.

GEOLOGY AND BUILDING STONES

The rocks of the West Riding as a whole spread in age across a vast length of time – from the Ordovician and Silurian of the north-west underlying Sedbergh to the Permo-Triassic under York itself – perhaps four hundred million years. To demonstrate the bulk arrangement of the various rock formations it is useful to imagine them as a low pile of rugs or carpets, of diverse size, thickness and texture, lying upon a hard floor; and the whole assemblage tilted over to one side – which is the east – with the upper units displaced to the east as well. In places some of the carpets have been wrinkled up and worn away, so that the lower ones, and the floor below, can be seen through the holes. Finally, to complete the model, a great cut or fracture (a 'fault' to the geologist) has been made from west to east halfway across the pile in the north, and the 'loose' northern part raised relative to the rest. The geological labels attached to these imaginary carpets are the names of the individual rock units or formations, listed here in order of age from the youngest at the top down to the old 'floor': Triassic: New Red Sandstone; Permian: Magnesian Limestone; Carboniferous: Coal Measures, Millstone Grit and Limestone; Silurian, Ordovician and Pre-Cambrian: rocks of the floor almost completely covered by the others.

The geology of the northern half of the West Riding is discussed in *Yorkshire West Riding: Leeds, Bradford and the North*. The geology of the southern area described in this volume is a little simpler, omitting entirely the Carboniferous Limestone which defines the scenery of the Dales and beginning instead with the sandstone rocks of the CARBONIFEROUS era. These were formed between 360 and 308 million years ago, when the landscape was

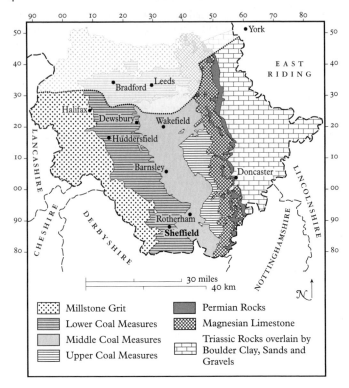

Simplified geological map of Yorkshire West Riding South

dominated by swamps and river deltas in which layers of sediment were deposited, a process which imparts considerable variation in the composition and thickness of the resulting stones. Here the oldest rock is the MILLSTONE GRIT, architecturally the most important, and topographically the most characteristic of all the West Riding rocks. This tough, massive, pebbly sandstone forms the real backbone of England here – the high, furrowed upland running down from Great Whernside and Hebden Moor above Grassington, to Embsay Moor, Rombalds Moor and Blackstone Edge, where it separates the great coalfields of Lancashire and Yorkshire, and separated also the cotton towns on the western Pennine slope from the woollen towns on the east.

Although it is a tough and often coarse stone to work, Millstone Grit has been used from the earliest times. Its qualities were recognized by the Romans, who quarried it at Thorner, NE of Leeds, for building in York. It was essential for large structures, notably in the long bridges across the main rivers, all liable to sudden flood, that cross the West Riding from the Pennine watershed eastwards to the sea. Many great castles (including Sandal and Pontefract) and churches were built of it, and even in the East Riding and Lincolnshire it was brought in for

p. 432

pre-Norman buildings. The gritstone country supports little but a sparse agriculture. Much of it is bare open moor with black furrowed crags and hollows, or 'slacks', where in winter the wind and rain go 'wuthering', eddying and howling – 'a waste of black, ill looking desolate Moors, over which Travellers are guided, like Racehorses, by Posts set up for fear of Bogs and Holes'.

Despite its widespread use, Millstone Grit is far from uniform in appearance with some variation across a spectrum from pale to dark shades of buff colours. They also often have a sparkly character imparted by the presence of mica and quartz grains. For construction the thickly bedded gritstone has been chosen, as this can also be carved or cut into ashlar. Alternatively, where cross-bedding has occurred, the rocks have thin layers than can be split into flagstones ideally suited for flooring or paving. Good sources of such stone include the East Carlton Grit quarried at Midgley near Mytholmroyd. As elsewhere in the West Riding the use of Millstone Grit in the medieval period was restricted to the locality of outcrops; so, for example, the church of St James, Bradfield, is built of the so-called 'Chatsworth Grit', a hard, coarse stone which outcrops in places from High Bradfield s as far as the border with Derbyshire and which was quarried in the Rivelin valley. This stone has few lines of weakness and could be worked in any direction as freestone. The exhaustion of supplies of timber for building by the end of the C16 greatly expanded the role for Millstone Grit as the principal building material for the spread of domestic buildings in the Pennine zone in the C17. In the area around Hebden Bridge, Mytholmroyd, Ripponden, Rishworth and Todmorden there is extensive use of the coarse-grained rocks from the Kinder Scout Grit group which outcrop on the w side of West Riding. Their character made them less useful for high-quality building work, but a finer-grained variety is that used for Sheffield Town Hall. It was the C19 expansion of the towns on the Millstone Grit which brought extensive quarrying of this stone.

From a higher layer in the Millstone Grit derives the Huddersfield White Rock, much used in the town and quarried still at Hillhouse Edge near Holmfirth. The most desirable stone was the Rough Rock in the upper strata of the Millstone Grit which is extremely thickly bedded, medium-grained and heavily cemented by quartz, resulting in stone of immense strength that could be cut into large blocks. In the northern area of the West Riding this is particularly well known by the name of Bramley Fall Stone (from the quarry of that name) but it is the same rock quarried elsewhere which provides much of the stone for buildings at Sowerby, Holmfirth, Langsett and other places. In the southern part of the West Riding there were especially important quarries for Rough Rock near Huddersfield at Crosland Hill (still active and the source for the material of, among other buildings, the Victoria Tower on Castle Hill, Almondbury).

A much larger area of the southern West Riding is covered by the COAL MEASURES, where the South Yorkshire coalfield is a damped-down or finer-grained version of the Millstone Grit country, with the same alternation of ridge and hollow and flat

moor: the two regions grade into each other, and the rocks are
often difficult to distinguish. All this country, whether true moorland or industrial spread, stands fairly high. As a geological unit,
it is grey shale and mudstone with bands of yellow, buff and grey
sandstone similar in colour and strength to the Millstone Grit
but finer in character. Many of these sandstones stand up in the
landscape as 'edges' or ridges in the Lower Coal Measure Formation, which runs N–S through our area from the S edge of Bradford, E of Halifax, through the E half of Kirklees, the W half of
Barnsley district and almost the whole of Sheffield district. The
lowest stratum is the Crawshaw Sandstone, which was quarried
on the W edge of Sheffield and which has a medium grain and
buff colour much used in the villas and public buildings of the
burgeoning C19 city. Lower Coal Measures sandstone from quarries at Spinkwell (now disused) provided the finely grained
walling for Wakefield Town Hall and the still active quarries at
Bolton Wood, Bradford, are now the best source. More often,
however, the Lower Coal Measures sandstones were employed
for rough walling and kerbstones, and the thinly bedded stones
were especially suitable for paving and roofing. Best known are
the Elland Flags, taking their name from Elland Edge near Brighouse, where the sandstone horizons were mined deep underground, but now a term more widely applied to sandstones
from across the West Riding. These flags are known to have
been quarried from the C12 but were at the height of popularity
from the late C19, when they were much used in Huddersfield
and Halifax. They were also exported widely from the early
C20. Flagstone quarries remain active around Northowram,
Southowram, Hipperholme and Brighouse.

Thicker-bedded sandstones suitable for building are more
common in the Middle Coal Measures, which underlie a wide
strip of landscape from Wakefield to Rotherham. These include
Mexborough Rock, notable for the purple-red colour caused by
proximity of the bedrock to younger Permian red sandstones,
which is employed in buildings in Mexborough itself but also in
nearby villages including Darfield, Denaby, Hooton Roberts and
Ulley (where it is still worked), and which also features in Pontefract and Rotherham (one of the local names is Rotherham
Red). The Upper Coal Measures occupy a tapering stretch of
territory S from Ackworth, where the local yellow-brown sandstone is much used in the village and nearby at Nostell Priory.
Other important quarries in the S were Wickersley (which also
supplied the grindstones essential to Sheffield's cutlery industry),
Dalton and Brierley. Many of these quarries were opened as a
by-product of digging for coal but a secondary extraction was
mudstone, which was utilized for brickmaking. Many places on
the Coal Measures (e.g. Wakefield) were from the C18 onwards
predominantly places of brick houses with stone reserved only
for the churches and the more important public buildings.

East of the Coal Measures lies the strip of MAGNESIAN
LIMESTONE (Cadeby Formation) of the Permian era, comprised
of dolomitic limestone that extends as bedrock as far S as

Nottingham. This rock, almost the youngest in our pile of carpets, rarely makes bare rock surfaces or 'scars', except where it is cut by rivers, e.g. in the gorge through which the Don runs at Doncaster. It is instantly recognizable for its white, cream or light grey colour – and is fine-grained with a distinctive crystalline character. As with sandstones the Magnesian Limestone is easily worked for carved decoration. Although often exceedingly porous, it has a long history of use as a building stone, beginning in the Roman period. The great minsters of York and Ripon have large quantities of it. The abbeys of Selby and Roche and the castle at Conisbrough are the most famous instances of its medieval use in the southern West Riding but it is also the material for numerous parish churches and major c18 and c19 buildings, including Brodsworth Hall and Scott's church at Doncaster – both buildings incidentally also demonstrating the stone's weakness in the face of industrial pollution. Many big quarries in this well-bedded rock lay along the Great North Road, and from them much of the stone was taken s, not always with good results, for care has to be taken (as with most rocks) to lay the blocks on their natural bed. If laid otherwise they will soon begin to scale and flake. The quarries at North Anston were important and supplied the rebuilding of the Palace of Westminster in the 1830s – a fact also indicative of the revolution in exporting stone further afield by rail and canal. It also provided superb building stone for the Vale of York, where stone was lacking. Quarries remain active at Cadeby. As the outcrop is quite narrow it is commonplace to find villages on the border between sandstone and limestone making good use of both (e.g. Ledsham, Swillington, Darrington, etc.).

A much thinner strip of younger PERMIAN AND TRIASSIC RED SANDSTONES provides a fringe to the Magnesian Limestone, but only in very isolated places do these rocks come to the surface, so this succession has produced little building stone. It is, however, the source of blocks of stone reused at Wistow church, close to the Ouse.

Eastwards, down the dip-slope of the Magnesian Limestone, the solid fabric of the West Riding disappears below loose morainic SANDS AND GRAVELS, and thick BOULDER CLAYS of glacial origin, in the Vale of York and the Humberhead Levels. Elsewhere the solid rock has been gouged away by glaciers coming down from the Pennine dales, and later buried by debris from the melting ice. From these great spreads of unconsolidated sand and shingle comes much of the material for modern building.

ARCHAEOLOGY
BY HUMPHREY WELFARE

The remains of the archaeological past are elusive in the s of the West Riding. In contrast to the rich prehistories of the Dales to

the N, and of the Peak District to the S, there is little that catches
the eye. Arable agriculture in the E, enclosure and the robbing
of stone monuments for walls, the growth of industry and the
spread of housing in the most habitable areas of the Pennine
valleys have all combined to remove or cloak earlier landscapes.
Some earthworks have survived on hilltops (Wincobank, Sheffield), on commons (South Kirkby), or in woods and parklands
(Scholes Coppice, in the park of Wentworth Woodhouse), but
elsewhere aerial photography, geophysics, laser-scanning and the
improved reporting of finds have filled out the picture and have
shown that the area was no less densely settled than other parts
of the historic county.

Flint tools from the LOWER PALAEOLITHIC period, found
around Hatfield, Cantley and Rossington, are the first, vestigial
traces of man in the southern West Riding. More substantial
evidence was left behind as the ice-sheets retreated farther and
farther N, at the very end of the UPPER PALAEOLITHIC, c. 8000
B.C., when individuals or families took advantage of the rock-
shelters within some of the limestone gorges, such as those in
Anston Stones Wood, Anston, near the border with Nottinghamshire. The ensuing MESOLITHIC period was still a time of
hunter-gatherers, whose characteristic minute flint tools have
been found throughout the area, from the Humberhead Levels
in the E to the high watershed of the Millstone Grit around Saddleworth and Marsden. No contemporary buildings have yet
been identified here, but elsewhere in northern Britain the post-
holes of small, lightly built sub-circular shelters have occasionally
been found in excavation.

The great construction projects of prehistory began in the
NEOLITHIC, at the beginning of the fourth millennium B.C.,
hand in hand with the establishment of agriculture and of more
settled communities. A small number of long barrows, for communal burials, have been identified on the Magnesian Limestone
to the W and SW of Doncaster, near High Melton, Sprotbrough
and Edlington. For larger gatherings, of the living, a sacred landscape was established in the early third millennium B.C. beside
the Aire at Ferrybridge, now in the shadow of the cooling towers.
A henge, enclosed by a circular bank of limestone rubble with
an inner and an outer ditch, probably served as a focus for a
scattered society. Excavation revealed that the henge overlay a
Neolithic round barrow, and the henge itself attracted the construction of smaller 'hengiform' monuments, circles of timber
uprights of uncertain function, and, later, Bronze Age barrows.
(The sanctity of this place lingered long, as there is evidence that
it was also the site of a shrine in the Iron Age, more than a thou-
sand years later.)

The southern part of the West Riding was not, however, one
where circles of stone were at all common in the BRONZE AGE.
A small possible example, now beneath the waters of the reservoir
at Walshaw Dean, near Hebden Bridge, was probably for burials
rather than for communal ceremonies on a larger scale. Many
contemporary burials were placed under the cairns that still

survive on the ridges of the Pennines, but other interments were made in simple cemeteries. Examples include that on Pule Hill, close to the watershed near Marsden, where inhumations and cremations were accompanied by food vessels, and that at Blackheath Cross, Todmorden, where the cremations were deposited in collared urns, enclosed by a low annular bank.

The SETTLEMENTS of the Bronze Age have proved hard to identify but, on Castle Hill, Almondbury (a special place which attracted activity from the Neolithic period onwards), the occupation in the late Bronze Age, *c.* 1000 B.C., was probably enclosed within timber palisades. The same initial form is also likely to have been taken by the sparse scatter of smaller HILLFORTS in the area, the defences of which seem to be evidence of a more fractured society. The palisades were eventually replaced by ramparts of rubble, derived from one or more external ditches. A timber frame, such as that found in excavation at Wincobank, in Sheffield, was sometimes used to provide these ramparts with additional stability. In contrast, the main defensive wall in the upland fort of Carl Wark, near Fox House, was of turf, faced with stone. (Such an unusual combination of materials offers no indication as to its date, whether Iron Age or post-Roman.) Not all hillforts may now be readily identifiable: from evidence elsewhere it is likely that some of the later castles may have started as forts in later prehistory; the defended knoll at Conisbrough might be an example of this. Down in the lowlands, at Sutton Common, near Askern, aerial photographs and excavation revealed a very unusual and short-lived 'marsh fort': two large IRON AGE enclosures, dated to the C4 B.C., and joined by a causeway. Within complex multivallate defences, the larger of the enclosures was found to contain about 150 densely packed structures, each supported on four stout posts, normally interpreted as granaries. Eventually, however, the site seems to have changed its function from a defended communal grain store to an undefended cemetery, underlining how close ritual significance could be to the core of everyday life.

Another glimpse of an aspect of Iron Age economic activity is provided by the industrial landscapes that still survive from the making of small hand-mill stones (querns), utilizing the outcrops of Millstone Grit at Wharncliffe Crags and at Rivelin on the western outskirts of Sheffield. Production seems to have continued intermittently from prehistory into the Middle Ages. An almost equally wide span may also be reflected in the construction and use of the great DYKES that dissect the countryside: for instance, the Bar Dyke, above Bradfield, and the so-called 'Roman Ridge' or 'Rig' – discontinuous stretches of bank with a ditch on the SE side – that extend along the N side of the Don valley from the environs of Wincobank, in Sheffield, to Kimberworth, Swinton, Greasborough, Thorpe Hesley, Wentworth and Mexborough. These major projects in early engineering are still little understood. They were probably lines of defence rather than boundaries, but whether they were thrown up against the Roman invaders, or against the Saxons, or both, is unknown.

By the late Iron Age, the landscape on the Magnesian Lime-stones, and on the Humberhead Levels between York and Don-caster, was characterized by small FARMSTEADS with round timber houses that would have had conical thatched roofs, walls of wattle-and-daub, and a central hearth. These houses often stood within small enclosures in the corners of much larger fields, the layout of which was increasingly systematic and regular: the so-called 'brickwork fields', the buried ditches of which have been identified on aerial photographs.

In the mid 50s A.D., only about a decade after the ROMAN INVASION on the south coast, the army had advanced as far N as the valley of the Don. At Templeborough, on the western outskirts of Rotherham, a fort was built to guard the river cross-ing. (The site was largely destroyed by the steel works in the C20 but some fragments of a granary were re-erected in Rotherham's Clifton Park.) With successive refurbishments it continued in occupation – probably intermittently – until the C3. To the NE, the great fortress at York was founded in about A.D. 71, establish-ing its pre-eminence in the later history of the region, a status that lasted until the C19. The area that became the West Riding was part of its Roman hinterland: first in a military context and then in a political and social one. Inevitably, some aspects of the early military history of the Roman period are clearer than others, so much having been revealed by the serendipity of excavations in advance of modern development. Thus a second large fortress, identified on air photographs at Rossington, SE of Doncaster, may also have been established in the C1, but little is yet known about it, whereas nearby, at the highest point to which the River Don was navigable, it is evident that a succession of forts was built, beginning in A.D. 71. Doncaster Minster now stands on the site. A large civilian settlement grew up on the S side of this fort, and occupation continued into the late C4, to be succeeded by the Anglo-Saxon *burh* and the medieval town. This pattern was probably repeated elsewhere. On the S bank of the Aire, just below its confluence with the Calder, the first fort at Castleford was also constructed, in the early 70s. It was given up a genera-tion later, but the associated civilian settlement continued. Most of the buildings in these extra-mural settlements were con-structed in timber, set in narrow plots, gable-on to the street, but at Castleford there were some more substantial stone buildings also.

These two centres, *Danum* and *Lagentium*, were at significant points on what became the main ROMAN ROAD to the far N – probably following the line of the initial invasion – that led from Lincoln to York, via Tadcaster and on to Catterick and (subse-quently) to Hadrian's Wall. This road survives as the Roman Ridge, just to the N of Cusworth, and as the A1, A639 and A656, through Barnsdale Bar, Pontefract, Castleford, and on to Aber-ford in the northern West Riding. Another major Roman road crossed the Pennines from Manchester to York and was policed from forts at Castleshaw, near Delph on the W flank of the hills to the SW of Marsden, and at Slack. At the site of the latter fort, now beside the M62 1¼ m. s of Stainland, there is now nothing to be seen. Occupied from about 80 to 140, it had a large civil settlement which lasted into the C4 but which was vulnerable enough to require defences. At Castleshaw, however, the earthworks of two distinct sites, a fort (active in the 80s) and a smaller, early C2 fortlet, have been excavated and displayed. The external settlement here was small, and did not thrive after the soldiers marched away.

In the lowlands of the Roman countryside the indigenous population continued to live in small communities of round houses within an enclosed agricultural landscape; however, some buildings were now rectangular in plan and were constructed of stone. In some cases these developed into simple examples of the characteristic VILLA, although few examples of the better-quality buildings have yet been found in the West Riding. A villa at Conisbrough is known to have had a set of baths, and the owners of another at Kirkby Wharfe, near Tadcaster, had sufficient means to afford a tessellated pavement. In the C3 a villa at Drax, on the site of the power station, had five rooms, with painted plaster walls, behind a veranda that opened on to a cobbled courtyard. Here, as at so many places, there is evidence of economic decline in the late C4, but elsewhere settlements seem to have survived into the Anglo-Saxon period and beyond.

THE MIDDLE AGES

Anglo-Saxon architecture and sculpture

ANGLO-SAXON relics are abundant in the West Riding, more numerous as carved crosses than as works of architecture. As a building the earliest and most important work that survives is at Ledsham. The date is probably *c.* 700 and it comprises the nave and chancel arch, the w porch later raised as the tower, and the s *porticus* remodelled as a porch. At Monk Fryston there is an Anglo-Saxon w tower, and at Laughton-en-le-Morthen the N doorway. Conisbrough has fabric from a large church possibly as early as Ledsham, and Burghwallis and Owston have distinctive herringbone masonry that is Anglo-Saxon or Saxo-Norman Overlap, i.e. Anglo-Saxon workmanship after the Conquest. Other churches that have features identified as Anglo-Saxon or Overlap, usually quoins and other masonry, are Bolton-upon-Dearne, Brodsworth, Dewsbury, Hooton Pagnell and Maltby. At Pontefract the foundations of very small church associated with C7 or C8 burials have been revealed close to All Saints. From the other end of the period two large carved Overlap FONTS, at Cawthorne and at Skelmanthorpe, must also be mentioned here.

At least twenty-eight sites with sculpted stones have been identified. These are mostly from free-standing crosses, sometimes from grave-slabs; three are cross bases. None of them is earlier than the C8. The earliest on the whole are the most interesting:

the Dewsbury Cross, of the late C8 or early C9, had a round
shaft and good figures. Of late work is the noteworthy group of
three rare surviving bases from the C11, with clear, crisp foliage
scrolls (Hartshead, Birstall, Rastrick), the Hartshead one perhaps
in its original location. The purpose of Anglo-Saxon crosses was
not always the same: some seem to have marked a sacred site
but most were probably private memorials erected in memory
of individuals, as the four at Thornhill with inscriptions show.

Norman parish churches and monastic foundations

The Norman Conquest was a disaster for the North, and building activity did not generally start again much before the end of
the C11. The Overlap herringbone masonry at Burghwallis and
Owston has been mentioned; that at Felkirk goes with the surviving stonework from an early Norman church of *c.* 1100, which
had, probably in its chancel arch, the fine decorated capitals later
reused in the tower arch. The most rewarding work occurs in the
E half of our area, where the most complete parish church is the
small church at Birkin, between Selby and Pontefract. Probably
of *c.* 1160, it has a rare rib-vaulted apse – the only Norman apse
in the whole West Riding – and also a W tower. The chancel arch
at Birkin is sumptuously decorated; other chancel arches include
those at Brayton, Hickleton and Hooton Pagnell and also those
at Edlington, Frickley and Rossington, which are curious for their
responds starting several feet above the ground, indicating the
existence of screens. The S doorway of Birkin is most sumptuous
too, and to this must be added the exceptional doorway at Fishlake. A little way behind come Brayton, Edlington and Thorpe
Salvin. Brayton and Fishlake are distinguished by their rare figurative decoration; Edlington is unusual in its continuous decoration uninterrupted by imposts. The usual decorative elements are
beakhead, chevron (on the wall surface and also at right angles
to it) and a few other geometrical motifs. Figured tympana are
rare too: lamb and lion at Emley, lamb and cross at Woolley, a
dragon at Austerfield, chequer-patterned at Wales, and with hap-
hazard rosettes etc. at Braithwell.

Norman W towers are quite frequent, the best those at Brayton
and Campsall. Piers, where there are aisles, are usually circular,
though the octagon also occurs. Most surviving arcades are Late
Norman to Transitional; indeed, the general impression one gets
in the absence of usable dates is that a large percentage of what
was done in the C12 in the area belongs to its second half. The
excellent arcades at Sherburn-in-Elmet are notable for the varied
decoration of their many-scalloped capitals and their hoodmoulds. At Conisbrough the later C12 arcades have very varied
capitals, one especially elaborate, and although the N arches are
round and the S ones pointed they cannot be very far apart in
date. The transition from the round to the pointed arch is surprisingly indistinct in the parish churches, and cannot be used for
the purpose of dating. Wadworth, a Late Norman aisled church,

illustrates this in its arcades and the tower arches into the aisles. Its other notable feature is the blank arcading, with round arches, in the porch and on the S aisle wall.

In the W side of the area, where churches were fewer and subjected to much greater rebuilding, only Elland (with its round chancel arch with beakhead reworked into a pointed one) and Hartshead (with reused chancel arch and S doorway) need mention.

MONASTIC ESTABLISHMENTS had of course existed in the North from an early date. One need only remember Holy Island (Lindisfarne) and Monkwearmouth and Jarrow. In the West Riding the earliest foundation of which buildings or parts of buildings remain is at the same time one of the grandest: the Benedictine monastery of Selby. This was founded c. 1070; in turn the priory at Snaith was founded from Selby c. 1100. The Benedictine priory at Ecclesfield, however, was a cell of the Abbey of St Wandrille, France, founded in the early C12; only the chapel of c. 1300 survives. Monk Bretton turned Benedictine in 1281 but had been founded c. 1154 as a CLUNIAC establishment. Cluniac too was the priory of Pontefract (c. 1090). The AUGUSTINIAN Canons were at Nostell (founded in the early C12) and Drax (1130s) but of these there are no remains except a barn at Nostell. The Templars had a preceptory at Temple Hirst, of which a few fragments remain, and another at Copmanthorpe, of which nothing survives. The Templars held the church at Kellington before suppression and it then passed to the Knights Hospitallers, who were at Newland near Normanton, but there too nothing of their buildings survive. Finally, as regards the mendicant orders, the Dominicans went to Pontefract in 1256, the Carmelites to the same town c. 1257, the Austin Friars to Tickhill c. 1260, the Franciscans to Doncaster before 1284, and the Carmelites to Doncaster in 1350.

In terms of MONASTIC CHURCHES associated with these foundations, the evidence is fairly slender except, as in the rest of the West Riding, for the Cistercians. The first Cistercian house in England was at Waverley (Surrey), founded c. 1128, but the first settlement by the order in the north of England was at Rievaulx, founded 1132 in the remote landscape of the North Riding, followed by Fountains (1137) in the northern half of the West Riding. Both typify the order's adoption of sites well away from external interference. The southern area of the West Riding did not offer the choice of secluded valleys provided by the Dales, so the surviving Cistercian buildings cannot compare in wealth and the more modest scale of Roche Abbey, which is placed in the valley of Maltby, is one more typical of the generality of Cistercian houses. The house was founded in 1147 by monks from Newminster, Northumberland (itself a foundation from Fountains). Cistercian nunneries existed in exceptional numbers: Kirklees (c. 1155), Nun Appleton (Appleton Roebuck, c. 1150) and Hampole (1170).

The plan of Roche is unusually well preserved and shows that it followed the type of its Yorkshire predecessors, which had been

p. 447

adopted from the order's second church at Clairvaux (begun in
1135), of an unaisled straight-ended chancel, transepts with
straight-ended E chapels separated by solid walls, and an aisled
nave. It is also, incidentally, the plan adopted by the Cluniac
order for the priory church at Monk Bretton in the late C12.

The structural innovations of the Cistercian order – in particular the introduction of pointed arches and pointed
vaults – derived from the Burgundian churches, where the
earliest surviving Cistercian abbey is Fontenay (1139–47). These
features appear at Fountains and subsequently Kirkstall
(*West Riding North*, 1152), where the more elaborate forms of
nave arcade piers combined with ribbed vaults are early instances
of devices also being developed from Anglo-Norman tradition
(notably Durham). The principal building campaign at Roche – to
which the largely surviving transepts remain – is believed
to have begun *c.* 1170, nearly twenty years after Kirkstall, and
represents the next stage for, although something of the traditional Cistercian austerity remains, the dependence on early
Gothic buildings in the north of France is undeniable in the
design. This is one of the earliest appearances of Gothic in the
north of England and roughly contemporary with Byland (*North
Riding*) and Ripon (*West Riding North*), so it is also necessary to
take account of the intercommunication of architectural ideas
between the establishments spread across Yorkshire and other
parts of the North. The introduction of the triforium is specially
characteristic, as are also the vaulting shafts rising from the
ground to carry transverse arches and ribs. Some of the shafts at
Roche are keeled, and that also is a French feature, appearing
there as early as *c.* 1130–50.

Excluded from this account of developments in the Cistercian
houses is the only other evidence of a great church: the Premonstratensian abbey of Beauchief, a fairly modest foundation now
recast as parish church for one of the outer suburbs of Sheffield,
which was begun in the 1170s or '80s. It consisted of a long
aisleless nave, transepts (the S one with two E chapels) and a
straight-ended chancel – i.e. broadly similar to Cistercian prac-
tise – but it also included a W tower.

In the employment of both round arches and pointed ones
in the transepts at Roche and other minor details (waterleaf
capitals, nailhead etc.) can be discerned the transitional style
from Norman to Early English. This change in style can also
be followed at Selby Abbey, where the first phases of building
works of the early C12 are Romanesque of the Durham style but
with the commencement of the major part of the nave *c.* 1170
the transition to Early English is made. Indeed on the W front
Late Norman and creative E.E. appear side by side, or rather
one above the other. Inside the story can be followed in detail,
and in the nave elevations there is a remarkable inconsistency
of treatment from one side to the other. Here also is evidence
of the changes taking place in pier forms away from standard
columns in Norman architecture towards ones of more complex

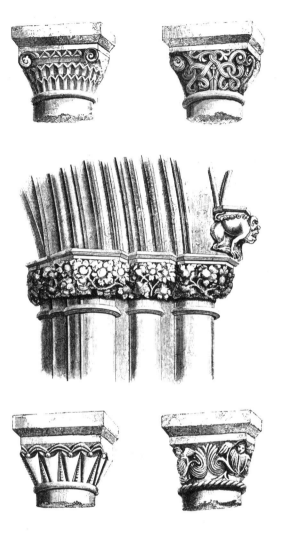

Selby Abbey, nave and choir capitals.
Engravings by O. Jewitt after J. A. Morrell, 1867

section and profile by the end of the C12. The lower parts of
the nave have the classic early C12 practice of alternation of
columns between bays, mostly of circular or composite form,
but then appears a compound form of pier with four major and
four minor shafts (there is a similar arrangement at Ripon, but
with keeled major shafts). But on the nave gallery at Selby there
is a charming arrangement with detached shafts round a core.   15

This was done yet earlier, probably *c*. 1180–90, in the chapter house at Kirkstall – on the strength no doubt of the crypt at York of *c*. 1170 – and in a simplified form in the parish church of Dewsbury.

p. 447   For the continuation of this story it is more profitable to look to the parish churches of the C13 and C14 (for which see below) and here conclude instead with the other MONASTIC BUILD-INGS. Only at Roche Abbey and Monk Bretton Priory are there substantial surviving remains. Except for the gatehouse, those at Roche stand to no great height, but they do give a very clear and almost complete plan of a smaller Cistercian establishment of the late C12, little altered after 1300. What one admires is the orderli-ness of the standard plan, one of course derived without break from the original plan of the Benedictine order. The plan for St Gall of *c*. 835 already has the clear axiality and logical distribution of ranges which we find at Roche. The arrangement is familiar, with its cloister, with chapter house and parlour in the E range, dormitory over the whole E range, refectory in the S range (one of the earliest in this new position), warming room and kitchen adjoining it, and premises for the lay brothers and storerooms in the W range. The abbot's or prior's lodging, which in other orders was usually in this vicinity, was transferred to a place to the SE of the cloister ranges. The apparently universal custom of breaking the axiality of the cloister ranges not only for the abbot's quarters but also for all the other appendages not so immediately connected with the church – that is, the reredorter or monks' lavatory, the whole group of the infirmary, the lay brothers' infir-mary to the SW of the W range, and the gatehouse – is followed. The gatehouse is significant as an early surviving example, with its separate archways to the inner and outer courts. Also at Roche the stream – the essential water supply, not only for cooking and washing, but also reversely for drainage – can be clearly followed, with the little tributary stream that served the abbot's buildings.

More still stands at Monk Bretton Priory, which follows essen-tially the same plan although the prior's lodgings are on the W. Much rebuilt in the mid C14 and extended in the C15, they, and the mainly C15 gatehouse, are especially impressive. Also of par-ticular interest are the exceptional formerly tunnel-vaulted chapter house and the well-preserved system of ashlar-lined drains.

Of the other religious houses listed earlier there are traces of their domestic and other associated buildings at only five: at Beauchief there is no more than an indication of the cloister and chapter house; at Kirklees Priory (Kirklees Park) the nunnery's early C16 timber-framed gatehouse remains near the home farm complex, which includes a C15 barn; at Nostell Priory part of the outer court ranges, probably from *c*. 1500, became farm build-ings; at Temple Hirst there is a reused Norman doorway from the Templars' preceptory; at Tickhill a fine late C15 two-bay arcade and other architectural features survive in a later house, but their place in the original friary buildings is unclear.

Parish churches, C13 and C14

For EARLY ENGLISH work, a delightful system of tall, slender arcading with continuous shafting which comprises the lancet windows was used in the chapel that Archbishop Grey built at his newly acquired palace at Bishopthorpe shortly after 1241. Another domestic chapel of the C13 is preserved at Ecclesfield, which has a window with three stepped lancet lights under an arch, a form of bar tracery typical of the late C13. E.E. piers exist in a variety of forms. The compound form of pier encountered in the nave at Selby has been referred to and the gallery pier with detached shafts round a core is also seen in a simplified form in the parish church of Dewsbury, where the N arcade piers have a circular core with four detached shafts. Adlingfleet is essentially 18 E.E. (under Lincoln rather than York influence) and has shafted piers with ring shafts; the C13 work at Arksey includes the altered crossing piers with attached shafts. At Cawood the S arcade has quatrefoil piers that have a new Gothic slenderness. The same applies often to the normal circular and octagonal piers taken over from the Norman style. With the tall circular piers of its arcades, an interior such as Darrington has in all simplicity a resilient erectness typical of the E.E. style. Tickhill has fine early C13 work in the lower part of the W tower: see the W doorway and also the deeply moulded arch to the nave with some keeling and filleting to the shafted responds.

For churches of the DECORATED STYLE – that is, the period from *c.* 1300 into the second half of the C14 – by far the most important monument is the choir of Selby Abbey. There are no 19, 23 complete Dec churches, so the Bridge Chapel at Wakefield of 20 *c.* 1350 must come first. Nearly complete are Anston and Barnby Dun; at Tankersley the chancel, at Thorpe Salvin the chancel and the N chapel, and at Wadworth the S chapel, are Dec. Special praise is due to the lofty and airy chancel of Fishlake, rebuilt after 1351, spatially among the finest effects of its century in the West Riding.

Window decoration can be followed from late Geometrical to the full freedom of flowing TRACERY, the grandest window of mature Dec design being the E window of Selby. The E windows at Anston, Fishlake and Hemsworth have excellent flowing tracery, but unfortunately we can only guess at the W window of Beauchief, Sheffield, which is deprived of its early C14 tracery. However, flowing tracery was not really popular in a county not much devoted to fantasy and the most usual form is reticulation, e.g. the E windows at Tankersley, and Hemsworth's S chapel. The same development from the moment when Geometrical tracery becomes restless and capricious to the licences of ogees of all kinds appears in the E window at Owston and the crazy 22 S chapel window at Wadworth.

Motifs to which attention ought to be drawn as guidance for the dating of churches and parts of churches are the sunk quadrant mouldings of arches and certain shapes of piers. OCTAGONAL PIERS of course continue as the standard form. QUATREFOIL

PIERS are more popular than they were in the C13; there are more of them than can be listed. Occasionally (Anston, Treeton) the shafts have fillets applied. Occasionally, too, a more dramatic form appears in which the four shafts are connected by deep hollows in one long, sinuous undulation (Wakefield Cathedral, Batley, Sandal Magna etc.). Exceptional pier forms based on the square are at Campsall and Marr. Straight-headed windows, although a motif typical of the late Perp style, were already in use before 1350 in the West Riding as in other northern counties (Acaster Malbis with very slim ogee-headed lights, Ryther, Anston, etc.).

Two rare and remarkable features of this time must also be mentioned. The double-helix staircase at All Saints church, Pontefract, exactly like Leonardo da Vinci's later drawing, is a very early example whose purpose remains unclear. The reason for the small arcaded gallery above the N chapel at Darrington is equally mysterious, and it seems to be unique.

Perp parish churches

Apart from the Selby choir there is nothing spectacular in the Dec style in our area, but with the PERPENDICULAR style it is different. The C15 and early C16 were a period of great prosperity in the districts connected with wool and cloth, and a number of large and important churches went up in the principal towns. Rotherham was begun *c.*1410, Wakefield *c.*1420, Halifax *c.*1430–55; Sheffield must be added, and Doncaster, before the fire of 1853 which caused its complete replacement by *Scott*'s *chef d'œuvre*. This list ought to be supplemented by Tickhill, with a W tower mostly of *c.*1375 – an early date for the Perp style in the West Riding – and Ecclesfield and Bradfield in Hallamshire, and perhaps Wragby. Hatfield *c.*1500 received a crossing tower so proud that it might stand in Somerset. Rotherham and Sheffield also have their big towers over the crossing, as did Doncaster, whose grandeur lives on in Scott's replacement.

Specialities in towers are the corbelled-out parapets where our area approaches the S and SE of Leeds (Batley, Birstall and Ledsham), and the curious and very pretty oriel in the W front of the tower at Royston. SPIRES are not frequent, although of the thirteen that J. E. Morris counted in the whole of the West Riding, twelve are ours. Among them are such important examples as Wakefield, Rotherham and Sheffield. A few churches have towers with octagonal tops: Pontefract's was on a large scale, more beautiful than its smaller C17 replacement; Laughton-en-le-Morthen has an interesting and personal composition, below a lofty spire; this was simplified at Anston, and appears with a spire also at Brayton. All these buildings belong to the E side.

Other specialities in the West Riding are not local. First, as for whole structures, the Bridge Chapel at Wakefield was followed by one of *c.*1483 at Rotherham. The architecturally treated cave of Pontefract (1368) can only with reserve be called a structure.

26,29
p. 269

28
26

20
p. 457

Then, regarding whole parts of buildings, a group of porches with pointed tunnel-vaults (Pontefract), usually with close transverse arches (Campsall, Darrington, Featherstone, Felkirk, Kellington etc.), one porch with a vault with ribs and ridge ribs (South Kirkby), vaulted tower halls (e.g. Laughton-en-le-Morthen and, with a fan-vault, Rotherham), and a few sunk vestries at the E ends of S aisles (Silkstone, Worsbrough, Bradfield) are worthy of note.

After that, individual elements. Of Perp piers one can safely say that about 90 per cent or more are octagonal. Of other forms no more need be noted than the transversely elongated lozenges with their triplet shafts against front and back at Rotherham and the three-eighths shafts connected by hollows at Tickhill. Windows are often straight-headed; grand displays of tracery are rare. Ecclesfield, Halifax and Silkstone play a pretty game with their buttresses, detaching them from the body of the wall and connecting them by slight, quite unstructural flying buttresses. Finally, panelled ceilings: among the best are Almondbury (dated 1522), Barnburgh, Bradfield, Halifax, Kirkburton, Rotherham, Silkstone, Thornhill and Wakefield. South Kirkby has the rarity of a coved panelled canopy above the site of the rood loft.

Parish church fittings and furnishings and church monuments

Of church furnishings down to *c.* 1300 a group of stone SEDILIA with arms only and no high backs or canopies (Arksey, Burghwallis, Campsall, Owston, Sprotbrough – all near Doncaster) need to be recorded. As to WOODWORK there are some good SCREENS in churches here and there, notably at Burghwallis, Fishlake, Kirk Sandall, Rotherham and Silkstone, and, with ribbed coving, at Campsall, Ecclesfield and Hatfield. Campsall's is distinguished by its rhyming inscription in English. The dado of an unusual stone screen survives at Laughton-en-le-Morthen. A very complete parclose screen of *c.* 1482 is at Batley, others are at High Melton, Rotherham and Wakefield. Of the early FONTS the best is the late Norman one at Thorpe Salvin, with [8] lively scenes under arches. The earlier one at Whitechapel church, Cleckheaton, has cruder carving of figures and ornamental motifs under intersecting Norman arches. The only worthwhile E.E. font is at Norton in the outer suburbs of Sheffield. Its unusual nine-sided bowl has carving, including a salamander, under four low trefoiled arches. At Aston the early [24] Perp font with a delightful and mysterious little man crouching at the foot must on no account be left out, nor should the font at Throapham with carving of three faces, one an African. There are a few Perp FONT COVERS to enjoy – lacy, lofty and quite spectacularly ornate. They are at Halifax, Almondbury and Selby.

Stalls with MISERICORDS are at Wakefield, Darrington, Ecclesfield, Loversall and Sprotbrough. BENCHES and bench-ends [25] usually have blank tracery in two or three tiers – or blank tracery and a shield and square tops (Birstall, Darrington, Edlington,

Rotherham, Treeton, Wakefield). The STALLS at Ecclesfield and
Rotherham have small carved figures instead of poppyheads.
There are few distinguished PULPITS. The best is C15, at Rossington (although perhaps originally in Doncaster), and is of wood
with traceried panels and an inscription. At Hooton Pagnell the
DOOR has a little C12 ironwork. The ancient door with medieval
hinges from Burghwallis is preserved at Doncaster Museum.
Worsbrough possesses a Perp door dated 1480 with tracery and
an inscription. Finally, an unusual and attractive piece of SCULP-
TURE, the head of a C15 Janus Cross at Sherburn-in-Elmet, ought
to find a place here – a Crucifixion of the type familiar on
churchyard crosses, but carved on both sides of the slab, which
is ingeniously pierced and traceried. The quality of the figures,
however, is not high.

Of STAINED GLASS there are many fragments, some of which
have been identified as from the great workshops at York. The
best was once the C14 Jesse window at Selby, of which only a
little remains, but Dewsbury has three C14 medallions with
delightful representations of figures, and the E window at Acaster
Malbis has exquisite work of the mid C14, almost certainly from
York. At Thornhill there is a remarkable amount of C15 glass,
some of it exactly dated. That in the Savile Chapel was probably
made at York but the very different chancel E window probably
came from Flanders. Bolton Percy has a number of early C15
figures and at Elland many of the twenty-one scenes of the life
of the Virgin have York glass of c. 1481. The Rokeby Chapel at
Kirk Sandall has superb glass of c. 1521.

The most important early MONUMENTS are those at Conisbrough and Throapham. The first is mid-C12, an extremely interesting coffin-shaped coped slab with rich foliage decoration and
also figures and scenes that ought to be better known. The coped
coffin-lid at Throapham is late C13 with naturalistic leaves. At
Treeton an early effigy of a knight from the same time is unfortunately in a poor state, but the early C14 semi-effigial slab at
Hickleton, unearthed in 1983, is in pristine state.

Of the early C14 a few other monuments of superior quality
have survived: at Birkin of knights, at Anston of a man with his
small daughter and three angels. The best of the C15 and C16 are
of alabaster – that is, not of local workmanship – and some of
them belong with those in the north of the West Riding, e.g. at
Harewood. The tomb-chests at Batley, Norton (Sheffield), Ryther
and Thornhill have their statuettes of mourners or angels along
the sides of the chest. In an alabaster monument of c. 1460 at
Wentworth the husband lies in the usual style, but the wife is
bundled up in her shroud. The three figures of the 4th Earl of
Shrewsbury †1538 and his wives in Sheffield Cathedral are especially richly carved. The Fitzwilliam monument at Tickhill, commissioned in the 1520s, is of exceptional importance for its
Renaissance-style decoration, by then fashionable around the
Court but not accepted in the North until very much later.

A few unusual compositions or conceits may be mentioned in
passing: a lid on which only the head and feet of the deceased

appear, framed by quatrefoil and trefoil, at Wadworth (cf. Moor
Monkton, *West Riding North*); three tomb-chests put up or kept
in the open (Lord Dacre killed in 1461 in the battle of Towton,
at Saxton, and the others at Loversall and Woolley); and the
Marshall monument (†1505) at Fishlake, where much play is
made with the black letter of the inscription on the tomb-chest.
Materials other than stone are rare and the area has only a few
interesting BRASSES. What would probably have been the finest,
at Snaith of *c.* 1559(?), survives only in the indent, but others
include Bradfield, Burghwallis, Marr, Owston, Sprotbrough and
Wentworth. Most unusual are two effigies of knights which are
of oak, not of stone. Such oaken effigies can be seen in various
parts of the country but they are nowhere frequent. An excellent

Burghwallis, St Helen.
Brass to Thomas Gascoigne †1554

specimen is at Barnburgh (early C14). But the most remarkable
wooden monuments are at Thornhill (1529) and Worsbrough
(†1534). They are (or were) 'four-posters', and in that at Worsbrough there are two slabs one on top of the other, with a grue-
some cadaver lying on the bottom slab.

30

Medieval secular buildings

In MILITARY ARCHITECTURE it is likely that the first simple
castles – usually in the form of RINGWORKS, and sometimes
reusing earlier fortifications – were constructed before the
Norman Conquest. Thereafter, many of the characteristic
MOTTES, bearing a timber tower and probably strengthened by
palisades, were thrown up in the late C11 and C12. Some castles,
such as that on the SW end of Castle Hill, Almondbury, and the
one beside the church at Laughton-en-le-Morthen, were sited on
high points with extensive views, and these locations were probably selected to dominate, subjugate and impress. Wherever possible the earthworks of the castle were economically carved out
of a ridge and made full use of any natural defences, as at Bradfield (Castle Hill), Conisbrough, Kimberworth, Mexborough,
Sandal Magna and Tickhill. For many others, the position chosen
was simply dictated by the lord's convenience. At Bradfield
(Bailey Hill), Laughton, Mirfield and Thorne, the castle survives
next to the church that the lord probably endowed, although
which building came first in any one case may be a matter of
debate. The forms of these early castles varied: many seem to
have been no more than a simple motte, surrounded by a quarry
ditch. Others had an attendant bailey to enclose the ancillary
buildings, or, as at Hangthwaite (Adwick-le-Street) and Lowe
Hill (Thornes, Wakefield), two baileys. (The same seems to have
been true at Doncaster, where the defences of the Roman fort
were utilized.) Many of the earthwork castles went out of use
relatively early on and were never rebuilt in stone. Although a
good number of them survive relatively unscathed, those at
Mexborough, Tickhill and Lowe Hill have all suffered modifica-
tion or enhancement in later landscaping.

1

Among STONE CASTLES, Conisbrough is the outstanding
example and has one of the most impressive of all English keeps.
Its buttressed circular tower dates from the early 1180s and is a
development of the polygonal form first seen at Orford (Suffolk)
in 1165–73. It was built by Hamelin Plantagenet, Henry II's half-
brother, who obtained it through his marriage to the heiress
Isobel de Warenne. In addition to its importance in the development of military architecture it is noteworthy for the outstanding
quality of its masonry and for the well-appointed private chambers on the top two floors. These are reached by a broad stone
staircase within the wall and have fine fireplaces and a little
rib-vaulted chapel in one of the buttresses. Tickhill was a royal
castle and had an eleven-sided shell keep dated to 1179–82 by
the Pipe Rolls. Although altered the motte is still impressive, as

16

is the heavily embanked and massive wall enclosing the bailey. The late CII gatehouse has four blind gables decorated with diaper-work comparable to that in a doorway tympanum in the tower of Chepstow Castle (Gwent) dated *c.* 1081–1093. In a Duchy of Lancaster document of 1562 the castle was described as an 'ancient monument' and was therefore considered worth maintaining, surely one of the earliest examples of official recognition of the historic importance of such structures.

Although there are few standing remains at Sandal Castle, excavations in 1964–73 clearly revealed the earthworks of William de Warenne's early C12 motte and bailey castle and the unusual plan of its stone-built successor. Rebuilding began in the late C12 *p. 470* and continued during the C13. As well as a new shell keep with four towers, a barbican tower was built on a rock outcrop in the widened ditch between the bailey and the motte. Drawbridges connected it with the bailey and with a twin-towered forebuilding to the keep, making the keep unusually secure. Sandal was improved by Richard III in 1484 as a northern stronghold, but was largely demolished in 1645. The famous and once-magnificent castle of Pontefract also suffered grievously from slighting after *p. 432* the Civil War and only the lower parts of its C13 keep's three large conjoined bastions remain.

Of FORTIFIED and SEMI-FORTIFIED HOUSES the battlemented stone gatehouse built by Archbishop Kempe after 1439 at Cawood Castle is the most impressive. Decorated with heraldic carving, it has a bay window on the outer side and a pretty oriel overlooking the former inner courtyard. The adjoining SE range, called the 'Banqueting Hall', is probably coeval, but of brick. At Steeton Hall, a semi-fortified house at South Milford, there is a gatehouse of *c.* 1360 and also part of a probably slightly earlier three-storey block whose windows include three reused Dec ones with reticulated tracery. Like Steeton, the C14 gatehouse at Hooton Pagnell Hall has both carriage and pedestrian entrances, and also an original oriel window, but the castellation is late C19 restoration. Although the moat remains, there are only scanty ruins of the C15 Savile mansion at Thornhill, and there are only fragments of the C15 courtyard houses of Cranford Hall, Darfield, and Old Hall, Denaby.

An isolated UNFORTIFIED HOUSE of stone is Campsall Old Rectory of *c.* 1400, a T-plan house which has a three-bay hall of uncertain purpose on the first floor and a private chapel with a traceried three-light window. At Bishopthorpe there is the long brick-built range added by Archbishop Rotherham (1480–1500), the work identifiable, despite later alterations, by the diaper pattern in vitrified brick. Also of brick is a staircase tower of *c.* 1500 at the house built after 1337 at the former preceptory of the Knights Templar at Temple Hirst.

After Leland visited Doncaster *c.* 1540 he wrote that 'the hole toune of Doncaster is builded of wodde' and this was true of the great majority of medieval houses in our area, even where stone was readily available. It is impossible to summarize the range that occurs across such a large and varied area but the main forms of

TIMBER-FRAMED CONSTRUCTION can be identified. The use of cruck frames is predominant in the SW upland areas and continued, at least for lower-status buildings, after the Middle Ages. Very few cruck-framed houses survived later rebuilding, but Pond Farmhouse, at Stannington near Sheffield, has two bays of a medieval house with crucks, and Manor Farmhouse, Midhope has a cruck frame within C17 stone casing. At Fulwood, Sheffield, Stumperlowe Cottage is a single-storey house with attached barn, both cruck-framed. Examples of barns of the C16 or C17 are at Almondbury, at Ingbirchworth, Gunthwaite, at Linthwaite Hall, Slaithwaite, at Upper Denby, and at Darfield, a rare example on the easternmost edge of the area of cruck use. Elsewhere, post-and-truss construction was usual, but there was a distinct difference in carpentry between the 'Highland' houses of the Pennine area, where the kingpost roof truss and the use of close studding and decorative diagonal strutting was normal, and the 'Lowland' areas to the E, where the collar-rafter roof was normal. There was considerable overlap in these forms, however, especially in the S part of our region, where both cruck-frame and kingpost-truss forms are found around the Sheffield area for example, and also between highland and lowland forms. The standard medieval plan of a hall, with a parlour at one end with a solar over, and kitchen and offices at the other end is followed for gentry houses. Lees Hall, Thornhill, is a good example of the highland type from the late C15 or early C16, with a fine kingpost roof to the hall, which retains its dais canopy. Other highland houses with good timber framing are Shibden Hall near Halifax, and the Old Queen's Head, with a jettied upper floor, Bishops' House with kingpost roofs to hall and later cross-wing, and Broom Hall, all in Sheffield, and Hopton Hall, Upper Hopton. Sharlston Hall, a house of complex development in the E part of our area, has crown-post roofs in the hall of *c.* 1425 and the cross-wing of *c.* 1450 with heated parlour and solar, although the early C16 W wing extension has a kingpost roof.

Other notable timber-framed buildings are the GATEHOUSE at Bolton Percy, dated by dendrochronology to *c.* 1501, which has close studding and a jettied upper storey, and the splendid aisled BARN at Whiston, the earliest part of which has timber dated to 1204. The mid-C16 Gunthwaite barn is of comparable scale and has a kingpost roof and decorative diagonal strutting.

Finally to URBAN PLANNING, where the survival of Bawtry's layout as a planned settlement is noteworthy. Dating from before the end of the C12, the grid pattern of streets survives on each side of the broad High Street, which includes the market place. Like Bawtry, the area's principal medieval TOWNS were almost all places that had direct or relatively easy access to river transport and the E coast, and most had markets and a borough charter or some form of self-government. Chief among them were Doncaster, Pontefract, Selby and Tickhill, their populations numbering about 1,000 adult taxpayers at the time of the West Riding Poll Tax returns in 1377–81. Sheffield and Wakefield were smaller, and Barnsley and Rotherham smaller still. Halifax, disadvantaged by its poor communications, cannot be ranked as a town until the C15.

ELIZABETHAN AND SEVENTEENTH-CENTURY

Churches and chapels, and their furnishings

CHURCHES AND CHAPELS of the later C16 and the C17 are few and far between. Nothing seems to be earlier than the accession of Charles I. In the West Riding as a whole, only St John, Leeds (*West Riding North*), built in 1632–4 and entirely Gothic in its details, ranks of national importance. In Sheffield, Attercliffe Chapel, which is dated 1629, is also Gothic in its detail with mullioned-and-transomed windows. Mullioned also are still the windows of the little church at Midhopestones, rebuilt in 1705, which has its pews and tiny gallery and Jacobean pulpit. Its old-fashioned character shows the same contrast of style with the ruined nave of 1684 at Wentworth that one sees in houses in the period of transition at the end of the C17. Wentworth has a symmetrical façade with Ionic pilasters to a pedimented s doorway and other classical details. The chapel at Great Houghton, distinctively battlemented with round-topped merlons, is said to date from 1650. Its windows also still have transoms with round-arched lights, and the interior is of great interest in its Puritan arrangement of the furnishings, which include the carved pulpit and box pews. The remote Independent chapel at Bullhouse Hall, Thurlstone, is as late as 1692. Here the interior is well preserved too and the windows have arched lights below and above the transoms. A tiny cottage for the minister is attached. The small Friends' Meeting House at Warmsworth dates from 1706, and originally had cross-windows. 44

Of other ECCLESIASTICAL FURNISHINGS not included with the exteriors mentioned above, the interior of the chapel made in the C17 out of the remains of the monastic church at Beauchief, Sheffield, is especially complete. The pulpit has below it the reading desk and the clerk's pew, facing the altar table. Elsewhere there is a diverse range of screens, pulpits, font covers etc., which help to enrich the interiors of medieval churches. It is not easy to single out particular examples. The elaborately carved rood screen by *Francis Gunby* at Wakefield Cathedral, dated 1635, is of a quality equal to the work attributed to him at St John, Leeds, its rich decoration including fleur-de-lys. Batley has a fine Renaissance parclose screen. The pulpit of 1604 at Rotherham with studded colonnettes is something special. The pulpit at Arksey is dated 1634 and has richly decorated arches. At Bolton Percy the tester of 1715 has cherubs' heads and pediments. The large group of benches surviving at Kirkburton is exceptional. One has the date 1584, dendrochronology has dated others to 1633; they have some carving and some have knobs on the ends. In the case of bench-ends, two sets best represent the

so-called Early Renaissance, otherwise absent from church furnishings: Drax is as early as *c.* 1535–50, and has both Gothic
tracery and Renaissance motifs; Sprotbrough can be dated to the
1550s, its busts in medallions including an African. The marquetry work at Felkirk is late Elizabethan. C17 bench-ends are still
square-topped, but often given two knobs as finials, e.g. at
Halifax (*c.* 1633–4). Examples of other C17 bench-ends include
Arksey, with acorns (and front pews with balustraded fronts),
Bolton Percy, which has a complete set of box pews, and Darfield, with acorn finials. Jacobean font covers are represented e.g.
at Bolton Percy and Greasbrough (originally at Rotherham), and
at Arksey with the date 1662 and flat boards shaped as large
volutes. As for fonts themselves, that from Edlington, now at
Dunscroft (Hatfield), is Elizabethan (1590), but the majority are
from the years immediately after the Restoration. The fonts of
the years 1661–3 are all very similar: small octagonal bowls with
a minimum of elementary decoration set in panels (Wakefield
1661, Batley and Ecclesfield both 1662, Kellington 1663, many
without dates).

From the end of the C17 there is the excellent communion rail
of 1698 at Halifax, and the gadrooned font at Emley. PAINTED
GLASS by *Henry Gyles* of York can be seen at Wentworth, with
flamboyant heraldry of 1685–95. Smaller examples, of 1679,
occur at Hickleton, and another heraldic medallion, probably by
him, is at High Melton. *Gyles* also made the stained glass sundial
dated 1670 at Nun Appleton Hall (Appleton Roebuck).

Church monuments

A field rich in good work. The most traditional types – the
recumbent effigy on a tomb-chest or sarcophagus and the kneeling figure – were still carried on confidently, the one following a
medieval, the other rather a C16 tradition. The Fitzwilliam Monument at Tickhill of *c.* 1530 with its Renaissance details has been
mentioned earlier. In contrast, the Shrewsbury Monument at
Sheffield, †1538, shows no signs of the Renaissance, but the
D'Arcy Monument at Brayton, †1558, combines Gothic arches
and cartouches with strapwork. There was evidently no real
conversion before the end of the century and the reign of Elizabeth I. The only really spectacular monument is that of the
celebrated 6th Earl of Shrewsbury, husband of Bess of Hardwick
and custodian of Mary, Queen of Scots. He died in 1590 and lies
buried in Sheffield Cathedral. The monument has a very large
architectural surround with a recumbent effigy. Other late C16
monuments worthy of note are Thomas Wentworth †1588 at
Wentworth, with alabaster effigies on a tomb-chest with Doric
columns, and John Freeston †1595 at Normanton, the latter
without effigies. After 1600 the scene gets livelier. There are the
splendid Savile monuments at Thornhill, that of Sir George
Savile †1622 by *Maximilian Colt*, in alabaster and marbles. At

Wentworth, Old Holy Trinity, monument to Thomas
Wentworth †1588 and Margaret Gascoigne †1593.
Etching by W. Cowen, 1831

Kirkheaton is the Beaumont monument (†1631), attributed to
Edward Marshall, also still with the traditional recumbent effigy.
Lady Mary Bolles †1662 at Ledsham (attributed to *Thomas
Burman*) lies in a shroud; recumbent too are Sir Thomas Went-
worth †1675 and his wife at Silkstone (attributed to *Thomas
Cartwright Sen.*). In the monument by *William Wright* at Ecclesfield (1640), the deceased lies stiffly on his side; the architectural
composition is odd. Other types of monuments have the very
common kneeling figures at a prayer-desk. An example of this at
Wentworth (1613) is given by Mrs Esdaile to *Nicholas Johnson*.
The next two generations of the Wentworth family in the same
church also have kneeling figures; one is of 1689, the other probably contemporary. The then very out-of-date composition must
be a deliberate family homage. A frontal demi-figure appears at
Cawood (†1628).

The old type of effigy was later translated to a new urbanity
and elegance when the alternative type created by the Italians
about 1500, with the effigy comfortably semi-reclining on one
elbow, was taken up. An absurdly stiff version of this of 1640 at
Ecclesfield has been noted. The new ease is apparent in the
Lewises at Ledsham (1677) by *Thomas Cartwright Sen.* and in the
monument at Wakefield to Sir Lyon Pilkington (†1714) attributed to *Francis Bird*.

Other rarer and more original types are the sombre Nevile
monument at Royston (†1673), where four white marble putti

carry a black marble slab without effigy, and the Beaumont monument at Kirkheaton †1692 with an urn between two busts, attributed to *John Nost*.

Public buildings

Of secular architecture there are some schools and some hospitals. The HOSPITALS or almshouses are Frieston's of 1595 at Kirkthorpe, Brian Cooke's at Arksey and Sir John Lewis's at Ledsham, 1670. Frieston's has a curious plan with an oblong hall in the middle of one side and the other rooms around it (cf. the circular Beamsley Hospital of 1593 (*West Riding North*)). Arksey, built after 1661, is more conventional, with three single-storey ranges round a quadrangle; Sir John's is a row of eleven stone cottages. At Arksey the school next door, built by a bequest of Sir George Cooke †1683, has a grand entrance with segmental pediment. Some other surviving SCHOOLS are also more ambitious than the usual one-storey cottage with a central doorway and one room on the l., one on the r., e.g. the late C16 one at Felkirk. Most important is the Grammar School at Wakefield, built by the Saviles *c.* 1596–8. It has big double-transomed windows and a large schoolroom with a fine kingpost roof. Of the equally fine Heath Grammar School at Halifax, completed in 1601, only the rose window survives in its successor. Other schools are at Laughton-en-le-Morthen, *c.* 1610, its two storeys including the master's house, and at Sherburn-in-Elmet, where the grammar school and Hungate Hospital were founded and built together in 1619.

Country and gentry houses

The greater stability and prosperity that prevailed at the end of the C16 and into the C17, as well as a rise in the number of gentry families, saw much rebuilding or new building and, despite some serious losses, the area still has a wide range of houses from this time. The conservatism of all but the greatest families is evident in the slowness with which the Renaissance was embraced and even in the post-Restoration houses there is a reluctance to adopt the classical style. First comes Manor Lodge, Sheffield, which the Earls of Shrewsbury developed from a C15 hunting lodge into a large C16 house with courtyard and long gallery. Now mostly demolished except for later C16 work, i.e. part of the w wing and the entrance flanked by brick-faced octagonal towers, and the contemporary summerhouse or standing, called the Turret House, built when the 6th Earl was custodian of Mary, Queen of Scots. Another such standing is the mid-C17 Ledston Lodge near Ledsham.

Then follow three houses all with associations with Robert Smythson. First Thorpe Salvin Old Hall, now a magnificent ruin with a tall, almost symmetrical front. Probably built in the 1570s, it seems influenced by both Chatsworth and the Earl of Shrewsbury's house at Buxton and is more important than known. The same is true of the Earl of Shrewsbury's New Hall, Pontefract, of 1591. Now demolished, this was also tall with an almost symmetrical front, which had raised angle towers. The hall lay in the middle but was entered at one end. Third was the Old Hall, *p. 311* Heath, also now demolished, a compact house of *c.* 1584–90 very similar to *Smythson*'s Barlborough Hall, Derbyshire, with a small inner courtyard and angle towers. Here the front was symmetrical, with a central entrance and the hall placed to its l., a departure from the traditional arrangement where the entrance was from a porch into a screens passage at one end of the hall.

Of the two principal large mansions of the earlier C17, both built by the Earl of Strafford, Wentworth Woodhouse of *c.* 1630 has all but disappeared – the only surviving fragment of importance being the South Court gateway, which has the sophistication one would expect. Ledston Hall, a remodelling begun *c.* 1629, shows fashionable symmetry in its great E front but its 39 finished appearance dates from the 1660s.

Below these come a number of houses of the middling and minor gentry that derived from the H-plan or hall-and-cross-wings house of the late Middle Ages and that are found in the Pennine areas. They show variety in their forms and plans: some have earlier timber-framed origins and were cased in stone at this time; others were altered, extended and improved during the period under consideration to meet changing requirements. Plans vary: F-shapes, with one projecting wing and a porch (Barkisland Hall, 1638; Wood Lane Hall, Sowerby, 1649), centre 38, 37 with two projecting wings (Oakwell Hall, Birstall), four ranges round a courtyard (Woodsome Hall, Fenay Bridge), or flat fronts. The plan is sometimes two rooms deep, with a second important room with big windows behind the hall and facing to the back. In elevation they always have gables, mostly straight and of low pitch. Their most characteristic feature is the very large hall window. It can have up to twelve lights and up to three transoms: e.g. Marsh Hall, Northowram, has twelve lights and two transoms; Pollard Hall, Gomersal, 1659, three transoms. In these long windows the number of lights is often subdivided by specially strong and deep mullions, or king mullions, so that ten may read five-plus-five and twelve four-plus-four-plus-four. Most have porches, usually two-storeyed, and some of these, from the 1630s and '40s, have charming rose windows – Barkisland Hall, Elland New Hall and Wood Lane Hall. Apart from fireplaces, the doorways of these porches are usually the only place where any classical motifs are found, e.g. the fluted Doric columns at Barkisland Hall and Wood Lane Hall.

The entry from the porch was commonly to a hearth passage, with the hall fireplace backing on to it, and large chimneys in the wall towards the passage are to be found at Woodsome Hall, Elland New Hall, Howroyde (Barkisland, 1642), Wood Lane Hall and Pollard Hall. While providing access to other rooms, the halls were principally used as reception areas and received the

most elaborate decorative treatment of fireplaces and ceilings.
Some, in the medieval tradition, are open through two storeys
and have galleries running round three sides (Pollard Hall,
Elland New Hall (1670)) or two (Woodsome Hall). At Oakwell
Hall, built *c.* 1583, the hall was remodelled *c.* 1630–40 from a
single-storey space to an open one with a new fireplace facing
the large new window and a screen with Doric columns where
the fire-hood against the passage had been.

This brings us to INTERIORS of this time. Kirklees Hall, a
house with a complex building history, has a fine Jacobean screen;
the Old Cock Inn, Halifax, has an overmantel with caryatids
dated 1581, Todmorden Hall another finely carved one of 1603.
Carbrook Hall, Sheffield, has a room with fine panelling and an
overmantel of 1623. The elaborate fireplace of *c.* 1585 from Heath
Old Hall is now at Hazlewood Castle (*West Riding North*). As
regards PLASTERWORK, the Turret House, Sheffield, has some
of *c.* 1575, there is Jacobean work at Carbrook Hall, and plaster
ceilings at Wood Lane Hall, Sowerby, Marsh Hall, Northowram,
Pollard Hall, Gomersal, and Howroyde, Barkisland.

The LATER DECADES OF THE SEVENTEENTH CENTURY were
a period of transition in the area and, although there are houses
that show acquaintance with the new styles of the South (almost
all in the E parts), the CLASSICAL STYLE was adopted very
slowly. The three principal houses of the most up-to-date style
have all been demolished. Wheatley Hall, Doncaster, *c.* 1683 for
Sir Henry Cooke, and Sprotbrough Hall, 1696–1700 for Sir
Godfrey Copley, were both three storeys with balustraded parapets; Kiveton Park, built by Thomas Osborne, 1st Duke of Leeds,

p. 720

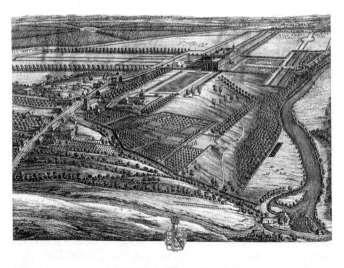

Sprotbrough Hall, perspective.
Engraving by L. Knyff and J. Kip, 1707

1698–1704, was brick with a pedimented centre and had sash windows. Surviving work includes Bishopthorpe Palace, where the hall was rebuilt by Archbishop Frewen in 1660–2 with pilasters to its strikingly rusticated brickwork (cf. the Banqueting House, Batley, with its decorative brickwork). The contemporary fragment of the former Hall at Acaster Selby is also brick, which was used for its original mullioned-and-transomed windows. It is the continued use of cross-windows that is the hallmark of the area's innate conservatism. They appear at Wentworth Castle in the N range of 1670–2 together with a central window with an open scrolly pediment, at Beauchief Hall in 1671, and at the brick Clarke Hall, Stanley, c. 1680, which has a symmetrical front but still spurned the double-pile plan. The latter was adopted at the ambitious Scout Hall, Shibden, of 1680, but even here the small oval windows are combined with cross-windows. Slade Hooton Hall, Laughton-en-le-Morthen, 1698, has a hipped roof, quoin strips and (according to Samuel Buck's immensely useful sketchbook, which recorded many houses in our area as they were c. 1720) a single sash window in the decorated central bay, the rest all being cross-windows originally.

In a period when the plain gable is commonplace, the memorable Dutch gables used by Sir John Lewis in his completion of Ledston Hall, probably in the 1660s, deserve mention, as do the large shaped gables at Woolley Hall, some of 1635, and another of c. 1680, and the curious, almost Baroque, great gable of c. 1690 crowning the front of Hellaby Hall, Bramley.

The same tentative encounter with classical motifs already seen in earlier INTERIORS continues after the Restoration. In PLASTERWORK, for example, in Archbishop Frewen's Great Hall at Bishopthorpe, Jacobean decoration is combined with Italianate wreaths, and at Clarke Hall, Stanley, the parlour ceiling dated 1680 has vigorous if rustic foliage. Beauchief Hall (1671) has a splendid alabaster CHIMNEYPIECE with pilasters and strapwork. The grandest STAIRCASES, with thick, lush openwork foliage scrolls, are the one at Wentworth Castle of c. 1670 and that from Wheatley Hall, Doncaster, c. 1683, now at Herstmonceux Castle, East Sussex. Unique in the area is the PAINTED PANELLING at Oakwell Hall, Birstall, with its rare *trompe l'œil* geometric patterns.

Yeomen-clothiers' houses

The late C16 and C17 stone Pennine houses on the W side make a distinctive contribution to the architectural character of our area, and their gables, decorated doorways and mullioned-and-transomed windows were the inspiration for the local Vernacular Revival style of the later C19. The larger houses of the gentry have already been discussed, but within the houses of the yeoman class are a large and distinct group, found almost entirely in the Halifax area of the Upper Calder valley, that merit special attention. Yeoman houses are of course found across our area – e.g.

Old Hall, Ackworth (early C17), Fulwood Hall, Sheffield (1620), and Thorncliffe Grange, Emley (*c.* 1623) – but in the Upper Calder Valley there were an exceptionally large number of wealthy yeomen who were building at this time. Their wealth derived partly from advantageous land-holding tenure in the huge Manor of Wakefield but especially from their involvement in the dual economy of agriculture and the textile industry. In his *Tour through the Whole Island of Great Britain* (1724–7), Daniel Defoe vividly described the area, with 'hardly a house standing out of speaking distance from another' and remarked on the busyness of the whole population, who found employment in the different stages of the industry.

Although weaving was mostly done by the poorer classes in their cottages, the houses of these yeomen accommodated other aspects of production and the storage of equipment, finished pieces etc. and this non-domestic use is reflected in both the plan and the appearance of their houses. These essentially follow the traditional tripartite medieval plan of three front rooms (invariably s-facing, or as near to s-facing as possible) with the house-body in the centre flanked by a parlour (sometimes in a cross-wing) and an unheated lower service end. Instead of the usual buttery etc. the clothiers' houses have their shops (i.e. workshops) at the lower end, most commonly separated by use of the hearth-passage plan. In this the housebody fireplace backs onto a through passage that isolates the lower end, e.g. Peel House, Luddenden (1598), Haigh House, Warley (1631) and Roebucks, Luddenden (1633). The lobby-entry plan, where the entrance faces the side wall of the housebody chimney and a small lobby has doorways to l. and r., is occasionally found in the southern West Riding, e.g. at Lower Old Hall (1634) and Fallingworth Hall (1642), both at Norland (cf. *West Riding North*, where the lobby-entry was much more common). The domestic functions of the lower end were displaced, and in the rare group of timber-framed houses of the late C15 to later C16 which have an aisled housebody (e.g. Dam Head, Shibden) this seems to have been the purpose of the rear aisle.

Where the housebody was used for cooking, the later houses sometimes have small service rooms on the N side but others, such as Peel House and Lower Old Hall have a rear kitchen, giving an informal double-pile plan. Kitchens might be added later, as at High Bentley, Shelf, which well illustrates the evolution of what was originally a timber-framed house of *c.* 1500. The upgrading of the housebody there once cooking was transferred is paralleled elsewhere, while at houses such as Lower Old Hall the original status of the housebody as a reception and superior living area is reflected in the quality of its plasterwork and its ornamental fireplace. The housebody and parlour windows are usually large, and the biggest yeoman-clothier houses have features such as mullioned-and-transomed windows and two-storey porches that are not so very different from those of gentry houses. The much plainer treatment of the shop ends, however, e.g. at Peel House and Lower Old Hall, reflects their industrial use.

THE GEORGIAN ERA

Country houses

The C18 has much less of a regional character than the C17; but that would be true of all counties of England where a regional character had held out so late. Nevertheless, it produced in our part of the West Riding, sometimes by means of Yorkshire architects, some of the best work done in England. The years from *c.* 1710 to *c.* 1740 or 1750 are less easy to summarize than the later ones, and that is due to what might perhaps still be regarded as a last sign of the resistance of the North to the South. In London, Lord Burlington's Palladianism had won the day by *c.* 1720–30. *Lord Burlington*'s style was introduced to York by his own pencil in the Assembly Rooms of 1731–2. Yet the West Riding was not converted to Palladianism until the 1st Marquess of Rockingham began work on the E front of Wentworth Woodhouse in 1730.

51

What represents EARLY EIGHTEENTH-CENTURY splendour before this is the BAROQUE style as seen further north in such mansions as Vanbrugh's Castle Howard in the North Riding and Seaton Delaval in Northumberland. Vanbrugh's only work in the West Riding is that curious little folly Robin Hood's Well near Burghwallis, *c.* 1720. We have the E range of Wentworth Castle begun *c.* 1710, and the W range of Wentworth Woodhouse begun *c.* 1724. Neither is English in any accepted sense. Wentworth Castle is very grand, the design of the Germanized Frenchman *Johann von Bodt* and Frederick the Great's architect *Johann Friedrich Eosander*, whom Lord Raby met when he was ambassador in Berlin in 1703–11. Their design is indeed of an unashamed *grand goût* with which little in England can be compared. The range is two-storeyed, and the whole upper floor is one *grande galerie* with a range of cabinets behind. The exterior also – with its arched windows, its profuse display of trophies and its top balustrade – smacks of Versailles or Berlin more than of the English countryside. At Wentworth Woodhouse, in contrast, the little known W façade is curiously reminiscent of Austria or Bohemia (K.I. Dientzenhofer's Villa Amerika at Prague). Here one finds the daintily garlanded, diagonally set pilasters which flank the doorway, here the fanciful shapes of the window pediments. One would like to know more of John Pertak, the Bohemian refugee whom Thomas Watson-Wentworth installed as curate at Bolsterstone in 1710 and who provided a personal link with that country. Yet these features might have been found in published sources and others, such as the fluted giant pilasters and the Venetian window, make close acquaintance with Vanbrugh likely. So the involvement of Yorkshire architects such as *William Wakefield* or *William Thornton* of York or his sons cannot be discounted.

p. 154
46
50

These two buildings are the supreme achievement of the Early Georgian decades. No other work by Bodt and Eosander in England is known, nor did Wentworth Castle find converts.

There is only one other house that is wholly Baroque, perhaps
influenced by Wentworth Woodhouse – Kettlethorpe Hall, Sandal
Magna, near Wakefield, of 1727, with its fanciful doorway and
window surrounds.

As to the INTERIORS of this period we have the names of some
of the craftsmen at Wentworth Castle, where *James Gibbs* was
responsible for the E range's interiors, fitted up between 1714 and
1731. There is carving by *Daniel Harvey*, and the Entrance Hall
has paintings by *Giacomo Amiconi* and *Andien de Clermont*.
Gibbs's Staircase has lavish stucco by *Francesco Vassalli* and an
iron balustrade by *Robert Bakewell*. The prodigious Long Gallery
includes carving by *Jonathan Godier*, a local man working for the
joiner/architect *William Thornton*, whose work at Wentworth
Castle compares with his interior joinery at Beningborough Hall
(*North Riding*). At Wentworth Woodhouse the W Entrance Hall
with its staircase, also with an iron balustrade, belongs to the
1730s, the doorway pediments showing familiarity with Roman
Baroque through published sources.

By 1750 PALLADIANISM had had its entrée into the West
Riding with unique magnificence. The E front of Wentworth
Woodhouse is the longest front in all England. It was designed by
the local architect *Ralph Tunnicliffe* sometime before 1734 on the
model of Wanstead in Essex and taken over by Lord Burlington's
protégé *Henry Flitcroft* in 1736. It thus represented what had been
new in the South in 1715–20. Building at Wentworth Woodhouse
went on after 1750 and we shall consider the magnificent interiors
in due course. Meanwhile the Palladian style was taken up everywhere, and the youthful *James Paine*, who came to Yorkshire
c. 1736 as executant architect for Sir Rowland Winn at Nostell
Priory, became its principal exponent in our area for over twenty
years. At Nostell he developed the purely Palladian design made
by the amateur architect *Colonel James Moyser* and derived from
that of the Villa Mocenigo; his own work, including Heath House
(1744–5), Hickleton Hall (1745–8), Cusworth Hall (1749–53),
Wadworth Hall (*c*. 1750) and Sandbeck Park (*c*. 1762–8) is more
dramatic and varied, and as we shall see many of his interiors have
lively Rococo decoration.

As Paine increasingly turned his attention to clients beyond
Yorkshire in the 1750s the man who was to be its leading architect
for over half a century began to establish his practice. *John Carr*
was born in 1723 at Horbury outside Wakefield and was the son
of a mason. In 1757 he became a freeman of York, in 1770 Lord
Mayor. When he died in 1807 he left £150,000. In 1754 he was
given the job of building the grandstand for the York Races, in
preference to a design of Paine's. His first major job in the field
of country house architecture was Harewood House (*West Riding
North*) from 1759. He erected or altered a very large number of
houses after that, and also buildings of other kinds. His style
remained essentially Palladian and, although his houses are not
ostentatious, they can be very refined in their reticent way. Sometimes they can be plain almost to the point of dullness, but he
excelled in providing the sort of gracious houses his many

Yorkshire gentry clients wanted. A shocking number in our area
have been destroyed. His best surviving work includes alterations
to Heath Hall, Heath, from 1754 and to Cannon Hall, Cawthorne, from 1764, Clifton House, Rotherham, 1783, and his
work at Wentworth Woodhouse, where he received an annual
salary from 1763 until his death. The losses include Campsall
Hall of 1762–70 and its fine lodge, neighbouring Campsmount,
1752–5; Stapleton Park, near Darrington, 1762–4, where only his
stables survive; and work at Byram Hall (Brotherton) and Ravenfield Hall from the 1760s.

The work of other architects, mostly local, up to the end of the
century must not be overlooked. *George Platt* (1700–1743) came
from Cheshire but established himself as an architect and builder
in Rotherham *c.* 1730* and with his son *John Platt* (1728–1810)
was responsible for Cusworth Hall 1740–5. John Platt's name
occurs subsequently as a mason and provider of interior
marble work, and he designed several smaller houses around
Rotherham. *William Lindley* of Doncaster (1739–1818) was Carr's
assistant before setting up on his own. His work, in a conservative
classical style, includes Owston Hall, 1794–5, and Cantley Hall,
1802. *Thomas Atkinson* of York appears at Bishopthorpe Palace,   57
where he made additions for Archbishop Drummond in 1763–9
in the Gothick style, a rare use in an C18 house in the area,
Hatfeild Hall, Stanley, which was Gothicized *c.* 1775, being the
other significant example.

Turning to the INTERIOR DECORATION of the Palladian
houses and their successors, we must first return to Wentworth
Woodhouse and its splendours. The ground-floor rooms on the
E front, completed 1735–8 for the family, are elegant but not
imposing, *Mercier*'s paintings of the 1st Marquess's children
adding an especially delightful touch. Above, the Saloon's spa-   53
cious galleried cube, designed on the pattern of Inigo Jones's
Queen's House at Greenwich, is as awe-inspiring as was intended
and the flanking rooms, with their dignified plaster ceilings and   52
fireplaces, are similarly magnificent. This must not lead us to
underestimate the quality of work in other houses. Many of the
interiors created by *Paine* and, in his earlier work, by *Carr*, have
rich Rococo plasterwork and fine chimneypieces and carving, e.g.
Paine's staircases and Dining Room at Nostell and the Great Hall
at Whitley Beaumont, Kirkheaton (dem.), Carr's Drawing Room
at Heath Hall. Paine's glorious Saloon on the upper floor at
Sandbeck Park is more 'classical', however, and this is partly the
influence of *Robert Adam*'s work. Adam began completing the
interiors at Nostell in 1766 and the Top Hall especially displays   55
his genius in combining the spatial forms of Roman architecture
with a delicacy of detail all his own. Adam's other major work
was the Library at Byram Hall (dem.). The influence of Adam's
sophisticated elegance is apparent in Carr's designs, especially
e.g. in the interior of the Rockingham Monument at Wentworth   61
Woodhouse and in his last major work there, the beautiful apsidal

*His brother *John Platt I* was one of the architects of St Paul's church, Sheffield.

staircase. None of this work would have been possible without skilled craftsmen such as the *Rose* family of plasterers to undertake it, and Paine and Carr in particular were fortunate in having men such as *Christopher Richardson*, the Doncaster carver, and *James Henderson*, the York plasterer, in the area.

Looking at the early C19 there is little to mention. Long after *Leoni*'s Grecian s front at Wortley Hall, 1742–6, the GREEK REVIVAL style was used for *John Rawstorne*'s alterations at Chevet Hall (dem.) and alterations at Bretton Hall by *Jeffry Wyatville* (*c.* 1815). The Gothic or castellated style was not especially popular and Thrybergh Park 1812–14 and Banner Cross Hall, Ecclesall, Sheffield, by *Wyatville* (1820), are almost the only examples.

These great houses of the C18 did not stand on their own, and they cannot be understood without their outbuildings and gardens and parks. Of the outbuildings the STABLES come first. *Carr*'s very large establishment at Wentworth Woodhouse with its inner courtyard is as exceptional as the mansion; those at Norton Hall are more typical. The GROUNDS of the great mansions are a special joy in the West Riding. Our companion area has been more fortunate in their survival, having in Bramham Park and Studley Royal some of the finest schemes in England, but painstaking restoration has brought back the extraordinary politically charged landscape of Wentworth Castle and rescued the monuments that proclaim Whiggery triumphant at Wentworth Woodhouse. The serpentine lakes and undulating lawns at Bretton Hall (Yorkshire Sculpture Park) are being reclaimed but *Capability Brown*'s landscape at Byram Hall has been lost to farmland and that at Whitley Beaumont to opencast mining, the little temple there a solitary survivor. *Repton*'s landscape at Wentworth Woodhouse was also undone by opencast mining.

Many richly varied structures, useful and useless, classical and Gothic, survive, however, and are an essential part of the pleasures to be derived from these gardens and parks. The earliest is Stainborough Castle, built in the grounds of Wentworth Castle 1726–30, a remarkably early example of romantic medievalism. Others range from follies such as the Needle's Eye at Wentworth Woodhouse, to lodges such as the *Adam* brothers' pyramidal Obelisk Lodge at Nostell (1776–7) and markers such as the 2nd Earl of Strafford's boundary obelisk at Birdwell (Worsbrough, 1775). The perfection of the landscape included such majestic buildings as *Carr*'s Rockingham Monument at Wentworth Woodhouse, and many temples, e.g. at Bretton Hall and Wentworth Castle. Orangeries remain at Bretton Hall, Byram Hall and, unusually, from a town house in Wakefield. Camellia houses are at Bretton Hall (1814) and Wentworth Woodhouse (1812). At Bretton Hall there is also a pretty shell grotto, and Wentworth Woodhouse has a bear pit. The Gothick style recurs in Wentworth Castle's Steeple Lodge, *c.* 1752, and the Menagerie House at Nostell Priory by *Paine*, 1765. In the same way that William Aislabie incorporated the ruins of Fountains Abbey into the Studley Royal landscape in 1768, *Capability Brown* used the Roche Abbey ruins in his landscape at Sandbeck Park, 1774–7.

Other housing, rural and urban

The numerous SMALLER GEORGIAN HOUSES, without large estates, that stand in the countryside or on the edge of towns were often built for men from the professional, manufacturing or merchant classes. Many, like *Carr*'s Pye Nest, built outside Halifax *c.* 1771 for the worsted yarn manufacturer Henry Edwards, have succumbed to urban expansion; remaining examples are White Windows, Sowerby, also by *Carr*, for John Priestley, a clothier (1767–8), and Page Hall, Firvale, Sheffield, by *John Platt* for the banker Thomas Broadbent, 1773. The best of the larger TOWN HOUSES are in Doncaster, along Hallgate and South Parade, where there are several by *William Lindley*, and in Wakefield, on Westgate. Wakefield also has the grandest of the new 'west ends', the late C18 speculative development of housing for the middle and professional classes. St John's Square, begun in 1791, has large three-storey terraced houses, but it was not a financial success and was not completed as intended. A later comparable development in Sheffield is much smaller but architecturally more ambitious – the remarkable Grecian terrace of private houses built by *William Flockton c.* 1832 at Broomhill and called The Mount.

As for WORKERS' HOUSING, something rare and special are the WEAVERS' COTTAGES, with a long, usually S-facing, mullioned window on an upper floor to light a handloom. The 64 windows are sometimes of as many as twelve or more lights, extending the full width of each cottage. These cottages belong mostly to the later C18 and to the early C19 and one finds them in the towns and villages all across the Pennine areas S and W of Huddersfield (Almondbury, Dobcross, Golcar, Holmfirth, Thurlstone etc.). They are so numerous that it is impossible to mention more than a fraction of them in the gazetteer, but they form a significant accompaniment to the earlier clothiers' houses of the same area that are similarly such a special building type in the history of the woollen industry. In areas where domestic weaving continued because people were still better than machines, especially for fancy-goods such as shawls, the building of weavers' cottages persisted until the later C19. Elsewhere, two- and three-light mullioned windows are almost universal in the smaller houses until well after 1800. These late mullions are of course much simpler than the C17 ones, having a rectangular section and no chamfer.

Churches and chapels

CHURCHES of the first half of the C18 are rare everywhere; one of the best in the whole Riding was St Paul, Sheffield, in baroque style by *Ralph Tunnicliffe* with the first *John Platt*, built 1720–1 and demolished in 1937. Otherwise examples are slight: St Giles, Pontefract, has Gibbsian touches outside and Doric columns 5 inside; the tower at Bawtry was rebuilt in 1712–13. In the second

half of the C18 many more churches and chapels were built.
These were classical, with the two exceptions of Ravenfield
church and alterations to Dewsbury parish church, both by *John
Carr*. Ravenfield, 1755–6, is small with ogee-headed windows, a
characteristic motif of the earliest Gothic Revival; Dewsbury in
1765 received a new Gothic tower and doorways under heavy
ogee arches. The majority of the classical churches are small – only
a few are large and serious and splendid. Sowerby of 1761–6,
based on William Etty's Holy Trinity, Leeds, of nearly forty years
earlier, has an elegant interior with giant Corinthian columns,
and a Venetian window and lavish plasterwork by *Giuseppe
Cortese* in the apsidal chancel. This was followed by the finest of
all – Horbury, built in 1790–4 by *John Carr* at his own expense
to commemorate his birth in the little town. This has an interesting plan, a majestic transeptal front with giant columns, and a
stately w tower. Inside are giant pilasters and columns and a
ceiling with plasterwork by *Henderson & Crabtree*. A little later
came Rastrick, 1796–8, with a domed cupola and three galleries
on thin Doric columns. With these go the chapels of ease that
were needed in the rapidly developing industrial towns and were
always in those parts in which well-to-do houses went up too. In
Sheffield, St James (dem.) was built in 1786–9; in Wakefield,
St John, 1791–5, formed the elegant centrepiece of a residential
square; Holy Trinity, Halifax, 1795–8, had an unusual plan
with the longer sides on the E and W and entrances flanking
the altar. All three had three galleries. At Wentworth Woodhouse
the chapel (1733–6) is simple and elegant and pious, but at Cusworth Hall *Paine*'s chapel, 1749–53, has paintings and lavish
plasterwork.

Elsewhere, e.g. at Friarmere (1765), Dobcross (1785–7),
Lydgate (1788), Meltham (1785–6) and Slaithwaite (1789), the
churches were simpler versions of these – oblong boxes with
rectangular or arched windows (often in two tiers where there
were three galleries), no distinctive chancel or a small chancel,
perhaps a Venetian window, and sometimes at the w end a bellcote or a tower with a little domed cupola.* The sides were
sometimes given more harmony with the Georgian sense of symmetry by adding a central transeptal projection in the manner of
Horbury, or entrances in the first as well as the last bay like
Sowerby and Rastrick (e.g. Holmfirth and Meltham). Most of
these churches were altered in the C19, especially with new or
larger chancels; Friarmere best shows their original form. Wortley
church (*c.* 1811–15), which has chancel chapels separated by
round arches from the chancel and the nave but Gothic windows,
is the latest of this group.

There was hardly any ornament inside these churches, and
MONUMENTS (*see* below) took their place, but among C18 FUR-
NISHINGS generally there is some Georgian STAINED or
PAINTED GLASS by *William Peckitt* to be mentioned, e.g. at High

---

*Lightcliffe church (1744–5), demolished except for the tower, had cast-iron
columns inside – a remarkably early case.

Melton for John Fountayne (where Peckitt also reused medieval glass he acquired from Oxford), and at Ravenfield in the E window of 1811. The gadrooned wooden FONT at Thurnscoe is noteworthy.

Moving into the PRE-VICTORIAN NINETEENTH CENTURY, from about 1810 the churches turn Gothic, and are larger and serious. They belong to the great church-building activity of the early C19, not to the playful Gothicism of the C18, and their purpose was to counteract the popular attraction of Nonconformity and cater for a rapidly growing population, especially in the industrialized areas. Liversedge, built at the personal expense of the Rev. Hammond Roberson, 1812–16, was a model for the churches provided with funding from the 'Million Act' of 1818, and its architect, *Thomas Taylor* of Leeds, designed five of the ten built in our area between 1821 and 1829 under the first grant from the Church Commissioners.*

Another forty-eight Commissioners' churches (of eighty-one in the whole Riding) were built between 1826 and 1855 with help from the second grant, but many others were built independently: at Huddersfield, for example, six new churches (St Paul, Highfields, Lindley, Lockwood, Paddock and Sheepridge) were built between 1816 and 1831, but Holy Trinity, Highfields, where Taylor reworked his Liversedge design, and his Christ Church, Sheepridge, were funded independently. In the period we are considering, these new churches were invariably Gothic, *Samuel Sharp*'s plain classical design for St James, Thornes (1829–30), in Wakefield being a notable exception. The smaller, more rural ones were often in an unelaborate lancet style, e.g. the Commissioners' church at Hebden Bridge (1832–3), but in the towns they were large and more elaborate and sometimes more scholarly. Where they survive, their battlemented or pinnacled towers and naves still make a distinctive contribution to our urban townscapes, e.g. Christ Church, Sowerby Bridge, by *John Oates* (1819–21) and St George, Sheffield, by *Woodhead & Hurst* (1821–5). Only the larger of these churches have aisles; otherwise a wide and relatively low nave was given three galleries, often on slender cast-iron supports. The chancels, when they existed, were small and had as a rule to be lengthened or rebuilt by the more ritualistically minded Victorians. 66

The earlier NONCONFORMIST CHAPELS of this period were still small, as those of the C17 had been, e.g. the Unitarian chapel at Fulwood (Sheffield), with its plain windows with a single mullion. The charming Underbank Chapel built for Dissenters at Stannington (Sheffield) in 1742 (now Unitarian) is more ambitious, and that for the Presbyterians at Wakefield, 1751–2 (also now Unitarian), much more so. It has a pulpit of 1737 from its predecessor. Its pedimented front presages those of the much larger galleried town chapels, such as the former Square Congregational Chapel at Halifax of 1771–2, which is red brick with 48

---

*He also designed two of the other six in the West Riding (*see West Riding North*).

Rotherham, Bunting Croft Octagonal Chapel.
Engraving, 1879

arched windows and little enrichment other than a Venetian window. Later examples of these big 'preaching boxes', which multiplied after 1800, are the fine former Methodist chapels in Carver Street, Sheffield, 1804, and Queen Street, Huddersfield, 1819. Numbered among the huge losses of town chapels is one of the noblest of those in the Grecian style, introduced in the latest Georgian years, i.e. the Brunswick Methodist Chapel, Sheffield, which had a portico with Greek Doric columns and dated from 1833. The former Ebenezer Wesleyan Chapel of 1823 in Sheffield, is, however, Gothic, and in this heralds a gradual change of style which the Victorian Age was to effect in chapels. Lastly, the octagonal Methodist chapel at Heptonstall must be mentioned. Built in 1764 it followed soon after the octagonal chapel (Bunting Croft) built at Rotherham in 1761 (dem.) and although not in its original form it is a rare example of a form that Wesley himself favoured.

Funerary monuments

For SCULPTURE we rely almost exclusively on church monuments. The most notable exceptions are *Rysbrack*'s statue of the 1st Earl of Strafford (second creation), dated 1744, originally inside the sham castle at Wentworth Castle, and now standing beside the mansion, and *Nollekens*'s statue of the 2nd Marquess of Rockingham at Wentworth (1790). Around him in the Rockingham Monument are busts of his political allies, four also by

Nollekens and the others by *John Bacon Sen.*, *Giuseppe Ceracchi* and *John Hickey*.

In CHURCH MONUMENTS the types are at first on the whole those created *c.* 1700. At South Kirkby is a very early *Rysbrack* tablet (Sir John Wentworth †1720), accomplished but minor. At Kirkthorpe the medallion portrait of John Smyth †1731 is attributed to *Rysbrack*. The standing figure of John Silvester †1722 between seated female figures at Darton is probably by *Andrew Carpenter*. Two busts by *Guelfi* on a sarcophagus with an impressive background by *William Kent* is the scheme chosen for the Stringer monument at Kirkthorpe (1732). The monument to Richard Beaumont †1704, at Kirkheaton, also erected under the will of the 6th Countess of Westmorland, has another bust by *Guelfi* (1731) in an equally elaborate composition. By *Nicholas Read* are the Finch monument (†1767) at Thrybergh with portrait medallions and another at Halifax †1776. Also at Halifax the monument to Mr and Mrs Hollins by *Henry Cheere* 1752, and another attributed to him again at Thrybergh. A final monument of these years deserving notice is the matronly figure of Mrs Ramsden †1745 at Adlingfleet by *Charles Mitley* and *Harvey*, not originally intended for this remote rural church.

As for the monuments of *c.* 1760–1800, all that can be accommodated here is a catalogue according to sculptors. By *Wilton* with *Joseph Panzetta* the standing statue of Archbishop Tillotson at Sowerby (before 1796), the monument's inscription by *Nollekens*, whose other work is all at Wentworth. There is one monument by *J. F. Moore* at Saxton (1783) and one tablet of *Coade* stone at Aston with a fine portrait medallion of the Rev. William Mason †1797. Those in the later C18 and early C19 who could afford a monument were fortunate in having a Yorkshire family of sculptors who could provide high-quality work with fashionable Neoclassical ornament, often using coloured marbles. They were the *Fishers* of York, *John Fisher I* (1736–1804) and his son *John Fisher II* (1760–1839); the work of the next generation, John and Charles, is not of the same standard. There are far more monuments by them than the gazetteer can accommodate and, like so many monuments, they are not always in a good state. Among the best examples are those at High Melton and Kirkburton. Another noteworthy local supplier was the architect and mason *John Platt* of Rotherham (*see* p. 35), who owned Derbyshire marble works.

After 1800 we have several by *John Flaxman*. They are his more Grecian ones, their style C19, not C18. At Campsall 1803 and at Rotherham †1806, with female figures, at Wragby 1806, and at Wortley †1797 and †1808. Flaxman's most popular successor was *Chantrey*, born at Norton (Sheffield). His earliest work, James Wilkinson †1805, is at Sheffield Cathedral, where there are two others, †1816 and 1823. Others are at Owston, to Mrs Frances Cooke †1818, free-standing, with a kneeling figure, and Bryan Cooke †1821, with a seated figure; at Wragby, 1823, to John Winn †1817, one of his best works; and at Snaith, 1837, with standing statue of John Dawnay, 5th Viscount Downe, †1832.

Public buildings

54
p. 216
Paine's Mansion House at Doncaster of 1744–9 is the principal CIVIC BUILDING of the C18, but it was built for a purpose unique to Doncaster for the mayor and corporation to entertain on a grand scale as well as to have rooms for official business. It was some time before other towns, without corporations, followed with buildings for local administration and for social gatherings. The first was Pontefract's Town Hall of 1785, by *Bernard Hartley*, which replaced the C17 Moot Hall and provided a room used for council meetings, courts and also assem-p. 514 blies. Sheffield's Old Town Hall, also in classical style, by *Charles Watson*, 1807–8, was built by the Town Trustees for themselves and with courtrooms for the Petty and Quarter Sessions. The great age of the town halls, however, had to wait until after the local government reform of 1835. Although not originally a public building, but rather a very private, outwardly unostenta-63 tious, commercial one, the Piece Hall, Halifax, must stand with the Mansion House as one of the area's foremost Georgian urban buildings. Little or nothing remains of the West Riding's other major halls for selling cloth, at Huddersfield, Leeds and Wakefield; fortunately the most magnificent of them all survives, the unique space of its great courtyard now open to all.

In the larger towns much was inevitably later replaced but other civic buildings from before about 1800 that survive include 5 the pretty Butter Cross of 1734 at Pontefract, Bawtry's obelisk and the more conventionally Georgian one at Tickhill (*c.* 1777) and at Sheffield the Infirmary of 1793–7 by *John Rawstorne*, which is the first hospital, in the modern sense, in our area. Examples of buildings that have gone are Sheffield's Assembly Rooms and Playhouse of 1762–3 and the Duke of Norfolk's Market Hall and Shambles (1786–90), *Carr*'s County Gaol of 1766–8 at Wakefield, and his Grandstand for Doncaster Races (1778).

More remains from the early C19, when a number of new building types, especially for civic and social purposes, make their appearance. Up to this period the quarter sessions for hearing criminal cases were generally held in existing town halls. The era of independent LAW COURT buildings began in the early 1800s and in the West Riding especially after 1806, when an Act was passed to allow the Justices of the Peace (magistrates) to 'provide convenient court houses for holding the General Quarter Sessions of the Peace' with sufficient offices and rooms for judge and jury to retire to. Thus at both Pontefract and Wakefield are court houses for the quarter sessions designed by *Charles Watson*, in a fine Neoclassical style with a full Greek Doric portico at Wakefield (1806–10) and an implied Ionic portico at Ponte-fract (1807–8). The preference for the Grecian style in public buildings is also especially evident in *Watson & Pritchett*'s Library, News Room and Music Saloon at Wakefield (1820–2) and at Sheffield in the Music Hall by *William Hurst*, 1823, and the

Doncaster, Racecourse Grandstand.
Engraving by A. Birrel after F. Nash, *c.* 1805

neighbouring Medical School, 1828, both demolished, and the Cutlers' Hall (1832).

At the beginning of this period CHARITABLE BUILDINGS were not very different from those of earlier centuries, e.g. Lady Betty Hastings's Orphanage at Ledsham, of 1721 – of three storeys and still with cross-windows, and not especially institutional in appearance. At Ackworth, Mary Lowther's Hospital provided a school and almshouses in a single-storey range in 1741. It was also at Ackworth, however, that the Foundling Hospital, begun in 1758, introduced a new formality and scale with its three ranges of buildings facing a great courtyard. It was not to be matched until the early C19. The Girls' Charity School of 1786 in Sheffield is domestic in character, but the Boys' Charity School opposite it, 1826, is strictly classical. After 1800 are Rishworth School by *John Oates*, 1827–8, quite sizeable but still retiredly Georgian, but *William Flockton*'s Wesley Proprietary School (now King Edward VII School) at Sheffield of 1837–40 is Grecian on the grandest scale – twenty-five bays wide with a central giant portico of eight Corinthian columns. Other schools preferred Gothic or Tudor Gothic clothes: the Proprietary School at Wakefield, 1833–4 by *Richard Lane*; *J. G. Weightman*'s former Sheffield Collegiate School, 1835–6; and *J. P. Pritchett*'s Huddersfield College of 1839.

Last come the buildings that go with the roads and canals that fed industry with fuel and raw materials and transported manufactured goods, and later coal, to markets at home and abroad. Fine stone structures include road BRIDGES by *John Carr*, who was one of the Surveyors of Bridges for the West Riding from 1761 to 1772, his best work the elegant three-arched bridge

carrying the Great North Road over the River Aire at Ferry-
p. 248 bridge, 1797–1804. Many new turnpike roads were made
throughout the period, linking all the towns with each other as
well as with the routes to London and York and to the ports of
Hull and Liverpool to E and W. Some of their numerous TOLL
HOUSES survive, typically single-storeyed with a projecting
canted front for observation in both directions, but with exceptions such as Ringinglow's tall Gothick octagon of *c.* 1795 on the
edge of the moors.

Knottingley on the River Aire was the West Riding's inland
port until the CANAL SYSTEM began in 1699 with the Aire &
Calder Navigation, which made the Calder navigable up to
p. 650 Wakefield by 1702. The Stanley Ferry cast-iron aqueduct,
1836–9, carrying the canal over the Calder, is its most significant
structure. The Calder & Hebble Navigation between Wakefield
and Sowerby Bridge opened in 1770, and Company warehouses
survive at Wakefield (1790) and at Elland Wharf, built from
c. 1820. The terminus at Sowerby Bridge, where the canal basin
has two three-storey warehouses of *c.* 1778 and *c.* 1796–8, became
an important transshipment centre when the Rochdale Canal
was built, the link to Liverpool via Manchester being completed
in 1804. Huddersfield was linked to the Calder & Hebble Navigation in 1776 by Sir John Ramsden's Broad Canal, but Halifax's
nearest access was a short spur opened in 1769 over a mile S at
Salterhebble Hill, until the Halifax Branch Canal, engineered by
Thomas Bradley, was completed in 1828. Huddersfield and the
Colne and Saddleworth valleys gained a direct trans-Pennine
route to Manchester when the Narrow Canal, a remarkable
feat of engineering by *Benjamin Outram*, was completed 1794–
1811, including the remarkably long tunnel at Standedge, near
Marsden.

In the S the Don Navigation was authorized by an Act of 1726,
promoted by the Cutlers' Company and the Town Trustees in
Sheffield to replace the slow road and river route for goods via
Bawtry to Hull and beyond with a faster river and canal access
to the Humber. The Navigation reached Rotherham in 1740,
Tinsley in 1751 and the centre of Sheffield in 1819, when the big
brick Terminal Warehouse was built. The Dearne & Dove Canal,
branching off at Swinton and completed in 1795, provided a link
to Barnsley.

In the E the River Ouse had always given Selby access to the
sea, and in 1778 the Selby Canal, linking the lower Aire to Selby,
offered an alternative to the winding river's slow route. This was
superseded by the Aire & Calder Navigation Company's 19-mile
Knottingley–Goole Canal, which opened in 1826 with two small
p. 2 docks beside the Ouse. Developed by their engineer *George
Leather* from proposals by *John Rennie*, the Company's scheme
marked the beginning of Goole's growth as a port and planned
new town, although only the Lowther Hotel, 1824–6, remains
from the earliest buildings.

VICTORIAN AND EDWARDIAN

Churches

The building of new churches that began in the second decade of the century accelerated in this period, especially in the S and W parts of the area, where there was the greatest urban growth and increase in population. Scores of new buildings appeared, some with help from the Commissioners, many with money from the Incorporated Church Building Society, others supported by the Diocesan Church Building Societies of Ripon and then Wakefield, when that diocese was created in 1888, and also York. A measure of the extent of the work can be gained from the fact that nearly forty new churches were built in Sheffield during this time. Together with this there were many restorations and enlargements of existing churches.

The styles used, or rather imitated, were almost invariably Gothic, at the beginning without the influence of Ecclesiological principles. This was usually a somewhat thin lancet style, seen for example at St Mary, Honley, a big, impressively galleried church with a small apsidal chancel, rebuilt by *R.D. Chantrell* 1842–3; *Pritchett & Son* used a more Perp-style tracery at St Edward, Brotherton, in the same years. A short Norman fashion also appeared about 1840, e.g. St George, Sowerby, by *Edward Welch*, 1839–40; Dodworth by *Benjamin Broomhead Taylor*, 1843–6; St Luke, Milnsbridge, Huddersfield, by *William Wallen*, 1845; and Whitley Lower by *Ignatius Bonomi*, 1842–6. These styles were soon replaced by something more substantial, in form as well as in learning. The earliest is St Andrew, Wakefield, 1845–6 by *Scott & Moffatt*, one of Scott's earliest Gothic revival churches and his second in Yorkshire, still in an E.E. style but showing Pugin's influence with nave, aisles and chancel all expressed separately in accordance with the Ecclesiologists' model. Later come more spectacular, more elevating churches. A paramount example of High Victorian church architecture is *Scott*'s Doncaster Parish Church of 1853–8. Its robustness is as characteristic of the 1850s and '60s as the greater refinement of *Pearson*'s church at Wentworth is of the coming of the Late Victorian style (1875–7). High Victorian also are the harshnesses of *Butterfield*'s small brick churches at Cowick, Hensall and Pollington, all of 1853–4 for Viscount Downe, and *G.E. Street*'s at Carlton, Barnsley, 1874–8. The Late Victorian desire for originality and unexpected effects is equally convincingly illustrated by *Sedding*'s small church at Netherton (1881). Churches were never built in a classical or Italianate mode in these years. In the last years of the century and in the Edwardian period, the most notable achievements are the noble E extensions to Wakefield Cathedral designed by *J.L. Pearson* in 1897–8 and executed after his death by *F.L. Pearson* in 1901–5 and the work of *Temple Moore*. He built the little church at Heck, 1894–5, but the great

67

69

p. 211

₉₂ brick church of St Peter, Barnsley, 1893–1911, with its uplifting interior, and the equally lofty and spacious E end of All Saints, Ecclesall, Sheffield, 1906–8, are among his most notable work of this time.

Looking at this period from the point of view of the ARCHITECTS, those mentioned so far are almost all of national standing. *G. G. Scott*, partly thanks to Edmund Beckett Denison, Lord Grimthorpe, did much: Doncaster has had its praise; he also did Cadeby (1856–60) near Doncaster, St Thomas, Longroyd Bridge, Huddersfield (1857–9), the majestic church at Mirfield (1869–71) ₇₀ and one – perhaps his best – at Halifax, or rather the model settlement of Akroydon, for Colonel Akroyd, the manufacturer (1856–9). To *Butterfield*'s small rural churches we can add one at Birkby, Huddersfield (1851–3); to *Street*'s St Michael, Thornhill, ₉₁ of 1877. *Pearson*'s distinguished parish church of Wentworth, built for the Fitzwilliams, is large, lofty and vaulted throughout; Hambleton (1881–2) is modest, Wakefield Cathedral sublime. *Bodley & Garner* are responsible for Horbury Junction 1891–3 and Skelmanthorpe 1894–5, and restorations at Cawthorne 1875–80, Hickleton 1870s–1880s and Womersley 1893–4. *Norman Shaw* only appears in a minor work at Hebden Bridge, 1874–6, *Sedding* at Netherton and at St Matthew, Sheffield, in 1886. Scott's horrible 'friend and tormentor', as he said, Beckett-Denison-*Grimthorpe*, the rebuilder of half St Albans Cathedral, not only patronized Scott at Doncaster but also designed churches himself (St James, Doncaster, 1858, and St Mary, Doncaster, 1885). *Henry Woodyer* designed the House of Mercy at Horbury.

Most of the churches, however, were the work of local architects, some of whom produced excellent work. In the N of the area, the Bradford architects *Mallinson & Healey*, who began their practice in the 1840s, were responsible for churches including Mytholmroyd 1847–8, Barkisland 1852–3, and Holy Innocents 1855–8 and St Mark 1862–5, both at Dewsbury. After Thomas Healey's death in 1863, James Mallinson worked with *W.S. Barber* of Halifax into the 1880s, while Healey's sons, *Thomas* and *Francis*, worked together. *William Henry Crossland*, a pupil of Scott, was in Huddersfield and Halifax, and before going to London *c.*1870 produced several fine churches e.g. Birstall 1863–70, St Stephen, Copley, 1863–5, and Trinity Church, Ossett, 1865. In the Sheffield inner suburban area the *Flocktons* and their partners were responsible for churches over a long period, from Christ Church, Pitsmoor, 1850 to their best work, St John, Ranmoor 1879 and 1888 by *E.M. Gibbs*. In the later C19 *John Dodsley Webster*, who had worked for Mallinson & Healey, was pre-eminent as church architect, and was appointed as a Diocesan Surveyor in the Diocese of York, with special responsibility for the Archdeaconry of Sheffield.

The new ROMAN CATHOLIC churches are all Gothic. Several in the S part of the area are by *Matthew Hadfield* of Sheffield and his son *Charles Hadfield*. Their practice enjoyed the patronage of their fellow Catholics the 14th and 15th Dukes of Norfolk, and Charles Hadfield was a lifelong friend of *J.F. Bentley*, who contributed designs for fittings for several of their churches. *Matthew Hadfield*'s first work is the small white brick church at Carlton, Selby, 1840–2. St Bede, Rotherham, 1841–2 with *J. G. Weightman*, followed and attracted favourable comment from Pugin himself. *Weightman & Hadfield*'s principal work is St Marie, Sheffield, 1847–50, now a cathedral, and notable for its beautiful E window and fine spire. The practice's later churches included St Peter, Doncaster, 1867 (now dem.), St Joseph, Wath-upon-Dearne, 1879 and St Joseph, Handsworth, 1881; the small but richly fitted mortuary chapel at Rivelin Valley, Sheffield, 1862, is also theirs. St Mary, Selby, by *Joseph & Charles Hansom*, 1856, is large with a prominent spire; Our Lady & St Paulinus, Dewsbury, by *E.W. Pugin*, 1867–71, makes a dramatic statement on an awkward site. Holy Rood, Barnsley, by *Edward Simpson* with *Charles Simpson*, 1903–5, is tall with a gloriously lofty interior. *p. 509*

There were, of course, many RESTORATIONS of medieval churches, some done with care and sensitivity, others regarded, even at the time, as vandalism. One of the most noticed was *Scott*'s restoration of the little C14 Bridge Chapel at Wakefield in 1848; he later regretted having replaced the exquisite, though decayed, W front with a copy. His restoration of Wakefield Cathedral from 1858 to 1874 was more successful, especially as his superintending architect was the scholarly *J.T. Micklethwaite*, who unravelled much of the church's early history during the work. The other major restoration in the area was that of Selby Abbey, begun by Scott in 1852 and continued by his son *J. Oldrid Scott* from 1889. Their work was partly destroyed by the fire of 1906, but work quickly resumed and included the rebuilding of the S transept, lost after the central tower's collapse in 1690, to *Oldrid Scott*'s designs in 1911–12. His designs for the completion of the W front, unfinished for nearly seven hundred years, were used by his son, *C.M. Scott*, in 1935. *20* *23*

Sheffield's General Cemetery is one of the earliest provincial CEMETERIES in the country, provided by a joint stock company and opened in 1836. Initially provided for Nonconformists, as few of the town's chapels had graveyards, its picturesque landscaping uses the hillside site to great advantage. *Samuel Worth*'s original chapel, gateway and offices are among the first in the Egypto-Greek style adopted in other cemeteries. Its non-Christian character was considered unsuitable for the Anglican chapel, which was provided by *William Flockton* in conventional Gothic style in 1850 for the additional, consecrated, area. Every town and even many of the larger villages had a cemetery by the end of the century, sometimes several in the big urban areas where the church and chapel yards were closed for public health reasons from the 1850s onwards. Where they survive – and the losses have been great – their chapels are mostly small and in a simple Gothic style, although Liversedge's, of 1903 with a little spired tower, is unusually ornate for its size. The larger town cemeteries typically have separate chapels for Church of England and Nonconformist use, often linked by a screen wall *p. 571* with an archway under a small tower. Good examples are those at Batley by *Walter Hanstock*, 1865, where there is also a cemetery keeper's lodge, and Burngreave Cemetery, Sheffield, 1860, by *Flockton & Lee*. At Mexborough the chapels, 1877–8, are separate but like so many are slightly different, one with a round apse and circular bellcote, the other with a polygonal apse and tower with spirelet. City Road Cemetery, Sheffield, by *M.E. Hadfield & Son*, 1881, has an imposing Tudor-style gateway flanked by offices for the Burial Board. Part of it was adapted as a columbarium when the Crematorium by *C. & C.M.E. Hadfield*, one of the earliest in the country and modelled on the Abbot's Kitchen at Glastonbury Abbey with a central chimney, was built in 1905.

Stained glass and furnishings

There are thousands of STAINED GLASS windows, their quality ranging from the superb through the competent but uninspiring to the downright hideous. A minority are by local firms, those by *Powell Bros* of Leeds being the most numerous but rarely noteworthy. The rest are by almost every firm who worked across the country, and space allows mention of only a tiny number of these here. The earliest decades include the chancel windows by *Thomas Willement* at Whitley Lower (1847) and *Pugin*'s large window at St Marie, Sheffield (1850), and one at Badsworth (1851), both made by *Hardman*. The dramatically colourful windows of this time include those by *Hedgeland* at Ecclesfield and Halifax (both 1855), by the *O'Connors* at Batley (1856, 1868) and Ossett (1865), by *William Warrington* at Halifax (1859–60) and Sowerby (1862), and the earliest of a number by *Capronnier*, at Christ Church, Doncaster (1858), and Rossington (1862). *William Wailes* occurs often from the 1850s onwards, e.g. at Cawthorne (1850), Ackworth (1855), Doncaster (1855) and Ecclesfield and Halifax (both 1860). The earliest of a number of windows by *Frederick Preedy* are those in Butterfield's three churches at Cowick, Hensall and Pollington, 1854. In a special category are the windows by *Morris & Co.* William Morris's first patrons in our area were the Spencer Stanhopes at Cawthorne (*c.* 1867, designed by *Burne-Jones*); then come Hoylandswaine (1870, also by *Burne-Jones*), the excellent windows at St Martin, Brighouse (1874), and St James, Brighouse (dem.; now at Bradford Museums), Woolley (1871), Flockton (*c.* 1872), Lockwood, Huddersfield (1878–9, by *Burne-Jones*) and Tankersley (1881, by *Burne-Jones*). Much later, four angels designed by *Burne-Jones* were used at Heckmondwike in 1912.

Of the leading firms who worked over several decades and whose work is widely spread, there are later windows by *Hardman* (Doncaster from 1859, Copley 1861–5, Birstall 1870s, Luddenden 1866–80 etc.), many by *Clayton & Bell* (St James, Doncaster 1860, High Green 1874, Mirfield 1870s–1880s, Rotherham 1890 etc.), by *Heaton, Butler & Bayne* (Sowerby 1879 onwards, Tickhill 1887, Arksey 1899 and the windows commemorating Louisa

Foljambe, e.g. Ecclesfield 1875 etc.), and by *Ward & Hughes* (Doncaster 1860s–1870s, Pontefract *c.* 1884–94, Cleckheaton 1890s and Selby Abbey 1885–1922 etc.). Around the 1880s there are several by *W.F. Dixon*, who had a following in the Sheffield area and for a time had a studio there, e.g. at Bradfield 1870–1890s, Ecclesfield and Sheffield Cathedral. In the later years especially there is work by *Burlison & Grylls* (Mirfield 1880s, Thornhill *c.* 1881–96, Marsden 1900–18 etc.), and much by *Powell & Sons* (Sheepridge, Huddersfield, 1902–24 and the large W window at Wentworth 1902), and by *Kempe* (a major group at Wakefield Cathedral 1873–1907, which brought many other commissions in the area: Clayton West 1891–1905, Harthill 1898, North Elmsall 1890s, Ecclesall, Sheffield, 1909–21, etc.). Windows by Kempe's student and admirer *Herbert Bryans* include those at Bawtry (1902–19) and Almondbury (1916–19).

As to FURNISHINGS, it is impossible to do more than mention a few highlights, beginning with *Pugin*'s reredos at St Marie, Sheffield 1850, sculpted by *Theodore Phyffers*. Near it is the oak organ case 1875, designed by *J.F. Bentley*, and carved by *J.E. Knox*. At Scott's church at Haley Hill, Halifax, the richly carved reredos, pulpit and font are by *J. Birnie Philip*, 1856–9, whose work can be seen elsewhere (e.g. Cadeby, Doncaster and Mirfield). At Cawthorne and Flockton the pulpits have painted panels by *J.R. Spencer Stanhope*; Cawthorne also has painted panels by *Evelyn De Morgan*, and Treeton has paintings by *Westlake*. Honley has a lofty oak pulpit by *C.E. Buckeridge & Floyce*, 1888, with painted panels, and a painted and gilded reredos by *E. Stanley Watkins*, 1905. Cantley is notable for *Comper*'s rich decoration and fittings from his restoration 1892–4 and later work. At Monk Fryston there is *Bromet & Thorman*'s very individual Art Nouveau Gothic traceried reredos and panelling of 1909. Examples of fine work in alabaster, marble, stone and oak by carvers of national repute other than those already mentioned, such as *Thomas Earp*, *Boulton* of Cheltenham and *Farmer & Brindley* can also be found. Work by local designers and carvers includes that by *George Shaw* of Saddleworth (Carlecotes, Friezland, Uppermill), *Arthur Hayball* and his daughter *Clara Keeling* of Sheffield (Bradfield, Ecclesfield), and *George W. Milburn* of York (Linthwaite). Anglo-Catholicism, a significant and perhaps surprising aspect of the area's religious character, is expressed in the rich furnishings of some Anglican churches, including reredoses, roods and even baldacchinos

Few of the vast number of MONUMENTS merit mention. Among several tomb-chests with recumbent effigies are Louisa Foljambe and her baby †1871 by *William Calder Marshall* at Tickhill, Charles Musgrave by *W.D. Keyworth* 1880 at Halifax, Charles Wood, 1st Viscount Halifax, †1885 and his wife, Mary, †1884 by *Farmer & Brindley* at Hickleton, and Bishop Walsham How †1897 by *J. Nesfield Forsyth* at Wakefield. The revival of MONUMENTAL BRASSES is best represented by those at Carlton for Col. Herman Stapleton †1847 by *Pugin*, made by *Hardman*, and at Horbury for Canon John Sharp †1903, both with kneeling figures.

Nonconformist churches and chapels

The strength of Nonconformity in the area in the C19, especially among the independent-minded inhabitants of the textile districts, is hard to exaggerate, and in many towns the chapels, by virtue of their number and size if not their architectural quality, were second only to the mills in prominence. Like the mills they too have been drastically reduced in quantity through redundancy, but similarly some have been saved by new uses. Although Gothic was, as seen in Sheffield, a permissible style as early as 1823, the simplicity of the Georgian tradition was mainly followed by use of classical and Italianate styles until Gothic became more frequent from the 1860s, with the so-called Free or Mixed Renaissance style gaining a hold later. Among earlier, classical, examples are the former St John's Methodist Church Birstall, rebuilt by *James Simpson* in 1846 with a simple pedimented front; Upper Chapel (Unitarian) in Sheffield, remodelled by *John Frith* in 1847–8 with an Ionic porch; Hope Baptist Chapel, Hebden Bridge, 1857–8, which has giant Corinthian pilasters to a pedimented three-bay front; and the equally dignified Wainsgate Baptist Church of 1859–60 above the town. The last three have fine galleried interiors. Batley's former Wesleyan chapel, 1861, has a plain pedimented gable front, but the larger and more prominently sited Central Methodist Church by *Sheard & Hanstock*, 1869, is more elaborately treated; it too has an excellent interior with an oval gallery. Selby's former Primitive Methodist chapel, 1862, is in a simple Italianate style, the large Baptist chapel near Heptonstall, rebuilt 1878–9 by *T. Horsfield* of Manchester, in a more elaborate one, its isolated hilltop site a reminder of how populous the uplands then were. None of these comes close in grandeur to the amazingly ostentatious former 68 Providence Congregational Church at Cleckheaton, by *Lockwood & Mawson*, 1857–9, one of the county's most powerful expressions of C19 dissent.

Contemporary with it, but in Gothic style, was the Crossley-endowed Congregational church at Halifax by *Joseph James* 1855–7, now represented only by its surviving tower and spire. At Todmorden the spire of the other great Gothic church, the sumptuous Unitarian church built by *John Gibson* 1865–9 at the cost of the Fieldens, is equally prominent in that town. At Heckmondwike *Arthur A. Stott* stayed with classical for the magnificent 93 porticoed front of the former Upper Independent Chapel 1888–90, but by the end of the century there is more variety of styles, with Free Gothic especially popular. At Hebden Bridge *Sutcliffe & Sutcliffe* gave the former Birchcliffe Baptist Chapel (1897–9) a grand Italianate front, but their Boulder Clough Methodist Chapel, Sowerby, is in an original Free Style that shows Arts and Crafts influence. *W.J. Hale* was equally inventive, going back to the octagonal form that John Wesley favoured and combining Perp Gothic with Arts and Crafts at Crookes Congregational Church, 1905, and at Wesley Hall, Crookes, 1907, both in Sheffield, while at Rawmarsh Methodist Church, 1907–8, his Gothic has an Art Nouveau flavour. *Garside & Pennington's* work shows similar elements in their Arts and Crafts Perp at Ossett Methodist Church, 1908, and Art Nouveau-influenced Gothic at Birkby Baptist Church, Huddersfield, 1910. The Oliver Heywood Memorial Sunday School at Lydgate Unitarian Chapel, New Mill, by *Edgar Wood & J. Henry Sellars*, 1910–11, displays their purer Arts and Crafts style.

Public buildings

The Victorian period is one of widespread MUNICIPAL REFORM instigated by multiple Acts of Parliament that passed powers to newly constituted, elected public bodies and which by the early C20 had given them authority over public health, drainage, gas, lighting, water supply, administration of the law, relief for the poor, education, policing, civic improvements, housing and transport.

The first significant change with an effect on the architectural character of several towns was the creation of Municipal Boroughs under the 1835 Municipal Corporations Act, which followed the reform of parliamentary constituencies in 1832. This brought about directly elected councils to govern the corporations already existing in the towns. Under the Act both Doncaster (with charter of 1688) and Pontefract (chartered from 1607) were reformed boroughs from 1836. At the same time, unincorporated towns could now petition to adopt municipal status. In s and w Yorkshire, as in other rapidly expanding industrial areas of England, newly important towns took this opportunity over the ensuing decades to replace existing systems of governance by Town Trustees or Commissioners: Sheffield (1843), Halifax (1848), Wakefield (1848), Dewsbury (1868), Batley (1868), Huddersfield (1868) Barnsley (1869) and Rotherham (1871).

The requirement for suitable premises for conducting council business and delivering services gave rise in most of these boroughs to the building of new TOWN HALLS: so, for example, Huddersfield's Town Hall of 1878–81 by the town's surveyor, *J.H. Abbey*. But these ambitious projects were subject to much argument over cost and delay, so for the premier examples there was often an interval of several years between the declaration of intent to build and the achievement of that intention. Halifax is a prime example (1859–63 by *Sir Charles Barry*), Wakefield (1877–80 by *Collcutt*) is another and Dewsbury (1886–9 by *Holtom & Fox*) a third. Pontefract and Sheffield already had premises for their Town Trustees (Pontefract's of 1785; Sheffield's of 1807–8 by *Charles Watson*, although in Sheffield one would be forgiven for identifying the Cutlers' Hall of 1832–3 as the likely seat of power) but both required enlarged premises as the new Corporation's functions multiplied, so Pontefract has a large addition of 1881–3 and Sheffield one of 1866.

Lower down the scale, the governance of the smaller towns was undertaken by Local Boards, who also built town halls. The finest of all is Todmorden of 1870–5, where the influence of

83
p. 273
84
85

wealthy local patrons and the involvement of *John Gibson*, who acted almost as the de facto town architect, produced the town's remarkable Neoclassical civic temple. More modest examples are Holmfirth (1842), Sowerby Bridge (1856–7 by *Perkin & Backhouse*), Lockwood (1862), Brighouse (1866–8 by *Mallinson & Barber*), Elland (1887–8 by *C.F.L. Horsfall*) and Cleckheaton (1890–2). These lasted until 1894, when the majority of the boards were formed into Urban District Councils; thus at Hebden Bridge (1897–8), Hipperholme (1898–9) and Meltham (1897–8) there are new buildings.

The 1889 Act produced the county councils that operated in England until 1974 and established the West Riding as a local authority with its headquarters at Wakefield, the historic county town that was raised to city status in 1888. Sheffield achieved the same status in 1893. From 1894 a series of county boroughs were created for places with no fewer than 50,000 people and were granted all the powers of the county council but independent of it. Those in our area of the West Riding were Sheffield, Wakefield, Barnsley, Halifax, Huddersfield, Dewsbury and Rotherham. From this moment flows a second wave of municipal buildings, purpose-built to address the expanding set of functions of each council. The effect on Wood Street, Wakefield, is remarkable and by the eve of the First World War had given it the character of a civic centre that no other Yorkshire town can rival. The style of the buildings erected in the last years of the C19 is demonstrably different from the manner of their mid-Victorian forebears. The two major projects in this area are the County Hall at Wakefield (by *Gibson & Russell*, 1894–8) and Sheffield Town Hall (1889–97) by *E.W. Mountford*. Both have high towers as the landmark accents and indulge in the styles and motifs of the Northern Renaissance, freely ornamented with sculpture and other decorative work on themes appropriate to the locale. At Sheffield every aspect of the city's trades and industries is represented by *F. W. Pomeroy* and at Wakefield the interior has a memorable series of gesso panels designed by *H.C. Fehr*, one of the artists most associated with the 'new sculpture' movement of the period *c*. 1900. Inside, both have fine council chambers and richly panelled rooms with plaster ceilings – that at Wakefield one of the best in England for its date.

The Act of 1846 introduced the system of COUNTY COURTS for hearing civil cases and resulted in the appointment of a surveyor to design new buildings in towns in England and Wales. Early results of this are to be seen at Sheffield (1854) and Dewsbury (1858–60), both designed by *Charles Reeves* as Italian palazzos, with the courtroom occupying the *piano nobile* above a rusticated basement of offices. The style may have been adopted as more suitable for the mercantile towns in which these courts were placed and as an intentionally different image from the Neoclassical severity of the existing criminal courts at Pontefract (*see* p. 434) and Wakefield (*see* p. 703). The style was continued by Reeves's successor, *T.C. Sorby*, architect of the buildings at Barnsley and Halifax. These are both of 1870–1, and slight variations on the same theme.

At the same time, purpose-built premises for the holding of PETTY SESSIONS – summary courts before Justices of the Peace and without jury – also proliferate in the second half of the C19. These might be accommodated within the new generation of large town halls, as at Halifax, but more generally they were independent buildings. Where this is so, it is interesting to see that they favour Gothic and Free Renaissance styles over the classical or Italianate of the higher courts. So, for example, at Barnsley (1878–9 by *Bernard Hartley III*), Goole (1887–8 by *J. Vickers Edwards*, County Surveyor), Castleford (1897) and Halifax (1898–1900, a very grand competition-winning design by *George Buckley & Son*), the last of which reflects accurately the need to relieve pressure for space in the major town halls by this date.

Several of the petty sessions courts are associated with POLICE STATIONS, a new building type from the mid C19 and one which in many places has an entirely domestic character, e.g. Hebden Bridge. After 1856 the boroughs had responsibility for policing, and early examples of purpose-built stations are at Barnsley (Westgate), 1856, and Goole (Aire Street), 1857. Most impressive are the Police Offices at Sheffield, added to the Town Hall in 1866 by *Flockton & Abbott*, and the building of 1878–9 at Wakefield (now the Magistrates' Court), and its successor of 1908 by *J. Vickers Edwards*. As the county town, Wakefield became the headquarters for the West Riding Constabulary from 1856 and from 1914 had grand new buildings in Laburnum Road (still in use), also designed by Vickers Edwards in a distinguished Neo-Georgian.

The other area of major importance over which the elected authorities obtained control in the C19 is that of SCHOOLS. For the first half of the C19 the Established and Nonconformist churches remained the providers of education in the towns and villages, supplemented by charitable foundations and grammar schools in several places, many of which were rebuilt or much enlarged in the C19, notably Doncaster's Grammar School (now Hall Cross Academy), rebuilt by *Scott*, 1867–9, in a Gothic not inappropriate for a foundation of the C14.

Large non-denominational BOARD SCHOOLS were built after the passing of the Education Act of 1870. This gave power to elected Boards to raise funds to erect new schools. The overcrowded industrial cities were among the first to grasp the opportunity and, beside Bradford in the northern half of the West Riding, Sheffield was the major pioneer. Outside London, it has one of the best collections of such buildings still in use. Thirty-nine were built during the thirty-three years of the Board's life. As with so many other aspects of public building in the West Riding, the preference was for local architects over national ones and so *C.J. Innocent*, of *Innocent & Brown*, architects of the first of the city's schools, was immediately appointed to the Board's staff and designed nineteen of the schools in his 'English Domestic Gothic'. p. 520 Although the majority follow common plans (usually of classrooms around a central hall) and are generally no more than two storeys tall, great care was taken to vary the elevations and achieve a picturesque grouping of parts. The scale of Sheffield's ambitions, however, meant that some of the designs were put out to competition and carried out by other – again local – architects, notably *W.J. Hale* and *Holmes & Watson*. But for the design of the Board's own offices in Leopold Street, the commission was given to *E.R. Robson*, architect to the London School Board, who also designed a suburban house for the Board's clerk.

Within the immediate environs of the offices at Sheffield developed too a wider variety of institutions for pupil training and Higher Grade education, offering more specialist education in science and art beyond standard elementary provision. The Higher Grade School in Halifax, 1882 by *Richard Horsfall*, is an early example and so too is Sheffield's Higher Grade School (the former Central Schools, by *Robson*), which was intended as a first step towards the higher education provided by Firth College (*see* below) on the adjoining site. Good examples of Board Schools and the varied styles adopted can be seen at Batley (by *Walter Hanstock*), Dewsbury (Eastborough School, by *Holtom & Connon*, with large windows of Geometrical tracery), Spring Grove School, Huddersfield (of 1879–80, one of the few adopting the Queen Anne style of the London schools), and Queen's Road, Halifax (of 1874 by *Horsfall* in a strikingly Neo-Baroque manner). After the 1902 Act, which passed school building to the local authorities, there is a notable expansion of schools specifically for the secondary education of girls, destined to increase the number of teachers in the system. Very good examples, and indicative of the turn architecturally towards a symmetrical Neo-Georgian style, are the Girls' High Schools at Barnsley (1909), Doncaster (1910–11) and Goole (1908–10).

Education was also communicated in the C19 through the large number of MECHANICS' INSTITUTES established in the towns and cities to educate working men in technical subjects. An early one is Wakefield's of 1842 – indeed, it is the first important civic building in the remarkable parade along Wood Street; another was Sheffield's (by *George Alexander*, 1847, but now demolished). The 1850s were a particularly fecund era for such establishments with examples of that decade still surviving – albeit in other uses – at Gomersal, Batley, Rotherham, Marsden and Halifax. Italianate styles prevailed in all of these: Batley is a quite ambitious example which became the Town Hall, and Halifax's institute has a *piano nobile* of Corinthian columns. Huddersfield's institute, however, by *Travis & Mangnall*, 1859–60, is of an altogether more adventurous character: Gothic of the Waterhousian stamp and little wonder that from 1883 this formed the core of what became the University of Huddersfield.

The same path was followed by other places of HIGHER EDUCATION. Several technical schools had been built in the 1880s (Sheffield, Huddersfield, etc.) but funding of technical education through local authority rates became possible from the 1890s and was pursued in the industrial towns, with new buildings appearing before the First World War. Examples include Batley's Technical School and Art School of 1893 and Doncaster's Technical College of 1913–15. Sheffield's University grew out of the merger in 1895 of its Technical School and Medical School with Firth College, established by the industrialist Mark Firth in 1879 as a purpose-built venue for the Cambridge University Extension Lectures, and with a façade designed by *Flockton & Abbott* consciously evoking the gatehouse of Clare College, Cambridge. The first buildings for the new University survive, by *E.M. Gibbs*, and in a traditional Tudor Collegiate style with a quad and octagonal library adjoining. Gibbs remained the University's architect for the new buildings for the technical schools and the excellent Wrenaissance-style Sir Frederick Mappin Building, 1912–13.

One major function of the educational institutes was to provide LIBRARIES and it is perhaps significant that those places with institutes were late adopters of the free libraries. These sprang up after the Act of 1850 made it possible to levy rates to subsidize the building, furnishing and staffing (although not stocking) of libraries. One of the earliest purpose-built examples standing in our area is Highfield Library in the inner southern suburbs of Sheffield, built in 1876 by *E.M. Gibbs*, an Italianate pile with Lombardic windows. But the majority of libraries belong to the period after about 1895, by which time much more generous financial support was being provided by benefactors such as Andrew Carnegie. His fund supported buildings at Castleford (1904–5), Batley (1906–7), Heckmondwike (1905–7), Swinton (1905–6) and Penistone (1913). Carnegie made no requirements about style, leaving local architects to express their individual flair, and many of these small institutes are a delight of the Free Baroque prevalent in the Edwardian years. Batley, by *Hanstock*, is one of the most impressive; among the other libraries of this date, Todmorden (1896–7 by *T.H. Mitchell*) and Wakefield (1905–6 by *Trimnell, Cox & Davison*) also stand out – the latter in the sweet C17 style favoured by Basil Champneys. Dewsbury's library is combined as a single design with the PUBLIC BATHS, a building type to be found in the more enlightened industrial towns. Many have been subject to conversion in the later C20 but at Sheffield the baths in Glossop Road preserve behind the façade of 1909–10 an exotic remnant of the tiled interior of the Turkish baths of 1877–9 by *E.M. Gibbs*.

WATER SUPPLY was also the responsibility of the Corporations eventually, but initially a matter for private companies. The offices of the Sheffield Waterworks Co. (established 1830) in Division Street are a particularly impressive palazzo by *Flockton & Abbott*, 1867. The water companies constructed RESERVOIRS in the catchment areas of the Pennines and Peak District to supply the major towns and cities. This was a potentially dangerous exercise and the collapse of the embankment at Bilberry Reservoir on the Holme in 1852 flooded Holmfirth, killing eighty-one. Many more were killed by the collapse of Dale Dyke in the Loxley valley in 1864. Precisely to avoid such calamities, engineers developed novel solutions to control overflow. At Butterley Reservoir, Marsden, created by Huddersfield Corporation in 1891–1901 (engineers *T. & C. Hawksley*), there is a dramatic

stone-stepped spillway built to carry excess water. Another of
c. 1900, more like a water chute, carries water from Tunnel End
reservoir at Marsden into the Colne river. Outflow was otherwise
controlled by valve towers. Widdop Reservoir, Heptonstall has a
valve tower like an Egyptian temple by *La Trobe Bateman*, c. 1876,
while at Sheffield Corporation's Langsett Reservoir 1888–94, on
the Porter (Little Don), the tower takes the form of a miniature
castle keep positioned against the immensely long dam. One of
the most remarkable attempts at beautification is the reservoir for
Halifax in the wild Luddenden valley where, in compensation for
the land taken from the Castle Carr estate, the Corporation paid
for the reservoirs to be designed as a water garden in 1864–70.

Of WORKHOUSES built by the Poor Law Unions after 1834
there is slender standing evidence, although a few survived first
in hospital use before conversion to residential accommodation:
for example, Pontefract's building by *Lockwood & Mawson* and
a small piece of Rotherham's workhouse by *Hurst & Moffatt*.
They were usually positioned slightly outside the then built-up
areas of the towns or districts which they served, although
suburbs later grew around them, as at the Sheffield Union's
workhouse of 1879–80 in the northern district of inner Sheffield
and at the Ecclesall Bierlow workhouse in the south-western
district of Nether Edge. Both survive because their infirmaries
were retained and expanded as HOSPITALS after the abolition of
the workhouses in the C20. These were general hospitals, but the
maladies of the C19 also saw an increase in specialist institutions
for the treatment of infectious diseases (Kendray Hospital,
Barnsley) and asylums for the mentally ill (the former County
Asylum at Stanley, Wakefield, begun in the early C19, and the
former Middlewood Asylum at Wadsley, 1869–72, in the outer
suburbs of Sheffield), as well as hospitals for women and children. The Children's Hospital at Sheffield is by *J. D. Webster*, 1902;
he also designed the unusual and innovative octagonal outpatients' building at the Sheffield Royal Infirmary in 1884. The
period ends with a flourish in the King Edward VII Hospital
(originally for disabled children) in the Rivelin valley near Stannington on the very edge of Sheffield. Designed by *A.W. Kenyon*,
this is a grand example of the Neo-Georgian style which came
to dominate much public building after the First World War.
CONVALESCENT HOMES also sprang up in locations away from
the polluted city, especially at Fulwood.

The movement to establish PUBLIC PARKS in most of the
largest towns has its roots in C19 legislation but their creation
was more often than not the benefaction of major industrialists
or landowners. An early anticipator of this desire for a health-
giving and educational ornament to a town was the Botanical
Gardens at Sheffield, which were opened in 1836 (landscaped by
Robert Marnock and with impressive glasshouses by *B. Broomhead
Taylor*), but free access was only available initially to shareholders
or subscribers. Genuine public parks begin instead with the
People's Park in the western suburbs of Halifax, 1856–7, donated
by Sir Francis Crossley and explicitly intended as a place of

recreation for the working men of the town. *Paxton* designed the layout. All the major towns have their equivalent, either laid out on land reserved during suburban development – as at Shroggs Park near Akroydon (*see* p. 289), the model industrial settlement at Halifax – or transformed from the grounds of formerly private houses: Rotherham's Boston Park (1876, also originally called the People's Park) and Clifton Park (1891); in Sheffield, Firth Park, 1875, and especially Weston Park, also opened in 1875. The last is an epitome of the Victorian ideal, with the site of the former Weston House taken for the museum and Mappin Art Gallery, emphasizing the park's role as a place of learning as much as recreation. Parks are also the location for much of the PUBLIC SCULPTURE to be seen in towns. Almost all the parks in our area are ornamented with statues of local worthies and benefactors, e.g. Sir Francis Crossley in his People's Park by *Joseph Durham* or Edward Akroyd at Akroydon by *J. Birnie Philip*. In more than a few instances statues now reside in the parks having been removed from the city centres as part of later replanning. An extreme case is the statue of Joseph Locke by *Marochetti* in the memorial park at Barnsley, which was cast for an unrealized ensemble of celebrated engineers to be erected in London.

Transport and industry

The RAILWAYS transformed south and west Yorkshire, complementing but eventually superseding the canals. An early line was the Sheffield & Rotherham Railway of 1838, which encouraged the first development of industry in the Don valley. There then followed the Sheffield, Ashton-under-Lyne & Manchester Railway, which reached Bridgehouses (Sheffield) in 1845 and was then extended through to Lincolnshire in 1848 as the Manchester, Sheffield & Lincolnshire Railway (MSLR). It continued in use as the Great Central Railway from 1897. The Great Northern Railway (GNR) had opened its line to York and moved its engine works to Doncaster in 1853, thus initiating that formerly agricultural centre's role as a place of heavy industry. By the end of the decade the GNR dominated much of West Yorkshire through lines to Halifax, Leeds and Bradford, and most of the major towns were served by more than one company, each with its own station. Many other early railway companies of the first boom were amalgamated as the Lancashire and Yorkshire Railway (L&YR) from 1847, itself absorbed in the C20 by the London, Midland & Scottish Railway. Sheffield had no direct route to London until 1870, when the Midland opened their line to the city.

In terms of RAILWAY ENGINEERING, there is the monumental stone viaduct of the MSLR at Sheffield by the local engineer *Sir John Fowler* and architects *Weightman & Hadfield*. Viaducts of *c.* 1845 also make an impressive intervention in the scene at Slaithwaite on the Manchester–Huddersfield line and the same is true for that by *George Stephenson* at Todmorden for the Manchester & Leeds Railway, which in 1841 achieved the feat of digging by hand the world's longest (1 mile) railway tunnel (the Summit Tunnel s of Todmorden, which burrows through the Pennines just across the Lancashire border). There are several viaducts criss-crossing the suburbs of Huddersfield and its neighbourhood, by *John Hawkshaw*, chief engineer for the L&YR. At Totley, on the far sw edge of Sheffield, the Midland Railway achieved a remarkable three-mile-long tunnel for their line to Manchester, second only to the GWR's Severn Tunnel. Also not to be forgotten is the splendid plate-girder Swing Bridge crossing the Ouse at Goole of 1869 by *T. E. Harrison* for the North Eastern Railway. The docks there also preserve some important railway structures, including hydraulic hoists for lifting wagons and tipping coal into boats.

75   Among early STATIONS Huddersfield is an outstanding example, still as designed in 1846–50 by *J.P. Pritchett*, grand Neoclassical with full Corinthian portico. Comparably impressive is Halifax's smaller Palladian-style station by *Butterworth* of Manchester, 1855. Among the branch lines, at Womersley is a delightful Swiss-style station house of 1848 for the L&YR. From the later period the best is Sheffield's station as rebuilt in 1905 by *Charles Trubshaw*, architect for the Midland Railway, with its excellent tiled refreshment room, and Hebden Bridge of 1891–3, its Victorian character carefully conserved.

The MILLS of the textile districts remain the single most important and widespread type of industrial building, despite demolition on a scale that is hard to imagine. The extent of the loss can only really be grasped by comparison of what exists now with photographs from say, the 1950s, not only of Dewsbury, Halifax, Huddersfield and the host of smaller towns but also of the valleys and hillsides of the rivers Calder, Colne and Holme and their tributaries. The mills' impact was not from architectural display – for beyond a grand Italianate entrance or a fancy-topped chimney that was reduced to a minimum – but their size grew to a prodigious degree. They were the largest buildings by far in the rural and semi-rural areas, and even in a town such as
74   Halifax the sheer scale of the Crossleys' Dean Clough Mills makes them an impressive rival to buildings like the Town Hall or Haley Hill church.

Although their buildings are similar, the different branches of the industry were mainly concentrated in different areas. The woollen area, producing plain cloth, often with a felted texture, was by far the largest, with Halifax and Huddersfield as its centres, although in the later C19 Huddersfield moved more into worsted, a lighter, smoother cloth. Todmorden and the w end of the Calder valley specialized in cotton, while the Batley and Dewsbury area was the centre of the heavy woollen district, producing blankets and coatings, and especially mungo and shoddy, made with recovered wool. The principal building types are multi-storey spinning mills, weaving sheds, warehouses and offices. Spinning mills were now built of fireproof construction, usually with floors on segmental brick arches and cast-iron beams and columns, until these were superseded by the use of concrete and steel after 1900. To accommodate the large and heavy power looms that replaced handloom weaving almost everywhere by 1860, weaving sheds were single-storeyed with north lights in sawtooth-profile roofs for even lighting. Shaw Lodge Mills, Halifax, is a good surviving complex dating from 1830–76 with all four building types; at West Vale are a group of four- to six-storey mills of the 1870s to 1890s, three by *Richard Horsfall*. Other big mills are at Elland, Huddersfield, Marsden, Queensbury and Slaithwaite. Oats Royd Mill, Luddenden, and Hollins Mill, 1856–8, beside the canal, and Frostholme Mill, 1896, both near Todmorden, are examples in rural surroundings. The most impressive warehouses, built off-site, are the Italianate and Venetian Gothic ones in Batley and Dewsbury, mainly from the 1850s to '70s, for rag merchants and shoddy and mungo manufacturers.

As for other industries, in Sheffield the traditional 'light trades' of cutlery and edge tools and the manufacture of silver and silver plate were still predominant in the town centre. A few large four- and five-storey works for the biggest firms such as Joseph Rodgers & Sons and Mappin Bros, which each employed hundreds of people, towered above the mass of small workshops and yards around them. The only survivor in Sheffield is the Cornish Place Works of James Dixon & Co., CUTLERY AND SILVERWARE manufacturers, with a courtyard partly enclosed by four-storey brick ranges of the 1850s. Other large complexes with courtyards are Butcher's Wheel, for cutlery and edge tools, 1850s, with a tall chimney, and Portland Works of 1877 by *J.H. Jenkinson* for

Sheffield, Rodgers & Sons razor grinders' workshop.
Engraving, 1866

cutlery manufacture, with well-preserved hand forges. Green Lane Works, for Henry Hoole's fire-grate manufactory, has a fine
78   triumphal arch entrance of 1860, with relief panels probably by his former designer *Alfred Stevens*. Little survives of Sheffield's early STEEL WORKS of the 1840s and 1850s in the Savile Street district, where architectural display was less conspicuous and a plain Italianate frontage, as at President Works, *c*. 1852, sufficed. Offices at later works, for firms such as Vickers with international connections, were more ambitious, at least inside; the River Don
98   Works by *Holmes & Watson* 1906 has a splendid marble-lined staircase and boardroom. Externally, the soot-laden air precluded sculptural display but cantilevered concrete balconies were included to facilitate window cleaning. Buildings for COAL MINING have vanished except at Middlestown, where the National Coal Mining Museum for England preserves the winding engine house and the heapstead building with headstock, 1876, of Caphouse Colliery. At Doncaster the GNR's ENGINEERING WORKSHOPS, called 'The Plant', have mostly gone, but *William & Joseph Cubitt*'s long original building, 1851–2, remains as offices, with the engine shop of 1853 behind.

Commercial and entertainment buildings

EXCHANGES for trading in goods were a well-established feature of the agricultural and textile towns. The southern area of the West Riding cannot now offer anything for the C19 as grand as the Corn Exchange at Leeds or the Wool Exchange at Bradford; its finest building in this class is, of course, the late C18 Piece
63   Hall at Halifax, which changing circumstances of trade rendered unwanted by the mid C19. Many corn exchanges were also surplus to requirements by the C20 and have disappeared, including Wakefield's first of 1820 and second by *W.L. Moffatt*, 1836–40, and the 15th Duke of Norfolk's great Tudor Gothic exchange of 1881 at Sheffield by *M.E. Hadfield & Son*. The outstanding survivor of the type is that at Doncaster of 1870–3 by *William Watkins*, which still dominates the market place and sits in the embrace of the earlier Market Hall, a serious late classical design, erected in 1846–9 by *John Butterfield* as part of a typically Victorian rationalization by the Corporation of the more chaotic outdoor market arrangements of previous centuries. This occurred elsewhere, and by the end of the C19 several towns had large covered markets. Not all have made it through to the present day, e.g. Sheffield's classical Norfolk Market Hall of 1851 and Huddersfield's grand Gothic Market Hall, which was demolished *c*. 1970, but the Borough Market at Halifax is characteristic of the most ambitious kind, built in iron and glass for the airy market hall but enclosed by street fronts of stone in a lavish Renaissance character. It is by *Leeming & Leeming*, 1891–6, and a forerunner of their City Markets at Leeds.

Every town has a variety of BANKS, many now in other uses, and invariably built in sober classical or Italianate styles until

Gothic ceased to be regarded as somehow less trustworthy. The best of the earliest ones is *Samuel Worth*'s fine Grecian Sheffield & Hallamshire Bank of 1838 in Sheffield. Later, in palazzo style, are the Royal Bank of Scotland by *Flockton & Abbott*, 1866–7, in Sheffield, the handsome Barclays Bank, by *Michael Sheard* in Dewsbury of similar date, and *Lockwood & Mawson*'s richly decorated Wakefield & Barnsley Union Bank of 1877–8 in Wakefield. *Perkin & Bulmer*'s ornate Yorkshire Bank, 1888–9, in Sheffield is one of the few in Gothic style, as the classical and, later, Baroque styles offered better opportunities for impressive display. Lloyds Bank, Halifax, by *Horsfall & Williams*, 1897–8, has a pedimented Corinthian portico and polished granite columns and a fine banking hall, and in Doncaster, which has especially good banks fronting High Street, once the Great North Road, there is *Demaine & Brierley*'s Portland stone former York City & County Bank of 1897 in Free Baroque, *F. W. Masters*'s Italianate palazzo for the Yorkshire Banking Co. 1885 and Lloyds Bank by *Sidney Kitson*, 1912, with giant Doric columns.

OFFICE BUILDINGS show more variety, and Gothic as well as mixed styles were widely accepted. Among the grandest offices is the Early Renaissance Venetian palazzo built in 1874 by *M.E. Hadfield & Son* for the Sheffield United Gas Light Co., which has carving by *Thomas Earp* and a glazed dome above the former general office by *J. F. Bentley*. *Crossland*'s Ramsden Estate Buildings in Huddersfield, 1868–70, are richly Gothic, with good carved decoration, and in Sheffield excellent carving by *Frank Tory* enlivens *M.E. Hadfield & Son*'s Tudor Gothic Parade Chambers of 1883–5, and Cairns Chambers of 1894. Goole has the Renaissance-style Bank Chambers, by *H.B. Thorp*, 1892, in red brick and terracotta, Halifax the Baroque Revival District Bank Chambers, 1907, with pedimented gables. Of the three Prudential Assurance buildings by *Alfred Waterhouse* and/or his son, those in Sheffield (1895) and Huddersfield (1899–1901) are in characteristic red brick and terracotta, while Doncaster's (1912–13) is in pink and purplish brick. One of the earliest uses of faience, the glazed terracotta that could resist the soot that coated every town, is on *Gibbs & Flockton*'s White Building, Sheffield, *c.* 1908, which has engaging relief figures by *Alfred & William Tory*.

SHOPS of this period still make a significant contribution to the character of all the towns but are so numerous and so varied in their size, date and style that it is impossible to do more than offer a few of the larger examples. Sheffield was the first to have department stores, but lost its most magnificent ones, Schofield's (1870s, 1897) and Walsh's (1899) to the 1940 Blitz and Cole Brothers (1869) to post-war redevelopment. Elsewhere, it was often the local Co-operative Society that built the largest and grandest town shops, a sign of the strength of the movement across the area. Dewsbury's Italian Renaissance pile by *Holtom & Connon* for the Dewsbury Pioneers Industrial Society, 1878–80 with later additions, is the most splendid. Barnsley has a group begun in 1885 with hall and reading room as well, and extensions up to 1938, Huddersfield a Renaissance block of 1886–1904, with domed and spired towers, and Wakefield a big brick Gothic block, with fine Edwardian shopfronts, begun in 1876–8 by *W. & D. Thornton* and extended more elaborately, with a large upper meeting hall, in 1899–1902 by *A. Hart*. Hebden Bridge has a plainer but prominent block of 1875–6 and 1889–90 with a clock tower, and Rotherham a block of 1900. Nowhere has ARCADES to match those of Leeds, and Sheffield's have gone, but Barnsley's, by *Wade & Turner*, 1893, and Dewsbury's, by *John Kirk & Sons*, 1899, have their own charm.

Notable HOTELS are few, the best being Huddersfield's George Hotel, 1848–50 by *William Wallen*, and the White Swan in Halifax, 1858, possibly by *Parnell & Smith*, both in palazzo style, the White Swan's long front especially richly decorated. Sheffield has the plainer Italianate Royal Victoria Station Hotel of 1862 by *M.E. Hadfield*, Barnsley the former Queen's Hotel by *Wade & Turner*, 1872, also Italianate with carved decoration, and Doncaster the Danum Hotel, by *W.H. Wagstaffe*, 1908, with a fine ballroom lined with mirrors.

Four fine THEATRES survive, three still in theatrical use. Barnsley's small Theatre Royal, by *Walter Emden*, 1898, is now a night club but retains its decorated interior with two galleries. Sheffield has lost *Frank Matcham*'s oriental-style Empire Palace, 1895, the Theatre Royal by *C.J. Phipps* 1880 and *Matcham* 1901, and the Moorish-style Alhambra, Attercliffe, by *G.D. Martin & A. Blomfield Jackson*, but has the Lyceum, originally by *Walter*
88   *Emden* with *Holmes & Watson* 1893, but with a beautiful interior from *W.G.R. Sprague*'s remodelling of 1897. In Wakefield is *Matcham*'s Theatre Royal, opened as the Opera House in 1894 and his smallest surviving theatre, which has jolly plasterwork decoration to the auditorium and circle and balcony fronts. Halifax's Victoria Theatre, by the local architect *W. Clement Williams*, 1897–1901, was built as a concert hall and has a fine exterior in late English Renaissance style and a splendid foyer with an imperial staircase under a stained glass dome.

Housing

Among the area's COUNTRY HOUSES there was one new one, at Brodsworth, and existing houses were altered in varying degrees to improve comfort and convenience, often with the benefit of new technology, or to follow fashion or ambition. Brodsworth
80   Hall was rebuilt in Italianate style in 1861–3, its obscure architect, *Philip Wilkinson*, incorporating novel ideas on planning and domestic efficiency, and creating interiors made more memorable by their Italian marble statuary. *E.W. Pugin*'s uncompleted
p. 161   scheme of 1871–4 at Carlton Towers was an ambitious project of medieval fantasy, but *J.F. Bentley* rescued Lord Beaumont
82   with sumptuous interiors that form his principal country house work. At Wortley Hall the Earl of Wharncliffe's new billiard room was richly decorated by *Edward Poynter* in 1871–83, and there and

at Sandbeck Park coachhouses were later converted to garages
fronted by glass-roofed canopies for car washing. While many
country house owners were busy rebuilding or restoring their
local parish churches, at Sandbeck a Gothic chapel by *Benjamin
Ferrey* 1869–70 terminated the now-demolished bedroom wing.
One may not mind that *Pritchett*'s Gothic chapel designed for the
South Court at Wentworth Woodhouse was not built, but the
demolition of *Pugin*'s ornate chapel for the Catholic Tempest
family at Ackworth Grange, 1841, is much to be regretted. At
Bretton Hall, *Basevi*'s weightily detailed stables, *c.* 1842–5, were
never finished; those in Gothic style at Rossington Hall by *W.M.
Teulon*, 1855, survived the fire that destroyed the house, which he
rebuilt in Jacobethan style *c.* 1880–2. In GARDENS new glasshouses widened opportunities for horticultural one-upmanship;   *p. 153*
of few survivors the best is the restored conservatory at Wentworth Castle of 1885. *Devey*'s remodelled gardens at Byram Hall
are mostly lost but the gardens at Brodsworth Hall have been
restored to their 1860s design. An ominous footnote to the story
of the country houses is the demolition in 1899 of Aldwarke Hall,
a classical house of *c.* 1720 (*see* Ripponden), beset by the industry
of Rawmarsh.

Much more numerous are the MANSIONS of the new commercial and industrial elites, mostly built in the suburbs, and
sometimes, like Colonel Akroyd's Bankfield (Halifax), little more
than a stone's throw from the works and the employees' houses.
A few men aspired to country retreats, such as Castle Carr (Luddenden), the remote sham castle built for J.P. Edwards by *Alfred
Smith* with *Thomas Risley*, 1859, and *John Hogg* 1868–72, which
stood on the moors above Luddenden, or Hesley Hall near
Bawtry, with its decorated Gothic chapel of 1891 by *J.H. Christian*.
In the earlier period the Italianate style was chosen by both steelmakers and textile manufacturers: in Sheffield by Mark Firth for
Oakbrook by *Flockton, Lee & Flockton*, *c.* 1860, and by Sir John
Brown for Endcliffe Hall by *Flockton & Abbott*, 1863–5; in Halifax
by Colonel Akroyd for Bankfield in the 1850s and its enlargement
by *J.B. & W.Atkinson* in 1867; and in Huddersfield by John Beaumont for Ravensknowle Hall by *Richard Tress* 1859–62. Endcliffe,
whose fireproof construction includes concrete floors, retains
interior decoration but is surpassed by Bankfield with its wall
paintings depicting classical mythology. The French villa style was
used for Sir Francis Crossley's Belle Vue (now Crossley House),
Halifax, by *G.H. Stokes* 1856–7, and Broadfold Hall, Luddenden,
1877. The full castellated mode had been introduced at an early
date in Sheffield for Samuel Roberts, whose admiration for Mary,
Queen of Scots was expressed in Queen's Tower by *Woodhead &
Hurst*, 1839, and was used at Dobroyd Castle, Todmorden, built   81
for John Fielden by *John Gibson* 1866–9. Houses in other styles
are St Catherine's Hall, Doncaster, by *John Clark* 1838–9 in Tudor
Gothic and the classical Meltham Hall for mill-owner William
Brook, 1841, attributed to *William Wallen*. At Batley the mildly
Gothic Woodlands (now the Bagshaw Museum) by *Sheard &*

Hanstock for the woollen manufacturer George Sheard, 1873–5, has interiors with unusual panelling and other joinery.

Every town has its MIDDLE-CLASS HOUSING, in the industrial districts usually on higher ground and to the w to avoid the smoke. In Sheffield it begins with the Italianate and Gothic and Tudor villas and semi-detached houses in Broomhall, Broomhill and Endcliffe; later comes Nether Edge, the plan laid out by *Robert Marnock* between 1851 and 1861. Huddersfield has the Italianate and Gothic villas of the 1850s and '60s in Edgerton; Halifax has Skircoat and later Savile Park with its fine houses by *Butler, Wilson & Oglesby* of Leeds, *c.* 1899, on Manor Heath Road. These bring us to the influence of the Arts and Crafts movement and the wide use of the Domestic Revival style, both in its more southern form with tile hanging and half-timbering and in the regional form drawn from local Pennine vernacular houses of the C16 and C17. Notable are the houses by *Edgar Wood*: in Huddersfield the Jacobean Briarcourt 1894–5 and Banney Royd, with Art Nouveau motifs, 1900–2; in Sheffield, The Dingle, 1904. In Barnsley, the rendered Moorland Court by *Percy Houfton* 1905–6 shows the influence of Voysey, seen again in north Doncaster e.g. in houses with roughcast by *Bunney & Makins* 1910.

There are excellent examples of WORKERS' HOUSING, some of advanced standards for their time. The earliest model settlement, which preceded the much better-known Saltaire (*West Riding North*), is at Copley, where Colonel Akroyd built three rows of back-to-back cottages beside his mill in 1849–53, with a school, library and canteen. Two further rows, *c.* 1865, are through-houses. Although tiny, these avoided the housing reformers' condemnation of back-to-backs, and Akroyd's much larger development in Halifax, Akroydon, begun in 1861, has only through-houses. Their domestic Gothic design is *Scott's*, amended by *W. H. Crossland*; at West Hill Park, Halifax, the smaller scheme promoted by John Crossley with Building Society support was won in competition by *Paull & Ayliffe* in 1863. Other housing built to higher standards than the ubiquitous speculative builders' terraces includes that provided by the Brook family at Meltham, and occasionally that provided through self-help, such as the Freehold Land Societies of Sheffield (who built in suburbs such as Walkley), the Co-operative Societies and the Oddfellows (who included cottages with their Hall near South Crosland in 1854).

The early C20 sees the first council housing on a scale to match Akroydon, notably in Sheffield at Wincobank, where the Flower Estate, planned on Garden City principles, was begun in 1900 and has Arts and Crafts-influenced cottage houses by both local and outside architects, including *Percy Houfton*. He also designed the earliest model village built for miners, at Woodlands, Adwick-le-Street, 1907–*c.* 1910, with cottage houses laid out spaciously around the church in the middle. The influence of Voysey is evident in their roughcast walls and tiled roofs; at Whitwood, Castleford, *Voysey* himself designed a smaller group of houses for colliery officials, built 1906–8.

p. 357
96
p. 294
99
p. 165

BUILDINGS AFTER 1918

So now we can proceed to the greater portion of the C20, beginning with the period BETWEEN THE WARS.

WAR MEMORIALS were erected in towns and villages within a very few years of 1918. Stained glass windows provide the vehicle for large numbers of individual memorials in churches, but for the civic memorials erected to the fallen the best examples are in the major towns. Sheffield's memorial in Barker's Pool by *C.D. Carus-Wilson* is one of the most original of the date, with a needle-like steel shaft soaring high above the base and good figure sculpture. Public parks were often deemed the most suitable location for these memorials, as at Weston Park, Sheffield, but also at Cleckheaton, Dewsbury and Doncaster. That at Cleckheaton is one of the best, by *George Frampton*.

At Barnsley the war memorial is incorporated into the Town Hall by *Briggs & Thornely*, 1932–3. The interwar period was the second great phase of grand CIVIC BUILDINGS, after the Victorian years. So at Sheffield the City Hall was opened in 1932 (although planned as early as 1920) and executed by *E. Vincent Harris*. As Pevsner wrote in the original volume for the West Riding: 'Mr Vincent Harris's buildings are of a higher order – within the Imperialist and revivalist categories' and Sheffield like many of his best works combines austerity in its massing with richness in interior decoration. In reference to Barnsley he wrote: 'it is of that bald grandeur which lacks the self-confidence of the Edwardians and feels forced to reach a compromise with the more functional and less verbose style of the C20'. This now seems unfair and is no more true of public building by architects working for the local authorities, who turned with some versatility to the Neo-Georgian or monumental stripped classical manner, e.g. the Mining and Technical Institute at Barnsley and the Library and Art Gallery at Huddersfield of 1937–40. The expanding responsibilities of the West Riding County Council (WRCC), especially over education and administration of the law, gave work to their County Architect, *P. O. Platts* (Court House and Police Station at Batley, court house at Rotherham, several buildings at Wakefield), and their Education Architect, *H. Wormald* (former Mining Institute at Dinnington (now Rotherham College), Ecclesfield School, Goole College and King's School, Pontefract). As a city, Sheffield made its own arrangements, supplying buildings for all the public services, mostly designed by *W.G. Davies*, the City Architect: e.g. notably the Library in the city centre and the City Museum at Weston Park. Then in the 1930s the Education Committee of the WRCC took a more progressive direction as part of their intention to raise the school leaving age while also attending to the social needs of the youngest children. This resulted in an entirely different Continental Modernist image for Whitwood Mere Infants' School, Castleford, where *Oliver Hill* was commissioned and produced a colourful and well-lit interior within a single-storey streamlined curved plan with continuous glazing that could be

103

105

retracted for open-air teaching. The prevalence of this idea – especially in polluted industrial areas – also directly informs the design of Newman School at Rotherham by *Geoffrey Raven* of the Borough Architect's Department, 1939, with classrooms in a series of linked pavilions with windows that could be drawn back for outdoor teaching.

Evaluating the INDUSTRIAL scene of these years is hard as so much of what was architecturally interesting for this period – e.g. the pithead baths erected at the collieries – has been swept away with the closure of the mines. Those at Caphouse Colliery (now National Coal Mining Museum, Middlestown) by *O.H. Parry* must now represent this vanished type. Among new building types for industry in the C20 the coal-fired POWER STATIONS are another class of structure rapidly vanishing from the landscape. At Ferrybridge the faience-decorated turbine hall etc. of 'A' station of 1926 was retired some years ago but has survived as offices. Its successors are unlikely to be preserved following closure in 2016. Technological innovation found its architectural representation in the more advanced stylings of the day and so the ticket hall of Doncaster Railway Station (by the *LNER Architects Dept*) is a sleek streamlined interior behind a restrained Neo-Georgian front.

After the First World War, HOUSING was a declared priority sustained by Acts of Parliament for expanding provision of subsidized housing as 'homes for heroes'. The character of the estates developed from that time was in some ways anticipated by the progress made in the design of purpose-built mining villages (*see* above) from before 1914, which followed many of the lessons of the housing reformers associated with the Garden City and Garden Suburb movements. Several initiatives were already in place before 1914 but further developed thereafter. Examples are at Armthorpe, Penistone (Cubley Garden Village for steelworkers, by *Herbert Baker*), Rossington, Ryhill and Thurcroft. At High Green the Miners' Welfare Hall is designed by *Barry Parker*, best known for his partnership with Raymond Unwin in popularizing the Garden City-style settlement.

Homes specifically for ex-servicemen include the Haig Memorial Homes of 1928–9 by *Grey Wornum* at Norton in the outer area of Sheffield, which were for disabled tenants employed in the workshops of Painted Fabrics Ltd founded by the artist Annie Bindon Carter in 1923. Rotherham was notably energetic in delivering new homes and had (unusually for the date) its own housing architect, who set out the East Dene estate in 1919–20. At Sheffield, the first major phase of council-built housing started in 1926, with low-density cottage estates begun in the outer areas of the city, e.g. at The Manor, and this programme continued through the 1930s at e.g. Parson Cross and Shiregreen. This space-hungry development was partly countered by designation of Sheffield's green belt in 1938, the culmination of a programme that had begun with the creation of a linear park from Endcliffe Park to the open Derbyshire moorland.

FLATS are something new in the more congested towns in the 1930s, although rare by comparison with the post-war experience. At Sheffield are two interesting schemes: the Edward Street flats of 1939–43 near the city centre and the Regent Court flats at Hillsborough, 1936.

Many of the new settlements, as well as expanding suburbs in the towns, were provided with new CHURCHES. Gothic was carried on into the 1920s and beyond but much the most interesting new churches are those which adopted an Early Christian style, favoured at this time as one which could be executed with economy of ornamentation in brickwork but would not disappoint in the creation of spatially interesting interiors with domes and round arches. The first important development is the Italianate church at Goldthorpe (1914–16 by *A.Y. Nutt*) for the very early use in England of reinforced concrete for the entire structure and the fittings. Why this should have been so ambitiously used at a time when there was little experience of building in this material in Britain is unknown. The other major design is the Church of the Resurrection at Mirfield, a Neo-Byzantine-cum-Romanesque design by *Walter Tapper* from 1911 but not implemented until 1924 and never fully completed. Even so it is a church of raw, monumental force, Albi-esque in the reliance on the massive sheer brick walls of the w front for its impact. *Adrian Gilbert Scott*'s Our Lady of Beauchief and St Thomas of Canterbury, Norton Woodseats, Sheffield, is the other important interwar church (1931–2) and one of Sheffield's best; its Greek cross plan, pantiled roofs and Romanesque details make it an elder relative of Scott's larger church of 1950–4 at Poplar in East London. Other very notable designs in this Romanesque manner are *C.F. Moxon*'s St Paul, Barnsley, 1936, which calls to mind Constantinople, and St James and St Christopher, Shiregreen, Sheffield, by *Stephen Welsh*, 1938–41, simplified Gothic with a mighty, flat w tower.

Of the traditional Goths, *Charles Nicholson*, pupil of Ninian Comper, is one of the most interesting exponents of the style, which he gradually transformed into a C17 classical manner. He was commissioned in 1919 to carry out the ambitious remodelling of Sheffield's parish church after it was given cathedral status. His scheme was gradually executed through the 1920s and 1930s but never fully implemented. Nicholson also had much to do in the parish churches of the southern West Riding, beginning with the church of St Paul, in the King Cross suburb of Halifax in 1909–12, and followed by two churches at Castleford (Holy Cross, Airedale, and St Michael and All Angels, Smawthorne) and St George, Lupset, Wakefield.

By and large if one is looking for variety and interest in the 1920s and 1930s in the southern West Riding it is to be found in some of the COMMERCIAL BUILDINGS, where the projection of an up-to-date image was given priority. As in the C19, one of the main sources of innovation was provided by the CO-OPERATIVE SOCIETIES, who were receptive to progressive styles and new materials such as glazed faience and glass block. One of the best examples in England is that at Doncaster, begun in 1939 by the local architect *Harry Johnson* in concert with *W.R. Crabtree*, principal designer of the Peter Jones department store in London, to which the streamlined style owes much. CINEMAS were the other new type of the interwar period and grow in scale and architectural ambition over the course of the era, starting out relatively modest as e.g. at the Abbeydale Cinema in the suburbs of Sheffield in 1920 by *Dixon & Stienlet*, but achieving a monumental scale by a decade later at Halifax's former Odeon (by *George Coles*) and Regal cinemas. Although more traditionally minded in matters of design, the BANKS in most towns are often the best buildings in the shopping areas. A walk up and down Doncaster's High Street demonstrates some of the best. At Barnsley, the Barnsley Permanent Building Society's headquarters of 1937–8 are of that breed of interwar classicism which employs giant orders of columns and has an unmistakably American character.

The SECOND WORLD WAR brought some destruction to the steel and engineering towns of Sheffield, Rotherham and Doncaster but left the textile-producing north largely unbattered. In Sheffield damage occurred in the centres of armament production along the Don valley, but devastated the High Street area and The Moor, which were left as bomb sites. REPLANNING was the watchword after 1945 and Sheffield at once opted for an ambitious scheme for complete rebuilding of the city centre, intending to retain little apart from the late C19 and interwar civic buildings. In practice less was done of such a comprehensive nature, but by the 1960s the city had given itself a very different image and skyline from that of 1939. Much of the new work was in the hands of the City Architect, *J.L. Womersley*. He revolutionized the design of PUBLIC HOUSING in blocks of flats at his Park Hill estate (designed by younger members of his department, *Jack Lynn* and *Ivor Smithson*): long winding blocks, coherent as a whole to the eye, and with elevated streets or decks running along the flats at every few storeys to take the place of the streets in old-fashioned estates of long terraces of cottages, where children could play and women could chat. From the 1950s an increasing proportion of the supply was being made in the form of high-rise towers. Sheffield had the natural advantage of topography to make something of the groupings of towers on the new estates such as Woodside (now largely demolished), memorably characterized by the chairman of the Housing Development Committee as 'having something of the fascination of the Italian hill towns'. The supreme, but often overlooked, achievement of Womersley's time is the Gleadless Valley estate (1955–62) which combined urban housing types and the natural landscape so effectively that it still looks stunning, especially on a bright winter's day.

Womersley's department also built many SCHOOLS in the outer suburbs and villages and commissioned others from good private architects, but sixty years hence all but a few have been replaced. The University of Sheffield did just as well. Their competition for new developments on their Western Bank campus had a commitment to Modernist architecture as a pre-requisite for successful candidates and was placed in the hands of *Gollins, Melvin, Ward & Partners*; it resulted in some of the best of all new English university buildings: the Arts Tower (1961–5) and the Library (1955–9), which looked to the   109 American functionalism of Mies van der Rohe and Skidmore Owings & Merrill for inspiration. Within the county of the West Riding before 1974, the design of schools in particular was in the hands of the County Architect's Department under *Hubert Bennett*, who arrived in Yorkshire from Southampton in 1945 and set about building a very large team under his charge until his departure for the equivalent post at the London County Council in 1956; schools were the priority and good examples remain at Batley (High School), Linthwaite (Colne Valley High School) and Todmorden (Community College), along with buildings designed by his successors *A.W. Glover* and *K.C. Evans*, e.g. Sherburn-in-Elmet. Of the Department's buildings at Bretton Hall little is likely to survive the redevelopments following the closure of the college there.

Other towns also set about replanning their centres, too often at the expense of their pre-Victorian heritage. Barnsley in particular, having grown in significance by virtue of its position at the centre of the south Yorkshire coalfield, indulged in extensive replacement to create a new civic centre, planned from 1951 by *Lanchester & Lodge*. Pontefract also remained largely intact until the 1960s, but then set about large clearances and obliteration of some of its medieval streets. The same is true of Wakefield, where much was sacrificed to indifferent new building. The port town of Goole similarly laid waste to many of its Georgian buildings. Doncaster – functioning without a proper town hall since 1846 – set about creating a civic centre on the s edge of its centre, commissioning *Frederick Gibberd* as architect. This proceeded fitfully over two decades and has been extensively reworked since *c*. 2010, with only a small portion of Gibberd's own architectural contribution remaining after redevelopment. At Castleford the Civic Centre of 1967–70 is a good representative of the drift towards a much more imposing Brutalist idiom by the end of the 1960s and the concentration of multiple functions into a single complex; it was originally complemented by one of *Henry Moore*'s sculptures, a personal gift to the town of his birth. Huddersfield's Civic Centre is almost exactly contemporary.

Bypassing is one theme for many town centres in the post-war years; Pevsner writing of Doncaster in the 1950s felt moved to warn against the danger of making a perambulation there after 7 o'clock in the morning in the face of traffic along the Great North Road –'England's Permanent Pandemonium Number One' – and by 1960 the bypass and ring road were in place; though not to the benefit of Scott's great minster church, which remains distressingly detached from the bustling town centre. Ring roads were a key feature of Sheffield's replanning (and the early C21 planners have had to work to undo some of the problems created for pedestrians) and in several other towns. It is a great discouragement at Huddersfield, where centre and inner suburbs are split apart. Yet other towns have kept their pre-C20 cores commendably intact in spite of the strategy of building a ring road. Dewsbury is one.

The results of post-war reconstruction in terms of COMMERCIAL BUILDINGS are exceedingly mixed, and late 1950s commercial buildings in particular suffer from an attraction to a stolid but watery classicism and Portland stone cladding. The Moor in Sheffield must rank, despite its great length, as one of the least interesting shopping streets in Britain. Much better to remember *Yorke, Rosenberg & Mardall*'s white-tiled Cole Bros store (1961–5) in Barkers Pool. In 1968 Doncaster provided itself with one of the national group of Arndale Centres (since remodelled), covered shopping malls accompanied by monumental groups of car parks and office slabs, almost always egregious and fifty years later usually, as here, re-clad to mitigate their baleful effect. At Huddersfield the office slab on a podium in New Street by *J. Seymour Harris Partnership* could stand for many others as the routine image of the replanned urban scene in England during the twenty years up to 1975. Yet the very same practice was responsible for one of the very best buildings in post-war Yorkshire, Huddersfield's Queensgate Market of 1968–70, with its thrilling concrete-vaulted roofs sailing above the top of the building. Two of the most impressive later C20 buildings are for the major banks: the former Midland Bank at Huddersfield (1968–72 by *Peter Womersley*) and the headquarters of the Halifax Building Society at Halifax itself (1968–74 by *BDP*), in which the sleekly glazed offices are jacked up above the street on massive concrete piers to provide a covered courtyard.

So far not much has been said about CHURCHES. That is because there is much less to say than in earlier sections. Until the removal of controls in the mid 1950s, architects were required to deliver buildings of considerable economy. That no doubt explains the use of bricks salvaged from the ruins of Clumber Park (Notts.) to build the new church of St Bernard at Parson Cross, Sheffield, in 1953. Also for the same estate, *Basil Spence & Partners* were commissioned and provided St Paul in 1958–9, an exceedingly simple design that follows the concepts of his little churches for Coventry's new estates at this time. Providing a bridge between Gothic and Modernism is *George Pace*, whose work in South Yorkshire includes St Leonard and St Jude, Doncaster, of 1957–63; the church of All Saints, Intake, Doncaster, immediately preceding this, and St Mark's church, Broomhill, in the inner western suburbs of Sheffield (1958–63). All have his characteristic motifs. In addition, Pace was consulted for the remodelling of Sheffield Cathedral in the 1950s but resigned in the face of the challenge.

Reordering of furnishings in response to the new liturgical movement begins in the mid 1960s. St Thomas the Apostle at Heptonstall is a notable instance of work undertaken by *Maguire & Murray*, one of the most significant post-war practices, in 1963–4, bringing the altar forward onto a dais and removing all the fittings of the C19 chancel. Also very worthwhile among the later churches are those for the Roman Catholics by *J.H. Langtry-Langton*, who seems to revel in austerity externally at St Mary Magdalene, Maltby, 1955, and the powerful Romanesque church of St Malachy (R.C.) at Ovenden, Halifax (1960), in order to surprise in the richness of the interiors, especially at the latter church, where a splendid spaciousness is achieved by the omission of columns from the aisles. A later work (by now *J.H. Langtry-Langton & Son*) is St Peter-in-Chains (R.C.) at Doncaster, 1972–3; its planning around a centralized altar under an octagonal lantern was dictated by the changes of liturgy introduced by the Second Vatican Council. Finally, in many places the post-war contribution is to be celebrated for the quality of the stained glass and in particular the work of *Harry Harvey*. But the 1960s were also regrettably a period of the abandoning of many churches and chapels, with demolition the eventual result, until protection was extended to churches without use but deserving of preservation, e.g. St Peter at Edlington, the first church to be vested in the Redundant Churches Fund (now Churches Conservation Trust).

The southern area of the West Riding has one of the very best of England's post-war houses: Farnley Hey (p. 243) designed by *Peter Womersley* in 1953–4. This is in the pre-war Corbusian and Miesian traditions of a pavilion in the landscape and an open-plan interior of rooms grouped around a core for the services. Houses of such distinction are rare for the post-war period and in the wider county the 1960s and '70s witnessed much DESTRUCTION OF COUNTRY HOUSES and other historic buildings, as the many footnotes in the gazetteer will attest for buildings lost since the first edition of *Yorkshire West Riding*. A most notorious abuse of the landscape around some of the major houses was the decision to permit opencast mining around and 'up to the door' of Wentworth Woodhouse. Houses such as Brodsworth suffered in other ways from industrialization, both from undermining and from acid rain attacking the limestone from which they had been built. Yet from 1977 one of the most celebrated achievements has been the repurposing of the landscape of Bretton Hall near Wakefield (itself in educational use from the post-war years until quite recently) as the Yorkshire Sculpture Park. Small efforts to conserve and preserve historic buildings can be traced in a variety of places. A remarkably early attempt to preserve a historic metalworking site was the purchase of the water-powered Abbeydale Works, now in outer Sheffield, in the 1930s, although it was not until 1970 that this pioneering industrial museum was opened.

The late C20 to the present day

It is remarkable now to see the confidence with which cities such as Sheffield emerged into the 1970s in the expectation of a prosperous future based on coal and steel INDUSTRIES. The following decade brought that to a rapid halt with recession, strikes and widespread closures. By the 1990s the effect on the Don valley in particular was severe, and widespread dereliction ensued among the stupendously large forges. In Sheffield there were also multiple sites of abandoned cutlery workshops. At Doncaster the Great Northern Railway workshops, known as 'The Plant' and where the Flying Scotsman and Mallard were built, have been largely demolished. In the Pennine districts the mills had been undergoing a slow but terminal decline ever since the end of the Second World War but this process moved more quickly from the 1960s and '70s in the face of technical improvements and lower prices from competitors abroad. Housing estates built in the flush of post-war optimism now began to take on a stricken aspect, seeming to fulfil Pevsner's assessment of Park Hill that 'The social idea is admirable, but these huge interconnected blocks are bound to lose very quickly their visual attraction by wear and tear, and will then be in danger of becoming slums.'

REGENERATION has taken a variety of forms across a range of building types. The pioneering spirit is represented by Akroydon on the edge of Halifax, where the complex of redundant carpet mills at Dean Clough was taken in hand by Sir Ernest Hall from 1982 and has been patiently revived as a centre for business and arts activities. Its counterpart in the northern West Riding is Salts Mill, Saltaire, but it took many years before the possibility of extending this model to other disused sites was fully grasped. More typical perhaps of the response to large tracts of land available for clearance were the new developments that spread along the Don valley NE of Sheffield from 1990 and that included not only the Meadowhall Shopping Centre but also large sports stadia and other sporting venues, of which some have already been replaced for a second regeneration effort. Elsewhere, redundant industrial complexes could be reborn as museums of the processes that had once made the fortunes of their owners. So Caphouse Colliery, which lies on the W edge of the Yorkshire coalfield and was worked out by 1985, has become England's National Coal Mining Museum, and part of the Templeborough steel works at Rotherham has been transformed into the Magna Science Adventure Centre with one of the arc furnaces as its showpiece. The Earth Centre at Denaby was an attempt to promote sustainable use of natural resources on the site of the former collieries. At Halifax the Eureka! Children's Museum of 1990–2 by *BDP* is a good reuse of former railway land and now incorporates the town's C19 station. Elsewhere, cleared sites have been turned over to new industrial, business and retail parks close to the major road networks.

Since the beginning of the new century much more attention has been given to reviving moribund city and town centres and

finding new uses for their historic buildings. CULTURAL REGEN-
ERATION brought about the changes in Sheffield city centre from
the 1990s, when a series of 'quarters' were identified for schemes
of repair, refurbishment and new build. Some of this new work
was more successful than other parts: the Peace Gardens, Winter
Garden and Millennium Galleries (2001–2 by *Pringle Richards*   115
Sharratt) are unquestionably a major asset to the heart of the city,
but the ill-conceived National Centre for Popular Music was a
short-lived venture that, fortunately for the likeable and unseri-
ous building by *Branson Coates*, has found a new use by Sheffield
Hallam University. Over nearly thirty years, more and more of
the small and medium-size complexes of cutlery works have been
given intelligent new uses while maintaining their distinct character. Yet more remains to be done.

In parallel with this, large programmes of replacement have
been taking place of the post-war housing schemes and schools,
and especially of higher-education buildings, where the provision
of accommodation for a greatly increased student population
seems now to be one of the dominant activities in Sheffield and
Huddersfield, where the University has played a key part since
1992 in giving life back to its C19 textile mill buildings. Some
mills have been converted to residential or new industrial use;
yet, as of the time of writing, there are well over 1,300 mill buildings in the West Riding as a whole that await some form of
productive reuse. At Sheffield, the Park Hill flats – in recognition
of their unique design – were listed in 1998, and since 2009 they
have been gradually but drastically transformed for continued
residential use. Even more remarkably, the preservation of Wentworth Woodhouse – for many years after the death of the last of
the Fitzwilliams a seemingly impossible task for any individual
to achieve – seems to have been secured by central government.
At Wakefield the success of the sculpture park at Bretton has
resulted in a permanent visitor centre and galleries, and it was
this success perhaps which emboldened the commissioning of
David Chipperfield Architects to design the Hepworth Wakefield
Gallery for a site in the former industrial area along the River   118
Calder s of the town centre. Finally, one must take encourage-
ment that the latest landmark building at Wakefield should be
West Yorkshire's History Centre.

FURTHER READING

The size and complexity both of the West Riding as a whole and
of its many urban areas deterred writers of the traditional
GENERAL HISTORIES of the C18 and C19 as well as more modern
authors from attempting coverage of the whole county or even
very substantial parts of it, and so studies have tended to focus
on specific parts – the individual cities and towns and local areas.
This is especially true since the abolition of the county in

1974, and so knowledge of the current administrative areas (i.e. counties and districts, *see* p. xv) is essential in tracking down the myriad publications that may only be available in the relevant local studies library. The major exceptions to the narrower focus are Joseph Hunter's scholarly two-volume *South Yorkshire – the History and Topography of the Deanery of Doncaster* (1828, 1831), whose area is almost coterminous with the modern county of South Yorkshire, and David Hey's *The Making of South Yorkshire* (1979), although that does not go beyond the C17. The wapentakes that cover our area are described in Volumes 5 and 6 of Thomas Allen's *New and Complete History of the County of York* (1831), which is not as comprehensive as its title promises. Unfortunately the *Victoria County History* of the West Riding (1913) is incomplete and has no detailed topographical volumes. Still useful, despite its dismissal or exclusion of most of the urban and industrial parts ('Huddersfield ... is absolutely without interest to the archaeologist'), is the handy summing-up of J. E. Morris's *Little Guide*, first written in 1911 (3rd edn, 1932). Among the most informative DIRECTORIES for the whole West Riding are E. Baines's (1822), W. White's (1837–8), and Kelly's (1881, 1905 and 1927, etc.). Others are less comprehensive, but no less informative, e.g. those for the Clothing Districts that include Halifax, Huddersfield and Wakefield with Leeds and Bradford (1858, etc.), and those covering much of the southern part of the area e.g. *Sheffield and 20 Miles Round* (1852). The *Yorkshire Archaeological Journal* (hereafter *Y.A.J.*) is the principal antiquarian periodical whose coverage includes the whole of the West Riding.

There are histories of the two CITIES and almost all the principal TOWNS. For SHEFFIELD there are J. Hunter's *Hallamshire – The History and Topography of the Parish of Sheffield* (1819; 2nd edn by A. Gatty 1875), M. Walton's *Sheffield: Its Story and its Achievements* (5th edn, 1984), D. Hey's *A History of Sheffield* (1998) and *The History of the City of Sheffield 1843–1993* (1993), ed. J.C.G. Binfield and others. The essays in M. Jones (ed.), *Aspects of Sheffield 1 and 2* (1997, 1999) are valuable, as are the *Transactions of the Hunter Archaeological Society*. WAKEFIELD has J.W. Walker, *Wakefield: Its History and People* (1939, 2 vols), K. Taylor, *The Making of Wakefield 1801–1900* (2008), and the essays in K. Taylor (ed.), *Aspects of Wakefield 1–3* (1993–2001).

BARNSLEY has R. Jackson, *The history of the town ... of Barnsley* (1858), B. Elliott, *The Making of Barnsley* (1988) and essays in B. Elliott (ed.), *Aspects of Barnsley 1–7* (1993–2007). DONCASTER has E. Miller, *The History and Antiquities of Doncaster* (1805), C. Hatfield's *Historical Notices of Doncaster* (3 vols, [1865]–70), B. Barber, *A History of Doncaster* (2007), and essays in B. Elliott (ed.), *Aspects of Doncaster 1 and 2* (1997, 1999). For HALIFAX there is J. Watson's *The History and Antiquities of the Parish of Halifax* (1775), J. Crabtree's *A concise history of the parish ... of Halifax* (1836), and *Halifax* (2nd edn, 2003) by J. Hargreaves. The *Transactions of the Halifax Antiquarian Society* cover the rest of Calderdale as well as the town. Malcolm Bull's 'Calderdale

Companion' website is a mine of information: *http://freepages. history.rootsweb.ancestry.com/~calderdalecompanion*. For HUDDERS-FIELD there is Taylor Dyson, *The History of Huddersfield and District* (2nd edn, 1951) and H.E.A. Haigh (ed.), *Huddersfield, a Most Handsome Town* (1992); for ROTHERHAM, *Historic Notices of Rotherham* (1879) by J. Guest, *Rotherham: A Pictorial History* (1994) by A.P. Munford, and essays in M. Jones (ed.), *Aspects of Rotherham 1–3* (1995–2002). The SADDLEWORTH area (now within Greater Manchester) has *Saddleworth Heritage* (1975) by B. Barnes, and *Saddleworth Villages* (2003) by N. Barrow, M. Buckley and A. Petford; and SELBY has *The History and Antiquities of Selby* by W.W. Morrell (1867).

For ARCHITECTURE there is no general survey of the whole area, but for the earlier period it is covered by P. Ryder's *Medieval Buildings of Yorkshire* (1982). B. and W. Armstrong's invitingly illustrated *The Arts and Crafts Movement in Yorkshire* (2013) covers both buildings and all the decorative arts. Again there are works that relate to some of the local government areas created in the reorganization of 1974. For those parts in West Yorkshire there is Derek Linstrum's classic *West Yorkshire Architects and Architecture* (1978). For Halifax and Calderdale there is I. Beesley and others, *Calderdale: Architecture and History* (1988); for Hud-dersfield *The Buildings of Huddersfield – An Illustrated Architectural History* (2nd edn, 2009) by K. Gibson and A. Booth and *The Villas of Edgerton; home to Huddersfield's Victorian elite* (2017) by D. Griffiths. Wakefield and its area has K. Taylor (ed.), *Wakefield District Heritage* (2 vols, 1976, 1979). Sheffield has *Sheffield* in this series, by Ruth Harman and John Minnis (2004), which covers the city centre and selected suburbs – and contains a fuller bib-liography including works on individual buildings. Across our area there are numerous local history and civic societies, many with websites that have valuable information about local build-ings. A far greater wealth of material relates to ARCHITECTS and to individual building types. The general sources of information for architects are Howard Colvin, *A Biographical Dictionary of British Architects 1600–1840* (4th edn, 2008) and more schemati-cally the RIBA *Directory of British Architects 1834–1914* (2nd edn, 2001) and *Edwardian Architecture: A Biographical Dictionary* by A. Stuart Gray (1986). As architects from Leeds worked in much of the northern part of our area, *Building a Great Victorian City: Leeds Architects and Architecture 1790–1914* (2011), ed. C. Webster, is also very useful, and is complemented by J. Holder's doctoral thesis, '"A race of native architects": the architects of Sheffield and South Yorkshire, 1880–1940' (University of Sheffield, 2005). Relevant biographies of architects include P. Leach on Paine (1988), B. Wragg on Carr (ed. G. Worsley, 2000), F. Beckwith on Thomas Taylor (Thoresby Society 1949), C. Webster on Chant-rell (2010), G. Stamp on Sir G.G. Scott (2015), P. Thompson on Butterfield (1971), A. Quiney on Pearson (1979), M. Hall on Bodley (2014), G. Brandwood on Temple Moore (1997) and P. Pace on George Pace (1990). For an industrial area the volumes of the *Biographical Dictionary of Civil Engineers*, for 1500–1830 by

Sir A. Skempton (2002) and 1830–1890 by P. Cross-Rudkin and
M. Chrimes (2008), are useful too.

For building types one can start with the GREAT CHURCHES
of the Middle Ages. For Selby Abbey see W.W. Morrell, *Selby
Abbey Church: with Notices of the Abbey and Town of Selby* (1876);
C.C. Hodges, 'The architectural history of Selby Abbey' in *Yorkshire Archaeological and Topographical Association: Records Series*,
13 (1893); G. Cobb, *English Cathedrals, the Forgotten Centuries*
(1980); R. Stalley, 'Choice and Consistency: The Early Gothic
Architecture of Selby Abbey', *Architectural History* 38 (1995).
Also 'The Romanesque Church of Selby Abbey' by E. Fernie;
'Observations on the Romanesque Crossing Tower, Transepts
and Nave Aisles of Selby Abbey' by S. Harrison and M. Thurlby;
and 'The East Window of Selby Abbey' by D. O'Connor and
H. Reddish Harris, all in *Yorkshire Monasticism: Archaeology, Art
and Architecture from the 7th to 16th Centuries* (1995) by L.R. Hoey
(ed.). For Roche Abbey there is the English Heritage guidebook
(2013) by P. J. Fergusson and S. Harrison and also P. J.
Fergusson, *Architecture of Solitude: Cistercian Abbeys in Twelfth-
Century England* (1984) and D. Robinson (ed.), *The Cistercian
Abbeys of Britain* (1998).

Coverage of PARISH CHURCHES is again mainly localized.
Exceptions are G.A. Poole, *The Churches of Yorkshire* (1844), a
selection with a delightful series of engravings, and *The Yorkshire
Church Notes of Sir Stephen Glynne* (ed. L. Butler, *Y.A.S. Record*
series 2007) – written mainly in the 1840s to '60s and especially
revealing for his accounts of churches before restoration, supplemented in this edition by useful references to the restorers'
work. For the C19 more generally one can start with M.H. Port,
Six Hundred New Churches (2nd edn 2006) on the Commissioners' churches. Giving invaluable coverage of large parts of the
area are P.F. Ryder's *Medieval Churches of West Yorkshire* (1993),
and his *Saxon Churches in South Yorkshire* (1982), which includes
a gazetteer of medieval churches in the county. A.R. Bielby's
Churches and Chapels of Kirklees (1978) and Canon W. Odom's
Memorials of Sheffield: Its Cathedral and Parish Churches (1922)
are useful for their areas, and the Heritage Inspired website
(*www.heritageinspired.org.uk*) has information on many churches
in and near South Yorkshire. The printed accounts of individual
churches are too numerous to list; some parishes have websites
that include excellent historical and architectural information
about their churches. NONCONFORMIST CHAPELS are covered
by C. Stell, *An Inventory of Nonconformist Chapels and Meeting
Houses in the North of England* (1994), supplemented by D.M.
Butler, *The Quaker Meeting Houses of Britain* (1999).

With regard to ecclesiastically related SCULPTURE, for the
Anglo-Saxon period see W.G. Collingwood in *Y.A.J.* 23 (1915)
and E. Coatsworth (ed.), *Corpus of Anglo-Saxon Stone Sculpture
in England: Western Yorkshire* (2008); for Romanesque see
R. Wood, 'The Romanesque Doorways of Yorkshire', *Y.A.J.* 66
(1994) and the Corpus of Romanesque Sculpture website *www.
crsbi.ac.uk*. For the later medieval alabaster tombs see P. Routh,

Medieval Effigial Alabaster Tombs in Yorkshire (1976). The post-medieval period is represented by M. Whinney, *Sculpture in Britain 1530–1830* (Pelican History of Art, 2nd edn, 1988), A. White, *A Biographical Dictionary of London Tomb Sculptors c.1560–c.1660* (Walpole Society 61 (1999)), with supplement in *Walpole Society* 71 (2009), and I. Roscoe, *A Biographical Dictionary of Sculptors in Britain 1660–1851* (2009; the associated database is also available online at *www.henry-moore.org/hmi/library/ biographical-dictionary-of-sculptors-in-britain*). For STAINED GLASS there is *The Medieval Stained Glass of South Yorkshire* (2003) by B. Sprakes; for the C19 M. Harrison, *Victorian Stained Glass* (1980) is a helpful introduction, and for individual manufacturers there are A.C. Sewter, *Stained Glass of William Morris and his Circle* (1974), the Kempe Society's *Corpus of Kempe Stained Glass in the United Kingdom and Ireland* (2000), and an online catalogue of windows by James Powell and Sons, available on the National Association of Decorative and Fine Arts Societies' website (*www.nadfas.org.uk/what-we-do/churches-recorded-nadfas* – see Useful Information).

For CASTLES see the six volumes of *The History of the King's Works* by H.M. Colvin (ed.) (1963–73) for Pontefract, and also for Sandall and Tickhill when in royal hands, and, generally, *The English Castle* by J. Goodall (2011). For Conisbrough there is the English Heritage guidebook (2015) by Steven Brindle and Agnieszka Sadrei.

For VERNACULAR and DOMESTIC ARCHITECTURE one can begin with A. Emery, *Greater Medieval Houses of England and Wales* I (1996); on the C16 and C17 gentry houses and yeoman farmhouses there is one still invaluable classic, L. Ambler's *The Old Halls and Manor Houses of Yorkshire* (1913), while C. Giles's *Rural Houses of West Yorkshire 1400–1830* (1986) includes an inventory of examples backed by an extensive archive of survey reports on individual buildings at Historic England's Archive at Swindon. For South Yorkshire there is P.F. Ryder's *Timber Framed Buildings in South Yorkshire* (1979). There are also survey reports for selected buildings in the whole area by members of the Yorkshire Vernacular Buildings Study Group, at the Yorkshire Archaeological Society, Leeds. On one particular aspect of the subject there is P. Leach, 'Rose Windows and other Follies: Alternative Architecture in the Seventeenth-Century Pennines', *Architectural History* 43 (2000); on one particular area *Saddleworth Buildings: a Guide to the Vernacular Architecture of the Parish of Saddleworth in the Pennines* (1987) by W.J. Smith.

For COUNTRY HOUSES a very informative picture of those existing in the early C18 is provided by *Samuel Buck's Yorkshire Sketchbook* (Wakefield Historical Publications, 1979). Regarding individual examples there are the usual articles in *Country Life*, including four by H.A. Tipping on Wentworth Woodhouse (1924). The Georgian landscapes and buildings of Wentworth Woodhouse and Wentworth Castle are studied in detail in Patrick Eyres (ed.), *New Arcadian Journal* 59/60 (2006) and 63/64 (2008) respectively. For Brodsworth Hall there is the English Heritage guidebook (2009) by C. Carr-Whitworth; for Nostell Priory the National Trust guidebook and E. Harris on Adam's interiors (2001). *Lost Houses of the West Riding* by E. Waterson and P. Meadows (1998) is a sad catalogue of what has gone. The industrialists' and merchants' VILLAS of the C19 are the main focus – despite its title – of A. Healey, *A Series of Picturesque Views of the Castles and Country Houses in Yorkshire* (1885), and the subject of G. Sheeran's analysis, *Brass Castles: West Yorkshire New Rich and their Houses 1800–1914* (2nd edn, 2006). For suburban housing in general there is S. Muthesius, *The English Terraced House* (1982). Some WORKERS' and SOCIAL HOUSING is covered by L. Caffyn, *Workers' Housing in West Yorkshire 1750–1920* (1986), and the final chapter of C. Giles and I. Goodall, *Yorkshire Textile Mills 1770–1930* (1992). For the C20 there is M. Glendinning and S. Muthesius, *Tower Block: Modern Public Housing in England, Scotland, Wales and Northern Ireland* (1994). It is set in a wider context by S.D. Chapman, *The History of Working Class Housing* (1971), J.N. Tarn, *Five per cent Philanthropy* (1973), and J.A. Jowitt (ed.), *Model Industrial Communities in mid-Nineteenth Century Yorkshire* (1986).

With regard to PUBLIC BUILDINGS, K. Grady, *The Georgian Public Buildings of Leeds and the West Riding* (Thoresby Society 1989) is very useful and C. Cunningham, *Victorian and Edwardian Town Halls* (1987) documents both the major buildings of Dewsbury, Halifax, Sheffield, Wakefield, etc., as well as many of the scores of other town halls in the area. Court buildings to 1914 are covered by *Ordering Law* (2003) by C. Graham; for schools there is M. Seaborne's *The English School* (1971 and 1977), supplemented for Sheffield by *Building Schools for Sheffield 1870–1914* (2012) by the Victorian Society; for hospitals *English Hospitals 1660–1948* (1998) by H. Richardson (ed.); for prisons *English Prisons: An Architectural History* (2002) by A. Brodie, J. Croom and J.O. Davies; for transport C. Hadfield's *The Canals of Yorkshire and North East England* (2 vols, 1972–3), M. Clarke, *The Aire & Calder Navigation* (1999), G. Biddle, *Britain's Historic Railway Buildings: An Oxford Gazetteer of Sources and Sites* (2003), and *Carscapes: The Motor Car, Architecture and Landscape* (2012) by K.A. Morrison and J. Minnis. Much useful information is now to be found exclusively online, e.g. for workhouses see *www.workhouses.org.uk,* and post offices *http://britishpostofficearchitects.weebly.com.* An increasingly large database of war memorials is held by the Imperial War Museum's UK National Inventory (*www.iwm.org.uk/memorials*). For PUBLIC SCULPTURE see B. Read, *Victorian Sculpture* (1982), S. Beattie, *The New Sculpture* (1983), and *Public Sculpture of Sheffield and South Yorkshire* (2015) by D. White and E. Norman.

For INDUSTRIAL and COMMERCIAL BUILDINGS the principal industry of the NW and W parts is comprehensively studied in C. Giles and I. Goodall, *Yorkshire Textile Mills 1770–1930* (1992), which has an inventory of examples and is backed by an archive of reports at Historic England's Archives. The Saddleworth area is covered by *The Cotton Mills of Oldham* (1998). For South Yorkshire industries *A Guide to the Industrial History of*

South Yorkshire by D. Bayliss (ed.) (1995) provides helpful gazetteers, while W. Taylor's *South Yorkshire Pits* (2001) gives more information about coal mining in the county. *Water Power on the Sheffield Rivers* by C. Ball, D. Crossley and N. Flavell (eds) (2nd edn, 2006) details over a hundred sites with water wheels used for the metal and other industries. For banks see J. Booker, *Temples of Mammon: The Architecture of Banking* (1990), for shops K.A. Morrison, *English Shops and Shopping* (2004), for market halls J. Smiechen and K. Carls, *The British Market Hall* (1999).

Finally regarding other disciplines, a review of the ARCHAEOLOGY of the area is T.G. Manby, S. Moorhouse & P. Ottaway (eds), *The Archaeology of Yorkshire: An Assessment at the Beginning of the 21st Century* (2003). For GEOLOGY see *Strategic Stone Study: A Buildings Stone Atlas for West & South Yorkshire* (2012) by Graham Lott, which includes a useful bibliography of works on the geology of the southern area of the West Riding.

For FURTHER RESEARCH there is a great variety of national and local resources, some available online. Knowledge of the different counties and local authority areas into which our area of the West Riding now falls is essential for using some of these (*see* p. xv). Detailed descriptions of individual listed buildings in the *National Heritage List for England* (NHLE) are available online (*https://historicengland.org.uk/listing/the-list*), and information from the Register of Historic Parks and Gardens is available there too. The website *www.heritagegateway.org.uk* gives access to the Historic Environment Records (or Sites and Monuments Records) databases for the City of York, Greater Manchester, and North, South and West Yorkshire. The equivalent records for the East Riding of Yorkshire are only available at the Humber Archaeology Partnership, Hull. Amongst the most useful PRINTED SOURCES are architectural periodicals and newspapers. The two main C19 periodicals are *The Builder* and *Building News* (later *Architect and Building News*); for the C20 and C21 there are the *Architectural Review*, *Architect's Journal* and *RIBA Journal*. The British Newspaper Archive is an invaluable online source of information, including an ever-increasing number of local newspapers from our area (*www.britishnewspaperarchive. co.uk*). There are separate Local Studies services, usually in the main Central Library or with the Archive Service, for all the different local authority areas, and some of these have subsidiary collections in local libraries. Most of them still have only card or paper catalogues for some older book stock, pamphlets, etc. Many have very useful online archives of photographs and other historic images (e.g. *www.twixtaireandcalder.org.uk* for Wakefield and its district).

As for PRIMARY SOURCES, the Historic England Archive at Swindon holds reports on individual buildings, including older ones produced by English Heritage and the Royal Commission on Historical Monuments, photographs, and other records. The research notes made for the earlier editions of this volume are held there, and those made for this revision will, in due course, join them. Other valuable national sources include the extensive archive of the Incorporated Church Building Society at Lambeth Palace Library, which includes records relating to new churches and to restorations and extensions (*see* online catalogue: *http://archives.lambethpalacelibrary.org.uk/calmview*, and copies of submitted plans: *http://images.lambethpalacelibrary.org.uk/luna/servlet*). The West Riding did not have a county record office and the situation for local archives and archive services is even more complicated than it is for libraries. The Districts of South Yorkshire each have their own archive service; the West Yorkshire Districts have separate archive offices in a joint service. The Wakefield office holds the West Riding County Council records. The North Yorkshire Record Office has archives for the Selby area, the East Riding Archives those for the Goole area, and Oldham Archives covers Saddleworth. The Yorkshire Archaeological Society at Leeds also holds archives. For diocesan records that include faculties for church work, the main archives are the Borthwick Institute, York (York diocese), Leeds Archives (Ripon), Wakefield Archives (Wakefield) and Sheffield Archives (Sheffield), but the picture is complicated as some parishes changed diocese two or even three times as new dioceses were created, and parishes on the edges of our area were or are in other dioceses – Lincoln, Southwell, Lichfield, Derby, Chester and Manchester.

GAZETTEER

ACASTER MALBIS

HOLY TRINITY, ¼ m. NE of the village. A church of the early
C14 (but with a Norman capital built into the E wall inside).
Aisleless nave, chancel and deep transepts, forming almost a
Greek cross. No signs of a crossing tower. Restored by
C. Hodgson Fowler, c. 1886. His are the pretty bell-turret
– weatherboarded with spire, replacing a similar structure – and
the roof. The fenestration is curious. Straight-headed windows
mainly of three lights (the W of five, the E of seven) set in deep
reveals, those to the ends of the arms under relieving arches
– bluntly pointed to N and S, segmental to E and W – springing
from a kind of simple bracket or shoulder, the others with
similarly bracketed lintels instead of arches. The lights are very
slim, ogee-headed and flush with the wall inside. In each of
the gables themselves also a foiled oculus, quatrefoils to W and
S, N a trefoil, E a heptafoil. Two-centred double-chamfered
doorways with continuous mouldings. In the chancel, brackets
for statues on the E wall, and a foiled, ogee-headed piscina:
further piscinas in the transepts. – PULPIT. Victorian, incorporating elaborate C17 Flemish panels. – FONT. Medieval tub.
– STAINED GLASS, in the E window. Outstanding work of the
mid C14, attributed to the workshop of *Master Robert* and
related to his masterpiece, the W window of York Minster.
Rearranged by *Peter Gibson* in 1977. Beautifully drawn faces.
The figures include Christ and St Bartholomew, carrying his
flayed skin over his arm. – Also some fragments arranged by
Gibson in the chancel N and S windows. – MONUMENTS.
Cross-legged knight, early C14, holding his heart in his hands.
Badly preserved. Presumed to be Sir John Malebisse †1316,
and possibly connected with the building of the church. – Medieval grave-slab with foliate cross.
In the grounds of the MANOR HOTEL, Mill Lane, the remains
of a FOLLY made of masonry and tracery from *Thomas Atkinson's* St Andrew, Bishopthorpe (q.v.), taken down in 1899. The
hotel is an C18 farmhouse extensively made over at about the
same time.

ACASTER SELBY

St John. Amid cedars in the middle of a field rumpled with medieval building platforms. 1850, an early work of *J.L. Pearson*. Aisleless nave and chancel; bellcote. Coursed sandstone with limestone dressings. Two-light windows with mouchette tracery. – FONT. Good C15 bowl on C19 stem.

The village is now just a few farms along the bank of the River Ouse. Chief among them is MANOR FARM, *c.* 1660–70, the former Acaster Hall, reduced in size and badly knocked about but once evidently a fine sight, the design related to Archbishop Frewen's work at nearby Bishopthorpe (q.v.). The main front was towards the river. Brick throughout, including the wildly unscholarly Ionic pilasters – tapering and thickly decorated – l. and r. of the (blocked) doorway, the plainer pilasters to the first floor, and originally the mullions and transoms of the windows (now all replaced). Two phases: the r. two bays with the door, and a further wider bay (now demolished) probably the earlier; the l. bay and the plain return façade, with former cross-windows, slightly later. Some earlier fabric perhaps incorporated at the back of this wing.

Dry MOAT, ¼ m. NE of the village. Adjacent is the site of the COLLEGE OF ST ANDREW, founded in the late C15 by Robert Stillington, Bishop of Bath and Wells and later Lord Chancellor, and a native of the township. It had a provost and three fellows. Ruins visible in 1748 included a chapel with transepts.

ACKWORTH

In three parts: High Ackworth, with the parish church, is a very attractive village, surprisingly rich in dignified Georgian houses; s of this the Quaker School and Low Ackworth; s again Ackworth Moor Top, mainly a later mining settlement. Local quarries were a source of high-quality sandstone.

St Cuthbert. The plain Perp w tower survived a fire in 1852; the rest is of 1855 by *J. W. Hugall*. Did he take his cue from the old church? Apart from the 'Perp' s porch with a stone roof on chamfered transverse ribs the rest is Dec. Spacious interior with wide, two-bay arcades with quatrefoil piers, N aisle and three-bay N chapel with a projecting sacristy. – FONTS. Under the tower, C12 square bowl from an earlier building, its base a section of quatrefoil pier. s aisle, dated 1663. Small, octagonal, with plain mouldings and inscriptions. – FURNISHINGS. Altars, stall etc. by *Martin Dutton* and *Robert Thompson*, mid-C20. – MONUMENTS. N aisle. Floriated cross-slab †1506. (Another, earlier, cross-slab in the churchyard.) – S aisle. Ann Bradley †1663, with decorated border and cusped head, beside plainer slab to Thomas Bradley, Chaplain to Charles I and Rector, †1673. – STAINED GLASS. E window by *Wailes*, 1855. The other two chancel windows probably also by him. – LYCHGATE, 1878, with beefy oak timbers.

ALL SAINTS, Wakefield Road, Ackworth Moor Top. 1888–9 by *Henry Curzon* of London. E.E. Small, aisleless, but with vestigial transept-like projections and well-detailed apsidal E end. The W end has an incongruous but delightful little shingled bell-tower with spire.

METHODIST CHURCH (Wesleyan), Barnsley Road. Gothic Revival, 1858 by *James Wilson*; restored after a fire in 1912 by *Garside & Pennington*.

ACKWORTH SCHOOL, Pontefract Road. Erected in stages 1758–65 as a Foundling Hospital, one of the provincial daughter institutions of Thomas Coram's London foundation. It closed in 1773 and was bought by Dr John Fothergill for the Society of Friends, opening as a boarding school in 1779. Its formal Palladian symmetry must certainly have looked impressive in contrast to the muddle of conforming public school buildings in the C18 and early C19. Only the colleges of the Roman Catholics – admittedly later than Ackworth – can compete with it. The original rigid segregation between boys and girls, separately housed and taught E and W of the central block, has disappeared.

The central range was built 1759–62 to designs by *Timothy Lee*, Rector of Ackworth. It has thirteen bays and two storeys with a three-bay pediment and a pedimented Ionic doorway. It faces a monumental forecourt enclosed to E and W by side wings, each also of thirteen bays and two storeys with three-bay pediments. The E wing, by *John Watson II* was completed in 1758. The W wing followed the central range in 1763. Both wings have cupolas; the weathervane on the E one displays the Foundling Hospital's emblem, reputedly designed by *Hogarth*. The wings were linked to the centre in 1765 by single-storey quadrants with colonnades. (Another low storey added 1856.) All columns are Tuscan, the most severe order, also used in additions for the Quakers, who maintained the austere classical character of the Hospital for nearly two centuries. Behind the E wing, a much smaller courtyard, built in 1786 as an entrance and partly covered exercise area and attributed to *William Lindley*. Colonnaded on two sides. The long E side, with the archway from the main road, was glazed in in 1976. Northwards is *J.P. Pritchett*'s entrance court with a colonnade to N and W linking a lodge and the school entrance to his impressive MEETING HOUSE, 1846–7. Plain interiors, with the exception of the original COMMITTEE ROOM in the three central bays of the main block with Rococo ceiling.

Later buildings, which Pevsner lamented as unenterprising, include FOTHERGILL HALL, 1899, the SCIENCE BLOCK AND GYM, 1911–12, a small LIBRARY by *Hubert Castle*, 1936, and the ANDREWS WING, 1953–5. A more imaginative note has been struck by the glazed staircase extension to Fothergill Hall, 1961, and the intimate clerestoried concert hall of the MUSIC CENTRE, 1993–4.

Opposite the entrance to the school, is a plain stone terrace of seven staff houses (Nos. 32–44 Barnsley Road) of 1847.

At High Ackworth, OLD HALL, w of the church, is a fine T-plan early C17 house with symmetrical s front of five bays with two big attic gables. Three-light mullioned windows. (Original entrance with Tudor arch at rear. Unusual small squint window in the w angle with rear range.) SE of the church, the handsome early C19 MANOR HOUSE, three bays with pedimented doorcase. It faces the CROSS on the green, a shaft (probably medieval) on octagonal stepped base, with Tudor ball on top. Across Pontefract Road is MARY LOWTHER'S HOSPITAL, founded in 1741 as almshouses and school. Pleasing one-storey front, the schoolroom in the three central bays. These break forward under a pediment. Doorway and windows have Gibbs surrounds. Two-storey schoolmaster's house with pyramidal roof behind the schoolroom. All restored as housing in 1985. A short distance E up Pontefract Road, on the s side, EDEN PLACE looks late C18 but its single-depth linear plan, end-on to the road, suggests earlier origins. Doorway with pedimented Gibbs surround. Tripartite sash windows either side. The l. return is a big two-storey bow with large tripartite sashes (cf. Ackworth Grange below). Humbler service range to the r., with single-storey pedimented garden house beyond. Coachhouse dated 1787. Further on, a small mid-C18 house (No. 126), stone, with quite a dramatic centre. Pedimented doorway, again with a Gibbs surround, but flanked this time by vertically halved Ionic columns with scrolled base, each with one volute and one scroll. Above this a Venetian window, and on the second floor a Diocletian window. Nos. 130–132, dated 1744 on a lintel but altered later, display more classical details on three storeys, e.g. Doric mullions on the canted bay to the road and a window with segmental pediment on brackets at the front.

ACKWORTH HOUSE, ⅓ m. s on Pontefract Road. Attributed to *William Lindley*, c. 1786. Three-storey N front has central pediment with medallion and swags; altered garden front has an open pediment above a first-floor Venetian window with balustrade and super-arch, flanked by tall canted bays.

In Station Road, the two-storey former BRITISH SCHOOL (Nos. 14 and 16), dated 1810 on the parapet of the slightly recessed centre. The outer bays have pediments above two large windows.

GUIDE POSTS. Ackworth has three of these distinctive tapering stone signposts, each about 10 ft (3 metres) high. On Pontefract Road, at Station Road, one dated 1805, hexagonal, with banded rustication, triangular cap and (restored) bell-shaped finial; at the junction with Long Lane, another dated 1827, octagonal with a ball finial. The third, on Barnsley Road at the Bell Lane junction, is undated and a column with conical cap.

ACKWORTH COURT (formerly Ackworth Villa), Villa Close, Low Ackworth. Early C19. Wide s front composed of three-bay centre under full-width pediment with attic lunette, flanked by wings with rounded ends. The wings both originally one storey, but the l. now two. Verandahs to both floors with outstanding Regency ironwork. The drawing room formerly had frescoed landscapes by *Agostino Aglio* (cf. Bretton Hall and Woolley Hall).

COLD BATH HOUSE, Mill Lane, Low Ackworth. Built over a chalybeate spring *c.* 1780 by *William Lindley* for Ackworth School. Converted to a house *c.* 1860.

ACKWORTH GRANGE, 1½ m. ese. Nice Late Georgian, with pedimented Doric doorway. Double-height bow to either side, with big tripartite sashes, like Eden Place, above. (Entrance-hall tiles by *Pugin*.)* South Lodge, Rigg Lane and the Priest's House are Gothic Revival, by *Matthew Hadfield*.

HESSLE HALL, 1 m. sw of St Cuthbert. Unpretentious gabled house nestling in a secluded valley. Tudor-arched lintel dated 1641.

HUNDHILL HALL. *See* East Hardwick.

ADLINGFLEET

8020

Small village, once a port, in the former marshlands where the broad courses of the rivers Ouse and Trent join together as the Humber. The confluence of the Don and the Trent was nearby, the Don's old course running along the village's e edge.

ALL SAINTS. Late C12 s doorway. Two orders of colonnettes with stiff-leaf and volutes to the capitals. The arch is pointed, but still with bold chevron on the face and at right angles to it. It was perhaps originally round and altered when re-set during the rebuilding of the church by John le Franceys, Rector in 1247–55, when Adlingfleet was one of the wealthiest livings in England. His work was uncommonly ambitious for a village church and although its transepts were not completed the interior is spacious. It remains essentially E.E., with most unusual details, derived from Lincoln. Nave with arcades of two bays, tower arch to its w, crossing with three arches to its e, and chancel arch a little further e than the crossing – all with shafted piers and responds with single shaft-rings, all with moulded capitals, and all with double-chamfered arches. The whole is like a reduced and thoroughly provincialized version of West Walton, Norfolk. The arcade piers are cruder than

18

*The JESUS CHAPEL by *Pugin*, 1841–2, for Mrs Elizabeth Tempest, was demolished *c.* 1966. He called it his 'Gem of the North'. The altar is at St Mary Magdalene, Campsall (q.v.), statues at St Leonard and St Jude, Doncaster (q.v.), and stained glass in the Chapter House and Galilee at Durham Cathedral.

those further E; the S capital has nailhead. Externally, too, the
E.E. style has left its marks, especially on the remarkable N
aisle window – two trefoiled lights and above it a large unfoiled
circle surrounded by three small trefoiled ones; the tracery,
hoodmould and clustered shafts (incomplete) in the reveals are
all filleted. This is latest E.E., say *c*. 1280. E.E. also the
N aisle's lancet and blocked W lancet, and the S transept's
blocked E lancet and two-light window. Next to this a window
with intersected tracery, i.e. again *c*. 1280. There is in the
church also both older and younger work, but its effect is
insignificant compared with the general impression. It must
not, nevertheless, be overlooked. The W tower's big four-light
W window is C15. Perp too its battlemented top and the S aisle
and the clerestory. The chancel was rebuilt 1792–4, using
original materials (see re-set piscina), but only half its former
length. Restoration by *William Fowler* of Winterton, 1827–8,
included re-roofing and box pews. The result, with whitewashed walls and arches, box pews and stone-flagged floor,
bathed in pure clear light, is like looking straight into an early
C19 aquatint.

SCULPTURE. Three C15 panels in the S aisle: Annunciation,
Coronation of the Virgin, and Assumption, the figures badly
worn. – MONUMENTS. Effigy of a lady with veil and wimple,
thought to be Margaret, wife of Thomas Egmonton, †1370.
Tomb-chest decorated with four shields in quatrefoils; the
quatrefoils set diagonally and with sharp barbs. – Francis Hal-
denby †1589. Very finely carved effigy dressed in armour, his
head resting on a crested helmet. Family procession on tomb-
front, ten sons kneeling behind their father, then three daughters behind their mother. Elaborate panel with inscription and
heraldic achievement on the back wall. – Mrs Ramsden †1745.
By *Charles Mitley* and *Harvey*, a London sculptor, 1755 (cf.
Tancred Robinson monument of 1754 at York). Excellent life-
size figure in amply draped costume, standing on wide base
with inscription between inlaid panels. Dignified reredos background with two fluted Corinthian columns, festoon and
cherubs' heads below segmental top, flaming urns above.
Veined grey and pink marbles. Oddly urbane in this remote
village church. The reason is that Mrs Ramsden had left her
fortune to St Catharine's College, Cambridge and that the
monument was intended for erection there.

50 yds S of the church is the altered fragment of a two-
storey domestic building, probably part of a rectory built by
John le Franceys; he erected a *camerum* or chamber in Adlingfleet, using stone from Whitgift church (q.v.), which he had
demolished *c*. 1250 in a dispute with Selby Abbey. On the w
side a re-set C12 doorway with chamfered round arch and
hoodmould.

In the village several pleasant C18 three-bay brick farmhouses and
houses, e.g. ELM TREE FARMHOUSE, 200 yds S and GRANGE
HOUSE, beyond.

ADWICK-LE-STREET   5000

St Laurence.* w tower, nave with N aisle, and lower chancel with N chapel. Of the Norman nave and chancel there are only the s doorway and internal evidence of a priest's doorway and two blocked chancel windows. The nave doorway, very worn and very restored, has three orders; the first and third plain and heavy, the second with plain shafts and roll-moulded arch. The w chancel window seems to have been cut into by the priest's door, the E one by the sedilia. This has two seats with a round shaft and round arches with a slight chamfer. It could be a little earlier than, or contemporary with, the N chapel added in the C13, which has lancet windows – at the E end two widely spaced ones with an oculus over – and a good arcade of two bays with quatrefoil pier, matching responds and double-chamfered arches. Early C14 N aisle arcade of three bays with standard elements. No E respond but a pier also carrying both the chancel arch, which is wider than the chancel itself, and an odd, angled, half-arch at the w end of the chapel arcade. The sequence here is confusing but it seems that a C14 plan to enlarge the chancel to the N was abandoned. Unusual C14 nave roof. The trusses have a series of posts, the sides of each post having alternate cusps to give a wavy effect. Original trusses at E and w ends, the other three copies of, 1967. Purlins have carved masks attached. The aisle N wall, with straight-headed windows, is late Perp like the tower. The church was over-restored by *J.M. Teale* in 1862, then in 1875 *W.M. Teulon* encased most of the nave s wall, adding the timber porch and also the curious, secular-looking gables over new windows. – STAINED GLASS. Nave s. Both by *Ward & Hughes*, 1875. – N chapel E lancets. Stories of St Francis, 1943 by *J.E. Nuttgens*. A charming set of roundels in the style of mid-C20 English book illustration. – MONUMENTS. Three tomb-chests. James Washington †1580 and wife, Margaret, †1579. Shields to sides include the family's stars and stripes; on top an incised alabaster slab with their figures and those of their twelve children. – John Fitzwilliam †1470 and wife, Amicia, †1477. The sides have quatrefoils carrying shields. – Leonard Wray †1590 and wife, Ursula. Undecorated.

    Rectory (now offices). 150 yds s. 1844. Gabled Tudor Gothic. Wall plaques from its C17 predecessor.

railway station (former). 350 yds NE. 1866, for the West Riding & Grimsby Joint Railway. Picturesque style with machicolated tower.

Woodlands Hall (Park Club), 1 m. s, across the Great North Road. Attributed to *William Lindley*, c.1791. Painted ashlar.

---

*Robert Parkyn, Curate 1541–69, left a diary containing a vivid chronicle of the effects of the Reformation on his rural parish, which included the Priory at Hampole (q.v.).

Five bays, two-and-a-half storeys. Plain three-bay pediment. Lower one-bay side wings have shallow blind arches to the ground floor (cf. Wyndthorpe Hall, Hatfield). Hipped roofs. Large C19 canted bays flank central doorway. Porch in similar style to r. return.

99   WOODLANDS, WNW of Woodlands Hall, is a model village laid out in two phases 1907–c. 1910 on the parkland of the house for the Brodsworth Main Colliery Co. The architect was *Percy Houfton* (cf. his pit villages at Bolsover and Creswell, Derbyshire). The houses are mostly in blocks, in an attractive and varied Arts and Crafts cottage style. Land between the first two phases of housing was allocated for communal buildings, including ALL SAINTS of 1911–13 by *W.H. Wood*, in round-arched style. Given by Charles Thellusson of Brodsworth, owner of the mineral rights. The distinctive needle spire is visible from Brodsworth Hall nearly two miles away. – PULPIT. C17. Panelled. – Tiny tiled IMMERSION FONT in the W baptistery. – STAINED GLASS. E, W and N chapel windows by *Leeds Modern Art Glass Co.*, 1920–2.

CASTLE. At Hangthwaite, 1¼ m. SSE, in low, level ground. A motte, surrounded by a ditch and a counterscarp bank. A bailey to the NNE, with a second one, less well preserved, to the E. (HW)

ADWICK-UPON-DEARNE

ST JOHN THE BAPTIST. Unusual in preserving its simple Norman form of small nave and chancel. S doorway, of one order, completely plain. Broad buttress-like W projection to support a gabled double bellcote. This also seems to be Norman and therefore a great rarity, but Glynne in 1860, before the church was pebbledashed, describes it with pointed arches and E.E., which is also the period of the S porch and chancel lancets that reuse three small Norman window heads. Y-traceried E window and nave S window, late C13. Chancel arch by *A.C. Martin*, 1910; its predecessor was round-arched with imposts i.e. possibly C12. – PULPIT. C19, incorporating carved pew panels *c.* 1600. – STAINED GLASS. E window by *Pitman & Son*, 1885.

POPLAR FARMHOUSE. 150 yds N. Early C19. Unusually formal three-bay front with quoins and a little central pediment.

DOVECOTE, 300 yds N. Early C18. Upper and lower doorways with massive stone surrounds.

AIRMYN

A charming village on the Aire just before it joins the Ouse. Airmyn's tranquil remoteness belies its earlier importance as one of the West Riding's principal ports and a ferry point to the East Riding. Founded by St Mary's Abbey, York before the mid C12 and allowed a chapel (of Snaith) in 1318. Promotion of the port by Hugh Smithson followed his purchase of the manor in 1656, and the family later involved the Aire & Calder Navigation Company in its development, but first the Selby Canal (1778) and then the Knottingley–Goole Canal (1826) enabled river traffic to bypass Airmyn. Now the brick houses and cottages along High Street face not wharves, warehouses and boatyards but a pleasant riverside walk along the tree-lined floodbank.

ST DAVID. Small, red brick, lying back from High Street. Nave built 1676, apparently by Anthony Smithson, whose arms adorn the w gable, but thoroughly remodelled by *Lockwood & Mawson*, 1858. w porch, double w bellcote,* two-light windows with four-centred heads and timber Y-tracery. Chancel and s organ chamber by *W. & R. Mawson*, 1884–5, reusing the E window with Dec tracery. – STAINED GLASS. E window by *Messrs Gibbs*, 1858. Five windows by *Powell Bros*, 1893, 1897, 1902. – MONUMENTS. Several to the Wells family, including Peter Wells †1845, by *W.D. Keyworth* of Hull, with broken column; William Wells †1854, by *Fisher* of York, with pedimented aedicule; and John Wells †1874, a medieval-style recess with cross-slab.

At the end of the village, 350 yds N, looking at first like the tower of a second, more ambitious church, the Gothic CLOCK TOWER by *H.J. Lockwood*, 1865–8. Built by villagers in honour of their landlord George Percy, 2nd Earl of Beverley and 5th Duke of Northumberland. Angle buttresses carry matronly angels with shields. Four big steep gables and a spiky steep pyramid roof.

AIRMYN HALL, High Street. Small country house with a chequered history; now three houses. Probably built by the Smithsons in the later C17, remodelled *c.* 1760, altered *c.* 1875 and C20. Two storeys. Brick; decorative eaves with paired corbels between bays. Hipped pantile roofs. Garden front has big, full-height central canted bay with pyramidal roof. Short polygonal-ended N wing with C20 extension; lower service wing to s. Rear to High Street divided into bays by narrow pilaster-strips.

BOOTHFERRY BRIDGE, ¾ m. NNE. By the *Cleveland Bridge & Engineering Co.*, 1926–9. A three-span steel girder bridge, the N span swinging open for shipping.

OUSE BRIDGE (M62), 1 m. NE, crossing the Ouse. Long, graceful, plate-girder bridge of twenty-nine spans with 1.5 km concrete deck. 1972–6 by *Redpath Dorman Long Ltd*, and *G. Maunsell & Partners* for *Costain Civil Engineering Ltd*.

'WHITE CITY'. 1¼ m. SW. An isolated row of eight rendered semi-detached houses, each originally with one-acre smallholding, built in 1921 for ex-servicemen.

---

* One BELL is by *Thomas Dekon* of York between 1375 and 1390, one of only three by him in England.

ALMONDBURY

High on a hill above Huddersfield and now the edge of that
town's SE suburbs. Close to the Norman castle of the de Lacys
on Castle Hill, the medieval village stood at the cross-roads of
packhorse routes and had a market charter from 1294, but its
local importance was gradually eclipsed as Huddersfield
developed.

ALL HALLOWS. Large, mostly Perp. The Perp parts are probably connected with an indulgence of 1486 for the repair of
   the church. But the long chancel has E.E. paired lancets as the
   N and S windows of its eastern end and there is a straight joint
   immediately W of the N pair. These windows are now only
   visible inside, as *W.H. Crossland* lengthened the side chapels
   in his restoration of 1872–6, when the chancel was much
   rebuilt and the chapels remodelled externally as continuations
   of the aisles. The C14 N (Kaye) chapel's original part opens to
   the chancel in two arches on moulded corbels, the eastern arch
   being Crossland's. Similarly, a matching third arch was added
   to the arcade of the late Perp S chapel. It has octagonal ribbed
   piers, with Tudor roses and fleurs-de-lys decorating the capitals. Crossland retained other windows, including the chancel's
   odd group of three E windows. The middle one is Perp with
   three cusped lights, the windows either side smaller with
   Y-tracery. Hammerbeam roof of 1876.
     Nave of five bays with straight-headed clerestory windows
   and large aisle windows with three-centred arches. Battlements
   and pinnacles of 1872–6. Big W tower has diagonal buttresses
   with many set-offs, three-light bell-openings, battlements and
   pinnacles. W doorway and three-light window over. The tower
   arch towards the nave dies into the imposts. Tall arcades with
   octagonal piers. Exceptionally good panelled nave ceiling, one
   of Yorkshire's finest. Its many decorated bosses, set diagonally
   and with stylistic foliage surrounds,* show the Instruments of
   the Passion, the sun, the moon, a grotesque face with two
   tongues, another with three eyes and two noses, etc. The long
   poetic inscription records the year 1522 and 'Geferay Daystn'
   as 'the maker of this'. – REREDOS. 1886, designed by *E.W.
   Lockwood*, carved by *John Roddis*. Caen stone, with painting
   and gilding, and alabaster figures in elaborately canopied
   niches. – SCREENS: CHANCEL. Almost wholly C19, but at the
   rear it carries the late medieval brattished ROOD BEAM, carved
   with roses etc. N CHAPEL (W arch). Perp, with traceried panels.
   ORGAN. Painted panels with angels by *A.O. Hemming*, 1890.
   – LECTERN. This is a gilded eagle, Early Georgian, and
   perhaps made for another purpose. – FONT COVER. Perp, and
   one of the best in the West Riding. 10 ft (3 metres) high.
   Painted and gilded. Three tiers of canopied arcades close

---

*Arnold Pacey has identified the similarity of their 'pierced leaf' ornament to that
found in some Cheshire churches, suggesting links with craftsmen there.

against the solid polygonal core. – STAINED GLASS. Restored figures of saints, probably early–mid-C15, incorporated in two windows by *Burlison & Grylls* in the N chapel, 1877–9. The E window has kneeling donors below, said to be named in the (lost) original inscription as John and Elizabeth Kay and their children. Chancel E windows 1876, and S aisle third from E 1881, by *Heaton, Butler & Bayne*. S aisle easternmost 1900, N aisle easternmost 1910 and the N chapel's third window 1892, all by *Burlison & Grylls*. S aisle fourth from E and W window both 1916, and N aisle fourth from E 1919, by *Herbert Bryans*. – MONUMENTS. N chapel. Arthur Kay of Woodsome Hall (Fenay Bridge) †1574, shown in armour on large incised slab. – William Lister †1701. Elaborate cartouche with cherubs' heads, drapery and flowers, attributed to *James Hardy* (GF). – Sir Arthur Kaye †1726 and wife, Anne, †1740. Standing monument with upper inscription in aedicule on gadrooned base. – Martha Allen †1804, by *William Bradley*, with draped urn.

KING JAMES' SCHOOL, St Helen's Gate. Grammar school founded in 1608. The two-storey Schoolhouse, rebuilt or substantially remodelled *c.* 1760, faces the E garden. Projecting to rear r. the Schoolroom, rebuilt by *Richard Armitage*, 1848–9, with a first-floor dormitory. Gabled N service extension to Schoolhouse and set-back S range, with large gabled classroom (now Library) projecting at front, by *W. Swinden Barber*, 1880–4. Multiple C20 and C21 additions.

S of the church in Westgate is WORMALL'S HALL (Conservative Club). C16 or earlier, timber-framed, with C17 stone-faced ground floor. The jettied upper storey has close-set herringbone strutting and three timber oriels with original diamond-pattern glazing bars. Carriage archway on the l. and the doorway, dated 1631, between seven-light mullioned windows. Grouped W of the church on Stocks Walk are the LIBRARY, 1905 by *K.F. Campbell*, Borough Surveyor; WESLEYAN SUNDAY SCHOOL, 1900; and former NATIONAL SCHOOLS by *E.W. Lockwood*, 1895–9. Behind the schools, the OLD CLERGY HOUSE, by *Edgar Wood*, 1898, once housed curates. It has his characteristic windows with square mullions and transoms set flush with the wall and two shallow canted bays with plain parapets breaking through the eaves. NE is the row of NETTLETONS' ALMSHOUSES by *W.H. Crossland*, 1861–4 and two later rows of 1931.

Some good large Georgian and later houses on the hillsides to the E and S, e.g. mid-C19 FENAY LODGE, Thorpe Lane, and mid-C18 FINTHORPE, Fleminghouse Lane. 50 yds W of the latter the very large C16 or C17 THORPE FARM BARN. Five bays, with cruck-trusses, the S side with exposed timber framing. Stone N aisle. On Fenay Lane FENAYWOOD, 1930s, in Pennine Vernacular style, is one of the best C20 houses. Also two experimental modular houses by *Peter Stead* with *David Lewis*, both set on two levels against the slope with big S-facing windows. No. 4 ARKENLEY LANE, 1957–63, has narrow-profile aluminium cladding. Nearby, No. 8 ALMONDBURY

COMMON (Branch Lane), 1957–9, retains original interior features such as a black Formica wall.

In the valley, along LUMB LANE, several WEAVERS' COTTAGES with typical long upper windows, e.g. Nos. 40–50, and one near Castle Hill, with a fourteen-light window.

CASTLE HILL, 1¼ m WSW, was a community focus for many centuries. There was activity here from the Neolithic but the most conspicuous element is the defensive ring of the Iron Age HILLFORT thrown around the crest. Probably beginning as a palisade in the late Bronze Age, a stone rampart was strengthened by an external ditch and a counterscarp bank. These defences were reshaped for the medieval CASTLE for which Henry de Lacy was granted licence to crenellate in the mid C12. A ditch was driven across the centre of the hillfort, creating an outer ward, entered from its NE angle, and a middle ward for which new cross-ramparts were provided. A smaller and higher inner ward on the SW summit took the form of a motte or ringwork; this was constructed from a substantial ditch, crossed by a causeway. Within the inner ward of the castle is VICTORIA TOWER by *Isaac Jones* of London, to commemorate the 1897 Jubilee. Broad and heavy, square with battered walls rising almost 100 ft (30 metres) to the embattled top, which has a still higher embattled stair-turret. S of the Tower is the castle's WELL, and two excavated sides of a medieval hall marked by modern walls. The castle walls were ruinous by the late C16. An attempt had been made to establish a small borough on the hill (a market was granted in 1294) but this failed and had gone by the early C17.

ALTOFTS

3020

ST MARY MAGDALENE. 1873–8 by *Adams & Kelly*. Rich Anglo-Catholic interior, with painted decoration. – REREDOS. Caen stone, with *Salviati* mosaic of the Crucifixion, after *Perugino*. – STAINED GLASS. E window (1885) and N aisle, first from E (1921) by *Kempe*. Also in the N aisle, one by *Mayer & Co.*, 1895. S aisle, one window by *Powell Bros*, 1887. W window to victims of a colliery explosion, 1886, with Shadrach, Meshach and Abednego in the flames.

ALVERTHORPE

3020

A Wakefield suburb.

ST PAUL, St Paul's Drive. 1823–5 by *Atkinson & Sharp*. Late Perp-style preaching box in a prominent hilltop position, its big W tower a local landmark. Chancel formed in the two E bays, 1906. Extensive crypt. STAINED GLASS. E window by *Heaton, Butler & Bayne, c.* 1920. S side, second from E, *c.* 1925, by *J. Eadie Reid*, who also painted the PULPIT panels, 1922.

ALVERTHORPE MILLS, Flanshaw Lane. The large mill, built 1870–2, was, unusually, single-storeyed, with planned layout. Only its Renaissance-style offices survive, with separate time office at l. end.

SILCOATES SCHOOL. *See* Wrenthorpe.

ANSTON

Village in two parts, on opposite sides of a valley. The parish church is in South Anston. In North Anston is an attractive enclave of C17 and C18 houses around and below The Green.

ST JAMES. Chevron and spiral moulded stones in the nave W wall and tower base are evidence of a C12 church, but what we see is mostly Dec. The chancel has a swagger five-light window with flowing tracery. It should be noted how the lights below the traceried head are not treated identically. Three reach up high, the other two are lower and ogee-headed. Aisles with straight-headed three-light windows with reticulation motifs. The S arcade with its filleted quatrefoil piers, moulded capitals and double-chamfered arches goes with all this. The chancel arch too is like this S arcade except in one respect, for its responds are red sandstone. The N arcade on the other hand has the standard elements of octagonal piers and double-chamfered arches. The capitals permit no date later than 1350. In the S aisle are a double piscina with cusped ogee arches and a simple recess. There is an identical recess in the N aisle. In the S recess stands the canopy of a niche, richly carved in red sandstone. When Glynne saw the church *c.* 1834 both aisle E windows had a canopied niche in the centre light and the N one wall brackets, presumably for lamps or images, to l. and r. In fact brackets remain beside both windows. Also Dec the chancel sedilia with embattled cornice; detached polygonal shafts between the seats.

The W tower is Perp, though well in keeping with the Dec architecture of the church. It is a smaller and simplified version of Laughton-en-le-Morthen (q.v.). Diagonal buttresses. The square tower turns octagonal halfway up the height of the bell-stage. Slender set-back spire. Embattled Perp clerestory of two-light windows. The bold head- and animal-stops of the hoodmoulds of these are again an echo of Laughton. – STAINED GLASS. E window 1915, N aisle E window 1919, both by *Kempe & Co.* – MONUMENT. Rare effigy of a man with a small girl by his side, no doubt father and daughter. Probably 1340s. The pillow of the man is held by two angels as usual, but a third angel reaches down to the child, while a fourth supports her from below.

LYCHGATE. By *J. D. Webster & Son*, 1919–20.

METHODIST CHURCH, 200 yds WNW. 1934–5. Neo-Norman, in Anston limestone. Decayed STATUE in the porch from the Palace of Westminster, rescued during restoration in 1973.*

MANOR HOUSE, 50 yds SW. Early C17. Two-storey gabled porch. Restored three- and four-light mullioned-and-transomed windows.

VICARAGE (former), ¼ m. NNE on Ryton Road. By *J. D. Webster*, c. 1890. Large, gabled.

5040

APPLETON ROEBUCK

ALL SAINTS. 1868 by *J. B. & W. Atkinson*, the daughter church of Bolton Percy (q.v.). Coursed sandstone outside, red brick inside. w gable bellcote. Geometrical tracery. – STAINED GLASS. N first from E, c. 1883 by *Mayer & Co.*; s, one window by *Kempe*, c. 1885.

WESLEYAN CHAPEL, Main Street. Dated 1818. Little hipped-roofed box. Two tall round-headed windows.

At HOLME GREEN, ⅜ m. s, BRICKYARD FARM, a restored yeoman's house of c. 1500 with close-studded and braced timber frame. Three bays, the l. rebuilt in brick, and a continuous outshut – not, apparently, an aisle. Lobby-entry plan, the entrance subsequently blocked. (Smoke-hood and common rafter roof with collars.)

(NUN APPLETON, 1½ m. s. Of the Cistercian nunnery founded in the mid C12 the only traces are some fragments of masonry in the grounds. Of the C16 mansion of the Fairfaxes, remodelled by General Fairfax c. 1650, an indefinite amount survives as part of the present, brick-built house created by a wealthy cloth merchant, William Milner, who bought the estate in 1711. The following year the antiquarian Ralph Thoresby recorded in his diary 'most of the house pulled down, and a much more convenient (though not quite so large one) erected by Mr Milner'. Large Victorian extensions by *E. B. Lamb* (1863) have been demolished, but further additions and alterations, including a tower at the w end, were made in 1920 by *B. Chippindale* of Bradford. Entrance side of seven bays and two-and-a-half storeys, with the centre projecting slightly in two stages. This might be the remodelled centre of the C17 house, which was also of seven bays. Thin quoins, framed windows, that in the centre with a more ornate surround. The porch is an unfortunate addition of 1920. The garden side by contrast has eleven narrower bays, with

---

*Between 1840 and 1844 nearly half a million cubic feet of limestone was sent from North Anston for the Houses of Parliament.

different window surrounds, and three full storeys. The central
bay is oddly singled out by two giant brick Doric columns
carrying a balcony to the second floor. Dentil and modillion
cornice, hipped roof. Main staircase behind the centre of the
garden side, with balusters indicating a date later in the C18.
Some good fireplaces, and some stuccowork. Sundial of
STAINED GLASS by *Henry Gyles* of York, dated 1670. In the
park a serpentine LAKE of after 1771.)
(WOOLAS HALL FARM, 1 m. NNE. Moated site, a grange of St
Mary's Abbey, York. Rendered range of no apparent antiquity
but retaining traces of timber framing inside, and a five-bay
kingpost roof, probably of the late C15. That roof type is exceptional in the Vale of York but was also used in the abbot's house
at St Mary's Abbey – now the King's Manor – of *c.* 1480.)

ARDSLEY   *3000*

Village destroyed by slum clearance and the road driven through
it in the 1960s.

CHRIST CHURCH, Doncaster Road. 1840–1 by *Hurst & Moffatt*.
The usual lancet style, but made Norman with round-headed
openings. Open bell-turret with a little pinnacle on the W
gable. – STAINED GLASS. E window by *Harry Harvey*, 1968. S
transept war memorial window, 1920 and nave N window, 1938
by *Powell & Sons*.
MANOR HOUSE, Doncaster Road. Looks C19 but probably
incorporates a hall house with cross-wings of *c.* 1639 (date on
demolished farm building adjacent). The infilled two-bay
centre is discernible by straight joints at the front. E elevation
has a five-light mullioned window to r. of doorway, under a
common dripmould.
ARDSLEY HOUSE, Doncaster Road. Small country house built
for Richard Micklethwait, who inherited in 1773. Plain three-
storey centre of five bays with asymmetrical two-storey wings,
swamped by hotel extensions. Staircase in the rear central bay
(now the front), lit by Venetian window with Doric screen. Is
it by *Carr* (cf. the stair at White Windows, Sowerby (q.v.))?
The 'FLAT TOPS', Scar Lane, are blocks of houses with flat
roofs, *c.* 1860, reputedly by a French architect.

ARKSEY   *5000*

ALL SAINTS. A sizeable cruciform building with a recessed
spire behind the battlements and pinnacles of its crossing
tower. Notwithstanding the spire and Perp clothing the basic
form of the church preserves its C12 appearance. Norman the

crossing piers (though confusingly added to later), Norman the lower windows of the tower, Norman a fragmentarily preserved chancel N window (see inside), and Norman the rubble masonry of the nave W wall (with some big quoins), the N transept N wall and the S transept S wall. Norman finally also the very simple unmoulded S doorway in the S transept. The E wall of the chancel looks Victorian – but it is original (see the rubble masonry low down), though much 'improved' in *Scott*'s restoration of 1868–70. Glynne described the E window in 1856 as 'poor, Perpendicular' – is it safe to assume that Scott found evidence for his boldly treated arrangement of three stepped windows with a vesica-shaped window above? There is one original late Norman capital on the S shaft of the now exaggeratedly rich-looking shafting inside. The church is thought to have been built in the 1120s but whether the Norman parts enumerated so far are all of one date cannot be said. It is certain that a further building campaign went on later in the C12, for the W window of the N transept is cut into by the E arch of the aisle, which is also still round-headed. It rests on cone-shaped corbels; a matching corbel supports the E arch of the N arcade. This has three double-chamfered pointed arches on circular piers with octagonal capitals. It could follow the opening of the E arch immediately or after a lapse of time.

The S arcade is clearly C13. Octagonal piers, double-chamfered arches. Other C13 contributions are the sedilia and half a window remaining in the chancel (the sedilia have no more than shaped arms – no back architecture; cf. Owston and Campsall). Again C13 the alterations of the crossing piers with the handsome fine attached shafts encircling the E piers to N, W and S, the graceful crossing arches in their present form, and the bell-stage of the tower. The fine, tall twin openings are in round-arched recesses with shafted jambs and have an oval hole in the spandrel – a kind of elementary plate tracery. The S doorway, reused when the aisle was widened later, goes with all this. About 1300 followed the N chapel: see its E window with intersected tracery; in the C15 or later the S chapel. Both chapels have one Perp arch without capitals towards the chancel. The S chapel projects beyond the chancel, and its S wall runs flush with that of the S transept. Rebuilt S aisle with buttresses and battlements and pinnacles like the S chapel. Low and wide Perp S porch with a four-centred arch on responds with lightly decorated capitals. A good arrangement of carved shields flanking the arch includes those of Sir Thomas Windham (†*c.* 1521) and his two wives. Finally Perp also the W front, except for its earlier masonry, the N walls of the N aisle and chapel and the short octagonal stone spire. Pretty tracery with mouchettes in the tops of the square-headed N aisle windows.

The wide interior is spacious and light, with C15/C16 roofs in the chapels and aisles and some excellent C17 fittings. – PULPIT with back-board and tester. Dated 1634. Panels with lozenges etc. in richly decorated arches. – NAVE PEWS. C17.

The ends have straight tops with big turned knobs on them, two to each end and spherical on the S side, acorn-shaped on the N. The fronts of the first row are open and nicely balustraded. – FONT COVER. Dated 1662. Its character is still Jacobean, but the design is unusual by the largeness of its members, and the fact that the eight conventional volutes are flat boards, set vertically, whose scrolly appearance is entirely due to their elaborately cut outlines. – SCREEN. Vestry. Is it the medieval former chancel screen? Mid-rail frieze has relief carving of quatrefoils and mouchettes. – SCULPTURE. Three C12 stones with chevron in the nave wall (NW corner). – Unusual cast-iron BENEFACTION PLAQUE, 1824. – STAINED GLASS. Some framed heraldic medallions and other early C14–C15 pieces are set in front of four windows. They are all that remain of what Hunter described in 1828 as one of the area's 'richest collection[s] of antient armoury ... still glowing in the windows in their original colours'. – E window by *Heaton, Butler & Bayne*, 1899. – MONUMENT. Sir George Cooke †1683. Excellent piece in black and white marbles. Bewigged portrait bust in oval niche framed by Ionic aedicule with broken segmental pediment and cartouche. Decorated with lushly carved foliage, flowers and fruit.

Side by side facing the W end of the church are the almshouses and school, both endowed by the Cookes of Wheatley (*see* Doncaster), who bought the Arksey estate in 1654. The ALMSHOUSES, built with a bequest from Brian Cooke (†1661), form three sides of a quadrangle. Mullioned windows. The steeply gabled ends are connected by a high wall along the street, its grand gateway, rebuilt in 1736 by Sir George Cooke, with similarly steep triangular pediment. The SCHOOL (now a shop) retains its walled yard in front. The Sir George Cooke who died in 1683 left money for it to be built. Plain rectangle with two two-light windows (later Gothicized) each side of the doorway. This already has a heavy 'Queen Anne' frame and a big broken segmental pediment.

Immediately SE of the church the former VICARAGE by *Woodhead & Hurst*, 1833–5. Good ashlar front, the gabled central bay set forward. Mullioned windows with Gothic-arched lights.

BEECH TREE HALL (CARE HOME), 250 yds NE. Formerly ARKSEY HALL. Plain rendered house, five bays square. Superficially Georgian, but with the irregular fenestration of an older house altered *c.*1820. (One fireplace has panelled wooden overmantel carved with lozenges and dated 1653.)

ARMITAGE BRIDGE

Mill village in the Holme valley. Mill, and church across the river, were built by the Brooke family, merchants and manufacturers involved in the valley's woollen industry since the C16.

St Paul. By *R. D. Chantrell*, 1847–8. Aisled nave, lower chancel and ambitious w tower. Dec style, quite lavishly done, costing over £6,000. In 1987 arsonists gutted the nave and chancel. Reordered by *Richard Shepley*, 1990, with FITTINGS by *Edward Wilcock*. – Gabled Tudor-style VICARAGE, Carriage Drive, also by *Chantrell*. He had designed ARMITAGE BRIDGE HOUSE (now flats), Stockwell Vale, for John Brooke in 1828. This has a distyle *in antis* porch with fluted Ionic columns. (Neoclassical interior decoration showing influence of Chantrell's teacher, Soane.) Temple-fronted SUMMERHOUSE, COACHHOUSE and BARN (all now housing)

BROOKE'S MILL. A large site, the best surviving example in our area of an early integrated woollen mill. Developed from *c.* 1816; closed 1987 and restored for office and commercial uses. Good range of original buildings includes: four-storey, thirteen-bay WAREHOUSE and OFFICES with pedimented gable and giant classical entrance arch to internal loading bay, an uncommon arrangement for transferring wool or cloth; at right angles to s, four-storey HAND-SPINNING and HANDLOOM-WEAVING SHOPS, extended 1825; plain five-storey fireproof MILL NO. 1, ten bays, built for water-powered fulling, scribbling and carding, its roof an early combination of cast iron (struts) and wrought iron (rods). MILL NO. 2, taller and deeper, was added 1828–9 for power spinning.

BERRY BROW, Carriage Drive. 1967–9. Single-storey house of elegant simplicity, designed by *Peter Stead* for himself, with the architect *Robert Clayton*. Timber-framed, with continuous rhythm of full-height mullions. Deep eaves to the flat roof, whose massive projecting beams replaced the aluminium space-frame roof originally intended.

ARMTHORPE

St Leonard and St Mary. Rendered exterior, save the stone dressings. Long narrow Norman nave, small lower chancel, n aisle and n chapel of 1885–6. The doorway and three small windows on the nave's s side are Norman. Two orders to the doorway, the inner one with a continuous plain chamfered arch, the outer one with renewed nook-shafts with moulded capitals and a chamfered arch. So the doorway is perhaps not older than *c.* 1200. The chancel arch, however, is early Norman. Unmoulded round arch, plain jambs and big chamfered imposts, oddly unmatched. The n impost is plain, the s one has on its n upright deeply incised vertical chevron and on the chamfer below a most unusual raised lattice pattern apparently overlying another, chip-carved, pattern that appears in the diamonds.

In extensive restoration by *C. Hodgson Fowler*, 1885–6, the n chapel was added and *Woodhead & Hurst*'s three-bay n aisle of 1826 rebuilt. Their small square bell-turret above the nave, E of the doorway, was removed. It stood over the curious unmoulded pointed arch across the nave which must have supported an earlier turret. The arch is of uncertain date but could be early C13. A larger, timber bell-turret with a steep pyramid roof, all attractively shingled, was placed over the nave w bay. Pretty drop tracery to the openings. – STAINED GLASS. By *Kempe* the E window, 1888, S chancel easternmost, 1889, and S nave third from E, 1888. – Miners' Memorial window by *Alan Moston*, 2004. – MONUMENTS. George Cooke Yarborough †1818 by *J. Lockwood*. Tablet conventionally orna-mented with garlanded vase, bands of paterae etc., but also a plate of communion bread.

N of Doncaster Road, ¼ m. w, is the VILLAGE for miners at Markham Colliery (1920–96). Spacious model layout around three concentric semicircles. Nearly 200 of the 1,000 proposed houses were completed by 1924, when coal was reached. Ground-floor bathrooms.

ASKERN

A popular spa resort from the late C18 to the early C20 (which explains uncharacteristically comfortable Victorian villas on Station Road and the substantial Arts and Crafts-style Railway Hotel, 1904–5) but its allure destroyed after 1911 by mining. The central boating lake remains as a welcome redeeming feature.

ST PETER. By *W.L. Moffatt*, 1848–52. Neat lancet style. Tall w bellcote. N aisle by *G. Fowler Jones & Son*, 1886. – STAINED GLASS. One by *Christopher Webb*, 1939.

ASTON

ALL SAINTS. Late C12 arcades with round double-chamfered arches except the easternmost arch on the S which is pointed. All the arches have hoodmoulds. Unusual too the polychro-matic effect of the dark red sandstone used for the outer orders and the light stone of the inner ones, the soffits of the N arcade also having traces of red painted decoration. Well restored in 1862–3 by *M.E. Hadfield*. One round and one octagonal pier on each side. The NW respond and nearest pier have a little leaf decoration. Dec chancel, of limestone ashlar, largely rebuilt before 1860. Blocked arch to former N chapel. SE squint. Flowing tracery in the E window, straight-headed side windows. The whole S side of the aisle also has straight-headed Dec windows. Much renewed, but big original hoodmould stops, also limestone. Perp s porch with two busts as hood-mould stops. Niche for an image above the outer doorway. w tower Perp with pretty openwork battlements and eight pinnacles. – Early Perp FONT. Octagonal, with battlements and elaborately traceried panels. Against the foot the unexpected seated figure of a little man with a sword. Thought perhaps to be Herod and an allusion to the slaying of the Holy Innocents. On the other side is an angel. – STAINED GLASS. e window by *Heaton, Butler & Bayne*, 1910. – s aisle e window. Darcy coat of arms (in 1831 in the chancel e window) and related heraldic medallions brought from Aston Hall in 1781, apparently saved from the C17 house. – MONUMENTS. Sir John Melton †1510. Now no more than the brass inscription and two shields. – John, Lord Darcy †1635 and three of his four wives, Rosamund †1606, Isabel †1623 and Mary †1624, erected 1628. Only the inscription and their kneeling figures, his in an altered marble aedicule, theirs in plain compartments below, remain from the splendid monument sketched by Nathaniel Johnston. Originally three-tiered and including four children, it was dismantled in 1756.* – Sir Francis Fane †1680, wife Elizabeth †1669 and family. Odd composition of short pilasters carrying a low flat-topped arch with heraldry. – Rev. William Mason †1797. Tablet by *Coade & Sealy* with fine portrait profile in a medallion, 1804. – s aisle: garlanded portrait profiles (plaster) of Thomas Gray 1771 and Mason 1800, originally in the Rectory summerhouse (*see* below).

ASTON HALL, 100 yds SE. Now a hotel. A large, square stone house of 1767–72 by *Carr* for the 4th Earl of Holderness, after the old hall burnt down. Before it was complete the Earl sold to Harry Verelst, former Governor of Bengal. Both the entrance (N) and the garden (S) fronts are of the same simple Palladian composition: seven bays of which the centre three form a canted bay. Rusticated ground floor and half-attic. The windows of the *piano nobile* have pulvinated friezes and cornices, balustrades below. The central pedimented window of the N front is the former doorway; curved stairs to it were removed *c*. 1825 (the date of the two-storey E service range) but the rustic entrance had probably already superseded this, as in 1776–7 *John Platt* inserted the staircase in the lower hall, set behind a screen of Doric columns. Wrought-iron balustrade. It produces a somewhat congested composition on the first floor, arriving against Carr's s screen of two unfluted Ionic columns. Adamesque decoration to library fittings and chimneypiece in ground-floor room with s bay.

STABLES (now residential). Also by *Carr*, altered 1826.

RECTORY (former), 50 yds NW. By *Carr*, 1770–1, for William Mason, cleric, poet and garden designer. Unpretentious stuccoed brick house of three bays with overwhelming C19

---

* It had a stylistic resemblance to the monument of Lady Margaret Osborne †1624, his third wife's sister, at Harthill (q.v.).

Italianate porch. Part of old rectory forms service wing.* Also
COTTAGES in Worksop Road (Nos. 20–24) by *Carr*, *c.* 1770
(originally six, altered). Second and fifth two storeys with
hipped roofs, the others one storey.

AUGHTON HALL, 1¼ m. NW. C18. Three-bay house with good
pedimented wooden doorcase below Venetian-style window.
Transformed by early C19 addition of big two-storey semicircular bays, both stuccoed.

AUCKLEY

6000

ST SAVIOUR. Simple Gothic former chapel/school by *William
Hurst*, 1837–8. Fine cast-iron tracery by *Marshalls* of Derby.

AUSTERFIELD

6090

ST HELENA. A small church, set far back in its long narrow
churchyard. At a distance its red tiled roof and porch and
Victorian double bellcote do not suggest great antiquity, so
its Norman S doorway comes as a surprise. Norman too the
chancel arch, both being clearly earlier than most decorated
Norman work in this part of the county. The doorway has two
orders of colonnettes with three block capitals and one double-
scallop one, their decoration elementary. Arch with crude
beakhead and chevron, and in the tympanum a representation
of a dragon (with an arrow-like tail-end) – a rarity in England.
Below is a raised band of semicircular merlons and below
that a row of paterae or rosettes and little domes. The chancel
arch has minimal ornament. Semicircular responds with block
capitals, each having a tiny man's face carved on the angle
looking into the nave. Outer order (W) with colonnettes. Soffit
roll and angle roll to the arch, faintly incised chevron on the
label.
   In the late C12 a N aisle was added. Arcade of three bays
with a piece of solid wall between the middle and W bays.
The two eastern bays have plain arches, a circular pier and
semicircular responds. The separating wall and the chamfered arch and semi-octagonal W respond of the third bay
suggest that it was an afterthought. Square capitals have bold
and varied waterleaf-type carving with leaf crockets. At the
SW corner of the pier's capital a sheila-na-gig, in an exceptionally patent position. Early C13 or so the W front with

---

*The SUMMERHOUSE containing commemorative urns to Mason and his friend
Thomas Gray has gone. The portrait medallions from its ceiling are in the church.

two small lancet windows and three buttresses. Late C13 E
window with intersected tracery. By the C19 the aisle was
demolished and the arcade walled up; it was rediscovered by
C. Hodgson Fowler, 1896–8, and the aisle rebuilt with funds
from the Society of Mayflower Descendants in memory of
William Bradford, Governor of Plymouth Colony, who was
baptized here in 1590. – FONT. Plain Norman bowl, tapering
slightly upwards. – COMMUNION RAIL. Humble, Jacobean,
with vertically symmetrical balusters. – STAINED GLASS. Nave
s wall E by *Herbert Bryans*, 1898. The other chancel and nave
windows by *C.E. Tute*, *c.* 1898. N aisle, middle, by *Sep Waugh*,
1989, commemorates William Bradford.

MANOR HOUSE, 300 yds N. William Bradford's family home.
L-shaped plan with late C16 cross-wing on E and two-bay
lobby-entry hall block added in early C17. Timber-framed,
with later brick infill. The timber posts are exposed at the
wing's front corners.

BADSWORTH

Pleasant village in the rolling countryside of its famous hunt.

ST MARY. Mostly C15, restored 1846–7, and *c.* 1877 by *John
Douglas* of Chester. A Norman impost with scallop decoration
and a voussoir with chevron are built into the NW corner of
the s aisle. Humble C13 N doorway (re-set). Humble early C14
chancel doorway. Good Dec chancel s windows. All the rest,
except the Victorian s porch, is Perp, of *c.* 1400. Tall, strong
W tower embraced by low aisles. On the s side the nave and
aisle are embattled. Clerestory. Three-bay arcades with the
standard elements. Panelled nave ceiling, fine chancel roof
with long moulded arch braces. Oak REREDOS and N chapel
SCREEN by *C.J. Ferguson*, 1902. N chapel reordered by *Sir
Charles Nicholson*, 1926. – FONT. Big, octagonal, Perp, with
traceried panels. From Barnsley Parish Church. – STAINED
GLASS. Some medieval fragments in the chapel E window.
Chancel s, second from E, by *Pugin*, made by *Hardman*, 1851.
By *Kempe* the s aisle w window, 1895, and two N aisle windows,
1901, one with St Hubert. The earlier window is clearly more
exuberant in its form. – MONUMENTS. Sir John Bright †1688,
attributed to *William Stanton*. Marble tablet with very big
achievement of shield, urn, two cornucopias and lush acanthus, carved as though draped with a fine veil. William Rhodes
†1777 with a portrait death mask. – In the churchyard, pyramid
to Osmond Alexander †1788, 'a native of Asia from the capital
of Hindostan'.

BADSWORTH HALL, a seat of the Brights of Sheffield, has been
demolished. The C18 stables were converted into a house in
1941.

THE OLD RECTORY. Main Street. Reputedly 1731, with E wing *c.* 1800. (One chamber, with C18 plasterwork, has walls apparently lined with cardboard. NHLE.)

BALBY *see* DONCASTER (OUTER)

BARKISLAND

0020

CHRIST CHURCH. By *Mallinson & Healey*, 1852–4. Modest, with Dec tracery and W bellcote. STAINED GLASS. E window by *Powell Bros*, 1883. N aisle first from E by *G. Cooper-Abbs*, 1963.

SCHOOL, 150 yds NW. By *Mallinson & Barber*, 1867–8. Simple Gothic schoolhouse with schoolroom to rear. Addition 1895.

BARKISLAND HALL, Stainland Road, ⅓ m. E. Dated 1638. A spectacular front of three storeys with three gables, a tall gabled porch with a rose window and very large mullioned-and-transomed windows arranged symmetrically. Built for John Gledhill, gentleman, the Hall is a large double-pile, F-plan house and is alone among the C17 'Halifax houses' in having a second floor. Its refinement and the correctness of its classical details also set it apart from them, perhaps because Gledhill, unlike the local yeoman-clothier builders, was university-educated, at Cambridge. Furthermore, it seems likely that his mason was either *Samuel Akroyd* or his son *John*. Both had knowledge of more sophisticated architecture outside the area, as Samuel's father and uncle had worked on the Bodleian Library and Merton College, Oxford, twenty-five years earlier, and John was apprenticed in Oxford.

The porch has fluted Doric columns on pedestals with lozenges and a straight entablature, its doorway a finely moulded Tudor arch, imposts and jambs. Second order with fluted Ionic columns; three-light window. The top window has seven circular lights, like that once at Bradley Hall, Stainland (q.v.), where Samuel's father, John Akroyd, was mason. Splendid twelve-light hall window, nine-light window above, the rest of six or eight lights. All with king mullions and elaborately carved stops, below the string course or to hoodmoulds. (Interior completely remodelled in 1920s; three C17 fireplaces remain, one dated 1605, another with well-carved balusters to the jambs. Good mock-C17 panelling in hall.) Bulgy GATEPIERS.

HOWROYDE, Howroyd Lane. Late medieval gentry house, timber-framed internally, altered in 1642 for William Horton and in the C18. Hall and cross-wings, hearth-passage plan. The hall is open through two storeys and has a large window of 3:3:3 lights with one transom. Slightly projecting gabled wings with sash windows. Entrance in the angle on the l. has moulded

Tudor-arched doorway with fluted Ionic columns and straight entablature, clearly copied from Barkisland Hall (*see* above), built by Horton's brother-in-law. Similar N doorway to passage, dated 1642, has Doric columns, again like Barkisland Hall. Sash windows to r. return, several formerly cross-windows. Kitchen in projecting two-storey rear wing originally had separate entrance. (Finely decorated hall has staircase and a gallery that runs round two sides and returns against the chimney-breast on the third. Fireplace flanked by fluted Ionic columns has overmantel with big royal arms in plasterwork and griffin frieze. Decoratively panelled ceiling centrepiece (cf. Wood Lane Hall, Sowerby). Painted glass in window, some panels dated 1641, some illustrating the senses.)

Downhill, ¾ m. E of the church, BARKISLAND MILL, late C19 (now flats), dominates a little clough. Long five-storey front punctuated by three staircase towers, their decorative *fin-de-siècle* tops with pavilion roofs incongruous in the wooded setting.

WORMALD FARMHOUSE, ¾ m. SE. Mid-C17, originally a three-room, through-passage plan but passage and lower end have gone. Good double-gabled front has mullioned-and-transomed windows to parlour and housebody and upper windows of three-over-five lights with carved stops to hoodmoulds. Rear kitchen wing and E gable entry with dated porch, 1693.

BARKSTON

BARKSTON TOWERS. Assertive Neo-Jacobean house 'considerably enlarged and beautified' in 1890. One tower over the entrance, another, with ogee dome, to the r.

TURPIN HALL FARM, SSE, in Saw Wells Lane. Unprepossessing rendered front hides a C17 building of hybrid construction, the outer walls of limestone but the partition demarcating the (truncated) rear outshut timber-framed (cf. Newlaithes Manor, Horsforth, *West Riding North*). Staircase in a panelled compartment with fluted frieze, several C17 doors.

BARLOW

CHAPEL (former), Brown Cow Road, opposite the site of Barlow Hall (dem. 1977). C17, restored and altered 1774 and late C19. Red brick with pantiles. Pretty lead-roofed W bellcote. One square-headed window with two cusped lights on each end plus a single-light S window. Will its fragile charm survive residential conversion?

BARNBURGH

ST PETER. Tall W tower. The lower half Norman with two slit-
windows, the S one blocked (but see the large round-arched
splay inside). C15 stages above, with two-light transomed bell-
openings and a low crocketed spirelet crowning the top behind
battlements and pinnacles. The rest of the church is all embattled too. N arcade of *c.* 1200, the S arcade later. Both two bays
with circular piers, semicircular responds, octagonal abaci and
double-chamfered arches. But the N pier base has a torus and
ring, while the other bases have broach stops. Dec chancel with
quadrant-moulded chancel arch and renewed reticulated
tracery in the S windows. Almost all the rest is Perp, including
the S porch with its chamfered transverse arches, most windows,
the clerestory, and the splendid roofs in the nave, chancel and
S aisle (E end) with moulded beams and carved bosses. N
chapel arcade inspired by Southwell's Chapter House, the pier
with two polished shafts and leafy capitals. The opening was
probably enlarged during partial restoration of the chancel in
1848–9, perhaps by *T. C. Hine* of Nottingham, whose rectory
(dem.) was then being built.

SCREENS. Late medieval. Four rood screen dado panels,
much restored 1866–9, behind the S aisle altar. Two parclose
screens: N chapel (W end) and enclosing the S aisle chapel.
Two-light divisions with ogee heads. – Part of a PEW (?) with
traceried panels and frieze with foliate trail. – Curious NICHE
in N aisle W wall, the small recess lozenge-shaped. Like a reli-
quary, but its position is wrong. – SCULPTURE. Very interesting Romanesque shaft, 6 ft 6 in. (2 metres) high (cf. Thrybergh).
In two pieces but apparently almost complete. It may have
terminated in a sort of pyramidal or gabled top rather than a
conventional cross-head. A cross and foliage on one slightly
wider side, interlaced bands enclosing foliage on the other. The
narrower sides each have a standing figure; one is tonsured,
with a book. – STAINED GLASS. E window by *Drury & Smith*
of Sheffield, 1864. Three windows by *Herbert Bryans*: chancel,
second from E 1904, S aisle W 1906 and N aisle W 1914. S aisle
E window by *Powell & Sons*, 1946. – MONUMENTS. Oak effigy
of a cross-legged knight, probably Thomas Cresacre †*c.* 1346.
He is holding his heart. A figure of outstanding quality, gentle
in the attitude and the execution. – He lies on the canopied
tomb of Percival Cresacre †1477, now free-standing, but until
1830 in a wall dividing chancel and chapel (hence the odd, but
necessary, C19 cusped buttresses). The tomb has shields below
cusped arches; the canopy has a straight cresting and an almost
straight-sided depressed arch below. The arch is closely
cusped. On both tomb and canopy are an exceptional number
of Latin inscriptions.* – Alice Cresacre †1450. Floor slab with
carved rosaries and English rhyme. – John Vincent †1676.

*All transcribed in the *Little Guide* and by Hunter.

Handsome aedicule with fluted pilasters and swan-neck pediment below bold cornice and heraldic achievement.

BARNBURGH HALL was demolished in 1970. Its Tudor
DOVECOTE (300 yds NE) is an impressively large and sturdy
octagon of coursed limestone rubble with ashlar dressings and
octagonal stone lantern.

HICKLETON HOUSE, 200 yds NNE. Fine mid-C17 farmhouse
with small two- and three-light mullioned windows, plus one
of five lights.

BARNBY DUN

6000

A small lowland village beside the River Don, swamped by
housing in the second half of the C20. The church and churchyard are an oasis at the N end.

ST PETER AND ST PAUL. Except for the Perp w tower the
church is almost completely early C14 (cf. Anston). *Hadfield
& Goldie* rebuilt the chancel in 1859–62 but reusing stonework and fittings. Four-bay nave with aisles and clerestory,
the aisle windows straight-headed with reticulation. N and S
doorways and chancel doorway with double-quadrant mouldings. Uncommonly bold and animatedly carved gargoyles. In
one N wall buttress a large image niche with ogee head under
crocketed gable. Similar niches in the chancel E buttresses.
C15 tower has full-height angle buttresses, battlements and
pinnacles.

Arcades with quatrefoil piers and double-chamfered arches
with small broaches. S arcade has octagonal capitals to responds
and easternmost pier. At the E end of the N aisle wall, high
up, a mysterious large recess with an elaborate crocketed ogee
arch and flanking pinnacles. Next to it on the l. the window
has two brackets in the jambs carried by angels. A chantry
was recorded here. Tall chancel arch with keeled responds.
On its S side is an unusual cylindrical stair-turret to reach
not only the rood loft (see different stonework in doorway
position) but also the S aisle roof. The chancel is large and
slightly wider than the nave. Roof trusses on corbels carved
with angels playing musical instruments. Restored sedilia and
piscina with colonnettes and four cusped arches, the hoodmould springing from angels. The piscina is held up by the
head and outstretched arms of a man, an impressive figure,
well in keeping with the gargoyles outside, though considerably
less elegant. – The chancel FURNISHINGS, 1862, ecclesiological and in keeping, were complete until reordering by *R. G.
Sims*, 1985–90. The arcaded stone and marble REREDOS, sanctuary floor tiles and altar rail remain. The chancel SCREEN is
in the tower arch. – FONT. Perp. Octagonal. Band of nailhead

above panels with shields and leaf motifs. – STAINED GLASS.
E window and N aisle W window by *Hardman*, 1862. – N aisle
E window by *Powell & Sons*, 1937. – MONUMENTS. Francis
Gregory †1671. Incomplete standing monument. Stone. Upper
part with cartouche framed by scrolls and palms. Achievement
with garlanded mantling and three winged cherubs' heads,
both detached. – Roger Portington †1683. Stone. Large framed
plaque, painted black, with gold inscription and coloured
heraldry. – Sir Thomas Hodgson †1693 and daughter
Frances, 16th Countess of Sutherland †1732, erected after her
death. Marble standing monument, still very grand though
lacking the 'pyramid' Hunter mentions (1828). Raised black
sarcophagus with gadrooned vase finial. To l. and r. their busts
on scrolled plinths with shells. – Hon. James Bruce †1798. A
woman kneeling by a pedestal which carries an elegant urn.
Beside her a pelican with its young.

BARNSLEY

3000

On a hill above the River Dearne, with some dramatic townscape created by the little valley of the Sough Dyke that bisects
the centre. The medieval manor belonged to St John's Priory
at Pontefract, which developed a new town around the parish
church and obtained a market charter in 1249. Barnsley's position at the junction of the main road from London to Richmond
and the cross-Pennine salt trade route helped it to flourish. The
Dearne & Dove Canal opened in 1799 (closed 1953) and railways eventually reached the town in 1850. The population grew
from 3,600 in 1801 to 10,000 in 1831, reaching 41,000 in 1901.
Barnsley became a borough in 1869 and a county borough in 1913.
    Wire-drawing was the principal industry before the C19, when
the town became the centre of English linen weaving. A few
warehouses survive but the bleachworks and mills have gone, as
have the linen weavers' cottages with their basement loom shops,
necessarily damp. In the C20 Barnsley drew much of its trade
and importance from its position at the heart of the South Yorkshire coalfield. By the 1950s only the parish church's tower and
a few timber-framed buildings survived from before 1500 and
scarcely more from the next three centuries; thereafter, most
worthwhile architecture remaining from before 1850 and too
much from after it was systematically destroyed. Redevelopment
was mostly mediocre or worse and paid scant attention to townscape or context. The economic decline that followed the pit
closures of the 1980s and '90s prompted a new approach, dem-
onstrated by the ambitious regeneration masterplan produced
with *Alsop Architects* in 2002. Inspired by a Tuscan hill town, its
proposals – still unrealized – include a wall encircling the town
centre and major redevelopment of the market area.

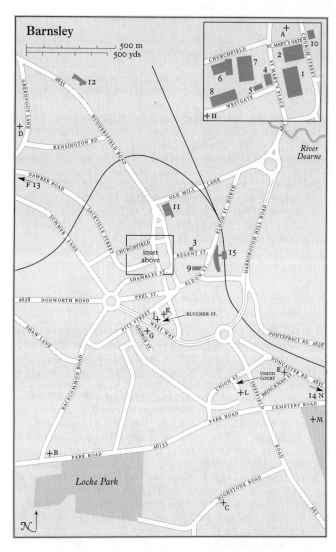

Barnsley

500 m
500 yds

inset above

River Dearne

Locke Park

N

A	St Mary	1	Town Hall
B	St Edward	2	Mining and Technical College (former)
C	St Luke	3	County Court (former)
D	St Paul	4	Magistrates' Court (former)
E	St Peter the Apostle	5	Police Station
F	St Thomas	6	Police Headquarters
G	Holy Rood (R.C.)	7	Magistrates' Court
H	Wesleyan Chapel (former)	8	Council Offices
J	Salem Chapel	9	Civic Hall
K	Hope House Church	10	Cooper Art Gallery
L	Buckley Methodist Church (Primitive Methodist)	11	Barnsley College
M	Cemetery	12	Girls High School (former)
N	Ardsley Cemetery	13	Barnsley District Hospital
		14	Kendray Hospital
		15	Transport Interchange

CHURCHES

ST MARY, St Mary's Gate. Plain Perp w tower of *c*. 1400, heightened slightly when the rest of the church was rebuilt by *Woodhead & Hurst*, 1819–22. The style is of *c*. 1300 with cusped
intersected tracery. Five-bay nave with clerestory. s porch.
Two-bay chapels, wider than the aisles. Their w bays are
higher than the E ones, with diagonal buttresses, giving the
impression of transepts. Buttresses, battlements and pinnacles
throughout. Nave arcades with tall thin clustered piers. Flat
panelled ceilings. The chancel arch is almost full-height, but
infilled above an inner arch to mask the slightly lower chancel
beyond. A second tall arch precedes the sanctuary in the third
bay. Shallow rib-vaults in both parts. *G.F. Bodley* restored the
church 1869–70 and was architect for some later windows
etc. – By him the REREDOS, 1891, and fine carved oak FIT-
TINGS (choir stalls, chancel screens, pulpit and pews),
1870–2. – ORGAN CASE. Good Baroque piece by *Thomas
Parker c*. 1741, made for St Peter's, Galby, Leicestershire, from
which it was bought in 1785. – C14 INSCRIPTION. Oak panel
commemorating Richard Haigh, Prior of Pontefract. It was
under the E window of the medieval church. – STAINED GLASS.
N chapel N window has figures of the four Evangelists from the
E window of *c*. 1821. By *Burlison & Grylls*: E window (with new
Perp tracery) 1870, w window 1873 and s aisle, second from
E 1882 (also, presumably, similar windows to l. 1877 and r.
1885). Several by *Ward & Hughes* (latterly with *T.F. Curtis*)
1891–7, including an impressively sombre group of seven in N
aisle. s chapel E. Both by *F.C. Eden*, who reordered the space
for his unconventional central WAR MEMORIAL, 1922. Hexagonal Gothic column, of painted and gilded wood, with
inscribed panels under pinnacled canopies.

ST EDWARD, Park Road, Kingstone. By *G.S. Packer* of
Southport, 1900–2. Amply proportioned, it stands prominently
on the hill near Locke Park. E.E. with Geometric tracery
to E and w windows. Big crossing tower with low pyramidal
spire, set back, and corner spirelets. Clerestory. Five-bay
nave arcades have polished black marble columns. – REREDOS.
By *Harry Hems & Sons* of Exeter. English alabaster with
marble figures against gold mosaic. – PULPIT. By *Norbury
Paterson & Co.* of Liverpool. Large, octagonal, ornately
carved in alabaster. Matching FONT. – STAINED GLASS. E and
w windows by *A.K. Nicholson*, 1936, the w a striking image of
the Ship of the Church. In the N and s aisles the two easternmost pairs are by *Percy Bacon*, *c*. 1919 (N) *c*. 1930 and *c*. 1933
(s).

ST LUKE, Highstone Road, Worsbrough Common. By *T.H. &
F. Healey*, 1872–4. Small, lancet style. w bellcote. – STAINED
GLASS. Chancel. Three good windows, two given by Samuel
Cooper of Mount Vernon.

ST PAUL, Greenfoot Lane. By *C.F. Moxon*, 1936. One of Barnsley's surprises. An unconventional essay in geometry with
something of the Near East. Nave a big cube with flat roof and

small copper dome behind parapet. The short chancel slightly lower and rectangular in plan, the sanctuary lower again and semicircular. Low arcaded s porch and the chapel, ambulatory and vestry around the e end. All flat-roofed. The sparse windows are narrow and round-headed except in the sanctuary, where they have square heads. Five stepped lights to n and s nave. Openings are punched through the plain brownish-yellow brickwork. Impressive interior spaces with a hint of Art Deco. Nave has big stepped dome on round arches in exposed brick. Good plain oak fittings. Additional w part not built.

St Peter the Apostle and St John the Baptist, Brinckman Street. By *Temple Moore*, 1893–1911. One of the great urban churches of the late C19. The brick exterior impresses with its scale and severity, the High Anglican interior with the uplifting quality of its light and space. Fitted onto a restricted and sloping corner site, with chancel and n chapel built 1892–3, se Lady Chapel 1900–1 and nave 1910–11. Its sheer walls rise high above the adjacent terraces, their plainness subtly relieved by double courses of thin bricks. Large windows at clerestory level, with varied Dec tracery. Short square bell-turret at nave's se corner. Lean-to chapels, the s with projecting polygonal end. Moore overcame the difficult slope by creating a small courtyard below street level at the w end, the entrances leading into a stone-vaulted narthex under the gallery. The narthex itself is set slightly above the level of the nave and has an open arcade to the e. It is an inventive and effective feature. Effective too the very wide nave, achieved by the use of internal buttresses with passage aisles, in the tradition of the 'town church'. Here it was also a very practical solution to the problem of building around an existing temporary nave of 1886. Aisle piercings slightly higher on the s than the n, one of several nice touches of asymmetry. Timber rib-vault on clustered columns. Vaulted chancel of almost equal height, creating a splendid vista from e to w. More intricate vaulting to the intimate s chapel. – REREDOS. By *Leslie Moore*, 1949. Large, canopied, with richly painted panels by *Douglas Purnell*. – REREDOS (s chapel). Continental Baroque, possibly late C17.

St Thomas, Church Street, Gawber. By *W.J. Hindle*, 1840–8. Neat five-bay lancet-style box with vestigial chancel. Arcaded belfry with stone spire over w tower-porch. Restored 1879 by *Dixon & Moxon*, who raised the sills and inserted Y-tracery.

Holy Rood (R.C.), George Street. By *Edward Simpson* with *Charles Simpson*, 1903–5. Very tall with continuous ridge to nave and chancel. Slightly lower transepts. Low outer projections for shrines and confessionals carry buttresses to lofty aisles. Small nw tower rises as octagonal belfry with stone spire. sw baptistery with apsidal end. Dec tracery. None of this prepares one for the glorious interior. Soaring stone arcades are set off by warm red brick walls, light descends from plain windows set high up. Aisles have transverse vaults in brick with stone ribs. The two easternmost bays of the arcades open into the transepts, which have similar but higher vaults. Chancel has polished marble shafts and good sculpted heads. Apsidal sanctuary with arcade. Above the central arch, in place of the E window, is a shallow niche for the Holy Rood, cleverly top-lit. – Rich FITTINGS in marble and alabaster. – HIGH ALTAR and REREDOS. Carved by *R.B. Wall*, with figurative panels and elaborate pinnacles. – STATIONS OF THE CROSS. By *Gabriel Pippett*, *c.* 1920. Marble and mosaic panels. S CHAPEL. Lined in white marble inset with pictures in *opus sectile*.

Simple classical front of porch from church of 1832 is reused as rear office entrance.

WESLEYAN CHAPEL (former, now Lamproom Theatre), West-gate. Built 1791–2 as plain rectangle. Arched windows on long N side flanked pulpit. Altered by *John Whitworth* of Barnsley, 1811, with new S entrance front, an elegant shallow bow of three bays between lower staircase wings. Further additions for conversion to school 1859.

SALEM CHAPEL, Blucher Street. Built for the Independents 1825, sold to Wesleyan Reform congregation 1857. Simple three-bay front with pedimented gable. Plain windows in two tiers. Good C19 interior with three-sided gallery on pencil-thin columns.

HOPE HOUSE CHURCH (formerly Wesleyan Protestant Meth-odist), Blucher Street. By *John Whitworth* of Barnsley, 1829. Alterations, including ponderous front extension, by *Herbert Crawshaw*, 1901.

BUCKLEY METHODIST CHURCH (Primitive Methodist), Union Court. 1875–6. Gabled front between big square staircase towers. Round-arched windows in two tiers. Well-preserved interior with round-ended gallery.

CEMETERY, Cemetery Road. By *Perkin & Backhouse*, 1860–1. Gothic-arched gateway flanked by lodge and tiny mortuary chapel with conical roof. Both chapels beyond mostly demol-ished 1983 but the arcaded screen wall between them remains.

ARDSLEY CEMETERY, Hunningley Lane. By *John Moxon*, 1886. Two small Gothic chapels. Only the Nonconformist one has its spired belfry.

PUBLIC BUILDINGS

TOWN HALL, Church Street. 1932–3 by *Briggs & Thornely*. A large and impressively sited building of Portland stone, its tall square tower a landmark in the district. The architecture of the twenty-one-bay front and also the back is classical re-revival; not Grecian, rather Imperial Roman, with not only something of the Imperial Parisian style of the Beaux Arts but also some motifs clearly derived from the English C18. Pevsner criticized the tower as 'of the bleak cubic kind which betrays a knowledge of the C20 style but a lack of courage to adopt it', carried 'uneasily' on a classical façade. The tower was an after-thought, which perhaps helps to explain some incongruity. The frontispiece is the WAR MEMORIAL, 1925 by *W. T. Curtis*, sculptor *John Tweed*. Tall stone pedestal with infantryman in greatcoat, and relief of winged Victory at rear, both bronze. INTERIOR refurbished in 2012 for museum and archive centre. Staircase hall, council chamber, reception room and Mayor's parlour.

Immediately N is the former MINING AND TECHNICAL COLLEGE (Huddersfield University), also by *Briggs & Thornely*, 1929–32. The two principal floors in the centres of the front and sides are treated in similar style to the Town Hall and in Portland stone. The rest mostly plain brick.

COUNTY COURT (former), Regent Street. 1870–1 by *T.C. Sorby*. In a Cinquecento palazzo style more familiar from clubs or banks. Dignified and a little aloof. Seven bays. Rustication to the ground floor and blank panels in the outer bays above. Five arched upper windows with balustrades, between attached Ionic columns. Balustraded parapet. For its predecessor *see* Perambulation, Regent Street.

MAGISTRATES' COURT (former), St Mary's Place. By *Bernard Hartley III*, County Surveyor, 1878–9. Gothic, its sternness relieved by a little octagonal tower with spire. The ground floor was originally a drill shed open to the yard of Westgate POLICE STATION (1856) behind. A double row of massive cast-iron pillars supports the upper floor, the outer one still exposed.

The first phase of the uncompleted CIVIC CENTRE around Westgate, planned in 1951, with buildings by *Lanchester & Lodge*, was the dull POLICE HEADQUARTERS, Churchfield, 1963, and immediately S of this the MAGISTRATES' COURT, Westgate, 1977, a large square block sitting low into the slope on a brick plinth with aggregate-panelled upper storey over-hanging.* W are COUNCIL OFFICES (Westgate Plaza One) by *Associated Architects*, 2006–7. Five storeys, the top one set back under the roof canopy. Mostly glass, with stainless steel wire-mesh screens in front. The rest has matt black ceramic facing. It frames the recessed entrance to the double-height reception area.

CIVIC HALL, Eldon Street. By *Hill & Swann*, 1877–8, for Charles Harvey of Kendray as a public hall with School of Science and Art and Mechanics' Institute. The big keystone of the elaborately carved double-height entrance bears Harvey's portrait. Ebullient Baroque attic storey. Large hall block at an angle behind. Given to the town in 1890. Refurbished and altered by *Allen Tod Architecture*, 2006–9.

COOPER ART GALLERY, Church Street. Originally the Grammar School, founded 1660 and rebuilt 1769. Altered and extended *c.* 1887 when elaborate, rather Mannerist, two-storey bay windows were added to the adjoining schoolmaster's house of 1726 (now offices). Converted as the gallery 1912–14, the gift of Samuel Cooper, who also donated many of the paintings.

*The third element, the CENTRAL LIBRARY (1973–5) between Westgate and Shambles Street, has been demolished.

Decorative pedimented porch to plain three-bay front. Refurbishment 2000–1 created the projecting triangular entrance in glass and steel and a matching bay window in the outer bays.

BARNSLEY COLLEGE, Church Street. Old Mill Lane Campus by *Jefferson Sheard Architects*, 2009–11, replacing buildings by *Lyons, Israel & Ellis*, 1957 and 1964. Both the SIXTH FORM CENTRE on Westgate and the CONSTRUCTION CENTRE, N of Old Mill Lane, are by *Bond Bryan*, 2015.

GIRLS' HIGH SCHOOL (former), Huddersfield Road. By *Buckland & Haywood-Farmer*, 1909; converted to flats, 2005–6. Free classical style in red brick with good ashlar details.

BARNSLEY DISTRICT HOSPITAL, Gawber Road. Opened 1977. Two large rectangular blocks, five and eight storeys, dominate the town's N skyline. Crisply clinical with alternate bands of windows and white cladding.

KENDRAY HOSPITAL, Doncaster Road. By *Morley & Woodhouse*, 1889–90. Built for infectious diseases. Small decoratively gabled administrative block, the two outer bays each side originally single-storeyed.

LOCKE PARK, Park Road. Opened 1862, as a memorial to the railway engineer Joseph Locke (1805–60), with bronze STATUE of Locke, by *Marochetti*, 1866.* At the top of the park an elaborately decorated four-stage circular TOWER by *R. Phené Spiers*, 1877. The lowest stage has a peristyle of Ionic columns supporting a wide balcony, the upper stages rise to an arcaded timber belvedere with conical roof. Octagonal cast-iron BANDSTAND by the *Lion Foundry Co.*, Kirkintilloch, 1908. Also four tall fluted IONIC COLUMNS from Commercial Buildings (dem.), Church Street, by *W.J. Hindle*, 1837, re-erected here in 1879.

TRANSPORT INTERCHANGE, Eldon Street. By *Jefferson Sheard Architects*, 2006–7; to date one of the few elements of the 2002 Masterplan completed. Attractively curvaceous in plan and form. Light and spacious interior with glazed roof and E front facing the buses and the railway station; the solid street side enlivened with blocks of colour.

PERAMBULATION

The most rewarding streets are near the Town Hall. In CHURCH STREET, Nos. 41–43 are the sole survivors of Barnsley's medieval secular buildings, part of a town house and cross-wing dated by dendrochronology to *c*.1463. Extensive, though incomplete, timber framing exposed inside. Restored 2002 by *Nuttall Yarwood & Partners*. On the N corner of Regent Street the Barnsley Permanent Building Society by *J.R. Wilkinson*, 1935–8, takes its classical cue from the Town Hall, with giant Corinthian columns to the side and canted corner. Downhill,

* Intended originally for a site near the Institution of Civil Engineers, Westminster, London, as part of a group including Brunel and Robert Stephenson. Brought here after the scheme was aborted.

the Royal Bank of Scotland with corner entrance, 1914. Classical. Rusticated ground floor, elaborately pedimented windows above.

REGENT STREET, from the Town Hall, was created in the 1830s and still has the town's best array of Victorian buildings, including the former Post Office (s side) by *James Williams* of *H.M. Office of Works*, 1881–2, Italianate with two elaborately treated entrances, and the former County Court (*see* Public Buildings) set back on the N side.* Below this, a pair of former houses (Nos. 14–16) of *c.* 1840, probably by *John Whitworth*, who lived in one. Their doorcases have fluted Doric columns with entablatures and modillioned open pediments. Good modest quartet opposite with pedimented doorcases, *c.* 1847. At the far end the former Queen's Hotel by *Wade & Turner*, 1872, is a three-storey pile boldly carved with good keystone heads, lions and garlands, facing the former Court House (now a bar) by *Charles Reeves*, 1861. Italianate, heavily detailed. Vermiculated rustication, keystones and panels. Behind in COUNTY WAY the striking DIGITAL MEDIA CENTRE by *Bauman Lyons*, 2005–7. The E side, visible from afar, reads as three tall towers, their faces recessed within narrow stone frames. Slightly staggered on plan. Gabion-walled base, with bronze cladding above to E and W and sandstone veneer rain-screen to N and S. Randomly placed windows. Inside, a large light atrium is surrounded by glazed balconies on five floors of offices. Diagonal second-floor bridge.

THE ARCADE leads from Eldon Street up to Market Hill. Created as a continuation of Guests Yard, the top end, by *Wade & Turner*, 1893, has a glazed roof on decorative cast-iron trusses. The flanking blocks with curved corners were originally a matching pair, their shopfronts elegantly framed by cast iron columns with Composite capitals. Made by local iron-founders *Qualter & Hall* and dated 1891. The market place once occupied MARKET HILL's generous width. On the W side a Late Georgian survivor at No. 7. Three storeys. Another at No. 15, one bay. Pedimented gable with lunette. Opposite, NatWest Bank (originally Sheffield Bank), 1915. Well-detailed, asymmetrical, classical front with giant attached columns. Ionic order. Below, the Yorkshire Building Society, originally the Yorkshire Penny Bank, 1903. Corner entrance with canted oriel over, prominently topped with clock in aedicule with broken pediment. Decorative aprons were removed to make the façade match the plainer five-bay extension along Eldon Street, 1923–4.

At the end of QUEEN STREET, No. 1, *c.* 1839, is only one bay. Venetian window and modillioned pediment. Then PEEL SQUARE, with a creditable three-storey Italianate block along the N side. It begins on the Market Hill corner with the Yorkshire Bank, built in 1857 as the Coach and Horses inn. Round-arched windows on the first floor have pilasters and decorated spandrels. Converted 1912, when the shapely little lead dome was added above the new entrance. Seven plainer bays on l. Then the three-bay front of the White Hart Hotel, a later C19 copy of the bank part. The final four bays are another convincing replica, this time *c.* 1924. On the square's w side a tall block, now a bar, built for the Barnsley Chronicle by *Dixon & Moxon*, 1876–7. Two-storey Gothic oriel on the corner with spirelet above.

PITT STREET provides the most glaring indictment of the late C20 town's neglect of its buildings. Of the Regency development planned with *John Whitworth*'s assistance only the former Oddfellows Hall (now offices) by *W. J. Hindle*, 1836–7, is a survivor. Grecian, with two fluted Ionic columns *in antis*. Weak imitation as an extension. The relief road cut through Pitt Street *c.* 1986. Across it remnants of the residential area around St George's church (by *Rickman*, 1821–2; dem. 1993), e.g. No. 36. This was the w end of ST CATHERINE'S TERRACE, originally four houses, *c.* 1833. Three bays with fine pedimented doorcase. In York Street the Gothic former PUBLIC BATHS (now flats), by *Wade & Turner*, 1872–4. Symmetrical front. Gabled centre bay projects. Corbelled frieze and pierced parapet with pointed arches.

Back to WELLINGTON STREET, s of Peel Square, too narrow properly to appreciate the pedimented front of the THEATRE ROYAL (now night club) by *Walter Emden*, 1898. It rises abruptly from the pavement, its round-arched entrances without display or panache. Jollier interior has two horseshoe-shaped galleries with cast-iron columns and decorated fronts. The s end of MARKET STREET, parallel to the E, was the empire of the Barnsley British Co-operative Society, founded 1862. On the w corner with Pall Mall, three-storey offices with hall and reading room, 1885. Round oriel with crested spire over the entrance. Mullioned-and-transomed windows. Long extension to l. along Pall Mall, 1938 (now the CENTRAL LIBRARY). On the E corner of Market Street and Pall Mall, the large grocery department, 1911. Exuberant Baroque in honey-coloured faience, with details in celadon green. Former shopfronts horribly altered.*

Now w and N of the Town Hall. In ST MARY'S PLACE a former early C19 linen warehouse. Three storeys, six bays. The E bay, with separate entrance, was probably offices. Pedimented coachhouse and stable. N, in BERNESLAI CLOSE the former Cooper Nurses' Home from Beckett Hospital (dem.). By *R. & W. Dixon*, 1905. Three-bay front well dressed in stone with semicircular oriel over porch and oculus under open pediment above that. Large addition to l. 1938. In SACKVILLE STREET to the w some Early Victorian middle-class housing, e.g. Providence Villa with wavy bargeboards, 1851,

---

*The drapery department block on Pall Mall and New Street 1886, extended 1903, with two sections of decorative cast iron frontage 1903, was demolished after a fire in 2016.

Temperance Terrace, 1856, and Nos. 68–74, Gordon Terrace, three storeys, doorcases with Corinthian pilasters, windows with lugged architraves.

The later N suburbs begin at the junction of HUDDERS-FIELD ROAD and VICTORIA ROAD. First, on the corner, the N.U.M. HEADQUARTERS, built for the South Yorkshire Miners' Association by *Wade & Turner*, 1872–4. Like a large villa in mixed Gothic and French chateau style it asserts equality with its middle-class neighbours. Boldly rounded corner and adjacent turret have conical roofs. Three-storey tower with pyramidal roof beside entrance bay. First-floor council chamber, its semicircular end in the corner tower. Two well-appointed officials' residences, with bathrooms, were included, their standard an exemplar for members. Large meeting hall in Edwardian ballroom style added behind adjoining villa in Victoria Road, 1912. To the NW is a good range of houses, mainly detached or semi-detached on the principal roads with some superior terraces behind. Built from the 1870s to *c.* 1910 in the usual variety of styles. An exception is the earlier Cockerham Hall, No. 17 Huddersfield Road, a villa with Doric portico, *c.* 1830. Carriage house and a mounting block with kennel. The best of the later houses is MOORLAND COURT, No. 33 GAWBER ROAD. By *Percy B. Houfton*, 1905–6. In the Voysey style; rendered, with broad gables and dormers. Other good villas, mid-Victorian, in DODWORTH ROAD.

HONEYWELL ESTATE, Honeywell Lane. By *Dept of Architecture and Planning, Barnsley Council* (project architects *J.B. Price, M.J. Clover* and *H.W. Adams*), *c.* 1982. 142 houses, mostly in terraces ingeniously built along the contours of the site and against its steep slope to allow level access to three storeys. Some top-floor houses are reached by bridges from landscaped paths between the rows.

NEW LODGE, Wensley Road, 1½ m. N. Now a residential home. Built by *John Carr* for himself, 1795, but occupied by his nephew John Clark a few years later. Three bays by four, very plain. Doorway with rusticated surround, detached Doric columns and dentilled pediment with fluted frieze. Interior destroyed by vandalism and fire. Octagonal lodge on Wakefield Road, apparently inspired by the Temple of the Winds, demolished 1957.

97   BARNSLEY MAIN COLLIERY (former), Oaks Lane, 1¼ m. E. Brick ENGINE HOUSE with high blind base. Steel-framed HEADGEAR with pulley wheel. *c.* 1970s. Preserved as solitary representatives of structures once numerous in the area.

OAKS COLLIERY DISASTER MEMORIAL, Doncaster Road, 1¼ m. SE. By *Wade & Turner*, 1913–14. Tall obelisk with a bronze winged Athene carrying a wounded warrior (a copy of *M.J.A. Mercié*'s 'Gloria Victis', 1874), commemorating the rescuers, most of whom were killed, in England's worst pit disaster, 1866. The total death toll was 361.

Barnsley, Oaks Colliery disaster.
Engraving, 1866

BATLEY
(including Batley Carr and Stainforth)

2020

Queen of the West Riding shoddy towns, crowded into the little valley of Batley Dyke with Birstall at its head and Dewsbury at its heels. Batley's unique contribution to the textile industry was the invention, *c.* 1813, of a complex process of wool recovery, from the pulling apart of rags and waste fabric to their reincarnation as heavyweight cloths used extensively for military and civilian uniforms. Batley's population increased from 2,574 to 9,308 between 1801 and 1851, and leapt to 36,389 by 1911. Borough status was granted in 1868. The mills that Pevsner saw, 'closing in everywhere and taller and bigger than any other buildings', have mostly gone.

RELIGIOUS BUILDINGS

ALL SAINTS, Stocks Lane. Low and smallish. The narrow nave and the aisles are unembattled but the stocky Perp W tower has the corbelled-out crenellated parapet of the region (cf. Birstall). Dec s arcade of three quatrefoil piers with the recession between the shafts worked in one deep undulation. Double-chamfered arches. Dec also the s doorway with a sunk quadrant moulding. All windows Perp, and most of them straight-headed, with round-arched lights and sunk spandrels. Those of the clerestory (two-light, plain mullioned) seem latest. N arcade Perp (octagonal piers, double-chamfered arches). A piece of wall is left standing between the E responds of the arcades and the chancel arch. In it on the S side the rood stairs, with ogee-arched doorway. Perp chapels of two bays with octagonal piers, the N arches with two hollow chamfers. – Oak PULPIT in elaborate Jacobean style *c.* 1905. – FONT. 1662. Octagonal. Crude chalice shape with ribs dividing the bowl into panels. – PARCLOSE SCREENS. N chapel, founded *c.* 1485, has completely preserved screen. – S chapel. Fine Renaissance screen with mermen and dragons in the frieze and double cresting, all pierced; restored in 1852 using cast iron. – STAINED GLASS. Fragment of a Crucifixion in a S aisle window. E window by *Michael & Arthur O'Connor,* 1856. S chapel E and S aisle easternmost by *Francis Spear,* 1954. S aisle, third from E and W windows by *W. G. Taylor,* 1890s.

MONUMENTS. Beside the porch a much battered C13 effigy of a civilian. Straight-legged. – Tomb-chest, the alabaster effigies almost certainly Sir William Mirfield †*c.* 1508, in armour, and his wife, Ann Fitzwilliam. On the very damaged E and S sides figures of ladies and gowned (?) men, holding shields. They stand under crocketed ogee canopies (cf. Harewood (*West Riding North*) and Thornhill).

CHRIST CHURCH, Staincliffe Hall Road. By *W. H. Crossland,* 1866–7. Prominent on the W ridge. Style of *c.* 1300. Five-bay aisled nave; narrow clerestory with windows of three trefoils; three-bay chancel. Big W tower, made top-heavy by pinnacles whose crockets, like other exterior details, remain as uncarved blocks. A slender spire was also intended. (REREDOS, ALTAR and sanctuary PANELLING 1916–17, and screened N aisle CHAPEL 1919, by *Charles Nicholson.* – STAINED GLASS. Three chancel S windows by *Powell Bros,* 1902.)

Almost opposite, gabled STAINCLIFFE HALL, with doorway dated 1709 and 1817. Early part has seven-light hall window with transom; Victorian alterations and additions.

HOLY TRINITY, Upper Road, Batley Carr. By *Chantrell,* 1840–1. Pinnacled W tower with plain parapet. Low, broad six-bay nave, tall chancel. Dec tracery. N aisle with one-bay chancel 'transept' by *W. S. Barber,* 1894–5. Aisle and four western bays of nave now separate community spaces. – Good carved oak REREDOS and chancel PANELLING and painted and gilded WAR MEMORIAL, including panels with St Michael and St George, by *Temple Moore* and *Mary Moore,* decorated by *Head & Sons,* 1918–19. – STAINED GLASS. E window and chancel N window by *Powell Bros,* 1899.

ST ANDREW, Denison Street, Purlwell. 1909–10. Edwardian Gothic Revival style. Intended tower not built. (STAINED GLASS. E window by *Kempe,* 1911.)

ST JOHN THE EVANGELIST, Ealand Road, Carlinghow. By *Sheard & Hanstock,* 1878–9. E window with Geometric tracery. Base of unbuilt tower forms tall buttressed porch at western bay of S aisle. (Parish centre, 2000, in W half of nave. ROOD, 1929. – STATIONS OF THE CROSS by *Stuflesser,* 1952.)

ST THOMAS, Grosvenor Road. By *Sheard & Hanstock*, 1867–8. E.E. style. Large SW tower whose set-back stone spire is a landmark on the E ridge. – STAINED GLASS. E window by *A. & W.H. O'Connor*, 1868.

ST MARY (R.C.), Upton Street. By *Adams* & *Kelly*, 1869–70; small transepts by *Kelly*, 1884. Gothic Revival style with simple Geometric tracery in windows under relieving arches. Five-bay nave and chancel under one roof; the chancel is apsidal-ended and has two-bay chapels. (Richly fitted sanctuary with marble altar, 1929, in original position, and mosaics, 1952, in tall blind arcade below high-set windows.)

CENTRAL METHODIST CHURCH, Commercial Street (Zion Chapel, United Methodist). By *Sheard & Hanstock*, 1869. Large, its fine classically detailed ashlar front facing the civic buildings. So many of the town's manufacturers worshipped here it was nicknamed the 'Shoddy Temple'. 1:3:1 bays. Corinthian pilasters, bracketed cornice and central pediment with enriched tympanum. Three round-arched entrances, the windows above with pediments on elaborate consoles. Seven-bay returns with two tiers of windows above basement storey on the slope. (Excellent interior with oval gallery, elaborate organ case and pulpit, and box pews.)

CEMETERY, Cemetery Road. By *Walter Hanstock*, 1865. Dec CHAPELS with a linking range that has an archway in a TOWER with decorative octagonal third stage and tall slender spire. Good carved details. LODGE with towered entrance bay, 1866.

MADINA MASJID, Purlwell Lane. 1989. Batley's first purpose-built MOSQUE, for a community of Gujarati origin. Wide single-storey front to courtyard, flanked by slender tiered minarets. Small dome. To l. large MADRASA, *c.* 2012. Curving red brick front detailed with Islamic arches in buff brick.

PUBLIC BUILDINGS

TOWN HALL. One of the fine group of buildings close to the steeply sloping Market Place. Originally Mechanics' Institute and Public Hall, 1853–4, bought by the Town Council in 1874, and rebuilt and extended after a fire by *Arthur Hanstock*, 1905. Well-detailed Italianate style. Original three-bay front on Commercial Street, with heavy rustication to blocked entrance. Pedimented centre to seven-bay main front, with small balcony over round-arched doorway flanked by Ionic columns. Above, the plain classical COURT HOUSE and POLICE STATION by *Percy Platts*, West Riding County Architect, 1927. Symmetrical two-storey front. Blind ends flank separate entrance bays finished with heavy parapets. Opposite, the former POST OFFICE by *Henry Hawks*, 1906, in simple but considered Edwardian Renaissance style, and the imposing CARNEGIE LIBRARY and ART GALLERY by *Hanstock*, 1906–7. Free classical style with tall domed clock tower. On the hilltop the WAR MEMORIAL GARDENS, 1923, and former

METHODIST CHAPEL (Independent), *c.* 1885, with twin pediments. Beyond, in Cambridge Street, the PUBLIC BATHS by *Walter Hanstock*, 1893, in Free Renaissance style with good ashlar details. Entrances in tall centre block; single-storey wings with balustraded parapets and decorated oculi. Former TECHNICAL SCHOOL and SCHOOL OF ART opposite by *H. Bagshaw Buckley*, 1893, with l. addition 1898. Front crowded with big mullioned-and-transomed windows, two breaking through the eaves as tall pedimented dormers.

BAGSHAW MUSEUM (formerly The Woodlands), Wilton Park. Large house by *Sheard & Hanstock* for George Sheard, woollen manufacturer, 1873–5. Slightly Gothic, with tall pyramidal-roofed entrance tower. Excellent interiors.

BATLEY GRAMMAR SCHOOL, Carlinghow Hill. Founded 1612. By *Walter Hanstock*, 1875–8, won in competition. Plain Gothic Revival style. Single-storeyed, with big canted porch. Gables to l. return. Headmaster's HOUSE to r. Rear additions include assembly hall by *H. Wormald* for WRCC, 1943, and extension by *Dex Harrison*, 1959.

GIRLS' HIGHER GRADE SCHOOL (former, now Pupil Referral Centre), Batley Field Hill. By *H. Bagshaw Buckley*, 1905. Edwardian Free Style. Broad recessed arched entrance under two semicircular windows in decorative gable. A big double-transomed window either side. Others to r. return overlooking the valley, above arcaded lower ground floor. Plainer rear additions.

UPPER BATLEY HIGH SCHOOL, Batley Field Hill. By the *County Architect's Department*, as a Boys' County Secondary School, 1959. Main classroom block three storeys with long strip windows between brick ends. Other buildings single-storeyed. All flat-roofed. Later additions.

Two large BOARD SCHOOLS by *Walter Hanstock*: PURLWELL SCHOOL, Purlwell Lane, 1873–4, has long single-storey front with large and small gables, small central bell-tower and distinctive striped slate roof. PARK ROAD SCHOOL, Bradford Road, 1876, two storeys, tightly grouped.

COTTAGE HOSPITAL (former), Carlinghow Hill. By *Walter Hanstock*, 1881–3. Free Renaissance style with big transomed windows and gables. Symmetrical seven-bay front; two storeys, with balconies.

THE TOWN. Not enough for a perambulation, but HICK LANE and then STATION ROAD are worthwhile, starting with the fine former bank with three-storey manager's house by *Sheard & Hanstock*, 1877. Gothic Revival style, with lots of richly carved capitals to nook-shafts. Opposite, the sober classical former WESLEYAN CHAPEL by *James Simpson*, 1861, with pedimented gable front, and clumsily detailed former SUNDAY SCHOOLS, 1875. Then two former BANKS. First, the palazzo-style Midland, 1890s, heavy with rustication and bracketed cornices. Four good carved heads as keystones. On BRADFORD ROAD, NatWest by *Ernest Newton*, *c.* 1905. Modest Edwardian classical in ashlar, the two French windows with iron balconies hinting at Beaux Arts style.

STATION ROAD is notable for the three-storey shoddy WARE-HOUSES and SHOWROOMS that line the route up to the railway, a main arrival point for both rags and shoddy buyers. Built in the 1860s and '70s, they are by a variety of architects, including *Sheard & Hanstock*, in Italianate and Venetian Gothic styles. Other former warehouses and MILLS on the long BRADFORD ROAD towards Dewsbury. ¾ m. s, on the w side at the corner with Mill Road, the former BATLEY CARR MILLS, now housing, with two chimneys isolated like obelisks in the car park. The six-storey, twelve-bay mill with a Venetian window in its SW gable is of 1845, by *James Radcliffe* of Huddersfield. The adjoining three-and-a-half-storey mill is of 1838–40, and the four-storey, L-shaped loom shop on Bradford Road was in existence by 1832.

BANQUETING HOUSE, Old Hall Road, ⅔ m. N. A Batley surprise. Small, C17, brick. Two storeys, with small mullioned-and-transomed windows. Upper walls on E and S sides decorated with vertical bands of lozenge-patterned brickwork in sunk panels. Now residential.

BAWTRY

Attractive small town beside the navigable River Idle, which forms the boundary with Nottinghamshire, and the main East Coast railway (1849). The Great North Road passes through it and the first house at the s entrance to the town has long had the distinctive address 'No. 1 Yorkshire'. Bawtry is a good example of a medieval planned settlement, its grid pattern of streets still evident either side of the broad High Street with its market place. Founded before 1199, when it belonged to a member of the de Busli family, it had a market and fair by the mid C13 and prospered until the mid C19 as an inland port, trading goods including Sheffield metalware that were transported via the Trent to the Humber and North Sea. Bawtry experienced little economic development after this and High Street still retains the character of a small Georgian market and coaching town.

ST NICHOLAS. A chapelry of Blyth (Nottinghamshire) from the later C12 to 1858. Situated aside from the High Street, its origins may lie with a riverside settlement that preceded the planned town. Its location next to the vanished wharves along the old course of the river near the E end explains its dedication to the patron saint of sailors (cf. Thorne). The building has several unexplained details and some well-meant but unscholarly work of the C18 and early C19 that, unusually, survived restoration by *C. Hodgson Fowler*, 1899–1901.

The earliest work is on the N side, where a farrago of disjointed elements starts at the W end with a blocked doorway of
c. 1200. One order with label. Slender shafts, capitals with leaf
volutes (l.) and waterleaf (r.), arch with keeled angle roll. Then
a window of two lights with shouldered heads and a small
blocked doorway of *c.* 1400 cutting into a partly blocked
window. The N chapel has a four-light C17(?) window, a partly
blocked straight-headed one of two lights with reused image
niche and finally a round-arched doorway, with headstops to the
hoodmould, inserted in 1839 by *John Youdan*, a builder. The
earliest work inside is the N arcade, which goes with the Transitional doorway. Three bays with circular piers, octagonal abaci
and double-chamfered arches. There is no chancel arch, and a
fourth bay, resting still on one of the circular piers, starts the N
chapel arcade. The E and W responds have corbels with restored
(in the C18?) masks. Later second arch to the chapel arcade. The
S arcade is Perp. Two-bay S chapel. The pier has an odd section,
quatrefoil set diagonally with four spurs in the main directions.
No respond at the E end. The chancel E window is of C13 origin.
The jambs inside, each with a slender keeled shaft and nailhead
border, inspire confidence. But is the dogtooth outside genuine?
There is a mismatch between the interior and exterior heads,
and the two bald mullions without any arches or tracery cannot
be accepted as C13 work. N chapel E window of *c.* 1300 (intersected tracery). The S clerestory windows may be post-
Reformation, and perhaps a C17 or C18 repair. The N clerestory
is early C20. The W tower collapsed in 1670 and was largely
rebuilt in 1712–13: see the odd treatment of the tracery of the W
window and the responds of the tower arch – an interpretation
of Gothic still robust and decidedly pre-Rococo. The tower's
top parts look like C14 work reused. – SCREEN. S chapel. A fine
C18 wrought-iron garden gateway, perhaps from Bawtry Hall
(*see* below). – FONT. Early C18? Gadrooning to bowl. – STAINED
GLASS. Three by *Herbert Bryans*, 1902, 1909, 1919. – N aisle by
Kempe & Co., 1921. – MONUMENTS. A good C18 to early C19
collection, including five to members of the Acklom family
(†1700–1772) and three by *Joseph Lockwood*, including Gilbert
and Kitty Hill †1827, with theatrically draped inscription above
garland with scythe.

CHAPEL of the HOSPITAL of ST MARY MAGDALENE (now
Masonic Hall), Tickhill Road, 300 yds W. Of C13 origin, rebuilt
1839. Lancet style. Four bays, rendered. On the E wall, outside,
an image niche, *c.* 1400, with richly ornamented canopy.

BAWTRY HALL, 300 yds SW. *c.* 1780–5. Attributed to *William
Lindley*. Its imposing gateway is immediately S of the Market
Place. Brick with painted stone dressings. Two storeys. L-plan.
E front of seven bays, the wide end bays set forward. Three-bay
pediment on two fluted brackets. Tetrastyle Doric porch with
pediment. Sill bands; balustraded aprons to first-floor sashes.
Low hipped roofs behind parapet. Broad S front has two-
storey canted bays flanking centre with C20 concrete portico.
Alterations and additions by *Demaine & Brierley c.* 1905
include large NW wing with service courtyard and water

tower. Georgian cantilevered stone staircase with wrought-iron balustrade.

PERAMBULATION. The spacious HIGH STREET, N from the gates of Bawtry Hall, has some good buildings of the 1780s–1830s, mostly three storeys, mostly rendered. No. 32, on the E side of the Market Place, has a pedimented two-bay front and two-storey shallow bow windows, the upper ones with wrought-iron balconies. To the l. and r. are archways in low wing walls topped by urns; original doorway in r. return. The w side is more mixed. Near the MARKET CROSS, an C18 obelisk, is an eight-bay house (TOWN HOUSE) dated 1691, later Georgianized. Two stone plaques carved with lions, on the front wall, are said to have come from the medieval St George's church, Doncaster. Then the former TOWN HALL, built in 1890 in flaming red brick (now painted) with a big shaped gable and octagonal timber cupola. Also a fine scrolly top to the arch to a former wine, spirit and seed merchants' premises in the following range, which ends with the only older (C17?) building in High Street, with gable-end to the street (now with half-timbering) but stone behind. Beyond it, the rather bland long low front of the CROWN HOTEL, Bawtry's principal posting house from at least 1772. Doorway and carriage arch in full-height blind arches. Probably older behind. Narrow rear yard has a canopy on large cast-iron columns along l. side. At the top of High Street the Gothic METHODIST CHURCH (Wesleyan), 1903, closes the view. The Great North Road, diverted through the new town in the C12, swings l. here to rejoin its original route 150 yds w.

In WHARF STREET, to the E of High Street, the Dutch House, brick, c. 1690, has its original shaped gable and C18 front facing the church.

SOUTH PARADE, continuing High Street's line s of Bawtry Hall, has a handsome brick terrace of three storeys with quoins, c. 1800, and just beyond, No. 1 Yorkshire, which has a good pedimented doorcase with fluted pilasters and frieze and a little canted bay on the s side.

HESLEY HALL (Adult Residential Centre), 2¾ m. NW.* Large, mildly Italianate brick house, dated 1887, with a tower. Small Gothic Revival chapel by J.H. Christian, 1891, with rich interior. WALL PAINTINGS in chancel (1897) and baptistery (1900) and STAINED GLASS (1891–9) all by Powell & Sons.

BEIGHTON

4080

Former agricultural and mining village on the E side of the River Rother, in Derbyshire until 1967.

ST MARY. Of Norman origin, altered in C14 and C15, mostly rebuilt in restoration by Samuel Rollinson of Chesterfield,

*In Nottinghamshire until 1974.

1867–8. Reordered 2007. Perp w tower of two stages with diagonal buttresses, battlements and eight pinnacles. The tower arch towards the nave, perhaps C13, has coarsely ornamented capitals with nailhead bands and masks, not a usual thing in the county. C14 nave arcades of two bays with octagonal piers and arches with sunk quadrant mouldings. Perp N aisle has w window with label. Nave, with quatrefoils to low clerestory, s aisle, and chancel with N chapel, all Victorian. Dec tracery to E window. Chancel arch in Norman style, based on remains of the arch found during restoration. REREDOS. Very fine alabaster panel of the Last Supper carved by *Farmer & Brindley*, 1892, from Neepsend church, Sheffield (dem.). – Ogee-headed PISCINA (another in s aisle). – ROOD. By *Comper*, 1950, from All Saints, Emscote, Warwick, installed 1969. Medieval rood-loft doorway.

MANOR HOUSE, High Street. Early C18, five bays, altered. Moulded doorway with segmental pediment, moulded window surrounds.

BENTLEY

5000

ST PETER. 1891–4. A remarkably competent design by *John Codd* of London, who had been Pearson's assistant. Tall s porch-tower with broach spire with lucarnes. w front with four buttresses and three tall windows with Geometrical tracery. Lofty interior has narrow passage aisles through cross walls which are really buttresses drawn inside the building. The attached piers forming the arcades are a mixture of round, octagonal, and triple round- and octagonal-shafted form. – Carved alabaster REREDOS, 1900. – STAINED GLASS. E window by *Clayton & Bell*, 1897. N aisle westernmost by *Harry Harvey*, 1971.

ST PHILIP AND ST JAMES, New Bentley, 1 m. N. By *F. Norman D. Masters*, 1915, for the South Yorkshire Coalfields Mission for the colliery village (cf. Edlington, Maltby and Rossington). Brick. Simple Romanesque style. Exterior w PULPIT. Attractive, well-preserved interior. – STAINED GLASS. Baptistery windows by *Francis Spear*, 1960.

BESSACARR *see* DONCASTER (OUTER)

4000

BILLINGLEY

BILLINGLEY HALL, Back Lane. Handsome three-storey stone house dated 1744. Three widely spaced bays. Segmental pediment to doorway. Quoins.

BIRKIN

Small village in flat countryside just N of the Aire.

ST MARY. C12. One of the most impressive and complete
Norman village churches in Yorkshire (cf. Adel, *West Riding
North*). Ashlar-built, of W tower, nave, chancel and apse, the
survival of the apse making it a great rarity. There has been
little alteration other than a C14 S aisle and a Perp tower top.
The building is done with some ambition and although probably dated to the 1150s or 1160s might even be as early as the
1130s if a French craftsman was directly involved. Birkin seems
a tranquil backwater today but both Pontefract, with the
important de Lacy stronghold and a Cluniac priory (consecrated 1159), and Selby Abbey are nearby, and York is not far.
The S doorway has similarities with that at Brayton (q.v.).
Although the Templars were in the parish at Temple Hirst
(q.v.) from 1152, it is unlikely that they had any responsibility
for the church. The family associated with Birkin in the C12
are the somewhat shadowy de Birkins. Their estates passed
through marriage in 1230 to the Everinghams but significantly
it is the de Birkin arms of a fess and label that were carved
twice on the tower in the C14. More controversially, one of the
S doorway capitals has a label-like carving – if original it would
be an astonishingly early use of heraldry.

The tower is tall and unbuttressed, with a tall plain arch to
the nave (obscured by the organ). This arch has plain imposts
and two shafts with scalloped capitals in the angles of the
responds. The tower's Perp belfry stage has gargoyles, battlements and pinnacles, with the de Birkin shield on the battlements on the N and below the string course on the S. Viewed
from the N the Norman building appears in its entirety,
the nave and chancel each with one large shafted window set
high up above a sill band. Nave, chancel and apse have
their original corbel tables, with a variety of heads, mostly of
animals real and fantastic but with some human faces among
them. On the S side is a sumptuous Romanesque doorway,
re-set in the later aisle and preceded by the timber porch added
in *J.O. Scott*'s restoration of 1882. The doorway has four
orders, with colonnettes to the three outer arches and twin
half-shafts on the jambs of the fourth. Their capitals are scallops with carved decoration, mostly of finely intertwined
bands, but two are plainer, one of these having carving similar
to the de Birkin label on both faces. Is it C12 or was it re-cut
in the C14 when the doorway was re-set in the new S aisle?
Imposts with scroll and interlace. The outer order has variously decorated medallions with concentric circles, triangles
etc., an Agnus Dei and other animals and a grotesque mask
with its tongue out. The second order has chevron, the third
beakheads with three bearded human faces among them, the
fourth roll moulding.

Inside, the view through the chancel arch to the arch of the apse and then to the E window with its halo of chevrons is a treat rare in an English parish church, though here tinged with regret at the window's unfortunate Dec tracery. The chancel arch is taller still than the tower arch. Three shafts in the responds, mostly scalloped capitals, one with volutes, much chevron in the arch. The chancel windows are shafted inside as well as outside. Then the apse. The W arch, with a bold roll moulding, is undecorated but again has shafts in the angles of the responds. There are three original windows, of even size. They are enriched outside, the N and S ones still by shafts with scalloped capitals, and all three in the arches by chevron (N), beakhead (E) and ornamented medallions (S), under hoods decorated with little domes. Between the windows are broad, strongly projecting pilaster-strips, no doubt to make sure that the vault inside would be safe. Transverse arch and two ribs of heavy section: three rolls. No keystone. The ribs stand on shafts inside with scallops and primitive volutes. The chancel doorway, finally, is small and has a plainly diapered tympanum. The only addition to the Norman church before the Perp tower top was a wide S aisle, probably connected with the chantry founded in 1328 by Sir John Everingham. Good ogee-headed piscina. Windows of various shapes with excellent curvilinear tracery, two-bay arcade with tall, wide arches on slim octagonal piers, double-chamfered arches.

FONT. Dated 1663. Cup-shaped with octagonal top; ornamented with raised semicircles. – PULPIT. A pretty C18 piece with a big, elaborately carved tester (cf. Bolton Percy). – STAINED GLASS. Fragments of the C14 glass in the S aisle E window. Nave N window by *Heaton, Butler & Bayne*, 1903. Apse and chancel windows by *Powell & Sons*, 1897 to 1917. – MONUMENTS. In the nave N wall a recess and in it an effigy of a cross-legged civilian holding his heart in his hand; early C14, and with unusually bold, unconventional draperies. Attributed by Richard Knowles to the Yorkshire workshop of the 'Sleeve-Master' or 'Cheyne Atelier'.* – Thornton family, rectors for three generations, 1612–1718. A shapely scrolled cartouche erected *c.* 1718. – Elizabeth, wife of the Rev. Thomas Wright, †1783 by *J. Fisher I*. Fine Neoclassical piece with large urn and obelisk. Rhyming inscription by *William Whitehead*, Poet Laureate. – John Bower †1844. Elaborately Gothic with ogee arches. – Rev. Thomas Hill †1875 by *J. Forsyth*. Neo-Norman style in alabaster and marble, including arch with chevron.

GATEPIERS of Birkin Hall (dem.) next to the churchyard. *c.* 1700. Tall, with pulvinated frieze and deep cornice (ball finials lacking).

Yorkshire Archaeological Journal 57, 1985.

BIRLEY EDGE *see* GRENOSIDE

BIRSTALL

Village immediately NW of Batley, in the same small valley. Its ancient parish was extensive. Very few textile mill buildings remain.

ST PETER. Early C12 W tower – see the small N and S windows and much-restored plain round arch to the nave. Top stage and buttresses Perp, with heavy quasi-machicolation and battlements like Batley (q.v.). The rest by *W.H. Crossland*, 1865–70, in the late Perp style of its medieval predecessor and even larger, with double nave aisles embracing the tower. The inner, lean-to, aisles continue to the E end as three-bay chancel chapels (S chapel is vestry and organ chamber). Inner nave piers short and octagonal; quatrefoil piers to the longer outer arcades, of seven bays with a different rhythm; more elaborate quatrefoil piers in chancel. Foliate capitals. Excellent carving in the chancel by *Samuel Ruddock*. – Caen stone REREDOS with Last Supper, 1893. – CHOIR STALLS and PEWS by *Rattee & Kett*. – Huge Caen stone PULPIT with Apostles and diaperwork, by *Farmer & Brindley*. – FONT. Octagonal, Perp, with much decoration, heavily restored 1840. – MURAL. 'Christ in Glory' above chancel arch by *E.R. Frampton Jun.*, 1901. – C20 oak ALTAR etc. by *Robert Thompson*. – S aisle 'MUSEUM' includes: FONT BOWL. Said to be C12. Round with a band of tegular decoration at the base and four corner stops to square plinth. – BENCH-ENDS. Eighteen, square-topped, with tracery; some also have tools of trade, e.g. shears. Mostly pre-Reformation, it seems, but one, with a six-petal flower in a circle, is dated 1616. – SCULPTURE. Rare, though incomplete, decorated Anglo-Saxon cross base, its front filled by a fine bush-scroll, the broken sides with interlace. Late C9–C10 (cf. Hartshead and Rastrick). – Incomplete Norman grave-slab, with close lozenge pattern.
STAINED GLASS. Chancel S chapel easternmost: Resurrection, probably 1812, from the old E window. Seven by *Hardman*, all 1870s; three by *Kempe*, 1881, 1896 and 1898. Four by *Clayton & Bell*: N chapel easternmost 1890s(?) and N aisle first three from E c. 1882. Two by *Capronnier*: N chapel E 1872 and S aisle westernmost 1885. Aisles' E windows by *O'Connor*, 1870. N chapel second and third from E by *F.X. Zettler* of Munich, 1879.
MONUMENTS. Chancel. Canon John Kemp †1895. Brass with half-figure by *Jones & Willis*. – 'Museum'. Mrs Elizabeth Popeley †1632. Brass with her lying in her shroud. – In the tower and on its interior walls a sadly unloved gathering (nearly forty), including three medieval cross-slabs and John Green Jun. †1674. Finely lettered brass in big slab with good scrolled border.
ST SAVIOUR, Brownhill. By *Michael Sheard*, 1870–1. E.E. style.

St John's Methodist Church, Huddersfield Road (offices). Rebuilt 1846, by *James Simpson*. Simple classical front, central pediment and big clasping pilasters. The diminutive brick building in the chapelyard was the 'study' of John Nelson, Wesley's friend and helper, 1751.

National School (former), Kirkgate. By *Thomas Taylor*, 1818–19. Of the same date and design as Liversedge school (q.v.).

In the Market Place, bronze statue of Joseph Priestley, born at Birstall, by *Frances Darlington*, 1912.

Oakwell Hall (Kirklees Museums), ⅔ m. n. An excellent and sizeable hall-and-cross-wings house, built for John Batt from *c*. 1583 (date on porch), but with significant C17 alterations. Well known by Charlotte Brontë, it became 'Fieldhead' in *Shirley* (1849).* Front with impressive full-height Hall window of five-plus-five lights with two transoms. Large two-storey porch in angle with gabled E wing, which has transomed six-light window with transomed five-light window above. In the farther-projecting W wing the Great Parlour has a transomed six-light window to front and to r. return, the chamber above the same to the front and a five-light window on the return. Both wings have service rooms at the back. Kitchen in E wing has massive stack on r. return and seven-light transomed window. W wing, with rear W projection, has eight-light transomed window to buttery(?) and a three-light window later marked 'Diry'.

The Hall was originally single-storeyed with a chamber above and with a fire-hood against the passage. Remodelling *c*. 1630–40 created an open-hall with W and N galleries, their balustrade with vertically symmetrical balusters. New fireplace on N wall, the staircase which projects slightly on the exterior, running up beside it. Original dog-gate; balusters of the flat openwork type. Original plasterwork left only on the underside of the gallery. Panelled screen to passage with paired Doric columns flanking two round-arched openings. The Great Parlour has lost its 1630s ceiling but retains small plaster panels with figures in the jambs of the windows and rare later C17 *trompe l'œil* painted panelling, with a stencilled and scumbled geometric pattern. Similar in the Painted Chamber with large ovals and grained like walnut. The Great Parlour chamber and E wing parlour and chamber have original oak panelling.

BISHOPTHORPE

The location of a residence of the archbishops of York since the mid C13, on the bank of the River Ouse just s of the city.

---

*Ridings Hall in Huddersfield Road was the home of Brontë's friend Ellen Nussey and became 'Thornfield' in *Jane Eyre* (1847).

ST ANDREW. 1898–1903 by *C. Hodgson Fowler*, replacing the old
church S of the palace (*see* below). Large, with a W tower, in
limestone ashlar with red tiled roofs. Perp style, the windows
mainly straight-headed. – REREDOS and integral chancel panelling. Boxy free Gothic by *G. G. Pace*, 1960. – FONT. Medieval, said to be from St Crux, York (dem. 1884 etc.). The
steepling COVER by *Pace*. – STAINED GLASS. Includes three
aisle windows by *Harry Stammers*, 1949–53.

BISHOPTHORPE PALACE. To a first view the palace merely hints
charmingly at antiquity rather than demonstrating it directly;
but beyond that its starting point is the house built by Archbishop Walter de Grey (†1255) after he had bought the manor
from Kirkstall Abbey in 1241. This consisted of a great hall
backing onto the river bank; a chapel at right angles at the
upper (S) end, projecting to the W; undercrofts below both of
these; and a continuation N of the hall range which probably
contained offices below and the archbishop's rooms above (cf.
the mid-C12 Bishop's Palace at Lincoln). Of later medieval
works, the most significant was the addition by Archbishop
Rotherham (1480–1500) of a long brick-built wing, running W
from the N end of the C13 house. So the palace was never
particularly large by medieval magnates' standards, a reflection
perhaps of the fact that the medieval archbishops had several
other residences, including the castle at Cawood (q.v.). Its
building history in the C17 and C18 has parallels with those of
Lambeth Palace and the Bishop of Durham's at Bishop Auckland. Alienated from the church under the Commonwealth, in
1647 the 'ruinated' palace was sold to Colonel William White
(*see* Bashall Hall, *West Riding North*) – a clerk in the Court of
Wards, member of the Long Parliament and secretary to Sir
Thomas Fairfax – who made the N wing into a self-contained
house; but the hall was rebuilt in 1660–2 by Archbishop
Frewen in the brick manner of the period.* Then in 1763–9
came the delightful additions in the Gothick style by *Thomas
Atkinson* for Archbishop Drummond: the entrance range,
facing W, backing onto the W end of the Chapel and a little in
front of the hall; and the detached gatehouse, symmetrically
aligned on its centre. Subsequent phases included a restoration
of the chapel by *Ewan Christian*, 1892, and various adjustments
of *c.* 1894 by *Demaine & Brierley* of York.

   Atkinson's Gothick work is of Magnesian limestone ashlar,
much of it from the ruins of Cawood. The GATEHOUSE, of
1763–5, is square and of two storeys, the lower with a heavily
moulded three-centre-headed entrance archway under an ogee
hood, the upper with four-light flat-arched windows to front
and back, with intersecting tracery. Angle buttresses topped by
pinnacles, low-pitched gable with miniature battlements. The
present bell-turret is of 1895. Battlemented and buttressed
screen walls to l. and r. pierced by pedestrian gateways and

---

* Bishopthorpe was now the archbishops' only residence, Cawood having suffered
even more severely during the Civil War.

cruciform arrow loops. Further to the l. the former stables (*see* below). The ENTRANCE FRONT, 1766–9, is characteristic of its particular stage of the Gothic Revival in that, if stripped of its Gothicisms, it would be a normal classical design. Two storeys over a semi-basement, seven bays. Main windows depressed-arched, with ogee hoodmoulds and intersecting tracery sashes. Parapet of delicate openwork battlements, rising to a pediment in the centre. Diagonal corner buttresses. Porch of three narrow pointed arches across the front and one to each end, with Gothic shafts instead of columns and pinnacled ogee gablets. Fan-vault inside. Until 1929 the centre above it had a similarly jewel-like bay window. To the l. are two further bays, in brick and set well back, so that they are not read as part of the façade, and then at right angles the w half of Archbishop Rotherham's N WING. This has all been re-windowed and otherwise altered, but the C15 fabric is readily identified by the fingerprint diaper pattern in vitrified brick, visible in many places. Colonel White in the 1650s made the w half of the s side into an approximately symmetrical entrance front for his house: a gabled return block at the w end was extended further to the s, and a not-quite-matching projection was added about halfway along, at what is now the return to the C18 front. In the middle between the two a much-altered C15 canted bay in ashlar, with a later doorway through the lower stage. At the back a broad shallow projection said to be of the early C19 but incorporating a pair of bullseye windows.

The C13 building, again of limestone ashlar, can be seen from the river terrace along the E side, and from the s. The CHAPEL is the main part surviving. Five tall double-chamfered lancets on the s flank, three by *Christian* to the E, replacing a window of *c.* 1500. Gabled buttress at the SE corner (with a rib-vaulted garderobe contrived within the lower stage), gabled staircase projection at the NE. Undercroft altered. Also a top storey probably first added *c.* 1500 (*see* below) but much remodelled, with some more of Atkinson's Gothick windows. To the N is the HALL RANGE, a picturesque combination of C13 stone and C17 and C18 brick. The undercroft retains four original lancets. Then above is Archbishop Frewen's rebuilt Great Hall, with a rainwater head dated 1662. Three bays, with corbelled-out pilasters and – the outstanding feature – brick rustication (cf. e.g. Pendell House, Surrey, 1636; Wilberforce House, Hull, *c.* 1660; and, in stone, Bishop Cosin's contemporary work at Bishop Auckland). Large windows of unequal width, with wooden mullions and transoms, the middle one a canted oriel. They were evidently modified in the C18 and C19 but appear to be in essence the original scheme. Above again are a plain attic stage, backing against the C17 roof, and three gables with tumbled brickwork, all perhaps part of a phase of alterations of *c.* 1704 for Archbishop Sharp, supervised by the clergyman amateur architect *Heneage Dering*. N of the hall is the masonry of the C13–C14 low end, with all the window openings heavily modified; and finally a two-gabled projecting element, wholly re-windowed, of which the first part may represent the C13 kitchen and the second is the E end of the N wing.

Inspection of the interior again starts with Atkinson's Gothick entrance range. The ENTRANCE HALL has a plaster rib-vault on clustered wall-shafts, crocketed ogee-arched door-ways and niches along the sides – the doors with tracery enrich-ment – and three taller arched recesses at the far end, with traceried heads: very pretty. The DRAWING ROOM to the l. is rather more lush, dominated by the elaborate Gothick ceiling executed by *Cortese*, a diagonal grid of moulded ribs with circular tracery patterns occupying the compartments. Complementary doorcases and marble chimneypiece, simpler plaster wall panels. Off the entrance hall to the r. by contrast is de Grey's CHAPEL, where the lancets seen previously are integrated into a system of continuous wall arcading with moulded arches on slender shafts. The w wall has three taller arches which contained lancets that were blocked by Atkin-son's entrance range, flanked by two of those awkward asym-metrically climbing arches of which E.E. designers were so fond (cf. Fountains Abbey Presbytery); but on the N wall, which adjoined the hall range and so had no windows, the arcade is of a simpler design with the components all cham-fered. Flat timber ceiling with thin mouldings, probably of *c.* 1500, the present colouring *Christian*'s; at the NE corner a corbel which may have supported the original roof. Christian also lowered the floor level by ten inches. Piscina and sedilia 1920 by *W.D. Caröe*, in positions where traces of medieval predecessors had been found; dado also designed by him, incorporating C17 woodwork; REREDOS occupying the arches at the w end, made in Oberammergau in 1898; STAINED GLASS by *Kempe*, 1892.

Straight ahead from the entrance hall is Frewen's GREAT HALL; but first, in a passage to the l., behind the Drawing Room, what was the outside of its front wall can be seen, with the same system of pilasters and brick rustication as on the E elevation, and blocked mullioned-and-transomed windows. The rustication also extends to the s wall of the passage: so there was evidently a porch here, which the inner half of the Entrance Hall replaced. The Great Hall itself is a noble room, with a ceiling in a style halfway between the traditional early C17 manner and that of Inigo Jones. The framework is a com-partmented scheme with broad moulded beams and circular and oval wreaths in the panels, but the enrichments – foliage trails on the beams, pendants etc. – are more Jacobean than Italianate, as is the elaborate frieze, with flowers, strapwork and heraldic devices. Pedimented doorcases, wall panels and a handsome marble fireplace with free-standing Doric columns, all of the mid C18. In the windows heraldic STAINED GLASS – the arms of various archbishops – mainly of the 1760s by *William Peckitt*, with two by *J.W. Knowles*, *c.* 1890, and one by *Kempe*, *c.* 1892. The next room to the N retains one bay of a

42

similar ceiling; then in the N WING are details of various dates. In the S wall of the E part, now facing into later infill, is the only unaltered C15 window – straight-headed, of two depressed-arched lights – and nearby are a number of four-centre-headed doorways, a plain brick medieval fireplace and a little stone-carving. At the W end two panelled rooms, perhaps of Colonel White's time, and a fine mid-C18 coved Rococo ceiling over a vanished stairwell. Part of the C15 roof structure remains, including two trusses with cambered collars, one of them with arched braces. Lastly there is the UNDERCROFT to the hall range and Chapel. It is not vaulted and the main features are the C13 and C14 rere-arches of the windows. In the part under the hall some Norman and early C13 masonry retained from the previous house on the site.

GROUNDS. De Grey's fish pond, S of the palace, was drained in the C19. On the river terrace to the SE an C18 SUNDIAL on a moulded cylinder of medieval masonry. To the N are remnants of an Italian garden of c. 1850 by *W.A. Nesfield*, and beyond it in a wood a derelict Gothick round TOWER of the C18. The former STABLES, N of the gatehouse, were built in 1761–3, perhaps by *Peter Atkinson Sen.* (no relation of Thomas). Of an originally quadrangular scheme only the N range remains. Brick with stone dressings, two storeys, but busily sub-Palladian rather than Gothick. Pedimented centre with over-arched Venetian window rising through the cornice, and above it a dovecote stage with a segmental pediment. Half-elliptical-headed coach entrances with blocked jambs and voussoirs, similarly blocked quoins. End bays again with Venetian windows but gables rather than pediments: are they the cut-off ends of the wings remodelled?

OLD CHURCH. Rebuilt 1766, presumably by *Thomas Atkinson*. Only the pretty Rococo Gothick W front remains (restored 2002), with niches l. and r. of the doorway, a bellcote and two tall pinnacles. The rest was taken down in 1899. The E window was said to have been real Perp work brought from Cawood Castle. W of it, facing the palace grounds, a few pleasant Georgian houses, including THE CHANTRY – the former vicarage – of 1737, five bays in painted brick. The rest of the village rather suburban.

THE GARTH, Sim Balk Lane. 1908 by *Walter Brierley*, an interesting example of a picturesque early C20 design, of brick with leaded casements and the roofs coming very low down. Low separate range along the street with entrance archway in the centre. *Gertrude Jekyll* made designs for the garden.

BLACKSHAW HEAD

Hilltop hamlet on the fringe of the moors with a Wesleyan CHAPEL of 1815, its interior refitted in 1899 and new E entrance made. Several good C17 FARMHOUSES. HIPPINS, ¼ m. S, dated 1650, is the best but also notable is FIELD HEAD, ¾ m. NNW, with polite seven-bay refronting of 1765 (the through passage determining the pedimented doorway's off-centre position) and HIGHER MURGATSHAW, ¼ m. N, with small Venetian windows in the mid-C18 rebuilt service end.

BOLSTERSTONE   2090

Small Pennine village on a ridge between the valleys of the Little Don and Ewden Beck.

ST MARY. By *Joseph Fawcett* of Sheffield, on the site of a medieval church. Chancel and W tower 1873, nave 1878–9, replacing that of *c.* 1791. Perp tracery. Ashlar interior. Nave arcades have headstops carved with portraits of previous vicars. STAINED GLASS. E and W windows, two chancel S windows, and N aisle easternmost all by *Dixon & Vesey*, 1879. Chancel N window by *Harry Harvey*, 1967.

Near the lychgate a gigantic rectangular STONE with two sockets, lying on another huge stone. Comparable with that at Ecclesfield (q.v.), so possibly a pre-Conquest cross base.

Incorporated into a C19 village meeting room, 75 yds E, are fragments of the gatehouse of a C14(?) CASTLE of the de Sheffield family: the jamb and the springer of one arch of a gateway, also a small doorway with a shouldered lintel, perhaps originally to a porter's lodge or guard chamber. C19 windows in keeping. CASTLE COTTAGE, 75 yds further E, is partly C16 or early C17: see the big ashlar masonry of the W wall and S gable, with Tudor-arched doorway and cavetto-moulded mullions to blocked windows. Also thought to survive from the castle/manor house, which then belonged to the Earls of Shrewsbury.

VILLAGE HALL, facing the little square. Gothic, former National School, 1852.

BOLTON PERCY   5040

Small leafy lowland village with a large and handsome church.

ALL SAINTS. Perp, of white Magnesian limestone, built apparently in two phases by the Rector, Thomas Parker, who died in 1423, and consecrated in 1424. Restored 1905 by *John Bilson*, the authority on the Durham Cathedral vaults. The earlier part, it seems, is the beautiful chancel – see the mismatch between the E responds of the nave arcades and the arcades themselves – with battlements, pinnacles, tall three-light windows and an excellent E window of five lights. Cross on the E gable, apparently not its original position, with a Crucifixion on one side and the Virgin on the other. W tower with straight-headed bell-openings of three lights, more battle-ments and slender pinnacles. Thin angle buttresses at the NW and SW corners only. The W window and aisle windows simpler than those of the chancel, each of three stepped lights under depressed arches. The interior has a fine feeling of space, thanks chiefly to the chancel, which registers as tall and wide. Nave arcades of four bays with octagonal piers and double-chamfered arches; but the E responds more elaborate. Sedilia with three gables, piscina with an angel at its base.

ALTAR. C17 communion table. The C15 MENSA under it. – CHOIR STALLS. The W return stalls are medieval. – PULPIT. 1715. Big tester adorned with cherubs' heads and open pedi-ments. Moved in 1905: the staircase is of this date. – READER'S DESK. C17, the former pulpit. – PEWS. A complete set of C17 box pews, plain, with knobs on the ends. – FONT. Norman tub, with very handsome C17 COVER, octagonal with openwork tracery and scrolly top. – ORGAN. Built in 1847 by *J. W. Walker* as a chamber organ for Nun Appleton, Appleton Roebuck (q.v.). – STAINED GLASS. The E window retains its excellent original glass of the early C15, though much restored by *William Warrington* in 1866. The Virgin and saints, includ-ing five archbishops of the North in the lower tier. – N and S chancel windows also by *Warrington*, 1866, with genuine C15 angels in the tracery of the E pair and pinnacled niches copied from the medieval window. – N aisle second and third from E by *Burlison & Grylls*, 1880 etc.; N aisle E by *Kempe*, 1907; N aisle NE by *Morris & Co.*, 1909; N aisle W by *Tom Denny*, 1999.

MONUMENTS. C15 gravestone at the W end, reputedly a prioress of Nun Appleton called Ryther. Faint outline of her form. – Ferdinando, 2nd Lord Fairfax (the elder general) †1648. Wall-mounted with heavy original railing. Bulgy sar-cophagus with a pedimented top. Reredos architecture above, with two columns. No effigy. – A number of Fairfax wall tablets. – Selina Milner †1805 by *John Bacon Jun.*, 1807. Dainty hanging monument with an urn on which is a medal-lion of Lady Milner and her two children in a pretty group, but no mention of her name. – In the churchyard an impressive Elizabethan SUNDIAL, a Doric column crowned with an obelisk and ball finial.

GATEHOUSE to the curtilage of the former Rectory. Dated by dendrochronology to *c.* 1501. An exceptional building for Yorkshire in both its form and the details of its structure. Timber frame with jettied upper storey, close studding and tension braces, on an interrupted sill. Originally of five bays, the two to the l. of the entrance demolished. Extensively restored 1972–4 by *Brierley, Leckenby, Keighley & Groom*. Much of the frame was renewed, post-medieval alterations expunged, new windows made; but some carved timber survives, especially the excellent dragon posts with grotesques. (Handsome upper room with jowled posts and knee-braced tie-beams, spandrels decorated with Tudor rose and other motifs. Trenched- and collar-purlin roof.) Sadly the original lath and limeash floor was destroyed in the restoration.

For the former RECTORY itself a licence to crenellate was granted in 1293, but the present house is said to have been built in 1698, a double pile with housebody and through passage in the traditional manner – Thoresby in 1711 called it 'a very curious parsonage'. Ashlar and some brick, now largely roughcast, with a steeply pitched roof. Eight-bay front, with the off-centre entrance in a keyed architrave surround, and two C19 bay windows. One beamed ceiling, in the former parlour, and the staircase – renewed in the C19 – still in the old-fashioned position behind the upper end of the housebody. Awful little modern extension against one side. Nearby was a tithe barn (dem.).

BOLTON-UPON-DEARNE   *4000*

St ANDREW. The nave is Anglo-Saxon, one of the very few pre-Conquest churches surviving in the s part of the Riding. Probably late C10 or early C11. Original features are its proportions, s and NW quoins and former s openings. The walls are some 30 ft (9.4 metres) long internally but over 21 ft (6.5 metres) high and only 2 ft 9 in. (0.85 metres) thick. 'Three of the original quoins survive of exceptionally massive long-and-short construction, a rarity in the north and the northernmost example in England' according to H.M. Taylor. High in the s wall is a small round-headed window with single splay, cut through a single sandstone slab. Double rebate outside. Traces of two much larger openings are just perceptible either side. To the w the jambs, imposts and first voussoirs of an arch 6 ft 11 in. (2.1 metres) wide, probably the s doorway. The jambs are of side-alternate construction. Between them are the jambs of a later medieval doorway, the heads of both openings being destroyed by the insertion of a window (two-light with Y-tracery). Of the E opening only the lower stones remain, with a four-light Perp window above. Side-alternate jambs again. The arch probably opened to a s *porticus*.

N arcade of *c.* 1200, two bays, circular pier, capital with primitive angle crockets, octagonal abacus, recessed-chamfered arches. Chancel early C14, its E window with three trefoiled lights and three unencircled quatrefoils over, one above the other two. The design comes from the nave of York Minster. Of similar date the broad arch to the N chapel, with double-quadrant moulding and very short responds. A N chantry was founded in 1328. N doorway also early C14. Perp w tower with tall tower arch. Four square-headed windows, probably C17,

survived much renewal in 1854 and by *E. Isle Hubbard, c.* 1894.
– PULPIT. C18. Octagonal, with marquetry-work. – ROOD. By
G. G. Pace and *Alan Durst,* 1955. Natural wood. – SCULP-
TURE. In the ringing chamber a reused FRIEZE of raised lozenges 1 ft 3 in. (38 cm.) high. It has no known Saxon parallel
but has been tentatively dated to the C11 as similar smaller-
scale patterns occur in the Overlap churches at Brodsworth
and Hooton Pagnell (qq.v.)

BRADFIELD

Village in the Loxley valley, its medieval church standing at High
Bradfield, where the graveyard offers glorious views southwards
across the Pennine moors of the Peak District. Low Bradfield
sits by the river, which has Sheffield's reservoirs upstream and
downstream.

ST NICHOLAS. Of fine appearance, entirely embattled. It is one
of the few medieval churches in this area, originally a chapel
of ease to Ecclesfield (q.v.) with a large moorland parish. The
W tower may be C14: W window and bell-openings of two lights
with Y-tracery cusped, the arch towards the nave tall, double-
chamfered in a continuous moulding. Dec also, curiously
enough, the N chapel E window. Simple flowing tracery. The
rest is all Perp. The E window of five lights with much panel
tracery, the S windows with nearly straight-sided depressed
arches, the N windows and the clerestory windows straight-
headed. The interior however holds no archaeological puzzle.
The solution seems the same as at Ecclesfield. Two N piers of
the four-bay arcades are circular, the rest are octagonal. Their
capitals were completely hacked off when galleries were
inserted. Their bases are high. They are no doubt reused
material of *c.* 1200. The chancel arch indeed still has complete
keeled responds of that date. The capitals are again hacked off.
Chancel chapels of two bays with octagonal piers. Double-
chamfered arches throughout. Good late C15 nave roof with
many large bosses; the chancel roof is of 1901. At the E end of
the S chapel an odd half-sunk former vestry with a fireplace.
Oak CHANCEL FITTINGS by *Arthur Hayball* and his daughter *Clara Keeling, c.* 1884–7, the REREDOS including medieval
panels with close tracery bought in Caen. – PULPIT with
figures of Christ and the Evangelists by *Clara Keeling,* 1887.
– LECTERN. Splendid oak eagle by *Robert Ellin & Co.* of New
York, a prizewinner at the Philadelphia Exhibition 1876. – FONT.
C12. Plain round bowl of Roche Abbey limestone on octagonal
stem. Pinnacled oak COVER, 7 ft (2.1 metres) high, by *Pace,*
1959. – SCULPTURE. Crude, complete CROSS, 3 ft 8 in. (1.1
metres) high, with five large bosses or blobs, one in each arm
and one in the centre. Probably C10–C11. – STAINED GLASS.

C15–C16 fragments in one N window. – E window by *Hardman*, 1872. – Most of the others by *W.F. Dixon* (some made by *Clayton & Bell*) viz. five on the S side and four on the N, 1870–90s, and the W window, 1875. – S chapel second from E by *Clayton & Bell*, c. 1875. S aisle third from E by *Joseph Bell*, 1897. – S aisle W by *J.E. Nuttgens*, 1930. – N aisle easternmost by *Comper*, 1911. – N aisle westernmost a copy of medieval panels at Cologne, c. 1880. – MONUMENTS. John Morewood †1647 and wife Grace †1647. Brass plate by *Francis Grigs* with their figures between nine sons and seven daughters. – Henry Rimington Wilson †1915. Brass plate (on a pew) with him and his family in Tudor dress.

WESLEYAN CHAPEL (former), Low Bradfield. By *W.J. Hale*, 1898. Well-detailed gabled front with Dec tracery to window and little flanking turrets (now a house).

Many good stone houses, e.g. (going anti-clockwise round Brad- field Dale): FAIRHOUSE, Annet Lane, 1687, with four-light mullioned windows and continuous dripmoulds. Attic. Two- room plan with end baffle-entry, service rooms in rear lean-to. (Original fittings, including panelling.) HALLFIELD HOUSE, off Mortimer Road, mid-C17, three storeys with two attic gables, some windows transomed. SUGWORTH HALL, Sug- worth Road, late C19 country house, originally a C17 farm- house with cross-wing, extended in keeping; wing with tower c. 1930 for Charles Boot, probably by *E. Vincent Harris*. Pros- pect TOWER, 1927, 350 yds NNW of hall. UGHILL MANOR, Tinker Bottom, early C18, five bays, has swan-neck pediment to doorway and architraves to windows. FOX HOLES FARM, Hoar Stones Road, mid-C19, with symmetrical castellated front facing High Bradfield across the valley. Also several CRUCK BARNS, e.g. at Ughill Manor, C17.

BROOMHEAD HALL, 2¾ m. NW of High Bradfield. The house, of 1831 in Tudor style, succumbed to dereliction in the mid 1970s. The fate of the fine early C18 staircase from Kiveton Park (*see* Wales, q.v.) is unknown. The matching STABLE BLOCK remains, its impressive front with a castellated tower flanked by gabled wings.

On Castle Hill, ¼ m. SE, is a small RINGWORK sculpted out of the end of a ridge, scarred by quarrying; an external ditch, except on the S. No bailey. Possibly a predecessor of Bailey Hill, NNE of the church: an unusually steep MOTTE, with a tiny summit, surrounded by a substantial ditch. Triangular bailey to the SW, bounded by a massive rubble bank and a ditch. A precipitous slope on the W obviates any need for defences there.

CARMELITE MONASTERY OF THE HOLY SPIRIT, Kirk Edge Road. By *M.E. Hadfield & Son*, 1871 and 1885, extended by *C. & C. M.E. Hadfield*, 1910–11. Originally a Catholic orphan- age built at the expense of the 15th Duke of Norfolk, who presented it to the Carmelites for a convent in 1910. Isolated hilltop group of plain stone buildings, attached around the tall, hipped-roofed, main residential block. The convent additions

included a 12-ft (3.6-metre)-high enclosing wall and a public
CHAPEL at the SW corner. Two-bay nave with lancets set high
up, transeptal S chapel. (Brick-lined interior, with nun's choir
N of sanctuary, behind a full-height grille.)

BRADSHAW

Upland village on the edge of Halifax.

ST JOHN, Pavement Lane. 1837–9 by *Charles Child*. Small, lancet
style, W tower and tiny chancel. W gallery. STAINED GLASS. E
window by *Ward & Hughes*, 1878; three S windows by *Mayer*,
1878–9.

BRAITHWELL

Attractive small village with limestone farms and cottages.

ST JAMES. Of the Norman church only the reused and incomplete S doorway survives, its tympanum an unsophisticated
arrangement of simple chip-carved rosettes, a rectangle with
crosses, and small roundels, all within a cabled frame. Soffit
has saltire crosses. Early C13 chancel arch on keeled semicircular responds. Pointed triple-chamfered arch. A puzzle is
another arch to the W, creating an intermediate bay between
nave and chancel, which are both of the same narrow width.
Double-chamfered, the inner order on corbels, with square
abaci similar to those of the chancel arch. Could a central
tower or belfry (perhaps of timber) have been intended or
indeed existed (cf. Armthorpe)? There is no evidence of one
now and the church has a normal Perp W tower with three-light
bell-openings, battlements and pinnacles. A later arch, on
corbels, opens into a S chapel with cusped ogee-headed piscina
and plain tomb-recess. The N arch, 1893–5, completed the
crossing, opening to *J.D. Webster*'s organ chamber/vestry.
Early C14 chancel, rebuilt by Lord Scarbrough in 1845. Simple
three-light E window with flowing tracery. In the N wall a
heavily restored Easter sepulchre. Crocketed arch with keeled
mouldings and unusual drop tracery. C14 S arcade of two bays
with standard ingredients; the aisle continues into the S chapel.
Divers Perp windows. – PULPIT, 1907, incorporates three
carved panels from its predecessor, one with a kneeling
priest in an architectural setting, another with elaborate initials
BS (Brian Sharpe, Vicar 1565–76). Painted copies of texts
dated 1574. – MONUMENT. Betta Sheppard †1766. Broken

segmental pediment with ball finials. Moulded cornice, egg-and-dart frieze.

CROSS, 300 yds SSE at the cross-roads. Possibly late C12 or C13. Stump of shaft, square base with re-cut Norman French inscription. Braithwell had a market charter in 1289.

OLD HALL FARMHOUSE, Holywell Lane, 300 yds SSE. Its rear wing is a two-storey house dated 1683, still with double-chamfered mullioned windows; continuous dripmould over former doorway and three-light windows. Two-and-a-half-storey N-facing range added 1771. Plain front of three widely spaced bays. Hipped roof. Quoined doorway.

MOAT HALL. ⅓ m. SE. Moated site, once a grange of Lewes Priory. Fragmentary walling and a solitary two-centred hollow-chamfered arch remain from a house rebuilt after 'Le Priorie' was leased to John Vincent in 1427. The arch appears to have opened into a passage between a W first-floor hall range and an E cross-wing with service rooms.

BRAMLEY

ST FRANCIS. By *J. Mansell Jenkinson & Son*, 1954–6. Brick with a stocky bell-tower.

METHODIST CHAPEL (former), Main Street. 1785. Very small; Wesley called it 'neat'.

BRAMLEY GRANGE. ⅜ m. N. The rear has fragmentary C16 timber framing. S front C17, five bays, two storeys, but altered *c.* 1700 and dated 1756. Buck *c.* 1720 shows the bolection-moulded doorway, with carved keystone and segmental pediment on consoles. Parapet with small central shaped gable. (Some C17 and C18 panelling, plasterwork with voluted pilasters and an early C17 plaster overmantel with figures. Another overmantel, dated 1637, has gone.)

HELLABY HALL, 1 m. E. An hotel since 1991. A curious and quite dramatic house of *c.* 1690 for Ralph Fretwell, whose wealth came from Barbados sugar plantations. Fine limestone ashlar front of five bays, with chamfered quoins, first-floor band and cornice. Two storeys plus attic in a full-width, bold, but unquestionably awkward, gable that starts on both sides with fat volutes issuing fruit and foliage and then rises in slopes and curves to a flat top. Three windows under it. All the windows have flat frames and plain aprons forming strips from plinth to gable. The windows are sashed but until recently two blind cross-windows survived in the gable. Doorway with moulded architrave and large keystone, framed by an open segmental entablature on Doric pilasters. Owing to the fall of the ground the three-bay sides and the rear, all rendered, have another, lower, storey. Rear attic has two gables. Windows in plain ashlar surrounds, mostly with original mullions and

transoms. One interior doorway has stone architrave with big
bolection moulding.

BRAMPTON BIERLOW

(including West Melton)

CHRIST CHURCH. By *Pritchett & Son*, 1853–5, partly funded by
Earl Fitzwilliam. Handsome, with good Dec tracery. Promi-
nent W tower has pierced parapet, its pinnacles removed.
Ribbed vaults; the interior stonework all painted. – Chancel
FURNISHINGS by *C. Hodgson Fowler*, 1904–5, with later ROOD.
– STAINED GLASS. E window by *Kempe*, 1908. S aisle: first from
E by *J.W. Knowles*, 1898, second by *Powell & Sons*, 1929. N
aisle: first from E by *Kayll & Co.*, Leeds, 1906.

WEST MELTON UNITED REFORMED CHURCH (Congregational), Melton High Street. 1799. Classically detailed. Two
Doric doorways with triglyph friezes; round-arched windows.
Doric Serliana at preacher's end, facing gallery with panelled
front.

BRAMPTON ELLIS SCHOOL, Brampton Road. Rebuilt 1791 by
Earl Fitzwilliam. Schoolroom with inscribed plaque and
sundial above central door. Three-bay, three-storey house
attached to r.

BRAMPTON HALL, Manor Road. C18 stone casing but the r. part
of the front range is a surviving bay of an E–W cross-wing of
c. 1500, with large arched fireplace. Two-bay S range is a
rebuilding of *c.* 1550 with cross-passage and two-storey hall
with W aisle, also two-storeyed. The form is unusually late.
Good roof timbers in both parts visible upstairs.

PEAR TREE COTTAGE, No. 1 Melton High Street, ½ m. E. By
Parker & Unwin, 1902–3. Square. Brick and render. Tiled
hipped roof with deep eaves. First-floor windows rise as hipped
dormers.

RAINBOROUGH LODGE, 1 m. W on B6097. Former N entrance
to the Wentworth Woodhouse estate (q.v.). By *John Carr*, 1798.
Impressive gateway with large piers topped by lions linked to
square lodges with pyramidal roofs. Round-arched openings.

BRAYTON

Village not quite attached to Selby, the church standing among
trees between them.

ST WILFRID. Its beautiful limestone steeple is a beacon to show
the way to Selby, if one comes from the S. Probably mid
C12, with some of the region's best Romanesque carving,

comparable with that at Birkin (q.v.) on the s doorway. Tall slender unbuttressed w tower of typically Norman proportions, with nobly scaled twin bell-openings; a billet frieze round the walls rises over them to form hoodmoulds (cf. Selby Abbey). The tympana are plainly diapered (cf. priest's door, Birkin). Norman corbel table. Above, the Perp top: battlemented parapet and an octagon with buttresses and tall two-light bell-openings, crowned by a slender ribbed spire. The bold combination of Norman and later work characterizes the whole church. Fine Norman s doorway of four orders, the outer three with colonnettes, the inner one on jambs with twin demi-shafts, all carrying intricately decorated capitals. Two are of different character with four figures under arches. Imposts with interlace, foliage trails etc. The arch's outer order has beakhead with three heads and two hares among them; the second order has seventeen medallions with human and animal figures, e.g. mounted knights with lances, two in combat, a huntsman with dogs, one attacking a supine boar, and others harder to decipher; the third order has chevron, the fourth angle rolls. The middle soffits have point-to-point chevron forming decorated lozenge bands.

Tall Norman tower arch with boldly scalloped capitals, the shaft bases also decorated. Remarkably wide and high Norman chancel arch. The responds here have four shafts on either side. The capitals again are intricately decorated, with intertwined bands, foliage and tiny human heads (two C19); on the inner faces are two wyverns (N) and two lions (S). The sculptural detail is still beautifully crisp. The arch has, to both w and E, chevron on the inner order and a roll and hollow on the outer order. Renewed hoodmould. The chancel itself was rebuilt or remodelled early in the C14. It is longer than the nave, its unusual length perhaps indicating the extent of an earlier chancel with an apse. Fine four-light E window with flowing tracery and side windows with still E.E.-looking bar tracery, restored by *Pearson* 1877–8. Rere-arches inside. Priest's doorway with double-chamfered continuous moulding. Piscina and stepped sedilia under renewed arcade with gabled pointed trefoiled heads.

Also early C14 the N and S aisles. Three-bay arcades, octagonal piers. The arches on the S side with double chamfer and a third slight chamfer, on the N side with the more usual plain double chamfer. Both sides have hoodmoulds. Trefoil-headed piscina in S aisle. On the N side the E and w responds are keeled; the cusped lancet in the w wall here the only original window remaining. The N and S windows of the aisles, as well as the clerestory windows, are straight-headed and Perp.

REREDOS. By *Pearson* 1878; Caen stone (moved to N aisle chapel 1937). – FONT. Plain circular Norman bowl, with faintly incised intersected arcading left uncarved. – STAINED GLASS. E window 1878, chancel second from E 1884 and s aisle E 1884, by *Ward & Hughes*. Chancel third from E 1895 and third from w †1899, by *Heaton, Butler & Bayne*. – MONUMENTS. George,

Lord D'Arcy †1558 and Dorothy, his wife, †1557. Mutilated and headless recumbent effigies. Splendid tomb-chest with shields on curly strapwork cartouches, divided by narrow panels still with two blank little Gothic arches one on top of the other (cf. the D'Arcy tomb of 1411 at Selby).

PUMPING STATION (former), Brayton Barff, 1¼ m. SW. 1908. For Selby Urban District Council by *P. Griffith* and *B.M. Gray*, engineers. At a distance easily mistaken for a folly. Pedimented centre with Venetian window, and wings with circular tops, their domes a novel feature that allowed access to the pumps.

BRETTON HALL
(Yorkshire Sculpture Park)

2010

The house sits low on the N slope of a valley which contains the River Dearne and forms the park. It was begun *c.* 1720 for *Sir William Wentworth*, and the design is attributed to him, assisted by *Col. James Moyser* (cf. Nostell Priory).* Described as 'now a building' in 1730 by the Earl of Mar, whose plans for improvements (a *piano nobile*, porticos to the E and W fronts and a S bow) were not implemented. This austere Palladian house is still distinguishable. Nine bays by five and two-and-a-half storeys high. It has windows with moulded architraves and a balustrade hiding the roof. In the century after its completion it was transformed into a grander and much larger classical house by a succession of architects. The first changes were for Sir Thomas Wentworth, who took the surname Blackett in 1777 after inheriting his uncle's Northumberland estates. Detached kitchens N of the house were rebuilt by *William Lindley* from *c.* 1790, his L-shaped block, including E-facing offices of two storeys plus semi-basement, linked to the house by a long corridor. Blackett died in 1792, making one of his illegitimate daughters, the formidable Diana, wife of Colonel Thomas Beaumont, his heiress. The Beaumonts spent a fortune on the house, first engaging *William Atkinson*, who added the tall entrance porch with four fluted Greek Doric columns in 1805. He probably gave the pediments to the S and E ground-floor windows while improving the five-bay S front with a big three-bay bow (two storeys, the third added later), and a terrace overlooking the valley. Its dies have marble panels with Italianate sculpture (cf. Archway Lodge below). A quadrant orangery that Atkinson added at the NW corner of the house, leading to hot and cold baths, a museum and a dairy, lasted less than a decade, being removed in a much more ambitious scheme of extensions by *Wyatville*, 1811–14. He filled the gap between the N end of the house and the offices with a square vestibule

---

* Of an earlier house, panelling and a bed of 1542 are are now at Temple Newsam, Leeds (*West Riding North*).

and a huge bow-ended dining room projecting to the E. On the
W a large ante-room, with bedrooms over, led to an irregular NW
range with library, music room and 'Young Ladies' Sitting Room'
linked to Atkinson's museum.

Colonel Beaumont died in 1829, his wife in 1831. Their son
sold the contents (and Mrs Beaumont's extraordinary domed
conservatory by *Loudon*, 1827) in 1832, apparently to obliterate
his hated mother's memory as much as for financial reasons,
and commissioned *George Basevi Jun.* to demolish Atkinson's
remaining work on the W side and replace the museum with the
ORANGERY, *c.* 1835. Seven bays, with square Doric piers; blocking course. On the E front the dining room was replaced *c.* 1841
with a smaller three-bay one on a N–S axis, projecting by only
one bay. Basevi reconfigured the necessarily shortened offices
with an additional NE bay and restored their symmetry with a
new seven-bay pedimented front with four giant pilasters.

The Palladian ENTRANCE HALL has at the far end three heavy
arches that screen off a groin-vaulted passage connecting two
staircases. The main one (N), also of the 1720s, has a fine
wrought-iron balustrade. Grisaille panels with Roman figures
and trophies both in the hall and at the foot of the staircase
may be C19. One room on the W side with original plaster
ceiling. The room to its N has a siena-and-white marble chimneypiece with pastoral scene by *William Collins c.* 1761. Coved
ceilings and dainty Adamesque decoration in the rooms W and
E of the staircase. There is compelling evidence that at least
the E one, the late C18 dining room, was altered by *Carr*,
1793–4. Its rich plasterwork is very similar to that at Farnley

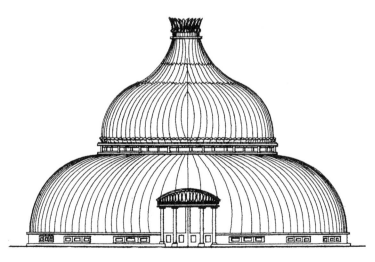

Bretton Hall glasshouse.
Drawing, 1833

Hall (*West Riding North*), and it has monochrome medallions like those painted at Farnley by Theodore de Bruyn.

The spectacular VESTIBULE N of the staircase is one of *Wyatville*'s finest spaces. Square, with cast-iron and yellow scagliola Tuscan columns supporting the upper stage. This rises up to an octagonal lantern on ornamented pendentives, the details all elegantly handled. Dramatically, a balcony opens from the staircase's half-landing into the upper level, where the walls are painted with striking architectural fantasies of classical ruins in the style of Panini and Piranesi. The side walls of the staircase have similar scenes. Attributed to *Agostino Aglio*, although one wall is signed by *Kitchen*.* These wall paintings must be among the last to use this theatrical depiction of ruins. The Regency-style Library is much denuded, but the Music Room retains some decoration. Segmental ceiling with rinceau panels and a shallow apse for an organ with clerestory of coloured glass panels (now blocked). Musical instruments painted in grisaille panels and in gilding on pilasters, and carved on good marble chimneypiece. *Wyatville*'s Ante-room was redecorated *c.* 1852 with a heavy Baroque ceiling with coffering and pendants. The Dining Room by Basevi received equally overwhelming Rococo plasterwork, its exuberant effect confused by much tamer wall panels and swags by *Guy Elwes*, *c.* 1930. Prodigious chimneypiece with vine scrolls, eagle and tigers' heads, 1841.[†]

The Hall and much of the estate were in college use from 1948 until 2007, with buildings by the *West Riding County Architect's Dept*, 1948–53 and 1960–3, set out N and NE of the mansion, greatly compromising its setting. Most college buildings were demolished in 2017 during the Hall's conversion to a hotel by *DLA Architecture*. Those retained for reuse include the 1960s library and the gym. Extensions to the Hall and associated uses for the stables and Camellia House are proposed.

STABLES and COACHHOUSE. By *Basevi*, *c.* 1842–5. Unfinished; partly demolished *c.* 1948, altered. Heavy rusticated ashlar, the details of the arched entrance curiously debased. Coupled giant columns with intermittent bands of vermiculated rustication, somewhat Frenchy dome. Colonnade to rear yard.

The GARDENS were mostly destroyed in the C20 but NW of the house is *Wyatville*'s CAMELLIA HOUSE, 1814. Glass walls with stone pillars without capitals and bases, but at the angles diagonally projecting arched and glazed bays with Tuscan columns – an excellent composition. Glazed hipped roofs whose decorative cast iron is dated 1871. To be restored as part of the conversion scheme.

The 500-acre PARK was first landscaped by Sir Thomas Wentworth. *Richard Woods* was consulted in 1764 but the extent of

---

*Information from BA dissertation by Gill Stark, Bretton Hall College, 1986, via Professor David Hill, University of Leeds.
[†]Some of the many chimneypieces removed in 1947 are at Bywell Hall, Northumberland.

his involvement is unknown. The UPPER LAKE was created by *c.* 1767, and the larger LOWER LAKE in 1776, beside a cut made for the river *c.* 1774. C19 landscaping extended the parkland. Much has been done to repair C20 neglect; the lakes, with their woodland and buildings were restored in 2009–11. CASCADE BRIDGE and weir, *c.* 1765, separate the two lakes. Immediately N the gently arched C19 cast-iron BRIDGE crosses the cut. Late C18 and early C19 pleasure grounds around Upper Lake have a rustic SHELL GROTTO with conical roof by *William Lindley*, a BOATHOUSE with roof on six stone columns, the OBELISK, an unfluted column, and a semicircular Doric temple SUMMERHOUSE. DAM HEAD BRIDGE crosses the cut at the E end of Lower Lake. Late C18. Triple-arched, elegantly detailed with wave scroll and rusticated panels; splayed ends with urns. Stone balustrade lost. LADY EGLINTON'S WELL, at Dam Head on the Lower Lake is dated 1685; probably altered in C18, perhaps as a small bath house. Built into a small rocky cliff, its doorway has paired engaged columns with fluted capitals and entablature.

Further afield within the park to the E of the house is the former CHAPEL (restored in 2013–14 as gallery space) of 1744, which replaced a medieval chapel of ease. Rectangular. Three-bay W front with bulgy Tuscan pilasters and pediment. Blank doorway between two arched niches. Square base to circular bell-turret with domed cap. S side five bays with plain end doorways, the E one blank. The angle pilasters again oddly bulgy. Venetian E window with Tuscan columns. Small W gallery with box pews. E of the chapel is THE PHEASANTRIES, the gamekeeper's house of 1749, probably by *Sir William Wentworth*. Five bays, two storeys, with three-bay pediment and giant Venetian window under. Other windows (altered) were still horizontal with plain mullions.

NORTH LODGE. *c.* 1811. Single-storeyed, square, under low pyramid roof with deeply projecting eaves. Sides of three bays, separated by panelled pilaster-strips. HAIGH LODGE (SE), *c.* 1860, is a copy. – ARCHWAY LODGE (E). By *William Atkinson*, 1804. Giant archway three bays wide and severely straight-topped. The arch is flanked by two fluted Roman Doric columns. Sculpted panel over the single sash to each side bay.

Since 1977 the park has incorporated the YORKSHIRE SCULPTURE PARK, brainchild of Peter Murray, a Bretton College lecturer, fulfilling Henry Moore's belief that 'sculpture is an art of the open air'. The VISITOR CENTRE (2002) and UNDERGROUND GALLERY (2003–5) are by *Feilden Clegg Bradley*, both placed with grace and sensitivity into the landscape. The Visitor Centre, on a precise E–W axis, has a strongly linear sculptural form. Its long, high, central corridor, naturally lit, leads from the entrance to the gardens. Wedge-shaped spaces for shop and balconied cafeteria on the S; meeting room, gallery and other spaces on two floors on the N. Exquisitely finished stonework within, complemented by glass and metal. The understated Gallery is set into the sloping lawn of the

Bothy Garden immediately w. Its grassed roof, with protecting ha-ha and line of flat skylights to the galleries below, make it virtually invisible at that level. The front, glass within a fine ashlar frame, faces a space enclosed by the Terrace Garden's yew hedge. The long concourse within is separated from three large galleries by screens that allow them to share its daylight or provide darkness needed for light installations. High on the s hillside at LONGSIDE, galleries and studio/workshops converted from three large modern barns by *Bauman Lyons*, 2001, retain an appropriately agricultural character.

Works by *Henry Moore* and *Barbara Hepworth* are always displayed. A small number of permanent works include 'Skyspace' by *James Turrell*, 2006, in the late C18 DEER SHELTER; three works by *Andy Goldsworthy*, 2006–7, including 'Hanging Trees', built into a ha-ha; and *David Nash*'s 'Seventy-one Steps', 2010, on the s slope of the valley.

At WEST BRETTON, on the N edge of the park, the ESTATE OFFICE, *c.* 1840, possibly by *Basevi*. Tudor Gothic, with spindly octagonal buttresses rising as pinnacles. Opposite, BRETTON LODGE, late C18, for the Agent. Brick. Pediment over central bay with giant blind arch and the two-storey canted bay each side. Similar three-bay pedimented centres to a house 100 yds N and the brick SCHOOL HOUSE, also late C18, flanked by single-storey classrooms. HOME FARM, *c.* 1842, displaced by Basevi's stables, has an attractive octagonal DAIRY with pyramidal roof. Just E, a row of four gabled ESTATE COTTAGES, 1860. Seven in BRICK ROW, ⅓ m. N, *c.* 1790. The centre and end ones have canted bay windows. Rear entrances. Unusually, two-bedroomed. – WAR MEMORIAL. 1921, using stone from *Wyatville*'s huge domed Menagerie House of 1811.

BRIERLEY

ST PAUL. By *John Wade*, 1869. E.E. Small, aisleless. w tower with spiky pinnacles and octagonal spire.

MANOR HOUSE, 1 m. SE. Evidence of the early C17, or possibly late medieval, house is a buttress on the NW side and a projecting oblong turret with spiral staircase to its l., now truncated, exposing a blocked doorway. (Cellar doorway with cambered head under the stair.) Late Georgian s wing.

BRIGHOUSE

Calder valley industrial town. The canal basin on the Calder & Hebble Navigation Cut was opened by 1768, the first railway station in 1840. Besides textile mills there were wire mills for card manufacturing and extensive flour mills. Local quarries shipped stone worldwide.

CHURCHES*

St Martin, Church Lane. 1830–1, by *F. Lees Hammerton*. Tall lancet windows with Y-tracery. No aisles, w tower. Restored and N and S galleries removed 1894–5; new chancel, organ chamber etc. built 1903–4 by *C. Hodgson Fowler*. Reordered 2002–6 by *George Pickles*. Spacious interior with very tall chancel arch and arcades. Elaborate REREDOS by *Wood & Oakley*, 1913, executed by *E. Bowman & Sons* with painted panels by *E. Stanley Watkins*. – Finely carved SCREENS, 1905–11. – PULPIT, 1913, with figures under ogee canopies, by *Bowmans*. – STAINED GLASS. N side first from E has excellent early *Morris & Co.* glass in four small panels, 1874, the two middle panels added 1897.   71

St Chad, Halifax Road, Hove Edge. 1911–12 by *C. Hodgson Fowler* and *W.H. Wood*. Simple Gothic. Low, with polygonal chancel and little spired bellcote.

St John, Gooder Lane. By *Nicholson & Corlette*, 1913–14. Tall, with single roof to nave and chancel. Low, flat-roofed aisles with five large clerestory windows above.

Central Methodist Church, Halifax Road. By *John Wills & Sons*, 1905–7. Arts and Crafts Perp. Square corner tower with little tiled spire. Large schoolrooms etc. attached.

Congregational church (former), Bridge End. 1854–6 by *Mallinson & Healey*. Large, robust Italianate with big pilasters and decorative eaves brackets. Adjacent MEMORIAL HALL, 1903–4.

Cemetery, Lightcliffe Road. Gothic CHAPELS with linking arch under short octagonal spire, 1873. By *William Gray* of Bradford, won in competition.

PUBLIC BUILDINGS

Civic Hall, Bethel Street/Bradford Road. Italianate of 1866–8 by *Mallinson & Barber*, as the Town Hall, providing offices and public hall over shops, whose fronts form a rusticated arcade.

Town Hall, Thornton Square. 1887 by *John Lord* of Brighouse, who won a local competition. Gabled clock of 1914.

Library and Smith Art Gallery, Halifax Road. Originally The Rydings, a distinguished classical house of *c.* 1841. It became the Library in 1898. Three-bay w front with columned porch. Original S front of four widely spaced bays, the outer ones with spacious bow windows, topped by low balconies of heavy cast iron. Three matching bays added to the r. in 1907 by *R.F. Rogerson* with the two top-lit art galleries to the NE. Carved oak panelling by *H.P. Jackson* is preserved in two rooms   102

---

*St James, Bradford Road, 1870 by *Mallinson & Barber*, was demolished 1973. STAINED GLASS by *Morris* and *Kempe* is at Bradford Museums.

(*ex situ*). It includes large grotesque faces and an overmantel with tiny figures rolling pastry, ironing, gardening etc. Also some of his furniture.

In the park, WAR MEMORIAL by *F.W. Doyle-Jones*, 1922. Granite column with bronze statue of winged Peace.

ASSEMBLY ROOMS AND MASONIC HALL, Owler Ings Road. 1906 by *Edward C. Brooke*. Idiosyncratic Vernacular Revival with mullioned-and-transomed windows but the upper lights pointed.

PERAMBULATION

The town centre is small. To the l. of the Town Hall (*see* Public Buildings) in Thornton Square is BARCLAYS BANK, a tall, handsome palazzo front of 1875. Then down Bethel Street, E of the square, on the l. the OLD SHIP INN, built 1926–7 with mock timber framing in C16 style, reusing parts of HMS *Donegal*, a battleship of 1858. The carved owls and heads are by *H.P. Jackson* (cf. Royal Oak, Halifax). Then the former BETHEL CHAPEL, 1811, like a three-bay Georgian town house, and the twin-towered Italian Romanesque former PARK METHODIST CHURCH, 1878, by *R.F. Rogerson*, its gal-leried interior fortunately retained. Large Sunday School behind. Round the corner in Bradford Road, NATWEST, 1895 by *C.S. Nelson*. Imposing gabled front with mullioned-and-transomed windows, oriel and good decorative detail.

s, in HUDDERSFIELD ROAD, THE CALDER pub, built as the Albert Hall, Theatre and Opera House by *Sharp & Waller*, 1898–9. Broad northern Renaissance gabled front with Vene-tian windows. Beside the canal, four-storey PERSEVERANCE MILL, dated 1831 in the gable. Across the road, on the canal's s side, near the entrance to the CANAL BASIN, is MILL ROYD MILL, a seven-storey former cotton mill *c.* 1875. Converted to flats *c.* 2000, with added penthouse storey and balconies.

SLEAD HALL, Halifax Road. (Hall and E cross-wing of 1636, additional wings 1718. Restored 1880s and arcaded w portico added. Wide mullioned-and-transomed window over this has reclaimed C17? stained glass, some apparently from New Hall, Elland.) Early C19 LODGE with pyramid roof and Gothic windows.

At HOVE EDGE, 1½ m. N, several early houses survive near each other:

GILES HOUSE, Lower Finkil Street. Dated 1655. Three even, low-pitched gables to front. Large mullioned-and-transomed windows to ground floor, wide mullioned ones above. Additions of 1723 created a double-pile house with second and third rear gables. C18 w range, enlarged in C19, connected with textile manufacture. (Parlour has carved wooden overmantel with enriched plasterwork frieze, 1655.)

NETHERHOUSE, Upper Green Lane. Late C16 timber-framed house encased in stone *c.* 1700. Linear plan with aisled housebody, originally open to roof, and through passage. The sixteen-light housebody window has timber mullions (numbered) and transoms, a rare survival made still more remarkable by the original leaded glass in the upper lights. Four-light fire window with timber mullions set diagonally. Inside, exposed structural timber, panelling, Tudor-arched doorways and doors with ogee-headed panels survive.

BRINSWORTH

St George (former). By *E. Isle Hubbard*, 1899–1900. Unhappily incomplete and now semi-derelict. Five-bay brick nave with bellcote, the arcades and E end encased in forbidding blind walls.*

BRODSWORTH

St Michael. The earliest surviving fabric indicates a small C11 church with nave and W tower built without any break in the N and S walls, as at Hooton Pagnell nearby (q.v.). The tower space was later absorbed into the nave, so the W wall's masonry, with occasional herringbone beside the tower arch, was the original tower's W wall. Its side-alternate angle quoins are visible outside. This tower's walls were thicker than the nave walls, as is evidenced by the set-back and disturbed stonework where its E wall met the nave N wall. In the late C12/early C13 the church was much enlarged, with a N aisle, extended chancel and new W tower. The N arcade consists of two clearly distinguished parts. The W opening, piercing the C11 tower wall, has heavy semicircular responds with square abaci. C19 arch. A small Norman window in the aisle N wall (possibly re-set) corresponds to this bay. The other two bays are slenderer, with semicircular responds and an octagonal pier with octagonal abacus. The capital has decoration developed from Norman scallops but they are now no more than little crescents or sausages. Pointed arches with one step and one chamfered step. The chancel has one Norman window (opening into later N vestry) and, outside the C15 pointed chancel arch, a few surviving voussoirs that apparently began a wide round C12 arch. C15 N chapel. Restored E window with three stepped lancets.

The tower, with later bell-stage, has on the upper S set-back a narrow band of reused Romanesque stones carved with a lozenge pattern (see too the coping of the adjacent nave wall).

*Canklow House, ⅜ m. E, by *John Platt*, 1767, was demolished 1965.

One-light bell-openings replaced by twin ones, but when? Three within four-centred arches, the E one within a round arch; some worn carving in the spandrels. Low single-chamfered tower arch on the simplest imposts, but pointed. S chapel, separately roofed, and S aisle with porch added in restoration by *C. Hodgson Fowler* for C.S.A. Thellusson, 1874–5. Structural restoration after mining subsidence, 1997–2003. – ROOD. By *W.H. Randoll Blacking & R. Potter*, with *Christopher Webb*, 1951–2. – PULPIT. 1696. Octagonal with marquetry panels and excellent carving typical of the date. Garlands, cherubs' heads etc. – STAINED GLASS. N aisle second from E by *Clayton & Bell*, 1919. – MONUMENTS. Many medieval cross-slabs. – Abigail Drummond †1766, with poetic epitaph by *William Mason*. Garlanded urn above finely carved aedicule. – Charles Thellusson †1815, wife Sabine †1814 and a son, by *Joseph Lockwood* of Doncaster, 1820. Simple pedimented tablet with draped sarcophagus.

BRODSWORTH HALL. Restrained Italianate mansion of 1861–3 by *Philip Wilkinson* for Charles Sabine Augustus Thellusson, one of the eventual beneficiaries of his great-grandfather's infamous will of 1796. It replaced the house nearby that had been rebuilt in the 1760s for Archbishop Hay Drummond. Two storeys in sandstone. The unconventional plan is compact and efficient, with a lower service wing extending N from the centre of the main block where the tall single-storey, top-lit billiard room and kitchen sit side by side. E front of 3:3:3 bays with large Doric porte cochère to projecting centre. Symmetrical thirteen-bay front to S garden. Crowning balustrades with elaborate urns on the dies.

The opulent mid-Victorian interior survived the gradual decay of the house in the C20 and since its donation to English Heritage in 1990 has been carefully conserved. Entrance Hall separated by a screen of paired Doric columns from the spacious top-lit staircase hall. Scagliola columns and pilasters, gilded plasterwork, and marbled wall panels in ochre, green and wine colours. The spaces are also distinguished by the large collection of Italian marble STATUARY (including works by *Pietro Franchi*, *Giuseppe Lazzerini* and *Pietro Magni*) bought by Thellusson at the 1865 Dublin International Exhibition.* On the S side of a long spine corridor from the stair hall is the Dining Room, with deeply compartmented ceiling and fine C18 marble chimneypiece, one of a number of fittings brought from the old Hall. Then the impressive South Hall, with yellow scagliola columns, C18 chimneypiece and mahogany doors with exuberant overdoors carved with putti and cornucopia. Lastly the gracious Drawing Room, in the style of the *dix-huitième*, with delicately painted ceiling; at both ends are

---

*Most were purchased from Chevalier Casentini of Lucca, and his undated drawings proposing the house's adornment with further sculptures have previously led to him being credited as its architect.

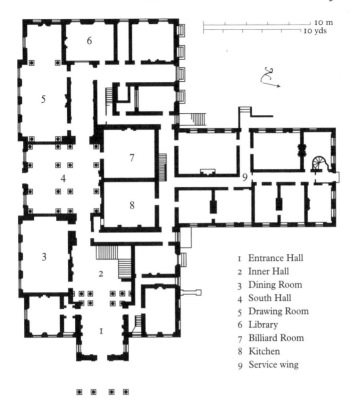

Brodsworth Hall.
Ground-floor plan

1   Entrance Hall
2   Inner Hall
3   Dining Room
4   South Hall
5   Drawing Room
6   Library
7   Billiard Room
8   Kitchen
9   Service wing

screens of white scagliola columns with gilded Corinthian capitals. The corridor vista here is most memorable: statues are set
against arcaded walls with mirrors framed by stencilled decoration and at the end *Giosue Argenti*'s 'Sleeping Girl' is bathed
in soft light from a prettily painted internal window.

The GARDENS have been restored to their 1860s design,
including formal terraces with statues, a tetrastyle Doric temple
SUMMERHOUSE on a mound above the ICE HOUSE, The
Grove, a former quarry, previously part of the old Hall's
gardens, and, in the archery range, the TARGET HOUSE, an
c18 pavilion with Gothic glazing to fine Venetian window and
picturesque roof of 1866.

At PICKBURN, ½ m. E, a row of attractive semi-detached estate
cottages, 1860s and ELM FARM, one of Thellusson's model
farms, with impressively vast quadrangle of gabled farm buildings, 1864.

BROTHERTON

Village on the Great North Road beside the River Aire. The area abounds with worked-out limestone quarries.

St Edward. Set into a steep slope, its w tower dwarfed by those of Ferrybridge C power station massed across the river (closed in 2015 and due for demolition). Rebuilt by *Pritchett & Son*, 1842–3, their last hurrah for the Commissioners' type of Gothic Revival churches. Tooled ashlar, surprisingly in sandstone, now blackened. The medieval tower survives as the core of its successor. Three-bay nave with galleried aisles under a broad, low-pitched roof; the aisles continue each side of the tower as porches with staircases. Transomed two-light windows with Perp cusped lancets. The lofty whitewashed interior is unusual for the greatly elevated E end, dictated no doubt by the site, not theology. Steps to chancel between balcony-like pulpit and reading desk, steps again to sanctuary and yet again to E bay of N chapel over Ramsden vault. – Stained glass. Nice original glass in the E window, all pattern-work except the small figure of Christ in the middle. – N chapel: first from E 1856, and E window 1858, both by *W. Holland* of Warwick. – Monuments. Notable group of the Ramsden family of Byram Hall (*see* below) in white and black marbles. – Sarah Ramsden, wife of John Ramsden, †1684. Attributed to *Thomas Cartwright I* (gf). Grand Baroque wall monument with good portrait bust in an oval niche. Segmental top. Two animated putti l. and r., apron with winged skull. – Sir John Ramsden †1690. Also attributed to *Cartwright* (gf). Fine, opulently shaped sarcophagus has swan-neck pediment strewn with flowers and excellently carved urn on top. No effigy. – John Charles Ramsden †1836. By *Walsh & Dunbar* of Leeds, with big flaming urn and pyramid on top. – Sir John Ramsden †1839. Large Gothic tablet with pinnacles and cresting, by *Walsh & Lee* of Leeds.

Independent Chapel (former) by *J.P. Pritchett*, 1837–8. Lancet windows with Gothic glazing.

National School (former), 250 yds NE. By *J.W. Hugall*, 1852–3. Limestone ashlar. Gothic. Rear schoolroom 1876.

Manor House, 200 yds NNW. Built 1664–6 as NW wing to a Tudor range now demolished; c18 etc. alterations. Limestone rubble, ashlar quoins. Six uneven bays. Sash windows, some with quoined, others with brick surrounds. Carved figure, possibly from old church, in small blocked opening in w gable.

Byram Hall, 1 m. E. Sir John Ramsden, 3rd Baronet, employed *Carr* in the 1760s to remodel and extend the existing c16 and c17 U-plan hall in plain classical style. The centre part between E and w wings collapsed in the 1930s; more was demolished in 1955. The former service wing now forms the w side of the stable courtyard, enclosed to N and E by *Carr*'s Coachhouse and Stables. Also probably by *Carr* the fine model Farm,

½ m. ESE. (Remains of GARDENS E of the Hall include a late
C18 ORANGERY (now a house), with Ionic pilasters and, inside,
a fine mid-C18 door with carved surround from Methley Hall
(*West Riding North*); a FOOTBRIDGE over the lake of lacelike
cast iron, inscribed and dated 1826, by *Sandford & Yates* of
Rotherham; and three elaborate gateways in Jacobethan style
by *George Devey* for the 5th Baronet, 1875.) – Remains of PARK
by *Capability Brown*, 1782, now farmland. In BYRAM PARK
ROAD a tiny square ashlar LODGE, one of a pair. Late C18,
possibly by *Robert Adam* who decorated the drawing room and
library of the house in the 1780s for the 4th Baronet.

BURGHWALLIS   5010

ST HELEN. The nave's side-alternate angle quoins and extensive
use of herringbone masonry in the nave and chancel S walls
indicate Saxon or Saxo-Norman work (cf. Kippax, *West Riding
North*). Plain S doorway, altered and restored, cut straight
through the wall. It has a not-quite-round flush arch above
what may have been a peaked lintel with a straight lower edge,
cut into by a later segmental doorhead. Norman W tower,
unbuttressed, with two round-headed windows below, but
pointed twin bell-openings above. Perp top. An unusual oculus
in a single square stone on the N side of the middle stage is
probably *ex situ* (another in the chancel N wall). The tower
arch's big semicircular responds are probably C12, the arch,
which is pointed, C13. A renewed C13 lancet in the nave S wall;
the chancel arch may be C13 too. The S porch, with stone roof
on chamfered transverse arches, and the one-bay chancel
extension are C14/C15. Late medieval stone bench sedilia with
shaped arms. There was extensive restoration by *J.L. Pearson*,
1883–5, parishioners' opposition having frustrated *J.M. Teale*'s
proposed scheme in 1864.

REREDOS. Marble and alabaster, 1885; with figures carved
by *Nathaniel Hitch* (painted in the 1950s). – ROOD SCREEN.
Yorkshire is not a county of screens. So Burghwallis's late
medieval screen, well restored in 1881, belongs to the first
class. Six wide bays, each with an ogee arch subdivided by a
pendant into two rounded arches and complex tracery above
the ogees (cf. Owston). Vaulted canopy, straight cornice with
rose trails, and cresting. Rood added 1938.* – STAINED GLASS.
E window by *Capronnier c.* 1869. – By *Powell & Sons*: chancel
S side, two easternmost windows 1898, nave S side easternmost
1891, and nave N side easternmost 1902. – MONUMENTS.
Several good medieval cross-slabs, that of William Adam
†1554 with rhyming English inscription. – Brass to Thomas
Gascoigne †1554. The figure, in armour, is 2 ft 10 in. (86 cm.)   *p. 21*

*The ancient South Door, with medieval iron hinges, is in Doncaster Museum.

long. – Nathaniel Sutton, Rector, †1702. Scrolled cartouche with winged cherub's head below.

RECTORY (former). By *Watson & Pritchett*, 1815. Rendered. Two storeys with pedimented porch to three-bay front. Pedimented r. gable with oculus; large extension to l.

BURGHWALLIS HALL. Two-storey H-plan house, probably early C16 but much altered, with additional s cross-wing, 1797. Limestone rubble with ashlar dressings. E front has large Gothic Revival entrance porch to original s cross-wing, and massive Tudor chimneystack between middle and r. bay of three-bay centre range. Stair-towers in the rear angles of this range. Mullioned attic windows, the rest mostly sashes. The C18 wing, originally stuccoed, was rudely medievalized c. 1820, its once-pedimented s front transformed by five small gables. From the late C16 the hall's owners were the Catholic Fenton and then Anne families; a priest's hiding hole survives near their attic chapel.

ROBIN HOOD'S WELL, 1 m. WSW, beside the Great North Road (A1(M) – E side). Square well-house by *Vanbrugh*, c. 1720, commissioned by the Earl of Carlisle (of Castle Howard). Three open arches, heavily rusticated, and a straight top of three steps. Rebuilding after 1960s road-widening diminished both its dignity and its proportions by omitting the two lowest courses of stone.

Burghwallis, Robin Hood's Well.
Engraving, 1831

CADEBY

St John the Evangelist (Churches Conservation Trust). A
sturdy little gem by *George Gilbert Scott*, 1856–60, for Sir Joseph
Copley of Sprotbrough. The model is St Giles, Skelton (North
Riding) but with one significant change, from E.E. to Scott's
favoured Dec. Nave and chancel, aisles and chancel chapels
all under one steep roof that falls low to meet the gables of
squat buttresses, to broad-bottomed effect. Gawky bellcote
over the nave and chancel junction (a replacement by *G.G.
Pace*, 1956). Cusped lancet windows have hoodmoulds with
foliate stops. Geometrical tracery in the E window. Tall gabled
s porch with arcaded sides. Delightful interior enriched with
virtuoso carving by *J. Birnie Philip*. Round nave piers with
naturalistic foliage capitals. Richly moulded arches. In the
chancel quatrefoil piers with even more elaborate capitals;
angel musicians as stops. Scissor-braced roof with pretty stencilled decoration between the rafters. – Octagonal panelled oak
PULPIT exquisitely carved with hawthorn, ivy etc. – FONT
COVER with ironwork scrolls, foliage and water-lily buds,
perhaps by *Skidmore*.

CAMBLESFORTH

Camblesforth Hall. Small double-pile country house of
c. 1700, attributed to *John Etty* on stylistic grounds. Red brick
with stone quoins. Two storeys, seven by three/four bays. Deep
modillioned eaves to hipped roof with central well. Pedimented
dormer windows. s front has doorway with broken segmental
pediment on finely carved brackets; the large sash windows are
vertically connected by slight projections in the wall (cf. The
Red House, Duncombe Place, York). E service entrance has a
heavy Gibbs surround with devil mask keystone, which must
be Early Georgian. Very large arched sash window to rear
staircase. This has a square open well and nicely rotund turned
balusters. Good original bolection-moulded panelling and fireplaces. sw bedroom has fine chimneypiece with swan-neck
pediment.

CAMPSALL

St Mary Magdalene. A large, complex building with a fascinating history, extensively restored by *Scott*, 1871–4. Its late
Norman w tower is the most ambitious of any parish church
in the West Riding. The earliest evidence is traces of E quoins

and herringbone work on the internal face of the nave s wall; this may be pre-Conquest although Domesday Book records no church at Campsall. Early Norman enlargement to create a cruciform church is attested by the rough masonry of the N transept and the blocked head of its N window (external voussoirs with faint chevron) plus that of a W window visible inside. This church was enlarged again *c.* 1170–80 by extensive works in ashlar masonry: W tower, aisles, new chancel. The tower is a piece of high display. Restored W doorway with three orders of colonnettes carrying scalloped capitals; chevron and lozenges in the arches. Above this a window with chevron enrichment set in a slightly lower blind arcade, the arches on stumpy shafts with block capitals. Above a shafted W window and then an impressive belfry stage with two twin openings on each side, their blank arches set wide apart and abundantly shafted. The aisles embrace the tower and must have been built with it for it has unmoulded arches on Norman imposts to N and S as well as to the nave. In the N aisle the E arch towards the transept survived C14 rebuilding. It cuts into the window mentioned above, thereby proving the two building phases. The arch has chevron decoration on face and soffit, and a few chevron-decorated stones are built into the W wall of the S transept, no doubt from the corresponding arch. Slightly later arches from the nave to the transepts are now pointed, but still have chevron on their inner faces. The N arch has dogtooth on the soffit, the S arch has angle rolls. The N respond of the tall and wide chancel arch is preserved and in the chancel one N window with shafts with scalloped capitals inside and out. (The carving to impost and hood does not look original.)

More work was done *c.* 1300 or a little earlier. The most interesting piece is the W bay of the S aisle, which was given a domical rib-vault (single-chamfered ribs). W window a cusped lancet. Above the vault is a heated chamber with small windows with shouldered arches to W and S. The W window of the N aisle is similar. In the N aisle N wall a recess with quadrant moulding, also typical of *c.* 1300. The chancel was extended, with new lancet windows of one light and of two (with Y-tracery).*

s buttresses with angle rolls. Keeled S respond of the chancel arch and E respond of the S transept – an amendment made at this time. See also the chancel S doorway with one continuous keeled moulding, the renewed sedilia with pointed trefoiled heads on plain shafts, and the two stone benches against the N and S walls further W, with arm-rests preserved at their W ends (cf. e.g. Owston). It is possible that this group of events actually belongs to two phases, one about the middle, the other at the end of the C13. Right in the C14, and typical of the Dec style, is the delightful S doorway with a shouldered lintel under a depressed two-centred arch, both lintel and arch, and the jambs, ornamented with big fleurons. Equally typical

*The Dec E window is of course *Scott*'s.

the S transept S window with reticulated tracery (a C19 replacement).

Finally late C14/early C15 Perp most of the aisle windows, the big three-light clerestory windows, the battlements and pinnacles to the clerestory and tower, the porch with a stone ceiling on chamfered transverse arches, and above all the three-bay arcades inside. Thin piers with four straight sides and big wave mouldings in the diagonals. The abaci were evidently made for semi-octagonal shafts. Tall two-centred arches of two quadrant mouldings. Of a date hard to determine are the two shallow recesses in the E walls of the transepts with low segmental arches. They are probably connected with reredoses of altars. But what can the purpose have been of the recess in the S transept S wall? It has a straight top on three heavy brackets, looking more military than ecclesiastical. – ROOD SCREEN. C15. Tall, of one-bay divisions; similar to Hatfield (q.v.). Its splendidly carved dado has a rhymed inscription in English.★ The upper tracery is gone, but the coving for the rood loft remains, with lierne ribs, and the prettily ribbed brackets for the former posts of the loft parapet.

ALTAR. In the S transept *Pugin*'s painted stone altar from Ackworth (q.v.). 1841–2. Elaborately carved, with angels in niches. – Oak PULPIT. C17. Octagonal, panelled. – SCULPTURE. Nave W wall. Small cubic capital *c.* 1090. Carved with a demi-rosette on the r. side and a lion entangled in foliage on the front. – N transept (loose). Norman carved stones including beakhead corbels and one with palmette, in excellent condition. Presumably found during Scott's restoration. Other pieces visible in the S aisle wall. – STAINED GLASS. E window by *Harry Harvey*, 1964. – N transept E window by *Heaton, Butler & Bayne*, *c.* 1920. – MONUMENTS. Richard Frank †1762. Broken-pedimented aedicule with coloured marbles. – Rev. Francis Yarborough †1770. Finely framed cartouche. – Thomas Yarborough, his wife and daughters by *Flaxman* 1803–6. Grecian relief of two young women giving alms to the poor and blind.

THE OLD RECTORY (former vicarage). Opposite the church. A T-plan building of *c.* 1400 with a first-floor hall, its original form and purpose unclear; the hall may have been for religious or secular meetings. Lower E and W wings at N end of hall block; extended on E side and altered *c.* 1800. Truncated extruded W stack indicates that the space below the hall was heated. (Full-height stud partition at N end of hall has two ogee-headed doorways on ground floor. Hall is three bays, divided vertically. N part, now with floor removed, has on E a moulded two-centred arched doorway of *c.* 1400, which must originally have led to an external staircase. S part has pointed vaulted ceiling and original window opening with hoodmould in S gable, now with Gothick sash. E wing has what was probably a private chapel on first floor. Three-light Perp E window

★The text is in Hunter's *South Yorkshire* and the *Little Guide*.

with panel tracery and hollow-moulded hoodmould; N window
with straight hoodmould. Original roofs visible in the attics;
the chapel has two-bay truss with arch braces forming a continuous pointed arch.)

The attractive older part of the VILLAGE lies SW of the church.
Very prosperous in the Middle Ages, it had a market charter
in 1293–4. Mainly C18 and C19 cottages along High Street.

CAMPSALL HALL stood 50 yds S of the church. Remodelled by
Carr in 1762, it was demolished in 1984. Only the Gothick
SUMMERHOUSE (now residential) by *Carr* and *William Lindley*,
1784, survives at Barnsdale, 1¾ m. WSW, as an eyecatcher
visible from the Great North Road (A1). CAMPSMOUNT,
¼ m. WSW of the church, also by *Carr*, for Thomas Yarborough, 1752–6, was demolished in 1959. The farmhouse of
Carr's HOME FARM remains (the rest mostly demolished 1962
and 1973). Canted S front flanked by single bays, originally of
one storey but now two, with parapets. Quadrant poultry
houses linked it to long ranges of essentially classical stables,
barns etc. enclosing the E and W sides of the farmyard in front.
The S end of the W range survives.

CANNON HALL *see* CAWTHORNE

CANTLEY

ST WILFRID. Medieval, pebbledashed except for the Perp W
tower. Norman priest's door has big lintel with segmental
doorhead under plain sunk tympanum defined by a narrow
semicircular chamfer. Of the C13 the E window's three stepped
lancets with continuous hoodmould and headstops, the trefoil
panel with sculpture above, and the S aisle E lancet; also the S
doorway, decorated with dogtooth. Three-bay S arcade Dec or
later. The church was first restored* by *William Eardley*, Vicar,
to his own designs in 1884, but is most notable for *Comper*'s
restoration and enlargement in 1892–4, and additional embellishment by him, especially after a chancel fire in 1905. The
chancel N wall arcade of two large arches with continuous
moulding is his and the interior rich with elaborately carved
and painted fittings, stencilled decoration and gilding. This
scholarly, and revolutionary, re-creation of an interior derived
from English late medieval precedent was widely noticed.
Comper's three-bay N aisle, however, was demolished in
1988–9 for *Donald Buttress*'s controversial extension, which
created the large 'second nave'. Although Comper's considered

---

*No evidence has been found to support claims of a restoration by *Scott* in the
1850s.

arrangement, with its two aisle chapels, has been lost, the jewel-box intimacy of his spaces remains. The FITTINGS include a correctly Gothic ROOD SCREEN (by *J. McCulloch*) with loft and rood, PARCLOSE SCREENS, REREDOS and HIGH ALTAR with enclosure of riddel-posts topped by angels under a large canopy with hanging pyx. This is Comper's second 'English altar', as described in his paper to the St Paul's Ecclesiological Society in 1893, and the first in a parish church. It was taken up as the new orthodoxy by Percy Dearmer in *The Parson's Handbook*, 1899. – FONT COVER 1904, ORGAN CASE 1905, both unpainted. In the 1980s extension a REREDOS by *Comper* with CANOPY by *Walter Tapper*, both from redundant churches. – STAINED GLASS. All by *Comper*, the former N aisle windows reused in the extension. – MONUMENT. John Walbanke Childers †1812. Large robed figure of Christ within marble aedicule with segmental pediment.

The church is surrounded by the later C20 Doncaster suburb of NEW CANTLEY which has its own church of ST HUGH by *Bernard Miller*, 1956.

CANTLEY HALL, ½ m. NE. Built for Childers Walbanke Childers, 1785; altered by *William Lindley*, 1802. Two storeys. Rendered. Parapet with balustrading. Seven-bay N front has three-bay pediment and large porch with paired Ionic columns. Good W front with two full-height canted bays. Single-storey ballroom/ billiard room of the 1890s on S side. Attached three-storey E bedroom/service wing. (Interior altered by *Garside & Pennington*, 1930. Cantilevered wooden staircase; galleried first-floor landing under domed lantern. Excellent Adamesque plaster ceiling in drawing room, with fan-shaped panels to semicircular ends. Ballroom has pine panelling, E minstrels' gallery and C18 bolection-moulded stone chimneypiece.) Georgian STABLES.

CARLECOTES

1000

CARLECOTES HALL. C17 origin (former N service buildings have a lintel dated 1696). Two parallel E–W ranges with E cross-wing and a third range behind with later eastward extensions. C19 two-storey canted bay with cusped lights and battlemented parapet added to S gable, probably by *George Shaw* of Saddleworth, who designed the chapel of ST ANNE in the gardens for John Chapman, 1856–7. Dec tracery. Delightful unaltered interior with elaborately carved oak fittings.

HAZLEHEAD HALL, off Lee Lane, 1½ m. E. Mid-C19. H-plan with gables and sashed windows. Two-storey crenellated N porch.

SHEEP SHELTER, 1 m. SE. C19. Square with diagonal walls under a pyramidal roof. Unusual.

CARLTON
Barnsley

3010

ST JOHN. By *G.E. Street*, 1874–8, and one of the grittiest of his churches. Dark stone tooled diagonally. Nave and N aisle, then a tower with a tall saddleback roof over the chancel's W bay. Its small circular staircase with conical top stands out on the S side. Varied Dec tracery, the tall W windows separated by a buttress. The chancel has a pointed tunnel-vault, stone under the tower, wood in the E bay. The decorative features are consistently of *c.* 1300: piscina, sedilia, low chancel screen wall, pulpit and font. – Elaborate three-stage pinnacled FONT COVER, from Wakefield Cathedral. – ROOD by *Cristi Paslaru*, *c.* 2006 (cf. St Luke, Grimethorpe). Additions by *Potts, Parry, Ives & Young*, *c.* 2008.

THE GABLES, W, is the former vicarage. *c.* 1878; possibly by *Street*. Stone, with tiled roof and gables, the three big ones at the front with decorative tile-hanging.

CARLTON
Selby

6020

ST MARY. Rebuilt for the Dowager Lady Beaumont by *J.B. & W. Atkinson*, 1862–3. Ornamented SW tower with stone broach spire on pyramidal base. Small chancel, narrow six-bay nave. Geometrical tracery. Tall arch-braced nave roof. – STAINED GLASS. E window by *Wailes*, 1863. Chancel S, first from E by *Preedy*, 1863. Nave S, first from E by *Powell Bros*, 1893. Nave N from E: first by *Lavers, Barraud & Westlake*, †1879, fourth by *Heaton, Butler & Bayne*, 1902. – MONUMENTS. Mary Errington †1696. Small brass with comical cherubs. – Nicholas Stapleton †1716 and second wife, Mary, †1735, erected 1738. Fine ornamented marble aedicule with fluted Corinthian pilasters and segmental pediment. – Miles Stapleton, 8th Baron Beaumont, †1854 by *Patrick Macdowell*. Marble. Inscription in classical frame with obelisks.

ST MARY (R.C.). By *M.E. Hadfield*, 1840–2. Founded by Lady Throckmorton, née Stapleton. Unostentatious, white brick. One-bay chancel with Perp tracery, narrow three-bay nave. Small SW gabled bellcote. Nave has high hammerbeam roof and W gallery. Restored chancel has elaborate painted and gilded REREDOS and panelling with blind tracery. – WALL PAINTINGS of saints flank E window. – Hanging ROOD (screen removed). – Elaborate SIDE ALTARS, 1904. – MONUMENTS. Brasses: Col. Herman Stapleton †1847 by *Pugin*, made by *Hardman*; Miles Stapleton, 10th Baron Beaumont, †1895, also by *Hardman*.

Tudor Gothic former PRESBYTERY attached. Former CONVENT, 1876, and SCHOOL, 1879, to rear.

METHODIST CHAPEL (Wesleyan). By *William Johnson* of Howden, 1898–9. Enthusiastic brick polychromy.

CARLTON TOWERS. A large country house with a weird skyline from most vantage points in the flat surrounding countryside. The staunchly Catholic Stapleton family were established at Carlton from the C14 and the w range is a house built in 1614 for Elizabeth Stapleton, with mid-C18 extension and alterations. Further work by *Thomas Atkinson c.* 1774–7 included the thirteen-bay E wing. After the family's long-dormant title was successfully reclaimed in 1840, Miles Stapleton became 8th Baron Beaumont; reverence for their lineage and their dashing medieval ancestors inspired his work on the house in 1842–5 and, more spectacularly, his son's Gothic re-clothing of the exterior as part of a scheme of extension by *E.W. Pugin* in 1871–4.

The tall, compact three-storey C17 block, its pilastered w entrance now a window, is still recognizably Jacobean. Shown with its original turrets and NE staircase tower in Buck's drawing *c.* 1720, its resemblance to Bolsover Castle, Derbyshire (for Elizabeth's uncle Sir Charles Cavendish) suggests that *John Smythson* may have been architect. The lower three-storey N extension, with an entrance in its canted centre, was probably added in the 1750s by Thomas Stapleton, who made interior alterations when he built the E wing as a chapel and stables in the 1770s. The 8th Lord Beaumont, probably acting as his own architect, absorbed the wing into the house, adding a bedroom range on the N. His wife and children being Protestant, he also converted the chapel to a music room. His heir re-embraced Catholicism and embarked on *Pugin*'s grandiose scheme, rendering the brick house in stone-coloured cement with obsessively regular horizontal grooving,

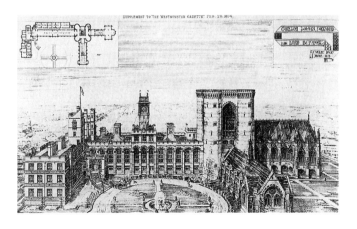

Carlton Towers, perspective, with proposed extensions.
Engraving, 1873

inserting mullioned-and-transomed windows and adding turreted chimneystacks. The W range's staircase tower was restored and a new, larger N staircase tower built; above the large-windowed E wing rose a taller and thinner tower, the square upper part for the clock decidedly odd in outline and details, with figures on the battlements. The best feature is the new S entrance in the angle, with talbot sentinels to its long curving staircase and a lushly ornamented porch.

Following a rift with his architect in 1874, Lord Beaumont abandoned *Pugin*'s crazy E extensions – a monster staircase tower, barons' hall and huge chapel – and turned to *J. F. Bentley* for the INTERIOR. This is his only major country house work and he designed every aspect of the furnishings and ornament, with painted decoration by *Westlake*, woodcarving by *J. Erskine Knox*, stained glass by *Lavers, Barraud & Westlake*, metalwork by *Longden & Co.* and fireplace tiles by *William de Morgan*. In the E wing his sumptuous state rooms – the galleried Inner Hall, Venetian Drawing Room, Card Room and Picture Gallery form an enfilade 195 ft (60 metres) long, their decoration a celebration of the family's heraldry. The best is the richly painted and gilded Drawing Room, with elaborately crested ebonized wall cabinets and panels painted with characters from *The Merchant of Venice*, upper walls with moulded plaster imitating embossed leather, splendid chimneypiece with coved top, and beamed ceiling. The Card Room has oak panelling matching the magnificent double doors, and stencilled walls and ceiling. The spacious Armoury and the impressive imperial N staircase link the E wing with the W range, where C18 work survives. (Three first-floor rooms have early C18 panelling and chimneypieces, one two-tier, with well-carved entablature. *c.* 1750s: the Dining Room (originally Great Hall) in Kent's style, with Corinthian-columned screen on line of screens passage, plasterwork frieze with Vitruvian scroll and fine wooden chimneypiece with caryatids; also the Harp Room with delicate Rococo ceiling in the manner of *Giuseppe Cortese* and prettily garlanded chimneypiece. In the Victorian Morning Room the chimneypiece has a relief of the Judgment of Hercules by *Rysbrack*. Above the dining room *Bentley*'s Library, 1876 (C17 Great Chamber), was formerly a drawing room and has a 1770s Adamesque ceiling and good marble chimneypiece.)

PARK. Landscaped by *Thomas White c.* 1765.

ESTATE HOUSES in the village include house and four attached cottages by *Bentley*, 1877. Brick. Single-storeyed with gabled attic dormers with decorative plaster panels. Very simple and excellent.

TOLL BRIDGE, ¾ m. S. 1776–7. Probably by *Carr*. Pair of tiny toll houses with lancet windows, and stone piers of Thomas Stapleton's wooden drawbridge over the Aire to Snaith. Superseded 1928.

CARL WARK *see* FOX HOUSE

CASTLEFORD

Industrial and former mining town on the s bank of the Aire, just below its confluence with the Calder; both rivers are navigable. Castleford stands on the site of the Romans' Lagentium/ Legiolium, the CI fort defending the river crossing and beside which the first civilian settlement grew. Pevsner's lament that 'There does not seem to be a single building in the centre of the town which would justify mention' is, alas, still too nearly true.

CHURCHES

ALL SAINTS, Church Street. Rebuilt by *H. Shephard*, 1866. E.E. Quite large and not immediately endearing. Central tower with corbelled quatrefoiled parapet. Spired octagonal stair-turret. The 'transepts' do not extend beyond the aisles. Five-bay nave with clerestory. Dec N aisle by *George Phillips*, 1852–3, reworked. Lofty Dec interior, all stone, some capitals still uncarved. – STAINED GLASS. s aisle westernmost and w by *Powell Bros*, 1892. – N aisle w by *Heaton, Butler & Bayne*, 1900.

ALL SAINTS, Hightown, Whitwood Mere. By *Bacon & Bell*, 1862–4. E.E. Squat sw tower/porch added *c.* 1888.

HOLY CROSS, Airedale. By *Nicholson & Rushton*, 1931–4. Unexpectedly impressive for this suburban estate. Its mining community salvaged the stone from Fryston Hall (dem. 1931)* and four giant Ionic columns from its portico are cleverly incorporated. Broad gabled roof embracing the aisles. Arcades of six round arches on round and square piers. Sturdy oak furniture by *Thompson* of Kilburn.

ST MICHAEL AND ALL ANGELS, Smawthorne, ½ m. SE. By *Sir Charles Nicholson*, 1927–9. Large. Brick. Gothic, simple but inventive. Single roof to the clerestoried chancel and the nave, spreading out over the three-bay aisles. Bellcote set sideways in angle of chancel and N aisle, above lower chapel. Very tall nave arcades. w organ gallery. Raked floor.

ST PAUL, Glass Houghton, ⅞ m. SE. 1898–1902, by *Demaine & Brierley*. Sturdy Gothic, in brick, not the more expensive stone intended. w tower not built.

ST JOSEPH (R.C.) Pontefract Road. By *Edward Goldie*, 1891. Sanctuary 1921. Gothic. Brick. Clerestory squeezed in above lean-to aisles. Spired bellcote.

AIREDALE METHODIST CHURCH, Elizabeth Drive, 1¼ m. E. 1929, by *Garside & Pennington*. Simple Gothic, with stone dressings.

CHRIST CHURCH (United Reformed, formerly Congregational), Carlton Street. 1863. Gothic. Porch, between shop units, 1934. Unspoilt galleried interior, delightful in its honest simplicity.

---

*FRYSTON HALL stood 2¾ m. ENE. It had been remodelled *c.* 1790, possibly by *William Lindley*. Stables (semi-derelict) and gatepiers survive.

PUBLIC BUILDINGS

CIVIC CENTRE, Ferrybridge Road. Won in competition 1964 by
the *Griffiths Lewis Goad Partnership*. Phase 1 1967–70, Phase 2
1970s.* Flat-roofed, stepped-back upper office floors. Strong
horizontal emphasis of the 'cornice' treatment plays against the
running rhythm of the window mullions. Pre-cast concrete
panels and purple-brown engineering brick.

105 WHITWOOD MERE INFANTS' SCHOOL (former), Methley
Road. Now a business centre. By *Oliver Hill*, 1939–40. An early
example for England of a school in the pure Modernism of the
years before the Second World War. One storey, flat roofs. Brick
with metal windows. Long curved range of classrooms, s-facing
to embrace the sun, has continuous windows opening onto a
covered terrace and clerestory lighting above its roof. On the
N side the higher assembly hall projects at the W end. The long
façade to the l. of this, divided by the main entrance, has
running along it a graceful frieze of green faience with incised
deer by *John Skeaping*.

BRIDGE, across the Aire. 1805–8. By *Bernard Hartley I*, built by
Jesse Hartley. Three segmental arches with guilloche frieze and
scrolled (E) and vermiculated (W) keystones. W of this a curving
FOOTBRIDGE by *McDowell & Benedetti*, 2008. 142 yds
(130 metres) long, its box-beam construction subtly engineered by *Alan Baxter Associates* and *Arup*. Supported mid-
stream on three pairs of slender raking A-struts. Useful,
beautiful and fun.

PERAMBULATION

In CARLTON STREET, the spine of the modest centre, the small
Baroque CARNEGIE LIBRARY by *G.H. Vernon Cale* of
Birmingham, 1904–5, refurbished and extended by *Niall
McLaughlin Architects* as Castleford Forum Library and
Museum in 2013. Next door, the façade of the MARKET
HALL, 1878–80. Italianate, with a small square tower on the
gable. On the corner of Bank Street, handsome Italianate
HSBC, *c.* 1895, its roof steepened by its narrow site. In BANK
STREET, the former POST OFFICE of 1901 by *Garside & Pen-
nington*. Plain stone front with double entrances. On the E side,
its larger Neo-Georgian successor, *c.* 1920 by *H.M. Office of
Works* has more presence. Brick. Three storeys, with giant
doorcase. In JESSOP STREET the Tudoresque POLICE
STATION AND COURT HOUSE, 1896–8, faces the vast
PICTURE HOUSE by *Arthur Hartley*, 1921. Partly white faience,
with classical motifs and four coloured faience panels with
comely Roman ladies.

In LOWER OXFORD STREET, No. 234, by *F. Scatchard*
1934. Modernist, rendered, semicircular tower-porch with
second-floor look-out.

---

*Formerly outside was a SCULPTURE (*Draped Recling Figure*) presented by *Henry
Moore* to his native town in 1980. Now in the museum.

Castleford, Whitwood, colliery institute and housing.
Drawing by C.F.A Voysey, 1904

WHITWOOD, 1½ m. SW, is a former colliery village with an attractive group of buildings in Whitwood Common Lane by *C.F.A. Voysey* for the Briggs family, owners of the colliery and his clients for Broadleys, Windermere.* The former MINERS' WELFARE INSTITUTE (now RISING SUN pub) and a terrace of nineteen double-fronted COTTAGES for colliery officials were commissioned in 1904, built 1906–8. They are roughcast, with stone trim and tile bands, and have big tiled roofs with tall chimneystacks, gables and deep-swept eaves. The window surrounds in particular are at once recognizable as Voysey. The institute, originally very pretty but now a little altered, is L-shaped and a long single storey, originally with open veranda (now glazed) between gables. At the corner a four-storey square tower for the manager's house with crenellated top around a pyramid roof and taller chimney at the corner. Some original panelling and fireplaces inside. The terrace is accented by seven gabled houses separating pairs with hipped dormers. Though modest their neat interiors demonstrate Voysey's genius for convenience and economy. The architect's simpler BRIGGS MEMORIAL HALL, behind the institute, was built in memory of Arthur Currer Briggs (†1906). Battered buttresses and a large lunette in the gable above the canted, flat-roofed entrance porch. Five similar windows at the sides.

CATCLIFFE

4080

ST MARY. By *J.E. Knight* of Rotherham, 1909–10. Perp revival, faced crazy-paving style with stone from Orgreave Colliery.
GLASSWORKS CONE, amid housing S of the church. Built *c.* 1740 for William Fenney, formerly of Bolsterstone glassworks, who supplied 1,076 sq. yds of window glass to Wentworth Woodhouse in 1755. Brick, on a battered stone plinth, *c.* 65 ft (20 metres) high.

---

*ST PHILIP, Whitwood Lane, 1865 by *Joseph Clarke*, was demolished *c.* 1975.

5030

CAWOOD

A little town on the w bank of the Ouse at a cross-roads and river crossing, split into two parts by the episcopal castle and its grounds. Cawood was promoted by medieval archbishops of York as a port, with a canal (Bishop Dike) to quarries at Sherburn, a ferry, market and brickworks.

ALL SAINTS. On a low rise beside the river at the far E end of the town, its lively Perp tower draws the approaching visitor's eye. The tower is set forward at the w end of the s aisle and has polygonal clasping buttresses ending halfway up in a cresting; above that diagonal buttresses, then battlements and pinnacles. Ogee heads to three-light w window and belfry openings. Canopied niche with statue of the Virgin and Child by *Alan Durst*, 1961. The nave's unassuming w doorway is late Norman with two orders of thin shafts and waterleaf capitals. Arch with two slight chamfers. Transitional also the s doorway with a double-chamfered round arch. E.E. chancel – see the s doorway with roll moulding and the two small lancet windows. In the wall a blocked opening to a short s chapel, pulled down. The five-light E window is Perp, as, outwardly, are the two-bay N chapel and four-bay aisles with straight-headed three-light windows. Inside, however, the s arcade belongs with the chancel. Fragile quatrefoil piers with moulded capitals, double-chamfered arches. The chancel arch has semicircular responds with moulded capitals. The N chapel and N aisle arcades are C14 with the usual octagonal piers and double-chamfered arches. – STAINED GLASS. C12/C13 fragments in a chancel s window. – s aisle: first from E by *Ward & Hughes*, 1889; second from E by *Kempe*, 1898. – N aisle, third from E (war memorial) by *T. Curtis* for *Ward & Hughes*, 1924. – MONUMENTS. George Mountain, Archbishop of York, †1628. Aedicule with free-standing columns and a life-size frontal demi-figure in an arched niche. Obelisks flank an elaborate cartouche above.

CAWOOD CASTLE. The architectural history is lamentably opaque. Cawood manor is said to have been given to the See of York by Athelstan in 937 and seems to have been the archbishops' favoured country seat from the C12, successive prelates creating the magnificent fortified palace that was the scene of Cardinal Wolsey's arrest in 1530. Already in decline before Parliament ordered its dismantling in 1646, there was further demolition in 1750 (some fabric reused in the Gothick gatehouse and entrance front of the episcopal residence at Bishopthorpe (q.v.) in 1763–9). The remains became a farm and all that now survives is the GATEHOUSE and attached HALL range, restored in 1985–7 by the Landmark Trust. The impressive three-storey battlemented gatehouse of limestone ashlar was built by John Kempe, Archbishop 1426–52, after he became a cardinal in 1439. Its sw front, facing the large open

Castle Garth, has a broad segmental arch over separate pedestrian and carriage entrances with four-centred arches. Tierceron star-vault of one-and-a-half bays. First floor has deep band with finely carved heraldic panels including Kempe's wheatsheaves and cardinal's hat, and a rectangular bay window with three stepped lancet lights under a depressed arch. Decorative cresting. On the former inner courtyard side a wide four-centred entrance arch and above a pretty canted oriel with more heraldic panels and windows with minimum panel tracery. Two-storey C18 stair-turret attached. The altered and much-restored brick SE range, called the 'Banqueting Hall', is probably also by Kempe. Partly buttressed. Front has blind ground floor, and six cusped lancets in straight-headed ashlar surrounds to upper hall. Courtyard side has similar windows on both floors, the lower five windows flanked by doorways with four-centred arches.

Attached NW of gatehouse a farmhouse, 1690, with C18–C19 alterations. Four bays, with Doric porch; central rear stair-turret.

SWING BRIDGE, crossing the Ouse on the line of High Street. By *Robert Hodgson*, engineer, 1870–2. Five spans of segmental-arched iron girders with latticework. The larger central span opens.

THE TOWN has many attractive brick and pantile buildings and also shows several signs of planned development e.g. in the regular single-row block of WATER ROW, now a delightful terrace along the riverside path with some good Georgian houses and a former C18 SCHOOL, the house and large-windowed schoolroom together under a hipped roof.

Handsome C17 houses include YEW HOUSE, nearby in Thorpe Lane. Three-cell, lobby-entry plan with pedimented two-storey porch and pretty Dutch end gables. Diagonal chimneystacks at l. end. C18 sashes. Rear stair-turret. Also THE GRANGE, Wistowgate, to S. Three-cell, direct-entry plan and a rear r. wing preserving some C16 timber framing. The gable-end windows have diamond mullions and straight heads with unusual alternately raised voussoirs.

In Church End, single-storey ALMSHOUSES, 1839, with central pediment and labels over Tudor doorways and diamond-paned windows. Further on, the excellent GOOLE BANK FARMHOUSE, early–mid-C18. Six bays with distinctive segmental moulded pediments to ground-floor windows. C19 doorway, the original baffle-entry between third and fourth bays blocked. Gabled rear stair-turret.

CAWTHORNE

2000

ALL SAINTS. Extensively restored and rebuilt by *Bodley & Garner*, 1875–80 for Sir Walter Spencer Stanhope of Cannon

Hall (*see* below). Old material retained includes the two N arcade piers of *c.* 1200 and the late C13 N chapel, which has lancet windows on the N side and intersected tracery in the E window. Also the late Perp N aisle windows with square heads and pinnacled w tower. The rest C19, that is the extended chancel with Dec E window and wagon roof, large new S chapel (vestry), nave with panelled wagon roof, S aisle, lengthened to overlap the tower, and both porches. Bodley's rich decorative scheme partly survives. – REREDOS. Alabaster, by *Bodley*, carved by *Farmer & Brindley*. – ORGAN CASE. By *Bodley*. – CHANCEL SCREEN. Carved lower panels Perp, from a pew in the N chapel. – FONTS. One C11, square, with sixteen carved panels, the other Perp, octagonal. – PULPIT. Painted panels by Sir Walter's brother *J. R. Spencer Stanhope*; the PAINTED PANELS that originally flanked the altar are by their niece, *Evelyn De Morgan*. – SCULPTURE. Late Anglo-Saxon. Cross-head, in E wall of N chapel (outside). In the centre originally a human figure. In a reconstructed cross W of the church, another cross-head (originally with a figure) and two shaft fragments with extremely primitively placed and carved decoration. – STAINED GLASS. E window †1880 by *Burlison & Grylls*. – N chapel. E by *Powell & Sons*, 1880, designed by *Spencer Stanhope*. N wall E †1867 by *Morris & Co.*, designed by *Burne-Jones*. – S chapel. Three by *Wailes* (in the chancel before 1875) †1850, †1857 and †1860. – w window has three figures of the Cardinal Virtues, the colouring predominantly white and yellow. By *Burlison & Grylls*, designed by *Spencer Stanhope*, 1873. – MONUMENTS. N chapel. In recess with depressed late C13 arch, a chest tomb with quatrefoil decoration, Walter Spencer Stanhope †1821, by *T. W. Atkinson*. – Several fine monuments, especially John Spencer (N chapel) †1729 by *W. Green*, 1732, with one of his disconcerting details – here a serpent emerging from a skull's eye-socket, carrying a golden apple in its mouth (cf. Darton). Also John Spencer †1776 by *John Hickey*, with two female figures.

S of the church the former GRAMMAR SCHOOL, 1639.

As well as some good C17 cottages and farms, Cawthorne has attractive C19 houses and other buildings for the Cannon Hall estate (*see* below). Mostly in Vernacular Revival style, with some half-timbering, by the *Swifts*, local stonemasons for three generations. N of the church in Church Street, a remarkable CROSS, 1866, with base of writhing serpents and decorative interlace on the shaft with fantastic beasts. Downhill THE GOLDEN CROSS, timber-framed with stone and brick infill. Hall range mid-C16, w wing possibly C15. To E in Darton Road, METHODIST CHURCH, 1895–6, with decorative shaped gables. In Taylor Hill the small MUSEUM, 1887–9. Partly timber-framed, including a reused cruck-truss. Downhill, Nos. 2–4, the Swifts' house, 1880, with sculpted details, the garden wall almost opposite incorporating pictorial panels by *Samuel Swift*. In Malt Kiln Row, the Gothic PRIMARY SCHOOL, by *Benjamin Swift*, 1871–2. On the N side SOUTH

LODGE, refronted early 1820s. Continuous hoodmoulds and sharp attic gable.

CANNON HALL, ⅝ m. WNW. Now a museum. Built *c.* 1698–1704 for John Spencer, a prosperous gentry ironmaster, possibly by *John Etty* of York (the joiner was *William Thornton*). The house was then five bays wide, two-and-a-half storeys high. Buck (*c.* 1720) shows a S entrance, dripstones instead of the cornices above windows and plain, not balustraded, parapet. Quoins, interrupted by nibs of cornice at the angles (cf. Heath Hall). In 1764–7 *John Carr* added the three-bay wings, heightening them to two storeys in 1790–4. His N and S fronts are virtually identical. Also by him the kitchen and stables, *c.* 1778–86.

Inside, small OAK ROOM with C17 (and possibly earlier) panelling and carved chimneypiece dated 1697. The two original S BEDCHAMBERS also panelled, the finest with Doric pilasters, fluted to the fireplace, and simply stellar-pattern plaster ceiling. Marble fireplaces with bolection mouldings. Other interiors by *Carr*, including ENTRANCE HALL (N), 1778, with Neoclassical frieze (repeated in NE bedroom) and pillared opening to the excellent early C18 dog-leg staircase. Chimneypiece probably by *John Hickey*. DINING ROOM (E wing). Accomplished Rococo ceiling with musical instruments, by *James Henderson* of York, 1767. Fine marble chimneypiece with Narcissus relief. Other good chimneypieces in the DRAWING ROOM, which has screen of fluted Corinthian columns and Adamesque frieze, and in the LIBRARY and BEDCHAMBER (W wing). The last have splendid carved overmantels, pedimented and festooned. 'Mr Tweedale' was the joiner in 1766–7. At the NE, BALLROOM, by *Sir Walter Spencer Stanhope*, assisted by *George Swift* of Cawthorne, 1890–1. Oak-panelled Neo-Jacobean interior, its chimneypiece by *Bertini* of Florence inset with paintings by *J. R. Spencer Stanhope*, *c.* 1896.

PARK. Landscaped by *Richard Woods*, 1760–5. WALLED GARDEN and Ionic pilastered PINERY (now a shell) E of the house and lakes and cascades with PALLADIAN BRIDGE to S. NORTH LODGES (pair) and GOTHIC FOLLY (Tower Cottage), New Road, 1789, probably by *Carr*.

BARNBY HALL, ½ m. E. By *T. W. Atkinson*, *c.* 1820. Large. Gabled. Good group of C18 brick barns and other farm buildings to NE, one originally a single-aisled hall house, *c.* 1500.

BANKS HALL, 1 m. S. Early C18. Fine S and E fronts of seven bays, almost identical, with ashlar dressings. Hipped roofs. S doorway with segmental hood (now on porch). Essentially as shown in Samuel Buck's view of *c.* 1720, but now without attic windows. Earlier rear ranges. (Original panelled hall has a splendid dog-leg staircase by *Jonathan Godier*.)

WOOL GREAVES, 1½ m. SW. 1672. Unusually intact example of a typical local farm. Well-detailed house with cross-wing and attached aisled barn.

CHAPEL HADDLESEY

St John. Greyish-white brick nave with lancet windows and box pews, 1836; chancel rebuilt by *W. M. Teulon* in E.E. style, 1878; NW tower/porch with broach spire by *Demaine & Brierley*, 1890–1. – FONT. By *G. W. Milburn*, 1883; a copy of the C13 font at All Saints, Leicester. – STAINED GLASS. E window by *William Glasby*, 1924.

Former RECTORY and SCHOOL, ½ m. NW. By *Teulon* 1874–5. Red brick with big slate roofs and timber-gridded panelling to gables.

CHAPELTHORPE

Small oasis in Wakefield's southernmost suburbs.

St James. Rebuilt 1771–3, attributed to *Carr* on stylistic grounds. The round-arched nave windows were originally pointed (cf. St Helen, Denton (*West Riding North*), also attributed to *Carr*). W front with pediment, in the pediment a quatrefoil (for a clock). Two pedimented entrances in giant blank arches. Round open bell-lantern with Doric columns and ogee top. The chancel by *W. S. Barber* 1882–3 reuses the C18 Venetian E window. All reconstructed within the walls by *Alwyn Waite*, after a fire in 1951. Carefully re-created interior, the chancel with panelled barrel-vault, and four giant Doric columns defining the chapels. – STAINED GLASS. By *Abbott & Co.*, reusing their designs for destroyed windows.

Chapelthorpe Hall. Immediately W. Two main façades, the earlier of a C17 house, much altered, the later of a taller, N-facing addition of 1847 that more than doubled its size. The seven-bay S front originally had three gables. Ground-floor windows, sashed early in the C18, have architraves, friezes and cornices. The central Doric porch, the Doric pilasters applied to the r. return and the hipped roof are part of the later work. N façade has five wide bays, the middle one slightly projecting and pedimented. Quoined angles. Ground-floor openings with cornices on consoles. W service range partly demolished 1903. (Two S chambers with C18 decoration and fireplaces. Early Victorian interiors in classical style include S hall and top-lit staircase.)

Old Hall, No. 2 Stoney Lane, ¼ m. SSE. The three-bay centre is the timber-framed housebody of a C16 linear house of hearth-passage plan, later encased in stone. Low walls, windows for two floors. The housebody was heated by a fire-hood, and the early plan-form supports the case that it was originally open (as restored). In the earlier C17 the lower (E) end, including the passage area, was rebuilt in stone as a two-storey cross-wing with heated parlour. The doorway l. of the parlour's five-light window replaced the passage entry. Matching w cross-wing is C19.

CHAPELTOWN

3090

Large village that developed with the former Thorncliffe mines, iron works and Izal chemical works of Newton Chambers & Co., founded 1793.

ST JOHN (now offices). By *Weightman & Hadfield*, 1859–60. Plain Gothic style; Geometric tracery. Porch in SW tower with broach spire with lucarnes. Steep, separate roofs. N aisle and chancel extension by *W.J. Sykes* of Hoyland, 1899–1901. S chapel dem. but REREDOS, other FITTINGS and STAINED GLASS retained. (Two W windows by *Francis Spear*, 1956 and 1959.)

    CHURCH SCHOOL (former), Loundside, facing the church. By *J.G. Weightman*, 1844–5.

MOUNT PLEASANT METHODIST CHURCH (Wesleyan; now house). By *Wilson & Willcox*, 1863–6. On the hill next to St John's, its prominent E tower has balustraded parapet, gargoyles and elaborate pinnacles, rivalling the Anglicans' spire.

FREEMAN HOSPITAL (now offices), Burncross Road. 1837. Row of six almshouses with small Reading Room in the centre with Gothic windows and high embattled parapet.

CHAMBERS NEWTON MEMORIAL HALL, Cowley Lane. By *Barry Parker*, 1923. Striking symmetrical composition, with big hipped roofs of red tiles. Stone hall has vertical window to tall gabled front. Columned entrance between set-forward single-storey wings, the effect spoilt by rendered additions.

COWLEY MANOR, Cowley Lane. Early C18. Pedimented doorway to symmetrical five-bay S front. Two-light windows with flat-faced mullions and surrounds; on both floors the lintels extend as a continuous band.

HOUSLEY HALL, Housley Lane. C15 core, remodelled in C18. U-plan. Symmetrical front. Ashlar centre of two bays, the entrance with consoled cornice. Two-bay cross-wings, of coursed rubble with quoins, have moulded architraves to front windows. (Internal C15 timber framing includes exposed crown-post roof trusses.)

(BARNES HALL, Bracken Hill. Rebuilt 1826. Large, handsome house of five bays; late C19 extension, in keeping. Good FARM BUILDINGS, grouped to N, include C16 or C17 timber-framed threshing barn, two-storey dovecote, 1740, and barn,

1824, being converted as a co-housing project at the time of writing.)

CHEVET HALL *see* NEWMILLERDAM

CHURCH FENTON

St Mary. Magnesian limestone. Cruciform with a low narrow s aisle, all essentially E.E., but the crossing tower Perp, broad and unbuttressed. Details from the C13 are the lancet windows in the transepts and the aisle – including a stepped group of three in the N transept end and a pair under a quatrefoil (i.e. forming plate tracery) on the s transept w side – and the shallow clasping buttresses at the transept corners. Other windows Dec and Perp, Dec in particular the E window and the s transept s window, both of four lights, the former with boldly flowing tracery, the latter reticulated: also the two-light window in the w gable. Perp e.g. the straight-headed windows to both sides of the chancel, those on the s side evidently done as part of a complete rebuilding of that wall. Inside, the tower is supported by powerful chamfered Perp crossing piers without capitals; and the aisle arcade was also rebuilt, presumably at the same time, in a curious way. The two w bays are entirely Perp, then there is a short stretch of wall, and then one-and-a-half bays – the half-bay next to the crossing pier – with a circular C13 pier reused. In the s transept a Dec ogee-headed tomb-recess, and within the reveal of the plate-traceried window two stiff-leaf corbels. Roofs, shallow s porch and s doorway from the restoration of 1844 by *G. Fowler Jones*. – In the N transept a SCREEN with a little panel tracery, heavily restored in 1844. – STAINED GLASS. Includes C14 fragments in the tracery of the E window and the s transept SE window. – MONUMENT. Recumbent effigy of a lady, early C14, with hands joined in prayer, on a low C19 base.

Two timber-framed houses partly preserved under later casings of stone, brick and render. N of the church CHURCH HOUSE, probably C16, originally aisled, with partially moulded aisle plate, straight braces and common rafter roof. Later wing to rear. Further NE, in Main Street, the OLD VICARAGE, a long low range of which the core is a two-bay open-hall, reinstated 1982, perhaps of C14 date, the w end the stump of a parlour cross-wing, probably C16 but truncated at both ends and re-roofed, and the E part probably C17. Posts, tie-beams and some close studding remain.

LEEDS EAST AIRPORT. Formerly RAF CHURCH FENTON. Fighter station constructed 1936–9 and further developed in 1940–1. Of the first phase two standardized brick-built hangars, of the second the concrete runways – the original ones were grass – and various defensive features: earthen fighter pens dispersed round the perimeter, an underground command post, a pillbox.

CLAYTON WEST

ALL SAINTS. By *Edward Hughes*, 1871–5. – STAINED GLASS. Twelve windows by *Kempe*, 1891–1905. – MONUMENT. Captain Charles Wintour †1916 at Battle of Jutland. Carved oak, by *Sir Charles Allom*, 1919. Trophies flank sarcophagus with relief of HMS *Tipperary*.

UNITED REFORMED CHURCH (Congregational), Church Lane. By *Pritchett & Son* 1864–6.

CLECKHEATON

Small town at the head of the Spen valley. In addition to its woollen industry, by the 1890s Cleckheaton was the world's principal producer of card clothing, leather sheets with wire teeth to disentangle wool before spinning. The Lancashire and Yorkshire Railway opened on the W side of the town in 1847–8, the London and North Western line on the E in 1900; they closed in stages from 1953.

CHURCHES AND PUBLIC BUILDINGS

ST JOHN THE EVANGELIST. All that survives of the Commissioners' church by *Peter Atkinson Jun.*, built 1830–2, is the narrow W tower with short gabled buttresses, its conical-capped pinnacles removed *c.* 1957. Two-bay chancel of 1864–5, with simple Geometric tracery, begun by *Mallinson & Healey*, completed by *Healey & Healey*. The nave was entirely rebuilt, with a clerestory and aisles with five-bay arcades, by *W.S. Barber* in 1886–8. – REREDOS. Caen stone, carved to *Barber*'s design, 1882. – CHANCEL SCREEN and PULPIT by *Jackson* of Coley, 1910. – STAINED GLASS. E window 1865 by *Hughes*, several others by *Ward & Hughes*, 1890s. – S aisle third from E by *Mayer & Co.*, 1887.

WHITECHAPEL CHURCH, Whitechapel Road. Of Norman origin, as a chapel of ease to Birstall (q.v.). Rebuilt 1820–1 by *John Casson* and restored by *W.H. Howorth* of Cleckheaton, 1887–8. Single-cell, six bays. Lancets with Y-tracery; E window with intersected tracery. Corbelled-out polygonal W bell-turret with spirelet. (W gallery. Barrel-vault with exposed roof trusses by *Sir Charles Nicholson*, 1934. – FONT. *c.* 1100, of tub shape, tapering slightly upwards, not downwards. Intersected arches and between them various elementary motifs of decoration, including human faces and a sheila-na-gig. Cable moulding at the top. – STAINED GLASS. E and W windows by *Booer* of Leeds, 1877.)

ST LUKE, Moorbottom. By *Medland Taylor*, 1887–9. Gothic Revival style. An odd composition of tall parts – nave with low clerestory and lean-to aisles, tower with broach spire forming SW porch, chancel with transeptal S vestry and organ chamber. Baptistery at the W end of the nave in a triangular apse. Simple Dec tracery.

ST PHILIP AND ST JAMES, Scholes. By *T.H. & F. Healey*, 1876–7. Four-bay nave with paired lancets; sexfoil window in W gable. Lower chancel. Intended spire added 1970 to a new design; four-sided, tall and thin, in steel and fibreglass.

68 PROVIDENCE CONGREGATIONAL CHURCH (former), Bradford Road. Rebuilt by *Lockwood & Mawson*, 1857–9. Amazingly ostentatious for Nonconformists; and one of the county's most powerful expressions of C19 dissent. Monumental portico front with giant Corinthian columns carrying five arches. Vermiculated rustication to frieze with big console brackets supporting modillioned pediment. In the tympanum an inscribed roundel with exuberant frame of oak and palm leaves. More wild vermiculation to rusticated angle pilasters and to the voussoirs of three central entrances. Five round-arched windows above, with Corinthian pilasters to jambs. Plainer nine-bay returns have heavily bracketed eaves and round-arched upper windows. Sunday School in semi-basement on the slope; additional classrooms etc. to rear 1886. (The splendid interior, now an Indian restaurant, originally seated 1,500, and has a horseshoe gallery on fluted cast-iron columns, a rostrum pulpit and organ gallery in a coffer-roofed apse at the end.)

CEMETERY CHAPEL, Whitcliffe Road. 1853. Small. Plain. Tetrastyle prostyle portico with Doric columns. Three bays deep, with round-arched windows and pilasters. Unused at the time of writing.

TOWN HALL, Bradford Road. By *Mawson & Hudson*, 1890–2. Asymmetrical, gabled front with a tower, in the style of Mountford and Collcutt. Mullioned-and-transomed oriel window in l. gabled bay; small balcony to shaped gable on the r. Good carved panels to all four bays, with strapwork, masks, griffins and other Renaissance decoration. Tower has broad external staircase to first-floor entrance, and gabled arcades against pyramidal roof finished with cupola. (Council chamber and reception rooms on first floor. In upper part of projecting rear range a large public hall. Proscenium-arch stage, rear gallery and narrow side galleries with four-bay arcades. Coved ceiling with decorative plasterwork.)

WHITCLIFFE MOUNT SCHOOL, Turnsteads Avenue. By *W.H. Thorp*, 1908–10, as a secondary and technical school. Long symmetrical two-storey front with gables and mullioned-and-transomed windows. Pretty timber clock turret with bell cupola. Main entrance in three-bay centre with Doric-columned loggia; pedimented entrances for girls and boys in end bays. Large additions to rear, mainly 1958 by *Abbey & Hanson*, and 1973. Edwardian range threatened with demolition at time of writing.

PUBLIC LIBRARY, Whitcliffe Road. By *J. G. Castle*, 1929–30. Given by the Mowat family, card-clothing manufacturers. Dignified single-storey stripped classical composition, the low roofs almost hidden by deep plain parapets. Centre block with tetrastyle portico *in antis*. Well-preserved interior, with some Art Deco details, has glazed dome to central space, and oak panelling and other fittings.

WAR MEMORIAL, King Edward VII Memorial Park, Greenside. 1922, by *George Frampton*. Magnificent Portland stone plinth with segmental pediments supporting finely sculpted seated male and female figures, who sit against a plinth carrying shields with lowered flags.*

VIADUCT, Station Road. *c.* 1899. Road viaduct, *c.* 150 yds (137 metres) long, built across the little river valley by the London and North Western Railway to give direct access to their Spen Bank station. Stone parapets to deck on six longitudinal brick jack arches with iron beams, the deck supported by twelve thin, insubstantial-looking, iron lattice piers carrying big transverse beams.

In the TOWN there is hardly enough for a perambulation. Starting from the park, narrow NORTHGATE is the modest main shopping street. First, BARCLAYS BANK (formerly Lancashire & Yorkshire Bank) by *W. H. Howorth*, 1898, with spired corner oriel, big transomed windows and wavy parapet with ball finials. On the l., set back, the former LIBERAL CLUB, 1897, by *Reuben Castle* of Cleckheaton. Three bays, the gabled centre flanked by decoratively topped pilasters and with balcony over arched entrance. Down Albion Street the former POST OFFICE by *Howorth & Howorth*, 1908. Baroque details, including segmental and shaped hoodmoulds with giant keystones. On the corners flanking the Town Hall two more banks. To the l., the HSBC by *Howorth*, 1890–1, in Northern Renaissance style. The canted corner and the end bays of the matching fronts have pedimented blind dormers with sculpted panels. Swan-neck pediments to upper windows. To the r. the small plain classical YORKSHIRE BANK, *c.* 1910, with tall round-arched windows and balustraded parapet.

Prominent on the W hillside, the four-storey PROSPECT MILLS, 1907, which made card clothing, is one of the largest surviving mills.

---

*The pompous Central Methodist Church, by *Reuben Castle*, 1875–9, that overlooked the park, was demolished in 1961.

CLIFTON

Set along the N ridge high above the Calder valley but too over-grown by housing in the late C20 to be recognized as the rural oasis described by Pevsner.

ST JOHN THE EVANGELIST, Towngate. 1859–60 by *Mallinson & Healey*. Small, cruciform, but with a funny tower with spirelet attached to the S transept. Style of 1300. – STAINED GLASS. Nave S side E by *Hardman*, 1870.

METHODIST CHURCH, Towngate. 1874–5 by *R.F. Rogerson*.

HIGHLEY HALL, Highley Hall Croft. Part of an early C17 house carefully remodelled in vernacular style as two cottages *c.* 1875. It is a puzzle. Symmetrical front, the r. porch with original lintel dated 1632. The gabled l. return has double-chamfered mullioned windows, twelve lights below, ten above, but both are offset. Are they *in situ*? Large former barn attached, partly aisled on SE side.

COLEY

ST JOHN THE BAPTIST, Coley Road. By *William Bradley* of Halifax, 1816–18, restored 1902 by *Hodgson Fowler*. A remark-ably serious design for its date. Prominently placed W tower with thin octagonal buttresses, short chancel. Windows of lancet character with intersected tracery above broad transoms for former galleries. Tall arcades with slender octagonal wooden columns. – VESTRY SCREEN. By the *Jacksons* of Coley, 1927 and 1951. – STAINED GLASS. By *Morris & Co.* the chancel E, N and S *c.* 1940, nave S third from E (upper) 1914, and nave N fourth from E (upper) *c.* 1940. Nave S second from E by *Kayll & Co.*

COLEY HALL, Coley Hall Lane. Picturesque if somewhat rustic gateway dated 1649. Segmental arch, openwork gable. Decora-tion with heads and animals which, in a church, one might easily call Norman. Beyond the gateway the S front, and the rooms behind it, handsomely Georgianized *c.* 1730. Nine bays, two storeys. The C17 back still with gables and seven-light transomed windows. (Reused doorway dated 1692 from demolished Langley House, Hipperholme, in C20 porch on E side.)

At CINDERHILLS, Denholme Gate Road, a rare late C15 timber-framed aisled hall survives as a cottage. C17 aisled barn attached.

No village, but going S and SE of the church are several good earlier C17 houses displaying a variety of common features in their gable and window treatments. Of special interest is WYNTEREDGE HALL, off Northedge Lane, *c.* 1642 with C19 alterations, which has a chamber with plaster overmantel – two

shields under arches and frieze of griffins and wreaths, and a
nice mid-C18 staircase.

At NORWOOD GREEN, 1 m. E, in Rookes Lane, two houses of
note: UPPER ROOKES. Dated 1589. Sensitively restored, with
added rear wing, by *G.R. Oddy*, 1929. Front with three gables,
the middle one smaller and steeper than the others. Hall with
eight-light window. ROOKES HALL is a large double pile.
Two-storey porch, the upper floor with sundial dated 1638
flanked by odd little fat columns or balusters. Small oriel in
angle to r. Parlour has sixteen-light mullioned-and-transomed
window (similar hall window altered). C18 textile warehouse
added to service end S of the through passage.

COLTON

COLTON LODGE. Mid-C18, perhaps built as a hunting lodge
– either by Sir Peter Leicester of Tabley Hall, Cheshire, who
sold the property in 1764 (a free-standing pigeon cote is dated
1748), or by his successor Bacon Morritt of Cawood. Brick,
three storeys. S front of six irregular bays, N with a large round-
headed staircase window in the middle and pedimented
entrance to the r.

STEETON HALL, ½ m. SW. Of the late C15 mansion of the Fairfaxes, a courtyard building with a gatehouse, virtually all that
remains is a two-storey range in limestone ashlar, running E–W.
Mullioned-and-transomed windows to front and back – presumably part of a phase of alterations of the late C16 – diagonal
buttresses with set-offs at the W end, Tudor-arched doorway.
(Also at right angles to this a low wall, apparently the residue
of another range, with a re-set C13 two-centre-headed doorway
reputed to be from a manorial chapel which was demolished
by 1873.)

CONISBROUGH

A small town set high above the Don valley on a spur of a Magnesian limestone ridge. To the NE where the river cuts through a
narrow gorge there are extensive quarries; N of the river mines
operated from the later C19 to the 1980s. Conisbrough means
'the defended *burh* of the King'; the name is recorded before
Harold Godwinson, its last Anglo-Saxon lord, became King. The
town has two of the West Riding's most significant medieval
buildings. The parish church is probably of C8 origin and may
have been an Anglo-Saxon minster. It and its many daughter
churches were given to Lewes Priory in the late C11. The Norman
castle with its imperious keep dominates the NE end of the town

and was celebrated, anachronistically, by Sir Walter Scott in
Ivanhoe as Athelstan's ancient Saxon fortress. The streets of Conisbrough are placed partly on the eminence around the church
and partly on the steep slopes in the dip between church and
castle and to the E. The historic core suffered extensive C20
demolition.

ST PETER. The noble exterior is mainly Perp, disguising internal
evidence of the nave and w tower or porch of the substantial
Anglo-Saxon church. This evidence includes the massive side-
alternate quoins at the NW and SW angles of the nave, the sills
and jambs of two blocked windows in the N wall of the nave,
and the E jamb of another on the S side. The nave's dimensions
(44 ft by 17 ft 4 in. (13.4 by 5.28 metres)) are very similar to
those of Ledsham church (q.v.). Above the tower's Norman N
and S arches are two small windows of cruder workmanship,
possibly C10 or early C11. Their jambs cut through a plain
internal string course perhaps indicating the heightening of an
earlier porch into a tower (cf. Ledsham).

In the C12 the chancel was altered or rebuilt and N and S
aisles made. The chancel arch ought perhaps to come first. It
need not be later than the mid C12 and although probably
interfered with in an over-zealous restoration by *J.M. Teale* in
1866–7 has features paralleled elsewhere (cf. Campsall).
Imposts with one engaged shaft in the w angles. Scallop capitals with decorative semicircles in low relief; lozenge bands on
the imposts. Both aisle arcades are of three bays, with low
circular piers, capitals with uncommonly substantial decoration, square abaci and unmoulded arches. The N arches are
round, the w one wider and higher; the S arches are pointed
and even, and perhaps a little later. The decoration of the
capitals is clearly not done by one man. The first on the N side
is conventionally multi-scalloped, the second has an outstanding display of sculptural artistry, almost unmatched in the
region (cf. the castle (below) and Selby Abbey). Richly carved
foliage, deeply undercut and in places free-standing, entwined
with figures (those at the angles unfortunately defaced). On
the S side the first capital has bold waterleaf, the second rather
solid foliage and crockets or volutes at the corners. The aisles
embrace the w tower, with plain round arches inserted to N
and S. Two small Norman windows in the N aisle were reused
when it was widened in 1866–7.

All that seems consistent with a date *c.* 1175–1200. Generally
speaking the style up to this moment is that of the castle keep
(*see* below). It would be surprising if they did not have features
in common. Late C12 S doorway, round-arched with renewed
shafts with crocket capitals, one keeled roll moulding in the
arch, and chevron. E.E. hoodmould with dogtooth. The S
porch entry would be in harmony with this phase or only
slightly later (dogtooth and billet), but was so renewed in
1913–14 that it can no longer be trusted.

Of the early C14 only a few scattered contributions: the
chancel N doorway (double-quadrant moulding), and the S

aisle E window (flowing tracery). It is always difficult to date straight-headed windows whose lights end in shouldered lintels. Such are those of the S aisle S wall. Are they Dec too? Later C15 tower top with two tall transomed two-light bell-openings. The arches below the transoms are blank. Decorative frieze above and then battlements and pinnacles. Perp too the clerestory of tall three-light windows with two-centred arches. Much later came the N chapel, built as an organ chamber in 1866–7 and converted by *G. G. Pace* in 1953, and the NE vestry by *J. D. Webster*, 1913–14.

FURNISHINGS. N chapel ALTAR. Medieval, brought from the castle *c.* 1953. – FONT. Perp. Octagonal on a square pillar with shafts at the angles. Carvings of the Resurrection and Christ enthroned in the E and W panels, shields in quatrefoils in the others. – PILLAR PISCINA. Beside the N aisle E arch. Square bowl on an octagonal shaft with angle volutes. Later C12 or a C19 copy? Above it a SQUINT aligned on the E end of the earlier shorter chancel. – STAINED GLASS. Chancel S, westernmost, has a jumble of late C15 glass including two good heads. E window by *H. Hughes*, 1866. Chancel S, easternmost, by *Alan Younger*, 1983. Chancel N 1943, and S aisle easternmost 1928, both by *Powell & Sons*. N aisle W by *Harry Harvey*, 1966. – SCULPTURE. E wall inside porch. Worn slab with small seated figure set in a niche with arched top. Probably C12, possibly Romano-British. Expert opinion is divided. – S aisle. Fragment of a cross-shaft with interlace; probably C10.

MONUMENTS. A most remarkable memorial with exceptional Romanesque carving, dated to *c.* 1140–60, and possibly for William de Warenne, 3rd Earl of Surrey †1147. Solid coffin-shaped stone with coped top. It is closely decorated with foliage, scrolls, figures and scenes and is unique for its date in this respect. On the front face are a standing bishop with crosier and a soldier fighting a big dragon trampling on a body. The top has on its front two knights on horseback in combat and animals in medallions, and on its back signs of the zodiac (Pisces, Sagittarius) and Adam and Eve with the serpent in the tree. – Chamfered coffin-lid with two birds, perhaps ravens, carved in unusually high relief, one much more complete. The date uncertain but possibly as early as the C12. – Nicholas Bosvile †1523. Restored tomb-recess with large finial to ogee arch. – Bosvile family (incomplete). Cartouche with flowery frame and on top a little trumpeting angel perched on a skull. Hunter dates it 1793.

75 yds NW is a medieval WELL-HEAD of limestone ashlar. Rectangular, with steeply gabled top. A rare survival.

CASTLE

The castle's position above the River Don is magnificent, and the keep is unsurpassed in England, in the beauty of its geometrical simplicity and of its large ashlar facing. There is enough left of the walls and towers of the inner bailey to make the castle the varied and composite picture of medieval might that inspired

Scott. Initially, however, the prominent but rather unstable limestone knoll was carved into a very substantial earthwork castle.
The summit was defended by a large bank (revealed in excavation), probably forming a ringwork; there certainly seems to have
been a Saxon phase, and a prehistoric predecessor (a hillfort) is
very plausible. The line of the bank was later followed by the
curtain wall. The interior was later made level, probably in the
C13. The whole was strengthened by a massive external ditch,
especially impressive on the s where a natural counterscarp bank
provided extra protection (and economy of effort). On the N, the
ditch is less impressive, little more than a terrace cutting through
the rock of the steep slope down to the Don; here the counterscarp bank is a minor affair. On the w, a small outer bailey.

At the Conquest, Conisbrough was presented to William
Warenne, subsequently 1st Earl of Surrey. As well as his southern
territories centred on Reigate, Lewes and Castle Acre, the Conqueror gave Warenne various important estates in Yorkshire,
including Conisbrough, Sandal (q.v.) and Wakefield. The C11
structures here, presumably of timber, were replaced by the
present buildings and, in so far as they were built by a half-
brother of Henry II, they are royal. He was Hamelin Plantagenet
(†1202), who obtained Conisbrough in 1163 through his marriage to Isobel, daughter and heiress of the 3rd Earl. Remarkably,
he built on his lands in Normandy a keep at Mortemer which is
identical in plan with that at Conisbrough. Neither is dated with
certainty and it is debatable which was first. Conisbrough can be
assigned to c. 1180–1200. It was at the forefront in its design,
technology and decorative fashion.

The inner bailey is enclosed by a battered wall of coursed rubble,
30 to 35 ft tall, with slender solid towers of D-shaped plan,
among the earliest in the country. The bailey is reached
through an ingenious barbican, i.e. a passage between high
walls which turns first 45 degrees to the r., and then 90 degrees
to the l. to face the gateway. The wall and barbican are probably slightly later than the keep, perhaps nearer c. 1200. The
towered gateway, which was altered c. 1300, has collapsed
forward into the inner ditch of the castle's extensive surrounding earthworks.

The KEEP is about 90 ft (28 metres) tall and circular, with
six mighty buttresses rising as turrets. The circular or polygonal shape of keeps in preference to the rectangular had been
introduced in France c. 1100 (e.g. Chateau-sur-Epte, Houdan)
and in England at Orford, built by Henry II 1165–73 (circular
inside, polygonal outside). It had obvious advantages, especially in avoiding those dangerous right angles at which sapping
and mining promised success. In addition, the buttresses at
Conisbrough allowed an unimpeded flanking watch from their
embattled top platforms over the stretches of wall between
them. Moreover, the foot of the keep has an uncommonly
strong batter, its diameter reducing from 66 ft at ground to
52 ft at first-floor level. In plan the buttresses taper towards

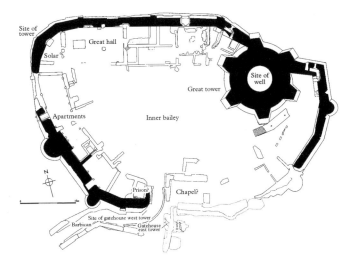

Conisbrough Castle.
Block plan

the outside. Their bases are battered too but appear more slender than they are, as the face of alternate courses of the sides slopes inwards and the stones below have a top chamfer – a remarkable aesthetic (and it can only be aesthetic) refinement. Again, the purity of the keep's form is not compromised by any forebuilding.

The keep has four floors, each a single room. Its only entrance, facing SE, is on the first floor, 20 ft (6 metres) above ground, and reached by a modern staircase replicating the original stone staircase, which had a drawbridge before the doorway. The doorway, and the window of the second-floor room, are placed symmetrically in the centre of the wall between the flanking buttresses. The doorway has a joggled lintel with relieving arch, and a very slight stopped chamfer. A tunnel-vaulted passage leads to the windowless first-floor room. Its floor is formed by the stone vault of the ground floor, a central circular aperture providing the only access, by way of a ladder, to the lower level. This has a well in the middle. To the r. of the passage is the first of the gently curving staircases set within the thickness of the walls. These are very thick (15 ft on the first floor) and the staircases accordingly by no means narrow (c. 4 ft), with steps whose height is easy on the legs.

The second floor was Earl Hamelin's principal chamber and was comfortably appointed. Its wooden floor, that of the chamber above, and the parapet walkway around a new conical timber roof were restored in 1994–5. The floor timbers are supported on a continuous ledge around the inner face of the ashlar walls, so each room is slightly larger than the one below. This construction had the advantage that in a fire the burning timber would cause less damage to the stonework than beams inserted in wall-sockets. Two-light window in a recess with stone seats and nearly opposite this a big hooded fireplace. This and the smaller one in the room above are the earliest known examples of hooded fireplaces. Their flues rise together in the wall straight to the top of the keep. Hood has joggled lintel on triple clustered shafts. Stylized leaf capitals (worn). Close to the fireplace a plain lavabo, and to the l. of the window recess a passage leading to a garderobe. The staircase, for reasons of defence, continues upwards opposite the entry from the lower staircase. The third floor contains the private chamber and the Chapel, which is ingeniously built within the wall and E buttress. The fireplace has triple shafts supporting the hood, the capitals are finely carved with undercutting and free-standing foliage sprigs (cf. NW capital in church). To the r. another lavabo, with trefoiled head. One-light window to the SW. The CHAPEL is opposite the fireplace, close to the entrance. Its tiny space is an irregular elongated hexagon, divided into two rib-vaulted bays. It has the keep's best display of decoration, some of it anticipating English Gothic. The diagonal ribs have quadrant chamfers and an applied demi-roll. In the nave SE rib a single dogtooth star. The transverse arch has a demi-roll between chevron mouldings. Foliate decoration on the capitals, including some waterleaf. Bosses in the vault. At the E end a tiny window under an arch with small shafts and chevron surround. To the l. and r. in the chancel quatrefoil windows (the latest-looking motif), decorated outside with pellets. Two separate piscinas with trefoiled heads. Small VESTRY to the N in the thickness of the wall. It has a trefoil-headed aumbry.

Access to the top floor from a doorway between lavabo and chapel. Before the stairs a passage leads to a garderobe corbelled out on a squinch-like arch to the NE. The top floor accommodated a much smaller guardroom and, surrounding it, the rampart walk. In three buttresses are cisterns and an oven; in the buttress above the Chapel is what was possibly a dovecote.

The remains in the inner bailey now have little to offer the architectural historian, being little more than the confusing footings of buildings mostly constructed against the walls. Some are perhaps post-medieval. The castle's single-aisled Hall was in the NW corner, the kitchen E of it. The private apartments were along the SW curtain wall, and what was probably the (C13?) chapel was immediately E of the gateway. It seems that little building work or repair was done after 1402 and a survey of 1537–8, when the castle belonged to the Crown, records *inter alia* that the curtain wall between gateway and keep had already fallen and one floor in the keep was gone. This made the castle unusable in the Civil War and further demolition after it unnecessary, allowing the keep and remaining inner bailey wall to stand preserved. Some landscaping took place in the C18 and C19.

WAR MEMORIAL. 350 yds E in Coronation Park. *c.* 1920. Square
column with statue of infantryman by *Tyas & Guest*, Swinton.
RED LION, Sheffield Road, ¼ m. S. Handsome turnpike inn,
c. 1800. Three-storey pedimented centre with one-bay single-
storey wings under half-pediments (cf. Midhopestones).
RAILWAY VIADUCT, ⅞ m. NE. Now part of a cycle path. 1906–7.
528 yds (477 metres) long. Designed by *Mr Kaye* of Leeds for
the Dearne Valley Railway. Twenty-one brick arches cross the
Don gorge, with a lattice-steel girder span over the river.

COPLEY

0020

In 1844 Colonel Edward Akroyd bought an unused mill beside
the Calder, S of Halifax, rebuilding it on a larger scale in
1846–7. The model industrial settlement which followed in
1849–53 (112 back-to-back cottages in three terraces) therefore
not only antedates the more famous Saltaire (*West Riding
North*) but is a precursor to Akroydon itself (*see* Halifax,
p. 283). There was a SCHOOL (1849; dem. 1980), LIBRARY
(1850, also dem.), allotments and a canteen serving dinners of
meat and potatoes. Finally, Akroyd paid much of the cost of a
church. The architect of all but the last is unknown. The mill
was demolished in 1974.

The first houses of 1849, in CALDER TERRACE (Nos. 25–42)
and ST STEPHEN'S STREET (Nos. 43–60), are in a picturesque
Pennine Vernacular style with small gables and mullioned
windows. They have two bedrooms, and originally had privies
in the front gardens. At the ends are projecting gabled cross-
wings to accommodate shops. Rents proved unacceptably high
however and the next two terraces, between ST STEPHEN'S
STREET and RAILWAY TERRACE were built more cheaply,
more plainly and smaller. Responding to criticism of the back-
to-backs in *The Builder*, 1863, there are two terraces of through-
houses built *c.* 1865 at the NW end of these streets. Yet they are
one room deep and with windowless rear elevations, as if a row
of back-to-backs had simply been split apart.

W of the railway embankment behind Akroyd's terraces,
COPLEY BRIDGE by *George Stephenson*, *c.* 1840, and N of that
the twenty-three-arched COPLEY VIADUCT, *c.* 1851.

SE of the houses, crossing the Calder, the former TOLL
BRIDGE, 1831, and adjacent octagonal-ended toll cottage,
c. 1833. This leads to the church of ST STEPHEN, 1861–5 by
W. H. Crossland, which stands against the wooded hillside.
Large and dignified, in Dec style with a decidedly French
flavour. Steeply pitched roof with only a bellcote between
nave and chancel. Five-bay nave with aisles and clerestory,
seven-sided chancel. Lancet windows, except in the aisles,
which have a row of cinquefoils, three per bay. Gabled porch
in W bay of N aisle. This side, facing the village, is the more
richly decorated. Excellent High Victorian INTERIOR, with

good-quality carving and fittings, though little of the original extensive PAINTED DECORATION by *Clayton & Bell* survives. One panel remains in the chancel vault, four figures on the N wall; the nave's scissor-braced roof and the aisles have stencilling. Unconventionally, the nave arcades are different – on the N round pillars and moulded arches, on the S big square piers formed with eight clustered shafts have square abaci supporting plain arches. REREDOS and PULPIT of Caen stone with mosaic panels by *Heaton, Butler & Bayne*. – STAINED GLASS. All by *Hardman*.

5040

COPMANTHORPE

St GILES. A chapel of ease of St Mary Bishophill Junior, York, until 1844. Small C12 single cell (cf. Askham Bryan and Askham Richard, *West Riding North*), with Norman-style chancel added 1889 by *C. Hodgson Fowler*. Rendered. W doorway with nook-shafts and scalloped capitals (W porch 1977), W bellcote, and stepped E windows reinstated in the new E end; but the other details, apart from a slit window on the S side, evidently from a previous C19 phase. Attached to the N a parish hall, 1992 by *R. G. Sims*, with arches opening into the church. – Reused C17 panelling round the sanctuary, and reused C18 ALTAR RAIL. – STAINED GLASS. E windows by *Kempe*, 1875.
MANOR FARMHOUSE, Main Street. Three-bay rendered front, with superimposed brick pilasters and other mouldings of later C17 character detectable under the render (cf. Bishopthorpe Palace and Manor Farm, Acaster Selby). Hipped roof and staircase with turned balusters consistent with that date. But inside there is also a timber-framed wall, and panelling and a door of early C17 origin; and the rear wing is of *c.* 1600, with narrow bricks and a pair of diamond-shaped chimneystacks.

6020

COWICK

HOLY TRINITY, East Cowick. By *Butterfield* for William Dawnay, 7th Viscount Downe, 1853–4 (cf. Hensall and Pollington). The form of the thin W tower must be drawn directly from St Mary, Lindisfarne, Northumberland, that is rising sheer on two big buttresses that tightly embrace the high W window in a deep stepped arch, and creating, with shorter buttresses beyond the narrow outer windows, a dramatic sense of strength and shadow (cf. also Cowthorpe, *West Riding North*). Plate-traceried belfry openings; short pyramidal spire. Five-bay nave arcades with chamfered and moulded arches dying into stout square ashlar piers. High arch-braced collared roof. Altered fittings include carved oak panelling to chancel, 1910. – Octagonal oak PULPIT with tester. – Big stone FONT, given by Lady Downe. Tapering sides with blind arcading. – *Minton* FLOOR TILES – STAINED GLASS. E and W windows by *Preedy*, 1854. S aisle: first two from E by *Powell Bros*, 1895; westernmost by *Powell & Sons*, 1908.

Butterfield's VICARAGE (former), S across the road, is similarly earnest, but far from dull. His SCHOOL, E of the church, is more altered and extended.

COWICK HALL (Croda International plc), ¼ m. SW. One of the most ambitious later C17 houses in Yorkshire, originally built *c.* 1670 by Sir John Dawnay, 1st Viscount Downe, to replace a medieval house. Restored from 1956 as offices, following use as a farm building. Two storeys with basement. Nine bays, with giant pilasters all round, Ionic on the N entrance front, Doric towards the garden and on the returns. Hipped roof with dormers. Comparison with Buck's view *c.* 1720, however, reveals that its fashionable post-Restoration appearance is misleading, for this is largely *James Paine*'s work for the 3rd Viscount Downe in 1752–60. He remodelled the front in ashlar, rusticating the basement, modifying the pilasters and replacing the enriched central bay (cf. e.g. late C17 Warmsworth Hall q.v.) with the large pedimented porch on Ionic columns in an elliptical-arched recess. Most dramatically he added, above the deep bracketed cornice, the steep three-bay pediment of convincingly C17 appearance, and flanking balustrades instead of the original rooftop one. The architraves to the sashes (originally cross-windows), with segmental pediments to alternate ground-floor bays, are more Palladian and would have been in keeping with *Paine*'s proposed wings, unexecuted due to Lord Downe's untimely death.

Changes to the S front, made with a lighter touch, are probably *Joseph Bonomi*'s work for the 5th Viscount in 1792–*c.* 1808; his interior modifications, less extensive than originally envisaged, were largely lost in radical alterations following the Hall's sale in 1869. These demolished an E wing of *c.* 1700 and created the present plan with central one-bay N and S entrance halls and more, smaller, rooms off a broad E–W hall and first-floor corridor with impressive flying staircases at each end. The W one is Bonomi's SW imperial staircase reworked, the balustrade wrought-iron latticework with scrolls, geometric panels and Greek fret. Paine's SW Library has intact C18 modillioned cornice and some joinery; other mid-C18 plasterwork, ornately carved window surrounds etc. and very fine doorcases survive, supplemented by some elaborate later C19 work. S and W halls have two tablets and fourteen roundels with classical reliefs attributed to *Flaxman*.

Former STABLES (altered). By *Bonomi*, 1804. Two-storey brick coachhouse has tripartite centre with ashlar pilasters and open pediment to top. LODGES. Probably by *Paine*.

BREWERY (former), Spa Well Lane, West Cowick, 1 m. W. Late C18/early C19 brick brewery and maltkin, behind a former inn;

to rear a big three-storey brewhouse etc. by *William Bradford*,
1892, with decoratively gabled roofscape.

CRAGG VALE *see* MYTHOLMROYD

CRIGGLESTONE

St John the Divine, Calder Grove. By *W. Swinden Barber*,
1893. Small stone mission church with bellcote. – STAINED
GLASS. E window by *Kempe*, 1893.

Blacker Hall Farm, 1 m. SSW. Good group, mainly C17.
Coped gables with shaped kneelers and other dressed stone
details. FARMHOUSE *c.* 1800. Symmetrical three-bay S front;
wing to rear, giving T-plan. Two big BARNS, restored. The
larger, dated 1635 or 1685, has stone roof sweeping down over
the N aisle. Interior impressively timbered, with kingpost
trusses. The W bay had a corn store on upper floor beyond a
closed truss. The derelict, early–mid-C17 MALT HOUSE is a
very rare survival.

CROFTON

All Saints. Sited prominently on a ridge and more impressive
from a distance than close to. It was built *c.* 1430 by Richard
Fleming, Bishop of Lincoln and founder of Lincoln College,
Oxford, who was born at Crofton and died in 1431. His
church replaced an older one on another site. Restored 1873–5.
The building's uncomplicated history gives it an unusual
uniformity. Small, cruciform, aisleless, with crossing tower and
S porch, all in plain Perp. Continuous plinth and plain gabled
parapet with roll-moulded top. The four arms have diagonal
buttresses at the angles and coped gables. The crossing arches
are double-chamfered and have continuous mouldings, a conservative design, employing a treatment usual a century earlier.
Small blocked doorway to a former rood loft at the SE end of
the nave, reached by an external circular stair. – SCULPTURE.
Remains of two Saxon crosses (N transept). One has the interesting motif of the bust of a bishop and on the opposite side
a bust of a horned individual upside-down (C11?), the other
(late C9?) scrolls, interlace and two intertwined quadrupeds.
Extraordinary polished granite Wilson family MAUSOLEUM,
1912, in the churchyard. Doric arcades on each side support
a ribbed, domed, roof like a rectangular umbrella. Railings
enclose a large marble angel, kneeling, by *Gaffin*.

Bedford Farmhouse, ½ m. SE, has an ogee lintel dated 1677.

CUDWORTH

St John the Baptist, Church Street. By *Smith & Brodrick*, 1892–3. Simple Dec, with an elaborate bellcote. – stained glass. Chancel s, 1949, and aisle w, 1951, by *Powell & Sons*. Aisle e by *Francis Stephens*, 1968.

Of the former bleachworks by *W.J. Hindle* of Barnsley, 1854–5, only a tall octagonal stone chimney and Tudor-style foreman's house survive.

CUMBERWORTH

St Nicholas. Rebuilt by *Edward Hughes*, 1879, except for lower stage of small c17 or c18 w tower, to which buttresses, belfry stage and pyramidal top were added. – font. c17(?). Octagonal with traceried panels. – stained glass. Excellent pair by *Morris & Co.*, 1939.

Nos. 4–6 Low Fold and Nos. 171–173 Cumberworth Lane, ¾ m. ne, are late c18 back-to-back weavers' houses. Three storeys with six-light upper windows.

CUSWORTH HALL

1¼ m. nne of Sprotbrough

A Palladian country house (now a museum) by *George Platt* for William Wrightson, 1740–5, completed by *John Platt*. The main block has five wide bays to n front. Basement, raised ground floor with quoins of even length, first floor and upper half-storey with Doric giant pilasters instead. The centre doorway and the window over are Venetian. Centre pediment; blocking course. Short quadrant corridors link five-bay kitchen (w) and stable (e) wings of one-and-a-half storeys to form an entrance court. The plainer seven-bay s front overlooks the park, the ground falling away to the lakes. The flanking pavilion wings (for Chapel and Library) are by *James Paine*, 1749–53. Low and pedimented, with a Diocletian window over a tripartite window with Ionic columns in the middle and niches on either side; on each return is a three-sided bay window. Paine's exterior alterations were limited: the central doorway with segmental pediment became a window and new entrances were made in the narrow corridor links; the basement was rusticated to match the wings; on both fronts the ground-floor window sills were lowered. More significant changes proposed by him for the s front, such as the giant columns and pediment illustrated in *Vitruvius Britannicus IV* in 1767, were not executed.

Excellent restored INTERIORS, those by *Paine* with plaster-work by *Joseph Rose* and carving by *Christopher Richardson*. Fine marble and Derbyshire marble (crinoidal limestone) chimney-pieces supplied by the *Platts*, 1742–4. ENTRANCE HALL has pedimented doorcases with pulvinated friezes and arcaded Doric screen to wide transverse corridor. Doric Serliana before N and S staircases. Paine's LIBRARY in N wing, later a billiard room, has joyous Rococo plasterwork to ceiling cove, corniced doorcases with acanthus friezes and chimneypiece by *John Watson*. BOOK ROOM by *John Rawstorne*, *c.* 1797–1803, with delicate Adamesque decoration. *Paine* enhanced the ceilings of the excellent Palladian SALOON and the BREAKFAST ROOM with Rococo decoration, adding a painted centrepiece of Endymion and Selene by *Francis Hayman* to the latter. The CHAPEL has especially sumptuous plasterwork. Panelled vaulted ceiling has central painting of the Ascension by *Hayman*, flanked by six grisaille paintings by *Samuel Wale*. Ionic columns and pilasters. Richly decorated Serlian screen with garlanded pediment to apse. Altar painting of the Good Samaritan by *Hayman* (now a copy). New DINING ROOM by *P. N. Brundell*, 1907, to N of chapel, has a lantern and a three-sided bay matching Paine's. Pretty plasterwork in keeping. N bedchamber has a very fine chimneypiece with mask by *Christopher Richardson* 1763.

ENTRANCE LODGE. Mid-C18. One-and-a half storeys. Quoins. Hipped roof. Openings to central tunnel-vault are tall continuous arches with alternate rusticated voussoirs.

Attractive small ESTATE VILLAGE. C17/C18 walled gardens near the site of the old hall include a SUMMERHOUSE or bowling green pavilion, 1727.

The PARK was landscaped by *Richard Woods*, 1761–5; the surviving part is now a Country Park. He created a river-like chain of three lakes with a picturesque rockwork cascade; beside the largest lake, at the foot of the hanging lawn, is a grotto-style boathouse. His 'Temple Hill' mound to the SW, now separated from the park by the A1(M), has been mistaken for a Norman motte.

4090   DALTON

Continuous with the eastern suburbs of Rotherham.

HOLY TRINITY, Vicarage Close, Dalton Parva. 1848–9. Single cell, with lancets and bellcote. – STAINED GLASS. E windows by *Baguley*, 1871. Three nave windows by *Heaton, Butler & Bayne*.

DARFIELD

ALL SAINTS, Church Street. Essentially Norman and Dec.
Unbuttressed early Norman W tower of two stages with battlemented Perp top; the tower arch narrowed at the same time,
concealing the Norman jambs. Two two-light bell-openings E
and W, three lights N and S. Also Norman a blocked round-
arched window (N aisle NW) and stones with chevron moulding
in the chancel S wall. The rest is nearly all Dec – the nave with
clerestory of two-light windows and arcades of three wide bays
with standard elements, the continuous S aisle and S chapel,
and the S porch entry and S doorway, both with quadrant
mouldings. In the N aisle, which has later straight-headed
windows, are two tomb-recesses. One has a tall, boldly cusped
arch with ogee head and pinnacles, the other fine C14 moulding. The chancel arch has typical Dec tripartite responds,
moulded capitals, and double-quadrant-moulded arch. Splendid curvilinear tracery in the S aisle and S chapel windows. The
chapel has a priest's doorway with ogee head, and against
the E wall an ogee-headed reredos rises above the foot of the
window. Perp work is at the E end – the E window and the N
chapel of two bays, its octagonal pier decorated with shields
in the capital.

The chancel presents several puzzles. The doorway through
the chancel arch's S pier must have opened to the rood-loft
staircase, the piscina beside the capital serving a loft altar. The
W arch of the S arcade has a deep soffit with double arch as if
over a tomb, and a fragment, perhaps of a canopy, in the l.
jamb. Part of what may also have been a canopy is in the
chancel N wall. Most curious are the upper windows, inside
the building, which are cut through by the E arches of the
arcades. Square-headed, they cannot be earlier than Perp, and
yet the S chapel seems consistently Dec. Were the arcades
altered after the Reformation, opening the chancel to former
chantry chapels? The S aisle and chapel have pretty painted
ceilings, the aisle panels bearing the Wombwell family's
emblem, a badge with a unicorn's head. The ceilings are
thought to be C18, so clearly major work was undertaken then.

COMMUNION RAILS (chancel and S chapel). Jacobean, with
vertically symmetrical balusters. – PEWS. A remarkably complete Jacobean set (cf. Great Houghton). Doors and ends have
carved ornament and acorn finials. Tiered in front of the tower
arch. S chapel. Bosvile family pew (*ex situ*). C15. Elaborately
carved panels, four with splendid Dec tracery and Thomas
Bosvile's name and initials. Equally good panels from the
Wombwells' pew with unicorn's head (S wall). – FONT. Octagonal, Perp. Alternating panels with shields and with two thin
blank two-light arches separated by a buttress. – FONT COVER.
Big, rather heavy Jacobean. – SCULPTURE. Three Anglo-
Saxon fragments. One outside, in W wall of S aisle, with two

volutes, C8–C9. Two inside, possibly from architectural features rather than cross-shafts and indicating an earlier church:
in the tower's s wall a petalled rosette and interlace C7–C8; in
s wall of N chapel, interlace C8–early C9. – In nave s wall above
E arch a dragon's head of unknown date. – STAINED GLASS.
By *Powell & Sons*, the E window (1915), and three in the s aisle
(1916, 1938 and 1922 (baptistry)). s chapel E by *T.F. Curtis,
Ward & Hughes*, 1900. w (tower) window is made up of figures
from former E window of 1849 by *Wailes*. Top lights in the
aisles and clerestory also by *Wailes*, 1849. – MONUMENTS. In
the s chapel an alabaster chest tomb *c.* 1400, the recumbent
effigies probably Sir John Bosvile and his wife, Anne. Rather
battered but some fine detail survives (see her jewelled head-
dress). – In the N chapel a low standing monument to Mrs
Godfrey †1658, the inscription surrounded by shields. – Several
good-quality C18 and early C19 monuments with urns, pediments etc.

MIDDLEWOOD HALL, ½ m. NNE. Three-storey rear part C17
with mullioned windows. The two-storey s front later Georgian with symmetrical arrangement of canted bays. Later C19
wing to r. has two unusual rounded oriel windows. Former
stables and large single-storey lodge in castellated Gothic of
c. 1800.

CRANFORD HALL (formerly NEW HALL), 1¾ m. WNW. The
central block is by *William Lindley*, 1787, later altered and
extended. Some intriguing fragments of a moated C15 courtyard house, including an archway with a four-centred chamfered arch with round-arched hoodmould and large Tudor
fireplace with a moulded round arch. NEW HALL FARM, s,
has a large C17 BARN with three cruck-trusses, rare this far E
of the Pennines.

TYERS HALL, off Doncaster Road, 2 m. NW. Four houses joined
in a row, the l. two C17, small, with some mullioned windows.
The others both three bays and three storeys, with sashes; the
first late C18 and wide-fronted, the last early C19 and tall and
narrow.

DARRINGTON

ST LUKE AND ALL SAINTS. Mainly of white Magnesian limestone and architecturally – by lucky accident more than con-
certed effort – one of the most satisfying village churches in
the West Riding. The sturdy w tower is Norman (if not
earlier – the use of imported sandstone blocks may indicate a
pre-Conquest date, cf. Laughton-en-le-Morthen) but with a
slightly recessed bell-stage probably added in the late C12.
Small two-light window on the N side, similar openings on the
s and E sides of the belfry. The aisles, embracing the tower,
were first built in the early C13 – see their w lancets, the N

doorway, which is still round-headed and has only one slight chamfer, and a lancet and a pair of lancets on the N side. The Dec contribution to the church was especially felicitous. The large S aisle windows have fine reticulated tracery and there is a good S doorway too, with three orders of shafts and a finely and deeply moulded arch. The porch could be as early, but perhaps need not be. Very tall entrance arch with continuous chamfer and tall octagonal pinnacles with miniature spires either side of the gable. Stone roof on two transverse chamfered arches. The chancel (rebuilt in the C13, though no more evidence remains than a N lancet now opening internally) has a Dec priest's doorway, but of the three S windows only the central one is genuinely of that period. Sir Stephen Glynne, writing in 1862, described the others as Perp, of three and five lights. They were altered before the restoration of 1879–80 by *A.W. Blomfield*. The E window is clearly Perp, and the enrichment of the base of the S wall by ornamental friezes is also a Perp habit. The l. part, simply quatrefoils in circles, is convincing. The r. part is less so. Its extreme r. block is limestone and has a design with an arch with quatrefoil head and fleur-de-lys finials. The rest is yellow sandstone, more crudely and deeply carved, and looks like a re-set section of an unusually ornate parapet (cf. Wakefield's Cathedral and Bridge Chapel). The N chapel was reputedly built by Sir Warin de Scargill and his wife (*see* below); it has a fine three-light E window of that date. Its square NW staircase tower has a blocked E door at the top, its round head cut from a single limestone block; nearby in the roof's W apex is a small lancet.

Inside, the Norman tower arch has responds with very substantial demi-shafts carrying many-scalloped capitals. The arch itself – semicircular, tall and unmoulded – was rebuilt in its original form by Blomfield; he specified the Saxon technique of using 'through stones' for the voussoirs. The three-bay nave arcades, noble in their upright proportions, have tall circular piers and double-chamfered arches. The responds at the W and E ends are characteristically (for the early C13) keeled, more tentatively on the N. The N chapel in some form must also have existed in the C13, for the E capital of its wide arch has nailhead decoration. Unusually, the wooden roof is carried on eight chamfered stone ribs. The most puzzling feature of all, and again one which turned out to be aesthetically a success, is the delightful little arcaded gallery running across the W end of the N chapel, high above the arch into the N aisle. It is unique, as far as we know, and what its purpose was and when exactly it was built is impossible to say. It could certainly be early C14. Only Sandal Magna (q.v.) has something similar, in the passage linking the NW and central tower staircases and overlooking the N transept. Here the gallery is accessed off the chapel staircase and it runs straight into the solid masonry of the early C14 chancel arch, so cannot have led, as is sometimes suggested, to the rood. Its three openings on each side have chamfered arches and little octagonal piers with broaches, and allow views into both the chapel and the nave and aisles.

FURNISHINGS. – BENCH-ENDS in the N chapel. Original Perp work with blank traceried arches in two tiers (cf. Wakefield Cathedral). The tracery is decidedly Flamboyant. – CHANCEL STALLS. Two are left, with MISERICORDS. – SCULPTURE. Chancel N wall. A crucifix under a round arch, c. 1200, from a farm wall at Cridling Park. The cross (of Lorraine) is clearly recognizable. – S aisle E wall, an ogee-headed niche with battlemented top. – STAINED GLASS. Fragments of C15 glass in the N chapel. – E window, 1879, S aisle E window and first from E, 1895, and W window, 1880, by *Burlison & Grylls*. S aisle second from E by *J.E. Nuttgens*, c. 1928. – MONUMENTS. Chancel N wall, in a simple recess, Sir Warin de Scargill †1326. Very slender effigy, cross-legged. Now separated in the N chapel, effigy of his wife, Clara, a Stapleton heiress. – William Farrer †1684. Ledger stone on four balusters, used as an altar in the S aisle. Fine inscription on a small brass plate set in a carved cartouche. – N chapel. Several to the Sotheran family, including William †1780 and Catherine †1812 by *Fisher*, and Frank †1839 by *Lockwood*. – N aisle, to Alexander Blair, a Scotsman riding to London, who fell from his horse in an apoplectic fit 1671. – N aisle (vestry), imposing tablet to the Faber family by *C. Fisher*, 1820. – LYCHGATE, by *Blomfield*, 1894.

In the churchyard former DOVECOTE, C18, square with pyramid roof and quoins. Two storeys. Converted to parish rooms in 1887, now a house.

STAPLETON PARK, 1¼ m. ESE, was demolished c. 1935. It had been rebuilt in 1762–4 by *Carr* for Edward Lascelles and Carr's STABLES survive. Main elevation to courtyard is seven bays, with round-headed archway in pedimented centre; clock turret and cupola added 1827. The Gothick CASTLE FARMHOUSE, 1 m. SE, might also be by *Carr*, built as an eyecatcher from the house.

At CARLETON, 1 m. W on the edge of Pontefract, ST MICHAEL by *Charles Vickers*, 1847–8, and CARLETON GRANGE, a large gabled Jacobethan brick mansion of c. 1879 for Thomas Tew, banker. Ornate interiors.

DARTON

Village on the Dearne extended by later mining settlements.

ALL SAINTS. Tall Perp W tower of two stages with diagonal buttresses. The SE buttress projects into the aisle. The body of the church also Perp, low and long, embattled, but without pinnacles. The rebuilding is said to have begun about 1480. A

bold inscription on its wall-plate records that the chancel was
completed in 1517 by Thomas Tickhill, Prior of Monk Bretton
and the church's patron. Five-light E window and three-light
chancel S window with transoms. The S window in design is
like those of the S aisle. The clerestory and N aisle windows
look yet later, straight-headed with two and three depressed-
arched lights respectively. The S porch, clerestory windows and
eastern windows have hoodmoulds with limestone headstops
(cf. Silkstone). Lofty nave of four bays with octagonal piers.
Sunk quadrant in the very tall tower arch and the arcades.
Rood stair in a projection from the wall of the N aisle. Chancel
arch with one chamfer and one sunk quadrant on corbels and
capitals with a little nailhead. Are they survivals from the
earlier building? Or could they be Victorian? Restoration by
Perkin & Sons of Leeds, 1867–8, occasioned correspondence
in *The Times* about the damaging re-cutting of interior mouldings. Chancel chapels of two bays with octagonal piers and
double-chamfered arches. Pevsner thought the capitals here
looked earlier too. Perp roofs throughout with good carved
bosses, some in the nave very large. – COMMUNION RAIL.
Early C18. Three-sided, the gates forming a semicircular projection in the centre. – Parclose SCREENS to N chapel and part
of S chapel. Simple, Perp, with one-light divisions. – Original
S DOOR. – PAINTING. N chapel. Virgin, demi-figure, Italian
Baroque, manner of *Gentileschi*. – STAINED GLASS. N chapel.
Small figure of Mary Magdalene, originally in the E window,
which was glazed in the 1520s for Thomas Tickhill. Monk
Bretton Priory was dedicated to the saint. E window by *A. O.
Hemming*, 1905. W window by *Powell Bros*, 1884. – MONU-
MENTS. Chancel. George Marsh †1689. Oval, with elaborately
scrolled frame. Thomas Cotton †1802 and wife, Rebecca,
†1816, by *George Walsha*, 1816. – S chapel. John Silvester of
Birthwaite Hall †1722. Convincingly attributed to *Andrew Carpenter* (Matthew Craske via GF). Imposing tripartite piece
against chapel's blocked E window. Life-size central statue
standing in a swaggering pose. A seated female allegorical
figure each side, the one on the r. with two small children.
From a family of master smiths, Silvester amassed a fortune
supplying the Office of Ordnance at the Tower of London.
The story that he made a long chain across the Thames to
obstruct the Dutch fleet seems to be apocryphal. – Rev.
Edward Silvester †1727. Ornate tablet with inscription on
marble drapery. – N chapel. Thomas Beaumont †1731 by
W. Green. Fine pedimented tablet with small seated cherub on
the gadrooned sill, its elbow propped on an hourglass. Green's
painted signature just discernible.

BIRTHWAITE HALL. ¾ m. NW. An impressive gabled house on
an H-plan, its complicated story not yet fully unravelled. A
medieval house is recorded here; the present three-bay centre
and W wing are a later C17 rebuilding, probably by Francis
Burdett, created a baronet in 1665. He sold Birthwaite to John

Silvester in the late C17 or early C18. The cross-windows were sashed in the C18; two- and three-light mullioned windows with dripmoulds survive in the attic gables. Samuel Buck's view from the S, c. 1720, shows assorted service buildings on the E side. Probably soon after Buck's visit, these were replaced by the E wing, matching its W counterpart, in major alterations, perhaps by Silvester's nephew and heir Edward Silvester, who died in 1727. These changes transferred the principal entrance from the S to the N side and the kitchen etc. to the W side. (N door has elaborate, almost Mannerist surround with a big segmental hood on richly carved brackets.) Forward of it the space between the wings was later infilled to make a one-storey outer hall. Its windows have sashes of sixteen over twelve panes so it was probably not much later. It is uncertain whether a similar addition on the S side, with Doric pilasters, dates from the C18 or the 1820s. Next, apparently, came the large single-storey W extension, its windows with architraves and cornices. It is attributed to *Robert Carr*, who was paid for work in 1746.

Mostly tenanted in the C18 and C19 and in dual occupation, the house was formally subdivided c. 1821. The W wing and extension were separated from the main house, whose five-bay E façade became its new entrance front, splendidly and surprisingly clothed in Georgian Gothick. Pretty tracery frieze, four polygonal buttresses rising as battlemented turrets, and battlemented parapet and middle gable.

(INTERIOR. Hall has bolection-moulded panelling and a very fine oak staircase, the lowest flight flying, the upper two cantilevered, probably contemporary with the new N entrance. W wing has C17 panelling and fine dog-leg staircase on upper floors. E wing has good Regency interiors, with Edwardian alterations.)

In the garden an early C18 former SUMMERHOUSE, shown in Buck's view. Brick, two storeys, with pyramidal roof.

Good range of C17 FARM BUILDINGS W of the house includes a doorway with one of those crazy lintels so popular around Halifax. This has two moulded bosses embraced by a shape like a letter E pointing down. Windows in chamfered surrounds, some mullioned, dripstone raised at intervals to form hoodmoulds.

(HAIGH HALL. Jebb Lane. 1¾ m. NW. Fine early C18 house for the Cotton family, iron masters. Five bays, with big hipped roof. Pedimented doorway; raised window surrounds and quoins. Rooms panelled in pine, good fireplaces. Brick SUMMERHOUSE probably by *Richard Woods* 1770s).

At STAINCROSS, 1 m. E, ST JOHN THE EVANGELIST by *R. Dixon* of Barnsley, 1896–7. Small, its plainness enlivened by a flèche and unchurchy half-timbered porch. S in Spark Lane two former chapels: METHODIST NEW CONNEXION CHAPEL, 1867, with dressed-up front and two tiers of round-arched windows, and the BETHEL CHAPEL, 1829, retaining a pretty wrought-iron gateway.

DELPH

A largely stone-built settlement in Saddleworth, with the remains of big mills along the main approach and the River Tame, which runs through the centre. Here interesting houses include No. 25 King Street, a good pair with mullioned windows, each doorway dated 1769. Many C18 and later houses and farms in the neighbourhood with rows of mullioned windows lighting weavers' workshops, of which a splendid three-storey example of *c.* 1800 is provided by Nos. 2–4 Oldham Road.

St Thomas, Church Street. Formerly St Hilda's mission church and school. Dated 1883, by *T.A. & G. Heys*. Very basic, of stone, with late C20 alteration.

Congregational chapel (former), Delph Lane. Of 1866, low-key, with paired lancets. By *Habershon & Pite*, replacing predecessors.

Shore Mill, Lawton Square. A former water-powered carding mill (for yarn preparation) of *c.* 1780, externally well preserved. Long rows of mullioned windows and an arch at the base for the tail race. Wheel pit inside, infilled.

Roman fort and fortlet, Castleshaw, 1½ m. nne. Beside the trans-Pennine Roman road from Chester to York, the slight rampart of a turf and timber fort, constructed *c.* a.d. 79 but given up a decade later. In the centre of its se side a much smaller double-ditched fortlet, occupied from about 105 to 125. (Its earthworks were restored in the 1980s.) Internal timber buildings included a small headquarters, a barrack, a large granary and a commander's house with a hypocaust. (HW)

DENABY

All Saints, Denaby Main. 1975–9 by *Kenneth Murta*.* Linked church and hall. Low, with roof clerestories and much plain buff brick. Small blind drum belfry facing road. – Miners' Memorial Chapel by *Jack Ford*, 1987–9, built with materials from local collieries. The altar, below a roof lantern representing a miner's lamp, displays a one-ton block of coal. – Stained glass by *Tony Banfield* and *Peter Fry*.

St Alban (R.C.). 200 yds se. By *Empsall & Clarkson*, 1897–8. Gothic Revival. Tall nave with aisles and clerestory; apsidal sanctuary. sw bell-tower, 1910, has decoratively panelled top and set-back shingled spirelet.

Old Hall, 1 m. wsw. Two cottages incorporating remains of a C15 courtyard house. In 1828 three sides were still standing.

*The previous church by *C. Hodgson Fowler* and *H.L. Smethurst*, 1899–1900.

On the ashlar N side is the head of a two-light window with pointed and cusped lights and to l. a projecting garderobe turret. This has on both floors two triangular-headed doorways (one on each level now visible externally).

KINGSWOOD DEARNE VALLEY EDUCATIONAL ACTIVITY CENTRE, ½ m. ENE by the River Don. Formerly the EARTH CENTRE, opened in 1999 on the sites of Cadeby and Denaby Main collieries and intended to demonstrate principles and technologies of sustainable living and development. Closed in 2004 but reopened for its present use in 2012, reusing most of the buildings completed to the masterplan by *Feilden Clegg Bradley*. They designed the timber and glass ENTRANCE PAVILION, linked to the stone-fronted, partly underground PLANET EARTH gallery by the SOLAR CANOPY, an elegantly complex timber space-frame supporting 1,000 square metres of photovoltaic collectors. Other buildings, also originally exhibits themselves, include *Alsop & Stormer*'s WATERWORKS, clad in ETFE cushions, demonstrating water recycling; the CONFERENCE CENTRE by *Bill Dunster*, set into the hillside, with intersecting circular gabion walls filled with reclaimed concrete and ventilation cowl finials to conical sedum roofs; and NATUREWORKS by *Letts Wheeler* of Nottingham, an observatory on pilotis over a pond.

DENBY DALE

Former textile mill village, renowned for pies.

HOLY TRINITY. By *H. Erskine Hill*, 1939. Small. A distinctive design in stylized Gothic with a dash of Art Deco.

METHODIST CHURCH (Wesleyan), Cumberworth Lane. 1799–1801. Broad pediment-gabled front of five bays with round-arched windows in two tiers. Additional rear bay 1839. Alterations by *Dixon & Moxon*, 1877–8, included organ apse, fine ashlar doorcase with Corinthian pilasters, and enriched plasterwork to ceiling. Gallery, floored in 1978, now forms worship space.

FRIENDS' MEETING HOUSE, High Flatts, 1 m. SW. Four-bay S front with porch and large sash windows, 1864. Developed from a barn; a lintel dated 1697 is the probable date of conversion. Interior fittings probably 1754–5.

RAILWAY VIADUCT. 1877–80, for the Lancashire and Yorkshire Railway. Magnificent stone curve with twenty-one round arches.

ROCKWOOD HOUSE, Barnsley Road. 1870 for Walter Norton, mill-owner. Castellated Tudor Gothic style with thin angle turrets.

DENSHAW

Part of Saddleworth.*

CHRIST CHURCH, Huddersfield Road. By *John Eaton* for the industrialist Gartside family, 1862–3. Big solid w tower with pierced parapet. (– STAINED GLASS. E window of 1863 by *Alexander Gibbs*, w window 1911 by *W. J. Pearce*.)

DENSHAW FOLD, Huddersfield Road. A group of C18 houses with rows of mullioned windows, probably lighting weaving workshops.

DEWSBURY

Like neighbouring Batley (q.v.), Dewsbury's C19 growth was based on the manufacture of heavy woollens, particularly mungo and shoddy (*see* p. 117). Its position on the Calder gave canal access across the Pennines via Huddersfield from 1811. New roads to Leeds and Bradford were formed in 1831 and 1833, and the railway to Leeds followed in 1848. The population was 6,380 in 1821, and by 1861 it had almost trebled to 18,148. Borough status was granted in 1862. The predominantly Victorian centre is well preserved and remarkably attractive, with an intricate network of streets centred on the Market Place. The ring road, begun in 1984, does less damage than at Huddersfield.

CHURCHES

ALL SAINTS (Dewsbury Minster). A site of Christian worship since Saxon times. Exterior C18 and C19, but older fabric survives inside. Four-bay nave with late C12 or early C13 arcades. N arcade has piers made up of a circular core and four detached shafts with shaft-rings (cf. Guiseley, West Riding North). Moulded capitals, double-chamfered arches (a section of wall above the two easternmost arches is thought to be C10). S arcade has simpler quatrefoil piers and double-chamfered arches. Flat wooden roof of 1895, but incorporating late C15 bosses. Extensively rebuilt in 1765–7 by *John Carr* in un-archaeological Gothic. Of his work there survives the w tower, with its typical pilaster-strips (the main windows probably altered; top C19) and the N aisle. The round-arched aisle windows have a transom with arched lights below; above, the mullions run straight into the main arch. The details of these windows may however belong to the extensive alterations of 1823 by *Joseph Nowell*. N and w doorways ogee-headed with

---

*In Greater Manchester since 1974.

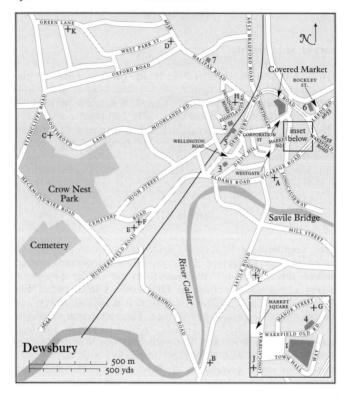

Dewsbury

500 m
500 yds

A All Saints (Dewsbury Minster)
B Holy Innocents
C St John the Evangelist
D St Mark (former)
E St Matthew (former)
F Our Lady and St Paulinus (R.C.)
G Baptist Church
H Unitarian Church (former)
J United Reformed Church
K Westborough Methodist Church
L Wesleyan Methodist
   (former; now mosque)

I Town Hall
2 County Court (former)
3 Public Library and Baths
   (former)
4 Post Office (former)
5 Railway Station
6 Eastborough School
7 Infirmary (former)

concave-sided pediments. In 1884–8, *A.E. Street* and *A.H. Kirk* pulled down the medieval E end and added the two-bay-deep transepts and a chancel with flanking chapels, and in 1895 they rebuilt Carr's S aisle. All this is in the Dec style. In a radical reordering begun in 1994, *R.G. Sims* divided the former chancel horizontally to create upper and lower halls. The reorientated nave is now entered from the N transept, the S transept has become a display centre, and the N chancel chapel a refectory. Timber stairs in the N transept lead to the upper hall, and to Sims's Paulinus Pilgrimage Chapel, an intimate centralized space, high up behind the chancel arch.

SCULPTURE.* Mostly displayed in the S transept, some discovered during the C18 rebuilding. – Three fragments of an important Anglo-Saxon cross with circular shaft. On one a seated figure of Christ blessing, inscribed IHS XPVS (this is now in the Paulinus Pilgrimage Chapel); on another, lower parts of two figures and heads of others under arches below (cf. Collingham, *West Riding North*); on the third, two standing figures. The overall subject was perhaps Christ and the Apostles (cf. Masham, North Riding). The date is late C8 or early C9. – Of the same date, and possibly linked with these three, a fragment of a cross-arm with a crouching figure clasping the feet of an angel. It may represent St Matthew and his man/ angel symbol. – Another equally interesting fragment comes from a square shaft and has on one side a Virgin and Child under an arch. Another fragment from a square shaft has the Marriage Feast at Cana and the Miracle of the Loaves and Fishes, with damaged inscriptions. These are also late C8 or early C9. – Fragment of a square cross-shaft with the lower part of a figure of Christ and plant scrolls on the sides, probably early–mid-C10. – Fragment of a cross-head with cusped arms (late C8 or early C9) and another with a domed boss in the centre (C10). – Fragment with a plant scroll on one face and part of a figure on another face, late C8 or early C9. – Two further fragments with plant scrolls, C9. – Part of a house-shaped tomb-cover, the roof carved to represent tiles, with plant scrolls along the sides and a cross in the gabled end panel. Not of the usual Danish, but of Anglian style, probably late C9. – Coved coffin-lid with a foliated cross and two dragons writhing to its l. and r. (cf. Kellington). Probably late C12.

FONT. Stone, octagonal, with crude carved ornament. – REREDOS. By *Temple Moore*, 1913, carved in oak by *R. Bridgeman & Son*. Now in the N transept. Christ flanked by ranks of Apostles and saints in niches. – MONUMENTS. Base of tower: several C17 slabs against the walls; also John Murgatroyd, an aedicule with broken pediment and gadrooned base, 1736 by *Henry Watson*; S side of tower arch, Mrs Allbutt, a Gothic tablet by *R.D. Chantrell*, 1843; N aisle, several early C19 tablets, classical and Gothic, plus John Peables †1684, a good cartouche with heads of putti, attributed to *Edward Pearce* (GF). – STAINED GLASS. A window in the N transept made up of C14 fragments, and below them three delightful small medallions representing labours of three months: pig-killing, harvesting and threshing. Probably by a York maker. – Otherwise, the E parts have glass mostly dating from after the 1884–8 rebuilding. The E window by *Mayer & Co.* replaced a smaller one of 1853, with reticulated tracery by *J.A. Cory* of Durham and glass by *Wailes*; this is now in the Refectory. – Two 1930s

*The following account relies on Elizabeth Coatsworth's *Corpus of Anglo-Saxon Stone Sculpture*, vol. 8, Western Yorkshire (2008)

windows by *H. Victor Milner*, one in each transept. – The nave has glass transferred from St Matthew and St Mark (*see* p. 201): s aisle by *J. E. Crawford*, 1960, and *Gordon Webster*, 1948; N aisle by *Ward & Hughes*, 1889.

HOLY INNOCENTS, Savile Road, Thornhill Lees. 1855–8, by *Mallinson & Healey*. Well sited on rising ground above the Calder. Dec Gothic. Nave with clerestory and aisles, long chancel, s porch and a fine w tower and spire. Interior impressively tall and narrow, with five-bay arcades on filleted quatrefoil piers, and label stops in spandrels. – FONT. Octagonal, of Caen stone, with ogee arches on small Purbeck shafts and a spire-like wooden cover. – REREDOS. Rich blind arcading around the sanctuary walls, also of Caen stone; this and the font are contemporary with the building and were carved by 'Mr Mawer' of Leeds – probably *Charles Mawer*. – PULPIT. In the same style as font and reredos, but only introduced in 1877. – STAINED GLASS. A rich and comprehensive scheme. Windows in the chancel and tower are by *Wailes*, and were present when the church opened; aisle windows mostly 1860s, and at the w end 1880s, one of the latter signed *G. J. Baguley*.

Opposite stands the Gothic VICARAGE, and s of it the former SCHOOLS, both contemporary with the church and by the same architects. (Immediately s of the schools on Lees House Road is the single-storey former SAVILE ESTATE OFFICE, 1860s. CLEGGFORD BRIDGE – five masonry arches, built 1778, widened 1889 and 1929 – crosses the Calder to Dewsbury Mills, where the donors responsible for Holy Innocents had their textile business. Most conspicuous of the mill buildings is five-storey ANCHOR HOUSE, 1927, on the e side of Thornhill Road. Classical, with pairs of giant pilasters running through the middle three floors, and the top floor treated as an attic.)

ST JOHN THE EVANGELIST, Boothroyd Lane. 1823–7 by *Thomas Taylor*. A Commissioners' church. Nave with battlements, gabled buttresses and lancets with Y-tracery; the windows have label stops with carved heads, and there are more heads on the fronts of the buttresses. Battlemented w tower with crocketed pinnacles. Shallow, square chancel with intersecting tracery in E window. An impressive interior: no aisles, but divided into bays by attached octagonal columns between the windows. They have bulbous capitals supporting plaster rib-vaults down the sides, but the ceiling is flat in the middle. w gallery introduced 1855, the carved front with figures in niches added by *Herbert Read*, 1913. – PULPIT. Also by *Read*, 1927. Oak, Gothic, richly carved, but emphasizing the rugged strength of the material. – STAINED GLASS. Several windows of interest, but especially a dramatic memorial window, N, to the three woollen-manufacturing Fox brothers, 1912: they follow Christ up a steep path to the Heavenly City – one dressed as a pilgrim, two wearing armour (they were Knights of the Order of St John of Jerusalem) – while an angel hovers, ready to bestow a jewelled crown. This extraordinary performance was designed by *W.A. Chase* and made by *Lowndes & Drury*.

ST MARK (former), Halifax Road. 1862–5 by *Mallinson & Healey*. Dec Gothic, cruciform, with W tower and broach spire. Five-bay nave with aisles and round piers. The church has become a school, with the loss of some fittings, but only minor subdivision. – STAINED GLASS. E and W windows, plus another in the N aisle, all by *A.W.F. O'Connor*, 1867; S transept by *Powell Bros*, 1881; N transept and S side of chancel, three good windows by *Burlison & Grylls*, 1884.

ST MATTHEW (former), Huddersfield Road, West Town. 1847–8 by *Bonomi & Cory*; SE chapel added 1898 by *Holtom & Fox*. A remarkably convincing evocation of a medieval North Country church: massive, unbuttressed W tower with stepped battlements and few, small openings; low nave, aisles and chancel with stone-slated roofs of shallow pitch. Perp tracery. Converted to housing, but with virtually no external changes.

OUR LADY & ST PAULINUS (R.C.), Huddersfield Road and Cemetery Road. By *E.W. Pugin*, 1867–71. A memorably dramatic response to a challenging site (a hairpin bend, sloping steeply up from S to N and from E to W). Nave and polygonal chancel under one continuous roof, plus S aisle, chapel and vestry, all raised very high above a lofty basement containing hall, etc. The extraordinarily tall, narrow apse rises sheer from the bend of the road, like the prow of an oncoming ship. The proportions are almost as extreme inside: nine very tall, thin, two-light windows down the N side of the long nave, which ends with a soaring chancel arch. S arcade on short, round columns, with clerestory above. Entrance under W gallery, supported by a single segmental arch – the full width of the nave – filled with a traceried wooden screen. SW War Memorial Chapel, originally Baptistery. – STAINED GLASS. Apse: Annunciation, with St Paulinus Preaching and Celebrating Mass, 1887. – S aisle: memorial to American benefactors by *W.J. Booer* of Leeds, 1871, and five single figures of saints, *c.* 1914–19, some signed by *Kayll & Reed*, who also did the round window in the memorial chapel. The contemporary PRESBYTERY, W, also by *Pugin*, is as tall and narrow as the church.

BAPTIST CHURCH, Manor Street. 1871 by *Henry Holtom*. Very prominent, now that the ring road sweeps past in front. Gothic. A gabled front with unequal flanking towers: the shorter one, l., contains gallery stairs, the r. one carries a spire. Between them, an open porch of three arches. Long, two-light windows down the sides, rising above the eaves to form gabled dormers. A single-storey hall, l., has a triple-arched porch, echoing that of the church.

UNITARIAN CHURCH (now Madina Academy), Swindon Road. 1866, by *Mr Crawford* of Leeds. Gothic. Paired lancets down the sides and a W rose window with plate tracery.

UNITED REFORMED CHURCH, Longcauseway. 1882–4 by *Walter Hanstock*. Elaborate Dec façade: a pair of big traceried windows above a grandiose central door with cathedral aspirations: trumeau, carved tympanum and three orders of granite shafts. Galleried interior, completely preserved, with organ and pulpit in the shallow apse.

WESTBOROUGH METHODIST CHURCH, Green Lane. 1874–6 by *Holtom & Connon*. Dec. Shallow transepts and tall NW tower with splay-footed spire.

WESLEYAN METHODIST CHURCH (now Zakaria Mosque), South Street, Savile Town. *John Kirk & Sons*, 1875. Italianate.

CEMETERY, Cemetery Road, Dewsbury Moor. By *J. Marriott & Son*, 1860. Two identical Dec Gothic chapels, both derelict, one ruinous.

PUBLIC BUILDINGS

84   TOWN HALL. By *Holtom & Fox*, 1886–9. A latecomer – begun twenty-four years after incorporation – but a fine embodiment of municipal pride. 'Mixed Renaissance' style, with pavilion-roofed corners and a domed clock tower above the central entrance. The main interior is the Victoria Hall, with coved ceiling and horseshoe balcony. This, and the mayoral suite on the top floor, are reached by a generous dog-leg stair with stone balustrade and marble handrail. – STAINED GLASS. On the stairs and second-floor landing: St Paulinus Baptizing, with Edwin and Ethelburga, designed by *Lawrence Scott* and made by *Winfield's* of Birmingham; a female figure representing Commerce, also designed by *Scott*, but made by *Pape* of Leeds; and another representing Science, by *Powell Bros*. – On the first-floor landing, a charming window of 1952 by *J. Stansfield*, presented by the Chamber of Trade. It has vignettes of a couple doing the rounds of Dewsbury's shops, and is lovingly detailed, down to the shopkeeper demonstrating a vacuum cleaner. In front of the Town Hall, a STATUE: The Good Samaritan, 1991 by *Ian Judd*: two over-life-size figures, roughly hewn from a single block of stone.

COUNTY COURT (former), Eightlands Road. 1858–60, by *Charles Reeves*. Six-bay palazzo with deep cornice on paired brackets. Converted to flats.

PUBLIC LIBRARY and BATHS (former), Wellington Road. 1896 by *G.E. Laurence* of London. Asymmetrical, with shaped gables and a lead-covered cupola. Some windows mullioned and transomed, others large and round-arched.

POST OFFICE (former), Wakefield Old Road. 1907 by *Walter Pott* of *H.M. Office of Works*. Sited where the street bends, so the front is slightly canted. Central entrance under a baroque aedicule with steep pediment. Three-bay wings with ground-floor Diocletian windows and balustraded parapets.

RAILWAY STATION, Wellington Road. Of the original LNWR station of 1848, probably by *John & Henry Paul Child*, only the centre survives, converted to a pub. It has a shaped gable and Tudor windows. The present booking hall at the NE end is of 1888–9 and also Tudor, but simpler. Immediately NE of the station, a short but impressive stone VIADUCT: ten round arches, and a wider elliptical one over Bradford Road.

EASTBOROUGH SCHOOL, Rockley Street. A large Board School of 1879 by *Holtom & Connon*. Gothic, with an octagonal tower and spire, and windows of Geometric tracery.

INFIRMARY (former), Halifax Road. 1881–3 by *A.H. Kirk* of *John Kirk & Sons*. T-plan, with the entrance – unexpectedly – in the short end of the cross-bar, at the base of the high clock tower. The main ward block extends s, with two diagonally set corner sanitary towers under steep pavilion roofs. The style is Gothic, the clock tower Flemish-looking, with gabled dormers in its steep roof.

CROW NEST PARK, Cemetery Road. Crow Nest is a five-bay C18 house of three storeys with a three-bay pediment and older re-set mullioned windows at the back. It appears on a map of 1761. Inside, central staircase with carved balusters; panelling in some rooms. s of the house, a square C18 summerhouse of one bay, quite elegant. The grounds became a public park in 1893, laid out with lake etc. by *William Daniels*. On the N side, WAR MEMORIAL, 1923–4 by *William Naseby Adams* and *Eric Ross Arthur*. A cylindrical temple with square columns embedded in the wall for half their height, then becoming free-standing with the roofless entablature silhouetted against the sky (a motif derived from St George's Hall, Liverpool, where the architects trained). NW of the memorial, facing into the park but entered from Boothroyd Lane, the FLETCHER HOMES by *F.W. Ridgway*, 1900: three pairs of almshouses with hipped roofs. Mullioned-and-transomed windows under pedimented gables with Queen Anne details.

SAVILE BRIDGE, Wilton Road. 1936. A single span of reinforced concrete by the *Yorkshire Hennebique Contracting Co. Ltd*, with Art Deco sandstone parapets.

PERAMBULATION

The MARKET PLACE is the historic centre, overlooked from the E by BARCLAYS BANK, a handsome palazzo of 1856–8 by *Michael Sheard* for the West Riding Union Bank. On the N side is the Renaissance façade of the ARCADE, 1899 by *John Kirk & Sons*, a simple glass-roofed avenue of two-storey shops. It leads to CORPORATION STREET, with more 1890s shops on the N side by *Holtom & Fox*, and the COVERED MARKET on the corner of CRACKENEDGE LANE, of 1904 by *Henry Dearden*, Borough Engineer: a parallelogram of part-glazed ridge-and-furrow roof on cast-iron columns, with a lower, open-sided extension along Crackenedge Lane. Opposite the extension is the triple-arched classical façade of the former CENTRAL STATION, 1880 by *James B. Fraser*, now incorporated into the retaining wall of the 1980s ring road. In WHITEHALL WAY, the mildly Baroque STATION HOTEL looks c. 1900: three-storey gabled centre with framing chimneystacks, plus a single-storey bar, r., sweeping round the corner towards the former station. Whitehall Way continues NW to the five-storey CLOTH HALL MILLS, 1874. Completely utilitarian apart from the short W elevation, ornamented with four carved heads by *John Allen* showing the mills' owners, Robert and William Machell, along-side Disraeli and Cobden. Facing this is the Italianate former SALEM CHAPEL (now a mosque) on BRADFORD ROAD, 1863 by *William Hill*. Bradford Road is joined here by HALIFAX ROAD, dominated by the majestic Italian Renaissance build-ing of the co-operative DEWSBURY PIONEERS INDUSTRIAL SOCIETY, 1878–80 by *Holtom & Connon*. With its triumphant domed tower, it might be taken for the town hall. Extended N by *Holtom & Fox* in 1896, and again in 1914. The 1896 addition is simpler, with a continuous band of first-floor glazing; that of 1914 more exuberant, curving into Wellington Road with canted bay windows bursting out on the first floor.

Halifax Road continues S as NORTHGATE, with early C20 shops on the E side incorporating two more glass-roofed arcades. Northgate leads back to the Market Place and the former Huddersfield Banking Company (now HSBC), a sumptuous palazzo of 1857–9 by *William Cocking*, with abun-dant carved decoration including several rams' heads. From the SW corner of the Market Place, WESTGATE leads to DAISY HILL, which winds attractively as it rises. Off to the l., in SCHOOL STREET, the former CHURCH OF ENGLAND SCHOOL of 1843 by *R. D. Chantrell*: paired lancets down the sides and five stepped lancets in the gable. Higher up on the r., the WESLEYAN CENTENARY CHAPEL (now Elim Pente-costal Church) of 1840. A plain but elegant classical box, set above the street in a railed enclosure. From Daisy Hill, NELSON STREET leads to WELLINGTON ROAD. Here, and in the streets running obliquely downhill – WELLINGTON STREET, BOND STREET, CROFT STREET and BRANCH ROAD – are impressive woollen warehouses of the 1850s, '60s and '70s, mostly classical, but turning Gothic later.

Beyond the ring road, BRADFORD ROAD is also lined with WAREHOUSES, specifically associated with the trade in rags for the mungo and shoddy industry. Dating from 1860 to 1885, they typically have dignified three-bay fronts containing offices, and utilitarian rear parts for storage and processing. A good example is No. 128 by *William & Stead Ellis*, dated 1863, with a round, cusped window and vigorously carved head above the door. For the former Batley Carr Mills, *see* p. 121.

5080

DINNINGTON

Village which mushroomed after the sinking of the colliery in 1902. The population leapt from 258 in 1901 to nearly 5,000 by 1911.

St Leonard. By *R.C. Sutton* of Nottingham, 1867–8, paid for
by John Carver Athorpe. Geometrical tracery. N aisle and W
bay of the nave added 1906. Chancel extended, reusing E
window, by *Sutton & Gregory* 1910–11. – Miners' Memorial Screen. Mosaic panels by *Janette Moon, Russell Morris*
and local people, 1994. – Stained glass. E window by *Mayer*
of Munich, 1881. N aisle, three by *Kempe*, 1896 and 1901
(easternmost).

Rotherham College, ½ m. NNE. Former Mining and Technical Institute by *H. Wormald*, County Education Architect,
1927–8. Plain institutional classical style with small pediment
to centre of long symmetrical front range. Prominent clock
tower with domed cupola.

Dinnington Hall, 200 yds S. An interesting C18 house with
earlier core, remodelled for Henry Athorpe. A rainwater head
dated 1752 probably indicates completion of building. Accounts
record payments from 1754 to *c.* 1757 to *Gervase Ledger* and
Thomas Ledger, plasterers, *Christopher Richardson*, carver, and
Francis Fenton, painter, all craftsmen employed elsewhere by
James Paine. The five-bay entrance front has an indifferent
early C19 infilling of the centre, with a porch between bay
windows. To the l. and r. are single-bay wings that have all the
characteristics of *Paine* – rusticated ground floor, niches l. and
r. of the upper window, relieving arch and broken pediment.
One would dearly like to know what the whole of this composition was originally like. The S front is late C18. Big canted bay
window with round-arched windows to ground floor, one bay
on either side. (C19 stair hall has a Doric-columned screen,
and an oval lantern above the staircase. The dining room, a
fine circular room with the bay window, and the drawing room
both have decoration in the style of Carr, perhaps by *William
Lindley*.)

DOBCROSS*

(including Diggle)

Many examples of farms and houses with weavers' workshops lit
by long rows of mullioned windows can be found in the village
and scattered over the hilly hinterland.

Holy Trinity. Erected by public subscription in 1785–7. Thin
Italianate tower dated 1843 by *David Bellhouse*, perhaps the
contractor rather than the designer. Two tiers of round-arched
windows; round-arched Venetian E window. Three galleries
with panelled fronts supported on stone Tuscan columns,
pretty ceiling plasterwork. – Gallery Seating. Part of the
original joinery scheme by *Henry Platt*. – Stained glass. S

---

*Part of Saddleworth, in Greater Manchester since 1974.

window, The Prodigal Son, *c.* 1895, probably by *Heaton, Butler & Bayne*. W window also probably theirs.

The stone buildings of Dobcross VILLAGE are arranged higgledy-piggledy up a slope. The main street widens to a square where LANE END HOUSE has a rainwater head dated 1780 and the SWAN INN is dated 1765. It had an assembly room, said to survive inside. CHURCH FIELDS lies SW, with an C18 group of three storeys with ranges of windows lighting former loom shops, including three sets of five-light mullioned windows divided by king mullions crammed along the top floor. Nearly opposite, MANOR HOUSE is quite grand, probably latest C18: symmetrical front with tall two-light mullioned windows; back with a central pediment above a Venetian window with intermittent rustication. Off Sugar Lane, WOODS HOUSE (dated 1791) displays a symmetrical front with stepped tripartite windows.

HARROP GREEN, Diggle, 1½ m. NNE. A group typical of the area, late C18 houses and loom shops lit by long rows of mullioned windows. Tiny No. 15 is one-up and one-down.

WARTH MILL, Huddersfield Road, Diggle, beside the Huddersfield Narrow Canal (*see* p. 44). Early C20 woollen mill converted for cotton weaving, now retail units etc. Imposing, of stone, with a big square water tower.

LOOM WORKS (former), Huddersfield Road, Diggle. Started in 1861, of stone, including a water tower and chimney. Large ornate Gothic office block of 1890.

WOOLLEN MILL (former), Brownhill Bridge, ½ m. SE of Dobcross. Of 1772, three-storeyed, with the arched opening for the tail race in the ground floor and ranks of twelve- and thirteen-light mullioned windows in the upper floors.

(GREAVES FARM, 1 m. NW of Dobcross. A set of stone TENTER POSTS about 6 ft (1.8 metres) high, for stretching and drying cloth. An unusual survival, dating from *c.* 1840; cf. Marsden.)

DODWORTH

ST JOHN THE BAPTIST. By *Benjamin Broomhead Taylor*, 1843–6. Eccentric Neo-Norman. W tower, galleried nave, very short chancel. Monstrous pinnacles at the angles. E window by *J.W. Knowles*, 1872.

METHODIST CHAPEL (Wesleyan), ⅛ m. NE. By *George Moxon*, 1903. Gothic, with spirelet.

DODWORTH GRANGE, ¼ m. SSW. 1710. Doorway has good moulded surround with truncated swept head and bracketed cornice. Two fielded panels run across front, below eaves.

DONCASTER

INTRODUCTION

Doncaster's name reveals its association with the river and the Romans, who in *c.* A.D. 71 founded a fort called Danum at the crossing point of the Lincoln–York road, outside the walls of which a civilian settlement was established, succeeded by the Saxon *burh* and the medieval town. The town's architectural character, however, owes much to three other Rs – the Great North Road or A1, racing and the railway. By far the oldest is the road, the centuries-old route between London and the North, travelled by king and commoner and connecting the town with the wider world in a way denied to much of the West Riding. Until 1960, when the bypass relieved it of England's Permanent Pandemonium Number One, Doncaster's High Street formed part of the A1; the banks especially put on as good a show as one can find in any provincial town to impress those passing by. Rivalling York, Doncaster races became pre-eminent in the northern racing and social calendar from the C18 and racing remains part of the lifeblood of the town. The route to the race-course has some of the West Riding's handsomest Georgian town houses. Together road and racing have done much to give Doncaster the enduring feel of a county town.

Until C18 and early C19 improvements gradually extended the waterway to Sheffield, the Don was navigable only up to Doncaster and river trade, from the wharf near Fishergate, was important in the town's economy from medieval times until the later C19. As an agricultural market town, however, its trade did not create the industrial and commercial waterfront that developed in Wakefield, for example, and little now remains of the canalside infrastructure. It was the coming of the railway in 1848, rivalling the road connection between London and the North, and, more especially, the establishment of the Great Northern Railway Company's workshops in 1852, that introduced large-scale industry to the town. The 'Plant' – that vast array of maintenance, repair and locomotive-building facilities – was brought here at the insistence of the town's powerful champion Edmund Beckett Denison, GNR chairman and West Riding MP, and cemented a close and fruitful, if sometimes uncomfortable, relationship with that formidably influential family. In the early C20

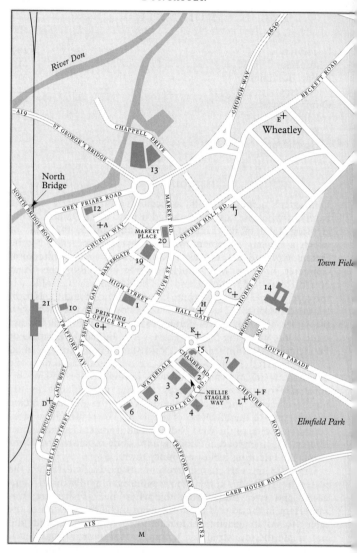

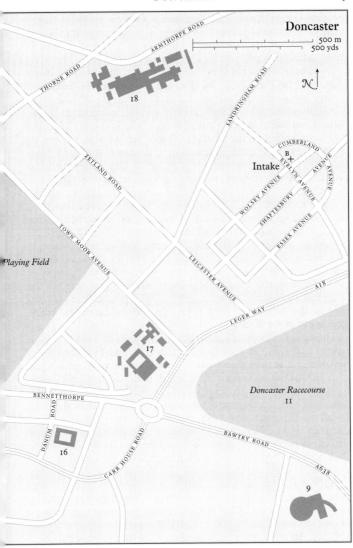

1   Mansion House
2   Civic Office
3   Cast Performance Venue
4   Crown Court
5   Quarter Sessions (former),
    Magistrates' and Coroner's
    Courts and Police
    Headquarters
6   County Court (former)
7   Museum and Art Gallery
8   Public Baths (former)
9   The Dome Leisure Centre
10 Grand Theatre (former)

11 Racecourse
12 Technical College (former)
13 Doncaster College (The Hub)
14 Hall Cross Academy
15 Girls' High School (former)
16 Central Schools (former)
17 Yorkshire School and College
    for the Deaf
18 Doncaster Royal Infirmary
19 Market Hall and
    Corn Exchange (former)
20 Wool Market (former)
21 Railway Station

the rapid development of Yorkshire's eastern coalfield transformed many local villages into large mining communities and
brought further diversification of the town's economy, as well as
strengthening its position as a sub-regional centre.

Doncaster had some borough rights by 1139, its status being
confirmed and extended by Richard I's charter of 1194 and
further enhanced in 1467 by Edward IV's grant of municipal
borough status. The town's former motto, 'comfort et liesse'
('liesse' meaning 'ease'), was that of King Edward. After the
Corporation bought the Manor of Doncaster in 1505 it controlled
all the rights that gave authority over the town and used these
for more than four centuries to develop its facilities, wealth and
position. In the C18, in addition to supporting the races and
providing the Mansion House for the entertainment of racegoers,
it built a theatre (dem.), by *William Lindley*, 1775–6, and improved
the streets, instigating a policy of insisting on rounded corners,
apparently entirely for aesthetic reasons and without legal
authority, that continued into the C20. Market improvements
included new Shambles (dem.) by *John Platt* in 1756 and extensive new buildings in the mid C19, when, with the benefit of
railway transport, Doncaster's cattle market was one of the
largest in Yorkshire. The railway brought larger numbers of visitors to the races too, with over eighty daily excursion trains
arriving in Race Week.

The resident population, however, grew slowly until the C20,
rising from 5,697 in 1801 to 12,052 in 1851 and 28,932 in 1901,
the increase mainly due to the 'Plant', which employed 3,500
men by 1913. The earliest suburbs, dubbed 'Plant Town', were
for its workers, at Hexthorpe and immediately E across the
railway. Their development followed Doncaster's first Building
Bye-laws, introduced in 1852, and so the town largely avoided
the grim back-to-back housing of other West Riding towns. Later
C19 expansion was SW, absorbing the village of Balby, SE to Hyde
Park and NE beyond Nether Hall and along Thorne Road. By
1921 the population had reached 54,700 and in 1927 Doncaster
became a County Borough. Interwar suburbs developed NE at
Wheatley and Intake; post-war estates were further out, SE
at New Cantley and West Bessacarr and NW across the river at
Scawsby and Scawthorpe. In 2011 the population was nearly
128,000. In the early C21, Lakeside, SE of the town, an airfield
and landfill site reclaimed with parkland and a 50-acre artificial
lake by *Skidmore, Owings & Merrill*, completed 2002, provides
space for retail, office and leisure developments and new housing.

CHURCHES

MINSTER CHURCH OF ST GEORGE. By *George Gilbert Scott*,
1853–8. A landmark to travellers on the East Coast railway, St
George's is the proudest and most cathedral-like of this fabu-
lously busy and successful architect's parish churches. Scott
was commissioned to build it after the splendid medieval
parish church, which was famous for its crossing tower, was

Doncaster, St George.
Drawing, 1855

destroyed by fire in 1853.* At the Rebuilding Committee's request Scott largely replicated the old church's form and proportions and kept to its Perp style for the tower; for the rest he decided on a 'better', i.e. earlier, style, the late Geometrical to early Decorated. Scott endured considerable interference in his designs from one of the building fund's principal donors, Edmund Beckett Denison Jun., later Lord Grimthorpe, the venomous, pompous, righteous bully of St Albans notoriety.

The church has a five-bay nave with two clerestory windows to each bay, two-storey S porch, transepts projecting only slightly beyond the aisles and straight-headed three-bay chancel with chapels. It is 169 ft (51.5 metres) long and the nave is 75 ft (22.9 metres) tall. The majestic crossing tower, 170 ft (51.8 metres) tall, can compare in height with e.g. that at Wells. Its upper stage has two three-light openings on each side, divided by broad transoms. The exterior is richly decorated, more especially on the S side. See, for example, the profusion of liberally crocketed pinnacles and gablets (those on the tower buttresses of nodding ogee form), the pierced parapets and the gargoyles and grotesques. The windows display *Scott*'s extensive repertoire of Geometric tracery. The impressively lofty interior is an exceptionally satisfying example of his genius, 69 enhanced by the skills of craftsmen in stone and wood and metal and glass. Compound piers and richly moulded arches, wall-shafts articulating the bays and half-bays of nave and clerestory, open arches under half-arches in the aisles with pierced cinquefoils in the spandrels. The sculpted ornament is

---

*The vaulted CRYPT survived and is below the N chapel.

by *J. Birnie Philip*, e.g. exquisite naturalistic foliage capitals, busts of Old Testament figures in roundels (nave) and of the Apostles in quatrefoils (chancel) and angel corbels. s (Forman) chapel has a stone rib-vault, a wall arcade with serpentine shafts, and excellent *Minton*-tiled floor.

FITTINGS. Elaborately carved and gilded SANCTUARY WALL ARCADES on shafts of Spanish marble, five taller crocketed canopies forming the REREDOS. Its richly painted figures of Christ and the Evangelists are by *Clayton & Bell*, 1868. – Forman Chapel: marble and alabaster REREDOS by *Harry Hems & Sons*, 1913. FONT. Huge serpentine bowl on seven marble shafts. – Large circular stone PULPIT. Marble colonnettes to open arcade and staircase balustrade. – Stone READING DESK. Vaulting and diaper-work to front. – Excellent WOODWORK by carvers from *Ruddle* of Peterborough, who had the fittings contract: CHOIR STALLS and MAYOR'S PEW with poppyheads, the nave PEW panels and finials a botanist's delight. – METALWORK. Painted and gilded s chapel and organ screens by *Skidmore* (ORGAN by *Schulze*, 1862). – STAINED GLASS. An instructive collection by several of the principal Victorian firms. After a gas explosion in 1896 four damaged windows by *Capronnier*, 1858, and *O'Connor*, 1870, were replaced. E window of eight lights, 44 ft (13.4 metres) high, by *Hardman*, overseen by *Scott*, 1862. It was shown at the 1862 Exhibition. – s (Forman) chapel windows by *Wailes*, 1858; the E window designed by *Alfred Bell*. – s transept s window by *Clayton & Bell*, 1870. – s aisle s windows, E–W, by *Wailes* 1858, by *Holland* of Warwick 1857, by *Hardman* 1860 and by *Ward & Hughes* 1863. – N and s aisle w windows by *Shrigley & Hunt*, 1896. – w window by *Ward & Hughes*, 1873. – N aisle windows, W–E, by *Clayton & Bell* 1864, by *Ward & Hughes* 1866, by *Hardman* 1859, and by *Wailes* 1865. N aisle easternmost and N transept N window by *Shrigley & Hunt*, 1897, designed by *Demaine & Brierley*. – MONUMENTS. Robert Thwaites †1698. Carved and painted wood with pediment and open twist columns and the badge of the Mercers Company. – Yorkshire Imperial Yeomanry (South African War): copper repoussé plaque by *W. Bainbridge Reynolds*, 1903.

ALL SAINTS, Evelyn Avenue, Intake. Built 1951–6 on the foundations of a church by *Morris Thompson* begun 1938–40. Unmistakably by *G. G. Pace*, with his signature small windows in a grid across the entire main (ritual) N wall – 115 in total. Pace reversed the conventional plan, making a large sanctuary area with forward altar in the intended w end. Brick, of barn-like form (cf. St Edmund below) with asymmetrically gabled roof and blind 'E' wall to the sanctuary. 's' aisle with square brick piers, 'N' passage aisle through transverse walls. (White walls contrast with the unusual rippled ceiling painted a dramatic dark blue. Striking MURAL by *Harry Harvey*, 1964, surrounding a hanging rood.)

CHRIST CHURCH, Thorne Road. By *Woodhead & Hurst*, 1827–9, as the town's first chapel of ease; made redundant in 1989 but reopened for worship in 2004. Comparable in size and plan with Commissioners' churches but its Gothic style treated more freely and elegantly. The s (ritual w) tower especially is free of immediate period precedent. Square below, but at the height of the nave roof turning octagonal with mediating pinnacles and flying buttresses. Then two recessed stages before the spire: the lower with two-light bell-openings between delicate pinnacled buttresses, the upper with lancets under crocketed gables. Short copper-clad spire of 1938; the original had been removed in 1919.

The battlemented sides have six bays separated by prominent buttresses with the lofty diagonal pinnacles (now unhappily truncated) so beloved of the period. Tall three-light lancets with intersected tracery. Pierced quatrefoil panels in transoms at gallery level. *Scott* redesigned the E window with Geometrical tracery in 1858 but his plan for enlarging the shallow rectangular chancel was not implemented until 1862–3, by *Brundell & Arnold*. It was extended eastwards, apparently reusing the original walls, to make an awkward canted end, with the new chancel aisles finishing on the diagonal. Attractive interior. Nave galleries on three sides, their fronts with traceried panels and an odd dogtooth frieze. Tall, slender compound shafts, graceful arches. Flat panelled ceiling. Plaster rib-vaults over the aisles. Chancel arcades of two bays with octagonal piers. Richly carved capitals, probably by *J.B. Philip*. – STAINED GLASS. Brightly coloured, all by *Capronnier*. E window with *Scott*, 1858.

ST AIDAN, Central Boulevard, Wheatley Hills. By *Bernard A. Miller*, 1955–6. Brick. Nave with NW and SW porches, five-bay aisles and attractive triple W bellcote rising from buttresses but badly compromised by *Shepherd Fowler & Robinson*'s pitched roof of 1987. Inside shallow-arched arcades with sunk panels to concrete piers and soffits. Shallow lamella vault over nave and chancel; matching transverse vault to each aisle bay.

ST EDMUND, Anchorage Lane. Old stone barn sensitively converted to chapel by *G.G. Pace*, 1954 (redundant since 2009), with grid of windows inserted and clerestories made with glazed strips along eaves.

ST JAMES, St Sepulchre Gate West. Built 1857–8, for the workers in the Great Northern Railway workshops, at the instigation of the chairman, Edmund Beckett Denison Sen. Subscriptions were extracted from fellow board members. Notionally designed by *Scott* but with the advice and under the supervision of *Edmund Beckett Denison Jun.* (cf. Minster Church of St George). The church's odd two-naved form was determined by the Denisons' antipathy to High Church practices, the deeds specifying 'no processing or other forms of popery'. The Geometrical style (which the younger Denison called 'the exact climax of the Gothic styles') allowed plenty of self-conscious differences in the details of the four virtually equal ends. Blind arcade to the (ritual) NE gable with rose window above. The organ stands against it inside, the N nave serving as an aisle. Sitting roguishly partly between the w gables and partly on the N one is an octagonal bell-turret, as redesigned by *Denison* and *J.M. Teale* in 1860 with elaborately moulded arcade and taller stone spire. Interior has central arcade of four-plus-two bays, with compound pier between. This has shafts supporting arch-braced trusses in both parts. Nave piers circular, the chancel pier octagonal. Good foliate capitals, probably by *J.B. Philip*. – REREDOS. Painted stone. Blind arcading with big quatrefoils and granite colonnettes, *c.* 1874. PEW-ENDS along main aisle have hinged seats. – STAINED GLASS. E window by *Clayton & Bell*, 1860. A testimonial to the church's founder. – Second from E on S by *Heaton, Butler & Bayne, c.* 1902.

108 ST LEONARD AND ST JUDE, Barnsley Road, Scawsby. By *G. G. Pace*, 1957–63, and one of his most uplifting and memorable church interiors, the parabolic laminated timber arches of the chancel soaring even higher than those of the nave. Yellow-buff brick. Tower with steep saddleback roof and pointed belfry openings rises from flat-roofed w narthex. Low-pitched nave roof, the gable filled with narrow transomed windows. The chancel roof is steeper; from windows in its w gable light falls onto the altar, set forward of the choir, with the plain white E wall as a dramatic backdrop.

ST LUKE, Broachgate, Scawthorpe. By *Maguire & Murray*, 1965–6. Small windowless box in white-painted concrete blockwork. Light comes from glazing along the S face of the asymmetrically gabled roof, illuminating the altar in a tiny N apse. Linked hall and curate's bungalow, also blockwork; the trio cost only £16,000.

ST MARY, Beckett Road, Wheatley. By *Edmund Beckett Denison Jun.*, 1884–5; chancel and w entrance by *P. N. Brundell*, 1912. Rock-faced ashlar enlivened by contrasting pale ashlar dressings. Six-bay nave with aisles under one roof. Buttresses between each bay. Paired cusped lancet windows. w porch and bellcote. There were originally two w doors and the pews had no central aisle, no doubt dictated by the architect's abhorrence of popish processions (cf. St James p. 213). The five-bay arcades have exceedingly thin and highly incorrect polygonal cast-iron piers, as if the church had been designed in 1834 and not 1884.

ST PETER-IN-CHAINS (R.C.), Chequer Road. By *J. H. Langtry-Langton & Son*, 1972–3. Buff brick. Large and impressive central nave and sanctuary in a clerestoried octagon that opens into glazed flanking bays and two apsidal side chapels, the octagon rising above these and the narthex and vestries also grouped around it. Flat-topped pyramidal roof with bold pierced parapet. Some of the fittings were brought from the church in Prince's Street (1865–7 by *M.E. Hadfield & Son*), e.g. the Lady Chapel reredos with STATUE by *Theodore Phyffers*, 1867 and Blessed Sacrament Chapel fittings by *J.F. Bentley*, who was born at Doncaster; the marble and alabaster ALTAR has a painting by *Westlake*, 1867; enamelled TABERNACLE 1867; curved Caen stone REREDOS, 1875, with traceried alabaster panels between four *opus sectile* panels with figures of Abel, Noah, Melchizedek and Abraham; sections of wrought-iron ALTAR RAILS, 1883 (to rear of pews). – STAINED GLASS. Six figurative lights by *Patrick Feeny (John Hardman Studios)*, 1973. A window (St Peter) by *Bentley* and executed by *Clayton & Bell*, *c*. 1894, is kept in the church.

PRIORY METHODIST CHURCH (Wesleyan), Printing Office Street. By *William Hurst*, 1832. Stately and ponderous, a five-bay front with arched upper windows and a heavy attic, raised over the centre. Projecting arched triple entrance by *J.G. Walker*, 1881. Galleried interior entirely subdivided for community use in 1979, the chapel reduced to the rear ground-floor bay.

ST ANDREW'S METHODIST CHURCH (United Methodist), Beckett Road, Wheatley. By *George Baines & Son*, 1915–16 and in their typical Gothic style.

METHODIST CHURCH (former, Wesleyan), Nether Hall Road. By *Gordon & Gunton*, 1902–3. Arts and Crafts Gothic in brick with a fine tower. Carved stonework by *Thomas Scrivens*. The church's gabled front, now screening flats, has lost its window tracery to flimsy-looking infill.

UNITED REFORMED CHURCH (Congregational), Hallgate. 1804, altered and enlarged 1874, interior remodelled by *J.G. Walker*, 1896. Set back from the street frontage, beyond small former burial ground. Arched windows like Priory Methodist Church, but here a looser assemblage of classical elements. Three-bay ashlar front with quoins, modillioned cornice and balustraded parapet flanking heavily framed inscribed panel. Single-storey front extension, full width with canted corners, has balustraded top and low pediment over double doorway. This handsome C19 front is marred by the asymmetrical and suburban-looking church room set in front *c*. 1970. (Interior has curved gallery all round, on slim cast-iron columns.)

TRINITY PRESBYTERIAN CHURCH (former), Waterdale. By *Herbert Athron*, 1890–2. Low and unassuming. Attached hall by *Athron & Beck* 1903.

BAPTIST CHURCH, Chequer Road. By *Herbert Athron*, 1893–4. Gothic style. Sombre red brick with yellow terracotta dressings. Prominent corner site with well-placed tower.

HYDE PARK CEMETERY, Carr Lane (semi-derelict at the time of writing). An early example of a municipal cemetery outside London, opened 1856. Lodge, gabled gateway and two small chapels, the N one Anglican, the S one Nonconformist, in limestone ashlar. By *Robert J. Johnson*, 1855, in Decorated Gothic style. Unusually the chapels are set at right angles to each other and are linked by a tower rising above a tall open archway which forms a shared porch. The picturesque tower turns from square to octagonal and carries a stone spire.

PUBLIC BUILDINGS

MANSION HOUSE, High Street. By *James Paine*, 1744–9 for
Doncaster Corporation, as a suitable venue for the mayor to
entertain in at the time of the race meetings. The painted stone
front is three bays. It has a rusticated low ground floor with a
curiously cavernous recessed entrance, in which two pairs of
Ionic columns, heavily blocked four times, are set behind each
other. The *piano nobile* has coupled Corinthian columns, a
beautiful Venetian window in the middle, and pedimented
windows below grapevine festoons in the side bays. It is copied
almost exactly from one of Inigo Jones's designs for Whitehall
Palace, published by William Kent in 1727. The front's original
full-width pediment was replaced in 1801 by *William Lindley*'s
faux-attic parapet topped with urns, cornucopia and an
achievement with Edward IV's emblem of a golden lion and
standard.

The ENTRANCE HALL has an Ionic screen and doors with
corniced architraves leading to plainly decorated rooms originally used by Corporation members and as the Gentlemen's
Dining Room. Paine's flair for embellishing an essentially Palladian scheme with Rococo flourishes is revealed in the increasingly sumptuous interior. The grand stone imperial staircase
has fine scrolly wrought-iron balusters, similar to those at
Nostell (*see* Wragby), and a richly decorated upper space with
panelled walls, coved ceiling with Rococo centrepiece and
Corinthian columns to the landing. The magnificent BALL
ROOM or Banqueting Hall occupies the whole front on the
first floor, its space a double cube 60 ft (18.3 metres) long. The
central doorcase has Corinthian columns and a large broken
scroll pediment, the other two doorcases matching columns

Doncaster, Mansion House and Betting Room.
Engraving by J. Rogers after N. Whittock, 1829

and straight but equally elaborate entablatures, all painted and gilded. Above the central doorway is a little balustraded musicians' gallery; between it and the outer doorways are two excellent corniced chimneypieces of grey marbles carved with grapes, their angled ends on Ionic columns. Plain cove to the ceiling (which Paine's published designs showed with decorative paintings) and rich Rococo decoration on the central flat. Accomplished stucco wall and ceiling panels, with masks, dolphins, musical instruments, grape vines etc., by *Thomas Perritt* and *Joseph Rose*. Elegant reception rooms with fine chimneypieces and doorcases behind, the Drawing Room to the E of the staircase and the Salon to the W, the latter altered in 1806 by Lindley and again by *William Hurst* in 1831, when its roof lantern above the double cove was made. Lindley's large rear BANQUETING HALL was also added in 1806 as 'accommodation [for] the nobility and Gentry attending Doncaster Races'. It has restrained Adamesque plasterwork and a recessed musicians' gallery set behind paired Corinthian columns. The staircase's rear landing was made in 1865 to allow direct communication between Banqueting Hall and Drawing Room, and the original Venetian window was copied. Its stained glass 'Peace window' is by *Harry Harvey*, 1986.

CIVIC AND CULTURAL QUARTER, Waterdale. After the demolition of the Town Hall in Market Place in 1846, the Corporation made do with the Mansion House and offices around the town. A town hall in South Parade was proposed in 1938, but post-war plans were made for a new civic centre at Waterdale on the town centre's SE edge. This was designed and redesigned 1955–73 by *Frederick Gibberd* with the Borough Architect, *L.J. Tucker*,★ and although further revised and still incomplete the essential scheme has, over more than half a century, slowly been implemented, most recently to a more extensive Masterplan of 2009 by *Cartwright Pickard*, who created SIR NIGEL GRESLEY SQUARE, completed 2012. In the first phase of redevelopment they are also the architects of the CIVIC OFFICE, 2010–13, Doncaster's first purpose-built town hall, placed on the N side of the square and on the site of the Technical College (1955–65). Its brightly coloured acute-angled corner, with stripy rows of vertical faience baguettes, mainly in blues, makes a striking statement in the square. The rest is a large, five-storey rectangular block with clean lines, its gridded frame clad in grey ceramic tiles. Corner entrance to double-height public area behind recessed glazed front. Kite-shaped COUNCIL CHAMBER above, overlooking the square, is also double-height, with semicircular public gallery. Light oak fittings. Spacious galleried atrium to offices.

★The cruciform shopping precinct between Waterdale and Cleveland Street also formed part of *Gibberd*'s scheme and was built to amended designs by *Morgan & Branch*, 1965–7, incorporating the Central Library facing Waterdale. Two-storey balcony-access flats project over the shopfronts, forming canopied walkways.

The other principal public buildings are also set around or near the square. For convenience they are described as a group, followed by other public buildings:

CAST PERFORMANCE VENUE. By *RHWL Architects Arts Team*, 2010–13. Visually the key building in the Square, its strong form fills the long E side with simple, almost classical, dignity. The tall glazed façade is set deeply within a bold, simply moulded artificial stone frame with angled sides, like a giant proscenium arch. Off-centre, a strikingly large two-storey projection, clad in copper, bronze and brass, is cantilevered over the main entrance and rises through the frame. The 'Main Space' is a 620-seat proscenium-arch theatre with a circle whose sculpted exterior form billows over the front café-bar area. It is complemented by a 200-seated/300-standing flexible 'warehouse' studio space with three-sided balcony, a double-height dance space, and smaller flexible meeting and drama spaces in the front projection.

QUARTER SESSIONS (former), MAGISTRATES' AND CORONER'S COURTS and POLICE HEADQUARTERS, College Road, E of the Square. By *Frederick Gibberd & Partners* with *L.J. Tucker*, Borough Architect, 1969. Adjacent blocks, almost square and powerfully if forbiddingly fortress-like but with well-modelled polished pre-cast concrete panels. The panels are structural and two storeys high, designed on a single and double 4 ft 6 in. (1.4 metres) module. The COURTS have a sloping plinth, and deep-set windows, those to the first floor a narrow mullioned strip. Low towers, with inward-facing roof-lights, rise over the higher spaces of the courtrooms. The POLICE HEADQUARTERS has a battered wall around a dry 'moat' providing light to semi-basement cells.

CROWN COURT, College Road. By *Property Services Agency* and *Fletcher Joseph*, 1989. Postmodern classical, visually more appealing than its counterpart opposite (*see* above), the solidity of the ground floor is lightened and given interest by pale banded concrete facing blocks. In contrast the first floor has continuous strip windows set under the deep eaves of a hipped roof, their strong horizontal emphasis relieved by projecting mullions. Two top-lit courtrooms on the upper floor.

COUNTY COURT (former), Waterdale/Trafford Way. 1936. Big open pediments/gables to three courts in T-plan arrangement off central hall, with offices (originally single-storeyed) to front. Entrance and hall have original buff faience facings and black Art Deco-ish doorcases.

MUSEUM AND ART GALLERY, Chequer Road. by *L.J. Tucker*, Borough Architect, 1962–4. Unassuming, simply detailed flat-roofed block with pilotis before deeply recessed entrance. Almost windowless first floor faced in random marble slabs. The foyer's terrazzo floor incorporates polished marble pebbles. Free-standing staircase from ground-floor museum to upper art gallery.

PUBLIC BATHS (former), Waterdale. Closed since 2013. By *R.E. Ford*, Borough Estates Surveyor, 1932. Sober brick front range with square Doric and fluted Ionic columns to tetrastyle portico. Large top-lit swimming pool hall behind, with balconies on three sides. The pool has square portholes along the sides for underwater lighting, the first public pool in England with this safety feature. Until 1964 the pool was floored over in the winter for use as a ballroom etc. (Turkish baths suite in the basement has mosaic tiled floors and walls with stylized red and cornflower blue flowers.)

DOME LEISURE CENTRE, Bawtry Road. By *FaulknerBrowns*, 1986–9. Complex and highly visible roof structure of white-painted steel trusses and tubes, supporting rows of sloping glazed ridges, contrasts with solid banded blockwork walls in white and grey. Broad spine walkway gives views into activity areas and expands into huge circular pillared atrium with glazed dome. More open s-facing side connects with reclaimed parkland.

TECHNICAL COLLEGE (former), Grey Friars Road. By *Schofield & Berry*, 1913–15. Good Edwardian Baroque front of thirteen bays facing the churchyard. Red brick with generous stone dressings. Two storeys and basement. Long extension of 1934 to r. for the College of Art, in stripped classical style, has blind upper floor to studios with N lights. Matching two-storey extensions, partly flat-roofed, face Grey Friars Road.

DONCASTER COLLEGE (The Hub), Chappell Drive. By *DLA Architecture*, 2004–6. A silvery-grey and glass citadel for almost 12,000 students forming part of the Waterfront regeneration beyond the approaches to St George's Bridge. Two four- and five-storey blocks set side by side. Triangular E block; w block is bisected by full-height galleried atrium and has canopied glazed front to Learning and Resource Centre looking across to the E end of the Minster.

HALL CROSS ACADEMY, Thorne Road. The former Grammar School (founded before 1350) by *George Gilbert Scott*, 1867–9, but *Edmund Beckett Denison Jun.* was an Old Boy and is said to have claimed credit for the design. Lofty seven-bay schoolroom set above undercroft (originally open), like a medieval guild-hall. Red brick with stone dressings. Tall buttresses. Geometric tracery in large gable-end windows, mullions and transoms to the sides. Awkward octagonal angle turret topped with ashlar arcade and spirelet. Hall-like schoolroom (now library) has magnificent black timber arch-braced roof, s gallery and elaborate wrought-iron chandeliers (possibly by *Francis Skidmore*). First World War Memorial stained glass N window by *C. Rupert Moore*, 1927 and 1937, unveiled 1938. Attached additions, set back to r., by *Julian Leathart* 1937–40, are in the Dudok style but acknowledge Scott's work with pointed-arched windows to ground floor. Main ten-bay front to classroom quadrangle has tall asymmetrical entrance/water tower at s end.

GIRLS' HIGH SCHOOL (former), Waterdale/Chequer Road. Unused at the time of writing. By *J.M. Bottomley, Son & Wellburn*, 1910–11. Free Renaissance style in red brick and Burmantofts 'Marmo' white faience. Two storeys. Butterfly-plan to fit the site. Corner entrance front with semicircular Doric porch is flanked by domed stair-turrets. Extended 1922 and 1937, when the side wings were heightened; rear parts demolished.

CENTRAL SCHOOLS (former, now Carr House Conference Centre), Danum Road. By *Athron & Dyson*, 1931. Brick with classical dressings in artificial stone. Two-storey front to large lawned quadrangle of single-storey classrooms Three-bay main entrance has giant Doric columns and pilasters, and pedimented doorway.

YORKSHIRE SCHOOL AND COLLEGE FOR THE DEAF, Leger Way. The first school for the deaf in Yorkshire, founded 1829 in Eastfield House (dem. 1959), overlooking the racecourse; largely rebuilt and extended by *Walker & Thompson*, 1933–5 and 1939–40. Main blocks in a very large, mainly two-storey, quadrangle in brick with stone details. Staid Neo-Georgian style, the long front enlivened by its Palladian centre with first-floor tetrastyle Doric portico and balustraded balcony. Earlier additions to NE include single-storey school hall flanked by classrooms, with lively shaped gables, by *J. G. Walker*, 1901–2. Extensive additions 1963–6.

DONCASTER ROYAL INFIRMARY, Thorne Road/Armthorpe Road. By *W.A. Pite, Son & Fairweather*, 1926–30; additions by the same practice (*George, Trew, Dunn & Co.* from 1959). A large site with a linear agglomeration of buildings, originally planned as a 300-bed pavilion-plan hospital to replace the Victorian infirmary in Wood Street. Only partly completed when opened in 1930, with four flat-roofed, four-storey brick ward blocks on a Greek cross plan. Hipped pantiled roofs to staircase and sluice-room towers lend an incongruously Mediterranean air. Open-air end wards now enclosed. Post-war additions have created a major 800-bed hospital.

MARKET HALL, Market Place. The imposing Market Hall by *John Butterfield*, architect to the Corporation, 1846–9, was the centrepiece of redevelopment of the markets, which necessitated demolition of the Town Hall and Shambles and the removal of the Butter Cross. Its style is late classical, without yet any solecisms. High rusticated base, upper stage with round-arched windows. Paired Tuscan pilasters flank small windows over the entrances, which are marked by big stepped parapets interrupting the blocking course. The central one in the long main front formerly had a statue of Ceres on top. Originally an L-plan, altered to a U-plan when the r. return was extended from three to six bays in the 1870s as part of the scheme for the Corn Exchange (*see* below). Interior has cast-iron columns and thin trusses with boarding under low hipped roof. The front elevation is now largely hidden by the thoughtfully designed single-storey extension by *R.E. Ford*, Borough Estates Surveyor, 1930, which has square Tuscan columns to its open front and sides.

The CORN EXCHANGE is by *William Watkins*, 1870–3, and sits between, and extends forward of, the Market Hall's side wings, facing the large open market area. A very busy front in a Free or Mixed Renaissance style, with Tuscan columns of pink Aberdeen granite and red sandstone, balustrades, and parapet piers with pilasters and acroteria. Sculpted tableau by *C.H. & J. Mabey* above main entrance, representing agricultural produce. Towering behind the façade like a railway shed is the round-arched and pedimented front of the hall's roof. Its spectacular galleried interior is a feast of decorative cast-iron work. Partly glazed roof on semicircular trusses with smaller flowery arches supporting a ridge light. Round-arched arcades to side galleries, which have elaborate half-arches under lean-to glass roofs. As a hall for concerts and public meetings the space could hold 2,000 people. Now a market and tea room.

WOOL MARKET (former, now General Market), Market Place. By *John Butterfield*, 1861–3. Large covered market with open cast-iron arcades to N and W.

GRAND THEATRE, Station Road. Disused at the time of writing. By *J.P. Briggs*, 1899, inexplicably discarded by planners in the remnant of Station Road sandwiched between Trafford Way and the Frenchgate centre. Curved three-storey front of painted stucco with arched openings and giant Ionic pilasters, and first-floor balcony with decorative ironwork. Elaborate top has balustraded parapet, central pediment, urns and finials. Interior has *c.* 800 seats. (Rich Baroque plasterwork to pro-scenium arch and curved fronts of dress circle and balcony. Adamesque decoration applied to auditorium in 1930s.)

RACECOURSE, Leger Way. Races were held on Doncaster Moor, a common on the E side of the town belonging to the Corporation, as early as the C16. By the C18 meetings had become more formalized and Doncaster was established as the principal course in the north of England. The St Leger, the world's oldest classic race, was first run in 1776 and in the same year the 2nd Marquess of Rockingham and other patrons instigated the present course. The grandstand by *John Carr*, 1778, sur-   *p. 43*
vived in much altered form until 1968. The present GRAND-STAND is by *Frank Whittle Partnership*, 2006–7. Five storeys, striking, with two enclosed balconied levels rising at the back of tiered seating, all under a huge projecting canopy. The CLOCK TOWER STAND, 1881, extended 1901, is an attractive and rare example of its time. Original l. part has colonnaded ashlar ground floor topped with balustrade to front of tiered seating, addition to r. has seating extending forward to ground level. Big hipped roof on arch-braced iron columns has square clock tower with decorative finial. Lower and plainer STAND, 1901, to r. – The BLOODSTOCK SALES ARENA is by *RMJM*, 2008. Main two-storey block with auctioneers' offices, restaurant, bar etc.; brick with glazed and timber-clad ends, the SW with a gallery overlooking the course, the NE fronting the main parade ring. Also covered parade ring, additional stabling for 390 horses and extensive ancillary facilities. Doncaster has a long tradition of bloodstock sales, the St Leger Festival Yearling sales being the oldest in the UK.

RAILWAY STATION, Trafford Way. 1873–7 for the GNR, and
1936–40 by *LNER Architects Dept.* The first permanent station
buildings of 1850 were replaced in 1873–7 by single-storey
canopied ranges in simple Italianate style on both the up and
down platforms, and a taller gabled entrance block. Major
track modernization begun in 1938 created a new up line separating the E platform buildings from the forecourt and necessitating a new entrance range. It is an impressive and formal
composition in a mix of spare Neo-Georgian and Modernist
styles. Five-bay centre with full-height booking hall and flanking pavilion blocks with offices etc., each with tall hipped roof
behind flat parapet. Red brick with artificial stone dressings;
large metal-framed windows. Booking hall has marble lining
to lower walls, dark-painted pilaster-strips above and decorative panels to ceiling lights.

NORTH BRIDGE, North Bridge Road. 1908–10. By *Edward
Parry*, engineer. A long-overdue replacement for the congested
level crossing where the railway crossed the Great North Road,
sometimes with a train every three minutes. Half a mile long,
it also carries the road over the canal and the River Don. Brick
arches reinforced with iron, steel girders over the canal and
railway. It was the largest improvement scheme the Corporation had then undertaken, costing over £100,000.

ST GEORGE'S BRIDGE. Completed in 2002 as part of the £44
million North Bridge Relief Road Scheme, spanning canal,
railway and river at high level.

PERAMBULATIONS

1. Town centre

The MINSTER (*see* Churches) sits on the sites of both Doncaster's Roman fort and its Norman castle; the thriving medieval
town later extended from the area around the church S to
Market Place and High Street, over the area of the Roman
vicus. Nothing of them survives except the stretch of ROMAN
WALL a few yards NE of the Minster and the medieval street
pattern within the encircling line of the town's defensive ditch;
street names preserve evidence of buildings such as the E
gateway at Sunny Bar and the Franciscans' friary, established
before 1284, near Grey Friars Road.

The Great North Road forms the backbone of the town's later
development and so we begin in the centre of HIGH STREET
at the Mansion House (*see* Public Buildings).* The lowly
group to the W at Nos. 4, 5 and 6 are the town centre's oldest
buildings; C17 and timber-framed within a later rendered brick
exterior. The first floor, with its two tall gabled dormers, was
jettied but has been underbuilt. From the later C18 small
properties and houses with large gardens gradually gave way

---

*Pevsner's advice to perambulate at seven in the morning, when the old A1 traffic
was least noisome, thankfully no longer applies.

to three-storey brick and stucco buildings with shops. Nos. 50–51, opposite, was built as a house *c.* 1775, but its distinctive bow-windowed shopfront dates from 1817 when it was taken by Parkinson's, the confectioners. Two smaller bows with floor-length sashes above, formerly with balconies like that to the l. It is the big C19 and C20 banks that have the big buildings, starting on the N with HSBC (originally York City & County Bank), inventive Free Baroque in Portland stone by *Demaine & Brierley*, 1897. BARCLAYS BANK next door, a five-bay Italianate palazzo by *F.W. Masters*, 1885, was built for the Yorkshire Banking Co. Opposite, LLOYDS BANK by *Sidney Kitson*, 1912, reserves its display for the upper floors, with enriched giant Doric columns and an assortment of classical details. On the corner, the former National Provincial Bank (now TSB), 1923–4, probably by *F.C.R. Palmer*. Well-detailed Greek Revival in Portland stone. Fluted giant Ionic columns, deep entablature, attic. Marble-lined entrance lobby with saucer dome. Excellent banking hall with grid-beamed ceiling and Ionic screen. NATWEST by *Walter Brierley*, 1924–8, surpasses all the others in grandeur, its single-storey front as high as its three-storey neighbours. Heavy grey granite plinth and end doorcases, Ionic columns, and tall round-arched windows alternating with straight-headed windows below garlanded panels. Spectacular double-cube banking hall 90 ft (27.5 metres) long has perimeter screen of fluted Ionic columns, big coved ceiling and luscious plasterwork. The former Doncaster Savings Bank next door is by *Hurst & Moffatt*, 1843. Originally just the three curved corner bays between paired giant pilasters, under a heavy bracketed cornice. Two-storey extension along Scot Lane by *F.W. Masters* in 1906, now lacking its cornice. Narrow two-bay addition on High Street, 1923, replicates the original Italianate style.

Across Scot Lane No. 17's plain stuccoed front, 1810, is a good example of an ordinary Georgian building complying with the Corporation's rounded corners policy. Standing with appropriate formality before the Mansion House are *Richard Perry*'s delightfully detailed stylized bronze rose trees, 2000. To the l. is No. 44, a mid-C18 four-bay brick house with fine rubbed brick lintels to the upper sashes and a very grand early C19 shopfront with urn finials above fluted columns and an eagle over the doorway. Richard Maw opened a draper's shop here in 1811. Next door, the small, elegant distyle *in antis* portico of *Woodhead & Hurst*'s SUBSCRIPTION ROOMS or 'Betting Rooms', 1826, is based on the temple on the Ilissus at Athens. For an annual subscription of a guinea these well-appointed public rooms provided betting facilities for racegoers as well as gaming.* Across the road No. 21, with eye-catching dentilled pediments to the first-floor windows,

* Off-course betting premises were banned in 1853; the Rooms closed in 1892; dem. 1974.

was remodelled in 1841 as the Victoria Rooms, a short-lived rival. Back on the s side Nos. 39–40, Westminster Buildings, retains the upper façade of one of the street's greatest Georgian town houses, by *William Lindley*, 1780. Its giant Ionic pilasters, pediment and balustraded wings remain but redevelopment in 1925 gave it the bizarre facing in marbled lapis lazuli blue, and gold, white and black mosaics. Lastly, on the corner, the DANUM HOTEL, by *W.H. Wagstaffe*, 1908, replaced The Ram, an old coaching inn demolished in 1904 for the widening of Cleveland Street. Long façades of brick above ground-floor ashlar, enlivened by attic dormers and the conical slated dome with lacy cast-iron lantern. Its well-appointed Edwardian interior, befitting the town's premier hotel, included a (surviving) mirror-lined ballroom with hydraulically operated rising wall separating its ante-room. The very Dutch-looking six-storey extension with Expressionist-style brickwork, ending the Cleveland Street return, was built in 1939 by local builders T.H. Jenkinson & Sons with *H.A. Hickson* as executant architect. On the other corner a tall block faced in white faience, 1910, fronts SILVER STREET with a huge second-floor oriel on reassuringly massive brackets and balustraded top with urns. Facing it on the Hallgate corner is the former PRUDENTIAL ASSURANCE building by *Paul Waterhouse*, 1912–13. The rounded tower-like stone corner, topped by a look-out, has bold Baroque details; the returns are in fine pinkish brick with purplish brick pilasters and window aprons.

w of the Mansion House is a large double-range former house with twin-gabled return, built *c.* 1805. The ground-floor front was rusticated and pilastered *c.* 1837 when an impressive new entrance with fluted Ionic columns and a pediment was made at the corner of PRIORY PLACE, created in 1831–2 over a garden and commemorating the Carmelite priory which stood here *c.* 1346–1538. The street's e side is Late Georgian; first *William Hurst*'s household offices etc. for the Mansion House, 1831, then a tall, very gently curved five-bay front, then a terrace of ten three-storey houses, designed in 1830 by *Woodhead & Hurst*, with elegantly long first-floor sashes. Only No. 4, which is three rather than two bays, still has its shallow ground-floor bow window. Priory Place Chapel closes the view at the s end; on the w is the POST OFFICE by *F. W. Masters*, 1885. Red brick. Five bays. Tudor Gothic style with big mullioned-and-transomed windows, those on the second floor reaching up into attic gables.

Now r. into PRINTING OFFICE STREET where the CENTRAL HALL by *Henry Beck*, 1904, has buff terracotta decoration and weird mullions. At the corner is a jolly shop and office block with square clock tower by *Gelder & Kitchen*, 1897–8. Brick with stone dressings, banded on the first floor. Excellent carved Renaissance-style decoration – see the griffins, the frieze panels, the attic's Dutch gables and the clock face's supporters. Opposite is the imposing former CO-OPERATIVE EMPORIUM and OFFICES (Danum House), built 1938–49 by *Harry*

Johnson of *T.H. Johnson & Son* with *W.R. Crabtree*, principal designer of Peter Jones department store in London. It is one of the best and earliest examples of the C20 style in the area, with all the curved glass and sweeping horizontals which the Modernist demands, with a central glazed stair-tower to the narrow symmetrical front and long asymmetrical returns to fit its wedge-shaped site. Steel frame with cladding of yellow brick and much pale blue-grey Vitrolite tilework.

The w side of ST SEPULCHRE GATE is dominated by the FRENCHGATE CENTRE (originally the Arndale Centre, by *Gray Birch Associates*, 1968) with its long curvy canopy. One of the country's earliest covered shopping centres, with multi-storey car park and six-storey office block, it was remodelled by *Leslie Jones & Partners*, 1984–5, with a glazed atrium and further extended by *Carey Jones* in 2001–6. More than holding their own on the E side are a nice variety of buildings, mostly built after street widening *c.* 1911–30. The former NAGS HEAD pub, by *T.H. Johnson*, 1930, displays his firm's enthusiasm for Art Deco. Intact ground floor clad in polished black granite with stepped top, bronze framing to central shopfront. Recessed tripartite window above has patterned metal glazing bars. Two attractively carved horses' heads below parapet. The YORK-SHIRE BANK'S plain sandstone façade of 1977 with its chunky window surrounds contrasts with the serious Portland stone front of the ROYAL BANK OF SCOTLAND, built for William Deacon's bank by *W. Cecil Jackson* of Chesterfield, 1923. Rus-ticated ground floor with two pedimented doorways; recessed upper floors strongly articulated by six giant Ionic columns. Then good ashlar fronts of 1912–13, by *Henry Beck*, with mullioned-and-transomed windows and double-height oriels, and finally a big curved corner block, also by *Beck*, 1912, con-tinues the Georgian tradition of balconies.* Ashlar front framed by rusticated end bays, attic with three Diocletian windows. Diagonally opposite, CLOCK CORNER by *J.G. Walker*, 1894–5, presents the cross-roads with a lively Free Renaissance front with sculpted details by *Samuel Auty*. Clock under a decorative lead dome with weathervane.

FRENCHGATE, once full of inns, carries the Great North Road onwards over the railway and canal, but is now truncated by the dual carriageway, which severs it from North Bridge (*see* Public Buildings). The Minster (*see* Churches) sits majestically alone to the NE; its separation from the town centre by Church Way seems unforgiveable but was the price paid to pedestri-anize the central streets. On Frenchgate's N side, between the corner and the site of *John Butterfield*'s GUILDHALL of 1847 (dem. 1968), is a stylish *Moderne* front, 1935, originally for Boots the Chemist by *Percy J. Bartlett*.

BAXTERGATE, widened in 1894, takes us N to the big MARKET PLACE which is dominated by the Market Hall and Corn Exchange, with the Wool Market at the NE corner (*see* Public

*Replacing *Woodhead & Hurst*'s Subscription Library of 1823.

Buildings). Until 1846 the Town Hall also stood in this space, itself converted originally by the Corporation in 1557 from the partly ruined chapel of St Mary Magdalene.*

The buildings enclosing the market place on three sides include remnants of once-handsome Georgian fronts on the SW side, e.g. Nos. 54–55 mid-C18 with bracketed cornice and pediment; 50–51, refronted in 1800 for the New Bank, with central blind arch rising into the second floor; and 47–48, early C19, with shallow first-floor bows. The better-preserved E side has the large mid-C18 WOOLPACK HOTEL, stuccoed, with later Georgian hooded entrance and broad flanking bow windows. Many taverns, including two examples of C20 'Brewer's Tudor' on the NW side, the BLACK BULL HOTEL, 1920, and the more showy OLDE CASTLE HOTEL, 1928. SCOT LANE, at Market Place's S corner, leads back to the Mansion House. The W side, rebuilt 1915–30 after street widening, has a series of commercial blocks in brick, whose giant pilasters, cornices and tripartite metal windows thoughtfully acknowledge their Georgian context.

2. East and north-east of the centre

HALLGATE running gently uphill from High Street to South Parade was once a distinguished thoroughfare. It retains a few good Georgian houses but has been badly disfigured by C20 demolition, redevelopment and shopfronts. Near the top, beyond the United Reformed church (*see* Churches), No. 26, with good doorcase and tripartite windows to full-height bows, and the plainer house adjoining its Prince's Street return, are by *William Lindley*, *c.* 1798. Opposite, Hallgate's largest house, Nos. 40–41A, has a pediment with decorative wreath and five simple iron balconies, while No. 39, five bays, has a full-width ironwork balcony with palmettes and Greek fret. Rusticated ground floor with big Doric porch.

SOUTH PARADE is wide and tree-lined with a sequence of pretty Regency houses along the route to the racecourse. Development began in 1779 and benefited from the public walkway created in 1793 when the Corporation erected the Hall Cross (*see* below) next to the new cutting that levelled out this stretch of the Great North Road. *William Lindley* bought land here in 1796 and probably designed Nos. 22–23A, completed *c.* 1808, which begins the S side. Seven wide bays, with Doric porch and central pediment on giant Ionic pilasters. Next the 'Pillared Houses', by *Lindley*, 1797, the most original design in the row. Three houses, 1:3:1 bays, the raised ground floor made into a loggia with six Doric columns supporting the upper floors. Prettily decorated doorway and a bow-fronted first-floor oriel to each house. Lindley lived in the larger middle one.

---

*Demolition revealed substantial remains of the Norman interior. Attempts to preserve them failed and the only relic is part of a pier in Regent Square (*see* p. 227).

No. 18, by *John Rawstorne*, *c.* 1798, has a more sophisticated Adamesque front of three bays, the central bay wider. Rustication below and paired giant Ionic pilasters above. Then two more houses by *Lindley*, the larger to the r. with two-storey bow and doorcase with cornice on fluted consoles, the house to the l. added after 1804. *Lindley*'s first enterprise was The Hall (No. 15, now Denison House), the only detached house on South Parade. Five bays with central pediment on giant astylar pilasters. Large Doric porch with triglyph frieze; full-width ironwork balcony. Original flanking carriage archway to r., its pair displaced by two-bay extension. (Screen of fluted Ionic columns between entrance and staircase halls; fine cantilevered stone staircase.)

The land opposite was bought in 1855 by local architect *W. L. Moffatt* and others for a development of large villas. After the scheme foundered REGENT SQUARE was made, with three sides around communal gardens laid out 1858–9, and developed with middle-class housing 1857–81. Local builder *Samuel Hawksworth* quickly built the E half, with two pairs of villas and two short terraces, all stuccoed; the first pair, No. 28 South Parade, with shared pediment, is probably by *Moffatt*. The W half is more varied, predominantly brick and stone including No. 10 (N side), Italianate, with sandstone ashlar front and decorative bargeboards, by *John Butterfield*. Part of a Norman column from St Mary's church (*see* p. 226), stands in the public garden. E of the square South Parade continues as before but the houses are raised on a narrow street above the main road: three storeys, mostly stuccoed fronts, mostly one-bay houses, with a variety of tripartite bow windows, ironwork balconies and decorated doorways with traceried fanlights. No. 8 is an exceptional Gothic Revival latecomer of 1869

Doncaster, Hall Cross Close, Regent Square, as proposed.
Drawing, 1856

by *John Athron* on the last plot available. Delicately carved stone dressings by *Thomas Scrivens*, Scott's foreman carver at St George's. The nice trio at Nos. 4, 5 and 6 have railed basement areas like London houses, an uncommon feature in the region. Lastly three large houses, No. 3 two storeys with lower one-bay wings and pedimented Doric porch, No. 2 with Venetian doorway and flanking windows all in recessed arches, almost identical to those at No. 1, built *c.* 1806. At the end is HALL CROSS of 1793 by *Lindley* and *Joseph Lockwood*, sculptor, a replacement for the C12 cross of Otto de Tilli which stood at the top of Hallgate. A circular shaft with four attached diagonal shafts, encircled by a copy of the medieval inscription. Octagonal pinnacle with acanthus urn finial and weathervane.

REGENT TERRACE opposite, three storeys, was begun *c.* 1819 with Nos. 1–2, which have simple Gothick doorways and first-floor oriels and a castellated parapet. The rest was completed by 1828, probably by *William Hurst*, who lived at No. 6, one of three elegant houses with fine ashlar fronts, stone Tuscan doorcases and elaborate ironwork balconies (cf. No. 39 Hallgate). Basement areas here too, the staircases across them supported on iron girders.

BENNETTHORPE has a more mixed character, but includes ELMFIELD HOUSE, a large stuccoed villa built *c.* 1803 for J.W. Childers of Cantley (q.v.), almost certainly by *Lindley*. Three-bay front with shallow bow windows; parapet with blind balustrading. The enclosed porch and ground-floor bows, which have overscaled consoles to cornices above Venetian-style windows, are later. Left return, to garden, has giant pilasters to first and fourth bays. The fine pedestrian gateway to South Parade, with a big broken segmental pediment, looks reused C17. The grounds became a public PARK in 1923; the WAR MEMORIAL, 1923 by *Ernest Prestwich*, made by *Messrs J. & H. Patteson* of Manchester, is a tall stone obelisk carrying a robed figure of Grief with laurel wreath.

Bennetthorpe continues for half a mile to the racecourse, its buildings of note less concentrated. On the N the former ROCKINGHAM ARMS HOTEL was rebuilt by *Allen & Hickson c.* 1923 with eleven-bay front in an unlikely and curiously anachronistic palazzo-style, the enlarged EARL OF DONCASTER HOTEL almost opposite following in 1933–8 in more stylish Art Deco. On the other side *Colin Harwood*'s unexpected and very individual BENNETTHORPE HOUSE, 1998–9, a discreetly sophisticated addition to the streetscape. On plan a slender lozenge, its four sides of white-rendered concrete are set off by the extensive glazing of the angles, ends and deep clerestory. Then on the S side THE WILLIAM NUTTALL COTTAGE HOMES by *Harry Slater*, 1930–1 ('For Aged Spinsters' now removed from the parapet inscription). Pleasantly varied group in red brick, four pairs each side of a terrace of eight, in a gently staggered crescent. Finally the GRAND ST LEGER HOTEL, formerly Belle Vue, 1811, intended as a hotel with training stables but used first as a house and later as accommodation for stable hands. Five bays with Doric porch and balconies, the original flanking l. gateway and one-bay, one-storey r. wing replaced by unbalanced C20 extensions.

HAMILTON LODGE, Carr House Road (300 yds SSW) by *B.S. Brundell & T. Penrice*, *c.* 1856, is a three-bay hipped-roofed villa. Distyle *in antis* porch with fluted columns. Tripartite bow windows have deep entablatures and blocking courses on elongated consoles.

The town's later C19 and early C20 middle-class suburbs developed NE from Christ Church (*see* Churches) along THORNE ROAD in piecemeal fashion. Characteristically red brick, at first mostly in variations of Queen Anne or Old English style. On its SE side Nos. 4–9, a terrace of three-storey balconied houses, *c.* 1829, was joined by CHRIST CHURCH HOUSE, by *B.S. Brundell* for himself, 1878. On the NW side Herschel Terrace, begun 1881, includes Nos. 25–39, three storeys with Gothic doorways by *Herbert Athron*, adjoining *J. G. Walker*'s ROSSLYN, 1886, at the corner of Christ Church Road. Further on the E side, ST VINCENT HOUSE (No. 46) by *F.W. Masters* for himself, 1888, is close to RUTLAND HOUSE, probably by *J. G. Walker*, 1876, and EDENFIELD, 1894, both overlooking the extensive Town Field, which became a public open space when Town Moor Avenue was made in 1895. Beyond Auckland Road, whose corner plots were taken in 1894 by *J. G. Walker*'s 'The Aucklands', and semi-detached 'Netherleigh' and 'Belvedere' with spired turrets, the influence of the Arts and Crafts style is more evident, especially in the Edwardian houses of the Town Field estate to the SE. Good examples, outshining the efforts of Doncaster's architects, are Nos. 115–121 Thorne Road, two similar semi-detached pairs by *Bunney & Makins*, 1910, and matching threesomes, with roughcast and half-timbered gables, by *Frank Tugwell* on the corners of Windsor Road opposite.

As land from the Highfield, Nether Hall, Broxholme and Wheatley estates was gradually released after 1875, the area NW of Thorne Road was mostly developed with decent-quality terraced housing, its size and value diminishing as the distance from Thorne Road increases. Especially attractive examples include *F. W. Masters*' houses between Christ Church Road and Broxholme Lane, 1892: white brick detailed in red brick; decorative timberwork supporting porches or continuous canopies over doorways and bay windows. On NETHER HALL ROAD to the N, W of Christchurch Road, is NETHER HALL, rebuilt by John Copley *c.* 1702 and still handsome, though hemmed in by C19 terraces. Brick, rendered. Two storeys, hipped roof with attic dormers. Originally seven bays, now five, the central openings replaced *c.* 1811 with tripartite entrance with Tuscan four-column porch; tripartite window over. Three-bay rear r. wing, originally a double-height music room, probably 1759. The l. wing and interior remodelled by *Walker & Thompson* for Doncaster Rural District Council, 1933–5, including the Ionic

screen to hall and impressive imperial staircase with tapering
barley-sugar balusters (some early C18?) and stained glass
windows depicting agriculture and coal mining; the former
council chamber has a domed oval lantern and limed-oak
panelling with Ionic pilasters.

OUTER DONCASTER

BALBY

ST JOHN THE EVANGELIST. By *Horace Francis*, 1847–8. Lancet
style. Nave of four bays with W bellcote. N aisle 1876–7 by
Herbert Athron. Additions to the E end by *Temple Moore*, 1908–
11, which, however, were not fully implemented – see the
bricked-up arches for the intended S chapel. No chancel arch.
Original triple-lancet E window reused, side by side with a
copy. 'English' ALTAR and ROOD by *Wood & Oakley*, 1937–9.
N chapel fittings by *G.G. Pace*, 1966, include REREDOS with
painted panels by *Harry Harvey*. – STAINED GLASS. Three by
T.W. Camm, 1897.

ST CATHERINE'S HALL, 1 m. S. Large house (now offices)
in bold Tudor Gothic by *John Clark*, 1838–9. Seven bays.
Central gable, big octagonal turret-like buttresses and battlemented porte cochère. Long garden front similar. Plain brick
ranges behind enclose small courtyard with battlemented
entrance tower. Some good Gothick plasterwork, joinery and
fireplaces.

BESSACARR*

Doncaster's most affluent suburb, developed from the early C20
on the E side of Bawtry Road, with covenants to ensure exclusivity. No. 3A ELLERS ROAD is by *Peter Aldington*, 1967–8. A
very private house tucked among back gardens. Single-
storeyed; concrete blockwork walls; flat roof. Almost windowless N entrance front with carport. All the rooms have window
walls looking into two intimate courtyards or the S garden, so
indoor and outdoor spaces flow into each other. A larger
courtyard, connecting with the garden, has a later glass roof
and fourth (W) side by *Aldington*. Interior of white-painted
blockwork, varnished timber board ceilings and tiled floors.
Carefully detailed fittings including folding screens between
dining and living rooms.

HEXTHORPE

Narrowly sandwiched between river and railway, Hexthorpe was
developed for employees at the Great Northern Railway workshops, known as 'The Plant', established from 1851 immediately
SW of Doncaster station.

---

*St Hilda's chapel by *G.G. Pace*, 1956–7, was demolished *c.* 1995.

ST JUDE, Hexthorpe Road. By *Herbert Athron*, from a sketch by
Lord Grimthorpe, 1893–4. Attractive exterior in red brick with
generous Ancaster stone dressings and tiled roofs. Spired
timber bellcote set diagonally. Unscholarly Geometrical
tracery. Capacious nave plain and open, the exposed roof
structure using iron ties as Grimthorpe intended. Narrower
short chancel, 1910.

Quirky brick CLOCK TOWER of 1937 in the road outside.

The WORKSHOPS have mostly been demolished. DENISON
HOUSE by *William & Joseph Cubitt*, 1851–2, is the original
building, later offices. Long two-storey brick range facing the
station. 4:38:4 bays, each bay articulated by plain pilasters
and projecting parapet. Ends set forward and pedimented. At
right angles behind, the ENGINE SHOP, 1853 with later additions. N are erecting shops in three gabled ranges with interior
brick arcades. Shorter twin-gabled boiler shop beyond the infill
range to S.

HEXTHORPE PARK. Opened in 1902. THE DELL, an enclosed
quarry garden with specimen trees and winding terraced walks
and rivulets around a central bandstand, was created in 1928–9
to designs by *R. E. Ford*, Estates Surveyor. An unusually imaginative and well-preserved example of municipal landscaping.

DRAX

6020

Small village in flat farmland beyond the power station, between
the converging Ouse and Aire rivers. The church gives some
indication of Drax's greater importance in the Middle Ages but
other evidence is scanty. A seat of the Paynels after the Conquest,
Drax had a castle which was demolished by Stephen in 1154, and
aspirations as a borough in the mid C13. An Augustinian priory,
founded by William Paynel in the 1130s, was suppressed in 1535.

ST PETER AND ST PAUL. Always the parish church, it was given
to the priory *c.* 1165. Norman work of at least three periods.
Building activity probably began in the C11 and must have
gone on to nearly the end of the C12. It needs further study.
First the plain chancel arch, of rough coarse ashlar. One step;
chamfered imposts with a quirk. With it go the remains of nave
windows on the N side, above the arcade. Then the big unbuttressed W tower (with Perp top and stone spire), which has a
tall first stage with ashlar quoins; its walls are mostly ashlar but
the lowest 8 ft (2.5 metres) or so are built of coursed rubble.
Was work interrupted, was an earlier tower partly rebuilt or did
funding improve? Two narrow round-arched W windows with
chamfered openings, the lower one the taller. The tower arch is
plain too but of much finer masonry than the chancel arch. One
shallow step and hoodmould; narrow chamfered impost band;
chamfered jambs. Lastly, the remarkably spacious N arcade.

The two E bays have a circular pier with waterleaf capital; the E respond has slender angle shafts. The arches have flat chevron, dogtooth and hoodmoulds. The W bay follows after a little solid wall; the details are almost the same. Small Norman W window to the aisle. Seven good Romanesque corbel heads are re-set in the S porch; it is a rare treat to view them face to face. E.E. chancel with finely spaced lancet windows (the E wall, with three lancets of even height, rebuilt in 1896 by *C. Hodgson Fowler*). Five lancets on the S side (and a priest's doorway with a shouldered lintel), and two on the N side. This E.E. work is dated 1230 (gift of Letticia, wife of Hugh Paynel, Baron of Drax). Next the Dec work. The S doorway has a filleted moulding resting on two fine leaf sprays. Four-bay S arcade with the normal elements, two piers anciently buttressed because of subsidence. Between 1330 and 1340 the N aisle was widened and a small chapel added. Ogee-headed aisle doorway, windows with reticulated tracery curtailed by their straight heads. The chapel's arch to the chancel rests on charming twisted-leaf corbels, one with a head.

Finally the Perp style, that is the bell-openings, parapet and fine recessed octagonal spire, but most remarkably the addition of an exceptionally ornate clerestory. Eight windows, matched to the four bays of the S arcade. Three lights under depressed four-centred arches, the individual lights with depressed heads too. The windows are so close together that they leave no plain wall. Elaborately decorated parapet with gargoyles and battlements, but the pinnacles are lacking. Inside, the ceiling rests on shafts which have a whole series of well-carved small figures set beneath them. The figures seem to be unrestored and are for that reason alone of considerable value. There are nineteen altogether and they represent the Apostles and other saints. The style is earlier than the late C15, i.e. still with heavy rounded folds – not yet angular in the C15 fashion of the Netherlands. The clerestory is said to have been built in 1540 and it is suggested that some stonework was brought from the priory. Replacement nave roof by *Sir Charles Nicholson*, dated 1932. Panelled, with carved bosses.

Good late C17 ALTAR RAIL. – BENCH-ENDS. A whole set (thirty-eight) of *c.* 1535–50 (cf. Sprotbrough). Engagingly carved, partly with Gothic tracery, partly with Renaissance motifs. Heads in medallions, the Instruments of the Passion, heraldry, a sow playing the bagpipes etc. – STAINED GLASS. E windows 1897, those adjacent on N and S 1900, all by *Powell Bros.* – Four S aisle windows by *Kayll & Co.*, 1900. – S aisle W by *Powell & Sons*, 1927. N aisle easternmost, commemorating Drax Grammar School Old Boys who died 1939–45, by *Harry Stammers*, 1951. – MONUMENTS. Tiny but elaborate cross-slab (?for a child). – Margaret Twistleton †1626 and numerous descendants etc. †1612–1716. Densely inscribed marble tablet below achievement; apron with shield between scrolls (early C18). – John Twistleton †1757. Blocked surround with flaming urn above cornice, in coloured marbles.

READ SCHOOL (formerly Drax Grammar School), 400 yds N.
Founded by Charles Reade in 1667. Rebuilt 1859–60 in white
brick. Altered five-bay schoolroom with Gothic windows and
central porch with bellcote. Headmaster's house behind. Main
block with entrance tower, originally for fifty boarders, by *T.S.
Ullathorne*, 1904–5. Large teaching block by *H.B. Thorp*,
1906–9. Both red brick in mongrel style with some mildly
Gothic and classical details. Further later C20–early C21 additions to rear.

READ CHARITY SCHOOL for girls and infants (former), 20 yds
W. 1849. White brick. Tudor Gothic schoolroom with Mistress's
house attached. Its red brick successor, 1894, is 100 yds S.

DRAX POWER STATION. The country's largest coal-fired power 4
station. Built in two phases (1967–74 and 1985–6) for the
CEGB by *W.S. Atkins & Partners* (executive architects, *Clifford
Tee & Gale*). Twelve COOLING TOWERS, six each end of the
turbine hall etc. Concrete CHIMNEY 850 ft (259 metres) high,
the tallest in the world when built. Since 2013 largely fuelled
by biomass, the wood pellets stored in four giant domed
containers.

EARLSHEATON 2020

ST PETER, New Street. Former National School, 1845–6, converted after 1971 (following demolition of the church of 1825–7
by *Thomas Taylor*). Tudor Gothic. The r. extension is by
William & David Thornton, 1872.

INFANT SCHOOL, Commercial Street, by *Holtom & Connon*,
1875. Gothic.

PROVIDENCE MILL, Syke Lane. Originally for blanket and rug
manufacture. Three-storey mill with small entrance block to
rear r., both *c.* 1820. Behind and to r., mill, chimney and
engine house, 1883.

EAST HARDWICK 4010

ST STEPHEN. By *Joseph A. Davies*, 1872–4. E.E. Cruciform, with
three narrow windows in gabled ends of each arm. Square SW
tower of 1927. Robust timber roofs. – STAINED GLASS. S transept: S windows by *Kayll & Co.*, 1893; E, two by *Adam Goodyear*, 2000.

HUNDHILL HALL, ⅓ m. WNW. *c.* 1800, possibly with C17 core.
Gracious symmetrical front of five bays and three storeys with
lower two-bay wings, set back. Ashlar, with hipped stone roofs
and bracketed eaves. (In the library is a fine carved timber
overmantel dated 1616, *ex situ*.)

ECCLESFIELD

Village on the N edge of Sheffield, whose suburban estates (e.g. Parson Cross p. 618) have encroached on all but the little oasis centred on the church and its large burial ground.

ST MARY. One of the southern West Riding's major late medieval churches, long known as the 'Minster of the Moors'. Of ancient foundation, it had, until the C19, a huge parish that stretched far into the Pennines, covering nearly 78 square miles (cf. Almondbury and Halifax). The church was granted to the Abbey of St Wandrille, Normandy, in the early C12, passing to the Carthusian house of St Anne, near Coventry, in 1386. Five-bay nave with clerestory and aisles, crossing with crossing tower, shallow transepts and three-bay chancel with shorter chapels, all embattled and, except for the aisles, pinnacled. Tower top has eight pinnacles (cf. e.g. Thornhill). Mainly Perp, but internally two earlier periods can be discerned. The nave piers and W responds are reused material of c. 1200. The responds are keeled, the N piers circular, the S piers octagonal. A small finely moulded arch of the same period is on display in the porch. The piers received new tall bases and new capitals to fit them into the proportions of the new church. This was started, it seems, with the crossing. The piers here have heavy semi-octagonal responds and the arches three sunk quarter-mouldings, a sign usually of the early C14. The Perp work is late (Dodsworth recorded inscriptions in windows of the chancel and chapels dating their glass to 1502–5) and quite ambitious. Externally the most original feature is half-detached buttresses and pinnacles connected with the body of the church by tiny flying buttresses (cf. Halifax and Silkstone). These occur at the S aisle and its SW angle, at the porch, and at the corner where the last bay of the S aisle has a shallow chapel-like projection to link it with the transept. The same projection in the N aisle. The windows all Perp and in the E parts transomed. The chancel chapels are of two bays with octagonal piers and capitals and double-chamfered arches just as in the nave. The chapels have restored ROOFS with good carved bosses. More bosses in the aisles. The church was restored over several decades by Dr Alfred Gatty, vicar 1839–1903, the chancel in the 1850s, the nave in the 1880s under *J.B. Mitchell-Withers*. The nave CEILING was replaced in 1964–9 by *George Pace*. The sculptural geometry of its grid of deeply sunk panels, in pale wood, seems wilfully alien. Will a future C22 reviser of this volume see it as a distinctive C20 contribution to the long continuum of alterations?

    REREDOS. Oak, carved with figurative panels, and sanctuary panelling, early C20. – Excellent early C16 chancel and chapel WOODWORK, restored by *Arthur Hayball* and his pupil *Harry Hems*: SCREENS. The rood screen has two-light divisions with close panel tracery and ribbed coving. Parclose screens of one-light divisions. STALLS. Four attached to the rood screen. They have misericords, two of these with heads, and heads carved on their arms. The bench-ends in front have small figures as finials, one either the Virgin and Child or St Anne with the infant Virgin (on St Anne, *see* above). – More BENCHES in the S chapel, several also with small figures instead of poppyheads, including St Catherine. One bench has on the back an inscription: 'Orate...pro bono statu Johannis Mountney et Johanne uxoris eius, qui hoc oratorium fieri fecerunt...1536' (Pray for the good fortune of John Mountney and Joan his wife who built this chapel 1536), another is dated 1564. – PULPIT. 1876. Octagonal, oak, by *Arthur Hayball*, with contemporary carved panels from Antwerp. – FONT. 1662. Octagonal on stout, heavily moulded plinth. The bowl's panels contain a heart, a rose, a fleur-de-lys, a lozenge and the four numerals 1–6–6–2. – SCULPTURE. S transept. Incomplete Anglo-Saxon cross-shaft, in a double-socketed base (cf. Bolsterstone). Plain, with a few roughly incised Latin crosses and other motifs on one face. Probably CII.

STAINED GLASS. In the N aisle westernmost window fragments of C15 and C16 glass, including an inscription referring to the Carthusian prior and monks of St Anne's 'qui istam cancellam et fenestram fieri fecerunt' (who had this chancel and window made). Notable and complete group of C19 and early C20 windows by leading firms. E window by *Wailes*, 1860. – Chancel S window by *Hedgeland*, 1855, still in a crudely coloured Nazarene style. – S chapel E window 1866, and first from E 1867, also N chapel first from E 1869, by *Hardman*. – N chapel E window by *Heaton, Butler & Bayne*, 1875, commemorating Louisa Foljambe (cf. Tickhill). – S chapel second from E and N chapel second from E by *Clayton & Bell*, 1874. – S transept window commemorating Dr Gatty's wife, Margaret, the children's author, designed by *W. F. Dixon*, made by *Clayton & Bell*, 1874. – S aisle easternmost by *W. F. Dixon*, 1882 (with some Pre-Raphaelite influence, but pale colouring). – S aisle second and third from E by *Kempe*, 1892 and 1895. – W window 1901, and N aisle third from E 1923, by *Powell & Sons*. – N aisle first from E, 1887, commemorating Dr Gatty's daughter Juliana Ewing, also a children's author.

MONUMENTS. S chapel. Sir Richard Scott †1638, by *William Wright*, 1640. He lies stiffly on his side, his cheek resting on his hand. The monument has its original iron grille but was restored in 1749. Was the composition then altered? Black columns l. and r., carrying two arches, and a taller column in the middle cutting across the figure. – Margaret Freeman †1783. Shapely but battered tablet by *John Platt*. – Maria Booth †1824. Chaste tablet by *William Hollins* of Birmingham. – Transepts. Thomas Rawson †1826 by *White Watson*. White marble, with fluted columns and a delicately carved urn. Beside it, a bust of Thomas Rawson by *Edward Law*, 1827, erected 1841. – John Rawson †1819 by *White Watson*. Unusual, the inscription on a scroll tied to a fluted column. – George

Byard †1813 by *John Blagden*, with sarcophagus and urn. – N
chapel (office). Francis Foljambe †1707 and family. Large
aedicule with broken segmental pediment, in grey marbles

PRIORY. The Benedictines of St Wandrille founded a cell here
in the early C12. Its medieval remains were restored by *Charles
Hadfield* in 1887–9 as part of the house called The Priory
to the N of the churchyard. First the tall chapel block, of
c. 1300, in rubble with quoins and later buttresses. Set above
a lower floor with an undercroft, the chapel has a three-light
E window with cusped stepped lancet lights, a paired cusped
lancet and a single lancet to the S, and a tiny look-out window
on the W side. (The internal W doorway, with the same sunk
quarter-moulding as the crossing arches of the parish church
leads into a set-back N–S cross-wing; there is a piscina below
the larger S window.) The walls of the two-storey cross-wing
are medieval, but the mullioned-and-transomed windows on
the E side are C16 or C17, and the windows in the S gable C19.
Attached to the W is ECCLESFIELD HALL, dated 1736, a plain
five-bay house of two-and-a-half storeys, built of large ashlar
blocks.

ECCLESFIELD SCHOOL, Chapeltown Road. By *H. Wormald*,
County Education Architect, 1928–31. Originally Ecclesfield
Grammar School. Stone. Staid, formal front of three storeys
with gabled end bays. Extensions 1954, and, to NW, the buildings of Ecclesfield Hunshelf County Secondary School, opened
1966. The schools amalgamated as a comprehensive school in
1967.

ECCLESFIELD PRIMARY SCHOOL, High Street. 1940 by *Sir
John Burnet, Tait & Lorne* for West Riding County Council as
a senior school. Good surviving example of the pre-war
Modern Movement style, in a spread-out L-plan. The entrance
and assembly hall form a N extension to the shorter classroom
wing at the angle, the gymnasium is a SE extension from the
longer wing. The forms are more rigid than they would have
been ten years later. Long bands of windows. On the S side
the upper floor of the longer wing is set on pilotis. Steel-
framed, with grey roughcast walls, which makes the building
look drabber than it ought to be.

WHITLEY HALL (hotel), ¾ m. NW. Essentially a two-storey
house completed in 1584 on an existing site, now much masked
by later alterations and additions. On the N side is a two-light
double-transomed staircase window to the r. of the main
doorway and a four-light king-mullioned window to the l. The
rest of the N front, with mullioned-and-transomed windows
and two-storey square bay to the l. gabled projection, is mostly
C19. Seven-bay garden front altered in the early C18: two
gables with oval windows, central doorway with broken segmental pediment on consoles. This front is enclosed by a
three-bay C17 l. wing, and double wings on the r., the inner
one of 1980 and the C19. The outer wing is C17 and has on its
E side two doorways dated 1683 with characteristic broad flat
rusticated surrounds, one now in late C20 extension. (Inside,

a doorway dated 1584 leads into the wing of 1683; one room has an original plasterwork ceiling.)

EDLINGTON

St Peter. The first church to be vested in the Redundant Churches Fund (now Churches Conservation Trust), in 1971.* Small, late C12, with some excellent Romanesque decoration, sadly worn in parts. Of chief interest is the very curious s doorway. This has chevron and beakhead round the arch, continued without any break by imposts or capitals right down the jambs. The hoodmould has roundels containing intricately detailed concentric circles. The nave and chancel are essentially Norman, as their N and S corbel tables prove. These display an engaging variety of human and animal heads. One quite large Norman window in the nave with much-renewed external shafts and chevron fragments in the arch (cf. Birkin and Campsall). The chancel arch has responds with shafts that start about 4 ft 6 in. (1.3 metres) from the ground, as if there had been a stone screen below (cf. Rossington). Capitals densely decorated with big stylized leaves and intertwined bands, beaded on the l., reeded on the r. Arch of two orders with chevron, and, on the face of the inner order, little round arches formed by a double row of arrises. N aisle and W tower added a little later, c. 1200. Two-bay arcade with circular pier, square abacus and double-chamfered pointed arches. Contemporary N doorway. The tower has at its original top a string course decorated underneath with semicircular scallops like tiny upside-down merlons. N and S windows still small and round-headed, but the arch towards the nave is again pointed, double-chamfered and rests partly on plain, round, cone-bottomed corbels designed on the model of Roche Abbey (q.v.). One capital square, the other semi-octagonal. Chancel has blocked C13 priest's doorway with shouldered lintel. In the mid C15 the N aisle was extended by a bay for a chapel, its arch to the chancel on semi-octagonal responds, and both nave and tower were heightened and battlemented. Most windows Perp too. The chancel's Dec-style piscina and credence table are Victorian. The roof is by *G. G. Pace*, 1971. – MONUMENTS. Decorated cross-slab carved with the heads of a woman and a man, early C16(?). – Lady Mary Cary †1672, wife of Sir Thomas Wharton. Good standing monument. Corniced panel with flowers and fruit, skull and hourglasses around frame for brass inscription (lacking); elaborate heraldic panel above.

---

* Redundant since 1962, the fittings had been removed and, by 1966, roofless and vandalized, the church faced demolition. The FONT, 1590, is at Dunscroft, Hatfield (q.v.). Benches are at St Mary, Sprotbrough (q.v.).

N is the former pit village of NEW EDLINGTON begun as a private development in 1911 by the Edlington Land & Development Co., but according to a plan and housing standards determined by the Staveley Coal & Iron Company. Most houses had bathrooms. The church (ST JOHN) is by *F. Norman D. Masters*, 1913–14, for the South Yorkshire Coalfield Church Extension Committee (cf. Bentley, Maltby and Rossington). Neo-Romanesque with a campanile at the SE corner beside the exterior pulpit. Light, attractive interior, its orientation successfully reversed in 1982 to make the apsidal E baptistery into the sanctuary and the matching W end into community space.

The VICTORIA PRIMARY SCHOOL of 1913 by *John Stuart*, West Riding County Education Architect, is a large and early example of the Council's single-storey quadrangular elementary schools with central lawn. Brick, well detailed with Baroque motifs; many-gabled.

MONUMENT, Edlington Wood. 1¼ m. NE. Large urn on inscribed pedestal, erected by Lord Molesworth to his dog, 1714.

EGGBOROUGH *see* WHITLEY

ELLAND

A small textile mill town on the S bank at a crossing point of the Calder, its medieval origins as one of the two chapelries of Halifax set it apart from other Calder valley towns. The church sits just above the river, with the town, which was later celebrated for its stone quarries, behind it. A market charter was granted in 1317. Although turnpike links began with roads to Rochdale by 1735 and Leeds by 1741, and the Calder and Hebble Navigation between Wakefield and Sowerby Bridge opened in 1770, real industrial growth only came in the C19 and early C20, with mills and works crowding the lower slope of the hillside that rises steeply to the ridge forming the watershed with the Colne valley.

CHURCHES

ST MARY. Essentially Perp, although of Norman origin. Long and low, and plain apart from the late corbel table. Mostly rubble. Chancel chapels roofed continuously with the aisles, which embrace the dark ashlar tower of *c.* 1490. The ashlar chancel extension, the E windows and the chapels' buttresses bearing the Savile owl also late C15. Sanctus bellcote on nave gable. Nave and chancel are of the same width, the broad chancel arch rebuilt using stones of *c.* 1180. Big soffit roll continued from semicircular responds, then a small roll, then beakhead. The similarities to Kirkstall Abbey (*West Riding North*) indicate masons in common. Late C13 arcades of two bays to chancel chapels. Four-bay nave arcades with octagonal piers and double-chamfered arches. Chancel has SE stair-case to sacristy or crypt below. – ROOD, and SCREEN now at nave rear, by *G.H. Fellowes Prynne*, 1917. – PAINTINGS. Two panels depicting Moses and Aaron, formerly flanking the altar. – STAINED GLASS. Important E window by York glaziers *c.* 1481. Life of the Virgin in twenty-one scenes; eleven with original glass, the rest from *Wailes*'s restoration, 1856–66. – S chapel S window by *Hardman*, 1876. N chapel E by *Hardman* 1874. S aisle second from E by *Wailes*, 1869. N aisle fourth from E by *Kempe*, 1893. – W window by *Wailes*, 1850. W windows of aisles. Jumbled fragments of medieval glass. – MONUMENTS. William Horton †1715 and sons William †1739 and Richard †1742. Hanging wall monument with bust in oval medallion. Several good later C17, C18 and C19 monuments, with aedicules, obelisks etc.

ALL SAINTS, Savile Road. By *G.H. Fellowes Prynne*. Designed 1896; the E half built 1900–3, completed 1915–17 to amended plans. Very large, and so quintessentially *c.* 1900-ish suburban that it would sit happily in a prosperous London suburb or near a south coast esplanade. Rock-faced exterior, tiled roofs, the long Butterfieldian profile broken only by a copper-clad flèche above the chancel arch. Small arcaded cloister on the N. Lancet windows. Lofty and handsomely proportioned interior; brick with stone dressings. Passage aisles. W arcade to raised baptistery. Chapels overlap the first two bays of the nave, the longer N chapel with polygonal apse to intimate aisled sanctuary. Excellent High Church fittings, especially the tall, elaborately carved and gilded REREDOS, 1928, the hanging ROOD, 1904, and the tiers of saints in the chancel arch by *Stuflesser*, 1912 – PULPIT. Oak, richly carved (from Chester Cathedral, 1967). – STAINED GLASS. E window and baptistry windows by *Percy Bacon & Bros*, 1916.

BETHESDA METHODIST CHURCH, Victoria Road. By *William Hill*, 1879–80. Slightly Gothic, with Geometric plate tracery in a large window in the steeply gabled front. Buttresses with decorative pyramidal spires. Buttressed returns have tall transverse gables to alternate bays. (Original galleried interior.)

SOUTHGATE METHODIST CHURCH (St Paul's United Methodist). 1914–15. Dec tracery to big window above paired doorways. Sturdy buttressed tower to l. has little stone spire, set back.

PROVIDENCE CHAPEL (former, Congregational), Huddersfield Road. 1822–3, altered 1856 and later. Thin stone 'bricks'. Simple but carefully composed front of three bays, with central recessed panel under a round arch rising into the gable and, at the angles, recessed 'pilaster' strips with coved ashlar tops. Plain round-arched windows. Later Doric porch. Larger and grander later C19 successor in BROOK STREET nearby has two doorways in pedimented centre of five-bay front and windows in two tiers.

TEMPERANCE CHAPEL (former, Methodist Free Church), Huddersfield Road. By *John Bedford* of Elland, 1875. Gabled front with Lombardic frieze and round-arched openings under Gothic heads.

WESLEY CHAPEL (former), Huddersfield Road. By *Waddington & Burnley*, 1891–2, for nearly 800 worshippers. Italianate style in stone 'bricks' with ashlar dressings. Prominent semi-octagonal ventilation towers with domed cupolas flank the central gable.

PUBLIC BUILDINGS

TOWN HALL. By *C.F.L. Horsfall*, 1887–8. Large, on a prominent corner site, comprising a 1,050-seat galleried public hall above ground-floor shops. Bald Italianate style in stone 'bricks'. Narrow giant portico to three-bay front, the cupola with clock above the pediment the better feature.

COUNCIL OFFICES, Southgate, Elizabeth Street. By *Horsfall & Williams*, 1895–6 for the new Urban District Council. Modest front with a little pediment and some Renaissance details; an addition to a plain existing house.

BROOKSBANK SCHOOL, Victoria Road. By *W.S. Braithwaite*, 1909–11, won in competition. Pennine Vernacular-style front with big double-transomed windows, the first-floor ones of three-over-five lights rising into the gables. The heavily pedimented porch with Ionic columns seems out of place. Additions include gable-ended classroom blocks with industrial-inspired ridge profile, by *Harrison & Seel* with *A.W. Glover*, West Riding County Architect, 1956–60.

PERAMBULATION

The medieval street pattern survives around the church, with four streets leading from THE CROSS. In NORTHGATE, facing the church a mid-C17 gabled house with short projecting wings and two upper windows of four-over-six with stepped lights. Steeply down to BRIGGATE, where the imposing former Halifax & Huddersfield Union Bank, by *E.W. Johnson*, 1893, faces the bridge. Richly decorated front with paired giant columns of Aberdeen granite and a seated figure of Britannia above the pediment. Across the river, off Gasworks Lane, ELLAND WHARF was built by the Calder & Hebble Navigation Co. from *c.* 1820. At the entrance a former single-storey, three-roomed lodge with hipped roof. Small former warehouse with gable to the canal has taking-in doors on two floors and attic; at its rear is the foreman and yard master's house with two-storey shallow bow window. Five-bay warehouse extension at right angles, *c.* 1840, has a basket-arched opening to each floor on the canal side and a big arched opening to a wet dock at the SW end. NE on Park Road, overlooking the canal, is the prominent block of VALLEY MILLS, a late C19 former worsted mill with Italianate details, converted to flats 2006. Three added glass-walled storeys compete with the stair-tower and the chimney for attention.

In WESTGATE a distinctive housing scheme by *Dewis Harper & B.H. Gilbert*, 1965–6, the first phase of the Harper plan for the town centre's redevelopment, shows sensitivity to the topography and the industrial skyline. Five-storey blocks in dark brick with monopitch roofs and strips of canted bay windows. Two-storey staggered terraced houses have integral garages. Facing Jepson Lane, the FLEECE INN is a good stone house, *c*. 1610. U-plan, passage entry. Transomed windows of 3:3 lights with king mullions to S parlours in the broad gabled wings and to the gabled housebody bay. This is squeezed by the (imported?) broad, two-storey gabled porch, constructed partly of big ashlar blocks and with arched upper lights. Projecting kitchen wing behind housebody.

On Dewsbury Road the plain PERSEVERANCE MILL, six and four storeys, is now flats but retains its tower and iron-banded circular stone chimney. Beyond, the four-storey MARSHFIELD MILL, *c*. 1910, has brick string courses arching over the windows. Converted 2007 as 'The Silk Mill' apartments, with three extra floors and balconies. Downhill, WELLINGTON MILLS, Quebec Street, now a business centre, was a steam-powered cotton-spinning mill. Five-storey block 1875, four-storey block by *Thomas Kershaw*, 1912; both of fireproof construction, replacing mills that burnt down.

NEW HALL, ¾ m. ESE. On the hillside off Whitwell Green Lane. One of the finest gentry houses in the area, built *c*. 1490 by Nicholas Savile of the lesser, Elland, branch of that mighty family. Two-bay hall and projecting cross-wings, hearth-passage plan. N front has original plain timber framing exposed on upper floor and gables. S front cased in fine ashlar 1656–7 with a nine-light double-transomed window and a crenellated parapet to the hall and a splendid porch with an 'apple and pear' rose window of six mouchettes (cf. Wood Lane Hall, Sowerby). Doorway below has fluted Doric columns and straight entablature, the arched inner doorway alternate blocks, like a vernacular Gibbs surround (cf. Barkisland Hall). N porch added about same time is partly timber-framed, matching N front. Other casing is in inferior stonework. (The hall, which originally had a fire-hood and a dais canopy, was preserved as an open space with roof timbers visible but remodelled with new stone chimneystack, staircase and gallery to N and W. Large and elaborate plasterwork royal arms above the fireplace is dated 1670. W wing has principal parlour with chamber or solar above, both heated by original extruded stone stack. Unusually, E wing probably also had heated 'lower parlour' to S from the beginning. Wings were re-floored in C16 to give parlours compartmented ceilings.) C18 extensions to E end have early C19 S workshop wing.

BLACKLEY BAPTIST CHURCH, ¾ m. SW. 1878–9. Big, typical isolated upland chapel, prominent on a ridge. First chapel, 1789, now cottages, adjacent.

ELSECAR

Village beside the collieries, iron works and other industrial enterprises developed in the C18 and C19 by the 4th and 5th Earls Fitzwilliam, who provided churches, public buildings and housing, well built in stone and, when appropriate, in simple classical style.

HOLY TRINITY, Church Street. By *J. P. Pritchett*, 1841–3. E.E. w tower with pinnacled buttresses and stone spire. Amusing headstops. Aisleless nave with w gallery on stone arcade. Small apsidal chancel. – STAINED GLASS. By *Morris & Co.*, 1920 (chancel; war memorial) and 1937 (nave SE).

SCHOOL by *Pritchett & Son*, 1851–2.

ELSECAR HERITAGE CENTRE, Wath Road. Complex of former workshops etc. around the IRON WORKS opened 1795. The three-storey ENGINE HOUSE with quoins and stone bands, retains its Newcomen Atmospheric Beam Engine of 1795. Mid-C19 two-storey GATEHOUSE with canted ends, and attached RAILWAY STATION for the 6th Earl, 1870. Large, aisled WORKSHOP with brick arcades on cast-iron columns, 1850. Long range on FORGE LANE has iron lintels and windows and very wide elliptical archway with brick head.

Off WENTWORTH ROAD is a quoined doorway to sloping ashlar-lined pedestrian TUNNEL (or footrill), probably for Low Wood Colliery, opened 1720.

Terraced cottages include STATION ROW by *John Carr*, 1796.

EMLEY

ST MICHAEL. Difficult to unravel. Modest nave and chancel, the nave's rubble masonry Norman but probably mostly reused in the C14 – see the tympanum with lion and lamb built into the s wall inside. Perp remodelling, with one-bay chancel chapel (E bay 1632, the arch on cruder corbels). The church was consecrated by Archbishop Scrope (1398–1405). Three-bay N aisle, of rough masonry, perhaps later. The big W tower, a commanding landmark, is mid–late C15 and possibly built by Byland Abbey, which exploited local minerals. The nave roof is unusual for the West Riding. Tie-beams, queenposts with cross struts. Two tiers of curved wind-braces. What is its date? Chancel ceiling C18, panelled. – FONT. Later C17. Goblet-shaped, the bowl with big irregular gadrooning. – Fine C18 PULPIT has tester with marquetry. – STAINED GLASS. E window, *c.* 1500, has Crucifixus with the Virgin and St John, the heads missing. In adjacent s window St George in armour and an angel. N aisle second from E by *Kempe & Co.*, 1910.

MARKET CROSS, Church Street. Medieval. Plinth and shaft (painted white). A market charter was granted in 1253.

(KIRKBY GRANGE, ½ m. N. *c.* 1606, altered and subdivided. Three-bay s front with e cross-wing. Entrance between first and second bays has lintel ornamented with scrolls and shields and inscription LAUS DEO. Wing is like another, similar, front. Its r. gabled bay, with attic storey, is part of a taller N range apparently of a different build. Mullioned-and-transomed windows to both fronts, of three, five and seven lights.)

THORNCLIFFE GRANGE, ¼ m. NE. Built by Brice Allot soon after 1623. Three-gabled front; U-plan. Porch to lobby-entry between w kitchen and housebody. Principal windows all transomed: six lights with king mullions to both front and rear of housebody, five lights to kitchen and front parlour, four to rear parlour and to chambers. (Huge fireplace in housebody; oak panelling in front parlour.)

EMLEY WOODHOUSE, 1 m. E. Handsome Late Georgian dower house for Bretton Hall (q.v.). Ashlar. Three by two bays. Entrance with attached Doric columns.

TELEVISION MAST, Emley Moor, 1½ m. w. by *Ove Arup & Partners* for Independent Television Association, 1969–71, a shapely landmark for miles around. 900 ft (274 metres) high, its reinforced-concrete walls taper in a fluid curve from an 80-ft (24.4-metre)-diameter base. Including the 184-ft (56-metre) antenna it is the tallest free-standing structure in the UK. It replaced a taller steel mast that collapsed in 1969.

FAIRBURN

4020

ST JAMES. By *Ebenezer Trotman*, 1846. Small and simple. s aisle extended by vestry, 1915. Dec tracery.

FARNLEY TYAS

1010

ST LUCIUS. By *R. D. Chantrell* for the 4th Earl of Dartmouth, 1838–40. Not of the normal lancet type, and of a village scale. Four-bay nave with small straight-headed three-light windows, their lights ogee-arched. Low, short chancel. w tower with a little octagonal spire on a splayed base. Wide nave with big queenpost roof. Alterations in 1904 included formation of a choir between organ and screened vestry in E bay, and carved FITTINGS in limed oak. – STAINED GLASS. Two N windows by *Harry Stammers*, in nave 1961, and chancel 1968.

FARNLEY HEY, Honley Road, ¾ m. w. One of the best post-war houses in England, designed by *Peter Womersley* for his brother, 1953–4. Much indebted to Le Corbusier and Frank Lloyd Wright for its setting and planning of the interior, the house is set on the edge of a steep wooded hillside and enjoys far-reaching views southwards down the Holme valley.

107

L-plan with N wing towards the road. Timber frame, with rough stone, pale brick and vertical teak slatting where a more solid closing than glass is desired. The management of the glazed and closed surface is most successful in its rhythms. So is the management of spaces and surface details inside – entertaining and music were important factors in the design, so the living spaces are arranged to promote openness and sociability. Small changes in levels, and fitted furniture, plant screens or curtains rather than conventional walls, define the rooms; the finishes are mostly wood, with stone and brick. Main living room, 12 ft 6 in. (3.8 metres) high, has glazed S wall, the external timber columns and overhanging flat roof forming a shallow loggia to the terrace; hardwoods to N wall, floor and ceiling, W wall brick. The open staircase, with marbled Formica side panels, rises from the living room to a mezzanine gallery/landing above the lower dining room to the E. The cantilevered S end of the gallery, now glazed, was originally an outdoor bedroom. A study/hall, with the front door, is at a slightly lower level N of the living room, the division a fitted hi-fi unit with built-in radio etc. The first bedroom is above the study. N of the dining room is the kitchen, with a door into a narrow passage under the N wing. Beyond the passage the garage; the two bedrooms etc. above this added in 1956 with slatted E and N walls, replaced the original projecting terrace. Beside these an addition containing a study and bathroom, added by *Arthur Quarmby* in 1964–5.

FEATHERSTONE

The setting of North Featherstone has changed dramatically since Pevsner saw it, as the colliery sites and mountainous coal tips have been reclaimed for agriculture and industrial estates. The separate C19 mining settlement of (South) Featherstone, which absorbed the old village of Purston Jaglin, lies in the valley about a mile S.*

ALL SAINTS, Ackton Lane, North Featherstone. Medieval, restored by *T.H. & F. Healey*, 1881–2. Small, rather low Perp church of blackened stone, much restored, especially on the S side. Nave of two bays with C15 three-bay S aisle, and chancel with S chapel, both of three bays, the chapel probably later C15. The nave, aisle and chancel are all battlemented, like the unbuttressed W tower. C15 S porch with stone roof on three massive single-chamfered transverse arches and crocketed

---

*FEATHERSTONE MANOR was demolished in the early 1960s and ACKTON HALL in 1969.

pinnacles either side of the plain gable. Inside, the s aisle and s chapel arcades have the standard Perp elements. The absence of an E respond to the latter suggests the E wall was at least partially rebuilt when the chancel's fine early C16 panelled ceiling was made. E window tracery very like that in Normanton's s chapel of *c.* 1519. Reordered, after fire damage, by *David Greenwood* 1999–2000, with new chancel furnishings, low E screen and full-height screens in the s chapel arcade. Also a w narthex with small gallery, in glass and wood. – FONT. Octagonal, Perp, with raised shields and an inscription commemorating Johes de Baghill and Katerina, his wife (he died in 1451). Said to have been brought from Pontefract in the Civil War.

ST THOMAS, St Thomas Road, Featherstone. By *Thomas Pollard*, 1876–8. Large, plain, buttressed church whose high nave roof stands up among Victorian terraces and C20 council housing. E.E. style. Wide, aisled nave of four bays with clerestory of large quatrefoils over very short paired lancets, chancel and N vestry. Arcades on short circular piers, with large, roughly cut stone blocks as capitals and hoodmould stops. Only the E responds with their arching stiff-leaf capitals and the half-finished chancel arch carvings show what was intended for them before funds ran out. – STAINED GLASS. Christ among the Doctors in the Temple by *Abbott & Co.*, *c.* 1917, and The Sower by *Morris & Co.*, 1938 (s aisle); five windows by *Kayll & Reed*, 1920s.

HUNTWICK LODGE, Huntwick Lane. Lodge to Nostell Priory, dated 1655, formerly with attached gateway. Ruinous at the time of writing.

PURSTON HALL, Ackworth Road. Sedate two-storey ashlar house of *c.* 1824 with five-bay s front. Matching N extension with open pediment, 1863.

FELKIRK

3010

ST PETER, Church Lane. Restored 1875 by *T.H. Healey*. The most impressive feature is the tower arch. Its responds are very fine Norman work probably reused from a chancel arch of *c.* 1100. In the tower's internal walls are many fragments of arch mouldings, presumably from the same source. The responds are paired shafts with a slimmer set-back shaft on the E and w. Scalloped capitals, with cable moulding at the base and friezes decorated with plain and intersecting round arches, stars and knots. The N capital has a head on the SE corner. Its frieze includes a row of faces (cf. those on the font at Skelmanthorpe (q.v.)). The tower walls include voussoirs with chevron and pieces of hoodmould with billets and stars. Other evidence of an early Norman church is the herringbone masonry on the N side at the E end of the S aisle, originally the external face of the nave S wall.

The buttressed W tower with its embattled top, gargoyles and pinnacles is quite stately, the rest of the church more humble. Short nave with low aisles and clerestory. Two-bay chancel, the E window lower and with more elementary tracery than its large W counterpart. Other windows mostly square-headed and late, possibly even C17 or C18. The S arcade with octagonal piers and three double-chamfered arches must be of the C13, probably late, and with that date goes the W lancet in the S aisle. The N arcade was built at the same time, but rebuilt in the Perp style, and higher, when the church was remodelled c. 1500. Its W respond was reused. This arcade also has octagonal piers and double-chamfered arches. Perp also the chancel chapels and the tower. The S chapel is of two bays. The N chapel is continuous with the aisle and has only one broad arch. E of it an earlier sacristy with a transverse pointed tunnel-vault, probably built c. 1400, like the S porch. This also has a stone roof, the slabs carried on massive arched ribs. – WINDOW HEAD. S aisle S wall. Made of one stone and with incised concentric lines round the arch. Another fragment of the Norman church? – PISCINA. S aisle, for a chantry chapel added here in 1285. Tiny, with ogee head. – BENCH. W end of S aisle. From the Galway pew, panelled, with late C16 marquetry. – STAINED GLASS. S chapel, second from E, by *Kayll & Co.*, c. 1902. – S aisle, W end, by *Frederick Preedy*, 1876. – MONUMENT. N chapel. Marble plaque to 4th Viscount Galway (†1810) by *Shout*.

OLD SCHOOLROOM. In the churchyard. Late C16. Small. Either side of the doorway one five-light window with Tudor-arched lights.

HODROYD HALL, High Well Hill Lane, ¼ m. E. C17, probably E-plan, remodelled and enlarged in C19. Main (W) front has three-bay centre with a double-height bay window in the middle. Projecting wings to N and S retain some early fabric. All are two storeys with attics and gabled. Some original windows with mullions and transoms. Large Victorian N porch, with tall staircase window to l.

FENAY BRIDGE
2¼ m. SE of Huddersfield

FENAY HALL, Fenay Lane. Of complicated development. Partly a C16 timber-framed house with a small single-storey hall and some good external decoration, altered in the C17 and late C18; partly late C18 with C19 extensions. S front has three bays of 1792 to r. and remodelled hall and gabled W wing to l. Both stuccoed, and with a Victorian veranda fronting the hall, these nevertheless retain their original form. (An exposed tie-beam in the wing, with tracery decoration and the initials of William Fenay suggests a mid-C16 date.) On the N, the wing has C18 stone casing and one surviving six-light mullioned window and, behind the hall, an adjoining addition with a gable hidden by a parapet. Left of this, above a later stone-built outshut, two pretty timber-framed gables of perhaps *c.* 1600, the r. one with the initials of Nicholas Fenay (†1616). Diagonal struts, tie-beams carved with foliage and vine trails (cf. Kirklees Priory gatehouse, Kirklees Park, q.v.), elaborate bargeboards and turned finials. Inside, the hall, apparently cruck-framed, has dates 1605 and 1660. Panelling with frieze of Latin aphorisms (Fear God, Love your spouse, Return a favour etc.) and a handsome plaster ceiling. Large star-motif, the points lily-shaped; individual floral etc. motifs in the compartments into which the star is divided. Rebuilt front of house, E of hall, has a projecting two-storey canted bay in the centre and pedimented entrance to l. C19 service range to rear r. w gateway dated 1617 to open N courtyard.

WOODSOME HALL, Woodsome Road (golf clubhouse). A picturesque and mellow Tudor manor house, high on the hillside in the little valley of Fenay Beck, rebuilt *c.* 1520 by Arthur Kay (1498–1574). Alterations and extensions were made by his descendants well into the C17 and the whole house was restored and altered in 1870–6 by the 5th Earl of Dartmouth.

Timber-framed open-hall with two-storey cross-wings, cased in stone in the C17. In the angle of the l. wing is a projecting gabled porch to the hearth passage, its moulded entrance dated 1600. A four-light mullioned-and-transomed window above, similar upper windows to the wings, all with labels. The hall has a large transomed five-light window with a narrow cross-window each side. A two-bay outer wing projects on the r., perhaps the chapel that in 1580 was 'devydid…into tow P(arl)lars for lakk of rowme'. Behind the hall range is a large paved courtyard, enclosed on all sides. On the N an early C17 wing of two storeys with attic, possibly built as lodgings. Three gables and two large mullioned-and-transomed first-floor windows to the courtyard; at the rear three big extruded stacks. w range with a C17 colonnade of short stumpy Tuscan columns. Much-altered s service wing may retain fabric of an earlier, s-facing, house.

The timber posts and arched braces of the Hall's original open roof are still visible, the upper part is ceiled. Carved in large florid letters on the bressumer of the broad fireplace the names Arthur Kay and Biatryx Kay, his first wife. Panelled walls; gallery opposite the windows with turned balusters and frieze decorated with wyverns. The parlour to the r. of the hall is also panelled and has a carved chimneypiece. Plaster ceiling has deep beams with acorns, grapes and pomegranates on soffits. To w is staircase with fine turned balusters, vertically symmetrical. First-floor chamber in C17 N wing has excellent plaster frieze of mermen between pairs of mermaids with mirrors, alternating with affronted wyverns.

FERRYBRIDGE

Halfway between London and Edinburgh on the Great North Road at the crossing of the Aire, the village was a major staging post until the mid C19.

St Andrew, Pontefract Road. The small medieval church (restored by *Ewan Christian*, 1878–9) was transferred here in 1952–3 from its lonely, often flooded, position at Ferry Fryston ½ m. N. Its limestone conceals a brick structure and in the process of rebuilding the N aisle was placed on the s side, and a third (w) bay added to the aisle. The former s doorway, re-set on the N side, is late C12 with one order of colonnettes with waterleaf capitals. Pointed arch of two slight chamfers and hoodmould with nailhead decoration. Further w two slit-like pointed late C12 windows on the staircase to the w tower, which is embraced by the nave. The tower arch is round with typical late C12 to early C13 imposts. Small pointed w window in larger internal splayed reveal with round head. So these w parts are of an early date. The chancel (with piscina) was rebuilt in the late C13 or C14, but has straight-headed windows with cusped lights like the rest. The tower top, the s aisle with its originally two-bay arcade of standard details, and the two-bay s chapel are C15 Perp. – FONT. Circular reeded bowl. Probably C12. – STAINED GLASS. Five windows by *Gordon Webster*, 1957–77, the figures all strong-featured, the colours clear, the leading bold. – MONUMENTS. Eleanor Crowle †1765, a cartouche with roses, and George Crowle †1744, aedicule with broken pediment, both finely carved in white marble, each with angel's head on the apron.

The old road BRIDGE, crossing the river ¼ m. NE, is a splendid design by *John Carr*, 1797–1804. Three graceful arches, the

Ferrybridge, bridge.
Engraving by J. Rogers after N. Whittock, *c*.1830

central one slightly wider and higher, and subsidiary arches over the w towpath. Ashlar, with smoothly rusticated voussoirs and piers. Bold cornice and blind balustrade. Contemporary Toll Cottage at s end.

FERRYBRIDGE POWER STATION. 'A' STATION beside the River Aire N of the bridge crossing, was built in 1926, closed in 1957 and is now offices, workshops etc. It is a significant piece of industrial design, even without its four chimneys, and a power-ful, symmetrical classical composition in red brick with white faience details over a steel frame. On the s front, the central bay projects, with a tall round-arched window above the entrance. On the E and w elevations full-height windows to the former boiler house and turbine hall. Overshadowing it to the w are the eight COOLING TOWERS of 'C' STATION (1962–8), which closed in 2016. A multi-fuel plant began operation in 2015.

FIRBECK

5080

ST MARTIN (formerly St Peter). Rebuilt 1820 by *Woodhead & Hurst* with tower, nave and short chancel in a queer lancet style. The windows are groups of three stepped lancets under one round arch. Alterations by *E. Isle Hubbard* in 1887 included the apsidal sanctuary with five large Romanesque windows and remodelling of an 1844 extension as a N aisle with hideous Neo-Norman arcade. w tower replaced in similar style at NW corner 1900. – CHANCEL SCREEN. Wrought iron. 1899. – FONT. Neo-Norman, arcaded, 1887. – STAINED GLASS. w window by *Willement*, c. 1847. – Sanctuary windows by *Wailes & Strang*, 1887. – Chancel s by *H.M. Barnett* of Newcastle, 1887. – N aisle by *Harry Stammers*, 1953. – MONUMENTS. Catherine Darcy, wife of William West, †1646. Oval black tablet with bay-leaf surround (SW corner). – John West †1659 and Frances West †1657. Inscription under large, very squarely and heavily detailed depressed arch on short pillars. – Faith, wife of Sir Ralph Knight, †1671. Black tablet with bay-leaf frame.

MANOR FARMHOUSE, NE of the church, partly c. 1600, with mullioned windows. Late C19 LODGE opposite the church, and two houses in *cottage orné* style, 1876, at SW end of the village, built for the St Legers' Park Hill estate (house dem. 1935).

FIRBECK HALL, ⅓ m. NE. The oldest part is late C16, two-and-a-half storeys with central canted bay window. To the l. is a large, square two-storey C18 house. Eight by seven bays. The E and s fronts have slightly recessed centres. The whole hall was then elaborately, if somewhat rudely, Elizabethanized by the addition of numerous steep shaped attic gables as part of improvements made in the 1820s and 1830s for Henry Gally Knight after his plans for a new house at Langold Park were frustrated (*see* Letwell). His architects were *Woodhead & Hurst*.

Remodelled inside by *Robert Cawkwell* of *Hadfield & Cawkwell*, 1934–5, for a country club; subsequently in hospital use and now semi-derelict. The C18 STABLES and WEST LODGE have large gables to match the hall. HOME FARM, N of the stables is a good early C19 model farm with quadrangular yard surrounded by linked barn, farmhouse and stables and detached piggeries and cowhouse.

6010

FISHLAKE

Fenland village in a tranquil backwater beside the Don. Once a small port, but now separated from the canalized river by flood embankments and spoilt by indifferent infilling and some pretentious late C20/early C21 houses. The church is tucked away in a corner among trees.

ST CUTHBERT. One of the most prosperous and spacious of the parish churches in the West Riding. The impression is of the late Middle Ages, ashlar-faced, with a tall, strong W tower, a large clerestory, and battlements everywhere. But the church's chief individual title to fame is not late medieval. It is the S doorway of *c.* 1170, perhaps the most lavishly decorated in Yorkshire. After the Conquest, Fishlake was part of Conisbrough lordship and in the late C11 was among the churches given by William de Warenne, 2nd Earl of Surrey to his father's Cluniac Priory at Lewes, East Sussex. The tradition that St Cuthbert's peripatetic body rested here in the C9 may explain the exceptionally elaborate sculpture on such a remote church and can be attributed to a Yorkshire team schooled in the Benedictine tradition that produced the Malmesbury Abbey (Wiltshire) S porch. Broad and low, with four orders of columns, now badly weathered. From the inner to the outer order the capitals and arches can be interpreted as representing first paradise, reached by entering the church, and then 'three stages, past, present and to come, in a history of salvation'.*

They are decorated as follows. First order: a series of stylized trees with tiny trunks and roots and large leaves of varied forms. Leafy capitals with beaded bands. Second order: also radially arranged, with leaves out of which grow tiny heads, mostly two to one stone and mostly human. Some are crowned, some winged. The apex voussoirs have two female figures and a single tonsured head, interpreted as the Salutation and St Peter. Capitals with centaur and dragon (l.) and two lion's bodies sharing a single head on the angle (r.). Third order,

---

*See Rita Wood, 'The Romanesque Doorway at Fishlake', *Yorkshire Archaeological Journal* 72, 2000.

Fishlake, St Cuthbert, s doorway.
Engraving by J. Swaine after Miss Foljambe, *c.* 1828

scenes relating to evil and the means of being saved from it.
The upper voussoirs contain several animals in profile running
up towards the apex and mostly filling two blocks of stone.
They include (l.) a bull, lion and goat and (r.) dogs, a wolf on
a leash held by a man wielding a knife, and a large lion. A leafy
stem trails round the arch along the angle. The capitals have
a monk in a boat and a demon trying to snatch a soul from an
angel. Fourth order: capitals (partly covered by the porch
walls) with opposing knights on horseback with lances (l.) and
confronted dragons (r.). On each side of the arch first a pair
of women (Virtues) vigorously spearing beasts (Vices), then,
descending from a seated figure of Christ at the apex, five
medallions with pairs of seated figures. This probably represents the Second Coming. The upper stones are the most
decayed and the r. halves of the two top r. medallions are
transposed. Nothing else remains of the Norman building,
except the modest chancel s doorway and some rubble masonry
around it.

Early C13 the lower part of the w tower (see the w doorway) and the nave arcades. These have five bays, circular piers with circular capitals, and double-chamfered arches. The w responds are three detached shafts, a handsome motif. Altered octagonal SE respond with two shafts. The s aisle still has its original w fenestration, three even lancets with hoodmoulds. The hoodmoulds have foliage, partly stiff-leaf, partly natural-istic. The windows must have been removed further w when the w bays embracing the tower were added (*see* below). C13 also was the former chancel N chapel (see the octagonal pier) which was already removed in the mid C14 when extensive Dec work was done. Its climax is the glorious chancel E window of seven lights with slender, elegantly flowing flame tracery (care-fully replicated in the 1854–7 restoration). This can be attrib-uted to a date later (though no doubt only a little later) than 1351. This window and the wide and tall chancel arch (and the absence of stained glass) give the whole church a feeling of generous space and the breathing of high, clear air. Dec also the w arches and tracery of the N and s chapels that extend the aisles, all N aisle windows (straight-headed with ogee-headed lights and a little flowing tracery above them), and the N doorway, gabled curiously into a buttress.

Perp divers other windows, the w bays of the aisles which embrace the tower (see their windows), and the splendid w tower and equally splendid clerestories. The nave clerestory has unusually tall three-light windows with tracery and of course battlements and pinnacles. The badges of Edward IV (falcon on fetterlock and rose and crown) on the tower's s side date it to 1461–83. It has a huge five-light w window with transom, a niche with a statuette of St Cuthbert above, two two-light bell-openings on each side, and again battlements and pinnacles. Soaring tower arch. C15 nave and chancel roofs, the nave's with one boss and traces of the ceilure in the E bay. Tudor arch from each chapel into the chancel.

FONT. Mid-C14. Octagonal. Richly carved, with nodding ogee canopies under which stand statuettes of saints. Angels beneath angle buttresses. – FONT COVER. Jacobean; rather rustic. – SCREENS. Restored chancel SCREEN *c.* 1500, also chapel SCREENS, all with one-light divisions. – MONUMENTS. Richard Marshall, Vicar, †1505, 'in whose time this chancel and vestry bildite was'. Big tomb-chest. The brass effigy lacking. On the sides are impressively big inscriptions – the lettering used as ornament, patterned decoration and carved chalices, books and bells. – Thomas Simpson †1704. Intricate frame with small Gothic arcades, faces etc. – John Gibson †1768 and wife Margaret †1759. Aedicule with triglyph frieze and broken pediment.

HALL FARMHOUSE, Main Street, 150 yds w. C18, five bays, the middle three set slightly forward, with stone angle quoins, keystones etc. Shield dated 1610 above altered doorway.

⅜ m. w, on Trundle Lane, the base and shaft of a late medieval CROSS.

FLOCKTON

ST JAMES. Rebuilt by *W.H. Crossland*, 1867–9. Unshowy Dec
style. W bellcote. Brick interior, including moulded arches,
now painted. – Later C19 traceried SCREEN with ROOD,
painted and gilded, and PULPIT with painted panels by *J.R.
Spencer Stanhope*. – STAINED GLASS. E window designed by
Eleanor Fortescue Brickdale, made by *Burlison & Grylls*, 1937.
W window has four lights of E window of 1869 by *G.J. Baguley*.
Nave: first from E by *Morris, Marshall, Faulkner & Co.*, *c.* 1872;
third from E by *Kempe*, 1902. N aisle second from E by *Kempe*,
1891.
ZION CHAPEL (former, Independent), ½ m. W. 1802. Five-bay
front with gable pediment; segmental-headed upper windows.
(Three-sided gallery; fine two-decker pulpit.)
DUMB STEEPLE, Grange Moor, 1¼ m. NW. A curiosity, rebuilt
in 1766 by Richard Beaumont of Whitley Beaumont (*see*
Kirkheaton). Small solid round tower with spire, in rough
coursed masonry. *c.* 23 ft (7 metres) high.

FOX HOUSE

Right on the Derbyshire boundary SW of Sheffield, where the C18
turnpike roads separate to go to Bakewell, Tideswell and
Hathersage.

The solitary moorland INN is said to have been built in 1773;
remodelled and enlarged by the Duke of Rutland as part of his
Longshaw estate in the 1840s in Jacobean Revival style (for
Longshaw Lodge see Hathersage, Derbyshire).
CARL WARK, ⅞ m. NNW. Sub-rectangular early FORT, undated
and unusual, on a wild moorland summit. Across the W access,
a massive turf rampart, faced with stone blocks; elsewhere,
drystone walling supplements the naturally defensive rock-
faces. In-turned entrance close to the SW angle. Later, mill-
stones were quarried here.

FRIARMERE

½ m. NNW of Delph

ST THOMAS (Heights Chapel; Churches Conservation Trust).
On a hill in a well-populated graveyard, commanding long
views, with only a pub (C17 etc.) for company. Dated 1765
above two doorways in the W wall. Nave, very shallow chancel,
later bellcote. Windows in two tiers, small and round-arched,

with Y-tracery. Galleries on stone Tuscan columns with panelled fronts of an 1880s refurbishment.

FRICKLEY

4000

ALL SAINTS. A small church, quite alone among fields, with no
trace of the medieval village. Good Norman chancel arch. Its
shafted responds stand on a plinth 3 ft (0.9 metres) high, so
there must once have been a screen (cf. Rossington). Double-
scallop capitals with sunk shields, one with carved face. Bases
with spurs. Chevron in arch to nave, one step to chancel. C13
the W tower and the N aisle arcade. The tower is plain and
unbuttressed and has small bell-openings with tracery typical
of *c.* 1300. Battlements and recessed stone spirelet. Two-bay N
arcade with standard elements. The N aisle windows are Perp,
the N chapel windows late Perp. Over-restored by *George Williams*, 1872–3, the busy S side extended with vestry, one-bay
transeptal S aisle, porch and SW baptistery. – Principal FIT-
TINGS by *Comper*, 1930–7, including the large and splendid
ORGAN CASE, much gilded and painted. – STAINED GLASS. E
window by *Comper*, 1909. – MONUMENTS. First World War.
Brass plaque by *Herbert Wauthier*, 1920. – William Warde-
Aldam †1925. Plaque with unusual ceramic portrait medallion
by *E. G. Rigg*.

FRICKLEY HALL, 700 yds N. Rebuilt *c.* 1760s; extended and
altered, with new ashlar facing, *c.* 1820, probably for Richard
Kennet Dawson. Two storeys with hipped roof. Five-bay N
front with pedimented Doric porch. Seven-bay E front, the
middle three bays set forward under a pediment enclosing an
oval window. The central French window has an architrave
with splayed base – an C18 detail, perhaps copying the original
doorway? Inner hall has cantilevered stone staircase with
square, fluted, cast-iron balusters, galleried landing and
lantern. Three-storey service range attached W.

PARK FARM, 350 yds ENE of Frickley Hall, is early C19 but
incorporates remains of C17 mullioned-windowed range associated with Frickley Old Hall (dem.) on adjacent moated site.

FRIEZLAND

9000

CHRIST CHURCH. 1848–50 with a tower and tall broach spire.
S transept 1847, N aisle 1860, all by the local architect *George
Shaw* for the industrialist Whitehead family. Idiosyncratic,
with gauche Dec style detailing typical of his work, and his
trademark 'S' tracery. His elaborate FURNISHINGS include
ALTAR, panelling, PULPIT and what look like choir STALLS,

actually seating for the donor family. – STAINED GLASS.
Chancel and s nave windows by *Willement*, dated 1850.

VICARAGE, w, also by *Shaw*. Of 1850. Gothic, asymmetrical, with groups of lancets with cusped or shouldered heads
and an oriel. Splendid c17-style stair with acorn pendants in
the balustrade.

WHARMTON TOWER, Oldham Road. *c.* 1861. By *Shaw* for John
Dicken Whitehead. Raw Gothic, the recessed centre with
narrow castellated porch-tower flanked by gabled wings with
oriel, castellated bay etc. on one side and big blunt castellated
tower on the other. (Magnificent stair, stair windows and hall
windows with stained glass, chimneypieces etc. all by *Shaw*.)

ROYAL GEORGE MILL (now flats), beside the Huddersfield
Narrow Canal (*see* p. 44). A fulling and scribbling mill of 1788
rebuilt from the early c19 by the Whiteheads. It produced felt,
flags, pennants etc. Remains include an early or mid-c19 classical entrance and a large late c19 block with a low clock tower.

GOLCAR 0010

ST JOHN. Commissioners' church by *Peter Atkinson Jun.*, 1828–9.
Lancet style. w tower with broach spire. One-bay chancel, in
keeping, 1862–6. Three galleries, the ORGAN filling the w one.
Sombre dark wood to panelled gallery fronts, tracery to the
queenpost trusses, and diagonally boarded roof panels, all part
of *J. Kirk & Sons*' restoration, 1885. – STAINED GLASS. Chancel
s 1910, and nave s second and third from E 1931, by *Jones &
Willis*. – Nave s fourth from E 1903, and nave N second from
E 1962, by *Powell & Sons*.

PROVIDENCE METHODIST CHURCH (New Connexion), ¼ m.
E. 1884. Handsome front of 1:3:1 bays divided by pilasters
and with urns above cornice and central pediment. Round-
arched openings, the upper window with blind balustrades.
Former Sunday School to r. by *Jonathan Shaw* 1878–9.

In the village, and the surrounding hamlets, are a large number
of c18 and c19 WEAVERS' COTTAGES. In Cliffe Ashe, below   64
the church, Nos. 22–24 (1845) and 26–28 have been restored
as the Colne Valley Museum.

GOLDTHORPE 4000

Large former mining village.

ST JOHN AND ST MARY MAGDALENE, Lockwood Road.
1914–16 by *A.Y. Nutt*, and funded by Lord Halifax to whom
the curious out-of-the-way Italian style must be due. It is also

of reinforced-concrete construction, on a beam raft to counteract subsidence. Aisled nave with tall windows set high up, alternately of two and three arched lights. Apsidal chancel with s chapel. Tall square sw tower with open belfry, surmounted by a clock cupola. Spacious, light interior, with passage aisles and slender, flat piers to the tall arcades. Big transverse tie-beams to each bay. Restored by *Andrew Wiles*, 2001–2. – Anglo-Catholic FITTINGS of 1921, also concrete, but the PULPIT C18, perhaps Flemish, bought in 1926.

GOMERSAL

ST MARY. By *Jeremiah Dobson*, 1850–1. Nave with lean-to aisles, pinnacled NW tower, chancel with transeptal s chapel. Good flowing tracery and carved detail, e.g. the angel corbels to the roof trusses and angelic orchestra on the chancel arch s capital. – More fine carving on the arcaded Caen stone REREDOS and the CHOIR STALL fronts. Most other fittings removed in reordering 2004.

METHODIST CHAPEL (Wesleyan), Latham Lane. 1827–8. Distinguished by its big ashlar bow front of four bays, which earned it the nickname of the 'Pork pie chapel' (cf. Barnsley Wesleyan chapel).

MORAVIAN CHURCH, Quarry Road. 1869–70 by *Mallinson & Bakewell*. Red brick with ashlar dressings. Slight Gothic details. The previous chapel was of 1751, for an offshoot of the congregation at Fulneck (*West Riding North*), and attached at each end are still the manse and girls' school, both of 1793, with plain ashlar quoins and dressings. To rear also COTTAGES, built c. 1800 for the settlement. Former SUNDAY SCHOOL to s, 1816–20. Round-arched windows with ashlar keystones. In Lower Lane, 300 yds SW, the 'SISTERS' HOUSES are a handsome row of three (Nos. 50–54) of four, three and four bays, the window heads of the middle house of rubbed brick with fluted keystones, the others of stone. Despite their harmonious appearance, the l. house appears to have been built by 1757, the middle one added for the Moravian sisters and the r. one in the mid C19.

PUBLIC HALL, Oxford Road. By *Jeremiah Dobson*, 1850–2, originally as the Mechanics' Institution. Good Italianate front in ashlar, the rest more pedestrian.

There are three houses of especial note in the older village:

POLLARD HALL, 350 yds NE of the parish church, is an exceedingly fine C17 double-pile stone house (now subdivided) that merits further study. It may have earlier timber framing. s front with four gables, and on the l. a projecting bay-windowed extension, 1889, in keeping. The two westernmost gables of the old house are the earliest part and have six-light windows on both floors, under continuous hoodmoulds. The gable to the r. has a projecting two-storey porch with door dated 1659 in its studding, and then the spectacular hall window, three-plus-three lights wide but so high that it has three transoms. The stonework of this gable and the end one is more deeply coursed than that of the earlier ones, but the end gable, with two four-light parlour windows, appears to be of yet another build. At the rear the hall bay has a porch to the hearth passage; above this a tall cross-window to the staircase, to the l. a big extruded stack. (The double-height Hall has a gallery on three sides; lovely plasterwork on the ceiling, also to the frieze above three-quarter panelling and under the gallery.)

RED HOUSE (Kirklees Museums) lies immediately N. Its core is one of the area's earliest brick houses, built by William Taylor, a cloth merchant, and said to date from 1660.* The four rear gables (rebuilt) preserve its form. The s front and interior were remodelled, probably in the 1740s, giving a fine entrance with semicircular fanlight opening into a spacious staircase hall. First floor has three double sash windows with single sashes between, the ground floor a single sash and a Victorian canted bay window to each side of the doorway. Additional l. bay 1920s.

PEEL HOUSE (also called MANOR HOUSE), Knowles Lane, ½ m. N. Large double-pile house with three-gabled front (now subdivided). Probably remodelled and cased in stone in 1651 (date in lost plasterwork), retaining earlier timber framing. Front ground-floor windows are all transomed. w gable has four-light window to Parlour and the original doorway, which opens into wide housebody with large window of four-plus-four lights. (Fireplace at r. end of housebody has panelled wooden overmantel carved with decorative lozenges.) Best Parlour or Dining Room to E has six-light window to the front and a four-light window to the side. (Incomplete decorative plasterwork ceiling with heraldry in lozenge panels and paired griffons on soffit of beams.)

GOOLE

In 1821 the hamlet of Goole on the banks of Vermuyden's Dutch River (the re-routed River Don) had barely 400 inhabitants. The town's history starts with the 1820 Act enabling the Aire & Calder Navigation Co. to build a 19-mile canal from Knottingley to the River Ouse, with two small docks at Goole. *George Leather*, the Company's engineer, developed the initial proposals by *John Rennie*; the company's architects were *Woodhead & Hurst* and the contractors *Jolliffe & Banks*. After the canal and the docks were

---

*Later the home of Charlotte Brontë's friend Mary Taylor, the house appears in *Shirley* (1849) as 'Briarmains'.

opened in 1826, the first part of the company's planned new town sprang up on their N edge. Regrettably little of this survives and few distinguished buildings have been put up at Goole since, but the docks, with their picturesque disorder, give the town a unique visual and historic interest. By 1931, two years before Goole became a borough, the population was some 19,000. Since then the town has hardly grown, but Goole maintains its role as the country's most inland port, over forty miles from the open sea.

St John the Evangelist. By *Hurst & Moffatt*, 1843–8, mostly funded by the Navigation Co. Remarkably large and stately, it sits at the head of the docks with sheds to the W and, if one is lucky, the prow of a ship just over the churchyard wall on the S. The ecclesiastical and the nautical rarely meet so intimately. Nave and transepts with pinnacled buttresses; crossing tower with flying buttresses supporting a fine tall spire. Tall two-light Perp windows, except for big five-light windows at the E, W, N and S ends. Less impressive close to, its only embellishment the jolly carved headstops, perhaps a hundred in all, including those in the plain interior. This is dominated by the overbearing, if inventively sculptural, plywood ceiling by *R.G. Sims*, 1988, the horizontal cladding of the once-open trusses especially intrusive. – REREDOS. 1908. Gilded oak, with painted panels under elaborate open-traceried gables. – STAINED GLASS. E window by *Mayer & Co.* of Munich, 1883.

St Thomas (R.C.), Old Goole, ¾ m. S. (disused). By *Goldie & Child*, 1876–7. PRESBYTERY and SCHOOL by *M.E. Hadfield*, 1870. Also small former CONVENT, 1877–8.

St Joseph and St Thomas (R.C.), Pasture Road. By *Lowther & Rigby*, 1912–13. Prominent tall corner tower with statue and separately gabled faces. Orange-red brick, liberally dressed with artificial stone (also used for nave arcades etc.).

Trinity Methodist Church (Wesleyan), Boothferry Road. By *H.B. Thorp* of Goole, 1899–1900. Red brick. Dec tracery. Tall gabled porch and gabled S transept towards the road. Polygonal E apse for organ. (Nearby, in a supermarket car park, is a striking tarred WINDMILL TOWER, *c.* 1820s.)

CEMETERY, Hook Road. By *William Watson*, 1875–7. Two chapels, unusually set at right angles to each other, linked by archway in low fussily gabled tower with small stone spire.

Civic and Arts Centre, Paradise Place. By *Henley Halebrown Rorrison*, 2007–9. Ingeniously adapted from a 1980s market shed. Lower half of long front is partly glazed and partly panelled in spruce plywood with timber mullions and has raised walkway sheltered by canopy with polished gold stainless steel soffit. Above, sombre slate-grey cladding follows the basic portal structure, echoing the dock sheds.

Magistrates' Court (closed) and Police Station, Estcourt Terrace. By *J. Vickers Edwards*, West Riding County Council Surveyor, 1887–8. Free Renaissance style. Red brick with good terracotta details to Dutch gables, keystones etc. Fourteen-bay front range of two tall storeys with hipped roof.

GOOLE HIGH SCHOOL, Boothferry Road. By *Willink & Thicknesse*, 1908–10, as the Secondary School. The most handsome of Goole's public buildings. Queen Anne style. Mottled yellow/ orange brick with red brick and ashlar dressings. Long front has main block with pedimented centre and projecting ends, and slightly lower, six-bay pavilion wings. Cranked-plan block by *East Riding of Yorkshire Council Architects' Department*, 2002, 2010, to N.

GOOLE COLLEGE, Boothferry Road. By *H. Wormald*, County Education Architect, 1930–7, as Goole Senior School. Pedimented centre with first-floor gymnasium, flanked by separate entrances for boys and girls. The rest single-storeyed.

THE COURTYARD (former Boothferry Road School). By *William Watson*, 1892–3, converted to community and social enterprise centre in 1995–7 by *Bramhall Blenkharn*. Red brick. Three-sided, with entrance in two-storey l. range under clock tower with ogee dome, and single-storey front and r. ranges, all with decorative gables. Landscaped rear courtyard with C20 verandas.

WAR MEMORIAL, Memorial Gardens, Boothferry Road. A half-size copy of *Lutyens*'s Whitehall Cenotaph, made by local mason *H. O. Tasker*. Portland stone; 18 ft (5.5 metres) high.

WATER TOWERS. Together with the church spire the two water towers are the town's landmarks. They date from 1881–3 and 1925–7 and represent the spirit of their respective ages convincingly. Of almost equal heights, the first (disused) is red brick with a slim panelled shaft and plain drum top with dome, the second a massive reinforced-concrete structure by *E. J. Silcock*, engineer. Nearly 160 ft (47.5 metres) high, its central tower has an outer framework of slender arches tied together and joined by radiating struts to the central shaft below a 90-ft (27-metre)-diameter tank.

GOOLE SWING BRIDGE, over the Ouse, 1½ m. NE. 1863–9 by *Thomas E. Harrison*, Chief Engineer, for the North Eastern Railway's Doncaster–Goole–Hull line. Five fixed spans with hogback plate girders, and towards the E end one swing span 250 ft (76 metres) long which rotates on a central column to open a 100-ft (31-metre)-wide channel on each side. Original octagonal glazed cabin for bridgeman above central pivot. Total length 830 ft (253 metres). Originally cast and wrought iron and wood; some later C20 and early C21 renewal in steel.

DOCKS. The docks of 1826 were extended as trade grew and larger ships needed to be accommodated; six, including Railway Dock, 1848, were added to the original Barge Dock and Ship Dock between 1836 and 1912. None of the original brick warehouses or offices etc. survives, but two large and fine SHIP LOCKS to the river remain: the ashlar Ouse Lock, 1835–8, for paddle steamers, and the much longer Victoria Lock, 1888 (*c.* 600 ft (180 metres)). Beside South Dock is a hydraulic

p. 2

79   BOAT HOIST of 1912, a type of structure unique to Goole and
     first developed *c*. 1862 by *William Armstrong & Co.* to transfer
     coal to ships from strings of compartment boats – metal tubs
     each holding up to 40 tons of coal. Originally one of five, it is
     a curious-looking contraption 90 ft (27.5 metres) high with a
     pyramidal steel girder frame topped by a semicircular-roofed
     control cabin with tapering domed turret. A cradle within the
     frame raised each compartment out of the water, tipping its
     coal down a chute into a ship's hold.*

     Nearby is the docks' last surviving HYDRAULIC ACCUMU-
     LATOR TOWER, later C19. Square, *c*. 50 ft (15 metres) high with
     pyramidal roof, re-erected with new cladding in 1997 after
     collapsing. Beside Railway Dock, at the end of one remaining
     bay of an arched railway viaduct, is a rare example of a
     HYDRAULIC COAL WAGON HOIST, made by *Tannett Walker
     Co.* of Leeds, 1906. Large five-stage open-trussed steel girder
     tower with a central well, where each loaded wagon was raised
     from the second-stage platform in a cradle and tilted to tip the
     coal down a chute into a ship.

A short PERAMBULATION starts at the bottom of AIRE STREET,
     the company town's main street, where the impressive
     LOWTHER HOTEL greeted those arriving by water. Built
     1824–6 for the contractor, Sir John Banks, and sold in 1828 to
     the Navigation Company, who used a spacious first-floor suite
     as board room and chairman's office. Both rooms have wall
     paintings (restored), *c*. 1828–30, including scenes of the docks
     and river, buildings (some proposed) and delightful details of
     dockside activity. Beyond is the only remaining three-storey
     terrace, of plain stuccoed or painted brick houses with a few
     original details and remains of nice later C19 shopfronts, but
     all dismally altered and run-down. Most of the Georgian
     company town, on the triangle of land extending to North
     Street, and only a third of what was originally envisaged, was
     cleared in the 1960s. At the wide top of Aire Street three-storey
     commercial buildings include a large block with stone-faced
     ground floor, by *Dobson & Chorley* of Leeds, 1869. Its Gothic-
     arcaded corner was originally the Leeds and County Bank.
     Adjoining, on Church Street, the former GOOLE STEAM
     SHIPPING CO. OFFICES, 1902–3, has a grand segmental-
     pedimented entrance in green-grey faience with frieze of sailing
     ships. Further up Aire Street, the former Leatham, Tew &
     Co.'s bank, by *Archibald Neill*. Before the corner with Booth-
     ferry Road, classical details and rock-faced stone give authority
     to the former COURT HOUSE and POLICE STATION, 1857;
     almost opposite, the ARCADE (closed) by *H.B. Thorp*, 1891–2,
     brick and terracotta, with two large and elaborate Flemish
     gables.

*This system, devised by *William Bartholomew*, the Navigation Company's engineer,
was in use from 1863 to 1986. The boats became known locally as 'Tom Puddings',
probably from their resemblance to a string of sausages.

By the later C19 the town's commercial focus had moved NW to the E end of BOOTHFERRY ROAD, where the CENTENARY CLOCK, 1927, now sits unceremoniously on a roundabout. Facing it on the E the Italianate former York City & County Bank, by *Atkinson & Demaine*, 1880. Ashlar, with four large semicircular clerestory windows to full-height banking hall and tall truncated pyramidal roofs to return bays. To the N on Estcourt Terrace, the MARKET HALL by *W. J. Tennant* of Pontefract, 1894–6, not completed to the design. Brick with ashlar Renaissance details. The best commercial building is BANK CHAMBERS to the SW, by *H. B. Thorp*, 1892, in red brick and red terracotta. Built for Beckett's Bank, with offices for shipping and coal companies, now altered and extended as East Riding Council offices. Excellent Renaissance fronts with two-storey oriels over arched entrances, but diminished by the loss of its lively roof-line with gabled dormers and corner turret. At the W end of STANHOPE STREET the Lancashire and Yorkshire Railway Co.'s offices, 1892, are also brick and terracotta. Boothferry Road, now the principal street, begins with some ambition, with ornate gables to ST JOHN'S CHAMBERS, 1890 and the one-bay TIMES BUILDINGS, 1894, opposite, both in rich red brick, but descends to ordinariness thereafter.

GOOLE HALL, 1¼ m. SSE. Handsome, upstanding house for Jarvis Empson, *c.* 1820. Two storeys, five by six bays. Red brick with painted ashlar dressings. Large balconied porch with fluted Ionic columns. (Interior with elaborate plasterwork, some good marble chimneypieces, and painted decoration, probably by *Elizabeth Empson*.)

GREASBROUGH

4090

Still rural former mining village separating the park of Wentworth Woodhouse from Rotherham, much expanded by later C20 housing estates.

ST MARY. By *Watson & Pritchett*, 1826–8. Earl Fitzwilliam contributed handsomely. Ritual W (i.e. N) tower with big pinnacles and lacy parapet. Low W porches. Nave with tall Perp two-light lancets. Ritual E (i.e. S) end raised above a schoolroom, exploiting the sloping site. High, wide interior, with Gothic W gallery on cast-iron columns. Chancel formed in 1909 by screens, reordered 1982 by *R. G. Sims*. – FONT COVER. A very interesting Jacobean piece of unusual shape, still essentially Gothic. It came from Rotherham parish church. Octagonal, two tiers, with round and ogee arches and flying buttresses with turned pinnacles. Corona of stylized pinnate leaves. Tall pinnacle. – WAR MEMORIAL. 1921. Panelled, with two mystical female figures painted by *Emily Ford* of Leeds.

WAR MEMORIAL, 150 yds W, is a distinctive triumphal arch by *James Totty*, 1925; sculpture by *F. Tory & Sons* of carved swags above a trabeated opening, containing a bronze lamp with eternal flame.

TOWN HALL, Coach Road. 1925. Modest single storey with an Arts and Crafts touch.

CHAPEL HOUSES, ¼ m. S, are single-storey Gothic cottages built *c.* 1828 with stone from the Holy Trinity Chapel succeeded by St Mary.

GLOSSOP LODGE, Cinder Bridge Road, ⅗ m. ESE. Tall stone hexagon with pedimented wings on three sides. Built 1845 at the start of the carriage road to Earl Fitzwilliam's railway halt at Parkgate (Rotherham), 1½ m. SE. The road used the route of the filled-in branch canal made by the Marquess of Rockingham in 1779–81 for his collieries.

BARBOT HALL, ⅞ m. SE. Handsome stuccoed house *c.* 1815. SW front has doorway with Doric columns and open pediment. Broad double-height canted bay on longer r. return.

ROMAN RIG. *See* Introduction, p. 9.

GREAT HOUGHTON

ST MICHAEL AND ALL ANGELS. Built by the Parliamentarian Sir Edward Rodes as a private chapel to Great Houghton Hall, which stood immediately to the E (built by Sir Francis Rodes *c.* 1580; dem. 1963). Said to date from 1650, and like the chapel at Bramhope (*see West Riding North*), a rare building for Presbyterian worship during the Commonwealth. Small, rectangular, in soft sandstone partly rendered. Nave and chancel in one. Gabled W porch probably added slightly later and W bellcote. Transomed windows of three lights with round arches to the individual lights. Battlemented N and S parapets with round-headed merlons. The gables have a frill of lobes rather than merlons. Roof with kingpost trusses. Well-preserved mid-C17 fittings: BOX PEWS facing E, their ends with decoratively carved upper panels and acorn knobs (cf. Darfield). The octagonal PULPIT, formerly opposite the N door (blocked), has its back-board and tester, all with good carving. A bookcase at the W end has panelling from the Rodes family pew, dismantled when the E end was reordered *c.* 1906. The chapel was conveyed to the Church of England in 1908. Restored and reordered by *G. G. Pace*, 1960–4; he added the N transept with attached church rooms. Re-set in the W wall of this extension one of the C17 N windows. – STAINED GLASS. E window. By *T. W. Camm*, 1911.

BURNTWOOD HALL, Moor Lane, 1¾ m. N. Late C18, remodelled and extended in second half of C19. Front has broad two-storey canted bays flanking central bay with pedimented Doric porch. Victorian SE wing has Doric loggia.

GREENFIELD*   *0000*

St Mary. Of 1875 by the local architect *George Shaw* for the industrialist Buckley family. In Shaw's chunky version of Dec, with slightly wild window tracery (cf. Friezland) and a tall broach spire. – FURNISHINGS by *Shaw* include the elaborate PULPIT. – STAINED GLASS. Several late C19–early C20 windows by *T.F. Curtis, Ward & Hughes* and one of 1892 by *Comère & Capronnier*.

METHODIST CHURCH, Chew Valley Road. Dated 1882. Symmetrical front, with a wheel window. (– STAINED GLASS. First World War memorial by *George Wragge*.)

WAR MEMORIAL. 1¼ m. NNE, high up among rock formations called Pots and Pans. Obelisk by *C.B. Howcroft*, dated 1923.

HEY TOP, Bradbury Lane. A row of forty-four mid-C19 back-to-back mill workers' housing perched on the hillside. Some earlier loom shops were incorporated, and projecting stones left in the terrace end for piecing in additions. It related to GREENFIELD MILL, in the valley below, an C18 scribbling and fulling mill, successively rebuilt and altered, C19 and C20.

KINDERS LANE. Nos. 1–5 is a very good C17 and C18 stone-built complex of several different phases; three- and four-storey weaving workshops, with arched cart entrance, rows of mullioned windows, upper taking-in doors and an external stone stair to the upper workshops. FOUL RAKE, a little to the S. A laithe, with three-unit house of unusual plan, formerly incorporating a dairy or still room, and an attached extended byre. Dated 1746.

GREETLAND   *0020*

Upland village, now joined to West Vale (q.v.).

St Thomas. By *Thomas Rushforth*, 1859–60, tower 1868. A curious mixture of Neo-Norman and Early Gothic: round and pointed arches, Geometric plate tracery, some feeble chevron, and big French Gothic capitals to the three-bay N arcade and the spindly shafts of the window rere-arches. – CHURCHWARDENS' PEW, 1889, with Romanesque arcading (from St John, West Vale).

SUNNY BANK, Sunny Bank Road, 250 yds SE. An important timber-framed house (now two), nestling against the slope. Mostly rebuilt *c.* 1550 by the Saviles of Bradley Hall (Stainland), but part is C15 or earlier. Hall and parlour, each gabled to front and rear; cross-passage with ogee-headed N doorway under a little gable; lower two-bay service end with a front and

*Part of Saddleworth, in Greater Manchester since 1974.

a rear gable. The gables have exposed kingpost trusses with V struts. s front has stone walls, much-altered window openings and some exposed timber posts. These posts and other timber members at s end of cross-passage provide evidence of the earlier house.

CRAWSTONE HALL, Dog Lane, ¾ m. WSW. Dated 1631 (but extensively reconstructed 1982). If the date is trustworthy the earliest flat-fronted house in the district. Informal double pile; three gabled elements. Best rooms probably on the first floor, where the large windows are transomed. Additional E (parlour) wing, c. 1700, has cross-windows.

CLAY HOUSE, Clay Park, ¾ m. E. Large, flat-fronted, with big mullioned-and-transomed windows and four deceptively identical gables. The second bay was probably built by the Clay family c. 1660 as a new parlour wing to a medieval timber-framed house. The hall, with a window of 5:4:4 lights with king mullions, and the service wing with rear kitchen were perhaps built c. 1675 (see painted glass in hall window). The carefully matched W wing and insertion of the two doorways with decorative lintels is c. 1700. Hall drastically remodelled as an open, galleried room in further alterations 1873 and 1920s.

GRENOSIDE

Village just above Sheffield's N suburbs, originally on the Halifax turnpike road (1777). In the C19 it specialized in file-cutting.

ST MARK. By J. D. Webster, 1884–5. Small, in simple E.E. style. W bellcote. – STAINED GLASS. E and W windows by Kempe, 1890–1.

Former administration building of WORTLEY UNION WORK-HOUSE, Salt Box Lane. By Aickin & Capes, 1850–2. Neo-Jacobean style with intimidating finials to shaped gable. Rest demolished 1992.

READING ROOM, School Lane. Built c. 1790 as a school. Central porch and, on each side, two round-arched windows with imposts and keystones.

At No. 2 TOP SIDE a rare CRUCIBLE FURNACE CELLAR, c. 1797, survives from Grenoside Steel Works. Narrow brick-vaulted passage, c. 20 ft long and 4 ft wide (6 metres by 1.2 metres) with five melting holes. The earliest known remaining example, especially unusual for its rural location (cf. Abbey-dale Industrial Hamlet, Sheffield p. 603).

BIRLEY EDGE is a hamlet ¾ m. S. BIRLEY OLD HALL (in Sheffield) is L-plan, the main part dated 1705. Handsome S front of four unequal bays with lintel bands to sash windows. Rusticated quoins of even length. Moulded doorcase with large cornice on scrolled brackets. Earlier timber-framed w cross-wing, remodelled, has upright two-light mullioned windows. Square gabled GAZEBO *c.* 1705.

Across the lane BIRLEY HALL FARMHOUSE and COACHHOUSE, a matching pair built between 1797 and 1827, have blind arcades of three arches to gabled fronts. BIRLEY HOUSE, to E, is a fine late C18 brick house with Doric porch and central parapet to its hipped roof.

GRIMETHORPE

Village for the former colliery.

ST LUKE. By *C. Hodgson Fowler*, 1902–4. E.E. Small spired NE turret. Impressive brick interior. – ROOD. By *Cristi Paslaru* of Romania, 2010, after Giunta Pisano's C13 Crucifix at Bologna. – STAINED GLASS. In the Lady Chapel, two by *Nathalie Liege*, 2009, of cast glass, using an innovative technique for creating the moulds from photographs of parishioners' faces, hands etc.

GRIMETHORPE HALL. Semi-derelict. *c.* 1669 with later alterations. On the front the parapet runs straight across between the gables. Vaguely Artisan Mannerist centrepiece of giant brick pilasters with faceted stones and elaborately moulded doorway.

GRIMSTON PARK

w of Kirkby Wharfe

By *Decimus Burton*, in his Grecian-cum-Italianate manner, *c.* 1840 for the 2nd Lord Howden and his Russian wife, Princess Catherine Bagration, a couple who had been prominent in Parisian high society: it has been suggested that the house incorporates some of the fabric of its C18 predecessor, but the epithet 'RESTAUR[AVIT]' accompanying the date above the entrance certainly overstates the case. The entrance front (N), approached axially between small cubic lodges, is restrained and formal, with an Ionic tetrastyle porte cochère, and big doorways and low screen walls l. and r.; but behind these, two unmatched Italianate towers are visible, one against the r. (W) flank, the other (l.) on the service wing. The long garden front is different again, reminiscent of a Regency terrace, with pedimented end pavilions, an Ionic colonnade between them, and iron verandas to the upper floors of all three elements. The composition is continued further W by a masonry-framed integral conservatory, now roofless. Interiors include two ornate drawing rooms with painted decoration in the *Louis seize* revival style of 1830s Paris: in one of them also fine Chinese wallpaper. Also a plainer library, an entrance hall with Doric columns, and a relatively modest staircase with rod-on-vase balusters which might be a survivor from the C18 house.

Formal Italianate GARDENS by *W.A. Nesfield* to the S and W, the bones of the layout surviving: on the N side a gazebo with Corinthian portico. E of the house, just beyond the service wing, a complex presumably by *Burton* consisting of Princess Bagration's RIDING SCHOOL and the former stables and coachhouse, all in a more rustic Italian style with heavy simplified detail. The riding school is a big impressive nine-bay rectangle, with pedimented three-bay centre, deep eaves and Diocletian windows high up. Defaced by other openings, and subdivided internally, mid-C20. Its S end partly occupies one side of the stable courtyard, with the stable and coachhouse ranges – smaller, with raised pedimented centres – to W and E. In the park, ½ m. SW, a slender tapering PROSPECT TOWER, doubtless also by *Burton*, with similar detail but including a mildly Egyptianizing doorway. On top a balcony on brackets (cf. Burton's two contemporary lighthouses at Fleetwood, North Lancashire) and an octagonal lantern. Further W, the main GATES opening onto the Tadcaster road, flanked by panelled piers and curved screen walls.

GUNTHWAITE

GUNTHWAITE HALL. The Bosviles' Tudor mansion was modestly rebuilt after an early C19 fire. – SUMMERHOUSE. 1688, with pyramidal roof. – Spectacular BARN, mid-C16, one of the finest in the country. Eleven bays, aisled, 163 ft by 44 ft (49 by 13.2 metres). Kingpost roof. Flattened ogee heads to S doorways beside the two outer cart entrances. The timberwork, above a high stone base, has diagonal strutting on the S side. STABLES to W, dated 1690. Farm buildings, E, 1701, have showy S gables with mullioned windows facing the hall.

INGBIRCHWORTH, 1 m. SW. The former BARN of Ingfield Farm, probably C16, has four tremendous cruck-trusses.

HALIFAX

0020

INTRODUCTION

The cloth trade of Halifax dates back to the C14 and flourished from the C16 into the C20. In 1566 there were about 2,600 inhabitants. The population in 1801 was 9,000, in 1841 20,000, and it peaked at 105,000 in 1901. There are now (2011) 88,000. Nature has done much for Halifax and the situation of the town is spectacular. The Pennine moors rise to the N and W while to the E the cliff-like slope of Beacon Hill confronts the town across the narrow valley of the Hebble Brook. To the S the River Calder runs at the foot of a steep wooded bank that separates it from the town's southern parks, and here the Hebble joins it. Nearby, a spur of the Calder and Hebble Navigation starts its 1¾-m. ascent to the basin below the Minster, parallel with the brook and with the railway of 1844 squeezed in beside it. Though much has changed since Pevsner first wrote, the steepest hills can still make car driving an adventure and their development-defying gradients have left bare moors overlooking the town. Roads still cross at different levels, the North Bridge of 1871 across the Hebble now dwarfed by the inner ring road's spiralling approaches and high-level bridge of Burdock Way, opened in 1973.

Of the medieval town only the parish church and one timber-framed building in Market Street remain. Though the town was small the parish was vast, covering more than 100 square miles of the upper Calder valley, and one of the largest in Yorkshire, with a church, now a minster, of appropriate grandeur. The development of the woollen industry in the C17 brought a significant increase in commercial traffic. Now the disadvantage of grand topography became more serious as the gradients of the surrounding hills, especially eastwards towards the markets of Wakefield and beyond, presented an obstacle to packhorses bringing in Lincolnshire wool and taking cloth out. The opening of the Calder and Hebble Navigation spur in 1828 brought some relief and two years later the Godley Cutting (*see* Shibden), a triumph of civil engineering, eased road access by removing part of Beacon Hill. As the valley filled with mills the town could only expand westwards and in the second half of the C19 Halifax's

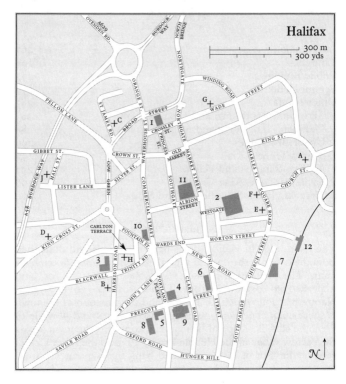

A   The Minster (St John)
B   Holy Trinity (former)
C   Ebenezer Methodist Church
D   Hanover Methodist New
     Connexion Chapel (former)
E   Square Congregational
     Chapel (former)
F   Square Congregational Church
     (former/part)
G   Sion Congregational Chapel
     (former)
H   Carlton United Reformed
     Church
J   Elim Pentecostal Church

1   Town Hall
2   Piece Hall
3   Magistrates' Court and
     former Police Station
4   County Court
5   West Riding Sessions House
     (former)
6   Drill Hall (former)
7   Eureka! Children's Museum
8   High School (former)
9   Swimming Pool
10   Victoria Theatre
11   Borough Market
12   Railway Station

impressive civic and commercial centre developed beyond the
secretly monumental C18 Piece Hall. That was built by the town's
manufacturers and Halifax owes much to them and their successors. In the C19 the greatest of these were the Crossleys and the
Akroyds. The Crossleys built two sets of almshouses and a large
orphanage and gave the People's Park; Edward Akroyd built
Akroydon and gave its church by Scott. If less architecturally
ambitious, it is also the manufacturers' mills, or at least those
that remain, that are still visually exciting and inspire awe. In the

c20 it was the vision of Sir Ernest Hall and others that ensured the survival of the monumental group of Dean Clough Mills by transforming them for new business and cultural uses.

CHURCHES

THE MINSTER (ST JOHN), Church Street. One of the stateliest parish churches in the West Riding and the largest in the W part of the county. Until the C19 it served a huge parish, with only two medieval chapels, at Elland and Heptonstall. Virtually all Perp. Nave of five bays with aisles, outer S aisle chapel of three bays (the Holdsworth Chapel), N and S porches and W tower. Chancel also of five bays and almost equal length to the nave, and of equal height. It has N and S chapels and an outer N chapel of two bays (the Rokeby Chapel). The church was apparently rebuilt throughout the C15. It was restored by *Sir (George) Gilbert Scott* and *John Oldrid Scott* in 1878–9.

Of the earlier, and sizeable, building some masonry of the N aisle in the bay containing the porch, and the two bays E of it, is attributed to the early C12. Reused chevron higher up in the same aisle and other C12 carved fragments around the building. The N aisle otherwise with its three (renewed) windows with Y-tracery must date from *c.* 1290. A SW tower was projected but then replaced by the much bigger W tower, built *c.* 1450–80. The tower has angle buttresses, battlements and pinnacles. The outline is oddly drawn in at the top, because the buttresses taper away just below the battlements. W doorway with two-centred arch and capitals still C14 in style.

The nave was building in 1437, the S choir aisle dates from some time between 1422 and 1470. The Rokeby Chapel was added in 1533 under the will of Archbishop Rokeby †1521 (cf. Kirk Sandall), the Holdsworth Chapel by Robert Holdsworth,

Halifax, the Minster.
Engraving by J. Rogers after N. Whittock, *c.*1830

the last pre-Reformation vicar, in memory of his father, c. 1554. The s aisle of the nave and the chancel and chapels are all embattled, the E parts with big crocketed pinnacles. The Holdsworth Chapel has buttresses with detached pinnacles connected to the wall by tiny flying buttresses (cf. Ecclesfield and Silkstone). Under the chancel is a crypt with low straight-headed mullioned windows. The windows of the church are mostly Perp and all large.

Inside, the nave and chancel arcades have octagonal piers, plain in the outer aisle chapels and the chancel E parts, with sunk panels in the w parts and the nave. Arches with double-hollow-chamfered moulding. Clerestory in the chancel (a later addition – see the two tiers of capitals in the chancel arch). Fine wooden ceilings in chancel and nave, paid for in 1636.

CHANCEL STALLS. Three late medieval stalls used as sedilia. From another church. Poppyheads at the ends and two small figures and two small animals. – COMMUNION RAIL. Paid for in 1698. Outstandingly fine. At the foot bulbous with leaves, above twisted of two strands. – FONT. Octagonal. C15. – FONT COVER. Excellent C15 piece of spire shape with two tiers of openwork arches and canopies (cf. Bradford, *West Riding North*). – BENCHES. Box pews in the nave and aisles, simple with knobs on the ends and a little ornamental carving. Made apparently about 1633–4 (cf. Bolton Percy, 1631). Reduced in height 1878. – ORGAN CASE by *J. O. Scott*, 1878, for the organ by *Snetzler*, 1766. – POOR BOX. A life-size bearded figure known as Tristram, probably C17, in spite of a date 1701. – STAINED GLASS. E window with large figures in glaring colours by *Hedgeland*, 1855. It was given by Col. Edward Akroyd. Chancel NE and SE windows by *Clayton & Bell*, 1857. Clerestory windows by *Shrigley & Hunt*, 1885–7. Holdsworth Chapel E window by *Hardman*, 1859. W window by *Wailes*, 1860. Rokeby Chapel windows by *William Warrington*, 1859–60. The leading in the glass of the s choir aisle and one window in the N choir aisle was given in 1652 and deserves notice. It forms close lozenge and star patterns. The w window, of 1657, has the same design. – MONUMENTS. A large and rewarding collection though nothing outstanding. The best include: s aisle, w wall. John Favour †1624, with bad frontal bust with hands. – N chancel chapel. Nathaniel Waterhouse †1645, large Early Georgian inscription to a philanthropist. Corinthian pilasters and semicircular top. – N aisle. Jeremiah and Mary Hollins, by *Sir Henry Cheere*, 1752. – Rev. George Legh †1776, by *Nicholas Read*. – John Royds †1781, by *John Fisher I*. – Jane Caygill †1806, by *R. Cooke* of London. Relief; she lies on a couch, an angel points upward ready to take her to heaven. – s aisle. H.W. Coulthurst †1817 with seated figure, by *Westmacott*. – John Rawson †1826, by *Westmacott*. – William Rawson †1828 by *Westmacott*. Relief of the Good Samaritan. – Under the tower. Archdeacon Charles Musgrave †1875, recumbent effigy on tomb-chest, 1880 by *W. D. Keyworth Jun*.

w of the parish church is the CHURCH SCHOOL, Gothic of 1865, eleven bays wide.

HOLY TRINITY (former), Harrison Road. 1795–8 by *Thomas Johnson*. Now offices. The first chapel of ease in the town, built by a special Act of Parliament obtained by the Vicar of Halifax. A good classical design, though unconventional in shape and plan. A tall rectangle, with the longer sides on the E and W and the tower on the S. The entrances are either side of the altar, which is, as one would expect, on the E side. This faces the town and has the most elaborate architectural treatment. Three wide bays, the middle one projecting and pedimented. Ionic columns here, pilasters in the side bays. Three-light E window with Ionic columns and balustrade under a large semicircular light. Similar upper lunettes on the N, W and S sides. Doorways on the E and small lower windows on the other sides have Gibbs surrounds. Tower with aedicules on the bell-stage and a low octagonal dome. The church was converted to offices in 1987 by *Oddy & Sykes* (project architects *Richard* and *Jill Wilson*). The spacious interior, with galleries on three sides, remains open, although the spaces under and in them are partly enclosed and an additional floor level has been added above them. The galleries are supported on Ionic columns, their fronts are panelled. – STAINED GLASS. E window, with lunette above, by *R. B. Edmundson*, 1863. E wall, N and S, by *Powell Bros* of Leeds, c. 1889. Other lunettes by *Ward & Hughes*, c. 1872.

EBENEZER METHODIST CHURCH, St James Road. By *Walsh & Nicholas*, 1922–4. Gothic, in ironstone. On a prominent but awkward site constrained by roads. Well-composed, rather narrow front with square corner tower and tall lancets over the paired doors. Shallow gabled 'transepts' towards rear. Upper part of galleried interior now forms the church, with meeting rooms etc. below. Large school behind, 1883, has rose window with plate tracery in the gabled front.

HANOVER METHODIST NEW CONNEXION CHAPEL (former), King Cross Street. 1834. Now the PLAYHOUSE. Front of three bays with broad strip pilasters and narrow pediment. Portico with two Greek Doric columns. Arched upper windows. Converted to a theatre by *Pickles Architects*, 1945.

SQUARE CONGREGATIONAL CHAPEL (former), Square Road. Now ARTS CENTRE. Attributed to *Thomas Bradley*, 1771–2. One of Yorkshire's greatest Georgian chapels, its size and grandeur set a new standard for West Riding nonconformity. Its name is thought to derive not from its plan, which is square, but from a new square of houses recently begun to the N. An early example of brick in Halifax, its deep, warm red is set off by the stone dressings. Five-bay Palladian front with central door with attached Doric columns and pediment. Venetian window above. The other upper windows are arched. Parapet and three-bay pediment above. Returns with similar windows to the front. Converted to a two-storey Sunday School when its more splendid Gothic successor opened in 1857, it closed with the church in 1970. After years of dereliction it was restored 1988–91 by *Allen Tod Architects*, with exhibition galleries and offices on the ground floor and a performance space above. Major new extension underway by *Evans Vettori*, 2016–17.

SQUARE CONGREGATIONAL CHURCH (former/part), Square
Road. 1855–7 by *Joseph James*. This was the most ambitious
C19 church in the centre of Halifax. Its C14 Gothic Revival
tower and slender pinnacled spire, soaring to 235 ft (70.5
metres), still dominate the town. They were the gift of Sir
Francis (Frank) Crossley and cost £1,500. The body of the
church was gutted by fire in 1971 and demolished 1976–7,
leaving only part of the s wall, including the transept's large
rose window with Dec tracery, and the magnificent adjoining
steeple. This was clearly influenced by Pugin's church at
Cheadle (Staffordshire). A new Central Library and Archive
by *LDN Architects* is being built on the site of the church in
2014–17, incorporating its remains.

SION CONGREGATIONAL CHAPEL (former), Wade Street.
1819. The imposing Greek Revival ashlar front has been incorporated into the Bus Station, by *Abbey Hanson Rowe & Partners*, 1989. Four fluted Doric columns *in antis* flanked by plain
entrance pavilions with tall doors and lunettes above the main
entablature. Incised Greek decoration in the fine ashlar. The
SION SCHOOLS building of 1846, originally alongside the
chapel, was moved to form the café etc. higher up Wade Street.
Single storey. Seven bays with Tuscan pilasters, arched
windows and a projecting central porch with Italianate belvedere tower. The screen wall of the bus station's E entrance on
Winding Road uses the classical façade of the school's JUBILEE
HALL, 1866.

CARLTON UNITED REFORMED CHURCH, Carlton Terrace.
1837 for the Congregationalists. Large, in sparse classical
design. Stone 'brick'. Entrances, either side of Venetian
window, elevated over semi-basement at front. Round-headed
windows to first floor. Central chimneystack above eaves at
front forms decorative date panel with anthemion, like a tiny
pediment.

ELIM PENTECOSTAL CHURCH, Hall Street. An inventive design
by *Colin Oldfield* of *C.F.L. Horsfall, Son & Partners*, 1970.
Single-storey square box, faced in Portland stone, with chamfered corners, containing a circular worship space under a
'pleated' copper roof with clerestory in the triangular openings
formed by the pleats. Open steelwork spire 40 ft (12 metres)
high. Meeting rooms etc. on the N side with abstract concrete
wall sculpture.

PUBLIC BUILDINGS

TOWN HALL, Crossley Street. 1859–63 by *Sir Charles Barry*,
completed after his death in 1860 by *E.M. Barry*. The story
of the conception and execution of the building in its present
form is long and complicated, in which the rivalry of Edward
Akroyd and John Crossley played a major part. As early as
1847, the year before incorporation, the Akroyd family had
been among those promoting a company to provide purpose-
built accommodation for the Town Trustees and other public
bodies. Nothing came of this before the Borough was created,

Halifax, Town Hall.
Engraving by I.S. Heaviside, 1860

and the new council used a converted warehouse on the corner of Union Street and Westgate as council chamber and offices. Serious consideration of a new building began in connection with the Halifax Improvement Act 1853 with inconclusive purchase negotiations for a site/land at Wards End. Improvements to the town's sanitary conditions took precedence until 1856, when John Crossley, then an alderman, offered to build a new town hall with Exchange News Room adjacent to his own redevelopment scheme S of Broad Street (*see* p. 279). His price for the site and building, a Palladian design by *Lockwood & Mawson*, was £11,500. Not only was this less than the real cost but he also undertook to build the tower at his own expense. Edward Akroyd responded with an imposing Gothic design by *George Gilbert Scott* for the Wards End site. Alarmed by its estimated cost of £20,000 the councillors obtained an inferior design from the Borough Engineer, *George Wilson Stevenson*. Akroyd then offered a generous contribution to the cost of his design but withdrew in 1859 and Crossley's second offer, of the present site on advantageous terms, won the day. The building was to be classical, in keeping with Crossley's surrounding development. *Barry*, initially brought in as adviser, was given the commission. It is regrettable that the site is too congested to take the building in as a monument of self-confident High Victorianism or for it to contribute much to the townscape of Halifax other than its tower and spire, which terminate the view from the S along Princess Street, Corn Market and Southgate.

83   The body of the building is rectangular, two storeys with a rusticated basement, and the angles expressed as pavilions. On the side elevations, arched windows in each bay, strongly articulated by attached columns, Doric on the ground floor, Ionic above, with plinths and entablatures. Above is a parapet, partly balustraded, with pinnacled dies. At the angles are domed cupola. *Barry Jun.* finished this free North Italian Cinquecento design with the steep crested mansard roofs. At the SW corner, boldly breaking forward on the axis with Princess Street, the three-storey tower. This is balanced by a more modest pavilion at the SE corner and between the two are two storeys of arcaded loggias. In Barry's original design the corner tower was of three unequal stages with a modest spire, but his son transformed it into a magnificent steeple, topping it with an 80-ft spire that defeats period categorizing. It has three tiers of dormers and a little balcony below the top to provide it with a desirable frayed outline. It took on an even more exotic appearance in 1869 when Barry Jun. designed the carved stone covering, finished like scales, to replace the original tiles. At the base of the tower, at the corner of Wesley Court, a big balustraded porch, with a feast of sculptural decoration, mostly by *John Thomas*, who worked for Barry on the Houses of Parliament, and completed after his death in 1862 by *Daniel Maclise*. In the spandrels of the arches of the loggias on the principal elevation and the SE pavilion, a troupe of clambering cherubs, bearing symbols of civic authority, art and industry. Two carry rolls of carpet. The tower has clock faces in aedicules, whose pediments have lions flanking allegorical figure groups of Europe, North America, Africa and Asia (by *Maclise*). Angels guard the corners of the spire.

The most striking feature of the INTERIOR is familiar from Barry's London clubs – the central (Victoria) hall with cantilevered gallery and gloriously coloured and patterned coved glass roof. An impressive, if rather extravagant, use of space, it has arcades on both levels with lots more cherubs, and a floor with encaustic tiles and coloured marbles. The first floor is reached by a domed imperial staircase in the tower. The Council Chamber was originally in the SE pavilion, with the Exchange News Room below. Next door, the Mayor's Parlour has a fine coffered plaster ceiling. After the Borough court and police moved out in 1900 the double-height courtroom, with its large oval ceiling light, was divided to create a larger Council Chamber with fine mahogany panelling and fittings on the new upper level.

PIECE HALL, Westgate. Yorkshire's only cloth hall to survive in its entirety, the Piece Hall is not only the most noteworthy architectural monument of Halifax but one of England's greatest Georgian commercial buildings. Built in 1774–9, after the inadequacies of its predecessor (first recorded in 1572 and rebuilt in 1708) prompted a group of cloth manufacturers to form an association for building a larger one. Both large-scale manufacturers and individual weavers joined; cloth merchants were excluded. The sloping site on the town's southern edge was given by John Caygill, a wealthy merchant and property owner. The building costs, which came to over £9,000, were raised by subscriptions of £28.4s., entitling the subscriber to a room in the building. *Thomas Bradley* of Halifax and *[Mr] Hope* are both credited in contemporary sources as architects, although *Samuel* and *John Hope* of Manchester provided detailed estimates of the building costs in 1775. The most plausible explanation seems to be that the youthful Bradley (he was only twenty-three in 1775) was author of the overall design, while the more experienced Hopes acted as executant architect and surveyor respectively.*

The principal entrance is in the centre of the N side, where it faced the town. Its lowness and narrowness is cleverly disguised outside by the false wooden doors that fill the tall arch under the pediment. Inscribed below the pediment is the date of its opening. The flanking walls have simple blind arcading. The S entrance, opening to fields, was originally equally small. The W entrance, more simply pedimented, was created in 1782 to relieve congestion at the N entrance. Its octagonal cupola, with bell and gilded sheep weathervane, was added in 1785. The exterior is otherwise entirely blank. Until the removal of buildings crowded against it, a visitor to the town could be forgiven for overlooking the building altogether.

Inside, it is an impressively large open rectangle 110 yds by 91 yds, enclosing a courtyard of European proportions, emulating a Roman forum. Colonnaded galleries surround the space, the two storeys of the W half increasing to three on the E as the ground drops away. The colonnades have square rusticated pillars below, decreasing in height towards the N and

63

*This account is indebted to Philip Smithies' detailed analysis of the building's design.

s entrances, and Tuscan columns above. Internal staircases at
each corner and beside the w entrance. The many small rooms
open onto the galleries. The design thus combines the large
enclosed courtyard of Leeds' Third White Cloth Hall, 1774–5,
and the long rows of separate cubicles in the Halls at Bradford,
1773, and Wakefield, 1778, providing both secure storage for
cloth and greater confidentiality for business transactions.

The building originally had 319 rooms, reduced to 315 when
the w entrance was created. Each measures 12 by 8 ft (3.6 by
2.4 metres) and has a door and window opening on to the
gallery. A room could be occupied by a single manufacturer
or weaver or shared by two or three with smaller quantities to
sell. Most rooms have been combined as larger spaces but a
handful survive unaltered, e.g. the upper one immediately N
of the w stairs. Trading was strictly regulated, with sales of
'pieces' (lengths of cloth about 27 in. by 24 yds (0.68 by 21.6
metres)) only allowed between the hours of 10 and 12 on
Saturday mornings.

From the 1820s demand for rooms steadily declined as
industrialized cloth production replaced handloom weaving
and cloth buyers dealt directly with mills. In 1868 the Hall was
given to Halifax Corporation and from 1871 was used as the
wholesale market for fruit, vegetables, fish and game. The s
entrance was enlarged and the magnificent cast-iron GATES by
George Smith & Co., Glasgow, were installed at that date. When
the market faced closure in 1973 the building was dilapidated
and the courtyard cluttered with sheds. The Hall's importance
had been formally recognized as early as 1928, when it was
scheduled as an Ancient Monument, and the champions of its
potential contribution to the town's regeneration prevailed.
Restoration as art and craft galleries, shops and cafés was first
completed in 1976 but a major restoration by *LDN Architects,*
including re-landscaping of the courtyard, has been underway
since 2013, for completion in 2017 as an attractive venue for
entertainment, specialist markets and other events.

MAGISTRATES' COURT AND (former) POLICE STATION, Blackwall, Harrison Road and Carlton Street. By *George Buckley &
Son* of Halifax, 1898–1900, following a competition. It replaced
the Borough Court and police accommodation in the Town
Hall. Large island block in Free Renaissance style. Mainly two
storeys plus attic with semicircular gables. The more elaborate
court-house frontage on Blackwall has a tall square tower with
octagonal stone cupola.

COUNTY COURT, Prescott Street/Portland Place. By *T.C. Sorby,*
County Court Surveyor, 1870–1. Dignified palazzo. Fine
ashlar, with smooth channelled rustication to the ground floor.
Balustraded parapet above modillion cornice with dentils.
Good decorative detail on the large porch in Coleridge Street.

WEST RIDING SESSIONS HOUSE (former), Prescott Street.
1889, for the new County Borough. Now flats. Two-storey
offices to the front, rather domestic in scale apart from the

three large, much-decorated Dutch gables. The courtroom behind has a high shaped gable overlooking Portland Place.

DRILL HALL (former), Prescott Street. By *R. Coad*, 1868–70. Gothic. Broad gabled front with corbel table. Massive porch flanked by rows of lancets, under large multi-foil round window. Now flats.

CENTRAL LIBRARY, Market Street. See Perambulation.

ARTS CENTRE, Square Road. *See* Churches, SQUARE CONGRE-GATIONAL CHAPEL.

EUREKA! CHILDREN'S MUSEUM, Church Street. By *Building Design Partnership* (project architects *Ken Moth* and *Alan Dunlop*), 1990–2. The site is a former railway goods yard, and the building a truncated triangle in plan, its curved E front following the line of the old tracks. Some of the station buildings (*see* below) are incorporated for offices and storage. Stone cladding to rear and sides and saw-toothed roof profile respect its context; the excitement is all reserved for the two-storey glazed front that enticingly reveals the contents. The entrance is in the angle of a triangular stone wall that slices through the building separating the exhibition areas from the restaurant and shop beyond. Inside, exposed parts of the building's structure and services, colourfully painted, are themselves exhibits. (At the time of writing plans to update the galleries, build a separate café and shop and develop an urban park on the site are being prepared by *Bauman Lyons* of Leeds.)

HIGH SCHOOL (former), Prescott Street. By *Richard Horsfall*, 1882, with S addition 1894. Spare Renaissance style. Built as a Higher Grade School, one of a few in the country providing secondary education before the 1902 Education Act. Long rectangular block with open play areas (now enclosed) below nine bays of classrooms either side of a spine corridor. A central screen divided the girls' school (N) from the boys' school (S). Each had separate entrances at the ends beyond taller bays with staircases to first-floor assembly hall, which has continuous clerestory each side. Converted to flats 2008–10.

SWIMMING POOL, Portland Place. By *F.H. Hoyles*, Deputy Borough Architect, 1964–6. Large flat-roofed block for the pool with smaller blocks attached at front and sides for ancillary spaces. Stone-faced with square ashlar slabs and local wallstones plus decorative aggregate panels to front. The pool hall has glazed E and S walls and a clerestory above the N gallery. Stylized tiled murals of British pond life by *K. Barden* with slate blue and pale green relieving the black, white and brown.

VICTORIA THEATRE, Commercial Street. By *W. Clement Williams*, 1897–1901. Built for the Halifax Concert Hall & Public Rooms Co. In late English Renaissance style with tall Baroque lanterns to the square towers. These flank the imposing curved corner with the canopied entrance. First floor has Ionic columns between bays, with two statues in niches, bands of ornament above and decorative balustrade. Elevation of seven bays to Commercial Street, the end ones pedimented. More decoration to upper storey over shopfronts. Plainer front to Fountain Street. The rich carving, which includes the names of composers, is by *R. Harvie* of Halifax. Ornately decorated foyer and imperial staircase under a stained glass dome by *William Pape* of Leeds. Auditorium, seating 1,512, has two semicircular cantilevered balconies, and panelled plasterwork to coved ceiling. Fly tower added in 1964 during refurbishment by the Council.

PLAYHOUSE, King Cross Street. *See* Churches, HANOVER CHAPEL.

BOROUGH MARKET, Market Street. 1891–6 by *J. & J. Leeming*, after a competition. A large and impressive block in a lively if undisciplined Northern Renaissance style. Three-storey street frontages with flats over shops, decorated with blocking to piers and arches, tourelles and good sculptured ornament, especially to Southgate. A fine display of dormers, chimneys, turrets and slated pyramids with finials to the roof-line. The hall is a glass and cast-iron construction with tall clustered columns supporting arches with decorative spandrels and a glazed clerestory. Ornamental ironwork and splendid entrance gates by *Walter MacFarlane* of Glasgow, other ironwork by the *Phoenix Iron Co.*, Derby. The four main avenues meet at an elaborate iron clock and lamp standard under a big octagonal dome 60 ft high. The building is a precursor to the Leemings' even more ornate City Markets in Leeds, 1904 (*West Riding North*). The scheme included THE ARCADE, linking the central market hall to Russell Street on the N and continuing as OLD ARCADE through to Old Market. Its entrance façades are as flamboyant as the rest, with mighty archways in rusticated surrounds and slated pyramid roofs to the top storey. Original shopfronts inside with thin iron frames.

RAILWAY STATION, Horton Street. By *Thomas Butterworth* of Manchester, 1855. Long, gently curving and dignified front of Palladian form. High central pavilion with pediment linked by six-bay, single-storey wings to projecting end bays. Rich, almost Baroque embellishments. Restored 1999–2001 by *Building Design Partnership* (project architect *Philip Ainsworth*), for use by Eureka! Children's Museum (*see* above). The present high-level access to the booking office and platforms, over the former goods yard, was created 1885–6 by *William Hunt*, architect to Lancashire and Yorkshire Railway Co.

s is a two-storey LOCOMOTIVE SHED, 1885 for the Great Northern Railway. Ten bays long, each bay with separately gabled roof. s again is a single-storey WAREHOUSE for covered transfer of goods, *c.* 1849, with railway access at E side of gabled N end and large cart entrances on building's w side.

Below the goods yard, on Berry Lane, a series of fifteen COAL DROPS, 1874, with metal doors to wooden bunkers. A rare survival.

NORTH BRIDGE, carrying the Leeds road over the Hebble Brook, was built in 1869–71, by *John Fraser*, engineer. It

replaced the high-level stone bridge of 1774. Cast-iron girder
structure 136 yds (122.4 metres) long with two wide arches.
Delightful Gothic tracery in the spandrels, and quatrefoils and
trefoils to the sides and balustrades. Castellated stone abutments. Running parallel are the flyovers of BURDOCK WAY,
carrying the ring road, erected 1970–3 by *West Riding County
Council.*

PERAMBULATION

Halifax has perhaps the best Victorian town centre in England.
The entire area s from the Town Hall to Wards End, between
Market Street and Cow Green, is satisfyingly intact. A start
can be made at the top of WOOLSHOPS, one of the medieval
town's principal streets, which ran from the market place
towards the parish church, where Nos. 2–3 on the corner of
Market Street is the only surviving timber-framed building in
the town centre.* Mid-C15, altered about 1670 and heavily
restored. Jettied to first and second floor, with close herringbone strutting and paired gables above.

Facing, on the w side of MARKET STREET, PALATINE
CHAMBERS by *W.H.D. Horsfall,* 1894, is typical of the town's
late C19 commercial buildings in mixed Renaissance styles.
More of this kind on both sides of OLD MARKET and along
NORTHGATE, although here the e side has been replaced by
the striking CENTRAL LIBRARY by *Calderdale Metropolitan
District Architect's Department,* 1981–3, with wide ashlar-clad
bays, separated by narrow strips of glazing and the contemporary District Council offices (NORTHGATE HOUSE) of 1981–2
by the same architects, a more-dominating five storeys in an
L-shape forming a public square.

Now w along CROSSLEY STREET, and the beginning of the
redevelopment of the town centre by John Crossley in the
1850s, planned by *Lockwood & Mawson,* who also designed
most of the fine classical and later Renaissance buildings that
provide the dignified setting for the Town Hall (*see* Public
Buildings). It is unfortunate that the view at the top of the
street is so unworthy of it. On the corners are matching buildings in Italianate style with rounded corners, that on the N built
as the Crossleys' offices and showroom. On the corner of
Wesley Court, opposite the town hall, a plainer palazzo of 1858,
for the Royal Insurance Co. Facing this, the former Mechanics'
Institute and School of Art of 1857, with a rusticated base and
upper storey of attached Giant Corinthian columns carrying
entablature blocks. Lavish carving in the tympana of the first-
floor windows. At the rear is a large first-floor hall with gallery.
Its neighbour, to the corner of Princess Street, is the former
offices of the HALIFAX PERMANENT BENEFIT BUILDING
SOCIETY by *Samuel Jackson* of Bradford, 1871–3, and opposite

---

* For another timber-framed house, moved from the town, *see* Shibden, p. 629.

that the former offices of the HALIFAX JOINT STOCK BANK, 1858. s extension, with decorated oriels and pediment of 1887. The w side of PRINCESS STREET has the long and rich frontage of the WHITE SWAN HOTEL, 1858, possibly by *Parnell & Smith*. Decorated as if it were John Crossley's own palazzo, with his arms above the first floor where the window pediments have lusciously carved consoles. The second floor has crosses and the top linked Cs framed by oak and palms. We have left the more correct classical style of Crossley Street and it is most instructive to follow its injection with freer, incorrect forms, resulting in what the age called the Mixed Renaissance, ending on the w side with an imposing five-storey block on the s corner. Opposite, a former BURTON'S of 1932, in the characteristic Art Deco of their architect, *Harry B. Wilson*; elephants' heads as capitals to pilasters.

CROWN STREET, w of Princess Street, was the town's high street. The landmark, in the angle with Silver Street, is the former Halifax Commercial Bank of 1880 by *W. & R. Mawson*. Venetian Gothic, three storeys high with steep roofed dormers, tourelles and windows with well-carved imposts and shafts, different on each storey. On the N side of Crown Street, the Baroque front of the SPORTSMAN INN by *W. H. D. Horsfall*, 1904. On SILVER STREET, other good late C19 commercial fronts including the former Halifax Equitable Bank, with its entrance on the corner with Central Street.

WATERHOUSE STREET, running N from Crown Street was laid out *c.* 1825, with Broad Street, to link Northgate to this area. On its w corner with Crown Street is NATWEST (originally National Provincial) BANK by *F.C.R. Palmer* (with *C.F.L. Horsfall & Son*), 1927, and a remarkably late example of the grandiose Baroque Revival prevalent in the Edwardian years. Portland stone, with rusticated ground floor and decorated arch to the corner entrance under a dome. On BROAD STREET, the former ODEON cinema (now Mecca Bingo Club) of 1938 by *George Coles*. Oddly jumbled composition, but over the entrance three faience-lined concave recesses with semicircular block-glass oriels. Tall fin tower at the corner.

6   COMMERCIAL STREET, s of Crown Street, was authorized by the 1853 Improvement Act but not laid out until 1880, as the last and highest of the three major streets along the town's contours. Where it meets George Street, crossing E–W, it becomes very wide, in an informal square, and here one receives the full impact of the town centre of *c.* 1900, with the imposing Baroque Revival DISTRICT BANK CHAMBERS, 1907, on the N side – symmetrical with pedimented Dutch gables and shallow bows to the end bays and tall chimneys – and in the centre of the square, the magnificent and sumptuously decorated LLOYDS BANK, by *Horsfall & Williams*, 1897–8, for the Halifax & Huddersfield Union Bank. To Commercial Street, a powerful pedimented Corinthian portico with paired columns in polished granite. To the outer bays and along the flanks, giant Corinthian pilasters between the bays

and expressing the angles, which also have panelled parapets
with segmental pediments. The banking hall has rich plasterwork. Immediately behind is SOMERSET HOUSE, built for
John Royds, a woollen merchant, in 1766 and restored in
2006–8.* Two-and-a-half storeys, topped by a modillion
cornice and balustrade, it was originally seventeen bays long
and included warehousing but the E end was curtailed to make
way for the bank c. 1897. So the handsome s front to Rawson
Street, the garden side originally, is now asymmetrical, with its
former centre section displaced to the r. This has a Doric
colonnade below a double-height first floor, of three bays, the
middle window pedimented. To its l., first a two-bay projecting
wing with pediment, then three bays and then another two-bay
wing, projecting more deeply and without a pediment, that is
obscured by later additions to s and N. The composition to the
r. of the centre was originally the same but after the E part was
demolished, the inner wing was extended s to the streetline
and its pedimented front re-set on the new line. (The walls
and coved ceiling of the central Saloon have fine Rococo plasterwork by *Giuseppe Cortese*, representing John Royds as
Neptune and his wife as Britannia over the fireplace. Some of
their children appear in medallions.)

At the corner of Rawson Street and Commercial Street, the
former Lancashire & Yorkshire Bank, by *Tarbolton & Tugwell*,
1892. Three storeys diminishing in height, with large pedimented attic gables. Opposite is the Gothic POST OFFICE of
1887 by *Henry Tanner* of *H.M. Office of Works,* with gables
flanked by tourelles, and the exuberantly eclectic Edwardian
POST OFFICE BUILDINGS adjoining on the r.

NE of these in Old Cock Yard is the OLD COCK INN, its
core thought to have been built by William Savile of Copley
c. 1581 on the doubtful evidence of a dated overmantel with
arched panels between caryatids in the impressive upper room,
which also has a 3:4:3 light transomed window, panelling and
a plaster ceiling. A plaster panel above the overmantel has the
Savile arms with royal supporters, probably 1630s, a more
likely date for the house.

E of here is SOUTHGATE, which has Borough Market (*see* Public
Buildings) filling the E side and, to the corner with King
Edward Street, the former ARCADE ROYALE by *Clement Williams & Son*, 1911–12, steel-framed with a facing of white and
green faience from the Leeds Fireclay Co. in stylized Baroque
with Art Nouveau details.

Back on Commercial Street, s of King Edward Street, more late
C19 and early C20 commercial architecture. YORK BUILD-
INGS, on the s corner, was built as a drapers shop by *Clement
Williams & Son*, 1904–5, but aggrandized as the headquarters
of the Halifax Permanent Benefit Building Society in 1919–21.

*The house is usually attributed to *John Carr* but this seems unlikely on stylistic
grounds. He designed a house in George Street for the Rawson family and they
owned Somerset House from 1807.

At ground floor, pairs of black polished granite Doric columns. Its extension of 1929–32, facing Alexandra Street to the s, is classical-cum-*Moderne*.

The entertainments area is concentrated at the s end of Commercial Street at the junction with Wards End and Fountain Street, dominated by the VICTORIA THEATRE (*see* Public Buildings). s, across Fountain Street, is the former PICTURE HOUSE (now a night club), by *W. Wormald Longbottom*, 1913. Stone front with Mannerist details and an octagonal domed tower set back between splayed wings embracing a curved portico. Opposite is the former REGAL CINEMA by *W.R. Glen*, 1938, built on the massive scale usual by that date and relying for effect on broad expanses of undecorated surfaces over a long curved stone frontage. But overshadowing everything here is the former headquarters of the HALIFAX BUILDING SOCIETY by *Building Design Partnership* (project architect *Harold W. Pearson*), 1968–74. Parallelogram plan with upper floors behind a sleek grid of brown smoked-glass curtain walling, carried on a deeply chamfered concrete floor deck over the entrance plaza and held by a square concrete pier at the corner. Within the plaza, steps and smaller volumes of glazed office space. As architecture it deserves the many accolades received but as townscape it is a brutal intervention. The line of St John's Lane is preserved behind with bridges passing over to a taller EXTENSION of 1987–90 by *Abbey Hanson Rowe* (project architect *Philip A. Thornton*) and *Clement Williams & Sons*, associated architects, in the ground floor of which the pedimented façade of the FREEMASONS' HALL, by *John Edwin Oates*, 1868–70, is exhibited like a stage set

The area w of here developed after Holy Trinity church (*see* Churches) opened in 1797 and remains a pleasant enclave of Late Georgian and Early Victorian buildings, the latter still classical in style, and including some good houses with Doric etc. porches. In HARRISON ROAD, s of the church, the WATERHOUSE ALMSHOUSES, whose unassuming two-storey sheltered housing, 1965–7, replaced the Tudor-style building of 1855 by *Charles Child*. N, beyond the Magistrates' Court (*see* Public Buildings), No. 10, with giant Tuscan pilasters, was originally the LITERARY AND PHILOSOPHICAL SOCIETY premises, 1834, and No. 11 opposite, with pedimented porch and upper windows, was the WEST RIDING MAGISTRATES' COURT HOUSE, c. 1859. The two l. bays were the police superintendent's house. Carlton United Reformed Church (*see* Churches) faces its r. return. At the bottom of Hopwood Lane, 150 yds NW, HOPWOOD HALL is a nice surviving Early Georgian suburban residence, built c. 1730 by William Hopwood. Three storeys, five bays, with rusticated ground floor. Segmental pediment to doorway. Front sashes, but mullioned and transomed windows at the back.

Now e along WARDS END. Its s side has Late Georgian terrace houses either side of THE COURTYARD pub, formerly Holly House, with a five-bay centre of 1751 and later Doric porch.

Projecting brick wings added in 1760–4 have Venetian windows in the attic gables. The larger E wing has been used as ware-housing. Next to it a three-storey terrace, returning into CLARE ROAD, with unusual porches with Doric columns and lintels inset under segmental arches. Opposite this, DIRTY DICK'S (former Royal Oak) by *Jackson & Fox*, 1929–31, is Vernacular Revival, using colourful ironstone with timber-framed gables and oriels. The timbers came from HMS *Newcastle* and have carvings by *H.P. Jackson & Son*, including a cavalcade of transport through the ages over the side door (cf. the Old Ship Inn, Brighouse). Down Clare Road is HOPE HALL, built *c.* 1765 by *James Green* for David Stansfield, a Leeds cloth merchant, and then called Hope House. Two storeys and five bays with a full-width pediment. Doric porch of four columns; Venetian window over. Lower projecting wings create a courtyard, their street fronts with open pediments. House's garden front, also pedimented, has big Venetian staircase window. In the N arm of Wards End, the THEATRE ROYAL (disused) by *Richard Horsfall & Son*, 1905, is formal Edwardian Baroque. Centre of five bays with giant Ionic pilasters and three-bay pediment set against attic storey. End bays have open segmental pediments with ornate oval windows.

Finally, down HORTON STREET, where Nos. 8–28 by *Walsh & Nicholas*, 1903, is an extensive and original Baroque Revival group. The lower part has shallow canted bay windows under segmental gables. Built as shops, offices, paper warehouse, bakery and café. For the thirsty the THREE PIGEONS Public House, Sun Fold, is 250 yds S in South Parade. By *Jackson & Fox*, 1932, it has a fine, modestly Art Deco, oak panelled interior with octagonal drinking lobby.

OUTER HALIFAX

The suburbs created from the mid C19 extend on all sides of the centre except to the E, where the precipitous slope of Beacon Hill naturally curtails development. As well as once-rural houses and hamlets swallowed up by the town's expansion, there are some still in isolated positions, especially to the NW.

AKROYDON, BOOTHTOWN AND DEAN CLOUGH

Halifax's earliest suburb, separated from the town centre to the S by the Hebble Brook and set out on the E side of the narrow valley of the Hebble and its northern tributary, Ovenden Beck. There was a hamlet here, Boothtown, but the chief architectural interest is the model village of Akroydon, planned in 1859 by Colonel Edward Akroyd following his experiments at Copley (q.v.). The wealth that funded his vision came from the family's vast worsted mills at Haley Hill and in the valley below at Dean Clough, where they sit alongside the even more extensive buildings of the Crossleys' carpet-manufacturing empire.

70 ALL SOULS, Haley Hill (Churches Conservation Trust). 1856–9 by *Sir George Gilbert Scott*, who wrote that 'It is, on the whole, my best church'. Given by Akroyd as the crown of his estate, though competition with the Crossleys undoubtedly played some part in the design and the spire is just a foot taller than that of their splendid Square Congregational Church in the town below (*see* Churches). The style is Scott's favourite late C13 Early Decorated and embodies his ideal of a traditional parish church. His later regret was that its size was not commensurate with the splendour of its execution (Akroyd spent some £100,000 on it) but it is nevertheless large, the commanding NW tower and octagonal stone spire the second highest in Yorkshire (after Wakefield) at 236 ft (71.9 metres). The tower has crocketed pinnacles, the spire three tiers of lucarnes. Large splendidly modelled bell-openings. Tall aisled nave of five bays, S porch, transepts and a square E end with S (founder's) chapel, N chapel and vestries, the whole beautifully composed. The rich sculptural decoration of both the exterior and interior, including the reredos, pulpit and font, is by *J. Birnie Philip*. There is much figure sculpture, a feature *The Ecclesiologist* welcomed as opening 'a new era of church art'. Outside, twenty-seven almost life-size figures include the Apostles on buttresses around the church; examples inside are the busts of the Fathers of the Church in the spandrels of the nave arcades. But in the choice of materials Scott unwittingly left a disastrous legacy by using Magnesian limestone and local sandstone for colour contrast, the former causing the latter to decay.

The lofty interior is as lavish as the exterior, the richness of decoration and materials increasing towards the E. Piers and capitals of French Early Gothic or Canterbury type. Marble and polished granite shafts to the clerestory arcade and elsewhere. Luscious, but naturalistic carved foliage of English, and especially Yorkshire, plants includes maple, ivy and hawthorn. The painted decoration is mostly lost but the Choir of Angels on the sanctuary ceiling, designed by *Clayton & Bell* and executed by *Marks & Russell*, survives as a reminder. – REREDOS. Alabaster, with marble inlays and six niches with figures. Exquisite wrought-iron SCREENS in the chancel by *Skidmore*, with floral spirals. – TILES. By *Minton*. – PULPIT. Large, octagonal, in richly carved Caen stone, on marble columns. Inlaid marble panels in the style of Cosmati work. – Huge circular FONT in the baptistery under the tower. Cornish serpentine on steps of polished red granite. – STAINED GLASS. E and W windows, chancel N and S, N chapel, S chapel and baptistery windows all by *Hardman*, 1859–60. Transept windows, central window of N aisle and the fifteen clerestory windows by *Clayton & Bell*, 1859. S aisle W window by *Wailes*, 1859. S aisle, three windows by *Jones & Willis*, 1928.

Behind the church is the substantial Gothic VICARAGE (now offices), also by *Scott*, also 1859.

ST THOMAS, Claremount Road. By *Mallinson & Healey*, 1859–61. An elevated landmark on the town's NE skyline, even more prominent before the spire was removed from the large SE tower in the C20. Dec. Four-bay nave with aisles and transepts. – STAINED GLASS. E window and one in S aisle by *Wailes*, 1872.

SACRED HEART AND ST BERNARD (R.C.), Range Lane. By *Edward Simpson*, 1895–7. On a dramatically steep site. Gothic. Tall, aisled, with rather austere exterior, the roof with single ridge. Sanctuary extended 1913. (Spacious interior with the windows set high up. Rich fittings include painted and gilded HIGH ALTARPIECE by *Mons Buissine* of Lille, early C20, and alabaster WAR MEMORIAL ALTAR by *Boulton & Sons*, 1919.)

BOOTHTOWN UNITED METHODIST CHURCH, Boothtown Road. By *C. F. L. Horsfall*, 1906. Large Tudor window with Perp tracery in gabled front, flanked by staircase towers with pavilion roofs.

SERBIAN ORTHODOX CHURCH, Boothtown Road. 1864. Originally Wesleyan, reopened 1954. Italianate, with bold pilasters and cornice to four-bay front with two central doors. Arched upper windows.

PERAMBULATION. S of All Souls, facing HALEY HILL, is a bronze STATUE of Edward Akroyd, 1875, by *J. Birnie Philip*, completed by *Ceccardo E. Fucigna*. Base by *W. Swinden Barber*, with bronze reliefs depicting scenes from Akroyd's public life from designs by *Samuel Baldwin* of Halifax. Erected in his lifetime by his fellow townsmen after he retired as M.P. for Halifax in 1874, it originally stood at North Bridge and was moved here in 1901. Opposite is the former SCHOOL built by Jonathan Akroyd, Edward's father, in 1839 and the Italianate LODGE, 1851, of his house (Woodside, 1825; dem.). Immediately behind the school were the combing and weaving sheds of the family's vast BANKFIELD MILL, 1836, extended 1856 (dem.) Its site is on the hill above their Bowling Dyke Mill in Dean Clough (*see* below).

N up BOOTHTOWN ROAD, on the E side is BANKFIELD, Col. Akroyd's mansion converted for a museum and library by the Corporation in 1887. The original villa of *c.* 1800, a modest three bays square, forms the W wing of the Italianate house created by Akroyd in the 1850s by adding single-storey loggias on the S and W and a morning room, chapel and kitchen to the SE, but the grand Italian Trecento to Quattrocento design that it is now is due to enlargement in 1867 by *J.B. & W. Atkinson*. Sumptuous interiors, especially the grand marble staircase from the porte cochère, its decoration inspired by the frescoes of Pompeii and Herculaneum, top-lit Saloon, and Library with ceiling with portraits of Chaucer, Shakespeare, Milton and Tennyson. (The oak staircase in the square tower has low plaster reliefs of Night and Day from sculptures by *Bertel Thorwaldsen*.) The gardens became AKROYD PARK in 1888. At the entrance, Italianate LODGE of *c.* 1851.

Further N, opposite the entrance to the mansion, is a Gothic GATEWAY AND SEXTON'S LODGE to All Souls' burial ground (1856).* Then follows the elaborate Gothic former STABLE BLOCK for Bankfield.

N of here and extending W of Boothtown Road, are the houses of AKROYDON, begun in 1861. They are arranged in straight blocks, mostly of six to ten houses, around a park, known as The Square, in the centre of which is the VICTORIA CROSS, modelled on the Eleanor Crosses, by *W. Swinden Barber*, 1875. The terraces and streets are named after English cathedrals. Akroyd originally turned to *Scott* for designs, but the intended residents took exception to what they considered the almshouse-like appearance of his domestic Gothic, so the scheme was modified and executed by *W.H. Crossland*. The style is Neo-Tudor with minimal ornament – hoodmoulds, spandrels with carved foliage, tiny quatrefoil windows in the gables. The overall effect is very pleasing. Thirty-eight houses were completed between 1863 and 1868 but of 350 planned only a fraction were erected by 1873 and the remaining land was sold off to speculative builders in 1894. The earliest are those facing the park on SALISBURY PLACE (which have the owners' initials on stone shields over the front doors) and RIPON TERRACE. Unlike Copley (q.v.) the houses are all through-houses and of two storeys with basements, except for one pair of three-storey semi-detached villas on CHESTER ROAD. All had a yard with water closet and ash place, one of which survives behind No. 40 Salisbury Place. The different sizes were intended to achieve a social mix and were not exclusively for Akroyd's employees. All were available for sale, in accordance with the principle of 'self-help' and to fulfil Akroyd's ambition to enfranchise the inhabitants through property ownership – ambitions largely unrealized. Behind York Terrace are allotments and on Boothtown Road is the former co-operative shop, provided in 1861.

BOOTHTOWN HOUSE, ¼ m. N in Hall Street North, is a survival of Boothtown hamlet. C17. Symmetrical front with two gables. Windows with ornamental hoodmould stops, those in the gable of five lights with three-light raised centres. Gabled returns.

W of the model village, by the Hebble, is the semi-derelict OLD LANE MILL, built by James Akroyd in 1825–8 as one of the earliest integrated worsted mills, using fireproof construction of cast-iron beams and columns and arched cast-iron roof trusses within a brick skin. Main range of six storeys and fifteen bays for spinning and weaving on steam-powered Jacquard looms, with a shallow pedimented wing at the SE corner containing the staircase, offices and storerooms. The W end has

---

*The MORTUARY CHAPEL by *Mallinson & Healey*, 1855–6, which doubled as the Akroyds' mausoleum, was demolished in 1968. *Joseph Gott*'s effigy of Jonathan Akroyd, 1863, and stained glass by *Hedgeland* were destroyed.

a tall/double-height window with rusticated surround and cornice for the beam-engine house.

DEAN CLOUGH, a little further downstream, is one of the most 74 impressive C19 industrial sites anywhere. In scale and grandeur at least, the complex of mills stands comparison with, say, the warehouses of Liverpool's docks. It grew from 1822, when John Crossley set up his own business, to fill the valley floor with 27 acres of mills and weaving sheds, employing some 6,000 people. By 1879, as John Crossley & Sons, it was the biggest carpet-manufacturing company in the world. After closure in 1982, the redundant site was bought by Sir Ernest Hall, who, inspired by the Dartington ideal of 'practical utopia', transformed it into a centre for business, education and the arts, a model of cultural and commercial regeneration (cf. the later conversion of Salt's Mill, Saltaire (*West Riding North*)).

The original water-powered Dean Clough Mill built in 1794 on the N bank of the Hebble Brook (its site now occupied by E Mill) was followed by two six-storey spinning mills: A Mill (1841) and B Mill (1844), built hard up against the valleyside below Old Lane. Seen from the S they read as one vast building. A MILL, at the E end, is seventeen bays long and has a pedimented staircase tower projecting in the centre with double taking-in doors at each storey. In the E gable-end a Venetian window. In the end bay on the S front the engine house window is tall, with a rusticated arched surround. (Wooden floors and beams on a single line of cast iron columns at near mid-span.) B MILL continues to the same design, creating a symmetrical front of forty-four bays in all and over 340 ft (104 metres) long, with a pediment over the centre four bays and another staircase tower balancing that of A Mill. (Wooden floors and beams as A Mill.) In front was C Mill, built in 1850, with extensive weaving sheds W and E but all demolished *c.* 1987–90. The resulting space, if unauthentic, nevertheless allows a better appreciation of the remaining buildings. These include the large D, E and F MILLS of 1854–8, designed by *Roger Ives* of Halifax in an unlavish Italianate style – bold modillion cornices below parapets, rusticated entrances and taking-in door openings, and privy towers with giant blind arches, paired round-headed openings to each floor and decorative top stages, which housed water tanks. All are of fireproof construction with segmental brick jack arches. Just to the W of F Mill is a great octagonal CHIMNEY, 297 ft (90.5 metres) high, dated 1857. Pointed cast-iron plates form the corona. On the S edge of the site the tallest block, G MILL, was completed in 1867. The last major spinning mill, H (dem.), finished a year later, stood behind it. Beside G is a WAREHOUSE built *c.* 1885 after the complex was linked to the Bradford railway line in 1874. Nearby is MILL HOUSE *c.* 1849, which replaced the Crossleys' home beside the old mill and provided offices.

E of D Mill the Hebble emerges from its culvert. James Akroyd bought a mill here in 1815 and the family developed what became the greatest worsted-spinning business in the country. On the N side of the brook is a four-storey spinning mill (FEARNLEY MILL) and a smaller warehouse (CROSSLEY MILL) to its W. Both were built by Jonathan Akroyd in 1836. The much larger BOWLING DYKE MILL replaced an older spinning mill that burnt down in 1847 and was built in two stages to allow production to resume without delay. E half of nineteen bays, completed in 1849, the W half, of seventeen, in 1851. Decoration is minimal. Thought to have been engineered by *Wren & Bennett*, engineers, of Manchester, who supplied the steam engine in 1849. Innovative features include an early use of Polonceau roof trusses, made entirely of wrought-iron sections.

OVENDEN, ILLINGWORTH, AND MIXENDEN

This area rises up to the moors NW of the town, with Ovenden Beck on the E and the Hebble Brook on the W. The older settlements of Ovenden, on the lower slope, and Illingworth, near the top, have lost any sense of separate identity or character among large pre- and post-war housing estates. The Hebble valley seems surprisingly rural now most of its mills, quarries and breweries have disappeared. Mixenden village towards its head was much expanded in the 1950s and 1960s by council housing, including point blocks beside the brook.

ST MARY THE VIRGIN, Raw Lane, Illingworth. First chapel built *c.* 1525, the present church mainly a rebuilding of 1777. Plain nave of seven bays with two tiers of arched windows and a W tower with little pyramidal pinnacles. Chancel with Venetian E window, 1887–8 by *T.H. & F. Healey*, and two-storey vestibule, vestry etc. extension, 1925, enclosing the tower. High and wide nave interior reduced to five bays when the galleried W end was walled off *c.* 1960. Richly classical chancel with arcades to side chapels and reused aedicule of the C18 E window with Ionic columns and swan-neck pediment. – REREDOS. By *Jackson* of Coley, 1920. – STAINED GLASS. All by *Ward & Hughes*, 1865 and later.

ST GEORGE, St George's Road, Ovenden. 1875–7 by *Jackson & Fox* of Halifax. Dignified E.E. Buttressed W tower over entrance at end of N aisle has pierced parapet and corner pinnacles. Steeply pitched roofs. Six-bay nave with clerestory, polygonal chancel with undercroft. – STAINED GLASS. Three in the S baptistery by *Kayll & Reed*, *c.* 1930. Big gabled VICARAGE, 1883.

ST MALACHY (R.C.) Nursery Lane, Ovenden. By *J.H. Langtry-Langton*, 1959–62. A bold and late example of stripped Romanesque. Large, in a bold interpretation of conventional forms and round-arched style. High, strikingly spacious interior. Gently arched beams spanning the full length of the nave support the clerestory, allowing the space to flow into the aisles without the interruption of an arcade. Good-quality original fittings. – STAINED GLASS in sanctuary perhaps by *Clokeys* of Belfast.

OVENDEN UNITED REFORMED CHURCH (Congregational), Keighley Road. 1837. A twin of Northowram URC (q.v.).

LEE MOUNT BAPTIST CHURCH, Ovenden Road. Large, Gothic *c.* 1910, with Sunday School behind.

SHROGGS PARK, Lee Mount Road. Instigated by Col. Akroyd as an amenity for his workers at Akroydon (*see* p. 283). Land-scaped at his expense from 1873, the designer *Edward Milner* (cf. People's Park, p. 295) and opened to the public in 1881. LODGE *c.* 1877. DRINKING FOUNTAIN with elaborate Gothic canopy.

A few relics of OVENDEN survive. Nos. 4–6 FRIENDLY FOLD ROAD, off Ovenden Road, is a small traditional Pennine house with a lintel dated 1709 and inscribed 'Iam mea mox huius sed posthac nescio cuius' (Now mine, soon his but after that I know not whose).* Further up Ovenden Road is OVENDEN HALL, a minor gentry house of *c.* 1662. Hall bay between projecting wings, all gabled. On the E gable is a curious square sundial. Recessed porch with moulded arch in the wider E wing. Deeply chamfered windows, all transomed, except over the hall and porch. The hoodmoulds to the upper windows have heavily ornamented stops, replicated on the C19 W wing.

HOLDSWORTH ROAD, 1 m. N, has one of the best groups of old houses and farms near Halifax. HOLDSWORTH HALL is prob-ably C17, with later alterations and additions. s front with two E cross-wings, both gabled, and long, plain mullioned win-dows.† On the r. LAUREL BANK, an C18 farmhouse with earlier barn. Then the best of the group, the splendid HOLDSWORTH HOUSE, dated 1633. Now a hotel. Asymmetrical but balanced s front of two gabled bays flanking a gabled two-storey porch, and a projecting E cross-wing also gabled. Porch has moulded doorway with shallow arch. Continuous dripstone above ground floor. Immensely long hall window of six-plus-five lights with transom; chamber window above has eight lights and E wing windows six, all with transoms. Rising into the l. gable a three-over-five-light window. Interior remodelled by *J.F. Walsh*, 1933. Walled garden with good C17 gatepiers with attached Doric columns and ball finials. Square two-storey gazebo at the SW corner. Single-storey range W of the house and large barn behind enclose a courtyard with entrance dated 1680. Rear extensions to house *c.* 1970, remodelled in more sympathetic guise by the *Arthur Quarmby Partnership*, 1984. W of the house HOLDSWORTH HOUSE FARMHOUSE is dated 1692. Long linear plan. Recessed porch with arched entrance and an oval window above. Eight-light mullioned windows.

---

*WHITE HALL, a late medieval aisled house noted by Pevsner was demolished 1970–2.
†FAR FIELD, noted by Pevsner, has been demolished.

At ILLINGWORTH, by St Mary's churchyard, the LOCK-UP, dated 1823. Arched doorway with lunette above, flanked by circular windows, all boldly rusticated. Between the upper-floor windows a large stone inscribed 'Let him that stole steal no more but rather let him labour working with his hands the thing which is good that he may have to give to him that needeth'. Unglazed window openings with vertical iron bars. On the l. the village STOCKS dated 1697.

POPPLES ALMSHOUSES, School Lane. Six tiny dwellings for women in Tudor Revival style, 1840.

NW of St Mary, in Mixenden Lane above the Hebble valley, THE FOLD, a late medieval timber-framed aisled house rebuilt in stone in the C16 with single-storey housebody. Its twelve-light transomed window is contained between the C16(?) w wing and a second, C18, E wing built in the angle of the main range and the first, C17, E wing. The N end of the added rear wing has a reused C16 window with five round-arched lights.

MIXENDEN HALL, Moor End Road, on the other side of the valley from Mixenden village, is mid-C18. Five bays. Plain ashlar dressings and doorcase with segmental pediment.

GRINDLESTONE BANK, in a rough lane below Scout Edge, has some puzzling features. The datestone 1603 does not go with the building, which must be later in the century. Main range has symmetrical three-bay front, the central entrance bay treated like a two-storey gabled porch but barely projecting. Gabled E cross-wing with similarly minimal projection. Uniform windows of five lights, the lower ones transomed. Rear elevation has three main gables, that is on the E cross-wing and on two additional N bays. The middle one, dated 1635, has a doorway with moulded surround. Through-passage bay has similar gable to s front.

UPPER BROCKHOLES

MOUNT ZION METHODIST CHURCH, Per Lane. Set in a large burial ground on the edge of the moors. Rebuilt 1815. Plain front with two windows between outer doorways and four windows above, all with round-arched heads. Above the oval date plaque a sundial from the previous chapel, dated 1773. Semicircular extension at rear for organ. Good galleried interior refitted in 1881 by *Leeming & Leeming*. Minister's cottage attached on W.

MOUNT TABOR

METHODIST CHAPEL. Typical moorland chapel of 1820, with simple gabled front with three round-headed windows. Large porch added *c.* 1860 and Sunday School rebuilt 1871.

Running back to Halifax on the W side of the Hebble valley there are several notable C17 and early C18 houses. In GIBB LANE,

½ m. E of Mount Tabor, No. 16 is a rare and early surviving example of the single-storey labourer's cottage. Two rooms with central porch dated 1708. Dwarfed by a barn attached slightly later. Steeply downhill to the S, Nos. 1–2, a farmhouse with simple mullioned windows, 1715. Further SE, in OVENDEN WOOD ROAD, SPRING LEA has a two-storey gabled porch dated 1625. Projecting E wing with mullioned-and-transomed windows, the upper one with heart-shaped label stops. C18 alterations include a tall transomed staircase window at E end. Then the incongruously suburban FOUNTAIN HEAD VILLAGE c. 2008–10 on a brewery site. The monumental MALTINGS remain, in splendid isolation. By *William Chambers* of London, 1900. Four storeys plus three, with triangular dormers in the big roof, set between two square towers with hipped roofs sweeping up to ventilators and a tall E tower forming a porte cochère for the railway. Converted to offices in 1989 by *Leach, Rhodes & Walker* of Manchester, and restructured internally. On the W, further on, LONG CAN is a C15 timber-framed house with aisle, rebuilt 1637 by James Murgatroyd of Warley (cf. East Riddlesden Hall, Keighley, *West Riding North*, c. 1648 and Kershaw House, Luddenden (q.v.), 1650). Big two-storey porch with very finely moulded doorway. To the l. a seven-light window plus two-light fire window and into the gable above these a three-over-five-light window. Several elaborate label stops. The bay to the r. of the porch incorporates a loom shop added in the late C16, with two-storey extension 1708.* YEW TREE, a little further S, is also by Murgatroyd, 1643. Simple linear plan, no gables. Housebody window similar to Long Can's. Decorative stops to dripstone.

WESTERN SUBURBS AND PELLON

On the W side Halifax goes on furthest as an urban personality, with the C19 streets of PELLON LANE, HANSON LANE, GIBBET STREET and HOPWOOD LANE leading almost in parallel from the centre. To the NW the older settlement of MOUNT PELLON grew separately until the town reached the area in the first half of the C20. QUEEN'S ROAD, running N–S through the W suburbs was created in the early 1860s by the Corporation to provide a link between Pellon Lane and King Cross (*see* p. 296), an early example of urban planning to foster development. Expansion was encouraged by the railway from the King Cross terminus to the Halifax–Bradford line at Ovenden, opened in 1890, and the introduction of trams from 1898.

PLACES OF WORSHIP AND PUBLIC BUILDINGS

CHRIST CHURCH, Church Lane, Pellon. 1853–4 by *Mallinson & Healey*. Dec. Four-bay nave with lean-to S aisle. Integral

---

*BROADLEY HALL, to the NW of Long Can, was noted by Pevsner but has been demolished.

battlemented tower over sw entrance. Separately roofed aisle
and Lady Chapel added on N side 1902–3, the former reconfigured with upper meeting rooms 1999. – STAINED GLASS. W
window 1912. The Te Deum, sixteen panels including an
American Indian. Large gabled VICARAGE, 1864.

ST HILDA, Gibraltar Road. by *C. Hodgson Fowler*, 1909–11.
Large, plain Perp. Nave and chancel under same roof. Small
square tower with pyramidal top at w end of s aisle. No clerestory. More impressive inside, spacious and well proportioned
with barrel roof. – STAINED GLASS. s chapel by *Edward Woore*,
1925.

ST COLUMBA (R.C.), Highroad Well Lane. 1933–4 by *Charles
Simpson*. Free late Gothic in stone. Single ridge to roof, with
bellcote on N side at junction of nave and sanctuary. No aisles.
Prominent gabled E end has massive polygonal buttress-like
projections linked by deep arch above tiny vesica-shaped
window. Below this, on a large plinth, a canopied niche with
sculpted figure of St Columba. – REREDOS. By *Thomas Earp*,
1865, from St Mary, Gibbet Street. Now painted. – PULPIT.
Also by *Earp*. Oak, the base lacking. – ALTAR RAILS and
GALLERY FRONTS. Carved oak panels with small open quatrefoils etc., their effect reminiscent of Moorish screens.

ST MARY (R.C.), Gibbet Street. 1836–9, rebuilt by *Ralph
Nicholson* of Halifax, 1864–5, enlarged (ritual) E end by *Clement
Williams & Sons*, 1923–4. An idiosyncratic but characterful
building in mixed Gothic. Powerful w tower embraced by the
aisles, with big pavilion-roofed porch, polygonal stair-turret
and large windows to the second stage. Three-bay nave with
tall arcades and tiny clerestory. The wider E half has three
wide bays, the piers in line with the nave aisle walls. Easternmost bay has transverse arches and forms sanctuary with
side chapels. Canted apse to sanctuary has patent glazed roof,
lighting the high altar in a most effective and unusual way.
Sanctuary and chapel screens and fittings in marble, elaborately
Gothic. Canted panelled ceiling, richly painted. – STAINED
GLASS. A varied collection with two especially good later C20
windows on the s side. E window by *Hardman*, 1860. N chapel
by *Earley* of Dublin, *c.* 1911; s chapel s window by *Alfred Fisher*
of Chapel Studios, *c.* 1973. Four-light s transept window and
N transept w window by *Sep Waugh* of York, 1985. s aisle, first
from E, and N aisle, third from E, by *R. B. Edmundson & Son*,
1865. Tower windows by *Waugh*, 1990s.

KING'S CHURCH. *See* Public Baths, below.

FAIRFIELD (PRIMITIVE METHODIST) CHURCH (former),
Queen's Road. 1890–1. Gothic, in stone 'brick'. Gabled front
articulated by buttresses, the outer ones forming little spiky
turrets.

PARK CONGREGATIONAL CHURCH, Hopwood Lane. Now
offices. By *Roger Ives*, 1867–9. Gothic, with Geometrical
tracery in the large window above the s entrance. Integral
tower to r. with octagonal belfry and slender stone spire
enhancing the prominent corner site. Aisle bays separately
gabled. Behind the church, extensive Sunday Schools, 1875.

PELLON BAPTIST CHURCH, Spring Hall Lane. 1913. Gothic, with big Perp traceried window in gabled front. Solid square tower set forward on l. Sunday School to r., 1875.

CENTRAL JAMIA MOSQUE MADNI, Gibbet Street. 1982–4, extended 2002. Squarish, with a pattern of arches in the ashlar facing. Small dome and three minarets, one taller. Attached Education Centre, 1994–5.

GENERAL CEMETERY, Lister Lane. Opened 1841. Only 3 acres, it has monuments of many of the town's leading families, including the Crossleys. At the time of writing the little Grecian mortuary chapel at the w end awaits restoration.

PUBLIC BATHS (former), Park Road. Now The King's Centre. 1858–9 by *G.W. Stevenson*, Borough Engineer. An early survival. Italianate, with a two-storey centre and low wings to l. and r. Doric pilasters and blind windows relieve the large blank walls of the top-lit pools. John and Francis Crossley contributed to the cost but insisted that there was no public washhouse.

CALDERDALE COLLEGE, Francis Street. The earliest building is the PERCIVAL WHITLEY CENTRE by *R.H. Pickles*, 1954–6. Seven storeys, stone-faced. The windows are given a rhythmical grouping. The Assembly Hall is attached to the s end of the tall block. It was built as an extension to the Technical College on Hopwood Lane (1895, by *Jackson & Fox*, dem.). To the s the CREATIVE & CONSERVATION SKILLS CENTRE, 2004, includes studios, a theatre and workshops for building crafts.

QUEEN'S ROAD SCHOOL (now Community Centre). By *Richard Horsfall*, 1874. One of Halifax's first purpose-built Board Schools. Single-storeyed. Extravagantly carved tympana in the pediments over the central infants' school and the projecting wings of the boys' and girls' schools. The handsome square entrance tower has a louvred belfry.

WARLEY ROAD PRIMARY SCHOOL, by *J.F. Walsh*, 1897. One of the earliest Board Schools in the country to be built with an indoor swimming pool. It is 27.6 ft (8.4 metres) long and 18 ft (5.5 metres) wide.

MOUNT PELLON ACADEMY, Battinson Road. By *C.F. L. Horsfall & Son*, 1903. Single-storey-plus-basement on lower side. Stone 'brick' with hipped slate roofs. Some canted bay windows, the others all with swan-necked pediments.

HALIFAX ACADEMY, Gibbet Street. By *Ryder Architecture*, 2010, behind the site of the former WELLESLEY BARRACKS, built 1875–7 under the Cardwell reforms (cf. Pontefract), by *Major H.C. Seddon*, Director of Design Branch, Inspector General of Fortifications' Dept. Entrance flanked by polygonal sentry boxes, then on r. forbidding three-storey square KEEP for the guardhouse, armoury etc. Attached at opposite corners two square staircase towers with machicolations and crenellated parapets. Behind is former parade ground overlooked on the w by OFFICERS' MESS and COMMANDING OFFICER'S HOUSE, their more domestic gables, mullioned windows and Gothic Revival details an acknowledgement of local styles.

PEOPLE'S PARK. *See* Perambulation below.

WEST VIEW PARK, Warley Road. Presented in 1896 by two Halifax manufacturers, Henry McCrea and Enoch Robinson. The SOUTH AFRICAN WAR MEMORIAL, 1904, is by *W. W. Longbottom*. At the top a granite drum has a stone frieze of cavalry by *A.F. Smith* and is surmounted by a bronze statue of a soldier surveying the veldt by *B. Sheppard*. The long balustrade in front was *E.M. Barry*'s screen for the Town Hall's basement (E side), moved here *c.* 1900.

PERAMBULATION

A start can be made immediately outside the city centre in GIBBET STREET, at the corner of Bedford Street North where the GIBBET's square stone platform was rediscovered in 1839. It was restored in 1973 with a replica of the 15-ft (4.5-metre)-high guillotine. Under manorial law Halifax retained an ancient right of summary trial and execution for the theft of goods worth 13½d. or more. The last beheading was in 1650. Fear of the penalty was voiced in the prayer 'From Hull, Hell and Halifax Good Lord deliver us'. A little further up is ST MARY (R.C.) (*see* Places of Worship and Public Buildings) with schools behind it in CLARENCE STREET by *Edward Simpson*, 1887, extended in 1894 by *J.F. Walsh*.

A few streets further W is John Crossley's WEST HILL PARK ESTATE, a model scheme supported by the Halifax Permanent Building Society to provide freehold houses for 'thrifty artisans, clerks and others' with church and school. A competition in 1863 was won by *Paull & Ayliffe*. The rules stipulated several

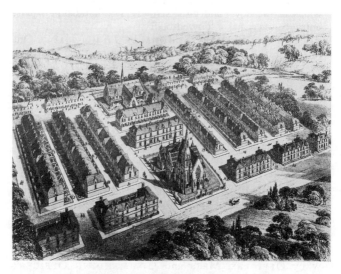

Halifax, West Hill Park Estate, workers' housing.
Artist's impression of the development as conceived

different sizes of houses, none back-to-back, and each with three bedrooms and separate yard and privy. By 1871 some 203 houses were built in terraces named after the heroes of Liberal nonconformity (Milton, Cromwell etc.) but not the church or school, and the social mix intended remained unrealized. The only amenities were the corner shops in the blocks of six larger, bay-windowed houses fronting Gibbet Street and in blocks of smaller houses on Hanson Lane to the N. Long terraces run between these two streets, five each side of Gladstone Road. The rear ones are paired and face each other across front gardens with only a communal central path between them. Gables relieve the steeply pitched roofs and front and back doors have fanlights, some under Gothic heads.

MILTON PLACE, across Lister Lane to the S, has two high-quality terraces of c. 1855, also built by Crossley, as a precursor to West Hill Park. In MARGARET STREET to the W is the first of (Sir) Francis (Frank) Crossley's own projects, twenty-six ALMSHOUSES, 1855, by *Roger Ives*. An impressively long range in Tudor Gothic with a battlemented tower in the middle and at both ends, they are built beside the main entrance to Crossley's mansion, Belle Vue (now CROSSLEY HOUSE offices), on HOPWOOD LANE, which was newly built when Crossley acquired it in 1845 or 1851, but is now as remodelled in lavish Louis XIV style by *G.H. Stokes*, 1856–7.* The inspiration for the elegant two-storey garden front comes from Parisian *hôtels particuliers*. Steep mansard roof with oval dormers in voluted surrounds and straight pavilion roof over the pedimented centre. Doric porte cochère on E and large apsidal-ended CON-SERVATORY on W with arcaded framing along the sides and a barrel-vaulted roof. (Interior has some lavish plasterwork, also boiseries, and spectacular top-lit marble staircase with arcaded landing.)

S across Hopwood Lane is the PEOPLE'S PARK, given by Crossley and laid out in 1856–7 by *Sir Joseph Paxton* (assisted by *Edward Milner*) so that 'every working man in Halifax' might 'go to take his stroll there after he has done his hard day's toil, and be able to get home without being tired'. Paxton applied some of the ideas used at Birkenhead Park, Cheshire, particularly in the use of picturesque mounds of earth, built up with rocks and planted with trees and shrubs, which screen the park from surrounding streets. At the higher, W, side a long formal terrace designed by *G.H. Stokes* (Paxton's son-in-law) allows views of the hills to the E. In its centre an Italianate pavilion, with arcaded loggia, holding a seated STATUE of Sir Francis by *Joseph Durham*, 1860. The terrace has marble statues by *Francesco Bienaimé* of Carrara, mostly c. 1857 but a few (Sophocles, Apollo (absent at the time of writing) and Italian Dancing Girl) added later. At the S end is Bienaimé's copy of the Medici vase, at the N end one of the Borghese vase. Below

---

*Stokes used an alternative design for the house, in François Premier style, for Battlesden, Bedfordshire, 1860–4 (dem.).

the terrace a central grassed area has a circular basin with the Venus fountain by *Durham*, *c.* 1855, from the winter garden at Somerleyton Hall, Suffolk, brought here in 1912. At the bottom of the slope serpentine lakes fed by a cascade and crossed by two decorative cast-iron bridges complete the transition from formality to informality that is modelled, albeit on a much smaller scale, on the Crystal Palace Park. Drinking fountain by *John Hogg*, 1859, the large sundial dated 1858, given in 1873 and splendid octagonal bandstand, 1897.

As part of the same scheme PARK ROAD was laid out on the E side and developed with six pairs of substantial Italianate houses by *John Hogg*, 1858–65. Handsome ashlar fronts with two-storey bay windows. At the park's SE corner, the former Public Baths (*see* Places of Worship and Public Buildings, p. 293). At the park's SW corner WEST HOUSE, a five-bay Georgian house. Ashlar S front with segmental pediment to doorway and a shallow bow window either side. Across King Cross Street, at the end of ARDEN ROAD, the magnificent JOSEPH CROSSLEY'S ALMSHOUSES by *Roger Ives & Son*, 1863–70. A very large open quadrangle with three ranges of picturesque Tudor Gothic buildings, looking more collegiate than charitable. Tall battlemented tower in the middle of the W side, with the N and S sides stepping up beside terraced gardens. Steeply roofed chapel on the S side.

About ½ m. N, between MIALL STREET and WILLIAMSON STREET, three large former worsted MILLS, which dominate the western skyline in views from Beacon Hill. All four-storeyed with basement, the oldest one to the N eleven by five bays, the largest, 1886, nineteen by seven bays, with parapet. Weaving sheds survive between it and the tall mill with gabled front on the corner of Battinson Road, dated 1896. A rare survival on Williamson Street are the thick walls that enclosed the former MILL POND, now a yard and car park. The outer face is battered, the inner one is lined with concrete to provide a reservoir some 6 ft (1.8 metres) deep.

SAVILE PARK AND KING CROSS

The SW suburbs are mainly part of the plateau at the S edge of town high above the Calder valley. At the centre is Savile Park, formerly Skircoat Moor. For centuries this area belonged to a branch of the Savile family and was not made available for development until the later C19, when the S and E parts became a fashionable suburb. King Cross, to the W, lay outside the Savile estate and, like the W suburbs to its N (*see* p. 291), was developed in the C19 with terraced housing.

CHURCHES AND PUBLIC BUILDINGS

ST JUDE, Savile Park Road, at the corner of Savile Park. 1889–90 by *W. Swinden Barber*. Restrained Dec, large and solemn. Prominent tower attached to W end of S aisle has ogee-headed bell-openings and pinnacles. Good-quality fittings include oak ALTAR AND REREDOS, 1920. – STAINED GLASS. N chapel E by *F. W. Cole*, 1972.

ST PAUL, King Cross Road. By *R. D. Chantrell*, 1845–7. Only the fine tower with broach spire remains. Used as a mortuary chapel from 1912 when the new church was built (*see* below), the body demolished in 1931.

ST PAUL, Queen's Road. 1909–12 by *Sir Charles Nicholson*, with *C. E. Fox* as superintending architect. The sturdy W tower was completed 1936–7 with a bell-stage with polygonal buttresses. Fine interior, well and uncommonly detailed. Octagonal piers; the arcade arches die into them and they are then carried on in shallow relief to embrace the large clerestory windows. Fittings by *Nicholson* include the REREDOS, lofty FONT COVER and BISHOP'S THRONE, the last two among other fittings executed by *H. P. Jackson* of Coley, *c.* 1912–29. – STAINED GLASS. E and N chapel windows by *Herbert W. Bryans*. Vividly coloured W window by *Hugh Easton*, *c.* 1937.

KING CROSS METHODIST CHURCH (former), Skircoat Moor Road. By *C. F. L. Horsfall*, 1878. Large. Geometrical tracery in the big front gable window (partly blocked).

HEATH UNITED REFORMED CHURCH (Congregational), Free School Lane. By *Horsfall & Williams*, 1890. Rather grand, with elevated front. Stepped lancets in a blind Gothic arch in the central gable, paired lancets in similar arches to the upper side windows. Big staircase towers either side have pinnacled parapets.

HEATH GRAMMAR SCHOOL, Free School Lane. Now Heath Training and Development Centre. By *Leeming & Leeming*, 1877–9, replacing the school built 1597–1601 under a royal charter of 1585. The land was given by the Saviles. The rose window of the original building, preserved in the gable of an outbuilding, is the oldest of the surviving Halifax rose windows. It has six mouchettes round a circle (cf. Wood Lane Hall, Sowerby and Elland New Hall). The high front gable of the central hall has a replica window.

CROSSLEY HEATH SCHOOL, Skircoat Moor Road. 1857–64 by *John Hogg*, additions 1883 and *c.* 1920. Formerly the Crossley and Porter Orphan Home and School. A magnificent testimony to the Crossleys' philanthropy. Large, free-standing, with a three-storey front and corner pavilions and an imposing central tower over the main entrance facing Savile Park. Free Northern Renaissance style with a definite French twist. Interior was divided into two matching ranges round small internal courtyards, girls to the N, boys on the S. Both had indoor, heated, swimming pools. Still in use, the boys' pool is the oldest non-municipal pool in the country.

ROYAL INFIRMARY (former), Free School Lane, by *Worthington & Elgood* of Manchester, in Renaissance Revival style, 1892–6. Converted to housing, 2003–4. The central ADMINISTRATION BLOCK and NURSES' HOME is the most impressive element. Three storeys with big attic gables. Strongly moulded string courses and chimneystacks. The admission building, with big glazed porte cochère, and service buildings lie behind. Original ward pavilions arranged symmetrically on arcaded basements (now enclosed). Wards nearest the road have cruciform ends with a big s-facing oriel window in the central gabled bay. The earlier additional wards, 1899 and 1910, are in similar style.

KINGSTON LIBERAL CLUB (former), Queens Road, opposite St Paul's church. 1894. Large, in eclectic style, with a wildly detailed doorway and canted balcony with arcade. Roundel with carved bust of Gladstone.

PERAMBULATION

SAVILE ROAD starts near the town centre and has some older suburban houses surviving among later C19 and C20 development. Nos. 21–23 look like a severe three-storey Georgian country house. They were started after 1769 and completed c. 1790. The street front has a recessed centre of eight bays between two-bay projecting wings. Distinctive centre doorway, of Serlian form, with fanlight in the arch but set under a wide pediment. The s, garden, front is eleven bays, the two outer bays each side defined by rusticated pilasters and quoins. Fine pedimented doorcase with engaged fluted Doric columns. Projecting s, the remains of single-storey brick w wing.*

Higher up, at the junction with SAVILE PARK ROAD, SAVILE HALL has a handsome early C19 E front of five-plus-one bays with pedimented entrance bay and Doric portico. At the far end of the road, downhill, SAVILE TERRACE, elegant three-storey houses, with a good ironwork balcony. The town's only Regency terrace.

⅛ m. s is SAVILE PARK, formed from a large area of Skircoat Moor, which was sold to Halifax Corporation by Captain Henry Savile in 1866 for a nominal £100. Apart from tree planting it was left as open space. LODGE by J. T. Hanson, 1880.

Facing the park are the best Arts and Crafts houses in Halifax, a block of three on MANOR HEATH ROAD – GREYSTONES, UPPER GREYSTONES and THE WARREN – and Nos. 1–6 QUEEN'S GATE, all by *Butler Wilson & Oglesby* of Leeds, c. 1899. The three are large and form a picturesque group with features of the Pennine Vernacular style. Some timber framing to Upper Greystones above a wide recessed porch with Doric columns. More timber framing, gables and pierced parapets to the three pairs of semi-detached houses.

Nearby, off Free School Lane, HEATH VILLAS is a serpentine, tree-lined private road with lodge and good, large midVictorian villas and semi-detached houses plus later pair of 1896.

---

*Kirby Leas, Savile Road, early C19, was demolished in 1979. Well Head House, nearby, attributed to *John Carr, c.* 1767, was demolished in 1976.

s of the park, the plateau of the sw suburbs is brought to an abrupt halt at ALBERT PROMENADE, which was created in 1861 by philanthropic industrialists as a public amenity for enjoying the spectacular views of the Calder valley and Pennine hills. In the view to the NW is the WAINHOUSE TOWER, at the top of SKIRCOAT MOOR ROAD. This is one of several buildings associated with the eccentric J. E. Wainhouse. The tower, of 1871–5, was intended as a chimney for his dyeworks down the hill but as he sold these in 1874 it was never used. It is octagonal, 253 ft (77 metres) high and so slim that from a distance it seems a column. Designed by *Isaac Booth*, but the flamboyant and fantastical Renaissance corona added by his assistant *R. S. Dugdale* after Wainhouse fell out with another of Booth's patrons, Sir Henry Edwards of Pye Nest (dem.), who took exception to his house being overlooked. The style seems curiously ahead of its time, almost like the version of the Renaissance cultivated by architects like Collcutt. It was designed with the staircase around the flue, so access to the top, reached by 369 steps (to the lower balcony) was always intended.

A little NW, on the side of the hill between BURNLEY ROAD and ROCHDALE ROAD, a curious VIEWING PLATFORM created from the rear gallery of WAINHOUSE TERRACE, a row of back-to-back houses built by Wainhouse in 1876. It is supported on a colonnade that allowed access to the underdwellings, and linked to a detached square staircase tower by a bridge. Almost immediately below, at the top of UPPER WASHER LANE, is WAINHOUSE TAVERN, built by Wainhouse as a house, Westair, in 1877. Idiosyncratic Jacobean Gothic. Wainhouse also embellished COTTAGES nearby with heavy stone porches.

Further down, on the still rural slope above the Calder valley are three older houses. In WASHER LANE Nos. 106–110 were originally OLD HALL, a good C17 house probably earlier than its porch dated 1690. Single-storey housebody with window of 2 : 4 : 4 lights with transom (l. end has door inserted). s crosswing with three-over-five-light window in the gable and the porch in the angle. This has upper window of two-over-four lights. To the SE in WOODHOUSE LANE, a large and excellent Late Tudor house, WOOD HALL, with symmetrical front. Two-storey gabled porch between two gabled bays with attic windows. Projecting gabled bays on the returns. Transomed windows, altered on the ground floor. The porch has the date 1589 in a spandrel, and transomed upper windows, the front of five lights.

WILLOW HALL, Upper Willow Hall, ¾ m. NW of King Cross, is dated 1610. Long gabled range with two-storey N porch. Arched lights to windows, with sunk spandrels. Altered, especially on the s (garden) front, which has sashes, two first-floor Venetian windows in adjacent gabled bays, and battlements at the w end.

ALLANGATE, Nos. 112–120 Rochdale Road. A much extended (and now subdivided) mansion which began as a Neoclassical villa, by *Bernard Hartley*, c. 1810. This forms the central three bays. Hipped roof and large two-storey bay in the centre. Large single-bay Italianate block added on w, c. 1845, beyond a lower link with two arched windows. Extensive service buildings with square tower further w. About 1870 Thomas Shaw M.P. added a matching Italianate block and link to the E and engaged *Christopher Dresser* to design several new rooms and their furniture in a Greek Revival scheme that made much use of black and gold.* These included a lower entrance hall in the new E wing, drawing room, library, dining room, billiard room and master bedroom. (Inside, fittings, stained glass and decoration survive, including the magnificent coffered drawing room ceiling painted in blue, black and gold with panels decorated with floral patterns in the Japanese style.)

SKIRCOAT GREEN, SALTERHEBBLE AND SIDDAL

The southern end of the town, down the Huddersfield Road, developed as a select suburb in the C19. Several of the Crossleys resided here among their peers but their mansions have been demolished.† It adjoined Savile Park (*see* p. 298) and the old hamlet of Skircoat Green above the precipitous N bank of the River Calder. To the E, across the Hebble Brook's narrow valley, the steep slopes of Salterhebble and Siddal housed workers from the mills below.

ALL SAINTS (Salterhebble), Dudwell Lane, Skircoat Green. By *Mallinson & Healey*, 1857–8. Nave and aisles extended by one bay to W in 1874 by *W. Swinden Barber*. Restrained Dec. N transept balanced on S by buttressed square tower with octagonal belfry and stone spire. Small clerestory windows alternately quatrefoil and cinquefoil. – Caen stone REREDOS with Purbeck marble shafts, elaborately carved by *Mawer* of Leeds. Pulpit and pews removed in reordering 1995. Decorative painting scheme by *Clayton & Bell*, 1859 and 1874, has been lost. – STAINED GLASS. Three windows by *Clayton & Bell*, 1874: N transept, N aisle third from E and S aisle fifth from E. The rest, except the clerestory, by *Ward & Hughes*, mainly 1859 and 1876. – MONUMENT. In the churchyard near the chancel a large Gothic tomb-chest. Arcaded sides with marble columns and elaborate carving.

ST MARK, Whitegate Road, Siddal. 1912–15, by *Walsh & Nicholas*. Simple Gothic Revival in Walsh's hallmark ironstone, except for the contrasting top stage of the massive NW tower facing the road. A last-minute donation to the building fund saved it from omission and it was executed less plainly than

---

* Dresser also designed carpets for the Crossleys.

† These were: Manor Heath, Skircoat Green Road, by *Parnell & Smith* for John Crossley, 1852–3; Broomfield, Broomfield Avenue, by *Roger Ives*, c. 1855 for Joseph Crossley; and Moorside, Stafford Road, by *H.J. Paull* for Louis John Crossley, 1870–2. Some lodges and outbuildings remain.

originally proposed. Long roof to chancel and nave, aisles with plain parapets. – PEWS, SCREEN ETC., 1920s by the *Jacksons* of Coley. – STAINED GLASS. Five-light E window, the Ascension by *Morris & Co.*, 1916.

STONEY ROYD CEMETERY, Whitegate, Siddal. Laid out by *Edward Milner* in the grounds of Stoney Royd, an C18 house, and opened 1861. The architect was *Charles Edwards*. The Anglican chapel is demolished, and only the broach-spired tower of the NONCONFORMIST CHAPEL remains. Small R.C. chapel added later. Gothic LODGE at the main entrance on WATER LANE has a funny little tower with over-sized conical roof.

PUBLIC LIBRARY, Skircoat Green Road. Halifax's first purpose-built library. A reticent single-storey classical essay by *A.C. Tipple*, Borough Engineer, 1926.

CALDERDALE ROYAL HOSPITAL, Dryclough Lane. The earliest part is the former Halifax Union Infirmary (St Luke's Hospital), on Dudwell Lane, which succeeded the workhouse infirmary at Gibbet Street. By *W. Clement Williams*, 1897–1901, and at that time among the largest outside London. It is still exceedingly impressive. The plans were exhibited at the Exposition Universelle at Paris in 1900. Impressive three-storey administrative block-cum-nurses' home, in Free Northern Renaissance style. Jacobethan details to first-floor loggia and gables. Central clock tower with cupola. The two original ward blocks that remain are increasingly rare examples of the late C19 vogue for circular buildings. Three storeys, with pyramidal roof and central chimney. Short corridors link them to their separate service blocks and sanitary towers. Most of the rest replaced by *RTKL*, 1998–2001, also with two very large drum-shaped ward blocks.

PERAMBULATION. SKIRCOAT ROAD leads S from the centre, on the embankment built when it was created in 1891 to improve the town's southern approach. At the junction with Heath Road is a small PARK with an equestrian STATUE of the Prince Consort by *Thomas Thornycroft*, 1864, cast in bronze by *Elkington* of Birmingham and elevated on a granite pedestal. It was transferred from Wards End in 1902. S of here, beyond the junction with Free School Lane, the street becomes HUDDERSFIELD ROAD. On the E side, set well back in a flat open park is SPRING HALL (Register Office), a mansion rebuilt in 1871 by *W. Swinden Barber* for Thomas Holdsworth, whose Shaw Lodge Mills are just across the railway to the E (*see* Siddal, below). Vernacular Revival style except for the octagonal Gothic tower crowned with pinnacles and battlements. Handsome painted wooden ceiling in the galleried hall.

Further S and to the W of Huddersfield Road, secluded in trees on the E side of Skircoat Green Road, the picturesque JOHN ABBOTT HOMES (or ABBOTT'S LADIES' HOMES), of 1876–7 by *W. Swinden Barber*. It has five pairs of semi-detached cottages and two single-storey dwellings spaciously set around a very large communal lawn. Gables and mullioned-and-transomed windows with varied decorative label stops. Lodge house at the entrance.

About ⅜ m. s is SKIRCOAT GREEN, raised on a slight eminence N of Dudwell Lane. Here are two C17 houses: WASKE HALL and DEAN HOUSE. The former, now altered and subdivided, has three gables to the front and a lintel dated 1675. Both houses have windows with decorative label stops. They are perched precariously on the edge of a deep cutting to the E taking Skircoat Green Road to the junction with Dudwell Lane. This was done for the trams' benefit in 1898. N of the Green an attractive jumble of C18 and C19 houses and cottages. On the w side RAVENSCLIFFE LODGE. This is C19 and served BERMERSIDE (off Greenroyd Close), which was rebuilt in 1872 for Edward Crossley, Joseph's eldest son, by *Roger Ives & Son*, in rather half-hearted Jacobean Revival style. (Attached to the service block a small two-storey OBSERVATORY, now a house.)

Nearby, to the E along DUDWELL LANE, All Saints Church. ½ m. NE of here, on the other side of the railway and the Hebble is SALTERHEBBLE. Off the E side of SALTERHEBBLE HILL is ROOKERY LANE. Built against the hill on the s side is THE ROOKERY, with a substantial front overlooking the Hebble Brook to the SE. C17. Deeply chamfered openings to six-light mullioned windows on ground and first floors (some altered), four-light ones on the second. No gables. Tall C18 staircase window.

At the foot of Salterhebble Hill a short spur of the Calder & Hebble Navigation, opened in 1769, provided the town's nearest access to the waterway until the HALIFAX BRANCH CANAL was completed in 1828. Engineered by *Thomas Bradley*, it led from here up to the town beside the Hebble, rising 100 ft (30 metres) in 1¼ m. with fourteen locks. Disused from the 1940s and now completely infilled (its course survives as the Hebble Trail). A little further s, at the junction of WAKEFIELD ROAD and HUDDERSFIELD ROAD, we reach the Calder valley and the main canal with LOCK COTTAGE, *c.* 1820, and BASIN.

Just N of the bridge taking Wakefield Road over the canal is BANK HOUSE, in Bankhouse Lane. It preserves the open housebody of a C16 timber-framed aisled house. Five-light transomed window has human faces (very worn) as hoodmould stops. (Inside, at the upper end, some surviving planks nailed to curved ribs provide rare evidence of a late medieval coved dais canopy.) Rebuilding in stone in the C17 created the present linear form with additions to N beyond hearth passage and a gabled cross-wing to s.

Back towards Salterhebble Hill and NE up the hill is BACKHOLD HALL in Backhold Lane. Handsome house with three gables. Dated 1668. Large windows, those to the housebody and parlour with transoms and king mullions. Three-light stepped gable windows have arched heads and sunk spandrels. Above them are projecting ledges for dovecote openings. Carved tablet over door has inscriptions in Latin and Greek. In the housebody and kitchen the large carved stone fireplaces are decorated with spirals; the plaster ceiling in the chamber over the parlour has panels with grapes, flowers etc.

Finally, SIDDAL running along the E side of the valley. Below WHITEGATE ROAD at the junction with Phoebe Lane is the PUMP HOUSE, 1828, built to keep the Halifax Branch Canal's many locks supplied with water from the river at Salterhebble. Tall arched window to the engine room at the W end.

The principal monument of Siddal is SHAW LODGE MILLS, on Shaw Lane by the Hebble Brook. It is an extensive and largely complete group with towering chimney. Developed from 1830 for John Holdsworth and Co., worsted spinners and manufacturers, it became the third largest mill complex in Halifax. Closed in 2008. Facing the narrow lane is a long run of weaving sheds of 1847 and 1852 on the W side and spinning mills and warehouse on the E. The earliest mill, with iron columns dated 1830, is at the S end, adjoining a larger block of 7:5:7:3 bays, 1850. Three storeys except in the five-bay section which has four floors with central loading doors (altered) under a gable. At an angle to the N, the impressively large five-to-six-storey, eighteen-bay warehouse dated 1862. Parapet with modillions. At the end of the weaving sheds, fronting a courtyard, timekeepers' office, 1876, with entrance under Italianate clock tower. Main offices to NW are a handsome five-bay block, 1865, possibly by *Charles Barry*. On BOYS LANE, behind the warehouse, a combing shed, 1876, and to the S the octagonal chimney, engine house and boiler house, all 1855. Here, because of the hill, the rear elevation of the mills reaches five storeys and the warehouse seven. Its attached Italianate privy tower is eight storeys.

HAMBLETON   *5030*

ST MARY. By *J.L. Pearson*, 1881–2. Modest. Dec tracery. Brick with stone dressings inside and out. The roof sweeps over low narrow aisles; shingled W bellcote with pyramidal spirelet. – STAINED GLASS. Four by *Ward & Hughes*, 1882–3. S aisle E by *Christopher Whall*, 1920.

METHODIST CHAPEL (Wesleyan) by *Hornsey & Monkman*, 1899–1900. Round-arched windows. Schoolroom adjacent, 1876.

OLD VICARAGE, 250 yds SSE. 1834, built by Theodosia Osbaldeston of Gateforth Hall. Gault brick. Three bays, hipped roof. Pedimented doorcase with Doric columns.

GATEFORTH HALL, ¾ m. S. Fine small Regency country house built for Humphrey Osbaldeston 1812–14, attributed on stylistic grounds to *Watson & Pritchett* (Christopher Webster). Gault brick with limestone dressings. Square plan with an impressive semicircular bow in the centre of the three-bay front. The bow is surrounded by giant unfluted Ionic columns carrying a low parapet. (Behind the entrance hall the top-lit staircase hall has a screen of two Ionic columns on the ground floor, Corinthian columns on the upper floor. Iron stair balustrade with anthemion enrichment.)

HAMPOLE

Hamlet notable for the site of St Mary's Priory, founded in 1170 for Cistercian nuns, and the shrine of the mystical writer Richard Rolle, who died here in 1349. Nothing visible remains.

Stubbs Hall, 4/5 m. NW. Late C17 L-shaped house, much altered. Tudor Gothic sw range added c. 1830 with embattled porch and parapet. Matching lodge.

HANDSWORTH

Former village on a hill ESE of Sheffield, which absorbed it in 1921. The widening of the former Worksop turnpike road (1764) in the 1960s destroyed its surviving character, leaving two important churches separated by a dual carriageway.

St Mary. Late C12, its exterior reveals little of its early history. The chancel, of coursed rubble with three stepped lancets at the E end and three single lancet windows on the N, is clearly E.E. The N chapel has an E window with intersected tracery, i.e. c. 1300. The three-bay N aisle, big and battlemented, with typical lancet windows, was rebuilt in 1833. The S aisle, with porch and vestry flanking the tower, was added by J.D. Webster in 1904, its E window, of four lights with panel tracery, being saved from the old S wall. It is recorded that rebuilding was in progress in 1492. The lower parts of the W tower, unpleasingly rendered, are of a similar date to the E end, but the impressive octagonal top and stone spire are a replacement of 1825. Internally more early work, late C12 to early C13, survives. In the chancel piscina and double sedilia with pointed trefoiled arches. N chapel, c. 1225, has unusual combined PISCINA and SQUINT with trefoil arch decorated with big semi-domes. A single broad arch on keeled responds opens from the chapel into the chancel. Capitals with a little nailhead in the abaci. The same keeled responds to the chancel arch, the arch itself rebuilt to correspond with the tower arch in M.E. Hadfield's chancel restoration of 1869–70. Fine N arcade of three bays, raised in height in 1833 for a gallery. The E pier round, the w one octagonal; the E respond keeled, the W one round; double-chamfered arches, the central one round. – ORGAN GALLERY and CASE in tower arch by *R. G. Sims*, 1989. – STAINED GLASS. E windows by *James Ballantine & Son*, 1873. S aisle E window by *Lavers, Barraud & Westlake*, 1875. S aisle, 1904, from E, by *Powell & Sons, Hawke* of Birmingham, and *Alfred Jeffery*. N chapel: three windows by *Christopher Webb*, 1935–44. – MONUMENT. John Smelter †1791 and family. The best of the wall monuments. Coloured marbles, with urn on shapely plinth.

RECTORY (now Parish Centre), S of church. C17 core, with some internal timber framing, the four-bay S front refronted in the early C18 with broad flat ashlar surrounds to sash windows. Later C18 pedimented wings.

ST JOSEPH (R.C.), St Joseph's Road. By *M. E. Hadfield & Son*, 1879–81. Built at the expense of the 15th Duke of Norfolk, with attached Presbytery to SE and School to N. Plain Perp style. Steep tiled roofs. Two-bay chancel over crypt; one-bay N chapel under same roof as five-bay N aisle. The W bay of the nave originally intended, with a S porch and a tower, was not built. In 1956–7 an impeccably matched W bay with choir gallery and S porch, and a small baptistery at the W end of the aisle were added by *Hadfield Cawkwell & Davidson*. Tall, full-width chancel arch; tall aisle arcade with arches dying into chamfered piers with battlemented coronas on the responds, probably inspired by Sheffield Cathedral's chancel arcades. Arch-braced wagon roofs. – REREDOS. 1949. Stone, elaborately carved, with figures of St Thomas More and St John Fisher. – STATIONS OF THE CROSS. Large relief panels by *E. de Fernelmont*, *c*. 1881. – STAINED GLASS. Chapel E window by *Hardman*, 1950.

BRAMLEY HALL, Bramley Hall Road. Early C18. Five-bay ashlar front with quoins and bracketed pediment. Doorway has eared architrave and tall broken pediment. Rear extension *c*. 1875.

HANGING HEATON 2020

ST PAUL. Commissioners' church by *Thomas Taylor*, 1823–5; a local landmark. Pinnacled W tower with open Gothic-arched parapet. High seven-bay nave with tall thin lancets with Y-tracery, hoodmoulds with morose headstops. Minimal chancel has E window with intersecting tracery; low flanking vestries added 1893–4 in restoration by *W. Swinden Barber*. Gutted by fire in 1916; restoration in 1920–3 omitted the parapets to the nave and the E gables.

METHODIST CHURCH (New Connexion), High Street. By *Sheard & Hanstock*, 1878. Broad front with three round-arched upper windows to gabled centre; flanking staircase bays.

HARTHILL

ALL HALLOWS. A very fine church with a tranquil rural village setting. Outwardly nearly all Perp, generously battlemented. Quoins of the original unaisled nave are visible at the W end, otherwise the oldest parts appear only inside. Short nave of three bays with arcades of *c.* 1200. Circular piers, octagonal abaci. The arches are round on the N side and have two slight chamfers, pointed on the S side with normal chamfers. Chancel C13 with one S lancet. E window from the chancel restoration by *W.S. Weatherley*, 1897–8. The N chapel is the mortuary chapel of the Osborne family, Dukes of Leeds. It was rebuilt in the early C18 with classical round arches but given a Gothic dressing in the later C19. N aisle rebuilt between 1807 and 1828; needless to say its horrible Neo-Norman windows are Victorian. The S chapel has a genuine Dec E window with reticulated tracery but its two-bay arcade has battlemented capitals and externally it is all of a piece with the remodelled Perp S aisle. Perp clerestory and large W tower. Tower arch, and vault with diagonal ribs and ridge ribs, 1850. – COMMUNION RAIL. C18. – Rich late C19 CHANCEL FITTINGS: ALTAR made from a reading desk which accompanied the Italian PULPIT and LECTERN with Renaissance-style carving by *Carlo Scarcelli*, 1887; walnut PANELLING, STALLS and ORGAN CASE, and marble PAVING by *Farmer & Brindley*, all 1897–8. – SCREENS. S chapel: wrought-iron N gate probably C16–C17; carved W screen adapted from *Scarcelli*'s chancel screen. – N chapel has C18 wrought-iron gate said to come from Kiveton Hall. – Octagonal FONT COVER. Jacobean, of an uncommon type. – STAINED GLASS. E window by *Kempe*, 1898. – S chapel E window by *Francis Stephens*, 1952. – Two windows elaborately signed by *Ulisse de Matteis* of the firm *Francini* of Florence: one a panel in the S aisle (easternmost), 1884, the other the N chapel E window, 1882. – W (tower) window by *J.F. Bentley*, 1876. – MONUMENTS. Chancel. Lady Margaret Osborne †1624. Attributed to *William Wright*. Kneeling figure in elaborate aedicule with black marble columns. Left and right of these small standing allegorical figures. Open pediment with obelisks, busts and heraldry. – N chapel. Sir Edward Osborne †1647. Wall monument with pediment and heraldic cartouche, set on pilastered base. Black and white marbles. – Thomas Osborne, 1st Duke of Leeds †1712. Large but otherwise unostentatious tomb-chest in black marble with long inscription on white marble side and end panels.

S of the church is the former RECTORY, *c.* 1716, and in the churchyard's SE corner is the old SCHOOLHOUSE, 1721; both designed by the Rector, *John Hewitt*. The school has cross-windows and a central gable, instead of a pediment, with an oculus. One cross-window survives on the N side of the handsome five-bay rectory; its doorway has bolection-moulded architrave and segmental pediment. Hipped roof with pedimented dormers.

At WOODALL, ¾ m. ESE, No. 4 Walseker Lane is a stone farmhouse of *c.* 1700 incorporating a late medieval timber-framed house of four bays. Above what was a two-bay open-hall are remains of a crown-post roof with decorated open truss (cf. Castlegate, Tickhill).

HARTSHEAD

1020

ST PETER. Isolated ½ m. NW of the village houses, with wide views to the Pennines. Mostly a Neo-Norman rebuilding by *W. Swinden Barber* in 1880–1 but the short battlemented W tower may contain some Norman or medieval fabric. The S doorway is genuine Norman work, probably mid-C12, with two orders of stout columns, decorated scallop capitals, abaci with chevron and pellets, much close chevron in the arch, decorated hoodmould. The chancel arch corresponds. Responds of two columns and one recessed colonnette to its W, one to its E. One-step arch. The inner arch has double chevron, intersecting to form lozenges, and even the soffit is decorated.

SCHOOL (former), in the churchyard. *c.* 1828; but perhaps originally a bier house – see the large blocked doorway in the gable-end.

WALTON CROSS, a few yards down the footpath opposite the W end of Second Avenue, ½ m. NW. Possibly early C9 and *in situ*. Massive cross base 4 ft 9 in. (146 cm.) tall and rectangular in section. The narrower faces (N and S) each have a panel filled with fine wiry interlace based on figure-of-eight knots. The E face has, within a broad double frame of interlace, scrolled decoration below two pairs of volutes on a stem, each volute containing a bird. On the upper part of the W face is a roundel with graceful loops of interlace around four heart-shaped segments, below this two affronted winged beasts (cf. Birstall and Rastrick).

HATFIELD

6010

Now a small town, its magnificent church and late C12 manor house reflect its former importance as the main settlement of Hatfield Chase. This medieval hunting ground, extending across some 180,000 acres of often watery peat moor to the E and into N Lincolnshire, belonged to the de Warennes (Earls of Surrey) from the Conquest until the early C14, reverting fully to the Crown in 1347. The royal connection ended in 1628, when

Charles I granted the manor to Cornelius Vermuyden, the Dutch
engineer put in charge of the first, and highly controversial,
scheme for drainage of the Chase. The area's later prosperity is
evident in the village's Georgian houses and the church's impressive collection of monuments. C20 expansion began with housing
W of the village for Hatfield Main Colliery, sunk 1911–17 and
closed in 2015.

ST LAWRENCE. A surprisingly large, dominating cruciform
church with a crossing tower so big and proud that it might
stand in Somerset. Exterior Perp, with battlements and pinnacles, except for the W front, which is Norman. Pebbly rubble
masonry with a (restored) portal of four orders, the inner one
with continuous angle roll, then three colonnettes, the third
keeled. Capitals with volutes, and a roll between two plain
chamfers in the arch. Also Norman the N aisle W window, the
S doorway (very plain, single-chamfered round arch; hoodmould with pellets) and some rubble masonry in the S wall.
So the Norman church already had two aisles. The arcades are
Transitional: five bays, piers circular with square abaci; double-
chamfered pointed arches. Some Dec windows in the aisles,
but the principal work is Perp. The crossing tower, nearly
100 ft (30.5 metres) high, carries shields of the Savage family.
Sir Edward Savage became Bailiff of Hatfield in 1485, his
brother Thomas was Archbishop of York 1501–7, making the
tower early Tudor. Very large four-light windows with panel
tracery give light to the crossing. Then two-light bell-openings
with transoms on each side. Perp probably also the odd and
impressive transverse arches struck in the N aisle from the wall
to each pier of the arcade. In conjunction with the big C19
buttresses (probably from *T.G. Jackson*'s restoration 1872) this
looks like a measure applied for security. It may be connected
with the erection of the tower and the big and daring clerestory
with its large three-light windows with two-centred arches (cf.
Fishlake).

Then followed the proud chapels, the N one with decorated
merlons. Each has cusped tracery, a slender octagonal pier to
the arcade and early C16 roof with carved bosses. Late Perp
the nave W, the chancel E and the transepts' N and S windows,
all with transoms and panel tracery, uncusped (as are also the
clerestory windows). The E front of the church is particularly
impressive with three large Perp windows all in a line yet all
different.

FITTINGS. – Tudor-arched DOORWAY to former charnel
house (chancel N wall). – Fine CHOIR STALLS by *Temple Moore*,
1912, have MISERICORDS carved traditionally with birds,
flowers, grotesques, a monkey etc. – SCREEN. *c.* 1500. Tall and
commanding. Richly traceried panels below, slender one-light
divisions above, each with two pointed arches and a pendant.
Larger pendant over the wider entrance. The rood-loft coving
with lierne ribs is preserved (cf. Campsall), and, more unusually,
the tall flanking styles topped with carved heads. – Traceried

PULPIT by *Smith, Brodrick & Lowther*, 1896, inspired by the screen. – FONT. Base *c*.1300, a thick shaft surrounded by four slimmer ones with moulded capitals, making a quatrefoil. Bowl 1872. – CHEST. C13. Dug out from one tree trunk. – STAINED GLASS. E window by *Ward & Hughes*, 1872. s aisle: easternmost window 1928, second from E 1904, by *Kempe*. N aisle: W window by *Powell & Sons*, 1872; fourth from E by *Kayll & Reed* of Leeds, 1925. N transept: Millennium window by *Sep Waugh*, 2000. – MONUMENTS. A good variety of C17 to mid-C19 wall monuments. – Tomb-chest with cusped lozenges carrying shields. Accompanying wall panel for brass plate (lacking). – Elizabeth Simpson †1671. Painted inscription, partly in Hebrew. – John Hatfield †1694 and wife Frances †1693. Standing monument with garlands, torches, tail-biting serpents, putto heads, etc. – William Oughtibridge †1728 and family by his son *Thomas Oughtibridge*, 'engraver'. Tall shapely standing monument with circular wreath framing inscription written in concentric curves. Big flowers, angels etc. boldly but ineptly carved. Its rustic interpretation of fashionable decorative ornament is attractive. – Thomas Johnson †1751 also by *Oughtibridge*, 'sculptor', with clumsy drapery. – Three others in similar style.

ST EDWIN (formerly Christ Church), Abbey Road, Dunscroft. 1964 by *Foster-Smith, Wallis & Anderton* of Doncaster. Striking octagon, with continuous clerestory, zigzag roof and needle spire. (FONT. From St Peter, Edlington. 1590. An unusual date and shape. Square with diamond-chamfered angles. Plain Roman lettering and geometrical ornament. Not at all Gothic Survival.)

CEMETERY CHAPEL, ¾ m. SE. By *Edwin Dolby*, 1884. Small, with apse and octagonal Gothic spirelet.

MANOR HOUSE, 200 yds S. Seemingly an unexceptional C18 house, hipped-roofed, sash-windowed and rendered. Its two-bay W range, however, is the stone hall block of a late Norman house and hunting lodge, later also an occasional royal palace, and so a very rare survival.* It has a small, square, medieval SE addition, possibly a solar block. Both were later extensively remodelled, adjoining timber-framed structures were demolished and a C17 and C18 range, which forms a larger E cross-wing, was built. The ground floor of the C12 part, probably an undercroft, has two small original windows, one W, one S (blocked). Traces remain of other S windows, the two upper ones probably of two lights. Evidence of W and upper N doors, the latter with external staircase. On the first floor of the addition the pointed-arched head of a doorway from the hall remains. In the later C16 the hall was apparently refashioned as a Great Chamber; some plasterwork and a Tudor-arched fireplace served by an enlarged N chimneystack survive. A similar, reused, C16 fireplace is in the present entrance hall

*Prince William, Edward III's second son, was born at the Manor House in 1336 and Edward Balliol and Elizabeth, Countess of Ulster were among a succession of temporary royal residents.

in the SE addition. The C17 E range, which has a parlour with very fine later C17 panelling and chimneypiece, received a three-storey N extension c. 1720, and together with the medieval parts was substantially remodelled during the C18. This work destroyed or obscured almost all pre-1700 evidence, until surviving medieval features were revealed in the C20.

The HIGH STREET stretches eastwards from the church, its S back lane surviving. The older houses and cottages are modest, mostly Georgian and invariably brick, which was made locally from the early C17, but is too often rendered. On the prominent corner near the church is the INGRAM ARMS, rebuilt in 'brewers' Tudor' by *Allen & Hickson*, 1924. Going S down MANOR ROAD to ASH HILL, ½ m. SW, is a trickle of larger houses, built or remodelled c. 1780–1830, and with grounds. THACKRAY HOUSE has rear part dated 1782, the larger three-bay front with central pediment and the handsome stable block slightly later. To its W the simple classical STABLES, 1789, of Hatfield House (dem. 1955).

WYNDTHORPE HALL (formerly Park Lane Hall), 2 m. SW. Small country house built c. 1826 for himself so presumably by *William Pilkington*. Stuccoed. An odd triple-pile composition, the gabled S end of the central range forming a big pediment with moulded triangle in the tympanum and on the W front a recessed bay for the entrance with Ionic columns and architrave and small raised pediment above eaves. Large central stair hall with Ionic columns and domed top light. Two chimneypieces look later C18; one with yellow marble and pastoral scene (damaged) carved in the manner of *William Collins*.

TOWER HOUSE, Mosscroft Lane, ⅔ m. SE. Early C19. Five-storey windmill tower, brick with stone base, crenellated top.

HEATH

The picturesque 'village of mansions' comes as a surprise barely a mile from the centre of a city the size of Wakefield. Heath's special quality was acknowledged as early as 1800 when John Housman, commentator on the Lake District, remarked that 'it is universally allowed to be one of the most beautiful [villages] in England', and the large and tranquil Common that provides the setting for the houses was preserved from enclosure in the 1840s. It falls into three distinct areas: the squarish N end faced by Heath House and Heath Hall; the middle section with the King's Arms and cluster of cottages overlooked by Beech Lawn; and the large, rougher S part. The impression of its size is greatly helped by the few cottages on island sites – often an effective, if rarely a self-conscious, means of composition. It is large enough for the houses around it to be taken in singly and not altogether;

Heath, Old Heath Hall.
Engraving by J. Rogers after N. Whittock, *c.* 1830

side by side, great and small are equal in their prospect of it and can equally be enjoyed from it.

In the 1950s the principal houses were in a parlous state through coal subsidence and neglect. The most important was OLD HEATH HALL, at the NW corner of the common, which was mostly demolished in 1960–1. Built *c.* 1584–90, its similarity to Barlborough Hall, Derbyshire (dated 1583–4) makes an attribution to *Robert Smythson* equally likely.* The entrance to its former drive is marked by C18 rusticated GATEPIERS with pineapple finials. OLD HALL COTTAGES are formed from its outbuildings, including the stables (which had been converted to a schoolroom with Gothic windows *c.* 1811).

The two other major houses remain intact and restored:

HEATH HOUSE, N side of the common, is by *James Paine*, who added a front range to a C17 H-shaped house in 1744–5. Although his very first proper architectural commission, its accomplished Palladian façade, based on Roger Morris's Marble Hill (London; 1724–9), became a template for several of his subsequent villas. Five bays, two-and-a-half storeys. The ground floor rusticated, with Victorian bay window on the l. Centre of three bays with a pediment on attached Ionic giant columns. At the angles of the house coupled pilasters and in the angles between the side parts and the centre odd quarter-columns. Segmental pediment on consoles to the central window on the *piano nobile*, triangular pediments to the outer windows, which have the splayed architraves that became one of Paine's hallmarks. A full-width subsidiary cornice linking

*The sumptuous Jezebel fireplace is at Hazlewood Castle (*see West Riding North*).

the window heads gives horizontal emphasis. The older house is distinguishable behind, its windows altered to sashes. (INTERIOR. Paine fitted a grand, top-lit stair hall into the central space between the old and new buildings. Cantilevered stone staircase with Victorian cast-iron balusters. Dining room in original house has fireplace dated 1656. Bedrooms in C18 attics have chimneypieces with later Georgian papier mâché decoration.)

HEATH HALL, on the E side of the Common, is a splendid mansion by *John Carr*, who about 1754–80 remodelled and enlarged an existing house, called Eshald House. This had been built, and probably designed, by *Theophilus Shelton*, who owned the Heath estate from 1694 to 1709. Its three-bay cube forms the core of the present house, which Carr created for John Smyth and his son, also John, who renamed the house after buying the Old Hall. Two storeys plus basement and attic. Eleven bays, counting the canted bay windows at the ends (of which Carr was so fond) as three windows each. He applied four attached Ionic giant columns and a pediment with carved achievement to the existing W front, adding a bay either side. The half-storey above was remodelled, its balustraded top being originally finished with vases. The N and S wings have arched ground-floor windows with splayed surrounds (cf. Heath House above), a detail dropped from Carr's vocabulary after the 1750s. The earlier house is evident on the simpler E front, where he set the narrow flanking bays back to leave its quoins and funny snippets of cornice at the angles undisturbed. The hierarchy of his roof-line was lost when *Salvin* added attic storeys to the wings (and a small N extension) in 1837–45. *Francis Johnson* restored the house in the 1960s. (INTERIOR. Entrance in the centre with the original asymmetrically placed hall on the l. retained, balancing the reused main staircase to the r. An open well with the early C18 twisted balusters but new carved Rococo tread-ends. DINING ROOM in N wing has a chimneypiece from *Carr*'s Castlegate House, York. Delightful circular STUDY behind. The DRAWING ROOM is one of Carr's finest spaces, using the S wing's entire ground floor and gaining extra height from raised bedroom floors above. With youthful daring his scheme combines a Palladian arcade, based on an unexecuted design by *William Kent* for Houghton Hall, with some of the most exquisite Rococo plasterwork of the period, possibly by *Joseph Rose*. Fine carved doorcases here and elsewhere by *Daniel Shillito*. SW bedroom above also has Rococo plaster ceiling, while other bedrooms have bolection-moulded panelling, cornices and chimneypieces of *c.* 1700.)

Screen walls link the house to handsome H-shaped service PAVILIONS, the laundry and brewhouse (S) and visitors' stables (N). Pedimented fronts, large lateral arches also with pediments and clock turrets crowned with Doric lanterns. Main STABLES to N with single-storey coachhouses as side pavilions. Restored as a house by *Francis Johnson*, 1984, with salvaged C18 fittings. The whole composition of the hall, pavilions and stables forms a magnificent front to the Common.

Impressive two-storey Palladian DEER HOUSE, Kirkthorpe Lane, ¼ m. NE of the stables. Early–mid-C18, possibly by *Robert Carr* or his son *John Carr*.

THE DOWER HOUSE, s of Heath Hall, has a simple restrained five-bay front of two storeys added in the 1740s to an older house. Shallow pediment supported on plain tablets between the outer bays. C19 bay on l. (Splendid carved STAIRCASE.) Very fine C18 GATEWAY, the ashlar piers pierced by arches with pilasters, keystone and voussoirs. Corniced tops. Decorative wrought-iron gates and overthrow. As at the Hall, an C18 HA-HA protects the front lawn.

A rich mixture of other houses etc. around the Common. The pre-1730 ones have, variously, mullioned windows, monolithic jambs and lintels (the earlier ones often massive), coped gables with kneelers, and string courses. The great Georgian building and rebuilding affected those of all sizes, the larger houses having many good interiors, some no doubt influenced by Heath House and the Hall and possibly by the same craftsmen. Limited later development complied with the Smyths' restrictions on the use of brick to chimneys and rear walls unless it was rendered. Some buildings, including THE KING'S ARMS, have panelling etc. said to be from the Old Hall. HIGHWAYS combines a pleasing house of *c.* 1800 and a slightly earlier cottage. Interior by *Francis Johnson*, 1978, includes fine C18 woodwork from a house by *Robert Carr* in Horbury. On the w side is the Gothic SCHOOL (former) by *W. S. Barber*, 1873, enlarged 1897 by *R. Kershaw*.

DAME MARY BOLLES'S WATER TOWER, further W and s of the site of the Old Hall is mid-C17. Square, five-stage tower, with pyramidal roof. Small windows in the second and top stages. Built over a spring and thought to have been part of a system for storing water and conveying it to Heath Old Hall. Possibly also used as a prospect tower.

HEBDEN BRIDGE

9020

Small, characterful town where Hebden Water joins the upper Calder, their scenic wooded valleys narrow and deep. An ancient bridging point below Heptonstall (q.v.), it developed after the opening of the Rochdale Canal in 1798 and in the C19 with textile mills specializing in fustian manufacture;[*] since their mid-C20 decline it has become a cultural centre and haven for those with alternative lifestyles.

---

[*]Fustian comprises various hardwearing cotton fabrics, some with a short pile, suitable for work clothing. This was also made here, hence the nickname 'Trouser town'.

St James, at Mytholm, ½ m. w of the centre. Commissioners' church by *Pickersgill & Oates*, 1832–3; chancel rebuilt in restoration by *R. Norman Shaw*, 1874–6. Pinnacled w tower. Lancets to broad five-bay nave. Lofty chancel with arcades, the s aisle remodelled as a chapel by *Sutcliffe & Sutcliffe*, 1903–4. – Painted and gilded REREDOS, 1934, by *F.C. Eden*; carved figures by *Alfonso Noflaner*. – Stone and marble PULPIT and dwarf SCREEN by *Shaw*. – One WALL PAINTING by *Heaton, Butler & Bayne* survives from *Shaw*'s rich decorative scheme, the disparate nave and chancel unified by the firm's set of STAINED GLASS windows, 1876–82.

St Thomas (R.C.), Fairfield (now flats). By *Walsh & Wrigley*, 1896. Plain Gothic nave with small sanctuary.

Hope Baptist Chapel, New Road. 1857–8. Large and dignified. Pedimented three-bay front with giant Corinthian pilasters, pedimented entrance. Full-height round-arched windows. Tuscan pilasters to five-bay returns. Good galleried interior with deeply panelled ceiling and later C19 fittings.

Ebenezer Baptist Chapel (former), Market Street. Now Arts Centre. 1777. Symmetrical two-storey front, handsome pedimented doorways flanking two central round-arched windows originally behind the pulpit. Cast-iron Doric columns support gallery (now floored).

Birchcliffe Baptist Chapel (former), Birchcliffe Road. By *Sutcliffe & Sutcliffe*, 1897–9, converted to conference/resources centre 1977. Set high uphill. Imposing Italianate front has almost full-width porch with five-bay arcade and balustraded top. Rising behind is a Palladian formation of three-bay pedimented centre with fluted Ionic pilasters, flanked by pavilions. These have pediments and parapets and contain staircases fronting aisles. Interior has floor at gallery level; the upper space, with round-arched arcades on red marble columns, tiered seating and clerestory with oculi, is largely intact.

Stubbings School, School Street. 1878. Long gabled front with open Gothic arcade to covered play space.

Railway Station. One of the county's best-preserved stations, as rebuilt 1892–3 by the Lancashire and Yorkshire Railway Co. Central booking hall block with attic windows in mansard roof to station master's flat, waiting rooms etc. in single-storey flanking ranges. Both platforms have fine glazed canopies with decorative cast-iron supports. SIGNAL BOX 1891.

PERAMBULATION. The OLD BRIDGE, rebuilt in stone *c.* 1510, carried the Halifax–Burnley packhorse route over Hebden Water. Two river arches and vast cutwaters; the third arch spanned the tail goit of BRIDGE MILL, now café, shops etc. Late C18 and *c.* 1820, three storeys; circular chimney. Across St George's Bridge (*J. Sutcliffe*, 1892–3) is the former Town Hall (and former fire station) by *Sutcliffe & Sutcliffe*, 1897–8. Northern Renaissance style, modestly scaled but well detailed. Off the refreshingly unpretentious St George's Square, The White Lion, altered from a C17 farmhouse with good decorative lintel dated 1657 and a seven-light rear window.

Prominent in the centre is a three-storey triangular island block between Carlton Street and Crown Street, built by the Hebden Bridge Co-operative Society, 1875–6 and 1889–90, with clock tower. Also in Crown Street the former LIBERAL CLUB by *Jesse Horsfall*, 1898–9, in livelier Northern Renaissance style with corner oriel. In Carlton Street, small but exuberantly Baroque former GAS COMPANY OFFICES, *c.* 1912. In Hope Street LLOYDS BANK fills a narrow triangular corner site, its style later C19 Italianate, with balustraded parapet; opposite Hope Chapel (*see* above) the domestic-looking former POLICE STATION, 1863, sports frilly bargeboards. NEW ROAD was made in 1806 to straighten the Halifax–Rochdale turnpike's route through the town. Facing Hope Chapel, the big classical PICTURE HOUSE by *J. T. Cockcroft*, 1919–21, with giant Doric columns flanking the recessed entrance and original decoration in foyer and auditorium. w, across the Hebden Water, MARKET STREET is lined with three-storey Victorian commercial buildings, some with original shopfronts. At Nos. 6–14, *c.* 1873, big first-floor windows, framed by decorative wooden arcades, lit sewing workrooms.

Up Keighley Road, N from the centre, NUTCLOUGH MILL, now offices and workshops. Early C19, with later C19 extensions for the Hebden Bridge Fustian Manufacturing Co-operative Society. Double-pile, five-storey main range of twenty-four bays; N tower topped by water tank under pyramidal roof. Nearby, some examples of the 'house-over-house' or 'double-decker' terraced housing that uses the steep hillsides to advantage, e.g. Nos. 52–68 Keighley Road, mid-C19 with basement entrances to the under-dwellings. Those in EIFFEL STREET and EDWARD STREET, 1890s, have four storeys facing the valley, the lower houses back-to-earth, the top two storeys the houses that face the upper street. Other variations include former back-to-backs and houses with access via iron balconies or bridges.

SE of the centre on the canalside at MACHPELAH, a fustian warehouse, *c.* 1840 and, almost opposite, Nos. 2–16 Burnley Road, a terrace of workers' cottages built 1805–*c.* 1820. The earlier, three-storey, end has a tenement courtyard behind and fustian cutters' workshops in the top floor and attic of Nos. 14 and 16, with fourteen- and fifteen-light windows extending across the gable.

s of New Road the former CANAL BASIN of 1893 and a C19 warehouse. Further w the impressive four-arched BLACK PIT AQUEDUCT, 1797, by *W. Jessop* and *W. Crossley*, engineers, carries the canal over the Calder, and ¼ m. w again, beside LOCK no. 11, a good example of a LOCK-KEEPER'S HOUSE, *c.* 1800, with corner windows.

GIBSON MILL (National Trust visitor centre), Hebden Dale, 2 m. NW, near Hardcastle Crags beauty spot. Unusual surviving example of small rural former cotton mill, built *c.* 1800, converted from water to steam power *c.* 1860.

WADSWORTH, 1 m. NE, is a plateau of farmland with two small settlements. At CHISERLEY, surrounded by C20 housing, CHISERLEY HALL has two E–W parallel ranges with gabled ends and its two-storey porch, dated 1617, on the E gable, a most unusual position. Further NW is a large green and OLD TOWN HALL, early C17, which has an arched gateway to its courtyard and large gabled porch with a transomed five-light window on the upper floor. Sixteen-light upper window to central rear wing. Altered and extended C18 range projects from r. front. Now cottages, but probably connected with the Mitchell family's woollen business before they built the steam-powered OLD TOWN MILL, immediately N, in 1851; a compact group including the two-storey spinning mill, tall warehouse 1889, and chimney of 1890. ¼ m. N in a wooded graveyard WAINSGATE BAPTIST CHURCH (Historic Chapels Trust) of 1859–60. Large and handsome, with pediment and quoins to three-bay front and moulded surrounds to two storeys of round-arched windows. Four-bay returns continued by plainer former Sunday School at rear. Very fine interior, with original gallery on cast-iron columns and box PEWS. Marble and alabaster PULPIT with carved panels by *Anthony Welsh*, 1891. STAINED GLASS by *Powell Bros.*

AKROYD FARMHOUSE, ¼ m. NW, has a late C17 hall range and the late C16 E cross-wing of its predecessor. (Inside, painted glass panels (C16?), Tudor-arched doorways, carved ceiling timbers and plank-and-muntin panelling in wing.)

PECKET WELL, ¼ m. N again, has a former METHODIST CHURCH (now a house) of 1834 opposite a Sunday School (1868) and a former fustian weaving MILL of 1873, striking in the landscape but spoilt by over-intervention in conversion to flats *c.* 2005.

HECK

5020

ST JOHN THE BAPTIST. By *Temple Moore*, 1894–5. Built as a chapel of ease for Hensall's Romish vicar. Nave and chancel in one, tiled roof, rendered walls, Dec E window. The square bellcote at the junction of nave and chancel the main feature of character outside; the large painted and gilded canopied REREDOS the principal one within.

HECKMONDWIKE

2020

'Hail Heckmondwike! Successful spot!' Thus G. K. Chesterton in his tongue-in-cheek ode to this little Spen Valley town. A stronghold of Nonconformity in the heart of the Heavy Woollen district, its weavers, and then mills, specialized in blankets and carpets. A Blanket Hall was built in 1811; *Perkin & Backhouse*'s pedimented second Hall, 1840, closed in 1866 and was demolished *c.* 1920. Following their later decline, the big mills have gone; smaller, more diverse industries remain.

ST JAMES. Commissioners' church by *Peter Atkinson Jun.*, 1830–1. Plain lancet style. W tower with ribbed broach spire. Chancel with chapel etc. by *C. Hodgson Fowler*, 1904–6; the former chancel arch, with narrow pointed side arches, forms a screen. E window of five stepped lancets by *Charles Nicholson* 1930. The chancel's ashlar interior, richly fitted, contrasts with the plain plastered nave. – Elaborate painted and gilded REREDOS designed by *Nicholson* 1921 (from St Saviour's church (dem.)). – S chapel REREDOS by *Temple Moore*, painted by *Head & Sons*, 1912, depicts Visit of Magi and Shepherds. – Fine chancel PANELLING, and chapel SCREENS and PANELLING, carved by *Herbert Read*, 1909–12. Also by Read, the ORGAN CASE, 1924–5. – Original triptych REREDOS (stored in W gallery), with Crucifixion painted by *E. Stanley Watkins*, 1906. – STAINED GLASS. E window by *A.K. Nicholson*, 1931. S chapel: four S lancets by *Morris & Co.*, with angels designed by *Burne-Jones*, 1912. S nave easternmost by *L.C. Evetts*, 1975.

CHURCH OF THE HOLY SPIRIT (R.C.), Bath Street. For Fr O'Connor[*] by *C.E. Fox* of *Holtom & Fox*, 1914–15. Not large. Byzantine style in red brick with grey faience dressings and decoration. Latin-cross plan; low central dome on octagonal drum above a square central space, with tall arches on columns of polished blue marble with cushion capitals, which was originally intended for a central altar.[†] Other parts barrel-vaulted. – STAINED GLASS. Three circular chancel windows by *Margaret A. Rope*, *c.* 1915.

UPPER INDEPENDENT CHAPEL (Congregational; now flats), High Street. By *Arthur A. Stott* of Heckmondwike, 1888–90, in a monstrously showy style. Giant distyle *in antis* portico with Composite columns and pediment. 93

HECKMONDWIKE GRAMMAR SCHOOL, High Street. By *Stott*, 1895–8, for the School Board. Plain Jacobean Revival style. Long symmetrical front with three big gables has large hall behind. Multiple additions since 1930.

PUBLIC LIBRARY, Walkley Lane. 1905–7. A Carnegie library, in simple Jacobean style. Two storeys, with decorative gables to three-bay front block.

FIRE STATION (former), High Street. By *James Saville*, Urban District Council Surveyor, 1901–2. Modestly Italianate, with entrance front to PUBLIC BATHS (dem.) on r.

MARKET PLACE is the town's centre, unhappily swamped by traffic and car parking. Its focal point is the DRINKING

---

[*] G.K.Chesterton's friend and model for his detective Father Brown.
[†] O'Connor achieved this at Our Lady and the First Martyrs, Bradford, 1934–5 – *see West Riding North*.

FOUNTAIN commemorating the Prince of Wales's marriage to Princess Alexandra, 1863, with small iron clock tower, 1904. Prominent on the corner the NATWEST BANK of 1928, for National Provincial. Down Market Street the handsome MASONIC HALL, 1851, has central pediment to restrained three-bay front.

OLD HALL, New North Road (now a pub). Altered and restored hall-and-cross-wing house with exposed (late medieval?) timber framing, and C17 stone casing, plasterwork and rear kitchen. Six-light mullioned-and-transomed window to single-storey housebody, six- and five-light windows to W parlour wing, all with hoodmoulds. The r. half of the S front and its gable-end was sliced off by the railway cutting in 1898. Housebody ceiling c. 1640, with pomegranates, birds etc. in lobes around square.

HEMSWORTH

ST HELEN. Quite large, with plain W tower with parapet. Exterior rebuilt by *J.L. Pearson*, 1865–7. He removed the clerestory and widened the N aisle. Only the five-light E window with its spectacular flowing tracery and the S chapel E window with reticulated tracery seem original. The interior had lost its Norman N arcade in 1812 but the three-bay S arcade, with standard elements and corbelled responds, is perhaps original. A similar N arcade overlaps the chancel arch, making it appear lopsided. In 1880 Pearson returned to open the second arch from the S chapel to the chancel, the W one created 1841. – STAINED GLASS. Six windows by *Lavers & Westlake*, c. 1885–95. – MONUMENTS. Catharin Gargrave †1631. Aedicule with black Corinthian columns and elaborate armorial top. – Robert Wrightson of Cusworth †1708 and wife Sarah †1717, erected 1720. Large cartouche with writhing scrolly surround, flying putti and skull.

THE ASCENSION, Kinsley, ¾ m. NNW. Now flats. 1904–7, by the garden designer *F. Inigo Thomas*, whose father had been Rector of Hemsworth. Simple but individual. Classically inspired round and segmental arches to openings, unusual for the date.

HEMSWORTH HIGH HALL (Hemsworth Arts and Community College), ¼ m. E. C17 manor house remodelled and extended c. 1770 for the Wood family, later of Hickleton. The older core forms the wide five-bay centre, made double-pile. Good porch with two pairs of Doric columns, otherwise plain. Low hipped roof. Grander three-bay wings are set back very slightly, their two storeys unconventionally a little higher. Balustraded parapets.

HOLGATE'S HOSPITAL, 1¼ m. WSW. Almshouses founded under the will of Robert Holgate, Archbishop of York, 1555,

and originally nearer the church and his Grammar School.
Rebuilt by *R. P. Pope* of London, 1858–60. Gothic, with quirky
details. Only the N and S sides of the intended quadrangle were
built. Red brick, strongly banded with blue; stone trim. Two-
storey S gatehouse, sharply gabled, with single-storey dwellings
either side (the end pairs 1913) penetrated by many tall chimneys. Similar N range, with the CHAPEL as its centrepiece with
diagonally set spired bellcote. – STAINED GLASS. By *Clayton
& Bell*, 1897.

VISSITT MANOR, 1 m. WSW. Possibly of Tudor origin. Several
builds; C18 remodelling. Older (E) end of two-storey main
front has two small mullioned windows among altered openings. Former housebody range to l. now two sashed bays
flanking doorway. Deep corniced lintel, dated 1721 below
swept moulding (cf. High Hoyland Hall). Heightened W cross-
wing, projecting to rear, with sashed openings.

HENSALL   *5020*

Small village just S of the meandering Aire. Until the C18 Weeland
nearby was at the river's navigable limit, its wharves etc. now
vanished.

The church of ST PAUL, and the former VICARAGE and SCHOOL,
½ m. SW of the village, are by *Butterfield* for William Dawnay,
7th Viscount Downe (cf. Cowick and Pollington), and form
an attractive brick group set among trees. The church is of
1853–4, very plain with steep slated roofs, the nave roof hardly
higher than that over chancel, vestry and narrow aisles. The
simplicity of outline is broken only by a big chimney-breast on
the S side and the NW tower-porch with its pyramid roof.
Three-bay arcades; round piers with moulded capitals. – Tiled
REREDOS *c.* 1870. – ORGAN CASE. By *Temple Moore* 1889.
– FONT. Octagonal, with elaborately carved cover. Given by
Lady Downe. – STAINED GLASS. E window, W window, and S
aisle E window by *Preedy*, 1854. – Two in the S aisle (1958 and
1969) by *Francis Spear*.
    Severely picturesque VICARAGE with big chimneys and
varied windows with timber mullions – an excellent precursor
of the style of Webb's celebrated Red House – while the
SCHOOL has the sharply roofed teacher's house with massive
chimneystack abutting the single-storey schoolroom.

METHODIST CHAPEL. By *G. F. Pennington*, 1902–3. Arts and
Crafts Gothic with half-timbered gables.

STATION HOUSE (former). 1848, for the Lancashire and Yorkshire Railway's Wakefield–Goole line (cf. Womersley). 'Swiss
cottage' style. Victorian timber WAITING ROOM. Rare surviving SIGNAL BOX by *E. S. Yardley & Co.*, 1875.

HEPTONSTALL

A very handsome village of dark stone houses on the hilltop
above Hebden Bridge. As well as the rarity of a dismantled
medieval parish church it offers all kinds of minor architectural
surprises.

St Thomas the Apostle. A large and prosperous-looking
edifice by *Mallinson & Healey*, 1850–4. Perp style, with three-
light windows and battlements and pinnacles. Big w tower,
six-bay nave and aisles, clerestory, chancel and chancel chapels.
Interior reordered by *Maguire & Murray*, 1963–4, at the time
a controversial act in which chancel fittings, screen and pews
were removed and the ALTAR brought forward to a dais in the
westernmost chancel bay. A PULPIT with discordantly Neo-
Jacobean blocked balusters and low movable BENCHES in light
wood furnish the nave, with new paving throughout. While
achieving the desired spaciousness the raised sanctuary and
chancel have been left bare and without purpose. Dividing the
shortened nave from a narthex/baptistery is the ORGAN SCREEN
with continuous loft, an open framework with twisted balusters
to the loft and two screened enclosures for vestries flanking
the central aisle. – Unusual eleven-sided FONT, probably
C13. – STAINED GLASS. s aisle, third from e by *Powell Bros.* N
aisle: easternmost by *Preedy*, 1873; third from e 1881, and w
window *c.* 1866, by *Mayer & Co.* of Munich.

The OLD CHURCH (St Thomas a Becket) to the N was damaged
by a gale in 1847 and left to stand as a roofless shell in 1854.
It is odd that its restoration was not preferred to a complete
rebuilding. Stubby w tower like a North Country tower house;
its lower masonry is C13, the windows and corbelled battlemented top of *c.* 1440. Broad, flat SE stair-turret. The body of
the church is low and exceptionally wide, having three aisles
all with e chapels, the inner N aisle being as wide as the nave
and its chapel like a second chancel. The chancel proper has
a sanctus bellcote over the chancel arch and ogee-headed
piscina. What was essentially a C15 church seems to have been
substantially remodelled in the late C16 or early C17, when the
four-bay nave arcades were renewed with short octagonal
piers, their rather crude capitals given a minimum decoration
of raised squares and circles. The narrow s aisle and s chapel
remained, also the s porch, with pitched stone roof on trefoiled
pointed transverse arches. The N side was extended. The aisle
was widened (note the altered s respond of the arch to its
chapel) and separately roofed, and a narrow low outer aisle
was added, reusing stonework from the old arcades in the new
one. Some late Perp tracery survives; the chancel and inner N
aisle e windows are both of five lights with transoms. Most
surprising is the transept-like cross-gable to the inner N aisle,
with a domestic three-over-five-light window to light galleries
built 1617. The hoodmould has stops decorated with curls.

Heptonstall, Old Church.
Drawing, 1845

The stops of the corresponding window on the s side of the nave survive, *ex situ*, on the aisle wall.

METHODIST CHAPEL (Wesleyan), Northgate. Built 1764 as an equal-sided octagon, the plan advocated by Wesley, who laid the foundation stone.* Altered 1802 to an elongated octagon with two-bay side walls, the N half rebuilt in its new position. Raised quoins at the angles; plain ashlar surrounds to windows in two tiers and to SE and SW doorways; window in original round-arched s doorway. Delightful interior has panelled front to gallery with canted ends, supported on stone Tuscan columns. – PULPIT ROSTRUM early C20. – Early C19 central and gallery BOX PEWS. – STAINED GLASS. E side, one by *S. Evans* of Smethwick. s window by *Forrest & Sons* of Liverpool. 59

The village's picturesque effect comes from the closely built, small-scale two- and three-storey C17 and C18 houses and cottages that line TOWN GATE, the steep cobbled main street, and its offshoots. Notable individually are LONGFIELD HOUSE, 1730s, five bays, two storeys, a good pedimented doorway, but still cross-windows, with stout flat-faced mullions and transoms. Tucked in a courtyard to the r. STAG COTTAGE *c.* 1580, has mullioned windows with arched lights. Off Northgate, preceded by a stone gateway dated 1578 on the mighty lintel, is WHITEHALL, a flat-fronted C17 farmhouse with three gables and mullioned windows. Beside a handsome

---

*The novel roof structure was made by carpenters at Rotherham, where an octagonal chapel (*see* p. 40) was built in 1761, see p. 40.

ARCHWAY, with the old GRAMMAR SCHOOL, 1771, beyond, is the 'CLOTH HALL', built as a single-storey extension to the Hall of *c.* 1550. Further on, SMITHWELL LANE is lined on both sides with early C19 WEAVERS' COTTAGES with typical long, mullioned windows.

BAPTIST CHAPEL, Slack, ¾ m. NW, standing prominently on the hill. Rebuilt 1878–9, by *T. Horsfield*. Like a big Italianate town chapel with galleried interior.

GREENWOOD LEE, 1½ m. NW. Large yeoman-clothier's house, probably mid-C17, with porch dated 1712. F-plan front, through passage and projecting rear kitchen wing. Gabled porch has acorn finials and large upper window of three-over-five lights with decorative hoodmould stops. The seven-light housebody window and several others have arched lights and sunk spandrels. A puzzling feature is the narrow, separate, two-storey space at the gable-end of the N service/shop rooms. It may have contained a staircase providing independent access to the upper floor, but it is also suggested that it housed a later C18 water wheel to power textile machinery there, a provision unknown elsewhere.

Other good C17 houses on the undulating plateau that stretches to the moors include COLDEN GREAT HOUSE, 1¾ m. WNW, mainly later C16, hall and cross-wings plan, with two-storey gabled porch set, unusually, side by side with E wing.

WIDDOP RESERVOIR, 4½ m. NW. Neo-Egyptian VALVE TOWER by *John La Trobe Bateman*, engineer, *c.* 1878.

HEPWORTH

1000

HOLY TRINITY. By *Mallinson & Healey*, 1862–3. Tower with stone broach spire set unconventionally in the angle of the chancel and N transept. – STAINED GLASS. E window by *Clayton & Bell*, 1880. – Nave and N transept windows by *Heaton, Butler & Bayne*, 1880–5. – S transept window a design by *Henry Holiday* of 1869, inserted 1924.

At Carr Farm on UPPERGATE a C17 former barn with two older cruck-trusses, perhaps as early as the C14.

HESSLE HALL *see* ACKWORTH

HEXTHORPE *see* DONCASTER (OUTER)

4000

HICKLETON

An attractive estate village, owing its distinctive character to the Wood family of Hickleton Hall.

ST WILFRID. Between the main Doncaster–Barnsley road and the drive from the lodge to the Hall.* The church is essentially Perp, with battlements and pinnacles. The chancel arch however is Norman. It has a nook-shaft in the responds, abaci decorated with lozenges (N) and chevron (S), and more chevron plus star-in-square beside the s capital. Reeded imposts (apparently trimmed). Arch of one order with chevron cut in steps, not as a roll moulding, and a double-cone pattern running almost at the angle. The windows of the church are mostly straight-headed, of different varieties and cusped as well as uncusped. Short s aisle rebuilt in the late C15 with one wide arch on corbels. Similar arch to the s chapel, which was added about the same time. Also Perp the w tower with a small recessed saddleback roof. In 1873–4 the mid-C16 two-bay N aisle was rebuilt with a new N chapel during restoration by *C. Hodgson Fowler*. The church is, thanks to the family of the Hall, exceptionally lavishly furnished. But most of what there is, and what makes the interior something of a minor museum, did not originally belong to the building. The transformation was begun by Charles Wood, 1st Viscount Halifax, who installed the sanctuary's black and white marble paving and its screens by *Bodley*, 1876–7. Much more was done by the 2nd Viscount, for whom *Bodley & Garner* built the vestry and decorated and furnished the interior in accordance with High Church principles in 1886–8. Of this date the REREDOSES (chancel and chapels), ROOD, CHAPEL SCREENS and ORGAN CASE. The chancel reredos is very tall, with painted and gilded statues. Halifax continued to ornament the interior until his death in 1934. The SCULPTURE includes: St Christopher, wood, German, early C16; a life-size bust of a bishop (St Wilfrid?) with church model, German(?), C18; large figures of St Peter and St Paul, Flemish(?), *c.* 1700; relief panels of the Passion, gesso and paint with metallic finish, German(?); as well as a plaster bust of G.F. Bodley †1907, probably by *T.J. Murphy*, 1911 (N chapel) and the marble busts of the 2nd Viscount and Viscountess Halifax by *Murphy*, 1926 (S chapel). – Chancel SCREEN by *Comper*, 1909. – CANDELABRA. Brass, 1746 by *William Howard* of Exeter. – FONT. C12 or C13. Cylindrical, with a frieze of four-petalled flowers. – PULPIT. Finely carved flamboyant tracery in the top panels.

STAINED GLASS.† Two heraldic medallions by *Henry Gyles*, 1679 (framed; suspended in N aisle w window). – N chapel N side, easternmost window by *Comper*, 1911. – The rest mostly 1886–8 by *Bodley & Garner*, made by *Burlison & Grylls*. – MONUMENTS. Rombard Haringel *fl.* early C14. Semi-effigial grave-slab in superb condition (unearthed in 1983). – Charles Wood, 1st Viscount Halifax †1885 and wife

---

*The ground below is unstable due to a geological fault and mining. In 1983–5 the church was ingeniously preserved from collapse by underpinning with a concrete platform, developed by *Ove Arup & Partners*, engineers, with *Hill Mawson Partners*, that can be re-levelled if further movement occurs.
†Many fragments of late C12 glass with painted grisaille decoration, excavated in 1983, are in Doncaster Museum.

Mary †1884. Tomb-chest with recumbent effigies in alabaster.
By *Farmer & Brindley.* – 11th Earl of Devon †1888. Bust in
Ionic aedicule. Alabaster (N chapel). – Lady Agnes Wood, 2nd
Viscountess Halifax, †1919. Tomb-chest with recumbent alabaster effigy. Designed by *Comper.* – Charles Lindley Wood,
2nd Viscount Halifax †1934. Large heraldic tablet (chancel
floor). By *Goodhart-Rendel.* – Edward Frederick Lindley Wood,
1st Earl of Halifax, †1959. Marble and alabaster tablet by
Esmond Burton, 1962.

HICKLETON HALL. Remains of a wall of the Elizabethan
house, with mullioned window, runs W of the churchyard
but the present Hall was built for Godfrey Wentworth of
Woolley. A plan dated 1745, by *John Watson* of Wakefield,
shows a rectangular house with single-storey N and S wings
with projecting semi-octagonal end pavilions. *James Paine*
took over its completion and decoration before its occupation
by the family in 1758. The basement storey largely conforms
to the plan but only the N wing was built, and probably not
until 1772 when a long N service wing was also added. This
extension (and slightly later interior alterations) is attributed
to *Carr.* In 1829 the estate was bought by Sir Francis Lindley
Wood of Hemsworth. Alterations made in 1858 by his son
Charles, 1st Viscount Halifax, included a single-storey extension across the E front with outer hall. The 2nd Viscount built
a rectangular chapel in the position of the intended SE pavilion,
c. 1889, altering the NE pavilion to match. From 1948 until
2012 the house was in institutional use. At the time of writing
there are proposals for its conversion, with the stables etc., to
flats.

The main house is a rectangle of seven by five bays and
two-and-a-half storeys plus basement. No columns or pilasters.
E front has three-bay pediment with shield flanked by palm
branches. Central window on first floor pedimented, the others
with floating cornices characteristic of Paine (S and W fronts
similar). The chapel and NE pavilion are each of three bays
with pediments to the central windows, deep blocking courses
and low pyramid roofs. Pilastered outer hall projects slightly
in centre of extension between them. On the l. return a balustraded terrace (1858) overlooks a sunken garden, the basement
being screened by an arcaded loggia. W doorway has segmental
pediment and architrave with splayed base. Round-arched
windows to NW pavilion.

The interior has a tripartite outer hall with Doric screens
and small glazed dome. Large Entrance Hall, 1740s, has a rear
Doric screen of four columns and dado with Vitruvian scroll
(cf. Wadworth Hall). Chimneypiece has tapered pilasters and
elaborate entablature with small pediment; plasterwork bust in
garlanded oval frame above. Full-height stair hall to W with
Ionic and Corinthian landing screens but the balustrade is a
replacement (early C20?) for the wrought-iron one by *Thomas
Wagg.* The Library, decorated in the finest Adam style, is an
oblong apartment connected by a screen of paired Corinthian

columns with a square one. The design of the smaller ceiling (circular, on pendentives) is derived from Plate XIV in George Richardson's *Book of Ceilings* (1774–6).* This is also the source (Plate VI) of the ceiling in a delightful room in the NW pavilion which has a marble chimneypiece with carved pastoral panel (possibly by *William Collins*). Elegant Saloon has chimneypiece with swan-neck pediment, elaborate friezes to doorcases and Adamesque ceiling. In the Chapel early C18-style panelling with bolection moulding. Is it genuine C18 work, reused? Reredos with fluted Ionic columns and broken segmental top.

STABLES. *c.* 1749. Attributed to *Paine*. Enclosing three sides of a large yard, with screen wall to E side. Simple Palladian S front with pedimented archway, giant recessed blind arches and niches. Interiors designed and executed by *John Billington*, carpenter.

EAST LODGE with GATEWAY in the form of a giant classical arch, in the style of Lutyens, *c.* 1910.

The lawned E GARDENS were laid out by *F. Inigo Thomas*, 1909, with semicircular drive, balustraded terraces, statues and urns. Some of the balustrades and urns are concrete (cf. Goldthorpe church). Two-storey square SUMMER-HOUSE overlooks site of maze. Brick with artificial stone quoins.

The VILLAGE is well preserved but unfortunately severed by the main road. Some C18–early C19 limestone and pantile cottages, former C17 school and attached schoolhouse, and picturesque mid-C19 cottages and houses with mullioned windows. Scattered throughout are eight large WAYSIDE CROSSES – some are canopied crucifixes – erected by the 2nd Viscount. They include the Edward VII memorial, 1910, and the war memorial of 1918.

HIGH GREEN

3090

Former mining village.

ST SAVIOUR, Mortonley Lane, 1871–2. An unpretentious work by *James Brooks* commemorating Parkin Jeffcock, mining engineer, who died leading the rescue attempt in the Oaks Colliery disaster, 1866 (*see* p. 116). Chancel E window by *Clayton & Bell*, 1874, with Shadrach, Meshach and Abednego in the fiery furnace (cf. Altofts). Porch remodelled 1995, interior reordered 2005.

MINERS' WELFARE HALL, Greno View Road. By *Barry Parker*, 1923. Simple Arts and Crafts style.

---

*Information from Ivan Hall.

HIGH HOYLAND

ALL HALLOWS. Now a house. Isolated N of the village, with
spectacular views to E and S. Stocky Perp-looking W tower,
added *c.* 1662–70 to the medieval church. A decorated inscription records completion. The rest rebuilt in the late C18 and
1906–8 by *Hodgson Fowler*, in plain Perp style. (Remains of a
C13 or C14 arch reused at the baptistery entrance. – SCULP-
TURE. Fragments of medieval carving including parts of C11
cross-heads are built into the N wall.*)
HOYLAND HALL, ¼ m. S. *c.* 1725. Very typical of that date and
very handsome. Stone with ashlar dressings. Pitched roofs, one
behind the other. Five bays, two-and-a-half storeys. Angle
pilasters to ground floor, quoins above plain band. Imposing
doorway with eared architrave and a frieze that curves up as a
truncated pyramid in the middle. Hood over, looking like a
deep segmental pediment without its base. The windows above
the doorway have moulded surrounds and are laced by an
ashlar panel, the rest have raised surrounds.

HIGH MELTON

ST JAMES. The small but unusually high nave, narrower than
the chancel, is perhaps of Saxon origin. Later Norman the
chancel arch and the two-bay S arcade. Both have completely
unmoulded arches. The chancel arch is tall with imposts
of the plainest type. Circular pier and semicircular responds
to the arcade, all with square abaci and multi-scalloped capitals. The two easternmost capitals have some nailhead. Slight
traces of medieval decoration in red paint e.g. on eastern arch's
S voussoirs. In the early C14 the church received its ogee-
headed S and (blocked) N doorways. The rest is Perp. Fine
ashlar W tower with transomed two-light bell-openings, battlements and pinnacles. On its E face is a curious small half-
octagonal chimney for a fireplace in the ringing chamber.
Chancel E window of four lights with shields on blank panels
below. – REREDOS, impressive SCREEN with gallery and ROOD,
and CHOIR STALLS by *Comper*, 1904–8. – S chapel PARCLOSE
SCREEN. C15. Tracery with mouchettes; delicate cresting.
   STAINED GLASS. Three windows with mostly C14 glass
acquired by *William Peckitt* and installed *c.* 1780 for the restoration of the church by his patron the Rev. John Fountayne,
Dean of York, of High Melton Hall. Chancel N: easternmost
includes three good figures, two from New College, Oxford,
painted *c.* 1390s in *Thomas Glazier*'s Oxford workshop; second

*The C11 font is at Skelmanthorpe (q.v.).

from E includes pieces from New College and possibly York Minster, *c.* 1335–1390s, plus fine later C17 heraldic medallion perhaps by *Henry Gyles.* – S aisle W, two C15 figures and fragments, probably from York Minster. – Nave N window and S chapel S windows by *Peckitt,* with distinctive thick yellow foliage and deep ochre colouring. S chapel easternmost window has Fountayne's coat of arms 1772, the other window four heraldic medallions in enamels, 1754 and 1759. – E window 1897, S chapel E 1886, S aisle easternmost 1887, all by *Kempe.* – W (tower) window by *Comper,* 1908. – MONUMENTS. Many to the Fountaynes: Thomas Fountayne †1710 by *Edward Stanton.* Long inscription in corniced aedicule with fluted pilasters and gadrooned base. – John Fountayne, the Dean's father, †1736; erected 1747. Open pediment above large decorated half-sarcophagus on giant winged and taloned feet. – Anne Fountayne, †1747 (first wife). Impressive standing monument, its consoled cornice supporting pedimented half-sarcophagus standing on giant winged eagle's feet. Tall black obelisk behind has heraldic cartouche with elephant crest. – Frances Maria Fountayne †1750 (second wife), Frances Maria Tatton †1777 (daughter), Anne Fountayne †1786 (third wife) and John Fountayne †1802. By *John Fisher* (erected *c.* 1786?). Paired urns against tall obelisk; fine details. Also by Fisher, Thomas Charles Fountayne †1780 (son), an elegantly decorated tablet with portrait medallion on the pedestal of an urn.

HIGH MELTON HALL (University Centre Doncaster). 100 yds W. Dated 1757. Attributed to *Paine,* whom John Fountayne employed at the Deanery, York. E wing enlarged 1878. Altered and extended 1949–52 as Doncaster's teacher training college. H-plan, the central range two-and-a-half storeys with seven-bay S entrance front. Square rusticated porch has paired columns with blocking. Two stone elephants on top. Window above has architrave with splayed base, blocked voussoirs and segmental pediment with date. Similar but simpler treatment to windows in second and sixth bays. Front wings originally two storeys. Long W side has full-height canted bay at end of central range, the front plane stepped slightly forward, a Paine device. Rusticated ground floor. Balustrades to the upper windows, two of which have floating cornices, also typical of Paine.

Tuscan-pillared entrance hall leads to circular staircase hall (staircase removed). Upper Venetian window with Ionic columns. Only two rooms with original decoration intact: an ante-room above the hall, with modillioned cornice and good doorcases with carved friezes, and the elegantly decorated former drawing room/ballroom extending W of it into the canted bay. End screens with fluted Ionic columns, carved doorcases with bracketed cornices and a panelled centre to the coved ceiling. Excellent carved marble chimneypiece with consoles and mask.

HILLAM *see* MONK FRYSTON

HIPPERHOLME

CHRIST CHURCH METHODIST CHURCH, Brighouse Road. 1870 by *William Ives*. E.E. style with plate tracery. On a prominent corner site.

LIGHTCLIFFE UNITED REFORMED CHURCH (former Congregational), Leeds Road. 1870–1 by *Lockwood & Mawson*. John Crossley of Halifax bought the site and Sir Titus Salt was principal financial contributor. Large, Gothic, cruciform, with tall, buttressed SW tower and soaring octagonal stone spire, it could easily be mistaken for the parish church. Converted to offices 1989 but the nave still open to full height. – STAINED GLASS. W window by *Heaton, Butler & Bayne*, 1877, a memorial to Sir Titus, †1876. Extensive Sunday School etc. to E, 1892–3.

LIBRARY, Leeds Road/Amisfield Road. 1898–9 by *J. F. Walsh* as offices for the Urban District Council. Jacobean style, and of a piece with the row of shops to its N. Rusticated columns support a little balcony over the entrance.

GRAMMAR SCHOOL, Bramley Lane. Endowed in 1648 and 1671 (see old lintel reused at rear). Rebuilt 1783–4 by *Joseph Jagger*. Single storey with hipped roof. Three large windows each side of tall porch with inscribed tablet. Bellcote on diminutive Doric columns added 1835. Venetian windows to E and W returns mostly blocked by additions of 1906–7. At the W end is School House, 1881–2, by *Richard Horsfall*, in scholarly Vernacular Revival style, with elaborately carved hoodmould stops.

NOS. 18–20 TOWNGATE. Late C17 house, altered later, now subdivided. Double pile. Display S front has two coped gables with linking parapet, each gable having a blind oval window in panel with sill and cornice. Stepped windows to chambers. House-body on l. has seven-light window with king mullion and, inside, a section of decorated plaster frieze. Original oak-framed doorway with Tudor arch and carved spandrels.

THE CRESCENT, off Leeds Road, was laid out *c.* 1863. Twenty-eight terraced villas with generous front gardens, in a horse-shoe around a central drive, originally gated.

BROOKVILLE, E of Brighouse Road. Workers' housing by *R. Fielding Farrar* for J. Brooke & Co., 1911, using their patent artificial stone, glazed bricks etc.

HOLMBRIDGE

ST DAVID. Beside the River Holme. Built 1838–40 using earlier plans by *Henry Ward* and overseen by *William Wallen*, who made alterations during restoration after the Holmfirth Flood

in 1852.* Plain lancet-style nave with battlemented w tower.
Corner pinnacles. Chancel etc. by *Edward Hughes*, 1885–7.
Two bays, with grouped lancets.

On the hillside to the N, scattered late C18–C19 WEAVERS' COT-
TAGES, some with windows of twelve or even sixteen lights.

AUSTONLEY HALL, ½ m. NW. C17 farmhouse, the S end rebuilt
with symmetrical front 1763. Three-light flat-mullioned sash
windows progressively diminish in size on each floor; l. return
with later sashes is, curiously, two, not three, storeys.

UNDERHILL, Holme, 1 m. SW. By *Arthur Quarmby* for himself,   115
1973–5. Pioneering earth-sheltered house, built almost invisi-
bly into the hillside. A 'living-garden', flanked by bedrooms,
opens onto a S terrace overlooking the moors; the main living
area behind has a top-lit central space with a circular swimming pool, enclosed by stone arches supporting the concrete
roof slab.

HOLMFIRTH   1000

Small town towards the head of the Holme valley, where the hills
close in both sides near the bridges. Evidence of the domestic
weaving industry survives in long-windowed stone houses on the
slopes; most of the later mill buildings along the river have gone.

HOLY TRINITY. Quite a large church, rebuilt in plain classical
style in 1782–6, probably by *Joseph Jagger*, who made estimates
in 1777 for rebuilding after flood damage. It stands beside the
river on a site granted in 1472 for a chapel of ease, hence its
curious position with the broad w gable facing the street and
the tower with battlements and pinnacles at the E end against
the steep hillside. Tiny chancel under the tower. The two-
storey nave has three galleries, on slender Doric columns of
stone and with original panelled fronts (W meeting rooms
1975). Low-relief centrepiece to simply panelled flat ceiling.
Screened w lobby with staircases, and most fittings (and the
chancel arch?) by *Mangnall & Littlewood*, 1875. To S, handsome former VICARAGE, later Georgian, with central three-
storey bow.

ST JOHN THE EVANGELIST, Upperthong. By *Edwin Shellard*,
1846–8. Cruciform plan; large battlemented tower as S transept. STAINED GLASS. Chancel N window 1873, and S side
second from E 1867, by *George Shaw* of Saddleworth. N transept N by *Kempe*, 1882. Nave N first from E by *Lavers, Barraud
& Westlake*, 1879, with two portrait photographs in tracery
lights.

R.D. Chantrell's design, 1837, was rejected by the Incorporated Church Building
Society.

LANE CHAPEL, Upperthong Lane (Congregational; now flats).
By *J. Berry* of Huddersfield, 1889–90. Italianate front of four
bays, the centre more elaborate.

CIVIC HALL, Huddersfield Road. 1842, built as the Town Hall.
Ashlar. Dignified plain classical façade of five bays, the
end bays projecting. Attached l. the mullioned-windowed
DRILL HALL, by *Joshua Barrowclough* of Holmfirth, 1891–2.
100 yds N, on a corner, the former TECHNICAL INSTITUTE,
1892–4 by *Joseph Smith*. Free late Gothic style with big double-
transomed upper windows rising into gables. Attached is small
bay-windowed POLICE STATION with house, 1857.

ALMSHOUSES (former), Nos. 78–86 Station Road. By *William
Hill*, 1856, won in competition. Two-storey gabled row in
simple Gothic style, the off-centre towered bay originally
spired. They commemorate the Holmfirth Flood of 1852, when
eighty-one died after the failure of the Bilberry Reservoir.

RAILWAY STATION (former), Station Road. Terminus of the
Lancashire and Yorkshire Railway branch line, opened in 1850.
Simple Tudor Gothic with distinctive octagonal chimneys.

DRUIDS' HALL (former), Station Road. 1851–2. Three tall
storeys. Centre of three bays, the projecting pedimented wings
each a one-bay house. Large top-floor hall for the Friendly
Society.

PICTUREDROME, Market Walk. Cinema by *P. Norman Brown* of
Holmfirth, 1912–13. Rendered walls with red brick piers;
inside a rare pressed-tin ceiling.

HONLEY

Large former textile village in the Holme valley, the historic
centre set on a knoll just above the river but comprehensively
redeveloped with social housing in the 1970s.

ST MARY. Rebuilt by *R.D. Chantrell*, 1842–3, on the site of
chapels of 1503 and 1759. Lancet style with buttresses. Very
tall thin W tower, seven-bay nave with clerestory, separately
roofed aisles, the S one with porches in the first and last bays.
Very small apsidal chancel. The interior, with three galleries
and open roof trusses, is impressively long and high; the tall
arcades have quatrefoil piers. Alterations by *Charles Hodgson
Fowler* in 1888 included furnishing the nave's two eastern bays
as a choir. The apse has slightly later STENCILLING (restored).
– Painted and gilded REREDOS TRIPTYCH by *E. Stanley
Watkins* 1905. – Excellent oak PULPIT on tall slender stem, by
C.E. Buckeridge & Floyce, 1888, with five panels painted in the
style of Van Eyck. – CHOIR STALLS and (reduced) low SCREEN
by *G.W. Milburn*, 1888. – STAINED GLASS. Three E windows by
Clayton & Bell, 1888. S aisle E window by *Burlison & Gryllls*,
1910. Five windows by *William Morris & Co.* of Westminster,

1939–52, the best one mostly hidden by the organ. N aisle sixth from E by *Frederick Cole*, 1969. – MONUMENTS. William Brooke †1846 and wife Anne †1840 by *E. G. Physick*. A pair of draped urns under a weeping tree, richly carved. – Sisters Anne Brooke †1846 and Elizabeth †1849, also by *Physick*. – Betty Leigh †1814 and husband Thomas †1825 by *H. Mares*. Urn with falling drapery.

On the valley's E slope, ¼ m. NE, two Regency houses built for the Brooke family (*see* Armitage Bridge). Main fronts in ashlar. NORTHGATE HOUSE has Doric E porch and three-bay S front with full-height canted bay to centre. NORTHGATE MOUNT has W porch with Tower of the Winds capitals to fluted columns (cf. Kirkburton Hall).

HOOK

7020

Village on a narrow hook of land in a loop of the lower Ouse, now almost attached to Goole.

ST MARY. C14 and C15. Limestone. Heavily restored 1844 by *Hurst & Moffatt* using sandstone; further altered 1873 and *c.* 1896. Modest nave with narrow aisles, lower two-bay chancel. W bellcote with twin openings. Rebuilt porch, single-chamfered S doorway. Arcades have octagonal piers. Perp W window, probably the E window until replicated in the C19; other windows mostly straight-headed. – STAINED GLASS. One of the chancel windows, by *Pape & Co.*, 1901, depicts Queen Victoria bespectacled and in a wheelchair, copied from the *Illustrated London News*.

HOOK HALL, ½ m. N. Built for the Sotheron family 1743. Brick. Square, with the usual five bays and two-and-a-half storeys, standing handsomely above flood level. Tall plain parapet, hipped roof. Identical front and back with pedimented doorways on consoles, returns almost blind. Fine interior lost in mid C20.

HOOTON PAGNELL

4000

One of the most attractive of the limestone villages, set high up along a ridge with the church and the Hall at its S end and enjoying a wide view towards the Pennines.

ALL SAINTS. Much of the masonry of a complete early Norman church is preserved, i.e. the coursed rubble with occasional herringbone in the S walls of the nave and the short chancel (see its E quoins) and in the W tower. The tower is the same width as the nave with no external break. More telling Norman features are the s doorway, plain except for incised motifs such as an arrow, a dagger and a key on several voussoirs, the plain tower arch of three orders (perhaps reconstructed in the C14) and the chancel arch, which has at least a fine angle shaft on each side, cable moulding and incised trellis on the heavy imposts and a simple roll in the arch. Enlarged in the late C12 or early C13 when a N aisle was added and the chancel extended. The two-bay N arcade has a big circular pier with decorated waterleaf in the capital and an octagonal abacus. Semicircular keeled responds. The arches are pointed with one step and one chamfered step. The two upper stages of the W tower seem Dec, but it is difficult to assign a date to the small round arch into the N chapel. It has boldly chamfered responds with big stops and could be C15.

Partial restoration in 1875–6 by *J.M. Teale* was superseded by *J.L. Pearson*'s more thorough scheme of 1885–6. Porch, roofs and most of the windows are his; the E end's group of three stepped single lancets with hoodmoulds linked to each other (cf. Brodsworth nearby) are shafted inside and have nailhead. – PULPIT. A nice C18 piece with marquetry. – N chapel. Stone ALTAR and REREDOS carved by *Esmond Burton*, 1936. – SCREEN. Two traceried sections of C15 rood screen dado (under tower arch). – S DOOR. The four central boards and middle ironwork strap are *c.* 1100; the bold C-strap hinges C19 reproductions. – STAINED GLASS. N chapel easternmost by *Comper*, 1930. Nave easternmost by *Ann Sotheran*, 2000. – MONUMENTS. Several medieval cross-slabs; one Romanesque, with incised cross bearing three pairs of volutes; another (rear of sedilia) has rare emblems of a penner and inkhorn to commemorate a notary (cf. Riccall, *East Riding*). – Lord John Stanhope †1627 and his wife, Lady Mary, †1661, erected 1674. Tablet against draped sarcophagus with skull.

HOOTON PAGNELL HALL. A C14 stone-built gatehouse range, with both carriage and pedestrian entrances, survives from a medieval manor house. Pretty oriel on NW corner overlooking the church. Extensive restoration 1894–1904 included two oriels to N entrance front, mullioned windows and much castellating. Three-storey S range by *William Lindley*, 1787, has shallow full-height bows to outer bays of garden front. N front continued by *Lindley*'s long E service range with off-centre pediment. (Fine late C17 staircase from Palace Yard, Coventry. Balustrade of lush foliage scrolls with birds and animals. Good Georgian decoration and chimneypieces in S rooms.)

Severe mock-medieval entrance GATEWAY with high walls and flanking turrets by *Granville Streatfeild & Frank Atwell* 1914–20.

Carefully conserved VILLAGE has good farms and cottages, many of C17 origin. One of the best is HOME FARMHOUSE, with gable-end to the road, doorway with massive Tudor-arched lintel dated 1688 and three-light mullioned windows with hoodmoulds. THE HOSTEL, almost opposite, is a distinctive exception. Arts and Crafts style with boldly timber-framed and jettied first floor and a cove above the porch; eyebrow dormer in the roof. Added in 1903 to the C18 cottage where the vicar had opened a hostel to help poor men prepare for theological training and university education.* Since 1916 the village hall and club/inn.

BILHAM BELVEDERE, 1¼ m. s. By *John Rawstorne, c.* 1800. Ruinous classical summerhouse, originally commanding extensive views. Curved front to two-storey centre, lower side wings. Now a conserved ruin.

HOOTON ROBERTS

4090

St JOHN THE BAPTIST. Small. Chancel and two-bay nave, both with a single-bay s chapel. Perp w tower with pinnacles. Much renewed, after a serious fire in 1700 and by *Wilson & Masters,* 1875–6. However, the round arch between chancel and s chapel proves a Norman date. Fat late C12 responds with Transitional capitals with crockets. All of one step and one chamfer. It is likely that this was the original chancel arch; the present one a C19 copy. Arch to the nave chapel double-chamfered and pointed, the capitals with some nailhead. The chancel and its chapel are embattled, except on the E gable, which has billet-moulded strips reused awkwardly as coping stones. – STAINED GLASS. E window by *W. F. Dixon,* 1884. Nave E: late C15 figure of a saint bishop, composite and much restored. The medieval parts include the head, that of a layman wearing a cap, with a mitre added on top. – MONUMENTS. Cross-slab of a priest *c.* 1200. – Charles Newby †1701. Splendid cartouche framed with tasselled drapery. Winged cherubs' heads and skull on the apron.

EARL OF STRAFFORD, Doncaster Road. The former hall, once the Wentworths' dower house, extensively remodelled in the late C18. Two storeys, double pile. Three-bay centre and single-bay wings, all with hipped roofs. The rear shows traces of the house engraved in 1740. Blocked Tudor-arched doorway and several windows with ovolo-moulded mullions. Two three-light staircase windows with transoms.

HORBURY

2010

A small town above the Calder valley whose centre retains its ancient, winding street pattern and much of its late C19 character.

---

*As St Chad's Hall it was licensed in 1904 by the University of Durham as their first independent hall and was the genesis of St Chad's College.

The local sandstone was generally preferred to brick. Horbury's development was due to the textile mills, mostly sw beside the river at Horbury Bridge, and local collieries. These were served by the river, improved in 1838 by the Calder & Hebble Navigation New Cut, and, from 1840, by railway facilities nearby. The population rose from 2,100 in 1801 to 7,500 in 1911. The strong Anglo-Catholic influence of the Rev. John Sharp, vicar 1834–99 and a militant Tractarian, is evident.

ST PETER AND ST LEONARD. By *John Carr*, 1790–4. One of his most elegant and distinctively original buildings, standing comparison with the London churches of Wren and Hawksmoor. Carr was born at Horbury in 1723 and is buried in a vault under the N transept. In 1790 he obtained permission to demolish the Norman church and build the new one at his own expense. The cost was £8,000. The inscription in the S pediment proudly announces to those inhabitants of Horbury who can read Latin: 'Hanc aedam sacram pietatis in Deum et amoris in solum natale monimentum … extruxit Johannes Carr architectus' ('John Carr, architect, erected this holy building, a monument of piety towards God and of love for his birthplace'). The church is in the classical style with an unconventional plan that is basically an elongated octagon with entrances in transeptal projections in the centre of the N and S sides. The transepts are three bays, the S having a portico with four attached Ionic columns at the main entrance. The roof is hipped. At the W end is an excellently scaled square tower that is a striking landmark for miles around. It surely owes something to Gibbs's St Martin-in-the-Fields and, perhaps, to the original tower of Etty's Holy Trinity, Leeds. Four diminishing stages, the lowest of smooth ashlar, the next rusticated, the third with coupled pilasters, the highest with recessed angle columns. Then a rotunda of columns and a conical fluted spire. Unconventionally, the pilasters and columns are all Doric. The sandstone ashlar has prominent graining, especially noticeable on the S portico columns, where it forms tiers of festoons. This quality may have influenced Carr in leaving the round-arched and square window openings without mouldings.

A small vestry in classical style added at the NE in 1884. At the SE the war memorial LADY CHAPEL by *H.C. Windley*, 1920–1, a brave attempt at keeping in keeping, but intruding on the effect of Carr's portico.

62   The INTERIOR is as successful as the exterior, intelligently enriched without losing any of its sobriety. Oblong nave of five bays with shallow segmental tunnel-vault. The polygonal ends to the E and W are represented inside by shallow segmental apses, the W with a gallery now filled by the organ. The transepts are screened by Corinthian columns; the walls otherwise have Corinthian pilasters. Their capitals are modelled on those of the Temple of Jupiter Stator, Rome – the innermost scrolls are intertwined. Columned screens at the E and W ends, shown on Carr's plan engraved by *Thomas Malton* in 1791, were

omitted. Elaborate entablature and panelled ceiling with bands enriched with fretwork and rosettes, by *Henderson & Crabtree* of York. – FITTINGS. Carr's pulpit and font were ejected by Canon Sharp, the box pews partly surviving as backs and dado panelling. Some of Sharp's replacements have in turn gone and at the time of writing the E end is barely furnished. – PULPIT. Octagonal, panelled oak, 1917. – FONT. Portland stone on marble columns *c.*1864. – MONUMENTS. Tablet to Harriet Carr †1841 by *J. Tilney* of York. With a kneeling allegorical figure by an urn. – Brass to Canon John Sharp †1903, in the medieval tradition, with his kneeling figure and depiction of his various buildings. – Marble tablet with border of fret and rosettes to Carr's parents, Robert †1760 and Rosa †1774, the inscription cut by *Thomas Waterworth Sen.*, and similar tablet but with guilloche border to Carr †1807.

ST JOHN, Mission Street, Horbury Bridge. By *J. T. Micklethwaite & Somers Clarke* 1883–4. Small, plain. – Sturdy oak ROOD SCREEN with plain square posts, 1926, in memory of the Rev Sabine Baring-Gould, who wrote 'Onward Christian Soldiers' here. – STAINED GLASS. E window 1884, chancel S 1908, nave S first from E 1906, second from E 1926, all by *Kempe*.

ST MARY, Daw Lane, Horbury Junction. 1891–3 by *Bodley & Garner*. Simple, low structure with Dec tracery. W bell-turret, another over chancel arch. Fine interior with quatrefoil piers to aisle arcades. Superb semi-octagonal oak SCREEN for font by *W. D. Caröe*, 1914, with elaborately carved coved top. – STAINED GLASS. By *Kempe*, thirteen windows in all including E and W windows and seven others 1893; four more 1898, 1907, 1910 and 1927.

Former ST PETER'S CONVENT, Dovecote Lane (now part of Silcoates school). By *Henry Woodyer*. Main S range 1862–4, with W range 1864; extension to E end of S range, with attached CHAPEL, 1869–71; E range 1883; tiny S CHAPEL attached to chapel 1898. Built as The House of Mercy, an Anglican convent, penitentiary and school, established in 1858 as one of Canon Sharp's religious enterprises. Brick with stone bands and other dressings. Quadrangular plan, two storeys, except for single storey N range. Windows of single or grouped lancet lights, some transomed. Gabled dormers to steep roofs. Stout tower with copper-clad broach spire in SW angle of courtyard. CHAPEL has apsidal sanctuary, N transept and S transept with gallery. Lancet windows, set high up. Lofty interior in brick with stone banding (painted). Good arch-braced roof. E.E. arcading at window level. W organ gallery above coved screen. – STAINED GLASS. Three by *Hardman*, 1871, originally in the apse, now first three from E on nave S. W wheel window 1871 by *Kempe*, and another ten by his firm 1888–1920, including the two S chapel E windows 1899.

Former WESTFIELD CONGREGATIONAL CHAPEL, Westfield Road. By *John Shaw* of Leeds, 1876. Three-bay gabled front with plain square pilasters, porch with two round-arched entrances.

Former HIGHFIELD UNITED FREE METHODIST CHURCH, High Street. By *Thomas Howdill & Son*, 1899–1900. Gabled front with Lombardic frieze, flanked by big square staircase bays. Almost facing this, at the Highfield Road junction, a handsome former BANK (United Counties), 1910. Classical details and an octagonal domed turret with open arcade.

Former TOWN HALL, Westfield Road, by *Walter Hanstock & Son*, 1902–3. Northern Renaissance style. Three-bay front has fine carving to gables with obelisk finials. Ionic porch with balcony over. Adjacent to r., CARNEGIE LIBRARY by *B. Watson* of Batley, 1905–6 in similar style. Single storey, with two decorative gables.

HORBURY HALL, Church Street. Unassuming in appearance, but an important timber-framed hall of a high-status gentry house, built by the Amyas family between 1478 and 1492 to replace an earlier hall, and originally attached to a large earlier cross-wing to the E (dem. 1938) (cf. Calverley Hall, *West Riding North*). It is the largest surviving medieval hall in our area. Later cased, partly in stone at the front, the rest in brick, partly rendered, and converted to cottages, now restored as a single house. (Three bays, the hall, now floored, of two bays. Evidence of a stair shows that the single W bay was always two-storeyed. The most impressive survivals are the hall's decorative roof timbers – a spere truss at the E end (showing that there was a screen and cross-passage), kingpost trusses with two intermediate trusses of arch-braced collar form, and a display of cusped wind-braces that are the only ones known in Yorkshire. An additional tie-beam towards the W end, which originally supported the top of a coved dais canopy, is brattished and has carved roses and shields with the Amyas coat of arms.)

CARR LODGE, New Street, formerly Sunroyd House. Built between 1770 and 1775. Plain five-bay brick house with pedimented Ionic porch. Bought by John Carr's nephew, also John Carr, in 1790.

ROCK HOUSE, Ossett Road. 1873–7. Tudor Gothic mansion for George Harrop of Albion woollen mills.

3000

HOYLAND NETHER

ST PETER. Gothic Revival by *Watson, Pritchett & Watson*, 1830–1, replacing an early C18 chapel. W tower with pinnacled buttresses and spire. Gabled N transept for organ, 1868. Interior restored 1880–1 by *W.J. Sykes* of Hoyland. Corseted with steelwork in 1924.

ST ANDREW, Market Street, in the little town, ½ m. ESE. By *W.J. Sykes*, 1889–90. Modest, with lancets. – STAINED GLASS. E and W windows by *Powell Bros*, 1900. Nave N: centre window by *Morris & Co.*, 1919; the flanking pair by *Harry Harvey*, 1955 (r.) and 1962 (l.).

SACRED HEART AND ST HELEN (R.C.), West Street. By *Empsall & Clarkson*, Bradford, 1928–9. Impressive Neo-Byzantine style.

HOYLAND LOWE STAND, ⅛ m. N on a prominent hilltop. Built 1750 by the 1st Marquess of Rockingham as a prospect tower with adjacent bowling green. Two-storeyed, square, with parapet. Higher stair-turret had low pyramidal roof. Ruined.

HOYLANDSWAINE   2000

ST JOHN THE EVANGELIST. By *W.H. Crossland*, 1867–9. Simple Dec. Sturdy buttressed W tower with gabled merlons and pinnacles. – STAINED GLASS. E window by *Morris & Co.*, designed by *Burne-Jones*, 1870. MURAL on E wall by *John Roddam Spencer Stanhope* 1869 (restored 2014).

NAILMAKERS' WORKSHOPS, No. 355 Barnsley Road. Row of three tiny early–mid-C19 forges.

HUDDERSFIELD   1010

INTRODUCTION

With high hills all around, Huddersfield has a spectacular setting. Situated where the valley of the Holme joins that of the Colne, it was originally a market for the domestic woollen industry of the surrounding area, but in the C19 it developed into an important manufacturing centre for textiles, engineering and chemicals. There were 7,000 inhabitants in 1801, 70,000 in 1871, 95,000 in 1901 and 132,000 in 1964; today the figure is over 160,000. Much of the town formed part of the estates of the Ramsden family until 1920, and their control largely shaped its development. In the late C18 it comprised little more than a single street, Westgate and Kirkgate forming the main axis, with the Market Place opening off. By 1826, however, several broad, straight streets (New Street, Cloth Hall Street, King Street, Queen Street and Cross Church Street) had been formed to the s, and Engels in 1844 noted the 'modern style of building' and called Huddersfield 'the most beautiful of all the factory towns in Lancashire and Yorkshire'. In 1776 Sir John Ramsden's Broad Canal gave access to other navigations E of the Pennines; in 1811 the Narrow Canal provided a trans-Pennine route to Manchester; and in 1849 the railway line from Leeds to Manchester via Huddersfield was completed. The following year the Ramsdens laid out a spacious New Town on a grid-plan adjacent to the magnificent new station, with advice from *Sir William Tite* helping to ensure high architectural standards. Pevsner described the smoking mills and blackened buildings in 1959 as 'impressive if bleak'. Many large C19 mills survive today, but most of their chimneys have gone, and everywhere cleaning has revealed the warm local stone. The town centre is tightly circumscribed by a dual-carriageway ring road, completed in 1973. It is a regrettable barrier to enjoyment.

TOWN CENTRE

CHURCHES

St Peter (the Parish Church), Byram Street and Kirkgate. A Norman foundation, but rebuilt at the beginning of the C16, and again in 1834–6 by *J. P. Pritchett*. Perp style. Nave and aisles under one roof, shallow chancel and broad, gabled s transept. The side windows are lancets with Perp tracery. High w tower with diagonal buttresses, panelling to the clock stage, openwork battlements and pinnacles. Polygonal vestries flanking chancel (the s one added 1879 by *Edward Hughes*). Interior with octagonal piers and three galleries. Gallery fronts incorporate what may be woodwork from the early C16 church: Gothic tracery, with roughly carved foliage and some animal heads in spandrels. Panelled ceiling with bosses and foliage sprigs at intersections. – FONT. Octagonal, chalice-shaped, crudely inscribed with the date 1570, royal cypher and arms of Elizabeth I. – ALTAR CANOPY. Classical, with four gilded Tuscan columns and statues of angels bearing tapers, 1921 by

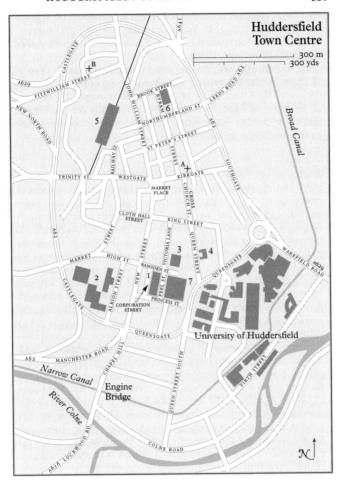

Huddersfield
Town Centre

300 m
300 yds

University of Huddersfield

Engine
Bridge

A St Peter
B Our Lady of Czestochowa

1 Town Hall
2 Civic Centre
3 Library and Art Gallery
4 Lawrence Batley Theatre
5 Railway Station
6 Open Air Market
7 Queensgate Market

Ninian Comper. By *Comper* also, the STAINED GLASS in the E
window: Christ in Majesty above, Risen Christ below, with
saints. – Other stained glass: s transept, w end, three lights
signed by *T. Willement*, 1852, and two lights including Three
Marys at the Tomb, †1858; other transept windows have older
armorial glass, re-set; s aisle, E end, Presentation in the Temple
and St Paul Preaching, †1886; s gallery, Agony in the Garden

and Four Evangelists, from the original E window by *Ward & Nixon* of London, 1836 but still in the C18 pictorial manner; tower, Christ Carrying the Cross, Renaissance style, by *Lavers, Barraud & Westlake*, 1876.

In the churchyard, an ARCHWAY facing Kirkgate, 1859 by *William Butterfield*, moved here from the SE corner.

OUR LADY OF CZESTOCHOWA, Fitzwilliam Street. By *Bowman & Crowther* of Manchester, 1853–4. Originally for the Unitarians. Dec Gothic. Nave with crocketed pinnacles on the corner buttresses and a lean-to N aisle.

PUBLIC BUILDINGS

TOWN HALL, Ramsden Street and Princess Street. It fills an entire block, built right up to the pavement on all four sides, with no civic space in front. Two distinct parts, both by Borough Surveyor *John Henry Abbey*. First came the Municipal Offices towards Ramsden Street, opened 1878: a two-storey palazzo with round-arched first-floor windows. This was followed immediately by the larger and more imposing part facing Princess Street, completed 1881 by *Ben Stocks*. Still only two storeys – offices below, concert hall above – but very high, so it towers above its surroundings. The style is what the Victorians called Free or Mixed Renaissance, with lavish carved decoration. Inside, the CONCERT HALL has sumptuous plasterwork. With horseshoe balcony and mighty organ, it looks like a Nonconformist chapel of exceptional grandeur.

CIVIC CENTRE, High Street. Three phases, opened 1967–77. Begun by the Council's own architects, but for the last phase, N, *Abbey Hanson Rowe* were consultants. Council offices plus combined Courts and Police Station, all stone-faced, flat-roofed and grouped around a paved area. They turn their backs on the old town centre to face the new ring road. The relationship between the three buildings was spoilt when an ill-matched fourth was later sited in the middle.

LIBRARY AND ART GALLERY, Princess Alexandra Walk. 1937–40 by *E.H. Ashburner*. A free-standing, severely rectilinear block in stripped classical style. SCULPTURE by *James Woodford*: a pair of seated figures flanking the steps, representing Literature and Art, plus allegorical reliefs on each side of the door. Entrance hall with imperial stair. On the first floor, five PAINTINGS of local folk tales by *Charles Reginald Napier* and students of the town's Art School, 1939–40, in a style reminiscent of Stanley Spencer.

LAWRENCE BATLEY THEATRE, Queen Street (former Queen Street Methodist Chapel). Possibly by *Charles Watson*. A fine classical building of 1819 with pediment, Venetian window and four-column Roman Doric porch. It forms a unit with two flanking pairs of terraced houses, enclosing a square on the E side of Queen Street (*see* p. 345). Said to be the largest Methodist chapel anywhere when it opened. A flexible theatre auditorium was inserted into the gutted C19 shell by *The Design Practice* (of Kirklees Metropolitan Council), 1994.

RAILWAY STATION. 1846–50, by *J.P. Pritchett*. One of the best   75
early railway stations in England. Classical, in the Corinthian
style, and composed like a Palladian country house. The two-
storey centre has a six-column portico with pediment, linked
by long, low, colonnaded wings to single-storey pavilions at
each end. Built for two clients, the Huddersfield & Manchester
Railway & Canal Co. (quickly absorbed into the London and
North Western Railway) and the Lancashire and Yorkshire
Railway Co. The centre originally contained both companies'
general offices, the pavilions their respective booking offices
and waiting rooms. There was only one platform until 1886,
when an island platform was added and the tracks roofed over.
w of the station is a colossal, five-storey WAREHOUSE of red
and blue brick, 1885 by the companies' own engineers. A
loading bay on mighty cast-iron Doric columns raised wagons
bodily into the warehouse; hydraulic power was supplied by
the Italianate ACCUMULATOR TOWER at the N end of the
goods yard. Another former warehouse – smaller and of
stone – adjoins the s end of the 1885 building and must be
earlier.

OPEN AIR MARKET, Byram Street. Built as the Wholesale
Market, 1887–8, by the Borough Surveyor, *R.S. Dugdale*; ironwork by the *Whessoe Foundry Co.* of Darlington. Light and
spacious: it fills almost an entire block of the New Town and
is open on three sides. Ridge-and-furrow roof on lofty cast-iron
columns, partly glazed between.

QUEENSGATE MARKET. *J. Seymour Harris Partnership* (project   114
architect *Gwyn Roberts*), 1968–70. Part of a comprehensive
redevelopment of the shopping area, it replaced an 1880 market
hall by *Edward Hughes* in King Street. The remarkable roof is
composed of twenty-one hyperbolic paraboloid concrete shells,
each rectangular in plan and springing, funnel-like, from an
off-centre column. Each column-and-shell is structurally independent, not braced by its neighbours, and the columns vary
in height, resulting in vertical spaces between the edges of the
shells, which are filled with clerestory glazing. The site slopes
steeply, and while the w end rises less than a full storey above
pavement level, the E end towers over the ring road. Here the
concrete shells project to form a deep, staggered canopy over
an external terrace. The blank wall below is stone-faced and
decorated with a series of nine large ceramic RELIEFS by *Fritz
Steller*, Articulation in Movement; inside, a black-painted steel
mural on the N wall, Commerce, is also by Steller.

PERAMBULATIONS

1. Within the ring road, north of Trinity Street, Westgate and Kirkgate

ST GEORGE'S SQUARE, in front of the Railway Station (*see*
Public Buildings), is the focal point of the New Town grid laid
out in 1850–1. Since grid and railway are not aligned, the
square is an irregular Y shape. It was sensitively landscaped
and repaved by *Whitelaw Turkington*, 2008. In the centre, a

bronze STATUE of Huddersfield-born Prime Minister Harold
Wilson, 1999 by *Ian Walters*, raised only slightly above pavement level, studiedly informal. Round the square are exceptionally good commercial buildings, all mid-C19 and all
classical, matching the high standard set by the station. The
GEORGE HOTEL, N side, 1848–50 by *William Wallen*, is a four-
storey palazzo with abundant rustication round the ground-
floor windows. The other buildings were originally offices and
warehouses for the woollen trade. Facing the hotel is the more
opulent BRITANNIA BUILDINGS, a palazzo by *William
Cocking*, completed *c*. 1858. Parapet with urns and balustrading, crowned with a statue of Britannia. Ground floor disfigured by overlarge windows, introduced in the 1920s, but the
original treatment survives on the shorter elevation to John
William Street, where there are keystones with excellent carved
heads. Back in the Square, No. 7 is probably of 1851 for the
woollen merchants J.W. & H. Shaw. It has three-quarter Ionic
columns on the ground floor, and the same treatment continues round the corner in RAILWAY STREET, perhaps built
in successive phases. Between here and the station is a particularly impressive block of *c*. 1856–7: a terrace of twelve repeating
bays to the square and a further four to Railway Street, all
under a continuous cornice. Doorways to Railway Street and
the square are barely distinguished from the round-arched,
ground-floor windows, but there is a grander entrance at the
rounded corner. Often ascribed to William Tite, though firm
evidence for this is lacking; the architect-builder *John Eastwood*
seems to have been involved, but in what capacity is unclear.

The E side of the square is closed by the LION ARCADE on
John William Street. Offices and warehouses over shops,
originally with a glass-roofed central court. 1851–3 by *Pritchett*,
whose design was modified by *Tite*. Still classical, but more
loosely composed than its neighbours. Quadrant corners, and
round-headed windows grouped in twos, threes and fours,
treated as arcades. The noble statue of a lion on the parapet
is a copy of the cast-stone original, which was by *John Seeley*.
JOHN WILLIAM STREET is the main artery of the New Town.
It has classical three-storey stone terraces on each side – shops
below, offices and warehouses above – all built 1851–8. Different architects were employed, their designs revised by *Tite*
to ensure consistency. The block on the E side between St
Peter's Street and Church Street is by *J.J. Roebuck*, 1851–3;
that at the rounded corner of Westgate by *William Wallen*,
1852. Interesting buildings can be seen in all the cross-streets,
described here from N to S. BROOK STREET, N, has a former
marble works at Nos. 1–2, simplest Gothic, dated 1863 above
the cart entrance. In NORTHUMBERLAND STREET, which
begins opposite St George's Square, the POST OFFICE is by
C.P. Wilkinson of *H.M. Office of Works*, opened 1914. Classical, with channelled rustication on the ground floor, giant
pilasters above and a semicircular Doric entrance portico
(good stone-faced rear extension, 1968). Directly opposite is

the previous Post Office of *c.* 1874–5 by *W.H. Crossland*: single-storeyed, bookended by taller office blocks, with minimal Tudor details. Further E on this side is the former MECHANICS INSTITUTION, 1859–60 by *Travis & Mangnall* of Manchester. Three giant round arches with blind tympana enclosing wreathed discs, and tripartite windows below. Rebuilt within the preserved shell by *Brewster Bye*, 2001, as live–work apartments (the new roof detracts from the imposing severity of the original design). Attached at the rear, facing the ring road, a five-bay house, probably late C18, and next to that the five-storey glazed MEDIA CENTRE, 2004–7, carried out by *Bradshaw, Gass & Hope* from a conceptual design by *Ash Shakula*. The next cross-street of the grid, going S, is ST PETER'S STREET. At its W end, on the corner of Station Street, is STATION STREET BUILDINGS, 1899 by *John Hatchard Smith*. An eclectic mix of C16 and C17 features: mullioned windows, shaped gables, pierced parapet and octagonal corner turret. Lower down, the building at the SW corner of St Peter Street and Byram Street incorporates the C18 façade of the former George Hotel (it stood on the N side of the Market Place until taken down in 1851 to make way for John William Street). Seven bays, with a central pediment. It faces REVENUE CHAMBERS, a palazzo probably of 1861 by *J.J. Roebuck*, with boldly chamfered quoins and voussoirs.

From here, BYRAM STREET runs S past St Peter's churchyard. The W side is filled by two matching commercial blocks of unusual ambition, and just round the corner at No. 5 Kirkgate is a third. The whole group is of 1879–83 by *W.H. Crossland*, and comprises offices above ground-floor shops in an exuberant Renaissance style. Sculptural decoration is by *C.E. Fucigna*. One of the shops, No. 4 Byram Street, has a stylish *Moderne* front by *Sharp & Law*, 1935. (A short detour E along Kirkgate leads to BEAST MARKET, where the BOY AND BARREL pub has a jolly rooftop statue, over life-size, perhaps *c.* 1900, of the eponymous Boy sitting astride his barrel and holding a lantern.)

KIRKGATE leads uphill, becoming WESTGATE after John William Street. The BYRAM ARCADE at Nos. 10–18 Westgate is by *Crossland* again, 1878–81 (but incorporating his earlier BYRAM BUILDINGS of 1870–5). Cliff-like façade with five gables, derived from north European medieval town houses. The entrance under the crowstepped central gable leads to four floors of shops, accessed from balconies around a top-lit court. Filling the block between this and Railway Street is *Crossland*'s very large RAMSDEN ESTATE BUILDINGS, 1868–70. As well as the Estate's own offices, it housed shops, a club and lettable office space. Full-blooded Gothic, with much naturalistic carving, machicolations, a traceried parapet and a roof-line diversified by gables and spirelets. The block on the NW corner of Westgate and Railway Street is four-storey classical of 1856, similar to its contemporary neighbours in St George's Square; Nos. 34–42 Westgate must be roughly the same date, but are richer, with Gibbs surrounds to the first-floor windows. For the s side of Westgate, *see* below.

Another pocket of interest lies just N of the station, where FITZ-WILLIAM STREET has two notable warehouses: No. 82, perhaps 1860s, is a three-storey palazzo with round-arched windows under Gothic hoodmoulds; No. 84, *c.* 1873 by *T. W. Helliwell*, is four-storey debased classical, with a short domed tower and a profusion of cast-iron balconies. In parallel BATH STREET, N, is the former Owenite HALL OF SCIENCE, 1839. A plain, classical front of five bays with a pediment.

2. *Within the Ring Road, south of Trinity Street, Westgate and Kirkgate*

The MARKET PLACE was the focus of pre-C19 Huddersfield and makes a good starting point. In the middle, a crudely detailed fluted COLUMN with ball finial, erected 1683 as a market cross. No. 27, s side, is a lavish five-bay palazzo of 1863–4 by *William Cocking* for the West Riding Union Bank. The parapet originally had balustrading and urns. On the w side, Chancery Court leads to CHANCERY LANE, where a late C18 warehouse survives at No. 13: gabled, four storeys, with taking-in doors flanked by pairs of two-light mullioned windows. Sweeping confidently round the corner of Market Place and WESTGATE is LLOYDS BANK, 1912 by *Gibson, Skipwith & Gordon* of London for the West Yorkshire Bank. Classical, with pairs of Ionic columns on the ground floor and carved figures of kneeling maidens above the entrance. Next to this is the remarkable WESTGATE HOUSE, a shop of 1923 by *Stienlet & Maxwell* of Newcastle. Its two elevations are almost completely filled by pairs of shallow three-storey metal-framed oriels and crowned by a hefty cornice. At the corner of Westgate and MARKET STREET, the former Bradford District Bank is by *W. Carby Hall*, 1913. Classical, with mildly Baroque decoration.

Returning to the Market Place, NEW STREET leads s, broad and straight. On the NW corner of Cloth Hall Street is the six-storey HSBC, 1968–72 by *Peter Womersley* for the Midland Bank, the best of Huddersfield's later C20 commercial buildings.* Its concrete frame emerges externally in pairs of projecting beam-ends. Opposite, the early C19 building on the NE corner of King Street was remodelled in 1925 for the National Provincial Bank by their in-house architects *Palmer & Holden*, with an impressive Greek Doric colonnade to the ground floor. Continuing s, the YORKSHIRE BANK at No. 40 is Portland stone classical of *c.* 1927 by *Chorley, Gribbon & Froggitt*: a single, lofty storey,

---

*At the top of Cloth Hall Street stood the Cloth Hall, Huddersfield's most famous and historically most important building. It was built of brick in 1766. In shape it was an oval with an open space in the middle with one cross-range and a second added at right angles in 1864. Pulled down in 1930. Fragments re-erected in Ravensknowle Park; see p. 362.

lit by an arched window. The next cross-streets are HIGH
STREET, W, and RAMSDEN STREET, E. Nos. 4–6 High Street,
1871–2 by *William Cocking*, were built as salerooms for the
auctioneers Eddison & Taylor. Polychrome Gothic, with polished granite shafts to the windows, doors and central cart
entrance. On the NE angle of New Street and Ramsden Street
is the Gothic former PRUDENTIAL INSURANCE, 1899–1901
by *Alfred Waterhouse*: characteristic red brick and terracotta
with a canted, gabled corner, the ground floor mutilated. On
the SE corner of New Street and Ramsden Street is RAMSDEN
HOUSE, an office slab above a podium of shops by the *J.
Seymour Harris Partnership*, mid 1960s. Its bleakness is relieved
by *Harold Blackburn*'s colourful MOSAIC frieze, illustrating the
development of the woollen industry from domestic production to the Industrial Revolution; another mosaic on the Princess Street front, by *Mural Consultants*, shows local vernacular
buildings.

Lower down PRINCESS STREET, opposite the Town Hall, are
the Tudor ST PAUL'S DISTRICT SCHOOL, 1846, and the
former COUNTY PRISON and COURT, domestic-looking
Georgian Survival of 1847 by *Edward Blore*, extended 1858.
Back on New Street, the W side of this stretch is all BUXTON
HOUSE, mid 1960s by *Bernard Engle & Partners*. A residential
tower above shops, pierced by a walkway with an abstract
mosaic by *Richard Fletcher*. The E side between Princess Street
and the ring road is filled by the former CO-OPERATIVE
STORE. The earlier parts, 1886–1904, are Renaissance, with a
short ogee-domed tower and higher clock tower with spire;
after these comes a striking addition of 1936 by *W.A. Johnson
& J.W. Cropper*, with horizontal window bands and stair bays
glazed from top to bottom: Pevsner described it in 1959 as
'modernistic, with Mendelsohn and other motifs'. The way the
ring road cuts off New Street at this point is jaw-droppingly
brutal, severing it from its historic continuations, Chapel Hill
and Manchester Road.

Another area of interest is on the E side of the town centre. Here,
CROSS CHURCH STREET and QUEEN STREET make a long
axis, the views N and S nicely closed by the transept of the
Parish Church (*see* Churches) and the spire of St Paul's (*see*
p. 346). The E side of Queen Street has the former Methodist
chapel of 1819, now a theatre (*see* Public Buildings), and the
former COURT OF REQUESTS, 1825, now a bar: a reticent
classical façade of five bays, recessed from the street, with a
pediment and a thin porch supporting the royal arms. A
handful of houses of similar date with columned doorcases
complete this side. Looming above the W side is the rear of the
J. Seymour Harris Partnership's PIAZZA SHOPPING CENTRE,
early 1970s: loading bay and ventilating tower combine in a
cliff-like mass, faced with stone and bands of dark brick. The
s end of Queen Street is cut off by the ring road – called
QUEENSGATE at this point – where two interesting C19 buildings by *William Wallen* survive opposite the University. The

former RIDING SCHOOL, built 1846–7 for the Huddersfield yeomanry cavalry, is much altered but retains its central arched entrance, flanked by reliefs of galloping horses. The ZETLAND HOTEL, next door and of the same date, has channelled rustication on the ground floor and paired Doric pilasters above. It looks old-fashioned in comparison with Wallen's George Hotel (*see* p. 342) of only two years later.

Finally, in OLDGATE, overlooking the ring road, three blocks of three-storey, balcony-access, former TENEMENT FLATS. Built 1914 by Huddersfield Corporation and apparently designed by the Borough Engineer, *K.F. Campbell*. The flats were for the very poorest: each had two rooms plus an indoor toilet.

3. University of Huddersfield

The University traces its origins to the Young Men's Mental Improvement Society, founded in 1841. This became the Huddersfield Technical School and Mechanics' Institute in 1883, and after further expansion and name changes achieved university status in 1992. It occupies a disparate campus of C19–C21 buildings – some purpose-built, some converted – immediately SE of the town centre between ring road and canal, and spreading latterly along the opposite bank of the canal.

Older buildings are concentrated along the w edge, overlooking Queensgate. ST PAUL'S HALL (for concerts and graduations) is a former Commissioners' church of 1828–31 by *John Oates*. Plain lancet style, but dignified and substantial. Nave and aisles, clerestory and w tower with recessed spire. Polygonal-apsed chancel added in 1883–4 by *John Kirk & Sons*, but it matches the rest. Inside, tall octagonal piers, and between them and the clerestory an odd E.E. blank triforium band. Panelled ceilings, almost flat; rib-vault over chancel. *Hugh Wilson* and *Lewis Womersley* converted the church to its present use, 1979–80, inserting a steeply raked bank of seats into the nave. – STAINED GLASS. Mostly later C19, including non-figurative medieval designs in the apse, and an Annunciation to the Shepherds signed by *S. Evans* of Birmingham in the s aisle; under the new seating and on the tower stairs, back-lit panels with heads of composers, brought from elsewhere. Just s of St Paul's is the JOSEPH PRIESTLEY BUILDING, 1936–40, probably by *W. Jaggar*, the Borough Engineer. Austere, symmetrical, classical in proportions, but without historicist details. Next to this, the RAMSDEN BUILDING by *Edward Hughes*, purpose-built 1881–3 as the Technical School, extended 1896–1900. Symmetrical late Gothic, with two full-height canted bays under steeply pointed roofs. On the first-floor landing, an unusual WAR MEMORIAL: a triptych of large paintings by *John Richardson Gauld*, 1924, entitled War, Death and Victory, with a wooden aedicule below inscribed Peace. The narrative scenes combine classical and medieval elements. On the S side of the Ramsden Building is the SIR PATRICK STEWART BUILDING, originally Milton Congregational Church, 1883–5 by *T.H. & F. Healey* of Bradford. Dec Gothic, with a square NW tower and large former Sunday School buildings behind, all now adapted for teaching performing arts.

Most impressive among C20 additions to the campus is the huge SCHWANN BUILDING by *Hugh Wilson* and *Lewis Womersley*, 1973–7. Buff brick with continuous bands of glazing to each floor. Roughly triangular in plan. The first floor overhangs, but those above step back as they rise, so that from some angles the outline is almost a ziggurat. Ten storeys on the side towards the town centre, but dropping a further three at the back, where the ground falls sharply to the canal. Through a gash in this side, external steps descend from a ground-floor concourse to the towpath, joined part-way down by a footbridge leading to University buildings on the far bank. Looking up from the canal, the cliffs of brick and glass are dramatic indeed, and the ascent from the bridge is like entering a medieval fortress. More recent buildings enclose UNIVERSITY SQUARE, an irregular open space in front of the Schwann Building, insulated from the ring road. They display a restless variety of forms and cladding materials. Most conspicuous is CREATIVE ARTS by *Darnton Elgee*, completed 2008. Curved in plan – concave to the road, convex to the Square – it has an atrium from end to end. A section of the two upper floors projects, supported on big V-shaped struts. A prominent building for Law and Humanities by *AHR*, currently (2016) under construction, will look outward to the ring road at the NE corner of the campus.

Across the canal footbridge is the BUSINESS SCHOOL, remodelled 2009–11 by *Farrell & Clark* around a quadrant courtyard with raked glazing. SW from here, two C19 textile mills have been adapted as teaching accommodation with striking success. CANALSIDE WEST (formerly Firth Street Mills) was converted *c.* 1995 by *Peter Wright & Martyn Phelps*, with minimal external changes. The six-storey fireproof spinning mill of 1865 is at the back of the site, beside the canal, while the octagonal chimney stands isolated on Firth Street, following removal of a linking boiler house (*William Cocking* designed a mill in Firth Street in 1865, which may have been this or neighbouring Larchfield Mills – *see* below); the repeating gables along Firth Street belong to a single-storey weaving shed of 1889. CANALSIDE EAST (formerly Larchfield Mills, 1865–6) was similarly converted by *Allen Tod Architects*, 1997–8, while LOCKSIDE, a northward extension of 2000–1 by *Farrell & Clark*, echoes the form of a demolished weaving shed. On the opposite side of Firth Street, the 3M BUCKLEY INNOVATION CENTRE, 2013 by *AHR*, is constructed partly within the walls of a two-storey C19 mill.

4. South and east of the Ring Road

The area round the River Colne and the canal remains a coherent
landscape of mostly mid-C19 industrial buildings, despite demolition and widespread conversion to new uses. A walk of
c. 1¼ m. along or near the canal takes in many of them. A
good place to begin is ENGINE BRIDGE, where CHAPEL
HILL crosses the Colne. Just w of the bridge, on the s bank,
is what remains of FOLLY HALL MILLS, established 1825 by
builder and entrepreneur Joseph Kaye. *Kaye* rebuilt the principal mill in 1844 after a fire: six storeys and seventeen bays,
with a central pediment enclosing an unconventional five-light
Venetian window, and smaller pediments over the end bays.
Architecturally, it is the most impressive of Huddersfield's C19
mills. It faces across the river to the town centre and was evidently designed to make a show. A smaller WAREHOUSE survives at right angles, plus a square, tapering CHIMNEY.

On the N side of Engine Bridge, COLNE ROAD leads E.
COLNE ROAD MILLS, N side, is mid-C19 with Italianate
details. It wraps around the corner into QUEEN STREET
SOUTH, where FAIRFIELD MILLS, just N of the canal bridge,
is dated 1855. A little higher up are the five gables of Thomas
Broadbent & Son's engineering works, early C20. The enor-
mously long side elevation to Milford Street – dated 1940, but
still stone-built – reflects the firm's expansion due to Second
World War work. On the opposite side of Queen Street South
is Broadbent's remarkable BATHS block of 1954–5 – a building
type more familiar in the context of coal mining. By *Abbey
Hanson* (designing architect *Andrew Buck*), its interlocking
cubic forms recall Dudok and Frank Lloyd Wright.

Returning to the lower end of Queen Street South, PRIEST
ROYD MILLS is on the E side at the junction with Firth Street.
Five storeys, rising to six for the pyramid-roofed corner tower
dated 1869. FIRTH STREET is all C19 mills on the N side. First
comes the Priest Royd Iron Works. A cast-iron entrance arch
– now detached – bears the date 1835, but the two surviving
buildings (converted to residential use) look later and substantially rebuilt. After this, the long front of COMMERCIAL
MILLS bends with the street. The round-arched ground-floor
windows have rusticated voussoirs and are tied together by
lengths of cornice, reading as an arcade. A short tower dated
1864 marks the entrance. Next are the University's Canalside
West and East buildings (*see* p. 347). Around this point the
Narrow Canal joins Sir John Ramsden's Broad Canal, opened
1776, the towpath of which leads NE to ASPLEY BRIDGE. At
the bridge's NW corner is a four-storey WAREHOUSE, described
as 'new' in 1778. Now converted to offices with numerous
additional windows, but the taking-in doors survive, overlooking the canal. NE of the bridge in ASPLEY PLACE is another
canalside warehouse of the same date.

300 yds N along the towpath from Aspley Bridge is a LIFTING
BRIDGE, dated 1865 but heavily restored. It crosses to QUAY

STREET, on the s side of which is seven-storey QUAY STREET MILL, dated 1846. Venetian windows in the gables. On the N side is TURNBRIDGE MILL, with an octagonal chimney dated 1872. The four-and-a-half-storey building adjoining the chimney appears to be of the same date, while the six-storey one behind is probably 1850s. Finally, back on the other side of the canal, Turnbridge Street leads E from the lifting bridge to ST ANDREW'S ROAD, where RAYNER'S MILL is set back on the E side, within the Cummins factory complex. The C19 mill was given an extra floor by *James Cubitt & Partners*, 1997–9. The lightweight metal structure has a curved roof in two sections, split lengthways down the middle, where a vertical glazed strip lets light into the heart of the space.

OUTER HUDDERSFIELD

BIRCHENCLIFFE

ST PHILIP, Halifax Road. By *J. N. Crofts* of Liverpool, 1876–7. Nave and N aisle with cusped lancets, chancel (added 1879–80) with geometric tracery. A short tower with saddleback roof rises from the w bay of the aisle; it has massive diagonal buttresses and was meant to carry a spire. Interior with round piers and open-timber roofs. – PULPIT. Gothic, with unusual arched panels of tiles, painted with foliage to represent the seasons. It was given in memory of Elizabeth Drury, whose son did the painting. – STAINED GLASS. All C20. E window, Christ in Glory with St Philip and St Stephen, 1934 by *James Powell & Sons*. Aisle windows by *Powell's*, 1934, and *E. Pickett & Co.* of Leeds, †1957. W window, Nativity and Christ Blessing the Little Children, 1935 by *Kayll & Reed*.

BIRKBY

ST JOHN, St John's Road. 1851–3 by *William Butterfield*. The E view with a SE tower crowned by a tall spire is impressive and varied. Otherwise the church is not one to show the originality of Butterfield's genius. Style of *c.* 1300. Five-bay nave – very high in proportion to its width – with quatrefoil piers and tiny clerestory openings. Parish room inserted at w end, 1978. Chancel with stalls. – PULPIT. Stone, octagonal. – STAINED GLASS. Chancel, E, Risen Christ with Saints, and N, SS Barnabas and Cecilia with King David, both 1922–3 by *James Powell & Sons*. The three w windows are of 1953 by *Frederick W. Cole* of *William Morris & Co.*, and they form a triptych: Christ in Majesty with saints and angels in the nave, flanked in the s aisle by portraits of Anglican clergy and in the N by local trades – a shepherd and his dog, a chemist with a bottle of dye, etc. – against a background of Huddersfield mills. Just N of the church in Osborne Road, a MEMORIAL by *Michael Disley*, 2010: a stylized tree carved in stone, with incised and gilded branches.

St Cuthbert, Grimscar Avenue. By *Hoare & Wheeler*. Consecrated 1926, when still unfinished. Gothic, with spare, refined details. Nave and chancel under one continuous, shallow-pitched roof, with lower s aisle. The gabled w front – not completed until 1956 – is quite plain apart from a tall, narrow arch enclosing the central door and a three-light window above. The aisle stops one bay short and has a niche in the gable, with a bell. Former HALL, e, 1913, with a hipped roof and big Diocletian window.

Birkby Baptist Church (now Buddhist Centre), Wheathouse Road. By *Garside & Pennington*, opened 1910. Gothic, with a low, battlemented nw tower under a pyramid roof, and overhanging eaves to the sw porch and aisles. Art Nouveau influence is evident in the sloping buttresses and the tracery of the w window. The Minister's House, n, with canted bay windows, makes a pleasing group with the church.

In St John's Road, two notable industrial buildings: the long single-storey Gothic front of the Albany Printing Works, 1888 by *J.G. Walker,* and the grandly Jacobean premises of the grocers Wallace's, 1896–7 by *John Kirk & Sons*. The latter – now derelict (2016) – included warehousing, stabling, a bakery and a jam factory. On the w side of Wheathouse Road is the 1904 office building of J. Hopkinson & Co.'s former engineering works (now flats): huge and mill-like, with pavilion roofs at each end. Off Miln Road is Bay Hall, C16, but heavily restored and divided in three. The middle gable survives from the original house. Its timber frame has closely set diagonal strutting (cf. Almondbury, Fenay Hall etc.). The w part is, externally, the result of restoration in 1895, as recorded in an inscription. Further ne in Wasp Nest Road is the former Hillhouse Board School of 1877, by *Henman & Harrison* of London. Gothic, with half-timbered gables and a clock tower with timber spire. The same architects added a rear wing for girls, 1881–2, which is less Gothic. The much larger, two-storey former Higher Elementary School (now Birkby Junior), s, followed in 1909.

Birkby Hall Road winds w from Wheathouse Road through an area of affluent housing. Birkby Grange, s side, is mid-C18, with unusually extensive outbuildings of the same date, some of three storeys. Further w, at the corner of Birkby Lodge Road, Azo House and Crendon are an asymmetrical semi-detached pair by *Edgar Wood*, 1903. Lower down Birkby Lodge Road is Birkby Lodge itself, mid-C19 with an addition of 1900 by *Wood*. His dining room interior with Arthurian frieze does not survive. (Further w on Birkby Hall Road, Rose Hill has interiors of 1909 by *Wood & J. Henry Sellers*.)

Finally, off Lightridge Road near the M62 is Fixby Hall (Huddersfield Golf Club), mid-late C18, of two storeys, with an e front consisting of a four-bay centre and two flanking canted bay windows. No interiors of special interest. STABLES w of the house. To the N, an ORANGERY (digging of the foundations is documented in 1790–1). Ashlar front with central pediment and seven tall, round-arched openings. The WEST LODGE on Bryan Lane is quite grand: two single-storey pedimented blocks flanking a big arch with heavy attic.

BRADLEY

ST THOMAS, Station Road. In secular use. By *W.H. Crossland*. Dec Gothic. Nave, chancel, s aisle and tower all 1859–63; short broach spire added 1865, N aisle 1879 (by *Mr Taylor*) and sw porch 1891. Earliest of Crossland's many Huddersfield churches, St Thomas's has eccentric details: the rounded pier growing from the sw corner of the w gable, the twin turrets flanking the E gable of the nave, and the wild ironwork of the w doors. Interior converted for its present use by dividing it horizontally just below the tops of the arches, cutting off the w rose window. The unusual N pier of the two-bay nave has a central column and four widely spaced granite shafts, supporting a massive, unmoulded block from which the arches spring. – STAINED GLASS. s aisle, Adoration of the Magi by *Albert O. Hemming*, 1903. Other windows damaged or obscured.

CROSLAND MOOR

ST BARNABAS, Church Avenue. 1900–2 by *C. Hodgson Fowler*. A large and prominently sited church, with nave, aisles and chancel. Dec tracery; clerestory windows square-headed. An intended w tower was not built, and the w front as completed in 1958 suffers accordingly, the steep pitch of the nave roof sitting oddly with the flatter aisles. The E end is more successful.

In Moorside Avenue, NW of the church, CROSLAND LODGE is an early C19 classical house. Its grounds are built over with interwar council housing, but two pyramid-roofed entrance lodges survive on Blackmoorfoot Road. ¾ m. sw along Blackmoorfoot Road, turn r. into Crosland Hill Road for CROSLAND HALL.* A timber-framed house, perhaps early C16, but completely encased in stone in the late C16 or early C17. The hall range lies behind and parallel to the twin-gabled façade, which has mullioned windows of five, six and seven lights (a cross-wing at the w end made a third gable until it was demolished in the early C20). The central door is flanked by two smaller ones, C17 or early C18, suggesting internal subdivision at an early date. The stone-built E wing was raised to two storeys in the late C17 and widened in the mid C18; it has a blocked taking-in door in the gable wall.

---

*This account is based on a report by the Yorkshire Vernacular Buildings Study Group.

EDGERTON

A district of large C19 villas set in wooded grounds on both sides
of the Halifax turnpike, which starts as EDGERTON ROAD and
becomes HALIFAX ROAD further on. EDGERTON HILL (No.
7 Edgerton Road) is the only one earlier than mid century: a
plain classical house of *c*. 1820, with a semicircular bow facing
E. Building activity really got under way in the 1850s, when
the release of land from the Lockwood, Thornhill and (in the
1860s) Fenton estates provided choice sites for speculative
developers and for the wealthy seeking to escape the town.
Construction seems to have peaked in the 1860s, and the
dominant styles are Italianate and Gothic. Local architects
were largely responsible, but outsiders were also employed. As
well as the main road itself, the most important locations are
Queen's Road, Kaffir Road, Bryan Road and Binham Road to
the N, and Hungerford Road and Thornhill Road to the S. Few
houses call for individual attention – it is the overall picture
that impresses, redolent of Victorian prosperity, domesticity
and social segregation – but the following are worth singling
out, roughly S to N. BREMEN HOUSE (No. 16 Edgerton Road),
dated 1868 and possibly by *William Cocking*, is good Italianate
with a tower. It was built for the wine and spirit merchant
Richard Rhodes. LUNNCLOUGH HALL off Kaffir Road is
Gothic of 1855, symmetrically planned around a circular
hall by *Pritchett & Sons* for the dyestuffs manufacturer Read
Holliday; *Willie Cooper* made asymmetrical additions in 1889.
STONELEIGH in Bryan Road is Gothic again, of 1860 for the
cigar manufacturer Edward Beaumont, but much altered
and extended. In a different class is BANNEY ROYD on Halifax
Road, 1900–2 by *Edgar Wood* for the accountant W.H.
Armitage. Largest and most impressive of Edgerton's houses.
Basically Neo-Tudor but with characteristic touches of Art
Nouveau, especially about the porch, with its diagonal buttresses. The interior has fittings of the highest quality, including three remarkable carved stone CHIMNEYPIECES, almost
certainly by *Thomas Stirling Lee*: that in the Hall has a maiden
with a scroll bearing a quotation from Longfellow, 'Each
Man's Chimney is his Golden Milestone'; in the Billiard
Room, a huntsman with hounds and a lady with a falcon; and
in the Dining Room, the Angel of the Rains, an attenuated
winged figure, filling the keystone, accompanied by sheaves of
corn and trees laden with fruit.

96

GREENHEAD PARK and SPRINGWOOD

GLEDHOLT METHODIST CHURCH, 1889–90 by *John Kirk &*
Sons. A more adventurous design than most Methodist chapels,
befitting its site at an important junction opposite the gates of
the new Greenhead Park. Classical, with a balustraded parapet
and a domed tower to one side. Former Sunday School, r.,
dated 1908.

GREENHEAD PARK. Opened 1884. Layout and architecture by
the Borough Surveyor, *R. S. Dugdale*. Among the buildings are
a pretty timber BANDSTAND (described as 'Japanese' in early
accounts) and the LODGE beside the main Trinity Street
GATES; the plain, rectangular CONSERVATORY only came in
1930. From the gates, a broad, straight path leads to a series
of raised terraces with Gothic balustrading. Dugdale intended
a two-storey viewing pavilion for this elevated site, but in
1922–4 Huddersfield's FIRST WORLD WAR MEMORIAL was
built here instead, a sombre and dominating presence, designed
by *Charles Nicholson*. It comprises a hemicycle of unfluted
Greek Doric columns, two deep, enclosing a taller pier with a
cross on top. Near the Trinity Street gates, the SOUTH
AFRICAN WAR MEMORIAL: a soldier leaning on his rifle,
bronze, 1905 by *Benjamin Creswick*.

The fringes of the park were soon developed with high-class
houses – some of the largest are in GREENHEAD ROAD, s.
Here too, in the grounds of Greenhead College, is a STATUE,
Welcome, 1961 by *Peter Peri*. An over-life-size female figure
made of 'pericrete' – a mixture of polyester and concrete – it
originally projected dramatically from high up on an external
wall, but is now free-standing at ground level. At the SE corner
of Greenhead Road and PARK AVENUE is the former ST
PETER'S VICARAGE, 1842 by *J. P. Pritchett*: a square, symmetrical Gothic villa with battlements and loopholes. SE of this, in
WATER STREET, the pedimented front of the former WATER
WORKS of 1828 faces down SPRING STREET, which has comparable Late Georgian terraced houses. Further s along Water
Street are the former premises of MESSRS CONACHER, organ
builders: a warehouse-like building, tall and narrow, rebuilt
after a fire in 1910, with big mullioned-and-transomed windows
to its four-storey gabled façade. s again is SPRING GROVE
SCHOOL, a Board School of 1879–80 by *Edward Hughes*, with
Queen Anne touches.

Finally, GLEDHOLT HALL, Gledholt Road. Two long ranges at
right angles. The s range has a central entrance under a C20
timber porch, with a lintel dated 1720, and sash windows of
various shapes and sizes, plus some with chamfered mullions.
Its regular garden front appears to have been refaced in ashlar
in the late C18 or early C19, with a columned doorcase and a
veranda right across. W wing with a variety of mullioned
windows; N extension probably later C18.

HIGHFIELDS

HOLY TRINITY, Trinity Street. By *Thomas Taylor* of Leeds, built
1816–19, and similar to his Christ Church, Liversedge (q.v.).
A tall, proud building. Nave and lean-to aisles with buttresses
ending in gabled pinnacles, chancel and four-stage W tower.
Windows with intersecting tracery. The interior with slender
octagonal piers and chamfered arches is exceptionally light and
lofty. It appears more so since removal of the N and s galleries

in a reordering of 1994–5 by *Peter Wright & Martyn Phelps*, who created a deep w gallery incorporating meeting rooms. – STAINED GLASS. A rich display. E window, Ascension with Works of Mercy below, 1885 by *A.O. Hemming & Co.*, who also did the easternmost windows in the aisles, 1888 and 1894. In the middle of the s aisle, Annunciation, 1981 by *Harry Harvey*. At the w end of the aisles, two matching windows of 1921 by *J.C.N. Bewsey*, with standing saints in Renaissance niches, putti above and good narrative scenes below: one shows the story of Ruth, the other – a war memorial – has a procession of marching Tommies accompanied by tanks and medieval soldier-saints on horseback. Under the w gallery, Christ Blessing the Little Children, 1897, and Entry into Jerusalem, 1901, both by *Heaton, Butler & Bayne*, the latter including portraits of the donors.

ST PATRICK (R.C.), New North Road. 1832 by *John Child* of Leeds. A simple Gothic box with shallow canted apse. Lancets down the sides. The more elaborate screen front has a higher centre framed by octagonal turrets. Narthex added 1962. Inside, ceiling with plaster rib-vault springing from corbels, and a very prettily ribbed apse, the ribs resting on thin, closely set wall-shafts. – STAINED GLASS. Three lancets in the apse showing the Crucifixion, 1874 by *Hardman & Co*. Nave lancets with single figures of saints, all by *A.O. Hemming*; two – more strongly coloured – are of 1888, the rest 1904. In the narthex, Ecce Homo, a powerful expressionist window by *Roy Lewis*, 1962. Attached Gothic PRESBYTERY.

HIGHFIELD CHAPEL (former), New North Road. By *Perkin & Backhouse* of Leeds, 1843–4. Late classical, quite an original composition. Entrances were originally in the advancing end bays, with giant Ionic columns under heavy attics. Windows unsympathetically altered for conversion to flats.

OLD INFIRMARY, New North Road (opposite the R.C. church). By *John Oates*. Disused. The nobly classical nine-bay nucleus with a Greek Doric four-column portico was erected in 1831. It was an important feature of the entry to the town from the N, but since the advent of the ring road it finds itself in a backwater. Many extensions of various dates. In front, a bronze STATUE of Edward VII, 1912 by *P. Bryant Baker*.

KIRKLEES COLLEGE: HIGHFIELDS CENTRE, New North Road. By *J.P. Pritchett*, 1839. Built as Huddersfield College, a non-denominational boys' school. Square plan, Tudor style, with battlements and square corner turrets. The centre rises higher, with clerestory windows originally lighting a three-storey hall.

CEMETERY, off New North Road. 1853–5. The Gothic buildings are by *Pritchett & Son*, the landscaping by *Joshua Major & Son*. *William Tite* apparently made minor changes to Pritchett's design for the LODGE. It is asymmetrical and unusually large, with a square, battlemented tower, a central archway (now blocked) and tripartite gateways to each side. On axis with it, paired Anglican and Nonconformist CHAPELS are linked by an arch which spans the central path (in fact there are narrow gaps between the arch and the chapels, concealed by buttresses: this was to placate the vicar of Huddersfield, who refused to consecrate a building physically connected to a Nonconformist place of worship). The chapels – derelict (2016) – have porches, pierced parapets, Dec window tracery and crocketed finials; the linking arch supports a spire with openwork lower stage. Paths nearest the chapels are symmetrical, but further away they wander more freely over the sloping site.

Highfields was an area of early–mid-C19 suburban expansion. Streets E of the College have a few short terraces and neat classical villas, including the somewhat grander CLAREMONT in BELMONT STREET. Near to this, Nos. 27–29 ELMWOOD AVENUE are C18, but the brick side elevation with mullioned windows suggests the re-casing of an earlier, timber-framed building. Longer mid-C19 terraces can be found in FITZWILLIAM STREET, WENTWORTH STREET and TRINITY STREET, near Holy Trinity church. VILLAS in a variety of styles spread along NEW NORTH ROAD in the 1850s: an observer in 1858 wrote of 'Grecian temples, Swiss Cottages, Gothic Castles and Italian Villas, all jumbled so closely together as scarcely to allow elbow room'. No. 73 is a *cottage orné* with Gothic bargeboards; Nos. 82–82A are semis with giant Doric pilasters and a shared pediment; Nos. 86–90, in existence by 1852, make up a short Tudor terrace by *John Kirk & Sons*.

LEEDS ROAD

ST ANDREW, Leeds Road. By *W.H. Crossland*, 1869–70. On a fine site above the road, but disused and boarded up (2016). Geometric Gothic. Nave with aisles and clerestory, chancel, S transept and S porch. The porch gable is carved with a figure of Christ in a mandorla surrounded by foliage.

JOHN SMITH'S STADIUM, Stadium Way. By the *Lobb Partnership*, opened 1994; final stand completed 1998. It incorporates conference and hospitality facilities, and was among the first of a new generation of all-seater, commercially orientated stadiums to be built in Britain, following notorious disasters at outdated football grounds in the 1980s. The architects paid great attention to spectator sightlines: each of the four stands is segmental in plan – shallower at the ends – so no seat is more that 150 metres from the furthest corner of the pitch. The arched roofs are suspended from four banana-shaped trusses of tubular steel latticework, springing from four-legged concrete bases at the corners. The buoyant curves of the huge, white-painted trusses and billowing bright blue roofs make a memorable landmark.

In Bradley Mills Road, NE of the Stadium, is what survives of BRADLEY MILLS, a fourteen-bay, five-storey block, early or mid-C19. Further uphill on Bradley Mills Road is DALTON GRANGE, 1871 by *John Kirk*, for the mills' owner, Henry Brooke: big, coarse Gothic, with a four-storey square entrance tower. On Leeds Road, ¾ m. NE of St Andrew's church, TRAFALGAR MILLS, 1896 by *John Kirk & Sons*. The long, two- and three-storey front block with central clock tower was offices; manufacturing took place in the vast single-storey weaving shed behind.

LINDLEY
(including OAKES)

ST STEPHEN, Lidget Street. 1829, by *John Oates*. Lancet style with aisleless nave and heavy w tower. Dec chancel added 1872 by *J.N. Crofts* of Liverpool. Inside, Crofts replaced the original nave ceiling with a hammerbeam roof to match his new chancel. Carefully reordered *c.* 1995 by *Peter Langtry-Langton*, who divided off the w end and brought forward the w gallery front. – STAINED GLASS. E window, the Ascension, 1872 by *Ward & Hughes*. Nave, s side, Elijah, 1887 by *Ward & Hughes* (combined with earlier scenes from bomb-damaged windows) and Christ the Sower, 1931 by *Kayll & Reed*. Nave, N side, Baptism of Christ and Presentation in the Temple, †1880, The Light of the World (after Holman Hunt) etc., 1913 by *C.E. Steel* of Leeds, and Christ Blessing the Little Children, 1902 by *T.F. Curtis, Ward & Hughes*.

METHODIST CHURCH, East Street. By *George Woodhouse* of Bolton, 1867–8. Gothic, with geometric tracery and a short sw tower with pyramid roof. In 1895–6 *Edgar Wood* made it more church-like by removing the side galleries and adding a CHANCEL. It has an arched wooden ceiling with bosses, panelling to the lower walls and a large E window with flowing Dec tracery. – COMMUNION TABLE. A highly individual design by *Wood*, with lively carvings in shallow relief illustrating Faith, Hope and Charity. – CHOIR STALLS, with pierced foliage decoration, presumably also by Wood. – STAINED GLASS. W window, New Testament women, 1893 by *Ward & Hughes*; E window, the Resurrection, 1895 by *Heaton, Butler & Bayne*; N side of nave, the Good Shepherd and St John, early C20; S side, war memorial, 1920 by *Jones & Willis* of Liverpool.

OAKES BAPTIST CHURCH, Oakes Road. 1867–8 by *George Woodhouse*. Italianate, unlike his Methodist church, with substantial porch and elaborately framed ventilator in the pediment.

SALENDINE NOOK BAPTIST CHURCH, Moor Hill Road. Rebuilt 1843. A large, pedimented rectangle, with round-arched first-floor windows and a Venetian window above the entrance. Single-storey classical porch, 1893 by *Ben Stocks*.

In the centre of Lindley, at the corner of Lidget Street and Daisy Lea Lane, is the CLOCK TOWER. By *Edgar Wood*, 1902, and

95

one of his *chefs d'oeuvre*. Tall, with diagonal buttresses, a pagoda roof and details so wilful that connections with Mackintosh and Glasgow must be considered. Sculptural decoration on the theme of Time by *Thomas Stirling Lee* includes a youth sowing and an old man reaping – oddly rustic imagery for an industrial village.

N of the Clock Tower on Lidget Street is NORMAN TERRACE, three houses by *Wood*, dated 1898. E, in OCCUPATION ROAD, is *Wood*'s earliest Huddersfield commission, BRIARCOURT, 1894–5, extended 1904 and 1906. Jacobean style. Dining room with painted frieze by *F.W. Jackson*. ACRE STREET leads SE from the Clock Tower to the HUDDERSFIELD ROYAL INFIRMARY, 1960–6, by *George, Trew & Dunn* with *P.B. Nash*; across the road, early C19 ACRE MILL has recently been converted to hospital use too. PLOVER ROAD goes SW from the Clock Tower to the imposing WELLINGTON MILLS. Two long, four-storey ranges follow the curve of the street, meeting below a mansard-roofed tower with iron cresting; the five-storey block behind is perhaps the original mill of shortly before 1864. Just E of the mills, in SCHOOL STREET, are the extensive buildings of the OAKES BOARD SCHOOL by *Charles Fowler*, 1873, added to by *Ben Stocks*, 1885. Part Tudor, part Gothic, with a pyramid-roofed tower. Now disused. NW of the mills in Low Hills Lane is GATEHOUSE, 1900 by *Wood*, the gate lodge to the Fieldhead estate. Picturesque Free Neo-Tudor composition with a short tower and arched carriage entrance, now surrounded by mid-C20 bungalows.

Huddersfield, Lindley, Briarcourt.
Drawing by Edgar Wood, 1895

LOCKWOOD and RASHCLIFFE

EMMANUEL (former), Woodhead Road. A Commissioners' church of 1828–9 by *R.D. Chantrell*. Lancets down the sides with Dec tracery; W front with octagonal turrets and a bellcote with crocketed pyramid roof. Chancel added by Chantrell, 1848. Now in residential use. (Window by *Morris & Co.* to a design by *Burne-Jones*, Enoch and Elijah, 1878–9.)

ST STEPHEN, St Stephen's Road, Rashcliffe. By *Blackmoor & Mitchell-Withers*, 1863–4. Disused. Dec, cruciform, with sloping buttresses. Tower with broach spire in the angle of chancel and S transept.

BAPTIST CHAPEL, Lockwood Road. Rebuilt in its present form by *John Kirk*, 1850. Classical, three bays, with pediment and first-floor Venetian window.

MOSQUE (former Methodist chapel), Bentley Street. *J.H. Abbey*, 1864. Single-storeyed, classical. Former Sunday School behind with large traceried window, 1884.

The centre of Lockwood is around BRIDGE STREET, which has a decent early C19 shop terrace on the S side. Round the corner in MELTHAM ROAD is the MECHANICS' INSTITUTE, 1865 by *J.H. Abbey*: three bays, the entrance between pairs of Doric columns, with round-arched windows above. The name appears in huge raised letters on the frieze. In SWAN LANE at the corner of North Street is the former TOWN HALL of the Lockwood Local Board (now a shop), 1866 by *William Cocking*: Italianate, with round-arched windows, rusticated ground floor and pediment. The E side of ALBERT STREET has C19 mills bordering the River Holme, including ALBERT MILLS: the Italianate block facing the street is of 1871 by *Mark Beaumont* (the date 1853 above the main entrance records the founding of the business); behind is a block of 1866 by *Leech & Beaumont*, plus the original six-storey fireproof mill overlooking the river. Improbably, Lockwood had a spa before it had mills: just off Albert Street, at the E end of BATH TERRACE, is the once-elegant façade of the LOCKWOOD SPA BATHS, 1827 by *John Oates*. Single-storey, with a pedimented portico and a niche at each end, framed by pilasters. It now fronts a warehouse, and the portico has had one of its Tuscan columns unceremoniously knocked out for a loading bay. It faces the former BATH HOTEL – three-storey ashlar – at No. 188 LOCKWOOD ROAD. Finally, ¼ m. SW of Bridge Street, the LOCKWOOD VIADUCT. Built 1846–9, engineer *John Hawkshaw*. A splendid monument of Victorian railway engineering, notable for the use of irregular squared rubble masonry rather than ashlar. Thirty-two narrow arches carry the line 122 ft (37 metres) above the Holme.

LONGROYD BRIDGE

ST THOMAS, Manchester Road. 1857–9 by *George Gilbert Scott* for the Starkey family, whose mills stood opposite. SW tower with broach spire of a rather tricky outline. Nave with aisles under separate roofs. Geometrical tracery, different in each window. Interior with circular piers. Chancel divided from flanking chapels by double arches with openwork tracery in spandrels. ROOD added by *Charles Nicholson*, 1920. Few original fittings: the church was comprehensively reordered *c.* 1990 to a scheme by the then parish priest, *Richard Giles*. Nave ALTAR and FONT by *Dave Haigh*, composed of rough-hewn stone blocks. Large enclosed parish room filling the W end, with a staggered front that steps forward and back to accommodate the nave arcades. – STAINED GLASS. One window by *Kempe* in the N aisle, 1884, the rest mostly *Clayton & Bell*. – MONU-MENT. W wall, contemporary with the church, commemorating three brothers of the Starkey family. Gothic, with naturalistic foliage and attractive angel corbels.

¼ m. E on Manchester Road is the preserved façade of the GRAND PICTURE THEATRE, 1921 by *Stocks, Sykes & Hickson*. White faience, giant Ionic columns. Opposite this, the very large new KIRKLEES COLLEGE by *Broadway Malyan*, opened 2013. A long, narrow building, end-on to the road. Designed to be seen from the canal, where its nine storeys step back dramatically in three groups of three. Each group is framed by a sort of square proscenium arch, two leaning inwards, one leaning out.

W of the church is the PADDOCK VIADUCT, 1848–9, engineer *John Hawkshaw*. Masonry arches at each end and wrought-iron lattice girders in the middle. It carries the line to Penistone and Sheffield in a curve over the canal, the River Colne and the road to Manchester.

LONGWOOD

ST MARK, St Mark's Road. By *John William Cocking*, 1876–7 (it replaced an C18 building, one Tuscan column of which survives in the burial ground, E). Dec. Five-bay nave with lean-to aisles and clerestory; chancel added 1882. High SW TOWER with diagonal buttresses, by *Oswald White*, commenced 1914. Interior with octagonal columns and open-timber roofs. – ROOD SCREEN. 1926, with pretty tracery. – STAINED GLASS. E window, Nativity and Resurrection, 1899 by *T.F. Curtis, Ward & Hughes*. W window, First World War memorial, by *Charles E. Steel* of Leeds. Other windows mostly first half of C20, by *Jones & Willis*, *A.L. Moore & Son* and *James Powell & Sons*. – MONUMENT. Chancel, S side, classical tablet, †1822, by *Williams* of Huddersfield, presumably from the old church. – SUNDIAL. S aisle, 1749 by *Joseph Miller*, but restored several times, most recently in 1993.

W of the church in Longwood Gate is DOD LEA HOUSE, 1841, but with a wing of 1674 with mullioned-and-transomed windows. ¼ m. S of this, in Grove Street, PARKWOOD MILLS is a mid–late C19 complex of multi-storey mills with a prominent square chimney of 1877. *T.W. Helliwell* designed at least one of the mills, in 1871. The two-storey office block is Gothic. Immediately NW of the mills in Parkwood Road is PARKWOOD METHODIST CHURCH, 1868 by *Joseph Balmford*. A gabled box with round-arched windows and classical doorcase. Further NW in Holmefield Road is HOLMEFIELD HOUSE. Italianate, mid-C19.

LOWERHOUSES

LONGLEY OLD HALL, Longley Lane, was owned by the Ramsdens from the mid C16 to the late C20.* It is a two-storey stone house with mullioned windows, externally of C17 appearance, but with a complex history dating back at least to the C14. By 1500 it had an H-plan, all timber-framed. Much framing survives within the later stone walls, but dates are uncertain. The E cross-wing may be C14 or C15, to judge by an ogee-headed lintel over an opening to the central range; the W cross-wing seems to have been an addition of the later C15, but includes one *ex situ* timber dated by dendrochronology to the 1380s; and the central range was possibly rebuilt in the 1540s, when William Ramsden is known to have obtained timber for repairs. Probably in the first half of the C17, the central range was extended forward to create the present flat S front, which was faced in stone (it is not clear if the whole house was encased at this time). Significant alterations are recorded in the early C19, but the appearance of the exterior today owes much to a restoration of 1884–5, the drawings for which are signed by *A.J. Taylor*: of this date are the four gables with balls on the kneelers. ½ m. N, off Dog Kennel Bank, is LONGLEY NEW HALL. John Ramsden built a house here in 1576–7, which became the family's Huddersfield base in succession to Longley Old Hall. It was last rebuilt by *W.H. Crossland* in 1871–5 and is now a school. Gables, battlements and mullioned windows, including a very large, curved one to the staircase, with glazing set directly into the stone. *Isaac Hordern*, the Ramsden Estate cashier, claimed authorship of the Gothic STABLE BLOCK of 1855. Between the two Halls, on both sides of HALL CROSS ROAD, council housing of *c.* 1930–31 with half-timbered gables.

MILNSBRIDGE

ST LUKE. By *William Wallen*, 1845, in Neo-Norman style. Redundant since 1982. The former VICARAGE, 1845, also probably by *Wallen*.

MILNSBRIDGE HOUSE, Dowker Street. Palladian mansion built *c.* 1750 for William Radcliffe, almost certainly by *James Paine*. In industrial use for many years but now partly restored. Fine

*Access was not possible at the time of writing. This account is based on a survey carried out by the Yorkshire Vernacular Buildings Study Group during renovation work in 1999–2004.

ashlar, much blackened. Nine bays wide, the five-bay centre of three storeys, the wings two storeys. Three-bay returns. The rather heavy composition has features Paine used elsewhere, e.g. full-width modillioned pediments, to both E and W, that interlock with the flanking half-pediments of the wings (cf. Serlby Hall, Nottinghamshire), the splayed base to the pedimented E doorway, and windows set in recessed round-arched panels or with floating cornices. W entrance altered, a garage door inserted beside it. The pediments, with Diocletian window to the W, Rococo cartouche on the E, rise into thin air above the C20 flat roof. Interior mostly gutted.

Surviving woollen MILLS include the four-storey BURDETT MILL, 1838, and taller sixteen-bay UNION MILL, 1861, both beside the canal and tidied up as flats. To the N the prominent COMMERCIAL MILL, 1864, with high stair-tower, has the twenty-arch LONGWOOD RAILWAY VIADUCT, 1845–9, as its backdrop.

MOLDGREEN AND DALTON

CHRIST CHURCH, Church Street. By *W. H. Crossland*, 1862–3. Five-bay nave and aisles under one continuous roof, with no clerestory. Two-light Geometric windows down the sides, and a bellcote at the E end of the S aisle. The CHANCEL was added in 1903–4 by *G. F. Bodley*, with *E. W. Lockwood* supervising the work. Its cliff-like E end rears above the street, taking advantage of the sloping site. Dec E window with two tiers of three lights, the lower tier blind, and three S windows above the flat-roofed vestries. Inside, Crossland's nave has arcades with short, round piers. The altar has been moved to the N side, while Bodley's chancel has, alas, been walled off and horizontally divided. – REREDOS. By *Charles Nicholson*, as late as 1944, but the blank wall below Bodley's E window suggests a reredos was always planned. Now displayed against the infilled chancel arch. Carved and painted wood, with standing figures of Christ etc. under Gothic canopies. – STAINED GLASS. In the upper part of the subdivided chancel, E window (Ascension) and S windows (Three Marys at the Tomb, Crucifixion and Nativity), 1904 etc. by *Burlison & Grylls*: large figures in Flemish Renaissance style, with no architectural framing, untypical of the firm's work for Bodley. S aisle, Crucifixion and Ascension, 1863 by *Evans Bros* of Shrewsbury, and Faith and Hope, 1894 by *Powell Bros* of Leeds. W window, Baptism of Christ and Christ Blessing the Little Children, †1926. N aisle, Light of the World and Good Shepherd, †1911, and Jesus Seeking the Wanderers, 2003 by *Adam Goodyear*.

ENGLISH MARTYRS (R.C.), Teddington Avenue, Dalton. 1969–70, by *John H. Black*. Square plan with flat roof. Walls of artificial stone, copper-clad parapet and full-height glazed strips at the corners. Entrance porch with barrel-vault, parallel to the body of the church. The altar is in a corner of the square, with the centre aisle along the diagonal.

On WAKEFIELD ROAD is Ravensknowle Park. It contains RAVENSKNOWLE HALL – now the Tolson Museum – by *Richard Tress* of London, 1859–62, for the textile designer and manufacturer John Beaumont. Italianate. Centre recessed, with an arcaded first-floor loggia above a columned porch. Large stable block – right beside the house – with top-heavy ogee-domed turret. Between the house and the road, some fragments of the CLOTH HALL of 1766 (*see* p.344), re-erected following its demolition in 1930 to form a pavilion: the cupola with its clock, some brick walls and arched openings, and some Tuscan columns from inside. ¼ m. further E on the opposite side of Wakefield Road are the ROEBUCK MEMORIAL HOMES, 1932 by *Clifford Hickson*. A composition of eight cottages in pairs, linked by loggias and a central pavilion. Classical, with hipped roofs and pedimented doorcases. Clearly inspired by Lutyens's Heathcote, Ilkley (*West Riding North*).

NEWSOME

ST JOHN, Jackroyd Lane. By *W.H. Crossland*, 1871–2. Chancel and nave of the same width, S porch and lean-to N aisle. No tower, but a very large bellcote on the W gable. S windows with cusped heads, Dec tracery in chancel and simple three-light windows to aisle. Single-storey addition at W end. Inside, alternate round and octagonal piers. – STAINED GLASS. E window, Faith, Hope and Charity, contemporary with the church.

NEWSOME MILLS in Ruth Street were established in 1827, according to an inscription over the gate, but the existing four-storey mill seems to be of 1886–7 by *John Kirk & Sons*. TOWER with clock and water tank – a landmark because of its elevated site.* NW of the mills, RIDGE STREET has curving terraces of timber-clad houses on both sides, 2006 by *Cartwright Pickard* for Yorkshire Housing. Their monopitch roofs make a sawtooth pattern and incorporate solar heating panels. RIDGE COURT, S, is part of the same development: a three-storey block of flats making a hollow circle, with an opening on one side. Steel access balconies on the outer face, and more timber cladding.

PADDOCK

ALL SAINTS (former), Church Street. 1828 by *John Oates*. Lancet style, with thin W tower and thin S porch. Chancel of 1879 by *John Kirk & Sons*, now in residential use. The nave is a roofless shell.

MOSQUE (former Methodist chapel), Church Street. 1872 by *Robert Boyle* of Manchester. Italianate. Gabled front with large, three-light window.

PADDOCK SCHOOL, Heaton Road. Board School of 1882–4, by *Henman & Harrison* of London. Two separate buildings, for

---

*Newsome Mills were largely destroyed by fire in 2016, but the tower survives.

Infants and Mixed departments. Mullioned-and-transomed windows.

QUARMBY

QUARMBY HALL, Quarmby Fold. C16, gabled, with mullioned-and-transomed windows of six and seven lights. On the SW front is a carving of a hart trippant, the badge of John Blythe, Lord of the Manor of Quarmby 1574–87.

SHEEPRIDGE

CHRIST CHURCH, Woodhouse Hill. 1823–4 by *Thomas Taylor*. Chancel 1901 (but presumably a chancel existed in 1824, when the church was described as 'cross-shaped'). Lancet style, with flat, shallow buttresses; W tower with broach spire. Thin S porch. Transepts; no aisles. Inside, flat ceilings with sloping sides and timber braces. The braces rest on pairs of slender wall-shafts, which end above the pews. Good early C20 wood-work: PULPIT, STALLS, ORGAN CASE and ALTAR RAILS. – SCREEN. A First World War Memorial with delicate Gothic tracery. – STAINED GLASS. Mostly by *James Powell & Sons*, including a fine E window, Christ in Glory with Angels, Saints etc., 1902, and others in the chancel, transepts and nave, 1902–24. N side of nave, Christ's Commission to the Apostles, by *Kayll & Reed*, †1872 (but probably early C20). W end, Temptation of Christ, 1965 by *Francis Skeat*, the figures set against large areas of clear glass. – MONUMENTS. Many tablets, including Thomas Starkey †1870, with marble organ pipes and music book, by *R. Garner*. Outside the porch, a MONUMENT to the factory reformer Richard Oastler, also by *Garner*, 1862. Only the inscribed base survives; it originally supported a Gothic superstructure rising to 14 ft (4.3 metres).

NEW HOUSE HALL, ½ m. NE of Christ Church, off Newhouse Road.* A stone manor house, described as recently built in the will of Thomas Brook I, 1553. The W (solar) wing appears to have been added or rebuilt in the early C17 by Thomas Brook IV, with eight-light mullioned-and-transomed windows on the ground and first floors, and a three-light window in the gable. The central hall range, probably rebuilt in the later C17, has six-light windows on both floors, and a high parapet with ball finials. The E wing is a rebuilding of 1865 and 1903. Inside, entrance hall with decorated plaster ceiling, the staircase opening off it, with twisted balusters of two strands and a more elaborate ceiling. All this is probably late C17. (A chimneypiece on the ground floor of the solar wing has the initials of Thomas Brook IV and his wife Margaret, †1615, while another in the room above has those of Thomas and his second wife, Dorothy, †1634.)

---

*New House Hall was severely damaged by fire in April 2017.

HUDDLESTON HALL
1¼ m. W of Sherburn-in-Elmet

An exceptionally perfect-looking manor house probably of the early C17: the property then belonged to the Hungate family, and some of the details are similar to those at Robert Hungate's School and Hospital at Sherburn-in-Elmet (q.v.), which was built *c.* 1619. Magnesian limestone* with chimneystacks of brick. H-plan, symmetrical, with mullioned-and-transomed windows of carefully graduated sizes – of five lights to the hall, the great chamber above it, and, on the W flank, to the main staircase; of three in the cross-wing ends, others of two. Also three-light mullioned windows in the wing gables and the further gable over the great chamber. Tudor-arched doorway l. of the hall window: another to the r. is an insertion of *c.* 1912, replacing a two-light mullioned-and-transomed window which lit the hall high end (cf. Woodsome Hall, Fenay Bridge). E flank less regular, with mullioned windows and massive projecting kitchen chimney-breast: another at the back, to the hall, originally flanked by two more of the two-light windows. (Interior largely devoid of features.) Behind the house two single-storey C17 service ranges at right angles to each other, that to the E greatly extended in C19; and W of these a C15 former CHAPEL built by the Langton family, now a barn, much altered but retaining its Perp three-light (ritual) E window and a segment-headed doorway. Behind again more farm buildings, C19 and C20. In the front garden wall late C17 gatepiers with ball finials.

HUNSHELF

HUNSHELF HALL. Mostly rebuilt 1746. Severely handsome three-bay front. Hipped roof. Long-and-short quoins, raised window surrounds. Doorway has bracketed cornice linked to window above by ashlar apron. Gateway to l. with segmental pediment, dated.

UNDERBANK HALL, Underbank Lane. Early C18 remodelling of a house with projecting W cross-wing. Symmetrical front to three parallel gabled ranges, 2:3:2 bays. The middle range, set back slightly, has good moulded doorway on r. Coat of arms above, beside (earlier?) intricately carved initialled panel. Sashes in plain raised surrounds. Pretty inlaid overmantel dated 1594, C18 oak panelling and two bolection-moulded fireplaces.

WORTLEY TOP FORGE, on the River Don, off Cote Lane. One of only three water-powered hammer forges surviving in the

---

*Quarries at Huddleston provided the stone for e.g. the earlier parts of King's College Chapel, Cambridge.

UK. Recorded as a finery in 1658, it was extensively remodelled in 1713 (datestone) as a heavy iron forge and further altered later. Rectangular, stone, with 'jack' roof. E wall has openings to pits for water wheels powering hammers. To l., set back, a two-bay arcade on cast-iron columns. W wall has four-bay arcade opening to continuous outshut, with attached housing for wheel driving the furnace bellows.

DEER PADDOCK, NW of the Forge. A rare survival, existing in 1746. Walls *c.* 6 ft (1.8 metres) high enclose about an acre.

KELLINGTON

ST EDMUND stands alone on a somewhat bleak knoll ¼ m. SW of the village. From the mid C12 it belonged to the Knights Templars (cf. Temple Hirst); after their suppression in 1312 it passed to the Knights Hospitallers. Excavations in 1990–1 associated with underpinning of the building against mining subsidence revealed a small late Saxon timber predecessor, as well as evidence for the development of the present church, which was originally of *c.* 1100 with shorter nave and chancel. The visible beginnings, however, are documented by one blocked Norman window in the nave S wall (interior) and a drawing of 1839 showing the former plain round chancel arch. By *c.* 1200 the nave had been lengthened, apparently absorbing a mid-C12 W tower (cf. Brodsworth), and a new, larger W tower had been built – see the nave S doorway with a round arch and decayed roll moulding but moulded capitals. The tower (two stages) was rebuilt in the early C13; its varied buttresses, all later, indicate continuing instability. Triple-chamfered tower arch on triple-chamfered responds, its hoodmould with a little dogtooth decoration. Probably at the same time the church was remodelled, the chancel being lengthened and a narrow N aisle added: see the nave's two S lancet windows and the three in the chancel, also the fine E.E. arcade. Five bays, with alternate round and octagonal piers with moulded capitals and bases, semi-octagonal responds, double-chamfered arches with hoodmoulds.

In the C14 the aisle was widened and a small N chapel added, its broad arch to the chancel springing from low octagonal responds. The chapel was extended in a late C15 rebuilding with a narrower second arch, three-light E window, and separate roof with coped parapet. Straight-headed N windows with cusped arched lights; similar windows to rebuilt N aisle. Below the chapel's E bay the excavations revealed a subterranean room, perhaps a sacristy, with a wall hearth (now in the tower). Also Perp the upper part of the tower, the clerestory with coped parapet, and the S porch. Low, broad, with coped gable and embattled sides, this has a stone roof on four single-chamfered transverse arches. Nave roof low-pitched with some original carved bosses to the (open) framework of ceiling beams; lead dated 1504 was found on the roof during extensive restoration in 1867–9 by *W. H. Crossland*. He rebuilt the N aisle and the chancel S and E walls, and inserted the E window with Dec tracery and chancel arch on clustered shafts with carving by *Farmer & Brindley*. – FONT. Plain, low, octagonal bowl dated 1663. – SCULPTURE. Serpent Stone (floor, N aisle). A very worn slab of 6 by 3 ft (1.8 by 0.9 metres), probably a coffin-lid, with a cross flanked by a winged serpent-like monster (l.) and a figure (a priest?) with a dog at its feet (r.). Probably C13. – MONUMENTS. Superb mid-C14 GRAVE-SLAB in pristine condition, discovered in 1990. Carved in relief with a sword beside a cross fleury on a trefoiled-arched base. – John Wallas †1819, by *C. Fisher* of York. Small corniced tablet with paterae.

KILNHURST *see* SWINTON

3090

KIMBERWORTH*

ST THOMAS. Lancet style by *Matthew Habershon*, 1841–3, as a four-bay nave with tall buttresses and (ritual) E altar recess. W bay and thin tower of 1860, the chancel, organ chamber and vestries of 1881–2 by *E. Isle Hubbard*. Interior enhanced by *Stock, Page & Stock*, 1892–3, including the tripartite roof with cusped rafters to side bays. W gallery reinstated, with narthex below, by *Robert Gordon*, 1992–4. – STAINED GLASS. W (gallery) window by *Christopher Webb*, 1935.

ST JOHN, Kimberworth Park, ⅝ m. N. By *J. Mansell Jenkinson*, 1957–8. Church and hall on the diocese's standard L-shaped plan. Detached (ritual) NW campanile.

CEMETERY, ¼ m. ESE. By *Blackmoor & Mitchell-Withers*, 1870–1, after a competition. Two small Dec chapels, their apsidal ends opposed.

MANOR HOUSE, ⅛ m. ENE. Dated 1694, the numerals on ashlar blocks above waterspouts each side of the three steep gables. Three storeys. Large quoins. Mullioned windows, still horizontal, and of two lights with flat frames. They are arranged symmetrically: five on the first floor, the middle one just one light. Flat lintel bands. Similar r. return of four bays under two gables. The gables all have small, blind, not-quite-circular windows with moulded surrounds. All this suits the date of the house. (Staircase with splat balusters.)†

CASTLE. Encircled by the suburban gardens of The Motte and Wilding Way, ¼ m. NE, a MOTTE, carved out of the end of the natural ridge. (HW)

---

*KIMBERWORTH HALL, C17, was demolished in the 1970s.

†Remains of a small C13 CHAPEL have disappeared.

Almondbury, Castle Hill (p. 92)
Whitgift, the River Ouse, and lighthouse, *c.* 1920 (p. 748)

3. Luddenden, Oats Royd Mill, 1847–87, with Stoodley Pike Obelisk, by James Green, 1856, on the horizon (pp. 395 and 680)
4. Drax, Power Station, from the SW, by W. S. Atkins & Partners, 1967–74 and 1985–6 (p. 233)

Pontefract, Market Place, with Butter Cross, 1734, and St Giles, with
w tower by Thomas Atkinson, 1790–1 (pp. 430, 436 and 437)
Halifax, Commercial Street, with the Halifax Building Society HQ,
by Building Design Partnership, 1968–74 (pp. 280 and 282)

7. Ledsham, All Saints, s doorway of w porch (now tower), *c.* 700, restored 1871 (p. 381)
8. Thorpe Salvin, St Peter, font, C12 (p. 662)
9. Conisbrough, St Peter, coped tombstone, *c.* 1140–60 (p. 179)

7 | 8
7 | 9

10. Campsall, St Mary Magdalene, w tower *c.* 1170–80 (p. 156)
11. Sherburn-in-Elmet, All Saints, nave interior, late Norman (p. 627)

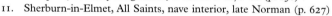

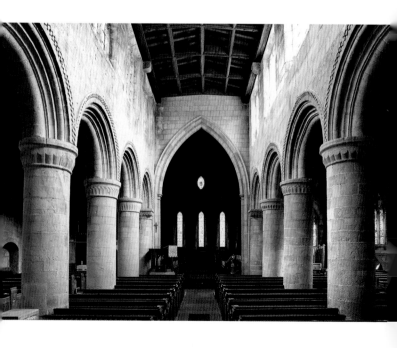

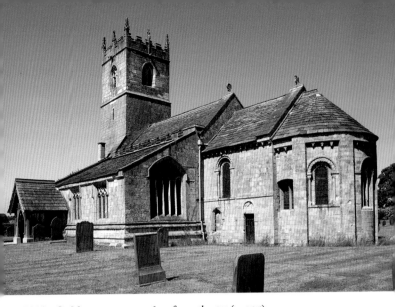

2. Birkin, St Mary, *c.* 1130s–1160s, from the SE (p. 125)
3. Rossington, St Michael, chancel arch, Norman (p. 451)

14. Selby, The Abbey, nave south side, C12 and C13 (p. 481)

5. Selby, The Abbey, nave north side, C12 and C13 (p. 481)

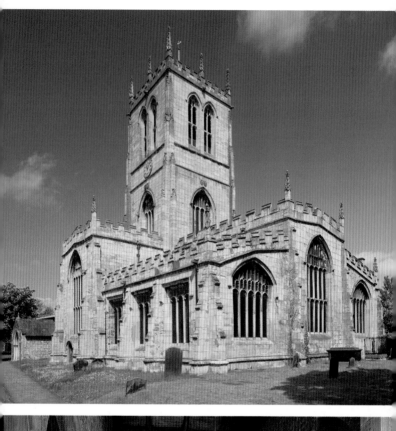

1. Shibden Hall, S front, c. 1490, W tower and E end with loggia, by John Harper, c. 1835 (p. 629)
2. Gunthwaite Hall, barn, interior, mid-C16 (p. 266)
3. Sheffield, Norton Woodseats, Bishops' House, c. 1500, with W cross-wing c. 1550 (p. 617)
4. Thorpe Salvin, Old Hall, probably 1570s, S front (p. 663)

39. Ledston Hall, E front, begun 1629, completed *c.* 1660s, from NE
    (p. 386)
40. Shibden, Scout Hall, 1680 (p. 630)

1. Stanley, Clarke Hall, parlour, 1680 (p. 650)
2. Bishopthorpe Palace, Great Hall, ceiling, 1662 (p. 131)

43. Thornhill, St Michael and All Angels, monument to Sir George Savile
    †1622, by Maximilian Colt, 1628, and effigy of knight (Sir John
    Thornhill †1322) (pp. 658–9)
44. Thurlstone, Bullhouse Chapel, interior, 1692 (p. 668)
45. Wentworth, Old Holy Trinity, painted glass, by Henry Gyles, 1685–95
    (p. 726)

50. Wentworth Woodhouse, w front, *c.* 1724–34 (p. 729)
51. Wentworth Woodhouse, E front, by Ralph Tunnicliffe and Henry Flitcroft, *c.* 1731–50 (p. 730)

2. Wentworth Woodhouse, Whistlejacket Room, with plasterwork by Joseph Rose, 1750s–60s (p. 733)
3. Wentworth Woodhouse, Marble Saloon, scagliola columns and pilasters by Charles Clerici, ceiling by Joseph Rose, 1750s (p. 731)

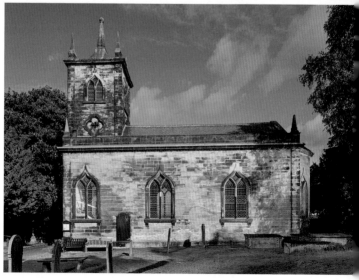

65. Wragby,
    St Michael
    and Our La[dy],
    monument
    to John Win[n],
    †1817, by
    Chantrey,
    1823 (p. 762)

66. Sheffield,
    St Mary,
    by Joseph &
    Robert Pott[er],
    1826–30,
    from the NW
    (p. 566)

IN THE VAULT BENEATH ARE INTERRED THE BODY OF
JOHN WINN, OF NOSTELL PRIORY, ESQUIRE,
WHO DEPARTED THIS LIFE AT ROME THE 17th DAY OF NOVEMBER A.D. 1817,
IN THE 2 4th YEAR OF HIS AGE.
THIS MONUMENT WAS ERECTED BY CHARLES AND LOUISA WINN,
AS A TRIBUTE OF RESPECT TO THE MEMORY OF
A BELOVED AND AFFECTIONATE BROTHER.
A.D. 1828.

7. Honley, St Mary, by R.D. Chantrell, 1842–3, interior (p. 330)
8. Cleckheaton, Providence Congregational Church (former), by Lockwood & Mawson, 1857–9 (p. 174)

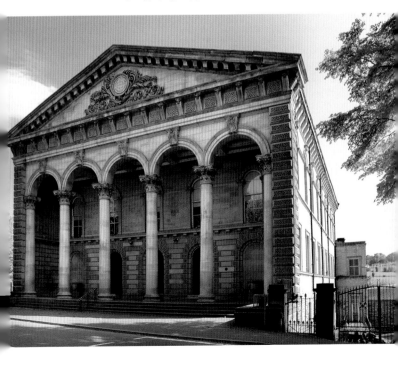

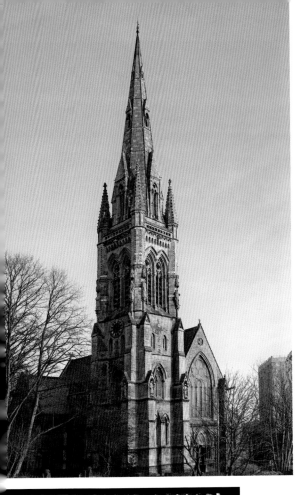

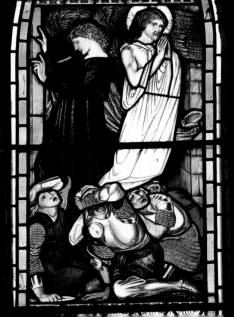

72	74
73	75

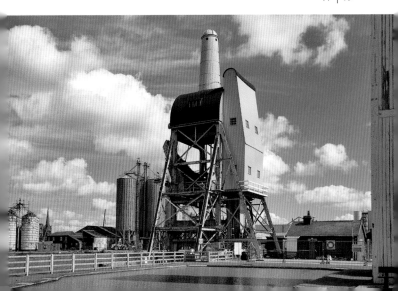

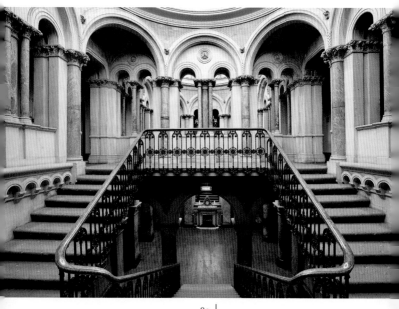

83. Halifax, Town Hall, by Sir Charles Barry and E.M. Barry, 1859–63, from the NW (p. 274)
84. Dewsbury, Town Hall, by Holtom & Fox, 1886–9 (p. 202)

5. Todmorden, Town Hall, by John Gibson, 1870–5 (p. 677)
6. Sheffield, Town Hall, by E.W. Mountford, 1890–7 (p. 512)

91. Wentworth, Holy Trinity, by J. L. Pearson, 1872–7, interior (p. 725)

2. Barnsley, St Peter the Apostle and St John the Baptist, by Temple Moore, chancel 1892–3, nave 1910–11, interior (p. 110)

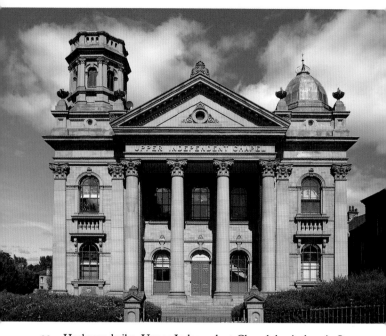

93. Heckmondwike, Upper Independent Chapel, by Arthur A. Stott, 1888–90 (p. 317)
94. Blackshaw Head, Wesleyan chapel, interior, 1899 (p. 132)

97. Barnsley, Barnsley Main Colliery, headgear and engine house, *c.* 197c
     (p. 116)

8. Sheffield, River Don Works, Brightside Lane, offices, by Holmes & Watson, 1906 (p. 558)

9. Adwick-le-Street, Woodlands model village, by Percy Houfton, 1907–*c.* 1910 (p. 88)

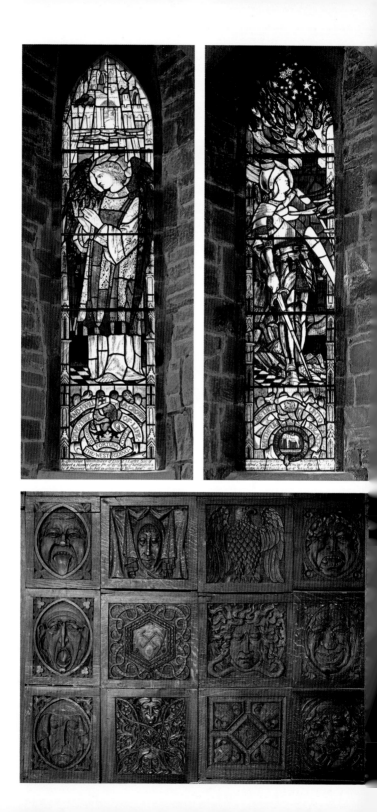

109. Sheffield, University
of Sheffield, Library
1955–9, and Arts
Tower, 1961–5, by
Gollins, Melvin, Wa
& Partners (p. 522)
110. Sheffield, Park Hill,
by J.L. Womersley,
Jack Lynn and Ivor
Smith, 1957–61;
before alterations
began in 2009
(p. 563)
111. Halifax, Swimming
Pool, by F.H. Hoyle
interior, tile mural
by K. Barden, 1964
(p. 277)
112. Sheffield, view
from Hemsworth
of Rollestone with
Holy Cross Church
by Braddock &
Martin-Smith,
1964–5 (pp. 610
and 611)

| 109 | 111 |
| 110 | 112 |

117. Penistone, Market Hall, by WCEC Architects, 2010–11, interior
(p. 427)
118. Wakefield, The Hepworth Wakefield Gallery, by David Chipperfield
Architects, 2007–11 (p. 717)

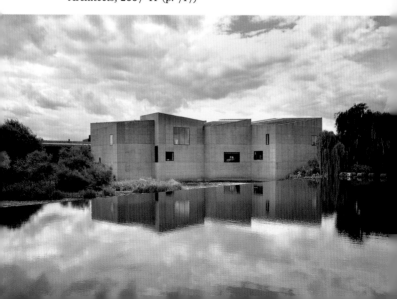

KIRK BRAMWITH

6010

Tiny village in the eastern lowlands, embraced by major water-ways. The River Don and the Stainforth & Keadby Canal are side by side to the s, the New Junction Canal runs arrow-like to the NE.

ST MARY. Small, in attractive wooded churchyard. Nave and lower chancel, narrow w tower. Norman s doorway close to the w end. Two orders of colonnettes. Many-scalloped capitals. Arches with outer order of beakhead, inner order of chevron. Wide chancel arch Norman too. Outer order with chevron; scalloped capitals. Hoodmould with lozenges. Roll mouldings to inner order and soffit, the responds paired demi-shafts with scrolled capitals. Tower *c.* 1300. Chancel s doorway early C14 (continuous quadrant moulding). Adjacent window has two lights with shouldered lintels; that may indicate the early C14 too. Perp tower top and E window. Flat nave ceiling with heraldic panels by *G. G. Pace* 1963–70. – FONT. An adapted medieval(?) cross base, unearthed in the churchyard in the 1940s. – The C15 octagonal FONT is outside, near the s door. – OAK FITTINGS with rustic finish (and twenty-six mice) by *Robert Thompson*, 1936–1940s. – STAINED GLASS. Five windows with coats of arms of various sovereigns and others connected with the Duchy of Lancaster, patron of the living. By *Reginald Bell*, 1936, and *Arthur Lucas*, 1942–5.

SWING BRIDGE. 300 yds s, crossing the Stainforth & Keadby Canal to South Bramwith. Early C19 ashlar abutment walls and C20 bridge platform. It allowed sailing keels to pass without lowering their masts.

AQUEDUCT, ⅜ m. SW, taking the New Junction Canal across the Don. The Canal, opened 1905, was the last commercial canal to be built in Britain and was especially used for transporting coal. Completely straight, it links the Don Navigation to the Aire and Calder Navigation 5½ m. NE. The aqueduct is unusual in being set at river level. Guillotine gates each end prevent floodwater from the Don reaching surrounding land.

BRAMWITH HALL, ¼ m. ESE at South Bramwith. Large stuccoed house said to have been rebuilt after a fire of 1838, but the pedimented doorway looks early C18, perhaps from the Countess of Sutherland's time (*see* Barnby Dun). Gothic GAZEBO *c.* 1800. Small square battlemented tower with first-floor balcony.

KIRKBURTON

1010

ALL HALLOWS. In a commanding position on a little spur above the former textile-manufacturing village. Essentially a church of about 1200. Good E.E. doorway re-set in slender Perp w

tower. It has a continuous filleted angle roll between very large
dogtooth motifs, like four-petalled flowers, up the jambs and
round the head of the doorway. Well-moulded arch with nailhead, on two slim shafts. Six-bay nave with lancet windows
along the s aisle and inside octagonal piers (except for one on
the N side which is round) with capitals typical of *c*. 1200. One
has crockets close to the core, others have separate stylized
leaves growing upward. Chancel arch with semicircular
responds with two shaft-rings. N aisle rebuilt in 1825, the
clerestory by *E.H. Shellard*, 1849–50. Long chancel with an E
window of three stepped lancets, carefully rebuilt with original
stonework by *W. S. Barber* in 1871. Tiny ambulatory restored
by *C. Hodgson Fowler*, 1907–8 with two rescued E.E. doorways
in stone screen. Large piscina, and in the chancel N wall a small
square opening, possibly originally into the cell of a hermit
recorded here in 1293. Good panelled nave ceiling with foliate
bosses, the beams dated to the 1520s by dendrochronology.
– BENCHES. A rare Elizabethan and Jacobean group, some
with plain oblong ends, others with knobs on the ends and
carved decoration. On one the date 1584 appears, others dated
1633 by dendrochronology. – REREDOS. *c.* 1920s. Painted
gessoed panel with the Nativity, designed by *Charles Nicholson*.
– Tulip FONT has elaborate COVER by *Nicholson* 1931. – Fine
oak war memorial TOWER SCREEN, 1920, carved by *Bowman
& Sons*. – SCULPTURE. Pieces of an incomplete CIO–CII
Anglo-Saxon CROSS, reconstructed with new stone. In the
head and down half the shaft the slender figure of Christ Cru-
cified. Interlace decoration below. – STAINED GLASS. E window
by *G.E.R. Smith* for the *A.K. Nicholson Studios*, 1938. s aisle
first from E by *Christopher Whall*, 1920. w window 1871, and N
aisle first from E 1908, by *Clayton & Bell*. – Three very fine
marble MONUMENTS by *John Fisher* to William Horsfall †1780,
his wife Elizabeth †1793 and their daughter Dorothy Bill
†1792, with urns and obelisks and exquisite ornament.

   WAR MEMORIAL, 50 yds N. By *W. D. Caröe, c.* 1920s. Slender
stone column with Calvary.

SPRINGFIELD MILLS, ½ m. NW. Former woollen/worsted mill
group, the oldest building *c.* 1820, the larger main building,
1834, at right angles to E. Both four-storeyed, with central
pediments and attic clerestories. Springfield House to the N
(now KIRKBURTON HALL) is a plain Regency villa built by
the mill-owner. Ashlar. Porch to three-bay front has fluted
columns with Tower of the Winds capitals.

STORTHES HALL, 1 m. WNW. Rebuilt by *William Lindley*
1787–90, for William Horsfall. Ashlar. Seven bays, two-and-a-
half storeys. Three-bay pediment. Porch with Doric columns
and segmental pediment. In the former grounds the derelict
gabled administration building with clock tower of the
STORTHES HALL ASYLUM, 1902–17 by *J. Vickers Edwards*,
West Riding County Architect. The rest demolished after 1991,
and part of the site redeveloped *c.* 2000 for Huddersfield University's STUDENT VILLAGE.

100–1

KIRKBY WHARFE

Church and a few scattered houses on the E approach to Grimston Park (q.v.).

ST JOHN. Heavily restored 1860 by *George Shaw* for the 1st Lord Londesborough, who had bought the Grimston estate in 1850. His are e.g. the aisle walls, in rock-faced Dec, the E window, the roofs and presumably the rebuilt Perp-style upper stage of the W tower. But there is much of antiquarian interest nevertheless, starting with the late C12 S doorway, round-headed with a double chamfer and a single order of colonnettes with waterleaf capitals. Also of the late C12 are the nave arcades, of three bays with cylindrical piers, very simply moulded capitals and pointed arches which are completely unmoulded (cf. Bardsey, *West Riding North*); but the SW respond still has a more traditionally Norman character. The tower and chancel arches have responds, with a single chamfer, which look to be Norman but pointed heads of different profiles, the former's double-chamfered – and perhaps coeval with the C13 lancets in the lower stage of the tower – the latter's triple-chamfered and probably later again: on the chancel S side are two Y-traceried windows, i.e. of *c.* 1300. Between them a straight-headed Perp window, and Perp also the N chapel, with similar windows, battlemented parapet and two-bay arcade to the chancel.

FONT (old). Plain cylinder, Norman. – SCREEN to the N chapel. C19, with a dado of bas-relief panels, probably C16, said to have come from North Milford Hall (*see* below), including the arms of the Leedes family, owners of the house, and depictions of various domestic scenes. – SCULPTURE. Roman sepulchral plaque, marble, with inscription and bas-relief figures. Found in a pigsty nearby. – Pieces of four Anglo-Saxon crosses, principally a shaft and part of a head with St Mary and St John l. and r. of a cross. Probably late C9. – Small Renaissance marble relief of the Adoration of the Magi, on the S wall of the N chapel above the arcade. Said to have been bought in Rome by Lord Londesborough. – STAINED GLASS. In two of the chancel windows C15–C17 glass collected by Lord Londesborough. In the S middle six panels of a C15 Austrian Life of Christ, installed in 1865 by *J. W. Knowles.* They have been linked to a workshop which glazed the nave of the Magdalenekirche at Judenburg in Styria *c.* 1420. In the SW an assortment, mainly C16–C17 Flemish and Swiss, the subjects biblical, but also a fox preaching, English C15. – N aisle middle, C14 armorials. – E window and N chapel E by *Capronnier*, 1860 and 1865, quite depressingly feeble. – MONUMENTS. Brass of a priest in canonicals, probably William Gisborne, Prebendary of Ulleskelf 1479–92. – Brian Leedes †1564. Small brass, an inscription and coat of arms. – Thomas Leedes †1602. Small stone tablet with incised kneeling figures of Leedes, in armour, and his wife and daughter.

w of the churchyard a curious SUNDIAL, a faceted ball on a short
shaft and domed base, perhaps C17, and a picturesque mid-C19
entrance lodge to the park.

NORTH MILFORD HALL, 1 m. S. Brick box of three-by-three
bays, probably late C17 but extensively Georgianized, with two
storeys of sash windows, complementary doorcase and a low-
pitched hipped roof. But the basement windows are stone-
mullioned; and those above, which were presumably of
cross-type originally, stand in shallow projections. They have
moulded stone sills, and there is a matching stone band at
first-floor level.

KIRKHEATON

ST JOHN. Of the medieval church only the w tower and the N
chancel chapel survive. The rest is a rebuilding of 1887–8 by
J.W. Cocking, following a fire in 1886 that destroyed the nave
of 1823 and the chancel. Perp tower with battlements and small
pinnacles; Henry Beaumont of Lascelles Hall bequeathed
money for a 'bell-tower' in 1468. The Beaumonts' chapel,
added in the mid C14, has one arch to the chancel; its short
and square octagonal w pier also supports the arch to the N
aisle and the E end of the nave N arcade. Opposite the arch a
window with flowing tracery, immediately E of that arch a
piscina. Is the long further part of the chapel, which has a
straight-headed E window with cinquefoiled arched lights, an
extension? The C19 work is low and spreading: three-bay nave
with clerestory; on the S, porch, narrow lean-to aisle with
straight-headed windows, transeptal organ chamber and vestry;
two-bay chancel; N aisle, like a second nave, overlaps the tower
and has pointed windows with Perp tracery. – Two FONTS. One
large, octagonal, with minimum panel decoration, thought to
be late C11 or early C12. The other (in porch) also octagonal,
finely carved marble, 1893. – LECTERNS. Fine Arts and Crafts
piece in brass with repoussé panels, almost identical to that by
Nelson Dawson, 1908, at Tickhill (q.v.). In the chapel – carved
wood, with doubly bulbous stem, C18.
   STAINED GLASS. Chapel E window has old fragments
including two with Edward IV's *rose-en-soleil* badge. – E window
and five others by *Samuel Evans*, 1888–1902. – S aisle westernmost by *A.O. Hemming*, 1888. – Tower window by *Lavers,
Barraud & Westlake*, 1888. – N aisle westernmost by *Comper*,
1908. – Chapel S window by *Powell & Sons*, 1900. – MONU-
MENTS. Very long coffin-lid with a shield and a sword, probably
C13 (in tower). – Beaumont Chapel. Sir Richard Beaumont
†1631, attributed to *Edward Marshall* (formerly thought to be
by Nicholas Stone). Recumbent armour-clad effigy on a panelled tomb-chest under a big round arch on Corinthian

columns. Black and other marbles with painted and gilded carving. Elaborately framed inscription within the arch; on the entablatures of the columns two small standing female figures. – Incomplete brass to Adam Beaumont †1655. Shown in armour, with wife and children; 14-in. (35-cm.) figures. – Richard Beaumont †1692, attributed to *John Nost* (GF). Two busts and an urn between, against a curtain background. Inscribed plinth with gadrooned top, cherubs and garlands; winged skull below. – Richard Beaumont †1704, first husband of Katherine née Stringer, later 6th Countess of Westmorland; erected in 1731 under her will (cf. Kirkthorpe). Sumptuous composition in white and grey marbles with bust by *Guelfi* under cloth baldacchino against an obelisk. Plinth with big scrolls and flanking urns with flaming tops, set on a fluted sarcophagus with lion's feet. – Charlotte McCumming †1813 and daughter Sarah †1815 by *Samuel & Thomas Franceys*. Aided by an angel, mother and child rise dramatically out of a broken sarcophagus, the inscription on it split apart. – John Beaumont †1820 and wife Sarah †1807. Plain tablet by *C. Fisher*. – Charles Beaumont †1814 and wife Martha †1827 by *Richard James Wyatt*. Grieving female kneeling before plinth carrying Neoclassical sarcophagus.

LASCELLES HALL, ⅓ m. SSE. A seat of the Beaumonts from the C15, rebuilt *c*.1800 by the Walkers, woollen manufacturers. Five-bay house with pedimented centre bay to plain ashlar front; matching two-bay extension to l. Distyle *in antis* porch with Doric columns and segmental pediment.

WHITLEY BEAUMONT, the principal mansion of the Beaumonts, stood 2 m. ESE. Demolished in 1953–5, the park, 1779–83 by *Capability Brown*, was then destroyed by opencast mining. Solitary BELVEDERE off Liley Lane, no doubt by *Paine*, probably contemporary with his redecoration of the mansion's Great Hall *c*.1752–4. Square, with recessed angles, originally domed.

KIRKLEES PARK

A wooded estate on the N side of the Calder valley. It belonged to a small Cistercian priory until the Dissolution and in 1565 was acquired by the Armytage family of Farnley Tyas who built the hall. KIRKLEES PRIORY was founded about 1155. It is situated in a sheltered little valley beside the Nun's Brook and must always have been a small house. At the Dissolution it had seven nuns, and annual revenue of £29. Of the medieval buildings only the gatehouse and the orchard wall survive. Excavations in 1863–4 and 1903–5 showed that the stone church was only 80 ft (24.4 metres) long and 21 ft (6.4 metres) wide. It consisted of a nave and a chancel of the same width, without aisles or transept. On its s side the cloister was a square of 40 ft (12.2 metres) with E.E. arcades. Living quarters were equally modest. The GATEHOUSE is partly early C16, with post-Reformation, i.e. Elizabethan or Jacobean, alterations and additions. It sits separately to the w, close to the farm. It is a sizeable building – it would in fact have filled the cloister had it been put there. The earliest part has a heavily timber-framed upper storey, with w gable over a four-light oriel window. Decorative detail includes a foliate scroll and hounds hunting hares on the tie-beam. The lower storey was probably open, forming the gateway, infilled later with large stone blocks. Additions in similar ashlar with mullioned windows. Former ORCHARD WALLS have gabled tops with Gothic roll-moulded coping.

w of the priory site is HOME FARM. The impressive C15 timber-framed barn with aisles belonged to the priory. Attached s is a large two-and-a-half-storey stable range with mullioned windows and hoodmoulds. Beside a label stop is a datestone 1620, not *in situ*. Other barns, cowhouse etc. are substantial stone buildings with quoins, coped gables with kneelers, and big stone lintels. Some originally timber-framed, encased in stone in the C17. Also a dovecote, now reduced from three to two storeys. Further w the large L-shaped malthouse. Late C17. Three storeys plus attic, with mullioned windows.

KIRKLEES HALL is about ¼ m. ENE. The complex history of its growth has not yet been unravelled. It is not even certain whether a house existed before the Armytages came. Parts of a probably Elizabethan house survive as s wings of the main (N) range, which is Jacobean. In 1753–4 Sir John Armytage employed *John Watson* to make survey drawings 'for *Mr Paine*'s perusal' and a payment to *Nathaniel Exley* for plastering is recorded in 1757, but details are lacking. George Armytage, succeeding his brother unexpectedly in 1758, initiated a series of significant alterations and additions completed *c.* 1788. He used a succession of architects, making payments to *Carr* (1759–60), *Joseph Jagger* (1773) and *William Lindley* (1777). Further alterations were made 1806–8 by *Charles Watson* and around 1900. The Armytages sold the house in the 1980s and it has been converted to separate residences.

The N front was built or remodelled in the early C17 (there is a reused sundial dated 1617). It is E-shaped, but the wings are no bigger than the porch. The three projections have three identical enriched parapets. The windows were all sashed *c.* 1776–80. Behind, the two older wings project considerably. The SW wing has on its E elevation a blocked doorway, and two large mullioned windows with two transoms. A large chimney rises above the steeply gabled s end. The more irregular three-storey SE wing contains a staircase tower in the former inner angle. The tower's lower stages are obscured by *Carr*'s two-storey entrance hall linking the wings, but its pretty top has two-light windows and an octagonal pyramid roof/little octagonal spire. This one would rather connect with the

Elizabethan than with the Jacobean house. This wing's E front includes a tall square projecting bay, like a porch, with hood-moulds over its sashes, perhaps an earlier entrance.

Running w from the Jacobean range is a ten-bay service wing built in the 1780s and heightened to three storeys with gables in 1903. It forms the N side of an attractive informal service courtyard enclosed to the w by a single-storey range and then two-storey Elizabethan or Jacobean STABLES that return on the s. They have mullions with ovolo mouldings and a coped E gable with finials and a little cupola.

The INTERIOR is as puzzling as the exterior. The porch of the N front led into a screens passage. The screen was walled up when the house was Georgianized and the Hall became the dining room, but revealed c. 1900. It has geometric inlay panels, richly decorated colonnettes and, standing above these against the balustrade of the arcaded upper gallery (which is blocked), armoured statuettes. The Hall filled the whole E part of the range including the NE arm of the letter E. Opposite, in the NW arm, there is also only one room. This was redecorated c. 1775–80 and may originally have been subdivided. Above the Hall the Music Room or drawing room is probably *Lindley*'s 'new room' of 1777. Good plaster ceiling and original music bookcase. Payments were made to *John* and *Ely Crabtree* for plasterwork 1779–88, and to *Bertram* (probably *Matthew Bertram*) for carving 'in the great room' in 1781. Good Adamesque chimneypieces in the dining room and a bedroom.

Behind the Hall *Carr*'s entrance hall of 1759–60 contains his impressively precarious flying staircase. It rises from a Doric colonnade with two flights meeting above the s front door and returning with a single upper flight (cf. his later, more daring, staircase at Arthington Hall (*West Riding North*)). *Maurice Tobin* was paid £249.15s. for reinforcing ironwork and the wrought-iron balustrade. (In the SW wing the former kitchen has a large Tudor-arched fireplace.)

The landscaping of the grounds was undertaken after c. 1760 to designs by *Richard Woods*. In the GARDEN was an ornamental pond crossed by an IRON BRIDGE by *Tobin*, of 1769 (i.e. ten years earlier than the bridge at Coalbrookdale). The gateway w of the hall has wrought-iron gates by *Tobin* of similar date. Incorporated within the park ⅜ m. SSE of the Hall, is CASTLE HILL, an earthwork enclosure defended by a bank and ditch. Plausibly prehistoric, but its excavator in 1904–5, Sir George Armytage, believed that it was Roman, and in honour of that he built the WATCHTOWER (based on those on Trajan's Column, in Rome) which survives in a ruinous state – an early example of such a reconstruction.

About 150 yds SSE in Nun Bank Wood is ROBIN HOOD'S GRAVE. According to legend the outlaw died at Kirklees in 1247 but the monument is an C18 stone and railed enclosure with Jacobean-style fluted columns with finials and a fragment of medieval grave-slab.

6000

KIRK SANDALL

A C20 deserted village, its church left poignantly alone beside a
bleak stretch of the River Don. From the 1960s, as factories to
the S crept closer, houses, school and farms were demolished.
Now the industrial tide has turned and C21 housing approaches
from the SE.

St Oswald (Churches Conservation Trust). Redundant from
1979. With its un-church-like tower and steep Victorian tiled
roofs the church does not at first strike one as a building of
venerable age and considerable antiquarian interest. Closer
acquaintance reveals a Norman nave and chancel of limestone
rubble and river cobbles. Probably earlier C12, but still Saxo-
Norman overlap with a little herringbone work in the W gable
and modest side-alternate quoins. Aisles were added in the
later C12. The S aisle has small Norman E and W windows. S
doorway with one order of colonnettes carrying moulded capitals; arch with two slight chamfers. Two-bay arcades have
semicircular responds and octagonal middle piers. Square
abaci, unmoulded round arches. W window of *c.* 1310, with
intersected tracery. Chancel windows C15. The low late medieval tower sprouts ridiculously from the S aisle's W bay, behind
the porch. Formerly two-stage: the battlemented and pinnacled belfry stage, rebuilt 1828, was replaced by the pyramidal
roof in 1935–7 by *Walker & Thompson*. – Plain round Norman
FONT. – STAINED GLASS. By *Powell & Sons*, 1935–58. For the
chapel glass, *see* below.

　　The *pièce de résistance* is the large, very tall, and finely detailed
N CHAPEL, referred to as 'new' in the will of William Rokeby,
Chancellor of Ireland and Archbishop of Dublin, a native of
Kirk Sandall and its rector before becoming Vicar of Halifax.
He died in 1521.* His MONUMENT is a finely carved marble
tomb-chest with canopied top with straight cresting. Tomb-
panels with cusped quatrefoils; canopy frieze of quatrefoils in
circles. Good moulded arches to chancel and aisle. Two large
late Perp windows of four lights under low four-centred arches.
27　　The STAINED GLASS, superb work of *c.* 1521 comparable with
Fairford (Gloucestershire), includes four large figures but
restored and rearranged in one window, 1981. Damaged image
niches l. and r. of similar five-light E window, now blocked
with the splendid but dominating monument of Sir Thomas
Rokeby †1699 by *William Stanton*. White, grey and black
marbles. Large oval inscription framed by big, lusciously
decorated brackets supporting open segmental pediment with
skulls, drapery and urn. Also a marble tablet for William
Rokeby †1662, with swan-neck pediment, heraldic achievement and skull and crossed bones.– Splendid C16 roof, not

---

*His will also ordained another chapel to be built in the Minster at Halifax (q.v.)
with a tomb for his heart and bowels.

originally made for the space, with large moulded and decorated beams and ribs and carved bosses. – CHAPEL SCREENS
(restored; original S screen now under chancel arch). C16.
Exquisitely carved. Dado with two lights in each panel, ogee-
headed and with dainty blank tracery above. One-light upper
divisions with little canopies projecting triangularly in front of
delicate four-light tracery. Vine trail in the cornice and lively
cresting. Traceried doors.

At LONG SANDALL, 1 m. SSW, in Clay Lane West close to the
canal, are two pairs of brick semi-detached gabled COTTAGES
by *John Butterfield*, 1867, for Doncaster Corporation. A very
early example of public housing.

PILKINGTON'S MODEL VILLAGE, ½ m. E. Uncompleted estate
for workers at Pilkington's glass factory (dem.), by *T.H.
Johnson*, 1920s. Neo-Georgian-style houses arranged in pairs
and fours around spacious squares and along broad straight
avenues.*

KIRK SMEATON   *5010*

Small village above the little valley of the River Went.

ST PETER. Of Norman origin, its appearance of antiquity compromised by external refacing in *J.B. & W. Atkinson*'s heavy-
handed restoration, 1862–3. Earlier evidence survives inside,
especially the late C12 chancel arch, a good piece, though
altered. Three shafts to each respond, the angle shafts smaller.
The capitals are still entirely Norman in style. The central and
SW ones have bands of interlace and leaves, the NW one beaded
bands and small angle volutes; the imposts have interlace and
scrolls. At the time of writing the details are lost under white-
wash. On the E side scalloped capitals and plain imposts. Three
roll mouldings in the arch, the large one decorated with
chevron on both sides. Yet the arch is tall and steeply pointed.
The unconvincing quality of the chevron compared with that
of the fine capitals makes it likely that it was heightened in the
C13. The tower arch is also pointed but its big plain responds
are Norman. The tower's lower stage probably Norman too;
its upper stage is Perp. The two W bays of the N arcade are
C13, with a quatrefoil pier and responds and arches of two
quadrant mouldings. Dec window with flowing tracery in the
nave, another in the N aisle (reused); Dec S doorway with two
continuous quadrant mouldings. The *Atkinsons* widened and
extended the aisle, inserting a third nave arch and including
the remodelled N chapel under a separate roof. – SEDILIA.

*The Kirk Sandall Hotel (dem.), by *T.H. Johnson*, 1934, was clad in the company's
pink and black Vitrolite, while its interior had glass walls, floors and ceilings, as well
as table tops, counters, mirrors etc., all in a wide range of colours.

Created 1862–3 with a large Dec piece from the chapel; three cusped ogee gables, pinnacles and much bossy foliage. – Norman FONT. Cylindrical, with an arcade of intersecting arches. – STAINED GLASS. E window by *Clayton & Bell*, 1895.

STUBBS HALL, Walden Stubbs, 1¾ m. E. Handsome L-plan C17 house of limestone but encasing an earlier timber frame. Main range has off-centre door with moulded surround, massive lintel and hoodmould. Armorial panel above with the arms of Francis Percy (*c.* 1554–*c.* 1634), a recusant who inherited his mother's estate, and his wife, Frances Vavasour. Mullioned windows but in the l. bay blocked windows with segmental brick heads, similar to the sashed staircase window on the l. return. One-bay r. wing has two five-light windows with wide hoodmoulds, three-light attic window above. Inside, a late C17 stair balustrade with luscious foliage scrolls and putti.

3020

KIRKTHORPE

ST PETER. C14 W tower. The rest Perp, extensively rebuilt by *Perkin & Backhouse*, 1850–1. The nave with N aisle was extended from three to four bays and the chancel with N chapel moved E but the survival internally of the arch of a Norman S door perhaps indicates a mercifully conservative touch. Spacious interior with open arcades. Nave piers of a characteristic but rare form, quatrefoil, but with the hollows between treated so as to give the whole pier a wavy outline. Abaci with fleurons. Three-bay chapel arcade has the more normal pier section of four shafts and four diagonal hollows. – FONT. Plain, octagonal, cup-shaped, 1718. – STAINED GLASS. N chapel E and chancel second from E by *Wailes*, *c.* 1851. N chapel N. Two by *H. W. Bryans*, 1896 and 1921. – MONUMENTS. A superb collection. – Thomas Stringer †1681 and Katherine †1707, erected in 1732 by the 6th Earl of Westmorland to his wife's parents under her will (cf. Kirkheaton). *Guelfi* was contracted for it in 1731. Two separate busts on a black sarcophagus with straight tapering sides and long inscription. Splendid architectural background by *Kent*, its frame starting from two big volutes and crowned by a broken pediment with coat of arms and grieving putti. – Sir Charles Dalston †1724 and infant daughter Anne. Aedicule with Corinthian columns and broken segmental pediment. – N chapel. Several to the Smyths of Heath Hall. – John Smyth †1731. Attributed to *Rysbrack* (GF). Two lively putti uncovering his draped portrait on an oval medallion. – Three monuments of the same design by *Flaxman*, 1799, all signed: Lady Georgiana Smyth †1799, two infants, and her husband †1811. John Smyth †1771 and his wife, Bridget, †1800. Sarah Caroline Smyth †1811 and her husband, John, †1822. Each a perfectly plain tablet with a band of Greek key and an attic above. A painted shield and some ornamental enrichment on this. – N aisle. Rev. John Leake †1741. Slender pyramid on elaborate base. – W wall. Dorothy Armitage †1683. Richly ornamented frame. – John Burton †1743. Frame with volutes and gadrooned top.

FRIESTON'S HOSPITAL, 80 yds SW. Now a house. Founded 1595 for seven poor men. An unusual conceit, its plan and form ingenious. Square, stone, with a rectangular top-lit communal hall surrounded on three sides by an 'aisle', divided into cells by timber-framed walls. The cells, slightly varied in size, each have a door under a massive stone lintel, and a two-light mullioned window. Only the hall was heated, by a large Tudor-arched fireplace at the N end, beside an entrance. Another doorway on the S side, off-centre. The cells are lower than the hall and covered by a pyramid roof, truncated over the hall by a lantern storey with mullioned-and-transomed windows, the front one under a gable, the others under dormers.

KNOTTINGLEY   5020

The town, on the S bank of the Aire at its highest naturally navigable point, was the West Riding's inland port until the Navigation opened up to Leeds in 1700. Pontefract Castle had a large three-storey warehouse here in the C16. The river route to Goole was superseded in 1826 by the canal, which cuts through the town. The old settlement along the river quay, E of the church and Town Hall, was mostly cleared in the 1960s. A few substantial houses survive, e.g. one with a good Georgian doorcase in Chapel Street and several in Ropewalk. The new focus, such as it is, is divorced from the river and lies further W at Hill Top, where BRIDGE HOUSE is perhaps early C18, with quoins and window surrounds that have odd triangular projections in the centre of each side.*

ST BOTOLPH, Chapel Street. A medieval chapel of ease to Pontefract, rebuilt as a plain classical preaching box c. 1755; in the W wall, and visible inside, is a window, probably later C12. Thin W tower, of limestone, added 1873 and heightened, with corner pinnacles, in 1887 by *Demaine & Brierley*. Chancel Gothicized and extended by one bay by *George Malcolm*, 1886. The whole interior is pleasing. Nave restored in 1887, the DADO PANELLING created from the box pews and the chancel arch also slightly heightened and narrowed at this time. – ALTAR. English altar with tall gold-winged angels on black and gold riddel-posts. – PULPIT and FONT. Both octagonal, in Caen stone (painted), on short marble columns, 1887. The pulpit

---

*Noted by Pevsner but since demolished: the White Swan Inn, in the E wing of the C17 Manor House, and The Hall, whose idiosyncratic mid-C19 mix of Jacobean and Georgian was 'a truly crazy performance'.

has alabaster figures of the Evangelists in hooded ogee
niches. – MONUMENTS. Chancel N wall, William Savile †1691.
Pedimented stone tablet (painted) with skull-and-crossbones
in each corner. Finely inscribed brass plaque in marble frame
recording Elizabeth Brown's gifts 1809–21. Nave S wall, Ann
Banks †1781. Large, of white marble, with obelisk and a stout
infant weeping over an urn. Another, similar, to Lydia Banks
†1792. – STAINED GLASS. E window by *Capronnier*, 1887, a
luridly coloured Crucifixion, in Pevsner's opinion 'doubly
hideous for a date when the art of glass staining had already
been so fully and widely improved'. Four nave windows by
Jones & Willis, c. 1887–1920. War memorial window by *Kayll
& Reed*, c. 1920.

WAR MEMORIAL, Chapel Street. 1921 by *G.H. Fairbairn*, with a
winged Peace in swirling gown holding a trumpet and a wreath
aloft.

KELLINGLEY COLLIERY, 1½ m. E. The last deep coal mine in
Britain, closed in 2015 (cf. Hatfield). Sunk 1959–65 by the
National Coal Board. Two Koepe WINDER TOWERS supported
by four-legged steel lattice frames. Flat-roofed brick surface
buildings.

LANGSETT

Just within the Peak District National Park.

WAGGON AND HORSES INN, on the former Wadsley turnpike
(A616). 1828 for William Payne, Lord of the Manor (cf. Midhopestones). Gabled front with Venetian window in attic.
The breathtaking RESERVOIR was formed in 1888–1904 by
damming the Porter (or Little Don) to supply Sheffield. With
a castellated VALVE TOWER (*William Watts*, engineer) and
LODGE for the water-keeper, with crowstepped gables and a
turret.

LAUGHTON-EN-LE-MORTHEN

Pleasant hilltop village, of considerable importance before the
Conquest. Edwin, Earl of Mercia, had his 'aula' or hall here.

ALL SAINTS. The church possesses one of the finest towers in
the West Riding, and one designed with considerable originality and ingenuity. It has angle buttresses, but they turn
diagonal halfway up the bell-stage (two two-light bell-openings
with Y-tracery on each side). On the same level the tower itself

changes from its square into an octagonal shape. Crowning battlements, behind which the recessed, thinly crocketed spire soars to 185 ft (56.4 metres). The diagonal buttresses rise above the battlements and at the base of their pinnacles connect with the spire by flying buttresses. Moreover, where these flyers touch the spire, another set of delicate shafts starts, ending again with pinnacles and again linked to the spire by diminutive flying buttresses. It results in an odd broken outline, which is, however, not without piquancy. Inside the tower has a vault with tiercerons – that is, star shapes. Perp arches to E, N, and S. Local tradition says the church was rebuilt in 1377, having been 'despoiled' in the 1322 uprising, and credits William of Wykeham with the steeple's design. Although Laughton was, from 1363, one of the numerous prebends held by that prelate, there is no certainty that the church enjoyed his architectural patronage. Its later C14 designer was, nevertheless, no ordinary village mason.

Evidence of the status of the pre-Conquest church survives at the W end of the N aisle in remains of a *porticus* with a blocked doorway 10 ft 2 in. (3.1 metres) high and some 3 ft 5 in. (1.05 metres) wide. It was recognized as Anglo-Saxon by Rickman, who drew it in 1835. Unmistakable features are the pilaster-strips accompanying the jambs at a distance, the blocks instead of capitals and abaci and the outer arched hoodmould strip (cf. Ledsham). The doorway's voussoirs are rebated. N and W walls of reddish sandstone, typical Mercian long-and-short quoins indicating the l. return (cf. Bolton-upon-Dearne). The church is not mentioned in Domesday, and its plan is uncertain. The quantity of sandstone reused (internally) in two major rebuildings in limestone indicates that it was substantial. In the first, in the later C12, the N doorway had a smaller one let into it. Norman also the chancel, with some sandstone used externally. One round-headed N window, shortened, and inside, to its W, a fragment of the head of another; indications of one S window and of a group of three in the E wall. Also the E jamb of the priest's doorway, part of its opening later incorporated in an odd arched recess inside. Some work was done in the earlier C14, for the nave S doorway is Dec. The church is otherwise largely the result of the later C14 remodelling. The Perp mason must have enjoyed figure-work for his aisle windows have hoodmoulds, and they rest on heads and figures which are, especially on the N side, given unusual prominence. In the first window (which overlaps the chancel) are an angel and a devil munching a human, then a queen and king, then a knight and a green man, and lastly a dragon and a lion.

Fine spacious interior without a chancel arch. Perp S arcade of three bays, the N of four, its uncharacteristically tall circular piers late Norman of *c.* 1190. Their capitals differ in design. One has simple leaf corners, one is still multi-scalloped, one is plain moulded. Abaci re-cut with rosettes and masks.

Evidence of a second N window suggests that the Norman chancel originally extended slightly further W (see also the strip buttresses which would have marked the middles of the N and S walls), its arch being removed when the nave was rebuilt. The S arcade has the usual elements. The N arcade was remodelled and extended with another E bay, probably reusing one old S pier and heightening all three with the other. A curious anomaly is the E respond with strong tripled shafts with fillets. This must be of the early C14. Renewed N arches match those on the S, the handiwork of Laughton's mason displayed again in the angels at the springers towards both nave and aisles. The tower is embraced by the aisles and the distinctive red sandstone walling inside the W bay on the S may indicate the existence of a second *porticus* here, rebuilt at a different time from the rest of the aisle. *G. G. Scott* restored the church in 1853, replacing the nave and chancel roof. Removal of plaster and re-pewing by *Milnes & France*, 1894–6. – SEDILIA. In round-arched recess. – FONT. Perp, octagonal, the bowl boldly embattled. Panels with cusped trefoils, circles with a wheel of three mouchettes, of four mouchettes and of other tracery motifs. – Dado of a stone ROOD SCREEN, also embattled. Fragment of a stone parclose of the same design re-set against the chancel S wall. – MONUMENTS. Blank panel between two kneeling figures on corbels, probably Ralph Hatfield and wife Margaret, both †1626. – Mary Beckwith †1702. Elaborate cartouche with cherubs and winged skull.

CASTLE. Immediately W of the church, commanding a wide view, a well-preserved MOTTE, with a bailey to the NE. (HW)

The SCHOOL, NE of the church, was built *c.* 1610. Two storeys, with mullioned windows of two to five lights. Single-storey classroom extension of same height, in keeping, 1845, by *Weightman & Hadfield.*

OLD HALL FARM, 200 yds ESE. Long C17 range of two builds, with well-carved mullioned windows, some transomed. Dripstones. N end has room with 1633 datestone. GATEWAY. 1742. Piers with blocked rustication, elaborately tooled. Cornice and vase finial. Motto and crest of the Hatfields of Laughton Hall (dem.). Samuel Buck's sketch, *c.* 1720, shows its SE front, with central pediment, giant pilasters and cross-windows, attached to C17 ranges.

SLADE HOOTON HALL, ¾ m. NNE. 1698. Fine classically designed house, one of the earliest in the area (cf. Darley Cliffe Hall, Worsbrough). Two storeys, with side dormers in the hipped roof. Five by four bays. Quoin strips at the angles, first-floor band. Excellent decorative central bay, the doorway and window with eared architraves flanked by finely rusticated strips, and a segmental pediment with carving in the tympanum. Eaves cornice carved with acanthus. Sashes in raised surrounds, some jambs with evidence of transoms. Buck's sketch *c.* 1720 shows cross-windows except in the central bay; two survive at the rear. STABLE BLOCK, 1702, has gables with giant volutes as kneelers.

LEAD

St Mary. Alone in a field, chapel of a medieval manorial complex of which otherwise only earthworks remain. Just the nave survives, 31 ft (9.5 metres) long internally; but excavation has revealed evidence of the chancel, a further 21 ft (6.5 metres) long, which is referred to in a will of 1421. The structure probably dates from the early C14: see the four windows, each of two cusped ogee-headed lights, the N and S straight-headed, the E and W arched with a pointed quatrefoil in the head. But the present E wall was built, and the E window re-set in it, when the chancel was abandoned. Round-arched S doorway, diagonal buttresses to the W, angle buttresses to the E, crude W bellcote doubtless later. Roof 1934, with brought-in old timbers. – ALTAR. 1931–2, incorporating a medieval *mensa* and part of a medieval grave-slab. – Simple boxy three-decker PULPIT in the NE corner, probably *c.* 1700, altered 1931–2. – Plain rustic PEWS, perhaps late medieval. – FONT. Round bowl tapering to a square base, possibly Norman but certainly pre-C14, so evidence of an earlier chapel. – Four panels of painted TEXTS expressing pious sentiments, probably late C18. – Four C13 GRAVE-SLABS of members of the Tyas family, who held the manor at that time, with shields and marginal inscriptions, and another with a floriated cross.

LEDSHAM

A small village with a number of buildings associated with the owners of nearby Ledston Hall (q.v.).

All Saints. A Saxon church essentially, which has been dated to *c.* 700 on the basis of both its plan and some of its details. It consisted of a nave, a two-storey W porch (cf. Monkwear-mouth, Co. Durham), a chancel, a S *porticus* (represented by the present S porch) and very probably a corresponding N *porticus* also. The W porch was raised into a tower in two phases, the first probably C11 – pre- or post-Conquest – the second C12, the chancel replaced in the C13, and any visible evidence of a N *porticus* lost when a Perp N aisle was built. Extensive restoration 1871 by *Henry Curzon*.

Coursed sandstone, with big side-alternate quoins, some of them re-set. The W porch-cum-tower has two small S windows, one above the other, of the type with arched heads cut from a single stone (again cf. Monkwearmouth etc.), and a very curious S doorway, the jambs and arch unmoulded but the imposts and an outer frame of stripwork decorated with interlace and vine scrolls. In its present form this decoration belongs entirely to the 1871 restoration and it is unclear to what extent, if at all, it replicates anything that existed previously; but a

7

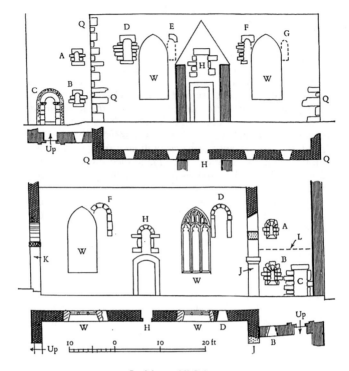

Ledsham, All Saints.
Measured drawing by H.M. and Joan Taylor, 1965

Upper diagram: exterior elevation of the south wall of the church, and a section through the side walls of the church.

Lower diagram: section through the centre of the church, looking southward so as to see the interior face of the south wall.

A	Original upper window of porch
B	Original lower window of porch
C	Original south doorway of porch, round-headed externally and square-headed internally
D	Surviving original window of nave
E, F	Partially surviving original windows
G	Window conjectured by analogy with windows in north wall
H	Partially surviving tall doorway, square-headed on south and round-headed on north
J	Norman tower-arch
K	Original chancel-arch
L	Conjectural original level of first floor in west porch, at same depth below window A as is ground floor below window B
Q	Surviving megalithic quoins of nave
W	Later windows of Perpendicular design

visitor in 1862 noted the existence of a stripwork frame and of 'some rude sculpture...on the jambs'. Also of 1871 the small Neo-Norman w window. The C12 top stage is in contrasting pale limestone ashlar, with two-light belfry openings (cf. Aberford, Bramham, *West Riding North*). Perp parapet with battlements and pinnacles, and Perp recessed spire. On the nave s wall two more of the Saxon windows, but blocked, together with one jamb of a C13 lancet and two three-light Perp windows providing the present fenestration. Between these the s porch, remodelled from the *porticus* probably in the C13. Outer doorway 1871, inner probably C17, straight-headed with a keystone, but above it another blocked Saxon opening which was presumably a doorway into an upper floor in the *porticus*. The two blocked windows are also visible inside, and in the N wall above the aisle arcade are the remains of four more. So perhaps there were four on the s side also. The tower arch is Norman, doubtless replacing a Saxon doorway, but above it is a Saxon window which would have lit the upper room of the w porch: within the tower the porch roof-line can be seen on the E wall. Saxon chancel arch, unmoulded, but with square imposts which are continued l. and r. as a string course and are decorated with a floral motif – again largely renewed in 1871, but with enough of the original surviving to testify to the accuracy of the restoration: the motif has parallels in C7–C8 work in France and Spain. To the l. a shouldered squint, C19. Chancel extensively rebuilt by *Curzon* – the lancets on the s side are his – the E window *c.* 1899. Perp nave arcade of three bays, chancel arcade of two: octagonal piers, double-chamfered arches, some capitals renewed. Chapel E window Perp; aisle N windows, straight-headed with uncusped arched lights, probably C16; others, and all the roofs, *Curzon*'s.

FONT (former). Cylindrical bowl with attached demi-shafts, C13. – SCULPTURE. Two pieces of an Anglo-Saxon cross-shaft, with interlace, built into the inner face of the N wall of the aisle. – ORGAN CASE. 1880, by *Curzon*. Oddly tall and narrow to fit its odd position at the SE corner of the nave. – STAINED GLASS. Nave SE, C15 fragments including an Annunciation. Chancel SW, three panels of the arms of Sir John Lewis, i.e. late C17, perhaps by *Henry Gyles*. – Tower w by *Lavers, Barraud & Westlake*, 1871; chancel SE, N chapel E and N aisle w by *Preedy*, 1872, 1873 and 1880; E window by *Shrigley & Hunt*, 1899. – MONUMENTS. Lady Mary Bolles, daughter of Sir William Witham of Ledston, †1662. Altar tomb with recumbent effigy in a shroud, white marble, attributed to *Thomas Burman*. A noble piece, the features peaceful, the draperies convincing. On the tomb-chest, of black and white marble, escutcheons and Ionic columns. – Sir John Lewis of Ledston †1671 and his wife, Sarah Foot. 1677 by *Thomas Cartwright Sen.*, who signs himself 'Londoni sculptore'. He received a fee of £100. Two parts, which unfortunately have become separated, both having had, evidently, a rather peripatetic history – a pedimented and pilastered backplate, with long inscription, which is now against the aisle N wall, and the body of the monument, which was moved from the N chapel to the W end of the aisle in 2009. Black and white marble. Two semi-reclining effigies, one set higher than the other. She rests on the surface of a bulgy-ended sarcophagus, he – dressed in armour, with his hand on a skull – on a plinth rising from the sarcophagus behind her. Commissioned by their two sons-in-law, for 'the best father of their wives'. – Lady Elizabeth Hastings, granddaughter of the Lewises, †1739. By *Peter Scheemakers*. She was a celebrated bluestocking *avant la lettre*, universally praised for her intellect, piety and philanthropy. Again the figure is semi-reclining, but slightly more upright and in classical dress, reading a book, raised high on a grey marble sarcophagus with straight tapering sides which itself stands on a tall plinth bearing the eulogy. Obelisk backplate. To l. and r. life-size standing figures of her two half-sisters, Lady Frances and Lady Anne, as Piety and Prudence. Nearby a framed brass plate giving her Instructions to Incumbents.

SIR JOHN'S HOSPITAL, N of the church. Almshouses founded by Sir John Lewis in 1670. Long low two-storey row of eleven units. Two-light mullioned windows, their stonework renewed. But the walls have been heightened – see the change in the stonework at the front and in the gable-ends – so presumably the first floor had dormers to start with. C20 timber porches.

THE ORPHANAGE, E of the church. Founded by Lady Elizabeth Hastings in 1721 as a boarding school for orphaned girls. Now flats. Only mildly institutional. A tall building of three storeys and seven bays with cross-windows – still unexceptional in the area at this date – and a broad central doorway with architrave surround and pulvinated frieze. Octagonal chimneystacks at the gable-ends, perhaps an early C19 alteration (*see* below). Former stair-turret at the back, opposite the entrance, later kitchen block adjoining.

MANOR FARM, SE of the church. C17. Three-bay range with mullioned-and-transomed windows, many of them C19 timber replacements. At the back a gabled stair-turret and a lower service wing. Good-quality panelling, fireplace and overmantel in the parlour. ¼ m. NW the OLD VICARAGE, 1821 by *Bernard Hartley II*. Ashlar, five bays under deep eaves, with pedimented tetrastyle Greek Doric porch. At the W end of the village a group of early C19 Tudoresque COTTAGES, the detail including diagonally set chimneystacks. Possibly designed by *Granville Hastings Wheler* of Ledston Hall and Otterden Place, Kent: a number of sketches in his hand for Tudor-style cottages are preserved in the Ledston archive.

LEDSTON LODGE, ¾ m. NNW. A distant appendage of Ledston Hall, in a setting still of park-like character, built by Sir John Lewis in the mid C17 as a hunting lodge or standing. Compact upright form typical of such structures. The main part is a three-bay, two-storey square with a flat roof, for viewing, and four taller corner towers. Battlemented parapet, lead ogee caps to the towers. Cross-windows, segment-headed doorway with hunting horn on the keystone, entablature and cartouche over.

Identically detailed blocks to W and N, probably early additions. On the E side a projecting chimney-breast, breaking the regularity of the plan. Most of each floor was occupied by a single large room, now subdivided. Stone spiral staircase in the NW turret.

LEDSTON LUCK COLLIERY, 1¾ m. WNW. Two strikingly architectural WINDING HOUSES, 1911 for the Micklefield Coal & Lime Co. Brick with stone dressings, flat Free Jacobean style, with mullioned-and-transomed windows of various sizes, vestigial corner pavilions, parapets. The machinery was electric-powered. Between the two the lower compressor house; in front typical former PITHEAD BATHS, 1951, low, blocky, much altered. Mine closed 1986.

NEWTON ABBEY, Newton Ings, 1½ m. SSW. Fragmentary remains – a few courses of masonry – not of an abbey but of a moated medieval manor house, the site now an island in a lake formed by mining subsidence.

LEDSTON HALL   4020

A big, impressive half-H-plan mansion, predominantly of C17 appearance, but behind that having a complicated and uncommonly interesting history which is reflected in some disjunctions between date and style. Its origins lie in a grange of the Cluniac Pontefract Priory, in existence by the mid C13, which was acquired after the Dissolution by the Witham family: they extended it into a compact house of quadrangular form which is represented by a rectangular projection at the back of the present building (W: the house faces E) and the S two-thirds of the main range as seen from the front. In 1629 the property was bought by Charles I's minister Thomas Wentworth, later Earl of Strafford, and the process of radical enlargement was begun by him; but it was cut short by his impeachment and execution in 1641 and completion was only accomplished, probably during the 1660s, by Sir John Lewis (†1671), a wealthy East India merchant who had bought the estate in 1653. So the question arises as to how much of the finished house was built by Strafford and how much by Lewis; and the probable answer is that the S wing is Strafford's but the (almost) matching N wing, together with the refacing and extension N of the main range, are Lewis's. Some further alterations were made probably *c.* 1720 for Sir John Lewis's granddaughter Lady Elizabeth Hastings (who occupied the house from 1705 with her two unmarried half-sisters), apparently by *William Thornton* of York.* Changes since have been

---

*His name appears in payments for work at Ledston and he travelled to London with Lady Elizabeth in 1720. A scheme for a more ambitious remodelling was produced by her neighbour *Robert Benson*, 1st Lord Bingley, of Bramham Park (*West Riding North*).

relatively minor; but part of the house was divided into flats in the mid C20.

39   Much of this is apparent in the monumental E FRONT. The front corners of the wings are marked by turrets with low ogee caps, which like the half-H-plan itself refer back to the forms of the early C17, e.g. at Hatfield House: so in repeating them on his N wing Sir John Lewis was favouring symmetry over up-to-date fashion. But Lewis's own signature was a memorable display of Dutch gables – there are no less than nineteen of them in all, on several different elevations – their crowning pediments alternately triangular and segmental and each pierced by one of the upright oval windows with four key blocks which are characteristic of the later C17. On the E front there are five along the main range, two on the return flanks of the wings and one to their ends – those on the S wing evidently replacing plain triangular gables of the Strafford period such as still remain on its S side. Below the gables there are three storeys, of which the first is the most important. Cross-windows to the ground floor; those above re-done c. 1720 – sashes in plain surrounds – organized as *piano nobile* and attic; and central doorway to the *piano nobile*, preceded by steps, also of that date, with segmental pediment and architrave ramped in the middle to carry a cartouche. Wrought-iron staircase handrail incorporating Lady Elizabeth's initials. The N flank of the house has four of the Dutch gables – and there are three more round the corner to the W – and retains all its C17 fenestration: cross-windows to the ground and first floors, smaller two-light mullioned above, quite irregularly disposed. The S has more of the C18 re-windowing. But on both flanks the corner turrets – now lacking their ogee caps – are repeated at the W ends, and they occur again at the corners of the W projection, where the lower stages of the SW one appear to be work of the Witham phase. So this feature is a particular constant in the building history. The projection is a storey lower than the rest of the house and was tidied up externally by Sir John Lewis, to produce an almost symmetrical W elevation with small plain gables next to the turrets. More cross-windows, some renewed in the C19; but on the S side also two straight-headed lancets, evidence of the medieval building.

    Inside, the complexities of the building history are immediately encapsulated in the HALL on the *piano nobile*, which runs S from the main doorway rather than lying symmetrically about it. The explanation will be that it was the hall of the Witham house – and possibly of the monastic grange too, which evidently also had its main rooms on the upper floor. Its present appearance dates from the phase of c. 1720: two storeys, with a plain coved ceiling and panelling to the lower stage only; but the panelling hides the remains of a big fireplace probably of the C16, and behind is its massive external chimney-breast, originally projecting into the small – and much encroached-upon – central COURTYARD. The one unambiguously medieval

Ledston Hall.
First-floor plan

part, probably early C13, is the SW corner of the W projection, SW from the courtyard, its lower floor an UNDERCROFT (now a chapel) lit by the lancets mentioned above, of three bays with segmental transverse arches, the upper (the so-called Lady Betty's Parlour) a room of uncertain original purpose, perhaps the monks' great chamber,* but fitted with Neo-Elizabethan decorative plasterwork, panelling etc. – confusingly dated 1588 – in the C19 and early C20. Both rooms had a C13 doorway, now blocked, on the N side, one above the other, the lower single-chamfered, the upper – which would have been reached by an external staircase – with a roll moulding. Possibly

*In the past it was assumed to have been a chapel but that now seems unlikely.

medieval fabric also extends E from the undercroft to link at right angles with the hall range: so the suggestion is that by the early C16 the building had the L-shape common among monastic granges. The two C13 doorways now give onto a confused area with a six-light mullioned-and-transomed window of the Witham period on the W side of the courtyard, which has been the kitchen at any rate since the mid-C17 phase; while on the N side of the courtyard at second-floor level there is another mullioned-and-transomed window of the Witham house but evidently re-set, and above it another of Sir John Lewis's shaped gables. On the S side is a two-bay Tudoresque loggia with enclosed corridor above, probably of the early C19 when more extensive alterations were contemplated by the owner, Granville Hastings Wheler (see Ledsham); and coeval with it is a staircase on the E side, in front of the hall chimney-breast. Behind them in the SE corner, alongside the chimney-breast, is a C17 staircase turret.

Of the other interiors in the main part of the house, S from the hall there are two further rooms of the c. 1720 phase, first an ante-room with a corner fireplace incorporating a stepped overmantel for displaying porcelain (cf. the china closets at Thornton's Beningbrough Hall, North Riding) and then, occupying the W end of the S wing, the DINING ROOM, with more enriched panelling and a handsome buffet – an arched recess housing a big marble basin, framed by panelled pilasters. The four overdoors by John Settrington, 1728, depicting the house and gardens, have been removed. E of the Dining Room was a saloon, subdivided in the 1960s, but on the ground floor one notable detail from the Strafford period has been uncovered: the remains of a stone fireplace similar to those in the keep at Bolsover Castle, Derbyshire, c. 1620. The part of the main range N of the hall takes the form of a double-pile block with a spine corridor, in which are some big stone doorcases probably also of the 1660s, but many of the rooms in the N parts of the house have only plain finishings of the early C19. The largest, perhaps a great chamber, on the second floor facing W, has a stone fireplace and more of the stone doorcases but was otherwise apparently never completed.

In the GROUNDS the most creative period was the early C18, when Lady Elizabeth Hastings consulted Charles Bridgeman about the development of the area E of the house. His plan, of c. 1716, shows a strongly axial layout with a hedged central walk aligned on the middle of the E front, preceded by semi-circular grass terraces stepping up the slope and flanked by woodland containing alleys, groves and bosquets. It appears that the scheme was executed, at least in part, but the features existing now are the product of a re-creation of the 1960s. Earlier elements, shown in Bridgeman's plan, are the STABLES, SE of the house, and a barn at right angles to them, both probably mid-C17, the former a squat H-shape with gables to the wings, cross- and mullioned windows, the latter similarly detailed. Behind it a big C20 extension for equestrian purposes.

w of these, at the beginning of a cross-axis running in front of the house, a GATEWAY flanked by square lodges set diagonally, probably all of the early C18 but built in two phases: the gateway appears to be shown by Bridgeman but not the lodges. The gateway is rusticated, straight-headed, with broken segmental pediment. Further away from the house at the N end of the axis a pair of tall C18 gatepiers crowned by big urns. W of the house, where the land falls away steeply, is a terrace with a PAVILION at its N end – in existence by 1728 as it is shown in one of the *Settrington* views – of brick with stone trim, principally a Serliana entrance. Below the SW corner of the terrace a LOGGIA of two-by-one round-headed arches, in the same materials.

LEPTON

2010

St JOHN. By *T.H. & F. Healey*, 1866–8, but the tower's upper stages finished 1876–7; short pyramidal spire removed 1929. Plate tracery E window.

LETWELL

5080

Attractive village along one street. Mainly C18 and of limestone with pantiled roofs.

St PETER. Perp W tower with C19 pyramidal roof. The rest largely rebuilt in 1820 as narrow three-bay nave all-in-one with apsidal-ended chancel of one bay. Medieval masonry survives externally as the W part of the nave N wall, with evidence of a blocked door. After a fire in 1867 left only the tower, vestry and outer walls standing, Sir Thomas Woollaston White of Wallingwells (Nottinghamshire) paid for restoration 1868–9. – The PULPIT and attractive pew POPPYHEADS were carved by his daughter *Mary White*; her sister *Fanny White* (*Lady Maitland*) sculpted the FONT. – STAINED GLASS. Three S windows in chancel and nave by *Henry Holiday*, made by *Powell & Sons*, 1870. W (tower) window by *Powell & Sons*, 1869. Nave N westernmost by *Harry Harvey*, 1979.
LANGOLD FARM, ¾ m. SE. Small Palladian house and three-sided stable block of *c.* 1760. Attributed to *Ralph Knight* of Langold Park,* who shared his friend Thomas Worsley's

---

*That house has been demolished but the lake and landscape praised by Repton are preserved in Langold Country Park, just across the border in Nottinghamshire. A house designed by *Wyatville* for Henry Gally Knight, 1814–17 was begun in 1818 but not proceeded with (cf. Firbeck Hall).

enthusiasm for amateur architectural design (cf. Hovingham Hall, North Riding), and probably part of his scheme for a new mansion (unbuilt). The house, perhaps intended as a summer or banqueting house, has matching fronts of a pedimented bay with a half-pedimented bay each side. On the s front a Venetian window below a Diocletian one, on the N a Serlian doorway.

LIGHTCLIFFE

St Matthew, Wakefield Road. 1873–5 by *W.S. Barber*. Perp. Transeptal-like N chapel, s baptistery, aisles and clerestory. Massive embattled NW tower with corner turret, the nave and chancel parapets and gables also embattled. (Richly furnished interior. Caen stone REREDOS by *J. Birnie Philip*; PULPIT and octagonal FONT similarly carved, the pulpit given by Sir Titus Salt, who lived at Crow Nest. – FONT COVER by *James Clinsty* of Huddersfield – WAR MEMORIAL. Finely carved oak panelling with Gothic canopy by *Jackson* of Coley, 1921. – STAINED GLASS. A good collection, nearly all by *Hardman*, 1875.)

350 yds E is the site of the OLD CHURCH of 1774–5 by *William Mallinson*, mason of Halifax, demolished in 1969 except for the W tower, with octagonal open rotunda and stone dome.

United Reformed church (former). *See* Hipperholme.

Primary School, Wakefield Road, ¼ m. w. National Schools of 1866–8. Symmetrical single-storey front between two-storey headteachers' houses as cross-wings, all with crowstep gables.

Cliffe Hill Primary School, Stoney Lane. By *Aedas*, 2009–11. One and two storeys on a vesica plan with an intimate central open courtyard. Continuous glazing to the classrooms and offices facing into this.

s of the parish church, the former VICARAGE of 1900–1 by *J.F. Walsh* in accomplished Vernacular Revival style and E along WAKEFIELD ROAD, two terraces, also Pennine vernacular, of 1868 (Nos. 102–116, s side; cottage-like with Gothic doorways) and 1885 (Grange Terrace, Nos. 139–151, with projecting ends, coped gables and finials). Further E HOLME HOUSE (No. 243), a handsome villa of 1820 with arcaded iron veranda across three-bay front.

150 yds NW of the church a C19 LODGE at the former entrance to CROW NEST (1788 by *Thomas Bradley*, dem.) with the arms of Sir Titus Salt, who bought the house in 1867. The PARK, with the lake he created, is a golf course.

On the adjacent land, CLIFFE HILL, a mansion built *c.*1780, extended 1854, now flats. Plain classical, with hipped roofs and large balconied porch.

Smith House, Smith House Lane. Early C16, timber-framed. Gabled cross-wing, cased in stone 1672 when the porch with round arch was added to create a lobby-entry. Unusually the one-and-a-half-storey housebody was retained as a high-status hall. Window of four-plus-four lights with transom. New E cross-wing for dining room and kitchen. Early C18 staircase added in rear wing when the hall was upgraded.

BOTTOM HALL RAILWAY VIADUCT, off Rookes Lane, 1850, by *John Hawkshaw* for the Lancashire & Yorkshire Railway. Eleven arches, 114 ft (34.7 metres) high. WYKE VIADUCT (former), ½ m. E, 1874–80 by *Hawkshaw & Meek*. Only nine of twenty-two arches remain after partial demolition, 1987.

LINTHWAITE 1010

CHRIST CHURCH. Commissioners' church by *Atkinson & Sharp*, 1827–8; its twin is at Golcar across the valley (q.v.). Lancet style. W tower with stone broach spire. Chancel, in keeping, by *Hodgson Fowler* 1894–5. Galleries, rebuilt in 1902, with timber arcades. – Fine painted and gilded oak REREDOS carved by *G.W. Milburn* 1902. – STAINED GLASS. E window by *Powell Bros*, 1896.

METHODIST CHAPEL (Wesleyan; closed), Lower Clough. Rebuilt 1867. Pediment-gabled front of four bays has central paired doorways with bracketed cornices. Six-bay returns.

COLNE VALLEY HIGH SCHOOL. 1953–6. Enduring good work of the *West Riding County Architect's Dept* under *Hubert Bennett*. Main block four storeys, all windows to N and S. Theatre block 1959.

LINTHWAITE HALL. *See* Slaithwaite.

LOW WEST WOOD MILLS, Low Westwood Lane (derelict at the time of writing). The oldest part is contemporary with the adjacent Huddersfield Narrow Canal, opened from Huddersfield to Marsden by 1799. Three three-storey ranges around a courtyard open on the E except for a smaller office building. Seven-bay W range is earliest, a water-powered scribbling, carding and fulling mill, built *c.* 1800, and altered *c.* 1824. TITANIC MILL, built for the Colne Valley Spinning Co., 1911–12 is starkly gigantic. Converted to flats and a spa in 2004–6. Six storeys high, twenty-six bays long, six deep. Centre of NW front, facing canal and railway, breaks forward under low parapet with dies; similar parapets to turret-like corners. Stair-tower rises on SE side.

LIVERSEDGE 1020

Not a town but an unfocused group of five settlements in the Spen Valley, viz. Mill Bridge and Littletown near the river and the parish church, Norristhorpe uphill ½ m. s, Roberttown higher on the hillside 1 m. ssw, and Hightown along a ridge 1 m. w.

CHRIST CHURCH. By *Thomas Taylor*, 1812–16, at the instigation of the redoubtable Rev. Hammond Roberson,* who obtained authority to build by a Private Act of Parliament and bore the entire cost of £7,474 himself. Set imposingly on a small knoll above the valley bottom. Big and serious Perp, with nothing of the papery thinness of so much contemporary Gothic work, it became an influential model for churches provided by the 1818 Million Act funds. Pinnacled w tower, five-bay nave with aisles and clerestory, chancel with big e window and crypt. Low battlements everywhere and, to nave, aisles and chancel, thin buttresses that rise as gabled pinnacles. Intersected tracery in the tower bell-openings. Other tracery a mix of Dec and Perp with much cusping. Tall arcades with octagonal piers and plain chamfered arches. w gallery added *c.* 1860. – Fine carved SCREEN with figures of northern saints by *Herbert Read* of Exeter, 1912. – Splendid hexagonal alabaster FONT, 1861, has panels carved with the symbols of the Evangelists. – STAINED GLASS. s aisle first from E 1905, and N aisle third from E 1908, by *Powell & Sons*.

The CHURCHYARD is remarkable for the consistency of its headstones, their simple, and egalitarian, gable-topped design stipulated by Roberson.

ALL SAINTS, Robertown. 1844–5. Designed by *Chantrell & Shaw*, executed by *Thomas Shaw*. Six-bay nave with w bell-cote, small chancel, both steeply roofed. Tall thin lancets between tall thin buttresses. (w gallery.)

ST BARNABAS, Hightown. By *W. Swinden Barber*, 1892–3. Four-bay nave has lean-to aisles with triple lancets, and low clerestory with cinquefoils. Gabled w bellcote instead of tower and spire originally proposed. Lower chancel.

LIVERSEDGE CEMETERY CHAPEL, Clough Lane. 1903. Unusually elaborate. Sturdy pinnacled tower with set-back spire; ogee hoodmoulds to tower and porch doorways.

SPEN VALLEY HIGH SCHOOL, Robertown Lane. Formerly Liversedge Secondary School, by the *West Riding County Architect's Dept*, 1957. Flat-roofed blocks in buff brick, one to three storeys. Windows in large timber grids with some coloured panelling. Later additions.

NATIONAL SCHOOL (former), Halifax Road. By *Thomas Taylor*, 1819, the same design as Birstall (q.v.) One of the earliest surviving purpose-built National Schools in the country, founded by Roberson. Symmetrical five-bay front. Wall behind gabled Gothic porch has large plaque and assertively battle-mented top with mini-turrets that rises above parapet. Large

---

*He appears as the Rev. Matthewman Helstone in Charlotte Brontë's *Shirley* (1849).

three-light mullioned windows have been lengthened and divided horizontally in two-storey residential conversion.

HEALDS HALL (Hotel), Leeds Road, ⅓ m. E, on the valley's N slope. Remodelled 1764. Ashlar front. Five bays, two-and-a-half storeys, with later one-bay, one-storey wings. Bracketed cornice and blocking course. Doorway has a segmental pediment on consoles, the window above a triangular one. The ground-floor windows originally had matching pediments, the outer ones segmental, the inner ones triangular. Hammond Roberson lived here from 1795.

SPEN VALLEY CARPET WORKS (former), Cooke's Mill, Wakefield Road. One of Liversedge's few surviving C19 industrial buildings. Long Italianate office range, c. 1870. Open segmental pediment to centre bay which has big round-arched doorway with rusticated voussoirs. Attached three-storey block with decorative entrance.

LIVERSEDGE HALL, Liversedge Hall Lane. Seat of the recusant Neviles, Lords of the Manor, in the C16. L-shaped plan probably preserves E wing and centre, much remodelled in the C19 and C20. Symmetrical NE front of three bays with tall plain parapet. Three-light mullioned-and-transomed windows; the same to double-gabled r. return, four-light windows to single-gabled l. return. (A traceried window with quatrefoil head, from the lost W wing CHAPEL, is reused in a fireplace.)

LOVERSALL

5090

ST KATHERINE. The only early evidence is the remains of a C12(?) window in the chancel S wall, E of the chapel arcade. The lower part of the W tower is of c. 1300 (see the mouldings of the doorway and the window above); the third stage's window and the fourth stage are Perp. The rest essentially all Perp too, though in *G. G. Scott*'s restoration 1854–6 the S aisle and nave walls were rebuilt, windows received new tracery and the nave a steeper pitched roof. *J. F. Bentley* was volunteer superintendent of the work. Original four-bay aisle arcade. Gabled S (Wirral) chapel built in ashlar c. 1530. Two bays, taller and wider than the aisle. It has windows with depressed arches and uncusped Y-tracery. – Norman tub FONT. – STALLS. C14, possibly from Doncaster parish church or Roche Abbey. Three pairs, two each having a MISERICORD with a finely carved face, one bearded, the other a green man. Third pair much altered. – Carved PANEL above S chapel arcade with Wirral and Wombwell arms. – STAINED GLASS. E window 1854, re-set 1856, and nave N middle window 1856, both by *Wailes*. – Chancel N easternmost by *Ward & Hughes*, 1868. – MONUMENTS. By far the most interesting is a narrow tapering tomb-chest outside, S of the chapel. Its sides are decorated with tracery of all kinds, as if an early C14 mason had gone to

his pattern book and copied current patterns: Y-tracery, intersected tracery cusped and uncusped, three lights and a foiled
circle, two lights with transom and shouldered-lintel heads. On
the lid a foliated cross. – s chapel. Early C14 effigy of a knight,
with sword and shield but without armour. – Tomb-chest,
probably John Wirral †1545. Black marble, with blank shields
in big quatrefoils between slender shafts. – William Dixon
†1783, by *Thomas Waterworth I* of Doncaster, with bust in front
of an obelisk. – Henry Overton †1799 and wife Mary †1800.
Elegant urn on draped pedestal with obelisk behind.

LOVERSALL HALL, 100 yds s. Rebuilt 1808–11 for James Fenton.
Now offices. T-shaped. Seven-bay front range, only one room
deep, in fine ashlar, simply detailed. Entrance flanked by Doric
half-columns and small sashes below plain cornice. Tripartite
window above. Blocking course. Narrower two-and-a-half-
storey part behind has Venetian staircase window on l. return.
Long rear service range.

DOVECOTE (restored), 200 yds sw. C17. Tall, rectangular, with
coped gables. Limestone rubble. Pretty octagonal timber
glover with lead roof.

LUDDENDEN

Small village in a long winding valley that rises from Luddenden
Foot, where Luddenden Brook joins the River Calder, up to the
moors 3 m. N.

ST MARY. Beside the river in the village. Rebuilt by *Thomas
Taylor* 1816–17, altered and chancel rebuilt by *Ralph Nicholson*
1866, third chancel bay 1910. Pinnacled w tower, mostly in its
original state. Also original the five nave N windows and the w
one on the s, with intersecting tracery. Dec tracery elsewhere.
Cavernous nave, the side walls stripped of plaster and an
equally bare stone wall separating the two-storey parish centre
created in the w bay in 1986. – FONT. Dated 1662. Octagonal,
with carved panels. – STAINED GLASS. E window by *Hardman*,
1866. Chancel N and s easternmost by *Heaton, Butler & Bayne*,
1910, s side second from E also by them, 1922. Six other s
windows by *Hardman*, 1867–80. – MONUMENTS. Abigail
Crosley †1721 and husband John †1730. Inscribed wooden
panel in good stone aedicule with round-arched pediment and
fluted Ionic columns. – Joshua Appleyard †1880, by *J.E.
Boehm*. Standing angel in canopied niche. – John Murgatroyd
†1880. Big marble panel including two seated angels by *William
Theed II*.

The VILLAGE s of the church has C18–C19 mullioned-windowed
houses, clustered picturesquely by the bridge across the Brook
and on the narrow valley's sides. The LORD NELSON INN is
dated 1654, above it the SCHOOL, 1825, enlarged 1856 and

1928, has two small Venetian windows in the gable and big upper windows. Off OLD LANE a row of early C19 one-bay cottages. Flat-faced mullions. The middle light of each five-light upper window is larger than the others, a typical detail repeated on the adjoining four-storey terrace, built as under-and-over dwellings (cf. Hebden Bridge).

KERSHAW HOUSE, ⅜ m. s on Luddenden Lane, is mainly of 1650 for James Murgatroyd. Large, many-gabled, and an exceptionally good example of its date. F-plan, with lobby-entry and rear kitchen. Two-storey ornamental porch, in ashlar, has scrolled plinth, finely moulded round-headed doorway and rose window with eight spokes and eight trefoiled heads (cf. East Riddlesden Hall, Keighley, *West Riding North*). Transomed windows of many lights, grouped in threes, to the parlours, chambers and to the hall, which has the largest one, of four threes.

OATS ROYD HOUSE, ¼ m. NW of the village on the valley's W side, has a fine mid-C19 E-facing ashlar range; five bays with Doric porch and pedimented ground-floor windows. It replaced the parlour wing of an F-plan house, built by James Murgatroyd and dated 1645, whose two gabled ranges, with ornamental porch, lie behind. Arched doorway very like that at Kershaw House (above), and similar large windows with king mullions, the hall window nine lights. Elaborate hood-mould stops, all different. A doorway (blocked) gave access to the porch's flat roof. N of this is OATS ROYD MILL (partly residential), an impressive example of a large rural steam-powered mill complex, set on the hillside and best appreciated when viewed across the valley. Begun in 1847 by John Mur-gatroyd, worsted spinner and manufacturer, the earliest part is the four-storey, twenty-seven-bay block on the W. N end demolished after a fire in 1989 that also destroyed a massive mill forming part of extensive additions made across the road in 1863 and 1886–7. Their survivors include single-storey weaving shed, 1887, adjacent engine house chimney and Ital-ianate office block. ¼ m. N is BROADFOLD HALL, a substan-tial villa in French classical style built for John Murgatroyd Jun., 1877.

The valley's E side has some of the best C17 houses. STOCKS LANE leads N from the village. Above it on the E off BUTTRESS LANE are HARTLEY ROYD and UPPER STUBBINGS, C17 with long mullioned windows and one of the typical C18 barns. In Stocks Lane itself PEEL HOUSE, where all the windows have arched lights. A fine house with datestone of 1598 on the two-storey porch. Hall and cross-wing, hearth-passage plan. Rear kitchen. Large, better quality masonry to front except to lower end on r. Mullioned windows with round-arched lights; the two central lights of the six-light windows to housebody, parlour and the chamber above all altered to one light in the Georgian period. Housebody originally had a fire-hood, replaced by a fireplace in 1691. Big projection to l. return combines a stack and garderobes to the parlour and chamber.

Shop end has plain mullioned windows, and taking-in door on r. return; oak screen to passage. ROEBUCKS, off Ubby Lane, 1 m. to S, 1633, has hearth passage plan. Double-gabled upper end, two-storey porch with ogee lintel. Plainer lower end probably a shop.

At LUDDENDEN FOOT, 1 m. S on Burnley Road, the former INDEPENDENT CHAPEL (now flats) of 1859. Unusual design in classical style, with long front facing the road. Five-bay chapel has central porch which rises as a tall, diminishing tower with decorative top stage. Tall round-arched windows, well detailed. Matching giant arches in the single pedimented bays that break forward at each end of the chapel and front the two-storey manse and vestries, the arches repeated on their four-bay returns. Rear similarly treated, above basement school set against the slope. Further N, off Station Road, near the crossing of the canal and River Calder, MILLBANK HALL, a three-bay-square villa (now flats) of *c*. 1805 with Greek Doric porch and on the bridge over the river the former MECHANICS INSTITUTE (now Civic Centre), a late example by *Sutcliffe & Sutcliffe*, 1914. About ⅓ m. NNW on Burnley Road, UPPER FOOT FARM of 1659. Hall and cross-wing plan. Continuous hoodmould over housebody and parlour windows, both eight lights with king mullion. Parlour chamber has three-over-five-light window.

BANK HOUSE, Bank House Lane, 1 m. N of Luddenden village. 1650, the earliest known surviving laithe house. Parlour and housebody with mullioned windows of six and seven arched lights, smaller rooms to rear. Barn to E, with an inscription in Gothic lettering over the doorway.

LUMB MILL, Lumb Lane, Wainstalls, 1½ m. N. A good example of a small hillside mill powered by a tributary stream. Built 1803 as a cotton-spinning mill, it was converted to worsted spinning *c*. 1833 and enlarged to accommodate the very rare cast-iron water wheel, 36 ft (11 metres) in diameter, that survives in the three-storey wheel house.

CASTLE CARR, in the moors 2 m. NNW, was a remote and over-ambitious Victorian castle with mixed Norman and Elizabethan features, demolished in 1962.* Begun in 1859 for Joseph Priestley Edwards, brother of Sir Henry Edwards of Pye Nest, Halifax. His architects were *Alfred Smith* of London, with *Thomas Risley* of Manchester as executant; *John Hogg* of Halifax completed it for his son, 1868–72. A fragment of the three-storey GATEHOUSE remains along with the WATER GARDEN, designed by *Hogg* and built 1864–70 as linked reservoirs for Halifax Corporation Waterworks. The decorative pools, with cascades and fountains, were compensation for using Edwards's land. ½ m. S on Low Lane, the LOW LODGE, 1860s, is like the house in miniature, a round arch with bold chevron linking

---

*The 'Talbot Fountain' from its courtyard is now in Trevelyan Square, Leeds (*West Riding North*).

the two turreted sides. ¼ m. ENE on Castle Carr Road the similar HEIGHT LODGE.

LUPSET *see* WAKEFIELD (OUTER)

LYDGATE*   *9000*

ST ANNE. Consecrated in 1788. Altered in 1888, with the addition or remodelling of the chancel and introduction of a Venetian window, designed for Dobcross church (q.v.) in 1880. Nave with small round-headed windows of 1788, reduced to one storey when galleries were removed in 1910–11. An organ chamber (chancel, N side) and vestries etc. (chancel S) were added at the same time. SW tower in Free Georgian by *R.B. Preston & F. Thorpe* of *c.* 1913, replacing a porch of 1910–11 – STAINED GLASS. E window, originally designed for Dobcross church, perhaps by *Capronnier.*

GROTTON HALL, Platting Road. A picturesque house dated 1686, with mullioned and mullioned-and-transomed windows. Much of the detail is owed to a renovation of 1844–7.

MALTBY   *5090*

Small former colliery town with undeservedly dreary centre. The pit, sunk 1907–11, was closed in 2013. Most surface buildings were demolished in 2014 but a few, including the PITHEAD BATHS by *W.A. Woodland* 1938 (altered) have been kept for reuse after reclamation of the site.

ST BARTHOLOMEW. Saxon–Norman W tower with Perp top, the rest rebuilt 1857–9 by *P. Boyce* of Cheltenham. The tower is CII to halfway up the third stage. Several original sandstone angle quoins. Some courses of herringbone masonry. Lower stage has N and S blocked openings also visible inside, the second stage three small round-arched windows with monolith heads. Perp mullions and tops to two-light bell-openings. Recessed ashlar spire. Boyce's church has a wide three-bay nave, the roof extending over narrow aisles. Geometric tracery. Chapels have transverse gables with circular lights in plate tracery. MONUMENTS. CI4 ALTAR TOMB with remains of inlaid brass cross (S porch). – Five good marble wall monuments, mostly 1770s, under the tower. S chapel monuments include one with Vitruvian scroll and urns to Thomas Fretwell

---

*Part of Saddleworth, in Greater Manchester since 1974.

†1753 and family, another by *Matthew Johnson* c. 1836.
– STAINED GLASS. E window by *T.W. Camm*, 1909. – S chapel
(vestry) E window by *Wailes*, 1861. – S aisle westernmost by
Harry Harvey, 1984. – N aisle westernmost by *Powell Bros*,
c. 1886.

ST MARY MAGDALENE (R.C.), Morell Street. By *J.H. Langtry-
Langton*, 1955. Plain, brick.

Fragments of the old village are scattered along BLYTH ROAD,
N of St Bartholomew. At the W end, in the junction with
Rotherham Road, is the medieval CROSS and below it a building with a resited lozenge-shaped plaque dated 1686 with
publican's joke – 'Come tomorrow and you shall have good
ale for nothing do not forget'. 250 yds SE the former METH-
ODIST CHAPEL (now Wesley Community Development
Centre), 1840s, has simple round-arched windows but also a
prominent gabled porch, 1914. Addition of 2005 for its present
use by *Burnell Briercliffe Architects*.

The COLLIERY VILLAGE lies SE, with some 400 houses by
Herbert Mollekin, a Maltby builder. Completed c. 1910. Garden
City influence evident in wide roads, some encircling an open
space with bandstand (now built on) beside the former
CHURCH OF THE ASCENSION (now flats) in Ascension Close
by *F. Norman D. Masters*, 1911–12, for the South Yorkshire
Coalfields Mission. Primitive Romanesque style with apsidal
ends (cf. Bentley, Edlington and Rossington).

5000   MARR

ST HELEN. A small church set a little N of the Barnsley–Doncaster
road and mercifully buffered from the traffic by houses. Nave
and lower chancel, narrow S aisle, and W tower carrying a
recessed spire. Nave and chancel are both early Norman – see
the herringbone masonry of their N walls and the head and
jamb of a blocked window above the priest's door. In the C13
the chancel was remodelled; the lancet windows and the
chancel arch, which has a double chamfer with broaches, are
sufficient evidence. Probably a little later, perhaps c. 1300, the
W tower was built. The tower is highly puzzling in that it has
shallow projections to N and S, as if the nave had been extended
to embrace it. Inside, in addition to the arch towards the nave
(with mouldings and details characteristic of c. 1300), there are
double-chamfered arches into these odd little recesses. If they
were for aisles to be built, the intention must have been
changed very soon for they were finished at the same time as,
or certainly not much after, the tower – see the lancets on the
S side and compare them with those on the W.

Now the arcade of the aisle. The pier and responds are of a
very unusual section, octagonal with broad sunk quadrant
mouldings in the diagonals (cf. Campsall). Their most likely

date is early C14. The arches are again double-chamfered. The
s porch is Perp, with chamfered transverse arches as so often
in this part of the country. C15 too the tower parapet and small
octagonal spire. – PULPIT. Given in 1579 by Christopher
Barker, the Queen's Printer, who was born in Marr. A royal
patent of 1577 granted him the exclusive right to print English
bibles. Panels in two tiers and simply carved shafts or columns
at the angles. Top centre panel has Barker's arms and initials
carved in relief; the rest plain. – FONT. Shapely octagonal bowl
on cruciform foot with four angle shafts. Octagonal base with
big broaches to connect with square plinth. Probably early C14.
– DADO. Reused box pews dated 1724. – SCULPTURE. Above
s pier. Mutilated Calvary over remains of cusped ogee-headed
niche with a figure (?). – PAINTINGS. Red foliage trails and
other patterns on the E arch of the arcade. – ROYAL ARMS.
George III, painted by *T. Curtis* of Doncaster, 1796. – MONU-
MENTS. Brass to John Lewis †1589, his wife, Mary (née
Reresby), and their children; the adult figures 2 ft 3 in. (68 cm.)
– Edward Lewis †1675. Finely carved black and white marble
aedicule with Ionic columns and cornice; coat of arms between
flaming urns above, drapery between consoles below.

MARR HALL, 300 yds ESE. Farmhouse with Georgian-looking s
front but incorporating a fragment of a large Elizabethan
mansion. On the w side the C16 porch (with moulded round
arch, pilasters, and armorial panel above the entablature) now
fronts a single-storey lean-to at the N end. To its r. the hall
window of ten lights of which eight belong to a two-storey
canted bay. A five-light window, also transomed, to the r. First-
floor windows similar. (Altered interior has plaque dated 1582
with names Lewys and Reresby.)

HALL FARM, 400 yds ESE, has good C18/early C19 former farm
buildings with two enclosed fold yards; the E elevation has a
fourteen-bay arcade to cartsheds; there is another at MANOR
FARM, 200 yds SW. From the C18 Marr was part of the Thel-
lussons' estate (*see* Brodsworth).

MARSDEN   *0010*

Large former mill village at the head of the Colne valley on the
county's w edge. The crossings over the Pennines from the valley
have been main E–W routes since at least Roman times.

ST BARTHOLOMEW. By *C. Hodgson Fowler* with *J.S. Kirk* of
Kirk & Sons. In Perp style, large and dignified, it is known as
'The Cathedral of the Colne Valley'. Six-bay nave with aisles
and clerestory 1894–5; long chancel with two-bay s chapel and
transeptal organ chamber 1898–9; w tower 1910–11. It replaced
a nearby chapel of ease of C15 origins, built to alleviate
Marsden's remoteness from the churches at Almondbury and

Huddersfield, and stands on foundations of a church by *W.H. Crossland* laid in 1866 but covered over after a dispute with the contractor. Fine ashlar interior with lofty chancel and tower arches, quatrefoil piers to arcades, and elaborate w arch to chapel. – High-quality FITTINGS. Elaborately carved oak REREDOS with alabaster panel of the Last Supper, 1924, and ROOD SCREEN, 1931 by *J. Harold Gibbons*, made by *Boulton & Co.* (rood stored until 1939). – Caen stone PULPIT carved by *George W. Milburn*, and FONT with Greek palindrome, both designed by *C. Hodgson Fowler*, 1895. – STAINED GLASS. E window 1905–18, and three s chapel windows 1900–9, by *Burlison & Grylls*. Good series of windows by *Powell & Sons*: five in s aisle 1913–19, w window 1916. N aisle: fifth from E, designed by *Harry Stammers*, 1940, installed 1945; fourth from E, designed by *Carl Edwards* and *E. Liddell Armitage*, 1952; third from E by *Ward & Hughes*, 1922; first from E by *F.C. Eden* and *A.K. Nicholson*, 1931. Three windows by *Leonard Walker*, 1950, 1951 and 1954, with his distinctive coloured glass and intense leadwork.

WAR MEMORIAL, Marsden Park, ¼ m. SE. 1922 by *Joseph Thewlis*, completed by *W.H. Wilkinson*. Classical. Portland stone. Pedestal with square pillar carrying eternal flame, flanked by lions couchant on side pedestals.

MECHANICS' INSTITUTE, Peel Street, by *John Hogg*, 1859–61. Italianate, but above the corner a timber clock tower by *Kirk & Sons c.* 1900.

On Brougham Road, the big ranges of NEW MILL, *c.* 1879–1910, some straddling the river (unused at the time of writing) and behind them, off Warehouse Hill Road, a row of stone TENTER POSTS, early C19, for the frames for stretching cloth (cf. Dobcross). s of Manchester Road the massive BANK BOTTOM MILLS on Wessenden Brook, redeveloped from 1876 and including a six-storey block of 1910, for J.E. Crowther, fancy woollen manufacturer. WORKERS' HOUSING 1907 (Ottiwells Terrace etc.) and DINING ROOM, 1905, near the entrance.

At TUNNEL END, ½ m. NW, is the portal of the Huddersfield Narrow Canal's STANDEDGE TUNNEL, built 1798–1811 (engineer, *Benjamin Outram*). The longest and deepest canal tunnel in the country at 3¼ m. (5.2 km) long. Above the canal tunnel's mid-point, 1¾ m. SW, is a late C18 ENGINE HOUSE (roofless), for a Newcomen-type engine used during construction.

Parallel with the canal is the RAILWAY and just before the horseshoe-shaped portals of its tunnels (1845–9; 1868–71 (both disused) and 1890–4) is an unusual steel-panelled AQUEDUCT, *c.* 1900, taking the Tunnel End Reservoir overflow across the tracks and thence down a curving stone cascade to the river below.

BUTTERLEY RESERVOIR spillway, ¾ m. s. 1891–1906 by *T. & C. Hawksley*, engineers. Impressive cascaded overflow in dressed stone, like a grand sweeping staircase *c.* 200 yds (180 metres) long and descending over 100 ft (30 metres) beside the reservoir embankment.

MELTHAM

Small town below the moors, developed in the C19 by the Brook family, owners of Meltham Mills, of which little survives.

ST BARTHOLOMEW. Nave 1785–6, probably by *Joseph Jagger.* Simple classical style. Ashlar. Six bays, with doorways in the first and sixth, and two storeys of windows. Of the church of 1651, no more survives than a datestone re-set near the entrance, the dated reading desk reused on the pulpit, and pieces of window mullions and round-arched heads in the churchyard. W tower and gabled N transept (forming a galleried aisle) by *J.P. Pritchett,* 1835. The tower has Tuscan pilasters on the tall bell-stage and a cornice with urns. Small chancel, of indeterminate Neo-Norman/Italianate style by *Edward Birchall* and *John Kirk & Sons,* 1877–8, when the interior was remodelled with W gallery, timber coffered ceiling and FITTINGS mostly in classical/Renaissance style. – REREDOS. Triptych by *J. Eadie Reid,* 1919. – STAINED GLASS. N aisle windows by *Powell & Sons,* 1953–7. – MONUMENTS. Four by *H. Mares.* Neoclassical. William Brook †1806 and wife Martha †1834. – Jonas Brook †1836 and wife Hannah †1868. Kneeling woman by an altar with portrait-profile relief. – William Wilson Brook †1836 and later relations. – Joseph Green Armytage †1841 and wife Ann †1819.

ST JAMES, Meltham Mills. By *Pritchett & Son* for James Brook, 1844–5. Cruciform, quite large. W tower with set-back stone spire. Altered by *Charles Pritchett,* 1860, including the organ chamber and vestry with traceried screens in new arches to chancel and transepts, oak FITTINGS, and TILES by *Maw & Co.* – STAINED GLASS. E window by *Lavers & Barraud,* 1865. Nave N third from E by *H.W. Bryans,* 1906. – MONUMENTS. Two by *E.G. Physick.* James Brook †1845 and wife Jane †1849. Graceful relief of Brook giving alms to a poor woman and child. – Charlotte, first wife of William Leigh Brook, †1847, with woman prostrate over broken column.

VICARAGE by *Pritchett* 1856.

CHRIST CHURCH, Helme. By *Pritchett & Sons,* 1859, in memory of Charles John Brook. A picturesque composition, not like the Pritchetts' usual work, that might sit happily in the Kent or Sussex Weald. Steep red tiled roofs to chancel and nave, the nave roof sloping more gently over the aisles. Pretty SW tower with little shingled splay-footed spire. Reticulated tracery. Ashlar interior with open-timber roof and painted texts on the chancel walls and around the chancel and arcade arches.

TOWN HALL, Carlile Street/Huddersfield Road. By *William Carter*, Clerk to the Urban District Council, 1897–8. Given by Edward Brook. Simple Tudor Gothic, its clock tower with pyramidal roof. Opposite, the former CARLILE (MECHANICS) INSTITUTE, 1891, by *J.S. Alder* for James Carlile, a former Brooks' director. Northern Renaissance style with good shaped gables. Interior retains high-quality plasterwork, joinery and marble mosaic floors.

MELTHAM HALL, Huddersfield Road (now flats). 1841 for William Leigh Brook. Attributed to *William Wallen*. Classical, with three-bay fronts and four-bay returns, the bays defined by giant pilasters with anthemion decorating their capitals. Parapet with some heavy balustrading and pedimented dies. Large hipped-roofed porte cochère in cast iron and glass, and three-storey W extension, not in keeping, both later C19. Landscaped GARDENS now a park.

HELME HALL, ¾ m. N. 1887, for Edward Carlile, in Pennine Vernacular Revival style.

The Brook family also provided the Gothic former CONVALESCENT HOME (now Woodlands, off Holmfirth Road, but part dem.) by *Edward Birchall* and *Kirk & Sons*, 1868–71; the PEOPLE'S PLEASURE GROUNDS in the glen below, landscaped by *Joshua Major*; and BANK BUILDINGS, below Mill Bank Road, a tall terrace of workers' houses on two levels in picturesque Tudor Gothic style built beside the stream *c.* 1860. Twenty-one bays long with paired gables between the projecting gabled end and centre bays.

(HEALEY HOUSE, Huddersfield Road, 1¼ m. NE. Fine classical house *c.* 1800. Three-bay centre has pediment to front and large two-storey bows to outer bays on garden front. Lower one-bay wings with Venetian windows. Single-storey wings beyond added *c.* 1850).

MEXBOROUGH

An architecturally unambitious small industrial town on the N bank of the Don in a former mining area. It was a property of a branch of the Savile family who lived here 1630–1718 when the estate passed to the Saviles of Methley (*West Riding North*) who were Earls of Mexborough from 1766. Their large, partly timber-framed house stood near the church and was demolished for the cutting of the Don Navigation in 1834. The town subsequently expanded W of the medieval settlement, which had grown up beside a ferry crossing on the river. Here, now, at the E end of both the town and the natural ridge above the river, are earthworks of a motte-and-bailey CASTLE, smoothed by landscaping.

ST JOHN THE BAPTIST. A rewarding building in an attractive setting, the churchyard sloping gently S down to the canal, but

it is a tragedy that highway engineers have so successfully
excised the church from the town centre to the NW. The Transitional N arcade of three bays reveals its C12 origins. Circular
piers with plainly moulded capitals, square abaci, round
unmoulded arches. Until the aisle was re-created in *E. Isle
Hubbard*'s heavy-handed restoration, 1890–1, the arches had
been filled in for many centuries. A doorway said to be of
c. 1260–80 was removed when they were reopened. E.E.
rubble-walled chancel: see the two S lancets, one with a little
billet decoration on the hood. Polygonal apse added in 1891,
with small windows set high up. The tower arch is hard to date.
It is small and may well also belong to C13. The tower plain
and topped with a set-back stone spirelet with little lucarnes.
Perp clerestory and battlements to nave and heightened
chancel. S aisle, including the arcade, and porch rebuilt 1891.
– REREDOS. By *Leslie Moore*, 1944–5. – SANCTUARY PANEL-
LING. Late C17. From Mexborough Old Hall, installed 1912.
– ORGAN CASE. By *Comper*.* – FONT. Dumpy octagon. C14?
– PULPIT. 1858, from Christ Church, Doncaster. – SCULP-
TURE. Incomplete C10 cross-shaft or slab with incised circles
in two small scrolls. – MONUMENTS. In the chancel four very
fine ones of the Saviles, all with black marble inscriptions.
– Samuel †1660. Tablet within coloured marble aedicule with
broken segmental pediment. – Samuel †1685. Elaborately
draped cartouche with gadrooned vase and cherubs above,
skull and bat wings below. – Margaret †1696. Curved tablet
between weeping putti, with winged cherubs' heads and skull
below gadrooned base. – Samuel †1724. Cabochon in carved
stone frame with urn finial and drapery held by large rosettes.
– Thomas Belton, curate, †1691. Vine-trail frame (top half
only).

UNITED REFORMED CHURCH (Congregational), Garden
Street. 1866–7. Tall thin lancets. Tower-porch, originally with
pyramidal spire.

CEMETERY, 2/3 m. NW. Gothic CHAPELS, 1877–8; one has round
apse and little circular bellcote, the other a small tower with
spirelet and polygonal apse interrupted by gabled E window.

RAILWAY STATION. 1871 and a standard design for the Manchester, Sheffield & Lincolnshire Railway. Single-storey range
with arcaded loggia, the gabled and bay-windowed parcel
office balanced at the other end by an attached house, similarly
detailed.

Beside almshouses in Church Street, an elaborate ARCH sculpted
by *Robert Glassby*, 1859, for John Reed, owner of Rockingham
Pottery and originally in the grounds of Reed's house in Market
Street. Semicircular, with a profusion of chevrons, beakhead,
gargoyles and other decorative features, some said to be copied

---

*Comper also designed the church of St George (1899–1902). This aspired to be
a cathedral for south Yorkshire but only the aisled chancel and part of the nave were
built. Demolished in 1980.

from local churches. Moved to its present position after restoration in 2015.

MICKLEFIELD

4030

Former colliery village strung out along the old Great North Road. The older buildings are to the N, the miners' housing, 1870s onwards, to the S.

ST MARY. 1860–1 by *H.F. Bacon*, replacing a C16 chapel of ease of Sherburn-in-Elmet. Nave, chancel, W bellcote. Rock-faced, geometrical tracery. (– STAINED GLASS includes E window by *Wailes*, 1861.)

HALL FARMHOUSE, NW of the church. Mainly later C17, altered. Cross-windows, and one mullioned-and-transomed window. Lower, older part to the r., with wind-braced kingpost roof.

MIDDLESTOWN*

2010

NATIONAL COAL MINING MUSEUM (CAPHOUSE COLLIERY). Shafts sunk in the 1780s. Closed 1985. Boiler house, with tall square chimney, winding engine house and heapstead building with headstock, of 1876 and later. Round-arched openings. – PITHEAD BATHS by *O.H. Parry*, 1938. Plain brick block, flat-roofed. Communal showers, accessed from separate clean and dirty changing areas with lockers. A very rare survival.

MIDHOPESTONES

2090

Pennine hamlet in the valley of the Little Don.

ST JAMES. Delightful small church of 1705, the nave and chancel in one. A medieval chapel of ease to Ecclesfield, it was rebuilt by Godfrey Bosvile of Gunthwaite, earlier rough rubble masonry surviving in the N and S walls. Little bell-turret with open pyramid roof. S porch has dated lintel with initials of Bosville and his wife, Bridget. Plain two- and three-light mullioned windows, the E one taller. – Octagonal Jacobean PULPIT

---

*St Luke, 1877, was demolished *c.* 1969. STAINED GLASS by *Kempe & Co.*, 1909–20, is stored at St Luke, Overton, near Wakefield.

with good decoratively carved panels. – BOX PEWS. – Small W
GALLERY has turned balusters to front and to its staircase.

On Manchester Road, ¼ m. N, MIDHOPE COURT flats, originally a turnpike inn built in 1811 by William Payne (cf. Langsett). Three bays, three storeys with pediment. One-bay,
one-storey wings with half-pediments. It makes a curious
effect, both homely and Palladian. Strikingly similar to the Red
Lion, Conisbrough (q.v.).

At UPPER MIDHOPE, 1 m. W, WELLBANK FARMHOUSE has
two C17 bays with gable-end on the lane and ground-floor
hoodmould to mullioned rear windows. C18 and C19 bays to
S. Cruck-framed front wing. MANOR FARMHOUSE, with three
cruck-trusses, has stone casing of 1671 (dated lintel) and C18
three-bay wing to rear r. Hoodmoulds with decorative square
stops to doorway and two mullioned windows on rendered S
front.

MILNSBRIDGE *see* HUDDERSFIELD (OUTER)

MIRFIELD   *1010*

Small industrial town on the Calder valley's N slope. The old
village centre was up Church Lane around the church. After the
Dewsbury and Elland turnpike (Huddersfield Road) opened in
1758–9, followed by the Calder & Hebble Navigation in 1776 and
the railway in 1840, the focus moved SW into the valley bottom.
Some large C17, C18 and C19 houses survive, but others like Blake
Hall (1745, extended by *Ignatius Bonomi* 1845, dem. 1955) have
succumbed to development. The C20 Church of the Resurrection is a prominent feature on the hillside.

ST MARY. Rebuilt by *G.G. Scott*, 1869–71. Its predecessor
replaced the medieval church in 1826, saving only the tower
(*see* below) and one round Norman pier now in the vestry.
Scott's church is much larger, its majestic W tower a local
landmark. Rich E.E. style with lancet windows and windows
with plate tracery. Spacious ashlar interior. Nave arcades with
alternate round and octagonal piers. Frosterley marble colonnettes to sedilia, and around piers of organ chamber
and S chapel arcades. Excellent carving by *Farmer &
Brindley*. – Opulent FITTINGS including the alabaster REREDOS
with Crucifixion by *Thomas Earp* (mosaics by *Salviati* added
1878) and PULPIT by *Birnie Philip*; he also designed the big
FONT with square green marble bowl inset with quatrefoil
figures representing the four rivers of Paradise. The old FONT,
1662, is octagonal, with simple foliate panels and fleur-de-lys
to tapering bowl. – SCULPTURE. Anglo-Saxon grave marker.
C10–C11. One side has figure with a cross, another a beast, and

two have interlacing, all badly preserved. – STAINED GLASS. E
window 1882, and most on S side 1880s, by *Burlison & Grylls*.
W window and most N side windows by *Clayton & Bell*,
1870s–80s. S aisle easternmost 1914, and N aisle fourth from E
†1916 and 1917, by *A.K. Nicholson*. S chapel easternmost by
Harcourt M. Doyle, 1958.

Outside, the medieval TOWER. Lower part C13; the belfry
stage C15, its embattled top replaced with a pyramidal roof by
Scott.

Immediately N of the church, in a commanding position, a
tall MOTTE, with an external ditch. By the C16 a manor house
stood in the bailey, now the churchyard; the medieval church
was outside the defences.

OLD RECTORY, Pinfold Lane, 150 yds SW. Probably early
C16; much restored and two rear wings added in the C20.
Four-bay main range, the ground floor stone, the upper floor
timber-framed. S front has moulded Tudor-arched doorway
and four- and six-light mullioned windows below, close studding and transomed timber windows above. Right end gable,
dated 1540, has diagonal strutting to first floor and to jettied
gable; close studding to penthouse, probably originally for a
staircase, on r. (Five sets of posts with kingpost roof trusses;
some moulded ground-floor ceiling beams, probably C17.)

CHRIST THE KING, Battyeford. 1972–3, extended 1982–3. Low,
spreading, unchurchy, in blockwork. It replaced *Ignatius Bonomi*'s Christ Church, 1839–40, destroyed by arson 1971.

ST PAUL, Eastthorpe. By *W. Swinden Barber*, 1881. Curvilinear
tracery. Prominent entrance tower with tall saddleback roof at
W bay of N chapel and a hall church appearance with nave,
aisles, chancel and chapels of equal height under steeply
pitched roofs. Arcades with polished granite columns and a
large octagonal black marble FONT with fine spired
COVER. – STAINED GLASS. Three E and three W windows by
Kempe, 1881. S aisle second from E by *Herbert W. Bryans*, 1919.

TRINITY METHODIST CHURCH (New Connexion), Huddersfield Road. Rebuilt 1877–8. Handsome, classically proportioned front with open pediment and giant pilasters with rich
foliate capitals. Fine interior with horseshoe gallery.

INDEPENDENT CHAPEL (former), Calder Road. 1829. Full-
width pedimented gable to five-bay front. Distyle *in antis* Doric
portico. (Good original galleried interior with box pews.)
Lower two-storey rear wing, later C19, accommodated vestry,
schoolroom etc. and, unusually, stabling and carriage house
for worshippers.

COMMUNITY OF THE RESURRECTION, Stocks Bank Road.
The mother house of this Anglican order, founded by Charles
Gore at Oxford in 1892. Fired by a mission to work in a northern industrial area, the Community moved to Mirfield in 1898,
six brethren taking over Hall Croft, a manufacturer's house
with extensive grounds.

Designs for a CHURCH to succeed the first chapel were
invited in 1907. Its (ritual) E parts, comprising the Resurrection

Chapel flanked by N and S chapels, were begun to *Sir Walter Tapper*'s grandiose Byzantine/Romanesque scheme in 1911, and completed in phases up to 1924, with temporary finishing of crossing and transepts, followed by the more economical aisled nave by *Michael Tapper*, 1936–8. The three E chapels are plain, in red sandstone, banded with white limestone. The Resurrection Chapel, almost as tall as the nave, has a five-sided apse with angle colonnettes and high-set windows in stepped reveals. Lower, shorter, semicircular-ended side chapels with slit-windows. All have set-back tunnel-vaults ending in half-domes. W of the central chapel a single bay, then the crossing, which was intended to carry a massive low tower with a dome, but is roofed by the copper-clad tunnel-vault that continues over the nave. Short transepts, mostly brick, finished differently. They were designed to have further projections; a lower N sacristy was added in 1958. Tall gabled brick porch, by *Francis Johnson*, 1973, between S chapel and transept. On N and S sides of crossing big Diocletian windows in arched gables. Five-bay nave with narrow aisles has white-rendered walls with brick pilaster-strips between bays. Clerestory with oculi, slit-windows to aisles, triplets to the undercroft. The imposing brick W front, with a giant niche and two small turrets, follows *Walter Tapper*'s design, derived from his Liverpool Cathedral competition entry and inspired by Tewkesbury Abbey.

Interior of cathedral-like proportions in Norman style, grandly ascetic and dignified, almost devoid of ornament. E piers and arches sandstone, elsewhere white plaster. The plan W of the chapels is highly unusual. The high altar stands in the groin-vaulted crossing. The transepts are two bays wide, each separated from the crossing by two arches on a circular pier. Another two arches on such a pier behind the altar to the E. This marks a kind of straight ambulatory behind the altar and the ambulatory is separated by yet another circular pier with two arches from the central chapel. So there is, seen from the nave, a sanctuary with two bays of arcading to its N, E and S, and behind the E arcading an indistinct glimpse of the long chapel. The nave, stripped to the essentials, has plain completely unmoulded piers and arches. Low arches between aisle bays. Controversial reordering by *Robert Harris* of *Harris McMillan*, 2009–12, diminished the eastward hierarchy of spaces by levelling the floor (N chapel steps retained) and replaced most C20 fittings. – Resurrection Chapel ALTAR. Caen stone; sculpted panels by *Nicholas Mynheer*, 2015. – S chapel SCREENS. Etched and engraved glass by *Mark Cazalet*, 2015. – STATIONS OF THE CROSS by *Joseph Cribb*, 1954–5.

A theological training COLLEGE was founded in 1902; it lies SE of the church with the residential accommodation to the N. This includes HALL CROFT, by *John Kirk & Sons*, 1875, with gables, token Gothic features and some good carved details. Grand staircase hall. Successive additions mostly three storeys and in an austere collegiate Jacobean style: tall W Dining Room wing by *Graham & Jessop*, 1905–6; the plain N extension to the house's service block is of 1906, designed by the *Rev. Caleb Ritson*, the Warden; attached to that in 1913–15 the long Retreat House for guests (extended 1926), with detached servants' block, by *H. S. Chorley*; lastly *Sir Hubert Worthington*'s gentler E block with flat-roofed attic dormers, 1932–3. The plain brick LIBRARY WING, 1956, links Hall Croft to the church, terminating in the lower stage of an intended CAMPANILE. At the time of writing a vesica-plan RESIDENTIAL BUILDING by *Harris McMillan* is proposed for the brethren (some twenty in 2015, the same number as in 1908), to be attached to the church on the NW.

The original COLLEGE, also by *Ritson*, 1902–5, is a modest two-storey, open quadrangle converted from the stable block, with addition of a big Gothic tower at the NW angle. W of this the separate Jacobean-style LIBRARY, by *John Bilson* with the *Rev. Chad Windley*, 1921, the only completed part of an ambitious building scheme to accommodate a hundred students. Attached N of the tower the six-bay REFECTORY by *Sir Hubert Worthington*, 1932–3. Narrow round-arched windows. Simple and serene interior, the walls rising as a depressed-arched barrel-vault; plaque by *Eric Gill* behind the high table.

QUARRY THEATRE. Dramatic amphitheatre cut into the rock, enlarged as stone was taken for new buildings. Used until the 1970s for evangelistic services, concerts and plays.

TOWN HALL (former), Huddersfield Road. By *John Kirk & Sons*, 1868. Simple Italianate front range with shops flanking entrance under pedimented gable; large public hall behind.

LEDGARD BRIDGE MILL, 400 yds SW of Town Hall, between river and railway. 1860s. The most prominent of Mirfield's few survivors, converted to flats 2004. Twenty-two bays, with large glazed extension forming SW gabled end.

BALDERSTONE HALL, ½ m. N. 1690, it is said; C19 alterations. Double pile, with central chimneystack. Five-bay front has full-width gable, which is probably C19. Original cross-windows to first floor and to l. return, sashes below. Central doorway has ornamental lintel with segmental moulding.

NORTHORPE HALL, ½ m. N. Early C17, with C19 alterations; restored late C20. Three-gabled front with two-storey porch between first and second bays. Tudor-arched lintel to outer doorway. Four-light mullioned windows.

DUMB STEEPLE, Cooper Bridge roundabout, 2 m. WNW. Obelisk, probably C18, of uncertain purpose. Square column of three reducing stages with ball finial. *c.* 15 ft (4.5 metres) high.

MOCK HALL, Leeds Road, 1½ m. WNW. C17. Three-bay house. Mullioned windows, the housebody window six lights with transom.

ROE HEAD, Far Common Road (Hollybank School). 1½ m. NW. Said to be 1740, altered and extended. House of two-and-a-half storeys, the W front two large bows with three-light windows; are the bows original or later Georgian? Five-bay r. return, the central doorway now a window. Early C20 two-bay extension to W front added a third, even broader, bow with five-light windows. Extensive C20 institutional additions. (Open central staircase; dining room with good C18 fireplace.) In 1830 it became a school, where Charlotte, Emily and Anne Brontë were pupils.

MONK BRETTON

3000

ST PAUL. By *L. & H. Solaini* of Liverpool, 1876–8. Dec. W tower with broach spire and apsidal chancel. The head of the W door is odd, with billets in a pointed arch. Moulded brick arcades with diaper-patterned outer arches in relief, all painted. Fittings of *c.* 1932–5 by *Faith Craft-Works*: ROOD and STATIONS OF THE CROSS, carved by *Charles Wheeler*. – STOUP (S porch). Possibly from the Priory. – STAINED GLASS. Chancel. By *W.F. Dixon*, *c.* 1880.

PRIORY, ⅞ m. SE. Founded *c.* 1154 as the small Cluniac monastery of St Mary Magdalene, colonized from St John's Priory, Pontefract, but it seceded in 1281 to become an independent Benedictine house. At dissolution in 1538 there was a prior and thirteen monks. The site, on a slope just N of the River Dearne and originally some 7 acres (2.8 hectares), was excavated in 1923–6.

The broad and impressive GATEHOUSE is mainly C15, incorporating earlier work in its lower parts. Off-centre gate passage has tall round arch with canopied niche for an image above. Porter's lodge to W, a large room to E, probably the almonry. Heated chambers above with straight-headed windows of two-lights, cusped. Projecting lobby at inner end of passage, again round-arched, with W stair-turret attached. E lies the large ADMINISTRATIVE BUILDING, *c.* 1300, with double gables to parallel roofs. Ground floor with row of three monolithic octagonal piers with moulded bases and capitals, carrying substantial timber plates. Upper room has C17 windows.

Of most of the rest only low walls remain. The CHURCH had a Cistercian plan: aisled nave, crossing, transepts each with two straight-ended E chapels and straight-ended presbytery. The S wall and E parts are later C12, except that the presbytery was lengthened soon after (the original piscina's sill is *in situ*). The few surviving details justify the dating. Triple shafts on the crossing piers. E entrance to the N aisle with semicircular responds. The transeptal chapels also had triple responds. About 1350 the N aisle and W walls were rebuilt with a wall-bench, partly surviving; the arcades had new responds. Nave has some original paving. The late C12 N arcade was taken to Wentworth church (q.v.). In the S transept remains of two staircases – a SW newel to the roofs and the base of the night stairs to the dormitory in the E claustral range. Fragments found during excavation show that the late C13 CLOISTER had

open arcades with clustered columns. On the E side the buildings are early C13 except for part of the W wall of the oblong
CHAPTER HOUSE, which adjoins the S transept. Unusually it
has no E projection. Some of the sloping stones or skewbacks,
on which the arch rested, remain from its tunnel-vault. C14
entrance with triple-chamfered jambs, paired colonnettes in
the jambs of flanking windows. INNER PARLOUR to the S, also
tunnel-vaulted. It opened onto a passage across which was the
WARMING HOUSE, vaulted from the central circular pier.
Above this range was the DORMITORY.

At its end is the separate mid-C13 REREDORTER, bridging
the ashlar-lined DRAIN on its S side. The bottom of the chute
from the westernmost latrine on the upper floor can be seen.
The priory's fine drainage system is uncommonly well
preserved.

S of the reredorter, slightly at an angle, was the GUEST
HOUSE, with a large hall. To the E was the isolated INFIRMARY,
its separate kitchen at the W end.

The S side of the cloister was occupied by the REFECTORY,
built soon after independence. Two tall two- and three-light
windows on the S side, with remnants of simple Geometrical
tracery. Triple shafts at the moulded doorway and at the
entrance to day stairs to the dormitory in the thickness of the
N wall. Between these openings are traces of the LAVATORIUM.
The narrow space at the E end, adjoining the warming house,
probably became a later, smaller, warming house. At the SW
corner a service hatch opens to a lobby attached to the contemporary kitchen with yard. A narrow kitchen drain runs into
the main drain under the attached scullery.

The impressive WEST RANGE or PRIOR'S LODGING stands
up highest. Part is the result of major alterations before the
dissolution, part of 1589 when it became a residence for
Edward Talbot, son of the 6th Earl of Shrewsbury, with C17
extensions for Talbot's daughter, Lady Armyne. The early C13
range comprised a small outer parlour N of a vaulted cellar
with a well. Extensive rebuilding for the prior in the mid C14
created a fine upper hall, with a galleried lobby at the slightly
lengthened S end, and a N chamber. A pier supporting a free-
standing hearth in the hall may have stood on the octagonal
base towards the N end of the storehouse below. Splendid
chamber fireplace with embattled lintel and moulded lamp
brackets. A small N door led to a stair or upper pew in the
church (cf. the Abbot's pew, Westminster Abbey). These apartments were extended in the mid C15, when a very tall, wide
chamfered arch, springing almost from floor level, was built
between the hall and chamber to carry the S wall of a new
second-floor chamber. The newel stairs against the W wall were
probably added in the later C16. The Talbots erected two new
buildings slightly further W. The nearer, with oriel window on
the N, was later linked to the prior's chambers by a block with
grand stone staircase rising to three floors. To create a continuous W wing the Armynes also built a GATEHOUSE between the

two Talbot buildings; part of the timber-framed E wall of the further one survives against it.

MONK FRYSTON

St WILFRID. Anglo-Saxon w tower of three stages, in rough masonry. The tall first stage has a small s window, possibly not original, the short second stage typical twin belfry openings with single round-arched lintels and mid-wall-shafts, then an odd feature – two corbel tables one above the other, the few feet of masonry between them hardly a stage. Perp buttresses, bell-openings, battlements and pinnacles; also the remodelled tower arch. E.E. arcades of three bays, with circular piers, broadly moulded capitals and double-chamfered arches. The w and E responds are keeled. The small chancel arch goes with the arcades; the unusual large round-arched squints either side are probably C15. The chancel itself was remodelled in the early C14. One N window with Y-tracery. Fine three-light E window with reticulated tracery; N and S windows with a simpler form (the s window preserved internally). Perp aisle windows and clerestory. Consecration is recorded in 1444.

The interior's character owes much to complete restoration in 1889–91 by *Robert J. Johnson* for the Rev. Benjamin Hemsworth of Monk Fryston Hall, with fine fittings and stained glass. – REREDOS and panelling by *Bromet & Thorman*, 1909, in their remarkable Art Nouveau Gothic. A profusion of roses and vines, sinuous tendrils entwining openwork frame, demented tracery (cf. Bramham, Otley and Tadcaster (*West Riding North*)). – ALTAR RAIL with stout balusters, 1644. – Excellent WOODWORK (poppyheads, bench-ends, roof bosses etc.) with carving by *Ralph Hedley* of Newcastle, 1889–91. – FONT. Square, perhaps C13. Two sides each have two very flatly carved crosses in circles with above each of these an arch-head with a fleur-de-lys. A little nailhead decoration below the rim. – STAINED GLASS. Old bits in the N and s aisle w windows, one with angels by *Kempe*. The rest, nine windows, by *Kempe*, 1891. – MONUMENTS. Large C19 and C20 tablets to the Hemsworths, including two polished white marble shields with leafy frames by *AlfredVerity*, 1891 – John David Hemsworth †1895. Arts and Crafts-style stone tablet by *Bromet & Thorman* with densely carved inscription and fruit tree with doves. – Elizabeth Duke †1926, alabaster, by the *Bromsgrove Guild*.

METHODIST CHAPEL (Wesleyan; now two houses), Water Lane. Built in 1845 as a hexagon, a unique plan for a Nonconformist chapel. Altered in 1875, with s schoolroom extension and entrance in gabled centre to E side. Two original sides form pointed N end, each with a tall round-arched sash set high up.

MONK FRYSTON HALL (hotel). A most interesting building, deserving further research. It originally belonged to Selby

Abbey, as the house of the Master of Works and the Agent who supervised the getting of limestone from local quarries. In the w end gable (concealed by later C20 extensions) is a two-light window of the later C13 with two cusped lancet lights and above a circle with an ornamented cross-head – a significant piece. The main four-bay s front is essentially late C16 or early C17, though with much-renewed windows and C19 doorway. Two storeys with attic. The projecting end bays are gabled and have five-light windows, the former hall window has eight lights with king mullion and transom. That would, if the medieval building followed a similar plan, make the C13 window a window of the solar. Bold E cross-wing in keeping, reputedly part of additions c. 1740, but all of a piece with alterations and rear additions by *Ernest George & Yeates*, who also remodelled the gardens, 1897. Altered interior includes galleried oak staircase and oak-panelled rear hall with carved inglenook fireplace. The extensive gardens (partly derelict) include loggia and terrace, Italianate garden, large meandering lake, picturesque wooden 'Lausanne Bridge' decorated with scenes from *The Ancient Mariner* painted by *Mrs Hemsworth*, and the 'Alpine Hall', a summerhouse with aviary.

PREBENDAL HOUSE, 50 yds S. Of C13 origin, disguised by render and much altered, but the central double-chamfered pointed doorway is medieval.

MONK FRYSTON LODGE, 1 m. WSW. Later C18. Attributed to *Carr*. Two storeys. Hipped roof. Five-bay s front with shallow central bow to ground floor, flanked by full-height canted bays. Tripartite entrance under Roman Doric portico. Hall with two-column screen against a spacious staircase behind. C19 and C20 alterations.

HILLAM HALL, ¾ m. SSE Tudor Gothic style, stuccoed. The cross-wing gables are dated 1827 and 1835 but this represents a remodelling of an older (perhaps C17) house for the Mouncey family. Now subdivided. At the edge of a small lake (now in neighbouring garden) a SUMMERHOUSE, like a tiny Gothic chapel, with pointy pinnacles.

MOSBOROUGH

Former mining village on Derbyshire's rural border, transferred from that county in 1967.

ST MARK. By *G.E. Statham* of Nottingham, 1886–7, after a competition. E.E. style. The tower's set-back pyramidal roof is discomposed by large gabled belfry openings added c. 1893. – REREDOS. Four wood panels carved in Renaissance style, said to be original Italian work given by the Sitwell family of Renishaw Hall nearby in Derbyshire.

TRINITY METHODIST CHURCH, Chapel Street. By *John Wills*, 1887–8. Small. Gabled front with rose window above the porch.

MOSBOROUGH HALL (hotel), Hollow Lane. An unusual-looking early C17 house, remodelled in the C18 and altered in the C19. Late C20 additions. Tall centre of three bays and three storeys; single-bay wings, the l. one also three storeys but lower, the r. one two storeys and slightly projecting. The house's original form, with recessed centre and projecting wings, probably gabled, was lost when the centre was filled in in the early C18 – see the broken pediment of the doorway, the raised quoins, the sash windows with sill and lintel bands and the balustraded parapet. Wings remodelled with sash windows and plain parapets, the l. wing with tall staircase window on w return. This wing retains fragmentary C17 dripstones. In the mid C19 the s entrance was replaced by a w doorway with flat stone hood on consoles. w stairwell with decorative plaster ceiling and C18 dog-leg staircase with vase and stem and twist balusters. Room to s has C17 panelling. Other rooms with C17 and C18 panelling. Late C17 staircase with turned balusters to rear of E wing.

ECKINGTON HALL (flats), Sheffield Road. 1868–70 for Joseph Wells, colliery owner. Large gabled and bay-windowed pile with some Gothic details. Tall entrance tower has decorative ashlar top storey with cast-iron cresting to pyramidal roof.

MOSS

5010

ALL SAINTS, at Haywood, 1¼ m. SSW. 1873–5. By *Charles Buckeridge* (†1873), executed by *J.L. Pearson*. Plain in form and outline. Parsimonious lancets. Handsome w tower with stone broach spire. Now a house.

MOSELEY GRANGE, ½ m. E of centre of village, has brick farm buildings, 1878, including an eye-catching three-storey dovecote. A very late example, perhaps for sporting, not culinary, purposes.

GLEBE FARMHOUSE, 1 m. E of church. Late C17. Limestone rubble. Quoins. Tall, with attic. Front has two (restored) mullioned windows to both floors. Rare for its date in the area.

MYTHOLMROYD

0020

Large, former textile mill village in the upper Calder valley, on the Rochdale Canal (1798) and the railway (1841).

ST MICHAEL. By *Mallinson & Healey*, 1847–8, s aisle and chapel by *T.H. & F. Healey*, 1887–8. Dec tracery. Big buttressed w tower with stone spirelet to NE stair-turret, five-bay nave with separately roofed aisles. The two-bay chancel is completely lined with MOSAICS by *Powell & Sons*, 1928–9. Biblical scenes, Apostles and northern saints, with much white and gold, set against a brilliant blue. – Unusual carved oak SEDILIA, 1931. – STAINED GLASS. S chapel E window 1934, and S window 1933 and 1950, also one in each aisle, by *Powell & Sons*. – S aisle third from E by *Shrigley & Hunt*, 1919. – N aisle eastern-most by *William Morris & Co.* of Westminster, 1955.

METHODIST CHAPEL (Wesleyan), Scout Road. Former Sunday School, 1872, with three-bay pediment-gabled front and round-arched first-floor windows.

BRIDGE, over the Calder. 1634, widened 1823–4. By this a SCULPTURE, 'Eye of the Needle' by *Nicolas Moreton*, 2010, commemorating Ted Hughes (1930–98), Poet Laureate, born in Mytholmroyd.

MYTHOLMROYD FARMHOUSE, 100 yds S of the railway viaduct (*William Gooch*, engineer). C17, with good late medieval timber framing within. Three-room plan; gabled housebody bay projects forward flush with gabled E parlour wing. Seven-light housebody window, the parlour's six lights. Both upper windows five lights, transomed, another in W gable. Decorative hoodmould stops.

REDACRE HOUSE, 350 yds NW of the church. Late C16, with F-plan front. Mullioned windows with hoodmoulds. Service and housebody bays are low-eaved, the housebody with gabled dormer window above. Porch and projecting E parlour wing are both two storeys and gabled. Probably Calderdale's earliest F-plan house.

BROAD BOTTOM OLD HALL, ¼ m. NW. A medieval timber-framed aisled hall, cased in rough ashlar blocks in the C16 (derelict at the time of writing). It nestles between a house of 1844 which replaced the W solar end and an early C18 farm, itself encasing older timbers. Doorway in two-storey gabled cross-wing; transomed hall window with three lights above four. (Aisles formed by two bays of post-and-truss construc-tion; hall, one-and-a-half bays, has kingpost trusses, the W wall truss with A-struts. Plank-and-muntin panelling below this, behind site of dais. Aisles have doorways to lost solar wing.)

Higher on the steep hillside, four fine late C16–C17 yeomen-clothiers' houses: GREAT BURLEES, to NW, has deep project-ing cross-wings and rear kitchen wing. Very large transomed housebody window of ten lights with king mullions; gabled dormer over, like Redacre House (above). LITTLE BURLEES, nearby, is of 1637, W parlour wing and porch give F-plan, the two-storey gabled porch, with round-arched doorway and oval window, added 1733. Another impressively large housebody window – nine lights, with two king mullions and transom. C18 barn with porch attached to service end.

BIRCHEN LEE CARR, ¾ m. E of Great Burlees, off Raw Lane, enjoys a commanding position. Large, three-room through-passage plan with rear kitchen wing added c. 1673. Excellent frontage, with the gabled housebody and parlour bays breaking forward; transomed housebody window of eight lights divided into twos by king mullions. Parlour has an unusual three-over-five-light window, the central upper light raised, with the hoodmould stepping up too.

WADSWORTH BANKS FARM, nearby, is a late medieval timber-framed house gradually stone-cased in the C17. High-quality projecting W cross-wing has big nine-light windows, transomed and with king mullions, to both parlour and parlour chamber. (Interior has rare surviving timberwork including late C15 board-and-muntin-panelled wall.)

STONEY ROYD FARMHOUSE, Bank Bottom, Ewood, ¾ m. NE of church. 1715. Traditional mullioned windows and upper taking-in door at rear for domestic textile manufacturing or storage, but tentatively uses more fashionable polite features. Double pile; symmetrical five-bay front, the centre breaking slightly forward, with quoined angles and an almost-a-pediment gable.

CRAGG VALE, 2 m. S. ST JOHN is a Commissioners' church by *Charles Child*, 1838–9, succeeding one of 1815. Plain four-bay nave with tall lancets, tiny chancel, pinnacled (ritual) W tower, all buttressed. W gallery. Oak REREDOS by *Jackson* of Coley. E window by *Powell Bros*, 1889.

CRAGG HALL burnt down in 1921. Its picturesque Arts and Crafts-style GATEHOUSE, 200 yds E, by *Edgar Wood*, 1906, remains. Arched gateway in l. bay, which has battered buttresses and decorative panel rising from upper window through gable. Flat-roofed canted bay with cross-windows to r.; mullions and transoms flush with walls. Opposite, large and very handsome gabled former VICARAGE in Pennine Vernacular Revival style, 1901. Above, OLD CRAGG HALL, 1617, restored in later C19. F-plan, with twin-gabled parlour bays and two-storey porch. Narrow housebody has six-light transomed window.

NETHERTHONG

1000

ALL SAINTS. Commissioners' church by *R. D. Chantrell*, 1829–30. Large six-bay nave with W entrance in a tall gabled projection flanked by staircase bays; very short lower chancel. Battlemented E and W gables and, at every angle, a big semi-octagonal buttress that rises as a battlemented turret. Ornate W bellcote with flying buttresses, rebuilt 1847. Lancet windows, their minimum Dec tracery probably from a remodelling by *W. Swinden Barber*, 1876–7. This removed the N and S galleries and lengthened the chancel very slightly while also extending it into the nave's E bay. A full-width traceried screen with tall pointed central arch marks the division. Nave W bay and gallery walled off and remodelled *c.* 2010. – STAINED GLASS. E window by *Powell & Sons*, 1877.

METHODIST CHAPEL (former), Haigh Lane, 300 yds N. 1769, the earliest Methodist chapel in the area. Built against a steep slope, the symmetrical two-storey front has two very tall windows that originally flanked a central pulpit, and entrances in the outer bays. Three upper windows. Openings all round-arched with ashlar surrounds, impost blocks and keystones.

NETHERTON

2010

St Andrew. By *J. D. Sedding*, 1880–1. Small, simple, but highly original. Nave and chancel in one. s porch and vestry, their hipped roofs meeting at a right angle. w bellcote on two but-tresses that rise from the baptistery projection. The side windows scarce and alternatingly narrow lancets with straight-headed lights and domestic-looking upright oblongs. At the E and W ends only one lancet, high up, with a slit l. and r. Boarded semicircular wagon roof in chancel, big open-timber roof with tie-beams on arched braces in nave. Arch braces between the wall-posts form side arcades, a successful effect, achieved economically. – STAINED GLASS. Three by *Kempe & Co.* E window and nave s, 1913, nave N, *c.* 1925.

NETHERTON HALL, ⅛ m. SW. *c.* 1775. Small gentry house, similar to but grander than Silcoates House, Wrenthorpe (q.v.). Compact three-storey main block, unusually only three bays, but with full-width pediment. The centre is emphasized by a giant blank arch that rises into the tympanum. Two-storey canted bays either side, with Diocletian windows above. Pedi-mented entrance. Double-pile plan with rear (SE) stair hall lit by tall round-arched window rising to top floor. Transverse corridor links small flanking service wings of two lower storeys. These originally had their own staircases. – Classical SUMMER-HOUSE, probably contemporary.

NEW MILL

1000

CHRIST CHURCH. Commissioners' church in lancet style by *Peter Atkinson Jun.*, 1829–30; larger chancel created in restora-tion and internal remodelling by *Frederick Moorhouse*, 1881–2. Original six-bay nave, lower chancel merely a shallow projec-tion, and substantial w tower, all with buttresses and plain parapets. Perp tracery probably also 1882. Chancel extends into easternmost bay of Atkinson's nave; organ and vestries to N and s. High, almost flat full-width arches on Purbeck marble shafts to chancel and sanctuary. Two westernmost bays of gallery converted to meeting room etc. by *Arthur Quarmby* 1972. – Good FITTINGS, 1882, include alabaster REREDOS,

SEDILIA and Caen stone FONT, all by *Farmer & Brindley*, and elaborate traceried oak PULPIT on very tall pedestal. – STAINED GLASS. E window 1882, third from E on N 1883 and fourth from E on S 1885, all by *Hardman*. – First three from E on S by *Clayton & Bell*, 1881–2. – Fifth from E on S (war memorial) by *E.R. Frampton*, 1920. – Fourth and fifth from E on N by *Ward & Hughes*, 1887.

LYDGATE UNITARIAN CHAPEL, Holmfirth Road, ½ m. NW. Rebuilt 1768; altered in 1848 and narrower, full-height E vestibule with organ loft above added, topped by pretty cupola with stone dome. Elevated late C18 PULPIT with tester between smaller Venetian windows (partly blocked) on W wall; BOX PEWS. E gallery 1786. To W, the former OLIVER HEYWOOD MEMORIAL SUNDAY SCHOOL by *Edgar Wood & J. Henry Sellers*, 1910–11. Stern Arts and Crafts front, partly in ashlar and sparely detailed. Single-storey full-width vestibule projects as a big bow, its recessed porch with deep lintel under tent-gabled parapet.

NEWMILLERDAM

3010

HARRISON'S ALMSHOUSES, Barnsley Road, opposite the Pledwick Well Inn. Three pairs of cottages with Flemish gables by *F. Simpson*, 1885.

NEWMILLERDAM COUNTRY PARK was part of the estate of Chevet Hall, seat of the Pilkington family from 1749 (dem. 1955). Large lake, dammed at the N end, with Tudor Gothic BOATHOUSE of *c.* 1830 and C19 LODGES at E and W ends of the dam onto the village road.

The Hall's E LODGE, ¾ m. E on Lodge Lane, is *c.* 1797, probably by *John Rawstorne*, who altered the Hall. Engaged Doric columns and fine gates. STABLES S converted to housing.

NORLAND

0020

Upland settlement of houses and farms scattered on the plateau and on the precipitous N slope down to the River Calder.

ST LUKE. 1866. E window by *R.B. Edmundson*.
A circuit NE from the church takes in the principal houses. First, in Norland Town Road, FALLINGWORTH HALL. Three-cell linear plan with rear kitchen wing. No gables. Lobby-entry through two-storey porch dated 1642. Large mullioned-and-transomed windows have hoodmoulds with decorative stops; three-plus-three lights with king mullion to parlour, two-plus-four lights to hall. Inserted doorway between, dated 1616, from Fields Farm (dem.). The only untransomed window, seven

36　lights, probably indicates the lower-end shop. LOWER OLD HALL is an impressive gabled F-plan house with the area's earliest ornamental porch, dated 1634, clearly the influence for Fallingworth's. Fluted Doric columns, straight entablature, gabled parapet with finials and waterspouts. Large mullioned windows, all transomed except to E end shop. Original rear kitchen, so the hall was exclusively a reception room. It is the most sumptuous of its type in the Calder valley with elaborate plasterwork attributed to *Francis Lee*. Overmantel displays royal arms, dated 1635, flanked by cartouches with arms of the Archbishop of Canterbury and the Earl of Derby. Arcaded frieze to two walls has pregnant women, pomegranate trails and putti. Fine stone doorways and two doors with linenfold panelling. Excellent parlour overmantel, again with royal arms. TOWN HOUSE on the r. is a mid-C16 timber-framed aisled house with C17 stone casing and alterations and extensions. N (rear) roof comes low over housebody aisle, which has long nine-light transomed window. N doorway, 1677, replaced a hearth-passage entry at the front when the two-storey addition under a low gable was built S of the housebody. Parlour window in original W cross-wing is nine lights with king mullions.

BINN ROYD, ½ m. ESE down towards the river, is a rebuilding of the previous house by *Jackson & Fox*, 1914, on hall-and-cross-wings plan, reusing mullioned windows with round-headed lights. Some of its lavish C17 plasterwork is in Bankfield Museum, Halifax (q.v.). Down London Road, UPPER WAT ING has a three-room plan with remains of timber framing. Triple-gabled flat S front; E bay label stops and housebody fireplace are dated 1638, indicating first rebuilding. W wing 1668. Altered and much added to. UPPER HALL (also known as NORLAND HALL) is a square plan with double-gabled S front right against the slope. E half, with front parlour, built *c.* 1600 as a stone wing to a timber house. This was rebuilt in 1690 and the whole S front handsomely refashioned in symmetrical form, in big ashlar blocks. Gabled porch, not quite central, has a one-over-three-light upper window. Decorative hoodmould stops to other windows. Old Norland Hall stood immediately W. It was pulled down in 1914 and parts taken to California by William Randolph Hearst in 1922.

In Spark House Lane the small former BETHEL CHAPEL (Baptist), 1865, has a pedimented front gable and plain sashes. LOWER SPARK HOUSE, 1677, nestles below the road. Three-over-five-light window in l. gable and elaborate hoodmould stops (painted). LANE ENDS FARM has main range, 1628, with eight-light hall window and C17 W cross-wing. C18 rear addition created double-pile house.

Returning uphill, SOWERBY CROFT on the r. has a two-bay C17 farmhouse with tall mullioned windows, much added to in the C18 and C19 with barns, workshops and cottages to create a small farming/cloth-manufacturing hamlet.

NORMANTON

A major railway junction from 1840 and then a mining town with brickworks, but without these industries a rather disjointed and characterless place.

ALL SAINTS, Snydale Road. A large blackish church, of Norman origin. Much restored and rebuilt in 1851–2, 1872–3, 1892 and 1906–7. The exterior is all Perp, with a good Latest Perp s chancel chapel of three bays, presumably the 'newe quere of our most blyssede Ladye' mentioned in George Freeston's will of 1519. Its E window is an imperfect copy of 1872 but characteristic of the style: five lights, round-arched without cusping; above each light two panels, rising slightly in height towards the middle so as to fill the space below a segmental arch. Inside, a very narrow mid-C13 N aisle. Its arcade has quatrefoil piers and four double-chamfered arches. On the E respond is a piscina for an aisle altar. s porch and aisle added next, the porch with two huge chamfered transverse arches, the arcade with standard later C14–C15 ingredients. The late C15 embattled W tower was built after the arcades – see the walling added to the W joining them to the new tower's diagonal buttresses. On the tower's W face is a small ogee-headed niche framed by crocketed pinnacles, above a carved angel bearing a shield (cf. Wragby). The clerestory followed after the tower. It has four, almost square, two-light windows each side.
    Few fittings have survived the drastic reordering in 1991. – FONT. A very interesting piece, octagonal, exquisitely carved with uncommonly dainty motifs – wheels with quatrefoils or four, seven or ten mouchettes, window heads with Dec tracery, etc. Possibly C15 but with a crispness almost like *Coade* stone, suggesting C19 recarving. – STAINED GLASS. Many old bits – all given before 1870 by Thomas Ward (of *Ward & Hughes*) – including grisaille of *c.* 1300, C15 figure-work and C17 Swiss medallions. The best fragment is a Pietà in the E window, late C15 and probably Flemish. – s chapel – darkly dramatic Fall of Jericho by *Heaton, Butler & Bayne, c.* 1920. – MONUMENTS. John Freeston †1595. A noble and restrained work, no more than a tall shrine, about 8 ft (2.4 metres) high, without effigy. Ionic columns, unfluted, with blank shields between them intended for his 'armes and pedigree'. Fine frieze with stars and rosettes. Several excellent C18 marble wall monuments.
ST JOHN THE BAPTIST (R.C.), Newland Lane. 1904–5 by *E. Simpson*. Urban scale in hard red brick with short SW spire.
BAPTIST CHURCH, High Street, by *John Peacock Kay* 1877–8, and the PRIMITIVE METHODIST CHAPEL, Wakefield Road, are brick with stone dressings and three-bay fronts, the former pedimented, the latter with decorative gable, and a porch added 1903. By the former, the modest TOWN HALL, 1889.

NEWLAND HALL, 1¼ m. w. The house, rebuilt *c.* 1745, was demolished in 1917. The ruinous former STABLES, dated 1745, are possibly by *Robert Carr.**

NORTH ELMSALL

ST MARGARET, Hall Lane. E.E. with a French flavour. 1896–7, by *A.H. Hoole.* – Sumptuous full-height Caen stone REREDOS of 1908. – STAINED GLASS. All by *Kempe.*

NORTH ELMSALL HALL, Hall Lane. Parts survive as farm buildings. Mullioned windows and a large C17 segmental-arched fireplace within a much larger (medieval?) arch of similar design.

NORTHOWRAM

Upland village, above Shibden Dale (p. 629), its older core of C17 and C18 houses recognizable among C20 housing.

ST MATTHEW, Back Clough. By *Walsh & Nicholas*, 1911–13. Large, free Gothic, with a blend of Dec and Perp tracery. Greyish sandstone, brightened by marmalade ironstone, in unevenly sized courses. The attached tower stands quite apart, giving the church more presence on the main road. Spacious ashlar-lined interior with high, full-width chancel arch. The arcade arches die into octagonal piers. Excellent oak FURNISHINGS in the Arts and Crafts tradition include REREDOS with figures of the Archangels, 1913, and ORGAN CASE 1914, both richly traceried, by *H.P. Jackson* of Coley; CHANCEL SCREEN by *C.H. Stevens*, 1938 (reduced, altered and moved eastwards in reordering 1996–2001). – STAINED GLASS. E window by *Gerald Moira*, 1913. – S aisle/transept, second from E by *Christopher Powell*, 1948.

UNITED REFORMED CHURCH (Congregational), Heywood Close, off Towngate. 1836–7. Founded by Oliver Heywood in 1672. The chapel stands in a large graveyard and has the monogramed datestone of its predecessor, built nearby in 1688, set in its S wall. Plain sandstone 'brick'. Tall, three-bay front, the entrance in a shallow arched recess which rises to the gable. Small windows in two tiers, their glazing of 1887. Rear organ chamber over vestry, 1853. Handsome interior, mainly of 1863 and 1894, with panelled front in grained wood

---

*In 1746 Carr was paid for work at Birthwaite Hall for Newland's owner, John Smith.

to gallery and organ loft. Heywood's C17 PULPIT preserved in
N aisle.

NORTHOWRAM HALL (now flats), off Northowram Green. By
Mallinson & Healey for Abraham Foster of Queensbury (q.v.),
1862–3, replacing the nearby hall of *c.* 1693. Two-storey stone
mansion with limited Renaissance details. Interior gutted by
fire in 1925. BATH HOUSE, 40 ft E. Probably mid-C18, now
entirely underground, the stairs sealed. Small circular cast-iron
roof-light. (Large plunge pool in barrel-vaulted chamber.
Smaller rooms off.)

Along the footpath between Hall Lane and Upper Lane a rare
surviving SLAB WALL, *c.* 1780, of over 200 upright ashlar slabs
about 3 ft (1 metre) high, with cast-iron linking plates.

MARSH HALL, Lands Head Lane. An important minor gentry
house (restored in 1990s). Mid-C16 hall range and E cross-wing
remodelled and upgraded in the 1620s–30s, when the upper
cross-wing replaced the original lower (W) wing, the kitchen
being transferred to a rear outshut. Doorway dated 1626 leads
directly into full-height open-hall, which has huge double-
transomed window of 4:4:4 lights. Transomed windows to
wings, those to upper parlour and chamber of four-plus-four
and six lights respectively. (Plasterwork: ceiling with flowers
and fruit in lower (E) parlour; panel with dragons, dated 1635,
in lower chamber; elaborate panelled ceiling in upper parlour;
frieze dated 1637, with coats of arms in arcade and lions and
unicorns in spandrels, in upper chamber.)

NOSTELL PRIORY *see* WRAGBY

OSSETT   *2010*

Small stone market town on a plateau high above the Calder
valley, and a centre of the wool-recycling industry from the C19
to the mid C20.

TRINITY CHURCH, Church Street. 1862–5 by *W.H. Crossland*.
Impressive, large stone church whose commanding crossing
tower and spire (226 ft (69 metres)) is a major landmark. Sited
on the edge of the town centre in the cemetery (1861), replacing an older chapel in Market Place. E.E. with some French-
inspired details. Compact plan of five-bay nave, low lean-to
aisles, single-bay transepts and two-bay chancel with small s
chapel. The emphasis is all upward – high nave clerestory,
steeply pitched roofs and soaring spire. Nave arcade with circular polished granite piers, alternately pink and grey, and
richly carved square capitals with angels and foliage. Clerestory
with tripartite arcade; triple marble colonnettes between bays.
Tall tower arches on round piers with pink granite colonnettes.

Scissor-braced roofs. – FITTINGS. REREDOS, PULPIT and
FONT all carved in Caen stone, the central panel of the reredos,
of the Last Supper, moved forward under an oak baldacchino
by *Charles Nicholson*, 1921 (cf. Carlisle Cathedral). – Old FONT,
small, octagonal, dated 1713. – STAINED GLASS. E window, the
Crucifixion in a riot of colours; W window, scenes after the
Resurrection, as vivid but better organized, both by *O'Connor*,
1865. – N transept, musical angels and the shepherds by *Clayton
& Bell, c.* 1870. Aisle W windows by *Clayton & Bell*, 1874.
– S chapel by *J. Eadie Reid*, 1925, uninspiring.

CHRIST CHURCH, Horbury Road, South Ossett. 1851 by *Mallinson & Healey*. Neat E.E., on a hillside. Cruciform, with
sturdy buttressed W tower. Three-bay nave, two-bay chancel.
REREDOS. Cusped panels with Christ and prophets in dreamy
oils by *Arthur Ellis c.* 1898. – STAINED GLASS. Five windows
by *Frederick Preedy*, E, 1863, chancel S (W), 1865, and S transept
S, 1865, all small scenes in medieval style. – Chancel N and S
(E) windows by *Powell Bros.*

ST IGNATIUS (R.C.), Storrs Hill Road, South Ossett. 1933 by
C.E. Fox. Round-arched style in red brick, nicely detailed.

METHODIST CHURCH, South Parade, Low Common. 1908, by
Garside & Pennington. Simple Arts and Crafts Perp with wide,
segmental-headed W (actually S) window, flanked by narrow
turrets with little spires.

TOWN HALL, Market Place. 1905–8 by *Walter Hanstock & Son*,
in eclectic Northern Renaissance style. Good carved decoration outside and Art Nouveau tiling and ironwork inside. Large
public hall with horseshoe gallery at rear.

WAR MEMORIAL, Market Place. 1928, a granite pedestal with
life-size infantryman in bronze by *R.L. Clark*.

OSSETT ACADEMY, Storrs Hill Road, incorporates PARK
HOUSE, *c.* 1870, a large Tudor Gothic mansion with much
ornate carving outside and within.

HOLY TRINITY PRIMARY SCHOOL, Church Street. 1875 by
Sheard & Hanstock. Standard gabled Gothic.

The town centre derives much of its character from late C19
commercial and institutional buildings near the pedestrianized
Market Place, mostly in coursed rock-faced stone and more or
less Italianate. The best is BARCLAYS BANK, Bank Street,
1870, ashlar, by *William Watson*; also several by local architect
W.A. Kendall – in Station Road the LIBRARY, formerly the
Mechanics Institute and Technical School, 1889–90 (altered),
and the former LIBERAL CLUB, 1893; also the former TEM-
PERANCE HALL, Illingworth Street 1887–8, and CONSERVA-
TIVE CLUB, New Street, 1881, the last with good portrait
keystone.

At Ossett Spa, GORING HOUSE, off Spa Croft Road, *c.* 1884.
The only villa built in tree-lined streets laid out for an ambitious but unrealized scheme to exploit local mineral springs to
create a 'Little Harrogate'.

OUGHTIBRIDGE

CHURCH OF THE ASCENSION. 1842–3 by *Joseph Mitchell*, who added the w gallery 1855–6. Plain five-bay rectangle with tiny chancel. Neo-Norman w doorway with zigzag, round-arched lancets. FONT like a scalloped capital.

OUGHTIBRIDGE HALL, ½ m. E. Timber-framed H-plan house with first-floor studding to truncated hall range, which has exposed central truss, *c.* 1400. Studding to gables of w cross-wing *c.* 1570. Post-1600 stone casing, alterations and extensions.

ONESACRE HALL, ½ m. w. Large, fine ashlar house rebuilt in two phases in C17. Hall-and-cross-wings plan; gabled attic storey. Projecting N wing built in 1630s by Nicholas Stead with E-facing parlour and unheated rooms to w. Thomas Stead rebuilt hall range *c.* 1660–70 but reversed it to face w, so s wing has kitchen to E and parlour to projecting front. Hall entrance in angle with s wing has bi-arcuated doorhead. Dripmoulds. Small cross-windows to front (hall window reduced), larger three- and four-light mullioned windows to double-gabled s side. Timbers of earlier house reused in second phase's roof.

OUTWOOD

ST MARY MAGDALENE, Leeds Road. Early Dec by *W.H. Dykes*, 1857–8; s chapel and s aisle by *Micklethwaite & Clarke*, 1887–8. – MONUMENT. Lt Kenneth Croft North †1914, bronze portrait profile by *Albert Bruce-Joy*, 1920.

PARKSIDE METHODIST CHURCH, Leeds Road. Economical Perp by *G.F. Pennington*, 1900–2.

OWSTON

ALL SAINTS. In the grounds of Owston Hall. An exceptionally interesting church revealing a complex building history. The story starts with the w wall of the nave, which has on its w face, both outside l. and r. of the tower and within the tower, the typical herringbone masonry of the early Norman period. High up are a pair of round-arched windows that now look into the tower and below them the original small w doorway that appears altered in its details. The tower was added in the C12, possibly in two phases. It is ashlar-faced and unbuttressed and has small, plain, round-arched windows in the two lower stages. Above are E.E. bell-openings each with a circular shaft between pointed chamfered arches, set within a larger pointed arch. Meanwhile a narrow N aisle was also added. Its rubble masonry remains and the three-bay arcade (the fourth bay is later). Circular piers and circular abaci and double-chamfered arches; keeled responds. The bracket with nailhead decoration at the E end of the S aisle must be a reused piece of similar date.

More was done c. 1300 and after, when both the nave and N aisle were heightened, the nave almost certainly lengthened by a bay, and the chancel rebuilt. This work is characterized by the use of Y-tracery and intersected tracery, mostly uncusped. Evidence is the W bay of the clerestory (the other bays have been made Perp), the N aisle N window, the nave S window (cusped), and in the chancel the three S windows, the N window and the spectacular five-light E window (cusped), which has in the apex of the intersections a circle with a wavy cinquefoil inside to break the regularity of the pattern. This is the latest of this group of windows. It looks as if the whole chancel belongs to c. 1290–1330. The tall chancel arch with its two continuous chamfers ought to be noted too, as well as the plain sedilia, just two seats with shaped arms (cf. Campsall), and the double piscina with trefoil heads. In the N wall is an elaborate tomb-recess or EASTER SEPULCHRE. It was originally open to a N chapel, probably contemporary with the chancel but later demolished, and is now bricked up outside. It has a moulded arch with pierced cusping and on each face a gabled hood with crockets and pinnacles. From the chapel there otherwise remains only a trefoil-headed piscina. The section of a Dec-style respond nearby is Victorian (see below).

The S aisle is also early C14 and has a three-bay arcade with standard elements; the S doorway has two quadrant mouldings. The short aisles suggest that the nave was originally three, not four, bays. Further, though inconclusive, evidence of changes at the junction of nave and chancel are the curious strip of stonework, with a headstop, that emerges from the plaster of the nave S wall just E of the S arcade, and traces of a window jamb on the chancel N wall immediately beside the chancel arch. The S aisle's straight-headed windows with reticulated tracery are perhaps connected with a chantry chapel founded here in 1333 (see also stained glass, below).

Finally Perp work: that is the tower top, most of the clerestory windows (see above), the S porch with steep stone roof and chamfered transverse ribs, and the nave's two-bay N chapel. This chapel absorbed the easternmost bay of the N aisle and extended the arcade. It has straight-headed windows with ogee-headed lights, daintily cusped. The date of this chapel may be known, for in his will made in 1417 Robert of Hatfield (see below) stated that he wished to be buried in the chapel of St Mary 'de novo constructa' (newly built).

The nave was restored by J.M. Teale in 1862–5, the chancel partly rebuilt by Sir (George) Gilbert Scott in 1872–3 with an impressive arch-braced roof and marble and Minton-tiled floor.

The proposed rebuilding of the lost N chapel was soon abandoned.

SCREEN. Very similar to the Burghwallis screen (q.v.). Six tall one-light divisions, ogee-headed, but subdivided by a pendant into two arches. Tracery with quatrefoils above the ogees and on the dado. Doors have the initials 'WA'. Perhaps a gift of William Adams (†1542). – MONUMENTS. Brass to Robert of Hatfield †1417 and his wife, Ada, †1409, with 2-ft (0.6-metre) figures holding hands. Inscription in French. – George Byard †1661. Panels from a tomb-chest include two with a horse and three grenades (below S aisle altar). – Henry Cooke †1717 and family, erected by the will of his son Anthony Cooke †1763. Excellent large cartouche with tasselled drapery and cherubs' heads. – Mrs Mary Cooke †1785, by *John Fisher I*. Corniced tablet with fluted pilasters. – Julia Cooke †1811 and her infant siblings. Tablet (incomplete) by *Fisher*. – Mrs Frances Cooke †1818, by *Chantrey*, 1820. Free-standing, with kneeling female figure on a tall plinth. An outstanding work of Chantrey's, with all the tender sentiment of which at that time he was capable. – Bryan Cooke †1821, by *Chantrey* 1830. Tall wall monument framed by (later?) Gothic arch. Seated figure in a thoughtful pose. Grecian detail. – STAINED GLASS. S aisle: upper lights of S windows have early–mid-C14 glass, some with a rinceau pattern found in windows of *c.* 1339 at York Minster. – E and W windows by *Powell & Sons*, 1865–6.

OWSTON HALL. A seat of the Cooke/ Davies-Cooke family, now golf club and hotel. Early C18, extended for Bryan Cooke with a new principal range by *William Lindley*, 1794–6. This is two storeys with basement. Plain rendered L-plan. Low hipped roofs. SE front of seven bays has three-bay pediment on giant Ionic pilasters. Tripartite entrance with fluted frieze, consoled cornice and small segmental pediment. SW garden front has full-height central bow between single bays, their ground-floor windows set in tall blind arches. Attached l. a large conservatory, 1854, with central canted projection. Behind, at a lower level, is the old hall, with wide NW front of five bays. Pedimented doorway. NE courtyard wall retains C16/C17 mullioned windows from an earlier hall.

Entrance hall with screen of two Corinthian columns opening towards a spacious cantilevered stone staircase lit by a Venetian window. Elegant former Library has curved ends and plaster frieze with quill pens, dividers and sheet music. Earlier library in old house has coved ceiling and crinoidal marble fireplace.

Repton produced designs for the PARK in 1792–3; the landscaping was altered in the 1920s for the golf course. – Former STABLES. Late C18, enclosing three sides of a courtyard. Pedimented central range. Arcaded exercise walk to rear. – LODGE, ¼ m. ESE. By *P.F. Robinson*, 1828. Small Greek Doric temple, tetrastyle prostyle. Lumpen C20 rear extension.

OXTON HALL

Early C18 brick-built house refronted in Magnesian limestone, it
is said in 1803. Seven bays, with three-bay pedimented centre
and a single-storey tetrastyle portico with slim Doric columns.
Side elevation with projecting end bays and a veranda between
them. (Good cantilevered staircase of the early C19, and panelled entrance hall.)

PENISTONE

Small Pennine market town, on the s fringe of the Yorkshire
textile district.

ST JOHN THE BAPTIST. Outwardly largely Perp. The tall pinnacled w tower, c. 1500, is visible for miles around. w doorway
with fleurons and masks in two continuous orders. The body
of the church is embattled, the clerestory in addition has pinnacles. C18 s porch. Simple Perp windows. Evidence of much
earlier origins inside. Fragment of herringbone masonry survives in the SE corner of the N aisle. Below it part of a cross-
shaft, probably C11, reused as a nave NE angle quoin. The nave
arcades of six bays are early C13. Alternating circular and
octagonal piers, characteristically simply moulded capitals,
double-chamfered arches. Chancel c. 1300, with intersecting
tracery in the restored E window and one s window. It was
lengthened later in the C14 and afterwards heightened – in
1691 according to a datestone outside, over its s door. One-bay
s chapel also c. 1300, with s gable. The s doorway too probably
of that date. Plainer N chapel rebuilt c. 1530, externally of a
piece with the N aisle. Splendid arch-braced nave roof, c. 1375,
on good figure-head corbels and with elaborately carved
bosses. Fittings from a restoration by *George Shaw*, 1862, have
been removed. Reordered by *Peter Pace*, 2006–8, with large
community space at W end.

    FONT. Medieval. Octagonal, with carved panels and taper-
ing base. – STAINED GLASS. E window by *Hugh Easton*, 1938.
s aisle. Third from E by *Frederick Cole*, 1962. w window by
Francis Hiley, 1914. – Clerestory s. Bosvile arms, from Gunthwaite Hall (q.v.). Enamelled glass by *Henry Gyles*, c. 1681.

BULLHOUSE CHAPEL. *See* Thurlstone.

PERAMBULATION. The small town centre around the church
barely justifies the name and few buildings display architectural aspirations. w of the church the former CLOTH HALL by
John Platt, 1763, was for trading the local coarse woollen cloth,
called Penistones. Pedimented face to Market Place. Originally
U-shaped, the hall probably had a partly open ground floor
and arcades in the seven round-headed openings at each side,

now glazed for shops. By the 1820s it had several other uses, and the open centre to Market Street (E) was infilled in ashlar with an open pediment. N is a handsome curved corner block by *J. D. Webster*, 1894–5. Built as a bank, Post Office and offices.

Down BACK LANE off Market Street is the splendid new aisled MARKET HALL, by *WCEC Architects*, 2010–11. Its dramatically soaring green oak frame, constructed by *Carpenter Oak Ltd*, is an interpretation of the area's traditional cruck construction and great medieval timber-framed barns. In Shrewsbury Road the TOWN HALL with former CARNEGIE LIBRARY, 1913 by *Henry R. Collins* in low-budget Baroque. The hall has been a CINEMA since 1915, its interior little altered.

WATER HALL, ¼ m. N. C17. S front of three gables, the r. pair with continuous dripmould to both storeys. Lower l. wing set forward. Late C19 sashes.

NETHER MILL HOUSE, ⅓ m. N. Tudor-arched lintel dated 1636. A four-light double-chamfered window each side. Seven lights with king mullion above. Large BARN to E has three crucktrusses, probably C16. Behind, early C18 FARMHOUSE with quoins and attached COTTAGE have double-chamfered mullioned windows.

NETHERFIELD CHAPEL (Congregational), ½ m. NNW. Now residential. 1788, overlaid with C19 extensions. The pedimented doorcase in the projecting gabled front of 1890, and adjacent moulded windows surrounds, may be from an earlier s front.

RAILWAY VIADUCT, ¼ m. NE. 1849–50. For the Lancashire and Yorkshire Railway's Huddersfield line. Twenty-nine arches, in a gentle curve 1100 ft (335.2 metres) long and 98 ft (29.8 metres) above the River Don's deep valley. An impressive adjunct to views of the town.

CUBLEY GARDEN VILLAGE, ¾ m. S. By *Sir Herbert Baker*, 1921–2. Built for the Springvale Steelworks. The first houses (Hackings Avenue etc.) are quite handsome gabled cottages in groups of two and four, some with low-sweeping rear roofs. Built of concrete blocks that look like stone, visible in those remaining unrendered.

POLLINGTON

6020

St JOHN'S CHURCH, VICARAGE and SCHOOL are by *Butterfield* for William Dawnay, 7th Viscount Downe, 1853–4 (cf. Cowick and Hensall). Of Spartan severity, the church is memorable for its great steep roof and the impressive W end with big buttresses, two-light windows between and the corbelled square brick and timber belfry turret with shingled spirelet. N porch with gabled roof breaking the eaves line, replicated by *Thorpe & Turner*'s vestry, 1910. Interior with no chancel arch; round arcade piers. Bleak rather than bracing, not helped by the tame oak REREDOS and sanctuary panelling of 1926. Big octagonal FONT given by Lady Downe (cf. Cowick and Hensall). – STAINED GLASS. E and W windows by *Preedy*, 1854. N aisle easternmost by *Francis Spear*, 1953.

Former VICARAGE and SCHOOL also typical of *Butterfield*'s free simplicity.

POLLINGTON HALL. Mid-C18. Impressively tall in the flat land-scape, its two-and-a-half storeys raised on a basement plinth. Five bays. Brown brick. Fine pedimented doorway. Flat-topped end gables with stone copings.

4020

PONTEFRACT

Medieval Pomfret, as it was long known, was one of the most important towns in England. It is sited on a commanding emi-nence SW of the crossing point of the Aire at Ferrybridge and its Norman castle, sited on a rocky spur at the NE end, controlled the main route to the N. The Saxon settlement, called Tanshelf, may have been at the foot of the rock, where there was a church and cemetery; the medieval town developed SW of the castle, the area around the present Market Place formerly being known as Newmarket. In 1377 912 adults paid poll tax (compared with 315 in Wakefield and 157 in Leeds). Pontefract's magnificent castle, renowned as a gaol for prisoners of the highest rank, was in royal hands from 1399, remaining the monarch's northern base until the Civil War. The two religious houses, the Cluniac Priory of St John at Monkhill and the Dominicans' St Richard's Priory, whose site is in Friarywood Valley Gardens, have no standing ruins. After the castle was demolished the town retained its pre-eminence as the capital of the West Riding until Wakefield assumed that role in the later C18.*

Pontefract's most famous industry, growing liquorice for sweets, developed in the C17 and lasted until the mid C20, but like the coal mining that dominated the town's N fringe from the 1870s to the 1980s it has left little physical evidence of its exist-ence. Pontefract's social and political importance ebbed away in the early C19, allowing much of the fabric of its earlier and rela-tively wealthy existence to survive intact until the mid C20. Although the losses in the 1960s and through later road schemes have been severe, the centre retains its medieval street pattern and some C18 buildings of real quality that give a lingering air of confident prosperity.

*The ruins of NEW HALL, Ferrybridge Road, the mansion of the 7th Earl of Shrewsbury of 1591, probably by *Robert Smythson*, were blown up in 1965.

CHURCHES

ALL SAINTS, South Baileygate. A large cruciform medieval church, and very dramatic in its still partly ruined state. It lies close to the castle rock, but on the E side of it, near a Saxon predecessor (*see* below). It was grievously damaged during the first sieges of the castle in 1644–5 and the only parts to be repaired before the C19 were the central tower and the transepts, which served as a mortuary chapel. What exactly was done to the tower is not recorded. One would like to know, because it is a splendid piece of architecture, with a tall square stage with pierced parapet and pinnacles and then a tall octagonal stage with battlements and pinnacles. This late C17 replacement is smaller than the original, even grander, octagonal lantern, which had eventually collapsed in 1660. In 1831–3 *Chantrell* converted the transepts and crossing into a usable church of strange shape, wider than it was long, by adding a small polygonal sanctuary and a matching W apse; the latter replaced by *G. G. Pace* in 1967 with a brick nave, inserted within the two eastern bays of the ruined nave.

In its complete state the church had a nave of four bays with aisles and clerestory, porches, transepts (the N one with two E chapels) and chancel with S chapel and NE vestry. The dating is not easy. Some C13 work probably survives within the nave and chancel but most of the medieval fabric is C14, with some C15 alterations. The chancel, the transepts, the tower's first stage with its remarkable double-helix staircase and the belfry are thought to have been complete when the nave aisles and N and S porches were built in the mid C14. The arcades are of standard details. N porch with pointed stone tunnel-vault and upper storey. The doorways still have their richly moulded surrounds. The clerestory, with two sunk windows for each bay set closely together under a continuous hoodmould, was added in the first half of the C15, when the W wall with its impressively large window was rebuilt. Its surviving Perp tracery was placed inside on the N transept N wall in 1906. At the E end much less remains and things are less clear. The wide, three-bay S chapel, however, is Dec; that can be said with certainty, for some reticulated tracery survives. Its S wall was raised slightly in the C15 and the parapet added to match the nave walls. Inside on this wall is a half-buried ogee-headed tomb-recess with multi-cusped arch. Burials within the ruined parts in the C17–C19 raised the ground level at least 2 ft (0.6 metres).

The most remarkable detail of the church is the NW STAIRCASE in the first stage of the tower, which runs up in two spirals of equal radius on top of each other. Its purpose is a mystery. Double-helix staircases are extremely rare and few appear so early. The most celebrated is that made as the spectacular centre of the Chateau of Chambord after 1520, and one was used for a practical purpose by Antonio da Sangallo the Younger in the well at Orvieto in 1527–37. Two others exist in

England, in the C15 tower at St Editha, Tamworth, Staffordshire and in the Prior's Lodgings of *c.* 1500 at Wenlock Priory,
Shropshire. That was a Cluniac house so could the idea have
come from Pontefract via the monks of St John's Priory?

Chantrell's interior is attractive Gothic Revival with the
original octagonal responds and arches of the crossing and
transepts plastered over and remoulded. The rib-vaults and
the hoodmoulds to the windows and blocked arcades have an
engaging portrait gallery of rather doughy-faced corbels and
headstops, some gilded. Several preserved in the nave may be
genuinely medieval. *Pace*'s nave, of brown brick and concrete,
fits unobtrusively between the nave walls, its steeply pitched
roof, with raised roof-lights, screened by the clerestory. Standing in the roofless aisles it is somewhat startling to see the
windows, with a pattern of small rectangular lights, in the
arcade openings. Plain plastered interior; W organ gallery.
– FONT. C19. A finely carved copy, with variations in the
details, of the medieval font now at St Giles (*see* below).
– STAINED GLASS. E windows by *Harry Harvey*, 1979. A boyish
Christ flanked by St Peter and St Paul, the figures set in clear
glass. N transept – six lights, each with a saint, by *Kempe*,
c. 1868. – MONUMENTS. Several marble wall tablets including
Elizabeth Rudd †1785, by *Fisher*, and Rev. John Atkinson
†1837, by *John Tilney*.

5 ST GILES, Market Place. Founded 1107 as a chapel of ease to
All Saints, it became the parish church in 1789. Externally
mostly Georgian, an engraving of 1777 shows the building in
its essentials as it is now except for the W tower of 1790–1 by
Thomas Atkinson (the medieval tower had already been rebuilt
in 1707), the E two bays of the chancel and aisles added by
Bernard Hartley I, 1792–4, and the inappropriate Gothic
tracery, of two cusped lights below a quatrefoil, inserted in
1868–9 by *George Malcolm*. The tower has, on the pattern of
All Saints, a big solid octagonal storey above the square. Here
the transition is achieved by rusticated broaches with large
urns at the corners. Above are arched openings with blank
balustrades, a cornice, and another balustrade with small urns.
The top with its huge urn finial has eight flying buttresses
forming an openwork dome, like a crown spire. Entrances in
the W bays of the aisles, with arched heads like the windows,
although on the N side these have keyed archivolts (as altered
1722–4) and on the S side, rebuilt *c.* 1742–4 in ashlar, very
heavy Gibbs surrounds.

The INTERIOR is stuccoed and painted, except for the stone
sanctuary of the 1860s. Five-bay N arcade of *c.* 1300, with
quatrefoil piers, moulded capitals and arches with two quadrant mouldings. Clerestory with straight-headed windows. The
very tall S arcade of high Doric columns, with oddly decorated
capitals that have lion masks on the necks at the cardinal
points, is probably contemporary with the rebuilding of the S
wall. The W gallery, with vestibule created in 1825 beneath,
dates from 1740. The chancel arcades, of 1792–4, have one

double-width segmental arch, equalling both the S arcade and
the C13-style sanctuary arch in height. The upper part of the
N arch forms the clerestory. The C16 panelled nave ceiling,
concealed by plaster in 1776, was revealed and extended above
the chancel in matching style when the chancel roof was
lowered in 1882. – REREDOS. 1870, stone, arcaded, with
marble colonnettes, and finials and crocketed gables, unfortunately painted. – FONT. C15, from All Saints. Octagonal, the
panels richly carved with quatrefoils with roses etc., and a
luxuriantly leafy frieze and base. – STAINED GLASS. S aisle: one
by *Henry Hughes*, 1879, and four by *Ward & Hughes*, *c.* 1884–94.
N aisle: one by *Curtis, Ward & Hughes*, 1899; three by *Powell &
Sons* 1900–3.

ST JOSEPH (R.C.), Back Street. *c.* 1806, a rare example of a
Catholic church built before the 1829 Catholic Emancipation
Act; later C19 alterations. Large plain rectangular building, not
obviously ecclesiastical. Rendered brick. Church on very tall
first floor has round-arched S windows, the N side towards the
town originally blind. Domestic-scale ground floor for presbytery and former school. (Church interior has flat ceiling,
apsidal sanctuary with half dome and W gallery. A little classical decoration.)

HOLY FAMILY (R.C.), Chequerfield Road. By *Derek Walker* of
Walker & Biggin, 1961–4 (closed 2008, still unused in 2017).
A far-sighted design, preceding the liturgical changes of the
Second Vatican Council and incorporating works of art as fittings. Walls of very light, very thin (2-in. (5-cm)) bricks, roofs
mostly flat. Tall rectangular central hall forms nave and sanctuary, with clerestory to nave and lantern over (ritual) W-facing
altar. Single storey side ranges for Lady Chapel etc. (N) and
confessionals, sacristy etc. (S). Exposed brick, concrete and
wood used in interior. – FITTINGS include ceramic 'Christ in
Majesty' by *Bob Brumby* on (ritual) E wall, and Lady Chapel
REREDOS of glass mosaic and a STAINED GLASS window by
Roy Lewis.)

SAXON CHURCH, The Booths, W of All Saints. Foundations only
of the nave and chancel of a tiny stone church, associated with
later interments in a nearby cemetery that was in use from the
C7 or C8.

CEMETERY, Skinner Lane. Opened 1859. Two chapels, each one
bay by three with steeply gabled roof over three-light windows
with Dec tracery. Smaller gabled vestibules link them to the
central archway, which has a little stone broach spire.

HERMITAGE AND ORATORY
Southgate

The hermitage was founded in 1386 and the licensing of hermits
continued until the Reformation. The oratory was built *c.* 1440,
but was sealed up *c.* 1539 and only rediscovered in 1854. Both
are cut deep into the sandstone rock with their entrances, a
few yards apart, in the cliff-like slope on the S side of the town,

just below Southgate. The hermitage's front was partly
obscured by a brick vaulted chamber when the road was
widened above it *c.* 1800, and both entrances were completely
covered when the Infirmary was built against the rockface in
1880 (they are now accessed via the hospital's basement).
Behind the hermitage's arched doorway and small window its
chamber is mostly filled with rubble, leaving only a passage
with twelve steps down to a spiral staircase. This has fifty-two
steps, and three niches for candles, descending to a shallow
basin at the level of the water table, 51 ft (15.5 metres) below
Southgate. The oratory, to the W, has a worn C13 lancet
doorway brought from St Giles *c.* 1870. A few stairs lead to a
single chamber about 12 ft (3.7 metres) square and 7 ft
(2.1 metres) high with an altar, a bench in an arched recess
and a fireplace all plainly cut from the rock. The space is partly
filled by a C19 brick pier.

PONTEFRACT CASTLE
Castle Chain

Situated on a rock NE of the town and a little W of All Saints. Of
its history little can be said here. The highlights are famous
enough: the death of the deposed Richard II in 1400 and the
sieges of the 1640s; after its slighting in 1649 its demolition was
swift and thorough. The castle was first built by Ilbert de Lacy
before 1086 and remained with the de Lacys until 1311. It then
passed to the House of Lancaster, and in 1399 became a royal
castle when John of Gaunt's son and heir, Henry Bolingbroke,
was crowned king. It was greatly strengthened and enlarged in
the first half of the C15. By the C16 it was one of the largest and
most impressive castles in England. Although it was little used
thereafter repairs were undertaken and it maintained its reputation as a stronghold for the Crown to the end, holding the last

Pontefract Castle.
Engraving by the Society of Antiquaries, 1734

Royalist garrison to surrender in the Civil War. After being used as a liquorice field for a time, the site was partly excavated and then laid out as public pleasure gardens *c.* 1880–2, with further excavations in 1982–6. Conservation of the remaining fabric has retrieved it as a historical site. One big chunk of walling survives at the s corner, but otherwise no more than the curtain wall up to various heights and inner walling laid out as excavated, though somewhat tidied up by the Victorians. The plan and C16 and C17 illustrations help remedy the deficiencies of the remains.

In 2015–17 further conservation of the ruins and improvements to their presentation, with a new visitor centre, were undertaken.

What is left represents the Inner Bailey. The Outer Bailey went downhill to the SE on two levels. The earlier stonework is limestone, while from at least the late C14 grey sandstone was used, sometimes with reused limestone when rebuilding was undertaken. The oldest remains are the foundations of St Clement's CHAPEL, which was endowed by 1090; the chancel apse is probably C12. The principal remaining elements of the late C12 to early C13 rebuilding in stone are parts of the CURTAIN WALL, most substantially on the SW, and the POSTERN GATE, with round-arched passage, in about the middle of the SW wall with flat buttresses flanking it. Early stonework is also evident in the lower parts of the early C15 GASCOIGNE TOWER and the TREASURER'S TOWER, both w of the postern gate, and in the s part of GATEHOUSE TOWER at the main E entrance. Next in time comes the C13 KEEP, called the Round Tower, placed in the SW corner and encasing the C11 motte. Three massive drum towers, of trefoil plan, project outside the curtain wall but the keep's inner-facing part is lost. It seems likely that the keep was originally a quatrefoil and similar to the contemporary Clifford's Tower, York, which was begun *c.* 1245. John Leland's description of it in the 1530s as having '6 roundelles, 3 bigge and 3 smaul' has, however, prompted suggestions that it had three inner towers. Connections with French lobed towers of a century earlier seem unlikely. The heightening of the keep, shown with its impressive battlements and corbelled turrets in C17 illustrations, was ordered by John of Gaunt in 1374.

Henry IV's building programme began with SWILLINGTON TOWER, 1399–1405, a strong rectangular tower in an unusual position outside the curtain wall on the NW, attached by a spur wall, probably with a drawbridge over a void. The outer half of the tower was demolished when North Baileygate was constructed in 1800. In the E curtain wall CONSTABLE TOWER was built 1405–*c.* 1412; further N the royal apartments in KING'S TOWER and QUEEN'S TOWER, linked by the GREAT HALL, are of similar date. Work begun in 1413 and continued under Henry VI included the extensive KITCHEN etc. range against the W side of the curtain wall and the GARDEN WALL, 1443–6, which runs across the bailey in front of the keep and has a rare stone seat. In the C16, probably between 1564 and

1581, a new CHAPEL was built against the E curtain wall between the constable and King's Towers.

PUBLIC BUILDINGS

TOWN HALL, Market Place. By *Bernard Hartley I*, 1785, replacing the Moot Hall of 1657. Modest but dignified, with a domed cupola. Of three bays and two storeys, the ground floor an open rusticated arcade with segmental arches (the centre arch now blocked), with two more open arches to the N side, facing Bridge Street, a visually most successful linking-up of two streets and two characters. The upper part has fluted Doric pilasters, coupled for the pedimented centre bay, and a second tier of smaller windows implying an attic storey. The large panelled room inside, which served as council chamber, court and assembly room, has a magistrates' bench with C19 panelled front at the N end, and above this a small, slightly bowed balcony with plain iron balustrade. White marble fireplace with fluted panels and sleeping lion. SCULPTURE. On the S wall, a huge plaster high relief of Nelson's death, by *J. E. Carew*, 1850, from which was cast the bronze for the plinth of the column in Trafalgar Square. Purchased for the town, amid considerable controversy, in 1855.

ASSEMBLY ROOMS AND REGISTER OFFICE, Bridge Street. By *Perkin & Bulmer*, 1881–3. Attached to the back of the Town Hall, with a tall, narrow front and a long return to Baxtergate on the l. Jacobean style in red brick, detailed in red sandstone. Large projecting central bay finishing as a pedimented dormer. Inside, the Assembly Room, with a stage and galleries on three sides. Transverse panels across the basket-arched roof are decorated to match the panelled gallery fronts, which have swags, cartouches etc.

MUNICIPAL OFFICES, Headlands Road. By *Tennant & Smith*, 1930–2. Plain Neo-Georgian, two storeys with attic. The centre of the nine-bay front is stone, with heraldry above the door.

COURT HOUSE (former), Corn Market. 1807–8 by *Charles Watson*. Plain Neo-Grecian, like his courts at Wakefield (q.v.) and Beverley. It is set hard to the street, without a plinth, and at an unhappy angle. Two-storey front of nine bays, all in banded rustication, with an Ionic portico, pediment and plain cornice. The back is much more interesting and inventive, with a wide, gently bowed, centre of five bays between canted ends, all in ashlar. Interior remodelled *c.* 1960.

MILITARY DEPOT (former), Back Northgate. *c.* 1859, succeeded by the Barracks (*see* below) in 1878. The crenellated stone gateway and flanking lodges survive, all now used as offices.

BARRACKS (former), Wakefield Road. Now offices. Of the extensive scheme by *Major H. C. Seddon* of the War Office, 1877–8, the principal survival is an imposing red brick mock fortress (for armoury, guard house and stores), like that at Bury St Edmunds, Suffolk. This has a three-storey, six-bay front with square, four-storey turrets at the corners, with slit-windows (lighting the stairs) and crenellated parapets above pretend machicolations.

WAR MEMORIAL, Corn Market. 1923. Tall, square granite cenotaph with angle pilasters, on a stepped base. Tiny dome with cross.

POST OFFICE, Ropergate. By *Garside & Pennington*, 1915. Symmetrical, rather severe six-bay front in Portland stone. Two storeys with attic. The five giant square pilasters have lost their Ionic capitals but over the projecting entrances are Egyptian Revival winged solar discs.

PUBLIC LIBRARY, Shoe Market. By *Booth Hancock Johnson & Partners*, 1975. Large, of two storeys with a flat roof, neatly fitted into the intimate streetscape. Broad horizontal concrete bands at first-floor and cornice level, between concrete panels with vertical ridges, textured with pinkish granite chippings. Double-height triangular window bays.

MUSEUM, Salter Row. The former Carnegie Library, by *Garside & Pennington*, 1904–5. An Art Nouveau treat. Bold, asymmetrical front with central entrance and two large projecting gabled bays (tall single storey on the l., slightly higher two storeys on the r.) that have the striking feature of big brick angle pilasters extending upwards as subtly battered and ornamented terracotta pylons with crenellated tops. In each gable, large Venetian windows with decorative tracery. Window dressings etc. have lilies with tall, sinuously twisting stems, and tulips. Inside, a beautiful hall with tiled dado and arches in pea green with pale blue flowers and emerald green trim, and mosaic floor with leafy border. Oak screen and doors with original brass fittings.

NORTH EAST WAKEFIELD (NEW) COLLEGE, Park Lane. The former Girls' High School, by *Henry R. Collins*, 1910–11, and a good example of the Wrenaissance style much used at that time. Front of fifteen bays, plus three each end originally single-storeyed. Large elaborately carved stone doorcase with scrolly pediment.

KING'S SCHOOL, Mill Hill Lane. Refounded in 1548. By *H. Wormald*, County Education Architect, 1932. Quadrangle and wings, mostly single-storey, in brick with hipped roofs and slight classical details. Additions including new hall, science laboratories, library, IT suite and classrooms 1997–8.

WORKHOUSE (former), Skinner Lane. 1862–4 by *Lockwood & Mawson*. Only the main building survives (now Northgate Lodge), converted to flats in 1994 and surrounded by new blocks. Three storeys, in red brick, with front of 1:5:3:5:1 bays, the end and central ones projecting, under pediments. The style hovers between classical and Gothic. Arched window heads in polychromatic brick with sill bands and continuous hoodmoulds in ashlar. The quoins on the projections, in pale yellow brick, are contrived to look like pilasters. Corinthian pilasters and other ashlar dressings to the doorway and its flanking square bays.

INFIRMARY, Southgate. 1880 by *J.A. Davis*, 1907 and 1924–5. Built as the General Dispensary. Tame red brick Gothic with two-storey gabled front of three bays plus a further three bays originally single-storeyed. Extended twice to the SW.

MARKET HALL, Market Place. *See* Perambulation.

RACECOURSE, off Park Road. Established *c.* 1720. Two red brick stands with half-timbered gables and glazed canopies, 1921; additions of 1983–91. The entrance incorporates four pairs of Georgian-looking stone Doric columns, perhaps survivors from *Bernard Hartley*'s grandstand of 1802. Little domed pavilion for displaying the results.

PERAMBULATION

5 The MARKET PLACE is long, rather a wide street than a square, with the Town Hall at its head. Now relieved of traffic, its character is still recognizable from Thomas Malton's view of 1777. Both sides are largely Georgian, of excellent quality, the usual pattern being three storeys in brick, sometimes painted or stuccoed, and three or five bays, with moulded stone or modillion cornices. Windows have flat gauged brick heads, moulded architraves with raised or fluted keystones or lintels with incised voussoirs, usually painted. The few late C20 intrusions are uniformly worthless.

The following should be noted. THE LIQUORICE BUSH (N side) has windows with splendidly dressed surrounds with quoins and corniced keystones, on the first floor also with pediments, and a pair of bows to the ground floor. Opposite, BARCLAYS BANK, the best house in the street, built *c.* 1750–5 and attributed to *James Paine*. It has his typical motifs of an

Pontefract, Market Place.
Engraving by S. T. Sparrow after T. Malton, 1777

open pediment above the three principal bays with the windows of the middle bay contained by an overarch, a splayed base to the pedimented window at first floor and floating cornices above the other windows. The house was altered as a bank *c.* 1800, this work attributed to *William Lindley* – see the moulded architrave to the second-floor window and the two bow windows and fanlights on the ground floor (like his work at Rotherham and Doncaster).

Opposite, THE RED LION, remodelled in 1776 by *Robert Adam* for Sir Rowland Winn of Nostell Priory, who had political interests in the borough. A refined brick front with a pediment, of five principal bays with tripartite openings in the wider centre that are framed at ground floor by engaged Doric columns and above by Ionic columns with fluted necks carrying an entablature with fluted frieze, paterae and dentilled cornice. The carriage entrance to the r. has a pedimented window under a super-arch. (Inside, the saloon has a fireplace with fluted pilasters.) Its neighbour is the splendid ashlar MARKET HALL, of 1859–60 by *James Wilson*, which reaches the same height by one order of giant Corinthian columns on vermiculated bases, coupled l. and r. of a central arch. Above this a tall pedimented gable (restored 1997) with deep arched recess, which originally fronted the high central roof of the hall (rebuilt 1957). In each of the outer bays, arches flanked by pilasters at the angles, with balustrades and corner urns above the richly carved entablature with pulvinated frieze. The keystones of the arches are symbolic of the building's original purpose as a meat market – giant bulls' heads, a brace of game birds and a hog.

Further w, No. 24 is an excellent early C18 house surviving above a white faience ground floor of *c.* 1910. It has a deep moulded cornice and chamfered quoins, and five tall, narrow sash openings on the first floor. Smaller ones above. The sills have unusual plump little brackets with gadrooning, on short flat stems. After a tall gabled and turreted block of 1902, the market place widens out with the handsome BUTTER CROSS in its centre outside St Giles (*see* Churches), an aesthetically excellent way of taking in a new vista. The Butter Cross was given to the town in 1734, replacing the ancient St Oswald's Cross. Three tall round arches on square, heavily rusticated piers to each side; the ends are in the form of a triumphal arch with a small niche either side above the impost band. Hipped roof, of 1763, replacing a flat roof with balustrade.

Near to this on the s side of Market Place, a large, three-storey building with four stumpy attached Doric columns supporting the second floor, in fact a refronting after 1777 of a jettied and gabled house of *c.* 1600. Between the columns a sash window in the narrow bay over the central passageway and a shallow tripartite bow on either side. Next to this, an elaborate Jacobean front in honey-coloured terracotta of *c.* 1896.

From the w end of Market Place narrow ROPERGATE continues sw. Set back on its s side is the solemn Italianate brick and stone front of HSBC, *c.* 1875, then further on some more good Georgian houses: No. 33 has a severe doorcase with strip cornice, railings and a rainwater head dated 1809; Nos. 37–41 has a central Venetian-like window on the first floor; and No. 43 is a very substantial five-bay house with pediment and three bays added to the r. with matching modillion cornice. The doorcase has engaged Doric columns and pediment. Next, No. 45 has an ashlar front, unusual here. Finally, on the n corner the former CRESCENT CINEMA, by *Hustler & Taylor*, 1926, dressed in white faience, with blue and gold mosaic panels.

From Market Place, BEAST FAIR runs NW into Corn Market, another long and wide market street, tapering towards the Court House (*see* above). Both continue in similarly attractive vein to Market Place, but with more late C19 and early C20 fronts, of very decent quality, and an especially good variety of pubs. On the n side of Beast Fair, Nos. 18–20 were originally one mid-C18 house with asymmetrical three-bay front. The upper floors have chamfered quoins and emphatic Gibbs surrounds with double keystones.

In CORN MARKET, where the scale is mostly two storeys, are two nice early C20 half-timbered pubs (THE PONTY TAVERN and THE MALT SHOVEL) both with tiled and terracotta ground floors. The cellar of the Malt Shovel, however, has two bays of sexpartite vaulting with massive, deeply chamfered ribs, possible C13 or C14; one boss has a carved mask. Another early survival in SWALES YARD immediately behind, a long range of three or four C16–C17 timber-framed cottages of different builds. Two storeys, the lower mainly stone with some brick, the upper jettied with close studding and some later brick infill. Back in CORN MARKET, a fine five-bay Georgian town house of *c.* 1745–50, attributed to *Paine*: central first-floor window with a cornice on fluted consoles, the outer windows with his simple floating cornices. All three have bracketed sills. Hipped roof with moulded stone cornice on brackets. Ground floor altered, except for the arched passage doorway with rusticated voussoirs, elegant architrave and pulvinated frieze. Beyond the Court House (*see* Public Buildings), the Jubilee Way dual carriageway has destroyed the w side of Front Street and separated St Joseph's church (*see* Churches) from the town centre. On the e side of Front Street, TANSHELF HOUSE (No. 40) is a good early C19 house. Three bays, the central one with the two-storey overarch which one sees in Wakefield. Well-detailed bow windows and doorway with arched head and pilasters. Only two more buildings require note. The former QUEEN'S HOTEL, 200 yds down Park Road, is an imposing turreted and gabled pile of 1898–1901, built near the racecourse and Tanshelf Railway Station. Yellow terracotta ground floor, with matching details to the red brick upper floors and attic. Canted central bay between the entrances. Behind the hotel, Nos. 6–8 CAMP MOUNT are a pair of stuccoed villas of *c.* 1850, with single-bay projections aggrandized with giant corner pilasters and pediments. About ¼ m. s THE MOUNT is a small enclave of later C19 and early C20 detached and semi-detached villas, the largest being the former Tudor Gothic red brick vicarage of 1882.

E of the Market Place, in BAXTERGATE, is a modest, outwardly Victorian house and shop with a very fine plaster ceiling of *c.* 1630 in the front room. A central diamond bordered by twining grape vines encloses oak leaves and acorns, while vine trails and bunches of grapes extend outwards from its corners (cf. the Nunnery, Arthington, *West Riding North*). Can it be *in situ*? The area between here and the castle was ravaged in the 1960s and is now dominated by the eleven-storey LUKE WILLIAMS FLATS of *c.* 1965 on the s side of Horsefair and Micklegate.* w of these, near the Castle entrance, Nos. 2–6 CASTLE CHAIN form a picturesque Gothic group, C17 or earlier, with C19 Gothic Revival embellishments. Formerly one large house with another to the l., and a late C18 cottage on the r. Original features include the base of the stair-turret, the coat of arms of the Duchy of Lancaster (and, inside No. 4, a fireplace of *c.* 1600 with Atlantes and caryatids on herms). The mullioned windows, hoodmoulds and other heraldry are Victorian. s, across Stony Hill, ROBSON'S ALMSHOUSES face SOUTHGATE. 1913. Single-storeyed, in brown brick and white artificial stone. Two dwellings, sharing a gable, each side of a more elaborately gabled central bay fronted by a semicircular screen with four Greek Doric columns.

STUMP CROSS, Ferrybridge Road, ¾ m. NE. Rectangular cross base, *c.* 1100, probably marking a boundary. Triple arcaded panel on each side. Two fragments of the shaft are in Pontefract Museum; one has a man on horseback.

CARLETON. *See* DARRINGTON.

QUEENSBURY   *1030*

Large s-facing village high on the ridge separating Halifax from Bradford (*West Riding North*).

HOLY TRINITY. By *James Mallinson*, 1843–5. Big nave with separately roofed aisles. Lancet windows. E end rebuilt in restoration by *T.H. & F. Healey*, 1884–5; rich E.E. style with carving by *Farmer & Brindley*. Landmark w tower dismantled and rebuilt at w end of N aisle in 1906–7, a seventh nave bay, forming a baptistery beyond a fine double-arched screen,

---

*Here were some of the better C18 houses. A severe loss was MICKLEGATE HOUSE, which had plasterwork attributed to *Giuseppe Cortese*.

taking its place. – STAINED GLASS. Several by *Shrigley & Hunt*, 1884 and 1909; others by *Kempe*, 1880 (N aisle), the style quite unlike his chancel S, and N chapel E, windows, 1906. S aisle SW by *Whall & Whall*, 1924.

BAPTIST CHAPEL, Chapel Lane. 1820. Simple symmetrical five-bay front with doorways flanking central Venetian window. (Three-sided gallery on cast-iron columns.) BAPTISTERY: small rectangular pool in burial ground.

VICTORIA HALL AND INSTITUTE. By *T.H. & F. Healey*, 1887–91. Lively Queen Anne style. Good stair hall has STAINED GLASS by *Powell Bros*, 1890.

ALBERT MEMORIAL FOUNTAIN, High Street/Brighouse Road. By *Eli Milnes*, 1863. Elaborate Gothic pinnacle with allegorical female figures in canopied niches.

Queensbury sprang up around BLACK DYKE MILLS, developed from 1835 by John Foster for his alpaca, mohair and worsted business, and still dominated by what remains of the buildings, closed *c.* 2000. The Fosters mostly used the *Healeys* and *Milnes & France* as architects. On Brighouse Road, the pedimented COUNTING HOUSE and GATEWAY, probably 1840s, with large bell in the pretty octagonal cupola. The immense, minimally Italianate, main range stretches W: first, the five-storey, fifteen-bay SHED MILL, 1840s, then its nine-bay extension *c.* 1848–51. Rounded S staircase projection at the junction. The slightly taller and deeper four-storey VICTORIA MILL, *c.* 1867–8, twenty-eight bays, has a giant through-arch with massive rusticated voussoirs in bays 4–6, and an off-centre roof tower. The later main gateway on High Street with Italianate LODGE and two-storey, nineteen-bay WAREHOUSE and SHOWROOM with decorative central parapet, are both *c.* 1870s. E of the cross-roads PROSPECT HOUSE, Sand Beds, *c.* 1827, John Foster's unassuming home. It faces his mid-C19 two-storey pedimented WAREHOUSE and CARRIAGE HOUSE, the front courtyard enclosed by STABLES.

PARK HOUSE, Park Lane. 1888, for John Foster Jun. Vernacular Revival style, with full-height square and canted bay windows and decorated gables.

LOWER NORTH ROYD, Green Lane, Shibden Vale, 1¼ m. S. It has a circular window above the doorway, and the date 1696 goes with that motif.

RASTRICK

Ancient upland settlement on the S side of the Calder valley, later developed as a suburb of Brighouse.

ST MATTHEW, Church Street. Handsome ashlar-faced building of 1796–8, replacing a chapel of 1603. Hipped roof. Short w

tower with low pediment to each side and circular cupola. The
N side towards the street is of five bays with entrances in the
first and last. Between the entrances small rectangular windows
in wide blank surrounds. The surrounds are arched and the
arches comprise the large semicircular upper windows. (Interior restored by *W. S. Barber*, 1874–9, retaining three galleries on
thin Doric columns. Apsidal chancel decorated with mosaics
(Kelly 1927). – STAINED GLASS. E window 1879 by *Powell Bros*.
Two in N aisle 1893, 1895, and two in S aisle, 1881, 1897, also
by *Powell Bros*. – S aisle first from E by *Hardman*, 1872, and one
by *R.B. Edmundson*, 1867.– MONUMENT. Greek Revival tablet
with figures to John Armitage †1828, by *Waudby & Sons*.)

In the churchyard, NW of the church, large square Anglo-
Saxon CROSS BASE. C9. Similar in style to Birstall and Hartshead (qq.v.). Scrolls with tri-lobed flowers on two sides, two
panels of wiry interlace on the third, the fourth plain. Nearby
(built into W face of boundary wall of No. 15 Crowtrees Lane)
is a MONOLITH of similar character. Probably C10 and carved
with a spiral motif.

PUBLIC LIBRARY, Crowtrees Lane. 1912. Single-storeyed. Symmetrical front with three pedimented gables.

A few older houses and cottages survive, mostly in the
vicinity of the church. SOUTH LODGE (No. 124 Rastrick
Common), was built 1879, partly with elements from a house
of 1659.

TOOTHILL HALL, at the top of the village, off Huddersfield
Road. Rebuilt 1823. Five-bay S front in fine ashlar with pedimented Doric porch. (In the garden a late C18 PAVILION
possibly by *Adam* for Nostell Priory and moved here in the
early C20.)

On Huddersfield Road a good variety of large houses of *c.* 1900
built above Brighouse's smoke, e.g. THE GATEHOUSE, on the
corner of Shepherds Thorn Lane, *c.* 1902 by *A.E. Kirk*, with
stone, roughcast and shaped gables.

RAVENFIELD

ST JAMES. On its own at the N end of the village, above the
grounds of the Hall whose owner, Elizabeth Parkin, commissioned the rebuilding by *John Carr*, 1755–6. Gothick taste with
classical touches. Nave of three bays, narrower flat polygonal
apse and embraced W tower. Plain parapet above cornice that
rises as a pediment over W entrance. Windows ogee-headed
with Y-tracery. Bell-openings ogee-headed too, and the form
used even in the lobes of quatrefoils below. The tower top has
spiky corner pinnacles and a curious stone spirelet with
concave-sided base and ball finial. The exterior is delightful,
the interior, refurnished in 1895, disappointing. Small W

gallery. – STAINED GLASS. Restored E window has coloured glass by *William Peckitt*, 1811. – MONUMENTS. George Westby †1686. Ionic aedicule with broken scrolly segmental pediment. Wreathed skull and bones below inscription. – Elizabeth Parkin †1766 and Walter Oborne †1778, side by side with elegant urns on matching bases, his, to l., by *Christopher Theakston* of Doncaster. Hers has a tall grey marble obelisk above, presumably his did once. Four smaller urns for later relatives. – Thomas Bosvile †1771 and wife Bridget †1793 by *Fisher* of York, 1804. Includes a pelican on a sarcophagus with rams' heads.

RAVENFIELD HALL. The house altered by *Carr* in 1767–74 was destroyed by fire in 1963. Surviving are Carr's imposing GATEPIERS and fine STABLES, their front of 3:3:3 bays with pedimented centre. Lower openings round-arched, the middle ones each side under large blind arches to match the central entrance (cf. Escrick (East Riding) and Ribston Hall, *West Riding North*).

RAVENSTHORPE

2020

ST SAVIOUR. Five-bay nave, wide S aisle and short NW tower with octagonal spired belfry, by *John Cory*, 1863–4; the rest by *C. Hodgson Fowler*, 1899–1901, the first phase of an ambitious, uncompleted scheme. Curvilinear tracery throughout.

RAILWAY BRIDGES. Two cast-iron skew-arched bridges on the Leeds–Manchester line, designed by *Thomas Grainger*, dated 1847.

RAWCLIFFE

6020

A river port on the Aire until the early C19. Pleasant ranges of unshowy brick and rendered houses, mostly Georgian, surround the attractive green.*

ST JAMES. On the green. 1841–2 by *Hurst & Moffatt*. White-grey brick. Lancets arranged in stepped groups of three. W tower with stone broach spire. Jarring red brick chancel, S chapel etc. by *Walter Brierley*, 1906–8 – his complete rebuilding was unrealized (see springers for nave arcades). W gallery (N and S galleries removed 1963) and original box pews. Excellent carved CHOIR STALLS. – MONUMENT. Ralph Creyke †1858. Pedestal with marble bust by *Matthew Noble*, 1859.

---

*RAWCLIFFE HALL, 1660, rebuilt 1899, was dem. *c.* 1996.

RAWMARSH

The parish church, overlooking the Don valley, is visible for miles. A dual carriageway and shopping centre erased the old village to its N in the 1960s; the late C19 centre is downhill adjoining Parkgate.

ST MARY. Aisled nave by *J.P. Pritchett*, 1837–9; W tower by *Blackmoor & Mitchell-Withers*, 1869–70; apsidal-ended chancel etc. by *Joseph Platts*, 1896–8. The tower's arched S entrance incorporates colonnettes and capitals from a Norman doorway of three orders; the inner capitals have crocket-like upright leaves. Tall, narrow four-bay nave has coupled lancet windows, the clerestory triple lancets, and the E end above the chancel three stepped single lancets. – FONT. Perp. – CROSS-SHAFT. C12. Badly weathered. – STAINED GLASS. W (tower) window by *Sidney Meteyard* of *H.H. Martyn & Co.*, Cheltenham, 1922. – Window over N door by *Camm* of Smethwick, 1921 and 1934. – MONUMENTS. John Darley †1617, kneeling with his family, on a large brass set in a moulded frame with heraldry above. – Lady Mary Middleton née Wentworth †1667. Fine marble aedicule with elaborate broken pediment and polished black Composite columns. – Rev. Rowland Hodgson †1796. Nice tablet with urn by *John Blagden*.

RECTORY (now flats), 25 yds E. 1752–3 and later. The design puts one in mind of *Paine*. Three-bay entrance front with full-width pediment, the slightly projecting and pedimented centre bay superimposed. This bay has a first-floor Venetian window within a tall blind arch. Huge rounded bay window to garden front, early C19.

ST NICOLAS, Ryecroft, ⅞ m. NE. By *W.H. Wood*, 1924–5. Plain, brick, incomplete. Three-bay nave with clerestory. Round-arched windows and arcades.

METHODIST CHURCH, High Street Centre. 1907–8, and a rare work by *W.J. Hale* outside Sheffield. Confident Art Nouveau Gothic.

CEMETERY, ½ m. NNW. 1908. Apsidal-ended brick chapels linked by square tower with Gothic archway and octagonal stone spire.

LIBRARY (former) Rawmarsh Hill. By *Joseph Platts*, 1904–5. Single-storey, five-bay front embellished with swan-neck pediments and obelisks. Adjacent villa-like OFFICES also by *Platts*, for the Local Board, 1892.

MINERS' INSTITUTE, Broad Street. 1914. Large, Renaissance style. Small central pediment, balustrades and other details in artificial stone.

PUMPING STATION (former), Westfield Road, 300 yds SSW. Gabled tower for a Newcomen engine, dated 1823 but possibly earlier. Attached boiler house and workshop. Built for one of Earl Fitzwilliam's collieries.

ALDWARKE STEEL WORKS (Tata Steel), 1 m. SE. Facing Aldwarke Lane, the former COMPUTER CENTRE (now Capgemini
offices) by *Gollins Melvin Ward Partnership* for British Steel,
1975. An elegant building, framed in black steel. Only the set-
back first floor, with its continuous glazing, is visible above the
sheltering container of a grassed embankment.*

REEDNESS *see* SWINEFLEET

RINGINGLOW

ROUND HOUSE. A tall, octagonal toll house built *c.* 1795 on the
edge of the moors SW of Sheffield, where the 1758 turnpike
road forked to Buxton via Fox House (q.v.) and to Chapel-en-
le-Frith via Hathersage. Crenellated parapet and Gothick
windows (several blind). Above each upper window a blank
quatrefoil.
NORFOLK ARMS. Early C19. Battlemented parapet and unusual
triangle-headed windows.

RIPPONDEN

Former textile mill village in the Ryburn valley.

ST BARTHOLOMEW. By *George & John Shaw*, 1867–8, replacing
a church of 1736. Dec style; flowing tracery. Tall SW tower
with slender broach spire. Six-bay nave; arcades with clustered
colonnettes. Aisle E bays transeptal. Clerestory.
CONGREGATIONAL CHAPEL (former), Oldham Road. By *Paull
& Robinson*, 1869–70. Asymmetrical composition, with attached
Sunday School, in early French Gothic style.
STONES METHODIST CHURCH, Rochdale Road. 1902. Gothic.
Broad gabled front. Paired doorways below stepped lancets
with tracery.
W of St Bartholomew, an C18 PACKHORSE BRIDGE across the
river and above this on Priest Lane the C18 VICARAGE, over-
looked by the tall CONSERVATIVE CLUB AND VICTORIA
HALL on Halifax Road, by *C.F. L. Horsfall & Son*, 1899–1900
with shaped gable overall. 150 yds SW, the former LIBERAL
CLUB and CENTRAL HALL, 1902–3, has a jollier Renaissance
front, with blocked pilasters and ball finials.

---

*ALDWARKE HALL, the Foljambes' mansion, *c.* 1720 with interiors by *James Wyatt*,
dem. 1899, stood nearby.

KEBROYD HALL, Kebroyd Lane, 4/5 m. N. Built by Samuel Hill, worsted manufacturer and entrepreneur, in 1739; alterations for John Hadwen of Kebroyd silk mills *c.* 1854. Plain four-bay front with projecting four-bay wings, the S wing enhanced with e.g. consoled cornices to the sash windows.

SWIFT PLACE, I m. SW. Fine house of 1626 altered and extended by Elkanah Hoyle 1698–1704 to form a domestic textile-manufacturing complex. Three-room, through-passage house has triple-gabled S front with two surviving four-light mullioned-and-transomed windows, other windows converted to sashes. Parallel rear range 1698. Two-bay E wing, 1704, projects to rear; front has cross-windows and big gable chimneystack. Similar W wing, connected to rear range, was lowered in late C19/early C20 and the house's W roof extended over it, creating a broad asymmetrical S gable. Alterations to house *c.* 1704 included relocation of S entrance and insertion of large rear staircase window. (Excellent carved stone fireplaces, one with Corinthian columns, one with Doric pilasters.) Splendid courtyard GATEPIERS *c.* 1704.

RISHWORTH

0010

Small village below the moors, in a tributary valley of the River Ryburn.

ST JOHN. 1927–8 by *Walsh & Maddock* after initial designs by *Austin & Paley*. Simple late Gothic, with stocky W tower and straight-headed mullioned windows. – STAINED GLASS. E window by *Veronica Whall*, its 'apple and pear' tracery copying rose windows in local C17 porches.

RISHWORTH SCHOOL, ⅓ m. N. Endowed by John Wheelwright, whose schoolroom of 1725 is now the CHAPEL. Four big mullioned-and-transomed windows, the fifth of 1960 in a sympathetic sanctuary extension which reuses the original E window. Painted glass shields in three windows. The SCHOOL, downhill, has two long ranges facing Oldham Road, one Late Georgian of 1827–8 by *John Oates*, the other less gracious Neo-Georgian of 1933. The first though severe is of impressive dimensions: semi-basement of big ashlar blocks; two-storey centre of seven bays with small pediment, lower four-bay connecting links, and three-bay angle pavilions (originally for dormitories) with attic storey and hipped roofs. Central range has colonnade to open rear quadrangle.

UPPER GOAT HOUSE, ¼ m. N. Late C16 through-passage house, altered, extended and subdivided. Original double-gabled front. Cross-wing (with rear gable) to l. has five-light window and inserted doorway, housebody has six-light window and two-light fire window. Windows are double-chamfered with plain hoodmoulds. Two-storey porch, 1624, set in angle with rebuilt service end to r., has fine Tudor-arched doorway and unusual transverse gable.

UPPER COCKCROFT, ⅔ m. WNW, above the village, near the moor. Two attached houses, sombre and impressive and quite stretched-out, with flanking barns to front. Farmhouse on the r., dated 1607, has double-gabled front with six-light transomed housebody window. Spiral stops to hoodmoulds. Porch, 1701, to entrance on r. return. House, 1642, has more regular gables to double-pile parlour and housebody bays. Transomed ground-floor windows, decorative label stops to upper windows. Two-storey gabled porch to through passage. Single bay with five-light windows links service end to farmhouse. (Some good fireplaces; parlour chamber has plaster overmantel with heraldry, 1644.)

RISHWORTH MILL (Rishworth Palace), off Oldham Road. Four-storey water- and steam-powered cotton-spinning mill, c. 1864. Nineteen-bay front with Italianate clock tower. Now flats. Italianate LODGE.

RISHWORTH LODGE, 1 m. SSW. Now flats. Steeply roofed and elaborately chimneyed shooting lodge by *W. H. Crossland* for Captain Henry Savile, c. 1870. Brawny C17 Revival style with Gothic touches.

ROCHE ABBEY

5080

Beautifully placed in a glen, Roche was a Cistercian house, founded jointly in 1147 by Richard de Buili and Richard Fitz-Turgis, who owned land either side of Maltby Beck, which runs from W to E across the site. The monks came from Newminster in Northumberland, settled in 1138 from Fountains (*West Riding North*). Roche's dedication to the Virgin Mary was distinguished by reference to its surroundings of cliffs of white Magnesian limestone as *Sancta Maria de Rupe* – St Mary of the Rock. The principal buildings lie on the N side of the stream, their layout following that of Fountains. The main building campaign in stone was from c. 1170 to the early C13, much of it under the fourth abbot, Osmund (1184–1213), who had previously been cellarer of Fountains.

Roche's unremarkable existence necessitated few later changes and the plan survives with exceptional clarity, even though mostly in the form of low walls only. Fortunately there is somewhat more of the CHURCH, especially at the E end. It has the standard Cistercian plan (cf. e.g. Fontenay in Burgundy 1139 etc., Buildwas in Shropshire, Kirkstall (*West Riding North*) etc.): that is, a straight-headed CHANCEL with two shorter straight-headed chapels each side and transepts. The only way in which Roche differs from this is that the chapels are

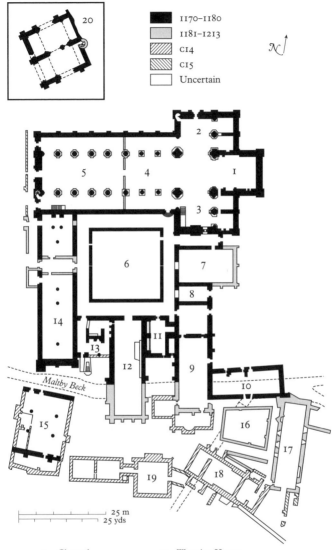

1170–1180
1181–1213
C14
C15
Uncertain

N

Maltby Beck

25 m
25 yds

1	Chancel	11	Warming House
2	North Transept	12	Refectory
3	South Transept	13	Kitchen
4	Monks' Choir	14	Lay Brothers' Quarters
5	Nave	15	Lay Brothers' Infirmary
6	Cloister	16	Infirmary Cloister
7	Chapter House	17	Infirmary Building
8	Parlour	18	Abbot's Lodging
9	Day Room	19	Abbot's Kitchen
10	Reredorter	20	Gatehouse (130 yds NW of Church)

Roche Abbey.
Plan

interconnected and that the chancel was linked to the first s chapel by a small doorway. The chancel is two bays and has in the w bay a blank triforium of two pointed arches close together. The shafts between have waterleaf capitals. Clerestory with a round-headed window in the middle. As at Fountains, all the constructive arches are pointed, while the windows are round-headed. e bay originally with three tiers of windows, the two lower tiers shafted with waterleaf capitals. In the C14 the chancel was refaced inside with tabernacle-work, subsequently robbed; on the n wall some crocketed finials remain to indicate what must have been a gorgeous piece. The former rib-vaults stood on single shafts that stand on conical corbels below the triforium sill. The shafts are tripled below the clerestory sill. Pevsner thought this indicated that only at that stage was rib-vaulting decided on. The inclusion of vaulting shafts in the compound CROSSING piers, however, makes a late change of plan most unlikely. The piers' shafts are keeled in the main directions. Extensive use of keeling is a feature of Roche. Shaft-rings at sill level.

17   The TRANSEPTS stand up almost to full height. Their e walls are divided in the elevation very much like the chancel walls except for the large openings into the chapels. Blank triforium arches, two to each opening below, plain clerestory window above. One thick vaulting shaft rises from the ground. It is joined just below the vault by two shafts on corbels. n transept n wall had three tiers of windows with a wall passage at triforium stage. The vaulted chapels survive most completely on the s. Diagonals on corbels. Simple bosses. In the inner chapel the window was altered later, but its tracery is broken out. Less survives of the second chapel, which has, however, a well-preserved s window.

It is the date of these remarkable e parts, which are unquestionably 'truly Gothic' (Bilson), that makes them so important. There is no documentary evidence but it is agreed that they date from the 1170s, possibly slightly earlier. Here a Gothic elevation, Gothic details and especially Gothic rib-vaulting are used with evident ease, making Roche not only one of the earliest buildings in the new style in the North but among the earliest in England. As the first Cistercian church in England to have a three-storey elevation and full rib-vaults Roche goes a decisive step beyond contemporary work at Fountains and Kirkstall. There is no specific source for its design but there are clear influences from NE France, particularly the Aisne valley in the Laonois. Close parallels for individual features occur at Nouvion, Bellefontaine (Oise) and Creil for example, and it is thought that the master at Roche must have had personal knowledge of the area.

The e parts have differences of detail typical of the period rather than indicative of different building phases. The capitals, for example, vary. In the n transept those from which the vault sprang have a sort of waterleaf. In the s transept they are moulded, the crossing piers have a mixture, and the chancel's

have stiff-leaf with semi-octagonal abacus. Roche has particularly fine stonework for its date, the regular ashlar blocks,
quarried on site, being part of its French character. It falls
short, however, in one important respect. The overall effect is
still of solid massing and it lacks the lightness of early French
Gothic, especially in the triforium's plain blind arches. The
vault was, however, carried without buttresses.

Of the NAVE and AISLES too little stands to enjoy them.
Eight bays, the piers symmetrical with four major and four
minor shafts. The vaulting shafts must therefore have been
corbelled out above. The monks' choir reached forward to the
w through the two E bays, the third forming the retrochoir. At
its w end the stone pulpitum (or rood screen?), its central
opening with nailhead decoration. Against it on the w two
pairs of chapels with side screens. Nearby the remains of a
tomb and several grave-slabs from lay burials allowed from the
C14 after the inclusion of lay brothers in the community ended.
w façade has three shafted doorways, the middle one with
three orders. A thin C15 Galilee porch in front continued
southwards to cover entrances to the w monastic buildings.
Bases of C14 buttresses outside the N and S walls indicate
concerns about the nave's stability.

THE MONASTIC BUILDINGS. The main buildings around the
CLOISTER follow the usual Cistercian plan. The w range is
probably the earliest, the rest completed by the 1180s. Fragments of the CLOISTER ARCADE (in the small site museum)
show that it had pointed arches on paired shafts with waterleaf
capitals. Doorway into the cloister from the E bay of the S aisle.
Along the E walk, first a PASSAGE, originally divided into a
small LIBRARY with larger SACRISTY beyond. The Sacristy
had a doorway into the S transept and, more unusually, into
the oblong CHAPTER HOUSE. This has two piers along its
longer axis, the w circular, the other with eight slender attached
shafts with deep hollows between. E part probably a slightly
later extension. Then the PARLOUR, and then the undercroft
of the Dormitory, with octagonal piers along its long axis. A
cross wall divides it into a square room with second doorway
on the E and the DAYROOM, originally three bays (see its SW
end buttress). A two-bay extension bridges the stream. The
DORMITORY ran all along the upper storey of the E walk and
communicated with the church by the night stairs inside the S
transept. The REREDORTER branched off the dormitory to the
E, over the stream. At the end of the dayroom, on the stream's
S bank, a rectangular room with large tiled fireplace and smaller
room to the w, probably built for cooking and eating meat after
dietary rules were relaxed in the mid C14. The principal room
in the S cloister range was the REFECTORY, at right angles to
the walk, possibly one of the first in this new position that the
Cistercians adopted from the 1170s. Like the dayroom it was
later extended across the stream, on another fine bridge. To
its E was the WARMING HOUSE, with two big fireplaces side
by side, and the day stairs to the dormitory; to its w the

KITCHEN, with free-standing hearths back to back. In the W range were the LAY BROTHERS' QUARTERS, with the REFEC-TORY in the S half, divided by a row of octagonal piers, and a passage with vaulted cellar beyond to the N. The DORMITORY occupied the upper floor, with night stair into the church's S aisle.

S of the stream was the LAY BROTHERS' INFIRMARY, divided by four circular piers into a hall with side aisles, and probably adapted in the C14 as guesthouse. In the site's SE corner an irregular secondary CLOISTER with part of the INFIRMARY (early C13) on the E and the ABBOT'S LODGING, rebuilt in the C14, on the S. The square ABBOT'S KITCHEN, C14, stands quite high up to the W, with bakehouse and brew-house beyond.

Roche has the most complete surviving early Cistercian GATEHOUSE. Built c. 1200. Only the lower of its two storeys survives but this has the order's distinctive triple portals to control access to both Inner and Outer Courts. Two bays. The NW one, with outer entrance arch, was a covered porch with porter's lodge. Vaulted in three equal parts: one wide part flanked by two narrow ones. Single-chamfered ribs, stiff-leaf bosses. The cross wall has two archways, one for carts and a narrower one for pedestrians, both originally closed by gates. The inner bay was a central vaulted gatehall with wide triple-chamfered SE arch opening to the Inner Court. The SW arch opened to a shallow unvaulted compartment forming a porch to the Outer Court.

Roche was dissolved in 1538, when there were fourteen monks. A vivid account of its immediate ransacking by local people was written in 1591. The site was landscaped in 1774–7 by *Capability Brown* as part of the grounds of Sandbeck Park, the contract directing him to create a picturesque setting for the ruins 'with Poet's Feeling and with Painter's Eye'. His destructive tidying up of the ruins occasioned criticism at the time, especially from Gilpin. Excavations in the late C19 and early C20 revealed most of the site but it has never been systematically excavated and the S parts of the site lie under terraces near *Brown*'s CASCADE from Laughton Pond.

Near the gatehouse is ABBEY HOUSE, appropriately Gothick. Probably c. 1807.

ROSSINGTON

ST MICHAEL. Rebuilt 1841–4 by *John Clark* for James Brown Sen. of Rossington Hall. The Norman S doorway and chancel arch and the limestone Perp W tower were retained. Chancel and narrow nave with new transepts in solid lancet style. Sandstone. Was the beakhead corbel table copied from the old church? Restored Norman doorway of two orders; the outer

has nook-shafts and an arch with beakhead. Hoodmould with
double billet. The chancel arch is more complex. Its shafts, one
strong, the other slender, are both exceedingly short, being set
above some 9 ft (2.7 metres) of bare imposts. That they start
so high means there must have been a stone screen (cf. Edlington and Frickley). The capitals have twisted and turned bands
or trails and at the corners heads and lion masks. Chevron in
the soffit and on the face of the arch, point to point, then
unusual mouldings between two rows of pellets, then foliage
trail on the hoodmould. – FONT. Norman. Cylindrical with
cable-patterned rim. – PULPIT. C15, reputedly from St Mary,
Doncaster (q.v.). Exceptionally ornate for Yorkshire, though
plain compared e.g. with Devon. Buttress-shafts at the angles,
traceried panels. – PEWS by *Robert Thompson*, 1959, other
WOODWORK by *Martin Dutton*, 1968. – STAINED GLASS. E
window by *Capronnier*, 1862. Four windows by *Powell & Sons*,
1890, 1903 and 1911.

75 yds W is the stuccoed former RECTORY by *William
Lindley*, 1801 as a school and schoolhouse, converted in 1804.
Five bays square, pediments to N and S fronts. The successor
SCHOOL and SCHOOLHOUSE, 75 yds E, is of 1857 by *W.M.
Teulon* for James Brown Jun. of Rossington Hall. Picturesque
cottage-style house with big half-timbered gables to first floor.
Attached school spoilt by later C20 alterations. Also by *Teulon*
the unusual Gothic former BUTCHER'S SHOP, 300 yds W, 1859;
and WELL-HOUSE, 1861, with lucarned spirelet, and, no
doubt, the picturesque FOUNTAIN COTTAGES with half-
timbered gables and big brick chimneystacks.

ROSSINGTON HALL (hotel), 1¼ m. SE. Also by *W.M. Teulon*
but *c.* 1880–2 for Richard J. Streatfeild after the earlier house
(originally 'Shooter's Hill') burnt down. Very large, three-
storeyed, five-by-five bays. Heavy-handed Jacobethan style in
brick with stone dressings. Some rich but unexciting interiors.
The former STABLES (Northern Racing College), 1855, are in
Teulon's picturesque gabled Gothic style.

NEW ROSSINGTON, across the railway line to the W, is the village
begun in 1912 when the colliery company began to sink the
mine (operational 1916–2006).* 800 houses were provided,
designed by the managing director, *Maurice Deacon*. Owing to
wartime labour shortages women were employed as bricklay-
ers' assistants in 1916 and 'proved quite satisfactory'. Main
grid of wide roads has central open space with three circular
roads around it. On the inner circle (cf. Maltby), the colliery
officials' semi-detached houses and the church of ST LUKE,
Neo-Byzantine style by *F. Norman D. Masters*, 1915–16 for the
South Yorkshire Coalfields Churches Extension Committee
(cf. Bentley, Edlington and Maltby). Its SW porch has an
outdoor pulpit over (tower not built). Later housing included

---

*The Chairman was Lord Aberconway, one of the most enlightened and far-sighted
industrial leaders.

the 'second circle' estate to the SE, built by the Industrial Housing Association 1922–5.

ROTHERHAM

INTRODUCTION

The spire of its splendid medieval parish church still dominates this small town, which even now has an urban centre of hardly more than a quarter of a mile across. Surprisingly, Rotherham can claim a longer history than Sheffield, for there was a substantial Roman fort with an associated settlement at Templeborough. Medieval Rotherham grew up on rising ground on the E bank of the River Don at a crossing point slightly downstream of its confluence with the Rother. There is no record of the earliest bridge but it carried the important route from London to Richmond, which crossed the ancient Sheffield to Doncaster road along the Don valley nearby. Rufford Abbey, Nottinghamshire, held the whole of the manor by 1283. Edward I's charter of confirmation the same year records an existing market that no doubt pre-dated a charter of 1208 granting an annual fair. Thomas Rotherham (1423–1500), who served as Lord Chancellor 1474–83 and was Archbishop of York from 1480, was a great benefactor of his native town. He founded the College of Jesus in 1483, its purposes including the education of boys unsuited to ecclesiastical careers as well as those aspiring to the priesthood. After its dissolution in 1547 its secular educational function was maintained by the town as a grammar school. Before the advent of modern local government the Feoffees of the Common Lands, a body established in the C16, managed most of the town's affairs.

The rich resources of iron ore and coal in the surrounding area were exploited from medieval times. After the Don Navigation reached Rotherham in 1740, with an extension to Tinsley in 1751, improved transport of goods via the Humber stimulated greater industrial development, including potteries, glassworks and breweries as well as engineering and metalworking. By the later C18 the Masbrough iron works established by Samuel Walker in 1746 were among the most important in the country, and

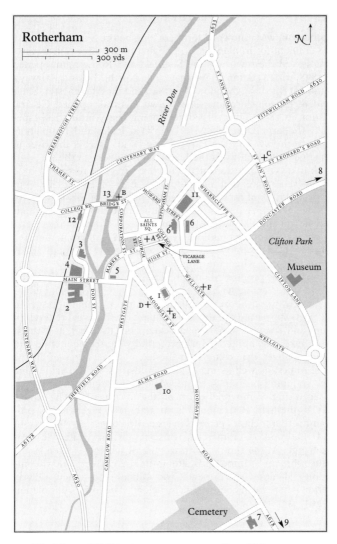

Rotherham

300 m
300 yds

A The Minster (All Saints)
B Chapel of Our Lady
C St Antony Coptic Orthodox Church
D Talbot Lane Methodist Church
E Unitarian Church of Our Father (former; now mosque)
F Primitive Methodist Chapel (former)

1 Town Hall
2 Civic Offices (Riverside House)
3 Law Courts
4 Police Station
5 Post Office (former)
6 College of Arts and Technology
7 Thomas Rotherham Sixth Form College
8 Clifton Community Arts School
9 Newman School
10 Workhouse (former)
11 Centenary Market
12 Central Railway Station
13 Chantry Bridge and Rotherham Bridge

Rotherham was renowned for them long before Sheffield became pre-eminent for iron and steel. The first of the three railway lines that served the town was the Sheffield and Rotherham, opened in 1838, with a station on Westgate. The North Midland Railway's station at Masbrough followed in 1840 and the Manchester, Sheffield & Lincolnshire line, later Great Central, opened Central Station in 1868. They served developing heavy industries, especially the large Don valley steel works at Ickles and Templeborough to the SW and the Parkgate works just across the river in Rawmarsh, as well as Rotherham Main Colliery to the S.

Until 1851 expansion of the town centre was restricted by a family settlement that prevented the Earl of Effingham from granting leases of more than twenty-one years on his land NE of College Street. A private Act of Parliament abolished the limit and he quickly laid out Effingham Street, Howard Street and Frederick Street for building. By 1871, when Rotherham became a borough, the population was 57,500. County borough status came in 1902, when the population had reached 61,000. The Council was progressive in providing housing after the First World War, starting with the East Dene estate in 1919 and erecting nearly 5,000 houses by 1939, twice the national average. In the post-war period the town did not escape the usual redevelopment and creation of new road systems but its effect, at least on the centre, was limited. More profound were the economic and social changes that came with the later C20 closures of all the local mines, as well as many local industries. At the same time new shopping centres at Meadowhall and Parkgate nearby had a depressing commercial effect on the town centre. The Council's Rotherham Renaissance is an ambitious regeneration programme that includes projects in six central quarters – Waterfront and Cultural, Commercial, Business, Civic, Lifestyle and Exchange. At the time of writing, several schemes – such as the refurbishment of Imperial Buildings in High Street, a new Community Health Centre, new Civic Offices and a new railway station – have been completed (*see* below). The town's population in 2011 was 110,000.

PLACES OF WORSHIP

26   THE MINSTER (ALL SAINTS). One of the largest and stateliest parish churches in Yorkshire, externally all splendidly Perp. The crossing tower with its soaring spire is the dominant motif of Rotherham, visible far and wide. Pevsner, using Bruno Taut's term, called it a true *Stadtkrone*. It is indeed the town's crowning glory and seems the more monumental when viewed from All Saints Square below, its elevated position an advantage not enjoyed by the comparable churches of Halifax, Sheffield and Wakefield.

A monition by the Archbishop of York of 1409 exists, pointing out that the parishioners have assigned rates and rents to the necessary rebuilding of the tower, warning those who have refused to contribute, and granting the others an indulgence.

The present church was probably started after the tower had gone up some way or even been completed. Only inside is there any evidence of its predecessors. The building is 147 ft (45.5 metres) long, the spire 180 ft (54.9 metres) tall. The tower has two four-light bell-openings in each face with two transoms. The lights above and below the transoms are arched, the bottom tier being blank. Angle buttresses with pinnacles that end just below the top of the square part of the tower. To the eye they are continued by the pinnacles at the corners of the tower. It gives the impression that the top of the tower is octagonal and not square. The spire, lightly crocketed, rises recessed behind the battlements. It is octagonal, and in its diagonals another set of shafts stand close to its body and end in yet more pinnacles. It is an original and successful design. The whole body of the church is embattled and pinnacled too. w front with a seven-light window and aisle w windows of four lights. The w doorway is relatively insignificant, although there is some blank panelling above it. Aisles with transomed four-light windows. The doorway within the s porch has a hood-mould on angel busts. Clerestory with three-light windows, transepts with six-light end windows and three-light w and e windows. The s chapel was built for the Chantry of Jesus founded by Thomas Rotherham in 1480, the year he became Archbishop of York. His College of Jesus was attached to the church. The chapel's tracery is uncusped. The N chapel, like-wise an addition, is not battlemented; the windows have trian-gular heads. Chancel clerestory of four bays, the windows as near continuous as they could be. It dates from 1508–12. The great e window is by *Scott*, who restored the church in 1873–5. He enlarged the opening and designed the tracery. Elsewhere his touch was lighter and some of the very competent and interesting external carving survives from an c18 restoration (e.g. the hoodmoulds' appealing figure-work).

The interior is as impressive as the exterior and until one reaches the chancel seems equally consistently Perp. The space under the tower is fan-vaulted, always a sign of Tudor rather than earlier Perp workmanship. Between the nave and the aisles arcades of four wide and high bays with very slender piers of lozenge shape, the long axis being at right angles to the axis of the nave so as to make the piers seem slimmer than they are. Towards nave as well as aisle three very thin shafts are attached to the piers. The capitals are very flat embattled bands above carved foliage hiding faces. The treatment of the crossing is the same, but capitals are here confined to the shafts. Excellent panelled nave ceiling with bosses. The similar chancel ceiling dates from 1510–12. But the chancel itself is clearly older than the rest of the church. The masonry is dif-ferent, the piers are octagonal, their capitals are simply moulded, and the arches are double-chamfered. The lower roof-line is visible inside against the crossing tower. The details look c14 and not too late, and the sedilia have indeed ogee heads on slim shafts.

FURNISHINGS. REREDOS. By *Burlison & Grylls*, 1877. – SCREEN. To the S chapel. C15. Only a fragment of a larger screen. Four-light divisions, four-centred arches. The middle mullion is stronger than the others and reaches up into the apex of the arch. – STALLS. 1452 (chancel). The ends with tracery. Poppyheads with statuettes (Annunciation, Adoration of the Magi), some very charming. – BENCH-ENDS. In the S chapel. Mostly with close tracery in two tiers. – Fine C18 ORGAN CASE. The organ is by *Johann Snetzler*, 1777. – PULPIT. 1604. An exceptionally accomplished piece with ornamental panels and angle colonnettes. C18 tester on two columns. All the columns are closely studded. – Spired FONT COVER. By *J.P. Seddon*, 1880. – STAINED GLASS. E window designed by *Scott*, executed by *Clayton & Bell*, 1874. – S chapel: E window by *Temple Moore*, 1921; second from E by *Harry Harvey*, 1963. S transept: E window by *Wailes*, 1867; S window by *Alexander Gibbs*, 1864; W window by *Camm Bros*, *c.* 1870. – S aisle east-ernmost window by *Heaton, Butler & Bayne*, 1876. – W window by *Clayton & Bell*, 1890. – N aisle: westernmost window by *James Bell*, 1875; third from E by *Powell & Sons*, 1934. – MONUMENTS. No big individual or family pieces but a good town collection, mostly gathered in the S transept. – N chapel. Tomb-chest in an arched recess with straight cresting, the arch no more than a horizontal carried by two small semicircles. On the back wall of the recess a brass depicting Robert Swift †1561 and his family. – Many small brasses, C17 and C18, on the chancel piers etc. – S aisle. Early C16 tomb-chest with three shields set in lozenges. – S transept. Mrs Buck †1778. By *John Platt*. – Samuel Buck †1806. By *Flaxman*. Group of standing females, sorrowful below an urn. – Samuel Tooker †1807. By *Joseph Lockwood*. Draped sarcophagus. – Memorial to Fifty Young Persons killed in the launching of a vessel at Masbrough in 1841. By *Edwin Smith* of Sheffield. Grecian figure of Faith. – Mrs Coward †1854. By *Edwin Smith*. An angel rising up. The style influenced by Flaxman.

CHAPEL OF OUR LADY, Rotherham Bridge. Begun *c.* 1483, when John Bokyng, school master, left 3*s.* 4*d.* in his will for the chapel 'to be built on Rotherham bridge'. Perp. Less celebrated than its grander companion piece at Wakefield (q.v.), but notable as one of only four surviving medieval bridge chapels in England. From 1547 to 1913 it survived as an alms-house, prison and finally a shop. Restored in 1924 by *J.E. Knight* of Rotherham and reconsecrated. Plain (ritual) W front with Tudor-arched doorway and two-light window above. Two bays long, with renewed three-light windows. Panel tracery. Renewed E window of four lights. Battlements and pinnacles. Plain interior with panelled ceiling. The tiny SW staircase led up to a gallery for priest's chamber. Tunnel-vaulted crypt below. – STAINED GLASS. E window by *Alan Younger*, 1975.

ST ANTONY COPTIC ORTHODOX CHURCH, St Leonard's Road. Formerly St Stephen by *T.D. Barry & Son*, 1872–4; SW tower completed, with stone spire, to original plans, 1910;

Rotherham, Chapel of Our Lady.
Engraving by J. Rogers after N. Whittock, *c.* 1830

executant architect *J.E. Knight*. Steep roofs, small aisle and clerestory windows and intricate tracery all typical of Barry's work. – STAINED GLASS. E window by *T.W. Camm*, 1910. Several in aisles also by *Camm*, *c.* 1890 and 1910.

TALBOT LANE METHODIST CHURCH, Moorgate Street. By *William Morley & Son*, 1902–3. Large, cruciform, in Geometrical Gothic style. E front has five-light window over paired entrances and tall tower with stone spire at SE angle. Impressive interior, galleried on three sides, seats 850 people. Good Art Nouveau electroliers. – STAINED GLASS. Apsidal chancel windows by *S. Evans* of Smethwick 1903.

PRIMITIVE METHODIST CHAPEL (former), Wellgate. 1851. The contrast between the pedimented simplicity of this and the elaboration of its successor of 1892–3 (Masonic Hall) to its l. is illuminating. Blatant red brick and terracotta front. Symmetrical now, but the angle tower originally had an octagonal turret with an ogee cap and pinnacles below, also with ogee caps.

MOSQUE, Moorgate Street. Former Unitarian church by *Flockton & Gibbs*, 1878–80. Tall, narrow nave with Dec tracery. Gabled doorway in decorative buff terracotta. Small NW tower has open arcade below 100-ft (30-metre) stone spire. – STAINED GLASS. By *W.H. Atkinson*, 1885.

PUBLIC BUILDINGS

TOWN HALL, Moorgate Street. Built as the West Riding Magistrates Court, 1928–9, by *Percy O. Platts*. Dignified Portland stone front with channelled rustication to ground floor and chimneystacks. Seven-bay centre with arched windows. Entrances in slightly projecting pedimented end bays have well-detailed Doric porches, also pedimented. Lower four-bay wings. Converted to Town Hall 1994–5, with rear extensions 1999.

TOWN HALL (former), Howard Street. *See* Perambulation.

CIVIC OFFICES (RIVERSIDE HOUSE), Main Street. By *Carey Jones*, 2009–11. Large block successfully composed as three parallel ranges of four, five and six storeys and different lengths. Simple window treatment complements fine red sandstone ashlar facing.

LAW COURTS (former), The Statutes. Magistrates', Coroner's and County Courts, by *Rotherham MBC Architects Department* (project architect *Steve Fryer*), 1990–4 but now disused. Set informally overlooking the canal, eschewing a grand civic statement. Irregular plan with advancing and receding blocks with low gables. Main entrance has double-height portico *in antis* with square piers. Buff brick with brick details including royal coat of arms.

POLICE STATION, Main Street. 1982. Red brick. Forbidding fortress-style, with internal courtyard. Four and five storeys, the ground floor mainly blind.

POST OFFICE (former), Main Street/Market Street. By *Walter Pott* of *H.M. Office of Works*, 1905–7. Wrenaissance style in pinkish brick and stone. Two pedimented entrance bays, the doorways with big segmental hoods. Doric columns as mullions to three-light windows on first floor.

COLLEGE OF ARTS AND TECHNOLOGY, Howard Street. By *A.F. Scott & Sons* of Norwich, 1930–1. Three-storey front with Portland stone centre. Modern style with a dash of Art Deco. Sculpted panel over entrance by *Bennett Ingram*, depicting the Fountain of Knowledge as inspiration for Art, Science and Technology. Subtly curved block opposite also by *Scott & Sons*, 1960.

THOMAS ROTHERHAM SIXTH FORM COLLEGE, Moorgate Road. By *Habershon & Pite*, 1874–6, as Rotherham Independent College for training Independent ministers. Tudor Gothic. Rock-faced sandstone with limestone dressings. Massive gatehouse tower, with two-storey oriel above the entrance. Gabled bays to flanking two-storey ranges, the l. one extended by two larger gabled bays, set forward. Many later additions for the Grammar School after 1890 and Sixth Form College since 1967.

CLIFTON COMMUNITY ARTS SCHOOL, Middle Lane. Originally the Girls' High School, by *Holdgate & Harrison*, 1908–10. Neo-Georgian, brick. Doric porch to single-storey entrance range between two-storey wings. Hall behind has big Diocletian windows between four pilaster-like chimneystacks. Adapted and extended by *Balfour Beatty*, 2003–6.

NEWMAN SCHOOL, East Bawtry Road. By *Geoffrey Raven* of the Borough Architect's Department. Completed 1939; opened in 1949, after war use, as the open-air school intended. Excellent example of the use of the International Modern style in an educational building (cf. Three Lane Ends School, Castleford). Seven separate south-facing classrooms, glazed on three sides. Clerestories above flat-roofed canopies. Linking curved corridor to rear; its N side, now glazed, was originally open. Assembly hall and administration wing to E. All in painted cement render with flat asphalt roofs.

WORKHOUSE (former), Alma Road. By *Hurst & Moffatt*, 1838–40, altered by *H.L. Tacon* of Rotherham, 1894. Severe Tudor Gothic. All that survives is the two-storey gabled E end of the NW range, and some single-storey attachments, now workshops.

CENTENARY MARKET, Howard Street. By *Gillinson, Barnett & Partners*, 1971. Two large halls, side-by-side, one with upper shop levels against the slope. Tubular steel framing with translucent plyglass and white fibreglass infill gives an exuberant interpretation of the traditional glazed roof.

CENTRAL RAILWAY STATION, College Road. By *Aedas Architects*, 2009–12. Cheerful upturned roof canopies on slender white trusses give a distinctive profile to upper booking hall and lower-level platforms. Attractive timber boarding underneath.

CHANTRY BRIDGE, Bridge Street. 1927–30, by *Vincent Turner*, Borough Engineer, with *Sir Reginald Blomfield* as consultant architect. Single span of 94 ft (28.7 metres). Reinforced concrete, with stone parapets to harmonize with the adjacent C15 ROTHERHAM BRIDGE. This had been widened and lengthened in the C18 and was restored to its original form as a linked footbridge. Four pointed arches, ribbed beneath.

PERAMBULATION

A walk around the modest centre reveals much of the medieval pattern of streets radiating out from the Minster. There were no extensive street improvements in the late C19, although Market Street was made in 1878 and the N end of Moorgate Street in 1879. The constricted junction of High Street and Westgate was opened up in 1905 and Corporation Street followed in 1913. The greatest changes came with the widening of Bridgegate, 1914–28, before widening and redevelopment in College Street and Effingham Street in 1929–32 culminated with the creation of All Saints Square below the church.

We start in the churchyard s of the Minster, overlooked on the E by mid-C19 commercial premises that replaced the old Vicarage. Three storeys, brick, in Late Georgian form with small pediment. Across CHURCH STREET is IMPERIAL BUILDINGS by *Joseph Platts*, 1905–7, an impressive island block of shops and offices in Jacobean Revival style. With its internal top-lit shopping courtyard it mirrors the plan of the Shambles previously on the site. Curved corners, extensive glazing and good Edwardian shopfronts (restored).

HIGH STREET, running downhill to the E, begins with a prominent three-storey corner with turret and gables (No. 36) a brick refronting of 1883 (see stone rear), with an elaborate clock (from the *Daily Express*'s Fleet Street offices c. 1920). Opposite, below the corner of Moorgate Street (*see* below),

No. 29 retains the two upper storeys of a plain five-bay house, probably *c.* 1770. Then comes the former Old Three Cranes Inn, timber-framed, with late C16/early C17 jettied front of three storeys, now rendered, and incomplete C15 rear wing, at right angles to the street. This part had an open-hall and retains half of a coved dais canopy, the only known example in this area. The building's l. half, a third bay with two more gables, was demolished in 1963. At the bottom of the hill the imposing ROYAL BANK OF SCOTLAND (originally Sheffield & Rotherham Bank) by *E. Isle Hubbard*, 1892. Recessed fronts with a giant Corinthian column in polished Aberdeen granite between each bay. Pedimented ground-floor windows. Heavy entablature with parapet. Good banking hall.

The bank turns the corner into WELLGATE. About 100 yds s is CLIFTON BANK, with a little enclave of nice Early Victorian terraced villas with a larger pair facing downhill at the top. Just before Hollowgate on the r. WELLGATE OLD HALL (Nos. 120–126) is the only C17 house in the town centre. During restoration in 1979 reused timbers dated to 1479, a Tudor-arched fireplace (displayed outside) and a 1679 date were found. They indicate the stone casing of a timber-framed house, retaining its older forms with small two- and three-light mullioned windows, but adding an up-to-date three-bay pediment with oculus.

Back now to the corner of DONCASTER GATE and the large curved front of a three-storey shop and office block by *Joseph Platts*, 1907. Fully glazed first floor, nicely patterned. Northern Renaissance style with gabled and balustraded top. Uphill to its l. is a more economically detailed companion, also by Platts but brick not stone. Uphill again is the CIVIC THEATRE, a converted Gothic Congregational chapel by a *Mr Shaw*, 1867. The w end originally had a square tower with spire. Alterations by *Hadfield Cawkwell & Davidson*, 1958–60, created a proscenium-arch theatre.*

COLLEGE STREET, n of High Street, begins with a former Burton's, by *Harry Wilson*, 1927–31, in the chain's usual white faience and stylized Ionic columns. Opposite, large three-storey HSBC (originally Sheffield Union Bank) of 1875. Restrained Italianate front with Ionic pilasters between seven ground-floor bays. Then the start of long, unexciting Neo-Georgian blocks that stretch down EFFINGHAM STREET. It includes, however, one important but completely invisible building: the remains of the College of Jesus, whose foundation stone was laid on 12 May 1483. These are incorporated into the shop fronting College Street. The College, which was described by Leland *c.* 1540 as 'sumptuusly buildid of brike' was used for secular purposes after its suppression, part as a C17 mansion (a doorway is at Boston Park – *see* p. 464). The SE wing survived into the C20 as the College Inn. Three outer

*The Rotherham Hospital and Dispensary opposite, by *Mallinson & Bakewell* 1869–72, was demolished in 2014.

walls, of two storeys with doorway and window openings, were preserved when its site was rebuilt in 1930 by *Flockton & Son*. They form one of the earliest brick buildings in the region and deserve to be properly revealed.

In Effingham Street the SCHOOL OF SCIENCE AND ART stands on the l. towards the N end. By *E. Isle Hubbard*, 1887–9, in a weak classical style with Ionic pilasters. Statue of Queen Victoria high on the pediment above the entrance bay. After 1931 the School was absorbed into the complicated palimpsest of two-storey buildings at the S end of the triangular block. These had been remodelled and extended in 1895–7 by *R.J. Lovell* as the Town Hall, Courts etc. Mixed classical/Jacobean Revival style, mainly in red sandstones. The upper façades were retained in conversion to a shopping arcade by *Hadfield Cawkwell Davidson & Partners*, 1990, but the ground floors were altered and the interiors lost. The corner building was the Mechanics' Institute, 1853; in 1897 its first-floor concert room became the Assembly Rooms. On the irregular Howard Street frontage the large Council Chamber window sits above remnants of the Local Board offices, 1853, and adjoining Savings Bank, 1851. The Borough Courts occupied the Frederick Street corner with plainer police headquarters extending NE.

Return towards ALL SAINTS' SQUARE, opened in 1933 and pedestrianized in 1972. On the College Street corner the attractive block with oriel windows was built as Davy's Tudor café and grocers in 1932 by *Chapman & Jenkinson*. Its splendid staring gargoyles include a ram, pig and bull. Across the square the W side of BRIDGEGATE starts with more Neo-Georgian, *c.* 1930, opposite two attractively detailed mock-Tudor fronts with timber oriels, 1928. The C18 house a little below was built for the lawyer Samuel Buck (†1749). Pedimented central bay with a first-floor Venetian window and a Diocletian window above that. At the N end of the street is the CHAPEL OF OUR LADY (*see* Churches).

S now to the top of CORPORATION STREET and the handsome former Sheffield Bank on the corner of Market Street by *M. E. Hadfield, Son & Garland*, 1892–4. Boldly detailed with Gibbs surrounds to door and windows. Balustraded top has ball-finialled dies. The big block at the top of the street, extending from Domine Lane into Westgate, was built for the Masbrough Equitable Pioneers Co-operative Society in 1900 and was the largest single shop in the town. Extension l. by *Joseph Platts*, 1909. Across the junction, on HIGH STREET, is the EMPIRE THEATRE by *Chadwick & Watson*, 1913 (a cinema from 1921; now a nightclub). Baroque style in white faience and quiet grey terracotta. Next to the Co-op, facing WESTGATE, is the house built for himself by *John Platt*, 1794. Three storeys (ground floor, originally with a porch, now a shopfront). Chaste ashlar front with cornice and blocking course. Recessed three-bay centre and, originally, two bays either side. The first bay was removed when Main Street was made *c.* 1865 and the l. return rebuilt in keeping. Further S, the CUTLERS'

ARMS, 1907 by *James Wigfull* for William Stones Ltd. Brownish-buff faience front has decorative armorial panels and raised lettering. Art Nouveau stained glass and well-preserved interior with green tiling and glazed screens.

The N section of MOORGATE STREET was mostly created from the garden of No. 29 High Street (*see* above), from 1821 home of the Badger family, a Rotherham legal dynasty. The street's initial development was promoted by Thomas Wright Badger and designed by *E. F. C. Clarke*; building continued in the 1880s and 1890s. The E side has an attractive series of red brick fronts with varied gable treatments and some nice Arts and Crafts details.

At the top of the hill THE CROFTS was the site of the town's cattle market until 1926. Behind the Town Hall (*see* Public Buildings), the former FEOFFEES' CHARITY SCHOOL by *John Platt*, dated 1776. Five bays, two storeys, three-bay open pediment. Doorway within round-arched recess, similar recess above rises into tympanum. Talbot Lane Methodist Church (*see* Churches) faces the Town Hall. A little further S, at the end of DOWN'S ROW is the former Unitarian chapel, built in 1706 as a Presbyterian meeting house and remodelled by *James Hill*, 1841, adding the plain two-storey Greek Revival porch. The r. return, with four round-arched windows, was the original front. The chapel's successor (now Mosque, *see* p. 457) is nearby on the E side of Moorgate Street. On the W side in GROVE ROAD, are the handsome former ROTHERHAM RURAL DISTRICT COUNCIL OFFICES, 1923. Three storeys in English Renaissance style. On the corner of MOORGATE ROAD the remains of Late Georgian service buildings of South Grove (dem.). Blocked entrance to Grove Road with Doric columns and three arches. On the E side the classical triple-arched form is repeated in the big open porch of the former PLYMOUTH BRETHREN'S MEETING ROOM, 1875. Red brick with stone dressings. The OLD GRAMMAR SCHOOL beyond (No. 11) was built by the Feoffees in 1857. After the school moved in 1890 (*see* Public Buildings) the large gabled school-room to the l. of the headmaster's house was altered to a house and the attached clock tower removed. Changes for office use have since robbed it of the octagonal bell-turret and attractive ogee-headed window tracery.

EFFINGHAM WORKS, Thames Street. Built in 1855 for Yates, Haywood & Co., ironfounders and prolific producers of stove grates, kitchen ranges etc., it was claimed to be the largest factory of its kind in the world. The first phase of the Centenary Way inner ring road, opened 1969, severed it from the town centre and took the r. end of its still immensely long frontage. 3:32:7:22 bays. The original four-storey centre has boldly rusticated pilasters and small pediment.

GUEST & CHRIMES' BRASS FOUNDRY (former), Don Street. 1857. Edward Chrimes Jun.'s invention of the screw-down high-pressure tap, patented in 1845, produced the modern domestic tap and the firm's fortunes. Brick, mostly three storeys. Entrance and office range, 2:5:2 bays, superficially aggrandized with arched window heads, rusticated pilasters, cornice and central parapet. Long r. and rear ranges, one with five-storey water tank tower. Multi-paned iron casements.

OUTER ROTHERHAM

CLIFTON, EAST DENE AND HERRINGTHORPE

St James, Cambridge Street, Clifton. By *J.J. Crowe* of *Crowe & Careless*, 1933–4. Sited where the late c19 suburb and the council estate meet. Substantial, cruciform. Brick with brick dressings, well detailed.

St Cuthbert, Sitwell Park Road, Herringthorpe. By *W.B. Edwards & Partners*, 1958. Light brown brick. Low-pitched roofs, zigzagging over (ritual) N vestries etc. Blind-ended sanctuary side-lit by blocks of tiny square windows.

St Mary (R.C.), Herringthorpe Valley Road. By *R.A. Ronchetti*, 1955. Large, plain, brick. Single ridge. Thin windows to clerestory and flat-roofed passage aisles.

Clifton Park, Clifton Lane. The Clifton Park estate was bought by the Corporation in 1891 and the grounds became a public park the same year. Clifton House, the most ambitious of Rotherham's c18 houses, was opened as a museum in 1893. It was built in 1783–4 for Joshua Walker, one of the sons of Samuel Walker. Two of his other sons had houses by *John Carr*, which puts a convincing stylistic attribution beyond doubt (cf. Middleton Lodge, North Riding). Two storeys, five by six bays, in plain ashlar. Front has three-bay pediment, and tetrastyle Doric portico with Venetian window above. First-floor band, and sill bands to windows, the upper ones with balusters below; no architraves. Full-height canted bay to rear; attached service range to r. The house is placed to enjoy the extensive views across the Don valley so the principal rooms face NE and NW.

Good c18 interiors with some c19 alterations. Extensive use of fine Derbyshire marble supplied by *John Platt*, viz. the crinoidal paving in the entrance and staircase halls and the cantilevered staircase. This has a pretty wrought-iron balustrade and a vaulted ceiling lit by four lunettes. Oval dining room at rear has chimneypiece with fluted Ionic columns by *Thomas Wolstenholme* of York. Drawing room has another chimneypiece by *Wolstenholme* and delicately painted ceiling *c.* 1840. Good friezes with anthemion etc., repeated on excellent doorcases. Octagonal room above dining room.

In the grounds a few remains of the GRANARY from the CI–C2 Roman fort at Templeborough. One whole Doric column and low footings of walls. The fort was excavated in 1877–8 and 1916, prior to destruction for the steelworks there.

Eastwood House. By *Carr* for Joseph Walker, 1786–7, dem. 1928. *Carr*'s fine gateway survives *ex situ* on Doncaster Road, opposite Middle Lane.

EAST DENE. By *Charles A. Broadhead*, Housing Architect. Large council estate begun in 1919 and built on Garden City principles at 10–12 houses an acre. Three-bedroomed, with bathrooms, and mostly of the parlour type. Semi-detached and terraces of four, mostly in brick, although other construction methods were tried. The first houses were occupied in May 1920. THE LANES, by *Gillinson, Barnett & Partners*, 1969–70 is a textbook contrast with East Dene. High-density low-rise scheme stepping down an E-facing slope. Ninety-seven bungalows, eighteen houses and 115 flats laid out on the Radburn principle in an intricate network of paths and alleys. Brick with flat and monopitch roofs.

BEEVERSLEIGH, Clifton Lane. 1970–1. Rotherham's only point block, on a prominent hillside. Forty-eight flats in twelve storeys, raised on pilotis. Unusual hexagonal plan. Brick facing, with non-structural concrete latticework forming a decorative cage.

MOORGATE

Suburb where Rotherham's Victorian manufacturers and professional classes built their houses, high above the industrialized valley.

CEMETERY, Boston Castle Grove. Well-preserved town cemetery, opened 1841. Three-bay chapel, originally only Nonconformist, with doors both ends. Round-arched windows. Clasping buttresses with obelisk pinnacles (shortened). Tudor Revival lodges.

BOSTON PARK, Boston Castle Grove. Opened in 1876 as the People's Park (22 acres). Previously known as Boston Woods, belonging to the Earls of Effingham. The 3rd Earl, a staunch sympathizer of the American colonists, built a shooting and pleasure lodge in 1773–4 and named it BOSTON CASTLE to commemorate the 'tea party' of 1773. It is said he would not allow tea to be drunk there. The park was opened on the centenary of the Declaration of Independence. The castellated square tower has a large upper room and commands panoramic views westward.

Set against a rock face 100 yds SE is an early–mid-C17 carved DOORWAY and aedicule with segmental pediment. Rescued in 1869 when part of the College of Jesus once used as a mansion by the Copleys was demolished; re-erected 1876.

MOORGATE HALL, C17, was the grandest suburban residence before the 1780s. Samuel Buck's sketch *c.* 1723 includes its original E-facing front. 1:3:1 bays and two storeys, plus a pedimented third storey in the quoined centre. The middle first-floor window, with segmental pediment, was formerly a doorway with external staircase. C18 alterations included moving the main entrance to the N side. S service extension probably by *John Platt*, 1764. (Good interior features include fine late C17 staircase.)

Notable C19 HOUSES in MOORGATE ROAD include (from N): No. 28, a pair in cream terracotta, 1878. MOORGATE GRANGE, stuccoed Italianate with belvedere, 1856, extended 1862. THE COTTAGE, 1840 in *cottage orné* style. OAKWOOD HALL (now hospital offices). Italianate mansion with Doric portico, balustraded parapet and (dem.) look-out tower, 1856–9. (SWINDEN HOUSE (formerly Red House), now Tata Steel conference centre. By *E. F. C. Clarke* for Thomas Wright Badger *c.* 1880 (cf. Moorgate Street p. 462). Elaborate Arts and Crafts Jacobethan style in sandstone and red brick with terracotta details.)

TEMPLEBOROUGH

Named from the Roman fort whose site was cleared for the steel works in the early C20.

MAGNA SCIENCE ADVENTURE CENTRE, Sheffield Road. By *Wilkinson Eyre Architects*, opened in 2001. A £46 million Millennium project; winner of the Stirling Prize 2001. Converted steel works with gigantic black shed, nearly ⅓ m. long, once typical of the area's industrial landscape. Steel, Peech and Tozer's Melting Shop, 1917, was built for fourteen 80-ton open-hearth furnaces, and altered 1960–3 to become the largest electric arc melting shop in the world. Its dark cavernous interior tells the story of steel and has innovative exhibition pavilions about Earth, Air, Fire and Water.

BRINSWORTH STRIP MILL (opposite). Brick, with huge windows, 1955–8.

MASBROUGH

Suburb whose separation from the town by the river, canal and railway was reinforced by the inner ring road.

ST PAUL, Kimberworth Road. By *Stock, Page & Stock*, 1901–2. E.E. S aisle and nave W end added in 1916 to the original apsidal chancel and incomplete three-bay nave. Gabled clerestory with multi-foil windows. – STAINED GLASS. S chapel. By *Christopher Webb*, 1937.

ST BEDE (R.C.), Station Road. 1841–2 by *Weightman & Hadfield*. In his *Present State of Ecclesiastical Architecture* (1843), Pugin praised Hadfield for having espoused 'true Catholic principles' and the designs, which he illustrated, for their 'correct style…in accordance with ancient models'. He explained the resemblance to his own buildings as a consequence of their common derivation. It does not look more distinguished in the engravings than in the original. Chancel and three-bay nave with bellcote at the junction. S porch. Dec tracery. Narthex, aisle with circular piers and baptistery by *C.M.E. Hadfield* 1920–1. – STAINED GLASS. (Ritual) E window seems original. The now plain interior enlivened by a series of colourful windows by *Pendle Stained Glass*, 2008–12.

Masbrough developed after the Walkers set up their iron and steel works in 1746, sited to take advantage of the new canal. By the end of the C18 the firm was a major supplier of cannon to the Board of Ordnance and an innovative manufacturer of cast-iron bridges. All that remains of their legacy apart from two fine C18 houses is the former INDEPENDENT CHAPEL, College Road, of 1777–80, largely at Samuel Walker's expense (gutted by fire at the time of writing), and their sadly neglected MAUSOLEUM in the graveyard behind it. The family built a 'vault' in 1776 but the architecture of the little mausoleum is too Grecian for so early a date.

FERHAM HOUSE, Kimberworth Road, was built for Samuel Walker's son Jonathan, c. 1787. Attributed to *John Platt* (cf. Mount Pleasant, Sheffield). Brick, with Palladian motifs. Three by five bays and two-and-a-half storeys. Centre bay is framed by a blank giant arch under a pediment. Tripartite doorway; Venetian window over. The l return has a full-height canted bay. (Good top-lit cantilevered staircase and some Adamesque plasterwork.)

3010

ROYSTON

A small town after the first mine was sunk in 1867.

ST JOHN THE BAPTIST. A very fine and interesting medieval church, on the s slope, not the top, of the hill. Noble Perp w tower with battlements and pinnacles. An unexpected and unique feature is the five-sided oriel projecting from the w wall above the big three-light window. Pyramidal stone roof and two small blank shields below each cusped light. Its only parallel is the oriel on the w porch of the Savage Chapel at St Michael, Macclesfield, Cheshire. Here its purpose was probably as a lantern to guide travellers.

The body of the church is long, with low chancel, all Dec or Perp. Nave of four bays with lean-to aisles, chancel of three bays with N and s chapels. The aisles and chapels have matching plain parapets, though of different builds. The s aisle has buttresses with pinnacle bases. Embattled and pinnacled s porch. The nave clerestory also has battlements and pinnacles, plus puny buttresses. Between bays one and two the buttresses are angled, like those at the E end, beside remains of corner gargoyles. This helps to explain the curious arcades inside. The first bay, with straight joints to the E, replaced an earlier tower. Its two arches are cut out of solid wall and are Perp, like the tower arch. All three arches have panelled corbels with Dec tracery. The remaining bays have octagonal piers elongated at right angles to the nave so that the diagonals are much longer than the main sides. Low four-centred arches dying against the piers. The arches' sunk panelling continues in the s, but not the N, piers. J.E. Morris in the *Little Guide* called all this Dec, but is it? The tall clerestory to these three bays has two-light windows with cusped Y-tracery. Splendid original roof with big decorative bosses, extended over the W bay, though this part has no brattishing at the wall-plate. So we seem to be in the transition between Dec and Perp and the nave extension and tower probably followed very soon after the nave's main arcades and clerestory. Nave N aisle has windows like the clerestory, the slightly later S aisle windows have three stepped, cusped lancets. Aisle roofs like the nave's. At the E end of the N aisle a rood staircase. The arches from the aisles to the chapels match the nave arcade, but are unmoulded. Perp S chapel of three bays, N chapel of two bays. Octagonal piers with rosette decoration in the capitals. The ogee-headed doorway from the sanctuary into the NE vestry is probably Dec. The E window's curvilinear tracery is by *J.L. Pearson*, who restored the church in 1867–9. – ROOD. *c.* 1933. – SCREENS to the N and S chapels. Perp, simple, with one-light divisions. Similar lower panels, with a gate, between the chancel and S chapel. All thought to be parts of the medieval rood screen. – FONT. Perp, octagonal, with tracery panels. – ROYAL ARMS. N chapel. Queen Anne, 1713, on wood. – WALL PAINT-INGS. C15? Two panels of text on nave walls. That between the N clerestory windows has a decorative frame. – STAINED GLASS. Medieval fragments in tracery lights of chapels. S aisle. Two easternmost windows by *Wailes*, 1869, the third by *Mayer*, *c.* 1902. W window by *Wailes*, 1871. – MONUMENTS. N chapel. Sandford Nevile of Chevet †1673. Attributed to *Jasper Latham* (GF). Remarkable free-standing piece consisting of two large black marble plates, the upper carried by four anguished and lachrymose putti of white marble. Original wrought-iron rail-ings. – W end of S aisle. William Blitheman †1660. Painted wooden panel with epitaph attributed to *Thomas Pecke*. Henry Broadhead †1754. Excellent Rococo monument, with a joyful putto riding on a garlanded cartouche. Three winged heads below. Black obelisk background.

RYHILL

3010

ST JAMES. By *J.P. St Aubyn*, 1871–4. Completed 1885–6 with vaguely French apsidal-ended chancel.

At HAVERCROFT, ½ m. E, off Cow Lane (East, West and South Streets, and Crescent Road), a spacious and open estate of model miners' housing by the Industrial Housing Association, *c.* 1925. Bathrooms were placed just inside the back door so miners could enter the house clean.*

---

*NEWSTEAD HALL, which stood ½ m. N of Havercroft, was built in 1708 and demolished in 1976.

RYTHER

ALL SAINTS. In dead flat fields beside the River Wharfe not far from its confluence with the Ouse. Nave, chancel and big S aisle, and pretty slate-hung W bellcote provided by *C. Hodgson Fowler* during his restoration of 1897–8. The oldest part is the chancel arch, late Saxon or early Norman, with irregularly shaped voussoirs, simple imposts of differing profiles and 'Escomb fashion' jambs; and in the nave N wall there are three small Saxon-style monolithic window heads reused as building stone, together with a block carved with trellis ornament.* Late Norman priest's doorway, plain with a slight chamfer; and built into the fabric at various points a number of beakheads, presumably from another Norman doorway. E.E. is represented by the nave W end, with two lancets and a central buttress, another lancet on the nave N side, and the (much-renewed) re-set S doorway, with colonnettes carrying moulded capitals. The S aisle, on a larger scale than the rest of the church and virtually as wide as the nave, was added *c.* 1300: see the Y-traceried S windows and the intersected tracery of the E window. Three-bay arcade to the nave, of the standard type with octagonal piers and double-chamfered arches. Dec chancel N and S windows, the latter straight-headed, and three-light window on the N side of the nave. Beside the chancel arch a large squint. Some rebuilding of the chancel in 1843, its E window 1897–8. – Five medieval ALTAR stones distributed round the church. – STAINED GLASS. C14 and later fragments in the S aisle E and W windows.

MONUMENTS. A remarkable group, all in the S aisle, although some of them at least are not in their original positions. – Recumbent effigies of a cross-legged knight and his lady, probably Sir Robert Ryther †*c.* 1327 and his wife. Limestone, of good quality, attributed to a York workshop. – Recumbent effigy of a lady wearing a horned head-dress and holding a heart between her hands: the head-dress indicates a mid-C15 date. Behind but unrelated is a tomb-recess with an ogee gablet framing a demi-angel. – Sir William Ryther †1475. Alabaster altar tomb with recumbent effigy, damaged but exceptionally fine, probably the product of a Midlands workshop: the alabaster monument to his grandparents, Sir William Ryther and Sybil Aldburgh, is at Harewood (*West Riding North*). He is in armour and has at his feet a dog and a human mask. On the sides of the tomb-chest male and female weepers holding shields, standing under crocketed canopies grouped in twos and threes. They are a pleasure to look at even in their mutilated state. – Altar tomb without effigies, probably Sir Robert Ryther †1491, son of Sir William: he stipulated that he should be buried next to his father. Elaborately foiled diamond

*Another is at the SW corner of the S aisle.

shapes enclosing shields, finely decorated base. – Also two brasses to C17 members of the Robinson family, inscriptions and shields.

SANDAL MAGNA

ST HELEN. Large and much rebuilt, with several puzzling features. It is cruciform, consistent with its probable Anglo-Saxon origin, but the w end's two bays are a lengthening by *Habershon & Pite*, 1872. This is Dec style and Dec are indeed the lower two stages of the crossing tower, the transepts with their (renewed) end windows and the very curious E end with two tall two-light windows and a (later?) smaller and wider window above. Tower battlements and pinnacles of 1888, but the upper stage with tall bell-openings looks Perp. So do the aisles, with strange windows that have shouldered lintels and shouldered heads to their lights, and the s chapel, enlarged in a rebuilding *c.* 1505. The E window of this is again very odd. It has in its panel tracery straight-sided arches, usually a post-Reformation motif. Probably the E end and the nave and aisles were extensively rebuilt in the late C17, when the roof is known to have been replaced, and further renewed in the C19.

Internally the evidence is more complex. The lower halves of the crossing piers are C12, though their plinths have odd corner blocks, like uncarved spurs. C12 too the base of the easternmost pier of the N arcade and the capital of the next one. C13 or early C14 the rest of the arcades – alternate octagonal and circular piers, double-chamfered arches and E responds with nailhead – but heightened in the late C17. The upper halves of the crossing piers are typically early C14: piers with shafts running into each other with wavy hollows, moulded capitals, and arches with quadrant mouldings. The little gallery in the N transept leading from a newel stair in the NW corner across the w arch to a tower stair seems to date from this remodelling (cf. Darrington). s chapel arcade, four bays of standard Perp elements. One capital is decorated with fleurons. The absence of any piscina or sedilia in the chancel suggests that the structure is post-medieval. Reordering in 1980–2 removed the chancel fittings and since 2004–5 the E end has been separate. – FONT. Dated 1662. Octagonal, with plain moulded sunk panels on bowl and stem. – SCREEN. s chapel. Perp. Linenfold panels, vine scroll and delicate tracery. – BENCH-ENDS. N aisle wall. *c.* 1530. Two, with traceried panels below heraldry of Joscelyn Percy. Straight tops. – STAINED GLASS. w window. Figures by *Hardman*, 1875, re-set in plain glass *c.* 1975. – MONUMENTS. s chapel. Two large cast-iron ledgers, one to George Beaumont's sons †1695, the other to his daughters †1695–1715. – Chancel. Two marble tablets with the usual mourning female figures: one by *Bacon & Manning*, *c.* 1820, has three portrait profiles for Thomas (†1771) and Margaret Gill of Kettlethorpe, and John Gill †1785; the other, Mrs Margaret Vaughan †1826, by *E.W. Physick*, 1828, with portrait medallion. – Also by *Physick*, 1838, Miss Margaret Vaughan †1836, her mourning brother seated before an urn. Many other C18 and C19 tablets, some signed.

St Peter and St Paul (R.C.) 1 m. SW. By *Michael Wingate*, 1991–2. The roof's E slope sweeps almost to the ground, with the apsidal sanctuary expressed as a small segmental projection with semi-conical roof.

Sandal Castle, off Manygates Lane, ⅜ m. W towards the Calder. The first timber castle was built by William de Warenne, 2nd Earl of Surrey, who acquired the Sandal estates along with the manor of Wakefield in 1107. The impressive earthworks, which determined the plan of much of the later phases, consist of a massive circular motte with a crescentic bailey on the SE, the whole surrounded by a rock-cut ditch and a counterscarp bank. The timber castle was replaced in stone, perhaps initially by Hamelin, 4th Earl (†1202 cf. Conisbrough) but predominantly in the mid- and later C13 by either the 5th or 6th Earls. Sandal remained important as a stronghold for Richard III. Excavations in 1878 and 1964–73 have revealed much of its

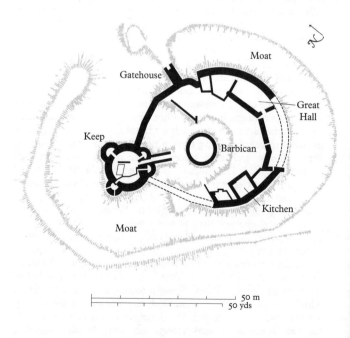

Sandal Magna, Sandal Castle.
Block plan

masonry and the unusual plan. Entrance was from the NE via
bridge and gatehouse into the bailey which contained the
principal buildings, including a hall, the constable's lodgings,
and a kitchen, around its SE curve; significant sections of wall
remain upstanding. On the bailey's NW side an irregular inner
ditch around a circular barbican tower which was reached via
a drawbridge. This barbican was connected with the keep on
its motte via a bridge across the ditch to a gatehouse with
massive twin towers and thence by ramp to a second gatehouse – also twin-towered – of the keep itself. This is circular
too and had two more attached towers to W and N, one semicircular (W), the other polygonal (N), creating a clustered
profile somewhat characteristic of other C13 stone castles. On
the SSE the earthworks of a defensive hornwork associated with
the siege by Parliamentarians in 1645, after which the castle
was untenable.

SANDAL MAGNA COMMUNITY PRIMARY SCHOOL, Belle Vue
Road, ½ m. N. By *Sarah Wigglesworth Architects*, 2009–10. Con-
figured as three linked rows, with social spaces between, taking
its cue from neighbouring terraced houses. Central hall stands
above single-storey classrooms etc. with varied façades. Brick
and wood cladding outside and in.

MONUMENT, Manygates Lane, ⅜ m. NW. A Gothic column by
Gerald Horsley, 1897, commemorating Richard, Duke of York's
death at the battle of Wakefield, 1460.

KETTLETHORPE HALL, 1⅛ m. SSW. Enchanting small Baroque   47
house of 1727, with an almost Viennese gaiety, rescued from
semi-dereliction in 1989–90. Two storeys, five bays and small
one-bay, one-storey adjuncts. Raised quoins, enriched modillion cornice. Parapet with vases, repeated on the wings. The
central chimneystack is made a feature. Doorway with an Italo-
Austrian style double-curved pediment, the ground-floor
windows have curved hoods on little ears and carving below.
Single-bay hall, with a large reception room either side extending into each wing. Rear stair hall.*

SANDBECK PARK

3 m. SE of Maltby

5090

The seat of the Earls of Scarbrough, Sandbeck enjoys a setting
in the Riding's rural SE corner that feels remote from its urban
and industrial parts. The house, of limestone ashlar, is by
Paine, c. 1762–8, and is one of his most dramatic designs. The
E garden front in particular, with its far-projecting portico with
Corinthian columns gathered in threes at the corners and
below this an arcade of three heavily rusticated arches to a

---

*Decayed remains of the medieval front of Wakefield Chantry Chapel (q.v.), used
in 1847 for a boathouse by the lake, are now at Thornes Park, Wakefield (p. 719).

Sandbeck Park, E front.
Engraving by J. Miller, *c.* 1767

shady loggia, is not easily forgotten. Above the portico a pediment, with Ceres and the Lumley coat of arms sculpted by
William Collins. Sandbeck's height is especially striking, with
one-and-a-half storeys rising above the heavily rusticated basement and more smoothly rusticated ground floor. This comes
from Paine's retention of the former compact three-storey
house of 1627 as the core of his work, broad single-bay pavilions being added to N and S. These pavilions are pedimented
front and back, giving the house its distinctive feature of triple
pediments to both fronts. The entrance front was originally
flat, the C19 adding the useful but unfortunate projecting
top-lit hall, which was extended even further forward in 1905
by *John MacVicar Anderson,* reusing the pedimented Doric
portico. Other later alterations included some internal remodelling by *William Burn,* 1857, and a N wing (dem. 1954).*

The most surprising feature of the house's plan is that its
principal room, the BALLROOM, is – as in Venetian palaces – in
the middle of the upper floor (or *piano nobile*) and runs from
front to back. It represents the C17 great chamber and is a most
unusual, if not especially convenient, survival. Double-height,
the Ballroom is among the finest C18 rooms in Yorkshire. It
has a superb coved plaster ceiling, perhaps the best in any
Paine house, probably by *Joseph Rose.* The style resembles
Adam's. With its mythological scenes, griffins and Neoclassical
vases it is emphatically no longer the Rococo of the Paine
decorations at Nostell or Doncaster Mansion House (qq.v.),
although it retains a Rococo spirit in its lively sprays of flowers
and its depth of relief. Fine marble chimneypiece with free-
standing Ionic columns, and relief plaque probably by *Collins.*
Unusual glazing bars of cast brass. To N, two bedrooms have
pedimented bed recesses with Ionic columns.

*Thankfully, *Anderson*'s 1907 proposal to insert a floor into the Ballroom to provide
more bedrooms was not implemented.

Some good C18 chimneypieces in ground-floor rooms, including in the E DINING ROOM, created out of two rooms by *William Burn* in 1857, and with later Ionic screen. DRAWING ROOM, which extends into the big full-height canted s bay and was originally elaborately fitted by Paine as the dining room, has chimneypiece by *Joseph Wilton* with elegant caryatids.   56

CHAPEL by *Benjamin Ferrey*, 1869–70. Large and serious in rich E.E. style. Apsidal E end. Nave of four bays divided by arches that carry the roof trusses and are set on elaborate corbelled shafts. W gallery, originally connected to N wing. – STAINED GLASS. One window (W end) with fragments of C14 glass from Roche Abbey. Five lancets by *Ward & Hughes*.

STABLES by *Paine*, 1765–6. Large quadrangle, mostly two-storeyed, with two square turrets guarding the W entrance, and a third above the archway. Diocletian windows to courtyard. THE LIMES, ¾ m. NW, is the former stables, remodelled as a gamekeeper's lodge *c.* 1760 by *Paine*, with bold rustication to pedimented centre. Other estate buildings probably by *Paine*, including S GATEWAY and LODGE, Four Lane Ends, and triumphal arch E GATEWAY, Malpas Hill.

Fine PARK landscaped by *Capability Brown*, 1762–74 (cf. Roche Abbey), includes two lakes, ha-ha (1771–3) and ICE HOUSE.

SAXTON
4030

ALL SAINTS. Perp W tower with corbelled-out parapet (cf. Barwick-in-Elmet etc. (*West Riding North*)) and big corner pinnacles. Late Norman S doorway with colonnettes carrying crude waterleaf capitals; a Norman window to the r. of it, another on the chancel N side and the remains of a third alongside it visible inside; and Norman chancel arch with one slight chamfer and the plainest of imposts. Big later C13 chapel on the S side of the nave, its roof-line raised, of three bays externally with bar-traceried two-light windows – much renewed and the head circles evidently added in an undocumented restoration of *c.* 1860 – and a two-bay arcade with circular pier and double-chamfered arches. Trefoiled piscina. Of the same date the nave N wall, with the same windows similarly renewed, and presumably the big plain round-headed squint to the r. of the chancel arch. Chancel lancets all from the mid-C19 restoration. Further interventions 1876 and 1907. – FONT. Plain irregular octagon, on a base probably of 1876. – SCULPTURE. Remains of an Anglo-Saxon cross-head, C10 or C11, at the time of writing on the chancel N side. – STAINED GLASS. Two very small medieval fragments, one in each of the nave N windows. – E windows, probably *c.* 1860. – Chapel S middle, 1895 by

Heaton, Butler & Bayne. – MONUMENTS. Four grave-slabs of members of the Hungate family, C17 and C18, three of them with armorial panels. – Chaloner Hawke †1777 and his infant nieces Catherine and Isabella †1780 and †1783. By *J.F. Moore* of London. Pedimented wall monument with an oval relief of an angel carrying the two children to heaven. – In the churchyard Ralph Lord Dacre †1461, killed at the Battle of Towton. An example of a type of outdoor memorial which rarely survives. Altar tomb with eroded escutcheons on the sides, surrounded by a kerb and railing added in 1883, the kerb carrying an inscription copied from the tomb-chest top, the original now illegible.

TOWTON CROSS, 1 m. N, on the W side of the road to Towton. C15 cross-head on a C19 shaft and C20 plinth, perhaps originating in an abortive scheme of 1483 to build a chantry chapel at Towton for those killed in the battle.

SCARTHINGWELL HALL, 1 m. E, was demolished in 1965. The CHAPEL attached to it survives (IMMACULATE CONCEPTION AND ST JOHN OF BEVERLEY (R.C.)), 1854 by *J.B. & W. Atkinson* for Henry Maxwell. Approximate Neo-Romanesque. (Ornate plaster-vaulted interior, with W gallery. – STAINED GLASS in the apse, by *Wailes*.) Immediately E of the chapel a sizeable LAKE, formed *c.* 1790–1 by *John Davenport* for the 2nd Lord Hawke.

Further N SCARTHINGWELL HALL FARM, originally a model layout for Lord Hawke and praised in 1793 as 'a completely convenient and elegant suite'. Three sides of a courtyard, the middle range a barn and the others stables etc. with granaries over. Arcaded projecting centres with pedimental gables, Venetian and Diocletian windows, many alterations.

SCAMMONDEN

Village mostly drowned by SCAMMONDEN WATER, the reservoir constructed in conjunction with the M62 in 1968–70.

ST BARTHOLOMEW. Rebuilt by *E.W. Tarn.* 1863–5. Small, compact and busy. Geometric tracery.

The section of the M62 MOTORWAY, ½ m. N between Saddleworth and Pole Moor, is the highest motorway in the UK (1,220 ft (372 metres)), by *West Riding County Council* (County Engineer *J.A. Gaffney*), and *Sir Alfred McAlpine & Sons*, contractors. Crossing its Deanhead cutting is the graceful precast concrete SCAMMONDEN BRIDGE, 1967–71, by *Col. S.M. Lovell*, County Surveyor. It was then the largest single-span fixed-arch bridge (410 ft (125 metres)) in the country, with flat piers in the open spandrels below the roadway (cf. Maillart's Salginatobel Bridge, Switzerland, 1929–30).

SCARTHINGWELL *see* SAXTON

SCISSETT

Former mining and textile village in Denby Dale, which grew up around the Norton family's fancy-goods mills.

St Augustine. By *Thomas Richardson*, 1837–40. Architecturally very poor. Lancet windows and w tower with stubby pinnacles. Apsed chancel by *John Kirk & Sons*, 1880, with chapels projecting oddly on the diagonal. (Nice and elaborate wrought-iron chancel screen, designed by *Hodgson Fowler*, 1910. – stained glass. e windows by *Lavers, Barraud & Westlake*, 1880. Nave s, one window by *Henry Payne*, 1901.)

Nortonthorpe Mills (former), Cuttlehurst. Two mid-C19 three-storey ranges face the mill pond. The engine house, 1885–6, retains its original *Pollitt & Wigzell* steam engine.

Bagden Hall (hotel), ½ m. ssw. By *Ignatius Bonomi* for George Norton, 1845–50. Large, gabled, with canted bays, mullioned-and-transomed windows and tall chimneystacks.*

Wheatley Hill Farmhouse, ½ m. sse. U-plan house with c16 timber-framed w wing, the housebody and e wing probably 1651 (dated doorway). Rear of w wing has good exposed framing with diagonal struts to first floor and gable.

SCOUTHEAD[†]

St Paul, Huddersfield Road, away from the settlement. Of 1886–9 by *Reuben Dransfield*, tall spire completed in 1912. Large, Dec style, with a polygonal apse. Converted to a conference and training centre in 2006–9 by *Halsall Lloyd Partnership*. In a group with a late C19 former Vicarage (stripped Tudor) and former School of 1878 by *John Wild* (Dec detailing).

---

*Joseph Norton, George's brother, used Bonomi's plans for Nortonthorpe Hall in 1846–8 (dem. *c.* 2005).

[†] Part of Saddleworth, in Greater Manchester since 1974

SELBY

THE ABBEY
(ST MARY AND ST GERMAIN)

It is very rare for an abbey church in England to have survived the Dissolution and the spoliations of later owners and to stand as a complete church in the C21 – provided the abbey church was not the National Shrine, as Westminster Abbey is, and was not converted into a cathedral, as, for example, Gloucester and Peterborough were.

The abbey's C12 historian relates that it was founded by Benedict, a monk from the French monastery of St Germain at Auxerre who, bidden in a vision by the saint himself, came to England, bringing the stolen relic of a saintly finger with him. In 1069 he settled as a hermit on the banks of the Ouse twelve miles south of York, subsequently becoming the first abbot of a new community. More certainty attaches to the Conqueror's foundation charter of 1070, which makes Selby earlier than any of the other great Benedictine houses in the N of England such as Durham and St Mary's, York. The venerated second abbot, Hugh de Lacy (1097–1123), began the present church c. 1100, abandoning wooden buildings on the river bank for a drier site. For its medieval building history we are lamentably short of dates – even of consecrations. However, we have the architectural evidence instead: an essentially Norman crossing and transepts, a Norman to E.E. aisled nave of eight bays (or rather four double bays) and a Dec aisled choir of seven bays. The total length is 304 ft (92.7 metres). The original E end, the transepts and crossing, and the first two bays of the nave are Abbot Hugh's construction. The design of this Romanesque work was clearly derived from Durham. The nave's completion, however, was an unusually protracted affair (cf. Romsey Abbey, Hampshire). Owing to both financial and disciplinary troubles there was a long hiatus after the 1120s, work then resuming, though not without further interruptions, from c. 1170 until completion c. 1230. The rebuilding of the chancel in two phases, in the late C13 and the early C14, ends the essential history of the building.

The story after the Dissolution is complex too. The abbey survived new ownership intact and in 1618 was officially made Selby's Parish Church. The central tower collapsed in 1690 and was rebuilt in 1701–2 with reconstructed Norman stages below a plain belfry stage finished with a balustraded parapet and handsome C18 pinnacles. The damaged westernmost part of the choir and its S aisle were repaired, with C18 tracery. The ruined Norman S transept, however, was cleared away and the gap between the nave and choir aisles made good under a low lean-to roof. In 1852 a long programme of much-needed restoration was begun by *George Gilbert Scott*; his work in 1871–3 included a new

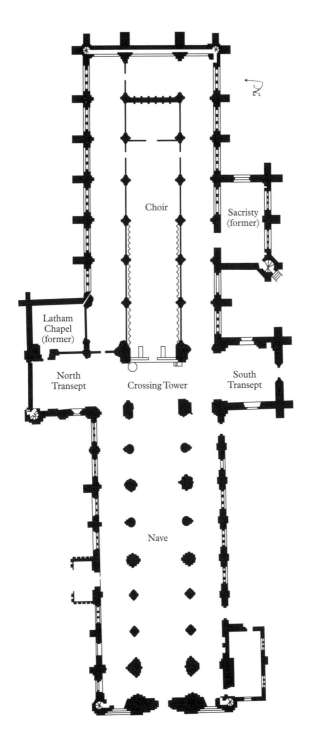

Choir

Sacristy
(former)

Latham
Chapel
(former)

North
Transept

Crossing Tower

South
Transept

Nave

Selby Abbey.
Plan

steeply pitched nave roof with an E.E.-style gable on the w front. Then in 1889–91 *J. Oldrid Scott* rebuilt the damaged s choir aisle bays. The c18 stage of the tower was removed in 1902 but, before *Oldrid Scott*'s plans to rebuild it more appropriately could be executed, a fire in 1906 consumed all the roofs and severely damaged the interior, destroying many new fittings by both the *Scotts*. Repairs began at once and, together with the new tower top, were completed in 1909. Rebuilding of the s transept to *Oldrid Scott*'s plans followed in 1911–12, and finally the w front, left unfinished in the c13, was completed in 1935 with N and s towers, by *C.M. Scott* using his father's designs.

Exterior

One cannot do better than start at the w FRONT. It is a summary of the three main styles of the building, Norman, E.E. and Dec, and of almost its whole construction history. The fine w PORTAL is obviously late Norman: see the waterleaf capitals of the five orders of slim shafts. It is part of the work, begun *c.* 1170, that completed the nave's ground floor. The arches all have exuberant geometrical ornament: point-to-point chevron with stylized leaf in the spandrels (first and fourth orders), net-like crossed chevron (second order), chevron only on the face (third order) and interlocked crenellations with inner triangular merlons (fifth order). There are no aisle portals, only one large shafted window on either side instead (the s one a copy, 1873), and the lower part of the wall is sheer and forbidding enough for a monastic church, which would only be approached from the w by laypeople. Four flat buttresses, shafted in the angles. Above the portal a blank frieze of trefoiled arches decorated with pellets. On the buttresses niches of the same shape for sculpture (cf. Nun Monkton, *West Riding North*), with statues of George V and Queen Mary and their archbishops as late additions.

Above that the mature E.E. style appears. The gap in time is filled in by work on the interior. Big centre lancet with two slim blank side lancets. Originally of two lights, the window has Perp tracery inserted in 1413. Purbeck shafts with two shaft-rings. Much dogtooth decoration. Sunk trefoils inset in the blank lancets l. and r. The side bays corresponding to the aisles start their E.E. display a little higher up. Two small lancet windows set in much larger blank shafted arches, the two arches gathered together by one big arch. Polygonal shafts of stone and Purbeck marble. Dogtooth and sunk trefoils again on the N side, pierced lozenges on the s side. *Scott*'s centre gable is also E.E, with a group of five stepped lancets, four blind. The aisles however at this stage turn Dec, with *Oldrid Scott*'s short towers. They are a little too short perhaps. Two two-light bell-openings with flowing tracery, battlements and crocketed obelisk pinnacles. It is clear from the strengthened aisle bays that towers were proposed in the c12, but until 1873 the w front was simply finished with a battlemented parapet and six lofty pinnacles, which were reused in 1935.

We must now turn to the NAVE, and start with the S, where the plinth moulding indicates that almost the full length of the aisle wall was completed under Abbot Hugh to separate the church from the cloister and monastic buildings. Restored flat Norman buttresses and corbel table. Blocked original doorway into the cloister in the second bay, an unconventional position; later doorways in the usual first bay and in the sixth, their outer mouldings late C12. The aisle windows here are early Dec, a pointed cinquefoil above three cusped lights. The clerestory has single lancets, two to each bay.

Now the N side, which takes us backwards in time to the N transept. The return of the tower bay is similar to its W face, then there is another surviving large Norman aisle window (jambs and arch with one step and one chamfer) and the beginning of the corbel table. After that altered aisle windows with late Geometrical tracery: three cusped lights with three unencircled quatrefoils above. The clerestory here has nothing more than one small lancet window for each bay – which is explained by the difference in interior design. The aisle is interrupted by the N PORCH, which must have been built a little after the ground floor of the W front. The N doorway which the porch covers is exactly in the style of the W portal. Four orders of detached shafts, and the arch with the same motifs as there. But the porch has inside and outside blank arcading with waterleaf capitals but pointed arches with a keeled roll moulding. The entrance however is again round-arched. Quadripartite rib-vault inside. The ribs are keeled in section, and there is no boss. Outside above the entrance are trefoiled niches as in the W front. Above these a frieze of blank arcading, but now with E.E. moulded capitals. Perp battlements and pinnacles. Before we leave the nave, a straight-ish joint and the plinth moulding's abrupt ending in the third bay mark the end of Abbot Hugh's work. Between the first two bays is a Norman pilaster-buttress, in the first bay a fragment of the original window head.

The Norman appearance of the TRANSEPTS can be partly deduced on the N. In the W wall there is one Norman window with a billet moulding along the wall rising to form a hood-mould around the window head – a motif familiar from the parts of *c.* 1100–10 at Durham and used locally at Brayton (q.v.). The window is set in a plain giant arch and another such arch is applied to the unwindowed bay beyond a flat buttress to the l. Above this blank arch two short strips of string course indicate the top and bottom of the Norman clerestory; the s end of the upper moulding survives in the angle with the nave as a stub of corbel table. Slit-windows to NW newel staircase. On the N side remains of a central pilaster buttress and the billet moulding again; on the E another fragment of clerestory string course, with half a round arch and an eaves corbel above. The clerestory, heightened *c.* 1340, has four-light windows with good flowing tracery. The N gable, with small three-light window with reticulated tracery, is of 1907–9. Very large and splendid Perp N window of seven lights with transom and much panel tracery. Attached to the E wall is the Latham

Chapel, with two five-light Perp windows. It was founded in
1476 by the will of John Latham.

Before we turn to the choir, we must have a look at the
CROSSING TOWER. This still has its splendidly solid two Norman
stages, partly repaired but mostly a careful copy of 1701–2. Both
have two windows to each face, the upper ones shafted and with
chevron to the arches. *Oldrid Scott*'s top parts could not be more
successful if they were original. The height is extremely well
calculated. Arcaded bell-stage with blind arches flanking triple-
lancet openings; much ballflower decoration; then quatrefoil
parapet and pinnacles. Four commanding parapet statues of
William the Conqueror (w), Abbot Hugh (s), Edward VII (n)
and Archbishop Maclagan (E), by *Robert Bridgeman*.

19   Now for the CHOIR. This with its aisles and the s addition
of a two-bay Sacristy is work of two phases: *c.* 1280–*c.* 1300
and *c.* 1320–40. The diversion of resources to fight the Scottish
wars may account for the interval. Building must have gone
on around the existing chancel and started with the stoutly
buttressed choir aisles, where the tracery is influenced by York.
On the N it is still decidedly late Geometrical: three quatrefoiled circles above three cusped lancet lights. That is, if anything, earlier than the nave N aisle alterations. The westernmost
window is from the second phase and repeats the clerestory's
normal Dec. In the s aisle the two westernmost windows are
Oldrid Scott's but he copied the blind tracery of the adjoining
bays against the Sacristy. These have three lancets again but a
large encircled cinquefoil above. With this work goes the
ground floor of the SACRISTY, which has simple cusped
stepped lancet lights. The later completion of the choir
included the clerestory as well as the interior. The rough
'tusking' stones for flyers on several clerestory buttresses
suggest that as with York Minster's nave a stone vault was
originally intended but abandoned. The tracery reflects the
changed style of the 1330s. The Sacristy's upper floor has
simple two-light windows with mouchettes, echoing the altar
screen's blind tracery (*see* below). The windows in the eastern
half of the s choir aisle and in the E gable window have reticulated tracery. Finally the E window, a glorious seven-light piece
of mature flowing style, one of the most beautiful examples in
the country. The influence now is not York but churches to
the s, e.g. Hawton, Nottinghamshire and Heckington, Lincolnshire. The N and s clerestory windows are all of that style
too. The aisle and clerestory parapets have an openwork
trefoil-cusped wavy line, a motif whose appearance again in
the clerestory wall passage dates it as original Dec work. It has,
as one more remarkable decorative enrichment, a variety of
carved figures seemingly standing along it like a half-heavenly
audience. These engagingly realistic people are a rare and
delightful conceit.* York Minster has such figures, as does
Beverley Minster, which has parapets of the same design. A

---

* Replacements for missing figures carved by *Alan Micklethwaite*, 2004.

remoter parallel is at the Marienkirche, Muhlhausen, Germany, where however it is a generation later. Rich crocketing to the buttress finials and the spirelets of four octagonal staircase turrets at the E end.

The Perp style, as was shown, did no more than the addition of one chapel and the enlargement of two key windows: W and N.

Oldrid Scott's S TRANSEPT is entirely Dec, with different tracery in all four clerestory windows. Above the S doorway (which would have been nonsense in a Benedictine church) is a very large six-light window, and above this, as on the N transept, a gable with flanking turrets. Wavy parapets.

Interior   *p. 15*

We can assume that the church was begun from the E. Excavations in 1890–1 indicated that the Norman E parts comprised a chancel with a small apse, flanked by straight-ended aisles or chapels, possibly apsidal inside. How close the connection with Durham was we can of course no longer decide. With the CROSSING and TRANSEPTS we come to remaining evidence. Of the crossing piers only the SW is completely in its original state. The SE one looks genuine but was rebuilt after failing in 1690. The E and W faces have flat projections flanked by shafts with scallop capitals; on the N and S the projections are corbelled high up, probably to allow for choir stalls. Taking the N TRANSEPT and the fragments of the S TRANSEPT together the following can be said. Both had an E chapel, the entrance arch with two orders of shafts with volute and scroll and scalloped capitals and two roll mouldings in the arch. End walls with central pilaster buttress, and (N) small plain round-headed doorway to NW stair. W sides with windows set in blank arches. The triforium, with four plain arches enclosing two sub-arches and chamfered string course at impost level, and the clerestory, with linking string course at springing level, can be reconstructed from fragments in the N transept, N and S of the E arches and in the C14 W wall passage, and in the S transept W wall, where there is a shaft with capital and evidence of an arch and sub-arch. From the S transept work progressed into the S aisle; the arch to the aisle has the triple shafting, plain steps and bold soffit roll all characteristic of the earliest Romanesque work, in which there is nothing that would necessitate a date later than *c.* 1100–10. As on the exterior the aisle wall has a chamfered plinth moulding (see also the N transept, crossing piers and N aisle). Near the W end, set high up, is a mysterious feature like a tall blind arcade with four small semicircular arches.

Now the NAVE, which makes a fascinating study. It is to be   *14, 15* warmly recommended to students. They ought to stop reading here and should not continue until they have found their own results. The basis of the design is, just as at Durham, the double bay, or alternation of supports, which the later designers respected, even into the C13. The arcades were started on the S side. Tripartite E respond still with volute and leaf-scroll capitals. Then a gigantic circular pier of the Durham type with an incised trellis all over its cylindrical surface. Circular capital with many scallops, some with foliage scrolls. Arch with heavy tripartite roll moulding. Rib-vault in the aisle with a half-roll moulding. The transverse arch has two rolls separated by a spur. To the designer this vault seemed irreconcilable with a cylindrical pier, and so, quite inorganically, four shafts are attached to a flat surface at the back of the round pier. The arrangement however is just as inorganic in the choir at Durham. The next pier, according to the principle of alternating supports, must be composite. The strongest of the attached shafts rises up to the ceiling. As there is only one such shaft, it does not look as if a nave vault was ever intended. With the arch between the Durham column and the composite pier a new motif with a great future arrives, chevron decoration. This makes its appearance in England c. 1110–15, and indeed at Durham at that time. Here it characterizes the later parts of Abbot Hugh's work. On the N side the chevron is there from the beginning, on both orders, with point to point on the inner one. The first round pier has no incised pattern (though may have had a painted one), its capital scallops without carving.

We must now examine the gallery above the arcades, for Selby, like Durham and most major Anglo-Norman churches, has a gallery. The first two bays on each side were originally the same, with a large twin opening with a short, heavy intermediate pier, under a big blank arch with chevron decoration; the tympanum has diaper-work. On both N and S, however, the opening in the first bay has later been infilled, leaving one much smaller shafted opening; the memorable distortion of the arches above and below on the N side explains/demonstrates the necessity. The cause was no doubt the tower, which we must turn to now as part of this work. The crossing arches that carry it are original on the N and W and have chevron on their outer orders; the rebuilt S arch has a W fragment. Above the crossing ceiling, in the ringing chamber, are much-restored parts of the lantern stage, i.e. the NW corner which was strengthened by the staircase, with one N and one W window each fronted by one arch from a four-bay arcade with wall passage. Below is a gallery originally with two arches on each side.

Back now to the nave's ground floor at the end of Abbot Hugh's church, indicated by straight joints at gallery level just W of the compound piers. A temporary wall here and a roof above the gallery would have allowed use of the completed parts when work stopped, probably by c. 1130. What happened next, i.e. some forty years later when work was resumed, is what makes Selby both special and especially instructive. Eschewing the options of replicating the existing work or creating an abrupt break by carrying on in contemporary style the monks took a middle path and maintained the Romanesque design, including the archaic form of gallery, but used a selection of up-to-date Gothic details as work proceeded over some five or six decades. Their choices display a cavalier attitude to contemporary theories of beauty that saw consistency as a virtue, especially between the N and S sides (they were not, of course, alone in this). The next double bays have an especially confusing mixture of elements, particularly on the N side, which make sense if their circular and composite piers (i.e. piers three and four) on both sides were constructed in the 1120s with those to the E; the character of the stonework supports this. Likewise the chevron on the inner and middle order of the third arch on the N is like that of the first and second arches, and these voussoirs may have been carved much earlier. The keeled angle roll of the outer order, however, clearly goes with the next arch and those on the S. It is in the next arch that the last chevron appears, perhaps to harmonize with its neighbour, but it is of a different and later variety, where the chevron is broken round a roll moulding, like a herringbone. The next double bay is no longer Norman. One might call it Transitional. Now, instead of the circular pier, a compound pier with keeled shafts, moulded capital and circular abacus. It is unusual in that all the shafts are the same size and that there are not eight but seven, plus a smaller trio at the back to carry the aisle vault. Finely moulded arches to the arcade. This system carries on to the W end, to both sides, but ending, as at Durham, with two compound piers in succession. On the capitals waterleaf now appears (cf. W and N doorways) and in the tower bay even crocket capitals, a yet later form. With the nave go the ground floor of the W front, the completion of the N aisle with the N doorway and the N aisle rib-vaults. These are square in section with hollow chamfers. The S tower bay has the same vaults as the N aisle and N tower bay, but the S aisle vaults, with ribs and arches of much finer profile, were apparently only put in when the S gallery was finally built.

Now to the N gallery, which must have followed straight on for again it has waterleaf capitals. From the third bay the twin openings of the Norman gallery are given up for a completely new pattern, with a single, cavernously wide arch of three orders to each bay, the same width as the arch of the bay below. With this anachronistic design one might think the Selby monks were looking back to their royal founder's church at Caen. Just as distinctive are the two intermediate piers, where a delightful solution was found to combine a weight commensurate with the sturdy piers below with a lightness now evidently aimed at. Instead of a solid circular pier there are now solid cores surrounded by completely detached shafts: the first has two concentric circles, an inner with six shafts, an outer with seven; the second has the core more simply surrounded by eight shafts. With circular plinth below and great circular abacus above they appear like carousels. Whether inspired by the York crypt piers with four detached shafts of c. 1170 (cf. also the retrochoir of Chichester of c. 1185) or that at St Mary's,

York, with sixteen, *c.* 1180–5, the designer gave Selby two uniquely inventive and happy features. The clerestory above must be left for the moment.

The s gallery, built with the s clerestory, harmonizes with the upper stage of the w front façade and may be dated tentatively *c.* 1225–30, so it was evidently begun quite some time after the N gallery was complete. It has one spectacular feature that, like the carousels, is an innovation unique to Selby. It starts, as on the N, at the third bay, but here more radical changes were made. Twin openings were kept, but each bay now has two pointed arches under one round arch. Pierced sunk trefoils in the spandrels. Many-moulded arches, inconsistent use of bold dogtooth, e.g. between the triple shafts, around the outer arches. What catches the eye is the system of shafts for the main ceiling beams. They are slender and hexagonal, with concave faces. One set rises up between the bays, while an intermediate set, balanced on corbels above the apexes of the nave arches, runs up quite free in front of the main gallery arches, dividing them in two.

The s clerestory has two shafted lancets in each bay, whereas on the N side the clerestory was given (no earlier, and probably later) three even blank arches in each bay with only one window in the middle bay and much dogtooth.

The panelled C15 NAVE CEILING was badly burnt in the fire, but quite a number of large square BOSSES were rescued and reinstated. They show birds, beasts, fish, a centaur, a mermaid, a wild boar under an oak tree, an elephant and castle, etc.

23 The richly Dec CHOIR offers harmonious consistency after the nave's stimulating variety of styles. The gap in time in its completion is only obvious where the blank arcading of the aisle walls and of the altar screen returns face each other. Tall arcades with piers of eight attached shafts, but in a typically Dec way the shafts are not separated from each other but connected by a long wavy moulding. Thick knobbly foliage capitals in which the distinction of the shafts disappears. Above the p. 15 capitals are statuary bases on excellently carved caryatid figures; grotesque types, sometimes single, sometimes in pairs. The statues (some missing, some replaced *c.* 1913) stand below elaborate canopies. Above the canopies the slenderest possible vaulting shafts rise to leafy capitals carrying stone springers for the vault, which was always wooden. In front of the clerestory windows a wall passage with wavy parapet. The openings of the passage through the wall have ogee heads with thick crocketing. Carved figures along the parapet, as on the exterior, look down into the choir: two at the w end on the N, above the organ, fragments of two more opposite, and of three above the sanctuary on the s side.

Now the aisles, whose blank arcading (and the blank lancets beside the windows) shows the influence of St Mary's Abbey, York, begun 1271. Arches with pointed trefoiled cusping and rich, solid foliage capitals. Their bossy character is already C14, but C13 in that individual species of leaves can still be recognized: ivy, vine, oak etc. Much of the carving is excellent imitation done by *Thomas Strudwick* of Selby after the fire; he also replicated the two w bays of the s aisle arcade. Keeled and filleted vaulting shafts. Vaults with longitudinal and transverse ridge ribs. No higher flights of fancy.

On the s is a double doorway to the SACRISTY, a wide, airy room, vaulted in two bays with longitudinal and transverse ridge ribs. In the wall under the sw window is a stone shelf with three small arched recesses, and to the r. a sink before a moulded arched recess for a cistern. Their purpose is not clear. The upper room, probably the SCRIPTORIUM or LIBRARY, has springers for a vault, but it is either lost or was never realized.

The junction of the new choir with the existing building was more complicated on the N side than on the s as the choir is wider than the Norman chancel was, the new centre line being set N of the old one. When the choir was completed the N TRANSEPT was remodelled, with its two E arches similar to the choir arcade, and the wall passage and wavy parapet carried on around it. After *c.* 1476 the northern arch opened to the Latham Chapel instead of the Norman one. As the seat of the 1906 fire, the chapel has much new masonry, some of the capitals being deliberately left uncarved.

FURNISHINGS. – ALTAR SCREEN. Behind the altar a solid screen wall to divide the altar space from the choir aisles and the ambulatory behind it. Mature Dec, with blank decoration to both sides. Two-light divisions with crocketed gables, and in the gables flowing tracery. Diapering between the gables, rich frieze above. The N and s returns are a little simpler. The style is connected with Lincoln and Southwell rather than York. Oak top 1909. – SEDILIA. Four seats, each with vaulted canopy, their tall pinnacled tops remade in 1892. – The CHOIR FITTINGS are a complete set by *Oldrid Scott*, 1908–9, in finely and elaborately carved oak, with some gilding: REREDOS with large carving of the Crucifixion by *Peter Rendl* of Oberammergau; metal COMMUNION RAIL with scrolls and trellis; CHOIR and CLERGY STALLS (canopies by *C.M. Scott*, 1937; SIDE SCREENS; CROSSING SCREEN with vaulted canopy; octagonal PULPIT with tester. – FONT. Plain C12 tub font, thought to have come from the medieval parish church. – FONT COVER. Splendid tall Perp piece, saved from the fire; restored. Two octagonal tiers with openwork tracery and a tall crocketed spire.

STAINED GLASS. In the easternmost choir N window are two fire-damaged C14 panels (?Judah and St John the Evangelist), restored in 1891, and a much-restored C14 panel of St John the Baptist and its fire-damaged 1891 replacement; also other medieval fragments. Further medieval fragments in the Sacristy E window. C14 glass from Ellerton Priory (East Riding) is in the N aisle, third from E. The great E window is a memorable work, with a Last Judgment in the tracery above the Tree of Jesse in the seven main lights. Although valuable in its own right it is, however, entirely a replica of the original window of *c.* 1340, made by *Thomas Curtis* of *Ward & Hughes* in 1906–9 with the benefit of drawings etc. from his restoration of 1891. Curtis subsequently received several other commissions, including the magnificent transept windows of 1914, the N of seven lights with forty-six scenes from the life of St Germain, the six-light S window with characters and events in the history of the abbey. There are several others by *Ward & Hughes*: W windows of the N and S aisle, 1885 and 1894; S choir aisle, fourth and fifth, 1897 and 1891; and N choir aisle E, 1911, and sixth (war memorial), 1922.

The rest are as follows: N choir aisle, from E: second †1914 by *J. Dudley Forsyth*, from Holy Trinity, Hampstead (dem.); third and fourth by *Wailes*, 1863, 1866. – S choir aisle. E window by *Hardman* 1917. From E: first by *Hardman*, 1926; second and third by *Wailes*, 1860; – N transept. W window by *Clayton & Bell*, 1892. – N aisle, from E: second by *Geoffrey Webb*, 1934; fifth by *Clayton & Bell*, 1871; sixth by *Heaton, Butler & Bayne*, 1866. Nave W window by *Heaton, Butler & Bayne*, 1866. – S aisle. First, fifth and sixth from E by *Hardman*, 1872–3.

SCULPTURE. A C15 alabaster panel of the Deposition, about 15 in. (38 cm.) high (N choir aisle). – MONUMENTS. All in the nave. Abbot Alexander †1221. Long, narrow tomb-slab with chamfered sides, the top edged with dogtooth and his name inscribed in large elegant letters. – Sir Hugh de Pickworth and his wife, Margery de Pickworth. Two worn early C14 effigies less than life-size (separate). He in armour, cross-legged, she under a crocketed canopy, holding two pendant shields. – Abbot John de Shireburn †1407. Large mutilated alabaster slab, with headless incised figure. – John, Lord Darcy †1411. Once-fine, but much abused alabaster tomb-chest, the effigy now a limbless chunk. One side with six angels holding heraldic shields, divided from each other by Perp panel motifs (cf. Brayton). – Abbot John Barwick †1526. Large incised tomb-slab with mitred and robed figure. – Richard Spencer †1691. Skull-and-crossbones above framed tablet with armorial shield. – John Audus †1809 and wife Jane †1830 by *W. Plows*, York (?1830). Large, with fussily decorated urn and tablet. – Hon. Catherine Petre †1830 by *Felix Austin*. Neoclassical, with dove and wreath. – Thomas Eadon †1835 by *M. Taylor*. Scrolled plinth with sarcophagus on lion's feet, chastely decorated. – John Dobson †1837 by *W. Bradley*, Selby. Draped urn and Vitruvian scroll. – Morley Wharrey †1797, daughter Sophia Buchanan †1817 and wife Elizabeth †1842 by *W. Plows* (?1817). Reeded tablet and finely carved sarcophagus with coloured marble. – Thomas Standering †1848 and family, with crocketed ogee arch.

The MONASTIC BUILDINGS have entirely disappeared. They extended as usual S of the nave and transept. The Great Gatehouse, W of the W front, was taken down only in 1792 and much-altered remains of a tithe barn in James Street to the SW in the 1960s. Beside the river, on the Abbot's Staith or wharf, behind later frontages in Water Lane is the large C15 or early C16 ABBOT'S STAITH WAREHOUSE (visible from The Quay). Two storeys, H-plan with long centre. Some double-chamfered window openings. Although much altered, its substantial ashlar masonry remains impressive.

THE TOWN

It is difficult to imagine Selby Abbey as an abbey, for the church stands at the heart of the unassuming brick-built C18 and C19 town. The burgesses saved the building and in the course of the centuries made it their own, the town gradually drawing nearer as the abbey precinct and its buildings disappeared. The demolition of the Great Gatehouse in 1792 brought the church's W front face to face with the market place. Selby has a long history as an important tidal river port, ranking as sixth largest town in the West Riding Poll Tax returns of 1377–81, but few traces of its riverside activities have survived their late C20 demise. Its modest Georgian and Early Victorian buildings best reflect its postmedieval heyday. From the completion of the Selby Canal in 1778 until Goole docks opened in 1826 it was the West Riding's principal port, and from 1792 the bridge across the Ouse increased through traffic and brought greater prosperity. The town's importance as a terminus for passenger steam packets linking inland Yorkshire with London and Hull was briefly reinforced when the Leeds–Selby railway opened in 1834, but disappeared once the line was extended to Hull in 1840. Although on the London–York–Edinburgh railway from 1871, the town was bypassed again in 1983 when the line was diverted around the new Selby coalfield, which closed in 2004. The population jumped from 2,860 to 4,600 between 1801 and 1831; in 1911 it was barely 9,000; in 2011 barely 13,000.

ST JAMES, New Lane. By *Newstead & Low*, 1866–7. Large, but surprisingly well hidden. W tower (spire demolished in RAF flying accident 1944), five-bay aisled nave with clerestory, chancel with transeptal vestry and organ chamber. Geometric tracery. Fine interior, following Ecclesiological principles. Chancel arch with clustered shafts of Devonshire marble, arcades with polished red Isle of Mull granite piers and richly foliate capitals. – STAINED GLASS. E window by *Heaton, Butler & Bayne*, 1867. W window 1873 and S aisle third from E 1884, by *Capronnier*. S aisle fourth from E by *Ward & Hughes*, 1927.

ST MARY (R.C.), Leeds Road. By *Joseph & Charles Hansom*, 1856, for the Hon. Mrs Petre. An attractive composition in sandstone with white limestone dressings. Big buttressed tower with broach spire at SW entrance. Five-bay nave with lean-to aisles, clerestory and transeptal S chapel, two-bay chancel. Dec tracery. Good details. Interior all painted. Three-bay arcade supports small w gallery. Octagonal former baptistery at sw corner. – ALTAR and REREDOS. Limestone, with richly carved figurative panels; similar in s chapel. – PULPIT. World War I memorial 1919, in keeping, has excellent sculptured scenes of St George, St Michael and Joan of Arc. – Remarkable NW octagonal GROTTO, 1931, inspired by that at Lourdes, with artificial rockwork. – STAINED GLASS. e window by *Wailes*, 1856. Nave chapel s window by *Bell*, 1856. – MONUMENT. Hon. Edward Robert Petre †1848. Plaque with elaborate brass, silver and enamel inlay.

KING'S CHURCH, New Lane. By *Pritchett & Son*, 1865–6, for the Congregationalists, incorporating fabric of a chapel of 1808–9. Tripartite brick front in French Romanesque style. Tall three-bay arcades with round arches and thin cast-iron columns.

CIVIC CENTRE, Doncaster Road.* By *Space Architects*, 2009–11. District Council offices and council chamber, built with the community HOSPITAL (on the site of *Leslie Moore*'s cottage hospital, 1926). Two-storey rear office range has long glazed N elevation. The hospital in brick, white render and jade green cladding.

TOWN HALL, Gowthorpe. Former Primitive Methodist chapel, 1862. Simple Italianate style.

COURT HOUSE (former), New Lane. Provided in 1855 by James Audus for his fellow magistrates. Domestic-looking.

RAILWAY STATION, Station Road. 1871 for the North Eastern Railway, on the site of the station built 1836–40 when the Leeds line was extended to Hull. Part-glazed canopies on decorative cast-iron columns to both platforms; single-storey brick range on up platform. At lower level to e the original simple brick terminus STATION of 1830–4 by *James Walker*, converted to a goods shed in 1841. The SWING RAILWAY BRIDGE for the Hull line is by *Thomas Harrison*, 1891.

SELBY BRIDGE. Swing bridge across the Ouse, by *E. W. H. Gifford & Partners*, 1969–70. Extensive use of timber as well as steel preserves the spirit of the picturesque wooden bridge of 1791–2 that it replaced – itself one of the earliest swing bridges in Europe; it pivoted on ball bearings like cannon balls.

PERAMBULATION. The broad paved MARKET PLACE extends from the churchyard railings towards the MARKET CROSS, a weathered Gothic pinnacle erected by the 9th Lord Petre, Lord of the Manor, *c*. 1790. GOWTHORPE, the main street, stretching westwards, includes an assembly of plain later Georgian houses, now shops, two- or three-storeyed, in brown brick or stucco with a varied roof-line. Also on the s side, the former LOCAL BOARD OFFICES, by *W.H. Thorp*, 1890–1, in red brick with good stone dressings, has a little spired oriel on the corner. At the end of Gowthorpe, 200 yds beyond the present

---

*Demolition of the previous Civic Centre, Portholme Road, by *Goad Burton Partnership*, 1977, is proposed at the time of writing.

Selby, bridge.
Engraving by W. J. Cooke after N. Whittock, 1831

Town Hall (*see* above), are two small squares each enclosed on three sides by simple two-storey brick ALMSHOUSES. Ten cottages in each square, the E one built by the Selby Feoffees in 1822, the W one given by James Audus in 1833 and distinguished by a grander centrepiece with ogee-headed archway. Then in LEEDS ROAD St Mary's church (*see* above), and GOWTHORPE HOUSE, a handsome early C19 sandstone ashlar villa with Doric porch. C20 school extension. Nearby at the S end of ARMOURY ROAD, by the level crossing, the former ARMOURY AND DRILL HALL, by *Edward Taylor* for the Selby Volunteers, 1864–5.

Lastly, from Market Place to the river along THE CRESCENT, a most successful piece of town planning embracing the S side of the abbey and designed as an elegant link between Market Place and the bridge. Initiated in 1792 by local merchant John Audus, who was enthused by a visit to Bath, it was completed *c.* 1829 by his son James Audus, who cleared unsightly Shambles from the Market Place and built a terrace of seven three-storey houses to balance the C18 Londesborough Arms Hotel opposite. The Crescent has two terraces, the first with ten mostly two-bay houses, now shops. Park Street intervenes. The centrepiece of its terrace, facing the park, is the pedimented front of the former PUBLIC ROOMS by *John Harper*, 1839. Rusticated ground floor and three tall round-arched windows above. The flanking two-storey houses, probably of the 1830s, retain their attractive doorways, some pedimented or paired. The Crescent's second terrace starts with one large house facing the park.

OUSEGATE faces the river. Once the town's main street, its former importance is evidenced by the early C18 CORUNNA HOUSE, the handsomest house in Selby. Brown brick. Eight bays, the third and sixth as raised panels in red brick. Hipped pantile roof; modillion eaves cornice. Doorway with semicircular hood on carved brackets.

SHARLSTON

St Luke. By *J. T. Micklethwaite*, 1886–7. Long, aisleless. Large buttresses and a spired bellcote mark the chancel arch. – STAINED GLASS. E window by *Kempe*, 1887.

Sharlston Hall, ½ m. SE. Timber-framed, but mostly hidden by stone casing and render. The core is the hall range of a linear hearth-passage-plan house of *c.* 1425. The hall was open, though relatively low, and heated by a fire-hood. Crown-post roof. Large five-light mullioned-and-transomed window to front and back. Gabled dormers, one large, one small, are early C18 when the upper part of the hall was floored. The w end was replaced *c.* 1450 with a three-bay cross-wing for heated parlour and solar, also with a crown-post roof and large external stack. A two-bay E cross-wing, with a collar-rafter roof, followed in the late C15, creating an up-to-date H-plan. The w wing was extended forward with a lower range in the early C16 (kingpost roof), possibly containing a chapel. Lower gabled additions on its E side slightly overlap the hall. A further E wing, also early C16, was built with a massive rear chimney-stack, probably as a kitchen. The most attractive feature is the porch, dated 1574, with decorative framing to its upper storey and gable. The crossed diagonal struts forming concave-sided lozenges are not at all a Yorkshire motif. – Good GATEPIERS with ball finials and obelisks, and DOVECOTE with pyramidal roof, probably all C17.

SHEFFIELD

INTRODUCTION

Sheffield is the largest city in Yorkshire in area and second in population (513,230 in 2001), yet its inhabitants still fondly refer to it as a big village. It is true that its centre seems modest when compared with those of Manchester or Leeds but none of the big cities of England has such majestic surroundings as Sheffield. The River Don flows down from the NW and turns to the NE where it is joined by the Sheaf; this and the Porter, the Loxley and the Rivelin descend in steep-sided valleys. The undulating hills between them are the city's greatest natural asset, accompanied by green swards that penetrate deep into the very edge of the city centre, which stands on a low hill, dwarfed by the surrounding landscape.

The district was known by the Anglo-Saxons as Hallamshire, a large parish including Sheffield, Ecclesfield and Bradfield (q.v.), with its church at Ecclesfield (q.v.). The medieval town grew up around the c12 castle sited defensively at the confluence of the Don and the Sheaf. This was the seat of the builder William de Lovetot, lord of Hallamshire, after 1116. On high ground to the SE was the manor's hunting park with the Lodge that in the c16 superseded the Castle as the preferred residence of the Earls of Shrewsbury who obtained the lordship in the early c15.

There was a thriving town by the late c13, when the burgesses were given a charter setting out their privileges and Town Trustees assumed responsibility for some local government functions. Weekly markets were established in Haymarket by a charter of 1296, and houses extended to Fargate and Church Street. Burgage plots on High Street were still evident well into the c19. Indeed, the city centre retains much of its medieval complexity, notwithstanding the two streets cut through in 1875, Leopold Street and Pinstone Street, and c20 additions such as Arundel Gate.

The town became notable for cutlery very early; the first reference to a cutler is in 1297 and Sheffield knives were sufficiently well known for Chaucer to refer to one in 'The Reeve's Tale'. The Cutlers' Company, formed in 1624, with its own hall from 1638, remains one of the principal institutions in the town. More than half of the town's water-powered industrial sites were used for grinding cutlery and edge tools but others powered iron works and by 1700 some ironmasters were also venturing into steelmaking using cementation furnaces to make blister steel. Benjamin Huntsman perfected his secret invention for making purer steel through the crucible process in 1751 and set up his first steel works at Attercliffe, NE of the centre. While blister steel was a mainstay of the industry, the production of high-quality crucible steel was Sheffield's dominant process throughout the c19. Raw materials were imported through Hull and came with coal via the River Don Navigation, which reached Tinsley (q.v.) in 1751 and was extended into the town centre in 1819. The improvements of the roads that were also needed to convey an ever-increasing range of goods out of the town began in 1756 with the Act to turnpike the road S to Chesterfield and London, and continued into the 1780s.

The c18 and early c19 was thus a time of sustained growth; the population expanding from 5,000 in 1700 to 20,000 by 1750 and 91,700 by 1831. Paradise Square was begun in 1736 and as streets were formed in the fields and meadows on the NW edge of the town, houses and workshops were built in the 'Crofts' or lanes around Scotland Street and West Bar Green. S of the town centre, Norfolk Street was created along the W edge of the manorial deer park, which was converted to farmland. Late c18 and early c19 expansion of the town was mainly to the S and SW, initiated by the Duke of Norfolk as Lord of the Manor of Sheffield, Earl Fitzwilliam as Lord of the Manor of Ecclesall, and the

Church Burgesses. Although they planned suburbs of a select character, in streets laid out on grid systems, in practice most of these areas were more mixed in character, with many domestic workshops. The new turnpike road W to Glossop stimulated development of the more substantial villas of Broomhill that mark the beginning of the middle classes' move to the higher western suburbs, escaping an increasingly polluted town. At the bottom of the town, either side of the Don, and to the N and NW, industry and poor-quality housing sprang up side by side, while from the early C19 middle-class suburban development spread on to the N slopes of the Don at Woodside and Burngreave, along the Barnsley turnpike road opened in 1835–6. With the suburbs came the four much-needed Commissioners' churches, only St George's and St Mary's now surviving, and numerous Nonconformist chapels, the noblest of which was the Doric Brunswick Chapel of 1833, lost like so many others as the inner suburbs lost their residents in the C20. Sheffield now also received a few monumental secular buildings: the Cutlers' Hall of 1832 with dignified Grecian front, the Gothic Collegiate School of 1835, and the large classical Wesleyan Proprietary School (now King Edward VII School) of 1837–40. 66

The Sheffield & Rotherham Railway arrived in 1838 with a terminus at the Wicker and that provided the impetus for the rapid development of the flat corridor of the Don valley N of the town for Sheffield's heavy steel industry, with the major firms – Cammell's, Brown's and Vickers' – moving out from the town centre to establish vast new steel works, expanding their range in the later C19 with production of bulk steel using the new Bessemer and open-hearth processes. In 1845 the Sheffield, Ashton-under-Lyne and Manchester Railway reached Bridgehouses, before the line was extended across the Don valley in 1848 and into Lincolnshire as the Manchester, Sheffield & Lincolnshire Railway, later (1897) the Great Central Railway. The first Midland Railway station, in Sheaf Street, opened in 1870 to provide a direct route S to London.

Sheffield became a municipal borough in 1843 but the Town Council had little effect on its appearance before 1875, when a vigorous street-widening programme was commenced. Three new streets were made, including Leopold Street, to create a linear commercial area from the markets and old Town Hall at Waingate to The Moor a mile to the S. The building of *Mountford*'s magnificent new Town Hall in 1893–7 followed these improvements, after Sheffield became a city in 1893.

By then its population was over 324,000 and the built-up area was greatly enlarged. Horse buses, and trams after 1873, had led to a boom in house-building to create lower-middle-class and working-class suburbs in the areas they served, spreading out to the S to include Highfield, Lowfield and Sharrow, and former rural areas such as Heeley and Meersbrook, and to the NW in Crookes and Walkley. Further rapid growth at the turn of the C20, encouraged by the electrification of the tramway network, was recognized by boundary extensions in 1900 to the NW at

Hillsborough and to the s at Norton Woodseats, and to the NE
with Tinsley (q.v.) in 1911. This suburban expansion mostly
comprised small terraced artisans' houses, decently built but of
dull appearance and set out unimaginatively. Among them,
however, stand schools, churches and chapels, and although
Sheffield's insular nature led to the almost exclusive use of local
architects, the Board Schools especially form a group of more
than local architectural significance. Noteworthy among the
churches and chapels are St John at Ranmoor and the three
chapels by *W. J. Hale* at Crookes. In the south-western suburbs
of Broomhill, Endcliffe, Ranmoor and Nether Edge the sumptuous manufacturers' houses such as the Italianate Endcliffe Hall
(1863–5) lost the exclusivity of their situation as more middle-
class villas surrounded them.

At the other end of the social scale, the older housing in the
town centre and areas like Park, built in the first half of the C19
on the E edge of the town, was increasingly unhealthy. In 1894
the Council obtained powers under the Housing of the Working
Classes Act 1890 to demolish the worst slums, in the Crofts area
around Campo Lane, and initiate the first of many public housing
schemes. Promoted by enlightened elements in the Council, the
Flower Estate at Wincobank, begun in 1900, was laid out on
garden suburb principles and marked the beginning of Sheffield's
adoption of progressive approaches to its developments.

Sheffield emerged prosperous from the First World War, for
which it had supplied much of the heavy armaments. The Corporation were still concerned that people in the inner city were
living in close proximity to heavy industry and in 1919 commissioned *Patrick Abercrombie* to prepare a Civic Survey and Plan
for zoning housing and industry and creating satellite towns
within a green belt. In practice, little was done other than clearance of houses from the industrial areas of the city centre. Of
greater significance was the attempt, again not fully implemented,
to create a Civic Centre comprising the city's major public buildings, including the City Hall by *Vincent Harris*, 1928–32, and the
Central Library and Graves Art Gallery by the City Architect,
W. G. Davies, 1929–34.

As interwar boundary extensions further increased the city's
area southwards as far as Dore, Totley and much of Norton, the
big council housing schemes for which Sheffield became notable
in the C20 were begun. The first major phase started in 1926 with
massive low-density cottage estates in the outer areas: The
Manor, Woodthorpe and Arbourthorne in the E; Shiregreen and
Parson Cross in the N. By 1939 25,000 council houses had been
built. The huge consumption of land for housing was partly
countered by designation of a green belt in 1938, the culmination
of a programme that had begun with the creation of a linear park
from Endcliffe Park to the open Derbyshire moorland.

In the Second World War the worst destruction was in the
city centre in High Street and The Moor, but after it the paramount need was to replace damaged and unfit housing stock in
continuance of the pre-war slum clearance programme. The

Parson Cross estate, left incomplete in 1939, was finished, and new estates at Ballifield, Birley, Stradbroke and Hackenthorpe (then outside the city boundary) and extensions of existing ones at Woodthorpe and The Manor were constructed. Under *J.L. Womersley*, City Architect from 1953, Sheffield's housing grew upwards. Schemes for comprehensive redevelopment in the inner areas were drawn up in the early 1950s. The most notable were Park Hill (1955–61) and Hyde Park (1955–64), which attracted unprecedented national and international attention to the city. In contrast were the more usual mixed estates: Lowedges (1953–9), Netherthorpe (1956–64), Gleadless Valley (1955–62) and Woodside (1960–2). All exploited the opportunities for picturesque planning provided by Sheffield's hills. Tower blocks were carefully placed to act as landmarks across the city and even from the Peak District. Equally significant was the visual relationship of one development to another. In all these schemes, Womersley applied his favourite maxim from Capability Brown: 'Flood the valleys, plant the tops'. Such dramatic townscape has been lost with the demolitions, particularly of most tower blocks, of the 1990s. Many of the post-war schools that accompanied the outer housing estates, by architects such as *Basil Spence*, were redeveloped in the early C21 under the national rebuilding programme for secondary schools. The churches, however, remain and several are significant examples of C20 ecclesiastical design.

The University of Sheffield's competition in 1953 was a seminal point in post-war British architecture: the first time that a competition for a major architectural project had a commitment to modern architecture as a prerequisite and as a focus for a debate about the form that architecture should take. *Gollins, Melvin & Ward*'s successful entries for the Arts Tower (1961–5) and Library (1955–9) looked to America and the functionalism of Mies van de Rohe and Skidmore, Owings & Merrill. Concurrent with this was the building of the Technical College (now Sheffield Hallam University) and the reconstruction of the city centre. Part of an inner ring road was built comprising Arundel Gate, Eyre Street and Charter Row, with a new focal point at Castle Square with an underground shopping centre (opened in 1968, now removed). The Moor was rebuilt as a principal shopping street in the 1950s and '60s with uniform designs with Portland stone facings and canted corners displaying little panache. At the time of writing some of these are being replaced.

In 1967 Sheffield's boundaries were extended to bring in part of NE Derbyshire, including Beighton, Mosborough and Hackenthorpe, which have seen the city's greatest housing expansion since the 1960s. In 1974 Sheffield became a Metropolitan District within the new county of South Yorkshire, as the historic West Riding was abolished. The next two decades saw serious economic and industrial decline as steel and engineering industries were hit hard by recession. In the Don valley, major works such as Firth Brown's and Hadfield's were closed and demolished. The consistent theme of the last four decades has been the need for economic regeneration, which has too often meant that opportunities for new development promising jobs have been seized, however mediocre the quality of new building and regardless of the price paid in loss of irreplaceable fabric of historic interest. In most of the Don valley the Sheffield Development Corporation had responsibility for economic and physical regeneration from 1988 to 1997, overseeing reclamation of derelict industrial sites and redevelopment for retail and sporting use, such as Meadowhall Shopping Centre, 1990. The huge expansion of the city's two universities has seen major new academic buildings and extensive residential accommodation for students, none architecturally noteworthy.

The scale and design of private flat developments such as the thirty-two-storey St Paul's Tower, which towers above the Town Hall nearby, remain controversial, but the imaginative conversion of historic industrial buildings to residential use has successfully ensured their future. In the Kelham Island area, conversions and new housing have brought life to the riverside; elsewhere footpaths and open spaces along the banks are allowing access to the once hidden and polluted River Don. Renewal in the city centre started in 1995 with the 'Heart of the City' project, which included the redesigned Peace Gardens, and the Millennium Galleries (2001) and Winter Garden (2002), both built with Millennium Commission funding. The regeneration of other parts was envisaged in a city centre Masterplan of 2000 by *Koetter Kim & Associates*, whose idea of ten Quarters has been partially realized. The Cultural Industries Quarter, the first one designated, now has an established identity, but development of the controversial Retail Quarter only began in 2016. Whether the conflicting demands of commercial developers seeking larger and ever taller buildings and those who value Sheffield's varied buildings and townscape and the more humane scale of earlier ages can be reconciled remains to be seen.

CITY CENTRE

The area of the city centre is broadly defined as the area bounded by the inner ring road on the E, S and W sides and the N bank of the Don to the N.

CHURCHES

Cathedral Church of St Peter and St Paul

The first post-Conquest church in Sheffield was probably contemporary with the castle built by William de Lovetot after 1116 and probably destroyed in 1266; fragments incorporated in the chancel interior are thought to be its only survivors. The dedication of another church is recorded in the 1280s but it was replaced *c.* 1430 by the church whose Perp chancel and splendid crossing tower and crocketed spire are visible today. The original cruciform plan began to disappear when the Shrewsbury Chapel was added to the SE *c.* 1520 by the 4th Earl and there is further evidence for other changes to the church at this time. By 1771 much of the fabric was in a ruinous condition and *John Carr* was engaged to remedy matters, refacing part of the chancel in a sympathetic and surprisingly convincing Gothic and supervising other repairs. *Thomas Atkinson* filled the NE corner in 1777 with a small vestry, with Church Burgesses' Room above, and after the N and S walls of the nave were rebuilt to match the chancel under the direction of *William Lindley* (Carr's former assistant) in 1790–3 the transformation to a rectangular plan was complete. Next the higgledy-piggledy accumulation of C18 private pews and galleries was swept away in a further rebuilding by *Charles Watson* (Lindley's former partner), 1802–5. The chancel and its aisles were walled off from the nave, and the nave arcades were heightened to accommodate new galleries on four sides. A major restoration was undertaken in 1878–80 by *Flockton & Gibbs*, with advice from *Sir George Gilbert Scott*. They added the N and S transepts and another bay, with porches, at the W end, and built new vestries on the NE side.

The parish church became the cathedral of the new Anglican diocese in 1914 and *Sir Charles Nicholson* was then engaged to transform it into one of cathedral-like proportions in 1919. His first proposal, approved in 1921, was to build a new nave and choir N of the existing church, changing the existing nave and chancel into a S aisle to be balanced by a corresponding N aisle with a matching steeple. Lack of funds placed any immediate start out of reach, and in 1936 Nicholson changed his plans to a more radical N–S reorientation of the building, which proposed the demolition of the nave, and the creation of a new chancel with a large nave extending S across the churchyard towards the Cutlers' Hall. The existing chancel was to become a (ritual) S transept, with the tower and spire replicated on the W ('N') side of the new nave. Work began in April 1937 and the new vestries, offices and Chapter House, together with a chapel linking them to the existing N transept, were completed the following year. Foundations of the new nave were begun in the churchyard but the contract was suspended at the outbreak of war, although work continued N of the existing nave. The 'S' choir aisle, crypt and adjacent passages were consecrated in 1942 and, although work on the Chapel of the Holy Spirit, which was to form the 'E' end of the new cathedral, was interrupted, it was eventually dedicated in 1948. At this stage no part of the existing church had been demolished. In the 1950s the plans were revived under Nicholson's successor, *Steven Dykes-Bower*, and from 1956 with new designs by *George Pace*. Constrained by cost, both resigned. The work of resolving Nicholson's incomplete scheme fell to *Arthur Bailey* of *Ansell & Bailey*, with a return to the old orientation, the replacement of Flockton & Gibbs's W end of the nave with a new W crossing entered through a towered porch and

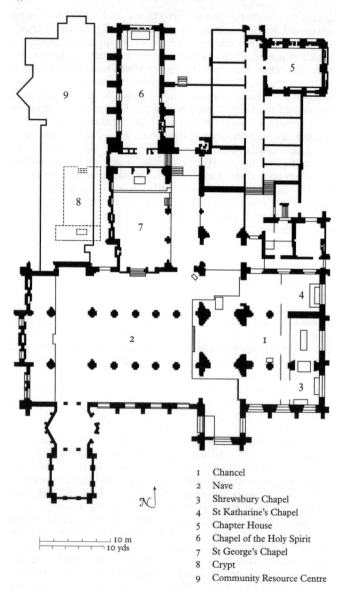

1 Chancel
2 Nave
3 Shrewsbury Chapel
4 St Katharine's Chapel
5 Chapter House
6 Chapel of the Holy Spirit
7 St George's Chapel
8 Crypt
9 Community Resource Centre

Sheffield Cathedral.
Plan

narthex, and transformation of the unfinished chancel into a
chapel. Dedication took place in 1966. More recently, the Community Resources Centre by *Martin Purdy* of *APEC Architects*,
2004–7, has been provided at the NW corner. Much less

satisfactorily, the latest work, part of a reordering by *Clive England* of *Thomas Ford & Partners* 2011–14, has seen the demotion of the s porch to a shop and a new entrance of deplorable insignificance in its remodelled link to the nave.

EXTERIOR. In spite of the several phases, the s side of the cathedral towards Church Street is consistent in style and its greyish gritstone ashlar. The tour starts with the wall of the s AISLE to the r. of the entrance. Four bays, rebuilt by *Lindley* 1790–3, set higher and slightly further out than the old wall in order to line up with the chancel. Pointed-arched windows of three lights with single transoms and panel tracery. Buttresses with details copied from Carr's work on the chancel (*see* below) and crocketed pinnacles. The nave clerestory, rebuilt 1805, has five two-light windows and can just be seen above the crenellated parapet. Next the gabled s TRANSEPT of 1880, the stone carefully matched with the older work, but the details clearly Victorian, with flowing tracery in the big five-light s window and the smaller windows to E and W. Big gabled angle buttresses, and narrower crenellation to the parapet, giving a more jagged effect than the C18 work. Behind the transept the superb C15 TOWER AND SPIRE rise above the crossing. Square tower, with large bell-openings, each of four lights with transom and flowing tracery. Above, the crocketed broach spire rises behind a crenellated parapet with corner pinnacles. The three bays of the s CHANCEL AISLE and its E wall (i.e. the E wall of the Shrewsbury Chapel) are as rebuilt by *Carr* in 1772–4. He seems to have left untouched (except for the parapet?) the wall of the adjoining CHANCEL, which had been restored in 1704 by Thomas Howard, 8th Duke of Norfolk. The differences in the stonework of the walls, tracery and plinths of the two bays are plain, even without the evidence of Howard's initials on the older work and those of Edward, the 9th Duke (†1777), on the later. Carr replaced the 'very decay'd' E window of the chapel with a careful copy of the chancel window, which has flowing Dec tracery. Was this in its turn copied from an original C15 window in 1704? The hoodmoulds of both windows have classical imposts. These and other details such as the little cusped arches and squat obelisks on pedestals carved on the buttresses are clues that the work is not the genuine Gothic it first appears. The illusion is maintained by *Atkinson*'s copy of Carr's work in the vestry added in 1777 at the end of the CHANCEL N AISLE. Rainwater heads, dated 1806, mark the completion of the rebuilding and alterations begun in 1772.

The single-storey VESTRY and CHURCH BURGESSES' ROOM, added in 1878–80 in the manner of a chantry chapel, bring us to the junction with the northward extensions, so from here the exterior is almost entirely C20 work. *Nicholson*'s additions of 1937–48 are heavy, rather sombre, late Gothic in plain ashlar blocks of buff sandstone. Deep moulded plinths and massive buttresses, with sloping parapets hiding flat roofs. The rectangular CHAPTER HOUSE at the NE corner of a two-storey range of offices has two-light pointed-arched windows set high up in deep recesses, except on the W wall which has a single large window with Dec tracery. Beyond a narrow gap the walls of the CHAPEL OF THE HOLY SPIRIT rise high above Campo Lane, its big gabled buttresses embracing the finely traceried five-light window at the N end. Aisleless, it has four slender two-light windows on each side.

Now we reach *Arthur Bailey*'s completion of Nicholson's scheme and his W extensions, which Pevsner thought 'depressingly traditional' for their date, but now seem acceptable and considerate. Free Gothic, with minimal tracery and closely set buttresses ending squarely above the roof-line. The AMBULATORY and the four bays of the CHAPEL OF ST GEORGE link the Chapel of the Holy Spirit to the nave. Their tall windows rise above the flat roof of the concrete HALL of 1966–7, and match those along the W end of the nave. The 1880 nave W window, with Dec tracery, was re-set in the N wall of the extension. Finally, at the SW corner of the Cathedral the towered PORCH projects confidently, trying at once not to be Gothic and not to be not Gothic, while harmonizing with the older work. Behind it, *Bailey*'s striking octagonal lantern sits above the W crossing.

INTERIOR. The entrance is the spacious W CROSSING, executed by Bailey in concrete and painted brick. Central lantern, whose lower structure forms an eight-pointed star, the dark Opepe hardwood mullions of the upper glazing descending into the space below as a 'Crown of Thorns'. As reconstructed in 1998–9, it has abstract glazing by *Amber Hiscott* with *David Pearl*, symbolizing darkness and light (replacing glass by *Keith New*). The concrete piers of the crossing match the octagonal piers of the NAVE of 1802–5 with their embattled capitals, which in turn are copies of the C15 chancel arcade (*see* below). Shields above the nave piers display the arms of the Lords of the Manor of Sheffield on the N side and the owners of the advowson since the Reformation on the S. Somewhat oddly, *Watson* retained the original arrangement of five bays in his rebuilding of the nave arcades and clerestory, even though the then newly rebuilt aisle walls have only four bays. The discrepancy must surely have been determined by a wish to retain the nave ROOF. This is a simple double-framed structure with billeted tie-beams which have carved and gilded bosses. Its low-pitched profile is matched exactly by the line of the later of the two earlier and lower roofs on the tower wall, suggesting it may have succeeded the original roof and was then raised in the C19.

The CROSSING PIERS are early C15. They have three orders of concave mouldings to the jambs and arches, with vestigial embattled capitals. The roof-lines of the original transepts can be seen on the N and S faces of the tower, and the S springer of the old N aisle survives on the NW crossing pier. Behind a doorway in the NE pier is the circular staircase to the rood loft, removed in 1570. The inner faces of the CHANCEL walls and its two-bay aisles are also early C15. Octagonal piers and responds with embattled capitals, and double-chamfered arches. The N aisle N wall and chancel E wall contain fragments of Norman masonry with chevron ornament. The two tiers of blind arcading with cusped arches on the chancel N wall are by *Robert Potter* 1841; other work of this date by him has gone. The chancel also retains its original steeply pitched hammer-beam roof. Moulded arched braces and collar-beams and large gilded angels with delicately outstretched wings.

The SHREWSBURY CHAPEL, built *c.* 1520, forms the E end of the chancel S aisle. Both chapel and aisle have a common roof, of similar style and pitch to the nave, although with more elaborately carved bosses. Similar roofs also in the tower aisles and the chancel N aisle, suggesting all are early C16. The chapel and aisle were restored as the LADY CHAPEL in 1935 by *W.H. Randoll Blacking*. At the same time Blacking supervised the alteration of the chancel N aisle and its E extension of 1777 to create ST KATHARINE'S CHAPEL. The cusped piscina in the S wall of the chapel originally served the pre-Reformation altar against the E wall, which was taken down in 1878–80. The tracery of its blocked five-light window was inserted in the E wall of the new N transept. Thought to be original C15, but its panel tracery matches that in the chancel S aisle windows so perhaps dates from Carr's restoration, even if copied at that date from surviving C15 work.

The N TRANSEPT of 1878–80 now forms part of the passage to Nicholson's extensions. The space N of the transept has a pretty painted panelled ceiling and was originally built as the sanctuary of the Chapel of Chivalry.

Adjoining to the W is the BURROWS MEMORIAL TRAN-SEPT. This would have been the 's' choir aisle to the high sanctuary, which was only partly built when work stopped in 1942. The triple arcades in Nicholson's conventional Gothic on the N and E sides of the sanctuary were eventually completed with Bailey's W wall of four bays and three high arched openings on the S, giving access from the nave. It became the CHAPEL OF ST GEORGE in 1966. The flat panelled wood ceiling with painted borders and gilded bosses is *c.* 1985. From the chapel there is an unexpected view through the N arcade to the upper part of the Chapel of the Holy Spirit. Nicholson intended this as the Lady Chapel of his Cathedral, visible yet separate from its functional 'E' end and set at a lower level.

From the Burrows Transept, steps lead down to the AMBU-LATORY. On the S side, under the Chapel of St George, is the CRYPT or COLUMBARIUM, a tiny stone-vaulted chapel three bays long and four bays wide. On the N side a doorway in a low screen wall under a high open arch flanked by narrow pointed arches leads into the CHAPEL OF THE HOLY SPIRIT. Chastely Gothic, it is tall and aisleless, with a quadripartite vault, the simply moulded stonework of the slender wall-shafts and ribs and bosses set off against the white plastered walls. The clear-glazed windows to E and W are set high up.

FURNISHINGS AND STAINED GLASS. After the 1880 restoration the interior was enriched with new furnishings and stained glass. Many of these and other fittings were altered and moved to new positions in the C20. Description is in the same order as the interior.

w crossing:*ROYAL ARMS above the sw door, 1805. – STAINED GLASS. N window (i.e. the re-set former nave W window). By *W.F. Dixon*, 1881. Six-light. In the upper lights an animated depiction of St Peter preaching to Cornelius. Smaller scenes from the lives of St Peter and St Paul below.

Nave: richly carved octagonal oak PULPIT of 1887, with figures in canopied niches. – BENCHES. 2014. – STAINED GLASS. N aisle window, scenes from the life of Joseph by *Thomas Baillie*, 1862; s aisle, four windows of the 1880s by *Dixon*. – MONUMENT. s aisle. Thomas and Elizabeth Harrison of Weston. A weeping figure seated by two draped urns, 1823 by *Sir Francis Chantrey*.

Chancel: oak CANONS' STALLS by *Temple Moore*, 1918, given by the Freemasons in 1920 as part of their war memorial. – BISHOP'S THRONE by *Nicholson*, 1937, coloured and gilded, its tall Perp spirelet terminating with a pelican. – SCULPTURE. Almost hidden in the SE corner wall a small and badly defaced medieval figure of the Virgin. – STAINED GLASS. Despite its earlier inscription the E window, by *W.F. Dixon*, is J.N. Mappin's 1880 replacement for the window he gave in memory of James Montgomery in 1857. – In the chancel s aisle, *Powell & Sons'* striking Vision of the New Jerusalem, 1928, its colours set off by pale gold and clear glass. – MONUMENTS. Chancel s wall. Lady Elizabeth Butler †1510, the earliest of numerous small brass plates on the walls, piers and floor of the E end. – In the arcade on the N wall, busts of three vicars. In the centre, Rev. James Wilkinson †1805, set against a pyramid draped with a pall. This is the first work in marble by *Chantrey*, who was born at Norton. – Thomas Sutton (l.) †1851 by *Edwin Smith*, and Canon Sale (r.) †1873, by *William Ellis*. – Chancel s aisle. George Bamforth †1739. Fine wall tablet with his bust against the foot of a tall obelisk.

Shrewsbury Chapel: ALTAR. Restored stone *mensa* of a pre-Reformation altar, discovered in 1864 in two pieces. – Painted alabaster REREDOS. 1935 by *W.H. Randoll Blacking*, the Crucifixion and figures of saints representing the seven altars of the medieval church. – STAINED GLASS. E window, 1871 by *Clayton & Bell*. – MONUMENTS. The 4th Earl (†1538) lies in effigy between his two wives, under a flat-topped, panelled arch with a heavy pendant and straight cresting open on both sides. The alabaster figures are exquisitely carved, probably by Italian craftsmen or by Nottingham alabaster workers in the Italian style, and the richness of their robes and other clothing is shown in detail. Lying with their hands folded in prayer, the

*A FONT of polished grey granite, 1881 by *Charles Green*, has been removed and is now at the Freemasons' Museum.

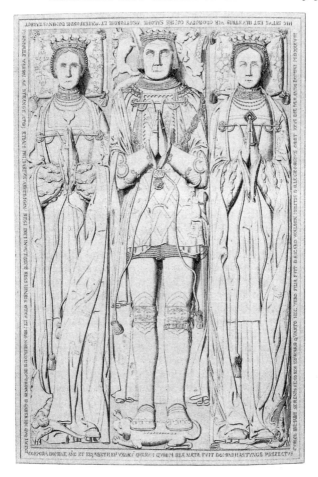

Sheffield Cathedral, monument to the 4th Earl of Shrewsbury.
Etching by E. Blore, 1819

two Countesses rest their feet on angels, while the Earl's are
supported by a talbot, the heraldic dog on the family's badge.
The Purbeck marble tomb-chest has panelled sides with
shields in quatrefoils and a twisted shaft at each corner. – 6th
Earl (†1590). On the s wall. A mighty alabaster standing monument, almost the full height of the aisle wall. His armour-clad
effigy lies on a straw mat under a very large, but not very
imaginative architectural surround, with a big heraldic achievement on top. His feet, too, rest on a talbot, and above the
columns on either side talbots flourish small banners. The
marble panel in the centre of the monument bears a lengthy
inscription in Latin by John Foxe, author of *The Book of*

Martyrs, reciting the Earl's family connections, honours and virtues. It refers to his long and loyal service as gaoler of Mary, Queen of Scots in Sheffield, but omits any mention of his estranged second wife, the formidable Bess of Hardwick.

St Katharine's Chapel: fine C15 canopied oak SEDILIA with cusped arcading on the back panels. – Pretty painted and gilded Baroque SCREEN at the w end, of 1937 by *W.H. Randoll Blacking*. – REREDOS in the form of a triptych by *Christopher Webb*, 1935. Painted and gilded mahogany panels surmounted by a figure of the Risen Christ carved by *W. Allen*.– STAINED GLASS. E window, 1935, also by *Webb*.* In the N wall *Harry Harvey*'s gentle scenes of works of charity, 1967, is less sentimental. – MONUMENT. William Jessop of Broomhall †1734. Fine marble tablet, the inscription framed by Corinthian columns and broken pediment.

S transept. STAINED GLASS. A fine series by *Clayton & Bell*, 1880, showing scenes of healing. – MONUMENTS. Rev. Alexander Mackenzie †1816. Moved here from St Paul's church (dem. 1938). Standing figures of Faith and Mourning either side of the inscription with a bust on top, carved in marble by *Chantrey*. – Archbishop Thomson †1890, a bust by *W.D. Keyworth*. – Archdeacon Blakeney †1895, also a bust, by *Onslow Ford*. – Tablet with medallion portrait of John Greaves †1828, and bust of Thomas Watson †1835, both by the local sculptor *Edward Law*. On the tower SE pier, centenary memorial with medallion portrait of the composer Sir William Sterndale Bennett (born 1816), carved by *Frank Tory & Sons*, 1920.

N transept: SCREEN between the transept and N tower aisle. C16, with Tudor flower tracery in the heads of its narrow openings. It originally separated the Shrewsbury Chapel from the S chancel aisle. Removed to its present position in 1933. – STALLS. Formerly under the crossing.

Burrows Memorial Transept: SCULPTURE. 'Sheffield Steel Nativity' by *Brian Fell*, 2012. – STAINED GLASS. N window. Installed in 1946, after removal from St Luke, Hollis Croft (dem. 1939). Four-light, an incomplete Tree of Jesse with eight robed figures, each with a canopy and entwined by part of the stem. Extensive grisaille and vivid colours of green, yellow, red and blue. These are panels originally made by *Henry Gerente* in 1853 for the w window of Butterfield's All Saints, Margaret Street, London, but removed from there in 1877 and obtained by the vicar of St Luke. – MONUMENTS. Bishop Burrows †1940, tablet by *G.G. Pace*, finely lettered by *David Kindersley* (another by Pace to Bishop Heaslett †1947 in the ambulatory).

Chapel of St George: unusual SCREEN on the E side of alternating swords and bayonets, the swords with points upwards, the bayonets downwards. – SCULPTURE. Four

---

*There are sixteen windows in the cathedral by *Webb*. Those in the N transept, Chapter House and Cathedral offices all relate to Sheffield's history and include a lively depiction of Chaucer's 'Reeve's Tale'.

painted and gilded stone figures of St Michael, St George, St Oswald and St Martin carved by *Esmond Burton*, 1937. – *HMS Sheffield* Memorial. Small anchor-shaped bronze with Christ as a ship's figurehead, by *Stephen Broadbent*, 2000.

Chapel of the Holy Spirit: richly gilded and painted REREDOS by *Temple Moore*, originally part of the chancel fittings given in 1920. Figure of Christ in the centre, with the Apostles on either side, all carved in half-relief and standing behind a low battlemented parapet. Masonic symbols on the lower end panels. The canopied SCREEN and OAK STALLS by *Sir Ninian Comper* came from the Missionary College at Burgh (Lincs.). Delicately stencilled decoration in green and grey on the screen and a vivid blue under the canopy. – STAINED GLASS. Te Deum window by *Christopher Webb*, 1948, his best work in the Cathedral, its brilliant colours dominating the N end of the lofty space.

Crypt. STAINED GLASS. A small window by *Keith New*, 1971, with pieces of coloured perspex rods set in a geometric pattern, giving a jewel-like effect.

The CHURCHYARD originally extended much further to the S, but was reduced in 1866–7 and 1891 for the widening of Church Street, and again in 1994. Closed for burials in 1856. Some of the headstones were laid flat as paving in a series of landscaping schemes which created the open forecourt to the S, the most recent by *Martin Purdy* of *APEC* in 1996 and revised in 2014–15, for a new approach diagonally across the yard from the SE corner to the new entrance beside the porch. Re-set to align with this are four gabled and crocketed stone GATEPIERS of 1890. On the E side a granite MONUMENT to James Montgomery (†1854) with life-size bronze statue by *John Bell*, moved from the General Cemetery in 1971.

Other Anglican churches

ST GEORGE (former), St George's Square. 1821–5 by *Woodhead & Hurst*, and an ambitious Commissioners' church, built with a fine ashlar facing in the Perp style. 140-ft (42.7-metre)-high W tower with pinnacles and ogee arches to openings and doors, long nave, short chancel, aisles and tall clerestory. Converted 1994 for the University of Sheffield by *Peter Wright & Martyn Phelps*. Lecture theatre in the nave with seating in the former W gallery. Three floors of student flats in the aisles. Former VESTRY HALL, 1965 by *John Needham & R.J. Claridge*, ingeniously built into the raised churchyard.

ST MATTHEW, Carver Street. 1854–5 by *Flockton & Son*. A simple building with an octagonal W tower and spire rising from the W wall with the entrance below. E end altered by *J.D. Sedding*, who designed a new chancel and E window in 1886. – Magnificent ALTAR and REREDOS by *Sedding* 1889–92, alabaster and timber (carved by *F. Tory & Son*), its centrepiece the Adoration painted by *Nathaniel Westlake*, 1890. Many

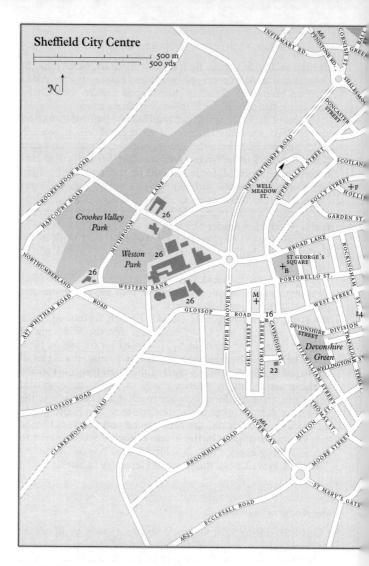

Sheffield City Centre

500 m
500 yds

A Cathedral Church of St Peter and St Paul
B St George (former)
C St Matthew
D Holy Trinity (now New Testament Church of God)
E Cathedral Church of St Marie (R.C.)
F St Vincent (former)
G Upper Chapel
H Methodist Chapel (former)
J City Life Christian Church
K Methodist New Connexion Chapel (former)
L Victoria Hall Methodist Church
M Catholic Apostolic Church (former)
N Central United Reformed Church

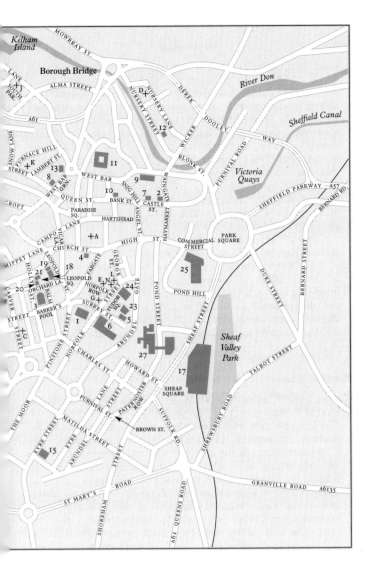

1	Town Hall	14	Fire Station (former)
2	Old Town Hall	15	South Yorkshire Fire and
3	City Hall, Barker's Pool		Rescue Headquarters
4	Cutlers' Hall	16	Public Baths (former)
5	Central Library and Graves	17	Railway Station
	Art Gallery	18	School Board Offices (former)
6	Millennium Galleries	19	Firth College (former)
	and Winter Garden	20	Pupil Teachers Centre
7	Police Offices (former)		(former)
8	Central Division Police	21	Bow Street School (former)
	Station (former)	22	Springfield School
9	South Yorkshire Police	23	Lyceum Theatre
	Headquarters and Magistrates'	24	Crucible Theatre
	Court	25	Ponds Forge International
10	County Court (former)		Leisure Centre
11	Law Courts	26	University of Sheffield
12	Coroner's Court (former)		(Western Bank)
13	Police, Fire and Ambulance	27	Sheffield Hallam University
	(now National Emergency		(City Campus)
	Services Museum)		

other furnishings by *Henry Wilson* (executed by *Henry Longden & Co.* of Sheffield), including CHOIR STALLS of 1897, inlaid with copper panels, low alabaster CHANCEL WALLS, and the GATES to chancel and chapel with copper panels in Arts and Crafts style. Wrought-iron GRILLES, based on those in Pisa Cathedral, separating S chapel from chancel, given by *Henry Longden*. – PULPIT and FONT, both of 1903, by *H.I. Potter* in oak with brass panels. Carving by *Tory*, metalwork by *Longden*. – ALTAR (N chapel). Gilded tracery and foliage decoration, 1958 by *George Pace*. – STAINED GLASS: E window by *Sedding*, 1884, the Incarnation with figures of St Matthew and other saints; W windows, N aisle given 1902, S aisle of similar date, both by *Lavers & Westlake*.

CLERGY HOUSE and Sunday School of 1896 by *J.D. Webster*. Red brick, Tudor Gothic with a large oriel.

HOLY TRINITY, Nursery Street. Now New Testament Church of God. 1848 by *Flockton, Lee & Flockton*, whose patrons insisted it copy Christ Church, Attercliffe (1826, dem.), hence the old-fashioned Gothic style. Thin spiky buttresses project above a crenellated parapet, tall lancets, short chancel and three galleries on iron columns – a church to incite Pugin's ire.

Roman Catholic

CATHEDRAL CHURCH OF ST MARIE, Norfolk Row. The finest Gothic Revival church in Sheffield. 1847–50 by *Weightman & Hadfield* in a rich and fluent Dec, strongly influenced by St Andrew, Heckington, Lincolnshire. Cruciform in plan, skilfully contrived to fit the confined site, and comprising a nave with clerestory, side aisles, S porch, transepts, and chancel flanked by side chapels. A mortuary chapel opens off the N aisle. In 1878–9 a chapel by *M.E. Hadfield & Son* was added and at the same time the sacristies at the SE corner were extended. Small crypt by *Vincente Stienlet* under the N transept, 1992. The church can only be viewed properly from Tudor Square to the SE, presenting a dignified and compact composition of high gables and steeply pitched slate roofs, with the slender stone spire that is its chief glory crowning the imposing square tower at the SW corner. The stone is coursed sandstone with ashlar dressings. The octagonal tower of the Lady Chapel, sprouting rather awkwardly from the S transept aisle, has a little spire with herringbone leadwork. SCULPTURE above the Norfolk Street door of the Annunciation, set in a niche with graceful ogee canopies, from *Thomas Earp*'s studio. To Norfolk Row gates and railings by *Maria Hanson*, 1997.

Subdued and spacious interior, with an uninterrupted view through the lofty, wagon-roofed nave to the chancel's great E window, following removal of the rood screen and choir stalls in major reordering of 1970–2. Seven clerestory windows were added in 1889 by *Charles Hadfield*, distinguished from the originals by quatrefoil tracery. Plain arcades with clustered

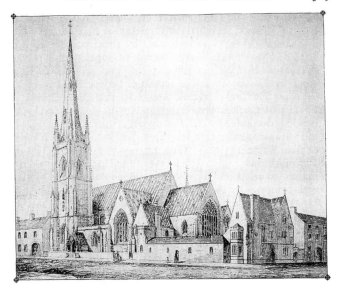

Sheffield, Cathedral Church of St Marie.
Etching by John Grey Weightman, *c.* 1850

quatrefoil piers and chamfered arches – carved headstops of male (s) and female (N) saints by *Charles James*. The narrow mortuary chapel opens off two bays in the N aisle, the capital of the massive central pier carved with a choir of heavenly angels. Unusual tiled dado *c.* 1886: a memorial to several priests with one shown at death with his angelic escort to heaven. Short N transept with Chapel of the Blessed Sacrament to the E.

The chancel has a magnificent painted and gilded arch-braced hammerbeam roof with ogee wind-braces and traceried spandrels. The angels are by *Arthur Hayball*. The stonework is more richly detailed here, mostly by *Charles James*, including the finely carved angel-stops to the chancel arch and the lusciously crocketed gables of the sedilia. The debt to Heckington is even more obvious in the E window's gloriously flowing tracery.

The Chapel of St Joseph, S of the chancel, was the Norfolk Chantry Chapel; *Minton* floor tiles include the ducal emblem and motto. Overlooking it is the tiny Lady Chapel, built as the Munster Memorial Chapel by *M. E. Hadfield & Son*, 1878–9. It is reached from the S transept by a winding stone stair. The open arcade of its octagonal shrine is supported on two piers of green Pyrenean marble, the other sides with richly sculpted blind arcades. These and the exquisite little lierne vault above were carved by *Thomas Earp*.

FITTINGS. Reordering by *Nicholas Rank* of *Buttress Fuller Alsop Williams* 2011–12 included a new CATHEDRA, forward

ALTAR, AMBO and FONT all of stone, and restoration of historic fittings. Chancel REREDOS 1850, designed by *Pugin*, sculptor *Theodore Phyffers*. (The high altar by them was replaced in 1921.) – The REREDOS in St Joseph's Chapel 1872, designed by *Charles Hadfield* in early C14 style and sculpted in Caen stone by *Thomas Earp*. The relievo of St Joseph's death is by *Theodore Phyffers*. – Marble ALTAR in the Lady Chapel by *Boulton* of Cheltenham, *c*. 1878. – ROOD of 1850 (now suspended) decorated by *H.T. Bulmer*, with figures by *Hayball*. – In the N transept two richly decorated SHRINES by *M.E. Hadfield & Son*. The SHRINE OF OUR LADY has a statue by *Johann Petz* of Munich *c*. 1850 with a base of 1868 including Frosterley marble columns and a carved and gilded oak canopy of 1872 with paintings by *Westlake*. Also the SHRINE OF THE SACRED HEART, 1879, the statue and marble-work of the base by *Boulton*, the oak reredos carved by *Thomas Earp* and gilded and decorated by *Lavers, Barraud & Westlake*. – ORGAN CASE 1875, designed by *J.F. Bentley*, carved in Austrian oak by *J.E. Knox*. – The wrought-iron entrance SCREEN to the Chapel of the Blessed Sacrament 1850 by *J. & C. Ellis*. – The crypt has GATES by *Giuseppe Lund* and CRUCIFIX and MOSAIC by *Fenwick Lawson*. – STAINED GLASS. E window. 1850, designed by *George Goldie*, made by *Wailes*. w window, 1850, designed by *Pugin*, made by *Hardman*. Both have sacred events in several tiers, but the superior quality of Pugin's design is patent. Other windows of the 1850s and '60s by *Hardman* and *Wailes*. – E windows of the Chapel of St Joseph, 1872 by *Lavers, Barraud and Westlake*, who also made the two windows on the Lady Chapel staircase to designs by *J.F. Bentley*, 1879 and 1884. – S transept w window by *Patrick Reyntiens*, 1982, to commemorate the new diocese, depicting the Virgin Mary as patroness and the Padley Martyrs executed in 1588. – MONUMENTS. Chancel. Effigy of Fr Charles Pratt †1849, holding a model of the church, by *Thomas Earp* as assistant to George Myers. – N transept. Matthew Hadfield †1887 by *Charles Hadfield*, with alabaster Pietà sculpted by *Frank Tory*, the design from a cast supplied to Matthew Hadfield by Pugin.

ST VINCENT (R.C.), Solly Street. Disused. 1856 by *Weightman, Hadfield & Goldie*. George Goldie was the probable designer and it was the first of his many churches to show French influence e.g. in the design of the shallow Continental-type apse. The S aisle and sacristy were only added during construction. Pretty Perp-style polygonal chapel on the S side of the aisle added in 1861 by *M.E. Hadfield*, who designed the porch and the lower part of the conspicuous SW tower, 1870. N aisle and N porch of 1898–9 and the tower's upper part, 1910–11, all by *Charles Hadfield*. The N aisle windows, which are accompanied by the parapet rising to form gables above them, are broad in comparison to those of the S aisle. The somewhat stark ashlar top stage of the tower again displays French influence in the paired tall thin belfry openings in each face and the delicate canted corners flanked by equally thin buttresses which contrast oddly

with the massive clasping forms of those at the base. The SE
Chapel of the Holy Souls of 1964 by *Hadfield Cawkwell
& Davidson* is in an angular style making few concessions to the
past. Lofty interior, now stripped of furniture and stained glass.
The six-bay nave has narrow arcading with octagonal piers and
carved angels as label stops. The S chapel, separated from the
aisle by a Perp-style stone screen has a vaulted ceiling and
arcaded stone altar. The N aisle quite different in character, with
arcading on round piers superimposed behind each window.
NW of the church, on SOLLY STREET, the former RAGGED
SCHOOL & ORPHANAGE, 1873 by *Flockton & Abbott*, and ST
VINCENT'S SCHOOLS of 1863. Gothic with an addition of
1892–7 with crowstepped gables. For the Presbytery *see* p. 546.

Nonconformist

UPPER CHAPEL, Norfolk Street. Sheffield's oldest Nonconformist chapel, now Unitarian. The congregation was formed
by followers of James Fisher, Vicar of Sheffield during the
Commonwealth, after he was ejected in 1662 for refusing to
subscribe to the Act of Uniformity. The brick side walls of the
first chapel, opened in 1700, are still discernible but heightened
in 1847–8 during extensive remodelling by *John Frith*, who
reversed the building to face Norfolk Street and extended the
E end to create a vestibule behind the handsome new pedimented stone front with its Ionic porch. The five arched upper
windows are flanked by Corinthian pilasters in the style of
Barry's Travellers' Club.
   The lofty interior with its three-sided oval gallery has been
enhanced by later additions and fittings (pews 1882, vestry
1900, organ console and central pulpit elevated on Doric
columns 1907, all by *E.M. Gibbs*). – MONUMENT. John Bagshawe †1721. Marble tablet, with cherubs and winged skull.
– STAINED GLASS. By *Henry Holiday*, 1899 and 1917–20, and
Hugh Easton, *c.* 1940.
METHODIST CHAPEL (former), Carver Street. Now a pub. 1804
by *W. Jenkins*. Large, with a three-bay pediment below a five-
bay gable. Arched upper windows set in blank surrounds, the
central one Venetian.
CITY LIFE CHRISTIAN CHURCH, South Parade, Kelham. The
former EBENEZER WESLEYAN CHAPEL of 1823 by *Joseph
Botham*, in a castellated Gothick style, with a S projection
formerly rising to a tower, and octagonal buttresses which rose
to short turrets. Window tracery of three lights, mildly flowing.
METHODIST NEW CONNEXION CHAPEL (former), Scotland
Street/Furnace Hill. Now flats. Dated 1828. Classical, brick of
five bays with a broad pediment. Adjoining, the LITTLEWOOD
MEMORIAL HALL of 1897 by *Flockton, Gibbs & Flockton*.
VICTORIA HALL METHODIST CHURCH, Norfolk Street. Big
red brick and stone front, the mix of Gothic and Arts and
Crafts styles less the product of *Waddington, Son & Dunkerley*'s

original design of 1906 than *W.J. Hale*'s reworking of 1908, particularly the massive Baroque top to the landmark tower. Carved decoration by *A.H. & W.F. Tory*, including portraits of the Wesley brothers in the gable. Glazed segmental-vaulted roof to central space, tall round-arched arcades, w gallery. Alterations, including removal of side galleries, and new fittings, 1965–6.

CATHOLIC APOSTOLIC CHURCH (former), Victoria Street. Built in 1850–1. Gritstone, rather fussy w façade with a miniature SW broach spire, a plain NW tower in three stages, the top one curiously stunted, and three lancets grouped together. All other windows lancets, the nave of five bays and an apsidal chancel.

CENTRAL UNITED REFORMED CHURCH, Norfolk Street. 1970, but thinly re-clad with stone and large, fragile-looking windows in 2002 by *Hadfield Cawkwell Davidson & Partners*.

PUBLIC BUILDINGS

86 TOWN HALL, Pinstone Street. Sheffield's grandest civic building, its design won in competition in 1889 by *E.W. Mountford* and constructed 1890–7. The final cost was over £134,000. The Derbyshire sandstone EXTERIOR is a lively interpretation of Northern Renaissance architecture. Mullioned-and-transomed windows, with small-paned casements, and a profusion of dormers, gables, pinnacles, turrets and chimneys form a picturesque composition which is enhanced by the tall asymmetrically placed angle tower at the junction of Pinstone and Surrey Streets. The symmetry and skilful articulation of the two-storey main front to Pinstone Street, raised on a semi-basement, gives a fitting dignity to the principal entrance, which takes the form of a gatehouse with first-floor balcony under a deep arch. At the N corner the clock tower, 210 feet (64 metres) high and topped by the figure of Vulcan by *Mario Raggi* 1896, is set slightly back in deference to the main façade and leads into the long elevation on Surrey Street. This rises to five storeys in the gables and is enlivened by the projecting porch, the oriel windows and the two-bay loggia on the second floor. The carving, devised by Mountford and *F.W. Pomeroy*, expresses pride in Sheffield's history and the art and skill of its workforce. The corner of the Norfolk Street return is marked by an octagonal tower with a turret and lantern, with a nearly identical tower at the southern end to Cheney Row, part of the L-shaped extension of 1923 by *F.E.P. Edwards*, the City Architect, a sensitive addition in matching style and materials.

The entrance VESTIBULE has wrought-iron gates, designed by *Mountford* and made by *J.W. Singer & Sons* of Frome. Walls are lined with polished Hopton Wood stone with Ionic columns of Irish marble on pedestals between the bays. The figures carved on the panels within the six blind arches depict 'Civic' and 'Eternal' virtues. The vestibule's sombre tone provides a dramatic contrast with the top-lit STAIRCASE HALL with its sumptuous confections of coloured marbles and limestone, executed by *E.E. Twigg & Co.* of the Ashford Marble Works, Derbyshire. On the inner face of the entrance arcade a carving of the local legend of the Dragon of Wantley and Sir Thomas More. Further carving, displaying the city's manufactures, arts and crafts, enlivens the frieze below the richly panelled plasterwork of the deep coved cornice. Magnificent bronze electrolier with four graceful winged figures, designed and modelled by *Pomeroy*, standing on a globe encircled with the signs of the zodiac. – SCULPTURES. 15th Duke of Norfolk, sitting in reflective pose, 1900, and a bust of Queen Victoria on a pedestal, 1898, both by *E. Onslow Ford*.

On the first floor S of the stair is the Ante-Room, with oak-panelled dado and chimneypiece with segmental top, the grate of hammered and raised copper. It leads to the COUNCIL CHAMBER, which is decorated in Northern Renaissance style with elaborate plaster ceiling with pendant bosses and delicate flowers and foliage in the panels. The half-height oak panelling, the Ionic aedicule for the Lord Mayor's chair and the floral carving on the Aldermanic bench all exquisitely executed by *Johnson & Appleyards* of Sheffield. The Chamber was lit on three sides until the 1920s extension was built, when a new public gallery replaced the windows on the E wall. The members' library and the conference room in the extension both have marble chimneypieces with early examples of stainless steel fireplaces.

The principal suite of three reception rooms extends along the main W front, opening off the marble-lined grand corridor. They all have carved oak panelling and were designed with oak dividing screens that ingeniously disappear into the roof space to create a single room. At the S end, the LORD MAYOR'S PARLOUR with an elaborate chimneypiece on the S wall standing on four columns of polished green Irish marble and with alabaster panels representing wisdom and valour guarding the gates of the city. The grate is from a design by *Alfred Stevens*.

OLD TOWN HALL, Waingate/Castle Street. Classical, built in three stages, the earliest by *Charles Watson* in 1807–8, to provide the Town Trustees with accommodation for the Petty and Quarter Sessions. Extension and remodelling by *Flockton & Abbott*, 1866, and further substantial additions, including a Police Court, made by *Flockton, Gibbs & Flockton* in 1896–7 when the new Town Hall was built on Pinstone Street (*see* above). Ashlar throughout, except for the rear elevations of the 1897 additions. Facing Waingate, Watson's building is symmetrical, of five bays. The ground floor is rusticated and has segmental-headed windows. The central three bays are brought forward slightly and emphasized by Ionic pilasters, above which the 1866 clock tower is perched rather uncomfortably. The entrance front on Castle Street was altered in 1866, when the parapet was rebuilt with a balustrade, and the Waingate front was extended by three bays, incorporating the Judge's

Sheffield, Old Town Hall.
Engraving by George Stow after N. Whittock, c. 1830

Entrance with enriched pedimented doorcase. The remainder
of the building is of 1896–7. Inside, a semicircular lobby with
Doric columns and entablature, leading to three courts, with
intact fittings. Currently awaiting reuse.

103   CITY HALL, Barker's Pool. 1928–32 by *E. Vincent Harris*. Among
the finest civic buildings of the interwar Classical Revival. Its
impressive massing achieved by large, compactly composed
blocks of unrelieved outline, constructed in reinforced concrete and brick and faced with Darley Dale stone. At the front
an entrance portico of eight giant Corinthian columns *in antis*
is flanked by the severe blank walling of the main elevation.
There is no pediment. The decoration of the entablature
originally proposed was omitted from the final design, leaving
only the simply dentilled cornice and narrow frieze of the
central block. This and the other stone-carving is the work of
Frank Tory & Sons. The apsidal N end, which contains the
semicircular Memorial Hall, has rusticated stonework and the
surprising feature of giant square pillars rising several feet
higher than the wall and carrying a heavy entablature on
Corinthian capitals. Three arched doorways with splendidly
crested wrought-iron gates.

Galleried ENTRANCE HALL. Above walls lined with bands
of Hopton Wood stone the vaulted ceiling has three saucer
domes and brightly coloured painted and gilded heraldic
decoration by *George Kruger Gray*. The inner doorways and the
balustrades of the little vaulted gallery are of veined black
Ashburton marble. The great domed OVAL HALL fills the
centre of the building and has two sweeping balconies at the
S end. It is lit by a magnificent elliptical lay-light set in an
elaborate radiating coffered ceiling, with a huge polyhedral

lantern suspended from the centre. Behind the stage, decorative iron grilles painted in scarlet and gold and set between Corinthian columns screen the *Willis* concert organ. Two Assyrian lions, carved by *John Hodge*, which originally flanked the central stage entrance were removed in 1962. The MEMORIAL HALL has a small curved balcony and a coffered ceiling. In the basement a grand ballroom with columned arcades and richly decorated beamed ceiling. An adjoining room also has giant Doric columns and painted decoration.

CUTLERS' HALL, Church Street. One of Sheffield's most important buildings, the Hall is the third for the Company of Cutlers founded in Hallamshire in 1624: the first (1638) was possibly, and the second (1725) certainly, on the same site. It presents a handsome dignified Grecian exterior to Church Street. The flat-headed archway to the l. and the front door, embracing two Giant Corinthian columns, distyle *in antis*, in Derbyshire sandstone ashlar, define the extent of the original building, the design for which was won in competition by *Samuel Worth* and *Benjamin Broomhead Taylor* in 1831 and built 1832. It is similar to the central part of the eastern front of Fishmongers' Hall, London, whose design it pre-dates by just three months. To the r., two more columns front an extension of 1888, won in competition by Worth's pupil, *J. B. Mitchell-Withers*. This addition altered the balance so that the main door now appears to be central, with the archway as an appendage. Above, the attic storey is an unfortunate excrescence by *Alfred E. Turnell*, 1928.

The ENTRANCE LOBBY AND HALL, with Doric columns heralding the main imperial staircase (doubled in size in 1865–7 when the Hall was extended by *Flockton & Abbott*), leads to a VESTIBULE on the first floor. Its sycamore and mahogany panelling, and electroliers, from the former White Star liner RMS *Olympic*, were installed here in 1936. This opens into a handsome RECEPTION ROOM, with bay windows at either end, both with pairs of Ionic columns. Across the vestibule is the OLD BANQUETING HALL. Giant Corinthian pilasters define three bays, the narrower end ones with shallow segmented glazed vaults over, the wider central one with dome on pendentives and lantern light. At the far end, a musicians' gallery, framed by a Palladian archway with Corinthian columns supporting entablatures either side of an uncomfortable depressed arch.

Flockton & Abbott's LARGE BANQUETING HALL, with ladies' and minstrels' galleries, was built on land to the W in 1865–7. Strident Italian Renaissance-style interior. A high black Belgian marble dado, incorporating pedestals supporting pairs of engaged scagliola Corinthian columns, single columns at the ends, dividing the large area of windowless walling into panels. On the frieze of a continuous entablature are key dates in the Company's history, a quotation from Chaucer's 'Reeve's Tale' and words from Ruskin in praise of Sheffield's workmanship. Above are clerestory lunettes in a coved ceiling. The

p. 516

Sheffield, Cutlers' Hall, Banqueting Hall.
Engraving, 1867

effect is unexpectedly overpowering and contrasts harshly with
the softer treatment of the Old Banqueting Hall. Connected
by further vestibules is the DRAWING ROOM in the 1888
extension, with gilded and impressive Grecian decoration; this
room in turn connects with the Reception Room (*see* above),
both rooms overlooking Church Street.

On the ground floor, the undercroft below the Large Banqueting Hall forms the HADFIELD HALL (formerly the Workmen's Hall), with eight free-standing Doric columns and
limited, plain decoration. Two murals by *Jean Clark*, 1954: one
celebrating the industrialist Robert Hadfield, the other, entitled Joy, commemorating the accession of Elizabeth II.

Then the small but dignified MUNIMENT ROOM and,
opposite, the NEILL ROOM – long, narrow and elegantly proportioned, entered at the narrower end, with, at the far end, a
Corinthian segmental-pedimented mantelpiece, under an arch
spanning the width of the room. Next, in the 1888 extension,
the Master and Mistress Cutlers' Rooms, built as a suite either
side of a spacious panelled foyer, of 1956–8 by *Hadfield, Cawkwell & Davidson*. The MASTER CUTLER'S ROOM has a richly
carved oak chimneypiece, with cartouches and strapwork,
dated 1623. Originally in Norton House (*see* p. 615), it was
rescued from Derwent Hall in 1919 and installed here in 1928.

CENTRAL LIBRARY AND GRAVES ART GALLERY, Surrey
Street. By *W. G. Davies*, City Architect, 1929–34. Originally
intended to form one side of a grand civic square, first proposed in 1924 by Patrick Abercrombie's Civic Survey as the
setting for civic offices, law courts and a college. The abandon-
ment of the scheme after the Second World War left the

building in an incomprehensibly insignificant position. Steel-framed, faced with Portland stone, with giant Ionic pilasters and a high parapet wall around the top-lit galleries on the third floor. Fine decorative carving by *A. H. & W. F. Tory*. The building is planned round a large central well above the ground-floor Lending Library, with the main reading rooms facing Surrey Street and Tudor Square on the ground and first floors. High-ceilinged, they are lit by tall windows and have oak fittings with restrained Art Deco details. From the marble-lined entrance hall the main staircase rises to the third-floor Art Gallery.

MILLENNIUM GALLERIES AND WINTER GARDEN, Arundel Gate and Surrey Street. 2001–2 by *Pringle Richards Sharratt*, both designs won in competition in 1995 and conceived as covered links in a new pedestrian route between the station and city centre, helping restore part of the urban fabric that had been unravelled by post-war road schemes and redevelopment. The MILLENNIUM GALLERIES present an elegant and quietly understated front to Arundel Gate, and are set into the slope of the hill with the galleries on the upper level over a service undercroft. The glazed front is set within a slender modular frame of white concrete and reveals the ground-floor café to Arundel Gate. Silver louvres screen the Long Gallery above. Inside, a light and spacious entrance hall has escalators to the first-floor 'avenue' which both serves as an indoor street to the Winter Garden beyond and gives access to the five galleries on its l. side. The roof comprises a series of lateral barrel-vaults, only partly visible externally, of fine white pre-cast concrete.*

The roof of the WINTER GARDEN is formed from twenty-one parabolic arches of laminated larch strips. Slender timber purlins and glazing bars create a fine framework between the arches to hold over 21,500 square ft (2,000 square metres) of glass. The primary arches are supported at ground level on sculptural steel cradles, while the intermediate arches finish at wall height and sit on elegant wooden raking struts. From the arches at each end, which lean outward to create canopies over the street entrances, they step up to the central section. This has allowed the taller species of trees, including Norfolk Island Pine and Eucalyptus, to reach an impressive maturity, creating a luxuriant canopy above the paving and planting below. 116

POLICE OFFICES (former), Castle Street. 1866 by *Flockton & Abbott*, contemporary with their remodelling of the (Old) Town Hall in Waingate (*see* above). Three storeys with attic and basement. Ashlar façade with a recessed centre, projecting bays at each end and a heavily rusticated ground floor. On the ground floor round-headed windows with chamfered surrounds; on the first, windows divided by shafts with Gothic acanthus capitals with a moulded foliage band continuing the

*Glass panels by *Keiko Mukaide* in the wall separating the last gallery from the Winter Garden have been removed and returned to the artist.

Gothic theme. Curious scrolls at the base of the projecting bays.

CENTRAL DIVISION POLICE STATION (former), West Bar Green. 1962–4 by *J. L. Womersley*. Well-composed group in engineering brick and curtain walling. Low front range and high slab for the former offices. (A hotel since 2014.)

SOUTH YORKSHIRE POLICE HEADQUARTERS and MAGISTRATES' COURT, Castle Street and Snig Hill. A combination of red brick and rough-textured ribbed concrete. The Police Headquarters, 1970 by *B. Warren*, City Planning Officer & Architect, has a prominent stair-turret. The taller Magistrates' Court (opened 1978) is entered at first floor from Castle Street across a footbridge. Courtrooms project from the Bridge Street façade. Coherent in design, if not particularly loveable.

COUNTY COURT (former), Bank Street. Now offices. Dignified and restrained palazzo by *Charles Reeves*, 1854. Painted *Coade* stone royal arms. The courtroom was placed on the first floor to leave room for offices below, a novel plan for its date.

LAW COURTS, West Bar. 1993–6 by *PSA Project Management*, succeeding the County Court in Bank Street (*see* above). A large and forbidding complex, as pompous as it is graceless. Alongside them, the FAMILY COURT of 2003 by *Aedas AHR* is slightly self-effacing and all the better for it. Red brick with a hipped roof and a strong horizontal emphasis achieved through a continuous band of glazing on the top (third) floor.

CORONER'S COURT (former), Nursery Street. Now business centre. 1913 by *F. E. P. Edwards*, City Architect. Red brick with twin gables enclosing a five-bay central portion and scrolls on both gables.

POLICE, FIRE AND AMBULANCE STATION (former; now National Emergency Services Museum), West Bar Green. 1897 by *Joseph Norton*. A somewhat confused façade of red brick with Venetian windows and rounded gables. Short tower, topped by cupola and ball.

FIRE STATION (former), Division Street. 1928 by the City Architect, *W. G. Davies*. Now a bar. Municipal Neo-Georgian with Art Deco detail. Three storeys with an attic in a pinky brick and ashlar facing to the ground floor. Engine doors recessed between two wings.

SOUTH YORKSHIRE FIRE AND RESCUE HEADQUARTERS, Eyre Street. 2009 by *BDP*. Smooth elevations of red and blue brick with curved corners. At the centre a slash of glass for the full height of the elevation, angled forward.

PUBLIC BATHS (former), Glossop Road. 1908–10 by *Arthur Nunweek*. Wrenaissance, well handled, with the entrances distinguished by rusticated giant pilasters with segmental open pediments above. Converted to residential and pub use but the sumptuous TURKISH BATH (dating from the rebuilding of the original baths in 1877–9 by *E. M. Gibbs*) has been restored for spa use. Octagonal cooling room with a mezzanine balcony and a hot room with deep arched recesses, both tiled and with mosaic floors.

JESSOP HOSPITAL FOR WOMEN (former). *See* University of Sheffield, p. 525.

RAILWAY STATION, Sheaf Square. Opened in 1870 for the Midland Railway but extensively rebuilt in 1905 by *Charles Trubshaw*, the company's architect. A one-off design, quite unlike much of his work of this period. Here the style is broadly classical, faced in fine ashlar with a large cast-iron porte cochère behind an arcaded and gabled stone screen. Notable refreshment rooms (SHEFFIELD TAP). The first class room has *Minton*-tiled walls and a mosaic floor; grill and dining room with Burmantofts faience on the walls inset with large mirrors. Parts of the 1870 station remain on Platform 2, used as offices. Rockfaced stone in the Italianate style. Good landscaping in front in the square, with cascading pool and SCULPTURE ('Cutting Edge') of 2006, in the form of a 90-metre (295-ft) steel wall by *Chris Knight, Brett Payne, Keith Tyssen* and *Keiko Mukaide*.

Schools and educational buildings

SCHOOL BOARD OFFICES (former), Leopold Street. Now the Leopold Hotel, converted as part of the Leopold Square development (*see* Perambulation 1). 1876–80 by *Flockton & Abbott* and *E. R. Robson*. Set up on a rusticated basement storey, with a prominent central doorway framed by Ionic columns and a broken pediment which embraces the moulded corbel of the slender semicircular oriel above. To the s an open arcade links to two blocks with a little bow-fronted link set back between them. At the corner with Orchard Lane the s block has a canted face with arched niches and delicately carved panels. This joins to the former CENTRAL SCHOOLS, facing Orchard Lane, which were executed as part of the same scheme. At the top of the lane, extensions of 1893–5 by *J. B. Mitchell-Withers Jun.*, including the Science School.

   Also part of the hotel, the FIRTH COLLEGE (former), West Street/Leopold Square. 1877–9 by *Flockton & Abbott* and *E. R. Robson*, designed as premises for the Cambridge University Extension lectures. Originally of two storeys with attached Ionic columns and pilasters (the third added 1891–2 by *Flockton & Gibbs*), its design loosely inspired by Clare College, Cambridge, and the centre of the West Street façade modelled on the Clare's E gateway (and cf. the School Board Offices nearby), with slender oriel window. Figures of Art and Science by *Onslow Ford*. Pretty festoons and other carving by *J. McCulloch*.

PUPIL TEACHERS CENTRE (former), Holly Street. By *H.W. Lockwood*, 1896. A rather busy front with polygonal roofed stair-turrets embracing the porch. Mullioned windows with arched lights. Converted to residential use as part of the Leopold Square development (*see* Perambulation 1).

BOW STREET SCHOOL (former), West Street/Holly Street. Opened in 1894. A big rectangular block, with rusticated

Sheffield, Springfield School.
Engraving, 1873

basement and flat Ionic pilasters at first floor. Entrances on
two sides. Formerly with a balustraded parapet, the present
attic storey added *c.* 2010 as part of the Leopold Square development (*see* Perambulation 1).
SPRINGFIELD SCHOOL, Cavendish Street. By *Innocent &
Brown*, 1875, and a particularly impressive three-storey example
of a Board School. Extensions 1891–2, and 1897 (on Bolton
Street) for infants. Gothic, but the motifs a mixture of secular
and ecclesiastical. Spired bellcote at the corner with Broomhall
Street.

Entertainment and leisure

LYCEUM THEATRE, Tudor Square. Opened in 1893 as the City
Theatre, designed by *Walter Emden* with *Holmes & Watson* but
substantially remodelled in 1897 by *W. G. R. Sprague*. Restored
and internally remodelled in 1989–90 by *Renton Howard Wood
Levin Partnership*, who reinstated the original AUDITORIUM,
where the stalls and cantilevered circle and balcony are flanked
by three tiers of boxes on either side, the whole space embellished by a glorious profusion of delicately gilded and painted
Rococo plasterwork created by *De Jong & Co.*
CRUCIBLE THEATRE. By *Renton Howard Wood Associates*, 1969–
71. It sits low to Tudor Square, its height increasing to four
storeys as the ground drops away behind it to Arundel Gate,
filling the irregular site with the subtly complicated geometry
of its octagonal form, executed in concrete blockwork. The
shape, expressing the plan of the auditorium, was influenced

by the ideas of 'theatre in the round' developed by the director
Tyrone Guthrie, whose associate *Tanya Moiseiwitsch* worked
with the architects, and it remains one of the most exciting
theatrical spaces in the country. Central thrust stage embraced
on five sides by a steeply raked bank of seating. Studio theatre
with seats entirely in the round. Refurbished by *Burrell Foley
Fischer*, 2007–9, with bold new entrance to Tudor Square, the
projecting first floor providing a canopy. Assertively right-
angled, the extension spurns the subtler form of the original
building.

PONDS FORGE INTERNATIONAL LEISURE CENTRE, Sheaf
Square. 1989–91 by *FaulknerBrowns* (project architect *Jon Igna-
towiez*) for the World Student Games. Along Sheaf Street, the
main body (enclosing the Olympic pool and the sports hall) is
elegant and restrained with a rough plinth, silver-grey powder-
coated aluminium panels and a shallow-arched roof with broad
eaves. But at the point where the leisure pool joins the main
building, the architecture goes into freefall with projections at
odd angles and a curving glass wall exposing the anarchic
activity of the pool to the outside world. At the entrance on
Commercial Street, a classical form is used with paired columns
and entablature represented in tubular steel and an encircling
masonry drum cut open to reveal a glass wall. Inside, the
Olympic pool is covered by a breathtaking shallow vault with
a diagrid structure of tubular steel trusses.

UNIVERSITY OF SHEFFIELD

The University began as Firth College (*see* p. 519) in 1879,
founded by the steelmaker Mark Firth, and amalgamated with
the city's Medical College and Technical School in 1895. Initial
plans drawn up in 1900 envisaged the entire university based at
St George's Square, but by 1902 approval for the purchase of a
site on Western Bank was given. Thus the split campuses of the
University have been a feature from the earliest days. Plans to
extend the buildings at Western Bank in the 1930s were only
partly realized. The University campus developed no further until
the post-war era, when the division of the two sites was complicated by the building of the inner ring road in the early 1970s.

1. Western Bank

The historic heart of the University is FIRTH COURT of 1903–5,
by *E. M. Gibbs*. It, together with the quadrangle behind, is in
the Tudor style, in hard Accrington red brick. Large mullioned-
and-transomed windows, with an oriel in the centre. Towers,
placed well back, at both ends. The central room on the first
floor (Firth Hall) has a fine scissor-braced oak roof with substantial pendants hanging from the trusses but much of this
work is now hidden by a suspended ceiling. Also on the first
floor, the WAR MEMORIAL, 1926 by *H. St John Harrison*, a

canopied shrine. Three rooms have decorated plaster ceilings. Those in the former Professors' Common Room and the Norfolk Room are genuine C17, much restored. The quadrangle behind has W and N ranges of the same Tudor and a particularly impressive N elevation of closely spaced buttresses and deep windows with arched heads. This was extended in 1914 by *Gibbs* with the intention of completing the quadrangle with an E range but this was only achieved in 2002–4 with the addition of science laboratories by *Bond Bryan Partnership*. The 1914 building continues eastwards, with an extension of 1938–41 by *Lanchester & Lodge* all in matching red brick, still nominally Tudor but less decorative than Gibbs's work.

Connected at the W end of the main façade of Firth Court is the octagonal former LIBRARY (now offices) of 1909, also by *Gibbs*, a little like a chapter house, in matching Tudor style with battlements and windows grouped in fours. Internally, radiating perimeter bays on two floors, the upper galleried. Arched arcading over the bays with carved heads by *Frank Tory & Sons*.

Facing Western Bank, set back, the FINANCE DEPARTMENT, 1962 by *Gollins, Melvin, Ward & Partners*, originally curtain-walled in black glass, but brick-clad in 1992 and given a cornice and a slated mansard roof, destroying the architects' intention of providing a neutral link between Firth Court and their ALFRED DENNY BUILDING of 1971, a very large, seven-storey slab with brick cladding to harmonize with Firth Court. Ground floor recessed behind pilotis.

To the NE, we come to the University's two set-piece buildings by *Gollins, Melvin, Ward & Partners*: the Library and the Arts Tower. Linked by a bridge at first-floor level, they are intended to be read together in a manner similar to the slab and podium of Lever House, New York (Skidmore, Owings & Merrill, 1950–2). The LIBRARY, a low square block given strong horizontal emphasis by bands of glazing and Portland stone on a base of blue brick, was built in 1955–9, and still deserves the prize for the best individual C20 building in Sheffield. The Reading Room faces Weston Park, its function indicated by the much higher bands of glazing. Inside, this is a handsome open space with two floors of book stacks (which incorporate ducts for partial air conditioning) along the internal wall, with four further floors of book stacks below, partly underground.

The twenty-one-storey ARTS TOWER, was built 1961–5 and in appearance is much indebted to the Seagram Building, New York (Mies van der Rohe and Philip Johnson, 1958). Concrete-framed, with an open ground floor, the frame exposed at ground level as sixteen columns supporting a five-foot-thick concrete slab with a bush-hammered surface. The tower is sheathed in glass curtain walling of rigid modular pattern based on the unit of the window bay with narrow corner bays. At the top, slender reinforced-concrete mullions extend to form a louvred screen around the motor room and plant. This provides a crisp termination and equates to an attic storey completing a classical tripartite form. The circulation areas on the entrance and lower floors are extremely generous in space with white Sicilian marble and Danish wood panelling together with stainless Sheffield steel handrails. Two underground floors contain nine lecture theatres.

To the NW on the edge of Weston Park in WINTER STREET is the GEOGRAPHY BUILDING by *William Whitfield*, 1968–71, exemplifying the move from the formalist planning by Gollins, Melvin, Ward & Partners to a looser, more organic approach. The need to incorporate large cartographic drawing offices produced a group of interlinked hexagons of varying heights, clustered around a central lift and stair-tower. Opposite, across Winter Street behind tall walls, the SCHOOL OF LAW built as the Borough Hospital for Infectious Diseases in 1877–81 by *S.L. Swann*. An open-ended quadrangle of central administration building with a spired tower and four bright red brick ward blocks in Ruskinian Gothic. The blocks are linked by glass-walled additions by *Race Cottam Associates*, 1995–6.

Retracing one's steps to Brook Hill, next is the DAINTON BUILDING (chemistry laboratories) of 1950–3, by *J. W. Beaumont & Sons*, in a depressingly institutional stripped classicism, surrounded by extensions by *Gollins, Melvin, Ward & Partners*. Those to the W, of 1960–4, are clad in blue glass, grey brick and small tiles with a neutral black glazed link to the earlier building. The large E block (Richard Roberts Building) is of 1955–64, remodelled in 2002 by *CPMG Architects* with a strikingly angled glass façade.

Moving now to the S side of Western Bank, via the CONCOURSE underpass of 1968–9 by *Arup Associates*, a highly successful unification of the two halves of the Western Bank campus. The earliest building on this part of the site was *Stephen Welsh*'s GRAVES BUILDING (originally the Student Union) of 1935–6, built of small Maltby bricks in refined but timid Neo-Georgian and now almost overwhelmed by more recent additions. The first of these was UNIVERSITY HOUSE of 1962–3 by *Gollins, Melvin, Ward & Partners*, built on a sloping site and broad rather than high. Very well composed with much glass and grey brick cladding but altered to its detriment with an additional storey in 1978–9, new lift tower in 1992 and the removal of the principal access bridge at first-floor level. The area between the entrance and the Graves Building was filled in quite a spectacular manner in 1996 by *Ward McHugh Associates*, who created further offices and a coffee shop linked to the existing building by an atrium with much display of its structural elements. The external curved glass wall of the addition contrasts uncomfortably with the rectangularity of the unaltered parts of the Gollins, Melvin & Ward building. The OCTAGON, also by *Gollins, Melvin, Ward & Partners*, 1982, is a multi-purpose Convocation Hall. Brick-clad with a quaint pyramidal roof topped by a finial and somewhat self-effacing.

Returning to Western Bank, to the E of the Student Union is the HICKS BUILDING, a nine-storey slab by *Gollins, Melvin, Ward & Partners*, 1962, re-clad in brick with a pseudo-classical cornice added. A free-standing bush-hammered five-storey lecture theatre block lies to the W. Opposite in Hounsfield Road, the COMPUTER BUILDING, 1974–6 by *Arup Associates*, was the only building from their 1970 campus plan to be built. Box-like with blockwork chamfered to look like rustication. N of this on Leavygrave Road is the INFORMATION COMMONS building by *RMJM*, 2006. Seamed metal cladding, the upper floors angled from the façade in sawtooth fashion along Upper Hanover Street.

PSYCHOLOGY BUILDING, Western Bank. 1972–4, by *Renton Howard Wood Levin Partnership*, in the firm's favoured concrete blockwork (cf. the Crucible Theatre, p. 520). V-shaped plan, its form determined by a need for a quiet interior, with the main entrance and lecture room set in the angle and much of the accommodation on the quieter N side. Adjacent to the NE is the WORK PSYCHOLOGY BUILDING of 1987–8 by the *Architectural Consultancy Service* (*David Bannister* and *K.H. Murta*). Steel-framed with two wings meeting at an oblique angle. While the strip glazing echoes its predecessor, a move to vernacular is evident in the buff brick cladding and the hipped roof.

For SCHOOL OF MANAGEMENT *see* p. 596.

2. St George's Square and neighbourhood

The other part of the University developed around the Technical School, founded in 1884 by Sir Frederick Mappin in the former Grammar School (*Woodhead & Hurst*, 1824) in MAPPIN STREET on the E side of St George's Square (for the church, *see* p. 505). Extensions were immediately made (*see* below) and the Grammar School subsequently demolished for the SIR FREDERICK MAPPIN BUILDING (originally the Department of Applied Science). Planned as a single entity but built in three phases 1902–13 by *Flockton & Gibbs* (*Gibbs, Flockton & Teather* after 1910), the style is a robust Wrenaissance, deriving its proportions and use of segmental-headed windows from Gibbs's earlier Technical School (*see* below) but treated much more elaborately, with pilasters and prominent quoins. The interior has, on the ground floor, the handsome JOHN CARR LIBRARY and, on the first floor, the MAPPIN HALL, oak-panelled with a good plaster ceiling in the Renaissance style, and carving by *Frank Tory & Sons*.

Immediately behind, and connected by a bridge at first-floor level, is the former TECHNICAL SCHOOL of 1885–6 by *Flockton & Gibbs*. Neo-Georgian, the central bay projecting slightly and given a parapet. *Gibbs* designed the MINING DEPARTMENT BUILDING in 1926 (extended 1951–7) in a virtually identical style and the plainer AMY JOHNSON BUILDING (formerly the Safety in Mines Research Station) on Portobello Street in 1928. E of this, the dull ten-storey SIR ROBERT HADFIELD BUILDING (Metallurgy Department etc.) by *J. W. Beaumont & Sons*, 1961–2, and N of these buildings along BROAD LANE, the PAM LIVERSIDGE BUILDING (Engineering Faculty) of 2012–14 by *Bond Bryan Architects*, replacing buildings of 1952. Brick with concrete bands, a throwback to the unadorned style of the 1930s.

There has been much new building around St George's Square since 1985. The best is ST GEORGE'S LIBRARY, Mappin Street, by *Building Design Partnership*, 1990–1, red brick and box-like but very sophisticated. Minimal classical references point to the influence of Aldo Rossi and Italian Neo-Rationalism. The Reading Room and book stacks on the first floor are lit by small square windows just below the eaves. On the ground floor, built into the wall, is a sculpted keystone of Hercules wearing the head of the Nemean Lion. Removed from the Caledonia Works (1873) formerly on the site.

To the W of St George's Square, on St George's Terrace is THE DIAMOND (Engineering Dept), by *Twelve Architects*, 2015–16.* Very large, with an all-over pattern of lozenges of varied sizes, it shrieks for attention in an unmannerly fashion. Formed by a deep-profile metal framework, the shapes are filled with white or clear glass, the largest ones in the windows lighting the full height staircase space facing the church. Abutting to the W, on Leavygrave Road, is the handsome former JESSOP HOSPITAL FOR WOMEN (now Music Dept) of 1878 by *J. D. Webster*, in a rather forbidding Gothic style. Two-storey oriel at the E corner of the building with elaborately carved base bisected by a plain buttress. The central tower lost its top stage in the Second World War. On the S side of Leavygrave Road, the ICOSS (Social Sciences) building by *CPMG Architects*, 2004. L-plan five-storey slab with seamed metal cladding and a pod projecting at first floor on raked and tapered metal stilts. Immediately W, providing some enclosure and protection from the inner ring road, the Y-shaped block of JESSOP WEST by *Sauerbruch Hutton* with *RMJM*, 2007–9, with multi-coloured cladding. Facing this is the rare survival in this area of a large plain brick villa (No. 34, now the University's HUMANITIES RESEARCH INSTITUTE) of *c.* 1830 with Doric doorcase. Round the corner in Gell Street, the SOUNDHOUSE (Music Dept practice rooms) of 2008 by *Carey Jones* and *Jefferson Sheard*, making a good joke out of the need for soundproofing with a black padded rubber exterior like buttoned upholstery.

The University has expanded to take in many buildings in Glossop Road. For these and university residences, *see* Broomhill (p. 584), Endcliffe (p. 588) and Ranmoor (p. 590).

---

*Part of it occupies the site of a wing of the Jessop Hospital, of 1902 by *Webster*, demolished despite its Grade II listing.

SHEFFIELD HALLAM UNIVERSITY
(CITY CAMPUS)

Sheffield Hallam University had its origins in the College of Technology, planned in 1948, established in 1950 and constructed on the present City Campus site to designs by *Gollins, Melvin, Ward & Partners*, 1953–68 (cf. University of Sheffield). It joined in 1969 with the College of Art in Psalter Lane to form Sheffield Polytechnic, and with the College of Education at Collegiate Crescent (*see* p. 580) in 1976. This institution became Sheffield City Polytechnic until University status was granted in 1992.

The site for the original College of Technology, rising steeply above Pond Street, was a difficult one and for which *Gollins, Melvin, Ward & Partners* designed an impressively simple and well-related group of three blocks. The focus is the twelve-storey OWEN BUILDING, E of Howard Street, a massive slab with concrete frame exposed and prominent stair-towers, approached from Arundel Gate by a pedestrian bridge and flanked by the lower HALLAM HALL (of the same date but re-clad in the 1990s and incorporated with the main entrance to the campus from Norfolk Street). On the E side, two spurs: one of five storeys (SURREY BUILDING), the other of eight (NORFOLK BUILDING) with its lower two storeys recessed behind pilotis, linked to the main block at first-floor level with access from Pond Street by stairs to a deck. Low workshop ranges, stepped up in terraces, stood to the N.

E across Pond Street on Harmer Lane, the ERIC MENSFORTH BUILDING, the former library of 1973 by *Bernard Warren*, City Planning Officer & Architect. Shallow window strips and deep concrete bands relieving the boxy brick exterior give it a pronounced horizontal emphasis. It is faced on its S side in red and brown brick to harmonize with its neighbour, the SHEAF BUILDING, a pitched-roofed teaching block, clad in powder-coated metal in the upper floor.* This dates from 1992–3 following a masterplan for the campus by the *Bond Bryan Partnership*, 1990. The buildings (by *Shepherd Design & Build* and *BDP*) include the concourse over Pond Street joining the two halves of the site and the HARMER BUILDING, with monopitch roofs falling towards the E and a five-bay façade on Pond Street with a ground floor set back behind columns that continue at first-floor level as buttresses, and the HOWARD BUILDING (by *BDP*) between the Owen and Surrey Buildings, clad in grey powder-coated panels and stepped down at the S end, providing lecture theatre and academic accommodation. On its S wall, visible from Surrey Lane, a stainless steel SCULPTURE ('Elements Fire-Steel') by *Brian Asquith*, 1965

---

* Refurbishment of the Eric Mensforth and Sheaf Buildings is underway in 2016, with a new atrium link between the two. Due for completion in 2017.

(originally for the Westminster Bank in High Street). On the end of the Owen Building the words of Andrew Motion's 'What If', 2007. Linking the old and new elements, and a successful focus for the campus, is the ATRIUM, a bright and airy quad covered by a space-framed monopitch roof on complicated tree-like struts. On the E side, teaching rooms (contained within the Harmer Building) cantilever into the space.

At first floor one can cross N to the ADSETTS LEARNING CENTRE, a library and media resources centre by *Faulkner-Browns*, 1997, on the site of the original terraced workshops whose stepped foundations now form a series of gardens, enlivened a little by *Laura White*'s 'Trilogy' of 1995 – three enigmatic sculpted stone blocks. The S front of the Centre dramatically falls away below, its face almost entirely concealed by solar shades and four cascading aluminium roofs shaped like aerofoils. Inside, at each level, the open-plan floors are cantilevered out for study areas, gradually receding at the highest level for a double-height space.

A short distance S along ARUNDEL GATE, on a large triangular site, the STODDART BUILDING (business school), 1994–7 by *Shepherd Design and Build* and *HLM Architects*, followed by the CHARLES STREET BUILDING by *Bond Bryan Architects*, 2016, and ARUNDEL GATE COURT. For the CANTOR BUILDING, Arundel Street, STUDENTS' UNION, Paternoster Row, and other buildings converted for student accommodation in the area SE of Norfolk Street *see* Perambulation 4.

PERAMBULATIONS

1. The Town Hall and central area

The Peace Gardens, S of the Town Hall, occupy the site of St Paul's church (begun in 1720, attributed to *Ralph Tunnicliffe* and *John Platt* of Rotherham), Sheffield's premier C18 church, which was demolished in 1937 after city centre slum clearance. The gardens were redesigned in 1997–8 by the City's *Design and Property Services* and incorporate artwork by *Brian Asquith* (metalworker), *Tracey Heyes* (ceramicist) and *Richard Perry* (stone carver), with a spectacular fountain and giant bronze vessels pouring water down cascades. On the E side is the MERCURE HOTEL, by *Weintraub Associates*, 2003, and contemporary OFFICES, both on the site of a 1970s extension to the Town Hall. These are broadly in scale with the Town Hall but rearing up behind, entirely indifferent to its setting, is the egregious ST PAUL'S TOWER, thirty-two storeys of flats, of 2010 by *Conran & Partners*, the tallest in the city centre and severely damaging views across it.* The buildings on the S and

---

*Associated with this, and of a similarly superficial character is the retail and gambling development on Arundel Gate, including the tacky crinkly façade of the multi-storey car park.

w sides of the gardens were all built in the 1890s, creating a harmonious group that defers appropriately to the Town Hall. Clockwise, first the SE corner block, built in two phases between 1898 and 1901 by *J. D. Webster*. Warm coloured brick with red sandstone dressings, an unusual combination for Sheffield. To the r., the distinctive deep pink brick and terra-cotta of the former PRUDENTIAL ASSURANCE COMPANY OFFICES by *Waterhouse & Son*, 1895, creates an imposing corner to Pinstone Street.

On the w side of PINSTONE STREET, on the lower corner of Cross Burgess Street, LAYCOCK HOUSE is an unusual block combining shops with 'better class dwellings' by *Flockton & Gibbs*, 1896. The corresponding corner block incorporates, on CROSS BURGESS STREET, the neglected red brick former SALVATION ARMY CITADEL by *William Gilbee Scott*, 1892, designed in the Army's usual castellated style. The other developments N along Pinstone Street's w side were, as was hoped, complete by the opening of the Town Hall. They include PAL-ATINE CHAMBERS by *Flockton & Gibbs*, 1895, with tall casements, projecting end bays and high roof which give it a decidedly French character, and TOWN HALL CHAMBERS, a worthy but slightly dull five-storey block of shops and offices by *J. B. Mitchell-Withers* built *c.* 1885 as part of the redevelopment following the street improvements here.

BARKER'S POOL, leading w from the Town Hall to the City Hall (*see* Public Buildings), was a small enclosed reservoir created in the C15 but filled in in 1793. The broad curve of its N corner with Leopold Street is the four-storey YORKSHIRE HOUSE by *Flockton & Gibbs*, 1883–4, for the cabinetmakers Johnson & Appleyards. Mixture of giant Ionic and stubby Doric pilasters on its first and second floors. Top floor and attic added in 1892. Next to this, NEW OXFORD HOUSE by *Hadfield Cawkwell & Davidson* in the standard 'International Modern' of the 1960s. Beside it is a tiny formal GARDEN given in 1937 to enhance the setting of the City Hall and preserve the view of it from the Town Hall. Set back behind the garden is the FOUNTAIN PRECINCT, nine-storey offices clad in buff and brown tiles by *Sidney Kaye, Firmin & Partners*, 1976, with open ground floor. At the front of its piazza, *David Wynne*'s delicately exultant SCULPTURE 'Horse and Rider', 1978, in stainless steel. In front of City Hall is the FIRST WORLD WAR MEMORIAL by *C. D. Carus-Wilson*, head of the University's School of Architecture, 1924–5. A highly unconventional design, with a 90-ft (27-metre) steel mast rising from an octagonal bronze base 18 ft (5.5 metres) high. Around it four almost life-size figures of soldiers, sculpted by *George Alexander*, with heads bowed and rifles reversed. Beside the City Hall, *Martin Jennings*'s SCULP-TURE 'Women of Steel', 2016, with two figures. It commemorates women who worked in the steel industry in wartime. On the S side of Barker's Pool, the scale of City Hall is matched by *Yorke, Rosenberg & Mardall*'s coolly confident JOHN LEWIS department store (originally for Cole Brothers), 1961–5. Clad in the architects' hallmark white tiles with panels of brown mosaic to the window bays. Innovative for its date in the incorporation at the rear of a ramped multi-storey car park communicating at each level with the store. Against this the bright red structural framework and mirror glass of the neighbouring former ODEON cinema by *Hadfield Cawkwell Davidson & Partners*, 1987, seems brash. (For buildings w of Barker's Pool *see* Perambulation 3.)*

Down CAMBRIDGE STREET is LEAH'S YARD, known in the 1880s as the Cambridge Street Horn Works. The two- and three-storey brick workshops around the yard are mid–late C19. Barely one room deep they have external wooden staircases to the upper floors and long casements to light the workbenches inside.

LEOPOLD STREET, running N from the Town Hall, was created in the 1870s as the link to Church Street (*see* Perambulation 2). On the w side is LEOPOLD SQUARE, formed in 2010–11 by refurbishment of the former School Board Offices, Central Schools, Firth College and Bow Street School (*see* Public Buildings) for residential, hotel and other uses on a site bounded by West Street (N), Holly Street (W) and Orchard Lane (S). Some limited and well-handled infill of new building and re-landscaping in the central courtyard by *AXIS Architecture*. At the top of Leopold Street's E side, on the broadly curving corner with Church Street, is the expansive Neo-Elizabethan LEOPOLD CHAMBERS, solicitors' offices of 1894 by *Holmes & Watson*. Striking shaped gables topped with spiky finials reflect the uneven rhythm of the bays, the three wider ones distinguished by double-height canted oriels decorated with strapwork. To the r., a more solemn front, designed as the Sheffield Medical Institution in 1888 by *J. D. Webster*. Northern Renaissance style.

Leopold Street superseded the inconveniently narrow ORCHARD STREET to its E, which has on the corner with Leopold Street a crisply detailed office block for the Abbey National Building Society by *Ronald Ward & Partners*, 1962. Grey marble panels to the five upper floors and rich green marble facing to the ground floor. Ahead is the entrance to ORCHARD SQUARE, a successful extension to the central shopping area by *Chapman Taylor Partners*, 1987, surrounded by a lively mix of new and old buildings, faced in red or yellow brick, and with consciously traditional features such as pitched roofs, casements and weatherboarded oriels.

E, along the N side of the Town Hall, is SURREY STREET, beginning with the MONTGOMERY HALL, built in 1884–6 as the headquarters of the Sheffield Sunday-School Union by *C. J. Innocent*, the Union's Honorary Secretary. There follows a modest former business training college by *T. H. Wilson*, 1887, and then CHANNING HALL, an elegant Italianate palazzo by

*At the time of writing, redevelopment of the S side of Barker's Pool for the new Retail Quarter is proposed.

Flockton & Gibbs, 1881–2 for the Norfolk Street Unitarian chapel (which lies behind, *see* Churches, Upper Chapel). Finally, to the corner with Norfolk Street, is the substantial HALIFAX BANK, designed by *J. D. Webster* in 1893–4 as shops, offices and a children's shelter on Norfolk Street. Prominent corner with a two-storey oriel window over the entrance. Along the s side of Surrey Street, after the Town Hall and hotel is the Winter Garden (*see* Public Buildings) and then up to the corner with Surrey Place, the former MASONIC HALL (now pub and health club), built 1875–7 of well-cut ashlar in a restrained Italianate style. Extended to the r. in 1888 and 1909–1912 by six bays, absorbing some three-storey Georgian houses, now stuccoed and with a new entrance with flamboyant doorcase with a big shell-hood on scroll brackets. At the end, the important survival of LEADER HOUSE of *c.* 1780, brick with pedimented Doric doorcase and a big canted bay window added in the early c19. Along Surrey Street's N side is the dignified Beaux Arts front of the Central Library And Graves Art Gallery (*see* Public Buildings), which overlooks TUDOR SQUARE to the w, created in 1991 and enclosed by the Crucible and Lyceum Theatres to N and E (*see* Public Buildings).

Now N along NORFOLK STREET, w of Tudor Square. First, at the corner with Surrey Street, No. 117 is Late Georgian with typical tall twelve-pane sash windows on the first floor. Attractive late c19 wooden shopfront and studio window which breaks through the eaves. The BROWN BEAR pub (No. 109) is the earliest surviving brick house in the central area, referred to as 'lately erected' in 1745. Plain, three storeys with pedimented doorcase. Next door, the carefully composed façade of the former Sheffield & Hallamshire Savings Bank (now a bar). By *Flockton & Son*, 1858. Though small – a two-storey cube of three bays flanked by single-storey entrance wings with projecting porticos – its rusticated stone front is skilfully articulated with round and square Corinthian columns on the ground floor and enriched with finely carved cornices, balustrades and urns. Next to this, a handsome building designed by *Flockton & Abbott* in 1876 for Hay's Wine Merchants.

Opposite, set well back in its landscaped graveyard, is Upper Chapel (*see* Churches). Further N, in NORFOLK ROW, is a row of late c18 and early c19 houses, now offices, facing the Cathedral Church of St Marie (*see* Churches). Its PRESBYTERY, facing Norfolk Street is by *C. & C.M.E. Hadfield*, 1903, in soft pink brick, its Gothic stone details sitting oddly with its sash windows. The headstop on the r. of the big canted bay is a portrait of Charles Hadfield by *Frank Tory*. Below, the boxy UNITED REFORMED CHURCH (*see* Churches) with a self-effacing entrance in Chapel Walk. The Victoria Hall Methodist Church (*see* Churches) next door with its mighty Baroque tower is much more assertive.

GEORGE STREET, up the side of Victoria Hall, leads NW to a small paved square. On the r. are the former ALLIANCE

ASSURANCE offices, 1913 by *Goddard & Co.*, a model of ingenuity in fitting a prestigious building onto a tiny site. Dignified and refined Baroque, in Portland stone, its single-bay front enhanced by exaggerated details which give it a monumental character. The CUTLERS HOTEL beyond, by *Mansell Jenkinson & Partners*, 1961–4, was built for the Sheffield Club. Four storeys, gradually diminishing in height, its steel and concrete structure expressed unusually creatively. Opposite, the CURZON CINEMA, adapted from the former buildings of the Sheffield Bank, who took over George's Coffee House in 1831. The three-storey building of 1793 still forms the core and the successive alterations and additions made for the bank can be traced in the changes in the brickwork. The l. extension in Portland stone is by *C. & C.M.E. Hadfield*, 1906. The three-storey offices to the r. (Nos. 12–14) are one of the rare instances of Venetian Gothic in Sheffield.

At the N end of George Street is HIGH STREET. On the N side, flanking the entrance to High Court, is a handsome classical stone block of 1887 which survived the 1940 Blitz, but much of the area E was destroyed and rebuilt post-war with shops and offices (*see* Perambulation 5). The upper W end escaped. KEMSLEY HOUSE, by *Flockton, Gibbs & Teather* for the *Sheffield Daily Telegraph* 1913–16, dominates the N side. White faience, now painted, with two tiers of giant arched window openings, Baroque details and a central square tower with light-hearted domed top. Original tempietto entrance has replica of Mercury by Giambologna, made 1856, on restored dome. W across York Street, dwarfed by its neighbours, a former BANK by *Holmes & Watson*, c. 1895, compensates for its smaller size with a front crammed with Renaissance details. Next to this PARADE CHAMBERS, designed for Pawson & Brailsford, printers and stationers, 1883–5 by *M.E. Hadfield & Son* in Charles Hadfield's favourite Tudor Gothic. Five storeys, its two principal elevations are a lively mix of mullioned-and-transomed windows, three-storey stone oriels and double gables, crowned with tall chimneys and two picturesque turrets with ornate leadwork. Stone-carving by *Frank Tory*, including garlanded portraits of Chaucer and Caxton. For the buildings around Cathedral Square, *see* p. 532.

Opposite Parade Chambers on High Street, FOSTER'S BUILDINGS is French Gothic of 1896 by *Flockton, Gibbs & Flockton*, and at the junction with FARGATE is one of their more exuberant *fin-de-siècle* essays with high mansard roof, designed as an auction house in 1895; in Fargate itself their versatility is shown by buildings erected after the street widening here – No. 14 of 1879 and No. 9 of 1889. The narrow gabled stone fronts reflect the width of plots preserved from much earlier development. Towards the other end of Fargate, close to the Town Hall, on the W side, Nos. 38–40 displays *J.D. Webster*'s economic handling of a late Gothic style decorated with carved panels above the first-floor windows and open quatrefoils in the parapets either side of the central gable. Built as a provision store for Arthur Davy in 1881–2, the carved animal heads advertise the hams, potted meats and pork pies for which it was famous. Above this the former National Provincial Bank, 1902 by *W.W. Gwyther*. It has a muscular metropolitan character with boldly rusticated end bays and a weighty stone dome on its octagonal Baroque turret. Opposite, curving round into Norfolk Row, the former YMCA of 1889–92 by *H.W. Lockwood*. Late Gothic style with gabled roof-line and carving by *Frank Tory* including six arched panels depicting the days of Creation and four to their r. showing the progress of Divine Law. Completing this side, curving round to Surrey Street, is the YORKSHIRE BANK, 1888–9 by *Perkin & Bulmer* for the Yorkshire Penny Bank. The five-storey building also had a temperance restaurant with hotel above. Late Gothic, ornately decorated, with elaborately carved winged lions and medieval figures. The gabled dormers and lofty chimneys above a crenellated parapet were sacrificed in the conversion of the hotel to offices after 1965.

2. The Cathedral area

EAST PARADE, along the E side of the Cathedral Square, was created as a thoroughfare in the 1790s and has a pleasing variety of C19 three- and four-storey buildings in brick and stone. An air of comfortable domesticity changes abruptly at the end of the Parade with the strict institutional demeanour of the former BOYS' CHARITY SCHOOL (or Bluecoat School), now offices. By *Woodhead & Hurst*, 1826. Correctly classical seven-bay front, built in a greyish gritstone ashlar, with a severely rusticated ground floor. Ungainly attic storey with dumpy Doric pilasters.

N, on HARTSHEAD, is OLD BANK HOUSE, the oldest surviving brick house in the city centre, dated 1728 on a rainwater head. Built by Nicholas Broadbent, a local Quaker merchant, whose grandson Thomas ran a private bank here from 1771 to 1782. Giant pilasters at the angles and either side of the central bay where they break through the cornice to the ramped coped parapet. Refurbished as offices in 1978–9 by *Hadfield Cawkwell Davidson & Partners*. N down FIGTREE LANE, No. 14 is a rather grand house of *c.* 1800; now offices. The imposing N elevation is set up on a high stone plinth and faced in ashlar, with giant fluted Ionic pilasters on the two upper storeys.

BANK STREET, at the bottom of the lane, was laid out in 1791. On the N side, the former COUNTY COURT (*see* Public Buildings) and further E a nice group of late C18 and early C19 three-storey brick houses and the bold Italianate stone front of the former *Sheffield Independent* offices by *John Frith*, 1861.

NORTH CHURCH STREET, W along Queen Street, runs steeply uphill to the Cathedral. On the E side, a large former SYNAGOGUE of 1872 in a simple Gothic style with narrow lancets. Hebrew inscription over the doorway. Converted to warehouses

in 1930, now offices. Almost opposite, No. 17, a small house
with a nicely proportioned ashlar front of *c.* 1830 with vermiculated rustication to the plinth. Immediately below, facing the
narrow WHEATS LANE, a grander red brick house with blackened stone dressings. Elegant front with projecting end bays
framed by pilasters and tapered architraves with pediments to
the doorcase and ground-floor windows.

Wheats Lane emerges at the NE corner of PARADISE SQUARE,
the most elegant survival of Georgian Sheffield, restored in
1963–6 by *Hadfield Cawkwell Davidson & Partners* with doorcases and other fixtures salvaged from demolitions elsewhere.
The earliest development was in 1736, when Nicholas Broadbent built the terrace of houses stepping down the hill on the
E side. Nos. 4 and 6 retain the most convincing original appearance. From 1771 to *c.* 1790 Thomas Broadbent laid out the
other three sides of the square. No. 18 in the centre of the N
side, projecting slightly forward of its neighbours, has a five-
bay front with balcony, French windows framed by columns
and an open pediment. Opposite, the higher S side has three
two-bay houses in the centre, Nos. 7–11 with elegant doorcases
displaying a variety of details that are repeated round the
square – eared architraves, reeded friezes, semi-pediments and
cornices.

SE of the square across Campo Lane, ST JAMES ROW has handsome three-storey brick houses overlooking the Cathedral and
the GIRLS' CHARITY SCHOOL (now offices) built in 1786, its
foundation recorded in the semicircular tablet set in the pediment above the three central bays, which project slightly
forward of single flanking bays. At the S end of the Row was
the vicarage, pulled down in 1854. In ST JAMES STREET,
adjacent to its site, the former Church of England Educational
Institute by *Flockton & Son*, 1860 (now Church House pub).
Double-gabled front in red brick with stone dressings, with
Geometric tracery in the big windows to the main lecture
rooms on the first floor. Concluding St James Row, open to
the Cathedral Square, the Gothic façade of GLADSTONE
BUILDINGS, designed as the Reform Club and offices in 1885
by *Hemsoll & Smith* but rebuilt as offices behind the façade by
Hadfield Cawkwell Davidson & Partners, 1976.

CHURCH STREET along the S side of the Cathedral forecourt
has the Cutlers' Hall (*see* Public Buildings), adjoined to its W
by the former Sheffield & Hallamshire bank, also by *Samuel
Worth*, 1838. Neo-Grecian in fine ashlar. Originally five bays
with four giant Ionic columns between plain pilasters, but
duplicated on the l. 1878 by *H.D. Lomas*, who also added the
Renaissance gateway. Splendid banking hall with Corinthian
pilasters and ornate plaster ceiling. E of the Cutlers' Hall is the
ROYAL BANK OF SCOTLAND, a sober mid-Victorian interpretation of the palazzo style by *Flockton & Abbott*, 1866–7.
Further W, ORCHARD CHAMBERS by *Gibbs & Flockton*, 1904,
cheerful Edwardian Baroque in red brick and stone. On the N
side, at the corner of Vicar Lane, the former CAIRNS

CHAMBERS, solicitors' offices by *Charles Hadfield* of *M.E. Hadfield, Son & Garland*, 1894, in a scholarly Tudor style. Stone-carving by *Frank Tory* with a richness and delicacy of detail including the imposing robed statue of the 1st Earl Cairns, Disraeli's Lord Chancellor, in the canopied niche of the central oriel. Lively roof-line of tall chimneys, square gable and crenellation.

3. West: the Devonshire Quarter

DIVISION STREET, W of City Hall, begins on the N side with the handsome former SHEFFIELD WATER WORKS CO. offices by *Flockton & Abbott*, 1867 (now a bar). Palazzo style, of seven bays. Ashlar façade, the remainder in brick. On the ground floor, round-headed windows are set back between attached columns, each arch with a carved keystone of a water god.

CARVER STREET crosses N–S. On the E side, the former NATIONAL SCHOOL, dated 1812 on a large plaque with a four-bay gabled centre with one-bay wings on each side. Two doorways with half-columns. KENDAL WORKS (No. 23) has a pedimented front range of *c.* 1830 and workshop ranges of the usual Sheffield type with a blank rear wall on to Carver Lane and large windows facing the yard. In the courtyard an early C20 scissor forge, single-storeyed with a hipped roof, large casement windows and two hearths. Part restored in 2003. Opposite, the lengthy and utilitarian façade of ALPHA WORKS by *Holmes & Watson*, 1900. For the former Methodist chapel to the N and St Matthew, in Carver Street S of Division Street, *see* Churches.

Further W, on the S side of DIVISION STREET, the former YWCA of 1939 by *J. Mansell Jenkinson*, Neo-Georgian with rounded corners, and the former Fire Station (*see* Public Buildings).

Devonshire Street is the W continuation of Division Street. S, in CANNING STREET, Nos. 4–14, a group of six former blind-back houses, *c.* 1830 with simple three-storey façades, some retaining sash windows. N in WESTFIELD TERRACE, fronting offices of the 1990s, the façade of the handsome MOUNT ZION CONGREGATIONAL CHAPEL, 1834, probably by *William Flockton*. Stone, of three bays with two giant Ionic columns *in antis*. To the S, in TRAFALGAR STREET is the ABERDEEN WORKS, occupied since construction in 1883 by Francis Howard, silversmiths. Incised lettering along the façade. One office has a big tripartite window in an ashlar surround, otherwise casement windows. In DEVONSHIRE STREET itself, Nos. 105–125 (S side), are a complete block of ten houses of *c.* 1840. Then, much further along on the N side is the former ware-house and showroom of John Armitage & Sons' Wharncliffe Fire Clay Works (Nos. 140–146). Dated 1888 and liberally decorated as an advertisement for the firm's speciality of fire-clay bricks and figures. This faces DEVONSHIRE GREEN, created *c.* 2000 from a former bomb site as the central space of the 'Devonshire Quarter', surrounded by developments, e.g. the WEST ONE group of apartments, bars and shops by *Carey Jones*, 2000–3, in brick, glass, coloured renders and dark blue glazed tiles.

W of Devonshire Green in CAVENDISH STREET is Springfield School (*see* Public Buildings) and the WILSON CARLILE COLLEGE OF EVANGELISM, of 1989–91 by *APEC Architects* in a low-key but attractive Neo-vernacular style in grey brick. W again in VICTORIA STREET, the BATH HOTEL, built as a shop *c.* 1870 at the corner of a terrace of similar date. Interior remodelled by Ind Coope in 1931, with a brown tiled counter front and slightly jazzy patterned obscured glass. GELL STREET gives an indication how this area must have looked when it was laid out from the 1820s. For buildings in Gell Street N of Glossop Road, *see* University of Sheffield (p. 525).

GLOSSOP ROAD, returning E to the city centre, has the SOMME BARRACKS of 1907 by *Alfred E. Turnell*, Quartermaster of the 1st West York Royal Engineers Volunteers. L-shaped Free Renaissance main block, canted on the corner with Gell Street with a large gatehouse as the focal point. Further E, on the S side, the former Public Baths (*see* Public Buildings) and opposite the SINCLAIR BUILDINGS of 2006 by *Project Orange*, all black brick with sinuous corner. Just behind in REGENT TERRACE, workshops of *c.* 1850, used for many years as a steeplejack's yard. Finally, on the S side, a former Birmingham District & Counties Bank, set on a difficult triangular site. Free classical by *Gibbs & Flockton*, 1906–7.

WEST STREET continues E. Following the opening of the turnpike in 1821 this was the principal NW exit from Sheffield, and today has the greatest concentration of Edwardian commercial architecture in the city, the result of street widening in 1907–10. Decorative faience is extensively employed and the result has a satisfying urbanity. On the N side, from the corner with Regent Street, BOOTS, 1906 by their usual architect *A.N. Bromley* and in their Free Renaissance house style, executed in light brown faience, with big Flemish gables, an open parapet and a cupola on the corner with a dome. A very long block follows E of Portland Lane: CAVENDISH BUILDINGS by *Hemsoll & Chapman*, 1907, extended 1910 and 1919, as garage and showrooms for the Sheffield Motor Co. Ltd with billiard saloons on the upper floors. Brick with buff faience dressings, including three over-sized broken segmental pediments on the front elevation, each with a large swagged plaque bearing the dates of building and extension, and obelisk finials. Immediately behind, on MAPPIN STREET, is the SHEFFIELD ROYAL SOCIETY FOR THE BLIND office, incorporated within a mundane block of student apartments of *c.* 2010. The stone doorcase of its predecessor building of 1938 (by *Hadfield & Cawkwell*) is retained; carved in *Moderne* style by *Philip Lindsay Clark*: on the l., a blindfolded person with prison bars behind;

on the r., a hand reading a book in Braille with the sun behind. Back on West Street, THE HALLAMSHIRE HOTEL of 1903 for Greaves & Co. has an exuberant rich brown glazed faience façade to the ground floor with a lettered fascia. Next, E of Orange Street, HUTTON'S BUILDINGS of 1885 for William Hutton & Sons, electroplaters. Plain red brick three-storey block on West Street with ground-floor shops and a very large works built around a courtyard behind, all now converted to student accommodation. Further on, TIGER WORKS (Nos. 136–138). Dated 1884. Narrow but ornate three-storey façade, embellished with two carved tigers. Then in succession: the large former Employment Exchange by *H.M. Office of Works*, 1934 in a weak, thin Neo-Georgian and the MORTONS BUILDING, a development by *AXIS Architecture*, 2003–4, incorporating the façade of CENTRAL WORKS (of Morton's knifemakers). The two w bays are of *c.* 1830, three storeys with a later C19 shopfront. These are dwarfed by the apartments built on the site of the workshop ranges behind of *c.* 1850.

West Street's s side was dominated from the 1830s until 1981 by the Royal Hospital, which grew out of the Public Dispensary. On its site, the massive ROYAL PLAZA apartments of 2000–2 by *HLM Architects*, followed by the seemingly interminable utilitarian interwar former REVENUE BUILDINGS by *Arthur Nunweek*, between Westfield Terrace and Rockingham Street. On ROCKINGHAM STREET is the former METHODIST SUNDAY SCHOOL by *H.W. Lockwood*, 1898, three storeys with a tall front gable. The tired Neo-Georgian block facing West Street is of 1927–9 by *W.J. Hale*. It was for the Methodist Chapel in Carver Street (*see* Churches).

E of Carver Street, the former SHEFFIELD INSTITUTE FOR THE BLIND (now a bar) of 1905 by *Edmund Winder*. Well proportioned in red brick with stone dressings. No. 49 (also a bar) was formerly the premises of J.W. Northend Ltd, printers. An expressive piece of Edwardian classicism of 1912–14 by *Chapman & Jenkinson* with some original detailing but the scale a little overpowering. Damaged in the Second World War but rebuilt to the original design. Diagonally opposite is Steel CITY HOUSE of 1927 by *H. T. Rees* of *H.M. Office of Works* as Post Office and Telephone Exchange. Triangular plan, clad in Portland stone with rounded corners lending panache. Massive fluted Greek Doric columns to the semicircular portico to the main (E) entrance. The upper floor bays are divided by giant Doric pilasters with the end bays brought forward slightly and given emphasis by pediments. For Leopold Square, s of West Street, *see* Perambulation 1.

Finally, N down Holly Street to TRIPPET LANE. On the corner, ANGLO WORKS, early C19, occupied for over a century by Walter Trickett & Co. Three storeys with an L-shaped plan incorporating a showroom. It has the closely spaced casements usual for workshops but with sashes on the ground floor denoting its superior status. WALSH COURT is the most striking building in the street. Built in 1906 as a furniture depository and workshops by *Gibbs & Flockton* for John Walsh Ltd, Sheffield's leading department store (*see* p. 540). Confident Edwardian Baroque in red brick and stone dressings with banded pilasters and outsized keystones.

A few buildings of interest lie outwith the areas of the perambulation:

MILTON STREET, SE of Devonshire Green. At the W end, Nos. 98–100, a group of four three-storey back-to-back houses built between 1850 and 1864, quite substantial with Late Georgian proportions and simple wooden doorcases. They adjoin the former BEEHIVE WORKS, its façade eighteen bays long with three-storey workshop range to the rear and a much taller four-storey shop, plain brick, at the rear. Large casement windows for the ground and first floors on the courtyard elevation. EYE-WITNESS WORKS is the only traditional integrated works still in operation. Front range of several phases: the l. part of five bays is *c.* 1852 with round-headed windows, a Venetian window over the cart entrance. Top floor added *c.* 1875, contemporary with the nine bays to the r. The final five bays are earlier and were also heightened *c.* 1875. Workshop ranges to the rear were used for grinding and an octagonal chimney provides evidence of steam power.

At the back of Eye-Witness Works in THOMAS STREET, TAYLOR's CEYLON WORKS, a specialized horn cutter's works. L-shaped, one three-storey range housing the offices *c.* 1875 rather like a pair of semi-detached houses with paired doorways and sash windows. At the rear a workshop block of *c.* 1850 with casement windows and a single- (formerly two-)storey warehouse. Horns were of high value, so it is windowless except for a skylight.

In MOORE STREET, the ELECTRICITY SUBSTATION by *Jefferson Sheard & Partners* 1965–8. A massive and totally uncompromising design well suited to its position on the ring road. In three stages, with a lower storey of thin concrete mullions, and two storeys of horizontal cladding divided by exposed vertical beams topped by a cornice of angled concrete panels. Detached glazed staircases at the E end. In complete contrast, almost opposite, part of the flamboyant Renaissance-style terracotta façade to J. PICKERING & SONS' cardboard box factory of 1908 by *C. & C.M.E. Hadfield*, retained in a 1990s office development.

4. South: Cultural Industries Quarter

HOWARD STREET, SE of Arundel Gate and now within the City Campus of Sheffield Hallam University (*see* p. 526) has some of the last surviving houses of the C18 development of Alsop's Fields on the Norfolk estate: Nos. 42–46 of 1788 are typical. ARUNDEL STREET, running SW, was one of the major streets on *James Paine*'s grid-plan layout of *c.* 1775 and the survivals here are more substantial: Nos. 105, 111 and 113 of 1791 are large and ornate with modillion eaves and the entrances emphasized by pilastered doorcases. No. 113 is plain brick, its neighbours were stuccoed later. No. 105 (Venture Works) has a rear courtyard with a workshop added *c.* 1840. On the other side of the street, COOPER BUILDINGS, the former Don Plate Works, a three-storey range (now Sheffield Hallam University Science Park), which occupies the entire block between Howard Lane and Charles Lane. Only the r. part is the original of *c.* 1880; that to the l. a replica. A chimney has been retained and the rear ranges sympathetically rebuilt. On the corner with Charles Street, the former St PAUL'S NATIONAL SCHOOL. Neo-Tudor of 1844. Opposite the SHEFFIELD INSTITUTE OF EDUCATION AND BUSINESS SCHOOL, 2015–16 by *Bond Bryan Architects.*

sw of Charles Street, SELLERS WHEEL (Nos. 151–167), is a former works with two L-shaped three-storey ranges around a courtyard, possibly of 1855. Externally plain, the front range with sash windows and a pilastered surround to the cart entrance, emphasized by tripartite windows above. Converted to student accommodation by *Cartwright Pickard*, 2014, with a new block inserted. Next to this the CANTOR BUILDING of Sheffield Hallam University, again by *Bond Bryan.*

Facing these is the colossal brick flank of BUTCHER'S WHEEL (or BUTCHER WORKS), formerly an integrated cutlery, edge tool and file-making works built up by William and Samuel Butcher *c.* 1855–60 and sensitively converted for mixed uses in 2007 by *Race Cottam Architects.* The austerity of the 130-ft (40-metre) four-storey façade to Arundel Street is atypical for its date in Sheffield, favouring casements of the type associated with the lowlier Sheffield workshop. Treatment of the buildings around the inner yard is uniform, with rows of closely spaced windows, round-headed on the sw side (the larger ones on the first and second floors illuminated the grinding hulls), segmental and straight-headed on the se and ne sides. The ground and first floors of the s range have fireproof brick vaults. In the centre of the flagged yard stands a chimney, surrounded at the base by privies enclosed behind a curved screen wall: a most unusual arrangement. The nw range is the Butchers' earlier premises of 1819–20, facing EYRE LANE. Brick-built of three storeys with sash windows and two cart entrances (now blocked) into the yard; ne extension (originally a house) in matching style probably built soon after. A wing extended into the centre of the yard and is irregular with low openings leading to steep steps up to workshops on upper floors. Hand forges had the characteristic split-stable-type door and window under a common lintel. sw of Butcher Works in Arundel Street, STERLING WORKS of *c.* 1870, again enclosing a large courtyard, have a slightly more pronounced architectural treatment with sash windows, round-headed on the first floor.

sw of Furnival Street is CHALLENGE WORKS, built *c.* 1883 for Louis Osbaldiston & Co., makers of steel, saws, files etc. Especially large segmental-arched doorway and an eaves cornice.

N of here in EYRE STREET is the MOOR MARKET, a traditional covered market of 2013 by *Leslie Jones Architecture*; brick but with remarkable panels of woven timber, like wattle hurdles, and on the front to The Moor an eye-catching quarter-circle roof, of glulam timber construction, with copper scales and diamond-shaped windows. The market is part of the same architects' masterplan for refurbishment of THE MOOR, one of Sheffield's principal shopping streets since the mid C19, which was completely redeveloped in the 1950s and '60s with dull, large flat-roofed Portland stone commercial blocks. The view sw is to MOORFOOT, the vast stepped red brick Government offices of 1978 by the *Property Services Agency*.

SE of Arundel Street, in MATILDA STREET at the corner with Mortimer Street, are the former TRURO WORKS for Joseph Cutts, manufacturers of silver plate and Britannia metal. The earliest buildings, of the late 1840s, are the three ranges to the SE surrounding a triangular yard. The works expanded to the N *c.* 1850–80 for Atkin Bros, cutlery manufacturers, with the four-storey block along Matilda Lane and further buildings within a courtyard to the NW. A four-storey thirteen-bay addition of *c.* 1900 to the N of the original offices forms a third phase. Converted to student flats, 1995 by *Capital Design Studio*.

E of here, in a blighted position on SUFFOLK ROAD, is COLUMBIA PLACE, the former Columbia Works. Ambitious stuccoed three-bay façade with first-floor paired pilasters and pediment. Built *c.* 1836, the large royal arms over the entrance dating from its time as the premises of William Wigfall & Sons, brush manufacturers, 1868–71. L-shaped workshop range to the rear. Extended and converted to flats 2002–4. On the E side of Suffolk Road, Nos. 35–37 (W. W. Laycock & Sons), also mid-C19, stucco fronted with vestigial pilasters and cornice. Of the same period on the w side further N, SCOTIA WORKS, with its name incised on the lintel keystones at first floor.

LEADMILL ROAD contained lead mills built in 1759, on the site of a 1730s cutlers' grinding wheel close to the River Sheaf. Demolished in 1910 for the TRAM DEPOT, whose twin octagonal towers, facing the junction with Shoreham Road, have been retained as a frontispiece to a development of student flats by *Bond Bryan Associates*. Opposite, filling a large site between Shoreham Street and Paternoster Row to the N is the SHOWROOM CINEMA and the WORKSTATION, built as Kennings garage and showroom in 1936. Imaginatively converted in 1993–8 by *Allen Tod* and *Tatlow Stancer* for four cinemas, café and office space. Steel frame with two floors of big windows and jazzy Art Deco cream faience cladding with black trim. The detail is echoed in the black faience piers of the new entrance foyer from Sheaf Square which opens into an atrium created from the original vehicle lift to the first-floor repair shop.

Facing are THE HUBS (Sheffield Hallam University Students' Union), converted in 2003 from the short-lived National Centre for Popular Music by *Branson Coates*, 1997–8. Four stainless-steel-clad drums surmounted by revolving ventilation cowls (apparently modelled on the nozzles of shaving foam cans).

w of the Workstation, in BROWN STREET, the PERSISTENCE WORKS, 1998–2001 by *Feilden Clegg Bradley* for the Yorkshire ArtSpace Society, a co-operative who first took over redundant industrial buildings in this area for studios in 1982. Constructed of *in situ* fairfaced concrete, industrial in scale (fifty-one studios) and austerely dignified in design with no surface decoration whatsoever. Two elements: a long low block facing Brown Street, with cantilevered first floor above a glazed podium and a parallel six-storey block behind, linked by an impressive glazed atrium through which large artworks can be removed. Screen of rippling glass panels along the façade by *Jeff Bell*,[*] perforated steel gates by *Jennie Gill*, blue circular lights with steel 'hairs' protruding from the façade by *Jo Fairfax* and reception area floor by *Jasia Szerszynska*. Opposite is the RUTLAND ARMS of 1936, for Duncan Gilmour & Co. and in their house style of applied faience decoration and bold lettering, probably the best example remaining in Sheffield.

5. North-east: Castle Square to Pond Street

The buildings of CASTLE SQUARE, a cross-roads at the E end of High Street close to the site of the medieval castle, are mostly post-war, a reminder of the extent to which the bomb-damaged heart of Sheffield's commercial area had to be rebuilt after 1945.[†] It lies at the N end of ARUNDEL GATE, one of the worst results of the car-orientated inner-city road schemes of the 1960s.

One of the only pre-war survivals is the former York City & County Bank (now Banker's Draft pub), of 1904 by *Walter Brierley*. Edwardian Baroque, carried off with panache. The most striking of the mid-C20 group is the former Walsh's department store (now POUNDLAND) by *J.W. Beaumont & Sons*, 1953, rebuilt with a splayed corner in the 1960s. In ANGEL STREET which falls sharply N, ARGOS was Cockaynes department store, also by *Beaumont & Son*, 1955–6. Opposite is CASTLE HOUSE (Sheffield Co-op), down to the junction with Castle Street. 1959–64 by *G.S. Hay*, originally for the

[*] Now covered by solid panels.
[†] As reconstructed in 1968 the square was made into a roundabout with shops below. This public space, known as the 'hole in the road', was filled in in the late 1980s for the tramway.

Brightside & Carbrook Co-operative Society as their headquarters and principal department store. Quite an impressive
granite front with a massively splayed corner. Inside, a stylish
cantilevered spiral staircase with stainless steel balusters under
a dome lit by circular glass bricks. At the top of this, mounted
on the wall, a metallic SCULPTURE of a bird. To the rear,
facing King Street, a 1962 block by *Hadfield Cawkwell Davidson & Partners* with a rather emaciated glass-fibre Vulcan
(1960) by *Boris Tietze*.

To the N the South Yorkshire Police Headquarters and Magistrates' Court (*see* Public Buildings) and next to the latter, in
SNIG HILL to the w, CORPORATION BUILDINGS, early
public housing above shops by *Gibbs & Flockton, c.* 1904. Big
gables and plenty of terracotta decoration. Half the block was
destroyed by bombing.

CASTLE STREET, leading E, has Nos. 9–11, 1868 by *Charles
Unwin*, its end wall with brick MURAL of a mineworker by *Paul
Waplington*, 1986. Opposite, THE CANNON (originally the
Cannon Spirit Vaults) 1902–3 by *J. R. Wigfull*, for William
Stones's brewery, Tudor Renaissance, with three big dormers,
the windows flanked by tapered pilasters and topped by seg-
mental pediments.

At the E end is WAINGATE with the Old Town Hall (*see*
Public Buildings) opposite the site of the Castle Market, one
of the city's post-war showpieces (1960–5 by *J. L. Womersley*,
dem. 2016 and superseded by Moor Market – *see* Perambulation 4). Waingate, s of Castle Street, becomes HAYMARKET.
The w side exhibits a variety of commercial styles. On the
corner is No. 32 Castle Street, 1904 by *Gibbs & Flockton*, built
as a shop, café and restaurant for Arthur Davy & Sons Ltd (*see
also* Fargate, p. 531). Effective Free Style with two large gables
linked by a circular tower, all in red brick with stone bands.

COMMERCIAL STREET has, on its E corner with Haymarket, the former YORKSHIRE BANK. Built as the Post Office
in 1871 by *James Williams*. Two storeys with an attic, in a classical style of such purity that it looks more like work of the
1850s, with heavily rusticated pilasters dividing each window,
two storeys with an attic and dentilled cornice. Superseded in
1910, see Fitzalan Square, below.

Next is CANADA HOUSE, one of the finest C19 buildings in
the city. It is of 1874 by *M. E. Hadfield & Son* as the offices of
the Sheffield United Gas Light Co. Symmetrical two-storey
Early Renaissance Venetian palazzo style, with paired columns
between the middle bays but with an unorthodox central attic
surmounted by an enriched pediment and a mansard roof,
broken by dormers, and corner turrets with niches and spires.
The entrance is off-centre with an open segmental pediment
supported by Atlantes, carved by *Thomas Earp*, and a pulvinated
frieze with bay-leaf decoration. Unduly prominent Portland
stone addition at the w end of 1938 by *Hadfield & Cawkwell*,
with sculpture by *Philip Lindsay Clark. J. F. Bentley* was

commissioned to decorate the general office. Glazed dome, pilasters with exuberant capitals, a deeply coved panelled ceiling and an ashlar doorcase with rounded pediment and delicately carved panels. The board room ceiling was the work of *Hugh Stannus*. Commercial Street passes over Park Square on the elegant SUPERTRAM BRIDGE of 1993.

The walk returns to FITZALAN SQUARE, which has in the centre a bronze STATUE of King Edward VII, 1913 by *Alfred Drury*. On the w side of the Square, the WHITE BUILDING (Nos. 6–12) by *Gibbs & Flockton, c.* 1908, one of the most original buildings of its date in Sheffield with a faience façade enlivened by figures in relief by *Alfred & William Tory* depicting Sheffield trades. The s side of the Square is taken up by the exuberant Baroque former POST OFFICE of 1910 by *Walter Pott* of *H.M. Office of Works*, now Sheffield Institute of Arts. Ashlar, with two long façades. The corner between the two is marked with a tower with a dome. Heavily rusticated entrance bays with giant pilasters and dentilled cornices with half-round pediments. Giant order engaged Ionic columns along the front to the square. The FLAT STREET elevation is a little quieter, continued by the red brick Queen Anne-style Post Office block of 1897 by *J. Williams*. Across Flat Street, the MECCA BINGO hall, formerly the Odeon cinema, by *Roger Bullivant*, 1956. Unusual single-storey wedge-shape glass foyer projecting in front of the brick-clad auditorium. Next, to the s, filling the site between Pond Street and Arundel Gate, is the massive multi-storey EPIC entertainment and shopping complex, originally of 1968–9 by *Jefferson Sheard & Partners*, exploiting the steeply sloping ground. Two large rectangular windowless blocks, clad entirely in panels of white tiles, the first built as a dance hall with conference suite (now O_2 Academy concert venue) and the other (now ODEON CINEMA with a gable-roofed foyer to Arundel Gate of 1992), built as a night club with twin cinemas under. The cinema perches above an open concrete framework.

In POND HILL is the oldest domestic building in Sheffield, the OLD QUEEN'S HEAD, traditionally known as the 'Hall-in-the-Ponds'. Probably C15, it has closely set studs and the first floor oversailing on a coved jetty. On the w façade, a bressumer with tracery and two figured brackets, one a queen's head, the other a male demi-figure. The windows with traceried wooded frames and curved jetties are restorations of 1993. A N cross-wing is shown on Gosling's plan of Sheffield, 1736, but had been removed by the early C19 and the rest further reduced by road widening later in the C19 when the N wall was replaced in brick and stone. Inside, on the first floor, two tiny mullioned windows of plaster set in a partition wall facing the foot of the attic stairs. Three carved heads in the bar. The adjoining early C19 brick building became the Old Queen's Head beerhouse *c.* 1840 and later incorporated the remains of the hall. Plain rendered addition of 1993. Further down Pond Hill is a GATEWAY (*c.* 1900) to the former forge of George Senior. The gate was moved here from Sheaf Street when the works were demolished for the PONDS FORGE INTERNATIONAL LEISURE CENTRE (*see* Public Buildings). s of Pond Hill, overlooking SHEAF STREET, the DIGITAL BUSINESS CAMPUS with the ELECTRIC WORKS of 2007–9 by *Dive Architects*, for multiple small digital, media and creative businesses. The massing is impressive. Inside, a tubular slide between floors is the most obviously modish feature.

6. *North: Wicker and Victoria Quays*

The perambulation begins at BRIDGE STREET, at the N end of Waingate (*see* Perambulation 5) by the Don, where the former EXCHANGE BREWERY (now offices) occupies a prominent site. Tennant Brothers Ltd moved here in 1852. The five-storey brewing tower is probably of that date but the offices and ornamental gates with reliefs of wheatsheaves are of 1867 by *Flockton & Abbott*. They also designed the stuccoed former LADY'S BRIDGE HOTEL which fills the corner of the site.

LADY'S BRIDGE across the Don was built in 1486 and had a chapel (dedicated to Our Lady Mary) on the town side until 1767. Early masonry is obscured by successive widenings, on the NW side in 1761 and on the SE in 1864 and 1909. Flanking the N end of the bridge is a mixed-use development of 1899–1900 by *Flockton, Gibbs & Flockton* for John Henry Bryars, an animal breeder and vet. The ranges along Lady's Bridge are of four storeys, on the l. ROYAL VICTORIA BUILDINGS, triangular in plan with a mansard roof and on the r. ROYAL EXCHANGE BUILDINGS. Both are covered in light brown glazed bricks with dark brown bands, and have crowstepped gables and finials. Facing the river is CASTLE HOUSE, originally multi-storey stables with iron frame and internal ramps, subsequently in factory and warehouse use but now converted as offices within the adjoining I QUARTER development of flats of 2006 by *Cartwright Pickard* that includes a sixteen-storey tower.

WICKER, the street running N from Lady's Bridge, begins on the W corner with RIVERSIDE COURT apartments (formerly the Lion Hotel) of 1879. Four storeys on the curve to Nursery Street, quite plain. Further W, AIZLEWOOD'S MILLS were built in the 1870s as flour mills for John Aizlewood Ltd, now converted to offices and workshops. Tall six-storey L-shaped mill, once linked at high level to the Bridgehouses goods yard, with a mixture of segmental- and round-arched windows and a tall rectangular chimney. Back on Wicker, on the E side are the former offices of Shortridge & Howell's steel works of 1853 (now COMMUNITY CENTRE). Tall, although of only three storeys, of brick with a richly decorated front in the Italianate palazzo style. The remainder of the frontage l. and r. was built in the early C20 for Samuel Osborn and Co.'s Clyde Steel Works. Plain red brick for shops with offices over. Opposite but further N is the former Sheffield and Hallamshire Bank (Nos. 87–91) of 1893 by *Flockton & Gibbs*, in French Second Empire style and the Edwardian former STATION HOTEL and former Sheffield Bank of 1893 by *M.E. Hadfield, Son & Garland*, Italianate, built of thin red bricks. Wicker is closed by the VIADUCT of the Manchester, Sheffield & Lincolnshire Railway and its fine classical BRIDGE over the street, known as the 'Wicker Arches', by *Weightman & Hadfield* with *John Fowler*, engineer, 1848. Broad segmental arch flanked by two narrow arches for pedestrians framed by pilasters and entablatures. On the E side of the bridge is the base of the Victoria Station (also by *Weightman & Hadfield*, 1851; dem.). E across the river is the ROYAL VICTORIA STATION HOTEL (Holiday Inn) 1862 by *M.E. Hadfield*, large but simple Italianate with tall chimneys. Enlarged in 1898 and extended to the rear over the former station site in the 1980s. Beside the hotel, the GREAT CENTRAL RAILWAY WAR MEMORIAL of 1922, formerly at Victoria Station. The original setting was within a Doric colonnade by *T.E. Collcutt*.

BLONK STREET, E of Wicker, is carried over the Don by BLONK BRIDGE, built to link Wicker directly with the Sheffield Canal basin, by *Woodhead & Hurst*, 1827–8. Altered *c.* 1913 with three elliptical rusticated arches and cast-iron balustrades. E across Furnival Road is the entrance to VICTORIA QUAYS, the former canal basin, which was created 1816–19 as the terminus of the link with the Don Navigation at Tinsley Wharf (*see* p. 675). Closed in 1970, but restored and the site redeveloped since 1992. Part of the site takes in the former coal yard of the Manchester, Sheffield & Lincolnshire Railway and close to the entrance are a handsome group of restored COAL MERCHANTS' OFFICES. Stone with steep-pitched roofs, they curve gently along the ramp to the yard and are of one storey to the ramp but two to the rear. The coal yard was built on a viaduct which crosses the N side of the basin quay and is now infilled by shops and restaurants. The earliest building associated with the canal basin is the TERMINAL WAREHOUSE of 1819 (restored 1994). It is of brick with a large stone dressed arched openings at ground floor, one forming a boat hole enabling goods to be hoisted from keels directly to the upper floors, the hoist extant on the top floor. Four storeys with a large gable incorporating a further storey, wide seven-bay pediments to the E and W elevations. Interior of timber construction but the middle two floors have a later steel framework. The roof is supported by a composite queenpost and kingpost with a truss span of over 66 ft (20 metres). A two-storey brick extension provided the original offices for the Basin. At right angles to the Terminal Warehouse a block built *c.* 1853 as the head office for the Tinsley Park Coal Co. To the N, a WAREHOUSE added in 1889 by the Manchester, Sheffield & Lincolnshire Railway, four storeys, brick with segmental-headed cast-iron casements and weatherboarded sack hoist towers. The STRADDLE WAREHOUSE of 1895–8 was a thoroughly up-to-date design. Steel frame with concrete infill supported on blue brick arches, red brick end walls and five docking bays. Restored by *Robin Hedger*.

A short walk N along the quayside leads to SHEAF QUAY, site of Sheaf Works, one of the earliest integrated steel works, built between 1822–6 for William Greaves, who produced cutlery, steel and edge tools. All that remains is the handsome office building, resembling a country house built of ashlar and coursed stone. Four storeys and nine bays, with a five-bay central pediment. Converted by *Carey Jones Seifert* in 1989, with a Postmodern W addition.

¼ m. E of the canal between Sheffield Parkway and BERNARD ROAD, are the remaining buildings of the NUNNERY GOODS DEPOT of the London & North Western Railway, opened in 1895, in blue and red brick with cogging. On the site of the terminus to the E is NUNNERY SQUARE, speculatively developed as a business park in 1993. Three office buildings were intended, facing a central oblong lawn but only two have been built. The first block, of 1993 by *Allies & Morrison*, is now occupied by South Yorkshire Police. Floor-to-ceiling glazing and white panels. A steel framework supports horizontal walkways for window cleaning, and sun shades wrap around it. The most prominent structure however is the ENERGY RECOVERY FACILITY on Lumley Street to the NW, by *FPCR Environment and Design*, 2007, a waste incinerator powering an electricity generator and district heating for the local area, with a tall chimney and stepped profile of blocks under curved roofs dictated by the internal functions.

7. North-west: Scotland Street and neighbourhood

A continuous perambulation of this district is not possible but amid a mixture of 1930s and later factories and a rash of mostly undistinguished student flats built *c.* 2010, there are numerous reminders of this area's past as a tightly packed mass of small houses and cutlery premises. In GARDEN STREET, climbing uphill, the CROFT HOUSE COMMUNITY CENTRE, which began as a Congregational Chapel of 1866–7 by *Innocent & Brown*. Large rose window with plate tracery. Converted in 1902 to a settlement house. Opposite, the former ST LUKE'S NATIONAL SCHOOLS by *H.D. Lomas*, of 1873. Brick with stone dressings on the ground floor and an open pediment over the central four bays. At the top of Garden Street, the eye-catching ROBENS BUILDING (Health & Safety Executive laboratory), 1993 by *PSA Projects* (project architect *Gordon Wilson*). The services are exposed externally, following the example of Louis Kahn's Richards Medical Research Building, Philadelphia, and culminate in a phalanx of sixteen flues forming a crest like organ pipes against the sky.

At the corner, facing SOLLY STREET, PROVINCIAL HOUSE is the former St Vincent's Presbytery by *M. E. Hadfield & Son*, 1878. It must have dominated what was a poor, largely Irish neighbourhood. Italianate, of considerable refinement in cut and gauged brick. Four storeys with a porch of red Hollington stone, a plaque and a niche formerly containing a statue of St Vincent. Apsed chapel at the rear. (For St Vincent's church, *see* Churches.) w, on the other side, is SOLLY HOUSE (student accommodation), pre-1850, three-storeyed and still retaining its small-paned windows. It was the front block of the Cambridge Works of James Lodge, cutlery and electroplate manufacturers. Further w are the EDWARD STREET FLATS by *W. G. Davies*, 1939–43. This was the largest interwar development of flats in the city centre and although the style is broadly Neo-Georgian, the influence of Dudok is evident in the pronounced horizontal emphasis given by the access balconies (since rebuilt in tubular steel), the streamlined staircase turrets and the large arched principal entrance. The flats encircle a green.

NE of the flats in UPPER ALLEN STREET, many large blocks of student apartments stepping downhill, but on the s side also the former works of Stephenson Blake Ltd, typefounders. C19 of three visually distinct periods, the earliest in the centre with curious flattened arches including a Venetian window above the cart entrance to the r. Behind the buildings opposite, facing WELL MEADOW STREET, is an important example of a mid-C19 integrated steel works of the type common in the city centre until well into the C20. This complex, now restored, was built by the steel and file-cutting firm of Samuel Peace. The front range retains a manager's or owner's house (the only part in existence in 1851), a three-storey workshop and a furnace with a crucible stack comprising six flues with a brick vaulted cellar below. In the yard behind three-storey workshops of *c.* 1853, probably used for file-cutting. Steelmaking ended in 1926. On the opposite side the former Well Meadow Steel Works (originally Well Meadow Place), incorporates one through house, two blind-back houses and three pairs of back-to-back houses. All pre-1820 with workshops and an early C19 crucible stack behind. (Derelict at the time of writing.)

LAMBERT STREET, ⅜ m. E, has late C18–early C19 houses which became part of the premises of John Watts's cutlery works. The houses have been rendered and have raised plaster lettering bearing the firm's name and manufactures. At the bottom of the street, on WEST BAR, MAYFIELD COURT is the former Common Lodging House of 1912 by *John Reginald Truelove*, whose father, Alderman Arthur Truelove, paid for the building. Tall and thin with a strikingly broad cornice, projecting centre and accomplished detailing of rusticated brick quoins, contrasting red and yellow brick and panels of tile and brick patterns. The public rooms on the lower floors were lit by the broad segmental-arched windows with slit-like openings to the three floors of bedrooms above, which were divided by a corridor into two rows of cubicles.

In SNOW LANE, the former SHEFFIELD METAL COMPANY works. Brick with round-headed windows built in a number of phases. In the 1890s the works took in three adjoining back-to-back houses of *c.* 1800, almost unique survivals of what was the most common form of the Sheffield working man's house in the early C19. Built of small irregular bricks and with their original small sill-less casement windows, only two are still recognizable while the third was refronted to match the round-headed windows of the remainder of the works.

In DONCASTER STREET to the w is preserved the only complete CEMENTATION FURNACE left in Sheffield, dating from 1848 and originally part of the steel works of Daniel Doncaster. Bottle-shaped like a pottery kiln and last heated in 1951, it now stands in isolation.*

8. Kelham and Neepsend

A former industrial area, along both sides of the Don, and separated from the city centre by the inner ring road (A61) which runs along SHALESMOOR, where the only building of note is the splendid SHIP INN, rebuilt for Tomlinsons in the 1920s. Particularly fine brown faience ground floor with a tiled picture of a galleon on the fascia and raised lettering to the 'Dram Shop'.

N of here is KELHAM and on ALMA STREET is a long rendered range, built as part of a cotton mill in 1805 but converted in 1828–9 as the workhouse for Sheffield township (the principal building was demolished in 1946–7 following bomb damage). Ibbotson Bros (of the Globe Works, *see* below) took over the site in 1882 and incorporated it within their GLOBE STEEL WORKS. All now cleared but for one range with a carved globe in the pediment of its façade to Alma Street. The works also occupied the large site to the NW between Alma Street and the River Don where there has been extensive rebuilding and regeneration for a low-carbon mixed-use development, still underway in 2016, known as LITTLE KELHAM, by the developer *Citu* and architects *Bauman Lyons*, *Hodson Architects* and *Cal Architects*. Incorporated within this are the restored former EAGLE WORKS, a riverside range of mid-C19 brick buildings on a stone base, the largest of four storeys with broad windows on the upper three. Immediately N of this in the river is KELHAM ISLAND, created by the goit for the medieval town mill. It is dominated by the KELHAM ISLAND MUSEUM, converted in 1982 from the former Tramway Generating Station of 1899.

---

*At Bower Spring, much less well preserved, are the remains of two cementation furnaces, built *c.* 1828 for Thomas Turton's Franklin Works.

GREEN LANE runs along the s side of the Little Kelham development. On the s side at the corner with Ebenezer Place, the former Ebenezer Wesleyan Chapel (*see* Churches). w is the most coherent stretch of industrial landscape in inner Sheffield. First, on the N side, incorporated within the second phase of the Little Kelham development, is the spectacular gatehouse of GREEN LANE WORKS. Built by Henry Hoole, a manufacturer of fire-grates, in 1860, although it looks at first a full generation earlier. It takes the form of a tripartite triumphal arch, constructed to commemorate Hoole becoming Mayor of Sheffield. Female keystone head over the central entrance. Over the pedestrian entrances are relief panels of Hephaestus and Athene, probably by *Alfred Stevens*, who designed for Hoole's between 1850 and 1852. Tall cupola on top. Principal workshop range to the rear along the Don, three storeys, twenty-six bays with very broad windows, now being converted for housing. Next is BROOKLYN WORKS (Alfred Beckett & Sons Ltd). Late C19, two- and three-storey buildings restored as offices and apartments in the 1990s, much of the remainder demolished. Good plaster signs on the front and the gable by BALL STREET BRIDGE across the Don (Gothic parapets of 1865 and widened in 1900; it was cast by the *Milton Ironworks*, Elsecar).

Filling a large site w of Ball Street and bounded N by the river and w by Cornish Street, are the CORNISH PLACE WORKS of James Dixon & Co. Its principal buildings, a mixture of brick and stone, were sympathetically converted into loft apartments by *AXIS Architecture*, 1998. James Dixon, who made Britannia metal, silver plate and cutlery, set up here in 1822. Only parts survive of that date, notably the office and workshop range (second floor added *c.* 1903) on Cornish Street, but the dominant part of the works are the four-storey red brick ranges with sequences of round-arched windows along Ball Street and the Don which were put up in 1851–4 at the time of conversion to steam power and continued s along Ball Street in 1857–9 (this part three-storeyed and originally containing a showroom and warehouse). In the courtyard is a tall circular chimney and an imposing staircase tower to the showroom block. Facing Green Lane, more elaborate treatment is given to the 1850s workshop block with the works name carved in stone on the parapet. The former plating shop adjoining this on Cornish Street is of a type particular to an electroplating works and has a tall single storey over a basement lit by large round-headed windows and a clerestory.

w are the unrestored WHARNCLIFFE WORKS. Three storeys over a basement, built *c.* 1861 for Steel & Garland, manufacturers of stoves, grates and fenders. Originally three ranges round a triangular yard, one demolished. Segmental arch over the cart entrance with a prominent decorative ashlar surround bearing the works name.

Beyond, facing PENISTONE ROAD, is the GLOBE WORKS of
1825 for Ibbotson & Roebank, edge tool manufacturers, with
a remarkably noble stone façade of nine bays, incorporating
the owner's house at the S end. Two storeys, except for the
three-bay centre which has another half-storey and a pediment. The first and last bays also pedimented. The ground-
floor windows arched, those on the first floor flanked by short
Ionic pilasters carrying shallow segmental arches – a personal
and successful rhythm. At the rear, the lower two floors are
deeply recessed in the central three bays, the top storey oversailing, carried on another shallow segmental arch. External
stone cantilevered dog-leg steps lead to a doorway on the first
floor. Behind the grand front block, much humbler three-
storey workshop blocks planned around the usual courtyard
but, in contrast to most Sheffield workshops, with coursed
stone façades, the other elevations mainly brick.

N of the Globe Works, where RUTLAND ROAD crosses the
Don, is INSIGNIA WORKS. Built in 1919–20 by *W. J. Hale* as
the spring shop for Samuel Osborn & Co.'s Rutland Works
(dem.). It was given its name, following conversion to offices,
from the Heart and Hand trademarks prominently displayed
on its walls. Large segmental-headed windows, of tripartite
form under gables on the riverside.

Across the Don is the industrial suburb of NEEPSEND. E along
the N bank of the river is BURTON ROAD with THE MALT-
INGS (now offices) *c.* 1870, formerly part of William Stones's
brewery. Three storeys with gable-end to road with segmental
arches to doors and windows and a circular window in the
gable. Next, the ALBYN WORKS of 1875 by *T. E. Watson*, built
for cleaning powders and knife pastes. To the S on NEEPSEND
LANE, the KELHAM MILLS housing development of 2003–6
by *Tatlow Stancer Architects* on the site of the Neepsend Rolling
Mills. The three-storey office block (Kelham House) of *c.* 1870
is retained. The central three bays slightly raised with a parapet
and given ornamental surrounds to the windows and rustication to the ground floor.

In MOWBRAY STREET there is a substantial pocket of surviving
small steel and edge tool works whose backs are visible from
Kelham Island, including LION WORKS with a crucible shop
on Ball Street with the stack facing the street. ¼ m. E at the
end of Mowbray Street on the l., massive stone retaining walls
of the 1860s are all that is left of the Manchester, Sheffield &
Lincolnshire Railway's Bridgehouses goods depot. BOROUGH
BRIDGE crosses the Don back to Kelham. 1853 by *Samuel
Holmes & Samuel Worth* as part of the improvements associated
with the opening of Corporation Street in 1856 for access to
the depot. S of the bridge, the UPPER DON WALK, opened
2003, runs along the river in both directions in front of
large groups of apartment and office blocks of little or no
distinction.

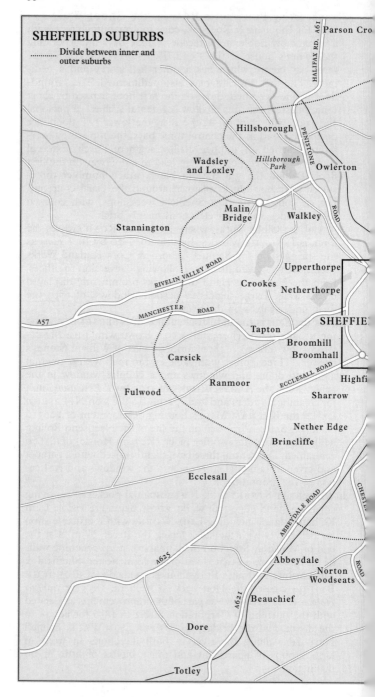

SHEFFIELD SUBURBS

.... Divide between inner and
outer suburbs

Parson Cro

HALIFAX RD. A61

Hillsborough

PENISTONE

Wadsley
and Loxley

*Hillsborough
Park*

Owlerton

Malin
Bridge

Walkley

ROAD

Stannington

RIVELIN VALLEY ROAD

Upperthorpe

Crookes

Netherthorpe

MANCHESTER ROAD

A57

Tapton

SHEFFIE

Carsick

Broomhill
Broomhall

Ranmoor

ECCLESALL ROAD

Highfi

Fulwood

Sharrow

Nether Edge

Brincliffe

Ecclesall

ABBEYDALE ROAD

CHEST

A625

Abbeydale

Norton
Woodseats

ROAD

A621

Beauchief

Dore

Totley

d Shiregreen

Concord
Park

Longley
Park

Wincobank

ROTHERHAM

Firth Park

TINSLEY

Crabtree Fir Vale

River Don

Brightside Carbrook

Grimesthorpe

Pitsmoor

Attercliffe

Burngreave

ATTERCLIFFE ROAD

Darnall

City
re map
506–7

Park
Hill

SHEFFIELD

Norfolk
Park

Manor
Park

HANDSWORTH

owfield

Woodthorpe

Arbourthorne

Richmond

eley

Meersbrook

Gleadless

Frecheville

BIRLEY MOOR ROAD

Hackenthorpe

A57

es
k

Oakes
Park

NORTON AVENUE

Norton

A6135

N

2 km

2 miles

SHEFFIELD INNER SUBURBS

NORTH

(Crabtree, Burngreave, Pitsmoor, Grimesthorpe, Fir Vale,
Firth Park and Wincobank)

CHURCHES

CHRIST CHURCH, Pitsmoor Road. By *Flockton & Son*, of 1849–50. Large and handsome in the Dec style, built to cater for an affluent congregation. The w tower has tall pinnacles and set-back buttresses. Large transepts. – FURNISHINGS of 1913, as are the mosaic floors in the chancel and baptistry. – STAINED GLASS. N aisle, works of Charity by *Kayll & Reed*, 1915. CHURCH HALL by *K.H. Murta* and *A.P. Fawcett* added to s wall of nave in the early 1980s.

ST CUTHBERT, Barnsley Road/Firth Park Road, Firvale. 1901–5 by *J.D. Webster & Son*. Set on a hill, its most dominant feature is its roof, a vast expanse of bright red tiles. E.E. style with transepts. Plain NW tower of 1959. Excellent STAINED GLASS by *Archibald Davies* of the *Bromsgrove Guild* 1920–22, 1938–47. s aisle window †1917 by *Kayll & Reed*, brighter colours and more conventional.

ST PETER, Lyons Street, Burngreave. 1980 by the *G.D. Frankish Partnership*. Circular, brown brick piers surmounted by a steel ring beam, low-pitched conical roof with lantern and skeleton spire. On the site of All Saints church (*Flockton & Abbott*, 1868–9).

ST THOMAS (former), Holywell Road (Greentop Community Circus Centre). By *Flockton & Abbott*, 1852–4. Geometric tracery. Nave with s aisle. SW tower/porch with splay-foot stone spire.

ST CATHERINE (R.C.), Burngreave Road. 1925–6 by *Charles Edward Fox & Son*. Red brick in the Early Christian style. Tall Romanesque campanile with a pyramidal roof. Nave arcading of round-headed arches on Carrara columns with decorated block capitals. Enormous BALDACCHINO on marble columns whose canopy bears a gilded figure of Christ the King.

TRINITY METHODIST CHURCH, Firth Park Road/Owler Lane. 1899 by *John Wills*, a conventional large Gothic chapel in rock-faced stone with a tall thin spire with pinnacles at the corners.

FIRTH PARK METHODIST CHURCH, Stubbin Lane. 1911 by *Chapman & Jenkinson*, built at the heart of the new suburb. Attractive Neo-Perp in red brick with a broad w window above a porch flanked by two short octagonal towers with spirelets. A flèche in the centre of the roof.

ST JAMES PRESBYTERIAN CHURCH HALL, Scott Road. 1911 by *H. L. Paterson*, in the mild Perp style much favoured for small Nonconformist chapels at the time.

SEVENTH DAY ADVENTISTS CHURCH, Andover Street. 1865 by *William Hill* for the Methodist New Connexion. SW tower with an octagonal broach spire. Straightforward Gothic. Interior with a gallery on three sides on cast-iron columns. SCHOOL of 1862 behind.

BURNGREAVE CEMETERY, off Burngreave Road. Opened 1860, the buildings, by *Flockton & Lee*. Mortuary chapels linked by an arch surmounted by a spire.

PUBLIC BUILDINGS

PUBLIC LIBRARY (former), Firth Park Road. 1937 by the City Architect, *W. G. Davies*. Superior Neoclassical with the central bays projecting, the doorway recessed behind Doric columns and the city coat of arms above, surmounted by a swag.

PYE BANK SCHOOL, Andover Street by *Innocent & Brown*, 1875. Gothic. Extended in 1884.

FIRS HILL JUNIOR SCHOOL, Barnsley Road. 1893 by *J.B. Mitchell-Withers*. Jacobean.

NORTHERN GENERAL HOSPITAL, Barnsley Road. Built as the Sheffield Union WORKHOUSE in 1876–80, by *James Hall*, of which only the N wing and central block survive, with some French Second Empire detailing in the mansard roof and circular dormers above the bays. To the w of the main block, H-shaped pavilion blocks were constructed for the workhouse INFIRMARY, most of which remain, albeit much altered. Dating from the separation of the infirmary is the Arts and Crafts-style LAUNDRY (1900), ADMINISTRATION BUILDING (1901–4) and NURSES' HOME (1899–1902), all by *E. W. Mountford*. Great expansion of the hospital has taken place since 1990. On the s edge of the site, by Herries Road, is the former Receiving House of the Cottage Homes for Children, 1894 by *C. J. Innocent*.

ABBEYFIELD PARK, Barnsley Road. Purchased by the Corporation in 1909, formerly the grounds of ABBEYFIELD, built in the late C18 for William Pass. It originally faced Barnsley Road but, following sale to Bernard Wake *c.* 1852, was reorientated to face enlarged grounds with a new N wing, followed by further extensions to the s, probably in 1883, the date of a prominent sundial. Ashlar-faced, asymmetrical with several canted bay windows, one on the principal façade and two more on the return.

FIRTH PARK was created from 35 acres of the Page Hall estate and given by Mark Firth in 1875. In Firth Park Road, the REFRESHMENT ROOM by *Flockton & Abbott*, 1875. Rock-faced stone with a fanciful Italianate clock tower linked to a single-storey pavilion which has had its roof extended at the front to form a loggia.

PERAMBULATION

The hamlet of CRABTREE lay NE of BARNSLEY ROAD. At its heart stands THE IVIES, in Crabtree Drive, surrounded by later housing. Late C17 vernacular, extended as suggested by three datestones inscribed HF 1676, JF 1841 (s wing) and

M 1948 (rendered N wing). JF was John Frith, a traveller and writer who acquired the estate in 1839. At the N end of Barnsley Road, NORBURY is a large Italianate villa of 1848 built for Thomas Blake of the typefounders Stephenson Blake.

Barnsley Road becomes BURNGREAVE ROAD. At the junction with Pitsmoor Road, TOLL BAR COTTAGE by *Woodhead & Hurst* for the Sheffield and Wakefield Turnpike Trust 1834–6. Classical with round-headed windows, mostly paired and a canted end.

BURNGREAVE's centre is the green at the top of SPITAL HILL. On the corner of Burngreave and Grimesthorpe Roads, the Tudor-style former VESTRY OFFICES of 1864, with the city arms carved on the porch and paired, banded pilasters providing a strong accent. S in GOWER STREET, the former LIBRARY (now mosque) of 1872 by *James Hall*, the first to be built in the suburbs. Classical and chapel-like with a pediment and round-headed windows. To the N, council housing in BRESSINGHAM CLOSE and DITCHINGHAM STREET of *c.* 1977 by *J. Winter*, Director of Planning and Design (project architect *John Guy*). An adventurous and attractive urban village concept of houses on winding pedestrian alleys that follow the line of the old streets. W of Spital Hill, the BURNGREAVE ESTATE of 1962–4 by *J. Mansell Jenkinson & Son*, maisonettes and flats of traditional brick construction.

Spital Hill leads down to the Wicker Arches (*see* p. 544). On the r. SPITAL HILL WORKS, occupied by edge tool manufacturers, John Sorby from 1823 and then Lockwood Brothers by 1849, the present buildings comprising two long ranges. The two-storey range, which has lunettes with ornamental grilles, is of 1864–5 by *M. E. Hadfield & Son*. They were also responsible for the front office block of 1878, three storeys with ornamental stone dressings. The taller range of 1891 by *M. E. Hadfield, Son & Garland* is of four storeys, part with vaulted brick ceilings, and set into the hillside.

CARR WOOD HOUSE, Grimesthorpe Road. A simple but handsome classical three-bay house *c.* 1835 in ashlar, pediment to the central bay.

PAGE HALL, Cammell Road, Firvale. 1773 by *John Platt* for Thomas Broadbent, banker. Coursed sandstone of two-and-a-half storeys with a three-bay ashlar front. Two canted bay windows flank the main doorway with pediment on attached Adamesque columns. Late C20 additions to the l. incorporate the arcaded front of the stables.

FLOWER ESTATE, High Wincobank. The land was acquired in 1900 by Sheffield Corporation, which held a national competition for the design of workmen's houses on garden suburb principles. It was won by *Percy Houfton* of Chesterfield, an architect much associated with improved miners' housing. *H. L. Paterson* won the competition to design further houses on the estate in 1906. The Yorkshire and North Midland Cottage Exhibition was then held in 1907, with prizes awarded for different classes of housing. The winning entry for the estate layout was by *W. Alexander Harvey & A. McKewan*, the architects of Bournville. In spite of unsympathetic modifications, all the early cottages may still be seen. In WINCOBANK AVENUE and HEATHER ROAD, are *Houfton*'s designs, built in 1903–4, laid out in long rows in an unimaginative grid. They are of two types, double- and single-fronted and with no rooms projecting at the rear. *Paterson*'s houses of 1906 in Heather Road, were built more cheaply and to a notably lower standard but have quite attractive elevations with decorative brickwork. The Cottage Exhibition houses begin at the N end of PRIMROSE AVENUE. At Nos. 65–67, by *Henry Webster*, a double-gabled design, which, modified, was used extensively by the Corporation in the 1930s on the Parson Cross Estate (*see* p. 618). Opposite, on the junction with Jessamine Road, one of the best designs, Nos. 59–63 by *Harvey & McKewan*, red brick with cogging below the eaves and tile-hung full-height bay windows.

HILLFORT, Wincobank Hill. On the summit of a discrete ridge, an Iron Age fort defended by a wall/rampart of rubble from internal quarry-scoops. The wall/rampart was strengthened by timber framing but was finally destroyed by fire. There is a second rampart on the SE, and on the SW where it guards the line of easiest approach; the principal entrance was probably here. There is another on the NE. For the ROMAN RIG *see* Introduction p. 9.

NORTH-EAST

(Attercliffe, Carbrook, Brightside and Darnall)

ST CHARLES BORROMEO (R.C.), St Charles Street. The only church in Attercliffe still in use. Plain Gothic style in coursed rubble-faced stone. Aisleless nave of five bays and the presbytery by *Innocent & Brown* completed 1868, with E and W extensions, including chancel and baptistery by *Innocent*, 1887. Oak pulpit, screen and stalls by *Harry Hems*.

ATTERCLIFFE CHAPEL, Frank Place/Attercliffe Common. The oldest building in the Don valley, opened in 1630. Restored to its present form by *J. D. Webster* in 1909 and *Martin Purdy* in 1993. Simple rectangular stone building with a late C18 king-post roof under stone slates. Coped gables with kneelers at E and W ends, four-light E window with trefoil heads and transom. Side windows square-headed. Simple slate pediments on carved brackets to the N and S doorways, the N one has a datestone of 1629.

LIBRARY (former), Leeds Road, Attercliffe. 1894 by *Charles Wike*, in red brick with stone mullions and transoms and three big coped gables.

BATHS (former), Leeds Road, Attercliffe. 1879 by Mr *Stovin*, of the Borough Surveyor's office, completed by Mr *Appleby*. Classical style, in stone, with pedimented upper windows and dentilled cornice. The return range plainer Italianate in brick with stone dressings.

CARBROOK SCHOOL (former), Attercliffe Common. 1873–4 by *Innocent & Brown*, in their usual Gothic. Symmetrical two storeys with a striking tall gabled front and a small stone spire above the central bell-turret. The open arcaded play areas on the ground floor of the rear cross-wing were later enclosed to provide additional classrooms.

OLYMPIC LEGACY PARK, Attercliffe Road/Worksop Road. Being developed from 2014 by *Ares Landscape Architects* on the site of the Don Valley Stadium of 1991 (itself occupying the site of Brown Bayley's steel works). Incorporated within the park is the existing ENGLISH INSTITUTE OF SPORT, 1999–2003 by *FaulknerBrowns* (engineers *Anthony Hunt Associates*) of eleven parallel bays, each spanned by an asymmetrical shallow curved roof, its trusses suspended from eight 165-ft- (50-metre-) high needle-like masts with fine rigging, and ICE SHEFFIELD, by *Building Design Partnership*, 2003. The massive OASIS ACADEMY and UNIVERSITY TECHNICAL COLLEGE, by *Bond Bryan*, opened in 2015.

SHEFFIELD ARENA, Broughton Lane. Hulking, dull, rectangular block with rounded corners. By *HOK Sport* and *Lister, Drew, Haines, Barrow*, 1991, for the World Student Games. Impressively vast and flexibly planned interior with 8,000 seats in raked blocks on three sides.

PERAMBULATIONS

1. Don valley

The industrial buildings along the valley are described working out from the city centre.

In SAVILE STREET, E side, the former DON STEEL WORKS with decorative pilasters and spiky finials, stylishly converted to a car showroom in 2002 by *Ward McHugh Associates*. Then ALBION HOUSE, 1902 with later additions. Long plain façade of brick with stone dressings. Stone-faced pedimented main entrance and square tower with French pavilion roof. The N side of the street is dominated by the colossal, but surprisingly elegant, grey steel-clad shed of Firth Brown's PRECISION FORGE. 1980 by *Husband & Co.*, 433 ft (132 metres) long and 51 ft (15.5 metres) high, it was built to house an innovative forging press with four hammers over 183 ft (56 metres) long and weighing 1,228 tonnes, processing ingots up to 8 tonnes. The forge partly occupies the site of Cammell's CYCLOPS WORKS by *Weightman, Hadfield & Goldie c.* 1845–52. Only a heavily rusticated Tuscan-style stone gateway (now blocked) survives on CARLISLE STREET.

Along CARLISLE STREET EAST all the older works have gone. On the N side, BESSEMER HOUSE by *Holmes & Watson*, 1901. The former offices of Henry Bessemer, facing the site where in 1859 he began the first commercial production of

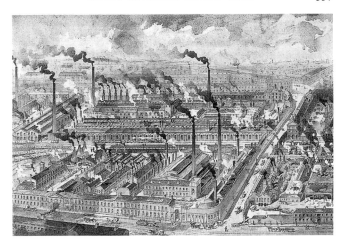

Sheffield, Cyclops Works of Charles Cammell & Co.
1887

cheap bulk steel from pig iron. Hard, smooth soot-resistant
red brick with stone dressings, five storeys dignified by a large
central porch with polished granite pilasters and three-storey
canted bays on either side.

Running parallel to the s is SAVILE STREET EAST. On the N
side, E of President Way, the former GATEWAY of the Norfolk
Works' Siemens melting shop of 1918 by *W. S. Purchon*. Rusticated ashlar and inscribed 'Thos Firth & Sons Ltd Siemens
Dept'. Beyond are two ranges of offices which typify the frontages of the mid-C19 steel works – modest but solid, two storeys
in a simple brick Italianate style with long sequences of arched
or segmental-headed windows. First, the twenty-bay former
QUEEN'S WORKS of 1853 for Armitage, Frankish and Barker,
and the slightly grander PRESIDENT WORKS of Moses Eadon
and Sons, *c.* 1852. E of this is a third range, built as the gun
shop of Firth's WEST GUN WORKS, 1863–4, for the manufacture of heavy artillery barrels. Long brick frontage with a
curved corner, the offices at the w end have been partly altered
with an oriel window while the workshops are lit by fifteen tall
round-headed windows below five blank lunettes, all with
stone sill bands.

BRIGHTSIDE LANE begins beyond Carwood Road. At the
northern end, at the corner with Hawke Street, E side, a former
MACHINE SHOP (now occupied by Rom) designed by the
English Steel Corporation Architects' Department, 1957, a gigantic
rectangular block of fifteen bays, 600 ft (183 metres) long and
168 ft (51 metres) wide. Steel-framed, faced in brick with
panels of yellow tiles and glass block infill on the N side. Series
of clerestories spanning the width of the shop. The three main

bays inside could accommodate 40-ton cranes with a span of 50 ft (15 metres).

The once-characteristic canyon effect of the valley's streets created by the works is best preserved at the RIVER DON WORKS (Sheffield Forgemasters) in the last stretch of Brightside Lane, originally developed by Naylor Vickers (Vickers, Sons & Maxim from 1897) who moved here in 1863. On the N side of the road the impressive four-storey classical Revival OFFICES (currently empty) by *Holmes & Watson*, of 1906. Steel-framed, with dirt-resistant, hard red brick walls and almost symmetrical façade of twenty-eight bays, with narrow balconies along the upper floors for window cleaning. An extension to the l., built 1911, has been demolished, leaving the ground-floor wall as a screen. The site also retains the best range of black steel-clad SHEDS in the valley. The group to the S includes the high, four-gabled gun heat-treatment tower of 1913 by *Sir William Arrol & Co*.

MEADOWHALL SHOPPING CENTRE, Meadowhall Way, by *Chapman, Taylor & Partners* 1990, extended 1999. The first and largest of the post-industrial developments in the Don valley, on the site of the East Hecla steel works, its green cladding roofs and glazed domes are a prominent landmark beside the M1 viaduct (*see* Tinsley).

2. Attercliffe and Darnall

On the S side of ATTERCLIFFE ROAD, E of Washford Bridge, the SPARTAN WORKS is a typical small Victorian crucible steel and wire-making complex of *c.* 1880 with a courtyard and workshops behind the long front range. Its window heads and other details display a rare and here slightly incongruous use of flowery terracotta decoration from the Wharncliffe Fireclay works. Further up, at the corner with Staniforth Road, is a former TRUSTEE SAVINGS BANK of 1899–1900 with three tall arched windows, fluted pilasters and balustrade with urns, abutting the former YORKSHIRE PENNY BANK of 1905, also in stone with oriel windows and decorative sculpture with children's heads. Then, a former branch of BURTON'S, 1931, in their usual white faience and Art Deco detailing, and, also in white faience, a former department store (1926–8 by *Chapman & Jenkinson* for John Banner Ltd, with extensions 1933–4).

The buildings grouped around the junction with WORKSOP ROAD still convey something of the character of Attercliffe in its heyday, in particular the handsome Renaissance Revival-style BANK on the l. by *Gibbs & Flockton*, 1902, with polished pink granite Doric columns. In the churchyard behind, the former NATIONAL SCHOOL by *Thomas Taylor*, 1824. Plain stone Gothic with lancet windows and open octagonal bellcote. Taylor also designed the parish church of 1826, demolished after bombing in 1940. On the corner opposite the bank is the

ZEENAT RESTAURANT, designed in 1904 by *A.N. Bromley* as a branch of Boots. Three storeys, in his usual gabled Jacobean Revival style, in caramel-coloured faience with a jolly mixture of decorative details. Further N, on VICARAGE ROAD, a second branch of BURTON'S of 1932 by *Harry Wilson*, again in white faience. Next to it the former ADELPHI CINEMA, by *William C. Fenton*, 1920. Baroque Revival front with the three central bays emphasized by a giant arch and projecting pilasters in faience. The little dome on the squat square tower above has four oddly large projections with oval windows.

In WORKSOP ROAD to the E of Attercliffe Road, THE BRITANNIA pub, with the date 1772 in steel figures on its gable, incorporates one of the area's oldest surviving houses, by tradition the home of Benjamin Huntsman, whose original works were nearby. Further E the road passes under the three-arched stone AQUEDUCT of 1819 for the Sheffield Canal, emerging as DARNALL ROAD. We end the walk a short distance on the r., at one of the most important steel-making sites in the country, containing a unique group of late C19 crucible shops. The western part of the works, mostly gone, was developed from 1912 by Kayser Ellison. Behind the offices, which face the road, is a large steel-framed and glazed workshop of 1913 in a state of shattered fragility, protected on three sides by corrugated iron sheeting at the time of writing. The site to the E was DARNALL WORKS, redeveloped in 1871–2 by *Sanderson Bros & Co.*, for bulk crucible steel production with 180 melting holes. The surviving buildings (unused) are the brick entrance lodge and weighbridge cabin flanked by high boundary walls, the villa-like offices and the brick CRUCIBLE SHOPS stepping up the hill along Wilfrid Road, their massive transverse stacks containing the flues for forty-eight melting holes. The large gabled shop set at a right angle in the top corner of the site had a group of twenty-four holes on each side of its impressively cavernous interior. The stacks are set longitudinally between the outer walls and the melting floor, creating narrow side aisles which were lined with shelves for storing crucible pots. Last used in the Second World War, the group is now the only surviving example of a crucible furnace with the capacity to produce large amounts of cast steel by the process that dominated the industry until the end of the C19.

CARBROOK HALL, Attercliffe Common. The surviving stone wing added *c.* 1620 to an older house, demolished in the C19, which was the seat of the Bright family. Now a pub with an unpromising and much-altered exterior, with some mullioned-and-transomed windows. Inside, a sumptuously decorated parlour for Stephen Bright, who was appointed Bailiff of Hallamshire in 1622. The geometric panelling is divided by pilasters carved with stylized sunflowers and foliage, below a frieze. Above this a moulded plaster frieze with foliage trails. Richly decorated ceiling divided by plastered beams, with sprigs of flowers and bold curled-up strapwork in curious frames. Carved oak overmantel, almost identical to the one from

Norton House, now in the Cutlers' Hall (p. 515), which is dated 1623. Its central panel has a relief of a figure in long garments stepping on a monstrous corpse with blown-up belly and a tail. A chamber above has stencilled wainscot panelling, an impressive Renaissance overmantel and some surviving plasterwork. It is probably by the same craftsmen who worked at Bolsover Castle, Derbyshire.

EAST

(Park Hill, Norfolk Park and Manor Park)

The SE side of Sheffield formed the hunting park of the lords of Hallamshire from at least the C13, a charter of 1296 confirming the right of Thomas de Furnival to hunt in his park. A survey of 1637 stated it to be 2,461 acres in size. The ruins of the Earl of Shrewsbury's hunting lodge survive (*see* below). The district known as the Park was developed from the late C18, followed by Norfolk Park, which was built up with high-quality villas in large grounds. By the interwar period the Park was a slum and subject to an early round of clearance, but the principal activity was delayed until after the Second World War and then took a form which has made Sheffield internationally famous for its public housing.

CHURCHES AND PUBLIC BUILDINGS

ST AIDAN, City Road/Manor Lane. 1932–3 by *Flockton & Son*. Cruciform, Perp style with a crossing tower and squat spire. Glazed timber cloister on the N side, part of the community centre by *Roger Barnes* of *Niall Phillips Architects*, 1999. Part of the nave has been turned into a hall. The chancel is a side-lit broad low recess under a Tudor arch. Fine FURNISHINGS in limed oak by *Andrew Skelton*, 1999. – STAINED GLASS: S transept (St Aidan preaching to the heathen), 1956 and others by *Alfred Wilkinson*. The VICARAGE adjacent, originally Manor Grange, early C19, plain three-bay classical.

ST JOHN, Bernard Street. Surrounded by the Hyde Park flats (*see* Perambulation, p. 564). 1836–8 by *M. E. Hadfield*. Re-roofed and restored by *E. M. Gibbs* in 1889–91. Predominantly Neo-Norman but the tower has a tall broach spire. Interior reordered c. 1971 by *K. H. Murta* and *J. B. Hall*, designers of the octagonal CHURCH HALL with projecting angled skylight, like Casson & Conder's Elephant and Rhino Pavilion, London Zoo.

VICTORIA METHODIST CHURCH, Stafford Road. 1899–1901 by *John Wills*. NW tower with a tall broach spire. Flamboyant Dec tracery in the E window, geometrical in the W, lancets elsewhere. Interior converted in 2003 with a two-storey space for meeting rooms etc. by *Bramhall Blenkharn*. STAINED GLASS. E window by *Abbott & Co.* of Lancaster.

CITY ROAD CEMETERY. Opened by the Sheffield Burial Board in 1881. *M.E. Hadfield & Son* created the imposing landmark of the tall Tudor-style gateway flanked by offices with full-height bay windows. Inside were Anglican (now demolished) and Nonconformist chapels of equal size but slightly different in design. The design of the CREMATORIUM by *C. & C.M. Hadfield*, 1905, is based on the Abbot's Kitchen at Glastonbury Abbey, with central flue for the chimney. The Roman Catholic chapel, also by *C. & C.M.E. Hadfield*, 1899–1900, in a free Gothic style, with hexagonal chancel and a lantern almost Early Christian in character, is now semi-derelict. – BELGIAN WAR MEMORIAL. 1921. Tapered octagonal cross-shaft with panelled sides and fleurons based on a C15 French example, commemorating the wounded Belgian servicemen and refugees who died while staying in Sheffield. BLITZ GRAVE of *c.*1941, a low wall enclosing a kidney-shaped enclosure and the WAR MEMORIAL cross by *Sir Reginald Blomfield, c.* 1920.

PARK LIBRARY, Duke Street. 1902. Watered-down Arts and Crafts style in red brick with shaped parapets and a tower to the rear. The grander side elevation originally gave access to baths.

MANOR LODGE SCHOOL (former), City Road/Manor Lane. 1877 by *Innocent & Brown*. A single-storey example of the first batch of Board Schools in the Gothic style. Additions by *Wightman & Wightman* of 1889 and, in the Renaissance style by *Charles Hadfield*, 1907.

SHEFFIELD CITY COLLEGE, Granville Road. By *Jefferson Sheard*, 2010. Three blocks, closely grouped with a full-height steel and glass atrium with curved profile in the centre, and topped by wind turbines. It replaced Sheffield College of 1958–61 by *J.L. Womersley*. The buildings to the S on Olive Grove Road by *Race Cottam Architects*, 2015.

MANOR LODGE
Manor Lane

The earliest documentary reference to a hunting lodge in the Park was in 1479–80, but its remains are few.

It is known to have comprised a rectangular structure in an outer courtyard with corner towers at the N ends, demolished in the second half of the C16, and successive structures have been found by excavations carried out 1969–79 under the C16 cross-wing and S courtyard. The lower stonework of the N half of the W front, known as the LONG GALLERY, is also late medieval. The upper part has the blocked remains of two four-light traceried windows.

Thomas Wolsey during his stay in 1529 lodged in a new tower, believed to be the block at the N end of the long gallery and now known as WOLSEY'S TOWER. The rebuilding of the upper story of the long gallery took place at the same time. A double courtyard layout emerged during the C16 with a smaller service court to the E. Much of the standing stonework in the s wing dates from the last half of the C16 and is likely to overlie and incorporate earlier structures. A cross-wing, dividing the two courtyards, underwent several stages of rebuilding and alteration in the C16. These works were undertaken as the Lodge was developed into the principal residence of the Lord of the Manor when Sheffield Castle fell out of favour.

The s half of the w wing represents a complete rebuild in the last half of the C16. This resulted in an imposing new entrance, flanked by brick-faced octagonal towers, a new courtyard and revised garden layout. It is possible that Bess of Hardwick, who was married to the 6th Earl of Shrewsbury (1570–84), may have had some hand in this and that the work was carried out to accommodate Mary, Queen of Scots, who was kept here under his custodianship. References are made in 1582 to 'the queens gallery there' and to 'the Quenes kitchen at the lodge'. After it passed (by marriage) to the Howards, the house was allowed to decay and it was largely demolished in 1708. Some surviving fragments (a piece of wall and mullioned window) were removed by Samuel Roberts about 1839 and re-erected in the grounds of Queen's Tower (*see* p. 565).

Architecturally more interesting than the scanty fragments of the main house is the Elizabethan summerhouse or stand-ing, called TURRET HOUSE, to the w. It was possibly begun in 1574 as there is a reference that may relate to it in a building account in the notebooks of William Dickinson, but is now as restored in 1873 by *M.E. Hadfield*, who reopened blocked windows and doors and removed others. Three-storeyed, of stone, with a higher circular angle turret of brick, it has diag-onally set chimneystacks and cross-windows. There are two rooms on each floor. The far room on the first floor retains a plaster ceiling with simple ribbed geometrical patterns. On the second floor, the most important room distinguished by a fine fireplace and elaborate plaster ceiling. The fireplace has an overmantel with two fat columns flanking the arms of George Talbot modelled in deep relief, the ceiling fashionably deco-rated in a pattern of eight-pointed stars with heads, leaves, flowers etc., all of the highest quality. The design incorporating a hand grasping a spray of flowers by the stems – a motif derived from Claude Paradin's *Devises heroiques* (1557) – rep-resents Mary Stuart's loss of freedom, reinforced by the depic-tion of Talbot dogs standing guard. It is possible that the decoration was carried out at the behest of Bess of Hardwick, who is symbolized in the choice of white briar roses or eglan-tine (the flowers on the Hardwick arms), and may be one of several examples of plasterwork with hidden meanings in buildings associated with her. Decorated frieze. The STAINED GLASS added during the 1873 restoration is by *J.F. Bentley* and was made by *Lavers, Barraud & Westlake*.

PERAMBULATION

One's first sight of the housing at PARK HILL is unforgettable.   110
It lines the eastern hillside above the Railway Station, providing a powerful if brutal horizontal accent that is visible from
much of the city centre. Topography is the key to understand-
ing why it was built and to the form of access that led to its
fame. The Park area identified by the City Council for building
the flats was the subject of the oldest outstanding slum clearance order in Sheffield, some of the land already having been
cleared in the 1930s. Proximity to the centre and to Don valley
industry, while remaining on the unpolluted windward side,
together with the topography of the land, made it suitable for
high-density housing at 193 persons per acre (net). The initial
idea evolved in 1953, when *J. L. Womersley* recruited *Jack Lynn*
and *Ivor Smith* to work on a housing scheme for Norfolk Park.*
When that was deferred, he gave them Park Hill and Hyde
Park to work on, assisted by *Frederick Nicklin*. The original
scheme was to have had blocks set at right angles to each other
on Park Hill with angled blocks for the development at Hyde
Park, higher up.

The go-ahead was given in 1955, work commenced in 1957
and it was completed in 1961. As built it comprises four blocks
varying in height from four storeys at the S end to fourteen at
the N, the sloping ground allowing the roof-line to remain level
throughout and all but the top deck to reach ground level at
some point. The blocks, which in plan resemble fragmentary
polygons, were linked by bridges at angles to enable the 10-ft
(3-metre)-wide access decks, provided on every third floor, to
shift from one side to the other so as to ensure that each got
as much sun as possible. The decks, each taking the names of
existing streets, were wide enough for small electric trolleys to
deliver milk, something that perhaps caught public imagina-
tion more than any other detail as 'streets in the sky'. The
decks were served by thirteen eight-person lifts located at the
ends of the blocks, together with three goods lifts, a total that
proved inadequate. On the ground floor was a shopping centre,
a laundry, a police station and four pubs. The blocks were so
arranged as to create courts within which a primary school and
a nursery school were eventually built, together with playgrounds. The playgrounds were provided with furniture (since
removed) designed by the abstract sculptor *John Forrester*, who
also advised on the modelling and colouring of the façades of
the blocks, street lighting and footpaths.

There were originally 994 dwellings for 3,448 persons in a
mixture of one- and two-bedroom flats and two- to four-
bedroomed maisonettes. The design was built around a

*The Norfolk Park Estate was built in 1967, along Park Grange Road, sw of Norfolk
Park, but cleared from 2004 and replaced with housing by *AXIS Architecture* and
HTA.

three-bay, three-storey unit with maisonettes at and above deck level and flats below, all dovetailed together with the front doors paired. To ensure quiet for the living rooms and bedrooms within each unit, internal back-to-back and interlocking staircases and halls were the only parts that abutted onto the decks. Within the grid of the elevations, the dominant motif is the concrete balustrades with closely spaced uprights that mark the decks and the balconies of the flats. Walls are of brick, differently coloured for each three-storey unit, which Pevsner found 'fussy'. Non-structural exterior and party walls could be varied as required enabling the complex internal arrangements of the flats to be expressed in the external grid. This expression of the structure fits the tough Brutalist ethos as much as the use of rough concrete, showing the impression of the timber shuttering used in its construction, praised by Reyner Banham for its 'gutsy finish', and the rejection of any attempt to hide function, most notably in the hammer-headed lift towers and exposed bridges.

From 2002, after an extended period of neglect and also the awarding of a Grade II* listing in 1998, refurbishment of Park Hill was commenced by the developers Urban Splash in collaboration with *Hawkins Brown*, *Studio Egret West* and *Grant Associates* for mixed-tenure housing and commercial uses in the lower floors. As part of the project, the communal social and commercial facilities have also been reintroduced and the landscaping restored. Still in progress in 2017, a substantial section of the building has been stripped back to the frame and refurbished with brightly coloured anodized aluminium panels in place of the original brickwork. The effect is unquestionably jollier and the elevational composition remains as before, with the exception of an arch opened through one end, but one must ask whether the fabric of pre-C20 listed buildings would be treated in this way.

HYDE PARK, which had 1,313 dwellings and was completed in 1966, was demolished in 1992. It rose to eighteen storeys with no opportunity to walk up from the level but it made a fine vertical counterpoint to Park Hill (compared by many in Sheffield to a castle keep). What remains, now isolated from each other, are the two lower blocks, CASTLE COURT and ST JOHN'S COURT, both re-clad, the decks glazed in and the entrances controlled by concierges. In their embrace is St John's church (*see* Churches). Immensely long blocks of three-storey maisonettes on HYDE PARK TERRACE and HYDE PARK WALK are equally unrecognizable today after refurbishment in 1990–1.

NORFOLK ROAD, s of Park Hill, begins with the SHREWSBURY HOSPITAL of 1825 by *Woodhead & Hurst*. A handsome group of almshouses in fine ashlar, Tudor, three ranges round a spacious court, single-storeyed with a taller central chapel. Ten more added to the E, again in Tudor style, in 1930, and between these and the road, two groups of pentagonal almshouses and a meeting hall by *Mansell Jenkinson & Partners*,

1976. Opposite, the CHOLERA MONUMENT, 1835 by *Weightman & Hadfield*, the Gothicist's equivalent for an obelisk. The rest of Norfolk Road is lined with substantial classical and Tudor villas from the 1830s to the 1880s. Nos. 72–74 are *c.* 1845 by *Weightman & Hadfield* for their own occupation, with bay windows on the ground floor. *Charles Hadfield* built Park Cottage (No. 84) for himself in 1875, but the house was much altered in the early C20. At No. 90, the Sale Memorial Vicarage of 1880 is a Gothic villa with an especially fine tall staircase window with wooden quatrefoils probably by *Flockton & Gibbs*, the architects of the Sale Memorial Church (dem.).

NORFOLK PARK ROAD has one house of significance, BEECH HILL. Described in 1831 as recently built, by *Woodhead & Hurst*. Tudor style with crowstepped gables and the Duke of Norfolk's coat of arms on the chimney. Extended in 1859 for the Duke's agent Matthew Ellison. The 15th Duke retained it as his Sheffield home from 1898. His previous house, The Farm, was another Tudor fantasy, demolished in 1967.

NORFOLK PARK itself was laid out for the public in 1841–8 by the 12th Duke of Norfolk and was by then all that remained of his manorial park. LODGES on Norfolk Park Road (1841) and Granville Road (1851), both pretty in the Tudor style with elaborate fretted bargeboards and tall chimneys. The screen wall on Granville Road of 1876 by *M.E. Hadfield & Son*, in C15 style with big octagonal stone piers and a long pierced stone balustrade incorporating quatrefoils. In front, an impressive Gothic iron gas LAMP. Presented to the City in 1912, and of this date, a restored Ionic stone ARCH, carved with an image of the 15th Duke. Originally the porch of a pavilion, it now forms the entrance to a viewing platform near to the CENTRE IN THE PARK of 1998–2000 by *DBS Architects*, single-storeyed, successfully blending with the contours of the park, in a continuous gentle curve which becomes sharper at one end. The other end is taken up with a drum.

EAST BANK ROAD, further SW, was a cul de sac of large houses built in the early C19 with leases from the Duke of Norfolk. QUEEN'S TOWER, 1839 by *Woodhead & Hurst*, is a remarkably romantic gesture by Samuel Roberts, a silver plate manufacturer and antiquary who was an enthusiast for Mary, Queen of Scots and who saw in the house a way of honouring her. The house, which was a wedding present for his son, also named Samuel, is inevitably a mixture of Tudor motifs with embattled walls, towers and turrets, and has a crenellated lodge. It was enlarged in the 1860s and converted to flats in 2003–4. Large stable court and an archway in matching style. In the grounds, laid out by *Robert Marnock*, were fragments of old wall and a mullioned window from Manor Lodge (*see* p. 562) which have now disappeared.

Off MANOR LANE, housing in SKYE EDGE AVENUE. Long low 1970s terraces of striking design, by *Ivor Smith & Hutton*, crown the ridge with spectacular views over the city.

SOUTH

(Highfield, Lowfield, Heeley and Meersbrook)

PLACES OF WORSHIP

HEELEY PARISH CHURCH (CHRIST CHURCH), Gleadless
Road. 1846–8 by *Joseph Mitchell*. A large and well-proportioned
cruciform church with the tower unusually over the N transept
rather than the crossing. Dec style with reticulated tracery in
the E and transept windows, ambitious flowing tracery similar
to that at Holbeach, Lincolnshire, in the W window. Nave
lengthened by one bay and N aisle and vestry added in 1890
by *J.D. Webster*. S aisle added in 1897. Large heads of kings,
queens and angels decorate corbels. Arch-braced principal-
rafter roof with kingposts in the nave, traceried spandrels in
the chancel braces and a timber vault in the crossing. The two
W bays have been enclosed for community use. – STAINED
GLASS. E window of 1913 and E window of S transept by *Mayer
& Co.* of Munich. Large OBELISK in the churchyard to John
Shortridge †1869.

ST BARNABAS, Highfield Place. 1874–6, by *Flockton & Abbott*.
E.E. with plate tracery, very tall aisles, an apsidal chancel and
a (ritual) SW tower with large openings on each face. Now
converted to housing.

ST MARY, Bramall Lane. 1826–30 by *Joseph & Robert Potter*. An
especially large and handsome Commissioners' church with
140-ft (43-metre) W tower with tall pinnacles. Substantial buttresses also with large crocketed pinnacles. Tall Perp three-
light windows divided by a deep transom with tracery below.
Grotesque headstops. Very short chancel. Damaged by
bombing, the W part was a pioneer conversion of 1950 by
Stephen Welsh into a community centre. The rigid division of
the church was softened by *APEC Architects* in 1999–2000,
who removed the 1950 work and created a new community
centre of two floors and a mezzanine filling all but the chancel
and the two E bays of the nave, which are still used for worship.
– STAINED GLASS. E window by *Helen Whittaker* 2008.

HIGHFIELD TRINITY METHODIST CHURCH, Highfield Place/
London Road. 1877–9 by *J.D. Webster*. An impressive early
work by this prolific local architect, most of whose work was
for the Anglicans, and designed to take them on architecturally.
Geometric tracery in the W window, the remainder lancets. A
range of large clerestory windows breaks through the eaves, the
resulting gables giving some vigour to the side elevations.
Tower with prominent angle buttresses extending to form pinnacles and tall spire. Interior rebuilt in the 1970s. Next door
in Highfield Place, the WESLEY INSTITUTE of 1905–6, in an
elegant Tudor style by *C & C.M.E. Hadfield*.

CHINESE CHRISTIAN CHURCH, Anns Road, Heeley. Formerly
St Andrew's Primitive Methodist church and Sunday School.
1895–7, by *J. Taylor*. Large, free Gothic, in rock-faced stone
on the street elevations and brick elsewhere. Two large windows

each of two lights with plate tracery in the gabled centre, four lancets below. Entrances in the bays l. and r. The school entrance on Anns Road is marked by a gable.

HEELEY INSTITUTE, No. 147 Gleadless Road. Former Wesleyan Methodist chapel of 1826. Simple, with three round-arched windows and coped gables, restored and extended in 2001 as a community centre.

SHEFFIELD ISLAMIC CENTRE MADINA MASJID, Wolseley Road. The first purpose-built mosque in the city, completed 2006. Brick with a pair of tall minarets.

PUBLIC BUILDINGS

MEERSBROOK VESTRY HALL (former), Meersbrook Park Road. Now flats. 1903–4 by *Joseph Norton*. Excellent Free Baroque in brick with ashlar dressings. Three-bay N façade with a bowed oriel. Small corner tower topped with a square timber cupola with balusters and a lead dome. At the rear is a hall with each bay divided by battered buttresses.

HIGHFIELD LIBRARY, London Road, of 1876 by *Flockton & Gibbs*. Florentine Renaissance style similar to the Upperthorpe Library (*see* p. 595) but with an oriel window at the N end and a house for the librarian attached to the rear. Figure sculptures representing Medical Science and Literature by *J. W. Cooper* flank a quotation from Carlyle above the entrance.

HEELEY SWIMMING POOL, Broadfield Road. The Public Baths of 1909 by *Arthur Nunweek*. Red brick and stone Neo-Baroque with a Gibbs surround to the entrance and a tall chimney to the boiler house.

BOARD SCHOOLS: LOWFIELD PRIMARY SCHOOL, London Road/Queens Road. 1874 by *Innocent & Brown* with two well-detailed Gothic single-storey buildings, one with a short tower and turret, squeezed into a restricted site. – HEELEY BANK COMMUNITY CENTRE, Myrtle Road, is the former Heeley Bank School by *E. R. Robson*, 1880. It blends the Sheffield school idiom with the style of his London schools in the use of Renaissance gables crowned with miniature pediments common to both. A pair of chimneys are each enlivened by a pediment halfway up and linked by a balustraded arch. – HEELEY BOARD SCHOOL (former), Gleadless Road and Hartley Street, remains a large and complete example of 1890–2 in Free Renaissance style by *C. J. Innocent*. Girls' department with cookery school added in 1899. Converted as Sum Studios in 2013 by *Gedye Studio* for Heeley Development Trust.

HEELEY STATION (former), London Road. 1901 by the Midland Railway's architect, *Charles Trubshaw*, in his characteristic style. Red brick with plenty of terracotta dressings (now overpainted).

DRILL HALL (former), Clough Road/Edmund Road. 1878–80 by *M. E. Hadfield & Son* for the 4th West York Artillery Volunteers. Red brick, Tudor style with tall gate-tower over the entrance with the arms of the Duke of Norfolk carved by *W. S.*

Gillman and a machicolated top stage. The 180 ft by 90 ft (55 by 27.5 metres) hall has shallow cast-iron lattice trusses by *Andrew Handyside*. The arch ribs spring from the floor in the manner of St Pancras Station, bearing on brick buttresses. Between each buttress is a shallow pointed arch. On the w side, stables and a riding school added by 1889.

BRAMALL LANE FOOTBALL GROUND. Founded as a cricket ground in 1855; home of Sheffield United since 1889. The earliest surviving stand, along Bramall Lane, was erected in 1966, the s stand by *Husband & Co.* from 1975 and the John Street Stand for 6,842 in 1996. E stand of 1982.

HEELEY CITY FARM, Richards Road. VISITOR CENTRE of 2001 by *Andrew Yeats* of *Eco Arch*. L-shaped energy-efficient range of buildings with rendered blockwork walls, overhanging eaves, super-insulated sedum roof and solar panels. A curved stable block has an arcade of rough timber posts in a self-consciously primitive manner.

PERAMBULATIONS

1. Highfield and Lowfield

LONDON ROAD begins at St Mary's Gate, with the former SHEFFIELD UNION BANK (now Ban Thai restaurant) of 1894 by *J. B. Mitchell-Withers & Son*. Lively Baroque with giant pilasters superimposed one upon another, tightly modelled with narrow window bays and heavily rusticated banding. Further s on the other side of London Road, the former LANS-DOWNE CINEMA (now Sainsburys) of 1914 by *Walter G. Buck*, Moorish style with suitably oriental arches in the windows and a splendid pagoda tower on the corner. Beautiful green and white faience. Nothing else of interest until further s of London Road in QUEENS ROAD, where the HEELEY BANK ANTIQUES CENTRE is a former Sheffield Savings Bank, dated 1900. The interior has a glazed office, counter and Art Nouveau tiling.

E and W of BRAMALL LANE was an industrial enclave. s of St Mary's church (*see* Churches) in CLOUGH ROAD, on the corner with Countess Road is CHAUCER YARD, the former Wardonia Works of Thomas W. Ward Ltd, which made razor blades. It shows the domestic scale of much of Sheffield's cutlery trade, with mid-C19 houses and a small cutlery works of *c.* 1879 (India Works) on Clough Road. Now small work-shops. w of Bramall Lane, STAG WORKS in JOHN STREET (now apartments) was built in 1877 by *J. H. Jenkinson* for Lee & Wigfull, makers of silver and electroplated goods. It has thirteen bays and is of three storeys with a mansard roof. Large rear yard, workshops with monopitch roofs. To the N in DENBY STREET, KENILWORTH WORKS of the late 1860s and early 1870s, occupied in the C19 and early C20 by George Tandy, manufacturer of horn and tortoiseshell combs. Its front range follows the curve of the road, behind is a yard and rear range.

Windows are the usual Sheffield workshop casements. To the
s in RANDALL STREET, at the corner of Hill Street, PORT-
LAND WORKS of 1877 by *J. H. Jenkinson* and built in one phase
for R. F. Mosley, cutlery manufacturer. Rounded corner with
a two-storey entrance gateway with rusticated pilasters and
window arches of cream brickwork contrasted with red. On
the ground floor of the w workshop range, there are the best-
preserved examples of hand forges in the city. These may have
been let separately and retain combined stable-type doors and
a window, under a rolled-steel lintel.

2. Heeley and Meersbrook

GLEADLESS ROAD was the heart of Heeley and opposite the
church and the former Board School (*see above*) in WILSON
PLACE is a survival of Heeley's rural past: No. 10, a simple
stone barn of *c.* 1600, with a cruck frame; it was used as a
foundry for much of the C20. ⅓ m. E in DENMARK ROAD,
DERBY PLACE and DERBY TERRACE are groups of four
stepped-back terraces of FLATS of 1978–9 by *Sheffield City
Council* (project architects *John Taylor* and *Peter Jackson*) on a
steep s-facing hillside. They look as though they have been
transplanted from California's Marin County or Laurel
Canyon. Elderly people live on the top two floors, families on
the ground floor, the latter enjoying private gardens. The flats
are deck-access and have extensively glazed façades articulated
by projecting greenhouse porches and rainwater spouts carried
forward on slim timber brackets.

sw of here, in LONDON ROAD s of the River Sheaf, a few items
of interest, including the WHITE LION (No. 615). Ground
floor and much of the interior 1920s. The back portion may
date from 1781 but was extended towards the road between
1877 and 1884. It still retains snugs and a private smoke room.
Green tiles and elaborate 1920s coloured glass. London Road's
continuation s of the Meers Brook and the railway is CHES-
TERFIELD ROAD. Here MEERSBROOK BUILDINGS was a
tannery built *c.* 1870 for Francis Colley & Sons, manufacturers
of machinery belts. Extensive front range, three storeys with a
central stone pediment, segmental arcading and pilasters.
Round the corner in VALLEY ROAD, the former MEERS-
BROOK SAW WORKS (now Meersbrook Enterprise Centre) of
Joseph Tyzack & Co. Built *c.* 1880. A long three-storey range
of twenty-one bays. The central pediment has the firm's three-
legged trademark.

w of the railway, in BROADFIELD ROAD, the former EXPRESS
DAIRY of 1939. One of the city's few Modern Movement-style
buildings. Well-mannered and restrained brick and rendered
design with a glazed semicircular stair-turret. To the N in
AIZLEWOOD ROAD, the former FINBAT WORKS conceals a
rare surviving Hoffman BRICK KILN. Built 1878–9 for the
Sheffield Patent Brick Co. Oval in shape with a vaulted tunnel

inside and a central service tunnel. Uniquely, it was converted for car production, as the paintshop for the Richardson Light Car, 1919–22. N on KILN STREET is the LOXLEY BROTHERS PRINTING WORKS. Classical façade with a raised centre, rebuilt in 1923 after a fire. Paired Doric columns with a projecting entablature and a deeply chamfered doorway with prominent rustication. To the W on ABBEYDALE ROAD is the former ABBEYDALE PICTURE HOUSE of 1920 by *Dixon & Stienlet*. The most impressive of Sheffield's surviving suburban cinemas. Built with a fly tower enabling its use as a theatre and refurbished for that purpose in 2008 but closed again in 2012. It also had a ballroom and billiard hall. Steel-framed with a façade in white faience, splendid if coarse decoration of swags and with a row of circular windows and a domed turret over the entrance. The disused interior retains much of its classical decoration.

MEERSBROOK PARK, Brook Road. Formed in 1886. Late C18 hall. Two storeys, brick, the N front of five bays with a canted bay window. The S front has pedimented wings and a recessed centre with a Venetian stair window. Modillion eaves. The house was extended to the W in the late C19 in similar style but treated more elaborately with stone bands and a triple-arched loggia forming a new entrance. Adjoining mid-C19 stone offices.

SOUTH-WEST

(Sharrow, Nether Edge and Brincliffe)

CHURCHES

ST ANDREW, Psalter Lane. 1928–30 by *T. A. Teather*. Built as a United Methodist church. Very traditional in Perp style with bulky towers flanking a broad W window. Reordered in 2002 by *Barlow, Wright & Phelps* to provide a narthex. – STAINED GLASS. E window of 2002 by *Rona Moody*, representing the Creation with light pouring from a golden source into a rich blue darkness.

MOTHER OF GOD AND ST WILFRID (R.C.), Abbeydale Road/ St Ronan's Road. Formerly a Congregational chapel and school by *Hemsoll & Paterson*. Schoolrooms built 1883–4, chapel 1899–1901. Both are large, of rock-faced stone, in free E.E. style.

BAPTIST CHURCH, Cemetery Road. 1859, by *Flockton & Son*. Strange Romanesque design with gable facing the road inset with a large rose window flanked by two octagonal turrets.

UNITED METHODIST FREE CHAPEL, Union Road. Classical, twin doorways with Ionic pilasters and a heavily modelled pediment

MONTGOMERY CHAPEL (now the King's Centre), Union Road. By *Wilson & Crosland*. Tall, Gothic, with a steeply pitched roof.

SHARROW VALE WESLEYAN REFORM CHAPEL (former), Sharrow Vale Road. 1902. Simple classical red brick. Now the Crowded House gospel church.

GENERAL CEMETERY, Cemetery Avenue. Built by the joint stock Sheffield General Cemetery Co. (formed 1834) and opened in 1836 as one of the first group of provincial cemeteries. It retains its original buildings, making it possibly the best pre-1850 cemetery outside London. The City Council acquired the cemetery in 1977.

Samuel Worth initially laid out the cemetery and its buildings for Nonconformists. The design, like all early British cemeteries, was influenced by Père Lachaise in Paris in its picturesque layout of sweeping drives among evergreens. Worth's use of an Egypto-Greek style is possibly one of the first examples in an English cemetery, followed shortly after by Bartholomew Street Cemetery, Exeter, in 1837 and Highgate Cemetery, London, 1839–42.

The principal entrance to the cemetery was from Cemetery Avenue, at the end of which is a GATEWAY with Greek Doric columns *in antis* which forms a bridge over the River Porter. The driveway then sweeps up the hillside in a gentle curve so as to draw the eye to the climax of the cemetery, the NONCONFORMIST CHAPEL, which has a Greek Doric tetrastyle portico with a triglyph frieze, Egyptian-style windows (originally iron-framed) and doorway and the bases of the former acroteria along the eaves. The processional route from the gateway to the chapel was designed to offer views across the Porter valley. To the N of the road, two curved tiers of CATACOMBS were built with massive battered retaining walls,

Sheffield, General Cemetery.
Engraving, 1836

punctuated by plain oblong openings, intended to be closed by iron gates. They were not a success: only ten were sold in the first ten years. The upper tier has a concrete balustrade added by *Hodkin & Jones* in 1936. The CEMETERY OFFICES in Cemetery Road have an austere ashlar façade with Doric pilasters, a pedimented gable on the road elevation and Egyptian windows on single-storey wings. The ENTRANCE to Cemetery Road nearby is again Egyptian with a behudet (winged sun motif) on the cornice.

By the late 1840s the cemetery was filling up and the Cemetery Company commissioned *Robert Marnock* to lay out a new Anglican cemetery to the E. The CHAPEL by *William Flockton* 1848–50 is Dec with a tall broach spire on a tower whose lower stage is open as a porch. Among the MONUMENTS may be mentioned those to William Parker of 1837, based on the Choragic Monument of Lysicrates; John Fowler, father of the engineer Sir John Fowler, of 1845, by *Edwin Smith*, with a relief of a dying tree in a niche below a rounded arch; George Bennet, a missionary †1850, also with a relief by *Smith* showing him leaning on a globe with a palm tree behind; Thomas Burch, 1870, a 15-ft (4.5-metre) column topped by an urn; the Nicholson family, *c.* 1872, a chest tomb with a statue of a woman praying on the top; and Mark Firth of 1869–76, a pedestal, topped by a draped urn and with railings made in his Norfolk Works.

PUBLIC BUILDINGS

BLUECOAT SCHOOL (former), Psalter Lane. Now housing. 1911 by *Gibbs & Flockton* (succeeding the first school in East Parade, *see* p. 532); College of Art from 1945 to 2008. Neo-Georgian, H-shaped, two storeys with the seven-bay N front relieved by the central three bays brought forward with an open pediment over the centre.

CLIFFORD SCHOOL, Psalter Lane. Dated 1832. Symmetrical Tudor style with an oriel window over a Gothic door. Extended 1896.

HUNTERS BAR INFANT and JUNIOR SCHOOLS, Sharrow Vale Road. By *A. F. Watson* of 1893, with a squat pyramidal tower, coped gables and C17 vernacular detailing. A second block of 1907 by the same architect is larger but plainer.

PORTERCROFT SCHOOL, Pomona Street. 1900 by *Holmes & Watson*. Elaborately Mannerist shaped parapets to the gables and buttresses that turn into pilasters above the ground floor.

NETHER EDGE HOSPITAL. *See* ECCLESALL BIERLOW WORKHOUSE.

ECCLESALL BIERLOW WORKHOUSE (former), Union Road. 1842–3 by *William Flockton*; E-shaped, Elizabethan style, of three storeys with gables, canted bay windows and a large clock above the entrance. To the rear, a screen, formerly part of a roofed arcade, of four-centred arches and with a battlemented parapet runs the length of the building. Enlarged with flat-roofed wings either side of the central block in 1894 and an infirmary block to the rear in 1895, both by *J. D. Webster*. Multiple other C19 additions for the workhouse infirmary etc. All built of rock-faced coursed masonry with lengthy sparsely fenestrated elevations punctuated by dormers and chimney-stacks. It became Nether Edge Hospital in 1929 and was converted to housing by *Gleesons* in 2000–3. Opposite the entrance on Union Road are the UNION OFFICES by *Holmes & Watson*, 1902. Neo-Georgian with a central open pediment and deeply moulded main entrance.

PERAMBULATIONS

1. Sharrow

SHARROW lies W of London Road (*see* p. 568). In SHARROW LANE, the former SHEFFIELD & HALLAMSHIRE BANK of *c.* 1890 has a semicircular corner porch with giant granite columns and a pediment incorporating a clock above. Red brick embellished with stone pilasters, enriched window surrounds, base and dentilled band. Beyond it is MOUNT PLEASANT, built in 1777 by *John Platt* for Francis Hurt and one of the best C18 houses in Sheffield. Brick-built, three storeys of five bays on the principal (E) façade, the central three brought forward and given a pediment. A Venetian window on the first floor is set in an arch with a balustrade below. Pedimented doorcase with Adamesque swags in the frieze and attached Corinthian columns. The S elevation has a full-height canted bay window. The arcaded stable block also has a Venetian window. The principal ground-floor room is an unequal octagon with scalloped niches in the two shortest walls and Adamesque ceiling.

N from here as far as Cemetery Road, four-storey deck-access maisonette blocks and three sixteen-storey point blocks of the LANSDOWNE ESTATE, built by the City Council in the 1960s. The towers have been re-clad. In their shadow on the N side of CEMETERY ROAD, the Gothic former VESTRY HALL of 1857. Uphill to the W, the Baptist church and General Cemetery (*see* above). S of the Cemetery, hidden behind later building, is SHARROW HEAD HOUSE (No. 311 Cemetery Road) believed to be by *John Platt* in 1763 for William Battie, an attorney. Brick, two storeys with an attic, the roof hipped and with a modillion eaves cornice. Diocletian window set within a pediment.

W, at the top of SHARROW VALE ROAD, is WESTBROOK COURT, the former Westbrook Mill of J. & H. Wilson, built in 1831. Plain, stone, three storeys with a pediment on the N façade, surrounded by many later additions. It was converted to offices after 1989 but still retains an oven room on the first floor with a round brick vault. Further downhill on Sharrow Vale Road, WESTBROOK HOUSE was built for the Wilsons in 1794–5. Brick of five bays on the N front, central doorcase with attached Doric columns linked to the first-floor window by a balustraded apron. Gabled rear with a Venetian window. Now apartments with C21 additions. The SHARROW SNUFF MILLS lie below the house to the NW, across the Porter Brook. A grinding wheel existed on the site by 1604 and Joseph Wilson introduced snuff grinding *c.* 1740. The mill of this date is of stone with strutted kingpost roofs, still domestic in scale. Although steam was introduced in 1796, the 19-ft (5.8-metre) water wheel is still in working order and drives sixteen weighted iron pestles around a post. The late C18 brick MANAGER's HOUSE has an open pedimented doorcase and modillion eaves. Adjoining, an early C19 COUNTING HOUSE, also in brick, completes what is a picturesque and well-maintained group. Behind these a complex of buildings built around a courtyard that include an early C19 warehouse and stable, the red brick New Mill of *c.* 1885 by *Wightman & Wightman* (doubled in width in matching style in the early C20) and a large L-shaped stable block built between 1819 and 1825 with pitching eyes, stone-walled to the N elevation, the remainder of brick.

NE of here towards Ecclesall Road, in POMONA STREET, are the Portercroft School (*see* Public Buildings) and BOW WORKS for the manufacture of steel measuring tape (invented by James Chesterman, whose firm moved here in 1864). The façades of the long street front are of 1891 onwards but the long narrow blocks behind, where the tape was made (akin to those employed in rope works), are of 1871 by *W. J. Hemsoll*. Restored and extended in an unexciting manner by *Hadfield Cawkwell & Davidson & Partners* in 1993.

ECCLESALL ROAD running SW from the city centre begins with the remains of the SHEAF BREWERY. Some stone buildings from the 1850s, a three-storey brick block converted from back-to-backs and the plain brick brewery tower of 1874 have been submerged within the Sheaf Island residential development of 2001–2 by *Finnegan Design and Build*.

2. Nether Edge and Brincliffe

A tour of NETHER EDGE might begin in KENWOOD PARK ROAD at the gates of KENWOOD (Marriott Hotel), built in 1844 by *William Flockton*, for George Wostenholm, one of the city's largest cutlery manufacturers. Relatively modest in size, the house is in the then favoured Tudor Gothic style in limestone quarried at Stanton, Derbyshire. The grounds were laid out by *Robert Marnock* and those parts nearest the hotel, which include a lake, survive. Enlarged 1882–3 with a large canted bay window by *Flockton & Gibbs* and many subsequent additions by *J. Mansell Jenkinson* following conversion to a temperance hotel in 1924. Imposing GATEHOUSE of *c.* 1868 at the junction of Kenwood and Kenwood Park Roads with a Gothic archway and lodge to the side. A coat of arms over the arch is by *Harry Hems*, Wostenholm's nephew.

Wostenholm named his house after a town near Oneida Lake, New York that had particularly impressed him. Inspired by this and other American suburban developments, he decided to emulate their pattern on land around Cherry Tree Hill. *Marnock* was employed in 1851–61 to lay out picturesquely curving roads, radiating from a rond-point outside the principal gate to Kenwood. Although many of the houses on the estate are smaller than Wostenholm had originally envisaged and are unspectacular, the layout is noteworthy as an example of a planned middle-class development. The largest houses were built over a thirty-year period on Kenwood Park Road, Kenwood Road and Priory Road and are generally Gothic, of two storeys with big attic gables and ornate bargeboards. Around 1900 a new style, less heavy and with plenty of applied half-timbering, is apparent. In KENWOOD PARK ROAD, unique in Sheffield and rare elsewhere, the cottage-like private LANTERN THEATRE, built *c.* 1893 by William Webster, a cutlery manufacturer who lived in the adjacent house.

In RUNDLE ROAD, STONEYGATE (No. 10) of 1925 by *J. Mansell Jenkinson* for himself, is the finest of his houses but submerged in extensions of 2003–4. Firmly in the Cotswolds Arts and Crafts tradition with leaded-light casements, stone-tiled steep-pitched roofs and uncoursed stone walling. KENWOOD CROFT, in Kenwood Road also by *Mansell Jenkinson*, 1925 displays many of the same features on a larger scale. Back in Rundle Road, No. 47 (SPRING LEIGH) is a little-altered classical villa of 1868 for Henry Booth, cutlery manufacturer. Extensive gardens laid out by *Marnock*.

To the E of MONTGOMERY ROAD, there are several roads laid out 1863–83 by the speculative builder *Thomas Steade*, who had worked closely with Wostenholm. Steade, who had set up an iron foundry in the late 1850s, used many cast-iron details: lintels in the shape of a pediment are the most distinctive. His houses are broadly Gothic with bargeboarded gables on narrow plots. To the S of this, in MONCRIEFFE ROAD, No. 16 of 1879 is an entertaining showpiece for the architectural joinery sold by its builder and owner, *John Johnson*. Good timber Gothic porch. SW of here, most of the roads were laid out from the mid C19 on the estate of the Newbould family, who owned virtually all the land known as Cherry Tree Hill. On the corner of Cherry Tree Road and St Andrew's Road, SHIRLE HILL (now hospital and school) of 1809 owned by John Brown while Endcliffe Hall (*see* p. 588) was being completed. His managing director, William Bragge, then occupied the house which, in 1865, he extended with a large Italianate wing by *Frith Brothers & Jenkinson* and refronted the older house to match. An odd mixture of rendered elevations, enriched stone lintels and rusticated giant pilasters which terminate in elaborate finials on the older part. A tall Italianate tower to the rear. Further SW, WILLIAMSON ROAD has some attractive villas. No. 7 with a squat pyramidal tower over the door was built by *John Law*, curator of the Botanical Gardens.

Due S, in MEADOW BANK ROAD, the Expressionist MERLIN THEATRE, completed in 1969 by *Black Bayes & Gibbs*, as part of a Rudolf Steiner centre in the grounds of TINTAGEL HOUSE, a Tudor villa by *Joseph Mitchell* of *c.* 1855. The entrance screen is derived directly from that of Steiner's Goetheanum in Dornach, Switzerland, and other doors and windows, together with the proscenium arch of the theatre, employ the distinctive organic forms favoured by Steiner. The ten-sided theatre is concrete-framed, stone-clad externally and brick within. Fly tower to the S. Its most distinctive feature externally are the eyebrow-like windows lighting the top floor, and the complex tiled roof.

MEADOW BANK AVENUE was laid out *c.* 1896 with a rectangular central lawn and gated entry but the houses are mostly unremarkable. Further S, in LADYSMITH AVENUE, THE EDGE is a rarity; a late C18 house probably by *Joseph Badger*, with an austere five-bay brick front, the rest in coursed stone. Canted two-storey bay at the rear with a full-height window.

The SW part of Nether Edge is characterized by a grid laid out by *Samuel Holmes* from 1853 on land rising steeply to Brincliffe Edge to the S, initially for the Reform Freehold Building Society. No requirements concerning the treatment of elevations were set out and the resulting houses show a pleasant if unremarkable profusion of styles. Many are small and quite plain three-bay detached houses, mostly of stone, many the work of *Scargill & Clark*.

The suburb of BRINCLIFFE, situated on high ground W of Union Road, is grander than Nether Edge, characterized by very large villas set in extensive grounds and rivalling Ranmoor (*see* p. 589) in their scale. The earliest was BRINCLIFFE TOWER, Chelsea Road, of 1852 for James Wilson, solicitor and Clerk to the Cutlers' Company. Highly picturesque Tudor house on a raised terrace with two gabled wings linked by a three-storey crenellated tower with a traceried oriel window. N of this and near the top of the ridge, CAVENDISH and OSBORNE ROADS have large houses of the 1860s and later with all the trappings of later C19 suburbia: laurels, monkey puzzle trees and pines. No. 6, THE TOWERS (formerly Brincliffe Grove), in Brincliffe Crescent, of 1874 for an accountant, Alfred Allott, is arguably the finest of the city's many late C19 Gothic houses. Almost certainly by *Innocent & Brown*, who are recorded as responsible for the substantial stables, it shares the skilled handling of Gothic detail, massing and picturesque skyline of the firm's Board Schools. The garden front is divided into two parts, that on the r. of twin gables clasping a rounded three-storey tower in the French manner with a high conical roof, balanced by that on the l., which has a lower tower. Extensive and finely executed carved decoration throughout; blind tracery above the windows, inset panels between storeys on the towers and gargoyles. Oriel window to the l. return and carved crest. The entrance façade has a big columned porch with birds carved on the capitals. The interior retains much of its Gothic character.

WEST

(Broomhill, Broomhall, Endcliffe, Ranmoor, Tapton and Carsick)

CHURCHES

ST AUGUSTINE, Brocco Bank, Endcliffe. By *J. D. Webster*, 1897–8, and in his usual E.E. 95-ft (29-metre) tower with a stair-turret, pinnacles, a pierced parapet and a spirelet. Three large openings on each side. The church has groups of triple lancets in the clerestory and single lancets in the aisles. Interior crudely divided in 1973 to create a hall from the rear three bays. Large arches for unbuilt transepts continue the nave arcading. – SCREEN (war memorial). Resited at the W end of the nave. 1920, designed by *Temple Moore*, carved by *F. Tory & Sons*. – STAINED GLASS. William Favell Memorial E window by *Kempe*, 1901; other windows by *Kempe & Co.* in N and S aisles. – MONUMENT. Mary Eddershaw, painting of the Angel in the Marketplace by the *Bromsgrove Guild*.

ST JOHN, Ranmoor Park Road, Ranmoor. Of the first church, by *E. M. Gibbs*, 1879, only the tower and spire survived a disastrous fire in 1887, and these were incorporated into the replacement, also by *Gibbs* (of *Flockton & Gibbs*), 1888. Opulent outside and inside, the church has an apsidal chancel, transepts, nave with N and S aisles, narthex, baptistery and vestries. The SW tower, with its large gabled bell-openings and tall spire, forms a porch. The walls are built in rock-faced Ancaster stone with ashlar dressings and articulated with sturdy gabled buttresses and decorative corbel tables below the slate roofs. The style is E.E., with Geometrical tracery.

The elegant proportions of the interior are matched by the outstanding quality and richness of its detailing and fittings, the only jarring notes some of the alterations made in the controversial reordering by *R. G. Sims* in 1991. At the W end the intimate space of the little baptistery, with octagonal rib-vault, opens off the narthex. From this a triple-arched opening gives access to the impressively spacious NAVE of five bays, heightened by the introduction of a triforium, a most unusual feature. It has two pairs of arches to each bay and continues across the W end below the big rose window in the gable. Plain round piers to the arcade and slender shafts to the upper stages, the exquisitely and densely carved capitals and corbels by *Frank Tory*. The octagonal chancel has blind arcades on each side; those to the N and S have sedilia under cusped arches. Slim wall-shafts with delicately carved capitals supporting the wooden ribs of the vault, which has flowing vine scrolls painted in red and green. Stone and marble REREDOS (Last Supper) by *Tory*, 1888. – Oak PULPIT, also 1888, on stone and marble columns. Elaborately carved arcades on each side with

figures of the Evangelists under nodding canopies at the corners. –
Stone FONT on a fat marble column, its carved base with
open trefoil arches on short marble shafts. Conical mahogany
and oak cover of 1975 suspended on wrought-iron stand by
Sims, 1991. – Superb brass LECTERN, 1892, with lions and
angels. – STAINED GLASS. Mostly animated groups of figures
in New Testament scenes, with architectural surrounds.
Chancel E windows all of 1890, the Crucifixion by *W. F. Dixon*,
flanked by the Entombment and Resurrection by *Heaton,
Butler & Bayne* and the Baptism of Christ and Christ Bearing
the Cross by *Powell Bros* – S transept (Lady Chapel). Good
Shepherd (1898) and Good Samaritan (1897) by *Clayton &
Bell*, who also made the chancel S window and three in the S
aisle. The other S aisle windows by *W. F. Dixon*, 1893 (Adoration
of the Magi) and 1894 (Christ Blessing the Children). Baptistery. By *Shrigley & Hunt*, 1888. – Rose window 1914 and two
in the N aisle †1915 and 1921 by *Victor Milner*.

ST MARK, St Mark's Crescent, Broomhill. 1868–71 by *W. H.
Crossland* but only the handsome Gothic tower with spire
(shorn of its crockets) and S porch survived bombing in 1940.
To this *George Pace* added a new church in 1958–63 that bril-
liantly succeeds in balancing a sympathy for Gothic form with
the smooth, hard, mechanical forms of Modernism. Concrete,
partly rubble-faced and with ashlar dressings, harmonizing
with the remains of Crossland's church. The shape is an irregular hexagon, with a nave of even width, but aisle or passage
spurs l. and r. and a broad area for the choir to the NE, which
produces the irregularity of outline. Slit-windows in two to
three tiers, the tiers jumping about, i.e. not all starting or
ending at the same levels, showing the influences of Le Corbusier's Ronchamp. The view from the narthex is one of serene
beauty, the light shining onto smooth walls, partly blocked by
a plain beam similar to Pace's use of the pulpitum in Llandaff
Cathedral to break the vista from the W door. – FURNISHINGS
by *Pace* include the choir stalls, font and a stone lectern and
pulpit. In the NE corner, a fine ORGAN CASE whose pronounced vertical bars act as a counterpoint to the E
window. – STAINED GLASS. Abstract W window, by *John Piper*
and *Patrick Reyntiens* 1963. E window (Te Deum) with good
Expressionist figures by *H. J. Stammers* 1963, both providing
brilliant colour to offset the predominantly white interior.

ST SILAS, Broomhall Street. Now redundant. By *J. B. Mitchell-
Withers*, 1867–9. Five-bay nave with a SW tower, generally E.E.
with plate tracery but with a four-light Dec-style E window.

ST ANDREW UNITED REFORMED CHURCH, Upper Hanover
Street, Broomhall. 1855–6 by *Flockton & Son*, originally for
Scots Presbyterians. Tall spire rising out of a short (ritual) SW
tower. The straight-headed side windows make much use of
trefoils in the tracery. Dec-style W window. Interior gutted in
1940. Its replacement is by *Teather & Hadfield*. – STAINED
GLASS. 1963 by *Donald Robertson*.

BAPTIST CHURCH, (former), Glossop Road. Now Sheffield University Drama Studio. 1871 by *Innocent & Brown*, the schools to the rear along Shearwood Road extended by the same architects in 1886. Large and impressive Gothic chapel with gabled aisles and a slim (ritual) SW tower and spire. Tripartite chancel arch with big piers, the spandrels above pierced by large openings. Converted to its present use in 1970 by *Alec Daykin*.

BROOMPARK CONGREGATIONAL CHURCH (former), Newbould Lane. 1864, by *Innocent & Brown*, enlarged with transepts, apse and vestries in 1870. A W porch and spire were intended but not built. Low (ritual) NE tower with pyramidal roof. The nave windows have plate tracery, the transepts rose windows and the apse, large quatrefoils. Now converted to housing.

TRINITY UNITED REFORMED CHURCH, Ecclesall Road. By *Mansell Jenkinson & Partners* 1970–1. Brutalist canted front of vertically ribbed concrete, tall, stark and almost windowless. Hexagonal worship space, partly top-lit. Linked to former brick church by *Hemsoll & Paterson*, 1900–01 on slope behind.

BROOMHILL METHODIST CHURCH, Fulwood Road. 1997 by *David Jones*. A tower to the l. with a Rhenish lantern sits unhappily in proximity to industrial metal cladding, red brick and stone dressings.

ENDCLIFFE METHODIST CHURCH (former, now The Well Baptist Church), Ecclesall Road. 1902–4, by *Joseph Smith*. Impressive with tall spire, clerestoried nave and apsed chancel. School of 1927.

CITY CHURCH, Wilson Road. Former Synagogue by *J. Mansell Jenkinson*, 1929–30. Classical, brick with faience decoration and a semicircular Doric portico. All rather heavy.

PUBLIC BUILDINGS

KING EDWARD VII SCHOOL, Glossop Road/Newbould Lane. Built in 1837–40 by *William Flockton* as the Wesley Proprietary Grammar School (later Wesley College), and a quite exceptionally ambitious piece of school design for its date. Twenty-five bays wide, with a pedimented centre of seven bays with eight giant Corinthian columns on a ground floor treated as a pedestal. The S entrance on the first floor reached by a big outer staircase. End pavilions of three bays, also with giant Corinthian columns. Low aisled entrance hall divided by eight timber Corinthian columns. Chapel behind, with semi-octagonal galleries. Interior gutted in 1905–6 by *Gibbs & Flockton* to provide additional height for classrooms in place of dormitories. A TEACHING BLOCK of 1996 by *DBS Architects* (project architect *Sue Williams*) slopes downhill on a curve with colonnaded front and walls of powder-coated panels. Refurbished and extended by *HLM Architects*, 2010–11, with SCIENCE BLOCK and SPORTS HALL at rear.

SHEFFIELD HIGH SCHOOL FOR GIRLS, Rutland Park. 1884 by *Tanner & Smith* for the Girls Public Day School Trust. Imposing but eclectic Free Tudor with Arts and Crafts detailing, its dominant motif is three big half-timbered gables with four chimneys flanking them. External covered staircase at the W end, central corridor with a spacious hall off it to the N, and a semi-basement that originally contained a gymnasium. Adjacent is No. 8 (formerly MOOR LODGE), a very large house of *c.* 1870 now incorporated into the school. Conventionally Neo-Tudor except for a massive machicolated tower and a third-floor room with an open ceiling, expressed externally by a loggia and lit by a large triangular window above it. Fine plaster ceilings in C17 style.

NOTRE DAME HIGH SCHOOL, Fulwood Road, Ranmoor. Neo-classical, red brick, of 1935 by *Henry C. Smart,* but incorporating OAKBROOK, the Italianate house designed by *Flockton, Lee & Flockton c.* 1860 for the steel manufacturer Mark Firth. Heavy porch and other additions made in 1875 by *Flockton & Abbott* when the Prince and Princess of Wales stayed here as Firth's guests on a visit to the city. Drawing room has a painted ceiling bordered by delicate Rococo plasterwork repeated in the panelling. In the library, fine bookcases removed from Page Hall. Oakbrook became a convent in 1919. The CHAPEL (now converted to a drama studio) by *Langtry-Langton,* 1955, is in a stripped Romanesque style. Arcading with round columns and Byzantine capitals.

SHEFFIELD HALLAM UNIVERSITY (COLLEGIATE CAMPUS) between Collegiate Crescent and Broomgrove Road, Broomhall. The MAIN BUILDING is the former Anglican Sheffield Collegiate School built in 1835–6 by *J. G. Weightman.* Perp style. It had a central hall with a large window and two flanking blocks, each having two bays brought forward. In 1911 *F. E. P. Edwards,* City Architect, raised the central hall by inserting a new ground floor, at the same time adding a first floor and extensions to the wings. Canopied niches flank a large window in the central hall. COLLEGIATE HALL, facing Ecclesall Road, is the former headmaster's house of 1837. Probably by *Weightman,* in a very convincing Tudor. Flanking it are substantial stone blocks, originally halls of residence, by *Gibbs & Flockton,* 1906, with additions by *Edwards,* 1911. Behind Collegiate Hall, the SAUNDERS BUILDING, refurbished in 2001 by *Michael Self Partnership.* Then the large, flat-roofed COLLEGIATE LEARNING CENTRE with a sweeping glass wall added in 2002 by *Jefferson Sheard* and the adjoining MARY BADLAND LECTURE THEATRE, 1976, by *Hadfield Cawkwell Davidson & Partners,* built as a library. Behind the Main Building, the HEART OF THE CAMPUS building by *HLM,* 2015, and NW of this BROOMGROVE HALL, a six-storey L-shaped slab by *Hadfield Cawkwell & Davidson* with reinforced-concrete grid-like frames with brick infill. WOODVILLE HALL by the same firm to the same basic design lies E on the S side of Broomhall Road adjoining the ROBERT WINSTON BUILDING of 2014 by *Race*

Cottam Associates.* The remaining buildings on the campus are converted villas in Broomhall (*see* Perambulation).

ROYAL HALLAMSHIRE HOSPITAL, Beech Hill Road/Glossop Road. *Adams, Holden & Pearson* won the competition in 1940 but only the concept of a tall slab with a low front block survived its long gestation period. The hospital as built comprises two main parts, a three-storey outpatients' department commenced in 1958 (completed 1971) and a massive eighteen-storey block for inpatients completed in 1978 (concrete, weathered to a dingy grey), with canted two-piece bay windows. Behind it, off Tree Root Walk, the JESSOP WING, 1993–2001, by *George Trew Dunn Partnership* in a rather incoherent, vastly enlarged domestic style, steeply pitched roofs with great overhangs and oddly truncated gables. The CHARLES CLIFFORD DENTAL HOSPITAL of 1951–3 by *Adams Holden & Pearson* in Wellesley Road is in the firm's familiar utilitarian red brick, extended with the UNIVERSITY SCHOOL OF DENTISTRY by the *James Totty Partnership* in 1989–91.

SHEFFIELD CHILDREN'S HOSPITAL, Clarkson Street. The hospital moved here in 1881. The earliest surviving building, on the corner with Brook Hill, is by *J.D. Webster*, 1902. Red brick, Tudor, with a tower with lantern over the main entrance; carved spandrels show a child receiving help. Extended in matching style in 1931. Stephenson Teaching and Research Unit (1968), the surgical block of 1976 and a massive extension to the rear of 1998 by *James Totty Partnership* are the principal subsequent additions. Major redevelopment along Clarkson Street for a new entrance to the outpatients' department by *Avanti Architects* is underway in 2016.

RYEGATE CHILDREN'S CENTRE, Tapton Crescent Road/Ryegate Road, Broomhill. 1978 by *Design Research Unit* (partner-in-charge *Kenneth Bayes*). Intended as a model in caring for the mentally ill in small units as an alternative to large institutions. Flat-roofed day-care unit quite dramatic with exposed beams, a first-floor balcony and three heating flues employed as a visual motif, very High-Tech for its date.

BOTANICAL GARDENS, Clarkehouse Road. 18 acres were purchased by the Sheffield Botanical and Horticultural Society in 1833 for about £18,000 from the Wilson family, owners of Sharrow Snuff Mills (*see* p. 574). Opened in 1836 with free access granted only to shareholders and subscribers. *Robert Marnock* won the competition for the design of the gardens, which were laid out on gardenesque principles i.e. an informal layout with the emphasis on small-scale features such as rock gardens surrounded by mounds planted with trees. The land rises gently to the N and sinuous paths weave through small dells which are interspersed with lawns. The buildings are believed to be by *Benjamin Broomhead Taylor*, who had won second prize in the competition. Fine Neoclassical GATEWAY

---

*There was a third, Marshall Hall, demolished to make way for the Heart of the Campus building.

with a portico supported on paired Ionic columns and a
rounded arch with a big keystone. It resembles Decimus Burton's Hyde Park screen of 1825. A lengthy curved screen wall
concealed single-storey offices and a caretakers house. The
three pavilion GLASSHOUSES originally had quadrangular
domed roofs of slender iron ribs and walls of Hathersage
sandstone with glazed panels separated by Corinthian pilasters. The central one is seven bays wide, the end pavilions only
three. They were linked by lower gabled colonnades, destroyed
before 1939 but reinstated during restoration by *Sheffield
Design & Property* in 2001–3. The Gardens have also been
restored to their original layout. Within them is a BEAR PIT. At
the time of writing, the CRIMEAN MONUMENT with a figure
of Victory by *Henry Lane* of Birmingham, the base by *George
Goldie* of *Weightman, Hadfield & Goldie*, is in storage. First
erected in 1863 on a granite column at Moorhead in the city
centre, it stood here 1957–2004.

WESTON PARK. Formed out of the grounds of Weston House,
formerly the home of the Misses Harrison, and laid out by
Robert Marnock in 1875. The SOUTH GATE on Western Bank
is by *E. M. Gibbs* but with terracotta piers (now painted) by
James Gamble. They incorporate pretty panels decorated with
putti designed by *Godfrey Sykes* and executed by *M. H. Blanchard.** Sykes died in 1866 and is commemorated in a terracotta COLUMN (painted), erected 1875. The column is a copy,
made by students of the National Art Training Schools, of
those originally made by Blanchard's for the main façade of
the South Kensington Museum of 1864–6 and ornamented
with bands, modelled by Sykes, of figure friezes depicting the
Three Ages of Man between fluted sections decorated by
foliage. The base of the column and an urn surmounting it are
by *Gamble*. The portrait of Sykes is based on that by *Gamble*
at the Victoria and Albert Museum and the railings around the
column are *Alfred Stevens*'s design for the Museum. Other
memorials include one to EBENEZER ELLIOTT, the Sheffield
poet, by *N. N. Burnard*, 1854, resited from High Street. – BOER
WAR MEMORIAL, 1903, by *J. D. Webster*. Bronze triptych with
Gothic tracery, the central panel giving the names of the fallen,
the outer ones depicting a soldier under a blazing sun. It was
removed from the Cathedral graveyard, Church Street, in
1957. Accompanying this, the impressive FIRST WORLD WAR
MEMORIAL of 1923. Its design is based on a sketch by *Francis
Jahn*, who taught modelling at the Sheffield School of Art,
translated into models by *G. N. Morewood* and *Roy Smith*, and
made by members of the school under the supervision of
Holmes & Son. An obelisk surmounted by a great winged figure
of Victory with two lifelike bronze soldiers on each side of the
shaft, one an officer holding a revolver by *Morewood*, the other

*Sykes was a student and a teacher at the Sheffield School of Design until he was
called to London in 1859 to superintend the decoration of the South Kensington
Museum.

a private soldier by *Smith*, who also modelled the regimental badges above the shaft's pedestal. Realistically rendered uniforms are piled up on the other sides of the stone base.

The WESTON PARK MUSEUM, at the SW corner of the park, incorporates the MAPPIN ART GALLERY, built by *Flockton & Gibbs* in 1885–7. Pevsner thought it 'an amazingly pure Ionic building – amazing if one considers its date. The pattern was no doubt Klenze in Munich rather than the English Greek Revival.' Ionic giant portico with pediment and an Ionic giant colonnade in the recessed parts l. and r. Semicircular apses at each end and very competent and elegant detailing. All but the façade and the two front galleries was destroyed by bombing in 1940. Weston House stood to the S of the art gallery and had been converted to a museum in 1875 but was replaced by the present building by *W. G. Davies*, City Architect, in 1937. Its stripped classicism blends well with the restrained art gallery. At the corner fluted Ionic columns *in antis* framing the entrance and panels carved by *F. Tory & Sons* of the Shrine of Knowledge with Crustaceans, Fishes, Reptiles Mammals and Birds in the order of their appearance. A second panel on the E side shows men working in the Sheffield trades. Behind this, sensitively handled additions by *Purcell Miller Tritton*, 2005–6 (on the site of galleries of 1961–5 by *J. L. Womersley*). Outside, SCULPTURE, 'Double Somersault': twisted interlocking stainless steel tubes by *William Pye*, 1976 (formerly at the Children's Hospital).

PERAMBULATIONS

1. Broomhill

We begin in GLOSSOP ROAD with a succession of handsome early C19 villas and terraces on both sides, interspersed with the buildings of the University and Hospitals, but the domestic highlight of Glossop Road is THE MOUNT, on the N side at the top of the hill, which like the King Edward VII School below has its principal front facing across the Porter valley. By *William Flockton*, c. 1830–2, it is a palace-fronted terrace of houses, seventeen bays long, with an Ionic giant portico of six columns carrying a pediment and end pavilions with giant columns *in antis*. Converted to offices with extensive additions to the rear of 1961 by *Mansell Jenkinson & Partners* and marred by a remarkably insensitive car park built into the rising ground in front of it. To the W of it, across Glossop Road, is No. 463 of c. 1836, a specially fine Grecian villa of three bays, the central one brought forward and with two giant fluted Ionic columns *in antis*, and corner pilasters. Its first occupant, *Samuel Worth*, was probably the designer.

To the N, beyond St Mark's church in BROOMFIELD ROAD, No. 11 is ornate Neo-Gothic, built in 1875 by the speculative builder *Francis Dickinson*, having a big canted bay, a tower and some especially elaborate bargeboards. No. 5 (and No. 2

Newbould Lane) are a pair of severe ashlar-fronted villas of
1840 by *William Flockton*, perfectly symmetrical, with only the
thinnest of Tudor veneers overlaying a classical plan. s of
Glossop Road in MELBOURNE AVENUE, MOUNT VIEW
(No. 1; Sixth Form Centre of Sheffield High School), a handsome classical s-facing villa, was built *c.* 1840 for David Ward.
Three bays, the central one brought forward slightly and given
a pediment. An Italianate tower-like N wing, probably 1860s.
Further down is the enormous MELBOURNE HOUSE (formerly St Mark's Vicarage and now Sheffield High's Junior
School), first occupied in 1885. The architect is not recorded
but was probably *W. H. Crossland*, who built the church; certainly the use of French motifs is characteristic of him.

To the sw, VICTORIA PARK, developed by William Fowler from
1854 with a great variety of substantial middle-class villas along
the curving Southbourne and Westbourne Roads. It includes
work by many prominent local architects, including *Flockton
& Abbott* at Nos. 28–30 SOUTHBOURNE ROAD and William
Hill's partner, *S. L. Swann*, at Nos. 21 and 23. Opposite the
end of Southbourne Road, in WESTBOURNE ROAD, a large
Gothic house, No. 60 (ASHDELL GROVE) of 1857, which had
a ballroom topped by a turret with an oriel and a castellated
top added in 1870 by *Flockton & Abbott* for Thomas Moore in
preparation for entertaining in his mayoral year. More Gothic
and Italianate villas in the upper part of Westbourne Road,
those on the SE side with their principal façades and gardens
facing away from the road. No. 21, *c.* 1854 by *T. J. Flockton*
for himself in a picturesque Italianate with a diminutive tower,
reminiscent of the cottages at Edensor, Derbyshire. At the s
end of Westbourne Road, ST CECILIA HOUSE (No. 65) of
1865 is by *M. E. Hadfield & Son* for William Stacey, a piano
dealer. Eclectic in style, a canted bay is embellished by a
medallion (depicting St Cecilia playing a portative organ)
designed by *J. F. Bentley* and carved by *Theodore Phyffers*.

On ASHDELL ROAD at the corner of Westbourne Road,
ASHDELL (now part of Westbourne School), a large villa with
an Ionic porch flanked by one slightly projecting bay on each
side, designed by *Samuel Worth* but completed by *William
Flockton* in 1840 following Worth's disagreements with the
client, John Shepherd. Follow Ashdell Road round to the NE
where on the N side is SUMMERFIELD, a formal arrangement
of communal gardens with two large terraces of 1869–70 by
James Hall, both with open pediments and big canted bay
windows and ASH MOUNT, Nos. 6–20, Ashgate Road, a handsome terrace of eight brick-built houses of *c.* 1860, still
classical.

w of Westbourne Road, up a long drive is CREWE HALL, formerly Oakholme, a three-bay house of *c.* 1828 (the heavy porch
added later in the C19). Restrained Neoclassical extension of
1936 by *John C. Procter* created three wings around an open
court as a Sheffield university hall of residence. Pretty mid-C19
Italianate stable. Behind it in Oakholme Road, STEPHENSON

HALL, centred around Carrysbrook, an Italianate house of 1869 almost certainly by *Flockton & Abbott*. The hall itself, by *J. W. Beaumont & Sons*, 1952, is large and clad in stone. A new wing added in 1989 by the *University Architectural Consultancy Unit (David Bannister)* has three linked blocks with a rusticated ground floor.

CROOKES ROAD goes up the hill to the N from Fulwood Road. ETRURIA HOUSE (No. 91) is of 1876 by *E. M. Gibbs* for John Armitage of the Wharncliffe Fire Clay company and incorporates much of his patented decoration. Of the streets to the w, in TAPTONVILLE ROAD there is HADOW HOUSE (No. 38), formerly Tapton Elms, built *c.* 1850 for John Hobson, who developed the road. Neo-Tudor, the principal room with a fine plaster ceiling and a black marble fireplace. Pretty lodge (No. 46), dated 1852.

To the w in MANCHESTER ROAD, KERSAL MOUNT NURSING HOME (formerly Castle Mount), Manchester Road. 1869 by *Hill & Swann* for Joseph B. Jackson, of Spear and Jackson, saw manufacturer. It has an oriel with a conical roof over the entrance, delightfully lively carving below the oriel of cherubs and a bird, and of animals along the elaborate cornice.

In TAPTON CRESCENT ROAD, HALLAM HOUSE (No. 92) is in the usual C19 gabled Tudor style but with a billiard room extension of 1908 by *Edgar Wood*. It has a flat roof and a broad rounded two-storey bay window with narrow mullions and transoms. The treatment is characteristic of Wood's work with slim buttresses projecting above a parapet and simple dentilled decoration between them.

2. Broomhall

HANOVER WAY marks both the boundary between the Broom Hall estate and Earl Fitzwilliam's lands, the historical and present-day division between the suburbs and the city centre. In this area WILKINSON STREET retains almost all the (mainly detached) villas mostly built between 1830 and 1840. They are all of two storeys and, in the main, very plain but with small variations of detail to keep the interest. PEEL TERRACE off the N side is a formal terrace of six houses of *c.* 1855, the central pair brought forward slightly for emphasis and with prominent quoins.

From Wilkinson Street, s down BRUNSWICK STREET, whose modest terraced houses belong to the 1850s and '60s but still largely in the Georgian tradition.

s off Broomspring Lane in GLOUCESTER STREET and DORSET STREET, a group of forty-three experimental houses designed by the *MHLG Research and Development Group* in collaboration with *Sheffield City Council's Architect's Department*. Built between 1962 and 1963, at a time when few industrialized techniques for low-rise housing were available. Structural timber and steel frames on a concrete slab, flat roofs, with concrete, timber or tile cladding. There are four types, including single-storey patio houses and five- and six-person houses with integral garages, a rarity for their date.

s again, immediately E of the redundant church of St Silas in Broomhall Street, is HANOVER SQUARE, not really a square at all but a wide cul de sac running s with four double-fronted semi-detached houses of the late 1840s, in red brick with hipped roofs, on one side, and a terrace of seven houses in identical style on the other.

In WHARNCLIFFE ROAD to the NW, small Neo-Jacobean houses, by *George Hague*, in short terraces as if to mark the boundary between the affluence of Broomhall Park and the merely respectable streets to the NE. The division is emphasized by the two- and three-storey brick-built 1840s terraces on the E side of the road and by the lodges at the junctions with Broomhall Road and Collegiate Crescent that once controlled the gates to the BROOMHALL PARK ESTATE.

Back on BROOMHALL ROAD, as we enter the Park, we move away from the formal grid-plan of the earlier parts to gently curving roads where we are immediately surrounded by an eclectic mix of large villas in generous plots. Unusually for Sheffield, there are no grand vistas because the estate is mainly on level ground with only a gentle rise to the N, which becomes more pronounced at its W end.

The most important house in the area is BROOM HALL on the N side of Broomhall Road. The medieval home of the de Wickersleys, it was gradually extended and passed through several families, most notably the Jessops. It was sold in 1826 to James Watson, who wished to remain at his family home, Shirecliffe Hall, and therefore let it out as three separate tenancies. The house remained divided and in a deteriorating state until it was restored in 1974–5 by *Mansell Jenkinson & Partners* for occupation as a workshop and home by the designer and silversmith David Mellor. The E wing is of *c.* 1784 by *Joseph Badger* for the Rev. James Wilkinson, Vicar of Sheffield. Hipped roof and a seven-bay ashlar façade, the central window given emphasis by an enriched surround and blind balustrade below. Broad and most handsome Adam-style fanlight above a door with sidelights. To the rear, however, is a significant survival: a timber-framed house, the earliest part tree-ring-dated to *c.* 1498, and extended *c.* 1614. It was built to a half-H-plan of central hall and wings projecting s. Much of the timber framing of the W wing survives. The N front has a projecting close-studded gable over a stone ground floor. Pretty carving with patterns, also of tracery. Attractive oriel and coving below the gable (cf. Bishops' House, Norton Woodseats, p. 617). The hall and E wing were rebuilt in stone in the C17 and the s front given an ashlar façade with a sundial and sash windows, probably at the time of construction of the late C18 wing. The roof of the W wing is one of a small group of hybrids which fall between the two major roof types found in South Yorkshire: principal-rafter-truss and common-rafter types. There is no ridge-beam and heavy kingpost roof trusses carry only a single purlin on each slope with hanging wind-braces from the back of the rafter as its only additional support.

Beyond Broom Hall, PARK LANE diverges to the NW. First, on the W, PARK HOUSE is an especially handsome three-bay house with pediment and Greek Doric porch. Then, completely hidden, the best post-war house in Sheffield, No. 1, 1961 by *Patric Guest* for David Mellor. A combined house and workshop, the design brief looked to Scandinavia but the influences of US examples, notably the Eames house and Mies van der Rohe's Farnsworth house, are evident. Long façade almost completely glazed, flat roof with a fine interior making extensive use of natural timber. Large studio at the W end, with extra height gained by a lower floor level on the sloping site. The house is little altered other than the replacement of the original galley kitchen with its folding bed and two bedrooms at the E end.

After buildings for Sheffield Hallam University on the S side (*see* p. 580), Broomhall Road joins the sweeping COLLEGIATE CRESCENT, where there are many more Tudor villas, some with tracery in the mullioned ground-floor windows. Two short culs de sac near the E end, Wilton Place and Mackenzie Crescent, have groups of smaller villas, symmetrical with Jacobean gables, the trademark of their builder *George Hague.*

W of the University campus BROOMGROVE ROAD developed from the 1830s. There is one outstanding house, No. 13, a Neoclassical villa of *c.* 1830 with a three-bay ashlar façade and Greek Doric porch. Low-pitch hipped roof topped by a platform with a timber balustrade.

At the top of Broomgrove Road, numerous pleasant mid-C19 houses on the S side of CLARKEHOUSE ROAD. Further W, Nos. 61–67 BROOMGROVE TERRACE is a group of four Italianate houses *c.* 1844 with shared doorcases. In CLARKE DRIVE, to the S, BELMAYNE HOUSE (Birkdale Prep School), a big Gothic villa of 1873, has carved dragons crawling around its door and a medallion of a dragon on the chimney. CLARKE HOUSE (also the Prep School), is a large three-bay brick villa of *c.* 1833 with a porch with fluted Greek Doric half-columns flanked by pilasters.

GEORGE WOOFINDIN ALMSHOUSES, Ecclesall Road. By *W. R. Bryden* of Buxton, 1898–9. Eighteen red brick cottages in a crescent picturesquely sited by the River Porter. Woofindin was a cutlery manufacturer whose bequest also paid for the Woofindin Convalescent Home at Fulwood (p. 609).

3. Endcliffe

A tour of this area should begin in ENDCLIFFE CRESCENT, an arcadian landscape of villas grouped informally around a large irregular green. It was developed by Thomas Asline Ward and eight others who in 1824 acquired part of the Endcliffe Hall estate and formed the Endcliffe Building Company. *William Fairbank* was commissioned to draw up plans for the development. Nos. 20–30 are the remains of four pairs of semi-detached houses of 1827–8 but the other houses in the crescent were built only sporadically from 1856 to 1881. Mostly large ornate villas, several in the favoured mix of Tudor and Gothic styles: Nos. 1, 3 and 5, by *Flockton & Abbott* of 1869–71; No. 4 is *Francis Dickinson* at his most flamboyant with bargeboards and big canted bays; No. 7 is of 1880–1 in the fashionable French style with steep-pitched roofs and rounded corners to the window surrounds; No. 11 by *Hill & Swann* of 1878–9 has a small open pediment and a most eccentric porch with Corinthian capitals and gross detailing.

Endcliffe is now dominated by the buildings of ENDCLIFFE STUDENT VILLAGE, developed by the University of Sheffield with halls of residence and communal buildings set in a grassy landscape. This began in 1923 with the acquisition of Endcliffe House of *c.* 1832 (now HALIFAX HALL hotel) on Endcliffe Vale Road. The tower added in 1891 by *Flockton & Gibbs* has a deep prostyle Greek Doric porch as its base: a strange addition to an otherwise chaste building. Inside, a library containing panelling from the White Star liner RMS *Homeric* installed in 1936. The surrounding campus of residential flats was created from the grounds of Endcliffe Grange (1867, dem.) in the 1960s but completely replaced in 2008 by *Halliday Meecham Architects* (cf. Ranmoor Student Village, p. 590) with a mixture of long ranges of cranked plan along the perimeter and standard blocks running downhill at right angles. Timber facings.

At the SW edge, ENDCLIFFE HALL, Endcliffe Vale Road, was built in 1863–5 by *Flockton & Abbott* for Sir John Brown. It is the largest and most sumptuous of all the steelmakers' mansions, estimated to have cost £100,000. Italianate, square with the central bays brought forward on each side, those on the W extended to form a tower (originally mansarded), those on the S with a canted bay window. Stone figures of the four seasons by *E. W. Wyon* above the porch. On the S front, two carved figures by *Papworth* representing Labour and Art. The house was of fireproof construction with iron joists and concrete floors. The windows were protected by retractable Belgian-made iron shutters (some of which survive), which in turn were hidden on the inside by large mirrors that slid into the walls. The richly decorated rooms include a 60-ft (18-metre)-long salon, built to house Sir John's art collection. Decorated by *John & Joseph Rodgers*, with the case for a water-powered organ in classical style at the E end. The dining room, like the other principal rooms, has a fine plaster ceiling by *Charles Green*. The chimneypieces are by *Joseph Hadfield* of the Norfolk Lane Marble Works. The drawing room has painted door panels and coving by the *Rodgers* and the ceiling has a central oval panel containing painted figures representing Music, Painting and Poetry, attributed on stylistic grounds to

Godfrey Sykes, who is also said to have done the murals (now overpainted) on the grand staircase. In 1913, the house was acquired for the Territorial Army, who remain in occupation. The Grand Conservatory, 160 ft (49 metres) long with a domed tower has been demolished save for part of the wall linking it to the house.

Part of the Endcliffe Hall estate was sold as early as the 1890s. In ENDCLIFFE HALL AVENUE, some interesting postwar houses: Nos. 50 and 54–58, of 1968–9 by *Peter F. Smith*, are set on falling ground; several are entered at first-floor level with ground-floor bedrooms. Very low-pitched roofs, the façades mainly glazed.

To the s, surrounded by large Victorian and Edwardian houses, is ENDCLIFFE PARK, which was acquired in stages by the City Council, who commissioned *William Goulding* in 1885 to adapt it for public use. Good Arts and Crafts PARK KEEPER'S LODGE of 1891 near the Hunters Bar entrance. Also two memorials to Queen Victoria – a bronze STATUE near the Lodge of 1904 by *Alfred Turner* with life-size bronze figures of Industry (an artisan holding a sledgehammer by an anvil) and Motherhood (with two children) on the sides of the base, which is by *E. W. Mountford*. Near Rustlings Road, an OBELISK by *Flockton & Gibbs*, originally installed in Fargate (*see* p. 531) to mark the Queen's Silver Jubilee in 1887 but later felt to be dwarfed by the new buildings there and removed to the park. NW of the Park at No. 89 GRAHAM ROAD is RIVERDALE, hemmed in by flats. Sumptuous Gothic of *c.* 1872, built for Charles Firth, the youngest brother of Mark Firth, and later the home of J. G. Graves, perhaps Sheffield's greatest benefactor. Fine lodge.

4. Ranmoor, Tapton and Carsick

Around St John's church (*see* Churches) in RANMOOR PARK ROAD, WEST LEA (No. 5) of 1870 and RANFALL of 1871 are both by *J. D. Webster* and both classical, showing how conservative Sheffield tastes could be. Both have pediments and large eaves brackets; West Lea has gained a big bay window and a billiard room. Off the N side of Fulwood Road, the much earlier and narrow lane RANMOOR ROAD climbs the hill. Although few of the buildings are of great individual architectural interest, they make a most harmonious assembly, varying in scale from vernacular cottages of the C17–C18 (e.g. No. 34) to the Neoclassical RANMOOR GRANGE, 1877 by *Flockton & Abbott*, with its centre emphasized by a heavy door surround and outsize segmental pediment which breaks through the eaves. To the s in RANMOOR CRESCENT, WHITE GATE (No. 9) *c.* 1908, Arts and Crafts with a half-hipped roof and tile-hung bay windows, and No. 15 (and No. 55 Ranmoor Road) also Arts and Crafts of similar date, especially attractive large semi-detached houses with white timber balconies, snecked masonry walls and Westmorland slate roofs, the chimneys roughcast.

At the top of Ranmoor Road, to the r., CLIFFE END (No. 45 Ranmoor Cliffe Road) is by *E. R. Robson*, 1879 for John Moss, Clerk to the Sheffield School Board. Riotously patterned half-timbering to the first floor, coved eaves and a big four-light dormer.

On FULWOOD ROAD, STORTH LODGE (No. 408) of *c.* 1860, Neo-Gothic, is by *Flockton & Abbott*. On the s side of Fulwood Road, Nos. 385, 389 and 389A, a group of three stone houses built *c.* 1939 by *J. Mansell Jenkinson* in his Arts and Crafts style. ESHOLT HOUSE (No. 381), brick with half-timbered gables, built *c.* 1897 for A. J. Hobson, Master Cutler that year, has a garden alcove, steps and potting shed of 1905 by *Edwin Lutyens*, carried out in stone, plain almost astylar.

Now N of FULWOOD ROAD to Tapton along TAPTON PARK ROAD. THORNBURY (now a hospital) was designed by *M. E. Hadfield & Son* for Frederick Thorpe Mappin of Thomas Turton & Sons Ltd, Sheaf Works (*see* p. 545) in 1864–5, in an ostensibly classical style, with two wings flanking a big two-storey bow and balustraded parapet, a steep-pitched roof, tall chimneys and gables. Two-storey porch and a large oriel with scalloped niches on the asymmetrical entrance front and large recent additions. The gardens were by *Robert Marnock* and the long sweeping drive and gardenesque clumps remain.

Immediately E is RANMOOR STUDENT VILLAGE by *Halliday Meecham Architects* (cf. Endcliffe Student Village, p. 588) for the University of Sheffield (on the site of the 1960s Ranmoor Hall of residence). E of that on SHORE LANE, TAPTON EDGE of 1864 by *Flockton & Abbott*, for Edward Firth, a younger brother of the steelmaker Mark Firth, Italianate with the entrance recessed behind a twin-arched loggia. A bowed oriel rises improbably from the centre of the loggia, the keystones of the arches doubling up as brackets for the oriel. Higher up Shore Lane, TAPTON HALL (now the Masonic Hall), *c.* 1855 by *Flockton Lee & Flockton* for Edward Vickers, one of the major figures in the development of Sheffield's steel industry. Also Italianate but a much more formal composition with a big rounded bay window, the roof concealed behind balustrades. Grand entrance hall with open-well stairs and arcading to the first floor. Large uncompromisingly modern extension with a meeting hall added in 1967 by *Hadfield Cawkwell & Davidson & Partners*. A large concrete mural by *William Mitchell* symbolizes the turmoil and chaos of the outside world.

NW Ranmoor and the suburb of CARSICK have several substantial and interesting houses, mainly of the early C20, spread out over steeply climbing hills.

On IVY PARK ROAD, PEMBURY (No. 37) is a large roughcast house of 1924 by *Arthur Nunweek* taking its stylistic cues from Voysey, notably in the chimneys and ashlar window surrounds. Built for Albert 'Bertie' Bassett, the sweet manufacturer, for whom Nunweek built a new factory at Owlerton in the same period.

At the northern edge of this area, THE TOWERS, Sandygate Road at the corner of Coldwell Lane, is an extraordinary Scottish Baronial fantasy by *Flockton & Gibbs*, 1895–6, for C.D. Leng, proprietor of the *Sheffield Telegraph*. Extended w in 1905. To the N, a U-shaped stable block and a charming lodge at No. 316 with a conical turret, also 1905.

SNAITHING LANE runs SE from near the top of Ivy Park Road. First, on the E side, BISHOPSCROFT, built as The Côte in 1912–13 by *Sydney L. Chipling* of Grindleford Bridge, an Arts and Crafts villa in random rubble with a turret and leaded lights, rather in the manner of Walter Brierley. Then, a group of large houses set back. TAINBY (No. 55) of 1909 is by *W. J. Hale* for his own occupation. Restrained s-facing garden front with two big gables flanking a narrow central bay and unusual heavy moulding to the door. THE CROFT (No. 57, originally Snaithing Croft) was built 1909–10 by *Briggs, Wolstenholme & Thornely* with a big half-timbered porch set between stone wings. Then SNAITHING GRANGE of 1904 for W. F. Osborn of the steel manufacturers Samuel Osborn & Co. Tudor style with a large staircase window. The s front generally symmetrical with three big square bay windows topped by carved panels with recessed gables above. Panelled hall with deep decorated foliage frieze. Finally, a rural survival, SNAITHING FARM with a long combined house and barn range *c.* 1700.

Further s in BELGRAVE ROAD, RANMOOR HALL (formerly Snaithing Brook), 1880–1 for William Wheatcroft Harrison, cutlery and electroplate manufacturer, in the usual Tudor style with a s-facing terrace. It was acquired in 1899 by Henry Andrew, steel manufacturer, who doubled the size of the house, building a new wing on the E side with a billiard room (elaborate plaster ceiling in the Tudor style) and a front porch which bears his initials.

Further w in SNAITHING PARK ROAD, the lodge to CARSICK GRANGE, Neo-Tudor of 1883, which is hidden up a long drive to the N. Then, RYDAL by *W. J. Hale*, built for his daughter on her marriage to Maurice Cole in 1921. Simple but well-proportioned roughcast exterior, battered chimneys and slate roof sloping low at the rear, not unlike Mackintosh's Windyhill, Kilmalcolm, Renfrewshire.

In CARSICK HILL WAY, QUARTERS, built as Carsick Hill Court of 1914 by *Hickton & Farmer*, combines half-timbering and tiling with a most elaborate stone porch and a three-storey tower, much altered. THE CROFT, No. 5 Stratford Road, of 1909 by *Briggs, Wolstenholme & Thornely* for the tool manufacturer James Neill is one of the larger houses in the area. Built in an attractive Arts and Crafts style with a stone ground floor, rendered above. The road front is symmetrical with a two-storey porch and twin gables, the garden front asymmetrical with two bay windows and an oriel. Tall chimneys and attic dormers.

Finally, STORTH OAKS (now a clinic) at No. 229 GRAHAM ROAD was originally built as a pair by *J. D. Webster*, 1869, but remodelled by *S. L. Swann* in 1875 for Alderman W. H. Brittain.

Double-fronted with a tower and offset entrance. The staircase ceiling is copied from a room at Clumber Park, Notts. Stained glass of foliage, flowers, fruit and birds by *Heaton, Butler & Bayne. Robert Marnock* undertook the landscaping of the garden.

NORTH-WEST

(Crookes, Walkley, Upperthorpe, Netherthorpe, Hillsborough,
Owlerton and Malin Bridge)

CHURCHES

ST MARY, Howard Road, Walkley. Two bays and a chancel of a mission church were erected in 1861. The nave was completed in 1869 when aisles and a ritual NW tower with broach spire were added by *J. G. Weightman* in association with *T. A. Wilson*. Simple Dec style. – Elaborate stone PULPIT of 1901 and Perp carved oak REREDOS, 1907. – Classical FONT COVER and LIGHT FITTINGS by *George Pace*, 1953. – STAINED GLASS. E window of 1893 and S chancel window 1896 by *Kayll* of Leeds.
   To the N, the former NATIONAL SCHOOLS (South Road Spiritualist Church) of 1871 by *T. A. Wilson*.

ST BARTHOLOMEW, Burgoyne Road, Walkley. 1991 by *David Greenwood* of *Ashfield Architects*, incorporating some arches and shafts of the former church (1882) by *J. D. Webster* and sited on the footprint of the former Sunday School. – STAINED GLASS by *Mark Angus* symbolizing the Four Gospels and the Five Wounds of Christ and some glass from the former church reused.

ST JOHN THE BAPTIST, Penistone Road, Hillsborough. 1874 by *J. B. Mitchell-Withers*. More picturesque in outline than most Sheffield churches of this period by virtue of its slender SW tower which has a traceried wooden belfry capped by a pyramidal slate roof. Lofty interior with tall chancel arch and scissor-brace roof. The 1994 reordering has left the chancel hidden behind the 1907 oak reredos. – STAINED GLASS. E window by *Kayll & Co.*, *c.* 1900; further *Kayll* window of 1898 in the S aisle; S and N aisles, windows by *Jeffrey & Foster*, 1900; N aisle, Mothers Union window of Virgin Mary with angel and dove of 1960 by *Harry Harvey*, angular, with a distinct Festival of Britain feel to it.

ST POLYCARP, Wisewood Lane, Malin Bridge. 1933–4 by *H. I. Potter* of *Fowler, Sandford & Potter*. Early Christian style. Attractive light interior. Sympathetic reordering by *David Greenwood* in 1992. New W porch and rear bay of nave enclosed.

ST MARK (former), Dykes Lane, Malin Bridge. 1904 by *John Wills & Sons* (Methodist New Connexion, now a Pentecostal church). Gothic and workmanlike. The adjoining WARD MEMORIAL SUNDAY SCHOOLS of 1930 are more striking. Late Perp style with canted bay windows.

St Stephen, Fawcett Street, Netherthorpe. 1856 by *Flockton & Son*. An imposing town church of cruciform plan with a tower rising from the centre with gallery at the w end. Nave lengthened in 1865. Extensively altered internally to provide a worship space at the w end, the remainder converted for community use. Further reordering undertaken in 2004.

St Thomas, Nairn Street, Crookes. 1839. Simple with w tower and nave lit by lancets. Drastically altered in 1979 when a long range by *Brandt Potter* incorporating meeting rooms was added across the end of the chancel and the e–w orientation of the church reversed. – STAINED GLASS. N window (St Michael) by *Morris & Co.*, 1900. s aisle, 1896 by *Ward & Hughes*.

St Timothy, Slinn Street, Crookes. By *J. D. Webster & Son*, 1910, a large church broadly in the Perp style, externally plain, built to cater for the expanding suburb. The gable faces the road. A sw tower and spire were intended but not built.

Sacred Heart (R.C.), Forbes Road, Hillsborough. 1936 by 104 *C.M.E. Hadfield*; one of the best interwar churches in Sheffield. Tower, w gallery and vestibules, nave and aisles of five bays, transepts, apsidal chancel. Portland stone tympanum by *Philip Lindsay Clark* above N door. The essence of the interior is the contrast between the superb quality of the plain brickwork and the richness of the decoration at the e end by *Eric Newton*, 1936, with a mosaic panel in the chancel apse of Sacred Heart with supporting angel and Ave Maria and Ave Joseph above the two chancel chapels. The reredos mosaics in the chapels added by Newton in 1961. – STATUES, STATIONS OF THE CROSS and FONT by *Philip Lindsay Clark*. – ORGAN CASE by *Albert Keates*.

St Joseph (R.C., former, now Sheffield Buddhist Centre), Heavygate Road, Walkley. By *M. E. Hadfield & Son*, 1871, as the chapel of a reformatory for girls, founded in 1861. Unified nave and chancel with a steeply pitched roof, apsidal nave and bellcote at the e end. Schoolrooms below took advantage of the sloping site. Attached to the e end the early C19 stone house with porch of paired Doric columns, taken over as a dwelling for the Sisters of Mercy.

Below the Chapel on the other side of Howard Road, the former St Joseph's School, 1889 by *Goldie, Child & Goldie*. E-shaped in coursed stone in the Renaissance style with mullioned-and-transomed windows. Restored and converted to offices 1990.

St Vincent (R.C.), Pickmere Road, Crookes. 2001 by *Jos Townend* of Manchester. Bright red brick with bands of buff brick and including meeting rooms and presbytery. Hipped roofs throughout and the church lit by a pyramidal lantern over the sanctuary. – FONT. C19. From St Vincent, Solly Street (*see* p. 510).

Crookes Congregational Church (former), Springvale Road. 1905 by *W. J. Hale*. Octagonal and particularly impressively sited on sharply rising land. Its height is accentuated by the prominent buttresses, some massive and battered, others slender, which lead the eye upwards from the rounded apse to the gables and thence to the lantern, which is surmounted by a flèche. The slender buttresses extend through the tracery of the E window. Carving probably by *Frank Tory*. Converted after 1988 to offices for their own occupation by the *Bond Bryan Partnership*.

CONGREGATIONALIST CHURCH, Carlton Road. 1910 by *Norman Doncaster*, almost domestic in its style, with an Arts and Crafts feel.

WESLEYAN CHAPEL (former), School Road, Crookes. Built 1836 by *J. Ridal*, mason, a typical chapel of the period of three bays with round-headed windows and a hipped roof. School wing added to the rear in 1843.

ST JOHN'S WESLEYAN CHAPEL (former), Crookesmoor Road/ Crookes Valley Road. 1889 by *C. J. Innocent*, an exciting composition perched on the side of a steep hill with a four-bay nave, aisles, transepts and an octagonal flèche with a spire. Rooms also below the church. Innocent's use of Gothic is highly original; the transepts each have rose windows set within pointed arches with the form of a cross created within the tracery and extended beneath the window as blind arcading. Converted to student flats in 2013–14.

ST LUKE'S METHODIST CHURCH (former), Northfield Road, Crookes. Now Hale Court (flats). 1900 by *W. J. Hale*. Conventional in form with four bays, an apsidal chancel and a segmental traceried window of five lights at the E end. The slender buttresses rise to form miniature towers. Sculpture by *Frank Tory*. School in similar but simpler style.

EBENEZER PRIMITIVE METHODIST CHAPEL (former), South Road, Walkley. Now student flats. By *W. J. Taylor*, 1890, and the epitome of the big C19 chapel. Massive E façade with pediment topped by ball-in-cup finials, giant pilasters rising up to dentilled eaves. SUNDAY SCHOOL AND INSTITUTE behind, 1904, also by *Taylor*.

HILLSBOROUGH TRINITY METHODIST CHURCH AND SUNDAY SCHOOL, Middlewood Road. 1901 by *John W. Firth* of Oldham, completed by his son. Gothic with ritual NW tower with octagonal lantern and short spire. Partly stone-clad, the rest in brick.

WESLEY HALL, Crookes/Carson Road. 1907 by *W. J. Hale*, and like his Congregational Church (*see* above) octagonal in plan but with radial wings flanking the porch and a pyramidal roof topped by a lantern. The massive buttresses culminating in ashlar caps and the shaped parapet provide a great impression of movement, while the broad seven-light windows spring directly from the buttresses rather in the manner of W. D. Caröe. The interior originally had shallow galleries on five sides of the octagon, with a platform rostrum and choir on the other three sides. Converted in 1992 by *Byrom Clark Roberts* to form a worship space above and a hall below, together with other facilities, thereby losing much of its character.

UNITARIAN CHURCH (former), Crookesmoor Road. Now student accommodation. 1915 by *J. R. Wigfull*, free Gothic red brick with a gabled front. – STAINED GLASS by *Henry Holiday*.

RIVELIN VALLEY CATHOLIC CEMETERY. Opened in 1862. CHAPEL of 1878 by *M. E. Hadfield & Son*. E.E. style with an apsidal E end, W bellcote and SW porch which has a niche above with sculpture of St Michael slaying Satan. Rich interior. – ALTAR of polished marble and veined alabaster with the dead Christ in white alabaster behind arcading; by *Boulton* of Cheltenham. – WALL PAINTINGS. E end. 1884 by *Charles Hadfield* and *Nathaniel Westlake*. – STATIONS OF THE CROSS. Terracotta, mainly paired below Gothic canopies. – STAINED GLASS. Three E windows by *J. F. Bentley*, executed by *Lavers, Barraud & Westlake*, c. 1878. W window of 1884 by *Hadfield* and *Westlake*.

PUBLIC BUILDINGS

CARNEGIE LIBRARY, Walkley Road. By *Hemsoll & Paterson*, 1905. Skilfully making the most of its corner site, it consists of two wings in a vaguely Tudor style linked by a rounded portico on paired columns with Ionic capitals.

ZEST HEALTHY LIVING CENTRE, Upperthorpe. A conversion of 2003 by *Tatlow Stancer Architects* of the red brick Jacobean PUBLIC BATHS, dated 1895, by *Charles Wike*, and UPPERTHORPE PUBLIC LIBRARY by *E.M. Gibbs*, 1874 (cf. Highfield Library, p. 567), in plain brick with Florentine windows. Sculpture by *J. W. Cooper*.

WALKLEY COMMUNITY CENTRE, Fir Street. Built as Walkley Reform Club, 1909 by *H.L. Paterson*. Small and in a minimal Art Nouveau with first-floor balconies.

WALKLEY AND HILLSBOROUGH DISTRICT BATHS (former), Langsett Road. 1926 by the City Architect *F. E. P. Edwards* with quite a sophisticated Neo-Baroque ashlar façade. Now a pub.

HILLSBOROUGH LEISURE CENTRE, Beulah Road/Penistone Road. 1989 by *William Saunders & Partners* for the 1991 Student Games. It comprises two parts, a sports hall and an Olympic-sized swimming pool, with a moving floor enabling its use for leisure or competition. Impressive exterior, dominated by the exposed roof trusses of the pool hall which extend outside the walls and are supported on external columns. Extensive glazing above masonry cladding.

ROYAL INFIRMARY (former), Albert Terrace Road. The first hospital in Sheffield and located in the fields when opened in 1793. It closed in the 1980s and, stripped of many later additions, was converted to office use in 1990. The original building of 1793–7 (now HERITAGE HOUSE) by *John Rawstorne* survives and with its central pediment and bows at each end resembles an enlarged country house. Under the Doric porch, niches with statues (now replicas) of Hope and Charity, very early work of 1802 by *Francis Chantrey*. Each floor had four wards extending the width of the building and stairs at each end. At the s end to the rear, *William Flockton* added the isolation wing (Recovery House) in matching style in 1839. Behind this is the ROUNDHOUSE, the octagonal former outpatients' department by *J. D. Webster*, 1884, with pyramidal roof with cupola. Roof of wrought-iron lattice girders with monograms in the spandrels. Round-headed windows light what was a tiled waiting room with consulting rooms radiating from it (extensions by *Young & Hall* of London, 1900). The other remaining buildings are a lodge (presumed to be by *Rawstorne*) and the large Nurses' Home (CENTENARY HOUSE) of 1897 also by *Webster*, with big bow-fronted end pavilions.

CROOKES ENDOWED SCHOOL (former), Crookes. Founded here in 1791 and developed in stages. To the l. is the earliest part. Probably early C19, classical of four bays with an open pediment enclosing a prominent plaque. Then a three-storey gabled addition dated 1880, a single-storey portion and the former master's house (Tudor) dated 1866.

BOARD SCHOOLS. NETHERTHORPE SCHOOL, Netherthorpe Street, and CROOKESMOOR SCHOOL, Oxford and Tay Streets, are by *Innocent & Brown*, 1873. From 1874 they were the architects to the Sheffield School Board and designed WALKLEY BOARD SCHOOL, Burnaby Crescent, in that year. The Gothic main part is now in residential use but the infants' department of 1906 built in a Renaissance style by *Hemsoll & Paterson* remains as Walkley Primary School. By the same architects is BURGOYNE ROAD BOARD SCHOOL, Walkley, 1881, a three-decker towering above the surrounding houses with additions of 1889 by *C. J. Innocent*. BOLE HILL SCHOOL, Bole Hill Road (now the Unity Centre), Walkley, is by *W. J. Hale* of 1896, one of only three schools designed by him. It has the characteristic large windows, powerful massing and buttressing of the other Board Schools but lightened by the use of Hale's favoured shaped parapets and crowsteps on the gables. Attractive carved lettering on a naturalistic background. HILLSBOROUGH SCHOOLS, Parkside Road, are of 1884 by *Wilson & Masters* for the Ecclesfield School Board. Rock-faced stone of one storey with diagonal nogging over the windows. MALIN BRIDGE SCHOOLS, Dykes Lane, are of 1905 (enlarged 1910) by *H. I. Potter*, four gables and a prominent ventilation tower.

MEDICO-LEGAL CENTRE, Watery Street. 1975 by *Hadfield Cawkwell & Davidson & Partners*. Notable as one of the first buildings in the UK to combine a coroner's court, public mortuary and university department of forensic pathology. Box-like, concrete-framed with good-quality brick cladding in appearance but few windows.

SCHOOL OF MANAGEMENT (University of Sheffield), Crookesmoor Road. 1977 by *William Whitfield*, a group of seven octagonal brick pavilions for the Law Department on a sharply sloping site linked at different levels by a cloister-like concrete passage, part glazed, part open, to a taller block with common room facilities.

HILLSBOROUGH BARRACKS (former), Langsett Road. 1850–4 by *H.M. Office of Works*, converted in 1990 by the *John Brunton Partnership* for office and retail use. In a simple Tudor Gothic style. Facing Langsett Road, a three-storey block for officers' mess and quarters. Central Tudor gateway. At the N end, a Gothic chapel (later used as an institute). Behind this the infantry parade ground (now a car park) and quarters. Set below that to the E, the cavalry quarters with stables flanking at right angles to enclose a second parade ground, now covered by a large supermarket. Enclosing the barracks is a wall, partly crenellated, with corner turrets.

HILLSBOROUGH STADIUM (Sheffield Wednesday F.C.), Penistone Road. The club, founded in 1867, moved to Hillsborough in 1899. Major works were carried out in 1913 but there is little left of *Archibald Leitch*'s South Stand other than a decorative football on the roof ridge and a central gable retained after redevelopment in 1993. The North Stand by *Husband & Co.* of 1961 was the first in Britain to have a cantilevered cover running the length of the pitch, the aluminium sheet roof suspended from a steel frame supported by pre-stressed concrete units. It was also the first to have entry on two levels, one entrance 12 ft (3.7 metres) higher than the other and accessed by spiral ramps. The West (Leppings Lane) Stand was built for the 1966 World Cup by *Husband & Co.* and the tragic loss of life here in April 1989 led to football grounds throughout the country becoming all seated. The East Stand or Kop was roofed in 1986 by *Eastwood & Partners*.

PERAMBULATIONS

1. Crookes, Walkley, Upperthorpe and Netherthorpe

CROOKES developed as a suburb somewhat later than its neighbours to the E; the 1853 Ordnance Survey map shows a village with farmhouses and cottages end-on to the eponymous main thoroughfare and only a few terraces with further scattered development along Commonside. From the 1880s there was rapid expansion, further encouraged by the extension of the electric tram route in 1901.

Owing to the influence of Freehold Land Societies, WALKLEY gained the reputation of being a place the artisan could aspire to; 'the workers' West End'. As with Crookes, there are a few surviving vernacular houses. THE OLD HEAVYGATE INN, Matlock Road, is the oldest building, with a 1696 datestone. Converted from a farmhouse, its appearance is ruined by an addition of the 1970s.

RUSKIN HOUSE, in Bole Hill Road, 1893 by *H.W. Lockwood*, was designed as a Girls Training Home. It incorporates to the N a small cottage in which the Ruskin Guild of St George's Museum was established in 1875. The museum moved to Meersbrook Hall (*see* p. 570) in 1890.

At UPPERTHORPE, in INFIRMARY ROAD, WHITE HOUSE BUILDINGS of 1904 by *H. I. Potter* in a vaguely Arts and Crafts style with brick, pebbledash panels, and shallow, three-storey canted bay windows.

Of the industrial area to the E of PENISTONE ROAD towards the River Don, known as Philadelphia, little survives except BATH STEEL WORKS, a small forge. Rendered buildings, one with a roof of stone slates. The two-storey forge building is lit by large unglazed windows with metal bars and wooden shutters for ventilation. Four steam hammers still in use.

NETHERTHORPE was cleared of its back-to-back housing from 1956 as part of a comprehensive redevelopment scheme over 120 acres. The new HOUSING of 1959–72 by the City Council was a mixed development of eleven point blocks (re-clad in brightly coloured metal 2000–1) running down the hillside in parkland along MARTIN STREET and three- and four-storey maisonette blocks arranged in interlocking squares with small flats on the ground floor for elderly people to live near their families. In recent years, many of these have been refurbished or demolished and replaced with two-storey houses. In MORPETH, BONVILLE and DOVER GARDENS, three blocks of flats of 1976, with flat roofs and access by tiers of steps, the prototype for a design fully developed at Heeley (p. 569).

2. Hillsborough, Owlerton and Malin Bridge

The natural centre of HILLSBOROUGH and OWLERTON district is Hillsborough Corner, where LANGSETT ROAD crosses the Loxley. Travelling S on LANGSETT ROAD, on the W side, the HSBC built for the Sheffield Union Banking Co., 1895 by *J. B. Mitchell-Withers* and completed by his son of the same name. Italianate red brick with stone dressings and pedimented windows. Uphill on FORBES ROAD, opposite the Sacred Heart church, the OWLERTON CHURCH WAR MEMORIAL HALL of 1925–6 by *Henry Webster*, pilastered with alternating bands of red brick and terracotta. Segmental-pedimented porch, heavily detailed, and the clock tower offset to the r. Back on LANGSETT ROAD, the vast bulk of the Hillsborough Barracks (*see* Public Buildings). By sad contrast on the N side on the corner of Hammerton Road, the horribly remodelled SOL-DIERS' HOME of 1907 by *George Malam Wilson*, Arts and Crafts, brick on ground floor, roughcast above, formerly with a turret. Then at No. 328, a former TOLL HOUSE in use between 1840 and 1857, stone with a bargeboarded gable and originally with a canted bay. From here housing of the 1980s rises steeply up the valley side.

REGENT COURT, Bradfield Road, E of Langsett Road and N of the Loxley, is a block of nine-storey balcony-access flats by *Edgar Gardham*, 1936, a rare example of flats in a working-class area erected by private enterprise. Lip service is paid to the Modern Movement in the flat roofs, strong horizontals and white rendering, contrasted with brick for the entrance and the balcony walls.

In the area between Middlewood Road and Penistone Road, BURROWLEE HOUSE in Burrowlee Road, was built for Thomas Steade in 1711 but incorporating an earlier house. Ashlar of five bays with a balustrade over the central three. Quoins and a band below the first floor, door surround with segmental pediment and the keystone bearing the date. In 1779, the Steades built HILLSBOROUGH HALL (now Public Library) nearby in Hillsborough Park. Three storeys, ashlar, of seven bays, the central three in a canted full-height bay window. The only decorative elements in an otherwise austere building are the central first-floor window, which has moulded architraves and a balustraded apron, a Venetian window in the W front and the dentilled cornice. Attractive stabling behind, incorporating a pediment with a Diocletian window. Three lodges at the entrances to the public park.

N of the park, on CATCH BAR LANE, at the junction with Middlewood Road, the former HILLSBOROUGH PARK CINEMA (now a supermarket) of 1919–20 by *P.A. Hinchliffe* for Sheffield Suburban Cinemas Ltd. Classical façade in red brick with much use of faience dressings.

MALIN BRIDGE lies SW of Hillsborough at a second crossing of the Loxley. By the bridge is the former MALIN BRIDGE CORN MILL, possibly *c.* 1850, with an undershot wheel and an L-shaped low stone range, rendered at the rear. E in HOLME LANE, the LA PLATA WORKS (Burgon and Ball since 1873, now the only British manufacturers of hand sheep shears). Rusticated ashlar façade to the offices, inscribed with the name of the works, with adjoining brick two-storey workshops.

To the N and W of DYKES LANE the City Council's WISEWOOD ESTATE, well maintained and little altered since completion in 1932.

OUTER SUBURBS

ARBOURTHORNE, WOODTHORPE AND RICHMOND*

ST CATHERINE OF SIENA, Richmond Road, Woodthorpe. By *Basil Spence & Partners*, 1956–9. Of convincing simplicity, the purity of its big plain E drum makes a powerful statement on the corner of Hastilar Road South. St Catherine's was built with War Damage compensation for the loss of Christ Church, Attercliffe, Spence's design following an earlier scheme by *Frederick Etchells*, who declined the revised commission for

*The following buildings in this area noted in the 2nd edition of *Yorkshire West Riding* (1967) have been demolished: ST PAUL, East Bank Road, Arbourthorne, by *Romilly Craze*, 1939; NORFOLK SECONDARY SCHOOL, Cradock Road, originally by *W.G. Davies*, City Architect, early 1930s; BROOK SECONDARY SCHOOL, Richmond Road, by *Hadfield, Cawkwell & Davidson*, 1953–4. MANSFIELD ROAD FIRE STATION by *J.L. Womersley*, 1961–3, is closed and superseded.

church, vicarage and hall. Buff brick. Oblong nave with rows of narrow slit-windows on the N and S sides and a continuous clerestory; semicircular chancel as wide as the nave. The campanile, just two gently convex brick walls connected by concrete ties, stands apart on the S, linked by a narrow glazed sacristy. Plain white plastered interior, the floors of black brick. Nave roof, with laminated timber beams supporting the joists, slopes slightly upwards to the E. The chancel, taller, has a W clerestory that bathes the apse in light, the focal point of the E wall a large CROSS with symbolic nails. – Simple ALTAR, now brought forward, and SEDILIA, of hardwood on black metal frames, by *Spence*. (PULPIT removed.) – Small cantilevered slate PISCINA. – Eggcup-shaped FONT of Derbydene marble, the cover's handle a dove by *Anthea Alley*.

w of the nave the lower HALL block, its folding screen originally allowing it to become a nave extension. Beside the S door the hall's slate facing has the church's name inscribed by *Ralph Beyer*, who carved the inscriptions at Coventry Cathedral. Campanile has bronze sculpture of St Catherine before Christ on the Cross by *Ronald Pope*, 1965. Covered walkways linking the VICARAGE form a cloister-like space on the N side. Later alterations include a fixed glazed timber screen at the rear of the nave to create a narthex, and a porch extension with a semicircular E window, 1999.

ST THERESA (R.C.), Prince of Wales Road. By *John Rochford*, 1958–60. (Ritual) W entrance in plain round stone tower with low roof; sanctuary in round brick tower with partly glazed drum and copper dome. Around the drum twelve sculpted panels of the Apostles by *Alan & Sylvia Rochford*. Blind E end, the sanctuary side-lit by windows in overlapping bays at the end of the brick nave. Seven tall thin clerestory windows above low aisles, transverse segmental vaults to both nave and aisles giving rippled roof-lines. Circular SW baptistery. – STATUES by *Philip Lindsay Clark* and *Michael Clark*. – STATIONS OF THE CROSS by *Philip Lindsay Clark*.

INTAKE CEMETERY, Mansfield Road. By *Innocent & Brown*, 1879. Two-bay CHAPEL with Perp tracery. Gabled LODGE with spired bell-turret (cf. Woodhouse Cemetery, p. 754).

SHEFFIELD SPRINGS ACADEMY, Hurlfield Road. By *Aedas*, 2008. Linear arrangement of flat-roofed angular blocks, two and three storeys, in brick and grey cladding, the E end a fearsomely acute angle on pilotis. On the site of Hurlfield Boys School (1952–6 by *Gollins, Melvin, Ward & Partners*; the Girls School, Hurlfield Road, 1952–4 by the *Architects' Co-Partnership* has also been demolished).

SHEFFIELD PARK ACADEMY, Beaumont Road North. By *Aedas*, 2006–8. Linked group of three-storey blocks, partly in red brick, partly with render or grey cladding. On the site of Waltheof School (*Architects' Co-Partnership*, 1956–60).

ACRES HILL PRIMARY SCHOOL, Mather Road. By *Hadfield, Cawkwell & Davidson*, 1951–2. Across the Parkway dual carriageway. Two-storey range with short projecting wings.

Low-pitched roofs. Brick, with diaper-work on the blind gable-ends.

BEAUCHIEF AND ABBEYDALE

Beauchief, the 'beautiful headland' on the E hillside of the Sheaf valley, was once Beauchief Abbey's land and then the Beauchief Hall estate. Part of it, now a golf course and park encompassing the Abbey's remains and the Hall, lies within Sheffield's s suburbs. Beauchief came into the city from Derbyshire in 1935.

St Thomas a Becket. The incongruous but very attractive combination of the w tower of the abbey church and a chapel-like nave of *c.* 1662. The tower and nave side walls represent almost the entire standing remains of the Premonstratensian abbey officially founded in 1183, but actually established between 1173 and 1176 when land in the parish of Norton was granted by Robert FitzRanulf. A daughter house of Welbeck Abbey, Nottinghamshire, Beauchief was a modest foundation; throughout its existence there were usually twelve to fifteen canons and an unknown number of lay brothers. After dissolution in 1537 the Abbey was bought by Sir Nicholas Strelley, passing by marriage to the Pegge family. It was Edward Pegge who used the tower and surviving nave walls to create a family chapel and took stone from the ruins to build the Hall. The abbey site and Pegge's church, which provided public worship from the beginning, were given to the City in 1931.

Excavations have proved that the medieval church was *c.* 200 ft (61 metres) long and consisted of a long aisleless nave 26 ft (8 metres) wide, transepts, the s one with two E chapels, and a straight-ended chancel. There was a small cloister s of the nave and E of this, adjoining the s transept, a chapter house with a polygonal E end and two piers. The tower lost its belfry stage in the C18. Against its E wall the steep line of the nave roof can still be recognized, with the top of the tower arch exposed below it. Against the s wall is the surprisingly high roof-line of the w range of cloister buildings. On the w the church's E.E. portal still exists, with the moulded capitals and the bases of five orders of colonnettes, the colonnettes themselves missing, and a finely and deeply moulded arch. Above is a very large window with deep reveals with hollow mouldings. The original tracery is lost but the stubs indicate that it was of the flowing early C14 variety. It was reglazed with plain concrete mullions in the 1960s. A small N doorway into the tower has an ogee arch and an ogee hoodmould with finial. Left and right of the tower are re-set doorways used as archways. The l. one is round-headed, i.e. probably of before 1200. Three orders of colonnettes of the same kind and in the same state as those of the w portal and a similarly moulded arch. The doorway to the r. is C14, with three orders of thin shafts on polygonal bases. Finely moulded arch. The C17 nave, less than half the 78-ft (24-metre) length of the medieval one, has restored/rebuilt coursed rubble walls to N and S, the N wall incorporating a C12 round-arched doorway converted to a window. Four-light E window with intersecting tracery.

The delightful INTERIOR still has its complete C17 FURNISHINGS. Octagonal PULPIT in the NE corner, and reading desk and clerk's pew below, facing the altar table. All have carved strapwork panels. – BOX PEWS, the largest (for Pegge's family) with more strapwork. – Four heraldic WALL PANELS, plaster, with foliage and putti. – MONUMENTS. Edward Pegge †1679. Tablet in grey marbles with segmental top and reverse scrolls, erected 1731. – Similar tablet to Christopher Pegge †1774. – Mrs Elizabeth Pegge Burnell †1844. Gothic frame and relief of two female figures representing Charity by *Henry Weekes*.

ST JOHN THE EVANGELIST, Abbeydale Road South. Nave and apsidal chancel in simple Gothic Revival style by *Flockton & Abbott* 1873–6; polygonal W baptistery 1926. In 1937 *J. Mansell Jenkinson* transformed the church's appearance with the addition of aisles in the form of paired transepts with stepped lancets and two W porches, giving a very broad front to the road. (Spacious interior, with two big arches to each aisle, and open roof with canted trusses.)

The church, set back, is somewhat upstaged by the former PARISH HALL by *Flockton & Gibbs*, 1893–4. Cruciform, in Gothic style, with four gables, lancets and pretty timber bell-turret. Mosaic panels above the entrance record its use as a hospital in the First World War.

BEAUCHIEF HALL, in the park SW of St Thomas. 1671, altered in 1836. A solid and stately seven-bay front of two storeys above a high basement. The first two bays and the last two bays are full-height canted bay windows. String courses. Hipped roof behind tall parapet. Central doorway reached by a grand, spreading staircase with heavy stone balustrading. The doorway is surrounded by mighty diamond-shaped ashlar blocks and has above it a Latin inscription with the date 1671. The porch with its lotus columns is of 1836. The timber balcony above is in the place of an original one, the window onto it has a surround which looks early C18. Above this (and above the parapet) an ogee gable dated 1836. Basement windows in their original state with stone mullions; the windows above altered in the C19. The jambs show that they were originally cross-windows; several cross-windows with stone mullions and transoms survive on the five-bay returns. The r. return has a plain straight staircase to a central doorway with Doric porch; a former central doorway on the l. return is partly blocked as a window and has a small stone balcony above. The N front, with less regular fenestration, is E-plan. Shaped gable to the middle bay; to either side two bays, each with a small attic gable. The main parapet returns around the side wings.

Inside, a sumptuous alabaster chimneypiece in the entrance hall (originally in the dining room). It has pilasters with close and intricate strapwork, a frieze with arabesques, and in the overmantel the demi-figure of a bearded man, richly dressed with a ruff and a chain of office and holding a book. Pairs of tapering pilasters l. and r. It was given by Adrian Mundy of Quarndon Hall, Derbyshire. Can it be of 1671? It looks more than a generation earlier. (Another, smaller, alabaster chimneypiece in the SE room has very curiously shaped pilasters and a vine frieze.) The original NW staircase, with simple turned balusters, looks still Jacobean. Early C18 main staircase, altered in the C19. Walled GARDENS have fine gatepiers of c. 1671 (to the E) and the C18 with C18 wrought-iron railings. STABLE BLOCK, partly of 1667, remodelled in 1836 with Jacobethan shaped gables, and partly late C18.

ABBEYDALE HALL (flats), Abbeydale Road South. Tudor Gothic villa, c. 1840s, with grander additions of 1860 by *Flockton & Son*, 1872 by *Flockton & Abbott*, and 1883 by *Flockton & Gibbs*.

ABBEYDALE INDUSTRIAL HAMLET (Museum), Abbeydale Road South, ½ m. W of Beauchief Abbey. Abbeydale Works was one of the principal water-powered sites on the River Sheaf and was in existence by 1714, possibly dating back to 1676, when a cutler's wheel was built in Ecclesall for Sir John Bright. From 1740 it was used for making scythes and other agricultural edge tools. After 1900 the works gradually became disused and in 1935 the philanthropist J. G. Graves bought them and presented them to the City for use as an industrial museum, eventually opened in 1970. Further restored in 2000–2.

Set NE of the 4-acre reservoir, the buildings form a quad-   73
rangle partly open to the N. All are of humble appearance and built of coursed rubble with stone slate roofs. The crucible shop, built in 1829 in order to make the steel required on site, has five melting holes and a substantial brick crucible stack. The melting shop floor is raised over a vaulted brick cellar (cf. Grenoside). The tilt forge was built in 1785, the grinding hull in 1817; both have gables with Venetian windows facing the courtyard. Four water wheels power the tilt hammers, a two-cylinder blowing engine, the grindstones and the horizontal boring machines. Secondary power is supplied by an 1855 single-cylinder horizontal steam engine outside the grinding hull. The yard's S side is a row of hand forges, each with its own doorway and a two-light window lighting the workbench. Three workmen's cottages were built by 1795, the manager's house is of 1830 and the coachhouse and stabling were added in 1840.

BENTS GREEN see ECCLESALL

BIRLEY see HACKENTHORPE

DORE

Village on the N slope below the moors at the end of the Sheaf valley, now a prosperous suburb. Transferred from Derbyshire in 1935.

CHRIST CHURCH. Rebuilt 1828–9 to designs by *Richard Furness*, village schoolmaster. W tower flanked by N porch and later vestry; tall and wide three-bay nave. Lancet windows, their tracery 1864. Two-bay chancel by *J.D. Webster* 1895–6, the Perp E window 1902. Queenpost roof dominates plain barn-like interior. – STAINED GLASS. E window by *Heaton, Butler & Bayne*, 1903. – Two chancel S windows by *Rosemary Smith Marriott* (later *Everett*), *c.* 1948. Nave S easternmost by *Mayer & Co.*, †1869.

PRIMARY SCHOOL, Furniss Avenue. By *W.L. Clunie*, 1963–5 (cf. Shooters Grove School, Stannington, p. 621).

In the VILLAGE centre, around the church, the plain former SCHOOL, 1821, and some older cottages. Others in TOWN-HEAD ROAD, one with datestone 1686.

LICENSED VICTUALLERS' ASSOCIATION ALMSHOUSES, I m. E on Abbeydale Road South, opposite the station. *By J.B. Mitchell-Withers*, 1877–8. Tudor Gothic style. Twelve dwellings in single-storey range with attics and two-storey gabled end wings; set forward in the centre the former chapel, with Dec tracery to large E window and octagonal lantern with spire. In front, a big steeple-like Gothic MONUMENT to Thomas Wiley †1853, brought from the previous Grimesthorpe site.

MOORWINSTOW, No. 99 Dore Road. By *Norman Doncaster* for himself, 1912. Considered essay in vernacular style drawn directly from Derbyshire manor houses of *c.* 1600, reflecting the local interest in vernacular architecture pioneered by S.O. Addy and C.J. Innocent. Grindleford stone with stone slate roofs. Three-storey N front has a central full-height gabled porch, with a broad gabled bay with plain mullioned windows to l., a large external chimneystack to r. Simpler two-storey garden front has a projecting gabled bay with transomed lower window. Sympathetic additions of *c.* 1950. (Original oak panelling and staircase, and reused carved overmantel *c.* 1600.)

DORE MOOR HOUSE (subdivided), Newfield Lane. By *A.F. Royds*, a pupil of Lutyens, 1906. Large stone house in vernacular style with gabled cross-wings, hipped attic dormers and small mullioned windows set flush with the walls.

ECCLESALL

(including Bents Green, Millhouses and Whirlow)

A prosperous SW suburb, stretching from the church on the hill between the Sheaf and Porter valleys along the new route (1812) of the Buxton turnpike down Ecclesall Road South and from that down to the River Sheaf. From the C18 the manor belonged to the Earls Fitzwilliam of Wentworth Woodhouse (q.v.). Their Millhouses estate was released for building in the early C20 but Ecclesall Woods, over 300 acres of ancient manorial woodland, was preserved when the City Council bought it from the 7th Earl in 1927 with help from J.G. Graves.

ALL SAINTS, Ecclesall Road South. A church of two halves, quite different from each other in scale and ambition. The w tower and five-bay nave were built in 1788 to replace a nearby chapel of ease that originated as a C13 manorial chapel served from Beauchief Abbey (*see* p. 601). In 1841–3 the church was completely remodelled by *Robert Potter* with lancet windows, a heightened tower and a Neo-Norman w door with chevron. A small chancel added in 1864 was swept away by *Temple Moore*'s bold and successful E end of 1906–8. This consists of chancel, chapels and transepts, and is, thanks to the fall of the site, placed on an undercroft that raises it to greater prominence. The undercroft has round-arched windows, the upper parts have lancet windows, but these are very different from the typical Early Victorian ones of the nave. E window of two tiers of three lancets, the upper ones taller and stepped, an arrangement Moore used elsewhere. s transept s window of five lancets, N transept N window of three. Clerestories to chancel and s transept.

Temple Moore's interior is impressively lofty and spacious. Full-height arch to chancel, which has a segmental-arched timber ceiling. The clerestory has arcades of eight tall, deep arches with shafts, the lower two-thirds blind and with a wall passage like a triforium. On the N side the three w arches open into the organ loft. The s chapel is taller than the N chapel and vestry and careful examination of Moore's disparate but not discordant treatment of the N and s sides is instructive. The taller s arcade has diagonally set piers with shafts at the angles, the N arcade unmatched clustered piers. Three finely moulded but unmatched arches each side: round, narrow pointed and wider pointed. The chapels open into the transepts with a narrow pointed arch and a broad round arch, the s pier clustered, the N octagonal. High above the s arches are three small clerestory windows, above the N ones an arcade of three tall arches opening into the organ loft. Continuous segmental ceiling to the transepts and crossing.

The intended rebuilding of the nave to a design by Temple Moore foundered on lack of funding. The arch between the nave and crossing, with big clustered responds on the w for the nave arcades, and narrow side arches for passage aisles, gives clues to his intentions. Eventually the nave's interior was remodelled by *G. G. Pace*, 1964–5. Tall columns of welded steel, aligned with the responds, carry a simple triangular-vaulted ceiling. Reordering by *Peter Wright & Martyn Phelps* in 1997–8 created a narthex below a new w gallery. – Carved oak SCREENS in chancel by *Frank Tory et al.* – Traceried SCREENS to organ loft 1926. – FONT by *Pace*, 1964. Tooled stone drum. – STAINED GLASS. In the E parts mostly by *Kempe & Co.*, notably the E window 1909–10, the vast s transept s window, with twenty figures associated with Britain's conversion to Christianity, 1911, and the N transept N window, 1921. Also the s chapel windows, 1912. – Two vestry windows by *Powell & Sons*, c. 1918 depict St Thomas a Becket and Robert

FitzRanulph shown with Beauchief Abbey. Also by *Powell &
Sons* the angels in the s transept e clerestory windows, 1931.
s transept w clerestory windows, 1864, the original chancel's
side windows. – MONUMENTS. Numerous opulent but conventional C19 tablets in the nave and transepts, several by
Edwin Smith. – Rowland Hodgson †1837 by *I. Greaves*, with a
Norman arch like the w doorway. – Mrs Penelope Parker
†1819, and Mrs Eliza Butcher †1833, and their children. Two
almost identical draped tablets by *Matthew Noble c.* 1833. The
huge graveyard has a great many C19 MONUMENTS, some very
large and elaborate.

ST OSWALD, Bannerdale Road, Millhouses. By *J.D. Webster*,
1909–10. E.E. style, with Y-tracery to clerestory. Very big, on
a sloping corner site, the e end above an undercroft. s chapel
with polygonal apse. Base of unbuilt sw tower and
spire. – STAINED GLASS. Three windows by *Kempe & Co.*:
five-light e window 1915; s chapel windows 1912 (e) and 1920
(s).

HOLY TRINITY, Grove Road, Millhouses. By *J. Amory Teather*,
1936–7. Built of random rubble in plain Romanesque style.
Rectangular NW tower. Simple, tranquil interior, the e parts
with tall round arches.

ST WILLIAM OF YORK (R.C.), Ecclesall Road. Chapel of 1904–5
by *C. & C.M.E. Hadfield*, re-orientated, with new nave and
aisle, in 1925 by *Hadfield & Cawkwell*, and remodelled by *John
Rochford & Partners* in 1970–1. Copper-covered roof has split
pitch to give continuous N clerestory that lights large open nave
and sanctuary. Sculpted steel CRUCIFIX on (ritual) e wall by
John Petts 1972. – STAINED GLASS. SE window by *Paul Quail*
1987.

BANNER CROSS METHODIST CHURCH, Ecclesall Road South.
By *W.J. Hale*, 1928–9. A late work by Hale, in stripped-down
style with bold massing, a monumental tower rising above the
paired round-arched entrances. The tracery has still a slightly
Gothic character. To rear, on Glenalmond Road, the former
church by *George Baines & Son* 1906–7, its gabled front with
Arts and Crafts touches to flanking turrets.

BENTS GREEN METHODIST CHURCH, Ringinglow Road. By
W.J. Hale, 1929, executed by *G.R. Bower* 1931–2. The pairing
of randomly coursed stone with red brick dressings makes its
appearance unusual.

MILLHOUSES METHODIST CHURCH (Wesleyan), Millhouses
Lane. By *J. Amory Teather*, 1936. Triangular corner site. Old-
fashioned Gothic style with tall lancets. Former chapel and
Sunday School by *J.D. Webster*, 1885–6, set transversely to
rear.

HIGH STORRS SCHOOL, High Storrs Road. By *W.G. Davies*,
Sheffield City Architect, 1933. Seen across the playing fields
the long w elevation, with its central clock turret and gymnasia
as end pavilions, is an impressive piece of interwar civic architecture in stripped classical style. Built as separate secondary
schools for girls and boys, each enclosing a central courtyard

and joined by an assembly hall and two dining rooms. Interior has Art Deco details.

HOLLIS HOSPITAL, Ecclesall Road South. By *Howard Chatfeild Clarke*, 1903. Founded 1703. Almshouses, replacing a city centre building. Cottage style in red brick with tiled hipped roofs, gables with mock timber framing and timber bay windows. Four blocks grouped around a lawn, the three single-storey ones more homely.

BANNER CROSS HALL (offices), Ecclesall Road South. By *Sir Jeffry Wyatville*, 1817–21, for General William Murray (formerly Foxlowe), on the site of the manor house. Stone, in Tudor Gothic style. Of moderate size, but all castellated and by picturesque grouping made to look more conspicuous. (Octagonal entrance hall. Plasterwork, joinery etc. with Gothick details. Board Room, originally Dining Room, has C17 carved wood festoons from Hayes Place, Kent (dem.), and fireplace and panelling from RMS *Mauretania*, scrapped 1935.)

MYLNHURST (Convent School), Button Hill. 1883. Large house for William Greaves Blake of Stephenson Blake, typefounders. Eclectic style, partly Gothic with cusped lancet lights and a castellated staircase tower but also with shaped early-C17-looking gables. (CHAPEL by *John Rochford*, 1962, has grisaille windows by *Patrick Reyntiens* and Crucifix by *Stuflesser*.)

WHIRLOW, still bordering countryside, was the choice of rich industrialists for their mansions as Broomhill and Ranmoor (*see* pp. 883 and 589) were overtaken by the suburbs. A few remain but only PARKHEAD, off Ecclesall Road South, by *J. B. Mitchell-Withers*, 1864–5, is still wholly residential. Entrance front overtly Gothic, the garden side, with a huge canted bay at each end, less so. Large square panels with good carved heads of mythological figures decorate upper walls. Enlarged in 1900 by *R. G. Hammond* and 1903 by *Wyngard, Dixon & Sandford* for Sir Robert Hadfield, steel magnate. CLIFFORD HOUSE, 1894, by *J. B. Mitchell-Withers Jun.* for Denys Hague, colliery owner, has good shaped gables and square and canted bay windows with balustraded parapets. WHIRLOW COURT, next door, for James Dixon Fawcett, cutlery and silverware manufacturer, early 1880s, is in a bold Tudor Gothic style. WHIRLOW BROOK HALL, for Percy Fawcett, 1906, is tamer but its big square bay windows are still castellated. The grounds, a fine example of a woodland garden created in the 1920s, opened as a public park in 1951.

The delightfully secluded WINFELL QUARRY GARDENS, given to the City in 1968, were made for Samuel Doncaster, steel manufacturer, in a small quarry in the grounds of 'Whinfell' (1897, dem.). *Clarence Elliott* designed the limestone rock garden in 1912.

WHITELEY WOOD HALL, 1¼ m. W of the church in the Porter valley. C17 house enlarged by *Sir Jeffry Wyatville* for William Silcock in 1822, dem. 1959. The STABLES remain (Girl Guides' centre). U-plan, including two-storey range and large barn; arcaded fronts. Nearby, the former WHITELEY WOOD

OPEN-AIR SCHOOL, Cottage Lane, a late C19 Gothic rural school adapted in 1909 as the city's first school for sickly children.

FRECHEVILLE

A large suburban estate, mainly of semi-detached houses, built by a company financed by the Sheffield builders Henry Boot & Sons Ltd. Originally all for rent, 1,540 homes were completed 1934–7, with shops and a community centre. Frecheville was in Derbyshire until 1967.

ST CYPRIAN, Churchdale Road. By *J. Harold Gibbons*, 1949–52. An unusual church, built with the compensation received for Derwent Woodlands church, Derbyshire, which was drowned by Ladybower Reservoir in 1945. Red brick with pantiled roofs; tiled eaves detail. Traditionally Gothic in plan if not appearance. Long continuous ridge to chancel and aisled nave. The N side, which deserves a more significant location than a minor residential road, is a fine composition with a NE bell-turret and transeptal chapel, and a gabled porch and a corresponding transeptal NW baptistery to the nave. Between the transepts the N aisle has its own narrow passage aisle and a clerestory. Gothic tracery to E window, narrow pointed-arched windows to transepts, other windows small and straight-headed with diamond leading. Tympanum above deeply recessed W doorway has carved panel depicting the waters engulfing Derwent Woodlands's steeple, the porch a sculpture of Our Lady and Child; both are by *James Wedgwood*. The intended NE tower succumbed to post-war brick shortages.

Plain spacious interior, all rendered and painted white, has features characteristic of Gibbons's work, e.g. shouldered arches and barrel-vaulted ceiling to nave and chancel. Two broad round arches to nave arcades. High-level cross-passage below E window. W organ gallery. – ROOD by *James Wedgwood*. – ORGAN, LECTERN and some PEWS from Derwent. – Most PEWS by *George Pace* 1964–72.

FULWOOD

Prosperous W suburb on the N side of the Porter valley, developed from the early C20. Some good detached and semi-detached middle-class housing, both in Vernacular Revival style, with roughcast walls and dormer windows, and in stone with classical details, e.g. Clarendon Road. Most, however, is standard inter-war semi-detached housing. To the W is farmland where the Porter valley linear park and the Mayfield valley rise to the edge of the moors and the Peak District National Park.

CHRIST CHURCH, Brookhouse Hill. 1837–9 by *Robert Potter*, in lancet style. Enlargements by *G. G. Pace* in 1953–5, and by *R. G. Sims* in 1979–82, render the original humble structure unrecognizable, only the w tower with obelisk pinnacles and the nave's crenellated n parapet remaining. It is Pace's work that makes the church noteworthy. Chancel with slightly canted-out e wall, completely windowless and sheer, rising as a low flat-topped e tower with n and s clerestory. Five-bay s aisle with huge mullioned windows separated by buttresses. Dramatic treatment of the space inside. e wall in pale brick, the other walls all whitewashed. The tall chancel arch, rising from near the floor, is plain, unmoulded and steeply pointed, a form Pace used in his first church design at Orpington, Kent, in 1939. Galleried n aisle by *Sims* follows Pace's lead, with large four-light, but transomed, windows. Arcade of tall skeleton piers with very shallow segmental arches. Overbearing w stair-turrets with half-hipped roofs flank the c19 tower.

St Luke (Ecumenical), Blackbrook Road. By *J. Needham* and *K.H. Murta*, 1965–7; church centre by *Alex Roberts*, 2001. Buff brick. Six-sided, with flat roof. Plain, non-prescriptive worship space, with three tall staggered windows each side of the e end. – STAINED GLASS. Foyer screen in abstract *dalle-de-verre* by *Pierre Fourmaintraux* of *Powell & Sons*.

Fulwood Old Chapel (Unitarian), Whiteley Lane. Dated 1729. Plain oblong, quite small. Quoins. Six bays, the second and fifth with doorways, the others with single two-light windows, higher than they are broad and with original leaded lights. Interior entirely c20. MINISTER'S HOUSE, 1754, adjoining to r., and tiny schoolroom, built soon after, attached to l.

Nether Green Junior School, Fulwood Road.* By *Holmes & Watson*, 1904, completed by *A.F. Watson* 1908–9. One of the best examples of the later Sheffield Board Schools, in Arts and Crafts style using classical motifs. For 700 pupils. Varied gables to eleven classrooms grouped around a tall central hall with arched bellcote and square flanking towers with wavy-topped parapets.

Royal Hospital Annexe (former), off Brookhouse Hill. By *Flockton & Gibbs*, 1908, built for convalescent patients. Neo-Georgian style, Brick. Symmetrical s-facing range. Centre block 3:5:3 bays, the three-bay sections with pediments; lower wings that originally had verandahs. Immediately e, the former Zachary Merton Convalescent Home by *J. Mansell Jenkinson*, 1938, in keeping. Eleven-bay range has pedimented centre with cupola. Lower wings project forward to l. and r. Hipped roofs. Both buildings converted to housing, with some unfortunate excrescences, as Mayfield Heights.

Woofindin Convalescent Home (former), Woofindin Avenue. Now flat. By *H.L. Paterson*, 1901. Queen Anne style. Brick. For seventy patients. Tall centre block with domed clock tower. Wings have balconies on columns that form

---

*Hallam School, Hallam Grange Crescent, by *W.L. Clunie*, 1963–5, has been demolished.

loggias to the ground floor; big semicircular pediments to outer bays.

COTTAGE HOMES (former), Blackbrook Road. By *A. F. Watson*, 1903–5. Additions 1911 included water tower with gabled and half-timbered top stage; assembly hall 1913. Twenty large semi-detached houses built by the Ecclesall Board of Guardians for children in their care. Stone, in plain domestic style varied with hipped roofs or half-timbered gables.

In STUMPERLOWE HALL ROAD some older houses. STUMPERLOWE HALL was rebuilt *c.* 1844 in plain Tudor Gothic style. Additions 1870. Front of three bays with a narrow gabled wing projecting each side. Enclosed porch in angle with l. wing. Parapet. The buttresses flanking the central bay are an odd feature. Immediately E is STUMPERLOWE GRANGE, a C17 five-bay farmhouse, remodelled in the mid C19 in Tudor Gothic style with battlemented porch and pointed windows to two gabled dormers. Taller addition to S, *c.* 1863, with big two-storey canted bay (now STUMPERLOWE HOUSE). N of the Hall, STUMPERLOWE COTTAGE, a restored C17 single-storey house with adjoining barn, both cruck-framed. 200 yds N THE GRANGE FARMHOUSE, partly C17 and early C18, has two- and three-light chamfered mullioned windows with hoodmoulds and two pairs of crucks. Former BARN has three cruck-trusses.

FULWOOD HALL, Harrison Lane. Datestone 1620. Fine former farmhouse on an older site. Three-bay hall range with parlour in projecting gabled wing to l. Mullioned windows, the hall and parlour windows both five lights with transom. Gabled cross-range to r. has smaller two- and three-light windows. (C17 and C18 fielded panelling in two rooms.)

GLEADLESS

CHRIST CHURCH, Hollinsend Road. By *M. E. Hadfield*, 1839, chancel rebuilt by *J. D. Webster*, 1883–4. Plainest lancet style. W tower with solid parapet and tapering pinnacles of four stages. Three-bay nave, two-bay chancel. Interior reordered by *G. Pace*, 1975, with glazed screen at chancel arch; chancel fittings removed. – MONUMENT. Thomas Dunn †1871, with oval portrait medallion by *E. & T. Smith*.

Almost opposite the church on Ridgeway Road, a crescent of five GRAVES TRUST HOMES of the usual designs (*see* Norton p. 616), 1937.

HOLY CROSS CHURCH, Spotswood Mount. By *Braddock & Martin-Smith*, 1964–5. Dramatically sited on the Rollestone hillside. Canted (ritual) E front, like a broad triangular prow, with a central concrete column dividing the E window and rising to form a cross. Roof sweeps steeply down behind. Plain white interior, dominated by the very striking full-height STAINED GLASS E window of *dalle-de-verre* by *John Baker*, made at Whitefriars Studio. Immensely tall figures of the Virgin Mary and St John and a Crown of Thorns above them.

Windowless walls; lighting by roof-lights at eaves. – Chunky rough-hewn FONT.

GLEADLESS VALLEY vies with Park Hill (*see* p. 563) as Sheffield's greatest contribution to the post-war development of public housing in Britain.* A mixed scheme for 17,000 people, its density of sixty-eight persons per acre (or, including open space and woodland, thirty-eight) contrasts with Park Hill's 192. Planned as a whole, it was begun in 1955 under *J. L. Womersley*, the City Architect, and completed by 1962. The valley, formerly entirely rural, is triangular in shape and rises to the S. It is the steepness of the slopes, averaging 1 in 8 and up to 1 in 4 in places, that really sets the development apart. There are views within, across and up the valley, and superb views from it, W to the moors and N to the city centre. So both enclosure and prospect co-exist.

A wedge of woodland divides it into three neighbourhoods, HEMSWORTH to the SW, HERDINGS to the SE and ROLLESTONE to the N, their names taken from farms and hamlets to establish continuity. The character of each neighbourhood differs accordingly in response to topography. Much of Hemsworth and Herdings resembles a new town with conventional terraces of houses, some in plain brick, others clad in timber on the first floor. What became known in the 1950s as 'people's detailing' is much in evidence in the low-pitched roofs and square windows. The layout is carefully designed, with traffic-free squares such as Raeburn Way. Rollestone, however, on the steep NE slope, is highly impressive, with chalet-like houses clustered on the hillside in a scene that is the antithesis of conventional estate planning. Some of the houses use similar elements to those employed by Span: warm red brick, tile-hanging and weatherboarding along the fascias of flat roofs.

Providing a focal point at the highest part of the estate are two (originally three) thirteen-storey point blocks off Raeburn Road in Herdings, now re-clad. At the lower end of the valley, on the estate's N edge, are a group of six towers, off Callow Road, Newfield Green, re-clad in Lincoln green.

Development took three forms: along and across the valley's contours, and on land with 'irregular contours', necessitating a variety of house types to fit specific locations. Along the contours, housing types include a reversed-plan design for steep slopes with a living room on the first floor e.g. in RAEBURN ROAD and six-storey maisonettes with bridge access at several levels. Other designs include flat-roofed houses with pedestrian entrances at first-floor level and garages underneath accessed from the rear, e.g. FLEURY PLACE. Across the contours, designs include narrow-fronted terraces with monopitch roofs, the houses staggered so that the access footpaths cross

112

---

*The following buildings have been demolished since the 2nd edition of *Yorkshire West Riding*: HEMSWORTH PRIMARY SCHOOL, Constable Road, 1955; GLEADLESS SECONDARY MODERN, Matthews Lane, by *J. L. Womersley*, 1958–61.

the contours on the diagonal (e.g. those on the E side of BLACKSTOCK ROAD by the shopping centre). Irregular contours designs are for sites where levels make terraced housing difficult and include cluster blocks of three-bedroomed houses with floor levels that can be varied to suit the slope, found throughout the area. These have flat roofs and back onto each other. Striking two-storey patio houses in SPOTSWOOD MOUNT, on a 1 in 5 slope, have an enclosed patio between each house and first-floor living rooms giving unobstructed views across the valley.

At Rollestone, PAXTON COURT is a group of ten energy-efficient houses by *Cedric Green* for the Solar Buildings Co-operative, 1984. Brick-clad with pitched roofs, they have much timber framing and very large S-facing conservatories for passive solar heating.

HACKENTHORPE

Village in Derbyshire until 1967, with much post-war Sheffield housing. Now part of the rural SE townships.

CHRIST CHURCH, Sheffield Road. By *J. D. Webster*, 1899. Small stone nave with porch, chancel unbuilt. Lancets. Steep tiled roof, W bellcote. Reordering by *Mitchell Proctor & Partners* 1999 reversed orientation, adding large transept-like NE entrance, E extension and linked HALL to S. Carefully matched forms, materials and details.

OUR LADY OF LOURDES (R.C.), Spring Water Avenue. By *Reynolds & Scott*, 1957. Large, plain and imposing, with a strong vertical emphasis. Modern style, in brick with flat parapets, but with Gothic echoes in some forms and details. Six-bay nave has tower-like (ritual) W end with octagonal turrets flanking the entrance, and tall windows above low aisles. Shallow transepts; polygonal sanctuary with blind E wall. (Reinforced-concrete frame expressed internally as slightly pointed arches.)

BIRLEY SPA HOUSE, off Birley Spa Lane. 1842. Hidden in woodland, a surprising and rare survivor of the often short-lived C19 spas that existed in unlikely places. A small combined bath house and hotel built by Earl Manvers as part of his ambitious but largely unrealized plans for commercial development of a spa first noted in 1734. Originally with seven baths, including cold plunge baths and a tepid bath, it was not profitable and by the late C19 offered only one plunge bath. A long rectangle of five bays set against the slope, the S front one storey, the N two. Rendered walls, ashlar details. Hipped roof to slightly projecting centre bays, exuberant shaped end gables with gadrooned urns as finials. (Gothick glazing bars to windows. Oval pool on ground floor.) Restored by *Peter Pace*, 2001–2, for community use but neglected at the time of writing.

MOSS WAY POLICE STATION. By *Sheffield City Council Building and Design Services*, 1993–6. Large, well-articulated block on a prominent corner site. Mainly three storeys. Golden brick with big hipped slate roofs whose deep eaves shade a continuous mullioned clerestory. Few windows to ground floor, but the effect is less forbiddingly defensive than the architectural manner of the South Yorkshire police in previous decades.

(RAINBOW FORGE PRIMARY SCHOOL, Beighton Road. 1953. For Derbyshire County Council. Prototype of the Derwent modular timber system, designed by *Samuel Morrison & Partners* for the building firm Vic Hallam Ltd during steel shortages. Single-storey classrooms with timber cladding and large windows.)

Little of the old VILLAGE remains. GREENSIDE, Beighton Road, is a plain Georgian stone house made more imposing by two buxom full-height ashlar bows added to the three-bay front *c.* 1840. The Staniforths lived here, their adjacent scythe and sickle works surviving as business units in plain C18 and C19 stone and brick ranges around a courtyard. 200 yds N, HACKENTHORPE HALL, Main Street, rebuilt 1875 in Tudor Gothic style with ridiculously steep gables.

JORDANTHORPE *see* NORTON

MEADOWHEAD *see* NORTON WOODSEATS

MILLHOUSES *see* ECCLESALL

NORTON

By far the most rewarding of outer Sheffield's villages, with the best medieval church and some good C18 stone houses. Transferred from Derbyshire in 1934 (except for The Oakes and its park, which came into Yorkshire in 1967), it is separated from the city's inner S suburbs by Graves Park and retains its village character.

ST JAMES. The oldest part of the church is in the porch: the S doorway, Norman, but over-restored (of the details only a little of the chevron in the arch and one capital original), and some heads saved from a corbel table. The W tower is E.E., except for the big W window and the top. The rest of the exterior is Perp, with battlements to the nave, S aisle and ashlar S chapel, which is called 'newly built' in 1524. It has straight-headed three-light S windows. The odd design of the aisle windows of three lights is by *Street*, who restored the church in 1881–2: the lights to the l. and r. lower than the centre light and with trefoils within circles over. Inside, the N aisle of *c.* 1200 with round piers and five double-chamfered arches. The E respond is simply one-stepped in section and has the plainest impost. The S aisle has octagonal piers. The E respond is altered to fit in an ogee-headed niche for an image. The aisle is shorter to the W than the N aisle and immediately continued by the S porch. *Street* restored a pier in each arcade, previously removed for galleries. Perp clerestory. Tower arch triple-chamfered.

The responds are double-chamfered, and the inner order is a semicircular shaft with a crocket capital. The chancel arch has semi-octagonal responds and crocket capitals, but is less tall than the tower arch. The Perp s chapel consists of two bays with octagonal pier and w and e responds formed as corbels with traceried panelling.

FONT. E.E. with four supports of three shafts each and a nine-sided bowl with four low pointed trefoil arches. Carving within the arches, including an angel's head and a salamander (cf. Ashbourne, Derbyshire). – MONUMENTS. William Blythe and his wife, Saffery, alabaster monument, erected by their son, Bishop Blythe of Lichfield, c. 1510–20. In the e arch between the chancel and s chapel. Recumbent effigies on a tomb-chest with many statuettes under crocketed nodding ogee canopies. – Two good incised floor slabs with figures, one to William Selioke †1512 and wife. – William Bullok †1667 and his son John †1683. By *John Bushnell* (GF). With a generously moulded sarcophagus top and winged heads of two putti. – Henry Gill †1716 and family. Good scrolled cartouche with achievement. – Richard Bagshaw †1750 and family. Tablet with broken pediment flanking an urn. – Richard Bagshaw †1776. Tablet carved as a scroll by the Fishers. – Sir Francis Chantrey, sculptor, †1841. Tablet with a portrait medallion by *James Heffernan*. – Samuel Gillatt †1862 and wife Sabina †1867. Tablet with portrait profiles by *Edwin Smith*. – STATUE (plaster) of Chantrey, seated, by *John Bell*, 1862. – STAINED GLASS. e window by *E.R. Frampton*, 1882. – s chapel windows commemorate the Cammell family, the e window *T. W. Camm* 1869, the rest 1882. – s aisle second from e by *Mark Harvey*, 2003. w window by *Ward & Hughes*, 1882. – Four windows by *Heaton, Butler & Bayne*, 1889–1935.

Former RECTORY, SE of the church, 1714–18, has three-bay pedimented centre with bolection-moulded doorway. Blind n bays added slightly later. To the s, beside Norton Lane, a plain granite OBELISK, 1854, commemorates the sculptor Francis Chantrey, who was born at Norton in 1781. Designed by *Philip Hardwick*, it stands 22 ft (7 metres) high (cf. the Bellot Memorial, Greenwich, London). Chantrey's grave in the churchyard is marked by a massive granite slab, enclosed by railings, SW of the tower.

NORTON HALL (flats) is immediately w of the church. Large ashlar house, mostly rebuilt or remodelled shortly before 1815 by *Samuel Shore Jun.*, with Victorian n wing. Seven by five bays and two-and-a-half storeys tall, with low three-bay pediment to s front. Recessed one-storey loggia with Doric columns below. Blocking course. Raised quoins. Plain moulded window surrounds with keystones. Matching two-storey NW addition built 1853–7 by Charles Cammell, the steel and shipbuilding magnate, includes dining room with canted bay (sumptuously panelled in oak c. 1905) and orangery at end of long Doric colonnade projecting to the w. Earlier NE range, of two lower storeys, has wide e portico with four Doric columns.

The handsome former STABLE block N of the church is characteristic of *John Carr* (cf. his stables of 1753 at Arncliffe Hall in the North Riding), who is known to have done unspecified work for Samuel Shore Sen. in 1768–9, presumably at Norton Hall. Pediments over the second and sixth bays of a seven-bay ashlar front; round-headed windows in blind arches with impost band. To NE a long symmetrical range of former FARM BUILDINGS, *c.* 1802, possibly also by *Carr*. Brick. Twelve bays, with round-arched openings in recessed arches. Hipped roofs to two-storey central and end pavilions.

GRAVES PARK, extending W and NE over 220 acres, is the Hall's former parkland, purchased in two portions by J.G. Graves in 1925 and 1935 and given to the City. It is Sheffield's largest park.

To the E OF NORTON HALL'S STABLES is NORTON GRANGE, 1744, facing Bunting Nook. Seven closely spaced bays. Segmental pediment to central doorway; above, a pedimented dormer with ramped sides and a semicircular window (cf. Jordanthorpe House, below). Matching attic windows in return gables. C19 bay windows. 350 yds N on Bunting Close are JOHN EATON's ALMSHOUSES, 1938. Twenty-eight gabled bungalows in small blocks enclose a large lawned quadrangle. Two-storey Warden's House and Reading Room etc. flank W gateway.

Now S of the church on Norton Lane. NORTON HOUSE (Club), is deceptive, its five narrowly spaced bays and tall hipped roof looking early C18. Built in 1880 it replaced an altered C17 house whose fine chimneypiece is now in the Cutlers' Hall (*see* p. 516). SW is CHANTRY COTTAGE, the former school, *c.* 1740. The three-bay ashlar centre is the master's house of one-and-a-half storeys with Gibbs surround to the doorway. Low two-bay schoolrooms l. and r. with their own entrances. Below, a LODGE to Norton Hall's kitchen gardens, *c.* 1860, in *cottage orné* style. From 1896 to 1900 it was used by Norton Colony, an alternative community, who leased the gardens.

300 yds further S, JORDANTHORPE HALL FARMHOUSE, Cinderhill Lane, is mid-C18. (Cut off by Bochum Parkway are CHANTREY HOUSE, and also JORDANTHORPE HOUSE, altered, but with a Diocletian window in its pedimented dormer, both C18, and in the grounds of MOSSBROOK SCHOOL by *W.L. Clunie*, City Architect, 1969. Single-storey SCOLA-system buildings, designed as a pioneering school for children with spina bifida.)

Going E along Norton Lane, CLOONMORE DRIVE, to the S, has *Moderne* houses, 1937, mostly semi-detached, rendered, with rounded corner windows and three-storey stair-towers to flat roofs. Others in Henley Avenue, partly in brick. Then the drive to Oakes Park with Italianate LODGE by *Woodhead & Hurst*, 1833, and fine GATEWAY.

THE OAKES (holiday centre for children) is a country house built *c.* 1668, extended and remodelled in the C18 and altered again in 1811 and 1827. It was the home of the Bagshaws of

Wormhill, Derbyshire, from 1716 to 1987. Plain nine-bay s front of two-and-a-half storeys with Tuscan porch. The five w bays, with four-bay l. return, represent the original house, which no doubt had gables and mullioned windows. It was probably Richard Bagshaw Jun., who inherited in 1750, who brought the house up to date with sash windows in plain surrounds and a coped parapet, and added the four, slightly less deep, e bays (see rear set-back). The c19 alterations, for Sir William Chambers Bagshawe and his son William Bagshaw, gave the house its present form. There are drawings by *Lindley & Woodhead* and *Woodhead & Hurst*, but both sets show more ambitious changes than were actually carried out, and the exact chronology and authorship of some work is not clear. Accounts show *Joseph Badger*'s involvement in the earlier alterations. The porch and the blocking course to the centre bays probably accompanied the rebuilt or remodelled roof, dated 1827. The c18 addition was rebuilt in 1811 as two tall storeys with windows in a new e wall, leaving the front windows as shams. At the rear a tall single-storey kitchen and lower service buildings were added. Beside the c18 rear staircase window a full-height polygonal turret at the NW corner accommodated new plumbing in 1827.

Early c18 work in the w part, probably for Richard Bagshaw Sen. Entrance hall has grey Derbyshire fossil marble fireplace with bolection moulding. To rear l. an excellent oak dog-leg staircase with 'umbrello'-type balusters. Drawing room, l. of hall, has very fine oak panelling with fluted Ionic pilasters. Cross-beam ceiling has c19 plasterwork with guilloche on soffit; pretty c19 marble fireplace with downward tapering columns. Behind is a panelled parlour with Doric pilasters and another fossil marble fireplace. To r. of hall an ante-room with Adamesque plasterwork, then the splendid dining room by *Joseph Badger*, 1811, similar to that at Renishaw, Derbyshire. Neoclassical plasterwork and N apse with elliptical arch and fluted Ionic pilasters. Staircase by *Badger* with glazed dome and cast-iron balusters leads to former music room above, which has a Doric screen.

Terrace designed by *Chantrey*. Beyond its w end a GATEWAY with c18 wrought-iron gates with elaborate overthrow. Long rear range of former STABLES, c17, with addition of 1722. PARKLAND setting, with pleasure grounds within ha-ha.

In LITTLE NORTON, by the sw corner of Graves Park on Little Norton Lane, is a crescent of five standard GRAVES TRUST HOMES, 1937 (cf. Gleadless, p. 610) and sw, facing Meadowhead, the HAIG MEMORIAL HOMES OF 1928–9, by *G. Grey Wornum* of *de Soissons & Wornum* with *Robert Cawkwell*. Ten houses and four flats in frankly Neo-Georgian brick. Central range with an archway where one would have expected the chapel; lower wings have dormers and projecting pavilion ends. They were built for the Painted Fabrics Settlement set up in 1923 to employ severely disabled ex-service men in the production of luxury clothing and furnishings. The archway led to workshops behind.

NORTON WOODSEATS

Southern suburb, transferred from Derbyshire in 1900 and mostly developed from the later C19 into the 1930s.

St Chad, Linden Avenue. Gothic style, of heavy appearance, in coursed rubble with ashlar dressings; inventive tracery based on C14 examples. Nave of 1911–12 by *C. & C.M.E. Hadfield*, whose complete scheme included a low crossing tower. Three bays with low clerestory; transverse gables to s aisle, parapet to n aisle. Chancel extension, with traceried round e window, and s organ chamber and vestry, 1931–3 to revised design by *Hadfield & Cawkwell*. Parish room, 1975, on site of their unbuilt ne tower.

St Paul, Norton Lees Lane. By *J.D. Webster*, 1875–7. Lancets. Small nw tower with stone spire has octagonal top with carving by *Harry Hems*. Clerestory and wide four-bay aisles added by *C.B. Flockton* 1935, using artificial stone. Tudor-arched arcades. Straight-headed windows with four cusped ogee lights. n chapel and sw baptistery unbuilt. – STAINED GLASS. e, chancel and w windows by *T. W. Camm*, 1893–4. Reordered 2005–6 with community rooms at w end.

Our Lady of Beauchief and St Thomas of Canterbury (R.C.), Meadowhead. By *Adrian Gilbert Scott*, 1931–2. One of the city's best C20 churches. Italian Romanesque style in well-detailed brick with hipped Roman tiled roofs. The plan is a Greek cross with a small semicircular (ritual) e apse to the sanctuary and to each transept, and an elongated nave. Low crossing tower with clerestory. The re-entrant angles of the transepts are filled with small triangular spaces with lower roofs; on the w these have single-storey canted extensions for confessionals. Inside, these spaces add a complexity handled with mastery, their little vaults supported on four stone columns with Lombardic capitals at the angles of the crossing. Plain plastered walls and tunnel-vault to each arm. w organ gallery. Plain glazing. Simple stone and marble ALTARS and FONT. Small carved STATIONS OF THE CROSS, unframed, by *Imogen Stuart* 1961. The whole provides a perfect setting for the striking MOSAICS in each apse, designed by *George Mayer-Marton* and made by *Geoffrey Wheeler*, 1960–2. Attached PRES-BYTERY by *Adrian Gilbert Scott*, 1928.

Norton Cemetery, Derbyshire Lane. By *Flockton & Abbott*, 1868–9. A two-bay Gothic CHAPEL and a LODGE flank the entrance.

Bishops' House, Norton Lees Lane. The outstanding timber-framed house of Sheffield. The name is recent and there is no documentary evidence that bishops lived here. Post-and-truss construction, L-shaped and picturesque in appearance with closely spaced posts and much diagonal studding above a later stone ground floor. The hall block is believed to be *c.* 1500, the w cross-wing a rebuild of *c.* 1550 (one post of its predecessor survives). The hall and wing are of two bays each with kingpost roofs. In the early C17, a floor was inserted in one of the hall bays and a new chimneystack built to serve the parlour and chamber over it at the s end of the cross-wing. A stone extension was built on to the N end of the wing *c.* 1650, housing a wide dog-leg oak staircase and the 'New Chamber' (so called in an inventory of 1665). The rebuilding of the ground floor in stone dates from the same time. In the parlour, early C17 plaster ceiling with rose motifs and in the hall, wooden panelling carved with strapwork, inscribed 'WB [William Blythe] 1627'. A carved C17 overmantel from Greenhill Hall (dem.) has been installed in the chamber over the hall in recent years. In the chamber above the parlour, arcaded plaster frieze over the fireplace, decorated with grapes, vine leaves and figs. Further simple plaster decoration of two dogs' heads and paired tapered pilasters above the fireplace in the N wing's New Chamber.

NEWFIELD SECONDARY SCHOOL, Lees Hall Road, Norton Lees. Originally separate boys' and girls' schools by *J.L. Womersley* 1958–60; rebuilt 2007–9 by *HLM*. Boys' school demolished, girls' building to E incorporated into new school for 1,000 pupils. TALBOT SPECIALIST SCHOOL attached on upper side.

In LINDEN AVENUE, near St Chad, Nos. 18–20 (PREEN and WENLOCK) are an attractive architectural curiosity of 1921, whose front incorporates an elaborate timber-framed upper floor and jettied double gable salvaged from *Norman Shaw*'s Preen Manor, Shropshire (1870–2).

PARSON CROSS AND SHIREGREEN

Northern suburbs, largely interwar council estates planned on garden suburb principles: the Norwood estate, begun 1919; the Longley estate, 1,700 houses built from 1926 in tree-lined roads, the layout including concentric semicircles; Shiregreen, 1930s, low density with semi-detached houses; and Parson Cross, similar, built from the late 1930s and completed after the Second World War, extending into Ecclesfield (q.v.).

ST BERNARD, Southey Hill, Parson Cross. By *Frederick Etchells*, 1953. Built of bricks salvaged from Clumber Hall, Nottinghamshire (dem. 1938). Plain rectangular nave with pitched roof. On the s four tall round-arched windows rise to the eaves, their grid of metal glazing bars industrial rather than ecclesiastical in character. No chancel, the sanctuary just a blind recess.

ST CECILIA, Chaucer Close, Parson Cross. By *Kenneth B. Mackenzie*, 1938–9; closed 2011 and demolition proposed. Large stone church of traditional form in simplified Perp style.

Low battlemented w tower. (Impressively spacious nave with seven-bay arcades to passage aisles, the arches dying into rectangular piers. Three-bay chancel. Sanctuary in shallow square-ended apse without windows. Crypt chapel. – Large elaborately carved triptych REREDOS, 1924, from a church in Preston. – ROOD, 1949.)

ST JAMES AND ST CHRISTOPHER, Bellhouse Road, Shiregreen. By *Stephen Welsh*, 1938–41. Brick with Roman tiled roofs. A memorably individual design, displaying Arts and Crafts and Scandinavian influence. Ritual w end, facing the road, has imposing rectangular tower with transverse saddleback roof. To either side a narrow blind bay with similar gabled roof, and, lower still, a flat-roofed square porch. Five-bay nave with aisles and clerestory, tall gabled transepts to chancel bay, shallow blind-ended sanctuary. Three- and four-light windows with flat ashlar mullions. (Brick used internally for dado, square piers and PISCINA, SEDILIA and PULPIT.)

ST LEONARD, Everingham Road, Norwood. Brick. Very big. Rectangular forms, of two storeys, set along a slope. Lower stage hall etc. with round-arched windows, by *E.W. Meredith*, 1932–3, built as mission church/hall pending funding for upper church. Completed to revised design by *Leslie Moore*, 1939–51.* Six-bay nave with tall paired lancets in blind arches. Straight parapets. (Octagonal timber piers to arcades, which continue across two-bay transepts to e wall with arched opening to shallow sanctuary. No e window. FONT COVER by *Bodley*, from St Stephen, Sneinton, Nottingham. – STAINED GLASS. N transept chapel by *Harry Grylls*.)

ST PAUL, Wordsworth Avenue, Parson Cross (formerly Ecclesfield). By *Basil Spence & Partners*, 1958–9. Simple oblong, with a shallow segmental vault constructed of light metal. The e and w ends are entirely glass, following Spence's experiments in Coventry churches; the plain brick side walls, slightly zigzag inside, only have clerestory strips. The effect is as if the roof is floating. The detached campanile is just two brick walls joined by concrete ties, and is connected by covered pathways. A vertical slatted afrormosia screen behind the altar and the placing of the organ (1962) on a w bridge, a visually very successful motif, combine to emphasize the transparency of the building. Spence was responsible for the ALTAR and other FURNISHINGS of hardwood and metal, their simplicity matching that of the building.

ST PATRICK (R.C.), Barnsley Road, Lane Top. By *Robert Cawkwell* of *Hadfield & Cawkwell*; nave and chancel 1939–40, passage aisles, chapel and N tower 1955–6. Large, brick. Traditional form, in spare modern style. Round e apse. Flat tops to rectangular tower and parapets. Tall many-transomed clerestory windows.

SHIREGREEN CEMETERY, Shiregreen Lane. Opened 1927. Stone chapel 1934.

106

---

* *Leslie Moore*'s ST HILDA, Windmill Lane, 1938, has been demolished.

JEWISH CEMETERY (of United Synagogue, Sheffield), Colley Road. First burials in 1874 for Sheffield Hebrew Congregation. Extended several times in first half of C20. The BURIAL HALL by *J. Amory Teather*, 1935–7 is small but monumental. Yellow brick with distinctive Art Deco detailing.

LEARNING ZONE, Wordsworth Avenue. By *Schmidt Hammer Lassen*, 2011. Library and community spaces. Sombre two-storey rectangle with slightly sloping roof. Deeply recessed frontage in black and cream with resilient metal screens; dark timber cladding to sides and rear.

CONCORD PARK, Shiregreen Lane. Fine wrought-iron entrance GATES from Hayes Place, Kent, C18, dem. 1933 by the donor, Henry Boot. Restored early C17 CRUCK BARN, off Oaks Lane, used as store. Four pairs of crucks.

LONGLEY PARK SIXTH FORM COLLEGE, Horninglow Road. By *Ellis Williams Architects*, 2004. Consciously unacademic in appearance. V-plan. Prominent corner entrance in tall main block with striking angled profile; a two-storey range diverges along Barnsley Road, enclosing a s-facing triangular courtyard. (Generous social spaces within, with abundant daylight.)

CHAUCER SCHOOL, Wordsworth Avenue. Originally separate boys' and girls' schools; the E buildings, by *Yorke, Rosenberg & Mardall* 1960–4, remain, remodelled and extended 2001–6 by *Sheffield Design & Project Management*. Some original blue brick; re-cladding in white render with yellow brick. New build in the same palette with deep blue for accent walls. One- and two-storeyed; overhanging, gently monopitch roofs.

YEWLANDS ACADEMY, Creswick Lane. By *HLM Architects* 2007–9; replaced Ecclesfield Yew Lane School, 1956–7, by *Basil Spence & Partners*.* Mostly two-storeyed, grey brick below, white render above. Pleasingly clean and unfussy.

SOAR WORKS, Knutton Road. By *Architecture oo*, 2010–11. Enterprise centre with offices, light industrial units, workshops and studios, for community charity Southey Owlerton Area Regeneration. Three storeys, in striking angular forms. Security roller shutters controlled by individual tenants give a quirky dynamic to the façades, a virtue made cleverly out of necessity.

STANNINGTON

Village on the hill between the Loxley and Rivelin valleys, linked to Sheffield's NW suburbs by C20 housing on the E slope.

CHRIST CHURCH. Commissioners' church by *Woodhead & Hurst*, 1828–30. Broad five-bay buttressed nave with deeply set lancets under hoodmoulds. Large bell-turret with crocketed spirelet on w gable. No chancel, but the E window is flanked

---

*ECCLESFIELD COLLEY SCHOOL, Remington Road, 1954 by *Basil Spence & Partners*, has been demolished. HINDE HOUSE SCHOOL, Shiregreen Lane, by *Jefferson & Partners*, 1959–62, has been replaced by *Aedas*, 2006.

by very tall octagonal buttresses with battlemented tops. Rising at all the angles, they give the building an ungainly appearance. W gallery; N and S galleries removed 1965. Reordered 1992–3 by *K.H. Murta*. E window enlarged by *Pace* in 1967 for STAINED GLASS, 1911, from Neepsend church, Sheffield (dem.). – MONUMENT. Rev. Samuel Carver and wife Eliza †1842 in carriage accident. Pedimented tablet by *Thomas Denman*.

KNOWLE TOP METHODIST CHAPEL (Wesleyan), Uppergate Road. Rebuilt 1877–9 by *H.W. Lockwood*. Cruciform; round-arched openings. Gabled front has polygonal organ chamber between porches, and octagonal stair-tower to r. Single-storey SCHOOL 1866 attached to rear.

UNDERBANK CHAPEL, Stannington Road, ⅜ m. NW. A delight-   48
ful example of a modest yet neat and not unornamental chapel built 1742–3 for Protestant Dissenters, one of the finest of its period. Unitarian since the late C18. Enhanced by its setting, it still has its graveyard with ash and sycamore trees, the care-taker's cottage is attached to its angle, a school (of 1853) in a similar, simpler style lies opposite, and the whole group looks N over the Loxley valley. Six-bay front. The two centre bays with tall arched windows, the two adjoining bays with corniced doorways and circular windows over, the outer bays narrower and two-storeyed – a usual Nonconformist scheme. Bold but plain ashlar details – quoins, window surrounds, impost blocks, keystones. Big stone-flagged hipped roof. Two tiers of windows to N and E. Two tall W windows of 1866, when interior was remodelled, with central pulpit moved from S to W wall and only an E gallery remaining of three original ones.

FORGE VALLEY SCHOOL, Wood Lane. By *BDP*, 2011, for over 1,100 students. Four storeys, eschewing symmetry. Long window strips. Double-curve to N side. Big hooded roof-lights. Medley of materials – light and dark brick, silver-grey cladding, detail panels in greens. It replaced Myers Grove Comprehensive School by *J.L. Womersley*, 1961–4.

SHOOTERS GROVE PRIMARY SCHOOL, Wood Lane. By *W.L. Clunie*, City Architect, 1963–5. One and two storeys, flat-roofed. Brick. Big windows, with timber mullions and transoms, in long strips or evenly spaced (cf. Dore, p. 604).

KING EDWARD VII HOSPITAL (former), Rivelin Valley Road (Sheffield), ¾ m. SSW. 1911–16 by *A.W. Kenyon*, after a competition. Near the River Rivelin, originally the Hospital for Crippled Children; later an orthopaedic hospital; closed 1992, now residential. A very fine example of the Neo-Georgian style of before the First World War. Long frontage with large central block of five bays, lower wings set back and stepping down from two storeys to one. Projecting outer wings have loggias for patients with coupled Doric columns. Similar blocks behind with Doric colonnades. All have dormer windows in big hipped pantile roofs. Pilastered entrance hall has copies of the pedestal panels from the statue of Edward VII in Fitzalan Square, Sheffield (*see* p. 542).

Above the hospital REVELL GRANGE, Bingley Lane, is an older house with a Georgian ashlar refacing. Lopsided front of five bays has broad plain pediment to centre three bays and another, small, pediment to wide first bay. Squarish sash windows, the upper ones with pediments to first and third bays, cornices to others. Blocking course with acroteria. Returns have flat-topped parapets disguising double gables. Odd windows with three triangular-headed lights to l. return. Attached to rear l. a former Roman Catholic CHAPEL, rebuilt 1858 in Gothick style, with tall gabled front.

A few older houses in UPPERGATE ROAD and NETHERGATE, e.g. WHITEHOUSE FARMHOUSE, No. 70 Nethergate, mid-C17, with four-light mullioned windows. Inside, braced arcade post to outshut aisle and good plank-and-muntin partitions; evidence of smoke-hood. Also POND FARMHOUSE, No. 645 Stannington Road, whose two cruck-framed s bays remain from a medieval open-hall house. Later stone casing and N bays.

ROBIN HOOD INN (former), Greaves Lane. Built 1804 by Thomas Halliday, who landscaped the steep slope down to the River Loxley as pleasure grounds, now lost, called Little Matlock after the Derbyshire resort. Handsome three-bay gable front with quoins, bands and three attic oculi. Below, LOW MATLOCK WHEEL, one of several former water-powered sites on the Loxley. Originally a cutlers' grinding wheel, 1732. Rebuilt 1882 as a steel rolling mill, its cast-iron pentrough and overshot iron water wheel, 18 ft 6 in. (5.5 metres) in diameter and last used *c.* 1956, survive.

WOOD LANE HOUSE, Wood Lane (Sheffield). 1802. Handsome ashlar-fronted house of three bays with open pediment to Doric doorcase. Service extension to l., stable range to rear. Other farm buildings. Restored as countryside centre.

LIBERTY HILL and WOODLAND VIEW ESTATES are 1960s terraced houses, four-storey flats etc. built using *Wimpey*'s 'No-Fines' system of *in situ* concrete construction. Three fifteen-storey point blocks, re-clad in brick.

TOTLEY

At the head of the Sheaf valley, below the Derbyshire moors, this hillside village on the Baslow turnpike developed in the later C19 and the C20 as a prosperous Sheffield suburb. It was transferred from Derbyshire in 1935.

ALL SAINTS. By *Currie & Thompson*, 1923–4. Cruciform, in Arts and Crafts Neo-Norman style. Low crossing tower covered by a saddleback roof, the apsidal sanctuary, transepts and nave with narrow clerestory and aisles grouped tightly around it. Plain, except for an arcaded frieze at the sanctuary eaves, relying for effect on the combination of random rubble walls, stone roofs and small, high-set windows. Inside, plastered walls set off the plain stonework of square piers, arches and deep window reveals. Two-bay nave and aisles have transverse arches. Choir in crossing. Apsidal chancel vault with groins. – Simple, robust, mahogany PULPIT, SCREEN AND CHOIR STALLS.

ENGLISH MARTYRS (R.C.), Baslow Road. By *John Rochford & Partner*, 1963–4. Square, the interior set on the diagonal. Plain brick elevations with tall windows grouped in recessed dark brick panels. Flat-roofed, but for a pyramidal roof at the NE corner above the square sanctuary.

PRIMARY SCHOOL, Sunnyvale Road. 1951. Low, plain, brick, with additions. Above the entrance three sculpted stone panels of children.

TOTLEY TUNNEL. 1888–93, for the Midland Railway's Sheffield–Manchester line. Just over 3 m. long, until the C21 it was Britain's second longest railway tunnel. The company's engineer was *Percy Richards*, who lived at Totley Grove and died of the typhoid which affected his workforce in 1893.

TOTLEY HALL (flats), Totley Hall Lane. C17 house, dated 1623 above the doorway, altered and extended in Neo-Jacobean style by *J. D. Webster*, 1883 and 1894. To l. of the door two five-light mullioned-and-transomed windows one above the other, then a cross-wing with a two-storey Victorian bay window. The additions r. of the door have another bay window with a cross-wing beyond.

Along Totley Hall Lane older village buildings include the former SCHOOL, dated 1827. More to N across the main road e.g. Nos. 5 and 7 Hillfoot Road, with doorway dated 1704, and CANNON HALL, Butts Hill, a restored late C16 linear farmhouse, barn etc. with two cruck-trusses and early C17 cross-wing.

THE DINGLE, No. 172 Prospect Road, Totley Rise. By *Edgar Wood*, 1904, for the Rev. William Blackshaw. Small house in Wood's characteristic domestic Arts and Crafts style, with varied elevations in rubble stone from the site. Diagonal NW entrance in inner angle of two gabled bays, the W one with small flat-roofed two-storey bay. Longer S front to terraced garden has broad canted bay to r. Painted timber mullions, the windows flush with the walls. The lofty hillside site is now much reduced and hemmed in by later houses.

WADSLEY AND LOXLEY

WADSLEY CHURCH, Worrall Road. By *Joseph Potter*, 1833–4. Lancet style. Big ashlar blocks. Pretty, almost Gothick, W tower flanked by unfortunate additions. Pilaster buttresses, frieze to third stage and stone broach spire. Six-bay nave with plain parapet and deeply set windows. Very short chancel with three stepped lancets. Remodelled W gallery, the other two removed in reordering 2003, but their slender cast-iron piers and tall arcades remain. – MONUMENT. James Willis Dixon †1876 and wife Ann †1882. Marble panels with achievement by *G. Trojani* of Florence.

To N, just beyond the plain Tudor Gothic former SCHOOL, 1838, are WADSLEY ALMSHOUSES, 1839, endowed by Hannah Rawson for six poor widows. Single-storey row, in livelier Tudor Gothic.

WADSLEY PARK VILLAGE, Middlewood Road. Originally built as the South Yorkshire Lunatic Asylum in 1869–72 by *Bernard Hartley II*, West Riding Surveyor. Subsequently Middlewood Hospital, closed in 1996. Converted to housing with new building in the grounds 2001–6, but preserving the three-storey Italianate administration block, in brick and ashlar with porte cochère, pediment and clock tower, a huge brick ward range of 1878 with towers flanking the central entrance bays and projecting canted ends and large Gothic Revival CHAPEL (1873–5, presently unused).

WADSLEY HALL, Far Lane. Very handsome five-bay house of 1722 with well-detailed ashlar front including moulded door-case and window surrounds.

Above the Loxley valley, almost clear of suburban streets and houses, is LOXLEY HOUSE, off Ben Lane. Rebuilt 1826. Ashlar. Three-storey centre of three widely set bays, all the windows Venetian. Two-storey one-bay wings with Venetian windows only to ground floor. Hipped roofs, balustraded parapets. Heavy square porch with Doric columns. Outbuildings of 1795. Now flats.

LOXLEY CHAPEL, Loxley Road. Built in 1787 and despite neglect after its closure in 1993 well preserved until finally gutted by fire in 2016, with the loss of its galleried interior.

SHELF

Upland village along the Halifax–Bradford road with worsted mills and much C20 development.

St Michael and All Angels, Carr House Road. 1848–50, by *Mallinson & Healey*, paid for by the Hardy family of the Low Moor Iron Co. Dec. Modest five-bay nave with lean-to aisles, gabled w bellcote and N porch. – STAINED GLASS. S aisle first from E by *Charles Steel*, 1920. – N aisle first from E by *Harry Harvey*, 1964.

Bethel United Methodist Church, Carr House Road. Dated 1853. Plain square chapel of stone 'bricks' with pyramidal roof. (Interior has horseshoe-shaped gallery.)

British School (former), Carr House Lane. 1816. Schoolroom with arched windows set high up, altered for residential conversion. Inscribed tablet over the door of the teacher's house.

High Bentley, below the village in Green Lane on the corner opposite Riding Hill, is one of the best yeomen-clothiers' houses of the Halifax area, restored *c.* 1990. Its core is a timber-framed aisled hall of *c.* 1500 with gabled w cross-wing, separately framed. Originally of hearth-passage plan, the lower end probably used as the shop. The unheated E cross-wing was built in stone *c.* 1600, seemingly to increase the working area. In 1661 Richard Wade made major alterations and improvements, including stone casing. He dated the ornamental lintel of a new N lobby-entry and fine plasterwork in the housebody, which was upgraded as a galleried hall with twelve-light mullioned-and-transomed window and stone fireplace. Its kitchen function transferred to a new N wing, with separate service rooms in the former aisle. The original lower end was converted to a heated parlour while the E wing remained as workspace, its segregation from the living area maintained by the creation of a new through passage with door in the SE angle. Mullioned windows include one to r. of N door with three stepped lights with ogee heads; above that, in a little gable, another three-light with truncated-ogee top (cf. Kildwick, *West Riding North*).

Lower Fold Farmhouse (formerly High Bentley Farm) is nearby on Green Lane's E side. Mid-C17. The hall and projecting l. cross-wing have double-chamfered mullioned windows with hoodmoulds; the lower wing's windows are plainer. Triple-gabled rear with external stone stair to upper floor of projecting central wing. Lower down on the w, Low Bentley Farmhouse. Unusual plan with the doorway, dated 1600, at the side of the house. Perhaps a later remodelling. Double-gabled s front, rebuilt *c.* 1975, has transomed hall window of fourteen lights.

Lower Field Bottom Farmhouse, Coley Road, ¾ m. sw. Mid-C16 aisled hall. The main range and side wall of the cross-wing have integrated framing. C17 stone casing. Fourteen-light mullioned-and-transomed window in wing's upper chamber.

On Brackens Lane, N of the village, the GATEWAY of the LION BREWERY (dem.), 1897 by *J. F. Walsh*.

SHELLEY

EMMANUEL CHURCH. 1866–8, by *James Mallinson*, completed with *W. Swinden Barber*.

METHODIST CHURCH, ¾ m. WSW. 1784–5. One of our area's oldest Methodist chapels still in use, standing among fields. Small. Originally a simple rectangle with entrances flanking the central pulpit on the broad S front, where vestry with organ gallery above, 1842, now forms gabled projection. Two-storey addition to W gable, 1882, has Venetian window to upper meeting room. Delightful interior, with original pews to three-sided gallery; pulpit and panelled box pews downstairs 1860.

SHELLEY HALL, ⅓ m. W. C17. Double-pile plan. S front has a window of three-plus-three lights to l. of near-central doorway, and a four-light window to r., both transomed. A three-light transomed window on the r. return. Mullioned windows of two, three and four lights elsewhere. Continuous dripmoulds; that on the first floor of the returns runs from the moulded eaves cornice of the front. On the first gable of the r. return it drops down over a window set lower than those on the second gable, a most odd-looking reversal of the usual practice of rising over doorways.

SHEPLEY

ST PAUL. By *William Wallen*, 1847–8. Plain lancet-style nave. Chancel 1868, organ chamber by *Edward Hughes* 1880. – STAINED GLASS. E window by *Wailes*, 1868.

SHEPLEY FIRST SCHOOL, Firth Street. By *Ben Stocks*, 1896. Free Northern Renaissance style, unusually exuberant for a rural Board School.

SHEPLEY HALL, Station Road. 1608, much altered. Inside, a ceiling dated 1609 with mermaids and mermen in the frieze.

CLIFFE HOUSE (Study Centre), Lane Head Road. 1888–9 for James Senior, brewer. Good example of an industrialist's house. Half-timbered gables, mullioned-and-transomed windows. Some well-preserved interiors.

SHERBURN-IN-ELMET

Large village, now mainly C20, centred on a cross-roads: the church stands at the w end, crowning a low hill. The site of an early medieval residence of the archbishops of York which was demolished in 1361: earthworks – of building platforms, ditches etc. – remain, on the sloping ground N of the church. A charter for a market was granted to Archbishop Grey in 1223.

ALL SAINTS. Substantially late Norman, of considerable ambitions – a consequence doubtless of the archiepiscopal connection – with aisles and a sturdy w tower embraced by them;
but the handsome exterior reveals little of that date. On the
tower the only indications are the shallow clasping SE and NE
buttresses. Other detail all Perp – short bulky SW stair-turret
and deep diagonal NW buttress, three-light W window, paired
two-light bell-openings, battlements and pinnacles. Perp also
the nave clerestory with straight-headed three-light windows
and similar battlemented parapet. Chancel rebuilt in the C13,
but its present scholarly E.E. appearance, with steeply pitched
roof contrasting with the parapets elsewhere, is due to *Salvin*'s
extensive restoration of 1857, in which Dec and Perp windows
were abolished. Of the aisles, the s had been widened, and
a short s chancel chapel added, probably in the C14 – the
present arched Perp windows are *Salvin*'s, replacing Dec ones
shown in earlier views. Re-set Norman s doorway, with a single
chamfer and a hoodmould with a keeled roll, incorporating
C14 escutcheons; and rebuilt s porch rebuilt again by *Salvin*,
replicating the late Norman entrance – chevron, colonnettes
with waterleaf capitals, but a pointed arch – which had also
been re-set with C14 escutcheons introduced. Adjoining the
porch to the E is a gabled outer chapel with straight-headed
windows similar to the clerestory's, probably of the early C16:
the name of a vicar of that period was formerly visible over the
entrance from the porch. The N aisle has been heightened and
lengthened to the E, in the C15 or C16, but not widened – see
the change in masonry halfway up the N wall and one small
Norman window: so the Norman aisles were remarkably
wide; and a short stretch of curved wall visible inside at the
SW corner of the N chapel suggests that they were apsidal-
ended. Other N aisle windows late Perp, straight-headed,
uniform.

So to the interior and first the nave arcades, of four bays with
tall strong cylindrical piers carrying many-scalloped round capitals of varied design and elaborately moulded arches framed
by similarly variegated ornamental hoodmoulds. The responds
have square capitals, the SW with a (renewed) waterleaf motif,
the NE a volute-like decoration. The three tower arches are
simpler, of three chamfered orders with plain imposts; and the
space within has a rib-vault with single-chamfered ribs which is

11

probably a slightly later addition, as one of the corbels carrying it is of the crocket type characteristic of *c.* 1200. Above the E arch, facing into the nave, a Neo-Norman window, presumably inserted by *Salvin*; later C19 internal buttressing N and S. Tall E.E.-style chancel arch also largely *Salvin*'s, it appears. In the chancel Dec and Perp double-chamfered arches to the S and N chapels, and on the N side one C13 lancet and traces of others. In the S aisle three C14 tomb-recesses, a trefoil piscina and a curious window into the outer chapel, reminiscent of the wavy-shaped doorheads of the C17 Pennines and doubtless an alteration of that period. Nave and aisle roofs almost flat, with moulded beams: the arms of Sir William Hungate (†1634) on the SE nave roof corbel perhaps relate to a re-roofing. – SCULPTURE. A very rare C15 piece, the head of a Janus Cross – i.e. a cross with near-identical Crucifixion scenes on both sides. It was found in the churchyard and, most extraordinarily, as a result of an ownership dispute between the vicar and the churchwarden, was then sawn in half across its thickness to separate the two scenes. Moulded base, gablet over, two-light tracery between the cross and the flanking figures, encircled quatrefoils under the gable. – STAINED GLASS. Medieval and later fragments, assembled 1857 in the W window, with coloured background; chancel windows *c.* 1859, one commemorating the 1857 restoration; S chapel E, 1875 in the manner of Heaton, Butler & Bayne. – GRAVE-SLAB, under the E tower arch. Of a priest, C14, with foliate cross, chalice and missal. – In the churchyard a medieval CROSS-HEAD on a later plinth.

SHERBURN HIGH SCHOOL, Garden Lane. 1972–3 by *West Riding County Architect's Department* (County Architect *K.C. Evans*). CLASP Mark IVB. One and two storeys, with central courtyard.

At the central cross-roads the former HUNGATE HOSPITAL, grammar school and hospital founded under the will of Robert Hungate, 1619, now a doctors' surgery. Flat symmetrical front, now rendered, with gables at each end, central round-headed doorway with coat of arms over, cross- and mullioned windows. Similar detail at the back, where two wings project. C19 and C20 alterations.

SHIBDEN

Immediately NE of Halifax, where Godley Lane passes through the deep GODLEY CUTTING, completed in 1830 by the Leeds & Halifax Turnpike Trust to reduce the gradients of the main route through the valley of Shibden Dale. The S end is spanned by a handsome iron BRIDGE, carrying the old road, as rebuilt in 1900 by *E.R.S. Escott*, Halifax Borough Surveyor. Hefty stone Gothic piers with crown finials.

SHIBDEN HALL, E of Godley Lane, is *c.* 1490, with the best timber-framed work in the Halifax district. From the early C17 it was a property of the Listers, the last of whom, John Lister, was bankrupted in 1923 after which Halifax Corporation purchased house and grounds for public use. The hall has been a museum since 1934. The original house was H-plan, the two cross-wings gabled. The centre encased in stone with long low Elizabethan hall window of ten lights with king mullion and transom. Elizabethan N wing. The tall W tower was added *c.* 1835 by *John Harper* for Anne Lister. Also the arcaded loggia and former kitchen at the E end. The interior retains the original hearth-passage plan and some important C16 features. *Harper*'s alterations for Anne Lister in the 1830s were made with a sensitivity for the house's history unusual for the time. The hall, floored in the early C16, was restored to its open form with a new N staircase and gallery; the walls have oak panelling downstairs and mock timber framing above. The upper windows were retained; the great window below has a painted armorial panel of Robert Waterhouse, who inherited the estate in 1583, and his wife Jane Waterton, probably by *Bernard Dininckhoff c.* 1585; also many delightful late medieval or early C16 quarries with birds, beasts etc., similar to those in the Zouche chapel, York Minster, reused in the C16. In the W wing the S parlour's painted timber ceiling of *c.* 1504 has been restored, its bosses covered in silver leaf. Panelling, *c.* 1834. In the N Parlour, on the stud partition wall, is some late C16 polychrome painted decoration patterned with stylized flowers and foliage, a very rare survival. The small front room of the original service wing, later a study, has early C18 fielded panelling.

Fine early C17 aisled BARN to rear.

The S and W terraces, designed by *Harper*, were made when the PARK was laid out by *William Gray* of York (opened as a public park 1926). Gothic-arched GATEWAY, with castellated LODGE, Godley Lane, by *Harper* 1837.

TUDOR HOUSE (formerly Daisy Bank), ½ m. E on Leeds Road, is a fine merchant's house of *c.* 1500, known as the 'House at the Maypole', brought here from central Halifax and re-erected *c.* 1891 by *J. F. Walsh* for John Lister.* The pointed doorway's carved spandrels include the arms of the Merchant Adventurers of York. The upper storey, set on a new stone base, has close upright as well as diagonal struts. Three oriel windows on elaborate brackets, the middle window's front decorated with diaper-work and a fleur-de-lys.

SHIBDEN DALE is the secluded narrow valley to the N with many good houses, accessible from Godley Lane only by narrow lanes and tracks, several precipitously steep and some still

---

*Lister also saved a C15 timber-framed cottage from Cripplegate, Halifax, dismantled in 1872. Re-erected in the park of Shibden Hall, it became derelict and was demolished in 1971.

cobbled.* In Staups Lane, STAUPS HOUSE (Nos. 34–36) has a (renewed) keystone dated 1684 over its finely moulded arched doorway. Three bays, each with gable and large mullioned-and-transomed windows, the upper one stepped, three over five. SPA HOUSE, ¼ m. NW up the valley, is the former bath house for the Horley Green Mineral Springs, *c.* 1840. Italianate style. Two-storey centre with Venetian window, single-storey wings (the l. with sunken bath).

DAM HEAD, at the bottom of Whiskers Lane is an early C16 timber-framed house cased in stone and enlarged in the C17, but originally of linear plan with hearth-passage entry and a housebody with two aisles. The front one remains in the still open housebody, which has a twenty-light transomed window with central king mullion. (Inside is exposed decorative herringbone framing of the later C16 W upper wing. Also the plank screen to a dais bench.) Moulded surrounds to passage doorways have scrolled bases.

40   SCOUT HALL, ⅓ m. W, is an improbable and ambitious palace built in 1680. Stylistically it stands on the threshold of the new age of the Caroline house, adopting a double-pile plan and a nearly symmetrical façade, but retaining some traditional features. Three storeys. The eleven-bay S front has a curious rhythm of windows: 2:1:4:1:3, the three groups being divided by small oval windows. These have moulded cornices and sills; a continuous dripmould forms the cornice of the tall cross-windows. Very finely moulded door surround with frieze of a fox followed by hounds and huntsman. Prominent five-bay E return with central oval windows. First-floor windows with individual cornices. The hipped roof here is a C19 alteration: it originally had two gables, like the simpler W elevation, which reverts to old-style details in the hoodmoulds. Plain seven-bay rear.

SILKSTONE

ALL SAINTS. Large and noble. Externally it appears all Perp, and uncommonly impressive thanks to the delightful idea of providing it with low buttresses whose tall detached pinnacles are connected with the wall by flying buttresses. The lower ones are tiny, the larger upper ones project as grotesques, carved in limestone. This form of buttress lends gaiety to the somewhat sombre style of the Perp churches of the area and occurs also at Ecclesfield and St John, Halifax (qq.v.). Battlements to the clerestoried nave, aisles, S porch and chapels, and to the big pinnacled W tower completed in 1495. Mainly funded by the Cluniac Priory of Pontefract, it replaced a Norman crossing tower taken down in 1479. Inside, it is clear that the Perp church succeeded a late C12 cruciform building. Chancel arch on

---

*One of the lost houses is HIGH SUNDERLAND (*c.* 1629, dem. 1950), whose gateway and other fragments are at Bankfield Museum, Halifax.

sturdy semicircular responds with square capitals. Arch into the present N chapel, replacing a crossing arch, on matching, but shorter, responds. The circular piers of the nave arcades are probably also reused (cf. Ecclesfield and Bradfield). Five bays, with double-chamfered arches. The sunk quadrant mouldings of the E arches of the aisles and of the S doorway indicate an early C14 date. Nave and aisles have good roofs with numerous bosses (four heads chin to chin; two green men; angels with instruments of the Passion, etc.). Tall tower arch with rosettes on the capitals. Low Perp vestry E of S chapel, sunk by six steps (cf. Bradfield and Worsbrough). Chancel rebuilt with hammerbeam roof by *Salvin*, 1857–8, his restoration destroying Norman fabric described by Glynne in 1852.

SCREENS. Ornate Perp screens to chancel and chapels, all belonging together, all differing in details, all apparently somewhat altered. Very rich and dense carving. – ROOD STAIR in S chapel. – PULPIT and BOX PEWS. 1832–5. Gothic traceried panels. – ROYAL ARMS. Late C17 or C18. Wood, cleverly carved double-sided. – C18 PAINTINGS of Aaron and Moses (W wall). – STAINED GLASS. S chapel E. Well-preserved shield *c.* 1540. Chancel. All four by *A. O'Connor*, 1858. – N aisle. Easternmost by *Shrigley & Hunt*, 1876. N chapel. – MONUMENTS. Several, including table tombs, to the Wentworths, C17. The most sumptuous is Sir Thomas Wentworth †1675, and wife, attributed to *Thomas Cartwright I* (GF). Excellent recumbent effigies of white marble, his in armour. Big sarcophagus with trophies against the sides. Above, inscription cut on black marble by *Claudius Rene*, 1676. Splendid aedicule with open segmental pediment, urns and achievement.

WOOLLEY MANOR, ⅔ m. SSW. H-plan house, C17 and C19. Right cross-wing of two bays, gabled. Attic. Two-, three- and four-light windows under common hoodmoulds. Central range and l. wing outwardly C19 but in keeping, using doorway dated 1628 at rear.

NOBLETHORPE HALL, ⅔ m. SW. 1838, altered and extended by *William Hill* of Leeds 1856. Five-bay ashlar front. Small segmental pediment between vase-topped dies of balustraded parapet. Pedimented porch with paired Ionic columns.

KNABBE'S HALL, 1¼ m. S. Built by William Wood of Wortley Forge (*see* Hunshelf), *c.* 1658–74. Ashlar front of three gabled bays with two-storey porch, off-centre. Iron plaque with royal arms, dated 1674, over entrance. Double-chamfered windows, mostly transomed; the largest four lights with king mullion. (Panelling and plaster ceilings inside.)

SKELBROOKE

4010

ST MICHAEL AND ALL ANGELS. In a secluded position at a little distance from the hall and old cottages of this tiny village. Extensively rebuilt in Dec style by *Joseph Goddard*, 1871–2, after a serious fire, preserving some original fabric and features. Unbuttressed W tower has two-light bell-openings with traces of former (C12?) openings below. Long narrow nave with C14 canopied niche in N wall and rood-loft staircase on S. The two-bay arcade to a lost chantry chapel, 'newly built' in 1336, was opened up by Goddard for a tiny N chapel with four quatrefoil side windows and pretty PAINTED DECORA-TION with procession of angels and brightly patterned roof timbers. – STAINED GLASS. Fragment with saint's head, c. 1330s, in staircase window. E window 1872, nave N eastern-most 1922, both by *Heaton, Butler & Bayne*. W window by *Mary Lowndes* of *Lowndes & Drury*, 1894. Chancel second and third from E and nave S second from E by *Herbert W. Bryans* 1920. – MONUMENT. Henry Browne †1770. Crisply carved tablet with obelisk above, cherub below.

SKELBROOKE HALL. Large, plain house built in the early C18 by Captain Henry Brown, who served under the Duke of Marlborough. Limestone rubble, formerly stuccoed, with ashlar quoins. Three storeys; lower rear service range. Five-bay E front has early C19 enclosed Doric porch with pediment. (One room has rich plasterwork (including Ionic pilasters, and chimneypiece with bust of the Duke of Marlborough, trophies and eagle with wreath) some made from moulds used at Blenheim Palace.)

SKELMANTHORPE

2010

Large former textile village above the Upper Dearne valley with weavers' housing in several streets; it specialized in hand-woven fancy-goods into the C20.

ST AIDAN. By *Bodley & Garner*, 1894–5. Not large. Nave and chancel under one roof, with sturdy bellcote above chancel arch. Four-bay arcade to separately roofed N aisle, the S arcade built but not the aisle. – FONT. Large, square, latest Anglo-Saxon or early Norman, similar to Cawthorne (q.v.). On two sides, three interlaced arches, on another four tall arched panels filled with foliage scrolls, two of the panels with heads at the top. On the fourth side two panels, one blank, the other with foliage. – STAINED GLASS. E window by *Victor Milner*, 1895.

SLAITHWAITE

0010

Large village in the Colne Valley, by the Huddersfield Narrow Canal, still with some big mills dominant in the landscape. Industrial development was limited until the Earl of Dartmouth's estate management was modernized in the 1850s.

St James. Rebuilt 1789. Nave and short chancel with Venetian window and w tower. The nave has straight-headed windows in two tiers. Porches and gallery staircases of 1890–1 by *Kirk & Sons*, who remodelled the interior. The nave's e bay forms a square choir, with a big round arch on each side, and chapels n and s of this with round w arches. – reredos. Painted triptych by *A.O. Hemming* 1896, commemorating the 5th Earl of Dartmouth. – stained glass. e window by *David & Charles Evans*, 1859, to the 4th Earl.

Providence Strict Baptist Chapel, Hollins Row. 1816, refronted and extended by *Ben Stocks*, 1886. Six bays. Doric pilasters to plain outer doorways; round-arched windows. First-floor l. extension carried over graves.

Civic Hall, New Street. Former Liberal Club by *Ben Stocks*, 1883–4. Its three-bay gabled Gothic front has the usual balcony for speeches; the first-floor hall held over 700 people.

Crimble and Slaithwaite railway viaducts. Built *c.* 1845 for the Huddersfield & Manchester Railway; doubled in width *c.* 1886–90. Nineteen and fifteen arches respectively, e and w of the station, impressive backdrops to the village across side valleys on the n hillside.

Manor House (Dartmouth Estate Office), 75 yds wsw of the church. Late c16; slightly later extension. Quite small, perhaps a fragment. Back to hillside. Quoins. One six-light mullioned-and-transomed window, another of five lights to short gabled wing. Mullioned windows above. To l., two similar additional bays, with Tudor-arched doorway. Just w, the forbiddingly crenellated lock-up, 1834. Going e, the former Free School, founded 1721, rebuilt 1842 with Tudor Gothic front. Nearby in Lewisham Road several picturesque gabled Tudor Gothic cottages, Nos. 6–10 dated 1853.

Along the Huddersfield Narrow Canal (1794–1811), the long five-storey frontage of Globe Mill, 1887, towering over the towpath, and Spa Mill (cotton), its huge and sole surviving No. 4 mill, 1907, with tall octagonal chimney.

Linthwaite Hall, Linfit Fold. Just above Manchester Road on the valley's s side. Early c17 gentry house (now subdivided) with w cross-wing and two-storey front and rear porches. Big ashlar masonry. The hall has a seven-light mullioned-and-transomed s window, a six-light one to the n, the wing a five-light and two six-light transomed windows. Deep e end a slightly later build. Large former barn to e, *c.* 1600, originally five bays, has three massive crucks.

SNAITH

Attractive small town with a fine church standing above the pantile roofs of its brick houses. An important medieval manor and huge parish, Snaith had a market from 1223 and a port on the Aire nearby. Although in the 1379 Poll Tax assessment it

ranked eighth in wealth in the West Riding, later development
was limited and after the river was bypassed by the Selby and
Knottingley–Goole canals there was little change to Snaith's
Georgian character.

PRIORY CHURCH OF ST LAURENCE. A big, all-embattled
church with sturdy W tower and plenty of pinnacles. On a
probable Saxon site, the church was given in 1100 to Selby
Abbey, which founded a small priory here. Of the original
Norman building with aisles and transepts no more can be
seen than the plain pilastered W responds of the former arcades,
and some unmistakable cobble and rubble masonry in the
transepts' lower walls. The Norman church was shorter
towards the W than is the present one and when the tower was
added in the C13 was lengthened by one bay. The broad four-
stage tower has a W portal with four orders of colonnettes,
carrying restored moulded capitals, and a shafted W window.
The bell-openings are three double-chamfered lancets of even
height on each side. The corbel table below the unnecessary
Perp embattled parapet of c. 1598 has worn human and animal
heads: are they mid-C12, reused? In lengthening the nave, the
architect decided to embrace the tower with the aisles, and so
the tower opens in clearly E.E. arches to N and S as well as E.
These arches are triple-chamfered and, like the two arcade
arches, stand on tapering corbels, except on the W, where they
rest on heads, one crowned by a wreath of simple upright
stiff-leaf.

   Early C14 chancel, the restored E window with reticulated
tracery. The two original windows are of three stepped cusped
lancet lights under one two-centred arch, the N one partly
blocked by the small, slightly later vestry. Then the C15: major
work including renewal of the arcades, aisles and chancel arch,
also two-bay N and S chapels and clerestory. The five bays of
the arcades have octagonal piers and double-chamfered arches,
the need for strengthening perhaps explaining the fragment of
wall after two of them. The Norman transepts were made
senseless internally by this even Perp arcade and the wider
aisles (the S aisle only partly widened). In the SE respond a
niche for an image, inscribed *Sca sitha* (St Osyth?). Lower
doorway to rood-loft stair and trace of upper doorway S of
chancel arch. S porch, originally two-storeyed. Big, mostly
four-light windows to transepts and chapels; another, with
Selby Abbey's three swans on the label stops, at N aisle W end
to light the abbey's Consistory Court room. – STAINED GLASS.
E window by *Francis Spear*, 1936. S aisle: second from E by
Camere & Capronnier, 1893; third from E by *Powell Bros* 1899.
N aisle, second from E by *W.H. Constable*, †1877. – MONU-
MENTS. Sir John Dawnay †1493. Low tomb-chest with no
effigy. Painted shields on the S and W, on the N the head of an
applied moulded arch, apparently an opening to the family
vault before the tomb was moved and lowered. – Chancel
floor. C16 black marble matrix of a huge BRASS of a mitred

abbot in elaborate surround with pinnacled top. Probably
Robert Rogers, last Abbot of Selby, †1559. – Lady Elizabeth
Stapleton †1684, signed by *Samuel Carpenter* of York.
Alabaster. Frontal bust in a small niche within an aedicule with
garlanded pilasters and open segmental top. Inscribed tablet
below, with palm fronds; other decoration damaged. – John
Dawnay, 5th Viscount Downe, †1832, by *Chantrey*, 1837. Life-
size marble statue standing in Parliamentary robes, as if it were
taken out of the N transept of Westminster Abbey. – Matthew
Boynton †1795, by *John Fisher II*. Large decorated urn on a
garlanded and scrolled pedestal, set over a shaped tablet with
elaborately fluted top, all against an obelisk.

In the churchyard the much-altered former GRAMMAR
SCHOOL, founded 1626. By the churchyard E wall the TOWN
LOCK-UP, *c.* 1800, with two cells.

METHODIST CHURCH (Wesleyan), Wesley Place, ¼ m. E. By
Lockwood & Mawson, 1861–2. A brick twin of their chapel at
Harrogate (*West Riding North*), remarkably large and splendid
for a country town. Hexastyle temple front with Roman Ionic
half-columns and pilasters, modillioned cornice and modillioned pediment with scrolled cartouche in tympanum, all in
stone. Three round-arched entrances, arched and pedimented
upper windows. Plainer six-bay returns. Fine interior has continuous gallery on cast-iron columns, the panelled front with
Art Nouveau stencilling *c.* 1906. Panelled ceiling with shallow
barrel-vault. Original fittings include ornate raised pulpit and
box pews.

Good brick houses in High Street and Market Place, e.g. the
mid-C18 DOWNE ARMS, its later bow windows under half-
domes. Some larger houses on Pontefract Road to S, notably
SNAITH HALL, *c.* 1829, for William Shearburn, in large ashlar
blocks of fine creamy limestone. Three-bay N front, the central
bay with four-column Doric porch and pedimented attic
storey.[*]

E, towards Goole, some mid-C19 villas, e.g. EASTFIELD HOUSE,
c. 1840, grey brick with Tuscan porch, and FAIRHOLME, 1848
by *B. & J. Sykes*, Tudor Gothic with decorative chimneys,
both for the Shearburn family.

SOUTH BRAMWITH *see* KIRK BRAMWITH

SOUTH CROSLAND   *1010*

HOLY TRINITY. 1827–30 by *Peter Atkinson Jun.* Lancet style.
Nave, W tower. Lower chancel of 1860. Interior with three
galleries. E window by *Lavers, Barraud & Westlake*, 1878.

---

[*] Its conservatory, attributed to *Paxton*, has been replaced.

CROSLAND HALL, ¼ m. SW. Later Georgian, with canted centre to garden front.

At NETHERTON, ½ m. ENE, the grand-looking ODDFELLOWS HALL, 1854, with wings formed of workers' cottages.

SOUTH ELMSALL

ST MARY, Doncaster Road. 1910 by *J. Nicholson Johnston*. Unassuming Perp revival. Painted rood and ferro-concrete baldacchino.

TRINITY METHODIST CHURCH, Ash Grove. 1884–5. Gothic, with a little stone steeple.

SOUTH KIRKBY

A rather characterless village in the heart of a former mining area. The older vernacular buildings have mostly been demolished or heavily restored following subsidence.

ALL SAINTS, Barnsley Road. Externally Perp, mostly a rebuilding *c.* 1481. Four-stage W tower, with sandstone in the lower parts. In other limestone area churches this may indicate Norman or earlier fabric (e.g. at Darrington and Laughton-en-le-Morthen, qq.v.) and the W doorway has some dogtooth that Sir Stephen Glynne noted as 'anomalous' in 1860. Three-light transomed bell-openings. Diagonal buttresses with decorative gables. Ornate two-storey S porch with big gargoyles and pinnacles. Shields of local families and a canopied niche above the entrance. Renewed rib-vault inside with ridge as well as diagonal ribs. Battlemented S chapel has short buttresses supporting tall diagonal pinnacles with crocketed finials (cf. the Holdsworth Chapel in Halifax Minster, and Silkstone, qq.v.). N side much less showy, with plain parapets. The light and spacious interior is more complex. The nave arcades are no doubt early C13, though now have only two very wide and high arches where three might be expected. They were perhaps rebuilt to accommodate C18 galleries, lit by the square-headed clerestory windows. Circular piers, simple moulded capitals, double-chamfered arches with small broaches. The SW respond is keeled. Pretty oakleaf carving on the tower arch responds. Wide chancel, with blocked door to the N chancel chapel, which could be later C13. Two bays, octagonal pier. The S chapel is Perp, with a big head corbel on the two-bay arcade's W respond. In the nave a rare survival – a coved canopy above the site of the rood, comparable with the dais canopy found in some late medieval hall houses. It is panelled, with slender ribs and large square foliated bosses. No doubt the panels were originally decorated with paintings. Good lean-to roofs in the N aisle and N chapel, with carved bosses and corbels, including delightful figures of musicians in the aisle. In the N aisle wall a large niche, now the Shrine of Our Lady of the Pits, but what was its original purpose?

FURNISHINGS. PEWS and tower SCREEN by *Robert Thompson*, *c.* 1960. – STAINED GLASS. N chapel E window by *Heaton, Butler & Bayne*, *c.* 1920. – MONUMENTS. Excellent Wentworth family monuments in the N (Lady) Chapel, including Agnes †1668, with Ionic aedicule, and Sir John Wentworth †1720, signed by *Rysbrack*. An early work of his and indeed no more than a tablet with a finely cut inscription, a well-proportioned and well-detailed frame and a pediment.

Prehistoric SETTLEMENT, 1¼ m. WSW ON BRIERLEY COMMON, in a barely defensible position on a N-facing slope; enclosed by a substantial bank and an external ditch. (HW)

SOUTH MILFORD

ST MARY. 1846 by *G. Fowler Jones*. Nave, chancel and chapter-house-like octagonal NE vestry. W bellcote, cusped lancets.

STEETON HALL, ½ m. W. Remains of the semi-fortified house of the Reygate family. The only part which survives complete, or anything like it, is the gatehouse at the NE corner of the site, which is datable to *c.* 1360 on the evidence of the elaborate heraldic corbel table. Magnesian limestone ashlar. Gateway passage with segment-headed arches and ribbed vault, separate tunnel-vaulted pedestrian passage, battlemented parapet above the corbels. Upper chamber with, on the outer face, a shouldered window and a corbelled-out chimney-breast carrying an octagonal stack, on the inner an ogee-headed window, and reached by a spiral stair from a doorway on the inner face beside the main archway. External steps and another, ogee-headed, doorway on the inner face lead to a smaller room over the pedestrian passage. The house itself has not been studied fully. It was described in 1882 as a 'shattered ruin…altered in our own time', and presents an irregular front predominantly of late C19 appearance. The main medieval element is the three-storey r. half of a block projecting at the l. end – the other half is C19 – for which more heraldic corbels suggest a date slightly earlier in the C14 than the gatehouse's and which was perhaps a solar tower. On the N flank at ground-floor level three reused three-light Dec windows with reticulated tracery; other windows a mixture of paired and single lancets, trefoil-headed lights and, at the back, some C17 mullioned windows. Inside, the ground floor is rib-vaulted, the ribs single-chamfered, and has a piscina which must again be re-set, as although there was a chapel – the licence for it was renewed

in 1342 – this would be an unthinkable position for it. To the
r. of this block a length of screen wall with a C17 three-centre-
headed doorway under a hoodmould.

SOUTHOWRAM

ST ANNE IN THE GROVE. 1816–19 by *Thomas Taylor*.
Lancet style. Aisleless, with buttresses and simple w
tower. The lancets have (or had) Y-tracery. w gallery inside.
Chancel extended 1869; polygonal N baptistery added 1884–5.
– STAINED GLASS. By *Ward & Hughes*, 1879 and 1909–22.
– Baptistery windows by *Powell Bros*, 1885–6.

ASHDAY HALL, Ashday Lane, has a Tuscan doorcase dated 1738
and sashes, the S front altered *c.* 1830 with bows flanking an
(earlier?) doorway with pulvinated frieze.

LAW HILL HOUSE, Law Lane. Built *c.* 1771, three storeys with
paired sashes. Later a school, where Emily Brontë taught
1837–8.

SOWERBY

On a hill that falls steeply to the River Calder on the N and to
the smaller Ryburn valley on the E. From the later C18 Sowerby
Bridge (q.v.) developed at its foot and on the Calder valley's N
slope; the two places have no obvious division.

ST PETER. One of the best C18 churches in the Riding, an
uncommonly stately building of 1761–6, which replaced a
chapel of C16 origin. It was funded by local subscribers and
designed and built by *John Wilson*, master mason of Halifax,
whose drawings, provided in 1759, were closely based on
William Etty's Holy Trinity, Leeds. w tower with gallery staircase has belfry stage added 1781. Coupled pointed openings;
no parapet but plenty of prickly pinnacles. The rest presents
a grandly classical S front of seven bays with two-storey openings. Entrances with Gibbs surrounds in the first and last bays.
Between these are round-arched windows with square ones
above and attached giant Doric columns. Entablature. Parapet
with blind balustrading. Apsidal chancel with Venetian
window. The starkly plain N side is a shock – bald rectangular
buttresses instead of columns, no entablature, no parapet; even
the tower's w face has only a S angle pilaster.

60

The magnificent interior has giant Composite columns with
the panelled oak fronts of the galleries between them. Rich
entablature with modillion cornice; Greek key to soffits. Splendidly decorated apse with sumptuous plasterwork by *Giuseppe*

Cortese. The E window has Composite columns, and to each side two panels with elaborate lugged architraves, the inner with Moses and Christ in painted relief, the outer with the Ten Commandments in medallions. Above the window, ROYAL ARMS, dated 1766, flanked by garlanded cartouches (with MOSAICS by *Powell & Sons*, 1882) and two coats of arms, the l. one of George Stansfeld of Field House (*see* below), principal subscriber. Restoration by *John Middleton & Son* of Cheltenham, 1878–9, extended the chancel, creating an organ chamber and a vestry in the first aisle bays, behind classical arcaded screens with coloured marble colonnettes. – Fine FITTINGS. Sanctuary PANELLING, CHOIR STALLS, low marble CHANCEL SCREEN and richly classical PULPIT elevated on marble columns, go with this. – Also PEWS, reusing parts of original BOX PEWS, which remain in the galleries. – Good Gothic Caen stone FONT, 1862, and a curious medieval(?) FONT with pierced pedestal. – Very elegant STATUE of Archbishop John Tillotson (1630–94) standing in declamatory pose, in a pedimented niche. By *Joseph Wilton*, assisted by *Joseph Panzetta*, *ante* 1796, when Wilton gave the model to George Stansfeld of Field House, who commissioned the statue. Inscription by *Nollekens*. Tillotson was born at Old Haugh End (*see* below).

STAINED GLASS. E window 1862, and s aisle E window 1868, both painted glass by *Warrington*. Six aisle windows with similarly lettered dedications by *Heaton, Butler & Bayne*, 1879, 1883 (and others?, later). s gallery second from E by *J.C.N. Bewsey*, 1923. Two N gallery windows by *J. Eadie Reid*, 1907. – MONUMENTS. Mary, wife of George Stansfeld, †1799 by *William Stead* of York. Large pedimented panel with coloured marble inlay. – John Lea †1800 and wife Mary †1796 by *M. Taylor* of York. Good decorated tablet below draped urn against obelisk. – John Priestley †1801 and family by *J. Pritchett* of Halifax. Draped tablet. – Mary Ann Wilks †1817 by *C. Fisher* of York. Fine Neoclassical tablet carrying a sarcophagus. – Henry Longfield †1833 by *Hall* of Derby. Large, with seated woman grieving beside a broken column beneath a tree. – Robert Stansfeld †1855 by *Fisher* of York. Tablet with scrolls. – Crimean War Memorial, 1856, with draped weapons, also by *C. Fisher*.

ST GEORGE, Haugh End Lane (now flats). By *Edward Welch*, 1839–40. Neo-Norman style, with bald w tower.

There are an exceptional number of good houses in Sowerby; the Georgian ones merit more research. Most of the area's leading families were involved in the textile industry and had workshops, warehouses etc. adjacent to their homes well into the C19.

WOOD LANE HALL, ¼ m. N. One of the finest houses in this part of the West Riding, built for John Dearden in 1649. Double-pile, F-plan, it has a fine two-storey porch with a circular window and inside one of the few surviving open-halls. SE front with gables to upper and lower parlour wings, which have six-light transomed windows with king mullions.

Double-transomed hall window of nine lights grouped in threes and battlemented parapet. Large decorative hoodmould stops; also carved faces and animals on gutter spouts to l. return. The porch doorway has fluted Doric columns and a dated lintel with semicircles as decoration (cf. Stock Lane House, Warley, p. 721). The window above is one of the 'apple and pear' type, i.e. with six mouchettes, as at Heath Grammar School, Halifax and Elland New Hall (qq.v.). Unusually the porch has a battlemented parapet, not a gable (cf. East Riddlesden Hall, Keighley (*West Riding North*)). Sundial 1651. Elaborately carved finials. Sash windows on r. return. Three gables to rear and another two-storey porch with entrance to kitchen.

(The hall's Tudor-arched fireplace against the passage has attached fluted Ionic columns and, above, an oak panel with carved arcade and flowers. Panelling with carved frieze. Galleries on three sides, the balusters of vertically symmetrical shape. Ceiling has large plasterwork centrepiece, similar to Howroyde, Barkisland (q.v.), with central boss and subdivisions with pomegranates, shields etc. Original fireplaces, beams etc. in other rooms. Right wing, altered in late C18/early C19, has brought-in older staircase.)

WHITE WINDOWS, Fore Lane Avenue, ¾ m. E. By *Carr* for John Priestley, clothier, 1767–8. The house closely resembles Manor Hall, Bradford, 1707 (dem.). Seven by five bays, two-and-a-half storeys. Ashlar front stands higher, above rusticated basement, with double staircases to doorway with swan-neck pediment. Moulded architraves to windows. Manor Hall had the same unusual detail of panelled angle pilasters instead of quoins above the second-floor band. Truncated hipped roof with top balustrade. Single-bay hall; transverse corridor; rear dog-leg staircase with Ionic columns to Venetian window and wrought-iron balustrade. (Some plasterwork and a chimneypiece in main rooms.)

OLD HAUGH END, Haugh End Lane. Early C17, with a three-gabled front, with lean-to porch in angle with projecting r. wing. Mullioned windows, mostly with plain hoodmoulds; seven-light housebody window. One transomed window above. (One room has early C18 decoration commemorating it as Archbishop Tillotson's birthplace, including fine panelling and brought-in overmantel with battle scene in plaster.) HAUGH END HOUSE, set slightly uphill to r., was built for John Lea, merchant, *c.* 1760s and attributed to *Carr* but perhaps, like the church, from a skilful local copyist. Five-bay front with three-bay pediment. Ground-floor openings with pedimented architraves, the entrance set in a round-arched recess, the second and fourth windows with segmental not triangular pediments. Cornices to upper windows. (Good original interior features include plasterwork and chimneypieces, and especially elaborate doorways with Ionic columns to upper stair hall.)

FIELD HOUSE, Dean Lane, ⅓ m. S. George Stansfeld's stately Palladian house of 1749. Eleven bays, the centre three set forward under a pediment filled with an elaborately carved coat of arms. Rusticated quoins. Segmental pediment to doorway. Window architraves have pulvinated friezes and cornices. The paired outer bays, perfectly matched under separate hipped roofs, are later C19 additions. Three-bay r. return has central pediment and another entrance, with Tuscan columns and blocking course. Rear has four-light windows with flat-faced mullions. (Interior (divided in two) has fine entrance hall, plasterwork, door architraves and top-lit oval stairwell with galleried landing.) Detached former kitchen range has a very good late Perp window brought *c.* 1762 from the old Sowerby church, which had been rebuilt in 1622. Pointed head, five lights, two transoms. The individual lights round-arched. Perched above, on the gable-end and two very tall Doric columns, a curious columned and pinnacled cupola also from the church. Surrounding outbuildings, much altered, included a cloth-drying house and warehouses. On Rochdale Road a pair of pedimented LODGES by *Horsfall, Wardle & Patchett*, 1874.

At BOULDER CLOUGH, ³/₈ m. NW, a former METHODIST CHAPEL, by *Sutcliffe & Sutcliffe*, 1897–8, in a very individual Free Style with Arts and Crafts overtones. Four-bay arcaded loggia with dumpy Doric columns flanked by hefty conical-roofed round towers whose narrow transomed windows step up in line with the stairs.

At COTTONSTONES, 1¼ m. SW, ST MARY by *Perkin & Backhouse*, 1845–6. Plain lancet style, all tall and thin. W tower with stone broach spire.

SOWERBY BRIDGE

No more than a hamlet until the later C18, following completion of the Calder & Hebble Navigation from Wakefield in 1770 and the opening of the Rochdale Canal in 1804. The Lancashire and Yorkshire Railway, across the river from the town on the S bank, opened in 1840. Although most of the iron foundries and engineering works have gone, textile mills, many in new uses, are still dominant in the townscape.

CHURCHES AND PUBLIC BUILDINGS

CHRIST CHURCH. By *John Oates*, 1819–21. Chancel rebuilt 1873–4. A big church without any of the paperiness of so many churches of *c.* 1820. Typical pinnacled buttresses and battlements. W tower with three-light Perp bell-openings; two-storey porches with staircases to N and S, 1894–5. Six-bay nave has tall three-light Perp lancet windows with transoms and amusing headstops. Two-bay chancel. Horseshoe gallery with panelled front on thin iron piers of quatrefoil section. Nave has huge single-span hammerbeam roof with arcaded/traceried trusses, from restoration by *Horsfall & Williams*, 1894–5, after a fire. REREDOS. Caen stone. Rich ogee arcade with tracery, marble colonnettes and diapered panels, 1903. – Good carved oak CHANCEL SCREEN by *H.P. Jackson*, 1935. – Elaborate Bath stone PULPIT, designed by *C. Williams*, 1895. – STAINED GLASS. All by *R.B. Edmundson & Son*: E window and S aisle 1864, N aisle *c.* 1869.

SACRED HEART AND ST PATRICK (R.C.), Upper Bolton Brow. By *Richard Byrom* of *Byrom & Noble*, 1934. Simple Neo-Romanesque. Long aisleless nave has gabled (ritual) W front with giant recessed arch; three windows above doorway, mosaic tympanum. NW tower has small grouped openings, short bell-stage and pyramidal roof. Small apsidal sanctuary.

WESLEYAN CHURCH (former), Bolton Brow. 1832. An elegant and urbane ashlar façade, partly rusticated, of five bays, the recessed centre with a Venetian window below an arched tri-partite window above. Perched on a steep slope above the canal basin and originally four bays deep, a two-bay S exten-sion, 1868, created an immensely tall rear elevation accom-modating a two-storey canal warehouse below. The former SUNDAY SCHOOL alongside is by *C.F.L. Horsfall*, 1882–3. Italianate façade with tall pedimented centrepiece over paired doorways with Doric columns and shared entablature.

TOWN HALL (former; now Lloyds Bank). By *Perkin & Back-house*, 1856–7. Handsome Italianate building in a prominent position at the W end of Town Hall Street, its tall circular tower facing the bridge. The tower has a Venetian window on the first floor, an elaborate cresting above the parapet, arched openings with grilles to the clock stage, and a ribbed stone dome. Three bays to the r., palazzo style with rusticated quoins and segmen-tal pediments on consoles to upper windows. The large public hall which adjoined to the l. of the tower was demolished in 1963. Along Hollins Mill Lane to the W is a long plain range in rock-faced stone, comprising the former COUNCIL OFFICES, 1878–9, with former PUBLIC BATHS behind, the former FIRE STATION, 1904, and single-storey LIBRARY by *Samuel Wilkinson* of Sowerby Bridge, 1903–5, with Renaissance-style pilasters and frieze. The intended upper floor for a Tech-nical Institute was abandoned.

POLICE STATION (former), Station Road. 1894. Simple Tudor Gothic style with gables and mullioned windows. C20 addi-tions spoil front; rear intact.

POST OFFICE (former), Station Road. 1922–3 by *H.M. Office of Works*. Pennine Vernacular Revival style. Two storeys. Arched central entrance has doorcase with fluted pilasters. Big mullioned-and-transomed windows to l. bay, gabled r. bay.

PERAMBULATION

TOWN HALL STREET and WHARF STREET form the High Street, with handsome later C19 two- and three-storey shops near the Town Hall, and, towards Christ Church, some more modest, early C19 former houses with flat-mullioned windows. On the s side are surviving buildings of the extensive SOWERBY BRIDGE MILLS. To the w is the earliest, the pioneering water-powered GREENUP'S MILL (now flats), set below street level on the river bank. Four storeys, 4:3:4 bays with central gable. Built shortly before 1792, for scribbling and fulling, as part of the first known integrated woollen mill in Yorkshire.* The hand-powered processes, spinning and weaving, were carried on in adjacent buildings, now gone. Nearby, CARLTON MILL and its chimney dominate the street scene. Added as a steam-powered worsted-spinning mill c. 1865–70, now offices. Four storeys to the road, plus two lower storeys in the s half towards the river. Five-bay N front has twin coped gables with oculi. ENGINE HOUSE to w and 125-ft (35-metre)-high octagonal stone CHIMNEY, heavily braced.

To the E, s of Wharf Street, is the CANAL BASIN. Initially the w terminus of the Calder & Hebble Navigation, it became a vital transshipment centre when the Rochdale Canal was built, the length between Sowerby Bridge and Todmorden being opened in 1799 and the link to Manchester, and so to Liverpool, completed in 1804. Different lock sizes and depths on the two canals made through traffic impossible and goods had to be transferred between each system's boats. WARE-HOUSES were built from 1770, when the Navigation was completed, but the chronology of those that survive is not fully established. Semi-derelict by the 1980s, the basin and its buildings were restored for leisure uses in the 1990s; the Rochdale Canal, closed in 1952, was reopened in 2002.

The earliest is probably the easternmost, the WET DOCK, c. 1778. Three storeys, seven bays, with loading doors and two- and three-light flat-faced mullioned windows to front and rear and tall arched opening to internal dock at N end. The SALT WAREHOUSE, c. 1796–8, straddles the quay with central roadway arch, and is the only one placed to load/unload from both the basin and the Rochdale Canal. Three storeys, with two double-height, through-arched openings for basin wet docks, and loading doors to quay and canal at s end. At the head of the basin the large WEST WAREHOUSE, with s wing, is probably a mid-C19 replacement for the first warehouse of 1770. Loading doors on all elevations and a tall through wagon archway in bay 3. Stone springers above first-floor level on basin sides once supported a canopy. To the N, overlooking the basin is a handsome three-storey HOUSE AND OFFICES for the Navigation agent/manager, 1779. Also small entrance LODGE 1837, and mid-C19 WEIGH-HOUSE.

Nos. 43, 45 and 47 HOLLINS LANE. C19 stone casing or re-casing conceals remains of a late medieval timber-framed aisled house, of linear, hearth-passage plan, with C16 s parlour wing.

*In 1792 Benjamin Gott began building Bean Ing Mills, Leeds (dem.), the first steam-powered integrated woollen mill in Yorkshire.

No. 45 includes two-bay housebody, later floored, with decorative fireplace, 1688, which replaced fire-hood.

SOYLAND

Upland plateau above Ripponden, crossed by little valleys of the River Ryburn's western tributaries. No village, but rich in C17 yeomen-clothiers' farmhouses.

GREAT HOUSE, Great House Lane. Dated 1624 on the porch. Large, double-pile, through-passage plan with housebody and two front parlours in three gabled ranges. Transomed windows; decorative stops to upper hoodmoulds. Good coped gables have elaborate finials and tiny carved ledges to former pigeon lofts. E shop end rebuilt. Housebody has bressumer and plank-and-muntin fire-screen. Fine stone fireplace with arcaded overmantel in main parlour.

LOW COTE, Cote Road. Dated 1671 on the hoodmould of its fine two-storey gabled porch. It is long, of three rooms; LOWER MOOR, off Cote Road, earlier C17, is similar, but distinguished by the huge mid-C16 timber-framed aisled BARN attached W like a cross-wing. Its stone exterior is contemporary with the house, whose service end extends, most unusually, into the S bay of the E aisle.

FLAT HEAD, Cross Wells Road, 1627, has porches at both ends of its through passage. The back porch, in the angle with the rear wing, has the unique feature of an octagonal column carrying the upper storey.

N again, Nos. 2–4 and 6 LANE HEAD ROAD, dated 1627. Fine three-room front with five-, six- and eight-light mullioned windows, one with whorled hoodmould stops. (C17 oak staircase from the Manor House, East Hardwick, and panelling and door from Earlsheaton Hall, Dewsbury (dem.).)

To the W, CLAY HOUSE, Lighthazles Road, is a sympathetic rebuilding, 1915, of a house of 1662.

GREAT GREAVE, off Greave Road. Late C16/early C17. Hall and cross-wings, the through passage, unusually, in the E wing. Parlour wing is aisled, giving big asymmetrical W gables. Low windows with labels; the housebody window seven lights, plus a three-light fire window, both transomed. Unusual ovolo mullions, except to E wing, which is probably of a different build.

SPROTBROUGH

ST MARY. In the upper walls of the two eastern bays of the nave fabric from a small Norman church with a high, narrow nave.

The N arcade responds are late C12, reused, perhaps from the original chancel arch. On the E capital some fluted foliage and on one angle a large ovate leaf. Chancel rebuilt in the late C13, wider than the nave. In the E wall, visible inside and outside, remains of tall windows with filleted shafts. It also has the piscina, stepped sedilia and S doorway. The three S windows with uncusped Y-tracery are of doubtful reliability. In the N wall two odd two-light windows with bar tracery in the N wall, their oddity perhaps due to an Early Victorian restorer: large circle above the lights with three small circles inside, uncusped. Certainly the chancel was re-roofed not long before 1850, its angel corbels copied from Lincoln Cathedral. In the N wall an image recess, straight-headed with three crocketed canopies.

From the first half of the C14 the double-chamfered chancel arch with hoodmould and semi-octagonal responds, the S aisle with matching responds and pier, and the N aisle, its octagonal pier with differently moulded capital. Probably not long afterwards the church was lengthened with a third bay and the W tower built. The S aisle's W respond appears to have been reused. The tower's doorway is ogee-headed. Its two top stages are Perp – in 1474 William Fitzwilliam left £40 to the 'new' tower. Two two-light bell-openings with traceried panels below. Late C15 two-storey N chapel, now vestry. Later Perp the square-headed aisle windows, the clerestory and the nave and aisle battlements. Also their fine roofs, with carved and painted bosses. S aisle roof dated 1516.

In 1912–15 *Comper* restored and reordered the church, reinstating a Tudor-style E window, refashioning the chancel screen, pulpit and pews, and re-creating the S aisle chapel (see its original piscina and squint).

The high whitewashed interior sets off the FITTINGS, many rich in heraldry, especially of the Fitzwilliams, Lords of Sprotbrough until 1516. – COMMUNION RAIL. Jacobean, the entrance stressed by two small obelisks. – CHANCEL STALLS. Mostly *Comper*'s but preserving two misericords too mutilated to date. – SCREENS. The rood screen is very unusual in the West Riding and puzzling. Three-light divisions with moulded shafts and Dec or Flamboyant tracery, the divisions not arranged symmetrically. The shafts are decidedly pre-Perp in style yet the tracery looks early C16 rather than mid-C14. – PULPIT. Octagonal, on a slender pedestal; C16 panels with tiers of tracery; large C18 tester. – Excellent BENCH-ENDS. Two different sets, both straight-headed. The main group were box pew doors. Above tracery they have Early Renaissance motifs such as profile busts in medallions, one of an African. Initials WC probably Sir William Copley (†1556). The W block, from St Peter, Edlington (q.v.), have tracery in two tiers. – ORGAN CASE. Gothic. 1839. – SCULPTURE. In buttress W of chancel S door. Fragment, probably of an Anglo-Saxon cross-shaft, possibly c. 800. Incised decoration, like a Vitruvian scroll. – Mysterious STONE SEAT in the chancel, possibly a frith-stool. In general shape it strikes one as of venerable age, but the decoration, especially the tracery on the r. side and the caryatid bust of a bearded man, makes the C14 certain. Is it perhaps a reworking of a much older piece? (cf. the seats (late C7?) at Beverley Minster (*York and the East Riding*) and Hexham Priory (*Northumberland*).) – STAINED GLASS. S chapel. E window includes elaborately quartered shield *c.* 1541. S side easternmost by *Comper*, 1921. – MONUMENTS. S chapel. Two very fine C14 Fitzwilliam effigies. Under an elaborate ogee-headed arch with drop tracery, a knight in chain-mail, probably Sir William Fitzwilliam, †before 1342. Unusually for the date the legs are not crossed. – Under a C20 copy arch, a lady with delicately pleated wimple, probably his wife, Isabel Deincourt, †1348. – Chancel. Excellent brasses to William Fitzwilliam †1474 and his wife, Elizabeth, the figures 31 in. (0.8 metres) long. – Philip Copley †1577, and wife and children. Alabaster slab on tomb-chest, with incised figures (damaged). – Incised floor slab with figure of a priest, probably Thomas Fitzwilliam †1482, Rector from 1440. – Lionel Copley †1766. By *John Platt*, 1769. Large, black marble. Two oval inscription panels, one blank, below pediment and obelisk; apron with swag and putti.

Former RECTORY. 150 yds WSW. Late C17, remodelled by *H.F. Lockwood* in the 1840s with Tudor Gothic S and E fronts. Also in the village many mid-C19 Tudor Gothic ESTATE COTTAGES for

p. 30   SPROTBROUGH HALL, Sir Godfrey Copley's mansion, built *c.* 1696–1700 with the involvement of *John Etty*, demolished 1926. Mid–late C18 STABLES survive.

At SPROTBROUGH BOAT, ⅓ m. SSW, a BRIDGE spans the canal and Don, with small classical TOLL HOUSE of 1849. 350 yds NE the (derelict) PUMP HOUSE of 1703 for Sir Godfrey Copley's 'water engine' (*George Sorocold*, engineer), which filled a tank supplying the mansion, fountain and swimming pool, 150 ft (46 metres) above the river.

6010   # STAINFORTH

Large village beside the Don, granted a market charter in 1348. It prospered with the opening of the Stainforth & Keadby Canal in 1797 but scant built evidence of its history remains. Expansion followed the sinking of Hatfield Main Colliery in 1911 (closed 2015).

ST MARY. By *C.B. Flockton*, 1933–4. Weakly Gothic, in rock-faced stone, its bulky W tower with pyramidal roof clasped by castellations at the angles. Extended E end converted to community centre by *G.G. Pace*, 1974–7.

TOWN END FARM, ¼ m. ENE. Large three-bay brick farmhouse, probably the one Abraham de la Pryme called 'lately built' in

Sprotbrough, St Mary, monuments to Sir William Fitzwilliam
†before 1342 and Isabel Deincourt †1348.
Engraving by C.J. Smith after W. Cowen, *c.* 1828

1698. Double gables of roof disguised at front and rear by a big flat-topped gable in the Dutch fashion.

STAINLAND

0010

ST ANDREW. Built 1754–5 as a non-denominational chapel of four bays with tall round-arched windows but Anglican from

1840 when it was altered by *Charles Child*. Classical w tower
1860; the belfry stage with canted angles with considerable
batter; small dome. The two-bay chancel and the tower's pedimented wings by *W.S. Barber*, 1887–8; his is the Venetian E
window and inside the elliptical panelled chancel ceiling
carried on four giant Doric columns with stone entablature,
and oak screens enclosing organ chamber and vestry and the
W gallery on Doric columns. Nave PANELLING, 1932. –
STAINED GLASS. E window by *Clayton & Bell*, 1894. Nave N,
easternmost, by *Powell & Sons*, 1958.

Near the top of the village a former bank of *c.* 1930 (now
LIBRARY) with classical porch, improbably urbane among the
dark stone cottages. In contrast is the huge – and, to Pevsner,
revolting – former MECHANICS' INSTITUTE of 1883–4 by
Leeming & Leeming, now without its balustraded parapet and
flanking turrets. Below it ELLISTONES FARMHOUSE, early
C17, has gabled cross-wings, flush at the front. Both had heated
parlours. The aisled hall's eight-light window was originally a
five-light window and two-light fire window, the intermediate
light is C18.

At HOLYWELL GREEN, ½ m. ENE, the UNITED REFORMED
CHURCH by *Joseph James*, 1853, was a Sunday School.*
Mullioned-and-transomed windows and good shaped gables.
SHAW PARK is the former gardens of Brooklands (1865, dem.
1933), built for Samuel Shaw above the family's vast Brookroyd
woollen mills (dem.). Mock-castle GATEWAY and unusual
towered and turreted AVIARIES/FOLLIES built *c.* 1870. Shaw's
penchant for Gothic also found expression in CASTLE FARM-
HOUSE (or Carr Hall), ⅓ m. SW.

BRADLEY HALL, ½ m. N. Fragment (now incorporated in golf
clubhouse) of a large house built 1577–1604 for Sir John Savile
of Methley, whose mason was *John Akroyd*. Two-bay gabled
section of N front has five-light transomed window with five-
light window over and a two-storey semi-octagonal bay window.
This was probably part of work begun 1597 and perhaps formed
the r. part of a symmetrical front, similar to the Old Hall, Heath
(q.v.), with a central porch or tower. Small pieces of a rose
window with circular lights survive (re-set in clubhouse S wall).
They indicate that Bradley Hall had one of the two earliest
Halifax round windows, contemporary with, but different from,
that at Heath Grammar School, Halifax, and the model for the
later window at Barkisland Hall nearby (qq.v.).

STAINTON

ST WINIFRID. Small. The nave and chancel are essentially
Norman: see the unmoulded chancel arch on chamfered

---

*The church by *J.P. Pritchett Jun.*, 1872–4, was demolished 1978.

imposts, traces of a chancel s window and the rere-arch of the nave s doorway. The chancel s doorway, round-arched with one slight chamfer, is probably later. A cusped lancet in the chancel N wall goes with the late C13 Y-tracery of the chancel s window and the nave easternmost N window. Large, separately roofed Dec s chapel with a broad corbelled arch to the nave. Straight-headed windows, the E three lights with reticulated tracery of say *c.* 1380. Good piscina with cusped ogee arch. Perp W tower. – STAINED GLASS. s chapel. Fragments include two C15 heads. – MONUMENTS. Several good C18/early C19 monuments include: George Pashley †1664 and family †1680–1727. By *John Hancock*, probably erected 1708. Enormous tablet in aedicule with broken segmental pediment and urn.

STAINTON HALL. 50 yds N. Late C17. Four bays. Cross-windows in raised surrounds, quoins, hipped roof. Tall staircase window at rear originally with two transoms.

WILSIC HALL, 1½ m. NNE. Small country house, mainly *c.* 1740 for Thomas Tofield (now a school). Rendered. Two-and-a-half-storey, hipped-roofed centre block with unequal two-storey wings that have shaped gables on the returns. N front has later canted porch.

STAINTON WOODHOUSE, ½ m. E. Large C18–C19 house. SE front *c.* 1800 with full-height shallow bows.

LAMBCOTE GRANGE, 1 m. W. Dated 1747. Imposing three-storey, five-bay farmhouse with hipped roof. Quoins, first-floor band and sill band. Segmental pediment to doorway.

STANLEY

3020

ST PETER. Demolished in 2014 after structural problems. It stood above Aberford Road and was a Gothic Commissioners' church by *Atkinson & Sharp*, 1821–4, that had been extensively rebuilt after a fire by *W. D. Caröe*, 1911–13. The exterior with two large towers was more odd than beautiful. The interior, though also *outré*, as Caröe tends to be, had beauty.*

STANLEY HALL, 1¼ m. SSW. 1804–7, extended. Plain, rendered, with small pedimented Doric portico. Two-storey bow to E front.

HATFEILD HALL, ¾ m. SW. *c.* 1600, gabled. Canted outer bays. Its charm is its conversion *c.* 1775 with Gothick windows, and, originally, battlements to the parapet. One room has C17 plaster frieze with mermen and mermaids (cf. Woodsome Hall, Fenay Bridge).

CLARKE HALL, Aberford Road, 1½ m. s on the edge of Wakefield. An excellent brick house of *c.* 1680, with a rear wing built some twenty years later. It is of special interest as an early

---

*The fate of the FONT with very ornate tall spired COVER, 1916, and CHOIR STALLS with misericords, by *Jackson* of Coley, 1921–4, is unknown at the time of writing.

example of the new type of gentry house built with a symmetrical front but without the double-pile plan that was still to be accepted in the area. The N-facing entrance side is an E with canted angle projections and a square porch. Two-storeyed, the square windows with mullions and transoms. The tops of the angle projections have been altered; the porch is gabled. On the s side the wing of *c.* 1700 projects on the E. All windows are again of the cross-type. The entrance leads directly into the Hall, with the kitchen to the l. and the oak-panelled dining parlour behind a dairy on the r. The parlour has a swagger plaster ceiling dated 1680, with an oval centre and vigorous if rustic foliage, the plant forms possibly derived from oriental chintzes. The staircase ascends straight from the Hall, and there is a Great Chamber over. Much restoration was undertaken in the C20 and items such as fireplaces (one from Flanshaw Hall, near Wakefield) were put in. A shelter in the garden has parts of the columns from Wakefield's market cross.

LAKE YARD, ¼ m. E. Former canal depot for the Aire & Calder Navigation, 1802 (now residential). Long symmetrical range, originally a three-bay house with two pairs of cottages each side, hipped-roofed workshops beyond, set back, and open cart sheds at each end. Slight classical details.

STANLEY FERRY, I m. SE. AQUEDUCT, carrying the canal over the Calder. Thought to be both the world's largest cast-iron aqueduct and the first iron suspension aqueduct. Designed by *George Leather Jun.* 1834, constructed by the *Milton Ironworks*, Elsecar, 1836–9. The trough, 160/165 ft (48.8/50.3 metres) long, 24 ft (7.3 metres) wide and 8 ft 6 in./9 ft (2.6/2.7 metres) deep; the bowstring girders 155 ft (46.5 metres) wide. Each side has a Greek Doric colonnade with full entablature. The

Stanley, Stanley Ferry, aqueduct.
Lithograph by J. C. Bourne, 1834

stone abutments are masked by pedimented octostyle prostyle porticoes. Diminutive CANAL OFFICE beside nearby basin, *c.* 1839, has similar tetrastyle portico.

STOCKSBRIDGE

Small Pennine town in the Little Don valley, built beside the steel works that Samuel Fox established in 1842.

ST MATTHIAS. By *J. D. Webster*, 1889–90, in memory of Samuel Fox. Plain Gothic revival style. Very tall. Five-bay nave with N clerestory and aisle; W bellcote. Two-bay chancel. – STAINED GLASS. E window (part) by *Francis Spear*, 1961; unharmonious coloured glass in first and fifth lights 1990. N aisle easternmost by *Harry Stammers*, 1950. N aisle fourth from E by *Francis Spear*, 1959.

ST JOHN, Deepcar. Nave, N aisle and porch (in base of unbuilt NW tower) by *Ewan Christian*, 1877–8. Robust E.E. details. Tamer chancel and S aisle with matching arcade by *J. D. Webster*, 1894.

BOLSTERSTONE GLASSHOUSE, Pot House Lane. Small, altered, late C17 glassworks building. Voussoirs of large blocked arch to E, another arch to W beside fragmentary remains of external kiln. Converted to a pottery in mid C18, later agricultural, now used by adjoining house.

TATA STEELWORKS. Includes Italianate OFFICES, 1870s, and the long five-storey UMBRELLA BUILDING, 1850s, where a mainly female workforce assembled Paragon umbrella frames, patented 1852, which made Samuel Fox's fortune. Similar block to SW. Also stylish former CANTEEN, *c.* 1970s, with projecting first floor clad in stainless steel.

SWINEFLEET

Village on the S bank of the lower Ouse.

ST MARGARET. Small, brick. Chancel 1882–3, from the rebuilding of the medieval chapel by *Smith & Brodrick*. Nave rebuilt again, more boldly, in 1903–5 by *Brodrick, Lowther & Walker*. Four bays, W bellcote, brick interior. – STAINED GLASS. Three windows by *Harry Harvey*, 1959 and 1965–6, include St Margaret in brilliant yellow gown standing triumphant over a small blue dragon.

THE PARK. 100 yds E. Fine mid–later C18 house. Red brick. Five-bay W front, the central bay projecting. Deep modillion eaves cornice, hipped roof. Pedimented doorway with fluted pilasters and enriched frieze and tympanum. Sashes under rubbed brick heads with raised keystones. (Interior. Some good plasterwork and chimneypieces.)

REEDNESS HALL, 1½ m. NE. Mid-C18. Brick, five bays, pedimented doorcase with plain frieze, sashes under rubbed brick heads. (Some good decorated timber chimneypieces.)

4090

SWINTON

Small town straggling downhill from the church and old village to Swinton Bridge, an industrial area between the railway, canals and River Don. Development followed the completion in 1795 of the Dearne & Dove Canal linking Barnsley to the Don Navigation here.

ST MARGARET. Rebuilt after a fire by *E. Isle Hubbard*, 1897–9, keeping the W tower of its predecessor (1815–17 by *Watson & Pritchett*). This is ashlar, with Y-tracery belfry openings. Tall nave with clerestory and buttressed aisles partly embracing the tower. Paired lancet windows. Chancel has two-storey transeptal S vestry. Fine early Dec interior with hammerbeam roof in New Zealand pine. – STAINED GLASS. A good series by *Powell & Sons*. E window, centre light 1901, the others 1913. S aisle windows date from 1899 to 1945. – N chapel E (war memorial). Centre light by *Drake* of Exeter, 1923, two outer lights by *Harry Harvey*, 1966.

Outside the N chapel, fragments erected here in 1817 of a richly decorated S doorway and chancel arch of the Norman chapel, which stood 300 yds SE. Only much-decayed jambs now remain, the shafts and one scalloped capital of the doorway still recognizable. (Some carved voussoirs with a mask and chevrons are stored in the church.)

METHODIST CHURCH, Church Street. By *A.E. Lambert* of Nottingham 1909–10. Free Gothic with Art Nouveau touches.

CARNEGIE LIBRARY, Station Street. Now flats. By *J.E. Knight* of Rotherham, 1905–6. Low-cost Baroque. Brick striped thinly with stone, a two-storey bow at the end and a centrepiece with clock and angel encouragingly displaying 'Knowledge is power' over the entrance.

SWINTON BRIDGE SCHOOL (former), Marriott Road. E. By *Harry L. Tacon*, architect to Swinton School Board. Most unusual is the polygonal corner tower with a pyramidal roof crowned by a tall spired belfry linking the single-storey ranges with big gables.

SWINTON HOUSE, Fitzwilliam Street. Built *c.* 1756 for John Otter. Handsome five-bay front, now degraded. Doorway has broken segmental pediment, the window above it a moulded architrave, decorative apron and cornice. Top-lit staircase with good turned balusters.

SWINTON HALL, Fitzwilliam Street. *c.* 1800 for John Otter II.
  Seven-bay front with unusual arrangement of two-storey
  centre with three tall first-floor windows but three storeys
  either side. Doric loggia to r. return. Gutted for flats conversion *c.* 1980.

QUEEN's FOUNDRY, Whitelea Road. Long stone-fronted range
  built in 1893 as offices, showrooms and warehouse of Hat-
  tersley Bros, manufacturers of ranges, railway wheels, boilers
  etc. Two storeys. Large entrance arch under three-bay gable.
  Windows have round-arched ashlar heads with keystones and
  impost blocks.

ROCKINGHAM POTTERY, ⅞ m. WSW. Famous for the exquisite
  porcelain produced by the Brameld family, who took over the
  pottery in 1806. Insistence on perfection was their undoing in
  1842, despite financial assistance from Earl Fitzwilliam, whose
  armorial griffin they had adopted as their trademark. The
  c. 36-ft (17–metre)-high WATERLOO KILN (actually a bottle-
  shaped brick oven which housed a kiln) is the only complete
  survivor. It is thought to be the only C19 pottery kiln left in
  Yorkshire.

At KILNHURST, 1 m. S, on a site given by Earl Fitzwilliam, ST
  THOMAS by *Pritchett & Son* 1858–9, the chancel with Dec
  tracery by *T.W. Roome* of Rawmarsh 1884–5.

SYKEHOUSE   *6010*

Small strung-out fenland village between the Rivers Don and
Went.

HOLY TRINITY. Licence to build a chapel was granted in
  1434, as floods sometimes made Fishlake church (q.v.)
  inaccessible. Red brick. Skinny W tower dated 1721, its tall
  pyramidal-roofed top and all the rest in C13 style by *C. Hodgson
  Fowler*, 1867–9. Interior with stone and black brick bands.
  Stone piers to N arcade. – FONT. C15. Octagonal, with simple
  tracery to neck. – STAINED GLASS. Late C15 Crucifixion
  (incomplete).

THE OLD PRIORY, ¾ m. ENE. The BARN of 1703 is the area's
  earliest surviving dated brick building.

TANKERSLEY   *3090*

ST PETER. The N arcade remains from a church of *c.* 1200 (cf.
  Ecclesfield etc.). Two circular piers with broach-stopped bases
  and double-chamfered orders, the inner also stopped. One
  capital octagonal, the other round. Pevsner doubted the
  authenticity of the E respond's waterleaf capital and the aisle

was indeed rebuilt by *Charles Hadfield*, 1881. His windows have straight heads and ogee-arched lights. The two-bay chancel is genuine Dec, probably *c.* 1330–50, its arch on moulded conical corbels. Reticulated tracery in the three-light E window and priest's doorway (blocked), also ogee-arched. Beside it (outside) a fragment of a door or window jamb with shaft base, thought to be from the C11 church. Chancel S windows straight-headed with cusped ogee lights. The embattled nave was rebuilt in the later C15. Central door with cavetto moulding. Both three-light windows were enlarged and given reticulated tracery in 1881, their heads butting into the low clerestory, which has small two-light mullioned windows – C16 or C17. Much-rebuilt S porch with a tall ogee-arched entrance. Unbuttressed W tower with pinnacles. Original rood stair in nave S wall. – ROOD SCREEN by *Edwin Gray* of Sheffield, 1922. – BENCH-ENDS. Pair, probably C17. – PORCH GATE. Wrought iron, 1929. – STAINED GLASS. Nave SE by *Morris & Co.*, designed by *Burne-Jones*, 1881, with glowing gold and russets. Nave SW 1937 and aisle W 1938, by *Christopher Webb*. – MONUMENTS. In the chancel floor many incised slabs, with crosses and with swords, including Thomas Toytill, a priest, †1492. Further fragments in the porch.

To the N, the former RECTORY, 1871 and GLEBE FARM, on a moated site. Handsome (but derelict) three-storey DOVECOTE, 1735.

TANKERSLEY OLD HALL, ½ m. SE, just E of the M1. Gaunt fragment of an Elizabethan mansion that stood in a deer park created 1303–4. Abandoned after 1654 and demolished from the 1720s. What survives was a tower at the W end of the house, built of stone and brick. The ruin stands over two storeys high with large moulded fireplaces exposed and some cross-windows. Some stone was reused *c.* 1730 for the adjacent FARMHOUSE with attached N barn, which has lunette in gable over round-arched wagon entrance.

COAL MINES RESCUE STATION (former), ½ m. N at Birdwell. 1902. The earliest purpose-built example in England. Domestic appearance, with transport and equipment stores at the rear.

TEMPLE HIRST

Village in flat farmland along the N bank of the Aire.

ST JOHN (Wesleyan Methodist, now Anglican). 1842. Nice example of a rural chapel. Gault brick front with three lancet windows and Gothic porch.

TEMPLE MANOR (Care Home), ½ m. W. C17 brick house with ashlar quoins, a dentilled brick parapet and (later) sash windows. Incorporated, however, are fragments of a preceptory of the Knights Templar, founded *c.* 1152 on land given by Ralph Hastings, e.g. re-set in the two-storey s porch a battered late C12 doorway with one order of colonnettes, decayed leaf capitals with beading and a deeply moulded arch with keeled roll moulding and hoodmould. Attached to the E gable is an octagonal brick staircase tower of *c.* 1500 from the house of the Darcy family, who held the manor from 1337. It has a C20 battlemented parapet and tiled spirelet (cf. Riccall Manor House, East Riding) and may have been for viewing the gardens and deer park. The house is marred by C20 alterations.

THORNE

6010

A small market town in the county's eastern fenland, close to the lower course of the Don. The Norman castle and church were built on a low sandy ridge in the surrounding marshland of Thorne Waste and the town developed with trade on the river. Vermuyden's C17 drainage of Hatfield Chase brought further prosperity. In the early C19 a steam packet service from the former quay at Waterside, 1 m. NW, connected south Yorkshire with Hull, London and the Continent. Meanwhile completion of the Stainforth & Keadby Canal beside the town in 1793 had opened another route to the Humber via the Trent, and its commercial trade, now replaced by leisure traffic, sustained boatbuilding and repair. The colliery at Moorends, sunk 1909–26, closed in 1956 due to flooding; the peat-cutting industry continues on Thorne Moor. Varied C18 and C19 buildings, some with earlier cores, mostly brick-built, sometimes stuccoed, give the town character, although it is badly run-down at the time of writing.

St Nicholas. Dedicated to the patron saint of seamen (cf. Bawtry). A large church with imposing W tower overlooking the town, it stands just 50 yds s of the castle mound and may have originated as a chapel in the bailey. It was a chapelry until 1327, when quasi-parochial status was granted after a funeral party going to the mother church at Hatfield was drowned. No early work visible externally but in the chancel remains of C12 round-arched windows, two on the E (probably the outer pair of three) and two on the s. Five-bay nave. N and s aisles added *c.* 1200, embracing the tower. Their easternmost openings are separated from the arcades by piers of solid wall and the double-chamfered arches of this bay die into the masonry, an odd feature repeated elsewhere (e.g. s tower arch). The arcade beyond has slender circular piers with square abaci. Matching arches, again dying on the w. Contemporary round-arched s doorway, finely moulded with dogtooth decoration. Small blocked N doorway with plain round arch. Circular pier to N chapel arcade of two bays. Both inside and out this earlier work is characterized by masonry of rubble and river cobbles.

In the late C13, or more likely as part of rebuilding work recorded soon after 1327, the tower, then two stages and unbuttressed, was remodelled. Windows with Y-tracery. On the E side the window arrangement and old nave roof-line show that the church then already possessed a clerestory. The aisle windows were renewed with Y-tracery too, though it remains in only one; the others that survive now appear as lancets grown too wide. The tall corbelled chancel arch is no doubt also part of this phase.

The Perp work is distinguished by fine ashlar. The bell-stage of the tower has two two-light bell-openings each side, battlements and pinnacles. Plain parapets to the aisles and the heightened chancel and nave. Large windows to the clerestory, still with Y-tracery. Perp too the transeptal S chapel and the remodelled N chapel with large N window. Perp S porch, originally two storeys; it has a pretty three-light oriel window partly renewed. – ROOD SCREEN by *Sebastian Comper* 1947–8; ROOD carved by *William P. Davison*. – STAINED GLASS. E window by *Clayton & Bell*, 1862. Chancel S by *O'Connor*, 1873. S aisle w by *Hardman*, 1916. Three late works by *Henry Holiday*: S aisle second from E, c. 1912; N aisle second from E, 1915, and third from E, 1917. S aisle westernmost by *Frederick Cole*, 1964. – MONUMENTS. Edward Forster †1781 by *John Fisher* of York, 1784. Finely carved urn against sombre grey marble obelisk. – Mordecai Cutts †1787 and sister Elizabeth †1782. Nicely detailed pedimented tablet; small medallion with his portrait profile. – Striking Second World War Memorial depicting a crumpled uniform, by *Byron Howard* 1992.

Immediately N, on top of the ridge, the castle MOTTE, surrounded by a substantial ditch. Of the stone KEEP, still standing in the C16, only scraps remain.

Church Street runs downhill past the former TRAVIS CHARITY SCHOOL, by *Brundell & Arnold*, 1863. Gothic, with little spired bell-turret between twin gables. At the bottom, in MARKET PLACE, the WHITE HART, a Georgian front with shallow tripartite bow windows, dated 1737 but the core is earlier. Up KING STREET to the N a restored merchant's town house (No. 42) of three bays, dated 1747, the tall pedimented front of the METHODIST CHURCH (Wesleyan), 1826 but remodelled 1898, and the former BROOKE'S GRAMMAR SCHOOL, by *Brundell & Arnold*, 1861–2. Gothic, with 40-ft (12-metre) battlemented clock tower/porch in the angle between schoolroom and master's house. Opposite is the former BETHESDA CHAPEL (Methodist New Connexion) 1817, enlarged 1893. Brash polychrome front with pediment and pilasters. The surviving towered frontage of DARLEY'S BREWERY, c. 1902, dominates the view beyond.

In SILVER STREET SE of Market Place is another Georgian town house; five bays, wooden porch with fluted Doric columns, quoins. Beyond is THORNE HALL, later C18 (offices). Five-bay centre, two-and-a-half storeys, with full-width pediment. Quoins. One-bay wings, 1818(?) set back, with Venetian windows and hipped roofs. (Fine ballroom in l. wing.) E garden front has two big double-storey semicircular bows. Immediately SE is GREEN TOP SCHOOL, 1939, an attractive example of the *West Riding County Architect*'s pre-war Junior schools. Quadrangle of single-storey classrooms, roughcast walls, big hipped roofs of green-glazed tiles.

At MOORENDS, 1 m. N, ST WILFRITH by *C.M. Cooper*, 1934–5. Spare Romanesque style in well-detailed red brick. Large bell-tower above S chapel.

THORNHILL

2010

Village on the S hillside of the wide Calder valley, much expanded and now almost a suburb of Dewsbury.

ST MICHAEL AND ALL ANGELS. Noble W tower of two tall stages with diagonal buttresses, set higher on the slope than the body of the church. Outwardly Perp but perhaps with older fabric (see the ogee-headed stair doorway inside). Corbel table, battlements and eight pinnacles (cf. e.g. Ecclesfield). Perp E end. Three-bay chancel with clerestory and six-light E window 1499. The N chapel is the one object of major importance in the church. It was the Savile Chapel and contains a remarkable number of monuments. Two bays were built by Thomas Savile in 1447, another bay added by William Savile in 1493. Three-bay S chapel of 1491. Both have their original roofs. The nave, with clerestory, and aisles are by *Street*, 1877 (having been rebuilt already in 1777). In the Dec style, rather restrained externally except for the S porch. Its fine doorway has a rich frieze by *Thomas Earp*, who did all the decorative stone-carving. Compound nave piers with filleted shafts; intermediate shafts smaller. Fine arch-braced roof, surpassed by *Street*'s superb traceried chancel roof with angel corbels. – GATES and RAILINGS to the Savile Chapel, C18, wrought iron.

STAINED GLASS. In the Savile Chapel much of the original glass survives. It has inscriptions of uncommon interest. In the central N window, depicting Holy Kindred, 'Pray for the soul of Thomas Savile, Knight, who caused this chapel to be built, A.D. 1447' (in Latin). Kneeling figures of Sir Thomas and his wife below the Holy Family in the central light. Contemporary window to l. has the Crucifixion with the Virgin Mary and St John. The E window is a masterly and meticulous replica by *Jonathan Cooke*, 2012; the original glass, probably made at York, is preserved in a display case nearby. Long inscription 'Pray for the good prosperity, mercy and grace of William Savile, one of the Company of Grays Inn...[who] enlarged this quier at his cost...the which work was finished in the year of our Lord 1493'. William and four relations kneel below. The window, with much white glass, is not a conventional Doom window but depicts the Resurrection of the Blessed and their ascension to the shining Holy City, where angels reach out welcoming hands and stand on turrets blowing trumpets.

In the chancel E window a Tree of Jesse, probably made in Flanders, much restored. The lush foliage of the branches and the warm colours of the figures are very different from the chapel glass. It was given by Robert Frost, chancellor of Prince Arthur and parson of Thornhill, 'who hath made new est window, and also clerestoried and arched this quyer; finished the year of grace 1499'. Some C15 fragments in two S chapel windows. In the screen between the chancel and N chapel a large panel (*ex situ*), with the achievement of George Savile, 1st Marquess of Halifax (†1695), attributed to *Henry Gyles*. Aisle windows 1879, and chancel and nave clerestory windows (incomplete scheme) *c.* 1881–1906, all by *Burlison & Grylls*.

MONUMENTS. Nine pieces of C9 Anglo-Saxon CROSSES. All but one from shafts, and most have forms of interlace. Four are vernacular memorials with inscriptions in Old English naming those commemorated, three of these being written in runes (cf. Dewsbury). That inscribed 'Gilswiþ raised up in memory of Berhtswiþ a beacon on a hill. Pray for her soul' is thought to be a unique example of a cross commissioned by a woman. – Savile Chapel, chronologically. Cross-legged knight in chain-mail, almost certainly Sir John Thornhill †1322. His head, with restored face, lies under a canopy. Sir John Savile †1482, and his wife, Alice Gascoigne. Alabaster tomb with effigies. She is a graceful figure, her drawn-back hair flowing loose.* He is in armour, wearing a Yorkist collar, but in a break with convention the helm on which his head rests has the delightful 'maiden crowned' crest of the Thornhills and not the Savile owl. Tomb-chest with knights, ladies and three male civilians as weepers. Broad, low, crocketed ogee arches above them (cf. Harewood, *West Riding North*). – Sir John Savile †1504, in armour, between his wives, Alice Vernon and Elizabeth Paston. Erected in 1529. A rare example of an oak tomb-chest with effigies, which would originally have lain under a four-poster (cf. Barnburgh and Worsbrough). Panels with shields, bordered by ornate quatrefoils. Inscription 'Bones among stones lie full still, whilst the souls wander where God will'. – Sir George Savile †1614 and his wife, Anne Wentworth, †1633, erected after her death by her brother, later Earl of Strafford. Large, almost over-sized monument between chancel and chapel. Two recumbent effigies. Below, against the tomb-chest their sons, Sir George Savile, 2nd Baronet, †1626, comfortably reclining on the chancel side, and Sir William Savile, 3rd Baronet, †1644, on the chapel side, frontally kneeling. Both look later in style than the parents. Above the effigies a

43

---

*It has some similar details to the tomb at Llandygai, Gwynedd, e.g. the ladies' identical necklaces.

segmental arch, decorated with trophies, and to the l. and r.
pairs of Corinthian columns, one stone, one touch. These carry
an entablature with an armorial cartouche and two figures;
between the figures is a large panel with strapwork scrolls, the
N one with the Savile achievement. Third figure above. No
inscription. – Sir George Savile, 1st Baronet, †1622. By *Maxi-*   43
milian Colt, 1628, under his widow's will.* Alabaster and
marbles. Recumbent effigy in armour, excellently carved features. Excellent strapwork cartouche at the back between trophies. Columns l. and r., and on top two small obelisks and
two cartouches flanking an elaborate achievement. – Sir
George Savile of Rufford, 7th Baronet, †1743. By *William
Barlow*. Black and grey marbles used to effect. Small black
sarcophagus with backpiece set between volutes and crowned
by a pediment. – Sir George Savile, 8th Baronet, †1784. By
John Fisher I. Elegantly detailed tablet in different marbles;
Savile owl with skull. – Richard Lumley †1818. Austere tablet
by *Charles Fisher*. – John, 2nd Baron Savile, †1931. By *Amy
Lewis*; brought from Rufford Abbey. Alabaster baby lying on
its back and holding up a basin. Meant for a font. – s chapel.
Sir John Copley †1745. Pedimented tablet with volutes; black
pyramid above. – Tower. Sir Thomas Radcliffe †1679. Attributed to *Grinling Gibbons & Arnold Quellin* (GF). A very fine
gadrooned sarcophagus with putti and drapery. Luxuriantly
framed inscription above, large winged skull below.

OLD RECTORY. Of C17 origin, mostly rebuilt 1824. Three-
bay s front has projecting wings with big single-storey bows.

THORNHILL HALL. Fragmentary ruins of the Saviles' C15
manor house, on a moated site in the park E of the church and
old rectory. The house burnt down in 1648 after some of its
Royalist garrison accidentally blew themselves up while nego-
tiating surrender with Parliamentarian forces. After the Civil
War the Saviles made Rufford Abbey, Nottinghamshire, their
principal seat. All that remains is a big brick-lined fireplace
and the base of one buttressed wall. Two very decayed limestone eagles stand on the site of the gatehouse.

THORNHILL HALL, Hall Lane, ¼ m. ENE. C17 W range with
some original mullioned windows; two of five lights in N gable.
Extensions to E in keeping 1879. Behind, a very large C17 stone
BARN. The r. end, probably residential, has two storeys of
three-light mullioned windows with continuous hoodmoulds.

COMBS HALL FARMHOUSE, Combs Road, 200 yds WNW. C17.
Altered double-gabled front has ornamental rainwater head
dated 1661. Two Tudor-arched doorways. Mullioned windows
below string courses.

GRAMMAR SCHOOL (former), No. 169 Combs Road (restored).
1643. Four bays, single-storeyed, with cross-windows. Five-
light transomed window in each gable-end. s front has

---

*She was Savile's second wife, Elizabeth Ayscough, †1626; her own monument by
Colt at Horbury was lost when the church was rebuilt 1791–4.

projecting addition on r., linking parallel schoolroom, 1884, modelled on the original.

LEES HALL, 1½ m. NW. In the valley bottom beside the railway, in unappealing surroundings; unused at the time of writing. Late C15/early C16 timber-framed house. Hall and cross-wings, hearth-passage plan, the passage and original W wing lost. Built by the Nettleton family, Huddersfield clothiers who rose to gentry status and remodelled and extended it in the early C17. The alterations included the replacement of ground-floor studding with stone, rich plasterwork and an outer W wing. Restoration in 1962–4 reopened the Hall to its full height.

Two-bay E wing, separately framed, has diagonal strutting to N and S gables, giving lozenge effect; on E side a big extruded stack and close studding. Two ground-floor rooms, one a parlour. Above, a large solar with uncommonly fine C17 plasterwork. (Ceiling with small geometrical panels divided up into squares, lozenges and octagons, decorated with flowers, fleur-de-lys etc. Frieze of affronted unicorns and lions, continued on the cambered tie-beam of the central truss.) Pent staircase in rear angle of Hall and wing. Close studding to the Hall, which was reduced from two bays to one-and-a-half when the lower end was demolished. The fireplace against the C19 brick W wall is probably in the position of the original hearth against the passage. Very fine kingpost roof. Dais end has impressive full-width canopy. (Traces of painted decoration on the wall below.) The three-bay outer W wing, of stone, included a kitchen: see the big extruded stack on the N gable. The large chamber above, with a six-light mullioned-and-transomed window, had plasterwork similar to that in the solar. A C19 extension to the W wing has reduced the gap between it and the Hall.

THORPE HESLEY

HOLY TRINITY. By *J.P. Pritchett*, 1837–9. Five-bay nave with buttresses and tall lancets, chancel merely a shallow projection. Odd little (ritual) W tower with gabled belfry stage and octagonal stone spirelet. W gallery. Large Tudor Gothic VICARAGE, 1843.

THUNDERCLIFFE GRANGE, 1½ m. S. By *John Platt*, c. 1776–83, for the 3rd Earl of Effingham. Square, with seven-bay front. Ashlar. Originally two storeys with central pediments on the entrance and garden façades. Added to the latter are full-height shallow bows, perhaps by *William Lindley*, who worked to 'finish' the house for the 4th Earl, 1794–5. Main openings tripartite. Pedimented porch with Doric columns. When the third storey was added, probably 1832, the pediment between the bows was broken by a window and on the front the pediment is similarly overwhelmed by the attic, made more ponderous here by pilasters. Similarly heavy enclosed porch. Entrance hall has curved inner wall with niches. Central hall under large lantern has cantilevered stone staircase to arcaded landing (altered). Square-section cast-iron balusters, fluted. – In the garden a BATH HOUSE. Tunnel-like space under a round arch set into a bank, the front open. Fine ashlar lining. Small rectangular plunge pool at rear. Probably contemporary with the house.

KIRKSTEAD ABBEY MEWS, ¾ m. SSE. A farm, restored in 1900 by the Earl of Effingham and again for residential conversion in 1985. The site is associated with Kirkstead Abbey (Lincolnshire), which was granted rights to mine, smelt and forge local iron ore in 1161. Long two-storey stone range, with original house to l. Probably late C15 or C16 incorporating earlier fabric including reused roof timbers. Four small windows have trefoil heads. One round-headed window might be Norman.

NETHER FOLD FARM, Scholes Lane, ⅔ m. SE. Timber-framed house, c. 1495, with later rendered stone and brick exterior, much altered. Originally three bays, cross-passage plan, its central hall open with a smoke-hood. Late medieval staircase in the w bay.

KEPPEL'S COLUMN. See WENTWORTH WOODHOUSE, p. 738.

ROMAN RIG. See Introduction, p. 9.

THORPE-IN-BALNE

5010

MANOR HOUSE. A large and well-preserved moated site. Among the outbuildings is the two-bay chancel of a Norman CHAPEL, probably built by Otto de Tilli in the mid C12 and in use until 1556.* Coursed limestone rubble with ashlar quoins. One small s window high up. At the e end two of formerly three round-arched windows, cut into and partly obliterated by a blocked three-light one of c. 1400 with fragmentary panel tracery. Plain Norman N doorway with semicircular hoodmould and a tympanum with segmental underside; C13 window to l. (Inside, the C12 and C13 windows have roll-moulded arrises. C13 trefoil-headed piscina. Semi-octagonal e respond of a s chapel. No more than traces of the nave footings survive.)

---

*In 1452 Joan, wife of Charles Nowel, was forcibly abducted from the chapel by Edward Lancaster. A petition was made to Parliament for redress, the Act granting this including important general provisions that gave all women increased protection against ravishment by allowing coercive marriages and other contracts to be annulled.

5080

THORPE SALVIN

St Peter. Essentially late C12, with one of the most interesting Norman fonts in the country. Part of the nave, the N arcade, the chancel arch and the lower part of the w tower all remain. One window in the nave s wall (and evidence inside of another, blocked), plus a tiny one in the tower. Superb s doorway, especially well preserved thanks to the Tudor porch with timber-framed front, a rarity in the North. Three orders, the inner one with small sunk shaft, the outer two with larger attached colonnettes. Rings with rope carving. The middle capitals each side are scalloped, the others have waterleaf with volutes. The details match only on the outer pair. The richly decorated arch has in the first order a subtle relief carving of trefoiled lobes. Little hemispheres or domes embellish the inner edge (many lacking). Complex arrangements of chevrons in the other two orders, especially the second. Here double chevrons point to point on both the soffit and the face produce two rows of open diamonds either side of the hollow behind a free-standing band of solid diamonds at the angle. These have (or had) domes in their sunk centres. Pretty foliate fans in the spandrels of the chevrons and some edges beaded. Finally a kind of outer frieze similar to the first order. Altogether a sophisticated piece (cf. Askham Bryan, *West Riding North*). The capitals of the chancel arch are similar to those of the doorway – large and scalloped in the first order, smaller and foliate in the second, but the arch itself has two strong rolls instead of ornamental enrichments. The arcade is of two bays. The responds semicircular, the pier octagonal, the abaci large and square. Flat capitals of waterleaf type, and single-stepped arches (cf. Treeton). Finally the tall tower arch, which has some chevron and semicircular shafts with multi-scalloped capitals, but is pointed (cf. Campsall and Kirk Smeaton).

Early–mid-C14 the chancel, with the reticulated tracery of its E window, the 'low-side' lancet with a transom low down, and the sedilia with ogee heads, polygonal shafts and a pretty castellated cresting. N chapel of one bay, a chantry added in 1380. The capitals still have a little nailhead decoration. N door has ogee head and hoodmould, the three two-light windows mouchettes. The two larger nave windows, also Dec, have interesting tracery (three stepped and cusped lights under an ogee arch under a pointed arch under a square head). The easternmost window has in the l. jamb a tall and oddly placed niche with cusped head. Perp the tower top and the later clerestory. The windows in the N aisle are Perp too, but were brought from Worksop Priory when the aisle was widened c. 1847. Organ chamber s of the chancel added during restoration by *Flockton & Gibbs*, 1892.

8   FONT. C12. Large, cylindrical, carved all round with beaded arches below a frieze with wavy beaded stem and stylized leaves. More leaves in the spandrels. Arranged within seven

arches grouped around two-thirds of it are delightfully detailed scenes depicting the four seasons and a baptism. On the remaining third the arches are simply intersected. Whether that third was seen less (as now, against the tower screen) or whether the sculptor had run out of stories, it is impossible to say. The interpretation of the scenes and their symbolism is a matter of debate. They read best from r. to l. In the first of three arches a mask above two vertical bands of chevron, perhaps representing Aquarius and the beginning of life and the year or the baptized person breathing out light to banish evil. Then a man warming his legs before a fire for Winter and a sower for Spring. In the next two arches are a rider bearing a leafy bough, perhaps out 'a-maying', for Summer, and a man harvesting corn for Autumn. Finally two arches are used to show a baptism. The scenes are lively but can never have possessed the poignancy of such small work as at Moissac or Chartres.

Traces of PAINTED DECORATION at NW of chancel arch. – MONUMENTS. Chancel. Katherine Sandford †1461. Incised alabaster floor slab with figure wearing horned head-dress, under a canopy. Sons and daughters nestle l. and r. against the lower folds of her gown, a curious arrangement (cf. brass to Lady Anne Norbury †1464, Stoke D'Abernon, Surrey). There are two splendid and almost matching monuments erected by Dame Mary Portington (†1635) to her father and her husband, both attributed to *Christopher Kingsfield* (GF), and probably early C17: Hercy Sandford †1582 and his wife, Margaret (s wall). Two kneeling figures facing each other, with a shrouded infant son before three kneeling daughters in the 'predella'. Aedicule with coat of arms in segmental pediment. – Sir Roger Portington †1604 and Dame Mary (N wall). More elaborate surround with black marble columns. – STAINED GLASS. Chancel s window by *Lavers, Barraud & Westlake*, 1882. N aisle, easternmost, by *Clayton & Bell*, 1909.

OLD HALL. Only the tall s front of the manor house stands. The mansion was built by Hercy Sandford, probably in the 1570s, and sold to Sir Edward Osborne in 1636. His son Thomas, 1st Duke of Leeds, abandoned it after building his new hall at Kiveton Park (*see* p. 719) in 1698–1704. A little two-storey gatehouse forms a central entrance to the walled courtyard before the hall. One narrow bay, with stepped gable. Moulded Tudor-arched doorway with label, and carved heraldic panel above. Three-light upper window under a trio of decayed shields.

The hall is three storeys. Its front of nine bays is not long, so the height dominates. It would perhaps even more if we could still see the original skyline. The façade is quite plain and virtually symmetrical, with projecting porch and round corner towers. Just enough survives behind to indicate that it was a compact rectangle in plan with rear angle towers. All this shows the likely influence of two of *Robert Smythson*'s Elizabethan high houses, both in Derbyshire, viz. the Earl of Shrewsbury's at Buxton and his wife Bess's much larger house at Chatsworth. The rectangular porch has a four-centred doorway with small three-light window over and windows in two storeys above. Transoms and labels. Three-light windows to l. and r., then – an odd conceit – two wide bare chimney-breasts with an arcaded frieze at the top. The bases of the stacks above are diagonally placed. These stacks must always have played their part in the dramatic skyline. Then windows of three lights again, excepting the larger four-light ground-floor window to the l. Finally the towers, the SE intact with windows at the angle.

Unfortunately one can see hardly anything of the distribution of the rooms, so how a possible Elizabethan plan could have been developed behind this front remains obscure. Was there a tiny internal courtyard? On the ground floor two very large fireplaces, the taller to the W perhaps for the hall, with the large window beside the dais. The adjacent tower had a newel staircase. Closets in SE tower. Slightly eccentrically placed smaller fireplaces with four-centred heads in the upper storeys. The unusually large top-floor windows suggest that, as at Chatsworth, the gallery and great chamber were skied.

5080

THROAPHAM

ST JOHN THE BAPTIST (Churches Conservation Trust). Its rather isolated position just ½ m. from the church at Laughton-en-le-Morthen (q.v.) is puzzling. Dodsworth noted in 1631 that pilgrims once flocked to it at Midsummer, when there was a fair, leading Professor Hey to postulate that the church's existence results from the well near the chancel having anciently been a sacred site. The relative thinness (2 ft 2 in. (0.65 metres)) of the nave's E, S and N walls and several quoins at its NE angle indicate Saxon or Overlap fabric. Reused Norman S doorway with water-leaf capitals. Chronologically next the three-bay arcades. Circular piers, with moulded capitals. Octagonal abaci on the N, circular ones on the S. Keeled SE respond with minor shafts and dogtooth. Deeply moulded arches. All this points to c. 1200. The chancel arch corresponds. The corbels look like re-cut shafts. C14 arch from chancel to N chapel, on head corbels. The C15 W tower replaced the nave's fourth bay; the springing of the arches remains. The odd blocked half-arch at the N aisle's W end probably due to C16 rebuilding of the N wall: see the plinth outside. Perp S clerestory windows. Chancel rebuilt 1709, restored in the C19. – FONT. Octagonal, Perp. Castellated bowl with varied tracery in the panels. A brother to the font at Laughton. Small carvings on the underside include three faces; one is an African, a rare early representation. They are perhaps the Three Magi. – Former rood SCREEN; part under the tower, part between N aisle and chapel. Plain Perp. – MONUMENTS. Coped coffin-lid of the late C13. If only this were in a mint state! It must have been a delightful piece. Foliated cross and, to the

l. and r. of the cross, scrolls etc. with naturalistic leaves in high relief. – Floor slab. Robert Dynyngton †1393 and Alice †1430. Unusually early English inscription. – Brass. John Mallevorer †1620. Dressed in armour.

THRYBERGH

4090

St Leonard. Narrow nave and chancel, unbuttressed w tower with spire, the spire set back and sparsely crocketed. The rubble masonry of the nave E parts is early Norman, of Overlap character. The lower jambs of the s doorway remain. A fragment of herringbone work is visible at the w end of the chancel N wall. The nave was soon enlarged by a third bay, as is witnessed by the ashlar work and blocked Norman N doorway. The N porch has disappeared. The chancel is Dec (dedicated 1349), but much renewed. Its uneven E buttresses and the medieval coffin on the raised ground beyond suggest that the sanctuary was once longer. The appearance of the church is otherwise Perp; before restoration in 1871 the parapets were battlemented. Upper parts of tower and the spire of between 1439 and 1469, though wholly rebuilt by *C. Hodgson Fowler*, 1894. Lumpy sw vestry extension attached to porch, by *G. G. Pace*, 1970. – Stained glass. s aisle, easternmost, is early c16, restored and adapted. It includes several angels and two kneeling donors, one probably William Reresby, rector 1505–20, who gave several windows.

A remarkable number of impressive Monuments. Two defaced c14 effigies, one in the tower s wall, the other in the vestry corridor. Both represent priests. – s side, westwards from chancel: Jane Hedges †1783 and husband Rev. William Hedges, Rector, †1811, by the *Fishers*, York. Dove and draped urn against dark grey obelisk. – Projecting half-tomb with helmet and shields on the front, c17 (below window). – Sir Leonard Reresby †1748. Attributed to *Henry Cheere* by Rupert Gunnis (GF). Excellent, with three putto heads below, and above a disconsolate putto resting his elbow on a medallion with a portrait. – Ralph Reresby †1530. In an ogee-headed recess. Tomb with incised figure of a knight, shields on wall behind. – Louisa Fullerton †1818. By *Bacon & Manning*. Draped female figure ascending heavenwards, her eight grieving children gathered round a sarcophagus below. – Immediately to r., a matching monument, with urn and obelisk, for her husband, John Fullerton, †1847. By *Edwin Smith*, Sheffield. – Sir John Reresby I †1646 and wife Frances †1668, erected 1674. Inscription in gold on black marble within large pedimented frame.

N side, westwards from chancel: Lyonel Reresby †1558 and wife Anne †1587. The usual two kneeling figures, facing one another across a prayer-desk, each under an arch. Their seven sons and nine daughters in the 'predella' below include two

swaddled babies who died in infancy. Erected by their daugh-
ter Elizabeth, probably after her mother's death (cf. her similar
monument at Harrington, Lincolnshire, to her husband,
Francis Copledike, †1599 and their two children). – The Hon.
John Finch †1739 and his wife, Elizabeth, †1767, by *Nicholas
Read*. Large obelisk, tapering pillar with urn on top and ample
draperies (damaged) tumbling down around a weeping putto.
Medallion with two profile portraits. – Savile Finch †1788, by
John Bacon Sen. Fine figure of Benevolence seated in front of
an obelisk and holding a medallion with two profile portraits.
– Rev. John Hedges †1743 and wife Valentina †1743, also
Elizabeth Hedges †1810, by *W. & R. Fisher*. Erected by the
Rev. William Hedges to his parents and sister. Mourning
female figure with an urn, against a black obelisk. – Sir John
Reresby II †1689 and wife Frances †1699. An excellent and
striking piece in black and white marble with Ionic aedicule
with swan-neck pediment. Apron has armour and weapons
between grinning skulls. Gold lettering on black marble.

In the churchyard part of a mid-CII CROSS-SHAFT of
Overlap style. On one side a bust under pointed arch and
above an animal and the lower part of a human figure. On the
opposite side a shaft with acanthus foliage l. and r. On another
side interlace. In Three Hills Close ⅛ m. E, part of another
CROSS-SHAFT with crocketed edges, probably CI2.

THRYBERGH PARK (Rotherham Golf Club), ½ m. N. Splendidly
battlemented Tudor Gothic/Gothick house by *John Webb* for
Col. John Fullerton, 1812–14. It replaced a house immediately
N of the church, rebuilt in the CI7 by Sir John Reresby II; its
garden was celebrated for his plant collection. Five bays
square, two storeys. Symmetrical E front has tall polygonal
angle turrets, canted bay windows and arcaded porch with
monster pinnacles. Lower N service range finishes with a
square tower, set forward. The S side, asymmetrical, has some
Gothick windows and buttresses with castellated tops. Its l.
return is a surprise. The first two bays, gabled, have a large
full-height blind window with intersecting tracery, and are
framed by buttresses rising as spired turrets. Entrance hall has
rib-vault, the stair hall beyond a cantilevered imperial staircase
with thin iron balustrade of Gothic arches with quatrefoils.

THUNDERCLIFFE GRANGE
see THORPE HESLEY

THURCROFT

ST SIMON AND ST JUDE. By *Walker & Thompson*, 1937–9. Plain
Gothic in imitation stone.

The village sprang up after the mine was sunk in 1909. From
1913 some MINERS' HOUSING in Katherine Road, John Street

etc. by *J.E. Knight* for Rothervale Collieries Ltd. More spacious 'model village' development in The Crescent etc. by *Frederick Hopkinson* of Worksop, 1920s.

THURCROFT HALL, ⅞ m. ene. 1699 for William Beckwith. Remodelled as small mid-Georgian country house with half-storey replacing dormers. Plain stuccoed front of seven bays. Raised quoins and first-floor band, blocking course. Bolection-moulded doorway. Stonework of segmental pediment continues to architrave of window above. Motto on sill, date on pilasters beneath. (Interior has some ornate plasterwork. Cantilevered stone staircase with wrought-iron balustrade.) Charming c18 GARDEN HOUSE. Pedimented ashlar front with arched doorway flanked by semi-domed niches.

BRAMPTON-EN-LE-MORTHEN, ¾ m. sw. Pleasant rural hamlet with c17 to early c19 farms and cottages, a world away from the pit village. The MANOR HOUSE, c16 and c17, is timber-framed with jettied first floor. Cross-wing has eight-light window with king mullion and transom. BRAMPTON HALL, probably late c16, altered and restored, has projecting wings with tall, crowstepped attic gables and an oddly placed two-storey porch to l. of l. return, similarly gabled.

THURGOLAND   *2000*

HOLY TRINITY. By *Street*, 1870–1, replacing a church of 1843 by *Hurst & Moffatt*. Simple Dec. Not large, but attractively composed with gables to n porch, two-bay n vestry and transeptal s chapel. Tall bellcote above central buttress on w gable. e vestry by *Nicholson*, 1930–2. – REREDOS, PULPIT and FONT, by *Street*. – STAINED GLASS. All by *Hardman*, 1871 and 1875.

METHODIST CHURCH (former), Cote Lane. 1892–3 by *George Moxon* of Barnsley. Broad gabled front has attached tower with conical pinnacles. Lancets.

HUTHWAITE HALL, ½ m. sw. By *John Carr*, 1748. His earliest known work, with a good Palladian garden front. The rest is plain. Five bays, two-and-a-half storeys. Pitched roof. Ground floor heavily rusticated, with Gibbs surround to the pedimented doorway. Gibbs surrounds to the windows too. In an almost imperceptible trick their lintels, except for the keystone, are carved from one stone. Upper windows have moulded architraves, with friezes and cornices at the first floor. The window over the doorway is further enhanced with a swept base to its architrave and an ashlar apron below the sill band.

THURLSTONE   *2000*

ST SAVIOUR, ½ m. w of the village. By *C. Hodgson Fowler*, 1904–5. Dec. The w tower was unbuilt. Refined interior of red sandstone walls setting off tall limestone arcades. Glorious woodwork, executed by *Hawleys* of Penistone, especially the chancel's wagon roof. – REREDOS. Carved by *Clara Nokes*, the vicar's sister-in-law, 1917. – STAINED GLASS. E and S aisle E by *Bryans & Webb* 1905.

VICARAGE (former). By *Edgar Wood*, 1906, with his typical towering proportions to taller S side and rear, which have canted bay windows rising full height from basement. Gentler Pennine domesticity to the E front, with central canted bay window and deeply recessed entrance to l.

In the village several late C18 and early C19 three-storey WEAVERS' COTTAGES.

BULLHOUSE HALL, I m. SW. Good Pennine gentry house of the Rich family, built 1655 (dated door), extended 1688. Gabled two-storey front has three original bays, the middle one narrower. Now a bay window, it was probably a porch. Later, wider, bay on r. projects slightly. Doorway in the angle has massive lintel. Double-chamfered mullioned-and-transomed windows, the later ones larger, with king mullions. (Panelling inside, probably C18 but reusing C17 carved panels. Pretty SUMMERHOUSE, 1686.)

In the former grounds is BULLHOUSE CHAPEL, built by Elkanah Rich in 1692 and in continuous use for independent Nonconformist worship ever since. Plain, solidly built oblong with gabled porch in E front. Two two-light windows to each side. The windows have round-arched lights above and below the transoms. The NW vestry was the minister's tiny cottage. Original PULPIT, raised between the N windows, panelled with back-board and canopy crowned with scrolls. Box pews reused in dado panelling.

HARTCLIFFE FOLLY, I m. S, is a tall cylindrical tower of 1856 built by Henry Richardson, linen merchant, and fully restored in 1999–2000. Spiral stair inside.

THURNSCOE

ST HELEN. Not large. W tower faced in ashlar in 1729, preserving a W window with late C14 tracery. Quoins, and arched bell-openings above circular windows. Nave rebuilt by *E. Isle Hubbard*, 1887, the chancel and S chapel in 1897. – ROOD 1897. – FONT. C18. Unusual gadrooned wooden bowl and handsome cover carved with acanthus. – STAINED GLASS. Chancel NE by *Ward & Hughes*, 1885. – Nave S: westernmost by *Morris & Co.*, 1922. – Nave N: two by *Francis Spear*, 1955; a third after his design, *c.* 1990.

ST HILDA, Hanover Street. By *C.B. Flockton*, 1934–5. Substantial, in economical late Perp. Large tower unfinished.

THURNSCOE HALL, ⅜ m. SE. Seven-bay S front built between 1670 and 1701; attic storey added *c.* 1985. Middle bay framed by rusticated pilaster-strips and broken segmental pediment. Later C18 pedimented Doric porch.

Low Grange, Thornwood Close. Probably *c.* 1600, in red brick – an early use in the area – with blue brick diapering. Rear wing 1664.

THURSTONLAND

St Thomas. By *Mallinson & Barber*, 1869–70. Prominent s tower with spire, placed at the nave's easternmost bay, where it forms a porch with small gallery over. – STAINED GLASS. E window by *Wailes*, 1870.

SCHOOLHOUSE (former), opposite. 1766–7. Venetian windows to ground floor.

METHODIST CHAPEL (former, Wesleyan), ¼ m. SW. 1836. Pedimented.

TICKHILL

Tickhill was one of the famous castles in the north of England, but since the keep's demolition in the C17 the church has been the town's more impressive building. The medieval settlement N and W of the castle walls first occurs as a place in the Nostell Priory cartulary of 1109–16; before this Roger de Busli's castle and the honour it commanded were called after Blyth, Nottinghamshire, where he founded a priory in 1088.[*] With church, market, school, Augustinian friary and three hospitals, Tickhill ranked second in prosperity in the south of the West Riding in 1334. Decline followed the castle's obsolescence as a military and administrative centre and the suppression of religious houses; in the 1540s Leland called the town 'very bare'. Some revival took place in the C17 and in the later C18/early C19 with the rebuilding that gives the town much of its character; but without significant transport links or industry, and latterly even a market, Tickhill barely changed from the mid C19 until outer residential expansion began a century later.

St Mary. The proudest parish church in the West Riding, except for those of the big towns. Silvery-grey limestone, large and essentially Perp, though the church must in fact have possessed its present size from the early C13. Witnesses of that are the lower part of the W tower with the W doorway, and the chancel. On the W the tower has broad flat clasping buttresses

---

[*] It superseded the Anglo-Saxon borough of Dadesley, which probably lay near the vanished All Hallows church, I m. NNW of the castle.

that have keeled shafts set in hollow mouldings at their angles. Fine nailhead on the first string course, at a height above the apex of the portal. This has three orders of shafts and big dogtooth bands running between them down the jambs. The design of the richly moulded arch corresponds. The capitals and angle have a little nailhead. Inside, this E.E. tower has towards the nave a deeply moulded arch with very tall, strongly shafted responds with some keeling and filleting. The arch's outer mouldings have nailhead. Opening out of the tower to the N and S are lower arches of the same design, so it is certain that the C13 church had aisles. The responds of these arches carry plain moulded capitals as one would expect, but three capitals also have tiny foliate details reminiscent of Romanesque work. The nave arch capitals are foliate too, more C13 in character than Perp, though conceivably from a later heightening of the arch. Embedded in the S E side of this arch's S pier is a puzzling fragment of a round shaft with waterleaf capital; another such capital is incorporated into a bracket beside the S door. They perhaps indicate that the tower was the culmination of a building begun in the later C12 further E. Other early C13 work is a small round-headed tower-stair doorway in the S aisle's W wall and the simple doorway of the N aisle. The S doorway could be C13 or early C14. As for the chancel, E.E. evidence is limited to one lancet window and the small priest's door, both opening into the N chapel, and the r. jamb of another window to their l.

From the mid C14 the church was rebuilt and enlarged, beginning c. 1348 with the N chancel chapel: see its two N windows, one of four lights with flowing, the other of three lights with reticulated tracery. The E window with Y-tracery is probably reused (?from a vestry). Buttresses with little gables decorated with ogee details. Then rebuilding started in earnest. We cannot follow it documentarily in detail, but the arms of Castile and Leon on the W tower prove a date for these parts of between 1372 and 1399, when John of Gaunt, who claimed that kingdom through his wife, held Tickhill as Duke of Lancaster. Other heraldry is local, of a similar period. Work was still incomplete in 1429 when £5 and a cart and four horses were bequeathed 'to the makying of the stepell'. Stylistic evidence is not much more help in dating, except that the S side, with four-light aisle and chapel windows and plainer porch and buttresses, looks later than the rest. The N aisle and the clerestory have three-light windows whose tracery is of a piece with that of the belfry openings, and aisle, clerestory and tower all have decoratively gabled buttresses.

On the W tower, it is the change from clasping to angle buttresses and from concentrated to diffuse decoration that marks the change from C13 to late C14 work. The W window of five lights with a transom was of course broken into the C13 wall. Around it are plenty of nicely suspended shields, above are three statues. The middle one, in a splendid canopied niche, is Christ in Majesty; those to each side seem to be the principal donors, a knight with his little son l., a lady r. Similar canopied niches with statues to N, E (Virgin and Child) and S. Above, a frieze of blank quatrefoils and then the tall bell-openings, two of three lights on each side, with a stepped and embattled transom. Heightened to 124 ft (37.8 metres) this majestic tower is crowned by battlements with unusual pierced ogee arches under crocketed gables, gargoyles, and diagonal pinnacles with yet more crockets. The body of the church has battlements and pinnacles too. Very tall nave and considerably lower chancel. Low porches, the N, with ogee-gabled arch, decidedly the more decorative. Large aisle and clerestory windows (*see* above), with twice as many clerestory windows as there are bays (cf. East Anglia). In addition, at the E end of the nave, above the chancel arch is a five-light window.

The INTERIOR is light and spacious, light especially because of the window just mentioned. This is a far from usual thing in English parish churches, although examples occur in all parts of the country. The best known are probably those of the major Cotswold churches. Wide arcades of four bays with tall piers of an unusual section. Four semi-octagonal shafts in the main directions, four small hollows in the diagonals. Each arch carries an ogee gable with a crocketed finial that reaches into the clerestory zone. The capitals of the piers carry small bands of bossy foliage. It was also intended to vault the inside of the tower, but no more was done than the finely corbelled springers of the ribs in the corners. The chancel arch harmonizes with the arcades. Above it the demi-figure of an angel carrying the Eastfield arms and l. and r. again two suspended shields. In the N aisle the rood stair with one ogee-headed doorway above another; in the S aisle two piscinas, one with cusped ogee head, the other trefoil-headed, with adjacent aumbry. The N chapel has one double-chamfered arch to the chancel, on brackets. On the N wall an ogee-headed tomb-recess. Irregular S chapel arcade of three bays with octagonal piers and double-chamfered arches, but the E arch considerably narrower than the others and dying into the impost.

FURNISHINGS. PULPIT. Made up of reused Perp traceried panels; other panels reused as priest's stall etc. – SCREEN. Perp, to the N chapel. – LECTERN. Fine Arts and Crafts wrought brass by *Nelson Dawson*, 1908. – PEWS. 1844. The poppyheads are cast iron. – FONT. Perp. Octagonal. Shallow bowl, simply decorated with quatrefoils and shields, on four stubby shafts and deep moulded plinth with fleurons. – FONT CANOPY by *G. G. Pace*, 1959. A tall painted ciborium, with unsettling combination of stylized Corinthian columns and plain pointed Gothic arches, with a pinnacle on top. – STAINED GLASS. Good late C15/early C16 remains, including six Apostles, in the upper parts of two S aisle windows. E window 1883, W window 1886, nave E window 1896, all by *Powell Bros.* – N aisle second from E by *J. W. Knowles*, 1882. – S chapel E by *Heaton, Butler & Bayne*, 1887. – N chapel E window 1898, NE window 1896, by *Kempe*.

MONUMENTS. William Eastfield †1386 and wife Margaret. Tomb-chest with quatrefoil decoration. The brass inscription is on the chancel N wall. – Alabaster tomb-chest with effigies of Sir Thomas Fitzwilliam †1498 and his wife, Lucy Neville, †1534 (niece of Warwick 'the kingmaker'). It must have been commissioned by Lady Lucy in the 1520s and was moved from the Friary (see below) soon after the Reformation. Although damaged it is especially notable for having some of the earliest Italian Renaissance decoration in England, the style being a rustic development of that of Torrigiano's tomb of Henry VII. The two surviving sides have square panels with shields in close laurel wreaths. Shell-tops above the square panels. Colonnettes or balusters with acanthus leaves growing up them. At the W end the shield is held by two putti, just as in Torrigiano's design. Lady Lucy's son by her second marriage, Sir Anthony Browne †1548, copied the design for his own tomb in Battle Abbey (East Sussex). – William Laughton †1702 and wife Jane †1695. Large cartouche with exuberant heraldry. – John Laughton †1709 and wife Jane †1699. Elaborately draped cartouche with cherubs' heads and skull, surmounted by a putto bearing a mantled achievement. – Thomas Tofield †1779 and Joseph Tomlinson †1792, two large marble tablets by *John Coulton* of Braithwell, the earlier with broken pediment. – Louisa Blanche Foljambe †1871, by *William Calder Marshall*.* Alabaster tomb-chest with recumbent effigies – she cradles her baby son, Frederick, †1871. Canopied niches with heraldry to tomb-chest sides. (Moved from Haselbech, Northamptonshire in 1908.)

CASTLE. The castle has belonged to the Duchy of Lancaster since 1372, when John of Gaunt received Tickhill and other estates in exchange for the Earldom of Richmond. Roger de Busli built the early Norman castle, enlarging a natural sandstone knoll to form a motte about 75 ft (22.9 metres) high and 80 ft (24.4 metres) in diameter on top. The oval bailey of two acres lies to the NW. They are surrounded by a massive earthen rampart and an outer ditch some 30 ft (9.1 metres) wide that still forms a moat to the S and W. To the E, a counterscarp bank where the ditch was cut through the hill.

The first stone structure was the two-storey W GATEHOUSE, probably built in the late CII, now a shell. Central gateways with continuous round arches of two plain steps, the arch to the outer side mostly obscured by the remains of a CI5 barbican with its projecting side walls. The wall above this arch is decorated with four blind gables or pediments sitting on the string course, their tympana filled with diapered decoration of square stones set diagonally, each carved with a cross (cf. similar tympanum of the doorway in Chepstow castle's great

---

*In a singular display of devotion, her husband, Cecil Foljambe, commemorated her with twenty-five stained glass windows in churches with family connections in seven counties. Most are in East Sussex, Nottinghamshire and the West Riding. All were made by *Heaton, Butler & Bayne*.

tower, dated *c.* 1081–93 (Gwent)). At the bases of the gables and the tips of the first and second are very worn carved figures, originally some 2 ft (0.6 metres) high, identified l. to r. as: (too worn), a watchman, a male exhibitionist, a robed figure, a sheila-na-gig, (missing), and a standing man. The gatehouse's upper room has a good early C14 hooded fireplace with lamp bracket to l., an ogee-headed doorway and an Elizabethan ten-light transomed window with king mullion.

Probably in the early C12 the stone CURTAIN WALL was built against the earth rampart around it and a circular stone SHELL KEEP constructed. The foundations show that this was replaced by an eleven-sided TOWER with angle pilaster-buttresses in work by Henry II, 1178–82. Probably contemporary is the superb pilastered ashlar walling running against the motte on its SW (evidence of a spacious staircase on the internal face), and the only survivor of DOMESTIC QUARTERS in the bailey's NW corner – a first-floor fireplace in the curtain wall. Plain opening under a relieving arch and a fine joggled lintel comparable with examples at Conisbrough Castle (q.v.).

By 1564 the castle was only useful for Duchy estate administration. Parliament demolished the keep in 1648 after a peaceful surrender and the large three-storey house on the N side of the bailey is probably C17, but of more than one build, reusing stone, with C18 and C19 alterations. Large mullioned-and-transomed windows to rear and evidence of others on the massively buttressed E side and the set-back NW range. Ashlar front of two bays between projecting gabled bays, the l. narrower, the r. with shallow bow, heightened later in sandstone to two storeys, with upper Venetian window. Sash windows. Round, probably Georgian, archways remain at S and N (blocked) ends of former walkway through the four E buttresses, the spaces between now enclosed on the ground floor. Extensive repairs etc. were made to the house and castle by *Woodhead & Hurst*, 1820–1.

C18 and C19 landscaping of the bailey as a garden included demolition of the S curtain wall and the creation of a NE terrace within it and a rampart walkway outside.

THE FRIARY, Doncaster Road, ½ m. WSW. The house (now two) incorporates parts of the Austin Friars' establishment founded *c.* 1256 by John Clarel, an influential cleric and courtier, whose family mansion stood nearby, and suppressed in 1538. Medieval fabric survives in two ranges, both running E–W and connected at their SE and NW corners respectively. Both are two storeys, built of coursed limestone rubble with stone slate roofs. The extended NW range has on the N side three buttresses with parts of a string course above, and later (except one?) mullioned-and-transomed windows. Re-set in the porch of a further W extension is a doorway with rusticated surround dated 1663. At the E end, mostly inside an adjoining C19 range attached to the N side of the SE part, is a late C15 two-bay arcade, the N arch being partly outside. Short octagonal pier with embattled fleuron capital and two four-centred arches. Small angel in the spandrel. S respond with oakleaves and acorns. The S E range has on its W wall a triangular chimney projection supported on fine moulded corbelling and a slender shaft. To its l., above a C19 two-light window with Y-tracery, is the head of a blocked first-floor lancet. On the S wall evidence of a blocked ground-floor window of two lights with ogee heads and at the W end a blocked first-floor doorway. If, as is suggested, this range was the dorter and/or infirmary, the doorway may have opened into a garderobe.

In the garden, with attached walling, remains of a C13 archway with continuous bowtell mouldings. Dogtooth on the soffit between them and on the E face.

ST LEONARD'S HOSPITAL (Parish Rooms), Northgate. Remains of a hospital founded c. 1225. A fine timber-framed façade of 1470, restored in 1851 with new mock-timber-framed first floor. Ground floor of ten bays with polygonal posts on big moulded stone bases, carrying embattled capitals. Decorated rib-vaulted coving to carry oversailing upper floor.

LIBRARY, Castlegate. By P. N. Brundell, 1907–8. Neat gabled front; brick with decorative stonework and nice clock turret.

THE TOWN. The medieval plan is evident in the three broad streets extending N, E and S from the market place, and West-gate continuing W from the bottom of Castlegate. Back lanes survive, e.g. in Pinfold Lane and St Mary's Road, the latter still the W boundary of long narrow burgage plots fronting the N end of Castlegate. A handful of larger buildings aside, the town is characterized by pleasingly varied and unpretentious C17 to early C19 houses and cottages, generally of two storeys, the three-storey buildings being mostly near Market Place, which has as its focus the MARKET CROSS, given by the Vicar in 1777. Rotunda with stone dome on eight Doric columns; attributed to *William Lindley*. In CASTLEGATE, No. 31 with unpromising C19 and C20 brick front, preserves rare remains of a crown-post roof, probably later C14. In SUNDERLAND STREET the plain former Independent CHAPEL, dated 1801. Sideways on, with three tall segmental-headed sashes. Hipped pantile roof.

Tickhill's two grandest town houses, both S-facing, are ¼ m. E. First the elegant ashlar TICKHILL HOUSE, early C19, three bays, with wavy-balustered wrought-iron balconies. Next door SUNDERLAND HOUSE. Large, C18, the five-bay E side with consoled pediment an improvement, possibly by *Lindley*. W entrance with mid-C19 Doric porch.

LINDRICK HOUSE, ¼ m. S. Early C18. Five bays. Handsome front, rendered, with ashlar quoins and corniced doorcase.

TINSLEY

Once a small village with a Norman church. In part of the Don valley that became heavily industrialized in the C19, it was taken into Sheffield in 1911, although it is now physically separated by the M1 motorway.

St Lawrence. Rebuilt by *G.E. Street*, 1877–9. Dec style, with a light touch; reticulated tracery. Four-bay nave with narrow N aisle and gabled triple bellcote on E end. W front, to road, has three-light window flanked by lower false windows with blind tracery. – STAINED GLASS. E window by *Clayton & Bell*, 1878. W window by *Percy Bacon Brothers, c.* 1894. Chancel N and S windows by *Francis Spear*, 1958. – LYCHGATE by *Street*.

Tinsley Locks. Flight of eleven locks (originally twelve – two combined 1959) on the Sheffield Canal, which opened in 1819 and finally linked the Don Navigation with the Sheffield Canal basin four miles away (*see* p.544). Tinsley Wharf, the terminus since 1732, became obsolete.

Tinsley Viaduct. 1965–8 by *Freeman Fox & Partners*, engineers, and *Cleveland Bridge & Engineering Co.*, contractors. Two levels, carrying the M1 motorway above the A631 trunk road across the Don valley. ⅔ m. long. Reinforced-concrete decks on steel box girders, supported by seventeen pairs of steel columns. Its slightly weaving path negotiated the river, canal, railway and the steel works then below, as well as two power station cooling towers (dem. 2008).

TODMORDEN   9020

Small former mill town, deep in the Pennine hills where Walsden Water joins the infant Calder. The W part of the town and its wider area was in Lancashire until 1888.[*]

Todmorden owes its development to the Fielden family, whose modest beginnings with spinning jennies at Waterside in 1782 grew into one of the country's largest cotton businesses. In the 1860s the Fieldens employed *John Gibson* as architect for their own houses and for Todmorden's most conspicuous buildings, the Unitarian church and the Town Hall.

They and the town benefited from the ingenuity of engineers who defied the physical obstacles to trans-Pennine connections: the turnpike from Halifax, branching NW to Burnley and S to Rochdale at Todmorden, was made in piecemeal stages between 1760 and 1781; the Rochdale Canal, opened in 1804, completed Todmorden's waterway links with Liverpool on the W and Wakefield and the Humber to the E; what was (briefly) the world's longest railway tunnel and several impressive viaducts brought the Manchester & Leeds Railway in 1841; the Todmorden–Burnley line opened in 1849 and was linked to Preston a year later. With the Fieldens' encouragement, a Local Board was set

---

[*]The original county boundary followed the rivers through the middle of Todmorden. The Town Hall is built over the culverted Water, so in its ballroom one could dance from Yorkshire into Lancashire and back again all evening.

up in 1860 and borough status was granted in 1896. The population was 11,998 in 1871, peaking at 25,418 in 1901. In 2011, following industrial decline, it was 12,114.

CHURCHES

St Mary. An awkward marriage of simple Georgian classical and Victorian Gothic, never seen to best advantage in its position end-on to and above the street. Originally a C15 chapel to Rochdale, it was largely rebuilt in 1770. w tower has older fabric in lower part, round-arched bell-openings, and battlemented top stage of 1860. Symmetrical s side of wide nave has two tall round-arched windows in the centre flanked by doorways with bold rusticated surrounds and then two small Venetian windows, one above the other, to each outer bay. The tall two-bay chancel, almost overhanging the street, was added by *J. Medland Taylor* of Manchester in 1896, the transeptal organ chamber fudging the junction with the nave. Spacious interior has exposed barn-like kingpost roof. Good oak balustrade with fluted dies to surviving w gallery. – STAINED GLASS. E window by *Kempe*, 1897. Pair of s windows by *Heaton, Butler & Bayne*, †1915. Handsome VICARAGE, 1824.

Christ Church (former), Burnley Road. By *Vulliamy*, 1830–1. Lancet windows, deeply set and paired, typical of other Commissioners' churches, but Vulliamy's composition is more individual. Tall, plain, five-bay nave with aisles and low clerestory. Pinnacled w tower flanked by gallery staircases. The short, lower chancel by *Jesse Horsfall*, 1885–6, encumbered with vestries etc., also has lancets.

St Paul (former), Cross Stone, 1 m. NE. Commissioners' church in plain lancet style by *Pickersgill & Oates*, 1833–5; it replaced a C16 chapel. A prominent landmark high on the brow of the hill. Pinnacled w tower. Broad five-bay nave has heavy parapets and clasping buttresses that rise as square pinnacles with ungainly gables. No chancel; gabled porches flank the E window.

St Michael and All Angels, Cornholme, 2 m. NW. By *C. Hodgson Fowler*, 1902. Large, in very plain late Gothic style. w tower with set-back stone spire. Straight-headed aisle and clerestory windows with Tudor-arched lights.

St Peter, Walsden, 1⅜ m. s. The Commissioners' church by *Charles Child*, 1846–8, burnt down in 1948; only the tower with spire by *James Green*, 1864, and the lower aisle walls remain. Rebuilt by *Pace*, 1954–9. Nave has thin paired lancets, chancel a large mullioned-and-transomed window to each side.

St Joseph (R.C.), Wellington Road. 1928–9. Plain seven-bay buttressed nave with lancets; small apsidal sanctuary.

Unitarian church, Honey Hole Road (Historic Chapels Trust). By *Gibson*, 1865–9, and one of the North's most splendid Nonconformist churches, built as the Fielden brothers' memorial to their father, who had become a Unitarian. It stands a little above the town, set off by lawn and trees, its commanding spire rising to 192 ft (59 metres) and visible from valley and hill around. Dec style and entirely Anglican in form. Chancel flanked by transeptal vestry with organ chamber and mortuary chapel; seven-bay nave with separately roofed aisles and an open porch below the big spired tower on the w (ritual s) side. Opulent and intact interior, the lavish use of carved stone, marble and oak sending the church's final cost to £35,000. Vaulted chancel and transept roofs with bands of white and pink Mansfield stone; chancel arch and arcades on clustered marble colonnettes. Polished Devonshire marble columns to nave arcades; marble wall-shafts supporting fine oak roof. Everywhere are *Underwood & Co*'s richly carved headstops, angel corbels and capitals with flowers, leaves and fruit whose naturalistic detail is a delight. – Oak CHOIR STALLS with poppyheads. – Octagonal oak PULPIT on marble shafts. – FONT. Fine white marble bowl with carved passion flowers and delicate coloured inlay. – MONUMENTS. Three matching Gothic tablets to the Fielden brothers by *J. & H. Patteson* of Manchester. – STAINED GLASS. Chancel windows by *Capronnier*, 1868.

PUBLIC BUILDINGS

TOWN HALL. By *John Gibson*, 1870–5. One of Yorkshire's grandest town halls – the pedimented temple rising above the little town one of Calderdale's most memorable views – and not dissimilar to Birmingham Town Hall (by J. A. Hansom, for whom Gibson had worked). Seven by three bays with apsidal N end. Channelled rustication to the walls. The ground floor is treated as a base, the upper floor is provided with giant Composite columns, attached on the s end and sides, detached and fluted to the apse. Between these are large windows or arched niches and small circular attic windows, their detail typical of Gibson, classical yet with a certain crisp and sensuous elegance. Entablature has pulvinated frieze carved with latticework like warp and weft and Tudor roses; modillioned cornice. In tympanum of s pediment sculpture by *C.H. Mabey* representing Lancashire cotton manufacture (W) and Yorkshire metalworking/engineering, wool and agriculture (E). The grand stone-lined entrance hall in the apse has a semicircular arcade with Tuscan columns of polished Hoptonwood stone, painted ceiling and staircase with balustrade of copper, bronze and gilt. Upper hall/ballroom with elaborate plasterwork walls and coved ceiling by *J.J. Harwood* with medallions of Art, Music, Literature, Justice, Peace, Commerce, Science etc.

LIBRARY, Rochdale Road. By *T.H. Mitchell*, 1896–7. Three bays, single-storeyed, in Free Northern Renaissance style. Short octagonal tower to r. return has shapely ventilator dome.

COMMUNITY COLLEGE, Burnley Road. By *Hubert Bennett*, West Riding County Architect, 1951–5. A period piece in buff brick. Mostly three storeys and flat-roofed. Distinctive fenestration, different on each floor, on long r. return beyond glazed staircase bay.

CENTRE VALE PARK. Opened 1912, originally the grounds of West Vale (dem. 1953), a house of 1826–8 bought by John Fielden Sen. in 1848, and enlarged by *Gibson* for Samuel Fielden in 1871. The grounds were by *Joshua Major*. Bronze STATUE of John Fielden by *J.H. Foley*, 1863, originally outside the Town Hall. Formal WAR MEMORIAL GARDEN 1921 by *Norman Thorpe*, with fountain statue of St George and symbolic figures of two children by *Gilbert Bayes*. Jolly timber BANDSTAND with projecting canopy, a replica of the original burnt down in 1999.

CENTRE VALE SCHOOL (former), Ewood Lane, by *Gibson*, 1871–2, for Sarah Jane Fielden, Samuel's wife, an educational reformer. Gothic Revival style. Elaborate tracery to classroom windows.

FIELDEN INFECTIOUS DISEASES HOSPITAL (former), Lee Bottom Road. By *John Sutcliffe*, 1892 (now housing). Mostly single-storeyed, its plainness relieved by shaped gables.

PERAMBULATION

Despite losses of C19 chapels and housing, the town centre is almost entirely Victorian. To the s of *George Stephenson*'s towering railway VIADUCT of 1840, over Burnley Road, is the plain classical, partly glass-roofed MARKET HALL by *Frederick Rodley*, Local Board Surveyor, 1879. Nearby the three-storey former ODDFELLOWS HALL, 1842, with tall pedimented central window. Past the Town Hall and set back along Hall Street, off Rochdale Road, is TODMORDEN HALL, rebuilt 1603 by Savile Radcliffe, the lower w cross-wing retaining timber framing of *c.* 1500. Irregular gabled front of five bays; mullioned-and-transomed windows. The porch's tall two-light window above the doorway and the hall's pair of four-light windows are double-transomed. (In E cross-wing a panelled room with elaborate oak overmantel with columns and carved heraldry and foliage, dated 1603. Rear chamber has plaster frieze with mythical animals). Small early C18 NW extension to w wing has external stairs to rear taking-in door.

s across the canal on Rochdale Road near the approach to the Unitarian church (q.v.), a former TEMPERANCE HOTEL AND COFFEE TAVERN by *Jesse Horsfall*, 1880. Mullioned-and-transomed windows; second-floor gables altered *c.* 1913. 300 yds further s on the w side, is the only surviving building of the Fieldens' WATERSIDE MILL, built in 1827 beside the canal as a warehouse, offices and factory school. Three storeys with pedimented doorcase on the s front and small square clock tower (cupola removed). In 1898 it became the Technical Institute and Fire Station, with terrace of four FIREMEN'S HOUSES, 1900, to N in a very agreeable Arts and Crafts style.

In a commanding situation above Waterside to the w is DOBROYD CASTLE, by *Gibson* for John Fielden, 1866–9. Large and castellated villa, with five-storey tower and octagonal angle turrets. Dark gritstone without ornament. The windows have a typically Victorian shape: straight heads connected with the jambs by quarter circles. The most spectacular interior is the richly detailed Romanesque-style double-height central HALL with adjoining STAIRCASE HALL. Both are square, under large glazed domes with elaborately panelled pendants, the imperial staircase rising at the side through the hall arcade. Columns and pilasters of polished pink Derbyshire marble, the capitals intricately carved with scenes of hunting and rural sports. Tympana over four hall doorways have sculpture in Caen stone depicting cotton production and manufacture. Upper arcades, carrying the domes, contain twin arches with marble colonnettes to galleries, the capitals exquisitely modelled with flowers, fruit and birds.

About ⅜ m. NW from the centre along BURNLEY ROAD, opposite Centre Vale Park (*see* above), are the former offices of Mons Mill (dem.) by *Stott & Sons*, 1907–12. Single-storey with a little domed angle tower; blue and red brick and yellow terracotta. In Ewood Lane, N of the park, EWOOD HALL, early C19, and the eccentrically Picturesque WOOD COTTAGE *c.* 1840, dower house for the Crossleys of SCAITCLIFFE HALL, a much-altered house to N. Its four-bay S front has stonework and five-light mullioned windows of a house of 1666, the windows lengthened *c.* 1833 in remodelling in Tudor Gothic style with addition of embattled porch, deep parapet and slightly later octagonal turret to l., beyond Doric colonnaded arbour of 1782. Rear range *c.* 1738, making double-pile house, linked in 1835 to NW range of 1802 which has taking-in door. Varied mullioned, cross- and sash windows, the mullioned windows mostly with lattice glazing.

STANSFIELD HALL, Stansfield Hall Road, ⅜ m. NE from the centre, is of 1640, much extended by *Gibson* in 1862 for Joshua Fielden and now subdivided. Original house at E end, altered, has narrow hall bay between projecting gabled cross-wings, the r. one with two transomed seven-light windows, the l. with oriel window. Gibson's eight-bay range, sympathetic but grander in scale and more richly detailed, extends to the W. Big lateral stack to bay 2 and full-height hall window of five lights with two transoms in bay 4. Bays 5 and 6 break forward and are gabled. Labels with diamond stops to mullioned windows, most of which have lights with cusped ogee tracery in heads. Entrance in l. return has porte cochère, and two Gothic-arched windows flanking buttress under oriel to r. Good headstops and other carved details.

Sprinkled across the S-facing upland slopes to the NE, numerous other good C17 and C18 houses including BEAN HOLE HEAD, Cross Stone Road, dated 1638, which has an excellent plaster frieze in housebody with vine, pomegranates etc., an arcade and royal coat of arms, 1634. In the wall of its barn part of a C10 CROSS-SHAFT with long-tailed creature and interlace. HIGHER ASHES FARMHOUSE, Ashes Lane, ¼ m. N, is one of the area's best yeoman-clothier houses. Fireplace dated 1682 and entrance dated 1691. Hall range with rear kitchen wing and parlour cross-wings projecting to s. Entrance is in w wing with through passage, an unusual feature. EASTWOOD OLD HALL, Eastwood Lane, ⅞ m. ENE, is *c.* 1740. Essentially vernacular, but off-centre doorway into housebody has architrave, pulvinated frieze and pediment, and window above has enriched surround. Other windows mullioned. The back-to-hillside position allows separate rear entrance to first-floor weaving chamber or shop, which has long twelve-light N window

ROBINWOOD MILL, Lydgate, 1⅜ m. NW. By *William Fairburn*, begun *c.* 1837, bought unfinished in 1844 by John Fielden, who completed the huge six-storey building as a steam-powered cotton-spinning mill. The projecting s wing and most of the eleven-bay pedimented centre were deliberately burnt down in 1992. The surviving N wing, still impressive, has five-bay N elevation with round-arched windows to staircase bay. Below, on the hillside, the Fieldens built ROBINWOOD TERRACE, 1864. Thirteen model houses in simple Tudor Gothic style.

FROSTHOLME MILL, Cornholme, 2¼ m. NW. Former cotton-weaving mill rebuilt by *John R. Blacka*, 1896, after a fire. Four-storey stone offices and warehousing has long kerbside frontage of paired bays with gables. Large single-storey weaving shed to rear.

LUMBUTTS MILL, 1¼ m. SE, has a unique three-storey water-wheel tower, probably *c.* 1830, which housed three 30-ft (9-metre)-diameter overshot wheels, arranged vertically and fed separately by three surviving dams, producing over 50 horsepower. Rectangular plan; attached staircase spiralled around chimney; balustraded top.

HOLLINS MILL, Walsden, 1¾ m. S. One of the largest surviving in the area, built by the canal in 1856–8 as an integrated cotton-spinning and weaving mill. Triple-span roof to four-storey mill. Tall-windowed engine house, placed between mill and weaving shed.

TOLL HOUSE, Steanor Bottom, 2¾ m. S on the A6033. Georgian, unusually two-storeyed. Semi-octagonal front with round-arched windows. List of tolls 1822 (replica) over door.

3 OBELISK, 2¼ m. E on Stoodley Pike, 1,300 ft (395 metres) above sea level. A Crimean War Memorial by *James Green*, 1856. 120 ft (37 metres) high, its heavy corniced base carries a balcony 40 ft (12 metres) above the ground. It replaced a collapsed Napoleonic War monument of 1815.

TODWICK

ST PETER AND ST PAUL. Small. Altered CII nave in coursed red sandstone rubble, similar to the Saxon work at Laughton-en-le-Morthen (q.v.). Round-arched N doorway (blocked)

possibly pre-Conquest. The s doorway with one slight chamfer
later Norman, the round chancel arch with a step, much
restored, probably also initially Norman. Dec work is the
porch roof, the intersected tracery in the chancel E window
and the ogee-headed recess in the nave. A chantry was indeed
founded in 1328, but its N chapel is long gone. Trefoil-headed
piscina re-set in the chancel N wall, probably after C18 rebuilding. Pointed nave s windows have C18 flat-faced surrounds.
Perp w tower. – Jacobean PULPIT and BOX PEWS. – STAINED
GLASS. N window by *Kempe*, 1920. – Chancel. s side easternmost by *Sep Waugh*, 1976. – MONUMENTS. Thomas Garland
†1610. Small brass with kneeling figure. – Elizabeth Ixem
†1664 and sons. Tablet with swan-neck pediment. – John
Garland †1692. Garlanded cartouche and draped panel with
cherubs, set on black marble. – Elizabeth Ashley †1709. Cartouche with skull and bones.

HARDWICK GRANGE FARMHOUSE, 1½ m. NNW. Mid-C19.
Distinctive front, more urban than agricultural. Three bays,
the middle recessed and profusely quoined.

TREETON   *4080*

ST HELEN. The only church in Hallamshire recorded in Domesday Book. It is rewarding but confusing, with many phases of
building and rebuilding. The earliest work is of *c.* 1175–*c.* 1200.
Re-set s doorway with two orders of shafts with waterleaf
capitals. The arch however is segmental and has C13 mouldings. The N arcade of two bays has C13(?) octagonal piers but
C12 arches: round and with a step. The tower, chancel arch
and s arcade all have C13 features. Plain and unbuttressed, the
tower is oddly placed at the W end of the s aisle. The falling
ground immediately w may explain its location. Blocked
doorway to the nave with shouldered arch; matching newel-
stair doorways. The ground-floor lancet perhaps a later insertion. The chancel arch is strangely narrow, on tapering corbels
with square abaci. The s aisle arcade is of the same style but
more elaborate, probably late C13. Quatrefoil pier with fillets
and a handsomely decorated leaf capital with a little nailhead
in the abacus. Double-chamfered pointed arches. Responds on
head corbels like those of the steeply pointed tower arch. The
faint line of an earlier roof on the tower's E face suggests that
the aisle was always wider than the tower. Is it slightly later?
The junction offers no conclusive evidence.
    Early C14 chancel, as long as the nave, has sedilia with
pointed trefoiled heads that originally continued as arcading
to the W. Windows of two single pointed trefoiled lancets,
except the E window and one N window which have reticulated
tracery and are perhaps a little later. Of similar period the nave

window w of the N aisle. This is of three lights and has as tracery the motif of arches upon arches. The w end of the nave is C15, but more likely a rebuilding than an extension – the doorway into the tower does not look like an external one. Perp too the battlemented clerestory, the heightening of the chancel (which has a good roof with angels), the rebuilding of the s aisle s wall, the porch and the tower's limestone ashlar belfry stage. Early C16 s chapel opening into the chancel with one broad arch on corbels. Unusual squint in the chancel arch pier, with four openings. *M.E. Hadfield & Son* restored the chancel in 1865–9 and the practice worked there until 1897. REREDOS. Carved stone, inset with paintings by *Westlake*, 1866. – PULPIT. Carved alabaster, with heraldic panels by *J.F. Bentley*, 1878. S CHAPEL ALTAR and REREDOS with paintings by *Westlake*, 1892. – SCREENS. S chapel, plain, Perp, much restored. – BENCHES. Some Perp remains, one with Latin inscription commemorating William Holmes, Rector 1513–40. Ends with blank arches with tracery in two tiers. – STAINED GLASS. Chancel E, s and N (first and third) windows designed by *Bentley* and *Westlake*, made by *Lavers, Barraud & Westlake*, 1869. – S chapel. By *Lavers & Westlake*, 1892. Three others by the firm. – MONUMENTS. Mutilated late C13 effigy of a knight in chain-mail, nave w wall. Rare for the date. – Fine floriated cross-slab (behind pulpit).

A small HOUSE (No. 25 BOLE HILL), ⅜ m. NNE, dated 1655, has dormers with fancy pedimented tops and a delightful miniature oriel window under the eaves.

ULLEY

HOLY TRINITY. 1850–1. A small 'High Church' pioneer by *Weightman & Hadfield* for Sir Charles Wood, later Viscount Halifax. Good Dec tracery. – Richly Gothic AUMBRY by *Charles Nicholson*, 1926.

ULLEY HALL, 1718, and ULLEY GRANGE, 1722, are handsome five-bay houses, similarly detailed. Hipped roofs with three dormers, the middle ones under segmental heads. The Hall gateway has the entwined initials of John and Rebekah Clarke.

UPPER DENBY

ST JOHN. Rebuilt 1842–3 by *John Ellis*, builder, retaining w tower of 1627. Chancel and interior remodelling – arcades and shallow barrel-vault – 1900–1.

CRUCK BARN, Nether End Farm, 1¼ m. ENE. C16 or early C17. (Four complete trusses.)

UPPER HOPTON

ST JOHN. By *Bonomi & Cory*, 1844–6. Perp style, and appropriately scaled for its rural location. Stout w tower, with diagonal buttresses with many set-offs and small pyramid roof behind battlements; four-bay nave with N aisle; lower chancel. Unusual, uncompleted scheme of CHANCEL DECORATION. Full-height timber panelling has inset painted panels, on canvas, by *J. Eadie Reid*, including Synod of Whitby and Whitby Abbey ruins, 1906. Unexecuted panels have stencilled foliate decoration. – Good traceried SCREEN 1846, with ROOD, 1951. – Oak PEWS, the ends with well-carved linenfold panelling, 1926. – STAINED GLASS. E window and two S nave windows by *Powell Bros*, 1892–3. N aisle E and W windows each have two Evangelists from original E window by *Barnett* of York, 1846.

HOPTON HALL. Next to the church. C16 H-plan stone house on a moated site, much rebuilt in the C19, but with excellent surviving timber framing in the wings with herringbone, vertical and diagonal patterns of studs.

UPPERMILL

The largest of the Saddleworth villages.* An attractive stone-built centre alongside the River Tame. Moorland around with scattered C17–C18 farms, many incorporating former weavers' workshops lit by long ranges of mullioned windows.

ST CHAD, ⅝ m. NE, on the site of a medieval predecessor. Partly rebuilt in 1746, largely replaced in 1831–3. The plans are signed by *Abram Bentley*, a local builder, and the design owes a debt to Richard Lane's church of 1827–30 in nearby Oldham (Greater Manchester). Nave and chancel without structural division, very tall windows of three lights with intersecting tracery and transoms; E window of five intersecting lights and two transoms. E and W ends framed by polygonal piers probably originally with pinnacles. W tower mainly of 1846–7 by *Starkey & Cuffley*, mostly within the body of the church, with part of the formerly exterior S wall exposed, dated 1746. Splendid cantilevered stone stairs up to the three galleries. These are supported on polygonal piers with cast-iron cores, with tall pointed arches at upper level. Flat ceiling with ribs radiating from bosses to suggest vaulting. – Elaborate FURNISHINGS, including STALLS, sanctuary PANELLING, LECTERN, PULPIT and huge, intricate FONT COVER by *George Shaw*, c. 1872. He also did most of the STAINED GLASS. One N window of

*In Greater Manchester since 1974.

1871 by *Capronnier*, upper s window by *Bell & Co.*, dated 1896. – CANDELABRUM. Of 1717, brass, with a dove on top. – MONUMENTS. John Whitehead †1715, with scowling cherub supporter. – John Winterbottom †1838. With military accoutrements, by *Richard Westmacott Jun.* – A couple of mid-C19 monuments with sculpture, signed *Garner*.

HEARSE HOUSE, SW. Dated 1824 in an inscription with the words 'Know Thyself'. Paired cart arches, perhaps indicating it doubled as stables.

OLD PARSONAGE, Gellfield Lane, ½ m. s of the church. Early or mid-C17 with later attached barn. W.J. Smith identified it as one of the earliest surviving buildings of Saddleworth. It was originally a two-unit baffle-entry house, now reconfigured. Six-light mullioned window lighting the principal room, otherwise lesser windows, including a blocked fire window indicating the inglenook position. (Interior with corbels for a smoke-hood, heavy reused timbers in the queenpost roof structure and evidence for a spiral staircase.)

ST WILLIAM (R.C.), High Street. Former Ebenezer Congregational church acquired by the Catholics in 1966. Dated 1873, by *James Lawton*, George Shaw's assistant (*see* St Chad's House, below). Imposing frontage with a tower.

METHODIST CHURCH, High Street. Of 1912–13, attributed to Mr *Brocklehurst*. Large, Romanesque style, with a big octagonal tower and short spire.

CIVIC HALL (former Mechanics' and Literary Institute), Lee Street. By *George Shaw*, possibly with his assistant *James Lawton*. Dated 1859. Churchy window with Shaw's 'S' motif in the tracery. c20 additions.

RAILWAY VIADUCT. With twenty-three arches, of stone, skewed where High Street and the canal (below) are crossed. By *A.S. Jee* for the Huddersfield and Manchester Railway & Canal Co., which merged with the LNWR before the structure was completed in 1849.

HUDDERSFIELD NARROW CANAL. Of 1794–9, engineer *Benjamin Outram*. A good group beside the railway viaduct (above) includes an AQUEDUCT over the River Tame, BRIDGE, LOCKS etc. The canal continues on to Diggle (p. 206), where the Standedge Tunnel begins (*see* Marsden, q.v.).

ST CHAD'S HOUSE (now Library), High Street. A farmhouse rebuilt in the late C18. It was the family home of the architect and antiquarian *George Shaw*, who gave it a Gothic makeover in the mid C19. Shaw designed churches in the area (at Friezland and Greenfield, qq.v.) and further afield, as well as stained glass and church furnishings, made in workshops at this house. Inside, the stair, rich panelling, plasterwork, chimneypieces etc. are *Shaw*'s, incorporating some genuine medieval and later work. – Architectural fragments around the house were part of Shaw's collection and of a chapel (dismantled) he built in the grounds.

ALEXANDRA MILL, Mill Street. The best preserved of several former textile mills in Uppermill. Of 1864, for flannel production, converted to apartments late c20. Main block of four storeys with thirteen windows, arched to the ground floor; square chimney.

WADSWORTH *see* HEBDEN BRIDGE

WADWORTH

St John the Baptist. A large, important and in some ways surprising church. The first surprise is the s porch and the s aisle. Both have blank arcading of the late C12: round arches with a keeled angle roll and quirks, detached shafts, capitals mostly foliate. In the porch there are two such arches on either side, on low benches; in the aisle, E of the porch, there are six arches, the furthest with a piscina – all proof of a very ambitious and spacious late Norman church and a wealthy but unknown patron. This church also had a N aisle: see its plain round-arched N doorway and indeed the N arcade of three bays, which has circular piers, quite tall and slender, with square abaci. The capitals of the piers are plain, the semicircular responds have volutes. All this is typical of *c.* 1190–1200. The arches however are pointed and double-chamfered. Apart from the chamfer stops they are identical with the arches of the s arcade, which has octagonal piers of the standard later style. This would ordinarily lead one to think that the s arcade is definitely later than the N arcade and that round N arches were replaced. Yet the s responds are still semicircular, though more slender than on the N, and keeled, in the taste of *c.* 1190–1200. Moreover the arches by which the w tower opens wide and high into the w bays of the aisles are also pointed, and both these bays have on the inside of their w walls round-arched window openings (altered externally, the s to a lancet). The s doorway too has a pointed arch with headstops, but also an angle roll and nailhead decoration that may or may not be later than the N arcade. So need the s arcade be much later than the N arcade or the w bays of the aisles? The mixture of elements here and the extent of the work involved makes it likely that any distance in time may be small and that one phase led imperceptibly into another. The aisles have a common feature in the beaked string course on the N and s walls and both porches (altered) have pointed entrance arches, their capitals characteristic C13 work.

Hunter (1828) describes the chancel arch as 'circular' but it was replaced in 1864 by *J.M. Teale* with a wider and very tall arch that makes the interior exceptionally spacious. The chancel itself was remodelled *c.* 1300 with the addition of a N chapel and vestry. The latter have windows with Y-tracery, the chancel lancets in the side walls but a splendid five-light window in the E wall. The intersected tracery of this is characteristically interrupted at the top by a quatrefoiled circle. About a generation later the s chapel was built, wider than the

aisle. It was designed by a mason of great originality. The w
window and one s window still have simple bar tracery, but
the second s window displays a complex pattern of pointed
trefoils. And as to the e window, there is nothing like it anywhere else. Four lights. The mullions are carried on so high
that the first and third touch the arch. They are then at that
height connected by a horizontal, so that a rectangle is created
within the arched shape of the window. The spaces in this grid
are then filled by mouchettes all nodding towards the centre
mullion. The arcade of the chapel towards the chancel has two
uneven arches. Dec sedilia and double piscina in the chapel
with cusped ogee heads.

Finally the tall and slender Perp tower. Diagonal w buttresses to just above the tall first stage, the s one with a staircase
to a former upper chamber above the w bay of the aisle (cf.
Campsall). Past roof-lines remain for it and another on the n
side. Belfry stage with two transomed two-light openings on
each side, a wavy frieze above, and battlements and pinnacles.
Perp also two s aisle windows, and late Perp the clerestories,
the nave with battlements, the chancel with good gargoyles.

FURNISHINGS. REREDOS. By *W. M. Teulon*, 1882. Roche
Abbey stone. Traceried panels to base, arcade with red marble
colonnettes above. – FONT. Perp. Octagonal, with quatrefoil
band, arcading and finely moulded base. – CHEST. Long, with
a frieze of coarse foliage. – STAINED GLASS. s chapel. e window
by *Heaton, Butler & Bayne*, 1876. One of the many to Louisa
Blanche Foljambe †1871 (*see* Tickhill). – s wall: easternmost
by *Powell Bros*, 1904; second from e †1903 by *E. R. Suffling*.
– MONUMENTS. A large number. – Early C14 semi-effigy modelled by scooping out a hollow area around it. Only the bust
and feet of a praying figure (a priest?) are visible, in ogee-
headed recesses. – Another similar slab, formerly outside, with
a pair of very worn figures, the busts in quatrefoils (cf. Moor
Monkton, *West Riding North*). – Later C14 effigy of a bearded
huntsman with a hunting horn and a sword, perhaps a forester
of Hatfield Chase. The *Little Guide* says that the effigy is unique
in Yorkshire. – Edmund Fitzwilliam †1431, and his wife, Maud
Hotham, †1433? (no widow's veil). Alabaster, finely carved but
damaged. Two recumbent effigies, his in armour, hers with
elaborately dressed hair. On the sides of the tomb-chest simply
standing angels carrying shields, the same design as that of Sir
William Gascoigne †1419 at Harewood (*West Riding North*).
The Fitzwilliams were part of that intricate C15 family network
that included the Clarels and Gascoignes. – Edmund Fitzwilliam, son of the above, †1465, and his first wife, Katherine
Clifton, †1436. Tomb-chest with bold quatrefoils and inscriptions on top. – Josias Wordsworth †1780 and wife Ann †1814,
by *Theakston* of Doncaster. Tall black marble obelisk with urn.
(N chapel).

WADWORTH HALL, 250 yds NW. A gracious house of no great
size but nevertheless one of *James Paine*'s most dramatic

designs. The small estate, with a later C17 house,* was bought in 1748 by Josias Wordsworth III, a London merchant of Yorkshire antecedents, and inherited by his son Josias IV in 1750. Which of them began the new house is unclear but by 1750 Paine was ordering plaster for it. Approached between two very substantial LODGES with cyclopic, rather Vanbrugh than Gibbs, door surrounds. Screen walls, again in their treatment cyclopean, curve theatrically forward from the house itself. This is only three bays wide, but they are very amply spaced. Two storeys. Tripartite centre bay, the doorway with a big open pediment, its flanking sashes with moulded architraves and cornices. Above, a Venetian window, but the middle arch a blank niche. Ground-floor windows of outer bays have architraves with splayed bases (a Paine device) and segmental pediments like the attic dormers. The form of this front and its decidedly un-Palladian dormers must raise the question of whether something of the previous house was retained. Venetian staircase window to centre of l. return. The garden façade has a central canted bay, its doorway a round-headed sash with pediment. A blind Diocletian window over the sash above. Quadrant screen walls again, here with two heavily rusticated gateways, topped by pedimented Diocletian arches, that carry on the Piranesian mood of the house. (Entrance hall has chimneypiece with tapering pilasters, lion masks and pedimented cornice. Rococo roundel with cornucopia above. Staircase has wrought-iron scrolled balustrade with acanthus, festooned wall panels and excellent Rococo plasterwork ceiling (cf. Doncaster Mansion House and Nostell Priory, p. 762). Good doorcases with enriched friezes.)

WAKEFIELD

INTRODUCTION

Leland, writing about 1538, calls Wakefield 'a very quik market toune and meately large' and says that 'al the hole profite of the toun stondith by course drapery'. The town was indeed the centre of the Yorkshire woollen trade before the rise of Leeds and

---

*Beside it was Wadworth Old Hall, a Jacobean house belonging to the Copleys, demolished in the C19.

Bradford. In the 1720s Defoe spoke of Wakefield as clean, large, handsome and very rich – with a population said to be larger than that of York. That explains the size of its parish church and the large number of prosperous Georgian houses in the town and outside. Although overtaken by Leeds in the marketing of cloth, Wakefield remained the chief wool market of Yorkshire in the C18. It failed to become a major industrial centre in the C19 partly because of the short-sighted self-interest of its merchant aristocracy, who protected their businesses from competition by forbidding their apprentices from setting up on their own within seven miles of the town. The more enterprising were driven first to Leeds, and then, when the exclusion zone was extended to ten miles, to Bradford. Despite the decline of the cloth trade, however, Wakefield remained an important market town for grain and other goods brought inland by water via the Aire & Calder Navigation, which was for many years the most profitable waterway in the country. It made the Calder navigable up to Wakefield by 1702 and this was a major factor in the town's C18 and early C19 prosperity.

The cattle market was the largest in the north of England in the C19 and mills, malthouses and warehouses crowded the area between the town centre and the river. Most of these have succumbed to highway schemes and retail units. Collieries came in the neighbourhood in the later C19, at East Moor and Newton, but otherwise there was little suburban development until the interwar municipal housing estates at Eastmoor, Lupset and Flanshaw. Wakefield became a municipal borough in 1848 and from the C18 until 1974 was the county capital of the West Riding, a status reflected in the range and importance of its public buildings. In 1888 it was made the see of a bishop, but it has certainly not become a cathedral city. Commercially it has been in the shadow of Leeds for a long time and this helped it to retain many of its medieval and Georgian buildings in the centre until the mid C20. The developments of the 1950s and '60s that replaced so many of them offer little architectural attraction. The present population (2011) is 99,250, as against 4,300 in 1723, 8,100 in 1801 and 23,700 in 1901. Regeneration since 2008 has included: the new Trinity Walk shopping centre; the Merchant Gate scheme including the Wakefield One council offices with Library and Museum; the new Westgate railway station; commercial offices and flats; redevelopment and landscaping in the Civic Quarter around the Town and County halls; the Hepworth Wakefield gallery and restoration of warehouses in the first phase of the Waterfront project, and the refurbishment of Kirkgate station and the new West Yorkshire History Centre in Kirkgate. But there are still gardens attached to houses in immediate proximity to the centre, and, looking out, open country is surprisingly close. Above all Wakefield has, what few towns of England can boast, a distinctive skyline.

CATHEDRAL

CATHEDRAL CHURCH OF ALL SAINTS. In an elevated position at the top of Kirkgate in the heart of the pedestrianized shopping area. The Diocese of Wakefield was created in 1888, and the

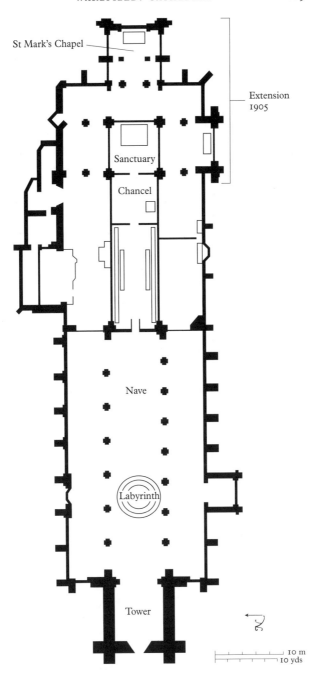

St Mark's Chapel

Extension
1905

Sanctuary

Chancel

Nave

Labyrinth

Tower

10 m
10 yds

Wakefield Cathedral.
Plan

church remains, in spite of the impressive early C20 E extension, a large and proud parish church like the cathedrals of Bradford and Chelmsford. The exterior, in local sandstone ashlar, is wholly Perp. The interior is more complex. Both owe much to *George Gilbert Scott*'s restoration of 1858–74, but there was enough evidence of medieval work left after C18 restorations to make Scott's work generally reliable. In recognition of the building's enhanced status, and as a memorial to its first bishop, *J. L. Pearson* designed transepts, a new sanctuary with retrochapel, and a chapter house 1897–8, executed after his death by *F. L. Pearson* in 1901–5.

J. T. Micklethwaite, Scott's superintending architect, worked out much of the early CHRONOLOGY of the building during restoration. A cruciform church with central tower is thought to have been built *c.* 1100, probably on the site of the Saxon church recorded in Domesday. Archaeological evidence for it has been found near the nave S aisle and the large block of masonry at the SW corner of the chancel S aisle is of this period. This contains a staircase (blocked up by Scott) and a door that gave external access to the tower via the S transept roof (cf. York Minster). A N aisle was added *c.* 1150, the S aisle in the early C13.

Much of the church was rebuilt a century after this, probably following the collapse of the tower. One can assume that the work was complete by 1329, when a chapel in the church was consecrated, but the tower was not reconstructed until 1420, when Joan de Thorp bequeathed 13s. 4d. for the 'nova fabrica campanilis' (new work of the bell tower). It was placed at the W end and the nave was extended by one bay to meet it. Then about 1458–1502 in a further, major, building programme, the nave aisles were heightened and a clerestory was added. The chancel was rebuilt, also with a clerestory, and was probably complete by 1475, when glass for the E windows was given.* The nave aisles were widened, their N and S walls being brought out to the line of the new chancel aisles, which took in the Norman transepts and changed the cruciform plan to a rectangle. Finally N and S porches were added, the S one with an upper room. The form of the church was then altered little until the Pearsons' additions, but its fabric was subject to alterations in the C18, notably the rebuilding of the S wall in 1724, using stone from the tower of the recently demolished Snapethorpe Hall. At this date the chancel S aisle was reduced from four bays to three and with it was lost the large six-light window of the former transept. The nave N wall was rebuilt in 1787, when the positions of the windows were altered to accommodate the N gallery. Tower and spire had been repaired or partly rebuilt several times before Scott's restoration, with advice from various architects including *Soane* in 1802. It was again the tower and spire that required most urgent attention when Scott started his restoration in 1858, before moving on to the nave and chancel in 1860–74.

The chief feature of the EXTERIOR is the stately W tower, re-cased in 1858. Four stages, with angle buttresses, two tall two-light

* Some panels of the C15 glass are in the Yorkshire Museum at York.

bell-openings on each side, and a much crocketed spire (rebuilt 1860) set back behind a battlemented parapet with crocketed pinnacles. Tower and spire stand 247 ft (75.3 metres) high, the highest in Yorkshire. Scott mistakenly restored the W door as early C14, initially thinking the tower a century older than it is. The only truly older feature outside is the N doorway with continuous mouldings, including a keeled one. Scott removed its C15 porch. The nave and chancel, restored 1860–74, share a continuous roof-line. The aisles and clerestory have parapets with blind arcading and pinnacles (cf. the Bridge Chapel, p. 695). The pinnacles, parapets and finials on the stepped buttresses are generously crocketed, the crockets very large and like epaulettes. Are they faithful C18 copies of the late C15 originals? The aisle windows are of four lights under segmental arches with some panel tracery. Their tracery was renewed by Scott, taking the design from a late C17 engraving of the church and suitable examples elsewhere. The clerestory has four-light windows in the nave, three-light windows in the chancel. Most of Scott's work at the E end was lost in 1901–5 for the extension, whose soaring height only becomes apparent from the lower level of Teall Street at the E end. The transepts and retrochapel are Perp, with very tall stepped buttresses that rise to form pinnacled turrets at the corners. Crocketed pinnacles like those on the older part of the church and even more blind arcading – on the buttresses, parapets and in the spandrels of the windows.

The INTERIOR presents a succession of progressively lighter spaces, from the nave's richly coloured glass, stone, and wooden panelled ceiling, through the rood screen to the chancel with its taller arcade and open-traceried screens to the aisles. Beyond is the delicate verticality of the retrochapel. Except at the E end, Scott's work in the interior was principally to sweep away post-Reformation fittings such as the late C17 nave galleries at the W end and in the aisles and to add new fittings;* there is no evidence that he reversed any of the C18 rebuildings of the S walls and nave N aisle wall. The NAVE arcades seem at first sight uniform in style, but are however far from it. The seven-bay arcade on the N has two round piers (third and fifth from the E) and four circular bases (first, third–fifth) from the original mid-C12 aisle. The piers of the early C14 rebuilding are of typically Dec section, quatrefoil, but the shafts connected by a continuous wave. The Norman piers were heightened and given new capitals at this time. The arches have double-quadrant mouldings, as do those rebuilt at the same time on the S side. Here, however, there are eight bays, the alternately round and octagonal piers those of c. 1220, also heightened in the early C14. On both sides the W bay, added with round piers when the tower was built c. 1420, has no hoodmoulds. Above, the mullions of the C15 clerestory windows were reduced to their uncomfortably fin-like proportions in the early C18 to let in more light. The nave's panelled ceiling with its carved bosses is late Perp. Scott removed the plaster from the aisle ceilings and

*Nave reordering by *John Bailey* in 2013 removed the pulpit and pews.

repanelled them to match, adding cast-iron bosses to the ribs.
LABYRINTH, based on the medieval one at Bayeux Cathedral,
France, inlaid in nave floor 2013.

The CHANCEL arch belongs to the early C14 and resembles
the early parts of the nave arcades. The doorway to the medieval rood screen survives in the nave wall immediately to its
NE. The chancel arcades are Perp – as we have seen, of
c. 1458–75. They have five bays, with octagonal piers and arches
with hollow chamfers. Panelled ceiling, more elaborately
carved than in the nave and chancel aisles. The bosses include
God the Father, the Holy Spirit as an angel carrying the Sacred
Heart, and Christ in C15 cap and jerkin. The SANCTUARY is
part of Pearson's stone-vaulted E extension, consecrated in
1905. SEDILIA, by *F.L. Pearson* and carved in Chilmark stone,
added 1912. The sanctuary is flanked by the transepts, the S
one dedicated as the Walsham How Chapel. At the E end ST
MARK'S CHAPEL has narrow arcades and aisles with very thin
long shafts supporting a gloriously complicated and high lierne
vault of stone. Below the transepts and chapel are the CRYPT
and CHAPTER HOUSE, accessed by stairs from the vestries
etc. beside the chancel N aisle. The Chapter House has a richly
vaulted ceiling, with piers on the same plan as those in the
chapel above it.

FURNISHINGS. REREDOS (high altar) 1896 by *John Oldrid Scott*.
Very tall, gorgeously painted, carved and gilded. Originally a
triptych, the side panels with figures of northern saints were
resited at the back, facing E, c. 1905. – ALTAR. By *F.L. Pearson*.
Oak, carved with the hierarchy of angels. – BISHOP'S THRONE.
Oak, by *George Pace*, 1974. – ORGAN CASES. The chancel case
by *Pearson*, 1905. In the chancel N aisle, the case given 1743
for the organ installed in the W gallery of the nave. Large, in
black oak with gilded cherubs, foliage and crowns, but now
without its clock and two carved muses on top. – CHANCEL
STALLS. No high backs, but instead simple Perp SCREENS
behind them. The screens in the two westernmost bays on each
side are C15, the rest are of c. 1870 with canopies and cresting
added by Pearson. The medieval stall-ends are on the S side.
They have poppyheads and other fine decoration with an owl
etc., and on one of them the arms of Thomas Savile of Lupset
and Margaret Bosworth, who married in 1482. Ten seats have
original late C15 MISERICORDS (nos. 1–3 N and 2–8 S), one
with the Percy badge of crescent and fetterlock. Fourteen of
the other misericords were added in the 1870s and the rest
c. 1905 – all of high quality and with convincingly 'medieval'
carvings, including a juggler with his head between his legs, a
pelican, a dragon and Tudor roses. – ROOD SCREEN. The
screen is an excellent piece of 1635 by *Francis Gunby* of Leeds
(cf. his screens at Slaidburn) and that at St John, Leeds, *West
Riding North*). It has long, slender, tapering pillars with tiny
Ionic capitals. The elaborate carving includes the fleur-de-lys
of the arms of Wakefield. The upper cornice is Scott's and
above this is a fretwork balustrade added with the ROOD by *Sir*

Ninian Comper, 1950. The doors of Gunby's screen are now fixed at the entrance to the Lady Chapel in the chancel s aisle. – In the Lady Chapel. One original BENCH-END with tracery in two tiers. – FONT. Dated 1661, one of many of the years immediately after the Restoration. Octagonal, carved stone, with CR II and the initials of the churchwardens in a kind of beaded lettering, with scrolls and coarse foliage. – SCULPTURE. In the s transept a replica of the shaft of the C10 Wakefield Cross.* – In the Lady Chapel, Madonna and Child by *Ian Judd*, 1986, a touchingly youthful mother, sitting cross-legged. – IRONWORK. Fine entrance gates, s porch, 1881.

STAINED GLASS. Nearly all by *Kempe*, a remarkable series of twenty-three windows demonstrating the consistently high quality of his work from 1873 to 1907. Among the best are the Old Testament Prophets (1886–91), nave N aisle, with more expressive faces and elaborate robes than the earlier Apostles and New Testament saints (1873) in the nave s aisle. The Creation of Angels (1894), nave N aisle W, has eight pairs of angels with golden curls and Kempe's lovely peacock-feathered wings; in the E extension mainly scenes from the life of Christ (1905–7), including E window Christ in Majesty (1905), using more white glass than the richly coloured earlier windows. Two later windows – in the chancel N aisle, second from E, the Empty Tomb (1907) and St Mark's Chapel chancel s Northern Saints (1911) – are attributed to Kempe and his firm. – W window by *Hardman*, The Resurrection of the Dead, *c.* 1868, an animated throng in richly detailed colours including many pale blues. – Three other windows by *Hardman*: chancel s aisle (Raising of Lazarus, 1867, rather faded), nave s aisle (Saint Barnabas etc., 1875, and the Baptism of Christ, 1874). – Chancel s aisle, second from E, the Nativity by *Ward & Hughes*, *c.* 1862. – Nave s aisle (Baptistery), first from W, the Infant Jesus and Christ in Majesty by *H.M. Barnett* of Newcastle, 1888, garishly coloured. – MONUMENTS. Sir Lyon Pilkington †1714. Reclining in an easy posture. Putti l. and r. Big reredos background with segmental pediment on which recline two allegorical figures. Attributed to *Francis Bird* (GF). – John Ingram †1780 and family, by *Joseph Wilton* 1782 (signed and dated). A delightful and very original tablet set against one of the octagonal piers of the chancel. Seated woman in an elegant, well-studied attitude. – Mrs Maude †1824 by *J.J.P. Kendrick*, to the design of Mrs Maude's husband. Tablet with the usual female figure bent over an urn. – Bishop Walsham How †1897. White marble effigy by *J. Nesfield Forsyth*. – Bishop James Seaton †1938. Tablet on chancel floor with lettering by *Eric Gill*.

BISHOP TREACY MEMORIAL HALL, with linking corridor, added N of the nave by *Peter Marshall*, 1981–2. A single-storey ashlar octagon, as if it were the chapter house, with two two-light windows or two blank bays on each side.

*The original is in Wakefield Museum.

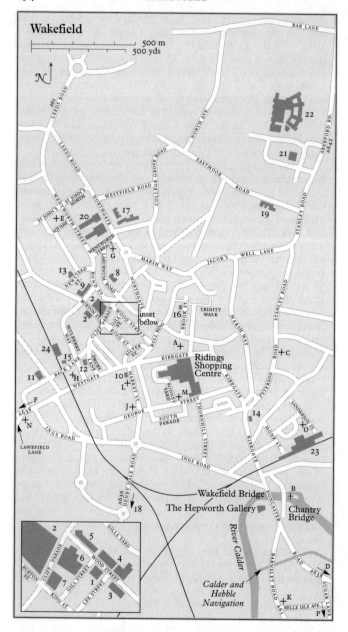

Wakefield

500 m
500 yds

N

BAR LANE

A61 LEEDS ROAD

LEEDS ROAD

WESTFIELD ROAD

NORTH AVE.

COLLEGE GROVE ROAD

EASTMOOR ROAD

A642 ABERFORD RD.

22

21

19

ST JOHN'S NORTH
WENTWORTH TERRACE
ST JOHN'S SQUARE
+E
20
NORTHGATE
17

WENTWORTH TERRACE
LABURNUM ROAD
+G
8
MARSH WAY
JACOB'S WELL LANE

STANLEY ROAD

13
NEWSTEAD ST.
9
BOND ST.
BURTON ST.
2
2
CLIFF PARADE
WOOD STREET
GILL ST.
KING ST.
SILVER ST.
BULL RING
inset
below

16
BROOK ST.
TRINITY WALK

A+

+C
STANLEY ROAD
MARSH WAY

24
15
MULBERRY WAY
BACK LANE
12
+H
DRURY LANE
WESTGATE
10
L+
MARKET ST.
KIRKGATE
Ridings
Shopping
Centre
RODNEY YARD
M+
THORNHILL STREET
KIRKGATE
PETERSON ROAD

14
SANDERSON ST.
+O

11
F

A638
+N
LAWEFIELD LANE
INGS ROAD
J+
GEORGE
SOUTH PARADE
STREET

MONK ST.
KIRKGATE
DONCASTER

23

INGS ROAD

A636 DENBY DALE ROAD
18

Wakefield Bridge
The Hepworth Gallery

B
+
Chantry
Bridge

River Calder

Calder and
Hebble
Navigation

BARNSLEY ROAD
ROAD
A638
A61
D
SUGAR LANE
BELLE ISLE AVE.
+K
P

2
5
GILLS YARD
BURTON ST.
CLIFF PARADE
6
WOOD STREET
4
GILL STREET
7
I
LEE STREET
3
KING ST.

OTHER RELIGIOUS BUILDINGS

BRIDGE CHAPEL (CHANTRY CHAPEL OF ST MARY THE VIRGIN), Chantry Bridge. Chapels on bridges, where masses said for travellers and the souls of the dead helped raise the money necessary for the bridge's upkeep, were a usual thing in the Middle Ages. A few remain in England (e.g. Derby, Rotherham (q.v.) and St Ives (Hunts)) but none is as sumptuous or as celebrated as Wakefield's chapel. The bridge was begun c. 1342, when Edward III granted the town the toll rights for three years to fund the replacement of the wooden bridge damaged by floods in 1330. It was presumably completed by 1345, when the town bought the rights for 40s. The chapel was licensed in 1356. As early as c. 1580 Camden called it much defaced, and it deteriorated even more during subsequent uses as warehouse, shop and offices. In 1848 the chapel was restored by *George Gilbert Scott*, who carefully rebuilt most of it as a copy of the original, including (to Scott's later 'shame and chagrin') the entire W façade.* The ill-chosen Caen and Bath stones rapidly decayed, necessitating extensive repairs by *Frederick Simpson* in 1890. Further restoration by *Nicholson & Rushton*

---

*Remains of the old front, which was re-erected in 1847 at Kettlethorpe Hall, Sandal Magna, are now at Thornes Park (p. 718).

with *H. Erskine Hill*, 1939–40, included another new front, this time in Derbyshire stone. More work has been required since.

The chapel stands on a small island on the downstream side of the bridge, and the corbelled courses of its base, which is medieval work, are bonded into the N pier of the central arch (*see* below). It is a small shrine, only 50 ft by 25 ft (15 by 7.5 metres), displaying the Dec style at its most profuse, at least externally. Façade of five bays with three small doorways. Five ogee arches within gablets, with elaborate blank flowing tracery and crockets. In the tall, battlemented parapet some fine reliefs, of the Annunciation, Nativity, Resurrection, Ascension and Pentecost: the last of these copies Scott's replacement for the sculpture of the Coronation of the Blessed Virgin. The top two stages of the spired buttresses have canopied niches, with statues only finally put in place in 1948. On the l. the Virgin, below St Paulinus and St Oswald; on the r. St Christopher, below St James and St Botolph.

The N and S sides each have three bays. Three-light windows with exquisite tracery, which may be Scott's own design. Quatrefoils and mouchettes around the main motif of a flowing cinquefoil or five-petalled flower. The window arches are placed under straight heads with pierced spandrels, again with flowing tracery. The headstops on the S side were carved for repairs in 1996 and depict local supporters of the work. Daintily decorated parapet with blank arcading. The E window is of five lights consisting of two of the three-light side units intersected. In the NE corner an octagonal stair-turret.

Simpler INTERIOR with panelled oak ceiling of low pitch and carved tie-beams with tracery over. The windows have inner hoodmoulds on headstops, those beside the E window are Edward III and Queen Philippa. To the r. a lavishly ornamented niche for an image contains a C19 statue of the Virgin and Child formerly in the external recess above the window. According to Walker a small two-light 'high side' window nearby in the S wall was lost in 1847–8. A light within it or before the image would have guided travellers at night. Below the E third of the chapel a crypt-like SACRISTY with slit-windows. It is connected with the chapel by a minute spiral staircase in the NE turret already referred to. – STAINED GLASS. Richly coloured E window by *John Barnett & Sons* of York, 1848, with scenes from the life of Christ and the Virgin. E windows on N and S sides also by *Barnett*. Central window on S side, 1848, by *Wailes*.

20   The BRIDGE is built of local sandstone. It is 320 ft (96 metres) long and has nine pointed arches with chamfered ribs on the underside. The base of the chapel (*see* above) forms an integral part of the buttressing on the E side, which is in its original form. The bridge was widened on the W (upstream) side, with round arches, in 1758 and 1797.

ST ANDREW AND ST MARY, Peterson Road. 1845–6 by *Scott & Moffatt*, one of Scott's earliest Gothic revival churches and his second in Yorkshire, after St Andrew, Leeds (dem.). Praised by the *Morning Post*,★ it was surely influenced by Pugin's church at Hulme. Small and sturdy in the E.E. style. Nave, aisles and chancel all expressed separately in accordance with the Ecclesiologists' model. Bellcote on the w gable; a w tower with 130-ft (39.6-metre) spire was intended and its double-chamfered E arch was built, making an odd feature on the w wall. Inside, the five-bay nave has plain round piers and an arch-braced roof. The chancel has a barrel roof with painted decoration in its panels, now very murky. E window of three stepped lancets. The original fittings were swept away in a reordering by *Richard Shepley*, 1978–9, which inserted a glazed screen in the chancel arch and two storeys of meeting rooms etc. in the nave w bay.

St CATHERINE, Doncaster Road. 1994–5 by the *Rev. Mike Croft* and *Ashfield Architects*. Orange-red brick under pitched slate roofs, with one- and two-storey ranges grouped either side of a multi-purpose worship space. Linking these is a glazed corridor that forms a projecting narthex with stumpy round belltower attached on its l. Large square worship space under a high pyramidal roof with central light. Inside, calmly serene; the axis is on the diagonal, leading from a low cruciform immersion font to the semicircular top-lit chancel, which has its own gabled roof. Central ALTAR formed from a massive gnarled tree trunk. Similar LECTERN and READING DESK. In the garden the ruined E end of its predecessor, 1877 by *William Watson*, burnt down in 1993.

St JOHN, St John's Square. Built 1791–5, by *Lindley & Watson* as the focus of the new square (*see* Perambulation 2 below). Interior rebuilt 1895–6 and chancel extended 1904–5, to designs made c. 1881 by *Micklethwaite & Somers Clarke*. Square w tower with pedimented Ionic doorway and hollow-chamfered angles. Octagonal top stage with domed cap. Five-bay sides, the three middle bays emphasized by coupled Doric pilasters. The upper windows round-headed, the small lower ones segment-headed and mostly blocked. Balustrade with urns. Original catacombs beneath the church. Micklethwaite & Somers Clarke's alterations were delayed after the tower was found to be unsafe and had to be rebuilt. The original E apse was replaced in matching ashlar with a two-bay chancel with Diocletian windows and E wall blank except for a niche with a statue of St John the Evangelist. Inside, N and S galleries with superimposed columns and flattened arches were replaced by much more elegant round arches on Doric columns. w gallery survives in the fifth bay. Flat ceilings. The chancel is tunnel-vaulted and straight-ended with side rooms l. and r. Big reredos *à la* Wren and Gibbons, panelling, choir stalls and pulpit all in dark oak by *J.E. Knox* of London, 1900–12. Massive square FONT of Frosterley marble 1886. Several elegant monuments in black and white marble, 1790s–c. 1815, by *George Walsha*.

★'... it is hard to believe that it is a church of the nineteenth century and not one of the thirteenth.' (28 Nov. 1846)

St Michael, Horbury Road. 1857–8 by *William Hey Dykes*. Small, neat Gothic Revival church built for the mill workers of Westgate Common and now unkindly stranded on a traffic island. Its best feature is the Geometric E window facing up Westgate. Gabled bellcote; the very large square base of the uncompleted NE tower is used as the organ chamber. Flat-roofed vestry, 1927. Large goblet-shaped FONT of Frosterley marble. – STAINED GLASS. Four-light W window 1883 by *Kempe* with a troupe of musical angels richly robed in green and gold with peacock-feathered wings.

St Austin (R.C.), Wentworth Terrace. Sideways on to this quiet residential street, it fits in unobtrusively, as was perhaps originally intended. Charles Waterton of Walton Hall was its principal benefactor when it was built in 1827–8 as a plain brick 'Mass house'. The designs by *Joseph Ireland* were simplified by the builder, *William Puckrin*. Extended 1852 and altered by *Austin & Delaney* in 1856, when the three nave sashes were given blank round-arched tops. In 1878–80 *Joseph Hansom* added the sanctuary, Lady Chapel, baptistery, sacristy and porch in a more overtly Italianate style with stone dressings. The tall, octagonal Lady Chapel with its dome is the most prominent of these. Inside, there is a W gallery on cast-iron columns. Corinthian columns to the chancel and a triple-arched screen before the intimate space of the Lady Chapel. An odd feature is the internal tracery to the sash windows in the nave.

Westgate Unitarian Chapel, Westgate. Built 1751–2 for the Presbyterians, replacing their first chapel of 1697 at Westgate Common. Its congregation included families from Wakefield's social, economic and political elite such as the Milnes and Gaskells. The Milnes were patrons of *John Carr* and it may be one of his early works, having similarities with his chapel of 1761 at Farnley (*West Riding North*). Amply proportioned, in red brick, with three-bay front under a full-width pediment. Pedimented entrances either side of a small Venetian window whose arch has a Gibbs surround like the windows above. The side elevations have three tall round-headed windows in recessed arches. The fine interior, which has a S gallery, was altered in 1881–2 by *J. W. Connon*. The carved walnut pews date from this time, as does the boarded and panelled pine ceiling. The high, canopied oak pulpit of 1737 and some panelling made of pew-ends were brought from the old chapel. – STAINED GLASS in the four windows on rear elevation by *Heald* of Wakefield, early 1860s. Below the W side of the building are CATA-COMBS. Three tiers of coffin spaces either side of a brick groin-vaulted passage, with a plainer extension of 1808 to the front wall, where there is a coffin chute.

New Life Christian Centre Pentecostal Church, George Street. Built for the Baptists in 1843–4 by *J. P. Pritchett*. An imposing chapel in brick with stone dressings, set back from the road and raised up on a tall basement. At the front Tuscan pilasters divide the first floor into three bays plus a windowless half-bay at each end and continue above the entablature on the attic. On top the gable forms a small pediment flanked by large scrolls and crude acroteria. The interior still has its curving gallery.

BAPTIST CHURCH, Belle Isle Avenue. 1939. Single-storey, self-effacing three-bay front in subdued two-tone brown brick with brick details, fitting in well with its semi-detached neighbours. Flat roof. The main space, on the r., has a tall, round bay window of five lights under a low gable. Prominent pale brick extension of 1998 to the l., on the corner of Barnsley Road, with a square pyramidal roof overhanging the corners of an octagonal meeting room.

UNITED METHODIST CHAPEL (former), Market Street. 1858. Large, its front dignified with ashlar quoins and four giant Corinthian pilasters supporting entablature and pediment.

ZION CONGREGATIONALIST CHURCH (former), George Street/Rodney Yard. Built 1843–4, replacing their chapel of 1782 here and designed by *William Shaw* as a large Italianate stone box of five by seven bays. Very tall, small-paned windows in arched openings. Pretty cast-iron frames, the margin lights with circles. Converted to residential use at the expense of the galleried interior *c.* 2005 with a large extension with pyramidal roof rising behind the parapet.

WESTGATE END CHAPEL (former; Wesleyan), Lawefield Lane. 1827, altered. Brick. Tall five-bay front has shallow central bow with Ionic pilasters to first floor and prominent gable entablature. Classical doorway *c.* 1870. Five-bay returns. Galleried interior with inserted C20 floor.

CENTRAL JAMIA MASQUE MOSQUE, Sanderson Street. 1995, extended 2007. Wakefield's first purpose-built mosque and madrasa.

WAKEFIELD CEMETERY, Sugar Lane. Opened in 1859. It had the usual composition of Gothic Anglican and Nonconformist chapels either side of an arched link, designed by *M.O. Tarbotton*, Borough Surveyor. The chapels were demolished *c.* 1991, leaving the centre as an odd-looking, heavily buttressed, square stone tower. Nearby the decayed stone monument to William Shaw †1859, a large square buttressed base covered in gablets and blind arcading, topped by an octagonal spirelet bristling with crockets.

PUBLIC BUILDINGS

The major public buildings of the town amount to a Civic Quarter along Wood Street. After the Town Hall and County Hall they are described in order S to N.

TOWN HALL. The site was acquired in 1854 for a successor to the Town Hall in the Crown Court (*see* p. 709) but not built upon until 1877–80, by which time offices for the School Board and a magistrates' court were also required; the design was won in competition by *T.E. Collcutt*. It is among his earliest works and though its form is in the Gothic Revival tradition it is, at least at the front, clothed in that eclectic mix of northern Renaissance decorative elements that marks the transition to the freer styles of urban façades in the later C19. The front is symmetrical, five bays, with three large oriels (whose debt to Shaw's Queen Anne-style New Zealand Chambers was noticed by the *Building News*) sticking up into the tall hipped roof as gabled and turreted dormers of Jacobean style. The central one sits over the main entrance, which projects forward under a balcony. Similar windows in the first bay to l. and r. returns. They all have panels of Renaissance ornament and bands of strapwork carved by *Walter Smith* of London in the building's Spinkwell sandstone. Only the main front and the prominent, asymmetrically placed tower, set back on the r., are fine ashlar. Rising to a total height of 190 ft (58 metres) the rectangular tower is crowned by a steep truncated pyramid roof, rather French in character. After the Cathedral's spire it is the most prominent feature of the city's skyline. Each side of the upper stage has an arched, belfry-like opening with balcony, below which is the face designed by Collcutt for *Sir Edmund Beckett*'s clock.

The building's long sides run back to the rear elevation on King Street and are much plainer – three storeys with ashlar dressings displaying Collcutt's liking for stressing the vertical and horizontal simultaneously with pilaster-strips and string courses. At the back is the second public entrance – over it a panel left uncarved when the Council reined in the budget as it climbed to £70,000, far exceeding the £35,000 originally allowed.

The ENTRANCE HALL is spacious but not grand and has Caen stone arches to the rear and the l. side where the main staircase rises to the first floor and the impressive double-height former COUNCIL CHAMBER. Lit by oriels on two sides this occupies two-thirds of the front range and is Jacobean in style. Half-height carved panelling in American walnut on the walls with elaborate plaster frieze above and richly decorated plaster ceiling divided by deep decorated beams. The tall pedimented chimneypiece and the screen below the public gallery are finely carved walnut. The BANQUETING HALL, on the floor above, under the roof, has a carved mahogany dado and more decorative plasterwork. The former COURT ROOM has lost its fittings but the lofty space retains its oak panelling. The mayor's drawing room, committee rooms and School Board room also have some good plasterwork, panelling and tiled fireplaces.

WEST RIDING COUNTY HALL (former, now Wakefield Metropolitan District Council offices), Bond Street and Cliff Parade. 1894–8, won in competition in 1893 by *Gibson & Russell*. One of the earliest and most palatial of the buildings commissioned, befitting the largest county council in England created by the 1888 Act. The style, described by the architects as 'Renaissance, with distinctly English detail as exemplified in such buildings as Kirby or Wollaton Halls', is also distinctively of its date, infused with 1890s Baroque Revival and emerging Art Nouveau forms. The lozenge-shaped PLAN is an ingenious response to the awkward site between Bond Street, Cliff Parade, Burton Street and Hardy Street. The outer ranges enclose an internal court, which is bisected by a central range containing the council chamber.

The EXTERIOR is in finely worked Grindleford stone, Hopton Wood stone being used inside. With no space for steps or a grand portico to mark the main entrance, Gibson & Russell placed it instead at the most important street corner, on Cliff Parade, where it can be seen in views N along Wood Street. This imaginative and highly successful position is emphasized by the polygonal tower above, which is crowned by a dome and cupola. This is the most Baroque element in the composition. It stands 130 ft (39 metres) high and makes no attempt to compete with the Town Hall's tower. Rather, after that and the Cathedral spire it forms the third main accent of the Wakefield skyline. The two principal façades either side are not symmetrical but in a nice balance and the obtuse angle allows a better view of them together. Both have big dramatic dormer gables over projecting bays at each end. The Cliff Parade side has on the first floor a series of oriels capped by a long balcony, the Bond Street range a six-bay loggia below the balcony instead. The ground floor is quite plain, but the two floors above have a well-integrated scheme of sculptured decoration by *W. Birnie Rhind* that must be among the most cheerful to be found on a major public building of this date. Among panels of Renaissance strapwork incorporating the council's monogram is an entire kindergarten of cherubs, while figures representing Science, Art, Literature, Music and Poetry in the gables hint at the more overtly Art Nouveau work inside. The main entrance has figures of Justice, Education, Progress and Health carved in low relief above it.* The Hardy Street and long Burton Street frontages are much plainer, both incorporating matching extensions of 1912–15.

INTERIOR. The interior offers a visual feast of colour, materials and textures, with woodwork, marble, plasterwork, paintings and metalwork of the highest quality. Beyond the porch, with its fine wrought-iron gates by *J. W. Singer* of Frome, is a small octagonal vestibule, the walls lined with black and white marble below a shallow domed ceiling with cherubs. Carved oak doors lead into the arcaded ENTRANCE HALL, which has the principal staircase on the l. Though the hall lacks the grand scale expected of late Victorian civic architecture, the octagonal stone pillars and procession of stone arches create a complex dignity to which the marble floor, oak panelling and pedimented doorcases, and red and white marble handrail and balusters, contribute a somewhat sombre opulence. Stained glass windows by *William Smith* of London and a dramatic

---

* Figures representing West Riding industries were removed from the niches on the Bond Street loggia in the 1960s.

painting on the staircase walls of a storm-blown Viking ship, representing the area's C9 Danish settlers. This and the *fin-de-siècle* mural paintings upstairs are by *Charles Grange Lowther*, a darkly atmospheric scheme in oils enhanced with gesso and highlights of copper and bronze. To the l. at the head of the stairs is a square, top-lit ANTE-ROOM, with oak panelling below richly modelled and coloured plaster friezes by *H.C. Fehr*. These depict four stirring scenes from the Wars of the Roses, including the Battle of Wakefield and the procession of Henry VII and Margaret of York through the town. The COUNCIL CHAMBER beyond is immensely impressive, 50 ft (15 metres) square and 40 ft (12 metres) high beneath a dome with central cupola, whose pendentives rest on four steel cross-beams clad in sequoia. On the pendentives low reliefs of Wisdom, Law, Learning and Power look down at Justice, Authority and Industry above the doors, which are set in fine mahogany panelling. The windows have stained glass by *Smith* with the arms of county families. Fixed seating in a semicircle, with the press gallery elevated above the Chairman's seat on columns of deep green Irish marble.

Returning to the stairs, the vaulted CORRIDOR leading to the committee rooms has *Lowther*'s symbolic murals including winged figures of debate and dictation, implements of the county's main trades and industries, and a serene figure of Peace, with doves and broken swords, beside her more buxom sister Plenty, presiding over an abundance of fruit and grain. At the end, outside the Chairman's room, is the lamp of knowledge between figures of art and science, with the book of history and flame of inspiration above. Along the Bond Street front the LIBRARY has panelling and bookcases in American walnut, a marble fireplace and a gilded plaster ceiling. The COMMITTEE ROOMS beyond also have walnut panelling and elaborate fireplaces, one with a plasterwork over-mantel depicting Education. All the principal rooms have superb Art Nouveau ELECTROLIERS in brass and copper. Their switch plates, decorated with ladies with, or sometimes without, swirling drapery, are indicative of the architects' attention to detail. Elsewhere are corridors with mosaic floors and decorative green and yellow tiled dados, and well-handled secondary staircases with wrought-iron balusters by *J.W. Singer*.

Gardens were created at the N end of the building in 2012 after the removal of a 1970s annexe and they open the view from Wood Street to an agreeable block of further Council Offices (WAKEFIELD ONE) of 2011 by *Cartwright Pickard*, incorporating the city's Museum and Library.

MECHANICS' INSTITUTION (former), Wood Street, s of the Town Hall. Now part of Wakefield College. Built in 1820–2 by *Watson & Pritchett* as a Library, News Room and Music Saloon, and intended to compare with the public rooms in Leeds. The style is the noble restrained Grecian much favoured at the time for such buildings. Five bays, rusticated ground floor with attached Ionic columns above and coupled pilasters at the angles. Large tripartite window to the saloon upstairs on s side, the n blank. No architrave to the entrance and no pediment. After 1842 the building became the Mechanics' Institution; *George W. Richardson* made alterations 1881–2. The staircase in the semicircular bay at the rear was reconfigured and the elegant saloon given a higher, coved ceiling with decorative plasterwork under a new roof. It was the city's museum until 2012, now at Wakefield One (*see above*).

POLICE OFFICES (former), opposite the Mechanics' Institution and Town Hall. 1908 by *J. Vickers Edwards*, West Riding County Architect. Lively Wrenaissance in stone and red brick. On the r. two-storey gabled blocks either side of gates to the rear yard. To the l. a more ornate block, of five bays, has a rusticated ground floor and stone oriels under open pediments in the projecting end bays.

COUNTY MEDICAL OFFICES (former), alongside the former Police Offices. Classical Revival, 1928–30 by *P. O. Platts*, West Riding County Architect, and dismissed by Pevsner as 'very tame after the Late Victorian flights of fancy'. Symmetrical front in Grindleford stone to match County Hall. Rusticated ground floor, fourth storey in mansard behind balustrade. Columns with Tower of the Winds capitals *in antis* above the entrance and corner. Figures of Justice and Wisdom originally enlivened the end pavilions.

COURT HOUSE (former). Between the Town Hall and County Hall. The first public building in Wood Street, 1806–10 by *Charles Watson* (competition 1804), and one of the finest early Greek Revival buildings in the West Riding, restored in 2015–16 after long neglect. Watson's earlier court house at Beverley (East Riding) is in the same style but this has a more forceful Doric order. Rectangular block five bays deep, both storeys rusticated, fronted by a deep and imposing tetrastyle Doric portico with the royal arms in the pediment and a figure of Justice on top. Single storey, one-bay wings also with banded rustication. A curious motif is the frieze above the door and windows of linked rings, uncomfortably suggestive of handcuffs. Additions of 1849–50, when a smaller, second court was formed to the n, and larger two-storey extension of 1883 on the s, all in matching stonework.

MAGISTRATES' COURT, Cliff Parade/Gill Street. Built 1878–9 for the police and fire services. Italianate style in stone and render with a heavy cornice on brackets at the eaves and above each window on both floors. To Cliff Parade a carved keystone with constable's head and friezes matching those on the Court House; to Gill Street a gable carving of firemen wielding hoses. The e façade is rendered and incorporates the remains of the TAMMY HALL, built 1777–8, whose s end was demolished to make way for the Town Hall. It was 30 ft wide and over 200 ft long (9 by 60 metres), with stalls for 200 traders in tammies and other worsted cloths.

COUNTY POLICE HEADQUARTERS, Laburnum Road. 1913–14,
probably by *J. Vickers Edwards,* West Riding County Architect.
Ten bays in a genteel Neo-Georgian style. Smooth red brick
with stone dressings, semicircular porch on Doric columns,
and a second floor in a steep, tiled mansard. To the l., two
pairs of well-preserved semi-detached POLICE HOUSES of
1912 with slightly Arts and Crafts details. The police also
occupy the former Education Dept offices opposite of 1961–2
by *A.W. Glover,* County Architect. Eight storeys, faced in
Crosland stone with bands of Westmorland green slate.

WAKEFIELD COLLEGE (City Campus), between Burton Street
and Bond Street. Formerly the Technical College and School
of Art. The oldest part is the handsome two-storey Wrenaissance range facing Burton Street, 1933–4, by *Louis Ives,* City
Surveyor. Behind this, the 1960s RADCLIFFE BUILDING,
transformed in refurbishment in 2013–14 by *Taylor Young* to go
with their routine HARRISON BUILDING, 2013, which
replaced another post-war addition. (*See also* Outer Wakefield – Thornes for Wakefield College, Thornes Park.)

Other public buildings

CIVIL JUSTICE CENTRE, Westgate. *See* Perambulation 1.

POST OFFICE (former), Market Street. By *James Williams,* 1876,
a tall, narrow brick front with well-detailed stone dressings.
The single-storey extension on the l. was Wakefield's first
automatic telephone exchange, 1926.

H. M. PRISON, Back Lane. 1843–7 by *Bernard Hartley II,* County
Surveyor, with later C20 additions. Hartley was the elder
brother of Jesse Hartley of Liverpool. The prison originated as
the county's House of Correction, established 1595, and the
present buildings are the successors of several purpose-built
gaols on the site. Since the late C18 it has been one of the
largest provincial prisons in England. Nothing of the pre-1843
buildings now survives apart from fragments of stone walls and
the clock from the new prison of 1766–70 by *John Carr* and
John Watson, which was resited on the tall square Italianate
tower in 1858. In brick with stone dressings, the clock tower
is the only building that can easily be seen over the roll-topped
stone perimeter wall of *c.* 1982. It stands above a central block
with four wings built on a radial plan in response to the Prisons
Act 1839. This brought in the 'separate' system of single-
occupancy cells as the standard, in place of the 'silent' but
communal accommodation of many older prison buildings.
Each wing, plainly built in red brick, is twenty-seven bays, with
cells either side of a central gallery. A and D wings were heightened from three to four storeys *c.* 1875, adding over a hundred
new cells. Improvements *c.* 1973–93 included enlargement of
the tiny cell windows and the re-dedication in 1992 of the
polygonal chapel at the s end of A wing, damaged by fire in
1979. New workshops etc. have replaced Carr's buildings and

extensive late C18 and early C19 additions, as well as some of the 1840s administrative blocks. The three-storey gatehouse of 1973, on Back Lane, is faced in blockwork and concrete panels and is as solid-looking as, though less forbidding than, Hartley's rusticated Doric triumphal arch at the old entrance on Love Lane, demolished in 1982.

PUBLIC LIBRARY (former), Drury Lane. Built 1905–6, the design by *Trimnell, Cox & Davison* selected in competition. A small but handsome Neo-Baroque building in Crosland Moor stone. Two round and two paired round-headed windows in each single-storey wing, either side of a taller gabled entrance with ornate cupola. The front reading rooms have barrel-vaulted ceilings decorated with bands of roses and vines in low-relief plasterwork. Plain but sympathetic extension for the junior library on the l. by *S. Hutton*, City Engineer, 1939. Converted in 2014 to artists' studios. The adjoining ART HOUSE in red and buff brick with Op Art tile decoration was built 2007–8, also originally as artists' studios but now serving a variety of related uses.

REGISTRY OF DEEDS (former), Newstead Road. The West Riding set up its deeds registry in Wakefield in 1704, prompted by the need of woollen manufacturers to raise capital for expansion by mortgaging their property. The building in Kirkgate was succeeded by the present large, solemn Neo-Georgian structure of 1931–2 by *P. O. Platts*, County Architect. Three-and-a-half storeys, the semi-basement in rusticated stone, the top floor set back behind a heavy stone parapet. To be succeeded by the West Yorkshire History Centre in Kirkgate in 2017.

WEST YORKSHIRE HISTORY CENTRE, Kirkgate. Purpose-built in 2014–17 by *Broadway Malyan* for the West Yorkshire Archives HQ, formerly at the Registry of Deeds, Newstead Road (*see* above). Simple of outline, appropriately like a huge box, except for the angled entrance front with overhang supported on V-shaped struts. Ground-floor public spaces, the two window-less upper floors providing environmentally controlled storage for parchment and paper archives including the West Riding Registry of Deeds. The perforated metal mesh wrapping finishes with an angular indented edge just above the ground floor windows, like a lifted lid.

HEPWORTH WAKEFIELD GALLERY. *See* Perambulation 3.

THE ORANGERY, Back Lane. A surprising and delightful survival in an urban setting. Built *c.* 1790 by Pemberton Milnes in a detached part of the garden of his house on Westgate (*see* Perambulation 1) but converted to a school for Westgate Chapel after 1849 and now an arts centre. Although much altered for later uses, the central five-bay stone arcade, its frieze decorated with garlands and paterae in an Adamesque manner, is still recognizable as an orangery. The arched openings between Ionic half-columns with feather necks (pilasters at the angles) were presumably glazed originally. They now have mid-C19 sash windows set in rendered brickwork, the central one tall and round-headed. Set slightly back on each side are C19 lower single-storey wings of five bays in rendered brick, with matching stone blocking courses and hipped roofs.

ELIZABETHAN EXHIBITION GALLERY. *See* Former Queen Elizabeth Grammar School below.

QUEEN ELIZABETH GRAMMAR SCHOOL (former), Brook Street. Built *c.* 1596–8 by the Saviles for the Free Grammar School founded in 1591. Restored 1980–1 by *L. R. Nutter*, Chief Architect (project architect *Malcolm Brown*) of Wakefield Council as the ELIZABETHAN EXHIBITION GALLERY. The original stone building was freed of later extensions apart from the small projection on the S. Five main windows each of five lights with two transoms. The back with equally large windows. Above the doorway a smaller five-light window, over a re-cut inscription around the Savile arms. The schoolroom has a fine kingpost roof. It is impressively large for its date.

QUEEN ELIZABETH GRAMMAR SCHOOL, Northgate. Built as a Proprietary school 1833–4, by *Richard Lane* of Manchester. A junior version of his Bluecoat School at Oldham, Lancashire, and the best preserved of all his schools. Symmetrical front in Tudor Gothic, with three high pavilions, l., r. and – the highest of the three – in the middle. This has a gable flanked by tall octagonal pinnacles. The single-storey linking ranges are four bays. All the windows have elaborately geometric cast-iron frames. The arcaded basement storey was originally open at the lower ground level to the rear to provide a covered playground. The buildings were taken over by the Grammar School in 1855, but additions since then have sensitively preserved the lawned setting at the front of *Lane*'s building. S of it *George Viall*'s laboratories and lecture theatre, 1891–3, survive, with E additions of 1910 by *Simpson & Firth*, who at the same time built the Junior School just N of Lane's building, again in stone in a sympathetic style. The SPILSBURY LIBRARY, 1929, forming a SE wing to Lane's building, is almost indistinguishable from the original. NE of this the buff brick ASSEMBLY HALL of 1958 has a gabled roof forming a porch over the deeply recessed centre; E of it Lane's headmaster's house of 1858 has been replaced by the pale brick SPORTS CENTRE, 1999. At the front, on Northgate, the original LODGE and railings survive. E of the lodge is the WAR MEMORIAL, 1921, by *W.H. Watson*, a classically detailed square stone column with bronze statue of a bugler.

CATHEDRAL ACADEMY, Thornes Road. Formerly the Cathedral High School, the best example of the city's secondary schools. 1964–5 by *Peter Marshall*, 1980s additions. The original buildings are flat-roofed, two-storey blocks in buff brick, the N-facing classroom blocks curtain-walled with large windows above maroon panels. Extensive one- and two-storey additions behind in yellower brick with very low-pitched hipped roofs. The red-framed windows run in continuous bands, broken by not quite full-height panels of solid brickwork and 'pilasters' of paired brick strips.

PINDERS PRIMARY SCHOOL, Eastmoor Road. Formerly Eastmoor School of 1877–8 by *William Watson* for Wakefield School
Board. Long, single-storey front in red brick with stone dressings and prominent gables. In the centre is the gabled end of
the school hall, flanked by separate entrances, the girls' under
a small gable on the l., the boys' to the r. in a big square clock
tower. A five-bay classroom at each end, their first and fifth
bays gabled.

WAKEFIELD GIRLS' HIGH SCHOOL, Wentworth Street. *See*
Perambulation 2.

CLAYTON HOSPITAL (former), Wentworth Street. Disused
since 2012. 1876–9 by *William Bakewell* in Flemish Renaissance style. Pavilion plan, the wards in two-storey gabled
blocks either side of the central administrative block, all in
stone. The entrance is in a square four-storey tower with
stepped gables and pinnacles.

WEST RIDING COUNTY ASYLUM (former), Aberford Road.
Subsequently Stanley Royd Hospital, closed in 1995, and now
Parklands Manor, a residential conversion and development of
2005 by *Spawforth Associates* that has preserved the original
buildings of 1816–18 by *Watson & Pritchett*. For its date the plan
is an interesting and innovative variation on the 'panopticon'
layout that permitted observation of both patients and their
attendants. Its form is an H with a central range for the entrance
and superintendent's accommodation, and cross-wings containing single rooms arranged along a gallery. All these ranges
are in an austere Late Georgian style; three storeys, in white
brick with stone sill bands and other details, and low-pitched
hipped roofs. The central range is eleven bays. The three middle
bays project forward and have a later attic storey above the
cornice instead of the original pediment. The similar, though
slightly later, three-bay extension at the rear retains its pediment. Above the central range is a two-tier cupola of eight tall
Doric columns with an entablature supporting a little dome
resting on eight very short square columns. It formed part of
the ventilation system. The four arms of the cross-wings are
each of seven bays, with pavilion ends. At the junctions of the
ranges are four-storey octagonal towers that originally contained spiral staircases with openings through which all the
corridors, wards and exercise yards could be discreetly observed.
The projecting ends of the central range were extended in
matching style in 1828–33. Of the later additions all have been
demolished except for an Italianate stone clock tower and the
large former DINING AND RECREATION HALL (now Destiny
Church), built in 1859. Its one-bay s extension of 1893, probably by *Bernard Hartley III*, provided a complete working stage,
including a grooved system for moving scenery; a unique survival. The CHAPEL (St Faith) of 1861, which stood on the
corner of Eastmoor Road, was demolished after an arson attack
in 2012. It had an odd plan of two equal, parallel ranges in E.E.
style, said to have been copied from Scott's and Lord Grimthorpe's plans for St James, Doncaster (1858), p. 213.

PINDERFIELDS HOSPITAL, immediately N of the asylum buildings on Aberford Road, is by *BDP*, 2012, on the site of the acute hospital for the asylum, built 1899–1900.

KIRKGATE STATION, Monk Street. Wakefield's first station, opened 1840 by the Manchester & Leeds Railway. Rebuilt in 1854 by *George Thompson & Co.* for the Lancashire & Yorkshire Railway on a grander scale in Italianate style in stone, with the rear and ancillary buildings in brick. The cost was £60,000. Long, almost symmetrical front. The tall pedimented entrance is linked by single-storey wings to end pavilions of three bays with hipped roofs.

WESTGATE STATION, Mulberry Way. Originally opened 1856 on the Great Northern Railway's Leeds–Doncaster line. The W platform buildings are by *J.B. Fraser*, 1867, the rest rebuilt 1969 and again, slightly further N, in 2013.

PERAMBULATIONS

1. Westgate

WESTGATE still preserves much of its ancient pattern of long, narrow building plots and intermediate yards or lanes running back from smarter street frontages. Beyond the medieval core most of these were substantial red brick Georgian houses, prompting Samuel Curwen, an American visitor, to comment in 1777 that Westgate 'has the noblest appearance of any [street] I ever saw out of London'.

Our route begins close to the Cathedral at the pedestrianized E end of LITTLE WESTGATE, where a pleasing mix of mainly three-storey C18 and C19 buildings survive on the N side, facing mediocre post-war commercial frontages. The first building of note is Peter Jones's shop, with its wooden dentilled cornice and finely gauged brick arches over the windows, a good example of the red brick Georgian development that gives Wakefield so much of its character. At the W end though, No. 38 is an early C18 three-storey house, of four narrow bays, with stone cornice, quoins and platbands, facing downhill. To the N, parallel with Little Westgate, is CROSS SQUARE, originally closed at its E end and with the market cross at its head from 1707 to 1866. On the S side, the narrow front of the BLACK ROCK pub, its arched entrance decorated with Art Nouveau tiles in browns and pinks. The Venetian window on first floor and the rear elevation in Bread Street betray its C18 core. Opposite, at the corner with Bull Ring, the exuberant Baroque former Grand Clothing Hall of 1906, by *Percy Robinson* of Leeds. Domed and gabled in stone-coloured terracotta, with giant keystones on the first floor and swags of fruit and flowers. Diagonally opposite, with its entrance on Wood Street, is a former bank, a handsome essay in red brick with classical stone dressings, by *James Neill & Son*, 1880–1. The smaller five-bay range to the r. was the manager's house, its entrance crowned with a very elaborate carved brick pediment. For the rest of Wood Street, *see* pp. 699 and 714.

Now back to the main part of Westgate via SILVER STREET, not much more than a wide passage separated from Westgate by an egregious set of mid-1960s shops and offices on the site of the Church Institute (High Victorian, by *A.B. Higham*) but also with the BLACK SWAN, a timber-framed early C17 house, its three-storey jettied front tantalizingly concealed by render. The small window in the attic under the big central gable has a Yorkshire sash. Next a detour into the series of streets and yards on the backlands N of Silver Street, beginning with KING STREET, which typifies the pre-C20 mix of domestic, commercial and industrial buildings that developed behind more prestigious properties. About 70 yds along on its r. No. 18 is the largest of the former wool warehouses in this area, where Titus Salt was apprenticed in 1820 to learn the raw wool trade. Four storeys in red brick, the upper two rendered. The giant arched entrance in the front of nine bays was made for the conversion to offices *c.* 2002. Beside it CHANCERY LANE leads into CROWN COURT, sensitively landscaped with stone seating and restrained planting in 2007. The three-storey stuccoed offices on the l. with rusticated ground floor were converted from a brick woolstapler's warehouse in 1840 by *W. L. Moffatt*, who added the pediments with console brackets over the windows and other Italianate flourishes. Also here the old TOWN HALL, a plain stuccoed building of two storeys with basement, built 1798 as the New Assembly Rooms. The Music Hall upstairs, lit by seven round-arched windows, was opened in 1801. It was the Town Hall only from 1848 to 1880.

On the other side of King Street is BARSTOW SQUARE, a narrow yard including an impressive late C18 three-storey terrace of brick houses with pediment, in the style attributed to *William Lindley* (cf. No. 136 Westgate and Wentworth House, Wentworth Street below). Eleven bays, the central one stressed by a tall blank giant arch and a tripartite window with columns. A very narrow passage on the l. offers the surprise of a tiny, rather scruffy yard, originally open to Silver Street, with a respectable (restored) mid-C18 house front and a C19 two-storey canted bay with fine stone Doric columns.

An archway from the S end of Barstow Square emerges into SILVER STREET. A few steps E No. 16's shopfront has two very fine Georgian Composite pilasters and part of a (salvaged) carved timber cornice. W in THOMPSON's YARD another example of the houses squeezed in behind the street. Three storeys, with a shallow two-storey bay, it was built with the shop in front *c.* 1830. W of this, the last of the back street detours, is CHEAPSIDE, remarkable chiefly for its continuous ranges of woolstaplers' warehouses, mostly built within twenty years of the street being laid out in 1802. They are perhaps the best surviving group of their kind in England. All are of brick and typically three storeys high and three or five bays wide, though the largest, No. 19, is four storeys and seven bays. The central bays have large openings for the woolpacks, some with hoist beams above.

Now for WESTGATE proper. At the junction with Silver Street, the street's impressive width still has the feel of the market place that existed here until the town's first corn exchange was built in 1820. On its site, the former Yorkshire Bank, *c.* 1930, a stone frontage with bulky rounded end, dull despite some Art Deco-ish details. Across Westgate, between Queen Street and Market Street, is a dismal block of shops and mid-1960s offices on the site of the lamented second Corn Exchange (1836–40 by *W. L. Moffatt*). W of Market Street, the much-altered Black Bull, built in 1772. Nine bays with a giant blank arch in the centre and a brick pediment (the rear also has a pediment). Two-storey canted bays at each end. Next to it, the former Wakefield & Barnsley Union Bank, an elaborately decorated Italian palazzo of 1877–8 by *Lockwood & Mawson* (now a night club). Ashlar front of seven bays, the tall ground floor heavily rusticated, with keystone masks of Mars, Diana, Bacchus etc. flanking William Stewart, Mayor in 1877. Opposite, the diminutive but perfectly detailed Beaux Arts-style HSBC, 1923, probably by *T. B. Whinney* for the Midland, in Portland stone.

Downhill on the S side again, Nos. 67–69 retain the appearance of a smart five-bay town house and were built in the early 1790s for Ingram & Kennett's bank. This discreetly occupied the two wider bays on the r. (the door now converted to a window), while the l. side was the manager's house. Three-storey brick front above a basement with area, the ground floor recessed behind a rusticated stone arcade. This is among the earliest surviving purpose-built provincial banks.

On the opposite side of the street is the former PICTURE HOUSE, 1913 by *Albert Winstanley*. White faience, now painted, the central and end bays with pilasters and pediments. Sparse classical decoration. Opposite again, between Bank Street and Smyth Street, is an extensive Gothic block in red brick and stone built for the Wakefield Industrial Co-operative Society and retaining its Edwardian shopfronts. The earliest, and plainest, part, by *W. & D. Thornton* 1876–8, has three storeys to Bank Street and short return to Westgate. The rest is an extension of 1899–1902 by *A. Hart* with gables, turrets and gargoyles. The meeting hall (Unity Hall) on the tall second storey has a large ogee-headed, traceried window to Westgate and nine round-headed windows along Smyth Street. Below the large window a prominent carved stone panel depicts a beehive and local industry and trade.

Facing it across Westgate is the THEATRE ROYAL, by *Frank Matcham*, opened as the Opera House in 1894. Restored by *TACP Design* (project architect *Roy Parker*) 1985–6. Tall Flemish-gabled front of two storeys in red brick with modest Jacobean-style decoration in cast concrete. Four heads of playwrights and composers in scrolled frames between the upper windows. Lower two-bay former shop with corner dome, 1905, now café, offices and additional dressing rooms. This is

Matcham's smallest surviving theatre, the delightful auditorium of a scale similar to his theatre at Cheltenham and the Lyric, Hammersmith, and typical of his earlier, more fanciful style. The horseshoe-shaped dress circle and gallery have rich though not very refined Rococo plasterwork on the balcony fronts, with scrolls, flowery swags, dolphins etc. Scrolled medallions on the ceiling and elaborate panels either side of the richly framed proscenium arch. Glass-fronted extension to the E for Centre for Creativity with studio theatre etc., by *Halliday Clark*, proposed in 2016.

W of here are some earlier survivors e.g. in DRURY LANE, N of the theatre, where YORK HOUSE, of two-and-a-half storeys, was built *c.* 1775 for James Banks, who provided the original Theatre Royal in 1775–6. The principal front, facing N, has finer bricks and a pedimented doorcase, the central doorway on the W front having a Gibbs surround. (Original interior features include carved chimneypieces, one with Ionic columns flanking a painted Chinese scene.) Opposite, the former Library and the Art House (*see* Public Buildings).

Returning to Westgate, a little further down on the N side after the CIVIL JUSTICE CENTRE (by *Hurd Rolland*, 2012) is the best of Wakefield's historic chapels, Westgate Unitarian Chapel, set back in its graveyard (*see* Religious Buildings). Its congregation included the wealthy Milnes family, who were woollen merchants with a lucrative trade supplying cloth to Russia. The only survivor of their four fine Georgian residences in Westgate is the smallest, PEMBERTON HOUSE, a three-storey brick mansion built just W of the chapel in 1752–3 by Pemberton Milnes. Five-bay S front right on the street and the entrance on the E. Two-storey canted bay with stone columns at the rear. Altered since 1864, when it ceased to be a residence. Its gardens extended N across Back Lane and included the Orangery (*see* Public Buildings), whose grounds were used as a graveyard after being given to Westgate Chapel in 1849. On the S side of Westgate, facing the chapel and house, a pleasant variety of buildings, including No. 105, with fluted frieze on its shallow Regency bay and, below, the excellent gabled ELEPHANT AND CASTLE pub, *c.* 1905 for Warwicks of Boroughbridge in red brick enriched with buff terracotta and Burmantofts warm brown tiles ornamented in green, all splendidly intact. Then another good Georgian brick front with giant arch in the centre and modillion cornice.

After this, regrettably, the railway cuts across Westgate and it takes some effort to try to visualize the remaining Georgian houses below the bridge as part of the same street. Nearly all have been ill-treated, some of them shamefully so. The best are on the N side, where No. 136 is the least altered. It has a projecting pedimented Doric porch with an Adamesque frieze prettily decorated with urns and garlands. Nos. 138–148 were originally a pair of houses of seven bays, their modest entrances in an arched carriageway within a giant blank arch. Stone frieze and eaves cornice. Long windows at the rear for identical staircases with stick balusters. The front windows have fluted triple keystones like those on the BLACK SWAN HOTEL over the road. Last is No. 160, nine bays and also originally a pair of houses with a central carriage arch. Still very grand, with an imposing pediment and a Venetian window with Ionic columns. It has too the typical blank giant arch in the centre and fluted keystones.

2. Northgate to St John's

Like Westgate and Kirkgate, most of the buildings of NORTH-GATE at the W end of the Cathedral have been sacrificed to banal post-war reconstruction, which also characterizes Northgate's junction with Bull Ring and Union Street. This was the Market Place, and has recently been re-landscaped to good effect around the cross-roads. The area to the N and E of Brook Street has also been redeveloped since 2008 as the TRINITY WALK SHOPPING CENTRE by *DLA Architecture* with two public squares, department store, shops and flats. A striking new MARKET HALL on Union Street by *David Adjaye*, 2008, replaced the 1960s one. Very tall angled black columns support a huge translucent polycarbonate roof on natural timber beams, providing a canopy over stalls at the open N end. Food hall and shops are set back at S end, enclosed by black timber panels.

The main part of Northgate to the N suffered grievously in the second half of the C20,* but on the W side No. 53 (Cow Shed restaurant, with gabled, timber-framed front of 1991) and Nos. 55–57 have extensive remains inside of a large timber-framed late C15 house including beams with painted chevron decoration, unique in the north of England, and a very fine, though altered, plaster ceiling dated 1596 on the first floor of No. 53. It is decorated with the royal arms, roses, grapes, pomegranates and mermaids. Only one other Elizabethan town house ceiling is known to exist in Yorkshire, in Coney Street, York. A two-storey range at the rear, in Gill's Yard, was the premises of Wright & Elwick, Yorkshire's leading cabinetmakers, from 1750. Further up is EGREMONT HOUSE, set slightly back, built *c.* 1811 but with early C20 stone doorcase. Then, beyond Rishworth Street, a good surviving group of two- and three-storey Georgian houses (Nos. 87–99) of two separate builds. Nos. 87–91 have reeded doorcases; No. 95 has two canted bay windows and a delicately decorated doorway with garlanded frieze and pediment. On the l. after Cardigan Terrace is WENTWORTH TERRACE with St Austin's church (R.C.) of 1827–8 set unobtrusively among the terraced houses (*see* Religious Buildings).

The next part of Northgate is dominated by the former Clayton Hospital (w side) and the Queen Elizabeth Grammar

*A major loss was HASELDEN HALL, a gabled C17 house.

School (set back on the E side), for which *see* Public Buildings. From here the tone becomes more suburban as Northgate becomes LEEDS ROAD. On the E side ST JOHN'S LODGE is a pleasant three-bay brick villa of 1827 with a pedimented doorcase.

Turning E, WESTFIELD ROAD leads to BISHOPGARTH, built 1891–3 as the bishop's palace, now part of the WEST YORK-SHIRE POLICE TRAINING CENTRE. A very large red brick mansion, with gables and mullioned-and-transomed windows. (The chapel has windows by *Kempe* and panels carved by *Ellen Frances Kenyon*, Bishop How's daughter, and *Mary Frances How*, his niece.) The outraged bishop burnt the first edition of Hardy's *Jude the Obscure* here in 1895. Then, on the S side, a row of six small ALMSHOUSES built 1887 for the Crowther Trust by *Arnold S. Nicholson*. Red brick and stone, with a high slate roof and large, very fancy gables above the mullioned parlour windows. At the bottom of Westfield Road a l. turn into COLLEGE GROVE ROAD leads into Wakefield's best Victorian leafy suburb, with the rather gloomy Gothic GROVE HALL *c.* 1875, large villas on EASTMOOR ROAD and substantial terraces such as those in WESTFIELD GROVE.

W of Leeds Road, however, is Georgian Wakefield's most impressive planned development and the only one that could possibly be called major. It comprises a single street, St John's North (originally St John's Street), linking Northgate with St John's Square, which has St John's church of 1795 as its focus (*see* Religious Buildings). This speculative residential scheme was begun in 1791 and promoted by local solicitor John Lee, who may have taken as his model the contemporary scheme for Park Square and St Paul's church in Leeds. The long terrace of twelve houses on the N side of ST JOHN'S NORTH was completed first, in 1795, the building lease and a design by the otherwise unknown *John Thompson* of Wakefield imposing uniformity of elevation and materials. Three storeys in red brick with 22:5:20 bays, the slightly projecting centre pedimented, with a modillion cornice to match the eaves. The houses are three or five bays and have substantial Doric porches, mostly pedimented, some for paired doors. The three-bay returns at the W and E ends each have two two-storey canted bays. At the front at the E end No. 2 has, perversely, added a big circular Victorian oriel. The N and W sides of ST JOHN'S SQUARE received similar treatment to St John's North, to designs by *Charles Watson*. The thirteen houses on the N side were completed 1799–1803, the eight on the W, where the end as well as the centre houses are larger, in 1801–2. Unusually in the West Riding they all have areas for front access to their basements, like London's grander terraces, many with original railings. Both terraces have projecting pedimented centres and on the N range the hipped-roofed ends also project, forming pavilions. Lee kept ST JOHN'S HOUSE, the largest dwelling on the W, for himself. Its elegant seven-bay pedimented front faces S instead of into the square.

The scheme was not a financial success and the s side of the square was never developed; the other streets that formed part of the scheme to the s were built up slowly in the C19, mostly with large villas, such as those in MARGARET STREET, where several are now occupied by the Girls' High School. Among them additions for the school include the HARTLEY PAVIL-ION, s of St John's House, 1995 by *Philip Lees Associates*, with six gently arching Glulam beams supporting a metal-clad timber roof, and across Margaret Street, pre-school MUL-BERRY HOUSE, in glass, wood cladding and metal, sensitively scaled, by *HLM Architects*, 2005. Further s, on the w side No. 15 is a good villa of *c.* 1830, five bays in red brick with angle pilasters and a prostyle Ionic porch with pediment. In SANDY WALK, a narrow lane just s of it, are CLIFF HILL HOUSE, an Italianate villa of 1839–40 and CARLTON HOUSE, also *c.* 1840, three bays in brick, with a deeply recessed central bay, porch *in antis* with square stone columns.

To the E, at the foot of WENTWORTH STREET, is WENT-WORTH HOUSE, a large seven-bay house built 1802–3 with a Doric porch with segmental pediment (cf. Barstow Square and No. 136 Westgate above, pp. 709 and 711). Occupied by the Girls' High School since 1878, its large back garden has various additions including the ASSEMBLY HALL of 1927–8 by *W. Wrigley* in plain brick, Neo-Georgian with gable pediment. N of Wentworth House, is FORREST BUILDING by *HLM Architects* 2004, three storeys in red brick, wood cladding and render with large two-storey window at the NE corner for the art rooms.

s of Wentworth Street BOND STREET provides a link to Wood Street, laid out at the same time as Lee's development as one of the principal streets of the town but now with only a few three-storey brick houses of *c.* 1830 on the E side facing the buildings of Wakefield College (*see* Public Buildings). Opposite County Hall (*see* Public Buildings), the CORONATION GARDENS, re-landscaped in 2012 around the focus of the WAR MEMORIAL cenotaph of 1921, and facing them BOND TERRACE, a three-storey brick terrace of 1840–1 by *William Billinton* with a cast-iron balcony at first floor abutting the former Police Offices (*see* Public Buildings). Associated with the gardens a square has been formed with the fine bronze STATUE of Queen Victoria, 1904 by *F.J. Williamson*, formerly in the Bull Ring.

Behind County Hall on BURTON STREET is the former SAVINGS BANK, 1834 by *Charles Mountain*. Square two-storey block of three bays, like a villa. Grecian style, ashlar, the front framed by giant Ionic pilasters changing to three-quarter-columns either side of the entrance. For the Wakefield One council offices *see* p. 702.

Finally, returning to WOOD STREET, opposite the Town Hall (*see* Public Buildings) are VICTORIA CHAMBERS, of 1905 with two large Dutch gables at the second floor.

3. Kirkgate and Waterside

KIRKGATE, S of the Cathedral, was the start of the ancient route S to London, via the town's only bridge across the Calder until 1933. The upper part, which continues the line of Westgate, is now pedestrianized. A few of its C18 and C19 brick buildings survive on the N side, but the S side was comprehensively redeveloped in 1955–7, implementing a long-planned street widening. In anticipation, a few shops, such as Boots and Marks and Spencer, rebuilt in the 1930s on the new building line and lost only an extended single-storey frontage. Behind the shops is the RIDINGS SHOPPING CENTRE of 1980–3 by *Chapman Taylor Partners*. Taking advantage of the natural slope of the site it has shopping on three levels, all accessible from adjacent streets. The upper level is top-lit and natural light reaches the lower levels from glazing over the heptagonal space where the malls are linked vertically. From an entrance off CATHEDRAL WALK the centre weaves round behind the upper Kirkgate shops to end lower down in a shopping development of 1968–71. The long blank rear elevation, which also screens a car park, has, however, created a lifeless edge, despite worthy attempts to enliven its brickwork with details drawn from the architecture of C19 mills.

S of the shopping centre in GEORGE STREET, on the corner of Thornhill Street, are CROWTHER'S ALMSHOUSES by *William Shaw*, 1838–63. A row of eight tiny stone dwellings in Tudor Gothic style nestling under high, steeply pitched roofs with stovepipe chimneys. The gabled central bays have a boardroom on the first floor. Completion of the building's shell was delayed for many years owing to the terms of Caleb Crowther's will. On the opposite corner, large red brick premises with a domed lantern, built for wine and spirit merchants *c.* 1893. To the W the former Zion Congregational Church (*see* Religious Buildings) makes an impressive statement but much of this area was cleared post-war and replaced by a series of TOWER BLOCKS, the first of which were the eleven-storey CARR HOUSE FLATS of 1960–1. Of greater value is SOUTH PARADE, S of George Street. This was Wakefield's second essay in Georgian town planning (*see also* St John's Square, p. 713) and is still one of its best-kept secrets. This long brick terrace, facing S across private gardens, was planned by *William Lindley* in the early 1790s, but was built in a piecemeal fashion over more than three decades and is not continuous. In spite of this a harmony is established in the houses' similar proportions and details, all three storeys and of three or five bays. No. 6 is large and has a stone porch with Doric columns, No. 10 is five bays again and has an Ionic porch with fine Regency iron balcony above and evidence of balconies to the first-floor windows. Some fine interiors survive. No. 6 has oak wreaths in the hall plasterwork and No. 10 has anthemion details on a stone fireplace and a doorcase. A design for WEST PARADE produced by *Charles Watson* in 1804 was for

a grand terrace of eleven houses in 15:5:15 bays with central
pediment, but it was not realized. Only West Parade Methodist
Chapel (dem.) and the two houses below it were built. The
mews behind these, overlooking the chapel's burial ground on
Thornhill Street, has at the end a strikingly different office
extension of 1995. Five storeys in white render under a curvy
roof, the oversailing corner of the upper three storeys supported
on a large tapering green column.

E of Thornhill Street, in TRINITY CHURCH GATE, is a solitary surviving Georgian villa, facing the TRINITY MEDICAL
CENTRE, built in red brick c. 2000 and of industrial scale.
Two storeys, pitched roof with deep eaves. Overhanging
gables and tall glazed porches supported on slender concrete
columns. Further down THORNHILL STREET is the former
METHODIST PRIMARY SCHOOL (Wakefield Resource Centre)
founded by West Parade Chapel in 1846. Handsome single-
storey building in Heath stone by *John Whitworth*. Originally
for 400 children in two rooms. Large tripartite window at
the front under the pediment and three similar but plainer
windows on the returns. To the r. is a group of early–mid-C19
industrial buildings ranged round a courtyard entered from
CHARLOTTE STREET. Three storeys, in brick, with all the
same details as the plainer domestic buildings of the same
date. The four-bay range facing Thornhill Street has wide,
sixteen-pane sashes. Charlotte Street leads back to Kirkgate.
The only building of note on the way is the former METH-
ODIST NEW CONNEXION CHAPEL in Grove Road on the r.
By *William Hill* 1866, converted to four floors of flats in 2005.
Coarse Romanesque in red brick with stone dressings, its
square corner tower originally sported a little spire.

Now E to KIRKGATE, just below the junction with MARSH WAY,
the early 1970s dual carriageway that skirts the city centre to
the E. This stretch of Kirkgate has been much knocked about
and is now undergoing regeneration. N of the junction is
mostly mediocre post-war redevelopment, characterized by the
group of four TOWER BLOCKS of 1968–71, now brightly re-clad
and given little pitched roofs. S of George Street some of the
C18 and C19 development survives between vacant sites. Contemporary with Marsh Way is CHANTRY HOUSE, built c. 1973
as offices for West Riding County Council and now disused.
Four storeys in an H-shaped block with long middle range, on
pilotis. Cream brick ends with glazing and blue panels between.
Next to this, the WEST YORKSHIRE HISTORY CENTRE (*see*
Public Buildings). More post-war housing to the S, up to
KIRKGATE STATION (*see* Public Buildings), which was built
on the original site of Joseph Aspdin's Patent Portland Cement
works. Patented in 1824, his product covers the exterior of the
WAKEFIELD ARMS, c. 1830, which survives just outside the
station. PRIMROSE HOUSE, W of the pub, was the second
block of flats to change the city's skyline, in 1962–3, but the
rest of the housing in the Primrose Hill clearance area to the
NE is low-rise.

KIRKGATE continues s, passing under the railway, and crossing the Calder at WAKEFIELD BRIDGE (1933 by *Sir Owen Williams*), which succeeded the medieval Chantry Bridge (*see* Chantry Chapel, p. 695). E of the road in NAVIGATION YARD are two buildings associated with the Aire & Calder Navigation, which terminated here. The surprisingly modest early C19 stone-fronted building to the r. was the company's head office until 1850. One storey, the central entrance with Doric columns *in antis*. Pediment above and two sash windows each side. On the l. a much-altered two-storey C18 brick warehouse with a square tower with pyramidal roof in the middle, like a look-out tower. s of the river is the w end of the long island created by the Fall Ings Cut, opened in 1761 for the Calder & Hebble Navigation, to bypass the weir above Wakefield Bridge. Since 2007 this former industrial area has undergone extensive redevelopment for mixed uses. In TOOTAL STREET the HEPWORTH WAKEFIELD GALLERY, 2007–11, designed by *David Chipperfield Architects* for original plaster and other sculptures by *Barbara Hepworth*, who was born in Wakefield, and the city's Art Gallery collections. A large, powerful and sophisticated building with walls rising sheer from the water on the riverside, it is designed to be viewed in the round. Its boldly angular form is a subtly composed cluster of eleven differently sized two-storey spaces, each trapezoidal in plan, and each formed with smooth concrete walls cast *in situ*. On the exterior the concrete is coloured grey with a mauve tinge and the colour is continued across the diversely angled roofscape created by the spaces' monopitch roofs. These have skylights; the walls have only one or two windows, some are blank. Inside, the central space of the cluster contains a top-lit staircase rising to the ten first-floor galleries; the ground floor spaces are devoted to public and staff uses. The galleries have plain white interiors and partial ceilings that screen the light from above. Nearby the RUTLAND MILLS, a worsted mill of 1871, to be restored as a creative centre with offices, shops and flats by *Hawkins Brown* from 2017. Off BRIDGE STREET the riverside warehouses and mills include the CALDER & HEBBLE NAVIGATION WAREHOUSE of 1790, converted to flats 2007–8.

118

OUTER WAKEFIELD

LUPSET

ST GEORGE, Broadway. By *Nicholson & Rushton*, with *W. Wrigley*, 1934–6. Built for the large new housing estate with seating for 450. Architectural salvage provided a solution to inadequate funds – the walls are reclaimed stone from the old Millfield woollen mill at Horbury Junction and the Registry of Deeds in Kirkgate, the exposed roof beams are the mill's. The church's form, with nave and (ritual) N aisle of equal size, is reminiscent of the C17 St John's, Leeds and St Faith (*see* p. 707), though the resemblance was unintentional as a s aisle, as well as a tower, was originally planned. Six bays, the windows with segmental heads and mullions. Set on a slope, with meeting rooms in the basement storey. The interior, divided by an arcade of six round arches, has an unresolved duality only partly addressed by the reordering of 1996–8. This placed the main altar on the N wall but left a worship space in the original chancel. Highly coloured painted and gilded reredos, 1915. Earlier gabled brick church hall, 1928 by *W. Wrigley*.

LUPSET HALL, Horbury Road, now a golf clubhouse. Dated 1716 over the doorway, it was built for Richard Witton, brother-in-law of *Theophilus Shelton*, who almost certainly designed it for him. There are obvious similarities with Shelton's Tong Hall (*West Riding North*). Plain seven-bay brick house of two storeys, with slight two-bay projections. Stone quoins, architraves and blocking course. The centre bay is distinguished by the elegantly framed doorway, the two Ionic columns and segmental hood around it, and ashlar facing above.

THORNES

ST JAMES, Denby Dale Road. 1829–30 by *Samuel Sharp*. Plain but pleasing classical style in sandstone ashlar. Short square tower over W entrance bay, the upper stage octagonal with paired Doric pilasters at the angles, under a domed cap. Five bays long with false entrances in the first, the doors and tall Georgian windows all straight-headed. The interior is light and austerely elegant. W gallery on very thin cast-iron columns, and a square chancel, which was added for Mrs Milnes Gaskell after she gave *Anna Tierlink*'s copy of Guido Reni's Crucifixion as the altarpiece in 1844. The chancel has Corinthian pilasters in the angles and a handkerchief vault with fluted centrepiece. It is lit from concealed Diocletian windows on the N and s sides.

WAKEFIELD COLLEGE, Thornes Park, Horbury Road. On the elevated site of Thornes House, built 1779–81 for James Milnes by *John Carr* and published in *New Vitruvius Britannicus* 1802. It was used by Wakefield Grammar School from 1922 until the house burnt down in 1951. The separate stables were demolished later. Two half-hearted Neo-Georgian blocks in brick, added 1922–5 for the school, survive. The school was rebuilt 1955–6 as Thornes House Grammar and Technical School by *J.N. Sedgewick*, City Engineer. Three- and four-storey flat-roofed blocks in brick and concrete with white panels.

THORNES PARK, Denby Dale Road and Thornes Road. One of the city's great public assets, this large park incorporates Clarence Park, laid out 1893 by *Backhouse & Son* of York, and the grounds of Holmfield and Thornes House, added in 1919 and 1923 respectively. Very large picturesque half-timbered BAND-STAND of 1927 with hipped and gabled tiled roof. The stage, facing Lawfield Hill, is shell-shaped to project the sound. HOLMFIELD, a large Gothic stone mansion, now a restaurant in the park, built by Major Barker of Thornes Mills *c.* 1865 and enlarged in 1877. The decayed remains of the medieval front of the Chantry Chapel (*see* p. 695), formerly at Kettlethorpe Hall, Sandal Magna, were re-sited here in 2014.

In Clarence Park, the overgrown earthworks of a motte and bailey CASTLE, known as Lowe Hill, sculpted out of the top of a short and narrow natural ridge. The motte was surrounded by a ditch and by a counterscarp bank, best seen on the N and W. A causeway on the NE gave access to and from a sub-rectangular bailey. The platform of a second bailey is in line to the NE. A third shelf, beyond, seems to be a product of the terraced paths that encircle the hill. This landscaping also levelled the banks that would have enclosed the baileys.

Substantial former VICARAGE in St James's Court. Stone, in Tudor Gothic style, 1840.

COTTON HORNE ALMSHOUSES, Horne Street, 1901 by *George Richardson*. Founded in 1647 and moved here from the original site in Almshouse Lane. Brick, seventeen bays, with gables over the ends and centre. The first-floor houses are set back behind an access balcony.

MAJOR BARKER'S ALMSHOUSES, Holmfield Avenue, 1887. A small single-storey row in stone with shaped gables at the ends.

WALES 4080

ST JOHN THE BAPTIST. Norman church of nave and chancel with plain Perp W tower. Reduced to the status of a N aisle/ chapel by the addition of a large new nave with S aisle by *C. Hodgson Fowler*, 1896–7. Chancel and S vestries by *Wood & Oakley*, 1933. C12 S doorway re-set within new S porch. One order of colonnettes with single-scallop capitals. Tympanum, its base broken by a later door, has chequer pattern under a lozenge band. Voussoirs with beakhead. Norman chancel arch. Primitive capitals, one pair with small volutes, the other with small heads instead of outer volutes. Arch with one roll moulding and one band of chevron. C15 nave roof. PULPIT with back-board, 1727. – STAINED GLASS. Three late C15/early C16 donor panels with kneeling female figures. – Chancel E window by *Francis Spear*, 1960. – MONUMENT. Sir Thomas Hewitt †1726 and wife Dame Francis Hewitt †1756. Large finely lettered arched marble tablet.

WALES COURT, ⅔ m. N. Complex house (now subdivided) with 1629 datestone. Late C18 alterations, further altered and extended *c.* 1870. Two-storey bay windows with distinctive copper spires.

KIVETON HALL, 1⅜ m. ENE, is an early C19 house on the site of KIVETON PARK, the magnificent brick house built 1698–1704 by Thomas Osborne, 1st Duke of Leeds, published in *Vitruvius Brittanicus IV* in 1739 and demolished *c.* 1812. Its

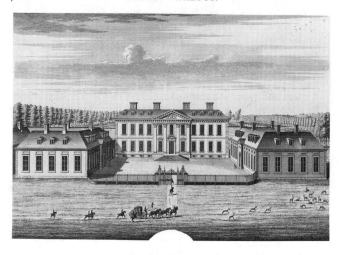

Wales, Kiveton Hall.
Engraving by W.H. Toms, 1739

authorship is unknown.* Surviving fragments include the
gatepiers reused for the present house and two quoined brick
panels with paired ashlar *œils de bœuf* (blind) in end walls of
former outbuildings at Kiveton Hall Farm.

KIVETON PARK COLLIERY, ¾ m. E. Opened in 1866, closed in
1994 and now re-landscaped as a country park. By the NW
entrance on Colliery Road, the former OFFICES of 1872–5 are
in an unlikely picturesque Gothic Revival style with clock
turret. The pithead baths, 1938, were demolished in 2013.

BEDGREAVE MILLS (Rother Valley Country Park Visitor
Centre), 1½ m. W. Former water-powered corn mills, converted 1983. OLD MILL is early C17 but unusually of medieval
form, single-cell. NEW MILL is *c.* 1768. Two storeys. Attached
brick engine house *c.* 1886. The park has been created from a
former opencast colliery.

WALTON

WALTON HALL (Waterton Park Hotel). 1767–8, on the site of a
C14 fortified house, its setting on a small island in a lake
delightfully picturesque. Eight bays, two-and a-half storeys.
Giant Tuscan pilasters with banded rustication at the angles
and defining the four centre bays, 1–2–1. Shallow pediment

---

*An unexecuted plan by *Talman*, *c.* 1698, exists. *John Fitch* was executant surveyor,
Daniel Brand the builder. Additions by *James Gibbs*, 1741, were unexecuted.

above with coat of arms and the Watertons' motto. One-storey, Tuscan four-column porch, early C19. Oak panelling and Jacobean overmantel in the entrance hall, probably from a previous house.

The island is reached by an extremely pretty, elegantly curved, cast-iron FOOTBRIDGE, *c.* 1800. Next to this the remains of the medieval WATER GATE. Near the house a SUNDIAL by *Charles Boulby*, 1813. Polyhedron with twenty triangular faces whose gnomons indicate times around the world. In 1821–6 Charles Waterton built a WALL around the park, some 3 m. long, excluding hunters and foxes from his bird sanctuary. Long stretches remain.

WALTON MANOR (formerly Walton House), Shay Lane. Five bays. Pedimented centre with four giant engaged Ionic columns. Entrance flanked by tripartite sashes.

WARLEY

0020

ST JOHN, on the steep hillside at Cote Hill, ½ m. E of the village. By *W. Swinden Barber*, 1877–8. Plain E.E. style with lancets in twos and threes. Prominent SW tower in angle of nave and aisle. Heavily buttressed lower stage, corbelled parapet, crocketed pinnacles. Ashlar interior has tall, full-width chancel arch and circular piers to four-bay arcade. – STAINED GLASS. E window by *Clayton & Bell*, 1878. – Two aisle windows by *Powell & Sons*, 1897, 1900. – W window by *E.R. Frampton*, 1896. Chancel N by *W.F. Dixon*, 1887.

In the VILLAGE, at the head of a little square, is the former CONGREGATIONAL CHURCH (Chantry House), rebuilt 1845–6 in Tudor Gothic style, externally much like Anglican churches of a decade or two earlier but without a W tower. S of this WARLEY GRANGE, a C17 linear, hearth-passage house with long nine-light windows to housebody and original service or shop end. Housebody window extended by two-light fire window beyond king mullion, the fire-hood replaced in 1711 by dated fireplace. Below, CLIFF HILL is probably mid Georgian, with early C19 additions. Five-bay S front with Doric porch and rusticated pilaster quoins. Plain ashlar window surrounds. Eleven-bay r. return. Good gate lodge.

Beyond the square, in Stock Lane, the former INSTITUTE AND CLUB by *J.F. Walsh*, 1904, in attractive Pennine Vernacular revival style. Given by Arthur McCrea of Warley House,[*] damask manufacturer, for whom *Walsh* built EDGEHOLME, almost opposite, in similar style in 1910. STOCK LANE HOUSE, ⅓ m. up the lane, looks early C19 but incorporates a two-storey porch of 1633, remarkable for the opposed semicircles in its lintel as at Wood Lane Hall, Sowerby (q.v.).

[*]This was of 1769, dem. 1964.

HOYLE HOUSE, Water Hill Lane, ½ m. SSW of the village. Built *c.* 1617 for John Ramsden, probably by his relatives the Akroyds. Three surviving gabled bays each with a five-light transomed ground-floor window. Ram's-head gutter spout between the gables of the two parlour bays. W service end rebuilt 1885 in keeping.

At FOUR LANES END, ½ m. NW of the village, a C19 crenellated gateway and crowstepped-gabled LODGE to THE HOLLINS off Raw End Road. *c.* 1810 with later C19 alterations and additions, including battlements and turrets and round tower as porch. Extensions by *G.F. Armitage* 1896. Long castellated front to former STABLES. (Early C19 bath house in garden.) HAIGH HOUSE, 300 yds E, 1631, has three-room linear plan and two-storey porch.

WARMSWORTH

5000

Small limestone village, ½ m. SW of the site of the Norman church and its C19 successor (dem.), and almost as far W of the C20 church now beyond the A1(M).

ST PETER. 1939–42 by *C.M. Cooper*, with *Grantham, Brundell & Farran*, engineers, to ideas of the then rector. Known as 'The White Church' its somewhat Hispano-Californian flavour makes a striking and exotic statement among the surrounding housing estates. White render; green pantiles to the big nave roof, the octagonal dome over the towering chancel and the semi-dome of the apse. Tall, white and starkly elegant interior. – SCULPTURE (N chapel) Excavated from the old church site: part of late C12(?) grave cover, fragment of a Norman(?) tympanum (cf. Braithwell), free-standing medieval piscina and floriated cross-slab. – MONUMENT. John Battie II †1724. Good scrolled cartouche with drapery enveloping cherubs.

WARMSWORTH HALL (hotel). Rebuilt *c.* 1702 by John Battie II, possibly incorporating part of a Tudor house which was enlarged *c.* 1670. Its H-plan, 2:3:2 bays, gives credence to this. Limestone rubble, partly rendered, its exterior motifs all typical of the rebuilding date: ashlar quoins, corniced first-floor band, hipped roof and gabled dormers. The centre bay has pilaster-strips with banded rustication and a big open segmental pediment; ashlar attic above with oval window and balustrade. Doorway with consoled pediment, now a window. The Doric porch to the entrance in the W wing is probably part of the early C19 alterations by *William Hurst*. (Good C18 wooden staircase with turned balusters.)

The attractive village has a regular street pattern with the Hall at its centre. This and the distance from the old church indicate a planned, possibly medieval, settlement. The BELL-TOWER, near the Hall's E gateway, is the church belfry, remarkable in being so far detached. Probably C16, possibly earlier. Square base with tall octagonal upper stage, restored arcaded timber cupola.

FRIENDS' MEETING HOUSE (former), Quaker Lane. Built by *William Aldam*, 1706. Simple three-bay front with central doorway. Flanking sashes were originally cross-windows.

CEMETERY, ½ m. NNE of the village. The GATES are mid-C19, formerly at the entrance to the park of Sprotbrough Hall.

WATH-UPON-DEARNE   *4000*

A small town, granted a market charter in 1312. Its importance increased with industrial development that followed the completion of the Dearne and Dove Canal in 1804, the opening of railway lines in 1840, 1849 and 1902, and large-scale mining from the 1870s. The canal was infilled in 1961 and the railways closed with the collieries in the 1980s. A nature reserve and lakes, a college, offices and vast retail distribution centres are their successors.

ALL SAINTS, Church Street. A fine, large church with a tall tower with spire and a transeptal N chapel with unusual W aisle. Nave N wall and two westernmost bays of chancel N wall have stonework of late Anglo-Saxon or Overlap date, both with mid-C12 arcades of the same design. Nave arcade of three bays. Circular piers, many-scalloped capitals and cross-shaped abaci. The round arches have a single step. High blocked doorway with square head at the E end, perhaps to an early rood loft. The original N chapel was probably an extension of the narrow aisle, with a lean-to roof – see the corbel heads. Norman also the plain W tower up to the blocked twin bell-openings. The tower arch seems a little later than the arcades and certainly later than the bell-openings. It has a double-chamfered pointed arch on semicircular responds with moulded capitals.

Then follows some C13 work. First the extended chancel with lancet and Y-traceried windows, then the larger N chapel of *c.* 1295. Its aisle has a quatrefoil pier with octagonal abacus. Keeled N respond, the square abacus with a little nailhead. Early C14 S aisle arcade has three arches with standard elements and a very odd half-round arch at the W end which has not been explained. Embattled S porch with typical double-quadrant moulding at its entrance. Stone roof on very heavy chamfered transverse ribs. Perp the tower top, with transomed two-light bell-openings and small recessed stone spire, and the battlemented clerestory. Excellent nave roof with carved bosses *c.* 1540. Considered restoration by *Hadfield & Son* 1866–71, the commission won in competition. S organ chamber 1868, enlarged 1920. Chancel restored by *Arthur Martin*, brother of the vicar (and botanist) W. Keble Martin, 1919–21 after a fire.

FITTINGS. REREDOS. 1871. Designed by *Charles Hadfield*, carved in Caen stone by *Thomas Earp*, though the central panel possibly by *Phyffers*; extended 1899. – PISCINA. In E respond of N chapel arcade, trefoil-headed. – Small FONT. 1726. Baluster-shaped bowl. Rim has Greek palindrome (NIPSONANOMHM A MHMONANOPSIN Wash my sins and not my face only). Charming wooden cover with dove 1839. – BENCH-ENDS. N chapel. Straight-topped with shields. Made for John Savile 1576, no doubt for his family pew. – Three CHESTS; one, probably C14, has iron straps with simple ornament. – Pair of brass CHANDELIERS in nave, 1810. – STAINED GLASS. E window (war memorial) by *Powell & Sons*, 1921. Chancel N: two windows with three small scenes surviving from former E window by *Wailes*, 1851. Two S aisle windows by *Lavers, Barraud & Westlake*, with medallions designed by *J. F. Bentley*, 1872. S aisle W window and three N aisle windows by *Clayton & Bell*, 1892. N chapel: three E windows by *Clayton & Bell*, 1893; N window by *Crookes* of Sheffield, 1854. – MONUMENTS. Several reused medieval cross-slabs, e.g. in N aisle wall. – George Ellis †1712, erected 1728. Elaborate cartouche with draped shield, cherubs' heads and scrolls. Skull spouting batwings at foot. – Thomas Tuke †1810. Wall monument with urn and coat of arms in coloured marbles by *Watson*, Bakewell. – Other C19 monuments include John Johnson †1862, by *Edwin Smith*.

VICARAGE (former), 150 yds NW. By *Arthur Martin*, 1910. Jacobean revival, reusing the foundations of *Lindley & Watson*'s 1793 vicarage.

ST JOSEPH (R.C.), Carr Road. By *Hadfield & Son*, 1878–9. Not large. Narrow five-bay nave and chancel under one roof, the division marked by an elaborate stone bell-turret with spire. Late C15 tracery. Very rich stone, marble and alabaster ALTAR and REREDOS designed by *Charles Hadfield*, 1886. – STAINED GLASS. Chancel E, S and N windows by *Lavers, Barraud & Westlake*, 1878. Nave N: easternmost by *E. R. Frampton*, 1885; third from E by *Lavers & Westlake*, 1904.

TRINITY METHODIST CHURCH, Church Street, SE of All Saints. 1893–4. Gothic. Large, with imposing three-stage corner tower. Good galleried interior, hardly altered. Adjacent, the former WESLEYAN CHAPEL, 1810–11. Pedimented three-bay front. Round-arched windows, the four each side originally full-height.

LOCK-UP (now a house), 150 yds W of All Saints in Thornhill Place. Early C19. Two windowless cells underneath heated constable's room, the room reached by attached rear staircase with external door.

WATH HALL. Immediately E of All Saints. 1770. Rendered, with decorative stone parapet and other C19 alterations. It became the Town Hall in 1891. Ionic porch. Entrance hall has Ionic screen to stone staircase under ornate plaster ceiling.

MAUSOLEUM, ½ m. S. 1834 for John Payne, a Quaker. Built in the grounds of his house, Newhill Hall (1785, dem. 1950s). Square, with chamfered quoins, cornice and stepped ashlar roof. On each side an arched recess with alternating chamfered voussoirs.

WENTBRIDGE

4010

A small former coaching village in a picturesque wooded valley presenting the steepest inclines on the Great North Road, now bypassed by the elegant pre-stressed concrete road VIADUCT of 1959–61, designed by *F. A. Sims*, engineer, of West Riding County Council. A 470-ft (142-metre) continuous beam carries the A1 high above the Went on two pairs of slightly tapering raking legs. 113

ST JOHN, Jackson Lane. By *A.W. Blomfield*, 1878. Small, upright, in C12 northern French style. Compact cruciform plan. Rock-faced, with red tiled roofs, the crossing tower's pyramidal top prominent against its woodland backdrop. Narrow three-bay nave with apsed chancel, the apse rib-vaulted like the crossing. – STAINED GLASS. By *Burlison & Grylls*, *c*. 1878–*c*. 1902.

WENTWORTH

3090

HOLY TRINITY. By *J. L. Pearson*. Designed 1866–72, built 1872–7. A very fine, sensitive and scholarly piece of Gothic Revival. Erected in memory of Charles and Mary Wentworth-Fitzwilliam, the 5th Earl and Countess Fitzwilliam, by their children, who could not have spent their money more judiciously. It cost some £25,000. High clerestoried nave, aisles, N porch, chancel, transepts and crossing, orientated SE–NW. The crossing tower with broach spire rising to 183 ft (56 metres) is a striking local landmark. The style is late C13 with Geometrical tracery. The building is rib-vaulted in stone throughout, giving the interior an impressive nobility. Pearson was the only architect at the time who so consistently insisted on vaulting. The nave has four-bay arcades and a blind half-bay w of the porch. Compound piers with richly moulded arches. Attached shafts rise between the arches to the springing of the vaults. Quatrefoil panels below three-light clerestory windows that are set within arches with dogtooth. More dog-tooth on the chancel and crossing arches. The crossing has an octopartite vault above a gallery of two twin arches on each side. – Fine MARBLE PAVING in the chancel. – STAINED GLASS. (Ritual) E window by *Clayton & Bell*, 1888. – w window 91 in memory of the 6th Earl Fitzwilliam by *Powell & Sons*, 1902. – s transept E window by *Clayton & Bell*, 1925. – N aisle: second from E by *Christopher Webb*, 1957; third designed by *G. G. Pace*, executed by *Harry Harvey*, 1968; fourth by *Harvey* 1972; fifth by *Sharon Troop*, c. 2004. The last three in memory of Agents to the Fitzwilliam Estate. – MONUMENTS. s transept. Wentworth-Fitzwilliam family C19 and C20. Carved stone frame with eight large brass panels under cusped heads. – A. H. Douglas †1936. White marble tablet by *Feodora Gleichen* (†1922). Without inscription, it incongruously depicts an elderly lady attended by angels.

OLD HOLY TRINITY (Churches Conservation Trust), 150 yds N. A poignant ruin except for the Wentworth Chapel, which comprises the chancel and N chapel of the medieval church. The w tower appears mostly to date from a rebuilding in the 1490s. It is unbuttressed, and the arch towards the nave with its two sunk quadrant mouldings seems Dec. The blunt top was left when the battlemented upper stage was removed in the C20. The nave was remodelled in 1684 by the 2nd Earl of Strafford, who spent £700 on the church. Only the classical s front with central projecting doorway remains. The projection has a pediment on Ionic pilasters. The four windows are tall and arched in oblong frames. Architraved square panels above once displayed heraldic symbols. The whole façade, fantastically decayed in its details, forms a theatrical Renaissance set-piece.

Dismantling of the old church followed an aborted scheme for restoration by *Pearson* and the subsequent completion of the new church. In 1878 the two-bay E end was converted to a mortuary chapel by *William Dickie* of Wentworth. Externally this looks rather earlier C17. Twin E gables, with crude pointed lights to tall three-light windows. Cavetto-moulded mullions. The other windows, though similar, have round-arched lights. The new w wall's windows (partly blocked) were probably salvaged from the N aisle. Panels like those of the nave above the E and s windows, their heraldic sculpture surviving. Interior has arcade of two bays with short octagonal pier. Double-chamfered arches. – COMMUNION RAIL with slim turned balusters and semicircular projection in the middle. – CHANCEL PANELLING. Some of c. 1684 with the monogram of the 2nd Earl of Strafford's wife, Lady Henrietta Maria Stanley, and acanthus foliage. – SCULPTURE. Vestry. Three large C12 scalloped half-capitals from Monk Bretton Priory (q.v.). Among stonework bought after the Dissolution by Thomas Wentworth and left in his will, 1546, for building an aisle. – Part of a panel with arcade of intersecting round arches and diaper with triangles. Probably from a C12 grave cover. – PAINTED GLASS. By *Henry Gyles* of York, 1685–95. Heraldic, with flamboyant monograms of the 2nd Countess of Strafford.

Numerous MONUMENTS include several impressive C16 and C17 Wentworth family memorials. – N chapel. C13 ledger slab with crossbow. Thought to be one of only three archers' memorials in existence. – Alabaster figures of a Gascoigne and his wife *c.* 1460. Only her head and shoulders remain. Though badly mutilated they are comparable with the fine effigies on contemporary monuments at Wadworth (q.v.) and Harewood (*West Riding North*). Two weepers from the tomb-chest, knights under crocketed ogee arches, are on the chancel s wall. The figures' identities are uncertain but Sir William Gascoigne †*c.* 1461–5 and his wife, Margaret Clarell, are strong possibilities.* – Thomas Wentworth †1588 and his wife, Margaret Gascoigne, †1593. Two excellent alabaster effigies on a simple tomb-chest with Doric columns. Skirted halves of two daughter weepers survive. – William Wentworth, 2nd Earl of Strafford, †1695 and his wife †1685. Erected by him in 1689, repeating the by then out-of-date compositional scheme of his grandparents' wall monument (*see* below). Large kneeling figures facing each other, framed by drapery. Big garlands in the Gibbons style round the inscription, a tender paean of praise to his wife written by the Earl himself. – Chancel. Sir William Wentworth †1614 and his wife, Anne, †1611. Erected in 1613. Alabaster, partly painted. Two kneeling figures facing each other in the usual way, under round arches within plain corniced frame. The kneeling children small in the 'predella', except for a larger one in the middle. This is Thomas Wentworth, later 1st Earl of Strafford. The monument is attributed by Mrs Esdaile to *Nicholas Johnson*. – Thomas Wentworth, 1st Earl of Strafford, †1641. Made at about the same time as his son's monument. Kneeling figure and surround very good. Arched frame with close, finely carved garland. Trophies in the spandrels of the arch. Two outer Composite columns carry a broken segmental pediment on which are two putti. – Sir William Rokeby †1665 and wife Frances, erected 1676. Alabaster frame with broken cornice, arms and helmet.

p. 27

VAULT. Made for the Fitzwilliam family in 1825, used 1834–79. Cast-iron railings enclose a large stone slab cover in the churchyard. Entered via steps from the N chapel vestry and an ashlar-lined passage. – Well-preserved CHURCHYARD with good carved headstones, some to servants and tenants of the estate.

WENTWORTH WOODHOUSE

Wentworth Woodhouse is not just one of Yorkshire's but one of England's greatest and most remarkable houses. Its ambitious Palladian E façade, extending 606 ft (185 metres), is celebrated for being the longest front of any English country house and its magnificent state rooms were intended for royalty. Just as remarkable as its size and grandeur is the contrasting architectural

*The Clarells, of Aldwarke (5 m. SE), were traditionally buried at the Friary at Tickhill (q.v.) and the battered state of these remains would be consistent with their rescue from there after the Dissolution.

character of its two fronts: the Baroque W front of *c.* 1724–1735 is gay and profusely decorated; the E front begun *c.* 1731 is staid, reserved and correct. Yet they were both designed and built for the same man, Thomas Watson-Wentworth, created Baron Malton in 1728, Earl of Malton in 1734 and Marquess of Rockingham in 1746. A devout Protestant and passionate supporter of the Hanoverian succession, he was the son of Thomas Watson-Wentworth, who was a grandson of Sir Thomas Wentworth, later 1st Earl of Strafford, who was executed in 1641. Strafford had rebuilt the house at Wentworth *c.* 1630 and it was this that Watson-Wentworth lived in from 1716 and inherited in 1723. The inception of his rebuilding scheme is shrouded in mystery, but an undated plan of the central part, from before 1724 and possibly several years earlier, shows that he intended to build it largely on the scale and in the form as completed, incorporating parts of the C17 house on the W side.

The name of Watson-Wentworth's first architect is unknown and the subject of much speculation. The style of the W façade is not like anything else in England and although English motifs of a Vanbrughian kind are not absent (Venetian windows, giant pilasters from ground-floor level), and some details are drawn from Rossi's *Studio di Architettura Civile*, published in 1702, there are also motifs which point more specifically to Austria and Bohemia.★ Among Yorkshire architects the similarities to other houses such as Beningbrough Hall suggest architects such as *William Wakefield*, or *William Thornton* or his son *Robert*.

The architect, or rather architects, of the E range are known. An engraving of the design by *Ralph Tunnicliffe* for the E front was published between 1728 and 1734. It is clearly derived from Colen Campbell's design for Wanstead House, Essex, the first great Palladian mansion of the C18 in England, as published in *Vitruvius Britannicus* in 1715. In 1734 Sir Thomas Robinson reported that the designs were to be submitted to Lord Burlington, high priest of English Palladianism, and after Tunnicliffe died in 1736 *Henry Flitcroft*, who was so obviously Lord Burlington's man that he was nicknamed Burlington's Harry, succeeded him as architect. Flitcroft made slight adjustments to the design of the central block, which was largely complete, and altered the design of the wings, but his most significant work at Wentworth is the interiors, for which he brought in some of the best craftsmen available. The interiors were unfinished when the 1st Marquess died in 1750, and work proceeded slowly under his son, the 2nd Marquess, the Marble Saloon not being fully complete even in 1772, when Walpole wrote about it. Rockingham, whose passions were politics and the turf, and who was Prime Minister

★To Pevsner 'the closest parallel is K.I. Dientzenhofer's Villa America of *c.* 1720 at Prague, the doorway especially, with its decorated pilasters set diagonally, and the window pediments point in that direction.' Should any significance be attached to Watson-Wentworth's patronage of a Bohemian Protestant refugee, John Pertak, for whom he procured the curacy of Bolsterstone chapel in 1710?

when he died in 1782, employed *John Carr* as his architect, as did his nephew and successor, the 4th Earl Fitzwilliam. After Carr's death in 1807 *Charles Watson* and then *J. P. Pritchett* and his sons served as estate architects, but the house remains essentially c18 with interiors of the highest quality.

Since the mid c20 the house's fortunes have been less than happy. After army use in the Second World War, the E side of the house was leased to the West Riding County Council as Lady Mabel Teacher Training College, later becoming part of Sheffield Polytechnic until closing in 1986. After the early death of the 8th Earl Fitzwilliam in 1948, the entail that kept house and heirlooms together was broken; following the death of the 10th Earl in 1979 the title became extinct and ownership of the house and its contents was separated. Paintings, furniture and sculpture associated with the family and often with specific rooms have gone, many being sold in 1948 and after 1979, with some going to public collections, others abroad. The house itself was sold in 1988 and again in 1999. At the time of writing, the Wentworth Woodhouse Preservation Trust have purchased the house to secure its future and allow its splendours to be universally appreciated and enjoyed.

EXTERIOR. Of Strafford's house of *c.* 1630 there is little to be seen. The most impressive survival is the ambitious Mannerist SOUTH GATEWAY in the screen wall of the S court. It has been ascribed to *Inigo Jones* but has obviously nothing to do with him. With its alternating blocked pilasters, broken pediment and heavy scrolly decoration it is an almost exact copy of the Doric archway in Dietterlin's *Architectura* published in 1598. In the inner courtyard between the W and E ranges there is a doorway in the altered stone W wall and another in the S wall, both no longer Jacobean in their details. There is a window between them, and one window on the first floor of the S range, facing S; these also are no longer of the many-mullioned Jacobean type. In the grounds, another c17 gateway is reused in the Bear Pit (*see* p. 737).

The exuberant but puzzling W front of 1724–34 is of brick with generous stone dressings and profuse decoration. Two storeys with semi-basement, nine bays wide. One-storey projecting wings. The centre is entirely stone-faced. Four giant Corinthian pilasters rising from the rusticated basement, the two middle ones carrying a broken pediment, surmounted by a statue. The pilasters are fluted and have at the foot pretty, leafy branches in the jambs. Doorway in a slightly concave recess with fluted pilasters in the curve and outer pilasters with garlands hanging down. These outer pilasters are set diagonally, one of the decidedly un-English motifs that suggest some European, or more specifically Bohemian, influence. A boldly carved macaw on the door lintel. The ground-floor windows have pediments of a fanciful shape, again more Continental than Vanbrughian Baroque; the first-floor windows are plain.

Central Venetian window on the first floor, the scrolly surround of the armorial shield above cutting into it. The heraldry, of Thomas Watson-Wentworth, makes a date between 1725 and 1728 certain. Lively surrounds and especially keystones of the windows in the wings. At the w end of the wings apses with curved Venetian windows, the staircase to the Gallery window added in 1793. To the l. of the l. wing three more plain bays of one storey, with the N service ranges set back beyond; to the r. of the r. wing the same. This s end forms a SW wing, which, owing to the fall of the ground, is two-storeyed. Three-bay s front with a doorway, E front of eight bays facing into the s court. This block has rainwater heads with the date 1743.

Work on the much larger and grander E range was well underway by 1734, when the w side was complete, the wings having been begun in 1730 and the central block by 1733. It was substantially finished when the 1st Marquess died in 1750, even though the interiors of the principal apartments were not and the Marble Saloon was not completed for more than two decades. The ashlar E front consists of a centre block of nineteen bays, with lower eleven-bay wings set back and connected by convex quadrants to higher, square angle pavilions with domed roofs and lanterns. The centre is clearly derived from Wanstead: rusticated ground floor, *piano nobile* and, in addition, in the nine-bay centre of the centre, another half-storey. The centre of this nine-bay centre has a portico of six giant Corinthian columns and a pediment. The portico rises on the *piano nobile* level and is accessible by two flights of stairs, from the l. and r. The ceiling of the portico is coffered. The *piano nobile* windows have alternating triangular and segmental pediments, but behind the portico the pediments are broken and originally carried busts. The centre doorway behind the portico has a swan-neck pediment on demi-columns. The main pediment has a coat of arms carved in 1740 in the tympanum, and a statue on top. Balustraded parapets with statues and urns.

The wings were originally only one-and-a-half storeys high and had plain broad five-bay pediments. They were heightened with another low storey by *John Carr* in 1782–4. He was responsible for the giant Doric columns and the three-bay pediments. The height of the quadrants was also raised. The angle pavilions however are original. Their lower windows and those of the quadrants have Gibbs surrounds.

The whole of this majestic if not imaginative E front screens the complex and irregular parts behind. They are of brick with stone dressings and except for the central part with C17 origins are extensive N SERVICE BUILDINGS around courtyards. The s wing has to its rear only a corridor and a staircase in a semicircular projection added by *Carr*. The CHAPEL, built in 1733–6, sits in the NE angle of the s court. Three bays, with s windows in two tiers, and a Venetian w window. The central courtyard, half-filled with the great blind drum of *Carr*'s staircase of 1801–6 has the Long Gallery, built in 1741–3, along its

N side. The Gallery's windows, on its N side, look into Basin Court. N again is the service court, arcaded all round and linked to the outer N court, which has an octagonal GAME LARDER by *Pritchett & Sons*, 1858, and a former FIVES COURT built in 1869 for the 6th Earl's Eton-educated sons.

INTERIOR. The interiors of Wentworth Woodhouse are of a quite exceptional value. They represent, with a few exceptions, the style of no more than one generation, but they represent it in a variety of shades, from the Viennese or Venetian gaiety of the West Entrance Hall, to the Palladian purity of the Grand Saloon. Between these two extremes there is some Rococo and much of Flitcroft's ornate Venetian style at its most splendid. A suite like that along the E front from the Whistlejacket Room at the S to the Library at the N end is not easily matched anywhere in England.

The usual entrance is on the ground floor in the middle of the E front into the PILLARED HALL. Five-aisled, low, with Tuscan columns. Niches with classical STATUES. To the S of the hall Flitcroft's suite of four family rooms completed 1735–8, with excellent doorcases and plaster ceilings and carved chimneypieces that all have overmantels with paintings of the 1st Marquess's children by *Mercier*. The PAINTED DRAWING ROOM has arabesque wall paintings, on canvas, depicting the five senses, attributed to *Andien de Clermont*, and an exceedingly fine chimneypiece with pedimented overmantel. The LOW DRAWING ROOM, originally a dining room, has an apsed W end with exquisitely carved festoons of fruit and flowers above two side niches. W of these rooms is a corridor with oak panelling of 1902–6 and a doorway into the CHAPEL. Oak architrave to the big Venetian window and oak fittings. Good set of PAINTINGS of Christ and the Apostles, in *Rubens*'s style, c. 1789. E gallery on fluted Ionic columns. The corridor's N doorway leads back into the Pillared Hall close to the beautiful top-lit STAIRCASE placed in a semicircular wall with niches for statues. It was added by *Carr* in 1801–6 and has plasterwork by *Ely Crabtree*. The staircase with its honeysuckle railing starts in one flight and then turns back in two following the apsidal curve of the wall. At the top of the staircase the magnificent MARBLE SALOON, the principal room of the house. This is 60 ft (18 metres) square and 40 ft (12 metres) high and has an upper gallery or balcony exactly on the pattern of Inigo Jones's Queen's House at Greenwich. Below the gallery attached Ionic columns, on the gallery-level Corinthian pilasters, of Siena scagliola by *Charles Clerici*. Restrained plaster ceiling, by *Joseph Rose*, in the Inigo Jones tradition: circular centre, surrounded by oblong and square panels. The same pattern is repeated in the inlaid marble floor which was added by the 5th Earl in 1856. The walls are marbled in different colours and have eight niches with statues. They were made for Lord Milton in Rome in 1749–50: Venus, by *G.B. Maini*; Flora and Germanicus, both by *Filippo della Valle*; Antinous, by *Bartolomeo Cavaceppi*; Apollo and the Clapping Faun, by

53

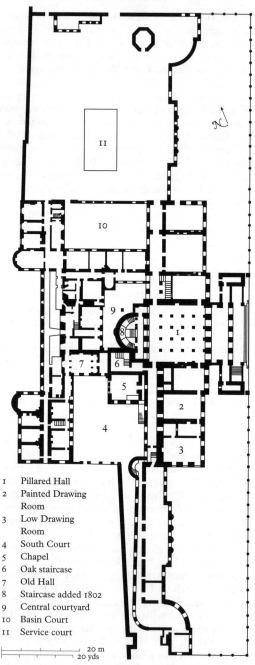

1   Pillared Hall
2   Painted Drawing
    Room
3   Low Drawing
    Room
4   South Court
5   Chapel
6   Oak staircase
7   Old Hall
8   Staircase added 1802
9   Central courtyard
10 Basin Court
11 Service court

Wentworth Woodhouse.
Ground-floor plan

Simon Vierpyl; the Medici Venus and a Faun, by *Joseph Wilton*. The panels above the niches were designed by *James Stuart*. The large reliefs above the fireplaces however were inserted as late as *c.* 1821 and are by *John Gibson*.

The state rooms N and S of the Saloon are in Flitcroft's grandest Kentian manner. The plasterwork is again by *Rose*, and much of the rich carving of doorcases etc. is by *Christopher Richardson* of Doncaster. To the S first the ANTE-ROOM or Supping Room. The plasterwork of the ceiling is here again divided in the Jones fashion, but the outer panels are filled with crisp decoration. Chimneypiece with two griffins, probably one of the several designed by *James Stuart* and made by *John Horobin* in 1763. Second the VAN DYCK ROOM or State Drawing Room. It has a gorgeous ceiling with heavily coffered coving and an oval middle panel. Frieze with flowers and fruit. Rich chimneypiece with caryatids to front and in profile, probably another of those by *James Stuart* and *John Horobin*. Overmantel with circular centre panel formerly framing van Dyck's portrait of Archbishop Laud. Finally the opulent WHISTLE-JACKET ROOM, so called after *Stubbs*'s portrait of Whistlejacket, the 2nd Marquess of Rockingham's most famous horse.* It was originally the Great Dining Room. Sumptuous gilded plasterwork, the ceiling with decorated panels round the polygonal centre, the elegant wall panels with luxuriant foliage around medallions with classical heads. Two panels, with swan-neck pediments, for paintings. Chimneypiece with an elaborate overmantel with a scrolly open pediment on Corinthian columns. N of the Saloon is an ANTE-ROOM, later the STATU-ARY ROOM. Wall with classical reliefs. Delicate fireplace in the Adam style by *John Fisher Sen.* 1783. Plaster ceiling of the reticent type of the Saloon. Scagliola floor. The next room is the STATE DINING ROOM (originally Grand Drawing Room). This has richer stucco decoration, not only in the ceiling but also in the wall panels and picture surrounds, which are like those in the Whistlejacket Room. After this, at the NE and NW corners of the E range the LIBRARIES, altered from a State Dressing Room and State Bedroom between 1801 and 1828. The first library has a splendid coved and coffered ceiling with a large oval centre panel. Griffins in the spandrels. The *enfilade* of doors from the Saloon is continued by a sham door in the N wall, i.e. the outer N wall of the centre block. Both libraries have fireplaces by *John Fisher Sen.*, made in 1768.

As one returns from here along a corridor towards the Saloon, one reaches a subsidiary staircase, immediately N of the semicircular staircase. It was one of the two principal staircases before *Carr* created the more impressive ascent to the State Rooms. Lyre-shaped wrought-iron balusters. Top-lit, with dome on a drum with Doric columns. From here one turns to the W into the GALLERY. This is 130 ft (40 metres)

52

*Now in the National Gallery.

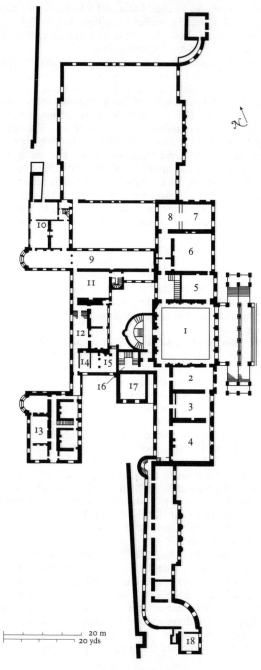

Wentworth Woodhouse.
First-floor plan

long, running E–W and is on the site of the C17 gallery (in 1741 'the old Gallery was rebuilt', in 1743 it was 'fitted up'). A screen of two Ionic columns separates the part of the gallery that extends into the projecting N wing of the W range (where it is at ground level), the Venetian window in the W apse opening to the staircase of 1793. It was renewed then with plate glass and exceedingly thin mahogany glazing bars. The ceilings have octagonal and circular panels with sparing Rococo decoration, very different from the Jonesian decoration of the E range. The plasterer was *John Bagnall*, who had worked for Lord Burlington at the York Assembly Rooms. Two chimneypieces with Neoclassical details, including Pegasus capitals, are clearly later than 1743.

In the NW wing N of the Gallery are the three rooms known as CLIFFORD'S LODGINGS, named for the family of the 1st Earl of Strafford's first wife, Lady Margaret Clifford. This was the last part of the C17 house to survive unaltered, being remodelled by *Carr* in 1762–3, with coved ceilings by *Joseph Rose*. The largest is fully panelled in pine, with finely carved borders and dado and skirting details. Ceiling with motifs which are classical (i.e. post-Rococo), but livelier than those of the E range. Charming fireplace, perhaps from Florence, has small *pietra dura* panels with flowers, fruit and birds. The other two ceilings with Adamesque decoration. S of the Gallery is the GREEN DINING ROOM, redecorated as a drawing room in the early 1790s with charming wallpaper. Probably French, it has pretty panels with festoons and wreaths of flowers, set within emerald green borders. Similar to papers by *Réveillon*, and to be compared with that at Moccas Court, Herefordshire. Chimneypiece by *John Fisher Sen.*, 1792, has swagged frieze and pilasters with rams' heads; an identical one was supplied for Milton, Northamptonshire.

Now S again into the WEST ENTRANCE HALL. The decoration here is of *c.* 1730 and in accordance with that of the W façade. Baroque door surrounds with fantastical scrolly pediments crowned by busts of Diana and ?Apollo, and friezes with

1	Marble Saloon	9	Gallery
2	Ante-room	10	Clifford's Lodgings
3	Van Dyck Room	11	Green Dining Room
4	Whistlejacket Room	12	West Entrance Hall
5	Ante-room	13	State Bedroom and
	(Statuary Room)		Dressing Rooms
6	State Dining Room		(originally Library)
	(originally Drawing Room)	14	Yellow Dressing Room
7	Library	15	Yellow Bedroom
	(originally State Dressing Room)	16	Oak staircase
8	Library	17	Chapel (gallery level)
	(originally State Bedroom)	18	South Pavilion Room

Bérain-style ribbon work and *bombe* ends. S doorway has half-pilasters with inverted Ionic scrolls in the manner of Borromini. Oddly unornamental cantilevered stone staircase in two narrow flights. Curvaceous iron balustrade. The two rooms E of the Entrance Hall are structurally part of the C17 house and face into the central courtyard. In the SW wing the STATE BEDROOM and flanking DRESSING ROOMS face the garden. They were originally the Library and were created in the 1820s. The S bedroom on the E side has Chinese wallpaper with birds and trees on a blue ground.

The S range, overlooking the South Court, also belongs to the C17 house. The YELLOW DRESSING ROOM and YELLOW BEDROOM are traditionally known as Strafford's Lodgings. Their mid-C18 fittings include panelled dados and, in the oddly ornate Dressing Room, fluted Ionic pilasters of wood and a Baroque chimneypiece that has a big overmantel with a bust under a draperied baldacchino. The Bedroom has a Doric screen. Below these two rooms is the panelled OLD HALL, which may be late C17. It has a three-bay arcade at the E and W ends. The arches rest directly on the capitals of the Doric columns and there are half-columns rather than pilasters at the walls. The E doorway, with segmental pediment, leads to the OAK STAIRCASE, which lies immediately N of the Chapel and was the other main staircase until 1806. Partly remodelled *c.* 1900. It is large, but not as important as might be expected. Wide open well, wide flights with wooden balustrade in the tradition of the late C17. Simple stucco ceiling and glazed dome.

On the SECOND FLOOR of the E front, N and S of the Marble Saloon's gallery, there are bedrooms with excellent coved ceilings, stucco decoration and carved chimneypieces with overmantels. One has fine Chinese wallpaper. In the BASEMENT is what is thought to be a FISH POND, probably for the 1st Marquess of Rockingham, whose many enthusiasms included breeding goldfish.

Finally the wings on the E side. The N kitchen wing was almost entirely altered in the 1950s. The S wing, known as Bedlam from the C18, had offices below and children's, guests' and servants' rooms above. At its far end, in the SOUTH PAVILION, is a delightful octagonal room with a Venetian window to the S and a bridge to the W gardens. Probably altered by *Carr*, it has a ceiling with Adamesque decoration and classical reliefs set in the walls.

STABLES and RIDING HOUSE. By *Carr*, 1766–89. A veritable equine palace, designed for eighty-four horses on a scale to emulate the house. It is the largest C18 complex in the country, originally surpassed only by the Duke of Devonshire's stables at Buxton, Derbyshire. Fifteen-bay front has rusticated entrance with coupled Tuscan columns, pediment and a cupola with an open rotunda of columns. Blank arches round each bay of the one-and-a-half storeys of windows. The fourth and twelfth bays have rustication and square hipped-roofed towers. Courtyard nearly 200 ft (31 metres) square with a big fountain in the middle. Fifteen-bay sides of one storey have a low square tower in the middle and pediments to the fourth and twelfth bays. Rear range has two-storey centre with carriage arches (altered). To rear r. the former RIDING HOUSE, built to exercise racehorses. Tall rectangular block, lit by lunettes high up.

GARDENS. W of the house, mostly lost to post-war opencast mining and neglect. CAMELLIA HOUSE by *Charles Watson* 1812. Nine bays, with Ionic columns and pilasters and glass walls between. At its back a pedimented SUMMERHOUSE with low wings. Doorway with columns with alternating blocking.

BEAR PIT. An odd garden ornament on two levels. Spiral stair inside. Domical vault. Exit below by a vaulted, grotto-like passage. The outer doorway is part of the architecture of *c.* 1630. Wildly ornamental pilasters and open segmental pediment. Nearby two bad STATUES of Roman soldiers of the same date.

The large PARK, which lies to the E and S of the mansion, was created in the C18 and was landscaped by *Humphry Repton* in the early 1790s. His scheme incorporated existing features such as the level E lawn, made from the 1760s as the old stables, kitchen garden, etc. were removed, and the series of lakes to the SE.*

Much of Repton's planting was destroyed by opencast mining from 1944 to the 1950s. Since the late C20 the reinstatement planting has been altered to restore some of his vistas and views, in which a group of notable follies and monuments, within and beyond the park, are important features.

ROCKINGHAM MONUMENT (MAUSOLEUM). An outstandingly fine and noble structure by *John Carr*. The frieze of the middle stage is inscribed 'To the memory of Charles Marquess of Rockingham this monument was erected by William Earl Fitzwilliam 1788' and detailed accounts record its building and decoration 1785–91. Notwithstanding its traditional name and the prominent sarcophagus, it is not a mausoleum but a cenotaph, for the Marquess was buried in York Minster in 1782. Of three tiers, it stands on a terrace facing the E front of Wentworth Woodhouse encircled with four diagonally placed obelisks. Its design was based on the Roman Tomb of the Julii at Glanum, Provence, France, dated *c.* 30–20 B.C. Square rusticated ground floor. Doorway and windows with attached Doric columns and pediments. Open second stage with tall round arches flanked by coupled Corinthian columns; sarcophagus within. Upper stage circular with Corinthian columns, four urns and dome. Interior with eight fluted Roman Doric columns carrying a dome, which has exquisite Adamesque plasterwork by *Thomas Henderson* and *Ely Crabtree*.

61

*His Red Book is at Milton (Peterborough).

Earl Fitzwilliam created not just a memorial from a grateful nephew but a celebration of Whig principles of government. Inside is an imposing life-size STATUE of Rockingham in ceremonial robes by *Nollekens*, 1790, surrounded by BUSTS of his political friends, paired in niches. John Lee by *Nollekens* 1789 and Lord John Cavendish by *John Bacon Sen.* 1793. Admiral Keppel by *Giuseppe Ceracchi* 1779 and Charles James Fox by *Nollekens* 1791. Sir George Savile by *Nollekens* and Edmund Burke by *John Hickey* 1789. The Duke of Portland by *John Bacon Sen.* 1793 and Frederick Montagu by *Nollekens*.

The obelisks, made in 1728 for the mansion's formal W garden, were placed here in 1793 at *Repton*'s direction. The monument was restored in 1989–90.

DORIC TEMPLE. By *Flitcroft*, 1744–5. On Temple Hill, SE of the house. Arcaded octagon with ashlar dome. Attached Doric columns with bands of stalactite rustication.

SOUTH TERRACE. S boundary of the W garden with a tremendous retaining wall, some 500 yds (450 metres) long, by *Ralph Tunnicliffe* 1735–6. Bastions at E and W ends, projecting viewing platform in the middle. At the W end the domed IONIC TEMPLE by *Flitcroft* 1736, with ten columns encircling a STATUE of Hercules fighting a monster.

NORTH LODGE, by *Carr*, 1793, and DORIC LODGE, early C19, probably by *Pritchett & Watson*.

EAST LODGE, Greasbrough. By *William Dickie*, 1868. Picturesque bargeboards.

NEEDLE'S EYE. Before 1728. Slender square pyramid *c.* 45 ft (8 metres) high. On the former private drive from North Lodge to Rainborough Lodge, Brampton Bierlow. Archway with ogee entrance arches and an ogee-vault. Urn finial.

RAINBOROUGH LODGE. *See* Brampton Bierlow, p. 140.

HOOBER STAND. By *Flitcroft*, 1746–8. A prominent tower of unusual form. Built in homage to George II, it commemorates the defeat of the Jacobite Rebellion of 1745 (and Rockingham's elevation from Earl to Marquess). Triangular, in ashlar with rounded corners, and tapering from a perpendicular base to a flat viewing platform at a height of 85 ft (26 metres). Small central hexagonal lantern above the spiral staircase. Spectacular views all round. Its counterpoint on a ridge at the S boundary of the park, about 2 m. S of the house, near Thorpe Hesley (q.v.), is KEPPEL's COLUMN by *Carr*, who produced several designs for the Marquess of Rockingham. The final form, a Giant Tuscan column with square abacus forming a look-out platform, was arrived at in 1776, and the acquittal in 1779 of Admiral Keppel, court-martialled on spurious and politically motivated charges, provided the impetus for its completion in his honour in 1781. At *c.* 115 ft (35 metres) high, it is still shorter than intended, explaining the too-bulgy entasis of the lower two-thirds.

Outside the main park entrance, beside OCTAGON LODGE, mid-C19, are the extensive Home Farm, early and mid-C19, and the former POWERHOUSE, *c.* 1905, with tall chimney. Electricity for the mansion was provided by generators powered by coal-fired boilers. Across Cortworth Lane, the large ESTATE BUILDING YARD with ranges of workshops.

Attractive VILLAGE, mostly along Main Street, without the formality of a model estate village. It was transferred to the Wentworth Amenity Trust by the 10th Earl Fitzwilliam in 1979. WENTWORTH SCHOOL, 100 yds NW of the church. By *Pritchett & Son*, 1836–7. Single-storey, H-plan. Cross-wing classrooms have pretty bargeboards and Tudor-arched windows with intersecting tracery. Former VICARAGE, 100 yds NE. Tudor Gothic, by *Pritchett & Son*, 1840–1. WENTWORTH HOSPITAL, Barrow, ¼ m. NW. 1725. Brick. Two-storeyed front range originally a school. Eleven bays, with gable and small timber bellcote to the centre bay. Single-storey almshouses enclose rear courtyard. Former MECHANICS' INSTITUTE, No. 9 Main Street, 1844–5, has battlemented parapet and turrets. The ROUND HOUSE, No. 47 Clayfield Lane, is the stump of a brick windmill *c.* 1745, castellated when converted to a house in 1793. The cottages and farms are mostly C17–C19, but some have earlier, probably C16, timber-framed cores.

In SCHOLES COPPICE, 1½ m. SSE, formerly in the S edge of the parkland, a SETTLEMENT of late prehistoric type in a non-defensive site close to a stream. Probably occupied into the Roman period, it was enclosed by a bank, topped by a palisade, and by an external ditch. One of the carefully graded C18 parkland walks crosses the SSW arc, probably utilizing the position of an original entrance on the S.

ROMAN RIG. *See* Introduction, p. 9.

WENTWORTH CASTLE
Stainborough

3000

One of the great C18 houses of Yorkshire, but neither a castle nor at Wentworth. It was known as Stainborough Hall until 1731. Like its rival, the even greater mansion of Wentworth Woodhouse (*see* Wentworth), it has both Baroque and Palladian fronts and incorporates an earlier house, here much more complete. The comparison, as was intended, extends to the gardens and park, which have one of the best surviving groups of buildings of their kind. Horace Walpole described it as 'my favourite of all great seats, such a variety of ground, of wood and water; almost all executed and disposed with so much taste'.

The house (now Northern College) sits high on an E-facing slope below Stainborough Low. The Everinghams held the estate from 1230, but by 1610 their lands and the house had been

acquired by Thomas Cutler, whose grandson Gervase rebuilt
the body of the hall in 1670–2. It is his house that forms the
NORTH RANGE. Seven bays, and originally two-and-a-half
storeys. Quoins at the angles and to a central porch, over which
is a window distinguished by an open scrolly pediment. The
windows had mullions and transoms, as those of the heightened
attic storey, with little pediment and hipped roof, still have. The
s front, its doorway with a frame of alternating blocks, now faces
into a narrow courtyard enclosed by later ranges. The first of
these was added by Thomas Wentworth, who purchased the
heavily encumbered estate from Gervase Cutler's son Henry in
1708. He held the title Lord Raby and the proximity of his purchase to the domain of his distant cousin, Thomas Watson-
Wentworth, at Wentworth Woodhouse was no coincidence. The
latter's good fortune in inheriting the family's historic estate
through the female line rankled deeply with Raby, who set out
to create his own Yorkshire seat on a scale grand enough to rival
that of his upstart relative and to support his aspiration to the
revived title of Earl of Strafford.

Raby was ambassador to Prussia from 1703 to 1711 and he
found in Berlin architects to help him realize his first ambition for Stainborough, the magnificent EAST RANGE. In a
letter of 1734 he named them as 'Monsieur Bott and Monsieur Eosander'. *Johann von Bodt* spent his youth in Paris and
later served William III as a military engineer, before entering
the King of Prussia's service in 1699. In Potsdam his buildings included the Arsenal. *Johann Friedrich Eosander* was
appointed court architect to Frederick the Great in 1699, for
whom he extended the Charlottenburg Palace (1702–4) and
completed the Königliches Schloss (1707–13; dem.). There is
no evidence that either man visited Stainborough and the new
range is their only known work in Britain. Plans are mentioned in 1709. Some have survived, which must be attributed
to them, although the design was revised with the addition of
a bay to each end pavilion and alterations to the window
treatment. *Thomas Archer* has been credited with these
changes but, although he offered advice, there is no firm
evidence for his greater involvement. With instructions from
Raby by letter, building began in 1709 under the supervision
of *Edward Reeves* and the structure was complete by 1714.
The façade was engraved in 1713, shown in a view by Knyff
of 1714 and illustrated in *Vitruvius Britannicus* in 1715. It is
all stone and its palatial splendour, uncommon in England,
derives more from Paris than from Germany, indicative of
Eosander's fluency in French Baroque vocabulary. It is fifteen
bays wide: 2:4:3:4:2 bays. The centre and the end
pavilions project slightly and have ground-floor quoins. Of
two even storeys with semi-basement and attic, it is, being set
lower, still the same height as the old house's three storeys.
Top balustrade relieved neither by a pediment nor by visible
roofs. The engravings show that statues on the dies were

intended. Ground-floor windows simple with recessed pilasters and straight hoods on corbels; their sills mostly lowered. The doorway arched without hood or pediment; garlands and trumpets in the spandrels, carved by *Daniel Harvey*. On the first floor the centre and pavilions have giant Corinthian pilasters. The windows are all given segmental pediments except for the three middle ones, which are much larger and arched like the doorway below. Above them a rich display of leaves and fruit and arms – richer than illustrated in *Vitruvius Britannicus* and again more Continental than English in character. Lord Raby was made 1st Earl of Strafford of the second creation on his return from Berlin in 1711. He then became Ambassador to the Netherlands and one of the negotiators for the Peace of Utrecht in 1712–13. But the death of Queen Anne, coinciding with the completion of the building, abruptly ended his career; denied any recognition by the Whigs, Strafford's celebration of his achievements and political loyalties found expression in the E range's interior and in the landscape. For these his architect was *James Gibbs*, a fellow Tory, a Scot and an associate of Jacobite sympathizers.

The SOUTH RANGE, built 1759–64 by William, the 2nd Earl, is far less grandiose, though of equal magnitude. It is purely English in its dignified and restrained Palladianism. It was designed by *Strafford* himself, and executed by *Charles Ross* of London. *John Platt* was employed as mason, and may have helped with the design. Thirteen bays, with six-bay W return. Two-and-a-half storeys, but set higher up than the E range, whose upper storeys and balustrade it matches. The rusticated ground floor is consequently rather low. Its centre has arched windows. Above these six detached Corinthian giant columns carrying a pediment with decoration carved by *Platt* in 1762. The end of the Baroque range was re-clothed as one bay plus the E pavilion, with a new Venetian window with detached Corinthian columns (matched plainly on the N end). The less emphasized parts between the ends and centre have pedimented windows in the *piano nobile*. In 1877 *George Devey* made plans for alterations, including a screen to the courtyard, but these were not executed. The W side was extended in 1897 with a matching L-shaped NW wing that almost joins the Cutler house. A full-height screen hides the gap.

The INTERIOR is confusing. The floor levels of the three main ranges are inconsistent and even with four principal staircases circulation is difficult. This partly arises from the alignment of the central axis of the E range on the cross wall of the double-pile Cutler house. Its main advantage was that the C17 house's staircase (remade in the later C19) easily brought one to the central entrance to the Gallery in the E range. The arrangement's symmetry may indicate that the 1st Earl, who mentioned a possible second wing, intended to create an H-plan house.

The NORTH RANGE has only a little original C17 work. The ENTRANCE HALL has some reused panelling, and two heraldic panels of the Everinghams in its large carved oak overmantel, which is otherwise probably a Victorian compilation. Good bolection-moulded stone fireplace with cornice. The splendid but ill-fitting STAIRCASE beyond seems genuinely late C17 but was clearly brought in, probably at the suggestion of *Walpole*, who gave advice to the 2nd Earl on alterations in the 1750s and '60s. Square open well formed by removing part of a floor. The balustrade thickly and juicily carved with trumpeting cherubs, leaves, flowers and scrolls in openwork. The room above the entrance hall has a rich frieze, and an eccentric fireplace with two caryatids, which is probably that designed for the Earl by *Richard Bentley* 'in the style of Architecture in the reign of James the first', and mentioned by Walpole in a letter in 1755. Excellent carved chimneypieces in the two chambers E and SE, probably from alterations *c.* 1730 and thus by *Gibbs*.

As for the EAST RANGE, this is as splendid in its interior as its exterior. It was finished in 1731, when Strafford changed the house's name. The centre of the ground floor is a full-depth ENTRANCE HALL divided into nine bays by four fluted Ionic columns, their capitals by *Daniel Harvey*, 1720. Ionic pilasters against the walls. Big doorcases of grey Derbyshire marble with bolection mouldings, one with Grinlingesque carvings in the spandrels. The central ceiling panel, painted on canvas, is by *Giacomo Amiconi*, who was paid £52 10s. for it in 1735. It depicts Morpheus and Endymion. The eight panels around it have charming grotesque paintings, also on canvas, by *Andien de Clermont*, their date uncertain. Two sets representing the seasons, derived from prints by Gillot and Watteau, with Bérainesque arabesques and ribbonwork and birds. One set, with central grisaille medallions, has Spring (S) and Bacchus/ Autumn (N) in the two larger panels. The corners have a *singerie* set with monkeys harvesting grapes, skating etc. The Queen Anne Suite to the S is an enfilade of ante-room, bedroom and S parlour, notable for their fine gilded joinery. *William Thornton*'s involvement is recorded from 1714 and the elaborately carved overdoors and bracketed cornices in the ante-room and parlour compare in quality to his work at Beningborough (North Riding). Giant Corinthian pilasters, rather ponderous for the size of the rooms, flank the former positions of the chimneypieces. Capitals and other decoration includes Strafford's initials and his earl's coronet. The parlour ceiling, by *Vassalli c.* 1731, has pretty Rococo decoration around a central figure of Fame, matched by Plenty in what was the corresponding room at the range's N end. The plan in *Vitruvius Britannicus* shows three rooms N of the Hall, but the first two were made into one large four-bay room, probably *c.* 1760. It was a drawing room when Arthur Young visited in 1768. Its decoration is purely English. Pedimented doorcases with gilded bay-leaf

friezes and mirrored tympana. Compartmented ceiling with
rinceau on the ribs. Later white marble fireplace with panel of
a lion cub eating grapes. In the early C20? the wall dividing it
from the N room was removed to create a large dining room.
At the NW corner is *Gibbs*'s remarkably ornate ITALIAN
STAIRCASE. Its cantilevered stone stairs succeeded two earlier
staircases, differently arranged, the space being enlarged for
the second. Lower N windows were inserted after the public
road passing the end of the building was moved ¼ m. N *c.* 1720.
Superb stucco by *Francesco Vassalli* 1729–31. White walls with
two large medallions of Fame and Perseus, portrait medallions
of the Earl and his son, and eight Roman busts on the cornice
between first floor and half-storey, the decoration all open to
Jacobite interpretation. In the centre of the painted ceiling a
giant Star of the Order of the Garter, which honour Strafford
received in 1712. Fine wrought-iron balustrade by *Robert
Bakewell*, an exact match with its contemporary at Bretton Hall
(q.v.).

The upper floor, one long room or GALLERY, is a showpiece
of almost megalomaniac magnificence. It is 180 ft (55 metres)
long from end to end, with fifteen windows, and was inspired
by the Colonna Gallery in Rome as a space to display pictures
and sculpture. Work had started by 1721. The joiner *Charles
Griffiths* was contracted for wainscoting in 1724. Other craftsmen recorded are the carpenter/carver *Jonathan Godier* and the
Derbyshire plasterer *Richard Huss*. *William Addinell* did painting and gilding. Set two bays in from the ends are screens of
two Corinthian columns of Carrara marble. Their gilded
wooden capitals must be those carved by *Harvey* in 1725. In
1720 he had agreed to carve four Corinthian capitals of Roche
Abbey stone for the gallery, for £50, but there is no evidence
of them. Rich cornice and generously coved ceiling. Corinthian half-columns to the Venetian windows and matching
pilasters between the central E windows and the facing W
doorway, all *c.* 1764. Two splendid marble fireplaces with pediments on coupled Ionic columns and three eagles perching on
each pediment. Originally they held gilded garlands in their
beaks.

The SOUTH RANGE is much less spectacular and much
more altered. At the W end of the *piano nobile* is Lady Strafford's apartment. The remainder is an enfilade of four rooms,
reached from the Gallery through an ante-room with
Continental-style corner chimneypiece with domed top, as
shown in *Bodt* and *Eosander*'s section. The first three rooms
had their ceilings lowered by some 6 ft (1.8 metres) in alterations by *Sydney Castle*, 1950, losing their covings and attic
clerestories, but retaining the flat centres intact. Geometric
panelling on the first ceiling, then the Roman Room, with a
design from Serlio in green and gold. Octagonal medallions
with delicate grisaille paintings of gods and goddesses on
frothy clouds, and half-octagons with sphinxes. The Canopy

Room beyond has panels with pretty garlands of roses – are they Early Victorian? The background looks C18. Lady Strafford's Bedroom, at the SW corner, has the best surviving Palladian interior. Exquisitely carved doorcases. Are the delicate garlands on the ceiling, in gilded grisaille, C18 or C19? Her 'Reading Closet' is a delightful small cabinet to the E. Frieze with green and gold swags on mirrors and a charming vaulted ceiling decorated as an arbour entwined with honeysuckle. The gilt trellis-work with its deep blue background has, however, somehow assumed something of the formality of coffering. The main staircase of this range is a simple cantilevered stone stair with plain Ionic screens of two pillars to ground and first floors.

At the N end of the house is a STATUE of the 1st Earl, dressed as a Roman general, by *Rysbrack*, 1744. It was originally placed by his son in the centre of Stainborough Castle (*see* below).

The 1st Earl laid out formal GARDENS S and W of the mansion, including the geometric wilderness known as the Union Jack garden, and an extensive PARK planted with a complex arrangement of avenues, mainly to the E and S. They are shown in Badeslade's perspective views of 1730, published in *Vitruvius Britannicus IV*, 1739. Much of his landscape and its ornaments can be interpreted as carefully thought-out symbols of Jacobite allegiance. Although the 2nd Earl replaced some of the formal scheme with more naturalistic planting, especially on the E slope, and added further monuments and buildings, Wentworth Castle is one of very few estates where so much of the early C18 landscape has survived, although part of the park was subjected to opencast mining. Since the late C20 it and the later work has been painstakingly restored, studied and interpreted by the Wentworth Castle and Stainborough Park Heritage Trust.

The 1st Earl's most important garden building is STAINBOROUGH CASTLE, a remarkably early and remarkably elaborate mock-medieval Gothic folly on the hilltop to the W. It was built 1726–30, but inscribed 'Re-built…in the Year 1730' to bolster Strafford's historic credentials. Circular embankment with castellated wall with four square towers, also castellated, one for each of his children. Big gatehouse with low, vaulted archway through and slight remains of the banqueting room above. Two of its original four round towers survive, one affording spectacular views across South Yorkshire. Below the castle is the needle-like OBELISK, erected by 1746 as the SUN MONUMENT with a reflective bronze disc on top. Later dedicated to Lady Mary Wortley-Montagu to commemorate her introduction of inoculation against smallpox into England in 1720. The inscription records that she got the idea from Turkey. Slightly SE is ARCHER'S HILL GATE, 1752, along the crenellated retaining wall and ha-ha. Canted screen with three arched openings. Ball finials. Rusticated outer face, the inner ashlar. W of the house the large and elaborate cast-iron CONSERVATORY, made by *Crompton & Fawkes* 1885, restored 2012–13. N of it the GUN ROOM, 1732. Small Palladian brick pavilion, probably a banqueting house originally. Enriched Venetian window with pediment. Very fine interior has apsidal ends, Corinthian side screens and rich plasterwork.

SW of the S terrace a little tetrastyle, prostyle Corinthian TEMPLE, 1766. *Platt* carved the columns.

The NE entrance to the park has a pedimented triumphal ARCH with rusticated quoins and ball finials, 1768. The drive leads uphill, crossing the N end of the Serpentine Canal begun in 1738 (unrestored at the time of writing) by the PALLADIAN or SERPENTINE BRIDGE, dated 1758. Beside the arch is the single-storey MENAGERIE HOUSE, 1720s. Stuccoed brick. E front of seven bays with good moulded architraves. Hipped roof. Pedimented two-storey rear wing, altered. (An UMBRELLO, built nearby in Menagerie Wood in 1759, is now completely ruinous. An imitation of the Market Cross at Chichester, it was designed in 1756 by *Walpole* and his protégé *Bentley*. A small Tuscan temple near this, also collapsed.) At the SE entrance a Gothic LODGE, 1733, and QUEEN ANNE'S OBELISK, 1733–4, dedicated by the 1st Earl to the memory of his patron. Its inscription can be interpreted as a coded statement of his loyalty to her Stuart successor, the 'Old Pretender' or James III. Domed ROTUNDA dated 1746. Modelled on the Temple of the Sybil at Tivoli, with a colonnade of fourteen Ionic columns. The DUKE OF ARGYLL'S MONUMENT was erected by the 2nd Earl in 1742 and then dedicated in 1744 as a memorial to his father-in-law, who died in 1743. A fluted Corinthian column, 60 ft (18 metres) high, topped with a statue of Minerva.

The HOME FARM and other service buildings are NE of the house, now converted to new uses. The STABLES and LONG BARN are parallel ranges with S gables, *c.* 1715? The stables have a symmetrical eleven-bay W front, facing the drive, with three corniced doorways, the middle with Diocletian window over. Triumphal-arch-like gateway to N, 1788. Between stables and barn the former ST JAMES'S CHURCH 1841–2. Gothic, with lancets. Pinnacled W tower, battlemented like the rectangular four-bay nave and chancel. W gallery. E window (*ex situ*) by *A.J. Davies* (*Bromsgrove Guild*), *c.* 1910. In the walled Kitchen Garden E of the drive a plain brick ORANGERY, *c.* 1728 (unrestored). Five rectangular openings beneath stone entablature. W of the drive the remarkable PILLARED BARN, *c.* 1715, a Dutch barn with sixteen tapering stone pillars and triangular ends. At the Lowe Lane entrance is the picturesque Gothick STEEPLE LODGE, *c.* 1752. Its embattled church-like tower is in three stages, with obelisk pinnacles, an ogee-headed doorway, quatrefoil windows, and windows with Y-tracery. Attached lodge also castellated.

WEST VALE

Later C19 mill settlement in the Black Brook valley.

ST JOHN. By *Thomas Rushforth*, 1880–2 (now offices). Its Neo-Norman style is unusual for the date. Decoration is confined to the splendid SW tower, which has, inconsistently, a Gothic belfry (cf. Greetland). – STAINED GLASS. E window by *Burlison & Grylls* 1882. W window by *Curtis, Ward & Hughes*, 1911 and 1920 (outer pair).

BAPTIST CHURCH (former), Rochdale Road. By *Richard Horsfall*, 1868–9. Pedimented tripartite front with Lombardic windows. Basement schoolroom.

PUBLIC HALL, Rochdale Road. By *Horsfall, Wardle & Patchett*, 1873–4, as Mechanics' Institute, Local Board offices etc. Italianate Gothic; the entrance in the tower with pyramidal roof; five-bay front has wider centre under gable with Lombardic frieze. Behind this, the PRIMARY SCHOOL by *C. F. L. Horsfall*, 1877–8, with reticulated tracery windows, a striking departure from the usual forms.

Several good textile mills in the vicinity: NORTH DEAN MILL, N of St John is a plain, four-storey woollen mill by *Richard Horsfall*, 1876–7, of thirteen bays with N stair/hoist tower. House and offices 1878; two-storey warehouse 1885. Fireproof S extension to mill by *William Hall*, 1919. Next to it, PROSPECT MILL by *Horsfall*, 1883, for worsted spinning. Five storeys, twenty-two by five bays, with distinctive ramped parapet each end. S on the main road is the impressive four-storey VICTORIA MILLS, as rebuilt in 1894–5 by *Horsfall & Williams* for cotton spinning. Decorative brick string courses arch over the windows. Early C20 five-storey water tower. The largest complex is WEST VALE MILLS, developed from 1850 as a worsted-spinning mill but converted to blanket manufacturing *c.* 1897. Six-storey, twenty-bay mill with pediment and pyramidal-roofed tower with cast-iron cresting. Just beyond, the stone RAILWAY VIADUCT, 1875.

CLAY HOUSE. *See* Greetland.

WHISTON

ST MARY MAGDALENE. A small C12 church forms the W part of the S aisle, the Norman window in its surviving W wall cut into by the arch of the mid-C13 tower. The rest by *John Oldrid Scott*, 1881–3, in Perp style, replacing a C15 chancel and N aisle. Elaborate tower top; the base retains C15 bell-frame posts. – PULPIT and other good oak furnishings by *Harry Hems*, altered and limed in reordering by *R. G. Sims* 1993–5. – STAINED GLASS. E window by *Clayton & Bell*, 1883. S aisle E window by

Burlison & Grylls, 1890. Four other windows by *Kempe*, 1883 to 1891. – MONUMENTS. Chancel. Rev. Thomas Atkinson †1896. Brass by *Hardman*.

WHISTON HALL BARN, ¼ m. w, on Chaff Lane. Magnificent medieval thatched aisled barn, the timber in the five SE bays dated to 1204. One of the earliest surviving secular buildings in the West Riding, comparable to barns in the south of England such as that at Cressing Temple, Essex. Early construction techniques such as aisle posts used as grown, not reversed, and notched lap-joints are evident. Originally with central entrance bay, it was altered and extended by three bays in the C16, and stone-cased in the C17. A C19 polygonal horse engine house breaks into the NE aisle.

MORTHEN HALL, 1⅞ m. ESE. Excellent early C18 house. Seven bays; five-bay pediment with oculus. Central bay embellished. Later wings, one-and-a-half storeys, also with hipped roofs. (Good interior includes plasterwork and fireplaces, one with Blue John inlay.) Other good houses in the hamlet.

WHITGIFT

8020

ST MARY MAGDALENE. Limestone. Rebuilt *c.* 1304, with octagonal piers (of uneven heights) and simple capitals to four-bay arcades. More finely moulded capitals to responds of wide, low chancel arch and S arcade. Tipsy W tower, its base and doorway partly sunk into once-marshy ground, its lower stage courses slanting. Pinnacled Perp top stages. Their inner face is of brick. Rendered brick aisles, rebuilt in the C16; the S aisle said to be dated 1589. Original Tudor-arched E windows; C19 three-light windows in four-centred arches; buttresses and battlements. Chancel rebuilt, nave re-pewed etc. by *Smith, Brodrick & Lowther*, 1898–9. – One unloved plain BENCH. C17 at the latest. – STAINED GLASS. E window and adjacent one on S by *Powell Bros*, 1899. – MONUMENTS. Elizabeth Romley †1746 and children. Unusual painted wooden board with segmental top.

WHITGIFT HALL, ½ m. E. Small country house of *c.* 1700, the most distinguished in the area, with some late C18/early C19 alterations. Red brick with good ashlar dressings. Five bays, two storeys raised on basement. Chamfered quoins, first-floor band, deep eaves cornice, hipped roof. The N centre bay projects slightly and is also quoined. Doorway with segmental pediment on fluted Ionic pilasters. Altered S front has porch with Doric columns carrying dosserets and open pedimented roof, and big full-height semicircular bows on either side. (Very fine original open-well cantilevered staircase. One room has a panelled overmantel with full-height fluted Doric pilasters to surround.)

2   LIGHTHOUSE, I m. E by the Ouse. *c.* 1920. An unexpected and
    engagingly maritime feature in a county that has no coast. Only
    46 ft (14 metres) tall, but high enough to give warning of a
    sandbank.

WHITLEY

ALL SAINTS. By *James Wilson* of Bath, 1860–1. Small, sturdy,
    stone church with apsidal chancel, perhaps inspired by Birkin
    (q.v.). Bellcote above chancel arch and Dec tracery. – STAINED
    GLASS. Three nave S windows by *T. W. Camm*, 1871.
EGGBOROUGH POWER STATION, 2¼ m. NE.* Closure of the
    coal-fired station announced in 2016. Built 1962–7 for the
    CEGB and then one of the largest power stations in the world.
    Landscaping by *Brenda Colvin* screens the clutter of ancillary
    buildings with tree-planted embankments, the turbine hall,
    chimney and eight cooling towers rising above this bosky base
    in vast and majestic simplicity. GALE COMMON, 1¼ m. W of
    Whitley, was designed by *Colvin* as the disposal site for ash.
    The now well-wooded N end of the hill is deceptively natural
    but the terracing, inspired by prehistoric lynchets, and the
    track spiralling to the gently sloping plateau top are deliberate
    clues to its artificial nature.

WHITLEY LOWER

ST MARY AND ST MICHAEL. By *Ignatius Bonomi*, 1842–6. Com-
    petent Neo-Norman with W tower and long raised chancel, the
    details inside and out all done with gusto. Chancel PISCINA
    and SEDILIA under an E.E. arcade. Neo-Norman stone FONT
    and excellent original carved oak CHOIR STALLS, PEWS,
    CHANCEL SCREEN and PULPIT. – Unusual standing angel
    LECTERN *c.* 1910. – STAINED GLASS. Chancel windows by
    Willement, 1847.

WHITWOOD *see* CASTLEFORD

*The station was built on the site of SHERWOOD HALL. The gateway of the house
noted in the 2nd edition of *Yorkshire West Riding* (1967) has been demolished.

WICKERSLEY

ST ALBAN. Perp w tower, the fourth stage C19. Wide three-bay
nave of 1832–6 by *John Lister*, his narrower short chancel
rebuilt as two bays by *E. Isle Hubbard*, 1886. The nave has in
the middle a slight projection with an embattled gable. Two-
light transomed windows with intersected tracery. Coved,
ribbed ceiling. – STAINED GLASS. E and w windows 1886, nave
windows 1885–*c.* 1888, by *Barnett* of Newcastle. – Chancel side
windows by *Barnett* of Leith, 1890. – MONUMENTS. Rev. John
Cox †1876, by *Hadfield* of Sheffield. Gothic.

INSTITUTE (former), Morthen Road/Gillott Lane. 1862, for
library, museum and lecture hall. Prominent polygonal corner
tower with spire.

CASTLE HOUSE, No. 51 Bawtry Road, ½ m. w. Brick, castellated. Built in 1930 for himself by Joe Lister, eccentric developer of the adjoining Listerdale estate.

WILSHAW

Small moorland village above Meltham, created 1863–74 by
Joseph Hirst for workers at his woollen mills (dem.).* His architects were *John Kirk & Sons*.

ST MARY. 1862–3, in an eclectic Italianate symmetrical ensemble
with Sunday School and Vicarage. A tall gabled entrance with
Lombardic frieze and huge central tower with steep pavilion
roof separates the nave from school and house. Round-arched,
the windows with Lombardic tracery. The Bishop of Ripon
swallowed his reluctance to consecrate a church of such unorthodox design when Hirst threatened to give it to the Method-
ists. Fine carved FITTINGS – STAINED GLASS. E window by
Clayton & Bell, 1863.

NATIONAL SCHOOL (former), 250 yds SE. 1870. Jacobethan
style with three nice shaped gables.

Three small groups of houses, two in simple Italianate style. ST
MARY'S COURT, opposite the school, is plain and steeply
gabled WORKERS' HOUSES of 1873, arranged 3:6:3 around a
courtyard with gardens on the open side. 50 yds SW of the
church ALMSHOUSES, 1871, paired in small villas, and 200 yds
NE, at Lower Greave, housing for foremen etc., with decorative
bargeboards.

---

* Hirst also partly built the model village of Thornton Hough, Cheshire.

WISTOW

ALL SAINTS. White limestone, and prominent beyond its real size in the flat countryside. Its history is more complex than it first appears; large reused red sandstone blocks, e.g. in the s aisle w wall, suggest origins even earlier than surviving fabric. Big Perp w tower with pinnacles. Doorway with two demi-figures of angels as hoodmould stops. Four-light w window with almost semicircular head. Like the tower, the s and N aisles, clerestory and rebuilt s porch are all embattled, the s aisle and clerestory being also Perp. But the s aisle's Y-traceried E window and the plain chamfered s doorway are of *c.* 1300, and with them harmonize the N aisle's w lancet, blocked N doorway and N window (intersected tracery cusped). Also its original E window, reused in the C19 N vestry. A little later the chancel: see its spectacular five-light E window with flowing tracery. The interior reveals a yet earlier period. Three-bay arcades with double-chamfered arches. The short circular piers and keeled responds of the s aisle, however, can hardly be later than the early C13. The wide chancel arch dies awkwardly into the wall on the s, but has a semi-octagonal respond with moulded capital on the N. The N arcade, with more finely moulded capitals to its octagonal piers, was clearly positioned after the chancel arch was in place.

Good chancel woodwork includes REREDOS and PANELLING by *W. H. Brierley*, 1911, and, especially, carved CHOIR STALLS by *Demaine & Brierley*, 1894, with linenfold and traceried panelling and poppyheads with angels. Also HAMMERBEAM ROOF from restoration by *James Demaine*, 1883–4. – PULPIT. Jacobean, restored. Octagonal, panelled, with enriched round arches. – SCULPTURE. ?C14 (damaged) figure of an anguished woman, kneeling. It is about 2 ft (60 cm.) high. – Small medieval figure of Christ enthroned. – STAINED GLASS. E window by *Lavers, Barraud & Westlake*, 1884. s chancel, first from E by *Kempe*, 1905, second from E by *Knowles* of York, 1875. N chancel, first from E by *C. E. Moore*, 1938, second from E by *Curtis, Ward & Hughes*, 1917. N aisle by *Harry Harvey*, 1955. – MONUMENTS. Early C14 coffin-lid with effigy of a woman under a crocketed gable with slender flanking buttresses. The gable is five-cusped and there are quatrefoils with the heads of a bishop and a civilian in the space between gable and buttresses. The Middle French inscription in Lombard lettering refers to Dame Margery. She was no doubt connected with the work in the church between *c.* 1300 and *c.* 1330. – Alethea, widow of Joseph James, †1768. Oval plaque on pedimented tablet with obelisk, with grey and yellow marbles. – Her father, Sir Richard Wynne, †1742, by *Atkinson* of York. Inscribed sarcophagus with pediment and tall grey marble obelisk. – Mrs Ann Poskitt †1802. Oval plaque on shaped tablet with urn. – Fragment of an C18 monument with death's head, hourglass and trumpets.

VICARAGE (former), 350 yds S. By *J.L. Pearson*, 1875. Red brick. Big, with projecting square bays, attic gables, tall decorative chimneystacks and large windows with timber mullions and transoms.

WOMBWELL

3000

ST MARY, Church Street. Large, dignified, Perp by *M.E. Hadfield, Son & Garland* 1896–8 (nave), and *C. & C.M.E. Hadfield*, 1903–4 (chancel) and 1913–14 (W tower). The squat tower was to have had a belfry and spire. – FRAGMENTS. Capital (nave wall SW), *c.* 1175 from an earlier church. A fragment of medieval arcade survives under the organ chamber. – STAINED GLASS. W window, 1919, by *Powell & Sons*.

CEMETERY. Chapels etc. by *Thomas Dobb* of Rotherham, 1868.

TOWN HALL, High Street. 1897–8. Renaissance revival. Clock tower and spired turret. BOER WAR MEMORIAL by local sculptor *G. Steele*, 1903. Downhill on Station Road, the LIBRARY by *A.B. Linford*, 1905. Free Jacobean.

WOMERSLEY

5010

ST MARTIN. Of white Magnesian limestone, distinguished outside by its beautifully strong broach spire on the crossing tower and memorable inside for *Bodley & Garner*'s High Church restoration. Evidence for a late Norman church here is no more than the W respond of the N arcade's three principal bays; it has stopped chamfers and plain abacus (renewed). These bays are otherwise E.E. Circular piers, semicircular E respond, moulded capitals. Double-chamfered arches with hoodmoulds, one with fragmentary dogtooth. Also E.E. is the additional W bay, its smaller arch dying into the walls. The plain lancet windows assure the date. So this Norman passage aisle was remodelled and lengthened in the C13. It must be assumed that the E.E. church had neither a W nor a crossing tower. Of its E parts only a small N chapel survived the rebuilding of the early C14. It is the contribution of those years – the crossing with its tower and the spire, the chancel, the S transept chapel and the S aisle – that gives the church its character. The tower has simple Dec bell-openings (now glazed) and stands on impressive piers with strong double-chamfered responds. The earlier chapel, rubble-built and slightly narrower than the tower (see the N crossing arch), forms a transept under a tall lean-to roof. It has a plain niche for an effigy. Straight-headed Dec windows, the N one with reticulated tracery. A small arch inserted at the E end of the N arcade smooths the connection of aisle with transept and crossing. The S transept is one bay

and has a piscina and a cusped tomb-recess. Entirely Dec the
S arcade, which is only two bays, starting further E than the N
arcade. The elements are standard. Dec too the S doorway,
which has a Norman French prayer carved on the r. jamb, and
probably the S porch. This has a continuous chamfer for its
entrance arch and a stone roof on chamfered transverse arches.
Dec windows in the clerestory, but those in the chancel and
the S transept (E window with reticulated tracery) date from
W. H. Crossland's restoration 1867–8. The S aisle window is
Perp and of odd design. Straight-headed, of three lights with
straight-sided arches and above each light a diamond, or, as it
were, a straight-sided spheric quadrangle or reticulation motif.
Late Perp, but much renewed, the big W window with panel
tracery. The church has no chancel E window – a great rarity.
In *Bodley & Garner*'s restoration for the 4th Countess of Rosse,
1893–4, it was removed to the S transept and the E wall strikingly dressed with a sumptuous deep crimson hanging that
complements the chancel's red and white marble floor by
Farmer & Brindley.

FURNISHINGS. A Catholic flavour was introduced by Lady
Rosse and her family with furnishings purchased from abroad,
including gilded standard CANDLESTICKS, C17 or C18, from
Rome, and a large TILED PANEL depicting the Last Supper,
C17, from Barcelona. – ROOD SCREEN with elaborate tracery
and carved figures, LOFT (with external staircase) and ROOD,
1895. Oak with some gilding but minimal colour. – C19 ROOFS
throughout have excellent richly painted decoration by *Bodley
& Garner*. – STAINED GLASS. Chancel: first from E designed
by *William Wallace*, made by *Cook & Co.*, 1874; second from
E by *Mayer & Co.* S transept: E window by *Kempe*, 1895; S
window (originally chancel E) by *Hardman*, 1868. Nave S
window by one of the *Gibbs* brothers, 1868. N aisle third from
E by *Kempe*, 1895. – MONUMENTS. Late C13 effigy of a cross-
legged knight in chain-mail with prick-spurs and shield with
the de Newmarch family's lozenges, perhaps Adam de Newmarch †*c.* 1287. – Tobiah Harvey †1720. Excellent cartouche,
lavishly scrolled, with putti under a canopy of falling
drapery. – Frances, wife of Stanhope Harvey, †1784 (incor-
rectly 1794). Fine Neoclassical sarcophagus with urn and
obelisk. – Elizabeth, wife of the Hon. Edward Harvey-Hawke,
†1824. Neoclassical tablet by *R. Blore* of Piccadilly. – Laurence
Parsons, 6th Earl of Rosse, †1979 and Anne, Countess of
Rosse, †1992. By *Simon Verity*. Grotto-esque aedicule with
swan-neck pediment, blocking with vermiculated rustication
and columns garlanded with oakleaves – the dense and exquisite architectural and botanical detail has an elfin quality.

WOMERSLEY HALL. Rebuilt *c.* 1705–10 by Tobiah Harvey, heir
of a London vintner, who bought the estate in 1680, but with
C17 mullioned windows of the older house surviving in the
basement. It passed to the Hawke, subsequently Harvey-
Hawke, family in 1798 and from 1870 to 2004 belonged to the

Earls of Rosse and their family. Harvey's two-storey, seven-bay double-pile house with single-bay l. wing, sketched by Samuel Buck, was remodelled by Col. Stanhope Harvey *c.* 1770. He added the r. wing, and a matching canted end to the l. one, a tall parapet screening the old-fashioned dormer windows, and the pedimented Doric portico. He probably first rendered the exterior. His architect is not known but the Dining Room (now Drawing Room) interior in the r. wing has been tentatively attributed to *Thomas Atkinson*. Double-height, its end screen of fluted Corinthian columns balances the apsidal window bay. Excellent ceiling with trophy in central roundel, rich cornice and fine doorcases. Chimneypiece has Ionic columns of Siena marble and relief copied from the frieze of the Temple of the Winds, Athens. Entrance Hall has Tuscan columned screen at each end and Greek Revival chimneypiece with draped female figures. In the l. wing is the Library, with Adamesque decoration and delicate enrichment to fitted bookcases (restored). Early C19 alterations, by the 3rd Lord Hawke, include the spacious Rear Hall with its fine mahogany staircase. The slender turned balusters are repeated as an unusual staircase dado and continued on the galleried landing, which stands on Corinthian columns. Curious carved roundels decorate string, balustrade piers and mahogany doors. Large stained glass window, mainly of reused C17 glass by *Henry Gyles*, includes busts of Roman emperors. Later alterations, by *J.B. & W. Atkinson*, included a one-bay N extension to the r. wing for a large oak-panelled Drawing Room (now kitchen), 1857, and a top-lit Billiard Room in the N court, 1869.

MANOR HOUSE, Station Road. Probably *c.* 1700, extended and restored. Limestone rubble with pantiled roof. Quoins. Three-cell, lobby-entry plan. One- and two-light windows with flat stone surrounds and mullions, regularly arranged.

STATION HOUSE (former). 1848, on the Lancashire and York-shire Railway's Askern branch line. Picturesque 'Swiss cottage' style.

PONTEFRACT GATE LODGE, ½ m. WNW. Probably *c.* 1867, when the parkland named Icehouse Park was laid out with a new drive. Gabled Tudor Gothic style.

WOODHOUSE

3080

Village above the River Rother on Sheffield's SE fringe.

ST JAMES. By *Innocent & Brown*, 1876–8. Gothic style. Geometric tracery. Nave has paired quatrefoils to minimal clerestory above S aisle, and wide triple bellcote with spirelet on E gable. Chancel with transeptal organ chamber. – Chancel FITTINGS and PULPIT by *Harry Hems*. – STAINED GLASS. Chancel N,

second from E by *Christopher Webb*, 1934. S aisle second from
E: centre light by *Francis Spear*, 1970, l. light by *Geoffrey Robinson*, 1985.

TRINITY METHODIST CHURCH (former, Wesleyan), Chapel
Street. Rebuilt 1878–9 by *G.B. Ford* of Burslem. Round-arched
style. Tall, ornate front with open pediment. The interior, with
continuous gallery on cast-iron columns, is largely original.
Adjacent SCHOOL, by *George Wilson*, 1861, now used as church.

WOODHOUSE CEMETERY, Stradbroke Road. By *Innocent &
Brown* 1878–9. Very small Gothic-style CHAPEL with two tall
cusped lancets under gabled dormers at the canted E end.
Picturesque single-storey LODGE with gabled attics and small
entrance tower with pyramidal top (cf. Intake Cemetery, Sheffield p. 600).

WOODHOUSE MEDICAL CENTRE, Tannery Street. By *Brenda
& Robert Vale*, 1990. Winner of the first 'Green Building of the
Year' Award in 1992. Long single-storey oblong in buff brick
with red and blue brick details. Giant battered buttresses
reflect the angle of the deep eaves under the super-insulated
roof.

Traces of the older village remain, e.g. the VILLAGE CROSS,
Market Place, a tall octagonal column of 1775 on a medieval
base, with sundial 1826. Facing it a former house of two bays
with lintel dated 1658. Nearby in Cross Drive, MANOR FARM-
HOUSE, 1690. L-plan with two- and three-light mullioned
windows and string course rising over the big lintel.

BADGER ESTATE, off Beaver Hill Road. Very high-density
development by Sheffield City Council, begun 1963, for 2,900
people. Mostly industrial system-built Hallamshire houses and
5M houses, with flat roofs and panels of brick, tile or timber
cladding. Staggered rows and stepped roof-lines on the slope
help relieve monotony.

WOODLANDS *see* ADWICK-LE-STREET

WOODSETTS

ST GEORGE. By *Hurst & Moffatt*, 1840–1, as nave and chancel
in one, with W bellcote and lancet windows. The E bay, apsidal
chancel and vestry added 1921–4 by *A.E. Turnell* of Sheffield,
also the Y-tracery and buttresses. Timber-framed S porch as
First World War Memorial. – STAINED GLASS. E windows by
Kempe & Co., 1924.

WOODSETTS HOUSE. Large High Victorian Gothic vicarage,
1869–71. Red brick banded in blue.

WOOLDALE

FRIENDS' MEETING HOUSE, Pell Lane. Late C17, largely rebuilt 1783; later alterations. S front has three large, many-paned windows to r. of entrance. Stone Doric columns support small W gallery with panelled front and shutters.

WOOLDALE HALL, built 1714 by Elihu Jackson, a Quaker. Five-bay front, originally with cross-windows. Mullioned windows to rear wing.

WOOLLEY

ST PETER, Church Street. First recorded in 1158 as a chapel of ease to Royston. The early font survives. So too a Norman tympanum with a lamb and cross in a border of foliage trails and a shaft with spiral decoration, both reused on the rood-loft stair in the S aisle. Now modest Perp throughout, the nave, N aisle, chancel and perhaps C14 N chapel having been rebuilt c. 1470–1520. At this time the W tower, and S chapel, aisle and porch were added. The chancel has a pretty carved frieze with flowers and animals; the porch has good timberwork. Restored by *J.L. Pearson*, 1870–1. – REREDOS. Oak, by *Robert Thompson*, painted by *Jan Edgar Evetts*, 1966. – SCREEN. S chapel. C16. Simple, Perp, with one-light divisions. – BENCH-ENDS. C16. Perp tracery in two tiers. – STAINED GLASS. E window by *W.F. Dixon & E.A. Vesey*, 1880. In the N chapel, and S chapel E window, fragments of C15 figures made up into new figures by *Clayton & Bell*. S chapel S window by *Lavers, Barraud & West-lake*, c. 1871. – S aisle. First and second windows from E by *Clayton & Bell*, 1871, third from E by *W.F. Dixon*, c. 1881, W window by *Morris & Co.*, 1871. Three outstandingly good figures with a background of white quarries with small yellow flowers. N aisle, first from E, by *Adam Goodyear*, 2001. – MONUMENTS. In the churchyard two shrine-like tomb-chests with pitched roofs. What can their date be?

E of The Green, THE OLD VICARAGE. C17 gables at the rear but smartened front with Tuscan pilastered entrance of c. 1810. Nearby the former SCHOOL, c. 1718. Plain, with two six-light windows one above the other. No influence from the classical style yet. S in New Road THE OLD COURT HOUSE retains C16 and C17 fabric, with much C20 restoration including five- and six-light mullioned windows. Fine stair balusters from Horton Old Hall, Bradford. MOUNT FARMHOUSE, dated 1719, heralds its rejection of the vernacular for the classical by pilastered gatepiers with obelisk finials.

WOOLLEY HALL, New Road. Described as 'newe' by its owner Michael Wentworth in 1635. It has an impressive number of large shaped gables, some original, some on late C17 and C18 extensions. The S front of the original H-shaped house survives, its recessed centre of three bays flanked by projecting gabled wings of two bays to which was added the gabled E wing of *c.* 1680 and a matching, if slightly wider, W wing of *c.* 1800. The rest is mostly the result of remodelling *c.* 1795–1800 in appropriately picturesque style, possibly by *Bernard Hartley I.* Nine-bay W front with a big central gable decorated with coat of arms. The N three bays are an earlier C18 extension, their l. return gabled. Centre of N front incorporates the outer half-gables of the 1630s wings, raised to three full storeys either side of a large canted bay. Another gabled bay beyond. The E side retains some C17 mullioned windows; its service extensions have plain gables. Fires in 1796 and 1806 destroyed much of the interior. (From the C17 only some oak panelling upstairs survives.) The dining room doorcases, which display Carr's influence, and several fine marble fireplaces look late C18. Other rooms, restored by *Charles Watson* in 1807, are Regency. Elegant drawing room with rectangular chain decoration on the door and window architraves and fireplace. Full-height landscape panels by *Agostino Aglio, c.* 1814, were destroyed *c.* 1900. *Watson*'s spacious hall, remodelled *c.* 1900, has a cantilevered imperial staircase with Tuscan columns below, Ionic above, and scrolly wrought-iron balustrade. Is it all original? – *John Webb* was consulted about the landscaping in 1811. – STABLES. *c.* 1808–10. Seven-bay N block with lower links to smaller E and W wings. All two-storey with central pediments; the N has a Diocletian window and a cupola. Detached S range, enclosing the yard. – GATE LODGES, New Road. Hexagonal with pyramidal roofs. By *Pritchett & Watson*, 1814. The ruinous GATEWAY on Barnsley Road is by *Wyatville*, 1820.

WORRALL

3090

Small village on the E hillside of the upper Don valley.

BRADFIELD SCHOOL, Kirk Edge Road. By *HLM Architects*, 2012. Linked flat-roofed blocks of two to three storeys set into the slope. Materials sensitive to the rural location, with natural vertical timber cladding above stone base.

MIDDLEWOOD HALL, Mowson Lane. 1808–13. Plain ashlar house of five by two bays. One-bay pediment. Porch with pairs of slender clustered columns, not the usual Doric ones.

WORSBROUGH

ST MARY. Norman chancel – see the one N window, and the
chancel arch, rebuilt in the C14. On the SE the impost of the
chancel arch has beaded arcading and the extradoses have
voussoirs with chevron, sunk rounds and arcading. Thin
unbuttressed Dec W tower (see the W windows) with Perp top
and small recessed stone spire. Chancel E window Dec with
reticulated tracery. The two big arcades Perp, slightly different,
the N one perhaps C14. Octagonal piers, double-chamfered
arches. Perp chapels of one wide bay each. E of the S chapel a
contemporary vestry, slightly sunk. Good panelled Perp ceiling
in the S porch. The embattled nave walls with transomed aisle
windows belong to a general heightening by *J. P. Pritchett*, 1838.
– ROOD SCREEN. C15. – Handsome S DOOR, 1480, with tracery
and a relief inscription with churchwardens' names. – Squire's
PEW 1722 (NW corner). – SCULPTURE. Norman stone with a
centaur-sagittarius (vestry). – STAINED GLASS. E window by
Wailes, *c*. 1848. Two in N aisle by *Powell & Sons*, 1920 and 1935.
S chapel easternmost by *Sep Waugh*, 1999. – MONUMENTS.
Thomas Rockley †1517. Tomb-chest with shields on cusped
quatrefoils, indents for brasses on top (N chapel). – Roger
Rockley †1534. Tomb-chest with shields, and above, on double-   30
decker bunks under a tester on four carved posts, two effigies.
The shrouded cadaver underneath, the knight above, as though
on his bier; crudely painted. Especially unusual in being oak
not stone (cf. Thornhill, 1529). – Several BRASSES, mainly C17
(chancel S pier) including Mary Edmunds †1678, heart-shaped.
Elizabeth Carrington †1710. Cartouche with scrolly frame,
cherubs and fruit.

ST THOMAS AND ST JAMES, Worsbrough Dale. 1¼ m. NNE. By
Flockton & Son, 1857–9. N chapel by *T. H. & F. Healey*, Bradford, 1879. E.E. High, aisled nave and a SE tower with broach
spire. – PULPIT. Caen stone on marble columns, sculpted by
Earley & Powell, Dublin, 1866. – STAINED GLASS. E and W
windows by *Barnett* of Leith, 1859. S aisle: two pairs by *Kempe*,
1896, 1901; middle pair by *Powell Bros*, *c*. 1894.

Square, domed MONUMENT to Swaithe Main Colliery
disaster, 1878 (in churchyard).

OUR LADY AND ST JAMES, Worsbrough Bridge (now R.C.),
⅔ m. NNE. By *T. H. & F. Healey*, 1901–2. Small, with lancets.
S tower forming porch to vestry has belfry stage and squat
leaded spire. Painted angels above chancel arch by *Powell Bros*,
1904.

WORSBROUGH HALL. C17. E-plan. Central range with two-
storey gabled porch, off-centre. Mullioned-and-transomed
windows to first floor. Wings added by *c*. 1700, the r. three-
storeyed. Later sashes, especially to long r. return. *John Platt*
designed the drawing room 1775. Several cross-windows and

gable of r. wing probably among alterations in convincing Jacobean style by *W.A. Nicholson* of Lincoln, *c.* 1840. Extensive service and stable ranges behind also by *Nicholson*.

CORN MILL (Museum), ½ m. N. Two-storeyed, built *c.* 1625 with C19 cast-iron overshot wheel. Three-storey additions, 1843. Projecting fourth bay housed steam engine. C18 miller's house.

DARLEY CLIFFE HALL, 1¼ m. NNE. Refined five-bay house of *c.* 1685. Hipped roof. Ashlar dressings. Entrance with segmental pediment on brackets. Pilaster-strips at angles, first-floor band. Raised window surrounds, originally with cross-windows. Rear matches front. (Bolection-moulded fireplaces and raised panelling.)

SWAITHE HALL, 2 m. NE. C16 timber-framed farmhouse with gabled stone wings flanking a narrow hall bay. A lost datestone, 1618, probably recorded remodelling. Substantial gabled N addition, *c.* 1870.

SWAITHE HOUSE, 1¾ m. NE. Polite house of five bays *c.* 1720. Three storeys. *Œil de bœuf* in pediment. Attached to a farmhouse dated 1680, with quoined doorway and mullioned windows.

BIRDWELL, 1¼ m. S. Tall OBELISK inscribed 'Wentworth Castle / 3 Miles / 1775', built for the 2nd Earl of Strafford.

ROCKLEY FURNACE, ¾ m. SW. In woodland E of Rockley Lane. Big stone stack built *c.* 1700. Slightly E a NEWCOMEN ENGINE HOUSE, dated 1813, for draining an iron ore mine. Four-storey square tower, crenellated.

ROCKLEY OLD HALL, ½ m. W. Long range with five uneven gables to W front. The middle three the earliest house, the N two possibly *c.* 1573. Mullioned windows, one to rear eight lights with transom. Dripstones. Flanking wings C17, the N later, with flat mullions.

HOUNDHILL, 1¼ m. NW. Fine H-plan house, the earliest part the timber-framed E cross-wing. The date 1566 on its S gable tie-beam conflicts with the 1606 date found in 1934 during restoration by *William Weir* for A.O. Elmhirst, younger brother of the founder of Dartington Hall, Devon. The later year is thought the more likely. Gables with A-struts. The principal posts descend to the ground floor, which is mainly stone. First floor has panels with close studding and herringbone bracing divided by horizontal mid-rails. Restored windows include pretty oriels. Late C17 W cross-wing and very narrow hall range, both in ashlar. (C17 panelling with decorated friezes.) Stout turrets at the site's SE and NW angles are Civil War Royalist defences. 200 yds further NW are DELF HOUSE and COTTAGE, formerly farm workers' cottages commissioned by Elmhirst from *Robert Hening*, 1933. Modernist (cf. the houses at Dartington).

OUSLETHWAITE HALL, 1¼ m. NNW. *c.* 1760. Two-and-a-half storeys. Five bays, with central ashlar panel. Raised quoins and window surrounds. Doric porch. Lower one-bay addition to r. with Venetian window, later C18. Extensive former farm buildings to E include four-storey tower dovecote.

WORTLEY

ST LEONARD. Nothing of the medieval chapel seems to survive. Written evidence suggests that the reticulated tracery of the former E window, now in the S chapel, is contemporary with the stained glass inserted in 1845. The earliest part is the sturdy W tower, built for Edward Wortley Montagu by *John Platt* of Rotherham, 1753–4. Four stages with embattled parapet. The chancel also rebuilt then but the present plain nave and chancel in one replaced it *c.* 1811–15. The nave windows have three stepped lights and Y-tracery. Are they original C13? Inside, the easternmost on the S side almost collides with the chancel's W wall. Semicircular chancel arch, likewise the unequal arches from the nave into the chapels, all on broad piers. The chancel arcades have two semicircular arches on a stubby column with wide abacus. Flat nave and chancel ceilings. – FONT. By *Butterfield*, 1845. – STAINED GLASS. E window by *Christopher Whall*, 1901. N chapel window has similar glass. – Excellent MONUMENTS. Edward Wortley Montagu †1761 by *John Platt*, erected 1778. Black and white marbles (Platt owned the marble works at Ashford, Derbyshire). Portrait profile framed by a snake biting its tail. Mary Wortley, Lady Bute †1794 by *Regnart*. Two figures in swirling drapery, by an urn. – John Stuart Wortley †1797 by *Flaxman*, with a child angel seated on a cloud and holding a book. – Margaret Stuart Wortley Mackenzie †1808 by *Flaxman*. Large seated woman in profile holding a book and looking up. The figure is dull. The surround a trefoiled arch on shaft supports under a round arch. – Archibald Stuart Wortley †1905 by his sister *Lady Margaret Talbot*. Unusual Arts and Crafts piece with silk embroidery in mahogany frame with decorative silver panels. – Rev. Thomas Thwaites †1802. Black marble with a vase. – A similar one to Benjamin Newton †1816 by *Woodward* of Bakewell, erected 1818. – Large Jacobean-style marble and mosaic wall monument to several members of the 1st Earl of Wharncliffe's family †1845–84. By *Powell & Sons*.

WORTLEY HALL. The former seat of the Wortley family, later Earls of Wharncliffe, on the site of a medieval house rebuilt by Sir Richard Wortley in 1586. The present hall was created in a piecemeal fashion in the C18 and early C19 by Edward Wortley-Montagu, who inherited Wortley in 1727 and was husband of the celebrated writer Lady Mary, their daughter Lady Bute, who succeeded in 1761, and her younger grandson, James Stuart-Wortley. Neither Wortley-Montagu nor Lady Bute lived at Wortley, and the character of the house and gardens owes much to Stuart-Wortley, who took up residence in 1800, and his grandson Edward Montagu-Stuart-Wortley-Mackenzie, who inherited in 1855 and became 1st Earl of Wharncliffe in 1876. The Earl, an art lover and socialite, commissioned alterations by *William Burn & John MacVicar Anderson*, 1867–73, and, on Millais's recommendation, paintings and decoration by *Edward Poynter* 1871–83. Following post-war neglect the hall became a Labour and trade union educational and holiday centre in 1951, and is now run as a hotel.

Although accounts record *Ralph Tunnicliffe*'s* involvement in building work in 1731–4, the earliest part is the good Grecian s front of seven bays by *Giacomo Leoni*, 1742–6. Ashlar, only one-and-a-half storeys, the centre with four attached Ionic columns and a pediment. Tympanum with coat of arms added after James Stuart-Wortley was created Baron Wharn-cliffe in 1826. Wide end bays and first return bays framed by coupled Ionic pilasters. Central doorway with cornice, flanking windows with pediments and cornices alternately. Balustrade to hipped roof. Five-bay l. return, with link to C19 two-storey wing set back on w. *John Platt* of Rotherham succeeded his father, *George Platt*, as builder and executant architect for Leoni's front and he also built the E entrance range, probably designed by *Matthew Brettingham*, in 1757–61. Set forward of Leoni's r. return bay, it has first a slightly pro-jecting quoined bay with an octagonal domed cupola added by *Burn*, then an arched doorway with Ionic columns and open pediment. Three further bays, with pulvinated friezes and cornices to ground-floor windows. Dentilled cornice and balustraded parapet. To r., three plainer bays, set back, then the N kitchen wing by *Platt* for Lady Bute, 1784–8, enclosing the inner courtyard. This wing, and *Platt*'s w service wing, 1786–8, replaced all remaining pre-C18 parts, but both were unfinished when a dispute with Platt stopped work in 1788. James Stuart-Wortley, Lady Bute's second son, consulted *John Carr* and his assistant *Peter Atkinson* in 1797 about completion and new stables, but it was left to the younger James Stuart-Wortley to finish the house, probably using *Atkinson*, whom he consulted in 1800.

William Burn's external alterations were minor, and mainly affected the extensive service quarters; he also made alterations to the principal interiors. The main rooms have opulent decor-ation with fine carved oak doorcases, oak and marble chim-neypieces and good plasterwork. The entrance hall has deeply beamed ceiling with heraldic panels painted 1856–7. The pan-elled Dining Room has Ionic columned screen and Rococo-style ceiling. The Large Drawing Room, divided by screen with fluted Corinthian columns, has pretty plasterwork with fes-toons and fretwork to wall panels and Rococo centrepieces to ceiling. Panelled w sitting room with Jacobean-style ceiling and carved frieze, shutters and doors. Magnificent former Billiard Room, with clerestory to central lantern, has decoration designed by *Poynter* as the setting for his four huge paintings, including Atalanta's Race and the Dragon of Wantley, painted 1871–9 and tragically now lost. Half-panelling and fluted Ionic pilasters in dark oak. Exotic decoration to lantern's coved

*He was then working at Wentworth Woodhouse (q.v.).

ceiling and to friezes, with parrots and vases among foliage and flowers in Renaissance style, all in red, gold and silver against a dark blue ground. Oak overdoor lunettes with peacocks, designed by *John Fisher* and carved by his students at the School of Art Wood-carving, Kensington. Long central hall with Doric screen leads to imperial staircase under oval lantern. Brass balusters. Spacious galleried landing with marbled Ionic columns and frieze with bucrania; window with heraldic stained glass by *Westlake*, 1872.

STABLES probably by *Atkinson, c.* 1800. Front range has pedimented centre with carriage entrance; five bays either side with blind round arches. Domed cupola like that on the house by *Burn.* Rear wings enclose yard, one with late C19 glazed canopy.

Early C19 GARDENS with balustraded terrace and arbour; pleasure grounds beyond with pond and ICE HOUSE, separated from former park by ha-ha. *W.S. Gilpin* had some involvement at Wortley. Mid-C19 LODGES.

A few ESTATE COTTAGES, 1850s, in the small village. Former VICARAGE by *Basil Champneys* for the Earl of Wharncliffe, 1878–80. Large, in good Jacobean Revival style, with gable to each bay and big transomed windows. S front has two-storey bay windows with pedimented parapets.

CARLTON HOUSE, 1 m. S. Early C19. Five bays, plain. Former dower house.

WHARNCLIFFE LODGE, Wharncliffe Chase, 2½ m. S (Stocksbridge CP). Commanding spectacular westward views it was originally a hunting lodge built by Sir Thomas Wortley in 1510, and until the C19 was often the family's preferred residence. Two storeys, nine bays, mostly C18 with C19 alterations.

WORTLEY TOP FORGE. *See* Hunshelf.

WRAGBY

4010

ST MICHAEL AND OUR LADY, off Doncaster Road. The church stands apart from the village, just inside the grounds of Nostell Priory (*see* below). Perp throughout, all embattled, and quite big. The chancel was built, according to an inscription on its wall-plates, by Prior Alured Comyn of Nostell in 1533.* Nave, aisles and S porch apparently rebuilt at the same time but the unbuttressed W tower may be C15. The nave clerestory is later – see original E and W roof-lines inside – but presumably not much. Its windows have late Perp square heads with hoodmoulds and three uncusped arched lights. Above the tower's W window is a small niche with ogee head and pinnacles between spiralled roundels. Nave arcade of four bays; continuous aisles – three bays to N chancel chapel, two to S chapel.

*The present boards are a C19 copy; the originals are stored at Nostell.

The elements of the arcades are standard; the massive octagonal piers at the E angles of the nave carry the arches springing in all four directions, as at St John, Halifax (q.v) and Whitkirk (*West Riding North*). Large chancel E window of five lights with transom. Chancel ceiling panelled, with bosses including a 'Green Man'.

Charles Winn of Nostell restored the church 1825–35, employing *Thomas Ward Sen.* to refurnish it in an antiquarian manner with fittings acquired by Winn. – REREDOS. Flemish, with a Pietà flanked by twelve saints carved in oak. – LECTERN. Incorporating a fine oak figure of a woman with a palm; 5 ft (1.5 metres) high. Perhaps German or Flemish C17–C18. – PULPIT. Octagonal, with six C17 Venetian panels in Turkish boxwood (not a set), the best the Scourging of Christ, in deep relief with perspective background, and a charming Nativity under the lectern. – FONT. Norman, cylindrical, with many large chevrons. From Auburn church, near Bridlington (East Riding), demolished 1731, it was brought here in 1830. – TOWER SCREEN. Incorporates elaborate C19 octagonal oak columns (also in S chapel screen) and panels with a man and woman, perhaps German C17. – ORGAN CASE. Georgian, with two carved masks among luscious foliage. Installed in the Top Hall at Nostell in the 1820s, transferred *c.* 1982. – SCULPTURE. An C11 stone panel in the chancel S wall, very worn but supposedly St Michael carrying Our Lady heavenwards. – Winn also assembled the unique collection of mostly Swiss PAINTED AND ENAMELLED GLASS, although it was not installed in the windows until the late C19. There are hundreds of mostly small panels and fragments, arranged tastefully, but rather like a stamp collection. The dated panels range from 1514 to 1751 and vary considerably in quality. Not one piece is of the first class but many have immense delicacy and charm and include biblical scenes such as the Garden of Eden with an elephant and unicorn, St George with a blue dragon with black spots, and contemporary secular figures and scenes. E window, including St Oswald, by *Thomas Ward Jun.* (later of Ward & Nixon) *c.* 1835. – MONUMENTS. Sir Rowland Winn †1765. By *Flaxman*, 1806, erected 1809. The relief, by no means large, with two seated figures and one standing figure, is Grecian and chilly (N chapel). – John Winn †1817. By *Chantrey*, 1823, and one of his best works. Very Greek. Two life-size mourning young figures, of his brother and sister, as on an Athenian stele (S chapel).

NOSTELL PRIORY

One of the great Palladian houses of Yorkshire, on the site of the early C12 Augustinian priory, its landscaped parkland seemingly untouched by the mines that surrounded and financed the estate.

The Priory buildings, dedicated to St Oswald, stood slightly S of the house; three ranges were incorporated into the C17 house,

Nostall Hall, most of which survived until the late 1770s. Of the rest, all that remains is a long farm building just w of the church, probably converted from a late C15 or early C16 part of the outer court of the Priory. s front of very large coursed stone blocks, originally only stone to first-floor level and timber-framed above the heavy dripmould. Several openings with four-centred arched heads and chamfered surrounds.

The new mansion was built for Sir Rowland Winn, the 4th Baronet, whose family acquired the estate in 1654. Returning from the Grand Tour in 1727, he planned a new house and by 1734 *Col. James Moyser* of Beverley had prepared designs. Their development and execution, however, was entrusted *c.* 1736 to *James Paine*, then only nineteen years old and here receiving his first commission. He remained architect until Sir Rowland's death in 1765, when the inside was still unfinished. The 5th Baronet called in *Robert Adam*. This was quite a usual thing to do then; for no-one was more fashionable, to design and supervise interiors. His work at Nostell from 1766 also includes an extension of 1779–80 designed with *James Adam*. It was still virtually a shell at the Baronet's untimely death in 1785 and was only made wholly habitable, by *John MacVicar Anderson*, in 1875–7. Given to the National Trust in 1954.

EXTERIOR. The house was intended to comprise an oblong with four square pavilions connected to it by quadrant colonnades framing the principal fronts, which face E and W. The designs, revised by *Paine*, were published in *Vitruvius Britannicus* in 1767. The idea came from Palladio's Villa Mocenigo by way of Moyser's friend Lord Burlington and Kent's Holkham Hall; there is an estate plan showing that the design was conceived as early as 1731. There is also a drawing by Colen Campbell for a house very similar to Nostell and it is possible that Moyser saw it, perhaps through Burlington, or that Campbell, who died in 1729, was originally going to undertake the professional role later entrusted to Paine. The building went up from about 1735 until 1750, when outside work stopped, with only the SE and SW pavilions built (the former was demolished in 1824). Despite the design's distinguished antecedents the result here is somewhat ponderous. The house is thirteen by five bays, of local stone (Brackenhill) and with a big hipped roof. Low rusticated ground floor. Pedimented surrounds to first-floor windows. The E side has a five-bay centre with attached giant Ionic columns and a pediment not sufficiently dominating the roof. On the garden side the columns are replaced by pilasters and the window architraves have scrolls. The W pediment's coat of arms was never carved.

After addressing the interior, *Adam*, as happened more than once, interfered with the exterior too. In about 1777 he created a grand entrance to the Top Hall at *piano nobile* level from a perron with curving balustraded staircases either side. More radically, he also proposed new wings flanking the E front. Only the N one was built, added solidly to the r. end of the main block

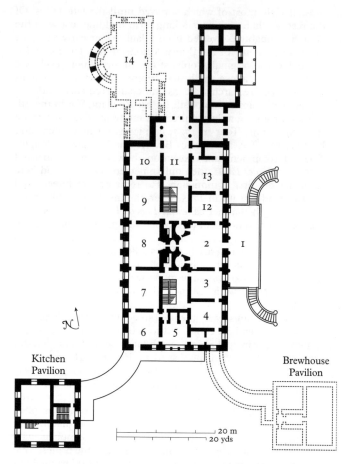

1	(Vestibule below)
2	Top Hall (Lower Hall below)
3	Breakfast Room
4	Crimson Room
5	State Bedroom (originally)
6	State Dressing Room (originally)
7	Dining Room
8	Saloon
9	Tapestry Room
10	Library
11	Billiard Room
12	Little Dining Room
13	Drawing Room
14	Proposed wing 1779

Wragby, Nostell Priory.
First-floor plan

with a three-bay link, 1779–80. Portico of four slender Ionesque giant columns; odd Ionesque angle pilasters. Their collared form of capital comes from Hadrian's villa near Tivoli. Enlivened by the portico's verticality and deft touches of decoration, carved by *Christopher Theakston*, the wing provides a contrast to the horizontal solidity of the main house, even if it makes a nonsense of the Palladian scheme. Behind, its appearance is confusing as the masonry incorporates the beginning of a link to one of a pair of corresponding w wings that Adam planned. His drawings, dated 1779, show these with large semicircular bays instead of porticos. As it is, the rather pedestrian sw kitchen pavilion survives from the original Palladian plan. Square, with a central chimney and a large pyramidal roof instead of the giant pediment of Paine's published design. The link to the house, originally an open colonnade, has been filled in.

INTERIOR. *Paine* planned and designed the interior and work started in the 1740s. By 1765 bedrooms and service rooms were in use but on the *piano nobile* only the state rooms in the s part were complete. The rest were left for *Adam* to create some of his finest interiors. This double helping of styles, changing from Paine's personal development of Anglo-Palladianism and mastery of ebullient Rococo to Adam's Neoclassicism, is an instructive experience, enhanced by *Antonio Zucchi*'s decorative classical paintings for Adam and accomplished stuccowork. The execution of Paine's designs is attributed to *Thomas Perritt* and *Joseph Rose*; *Adam* employed *Joseph Rose Jun. Thomas Chippendale*'s superb furniture and original colour schemes, restored in the late C20, are felicitous accompaniments.

The entrance is in the middle of the sub-structure of the outer staircase. Pedimented doorcase, added *c.* 1910. Adam's VESTIBULE, 1777, has apsidal ends, deep vaulted niches and detached Doric columns. Beyond an arcaded screen is the windowless LOWER HALL, again with Doric columns. From the broad lateral corridor behind rise Paine's two large symmetrically arranged STAIRCASES of *c.* 1747. The idea was taken from Kent's Devonshire House, Piccadilly. Both are top-lit. They have some of the earliest Rococo stucco in the north of England, of ascending complexity, and unconventionally richer on the N, family, stair (*see* below) than on the visitors' stair. The Vitruvian scroll and subdued fretwork panels here are possibly by *John Renison*. The more elaborate ornamentation, which includes touches of Chinoiserie in the mandarins with garlanded moustachios, is comparable with the plasterwork at Paine's Doncaster Mansion House (q.v.). Doorcases have his hallmark floating cornices. Iron balustrade with a double-S-shaped pattern.

Although all of *Paine*'s state rooms have later alterations, their coved ceilings are his, as are most of the door and window architraves (some of the latter with his splayed bases) and the chimneypieces. The BREAKFAST ROOM was restored after a fire in 1980, using designs in drawings by Paine. His Rococo-

Gothick chimneypiece with central ogee arch was brought
from a bedroom. In the CRIMSON ROOM, *c.* 1750, a chimneypiece with tapering Ionic pilasters to which *Adam* added rams'
heads, husks etc. The low-relief ceiling decoration is also by
him. Then two CLOSETS, now bathrooms, the first with early
C19 Chinese wallpaper, the second part of the magnificent
suite created in 1769–71 by remodelling the principal guest
bedroom and drawing room as STATE BEDROOM and STATE
DRESSING ROOM (although their titles have been reversed
since the C19). All three rooms have exquisitely hand-painted
Chinese paper with peacocks and other exotic birds among
luxuriant flowers. In Paine's Bedroom, Adam framed the bed
alcove with Ionic pilasters and flanking doorcases and added
the chimneypiece. In Paine's Drawing Room, his work is intact.
It is rich but not heavy. Exuberant Rococo ceiling with a centrepiece of putti playing musical instruments; fretwork frieze
and door architraves embellished with garlands of roses. Conservative chimneypiece with an elaborate carved overmantel
with scrolled pediment and more roses. Paine's most sumptuous work is the DINING ROOM, *c.* 1748–50. Rococo ceiling
with Ceres in the centre, vine frieze, marble chimneypiece with
heavy termini caryatids and cornucopia, and pedimented overmantel with big scrolls, dense swags and a painting by *Joseph
Nicholls c.* 1750. Ornately carved wall panels carrying eagles in
their pediments; framed roundels over the doors with shaped
cornice-strips. The side tables are among *Paine's* designs for
furniture for the house. Adam added the overdoor medallions
of putti and the arabesque panels, which were overpainted by
Thomas Ward in 1819.

55   The other principal interiors are *Adam's*. The TOP HALL,
executed 1774, is his grandest room, among his best in Yorkshire, decorated in half-Neoclassical, half-Etruscan style, and
painted in off-whites. He converted the back wall and the area
behind it into a dignified Roman composition of an apse, from
which three doors lead into oval vestibules. The two outer
vestibules are lit by open aedicules either side of the apse. This
tripartite composition is mirrored on the other walls, which
have central arched bays, flanked on the side walls by doors
and on the entrance wall by windows. Panels within the arched
bays repeat the triple arrangement. Delightfully crisp and
dainty decoration. The blank rectangular panels over the
doors, windows and chimneypieces were intended to contain
large-scale figurative subjects. Stone chimneypieces by *Christopher Theakston*. The central vestibule leads to the SALOON,
finished in 1776. As grand as the Hall, it has a smaller apse
adjoining the intermediate vestibule. Coved ceiling with superb
stuccowork, originally mainly in green and pink. Its principal
motif is semicircles, a somewhat restless device. Elsewhere
delicate anthemion, scrolls etc. abound. The central roundel
and the cameo-like medallions in the cove were sketched by
Zucchi, whose four wall panels are among the largest he ever
painted. White marble chimneypieces probably by *John Deval*

Sen. To the N the TAPESTRY ROOM was a drawing room. The ceiling, which achieves its effect with delightful painted decoration rather than the plasterwork, is especially successful. Central medallion surrounded by eight lunettes, depicting the education of Cupid by Venus and the Muses. Pilasters painted with arabesques were removed for the tapestries installed 1822–4. The statue of Flora and Zephyr is by *R. J. Wyatt*, 1834; the chimneypiece probably by *Deval*. N again, the LIBRARY, 1766–7, was Adam's first room at Nostell. Pedimented wall fitments for books, with Ionic pilasters; these and the friezes and pediments all closely and delicately ornamented. Now grained, they were originally painted in green, pink and white to match the ceiling. Marble chimneypiece by *Deval*, with relief in wood by *William Collins*. The massive library table is one of *Chippendale*'s masterpieces.

At the N end the inner part of the BILLIARD ROOM was decorated by *Adam, c.* 1771, and then extended in 1783 to form a T-shaped vestibule to his NE wing and its proposed NW counterpart. The extension has screened ends and a distinct change in style from the earlier rooms, with more restrained, Grecian, decoration. The reused central Venetian window was meant to look into a court between the wings. S chimneypiece has plaster bas relief with a scene from Dante, by *Richard Westmacott the Younger*, 1837. *Paine*'s lavish plasterwork on the NORTH STAIRCASE includes elaborately festooned frames and portrait medallions on the top floor. Luscious Rococo on the compartmented ceiling and tapering skylight mullions. Iron balustrade with acanthus ornament and tapered newels. In the LITTLE DINING ROOM, which was a dressing room in the C18, *Adam* decorated *Paine*'s doors with arabesques and charming little medallions. Venus and Cupid on the ceiling and painted paper decoration applied to the cove. Chimneypiece with marble inlay, part of *Thomas Ward*'s redecoration 1819–21. The DRAWING ROOM was originally a family bedroom, and like several on the second floor has a chimneypiece by *Paine*.

STABLES. Long, low quadrangle in classical style, with a complicated history of building and rebuilding and a rare combination of uses. Pedimented entrance in the centre of the N side by *Paine*, probably built in the 1750s. The tall clock turret with cupola, however, is from a drawing by *Adam*, 1776, used by *Watson, Pritchett & Watson* for the W entrance formed *c.* 1827. It was moved by *MacVicar Anderson* in 1875, when he built the E part of the N range and the E range. These parts retain many original fittings. The S and W sides by *Adam, c.* 1769–73. The RIDING HOUSE, in the centre of the S side, has a first-floor viewing gallery with Doric screen and is, unusually, integrated with the utilitarian space of the stable yard. Its S front has a tall semicircular loggia flanked by a GREENHOUSE on the E behind Doric colonnades and, originally, an outward-facing GARDEN ROOM on the W, both segmental in plan. These three quite separate 'polite' spaces were quite unrelated to the stables behind. End pavilions with pyramidal roofs and

Venetian windows. The Garden Room was rebuilt as a coach-house *c.* 1827 by *Watson Pritchett & Watson*. Adam's w range was altered internally when *MacVicar Anderson* built the NW corner and N range w of the entrance in 1904.

PARK and GARDENS. The deer park was landscaped between 1730 and 1820; some elements of the designs remain. The earliest plans are by *Stephen Switzer, c.* 1730 and *Joseph Perfect*, 1731; both included the grand AVENUE that runs E for a mile. Its width is that of the house with the quadrant galleries and pavilions. The three serpentine LAKES, w of the house, date from a more naturalistic scheme of the late 1750s. The Middle and Upper Lakes are separated by the Wakefield–Doncaster road, on a BRIDGE designed by *Sir George Savile*, 1759–61. Five elliptical arches, increasing in height and width towards the centre. In the GARDENS beyond the Middle Lake is the crenellated Gothick MENAGERIE HOUSE. Canted front by *Paine*, 1765, small wings added by *Adam, c.* 1776. At the E end of Lower Lake a small BRIDGE and BOATHOUSE, early C19. – OBELISK LODGE. On a low ridge N of the house. By the *Adam* brothers, 1776–7. A tall pyramid, also known as the 'Needle's Eye'. Formerly the principal entrance, on the route to York via Featherstone. The central archway, framed by Tuscan columns and pediment, cuts through the pyramid. – FOULBY LODGE, Doncaster Road. *c.* 1800, with gabled front facing the former drive. The *Adam*s' gateway, 1776–7, has gone. – WRAGBY LODGE, Doncaster Road. By the *Adam*s, 1776–7. Two plain square lodges with low pyramidal roofs and curved screen walls. – ESTATE YARD. Well laid out *c.* 1830–50, with residences, kennels, cartsheds etc.

WRENTHORPE

ST ANNE. By *J. T. Micklethwaite*, 1872–4. Most interesting inside, where black timber is used to effect in the roof and the full-height chancel screen of tiered arches. Big w window, the rest narrow lancets. – STAINED GLASS. By *Kempe* – the three E windows, 1874, and nave S, first two from E, 1875. They are among his earlier works and the style is indeed still without those characteristics that make it so easy to recognize his later windows.

RED HALL, ⅝ m. ESE. C17 brick manor house, much altered: Ground floor of main range, recessed behind later arcade of three round arches, has two chamfered mullioned windows, of three and four lights. (Similar windows at rear, under continuous dripstones, and in projecting l. cross-wing.)

SILCOATES SCHOOL, ½ m. SW. Founded as the Yorkshire Dissenters' Grammar School in 1820 and originally occupying SILCOATES HOUSE, a charming Wakefield suburban residence of *c.* 1748, now the headmaster's house. Brick with fine stone dressings. Two-and-a-half storeys, but not deep, hence the lower two-bay wings. The centre of the E front is stressed by a blank giant arch, in the way favoured in the area. Arched doorway within attached Doric columns set on sill band, fluted frieze and dentilled pediment. Either side are two-storey canted bay windows, the ground floor with columns and frieze matching the doorway, the upper more daintily decorated with Vitruvian scroll frieze. Pretty ogee lead roofs (cf. Netherton Hall). Attached to the S, the Hall, projecting by a bay, its pedimented front with giant Venetian window between paired Ionic pilasters and, beyond, a disconcertingly faithful copy of the C18 house, all by *Oliver & Dodgshun*, 1907–8, replacing 1870s additions destroyed by fire. To the E, in an L-plan, a new Hall and Chapel, each with big pedimented porch, by *W. Illingworth & Sons,* 1931. Confronting the older ranges across lawns a large block by *Garnett & Netherwood*, 1990–1, brashly attempting to fit in.

MELBOURNE HOUSE, ½ m. NNW. 1856–7 for Prophet Wroe, leader of the Christian Israelites, a sect inspired by Joanna Southcott. Stately stone house, seven by four bays, with giant Ionic pilasters. Distyle recessed porticos to front and r. return. Plain parapet. Inside: impressive cedar and mahogany staircase in one long flight.

GLOSSARY

Numbers and letters refer to the illustrations (by John Sambrook)
on pp. 780–787.

ABACUS: flat slab forming the top of a capital (3a).

ACANTHUS: classical formalized leaf ornament (4b).

ACCUMULATOR TOWER: *see* Hydraulic power.

ACHIEVEMENT: a complete display of armorial bearings.

ACROTERION: plinth for a statue or ornament on the apex or ends of a pediment; more usually, both the plinth and what stands on it (4a).

AEDICULE (*lit.* little building): architectural surround, consisting usually of two columns or pilasters supporting a pediment.

AGGREGATE: *see* Concrete.

AISLE: subsidiary space alongside the body of a building, separated from it by columns, piers, or posts.

ALMONRY: a building from which alms are dispensed to the poor.

AMBULATORY (*lit.* walkway): aisle around the sanctuary (q.v.).

ANGLE ROLL: roll moulding in the angle between two planes (1a).

ANSE DE PANIER: *see* Arch.

ANTAE: simplified pilasters (4a), usually applied to the ends of the enclosing walls of a portico *in antis* (q.v.).

ANTEFIXAE: ornaments projecting at regular intervals above a Greek cornice, originally to conceal the ends of roof tiles (4a).

ANTHEMION: classical ornament like a honeysuckle flower (4b).

APRON: raised panel below a window or wall monument or tablet.

APSE: semicircular or polygonal end of an apartment, especially of a chancel or chapel. In classical architecture sometimes called an *exedra*.

ARABESQUE: non-figurative surface decoration consisting of flowing lines, foliage scrolls etc., based on geometrical patterns. Cf. Grotesque.

ARCADE: series of arches supported by piers or columns. *Blind arcade* or *arcading*: the same applied to the wall surface. *Wall arcade*: in medieval churches, a blind arcade forming a dado below windows. Also a covered shopping street.

ARCH: Shapes *see* 5c. *Basket arch* or *anse de panier* (basket handle): three-centred and depressed, or with a flat centre. *Nodding*: ogee arch curving forward from the wall face. *Parabolic*: shaped like a chain suspended from two level points, but inverted. Special purposes. *Chancel*: dividing chancel from nave or crossing. *Crossing*: spanning piers at a crossing (q.v.). *Relieving or discharging*: incorporated in a wall to relieve superimposed weight (5c). *Skew*: spanning responds not diametrically opposed. *Strainer*: inserted in an opening to resist inward pressure. *Transverse*: spanning a main axis (e.g. of a vaulted space). See also Jack arch, Triumphal arch.

ARCHITRAVE: formalized lintel, the lowest member of the classical entablature (3a). Also the moulded frame of a door or window (often borrowing the profile of a classical architrave). For *lugged* and *shouldered* architraves *see* 4b.

ARCUATED: dependent structurally on the arch principle. Cf. Trabeated.

ARK: chest or cupboard housing the

tables of Jewish law in a synagogue.

ARRIS: sharp edge where two surfaces meet at an angle (3a).

ASHLAR: masonry of large blocks wrought to even faces and square edges (6d).

ASTRAGAL: classical moulding of semicircular section (3f).

ASTYLAR: with no columns or similar vertical features.

ATLANTES: *see* Caryatids.

ATRIUM (plural: atria): inner court of a Roman or C20 house; in a multi-storey building, a toplit covered court rising through all storeys. Also an open court in front of a church.

ATTACHED COLUMN: *see* Engaged column.

ATTIC: small top storey within a roof. Also the storey above the main entablature of a classical façade.

AUMBRY: recess or cupboard to hold sacred vessels for the Mass.

BAILEY: *see* Motte-and-bailey.

BALANCE BEAM: *see* Canals.

BALDACCHINO: free-standing canopy, originally fabric, over an altar. Cf. Ciborium.

BALLFLOWER: globular flower of three petals enclosing a ball (1a). Typical of the Decorated style.

BALUSTER: pillar or pedestal of bellied form. *Balusters*: vertical supports of this or any other form, for a handrail or coping, the whole being called a *balustrade* (6c). *Blind balustrade*: the same applied to the wall surface.

BARBICAN: outwork defending the entrance to a castle.

BARGEBOARDS (corruption of 'vergeboards'): boards, often carved or fretted, fixed beneath the eaves of a gable to cover and protect the rafters.

BAROQUE: style originating in Rome *c.*1600 and current in England *c.*1680–1720, characterized by dramatic massing and silhouette and the use of the giant order.

BARROW: burial mound.

BARTIZAN: corbelled turret, square or round, frequently at an angle.

BASCULE: hinged part of a lifting (or bascule) bridge.

BASE: moulded foot of a column or pilaster. For *Attic* base *see* 3b.

BASEMENT: lowest, subordinate storey; hence the lowest part of a classical elevation, below the *piano nobile* (q.v.).

BASILICA: a Roman public hall; hence an aisled building with a clerestory.

BASTION: one of a series of defensive semicircular or polygonal projections from the main wall of a fortress or city.

BATTER: intentional inward inclination of a wall face.

BATTLEMENT: defensive parapet, composed of *merlons* (solid) and *crenels* (embrasures) through which archers could shoot; sometimes called *crenellation*. Also used decoratively.

BAY: division of an elevation or interior space as defined by regular vertical features such as arches, columns, windows etc.

BAY LEAF: classical ornament of overlapping bay leaves (3f).

BAY WINDOW: window of one or more storeys projecting from the face of a building. *Canted*: with a straight front and angled sides. *Bow window*: curved. *Oriel*: rests on corbels or brackets and starts above ground level; also the bay window at the dais end of a medieval great hall.

BEAD-AND-REEL: *see* Enrichments.

BEAKHEAD: Norman ornament with a row of beaked bird or beast heads usually biting into a roll moulding (1a).

BELFRY: chamber or stage in a tower where bells are hung.

BELL CAPITAL: *see* 1b.

BELLCOTE: small gabled or roofed housing for the bell(s).

BERM: level area separating a ditch from a bank on a hill-fort or barrow.

BILLET: Norman ornament of small half-cylindrical or rectangular blocks (1a).

BLIND: *see* Arcade, Baluster, Portico.

BLOCK CAPITAL: *see* 1a.

BLOCKED: columns, etc. interrupted by regular projecting

blocks (*blocking*), as on a Gibbs surround (4b).

BLOCKING COURSE: course of stones, or equivalent, on top of a cornice and crowning the wall.

BOLECTION MOULDING: covering the joint between two different planes (6b).

BOND: the pattern of long sides (*stretchers*) and short ends (*headers*) produced on the face of a wall by laying bricks in a particular way (6e).

BOSS: knob or projection, e.g. at the intersection of ribs in a vault (2c).

BOWTELL: a term in use by the C15 for a form of roll moulding, usually three-quarters of a circle in section (also called *edge roll*).

BOW WINDOW: *see* Bay window.

BOX FRAME: timber-framed construction in which vertical and horizontal wall members support the roof (7). Also concrete construction where the loads are taken on cross walls; also called *cross-wall construction*.

BRACE: subsidiary member of a structural frame, curved or straight. *Bracing* is often arranged decoratively e.g. quatrefoil, herringbone (7). *See also* Roofs.

BRATTISHING: ornamental crest, usually formed of leaves, Tudor flowers or miniature battlements.

BRESSUMER (*lit.* breast-beam): big horizontal beam supporting the wall above, especially in a jettied building (7).

BRICK: *see* Bond, Cogging, Engineering, Gauged, Tumbling.

BRIDGE: *Bowstring*: with arches rising above the roadway which is suspended from them. *Clapper*: one long stone forms the roadway. *Roving*: *see* Canal. *Suspension*: roadway suspended from cables or chains slung between towers or pylons. *Stay-suspension* or *stay-cantilever*: supported by diagonal stays from towers or pylons. *See also* Bascule.

BRISES-SOLEIL: projecting fins or canopies which deflect direct sunlight from windows.

BROACH: *see* Spire and 1c.

BUCRANIUM: ox skull used decoratively in classical friezes.

BULL-NOSED SILL: sill displaying a pronounced convex upper moulding.

BULLSEYE WINDOW: small oval window, set horizontally (cf. Oculus). Also called *œil de bœuf*.

BUTTRESS: vertical member projecting from a wall to stabilize it or to resist the lateral thrust of an arch, roof, or vault (1c, 2c). A *flying buttress* transmits the thrust to a heavy abutment by means of an arch or half-arch (1c).

CABLE OR ROPE MOULDING: originally Norman, like twisted strands of a rope.

CAMES: *see* Quarries.

CAMPANILE: free-standing bell-tower.

CANALS: *Flash lock*: removable weir or similar device through which boats pass on a flush of water. Predecessor of the *pound lock*: chamber with gates at each end allowing boats to float from one level to another. *Tidal gates*: single pair of lock gates allowing vessels to pass when the tide makes a level. *Balance beam*: beam projecting horizontally for opening and closing lock gates. *Roving bridge*: carrying a towing path from one bank to the other.

CANTILEVER: horizontal projection (e.g. step, canopy) supported by a downward force behind the fulcrum.

CAPITAL: head or crowning feature of a column or pilaster; for classical types *see* 3; for medieval types *see* 1b.

CARREL: compartment designed for individual work or study.

CARTOUCHE: classical tablet with ornate frame (4b).

CARYATIDS: female figures supporting an entablature; their male counterparts are *Atlantes* (*lit.* Atlas figures).

CASEMATE: vaulted chamber, with embrasures for defence, within a castle wall or projecting from it.

CASEMENT: side-hinged window.

CASTELLATED: with battlements (q.v.).

CAST IRON: hard and brittle, cast in a mould to the required shape.

Wrought iron is ductile, strong in tension, forged into decorative patterns or forged and rolled into e.g. bars, joists, boiler plates; *mild steel* is its modern equivalent, similar but stronger.

CATSLIDE: *See* 8a.

CAVETTO: concave classical moulding of quarter-round section (3f).

CELURE OR CEILURE: enriched area of roof above rood or altar.

CEMENT: *see* Concrete.

CENOTAPH (*lit.* empty tomb): funerary monument which is not a burying place.

CENTRING: wooden support for the building of an arch or vault, removed after completion.

CHAMFER (*lit.* corner-break): surface formed by cutting off a square edge or corner. For types of chamfers and *chamfer stops see* 6a. *See also* Double chamfer.

CHANCEL: part of the E end of a church set apart for the use of the officiating clergy.

CHANTRY CHAPEL: often attached to or within a church, endowed for the celebration of Masses principally for the soul of the founder.

CHEVET (*lit.* head): French term for chancel with ambulatory and radiating chapels.

CHEVRON: V-shape used in series or double series (later) on a Norman moulding (1a). Also (especially when on a single plane) called *zigzag*.

CHOIR: the part of a cathedral, monastic or collegiate church where services are sung.

CIBORIUM: a fixed canopy over an altar, usually vaulted and supported on four columns; cf. Baldacchino. Also a canopied shrine for the reserved sacrament.

CINQUEFOIL: *see* Foil.

CIST: stone-lined or slab-built grave.

CLADDING: external covering or skin applied to a structure, especially a framed one.

CLERESTORY: uppermost storey of the nave of a church, pierced by windows. Also high-level windows in secular buildings.

CLOSER: a brick cut to complete a bond (6e).

CLUSTER BLOCK: *see* Multi-storey.

COADE STONE: ceramic artificial stone made in Lambeth 1769–c.1840 by Eleanor Coade (†1821) and her associates.

COB: walling material of clay mixed with straw. Also called *pisé*.

COFFERING: arrangement of sunken panels (coffers), square or polygonal, decorating a ceiling, vault, or arch.

COGGING: a decorative course of bricks laid diagonally (6e). Cf. Dentilation.

COLLAR: *see* Roofs and 7.

COLLEGIATE CHURCH: endowed for the support of a college of priests.

COLONNADE: range of columns supporting an entablature. Cf. Arcade.

COLONNETTE: small medieval column or shaft.

COLOSSAL ORDER: *see* Giant order.

COLUMBARIUM: shelved, niched structure to house multiple burials.

COLUMN: a classical, upright structural member of round section with a shaft, a capital, and usually a base (3a, 4a).

COLUMN FIGURE: carved figure attached to a medieval column or shaft, usually flanking a doorway.

COMMUNION TABLE: unconsecrated table used in Protestant churches for the celebration of Holy Communion.

COMPOSITE: *see* Orders.

COMPOUND PIER: grouped shafts (q.v.), or a solid core surrounded by shafts.

CONCRETE: composition of *cement* (calcined lime and clay), *aggregate* (small stones or rock chippings), sand and water. It can be poured into *formwork* or *shuttering* (temporary frame of timber or metal) on site (*in-situ* concrete), or *pre-cast* as components before construction. *Reinforced*: incorporating steel rods to take the tensile force. *Pre-stressed*: with tensioned steel rods. Finishes include the impression of boards left by formwork (*board-marked* or *shuttered*), and texturing with steel brushes (*brushed*) or hammers (*hammer-dressed*). *See also* Shell.

CONSOLE: bracket of curved outline (4b).

COPING: protective course of masonry or brickwork capping a wall (6d).

CORBEL: projecting block supporting something above. *Corbel course*: continuous course of projecting stones or bricks fulfilling the same function. *Corbel table*: series of corbels to carry a parapet or a wall-plate or wall-post (7). *Corbelling*: brick or masonry courses built out beyond one another to support a chimney-stack, window, etc.

CORINTHIAN: *see* Orders and 3d.

CORNICE: flat-topped ledge with moulded underside, projecting along the top of a building or feature, especially as the highest member of the classical entablature (3a). Also the decorative moulding in the angle between wall and ceiling.

CORPS-DE-LOGIS: the main building(s) as distinct from the wings or pavilions.

COTTAGE ORNÉ: an artfully rustic small house associated with the Picturesque movement.

COUNTERCHANGING: of joists on a ceiling divided by beams into compartments, when placed in opposite directions in alternate squares.

COUR D'HONNEUR: formal entrance court before a house in the French manner, usually with flanking wings and a screen wall or gates.

COURSE: continuous layer of stones, etc. in a wall (6e).

COVE: a broad concave moulding, e.g. to mask the eaves of a roof. *Coved ceiling*: with a pronounced cove joining the walls to a flat central panel smaller than the whole area of the ceiling.

CRADLE ROOF: *see* Wagon roof.

CREDENCE: a shelf within or beside a piscina (q.v.), or a table for the sacramental elements and vessels.

CRENELLATION: parapet with crenels (*see* Battlement).

CRINKLE-CRANKLE WALL: garden wall undulating in a series of serpentine curves.

CROCKETS: leafy hooks. *Crocketing* decorates the edges of Gothic features, such as pinnacles, canopies, etc. *Crocket capital*: *see* 1b.

CROSSING: central space at the junction of the nave, chancel, and transepts. *Crossing tower*: above a crossing.

CROSS-WINDOW: with one mullion and one transom (qq.v.).

CROWN-POST: *see* Roofs and 7.

CROWSTEPS: squared stones set like steps, e.g. on a gable (8a).

CRUCKS (*lit.* crooked): pairs of inclined timbers (*blades*), usually curved, set at bay-lengths; they support the roof timbers and, in timber buildings, also support the walls (8b). *Base*: blades rise from ground level to a tie- or collar-beam which supports the roof timbers. *Full*: blades rise from ground level to the apex of the roof, serving as the main members of a roof truss. *Jointed*: blades formed from more than one timber; the lower member may act as a wall-post; it is usually elbowed at wall-plate level and jointed just above. *Middle*: blades rise from half-way up the walls to a tie- or collar-beam. *Raised*: blades rise from half-way up the walls to the apex. *Upper*: blades supported on a tie-beam and rising to the apex.

CRYPT: underground or half-underground area, usually below the E end of a church. *Ring crypt*: corridor crypt surrounding the apse of an early medieval church, often associated with chambers for relics. Cf. Undercroft.

CUPOLA (*lit.* dome): especially a small dome on a circular or polygonal base crowning a larger dome, roof, or turret.

CURSUS: a long avenue defined by two parallel earthen banks with ditches outside.

CURTAIN WALL: a connecting wall between the towers of a castle. Also a non-load-bearing external wall applied to a C20 framed structure.

CUSP: *see* Tracery and 2b.

CYCLOPEAN MASONRY: large irregular polygonal stones, smooth and finely jointed.

CYMA RECTA and CYMA REVERSA:
classical mouldings with double
curves (3f). Cf. Ogee.

DADO: the finishing (often with
panelling) of the lower part of a
wall in a classical interior; in origin
a formalized continuous pedestal.
Dado rail: the moulding along the
top of the dado.

DAGGER: *see* Tracery and 2b.

DALLE-DE-VERRE (*lit.* glass-slab): a
late C20 stained-glass technique,
setting large, thick pieces of cast
glass into a frame of reinforced
concrete or epoxy resin.

DEC (DECORATED): English Gothic
architecture *c.* 1290 to *c.* 1350.
The name is derived from the type
of window tracery (q.v.) used
during the period.

DEMI- or HALF-COLUMNS: engaged columns (q.v.) half of
whose circumference projects
from the wall.

DENTIL: small square block used in
series in classical cornices (3c).
Dentilation is produced by the
projection of alternating headers
along cornices or stringcourses.

DIAPER: repetitive surface decoration of lozenges or squares flat or
in relief. Achieved in brickwork
with bricks of two colours.

DIOCLETIAN OR THERMAL WIN-
DOW: semicircular with two mul-
lions, as used in the Baths of
Diocletian, Rome (4b).

DISTYLE: having two columns (4a).

DOGTOOTH: E.E. ornament, consisting of a series of small pyramids formed by four stylized
canine teeth meeting at a point
(1a).

DORIC: *see* Orders and 3a, 3b.

DORMER: window projecting from
the slope of a roof (8a).

DOUBLE CHAMFER: a chamfer
applied to each of two recessed
arches (1a).

DOUBLE PILE: *see* Pile.

DRAGON BEAM: *see* Jetty.

DRESSINGS: the stone or brickwork
worked to a finished face about an
angle, opening, or other feature.

DRIPSTONE: moulded stone projecting from a wall to protect the
lower parts from water. Cf. Hoodmould, Weathering.

DRUM: circular or polygonal stage
supporting a dome or cupola. Also
one of the stones forming the shaft
of a column (3a).

DUTCH or FLEMISH GABLE: *see* 8a.

EASTER SEPULCHRE: tomb-chest
used for Easter ceremonial, within
or against the N wall of a chancel.

EAVES: overhanging edge of a roof;
hence *eaves cornice* in this position.

ECHINUS: ovolo moulding (q.v.)
below the abacus of a Greek Doric
capital (3a).

EDGE RAIL: *see* Railways.

E.E. (EARLY ENGLISH): English
Gothic architecture *c.* 1190–1250.

EGG-AND-DART: *see* Enrichments
and 3f.

ELEVATION: any face of a building
or side of a room. In a drawing,
the same or any part of it, represented in two dimensions.

EMBATTLED: with battlements.

EMBRASURE: small splayed opening
in a wall or battlement (q.v.).

ENCAUSTIC TILES: earthenware
tiles fired with a pattern and glaze.

EN DELIT: stone cut against the bed.

ENFILADE: reception rooms in a
formal series, usually with all
doorways on axis.

ENGAGED or ATTACHED COLUMN:
one that partly merges into a wall
or pier.

ENGINEERING BRICKS: dense
bricks, originally used mostly for
railway viaducts etc.

ENRICHMENTS: the carved decoration of certain classical mouldings, e.g. the ovolo (qq.v.) with
egg-and-dart, the cyma reversa
with *waterleaf*, the astragal with
bead-and-reel (3f).

ENTABLATURE: in classical architecture, collective name for the
three horizontal members (architrave, frieze, and cornice) carried
by a wall or a column (3a).

ENTASIS: very slight convex devi-
ation from a straight line, used to
prevent an optical illusion of con-
cavity.

EPITAPH: inscription on a tomb.

EXEDRA: *see* Apse.

EXTRADOS: outer curved face of an arch or vault.

EYECATCHER: decorative building terminating a vista.

FASCIA: plain horizontal band, e.g. in an architrave (3c, 3d) or on a shopfront.

FENESTRATION: the arrangement of windows in a façade.

FERETORY: site of the chief shrine of a church, behind the high altar.

FESTOON: ornamental garland, suspended from both ends. Cf. Swag.

FIBREGLASS, or glass-reinforced polyester (GRP): synthetic resin reinforced with glass fibre. GRC: glass-reinforced concrete.

FIELD: *see* Panelling and 6b.

FILLET: a narrow flat band running down a medieval shaft or along a roll moulding (1a). It separates larger curved mouldings in classical cornices, fluting or bases (3c).

FLAMBOYANT: the latest phase of French Gothic architecture, with flowing tracery.

FLASH LOCK: *see* Canals.

FLÈCHE or SPIRELET (*lit.* arrow): slender spire on the centre of a roof.

FLEURON: medieval carved flower or leaf, often rectilinear (1a).

FLUSHWORK: knapped flint used with dressed stone to form patterns.

FLUTING: series of concave grooves (flutes), their common edges sharp (arris) or blunt (fillet) (3).

FOIL (*lit.* leaf): lobe formed by the cusping of a circular or other shape in tracery (2b). *Trefoil* (three), *quatrefoil* (four), *cinquefoil* (five), and *multifoil* express the number of lobes in a shape.

FOLIATE: decorated with leaves.

FORMWORK: *see* Concrete.

FRAMED BUILDING: where the structure is carried by a framework – e.g. of steel, reinforced concrete, timber – instead of by load-bearing walls.

FREESTONE: stone that is cut, or can be cut, in all directions.

FRESCO: *al fresco*: painting on wet plaster. *Fresco secco*: painting on dry plaster.

FRIEZE: the middle member of the classical entablature, sometimes ornamented (3a). *Pulvinated frieze* (*lit.* cushioned): of bold convex profile (3c). Also a horizontal band of ornament.

FRONTISPIECE: in C16 and C17 buildings the central feature of doorway and windows above linked in one composition.

GABLE: For types *see* 8a. *Gablet*: small gable. *Pedimental gable*: treated like a pediment.

GADROONING: classical ribbed ornament like inverted fluting that flows into a lobed edge.

GALILEE: chapel or vestibule usually at the W end of a church enclosing the main portal(s).

GALLERY: a long room or passage; an upper storey above the aisle of a church, looking through arches to the nave; a balcony or mezzanine overlooking the main interior space of a building; or an external walkway.

GALLETING: small stones set in a mortar course.

GAMBREL ROOF: *see* 8a.

GARDEROBE: medieval privy.

GARGOYLE: projecting water spout often carved into human or animal shape.

GAUGED or RUBBED BRICKWORK: soft brick sawn roughly, then rubbed to a precise (gauged) surface. Mostly used for door or window openings (5c).

GAZEBO (jocular Latin, 'I shall gaze'): ornamental lookout tower or raised summer house.

GEOMETRIC: English Gothic architecture *c.* 1250–1310. *See also* Tracery. For another meaning, *see* Stairs.

GIANT or COLOSSAL ORDER: classical order (q.v.) whose height is that of two or more storeys of the building to which it is applied.

GIBBS SURROUND: C18 treatment of an opening (4b), seen particularly in the work of James Gibbs (1682–1754).

GIRDER: a large beam. *Box*: of hollow-box section. *Bowed*: with its top rising in a curve. *Plate*: of I-section, made from iron or steel plates. Lattice: with braced frame-work.

GLAZING BARS: wooden or some-times metal bars separating and supporting window panes.

GRAFFITI: see Sgraffito.

GRANGE: farm owned and run by a religious order.

GRC: see Fibreglass.

GRISAILLE: monochrome painting on walls or glass.

groin: sharp edge at the meeting of two cells of a cross-vault; see Vault and 2c.

GROTESQUE (*lit.* grotto-esque): wall decoration adopted from Roman examples in the Renaissance. Its foliage scrolls incorporate figur-ative elements. Cf. Arabesque.

GROTTO: artificial cavern.

GRP: see Fibreglass.

GUILLOCHE: classical ornament of interlaced bands (4b).

GUNLOOP: opening for a firearm.

GUTTAE: stylized drops (3b).

HALF-TIMBERING: archaic term for timber-framing (q.v.). Some-times used for non-structural decorative timberwork.

HALL CHURCH: medieval church with nave and aisles of approxim-ately equal height.

HAMMERBEAM: see Roofs and 7.

HEADER: see Bond and 6e.

HEADSTOP: stop (q.v.) carved with a head (5b).

HELM ROOF: see IC.

HENGE: ritual earthwork.

HERM (*lit.* the god Hermes): male head or bust on a pedestal.

HERRINGBONE WORK: see 7ii. Cf. Pitched masonry.

HEXASTYLE: see Portico.

HILL-FORT: Iron Age earthwork en-closed by a ditch and bank system.

HIPPED ROOF: see 8a.

HOODMOULD: projecting moulding above an arch or lintel to throw off water (2b, 5b). When horizontal often called a *label*. For label stop see Stop.

HOUSEBODY (Yorks.): main living room in C16–C17 yeoman houses, usually also used for cooking.

HUSK GARLAND: festoon of stylized nutshells (4b).

HYDRAULIC POWER: use of water under high pressure to work ma-chinery. *Accumulator tower*: houses a hydraulic accumulator which accommodates fluctuations in the flow through hydraulic mains.

HYPOCAUST (*lit.* underburning): Roman underfloor heating system.

IMPOST: horizontal moulding at the springing of an arch (5c).

IMPOST BLOCK: block between abacus and capital (1b).

IN ANTIS: see Antae, Portico and 4a.

INDENT: shape chiselled out of a stone to receive a brass.

INDUSTRIALIZED OR SYSTEM BUILDING: system of manufac-tured units assembled on site.

INGLENOOK (*lit.* fire-corner): recess for a hearth with provision for seating.

INTERCOLUMNATION: interval be-tween columns.

INTERLACE: decoration in relief simulating woven or entwined stems or bands.

INTRADOS: see Soffit.

IONIC: see Orders and 3c.

JACK ARCH: shallow segmental vault springing from beams, used for fireproof floors, bridge decks, etc.

JAMB (*lit.* leg): one of the vertical sides of an opening.

JETTY: in a timber-framed building, the projection of an upper storey beyond the storey below, made by the beams and joists of the lower storey oversailing the wall; on their outer ends is placed the sill of the walling for the storey above (7). Buildings can be jettied on several sides, in which case a *dragon beam* is set diagonally at the corner to carry the joists to either side.

JOGGLE: the joining of two stones to prevent them slipping by a notch in one and a projection in the other.

KEEL MOULDING: moulding used from the late C12, in section like the keel of a ship (1a).

KEEP: principal tower of a castle.

KENTISH CUSP: see Tracery and 2b.

KEY PATTERN: *see* 4b.

KEYSTONE: central stone in an arch or vault (4b, 5c).

KINGPOST: *see* Roofs and 7.

KNEELER: horizontal projecting stone at the base of each side of a gable to support the inclined coping stones (8a).

LABEL: *see* Hoodmould and 5b.

LABEL STOP: *see* Stop and 5b.

LACED BRICKWORK: vertical strips of brickwork, often in a contrasting colour, linking openings on different floors.

LACING COURSE: horizontal reinforcement in timber or brick to walls of flint, cobble, etc.

LADY CHAPEL: dedicated to the Virgin Mary (Our Lady).

LAITHE HOUSE: house and byre in the same range with internal access between them.

LANCET: slender single-light, pointed-arched window (2a).

LANTERN: circular or polygonal windowed turret crowning a roof or a dome. Also the windowed stage of a crossing tower lighting the church interior.

LANTERN CROSS: churchyard cross with lantern-shaped top.

LAVATORIUM: in a religious house, a washing place adjacent to the refectory.

LEAN-TO: *see* Roofs.

LESENE (*lit.* a mean thing): pilaster without base or capital. Also called *pilaster strip*.

LIERNE: *see* Vault and 2c.

LIGHT: compartment of a window defined by the mullions.

LINENFOLD: Tudor panelling carved with simulations of folded linen. *See also* Parchemin.

LINTEL: horizontal beam or stone bridging an opening.

LOGGIA: gallery, usually arcaded or colonnaded; sometimes freestanding.

LONG-AND-SHORT WORK: quoins consisting of stones placed with the long side alternately upright and horizontal, especially in Saxon building.

LOUVRE: roof opening, often protected by a raised timber structure, to allow the smoke from a central hearth to escape.

LOWSIDE WINDOW: set lower than the others in a chancel side wall, usually towards its W end.

LUCAM: projecting housing for hoist pulley on upper storey of warehouses, mills, etc., for raising goods to loading doors.

LUCARNE (*lit.* dormer): small gabled opening in a roof or spire.

LUGGED ARCHITRAVE: *see* 4b.

LUNETTE: semicircular window or blind panel.

LYCHGATE (*lit.* corpse-gate): roofed gateway entrance to a churchyard for the reception of a coffin.

LYNCHET: long terraced strip of soil on the downward side of prehistoric and medieval fields, accumulated because of continual ploughing along the contours.

MACHICOLATIONS (*lit.* mashing devices): series of openings between the corbels that support a projecting parapet through which missiles can be dropped. Used decoratively in post-medieval buildings.

MANOMETER or STANDPIPE TOWER: containing a column of water to regulate pressure in water mains.

MANSARD: *see* 8a.

MATHEMATICAL TILES: facing tiles with the appearance of brick, most often applied to timber-framed walls.

MAUSOLEUM: monumental building or chamber usually intended for the burial of members of one family.

MEGALITHIC TOMB: massive stone-built Neolithic burial chamber covered by an earth or stone mound.

MERLON: *see* Battlement.

METOPES: spaces between the triglyphs in a Doric frieze (3b).

MEZZANINE: low storey between two higher ones.

MILD STEEL: *see* Cast iron.

MISERICORD (*lit.* mercy): shelf on a carved bracket placed on the underside of a hinged choir stall seat to support an occupant when standing.

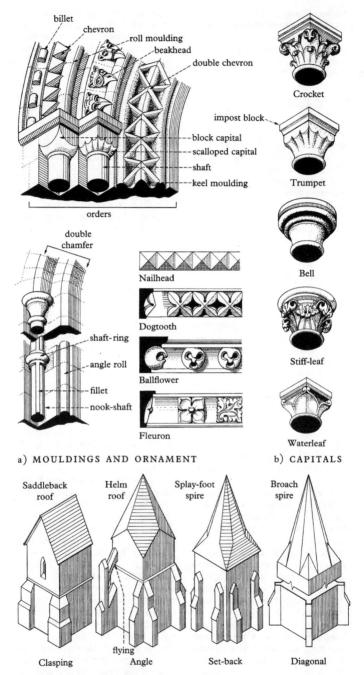

a) MOULDINGS AND ORNAMENT

b) CAPITALS

c) BUTTRESSES, ROOFS AND SPIRES

FIGURE I: MEDIEVAL

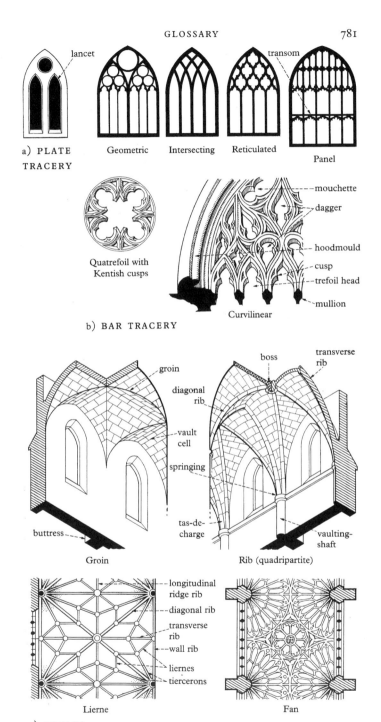

a) PLATE
   TRACERY

Geometric   Intersecting   Reticulated

Panel

Quatrefoil with
Kentish cusps

mouchette

dagger

hoodmould

cusp

trefoil head

mullion

Curvilinear

b) BAR TRACERY

groin

diagonal
rib

vault
cell

buttress

Groin

boss   transverse
              rib

springing

tas-de-
charge

vaulting-
shaft

Rib (quadripartite)

longitudinal
ridge rib

diagonal rib

transverse
rib

wall rib

liernes

tiercerons

Lierne   Fan

c) VAULTS

FIGURE 2: MEDIEVAL

ORDERS

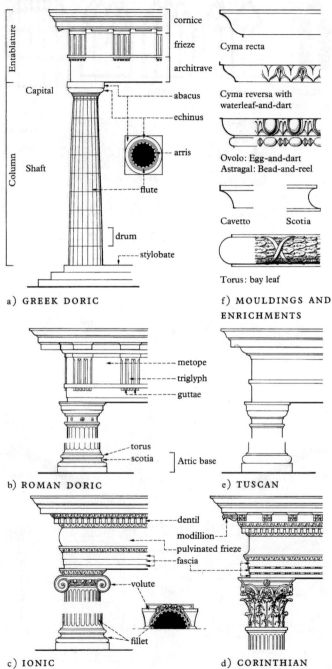

cornice
frieze
architrave
abacus
echinus
arris
flute
drum
stylobate

Entablature
Capital
Column
Shaft

a) GREEK DORIC

Cyma recta

Cyma reversa with
waterleaf-and-dart

Ovolo: Egg-and-dart
Astragal: Bead-and-reel

Cavetto   Scotia

Torus: bay leaf

f) MOULDINGS AND
ENRICHMENTS

metope
triglyph
guttae

torus
scotia

Attic base

b) ROMAN DORIC

e) TUSCAN

dentil
modillion
pulvinated frieze
fascia

volute

fillet

c) IONIC

d) CORINTHIAN

FIGURE 3: CLASSICAL

a) PORTICO

Distyle in antis   Prostyle

Anthemion & Palmette   Guilloche   Key pattern

Rinceau   Husk garland   Vitruvian scroll

Console   Diocletian window   Acanthus

Broken pediment   Lugged architrave

Segmental pediment   Shouldered architrave

Venetian window

Open pediment   Swan-neck pediment   Gibbs surround

b) ORNAMENTS AND FEATURES

FIGURE 4: CLASSICAL

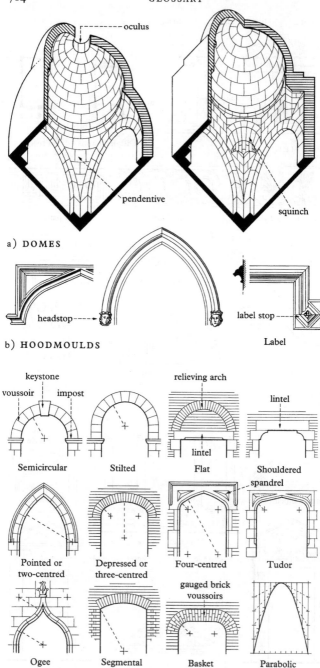

a) DOMES

b) HOODMOULDS

Label

c) ARCHES

FIGURE 5: CONSTRUCTION

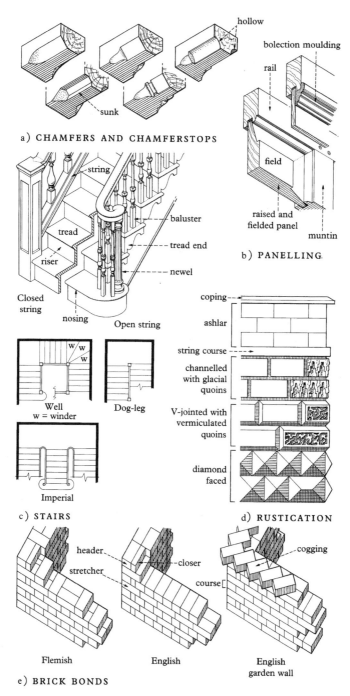

a) CHAMFERS AND CHAMFERSTOPS

hollow

bolection moulding

rail

field

raised and
fielded panel

muntin

b) PANELLING

string

baluster

tread

tread end

riser

newel

Closed
string

nosing

Open string

Well
w = winder

Dog-leg

Imperial

c) STAIRS

coping

ashlar

string course

channelled
with glacial
quoins

V-jointed with
vermiculated
quoins

diamond
faced

d) RUSTICATION

header

closer

stretcher

course

cogging

Flemish

English

English
garden wall

e) BRICK BONDS

FIGURE 6: CONSTRUCTION

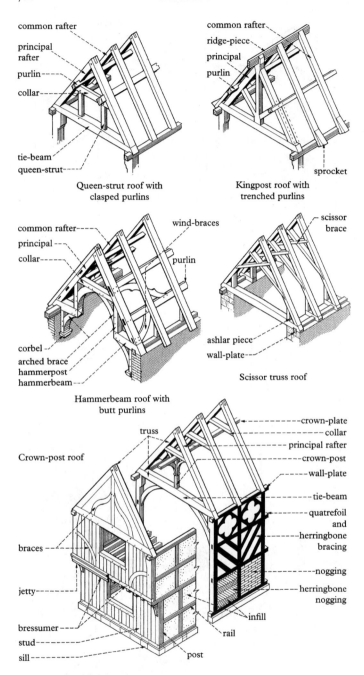

Queen-strut roof with
clasped purlins

Kingpost roof with
trenched purlins

Hammerbeam roof with
butt purlins

Scissor truss roof

Box frame: i) Close studding   ii) Square panel

FIGURE 7: ROOFS AND TIMBER-FRAMING

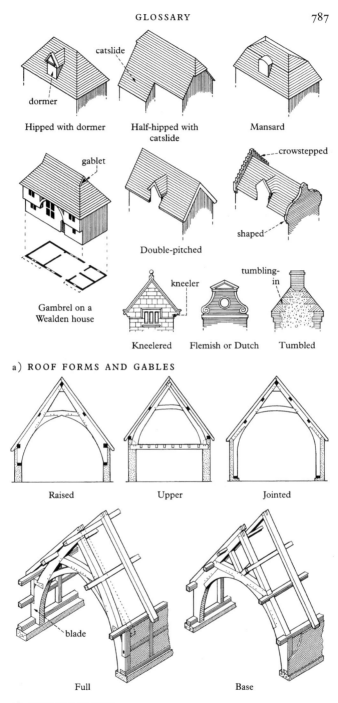

a) ROOF FORMS AND GABLES

Hipped with dormer

Half-hipped with catslide

Mansard

Gambrel on a Wealden house

Double-pitched

Kneelered

Flemish or Dutch

Tumbled

Raised

Upper

Jointed

Full

Base

b) CRUCK FRAMES

FIGURE 8: ROOFS AND TIMBER-FRAMING

MIXER-COURTS: forecourts to groups of houses shared by vehicles and pedestrians.

MODILLIONS: small consoles (q.v.) along the underside of a Corinthian or Composite cornice (3d). Often used along an eaves cornice.

MODULE: a predetermined standard size for co-ordinating the dimensions of components of a building.

MOTTE-AND-BAILEY: post-Roman and Norman defence consisting of an earthen mound (motte) topped by a wooden tower within a bailey, an enclosure defended by a ditch and palisade, and also, sometimes, by an internal bank.

MOUCHETTE: *see* Tracery and 2b.

MOULDING: shaped ornamental strip of continuous section; *see* e.g. Cavetto, Cyma, Ovolo, Roll.

MULLION: vertical member between window lights (2b).

MULTI-STOREY: five or more storeys. Multi-storey flats may form a *cluster block*, with individual blocks of flats grouped round a service core; a *point block*, with flats fanning out from a service core; or a *slab block*, with flats approached by corridors or galleries from service cores at intervals or towers at the ends (plan also used for offices, hotels etc.). *Tower block* is a generic term for any very high multi-storey building.

MUNTIN: *see* Panelling and 6b.

NAILHEAD: E.E. ornament consisting of small pyramids regularly repeated (1a).

NARTHEX: enclosed vestibule or covered porch at the main entrance to a church.

NAVE: the body of a church W of the crossing or chancel often flanked by aisles (q.v.).

NEWEL: central or corner post of a staircase (6c). Newel stair: *see* Stairs.

NIGHT STAIR: stair by which religious entered the transept of their church from their dormitory to celebrate night services.

NOGGING: *see* Timber-framing (7).

NOOK-SHAFT: shaft set in the angle of a wall or opening (1a).

NORMAN: *see* Romanesque.

NOSING: projection of the tread of a step (6c).

NUTMEG: medieval ornament with a chain of tiny triangles placed obliquely.

OCULUS: circular opening.

ŒIL DE BŒUF: *see* Bullseye window.

OGEE: double curve, bending first one way and then the other, as in an *ogee* or *ogival arch* (5c). Cf. Cyma recta and Cyma reversa.

OPUS SECTILE: decorative mosaic-like facing.

OPUS SIGNINUM: composition flooring of Roman origin.

ORATORY: a private chapel in a church or a house. Also a church of the Oratorian Order.

ORDER: one of a series of recessed arches and jambs forming a splayed medieval opening, e.g. a doorway or arcade arch (1a).

ORDERS: the formalized versions of the post-and-lintel system in classical architecture. The main orders are *Doric*, *Ionic*, and *Corinthian*. They are Greek in origin but occur in Roman versions. Tuscan is a simple version of Roman Doric. Though each order has its own conventions (3), there are many minor variations. The *Composite* capital combines Ionic volutes with Corinthian foliage. *Superimposed orders*: orders on successive levels, usually in the upward sequence of Tuscan, Doric, Ionic, Corinthian, Composite.

ORIEL: *see* Bay window.

OVERDOOR: painting or relief above an internal door. Also called a *sopraporta*.

OVERTHROW: decorative fixed arch between two gatepiers or above a wrought-iron gate.

OVOLO: wide convex moulding (3f).

PALIMPSEST: of a brass: where a metal plate has been reused by turning over the engraving on the back; of a wall painting: where one overlaps and partly obscures an earlier one.

PALLADIAN: following the examples and principles of Andrea Palladio (1508–80).

PALMETTE: classical ornament like a palm shoot (4b).

PANELLING: wooden lining to interior walls, made up of vertical members (*muntins*) and horizontals (*rails*) framing panels: also called *wainscot*. *Raised and fielded*: with the central area of the panel (*field*) raised up (6b).

PANTILE: roof tile of S section.

PARAPET: wall for protection at any sudden drop, e.g. at the wall-head of a castle where it protects the *parapet walk* or wall-walk. Also used to conceal a roof.

PARCLOSE: *see* Screen.

PARGETTING (*lit.* plastering): exterior plaster decoration, either in relief or incised.

PARLOUR: in a religious house, a room where the religious could talk to visitors; in a medieval house, the semi-private living room below the solar (q.v.).

PARTERRE: level space in a garden laid out with low, formal beds.

PATERA (*lit.* plate): round or oval ornament in shallow relief.

PAVILION: ornamental building for occasional use; or projecting subdivision of a larger building, often at an angle or terminating a wing.

PEBBLEDASHING: *see* Rendering.

PEDESTAL: a tall block carrying a classical order, statue, vase, etc.

PEDIMENT: a formalized gable derived from that of a classical temple; also used over doors, windows, etc. For variations *see* 4b.

PENDENTIVE: spandrel between adjacent arches, supporting a drum, dome or vault and consequently formed as part of a hemisphere (5a).

PENTHOUSE: subsidiary structure with a lean-to roof. Also a separately roofed structure on top of a C20 multi-storey block.

PERIPTERAL: *see* Peristyle.

PERISTYLE: a colonnade all round the exterior of a classical building, as in a temple which is then said to be *peripteral*.

PERP (PERPENDICULAR): English Gothic architecture *c.* 1335–50 to *c.* 1530. The name is derived from the upright tracery panels then used (*see* Tracery and 2a).

PERRON: external stair to a doorway, usually of double-curved plan.

PEW: loosely, seating for the laity outside the chancel; strictly, an enclosed seat. *Box pew*: with equal high sides and a door.

PIANO NOBILE: principal floor of a classical building above a ground floor or basement and with a lesser storey overhead.

PIAZZA: formal urban open space surrounded by buildings.

PIER: large masonry or brick support, often for an arch. *See also* Compound pier.

PILASTER: flat representation of a classical column in shallow relief. *Pilaster strip*: *see* Lesene.

PILE: row of rooms. *Double pile*: two rows thick.

PILLAR: free-standing upright member of any section, not conforming to one of the orders (q.v.).

PILLAR PISCINA: *see* Piscina.

PILOTIS: C20 French term for pillars or stilts that support a building above an open ground floor.

PISCINA: basin for washing Mass vessels, provided with a drain; set in or against the wall to the S of an altar or free-standing (*pillar piscina*).

PISÉ: *see* Cob.

PITCHED MASONRY: laid on the diagonal, often alternately with opposing courses (*pitched and counterpitched* or *herringbone*).

PLATBAND: flat horizontal moulding between storeys. Cf. stringcourse.

PLATE RAIL: *see* Railways.

PLATEWAY: *see* Railways.

PLINTH: projecting courses at the

foot of a wall or column, generally chamfered or moulded at the top.

PODIUM: a continuous raised plat-form supporting a building; or a large block of two or three storeys beneath a multi-storey block of smaller area.

POINT BLOCK: *see* Multi-storey.

POINTING: exposed mortar jointing of masonry or brickwork. Types include *flush*, *recessed* and *tuck* (with a narrow channel filled with finer, whiter mortar).

POPPYHEAD: carved ornament of leaves and flowers as a finial for a bench end or stall.

PORTAL FRAME: C20 frame com-prising two uprights rigidly con-nected to a beam or pair of rafters.

PORTCULLIS: gate constructed to rise and fall in vertical grooves at the entry to a castle.

PORTICO: a porch with the roof and frequently a pediment supported by a row of columns (4a). A portico *in antis* has columns on the same plane as the front of the building. A *prostyle* porch has columns standing free. Porticoes are described by the number of front columns, e.g. tetrastyle (four), hexastyle (six). The space within the temple is the *naos*, that within the portico the *pronaos*. *Blind portico*: the front features of a portico applied to a wall.

PORTICUS (plural: *porticūs*): sub-sidiary cell opening from the main body of a pre-Conquest church.

POST: upright support in a struc-ture (7).

POSTERN: small gateway at the back of a building or to the side of a larger entrance door or gate.

POUND LOCK: *see* Canals.

PRESBYTERY: the part of a church lying E of the choir where the main altar is placed; or a priest's resid-ence.

PRINCIPAL: *see* Roofs and 7.

PRONAOS: *see* Portico and 4a.

PROSTYLE: *see* Portico and 4a.

PULPIT: raised and enclosed plat-form for the preaching of sermons. *Three-decker*: with reading desk below and clerk's desk below that. *Two-decker*: as above, minus the clerk's desk.

PULPITUM: stone screen in a major church dividing choir from nave.

PULVINATED: *see* Frieze and 3c.

PURLIN: *see* Roofs and 7.

PUTHOLES or PUTLOG HOLES: in the wall to receive putlogs, the horizontal timbers which support scaffolding boards; sometimes not filled after construction is com-plete.

PUTTO (plural: putti): small naked boy.

QUARRIES: square (or diamond) panes of glass supported by lead strips (*cames*); square floor slabs or tiles.

QUATREFOIL: *see* Foil and 2b.

QUEEN-STRUT: *see* Roofs and 7.

QUIRK: sharp groove to one side of a convex medieval moulding.

QUOINS: dressed stones at the angles of a building (6d).

RADBURN SYSTEM: vehicle and pedestrian segregation in resid-ential developments, based on that used at Radburn, New Jersey, USA, by Wright and Stein, 1928–30.

RADIATING CHAPELS: projecting radially from an ambulatory or an apse (*see* Chevet).

RAFTER: *see* Roofs and 7.

RAGGLE: groove cut in masonry, especially to receive the edge of a roof-covering.

RAGULY: ragged (in heraldry). Also applied to funerary sculpture, e.g. *cross raguly*: with a notched outline.

RAIL: *see* Panelling and 6b; also 7.

RAILWAYS: *Edge rail*: on which flanged wheels can run. *Plate rail*: L-section rail for plain unflanged wheels. *Plateway*: early railway using plate rails.

RAISED AND FIELDED: *see* Pan-elling and 6b.

RAKE: slope or pitch.

RAMPART: defensive outer wall of stone or earth. *Rampart walk*: path along the inner face.

REBATE: rectangular section cut out of a masonry edge to receive a shutter, door, window, etc.

REBUS: a heraldic pun, e.g. a fiery cock for Cockburn.

REEDING: series of convex mouldings, the reverse of fluting (q.v.). Cf. Gadrooning.

RENDERING: the covering of outside walls with a uniform surface or skin for protection from the weather. *Limewashing*: thin layer of lime plaster. *Pebble-dashing*: where aggregate is thrown at the wet plastered wall for a textured effect. *Roughcast*: plaster mixed with a coarse aggregate such as gravel. *Stucco*: fine lime plaster worked to a smooth surface. *Cement rendering*: a cheaper substitute for stucco, usually with a grainy texture.

REPOUSSÉ: relief designs in metalwork, formed by beating it from the back.

REREDORTER (*lit.* behind the dormitory): latrines in a medieval religious house.

REREDOS: painted and/or sculptured screen behind and above an altar. Cf. Retable.

RESPOND: half-pier or half-column bonded into a wall and carrying one end of an arch. It usually terminates an arcade.

RETABLE: painted or carved panel standing on or at the back of an altar, usually attached to it.

RETROCHOIR: in a major church, the area between the high altar and E chapel.

REVEAL: the plane of a jamb, between the wall and the frame of a door or window.

RIB-VAULT: *see* Vault and 2c.

RINCEAU: classical ornament of leafy scrolls (4b).

RISER: vertical face of a step (6c).

ROACH: a rough-textured form of Portland stone, with small cavities and fossil shells.

ROCK-FACED: masonry cleft to produce a rugged appearance.

ROCOCO: style current *c.* 1720 and *c.* 1760, characterized by a serpentine line and playful, scrolled decoration.

ROLL MOULDING: medieval moulding of part-circular section (1a).

ROMANESQUE: style current in the C11 and C12. In England often called Norman. *See also* Saxo-Norman.

ROOD: crucifix flanked by the Virgin and St John, usually over the entry into the chancel, on a beam (*rood beam*) or painted on the wall. The *rood screen* below often had a walkway (*rood loft*) along the top, reached by a *rood stair* in the side wall.

ROOFS: Shape. For the main external shapes (hipped, mansard, etc.) *see* 8a. Helm and *Saddleback*: *see* 1c. *Lean-to*: single sloping roof built against a vertical wall; lean-to is also applied to the part of the building beneath.
Construction. *See* 7.
Single-framed roof: with no main trusses. The rafters may be fixed to the wall-plate or ridge, or longitudinal timber may be absent altogether.
Double-framed roof: with longitudinal members, such as purlins, and usually divided into bays by principals and principal rafters. Other types are named after their main structural components, e.g. *hammerbeam, crown-post* (*see* Elements below and 7).
Elements. *See* 7.
Ashlar piece: a short vertical timber connecting inner wall-plate or timber pad to a rafter.
Braces: subsidiary timbers set diagonally to strengthen the frame. *Arched braces*: curved pair forming an arch, connecting wall or post below with tie- or collar-beam above. *Passing braces*: long straight braces passing across other members of the truss. *Scissor braces*: pair crossing diagonally between pairs of rafters or principals. *Wind-braces*: short, usually curved braces connecting side purlins with principals; sometimes decorated with cusping.
Collar or *collar-beam*: horizontal transverse timber connecting a pair of rafter or cruck blades (q.v.), set between apex and the wall-plate.
Crown-post: a vertical timber set centrally on a tie-beam and supporting a collar purlin braced to it longitudinally. In an open truss

lateral braces may rise to the collar-beam; in a closed truss they may descend to the tie-beam.

Hammerbeams: horizontal brackets projecting at wall-plate level like an interrupted tie-beam; the inner ends carry *hammerposts*, vertical timbers which support a purlin and are braced to a collar-beam above.

Kingpost: vertical timber set centrally on a tie- or collar-beam, rising to the apex of the roof to support a ridge-piece (cf. Strut).

Plate: longitudinal timber set square to the ground. *Wall-plate*: plate along the top of a wall which receives the ends of the rafters; cf. Purlin.

Principals: pair of inclined lateral timbers of a truss. Usually they support side purlins and mark the main bay divisions.

Purlin: horizontal longitudinal timber. *Collar purlin* or *crown plate*: central timber which carries collar-beams and is supported by crown-posts. *Side purlins*: pairs of timbers placed some way up the slope of the roof, which carry common rafters. *Butt* or *tenoned purlins* are tenoned into either side of the principals. *Through purlins* pass through or past the principal; they include *clasped purlins*, which rest on queenposts or are carried in the angle between principals and collar, and *trenched purlins* trenched into the backs of principals.

Queen-strut: paired vertical, or near-vertical, timbers placed symmetrically on a tie-beam to support side purlins.

Rafters: inclined lateral timbers supporting the roof covering. *Common rafters*: regularly spaced uniform rafters placed along the length of a roof or between principals. *Principal rafters*: rafters which also act as principals.

Ridge, ridge-piece: horizontal longitudinal timber at the apex supporting the ends of the rafters.

Sprocket: short timber placed on the back and at the foot of a rafter to form projecting eaves.

Strut: vertical or oblique timber between two members of a truss, not directly supporting longitudinal timbers.

Tie-beam: main horizontal transverse timber which carries the feet of the principals at wall level.

Truss: rigid framework of timbers at bay intervals, carrying the longitudinal roof timbers which support the common rafters.

Closed truss: with the spaces between the timbers filled, to form an internal partition.

See also Cruck, Wagon roof.

ROPE   MOULDING: *see*   Cable moulding.

ROSE WINDOW: circular window with tracery radiating from the centre. Cf. Wheel window.

ROTUNDA: building or room circular in plan.

ROUGHCAST: *see* Rendering.

ROVING BRIDGE: *see* Canals.

RUBBED BRICKWORK: *see* Gauged brickwork.

RUBBLE: masonry whose stones are wholly or partly in a rough state. *Coursed*: coursed stones with rough faces. *Random*: uncoursed stones in a random pattern. *Snecked*: with courses broken by smaller stones (snecks).

RUSTICATION: *see* 6d. Exaggerated treatment of masonry to give an effect of strength. The joints are usually recessed by V-section chamfering or square-section channelling (*channelled rustication*). *Banded rustication* has only the horizontal joints emphasized. The faces may be flat, but can be *diamond-faced*, like shallow pyramids, *vermiculated*, with a stylized texture like worm-casts, and *glacial* (frost-work), like icicles or stalactites.

SACRISTY: room in a church for sacred vessels and vestments.

SADDLEBACK ROOF: *see* 1C.

SALTIRE CROSS: with diagonal limbs.

SANCTUARY: area around the main altar of a church. Cf. Presbytery.

SANGHA: residence of Buddhist monks or nuns.

SARCOPHAGUS: coffin of stone or other durable material.

SAXO-NORMAN: transitional Romanesque style combining Anglo-Saxon and Norman features, current c. 1060–1100.

SCAGLIOLA: composition imitating marble.

SCALLOPED CAPITAL: *see* 1a.

SCOTIA: a hollow classical moulding, especially between tori (q.v.) on a column base (3b, 3f).

SCREEN: in a medieval church, usually at the entry to the chancel; *see* Rood (screen) and Pulpitum. A *parclose screen* separates a chapel from the rest of the church.

SCREENS or SCREENS PASSAGE: screened-off entrance passage between great hall and service rooms.

SECTION: two-dimensional representation of a building, moulding, etc., revealed by cutting across it.

SEDILIA (singular: sedile): seats for the priests (usually three) on the S side of the chancel.

SET-OFF: *see* Weathering.

SETTS: squared stones, usually of granite, used for paving or flooring.

SGRAFFITO: decoration scratched, often in plaster, to reveal a pattern in another colour beneath. *Graffiti*: scratched drawing or writing.

SHAFT: vertical member of round or polygonal section (1a, 3a). *Shaft-ring*: at the junction of shafts set *en delit* (q.v.) or attached to a pier or wall (1a).

SHEILA-NA-GIG: female fertility figure, usually with legs apart.

SHELL: thin, self-supporting roofing membrane of timber or concrete.

SHOULDERED ARCHITRAVE: *see* 4b.

SHUTTERING: *see* Concrete.

SILL: horizontal member at the bottom of a window or door frame; or at the base of a timber-framed wall into which posts and studs are tenoned (7).

SLAB BLOCK: *see* Multi-storey.

SLATE-HANGING: covering of overlapping slates on a wall. *Tile-hanging* is similar.

SLYPE: covered way or passage leading E from the cloisters between transept and chapter house.

SNECKED: *see* Rubble.

SOFFIT (*lit.* ceiling): underside of an arch (also called *intrados*), lintel, etc. *Soffit roll*: medieval roll moulding on a soffit.

SOLAR: private upper chamber in a medieval house, accessible from the high end of the great hall.

SOPRAPORTA: *see* Overdoor.

SOUNDING-BOARD: *see* Tester.

SPANDRELS: roughly triangular spaces between an arch and its containing rectangle, or between adjacent arches (5c). Also non-structural panels under the windows in a curtain-walled building.

SPERE: a fixed structure screening the lower end of the great hall from the screens passage. *Spere-truss*: roof truss incorporated in the spere.

SPIRE: tall pyramidal or conical feature crowning a tower or turret. *Broach*: starting from a square base, then carried into an octagonal section by means of triangular faces; and *splayed-foot*: variation of the broach form, found principally in the southeast, in which the four cardinal faces are splayed out near their base, to cover the corners, while oblique (or intermediate) faces taper away to a point (1c). *Needle spire*: thin spire rising from the centre of a tower roof, well inside the parapet: when of timber and lead often called a *spike*.

SPIRELET: *see* Flèche.

SPLAY: of an opening when it is wider on one face of a wall than the other.

SPRING or SPRINGING: level at which an arch or vault rises from its supports. *Springers*: the first stones of an arch or vaulting rib above the spring (2c).

SQUINCH: arch or series of arches thrown across an interior angle of a square or rectangular structure to support a circular or polygonal superstructure, especially a dome or spire (5a).

SQUINT: an aperture in a wall or through a pier usually to allow a view of an altar.

STAIRS: *see* 6c. *Dog-leg stair*: parallel flights rising alternately in opposite directions, without an open well. *Flying stair*: cantilevered from the walls of a stairwell, without newels; sometimes called a *Geometric* stair when the inner edge describes a curve. *Newel stair*: ascending round a central supporting newel (q.v.); called a *spiral stair* or *vice* when in a circular shaft, a *winder* when in a rectangular compartment. (Winder also applies to the steps on the turn.) *Well stair*: with flights round a square open well framed by newel posts. *See also* Perron.

STALL: fixed seat in the choir or chancel for the clergy or choir (cf. Pew). Usually with arm rests, and often framed together.

STANCHION: upright structural member, of iron, steel or reinforced concrete.

STANDPIPE TOWER: *see* Manometer.

STEAM ENGINES: *Atmospheric*: worked by the vacuum created when low-pressure steam is condensed in the cylinder, as developed by Thomas Newcomen. *Beam engine*: with a large pivoted beam moved in an oscillating fashion by the piston. It may drive a flywheel or be *non-rotative*. *Watt* and *Cornish*: single-cylinder; *compound*: two cylinders; *triple expansion*: three cylinders.

STEEPLE: tower together with a spire, lantern, or belfry.

STIFF-LEAF: type of E.E. foliage decoration. *Stiff-leaf capital see* 1b.

STOP: plain or decorated terminal to mouldings or chamfers, or at the end of hoodmoulds and labels (*label stop*), or stringcourses (5b, 6a); *see also* Headstop.

STOUP: vessel for holy water, usually near a door.

STRAINER: *see* Arch.

STRAPWORK: late C16 and C17 decoration, like interlaced leather straps.

STRETCHER: *see* Bond and 6e.

STRING: *see* 6c. Sloping member holding the ends of the treads and risers of a staircase. *Closed string*: a broad string covering the ends of the treads and risers. *Open string*: cut into the shape of the treads and risers.

STRINGCOURSE: horizontal course or moulding projecting from the surface of a wall (6d).

STUCCO: *see* Rendering.

STUDS: subsidiary vertical timbers of a timber-framed wall or partition (7).

STUPA: Buddhist shrine, circular in plan.

STYLOBATE: top of the solid platform on which a colonnade stands (3a).

SUSPENSION BRIDGE: *see* Bridge.

SWAG: like a festoon (q.v.), but representing cloth.

SYSTEM BUILDING: *see* Industrialized building.

TABERNACLE: canopied structure to contain the reserved sacrament or a relic; or architectural frame for an image or statue.

TABLE TOMB: memorial slab raised on free-standing legs.

TAS-DE-CHARGE: the lower courses of a vault or arch which are laid horizontally (2c).

TERM: pedestal or pilaster tapering downward, usually with the upper part of a human figure growing out of it.

TERRACOTTA: moulded and fired clay ornament or cladding.

TESSELLATED PAVEMENT: mosaic flooring, particularly Roman, made of *tesserae*, i.e. cubes of glass, stone, or brick.

TESTER: flat canopy over a tomb or pulpit, where it is also called a *sounding-board*.

TESTER TOMB: tomb-chest with effigies beneath a tester, either free-standing (tester with four or more columns), or attached to a wall (*half-tester*) with columns on one side only.

TETRASTYLE: *see* Portico.

THERMAL WINDOW: *see* Diocletian window.

THREE-DECKER PULPIT: *see* Pulpit.

TIDAL GATES: *see* Canals.

TIE-BEAM: *see* Roofs and 7.

TIERCERON: *see* Vault and 2c.

TILE-HANGING: *see* Slate-hanging.

TIMBER-FRAMING: *see* 7. Method of construction where the struc-

INDEX OF ARCHITECTS, ARTISTS, PATRONS AND RESIDENTS

Names of architects and artists working in the area covered by this volume are given in *italic*. Entries for partnerships and group practices are listed after entries for a single name.

Also indexed here are names/titles of families and individuals (not of bodies or commercial firms) recorded in this volume as having commissioned architectural work or owned, lived in, or visited properties in the area. The index includes monuments to members of such families and other individuals where they are of particular interest.

INDEX OF PLACES

Principal references are in **bold** type; demolished buildings are shown in *italic*. Sheffield is indexed in three separate entries: 'Sheffield city centre', 'Sheffield inner areas' and 'Sheffield outer areas'. Outer areas of other cities are grouped together at the end of the entry.